Engaging Videos explore a variety of business topics related to the theory students are learning in class. **Exercise Quizzes** assess students' comprehension of the concepts in each video.

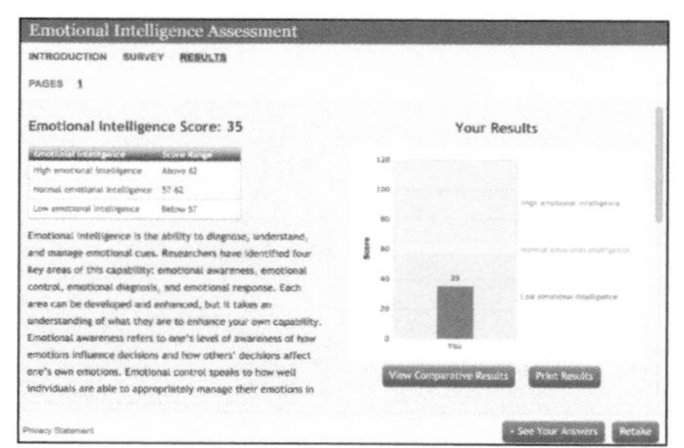

Personal Inventory Assessments is a collection of online exercises designed to promote **self-reflection** and engagement in students, enhancing their ability to connect with management concepts.

"I most liked the Personal Inventory Assessments because they gave me a deeper understanding of the chapters. I would read about personalities and then find out which category I fit into using the assessment."

— Student, Kean University

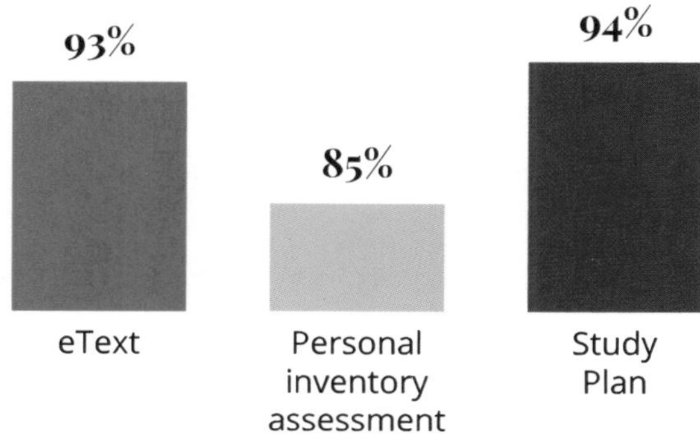

% of students who found learning aid helpful

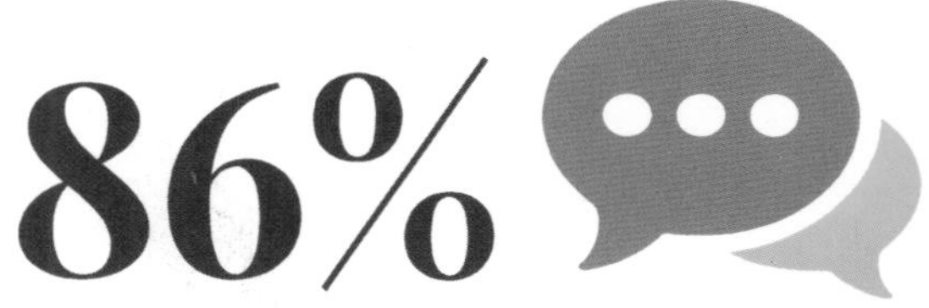

of students would tell their instructor to keep using MyLab Management

Pearson eText enhances student learning with engaging and interactive lecture and example videos that bring learning to life.

The **Gradebook** offers an easy way for you and your students to see their performance in your course.

For additional details visit: www.pearson.com/mylab/management

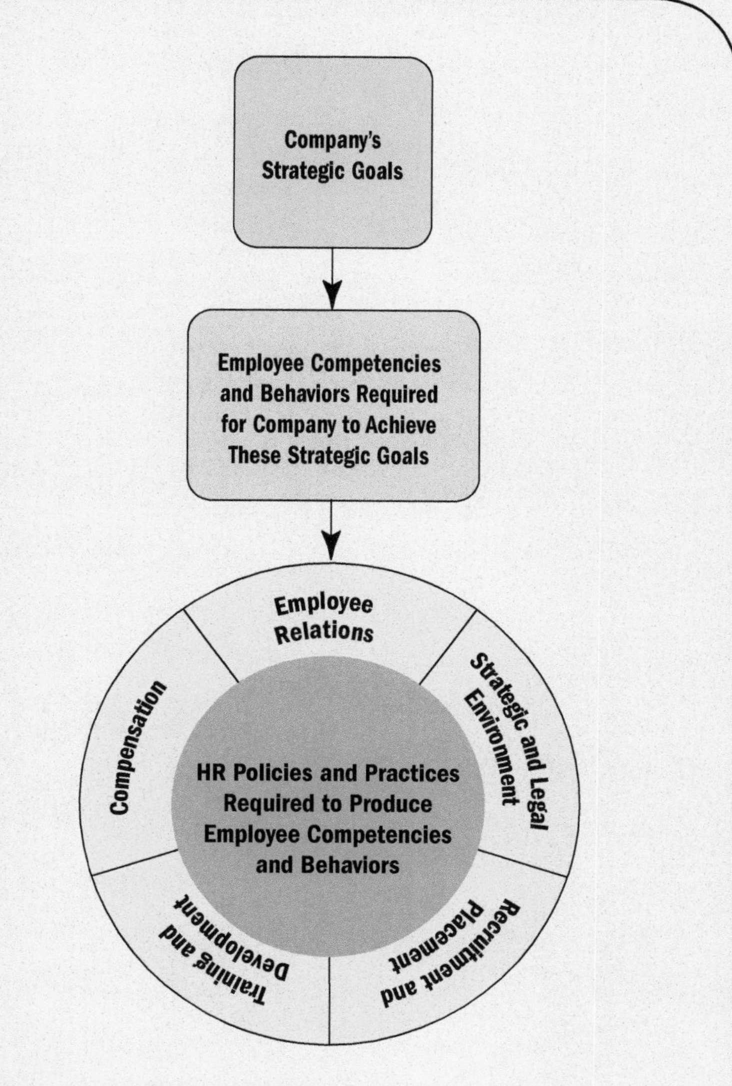

WHERE WE ARE NOW

The framework above introduces each chapter and makes the following point: That the firm's HR policies and practices should produce the employee skills and behaviors the company needs to achieve its strategic aims.

Human Resource Management

Sixteenth Edition

GARY DESSLER
Florida International University

FOR CLAUDIA

Vice President, Business, Economics, and UK Courseware: Donna Battista
Director of Portfolio Management: Stephanie Wall
Director, Courseware Portfolio Management: Ashley Dodge
Senior Sponsoring Editor: Neeraj Bhalla
Development Editor: Kerri Tomasso
Editorial Assistant: Linda Albelli
Vice President, Product Marketing: Roxanne McCarley
Senior Product Marketer: Carlie Marvel
Product Marketing Assistant: Marianela Silvestri
Manager of Field Marketing, Business Publishing: Adam Goldstein
Field Marketing Manager: Nicole Price
Vice President, Production and Digital Studio, Arts and Business: Etain O'Dea
Director, Production and Digital Studio, Business and Economics: Ashley Santora
Managing Producer, Business: Melissa Feimer
Content Producer: Yasmita Hota
Operations Specialist: Carol Melville
Design Lead: Kathryn Foot
Manager, Learning Tools: Brian Surette
Learning Tools Strategist: Michael Trinchetto
Managing Producer, Digital Studio and GLP: James Bateman
Managing Producer, Digital Studio: Diane Lombardo
Digital Studio Producer: Regina Dasilva
Digital Studio Producer: Alana Coles
Full Service Project Management: Pearson CSC, Ann Pulido and Roberta Sherman
Interior Design: Pearson CSC
Cover Design: Pearson CSC
Cover Art: Katty2016/Shutterstock
Printer/Binder: LSC Communications
Cover Printer: LSC Communications

Acknowledgments of third-party content appear on the appropriate page within the text, which constitutes an extension of this copyright page.

Library of Congress Cataloging-in-Publication Data

Names: Dessler, Gary, author.
Title: Human resource management / Gary Dessler, Florida International University.
Description: Sixteenth Edition. | New York : Pearson, [2018] | Revised edition of the author's Human resource management, [2017]
Identifiers: LCCN 2018036314 | ISBN 9780135172780 (casebound)
Subjects: LCSH: Personnel management.
Classification: LCC HF5549 .D4379 2018 | DDC 658.3--dc23
LC record available at https://lccn.loc.gov/2018036314

ISBN 10: 0-13-517278-0
ISBN 13: 978-0-13-517278-0

6 2021

BRIEF CONTENTS

Continued

CONTENTS

9 Performance Management and Appraisal 277

APPENDICES

PREFACE

NEW TO THIS EDITION

Adopters will find three main changes that are new to this edition:

Updated Chapters

To ensure a smooth transition for adopters from the 15th to this 16th edition, this edition's 18 chapter table of contents and the outline of all 18 chapters are basically as they were in the 15th edition, so in terms of teaching, the topic flow is about the same as the 15th edition. However, embedded in each chapter's paragraphs are dozens of new topics, practical examples, and research insights, all accompanied by hundreds of new endnotes from 2015–2018.

We've made sure to integrate the new text material into the book's accompanying PowerPoint slides, test banks, and other instructional supplements.

HR and the Gig Economy Features

It's not easy getting a handle on how many people are working in the gig economy, but the number is huge.[i] By some estimates, over 40% of all workers in America may soon be freelancers, and by another estimate about a third of all workers now do gig work on the side, such as teachers driving for Uber.[ii]

Whatever the exact number, the growth of the so-called gig economy has big implications for those who have to manage gig workers. New **HR and the Gig Economy** features show how companies manage gig workers' HR needs, for example how to recruit, screen, train, appraise, and manage the safety of gig workers.

HR AND THE GIG ECONOMY: *DISCRIMINATION IN THE GIG ECONOMY?*

Most companies use recruiters, supervisors, and/or HR professionals to do their hiring, so if an applicant suffers discrimination it's usually pretty clear who did it.[8] But what do you do when you're a gig worker, doing work through a gig economy company like Uber, Task Rabbit, or Fiverr? Here the people doing the "hiring" are usually Task Rabbit, Uber, or Fiverr users, and they're hiring based on reviews compiled from previous users, or from photos in your profile. What stops customers from illegally discriminating?

Unfortunately, the answer may be, "not much." For example, in one study of labor markets like Task Rabbit and Fiverr, black service providers got more negative reviews than did white ones. Because the rating algorithms are then based partly on prior customers' reviews, the black service providers were usually less likely to get new gigs. It's therefore a problem that gig companies (and customers) need to address.

New Cases

Application Case

Techtonic Group

Written and copyrighted by Gary Dessler, PhD.

It's been estimated that there are more than 600,000 unfilled technical jobs (systems engineers, programmers, and so on) in the United States.[182] Therefore, IT companies like Techtonic Group are continually battling for good applicants.

For many years, Techtonic outsourced app software development to Armenia; CEO Heather Terenzio flew twice a year to work with the people there. However, programmers' salaries in Eastern Europe were

Seven new end-of-chapter cases (for Chapters 2, 3, 5, 10, 12, 15, and 16) on Starbucks, Tesla, Techtonic, Uber, HubSpot, Vice Media, and a meatpacking firm have been added to the text. They replace older cases in these chapters. All other application cases have also been updated, as necessary, and I wrote a new Experiential Exercise ("Pearson Urgent Care") for chapter 12.

SOLVING TEACHING AND LEARNING CHALLENGES

Human Resource Management, 16th edition, provides students in human resource management courses and practicing managers with a complete and practical introduction to modern human resource management concepts and techniques in a highly readable form. This book has always emphasized giving all managers the

[i] https://www.bls.gov/careeroutlook/2016/article/what-is-the-gig-economy.htm, accessed June 29, 2018.

[ii] https://www.forbes.com/sites/karstenstrauss/2017/02/21/what-is-driving-the-gig-economy/#11e46e81653c; www.shrm.org/certification/pages/default.aspx#sthash.JRZQeAWR.dpuf, both accessed June 29, 2018.

skills they need to do their jobs. And today, with employers transferring more HR tasks to line managers, it's more important than ever that all managers—not just HR managers—be skilled in human resource management concepts and techniques. As the following figure sums up, you'll therefore find an emphasis here on the practical material you need to perform your day-to-day management responsibilities, even if you never spend one day as an HR manager.

The following tools especially help address teaching and learning challenges.

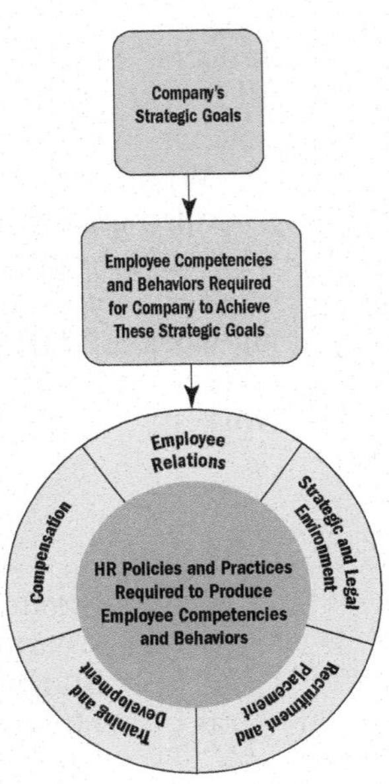

The Strategic HR Features

This book's Strategic HR features give students a bird's-eye view of how all the topics in each chapter fit together, and a tool instructors can use to illustrate these interrelationships.

As more employers transfer HR tasks to line managers, those managers need a "line of sight" that shows them how their HR actions impact the company's goals. This 16th edition therefore continues the book's emphasis on strategic human resource management and on improving performance, productivity, and profitability at work. This 16th edition also provides a comprehensive fully integrated treatment of strategic human resource management.

For example, tied to the chapter-opening scenarios, the **Strategic Context** features in Chapters 3–18 show how actual managers' HR actions produced the employee behaviors that were required to achieve the company's strategic aims.

IMPROVING PERFORMANCE: *THE STRATEGIC CONTEXT*

Wegmans Food Markets

Strategic compensation management means formulating a total rewards package that produces the employee skills and behaviors that the company needs to achieve its strategic goals.

Wegmans exemplifies this. It competes in the retail food sector, where profit margins are thin and where online competitors and giants like Walmart drive costs and prices down. The usual competitor's reaction is to cut employee benefits and costs.[55] Wegmans takes a different approach. Number 2 on Fortune's 100 Best Companies to Work For,[56] Wegmans views its workforce as an integral part of achieving Wegmans's strategic aims of *optimizing service while controlling costs by improving systems and productivity*. For example, one dairy department employee designed a new way to organize the cooler, thus improving ordering and inventory control.[57] The firm offers above-market pay rates, affordable health insurance, and a full range of employee benefits.[58] Wegmans's pay policies thus aim to produce exactly the sorts of high-productivity employee behaviors the company needs to achieve its strategic aims.

It's likely that its pay policies are one reason for Wegmans's exceptional profitability. For example, its employee turnover (about 6% for full-timers) is well below the industry's overall average of about 47%.[59] Its stores (which at about 120,000 square feet are much larger than competitors') average about $950,000 a week in sales (compared to a national average of $361,564), or about $49 million in sales annually, compared with a typical Walmart store's grocery sales of $23.5 million in sales.[60] As Wegmans's human resource head has said, good employees assure higher productivity, and that translates into better bottom-line results.[61]

MyLab Management Talk About It 2

If your professor has assigned this, go to the Assignments section of **www.pearson.com/mylab/management** to complete this discussion question. If Wegmans does so well with a high-pay policy, why don't more employers do this as well?

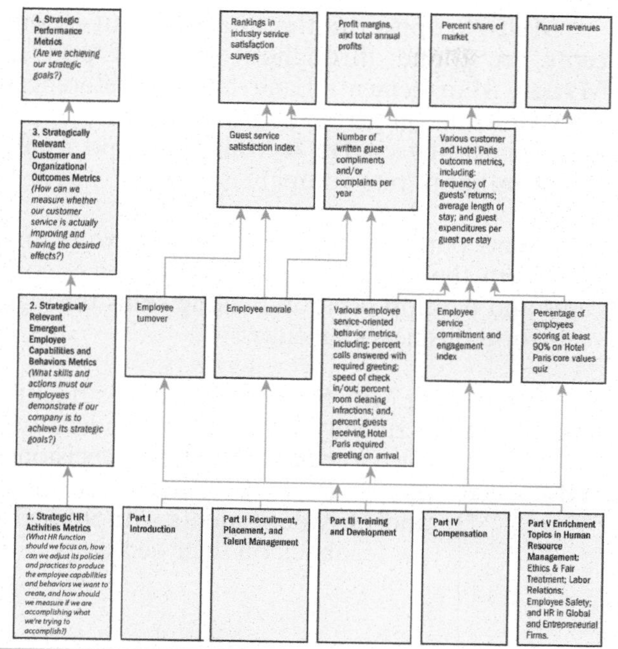

HR Scorecard for Hotel Paris International

Note: An abbreviated example showing selected HR practices and outcomes aimed at implementing the competitive strategy, "To use superior guest services to differentiate the Hotel Paris properties and thus increase the length of stays and the return rate of guests, and thus boost revenues and profitability and help the firm expand geographically."

The specialized strategy map for each chapter's Hotel Paris case is in the chapter's accompanying MyLab Management.

In addition, a **Fully Integrated Strategy Case and Strategy Maps** help to provide the most comprehensive treatment of strategic human resource management in a HR survey text:

- Chapter 1 introduces and Chapter 3 presents the concepts and techniques of human resource strategy.
- Chapter 3 onward, every chapter contains a **continuing "Hotel Paris" case** (identified by an "Eiffel Tower" icon), written to help make strategic human resource management come alive for readers. The continuing case shows how this hotel's HR director uses that chapter's human resource management concepts and techniques to create HR policies and practices that produce the employee skills and behaviors the Hotel Paris needs to improve its service and thereby achieve its strategic goals.
- An overall **strategy map** for the Hotel Paris on the book's inside back cover, and chapter-specific Hotel Paris strategy maps in the accompanying MyLab Management, help readers understand and follow the strategic implications of the hotel's HR decisions.

Building Employee Engagement

Each chapter's Building Employee Engagement features help to further integrate the chapter's topics and to make the book a more coherent whole. *Employee engagement* refers to being psychologically involved in, connected to, and committed to getting one's jobs done. You'll find practical examples and advice on how managers build engaged employee work teams and companies. *Employee Engagement Guide for Managers* sections in Chapters 1–14 show how managers use human resource activities to improve employee engagement.

HOW TO EXECUTE AN EMPLOYEE ENGAGEMENT STRATEGY Actually executing Kia UK's employee engagement HR strategy involved six steps (and these provide a roadmap for any such endeavor). First, Kia UK set *measurable objectives* for the program. These objectives included improving by at least 10% survey feedback scores for line managers' behaviors in terms of communication, the quality of appraisal feedback they gave their direct reports, the recognition of work done, and the respect between manager and employee.[79] Other objectives included reducing employee turnover employment costs (e.g., recruitment costs) by at least 10% per year.

Second, Kia UK held an extensive *leadership development* program. For example, it sent all managers for training to improve their management skills. Kia then tested the new skills with "360-degree" assessment tools (having managers' bosses, peers, and subordinates rate the managers' new leadership skills).

Third, Kia UK instituted new *employee recognition programs.* These included, for instance, giving "Outstanding Awards" to selected employees quarterly, and "Kia thank you" cards for jobs well done.[80]

To improve student results, we recommend pairing the text content with **MyLab Management**, which is the teaching and learning platform that empowers you to reach every student. By combining trusted author content with digital tools and a flexible learning platform, MyLab personalizes the learning experience to help your students learn and retain key course concepts while developing skills that future employers are seeking in potential employees. From **Mini Sims** to **Personal Inventory Assessments**, **MyLab Management** helps you teach your course your way. Learn more at www.pearson.com/mylab/management.

The **Chapter Warm-up** assessment helps you hold your students accountable for **READING** and demonstrating their knowledge on key concepts in each chapter before coming to class.

Homework: Chapter 5: Warm Up

Show completed problem Save

Score: 0 of 1 pt 1 of 12 (0 complete) **HW Score:** 0%, 0 of 12 pts

Warm-up 5.1.1 Question Help

The process of deciding what positions the company needs to fill and how to best fill them is known as ______.

- A. trend analysis
- B. alternative staffing
- C. workforce planning
- D. succession planning
- E. recruiting

Click to select your answer and then click Check Answer.

All parts showing Clear All Check Answer

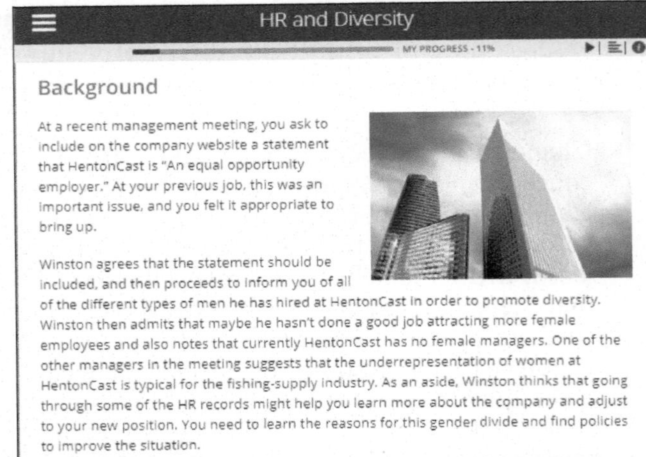

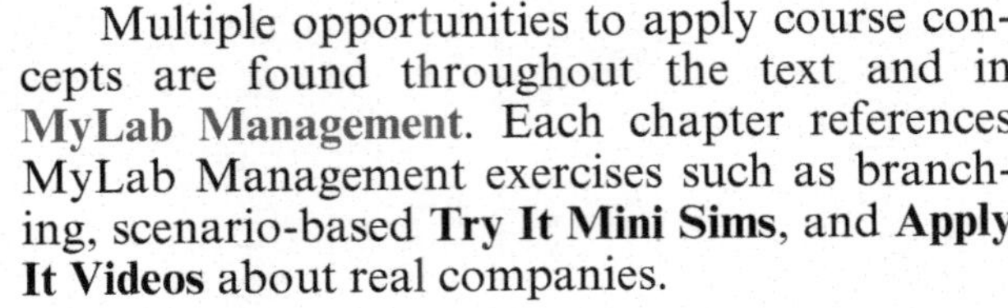

Multiple opportunities to apply course concepts are found throughout the text and in **MyLab Management**. Each chapter references MyLab Management exercises such as branching, scenario-based **Try It Mini Sims**, and **Apply It Videos** about real companies.

Mini Sims put students in professional roles and give them the opportunity to apply course concepts and develop decision-making skills through real-world business challenges.

These **branching** Mini Sims strengthen a student's ability to think critically, help students understand the impact of their decisions, engage students in active learning, and provide students with immediate feedback on their decisions.

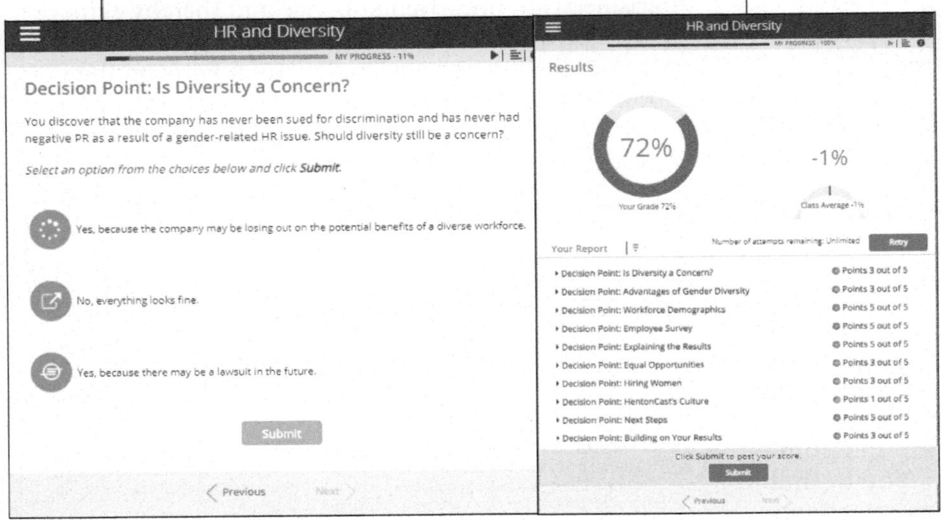

Engaging Videos explore a variety of business topics related to the theory students are learning in class. **Exercise Quizzes** assess students' comprehension of the concepts in each video.

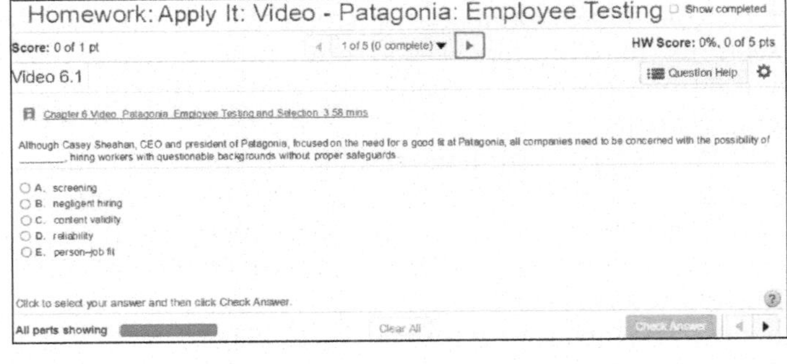

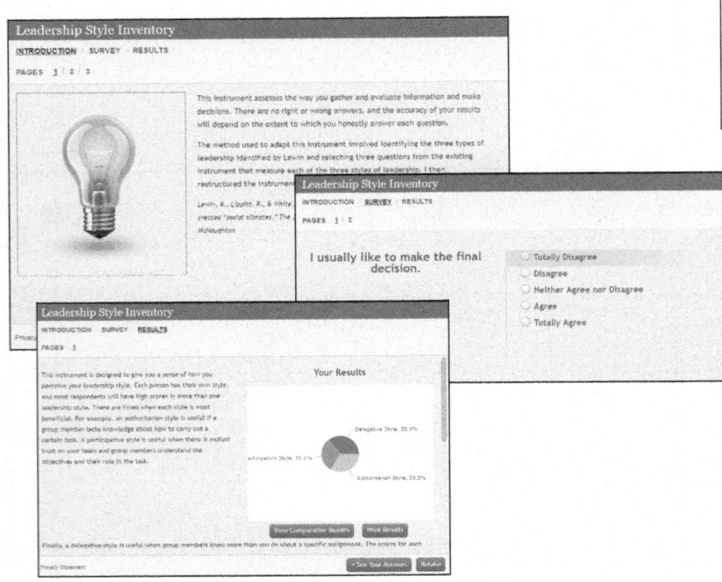

The author has recommended a **Personal Inventory Assessment** for most chapters, which is assignable in MyLab Management. These assessments help develop professionalism and awareness of oneself and others, skills necessary for future career success.

Personal Inventory Assessments is a collection of online exercises designed to promote self-reflection and engagement in students. It enhances their ability to connect with concepts taught in principles of management, organizational behavior, and human resource management classes.

DEVELOPING EMPLOYABILITY SKILLS

As noted earlier, every edition of this book has had the same aim: to provide all managers—not just HR managers—with the practical skills and knowledge they need to perform their day-to-day management responsibilities. A few examples of such skills you'll find here include:

Chapter 2: How to deal with a charge of discrimination

. . . You turn down a member of a protected group for a job. This person believes he or she was discriminated against due to being in a protected class, and decides to sue . . . What should you do?

Chapter 4: How to write a job description

. . . A job description is a written statement of what the worker actually does, how he or she does it, and what the job's working conditions are. This information is in turn . . .

Chapter 7: How to interview job candidates

. . . First make sure you understand the job andits human requirements. Then compose questionsbased on actual job duties from the job description . . . . Examples include (1) situational questions like "Suppose you were giving a sales presentation and a difficult technical question arose . . .

Chapter 14: How to discipline an employee

. . . Make sure the evidence supports the charge of employee wrongdoing. (Arbitrators often cite "the employer's evidence did not support the charge.") . . . Make sure to protect the employees' due process rights . . .

Know Your Employment Law sections within each chapter discuss the practical implications of the employment laws that apply to that chapter's topics, such as the laws relating to recruitment (Chapter 5), selection (Chapter 6), training (Chapter 8), and safety (Chapter 16) that all managers should know.

Diversity Counts features provide practical insights for managing a diverse workforce, for instance, regarding gender bias in selection decisions, bias in performance appraisal, and "hidden" gender bias in some bonus plans (Chapter 12).

Various *Improving Performance* features demonstrate real-world human resource management tools and practices that managers can use to improve performance. The discussion questions within each of these features are also in the accompanying MyLab Management. The *performance* features include:

IMPROVING PERFORMANCE: *HR AS A PROFIT CENTER*

Diversity can actually drive higher profits. In one study, researchers examined the diversity climate in 654 stores of a large U.S. retail chain. They defined *diversity climate* as the extent to which employees in the stores said the firm promotes equal opportunity and inclusion. They found the highest sales growth in stores with the highest pro-diversity climate, and the lowest in stores where subordinates and managers reported less hospitable diversity climates.[153] Another study found racial discrimination to be related negatively to employee commitment, while organizational efforts to support diversity reduced such negative effects.[154] When Merck needed halal certification for one of its medicines, it turned to its Muslim employees. They helped Merck bring the product to market faster and helped ensure its acceptance among Muslims.[155]

More than 50 of the largest U.S. companies, including GE, Microsoft, and Walmart, filed briefs with the U.S. Supreme Court arguing that affirmative action produces increased sales and profits. ■

Improving Performance: HR as a Profit Center contains actual examples of how human resource management practices add value by reducing costs or boosting revenues.

IMPROVING PERFORMANCE: *HR TOOLS FOR LINE MANAGERS AND SMALL BUSINESSES*

Chances are the EEOC won't file a suit, but getting a notice saying it's investigating is still scary. Whether you are managing one team or your own small business, every manager should know in advance what the EEOC will be looking for and what to do. A checklist follows.[141]

During the EEOC Investigation:

✓ *Conduct your own investigation* to get the facts.
✓ Ensure that there is information in the EEOC's file *demonstrating lack of merit* of the charge.

Improving Performance: HR Tools for Line Managers and Small Businesses explains that many line managers and entrepreneurs are "on their own" when it comes to human resource management, and describes straightforward HR tools such as work sampling tests that line managers and entrepreneurs can create and safely use to improve performance.

Improving Performance: HR Practices Around the Globe shows how actual companies around the globe use HR practices to improve their teams' and companies' performance, while illustrating the challenges managers face in managing internationally.

IMPROVING PERFORMANCE: *HR PRACTICES AROUND THE GLOBE*

Career Development at Medtronic[29]

Medtronic is a global medical technology company with more than 85,000 employees around the world. The company offers a wide range of career planning and development support tools aimed at helping employees understand their occupational strengths and weaknesses and reach their potential. These tools include customized development plans, self-assessment and feedback tools, mentoring programs, comprehensive on-site classes covering business, engineering, and science topics, tuition reimbursement scholarships, and online job listings so the employee can seek out new career opportunities within the company.

Trends Shaping HR Features

Just about every chapter again has one or more **Trends Shaping HR** features, each focusing on topics like Digital and Social Media, and other trends that affect HR practices.

TRENDS SHAPING HR: *DIGITAL AND SOCIAL MEDIA*

Sitedocs Digital Workplace Safety

Safety compliance usually has been managed centrally, by human resource managers or by a specialized safety unit. However, new digital mobile device–based safety systems now give managers and even employees more influence over safety. For example, the SiteDocs digital safety management system lets the employer digitize, move, store, work with, and access safety documents via mobile devices (iPad) and the Web.[55] Employees can login via the mobile device and view and complete their safety documentation (such as OSHA reports). These become available immediately to management. This enables management to monitor in real time whether employees are completing their documentation and to identify almost at once workplace hazards and incidents. ■

TRENDS SHAPING HR: *ROBOTS*

With more employees working alongside robots, safety standards are evolving. For example, industrial robots have speed and separation monitoring and safety stops so humans can "hand" them parts without the robot arm hitting them.[75] Many of the new so-called cobots have digital screen faces with human characteristics. For example, one cobot "glances" in the direction when it's about to pick something up, to forewarn its human "colleagues."[76] ■

TRENDS SHAPING HR: *LOCATION BEACONS*

Beacons—tiny devices that continuously transmit radio signals identifying themselves—are becoming valuable occupational safety tools. Employers use beacons to keep track of employees, particularly if they're in distress. Others use them to warn employees, such as when they're too close to a danger zone.[89] ■

INSTRUCTOR TEACHING RESOURCES

This program comes with the following teaching resources.

Supplements available to instructors at www.pearsonhighered.com	Features of the Supplement
Instructor's Manual authored by Susan Leshnower from Midland College	• Lecture Outlines • Chapter-by-chapter summaries—Where are we now • Examples and activities not in the main book • Annotated Outline • Teaching tips • Solutions to all questions, problems, and case problems in the book • Case Notes • Key Terms
Test Bank authored by Carol Heeter from Ivy Tech Community College	2,000 multiple-choice, true/false, short-answer questions with these annotations: • Difficulty level (1 for straight recall, 2 for some analysis, 3 for complex analysis) • Type (Multiple-choice, true/false, short-answer, essay) • Topic/Explanation (The term or concept the question supports) • Learning outcome • AACSB learning standard (Written and Oral Communication; Ethical Understanding and Reasoning; Analytical Thinking; Information Technology; Interpersonal Relations and Teamwork; Diverse and Multicultural Work; Reflective Thinking; Application of Knowledge)
Computerized TestGen	TestGen allows instructors to: • Customize, save, and generate classroom tests • Edit, add, or delete questions from the Test Item Files • Analyze test results • Organize a database of tests and student results.
PowerPoints authored by Patricia Buhler from Goldey-Beacom College	Slides include all the graphs, tables, and equations in the textbook. PowerPoints meet accessibility standards for students with disabilities. Features include, but are not limited to: • Keyboard and Screen Reader access • Alternative text for images • High color contrast between background and foreground colors

ACKNOWLEDGMENTS

Everyone involved in creating this book is proud of what we've achieved. *Human Resource Management* is one of the top-selling books in this market, and, as you read this, students and managers around the world are using versions translated into about a dozen languages, including Thai, French, Spanish, Greek, Indonesian, Russian, Chinese, and the Arab World edition.

Although I am responsible for *Human Resource Management*, I want to single out some people for their assistance. They include, first, faculty members who carefully reviewed the past few editions, and who made many useful and insightful suggestions:

Kimberly Pierre, *Houston Baptist University*
Oscar D. Munoz, *Miami Dade College*
Christopher McGraht, *Delaware County Community College*
Johnny Peppers, *Nashville State Community College*
Shamira Malekar, *CUNY – BMCC*
Robert Micera, *Stony Brook University and Seton Hall University*
Marcia Johnson, *Delaware County Community College*
Roger Liska, *Clemson University*
Michael Wayland, *Methodist University*
Melissa Bankroff, *Michigan State University*
David Gerth, *Nashville State Community College*
Evie Maxey, *Anderson University*
Paulette Holmes, *Coppin State University*
John Durboraw, *Columbia College*
Lisa Nieman, *Wesleyan University*
Brooke Sorrells, *Virginia College*
Craig Tunwell, *Troy University*
Kyle Stone, *Fort Hayes State University*
George Wynn, *University of Tampa*
Edward Ward, *Saint Cloud State University*
Daniel Grundmann, *Indiana University*
Clare Francis, *University of North Dakota*
John Durboraw, *Columbia College*
Mary Kern, *Baruch College*
Lucy Ford, *St. Joseph's University*
Leonard Bierman, *Texas A&M University*
Thomas J. Zagenczyk, *Clemson University*
Itoe Valentine, *Albany Technical College*
Pravin Kamdar, *College of Business and Management, Cardinal Stritch University*
Craig J. Russell, *Professor, Price College of Business, University of Oklahoma*
Matthew S. Rodgers, *The Ohio State University*
Carol Heeter, *Ivy Tech Community College*
Magdalem Upshaw, *Richland College Dallas*
C. Darren Brooks, *Florida State University*
Brian D. Lyons, *Wright State University*

I am very grateful to Susan Leshnower, Carol Heeter, and Patricia Buhler for their hard work on updating and improving the supplements for the 16th edition, and to the MyLabs team of Project Manager Kerri Tomasso, Gordon Schmidt (Indiana University/Purdue University Fort Wayne), Susan C. Schanne (Eastern Michigan University), Angela Boston (University of Texas), and Leslie Carnes, SPHR (Ivy Tech Community College).

At Pearson, thank you for the support and dedicated assistance of all involved. I particularly appreciate the insights, suggestions, and personal involvement of Editor-in-Chief, Stephanie Wall. Thank you again to my outstanding production team, with whom I've worked for many years: Ashley Santora, Director, Production & Digital Studio, and Yasmita Hota, my Content Producer. Thanks to Nicole Price, Field Marketing Manager, and the Pearson sales staff, without whose efforts this book would languish on the shelf, and to Neeraj Bhalla, Portfolio Manager, and Linda Albelli, Editorial Assistant. I want to thank everyone at Pearson Education, Inc. for successfully managing *Human Resource Management*'s internationalization. Development Editor Kerri Tomasso was extraordinarily helpful, and thank you to Roberta Sherman at SPi-Global. Separately, thanks very much to Billy Hunter for reviewing the book and for his suggestions about gig workers, and to Dr. James Scheiner for his many suggestions for possible new examples and updates.

At home, I want to thank my wife, Claudia, for her support during the many hours I spent working on this edition. My son, Derek, always a source of enormous pride, was very helpful. Samantha and Taylor are always in my thoughts. My parents were always a great source of support and encouragement and would have been very proud to see this book.

Antonio Guillem/Shutterstock

1 Introduction to Human Resource Management

LEARNING OBJECTIVES

When you finish studying this chapter, you should be able to:

1-1 **Explain** what human resource management is and how it relates to the management process.

1-2 **Briefly discuss and illustrate** the important trends influencing human resource management.

1-3 **Briefly describe** six important components or pillars of human resource management today.

1-4 **List** at least four important human resource manager competencies.

1-5 **Outline** the plan of this book.

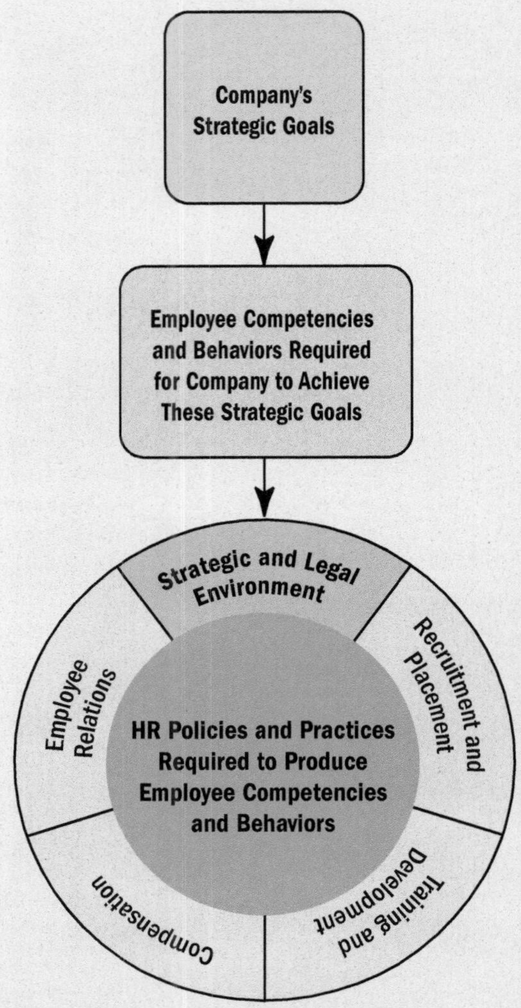

WHERE ARE WE NOW . . .

The purpose of this chapter is to explain what human resource management is, and why it's important to all managers. We'll see that human resource management activities such as hiring, training, appraising, compensating, and developing employees are part of every manager's job. And we'll see that human resource management is also a separate function, usually with its own human resource, or "HR," manager. The main topics we'll cover here include **What Is Human Resource Management?**, **The Trends Shaping Human Resource Management**, **The Components of Human Resource Management**, **The New Human Resource Manager**, and **The Plan of This Book**. The framework above (which introduces each chapter) makes this point: That the firm's HR policies and practices should produce the employee skills and behaviors the company needs to achieve its strategic aims.

For many people today, Upwork (www.upwork.com/) symbolizes much of what's new in human resource management. Millions of freelancers, from graphic designers to translators, accountants, writers, and customer service agents register on the site. Employers then use it to find, screen, hire, and pay the talent they need online in more than 180 countries.[1]

LEARNING OBJECTIVE 1-1

Explain what human resource management is and how it relates to the management process.

organization
A group consisting of people with formally assigned roles who work together to achieve the organization's goals.

manager
Someone who is responsible for accomplishing the organization's goals, and who does so by managing the efforts of the organization's people.

managing
To perform five basic functions: planning, organizing, staffing, leading, and controlling.

management process
The five basic functions of planning, organizing, staffing, leading, and controlling.

human resource management (HRM)
The process of acquiring, training, appraising, and compensating employees, and of attending to their labor relations, health and safety, and fairness concerns.

What Is Human Resource Management?

To understand what human resource management is, it's useful to start with what managers do. Upwork is an *organization*. An **organization** consists of people (in this case, people like Upwork's own in-house Web designers and managers) with formally assigned roles who work together to achieve the organization's goals. A **manager** is someone who is responsible for accomplishing the organization's goals, and who does so by managing the efforts of the organization's people.

Most writers agree that **managing** involves performing five basic functions: planning, organizing, staffing, leading, and controlling. In total, these functions represent the **management process.** Some of the specific activities involved in each function include

- ***Planning.*** Establishing goals and standards; developing rules and procedures; developing plans and forecasts
- ***Organizing.*** Giving each subordinate a specific task; establishing departments; delegating authority to subordinates; establishing channels of authority and communication; coordinating the work of subordinates
- ***Staffing.*** Determining what type of people should be hired; recruiting prospective employees; selecting employees; setting performance standards; compensating employees; evaluating performance; counseling employees; training and developing employees
- ***Leading.*** Getting others to get the job done; maintaining morale; motivating subordinates
- ***Controlling.*** Setting standards such as sales quotas, quality standards, or production levels; checking to see how actual performance compares with these standards; taking corrective action as needed

In this book, we will focus on one of these functions—the staffing, personnel management, or *human resource management* function. **Human resource management (HRM)** is the process of acquiring, training, appraising, and compensating employees, and of attending to their labor relations, health and safety, and fairness concerns. The topics we'll discuss should therefore provide you with the concepts and techniques every manager needs to perform the "people," or personnel, aspects of management. These include

- *Conducting job analyses* (determining the nature of each employee's job).
- *Planning labor needs* and *recruiting* job candidates.
- *Selecting* job candidates.
- *Orienting and training* new employees.
- *Managing wages and salaries* (compensating employees).
- *Providing incentives and benefits.*
- *Appraising performance.*
- *Communicating* (interviewing, counseling, disciplining).
- *Training employees* and *developing managers.*
- *Building employee relations and engagement.*

And what every manager should know about:

- Equal opportunity and affirmative action.
- Employee health and safety.
- Handling grievances and labor relations.

Why Is Human Resource Management Important to All Managers?

The concepts and techniques in this book are important to all managers for several reasons.

AVOID PERSONNEL MISTAKES First, having this knowledge will help you avoid the *personnel mistakes you don't want to make* while managing. For example, you don't want

- To have your employees not doing their best.
- To hire the wrong person for the job.

- To experience high turnover.
- To have your company in court due to your discriminatory actions.
- To have an employee hurt due to unsafe practices.
- To let a lack of training undermine your department's effectiveness.
- To commit any unfair labor practices.

Carefully studying this book can help you avoid mistakes like these.

IMPROVING PROFITS AND PERFORMANCE More important, it can *help ensure that you get results—through people*.[2] Remember that you could do everything else right as a manager—lay brilliant plans, draw clear organization charts, set up modern assembly lines, and use sophisticated accounting controls—but still fail, for instance, by hiring the wrong people or by not motivating subordinates. On the other hand, many managers—from generals to presidents to supervisors—have been successful even without adequate plans, organizations, or controls. They were successful because they had the knack for hiring the right people for the right jobs and then motivating, appraising, and developing them. Remember as you read this book that *getting results* is the bottom line of managing and that, as a manager, you will have to get these results through people. This fact hasn't changed from the dawn of management. As one company president summed it up:

> For many years it has been said that capital is the bottleneck for a developing industry. I don't think this any longer holds true. I think it's the workforce and the company's inability to recruit and maintain a good workforce that does constitute the bottleneck for production. I don't know of any major project backed by good ideas, vigor, and enthusiasm that has been stopped by a shortage of cash. I do know of industries whose growth has been partly stopped or hampered because they can't maintain an efficient and enthusiastic labor force, and I think this will hold true even more in the future.[3]

With global competition and economic pressures, that statement has never been truer than it is today. Human resource management methods like those in this book can help any line manager/supervisor (or HR manager) boost his or her team's and company's levels of engagement, profits, and performance. Here are two examples we'll meet in this book:

> *At one Ball Corp.* packaging plant, managers trained supervisors to set and communicate daily performance goals. Management tracked daily goal attainment with team scorecards. Employees received special training to improve their skills. Within 12 months production was up 84 million cans, customer complaints dropped by 50%, and the plant's return on investment rose by $3,090,000.

> *A call center* averaged 18.6 vacancies per year (about a 60% turnover rate). The researchers estimated the cost of a call-center operator leaving at about $21,500. They estimated the total annual cost of agent turnover for the call center at $400,853. Cutting that rate in half would save this firm about $200,000 per year.

YOU MAY SPEND SOME TIME AS AN HR MANAGER Here is another reason to study this book: *you might spend time as a human resource manager*. For example, about a third of large U.S. businesses surveyed appointed non-HR managers to be their top human resource executives. Thus, Pearson Corporation (which publishes this book) promoted the head of one of its publishing divisions to chief human resource executive at its corporate headquarters. Why? Some think these people may be better equipped to integrate the firm's human resource activities (such as pay policies) with the company's strategic needs (such as by tying executives' incentives to corporate goals).[4] Appointing non-HR people can also be good for the manager. For example, one CEO served a three-year stint as chief human resource officer on the way to becoming CEO. He said the experience he got was invaluable in learning how to develop leaders, and in understanding the human side of transforming a company.[5]

However most top human resource executives do have prior human resource experience. About 80% of those in one survey worked their way up within HR. The Society for Human Resource Management (SHRM) offers information on topics such as alternative career paths within human resource management.[6] Find it at www.shrm.org.[7]

HR FOR SMALL BUSINESSES And here is one other reason to study this book: you *may well end up as your own human resource manager*. More than half the people working in the United States work for small firms.[8] Small businesses as a group also account for most of the 600,000 or so new businesses created every year. Statistically speaking, therefore, most people graduating from college in the next few years either will work for small businesses or will create new small businesses of their own.[9] Small firms generally don't have the critical mass required for a full-time human resource manager (let alone an HR department).[10] The owner and his or her other managers (and perhaps assistant) handle tasks like signing employees on. So studying the techniques in this book should help you to manage a small firm's human resources more effectively. We'll address human resource management for small businesses in later chapters.

Line and Staff Aspects of Human Resource Management

All managers have always been, in a sense, human resource managers, because they all get involved in recruiting, interviewing, selecting, and training their employees. Yet most firms also have a human resource department with its own top manager. How do the duties of this human resource manager and department relate to the human resource duties of sales and production and other managers? Answering this requires a short definition of line versus staff authority. **Authority** is the right to make decisions, to direct the work of others, and to give orders. Managers usually distinguish between line authority and staff authority.

authority
The right to make decisions, direct others' work, and give orders.

line authority
Traditionally gives managers the right to issue orders to other managers or employees.

staff authority
Gives a manager the right to advise other managers or employees.

line manager
A manager who is authorized to direct the work of subordinates and is responsible for accomplishing the organization's tasks.

staff manager
A manager who assists and advises line managers.

In organizations, **line authority** traditionally gives managers the right to *issue orders* to other managers or employees. Line authority therefore creates a superior (order giver)–subordinate (order receiver) relationship. When the vice president of sales tells her sales director to "get the sales presentation ready by Tuesday," she is exercising her line authority. **Staff authority** gives a manager the right to *advise* other managers or employees. It creates an advisory relationship. When the human resource manager suggests that the plant manager use a particular selection test, he or she is exercising staff authority.

On the organization chart, managers with line authority are **line managers.** Those with staff (advisory) authority are **staff managers.** In popular usage, people tend to associate line managers with managing departments (like sales or production) that are crucial for the company's survival. Staff managers generally run departments that are advisory or supportive, like purchasing and human resource management. Human resource managers are usually staff managers. They assist and advise line managers in areas like recruiting, hiring, and compensation.

Line Managers' Human Resource Management Responsibilities

However, line managers do have many human resource duties. This is because the direct handling of people has always been part of every line manager's duties, from president down to first-line supervisors. One major company outlines its line supervisors' responsibilities for effective human resource management under these general headings:

1. Placing the right person in the right job
2. Starting new employees in the organization (orientation)
3. Training employees for jobs that are new to them
4. Improving the job performance of each person
5. Gaining creative cooperation and developing smooth working relationships
6. Interpreting the company's policies and procedures
7. Controlling labor costs
8. Developing the abilities of each person

9. Creating and maintaining departmental morale
10. Protecting employees' health and physical conditions

And we'll see that, if anything, social media tools like *LinkedIn hiring* are expanding many line managers' HR responsibilities. That's why in a recent survey, 49% of the employers were taking steps to "Improve line managers' people management skills."[11]

The Human Resource Department

In small organizations, line managers may carry out all these personnel duties unassisted. But as the organization grows, line managers usually need the assistance, specialized knowledge, and advice of a separate human resource staff.[12] In larger firms, the *human resource department* provides such specialized assistance. Figure 1-1 shows human resource management jobs in one organization.[13] Typical positions include compensation and benefits manager, employment and recruiting supervisor, training specialist, and employee relations executive. Examples of job duties include

- ***Recruiters:*** Use various methods including contacts within the community and print and online media to search for qualified job applicants.
- ***Equal employment opportunity (EEO) representatives or affirmative action coordinators:*** Investigate and resolve EEO grievances, examine organizational practices for potential violations, and compile and submit EEO reports.

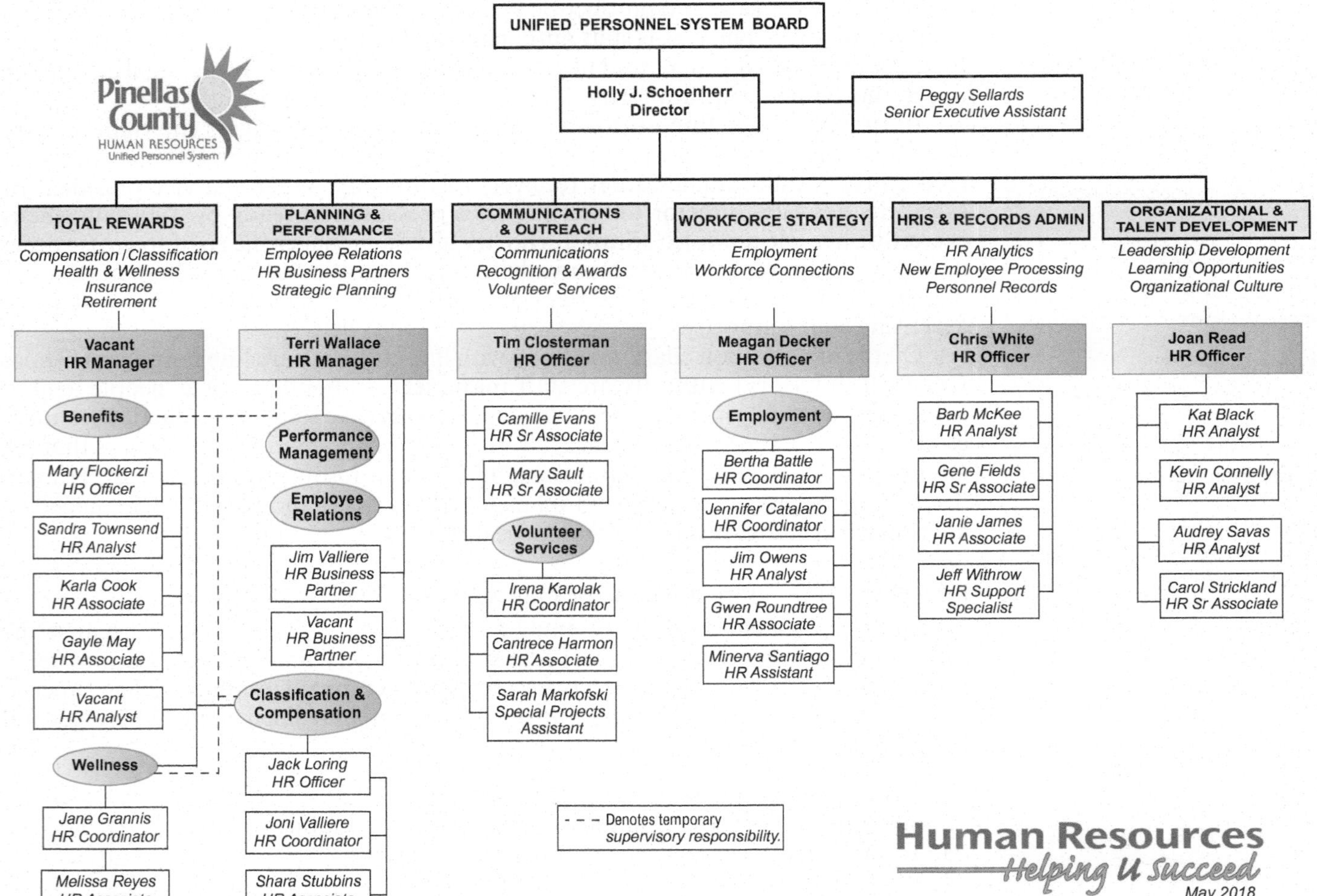

FIGURE 1-1 Human Resource Department Organization Chart Showing Typical HR Job Titles

Source: "Human Resource Development Organization Chart Showing Typical HR Job Titles," www.co.pinellas.fl.us/persnl/pdf/orgchart.pdf. Courtesy of Pinellas County Human Resources. Reprinted with permission.

- ***Job analysts:*** Collect and examine detailed information about job duties to prepare job descriptions.
- ***Compensation managers:*** Develop compensation plans and handle the employee benefits program.
- ***Training specialists:*** Plan, organize, and direct training activities.
- ***Labor relations specialists:*** Advise management on all aspects of union–management relations.

In practice, HR and line managers share responsibility for most human resource activities. For example, human resource and line managers typically share responsibility for skills training. Thus the supervisor might describe what training she thinks the new employee needs, HR might design the training, and the supervisor might then provide on-the-job training.

NEW APPROACHES TO ORGANIZING HR However, what HR departments do and how they do it are changing. Because of this, many employers are taking a new look at how they organize their human resource functions.[14]

For one thing, employers are changing how they organize and deliver HR services. For example, one survey found that 55% of firms surveyed were actively "reengineering" their human resource management processes, (for example, by moving recruiting from in-house recruiters to online and social media platforms).[15] Most are "actively seeking to transform" how they deliver human resource services, largely by adopting new HR technology tools (such as online training portals).[16] Many are using technology to institute more *"shared services"* arrangements.[17] These create centralized HR units whose employees are shared by all the companies' departments to assist the departments' line managers in human resource matters. These shared services HR teams generally offer their services through intranets or centralized call centers; they aim to provide managers and employees with specialized support in day-to-day HR activities (such as discipline problems).

You may also find specialized *corporate HR teams* within a company. These assist top management in top-level issues such as developing the personnel aspects of the company's long-term strategic plan. *Embedded HR teams* have HR generalists (also known as "relationship managers" or "HR business partners") assigned to functional departments like sales and production. They provide the employee selection and other assistance the departments need. *Centers of expertise* are basically specialized HR consulting firms within the company. For example, one might provide specialized advice in areas such as organizational change to all the company's various units.[18]

LEARNING OBJECTIVE 1-2

Briefly discuss and illustrate the important trends influencing human resource management.

The Trends Shaping Human Resource Management

Working cooperatively with line managers, human resource managers have long helped employers hire and fire employees, administer benefits, and conduct appraisals. However, trends are occurring that are changing how employers get their human resource management tasks done. The trends include *workforce demographic trends, trends in jobs people do, technological trends,* and *globalization and economic trends.*

Workforce Demographics and Diversity Trends

The composition of the workforce will continue to become more diverse with more women, minority group members, and older workers in the workforce.[19] Table 1-1 offers a bird's-eye view. Between 1992 and 2024, the percent of the workforce that the U.S. Department of Labor classifies as "white" will drop from 85% to 77.7%. At the same time, the percent of the workforce that it classifies as "Asian" will rise from 4% to 6.6%, and those of Hispanic origin will rise from 8.9% to 19.8%. The percentages of younger workers will fall, while those over 55 will about double from 11.8% of the workforce in 1992 to 24.8% in 2024. Many employers call "the aging workforce" a big problem. The problem is that there aren't enough younger workers to replace the projected number of baby boom–era older workers (born roughly 1946–1964)

TABLE 1-1 Demographic Groups as a Percent of the Workforce, 1992–2024

Age, Race, and Ethnicity	1992	2002	2012	2024
Age: 16–24	16.9%	15.4%	13.7%	11.3%
25–54	71.4	70.2	65.3	63.9
55+	11.8	14.3	20.9	24.8
White	85.0	82.8	79.8	77.7
Black	11.1	11.4	11.9	12.7
Asian	4.0	4.6	5.3	6.6
Hispanic origin	8.9	12.4	15.7	19.8

Source: U.S. Bureau of Labor Statistics Economic News Release, www.bls.gov/news.release/ecopro.t01.htm, December 19, 2013, and https://www.bls.gov/news.release/ecopro.t01.htm, accessed April 16, 2017.

retiring.[20] Many employers are bringing retirees back (or just trying to keep them from leaving).

With the resulting projected workforce shortfalls (not enough younger workers to replace retirees), employers are taking several steps. Many are hiring foreign workers for U.S. jobs. The H-1B visa program lets U.S. employers recruit skilled foreign professionals to work in the United States when they can't find qualified American workers. U.S. employers bring in about 181,000 foreign workers per year under these programs, although such programs face increasing opposition today.[21] Under the Trump administration the Department of Justice and the immigration service is enforcing H-1B rules more forcefully.[22]

Trends in Jobs People Do

There are three big trends in the jobs people do. First, work has shifted from manufacturing to service. Today over two-thirds of the U.S. workforce is employed in producing and delivering services, not products. By 2024, service-providing industries are expected to account for 129 million out of 160 million (81%) of wage and salary jobs overall.[23] So in the next few years, almost all the new jobs added in the United States will be in services, not in goods-producing industries.

ON-DEMAND WORKERS Second, today in companies like Uber and Upwork, most workers aren't employees at all: They're freelancers and independent contractor–gig workers, who work when they can, on what they want to work on, when they're needed.[24] The head of one such firm said employers view those workers as "mobile, independent bundles of skills."[25] Uber signs up thousands and thousands of new independent contractor drivers per month.[26] And people don't just do gigs full-time. About one-third of *all* workers do gig work on the side, such as teachers who drive for Uber.[27] The accompanying HR and the Gig Economy feature elaborates.

HR AND THE GIG ECONOMY *ON-DEMAND WORKERS*

Upwork (www.upwork.com)[28] symbolizes on-demand work. Millions of freelancers from graphic designers to translators, accountants, and lawyers register on its site. Employers use it to find, screen, hire, and pay the talent they need, in more than 180 countries.[29] These workers are part of a vast workforce comprised of contract, temp, freelance, independent contractor, "on-demand," or simply "gig" workers. Other on-demand sites include Amazon's Mechanical Turk, IKEA's TaskRabbit, and Handy (which lets users tap Handy's thousands of freelance cleaners and furniture assemblers when they need jobs done), and, of course, Uber.[30] Such workers may comprise half the workforce in the next 10 years.[31]

But freelance work goes beyond sites like Handy and Uber. For example employers are using more temp workers and contractors. Before it combined with Alaska Air group, Virgin America used contractors rather than employees for jobs including baggage delivery, reservations, and heavy maintenance.

Anyone using Uber already knows about on-demand workers. It is signing up tens of thousands of new independent contractor drivers per week, a rate that is doubling fast.

REB Images/Blend Images/Getty Images

A trucking company supplies contract workers who unload shipping containers at Walmart warehouses. And (somewhat amazingly) even Google's parent, Alphabet Inc., has about the same number of outsourced jobs as full-time employees.[32] We'll see in gig economy features like these that companies that rely on freelancers and other such nontraditional employees need special HR policies and practices to deal with them.

Gig economy work has detractors.[33] Some people who do these jobs say they can feel somewhat disrespected. One critic says the work is unpredictable and insecure. An article in the *New York Times* said this: "The larger worry about on-demand jobs is not about benefits, but about a lack of agency—a future in which computers, rather than humans, determine what you do, when and for how much."[34] Some gig workers are taking action. For example, some Uber drivers sued to unionize.

HUMAN CAPITAL Finally, more jobs are becoming "high tech." Jobs like engineer always emphasized knowledge and education. The big change now is that even traditional manufacturing jobs like assembler are increasingly high tech. Similarly bank tellers, retail clerks, bill collectors, mortgage processors, and package deliverers today need a level of technological sophistication they didn't need a few years ago. So in our increasingly knowledge-based economy, " . . . the acquisition and development of superior human capital appears essential to firms' profitability and success."[35]

For managers, the challenge here is that they have to manage such workers differently. For example, letting workers make more decisions presumes you've selected, trained, and rewarded them to make more decisions themselves. This means adjusting how you select, train, and engage these employees.[36] To paraphrase one recent headline, technology is useless without skilled workers.[37] The accompanying HR as a Profit Center discussion illustrates how one employer capitalized on its human capital.

IMPROVING PERFORMANCE: *HR AS A PROFIT CENTER*

Boosting Customer Service

A bank installed special software that made it easier for its customer service representatives to handle customers' inquiries. However, the bank did not otherwise change the service reps' jobs in any way. Here, the new software system did help the service reps handle more calls. But otherwise, this bank saw no big performance gains.[38]

A second bank installed the same software. But, seeking to capitalize on how the new software freed up customer reps' time, this bank also had its human resource team upgrade the customer service representatives' jobs. This bank taught them how to sell more of the bank's services, gave them more authority to make decisions, and raised their wages. Here, the new computer system dramatically improved product sales and profitability, thanks to the newly trained and empowered customer service reps. Value-added human resource practices like these improve employee performance and company profitability.[39] ■

> **MyLab Management Talk About It 1**
>
> If your professor has assigned this, go to the Assignments section of **www.pearson.com/mylab/management** to complete this discussion. Discuss three more specific examples of what you believe this second bank's HR department could have done to improve the reps' performance.

Globalization Trends

Globalization refers to companies extending their sales, ownership, and/or manufacturing to new markets abroad. Thus, Toyota builds Camrys in Kentucky, while Apple assembles iPhones in China. Free trade areas—agreements that reduce tariffs and barriers among trading partners—further encourage international trade. The North American Free Trade Agreement (NAFTA) and the European Union (EU) are examples.

Globalization has boomed for the past 50 or so years. For example, the total of U.S. imports plus exports rose from $562 billion in 1980, to about $5.2 *trillion* recently.[40] Evolving economic and political philosophies drove this boom. Governments dropped cross-border taxes or tariffs, formed economic free trade areas, and took other steps to encourage the free flow of trade among countries. The economic rationale was that by doing so, all countries would gain, and indeed, economies around the world did grow.

At the same time, globalization vastly increased international competition. More globalization meant more competition, and more competition meant more pressure to be "world class"—to lower costs, to make employees more productive, and to do things better and less expensively. Today a loss of jobs and growing income inequities are prompting some to rethink the wisdom of globalization.[41]

So globalization hasn't been without significant cost. As multinational companies jockey for position, many transfer operations abroad, not just to seek cheaper labor but also to tap into new markets. For example, Toyota has thousands of sales employees based in America, while GE has over 10,000 employees in France. The search for greater efficiencies prompts some employers to *offshore* (export jobs to lower-cost locations abroad, as when Dell offshored some call-center jobs to India). Some employers offshore even highly skilled jobs such as lawyer.[42] Managing the "people" aspects of globalization is a big task for companies that expand abroad—and for their HR managers.[43]

Economic Trends

Although globalization supported a growing global economy, the period from roughly 2007–2015 was difficult economically. As you can see in Figure 1-2, gross domestic product (GDP)—a measure of the United States of America's total output—boomed between 2001 and 2007. During this period, home prices (see Figure 1-3) leaped as much as 20% per year. Unemployment remained docile at about 4.7%.[44] Then, around 2007–2008, all these measures fell off a cliff. GDP fell. Home prices dropped by 10% or more (depending on city). Unemployment nationwide soon rose to more than 10%.

Why did all this happen? It's complicated. Many governments stripped away rules and regulations. For example, in America and Europe, the rules that prevented commercial banks from expanding into new businesses such as investment banking were relaxed. Giant, multinational "financial supermarkets" such as Citibank emerged. With

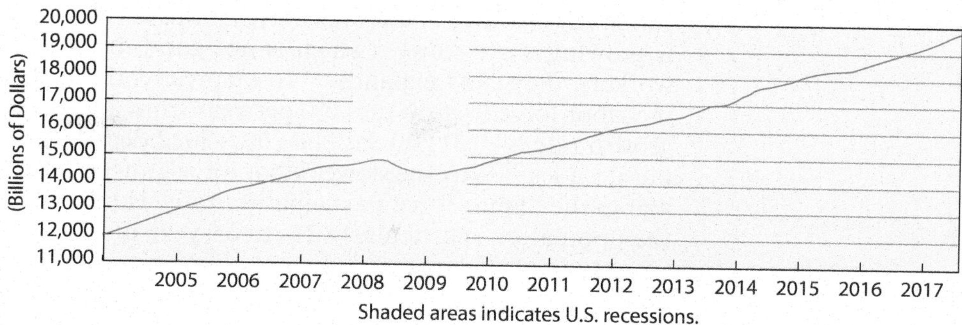

FIGURE 1-2 Gross Domestic Product, 2005–2017

Source: St. Louis Federal Reserve Bank, https://fred.stlouisfed.org/series/GDP, accessed March 9, 2018.

fewer regulations, more businesses and consumers were soon deeply in debt. Homebuyers bought homes with little money down. Banks freely lent money to developers to build more homes. For almost 20 years, U.S. consumers spent more than they earned. The United States became a debtor nation. Its balance of payments (exports minus imports) went from a healthy *positive* $3.5 billion in 1960, to a huge *minus* (imports exceeded exports) $497 billion deficit more recently.[45] The only way the country could keep buying more from abroad than it sold was by borrowing money. So, much of the boom was built on debt.

Around 2007, all those years of accumulating debt ran their course. Banks and other financial institutions found themselves owning trillions of dollars of worthless loans. Governments stepped in to try to prevent their collapse. Lending dried up. Many businesses and consumers stopped buying. The economy tanked.

Economic trends have moved up today, and hopefully they will continue to do so. For example, the unemployment rate had fallen from a high of more than 10% a few years ago to around 5% in 2015, and to about 4% in 2018, and GDP was growing at about 4.0% in 2018.[46]

However, that doesn't necessarily mean clear sailing for the economy. For one thing, the Federal Reserve Board, which supported economic expansion after the Great Recession, began raising interest rates as a guard against inflationary pressures. For another, productivity is rising more slowly than in the past, which may further retard economic growth.[47] (Automation may change that. In Asia robots are replacing human labor in clothing factories, and many experts predict automation will soon replace jobs ranging from bookkeepers and telemarketers to cashiers, retail salespeople, and, alas, human resources assistants.)[48] And after the experience of 2007–2009, it's doubtful that the leveraging and globalization that helped drive economic growth for the previous 50 years will continue unabated. Add it all up, and the bottom line could possibly be slowing economic growth ahead. Overall, the Bureau of Labor Statistics and the Congressional Budget Office project that gross domestic product (GDP) will increase by about 2.0% annually from 2020 to 2026, slower than the 3% or higher that more or less prevailed from the mid-1990s through the mid-2000s.[49]

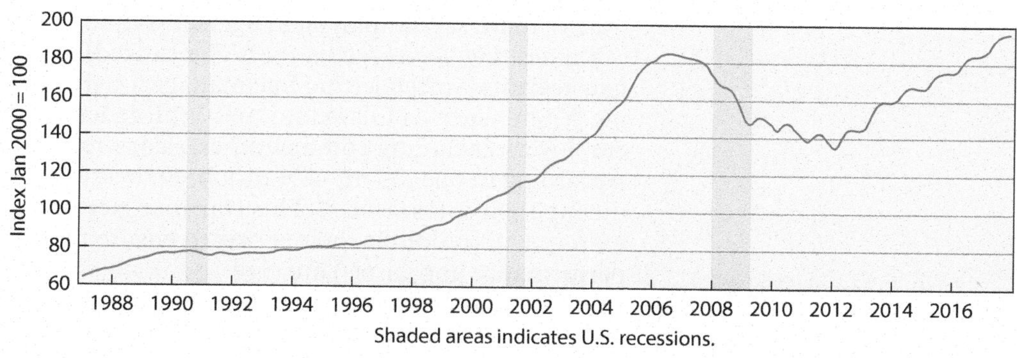

FIGURE 1-3 Case-Shiller U.S. National Home Price Index, 1988–2016

Source: St. Louis Federal Reserve Bank, https://fred.stlouisfed.org/series/CSUSHPINSA, accessed March 9, 2018.

LABOR FORCE TRENDS Complicating all this is the fact that the labor force in America is growing more slowly (which is not good, because if employers can't get enough workers, they can't expand).[50] To be precise, the Bureau of Labor Statistics projects the labor force to grow at 0.6% per year from 2016 to 2026. That's up from an annual growth rate of 0.5% during the 2002–2012 decade, but is much slower than in previous decades.[51] Why the slower labor force growth? Mostly because with baby boomers aging, the "labor force participation rate" is falling—in other words, the *percent* of the population (particularly 25- to 54-year-olds) that wants to work is way down.[52] One study of 35 large global companies' senior human resource officers said "talent management"—the acquisition, development, and retention of talent to fill the companies' employment needs—ranked as their top concern.[53]

THE UNBALANCED LABOR FORCE Furthermore, demand for workers is unbalanced; for example, the unemployment rate for, say, recent college graduates in general was higher than that of software engineering graduates.[54] In fact, almost half of employed U.S. college graduates are in jobs that generally require less than a four-year college education.[55] Why did this happen? In brief, because most of the jobs that the economy added in the past few years don't require college educations, and the Bureau of Labor Statistics says that will probably continue. Occupations that *do not* typically require postsecondary education employed nearly two-thirds of workers recently.[56] Similarly, about two-thirds of the occupations with the largest projected employment growth from 2014 to 2024 typically do not require postsecondary education for entry.[57] Such imbalances are complicated by a skills gap. For example, the manager of a PPG paint and coatings plant in Wisconsin, says they're "always short people" because they can't find enough skilled workers.[58]

The result is an unbalanced labor force: in some occupations (such as engineering) unemployment rates are low, while in others unemployment rates are still relatively high; recruiters in many companies can't find candidates, while in others there's a wealth of candidates;[59] and many people working today are in jobs "below" their expertise (which may or may not help to explain why about 70% of employees report being psychologically disengaged at work). In any case, the bottom line is more pressure on employers (and their human resource managers and line managers) to get the best efforts from their employees.

Technology Trends

Technology is changing human resource management in two main ways. First (as we saw), technological change is affecting *the nature of jobs*.[60] When someone thinks of "tech jobs," jobs at Google come to mind, but technology affects all sorts of jobs. At an Alcoa plant in Iowa, a computer at each workstation helps employees control their machines or communicate data. Employees type their commands into computerized machines that create precision parts.[61]

Second, technology is changing *how employers get human resource management tasks done*. In one survey 41% of companies were designing mobile apps to deliver human resource management services, and about a third were using artificial intelligence.[62] Several technologies are important here:

- Employers use *social media* tools such as Twitter, Facebook, and LinkedIn (rather than, say, employment agencies) to recruit new employees. Accenture estimates that social media tools like LinkedIn will soon produce up to 80% of new recruits—often letting line managers bypass HR and do their own recruiting.[63] Sites such as Glassdoor and JobBite let their members share insights into employers, including commentaries, salary reports, and CEO approval ratings. According to one report, 48% of job seekers surveyed said they've used Glassdoor during their job search.[64] This transparency prompts sensible human resource managers to redouble their efforts to ensure that their internal processes (such as performance appraisals) are civil.
- Employers use *mobile applications*, for instance, to monitor employee location and to provide digital photos at the facility clock-in location to identify workers.

- Web sites such as Knack, Gild, and True Office enable employers to inject *gaming* features into training, performance appraisal, and recruiting.
- *Cloud computing*–based tools enable employers to monitor things like a team's goal attainment and to provide real-time direct evaluative feedback. Others use cloud-based systems to track employee engagement in real time via quick surveys. SAP and Kronos offer cloud-based systems for in-taking, tracking, and scheduling freelance gig workers.[65]
- *Data analytics* basically means using statistical techniques, algorithms, and problem solving to identify relationships among data for the purpose of solving particular problems (such as how can I tell in advance which of my best employees is likely to quit?). When applied to human resource management, data analytics is called *talent analytics*.

  As one example, an employer operated for many years on the assumption that what mattered in hiring was the school the candidate attended, the grades they had, and their references. A retrospective talent analytics study showed that these traits didn't matter at all. What mattered were things like: their résumés were grammatically correct, they didn't quit school until obtaining some degree, and they were able to succeed with vague instructions.[66] At GE, an analytics tool helps management identify when key employees are likely to leave GE.[67] When executives at Shell needed employees with expertise in car maintenance, it used its analytics-based talent search algorithm to scan current Shell employees to find those with the right skills.[68]
- *Artificial intelligence* (AI) basically means using computers to do tasks in human-like ways. For example, companies use AI for: scanning and transferring customer address changes from e-mails to the company's data records ("automation"); and to "learn" and predict which job applicants will succeed, and which are most likely to leave ("analysis"). And, when you call an airline and find yourself answering questions from an automated system, they're using AI to "engage" with customers.[69] At one insurance firm in Japan, IBM's Watson artificial intelligence system enables inexperienced employees to analyze claims like experts.[70]
- *Augmented reality* (AR) transforms huge amounts of data and superimposes digital summaries and images on the physical world. For example, if your car shows the car's speed and direction directly on the windshield, you're experiencing AR. Employers use AR for human resource management too. For example, Boeing uses AR to help trainees learn the 50 steps required to assemble an aircraft wing section.[71]

LEARNING OBJECTIVE 1-3
Briefly describe six important components or pillars of human resource management today.

Important Components of Today's New Human Resource Management

A Brief History of Personnel/Human Resource Management

"Personnel management" is not new.[72] Ancient armies and organized efforts always required attracting, selecting, training, and motivating workers. But personnel tasks like these were mostly just part of every manager's job, something that lasted in most countries until the late 1800s. At that time, labor problems (having to hire and assimilate large numbers of workers, for instance) began arising in many of the post–Industrial Revolution's new factories. Soon employers were setting up "welfare offices" and "welfare secretaries" to manage activities like factory washrooms, and "safety bureaus" to oversee plant safety. By 1900, employers set up the first "hiring offices," training programs, and factory schools. Personnel management had begun.

In these early firms, personnel managers took over hiring and firing from supervisors, ran the payroll departments, and administered benefits plans. As expertise in testing emerged, personnel departments played a greater role in employee selection and training.[73] New union laws in the 1930s added "Helping the employer deal with unions" to personnel's tasks. New equal employment laws in the 1960s made employers more reliant on personnel management to avoid discrimination claims.[74] By the 1970s globalization made gaining a competitive edge through engaged employees—and therefore personnel management—increasingly important.

Today economic and demographic trends (recall the aging population, for instance) make finding, hiring, and motivating employees more challenging, while at the same time more high-tech jobs means employers must excel at managing employees' knowledge, skills, and expertise (human capital). Furthermore, as we've seen, technological trends including mobile and social media are changing how employers recruit, select, train, appraise, and motivate employees.[75] In a sense, a new human resource management is emerging, one built on six main components or pillars.

Distributed HR and the New Human Resource Management

First, thanks to technologies like social media and cloud computing, more human resource management tasks are being *redistributed* from a central HR department *to* the company's employees and line managers.[76] For example, employees at Washington-based LivingSocial use a digital tool called Rypple to comment on each other's work. LivingSocial then uses these comments as an input to its formal employee appraisals.

Some experts say that if current trends continue, many aspects of HR and talent management may become "fully embedded in how work gets done throughout an organization [distributed], thereby becoming an everyday part of doing business."[77] So, somewhat ironically, we seem to be shifting in some respects back toward the time before the first personnel departments when line managers did more of the personnel tasks. As an example, Hilton Worldwide is placing more HR activities in the hands of employees, while redirecting the savings thus attained to building up the more strategic aspects of what its human resource managers do.[78] In the following chapters, we'll use Trends Shaping HR discussions like the accompanying one to present more examples.

TRENDS SHAPING HR: *DIGITAL AND SOCIAL MEDIA*

Digital and Social Media Tools and the New Human Resource Management

Digital and social media tools are changing how people look for jobs, and how companies recruit, retain, pay, and train employees. In doing so, they've created, in a sense, a new human resource management.

For example, career sites such as Glassdoor, CareerBliss, CareerLeak, and JobBite let their members share insights into thousands of employers, including company commentaries, salary reports, and CEO approval ratings.[79] According to one report, 48% of job seekers surveyed said they've used Glassdoor during their job search, including checking before applying for employment at a company.[80] Among other things, this prompts sensible human resource managers to make sure their internal processes (such as promotion decisions, pay allocations, and performance appraisals) are fair, and that their recruitment processes are civil—for instance, by getting back to rejected job candidates.

Recruitment is another familiar way social media revolutionized human resource management. For example, managers use LinkedIn to find passive employment candidates (those not actively looking for jobs), and to check out active candidates. Another site, Gild, lets managers find skilled software engineers by searching the Web for open source code; they then evaluate the code's programmers by scanning technology forums to assess the programmers' reputations. ■

A Quick Overview

We can summarize a quick overview of our discussion to this point as follows:

- One big consequence of globalized competition, economic and demographic trends, and the shift to high-tech and service jobs is the growing need for employers to get the best from their "human capital," in other words, from their workers' knowledge, education, training, skills, and expertise.

antoniodiaz/Shutterstock

Like many employers, Hilton Worldwide is "distributing HR"—placing more HR activities in the hands of employees.

- This requires, among other things, using human resource methods to improve employee performance and engagement.
- Thanks to digital devices and social media, employers are shifting (distributing) more HR tasks from central human resource departments to employees and line managers.
- This gives many line managers more human resource management responsibilities.
- And this means that many human resource managers can refocus their efforts *from* day-to-day activities like interviewing candidates *to* broader efforts, such as formulating strategies for boosting employee performance and engagement. Figure 1-4 illustrates this.

FIGURE 1-4 **What Trends Mean for Human Resource Management**

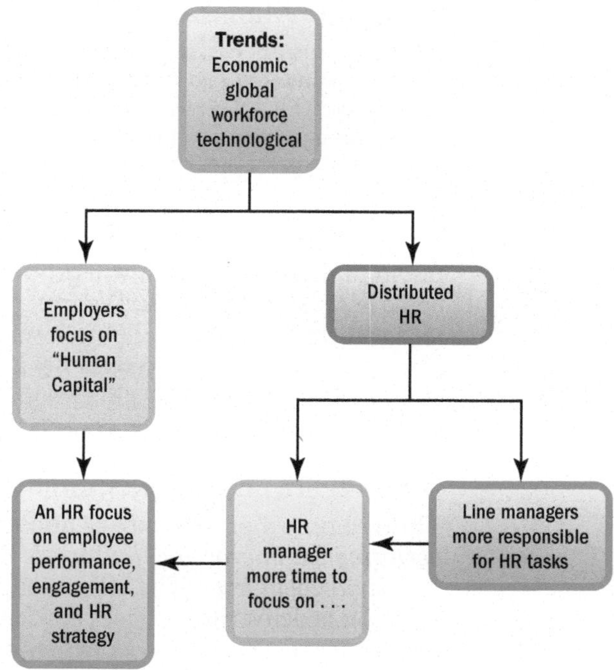

Strategic Human Resource Management

strategic human resource management
Formulating and executing human resource policies and practices that produce the employee competencies and behaviors the company needs to achieve its strategic aims.

A second pillar of HR today is that today's human resource management is more involved in longer-term, strategic "big picture" issues. We'll see in Chapter 3 (Strategy) that **strategic human resource management** means formulating and executing human resource policies and practices that produce the employee competencies and behaviors the company needs to achieve its strategic aims. We illustrate this throughout this book with Strategic Context features such as the accompanying one.

IMPROVING PERFORMANCE: *THE STRATEGIC CONTEXT*

Building L.L.Bean

Strategic human resource management means formulating and executing human resource policies and practices that produce the employee competencies and behaviors the company needs to achieve its strategic aims.

L.L.Bean illustrates how companies do this. The heart of L.L.Bean's strategy has always been offering great outdoor equipment with outstanding service and expert advice. As its company history said, "L.L.Bean, Inc., quickly established itself as a trusted source for reliable outdoor equipment and expert advice. The small company grew. Customers spread the word of L.L.Bean's quality and service."[81]

To provide such service, L.L.Bean needs special people as employees, ones whose love of the outdoors helps them deal knowledgably and supportively with the company's customers. To paraphrase its Web site, L.L.Bean is looking for special employees, "innovative professionals with a love for the outdoors, a commitment to service and a shared excitement for the future."[82]

L.L.Bean's HR policies and practices attract and develop just such employees. For one thing, the company knows just who to recruit. It wants passionate, sociable, friendly, outdoors-oriented applicants and employees.[83] To attract and cultivate these sorts of employee competencies and behaviors, the company uses multiple interviews to screen out applicants who might not fit in.[84] And L.L.Bean offers an outdoors-oriented work environment and competitive pay, and benefits that include outdoor clubs, sporting equipment to borrow, and outdoor courses and tours.[85]

To help encourage great employee service, L.L.Bean also provides a supportive environment. For example, when its Web sales for the first time exceeded phone sales several years ago, L.L.Bean closed four local call centers, but arranged for the 220 employees to work from their homes. And instead of sending jobs abroad, the company keeps its jobs close to the town where Leon Leonwood Bean started his company almost 100 years ago.[86] L.L.Bean's managers built the firm's strategy and success around courteous, expert service. They know that having the right employees is the key to its success, and that it takes the right blend of human resource practices to attract and support such employees.

MyLab Management Talk About It 2

If your professor has assigned this, go to the Assignments section of **www.pearson.com/mylab/management** to complete these discussion questions. What would you say are (1) L.L.Bean's strategic aims, (2) its required employee behaviors and skills to achieve these aims, and (3) HR policies and practices it needs to produce these necessary employee behaviors and skills?

As in the Strategic Context feature, today's employers want their HR managers to put in place practices that will produce the employee behaviors that help the company achieve its strategic aims. We use a model opening in each chapter to illustrate this idea, but in brief the model follows this three-step sequence: Set the firm's strategic aims → Pinpoint the employee behaviors and skills we need to achieve these strategic aims → Decide what HR policies and practices will enable us to produce these necessary employee behaviors and skills.

Performance and Human Resource Management

Third, employers also expect human resource management to spearhead *employee performance-improvement* efforts.[87] Here HR can apply three levers. The first is the *HR department lever*. The HR manager ensures that the human resource management function is delivering services efficiently. For example, this might include outsourcing certain activities such as benefits management, and using technology to deliver its services more cost-effectively.

The second is the *employee costs lever*. For example, the human resource manager takes a prominent role in advising top management about the company's staffing levels, and in setting and controlling the firm's compensation, incentives, and benefits policies.

The third is the *strategic results lever*. Here the HR manager puts in place the policies and practices that produce the employee competencies and skills the company needs to achieve its strategic goals. That's what was done at L.L.Bean, for instance.

HR AND PERFORMANCE MEASUREMENT Improving performance requires measuring what you are doing. For example, when IBM's former chief HR officer needed $100 million to reorganize its HR operations several years ago, he told top management, "I'm going to deliver talent to you that's skilled and on time and ready to be deployed. I will be able to measure the skills, tell you what skills we have, what [skills] we don't have [and] then show you how to fill the gaps or enhance our training."[88]

Human resource managers use performance measures (or "metrics") to validate claims like these. For example, the average number of HR employees per 100 total employees is 2.57.[89] We'll address this in Chapter 3.

HR AND EVIDENCE-BASED MANAGEMENT Basing decisions on such evidence is the heart of *evidence-based human resource management*. This is the use of data, facts, analytics, scientific rigor, critical evaluation, and critically evaluated research/case studies to support human resource management proposals, decisions, practices, and conclusions.[90] Put simply, evidence-based human resource management means using the best-available evidence in making decisions about the human resource management practices you are focusing on.[91] The evidence may come from *actual measurements* (such as, how did the trainees like this program?). It may come from *existing data* (such as, what happened to company profits after we installed this training program?). Or, it may come from published *research studies* (such as, what does the research literature conclude about the best way to ensure that trainees remember what they learn?).

HR AND ADDING VALUE The bottom line is that today's employers want their human resource managers to *add value* by boosting profits and performance. Professors Dave Ulrich and Wayne Brockbank coined the phrase "HR Value Proposition."[92] They say human resource management's aim is to add value. *Adding value* means helping the firm and its employees improve in a measurable way as a result of the human resource manager's actions. Particularly today, adding value does not just mean cutting costs. It also entails improving the company's processes, aligning HR's activities with the company's strategy, and fostering employee engagement.[93] We'll see in this book how human resource practices do this.[94] For example, we'll use, in each chapter, HR as a Profit Center discussions (as on pages 9–10), as well as special employee engagement, and human resource strategy discussions and cases to illustrate this.

Sustainability and Human Resource Management

Fourth, in a world where sea levels are rising, glaciers are crumbling, and people increasingly view financial inequity as offensive, more and more people say that businesses (and their HR teams) can't just measure "performance" in terms of maximizing profits. They argue that companies' efforts should be "*sustainable*," by which they mean judged not just on profits, but also on their environmental and social performance as well.[95] As one example, PepsiCo has a goal to deliver "Performance with Purpose"—in other words, to deliver financial performance while also achieving human sustainability, environmental sustainability, and talent sustainability. PepsiCo wants to achieve business and financial success while leaving a positive imprint on society (click www.pepsico.com, then click *Sustainability*, and then *Performance with Purpose*). As another example, the giant French materials company Saint-Gobain recently opened new offices in Pennsylvania. Its human resource management department took a lead in creating sustainable offices, for instance, in terms of indoor air purity monitors.[96] In one survey, about 80% of large surveyed companies report their sustainability performance.[97]

Employee Engagement and Human Resource Management

employment engagement
The extent to which an organization's employees are psychologically involved in, connected to, and committed to getting their jobs done.

Fifth, **employee engagement** refers to being psychologically involved in, connected to, and committed to getting one's jobs done. Engaged employees "experience a high level of connectivity with their work tasks," and therefore work hard to accomplish their task-related goals.[98] Employers expect HR to help achieve employee engagement today.

Employee engagement is vital to employers today because it drives performance. For example (as we will discuss in Chapter 3), based on one Gallup survey, business units with the highest levels of employee engagement have an 83% chance of performing above the company median; those with the lowest employee engagement have only a 17% chance.[99] A survey by consultants Watson Wyatt Worldwide concluded that companies with highly engaged employees have 26% higher revenue per employee.[100]

The problem for employers is that only about 21–30% of today's employees nationally are engaged.[101] In one survey, about 30% were engaged, 50% were not engaged, and 20% were actively disengaged (antimanagement).[102]

We will see in this book that managers improve employee engagement by taking concrete steps to do so. For example, a few years ago, Kia Motors (UK) turned its performance around, in part by boosting employee engagement.[103] As we will discuss more fully in Chapter 3, it did this with new HR programs. These included new *leadership development* programs, new *employee recognition* programs, improved *internal communications* programs, a new *employee development* program, and by modifying its *compensation and other policies*. We use special Employee Engagement Guide for Managers sections in most chapters to show how managers use human resource activities such as recruiting and selection to improve employee engagement.

Ethics and Human Resource Management

ethics
The principles of conduct governing an individual or a group; specifically, the standards you use to decide what your conduct should be.

Finally, **ethics** means the standards someone uses to decide what his or her conduct should be. Regrettably, news reports are filled with stories of otherwise competent managers who have run amok. For example, prosecutors filed criminal charges against several Iowa meatpacking plant human resource managers who allegedly violated employment law by hiring children younger than 16.[104] Behaviors like these risk torpedoing even otherwise competent managers and employers. We will see that many ethical issues—such as workplace safety—are HR-related, and that HR plays a big role in cultivating organizational ethics today.[105]

LEARNING OBJECTIVE 1-4
List at least four important human resource manager competencies.

The New Human Resource Manager

All this means that it's more complicated being a human resource manager today.[106] Tasks like formulating strategies and making data-based decisions require new competencies and skills. HR managers can't just be good at traditional personnel tasks like hiring and training. Instead, they must "speak the CFO's language" by defending human resource plans in measurable terms (such as return on investment).[107] To create strategic plans, the human resource manager must understand strategic planning, marketing, production, and finance. As companies merge and expand abroad, HR managers must formulate and implement large-scale organizational changes, drive employee engagement, and redesign organizational structures and work processes. None of this is easy.

When asked, "Why do you want to be an HR manager?" many people basically say, "Because I'm a people person." Being sociable is certainly important, but it takes much more.

What does it take to be a human resource manager today? The Society for Human Resource Management (SHRM) introduced a "competency model" (called the SHRM Body of Competency and Knowledge™); it itemizes the competencies, skills, and knowledge and expertise human resource managers need. Here are the *behaviors or competencies* (with definitions) SHRM says today's HR manager should exhibit

- ***Leadership and Navigation*** The ability to direct and contribute to initiatives and processes within the organization

- ***Ethical Practice*** The ability to integrate core values, integrity, and accountability throughout all organizational and business practices
- ***Business Acumen*** The ability to understand and apply information with which to contribute to the organization's strategic plan
- ***Relationship Management*** The ability to manage interactions to provide service and to support the organization
- ***Consultation*** The ability to provide guidance to organizational stakeholders
- ***Critical Evaluation*** The ability to interpret information with which to make business decisions and recommendations
- ***Global and Cultural Effectiveness*** The ability to value and consider the perspectives and backgrounds of all parties
- ***Communication*** The ability to effectively exchange information with stakeholders

SHRM also says human resource managers must have command of *the basic knowledge in the functional areas of HR*, such as talent acquisition. The basic knowledge of each function's principles and practices they need here include, according to SHRM

- Functional Area #1: HR Strategic Planning
- Functional Area #2: Talent Acquisition
- Functional Area #3: Employee Engagement & Retention
- Functional Area #4: Learning & Development
- Functional Area #5: Total Rewards
- Functional Area #6: Structure of the HR Function
- Functional Area #7: Organizational Effectiveness & Development
- Functional Area #8: Workforce Management
- Functional Area #9: Employee & Labor Relations
- Functional Area #10: Technology Management
- Functional Area #11: HR in the Global Context
- Functional Area #12: Diversity & Inclusion
- Functional Area #13: Risk Management
- Functional Area #14: Corporate Social Responsibility
- Functional Area #15: U.S. Employment Law & Regulations

HR Manager Certification

Many human resource managers use certification to demonstrate their mastery of contemporary human resource management knowledge and competencies. Managers have, at this writing, at least two testing processes to achieve certification.

adamgregor/123RF

HR managers can't just be good at traditional personnel tasks like hiring and training, but must "speak the CFO's language" by defending human resource plans in measurable terms.

The oldest is administered by the HR Certification Institute (HRCI), an independent certifying organization for human resource professionals (see www.hrci.org). Through testing, HRCI awards several credentials, including Professional in Human Resources (PHR), and Senior Professional in Human Resources (SPHR). Managers can review HRCI's Knowledge Base and take an online HRCI practice quiz by going to www.hrci.org and clicking on How to Get Certified and then on HRCI Practice Exams.[108]

SHRM offers its own competency and knowledge-based testing and certifications, for SHRM Certified Professionals, and SHRM Senior Certified Professionals, based on its own certification exams.[109] The exam is built around the SHRM Body of Competency and Knowledge™ model's functional knowledge, skills, and competencies.

We've summarized separately the SHRM and the HRCI knowledge bases in Appendices A and B of this book (pages 614–634). One covers SHRM's functional knowledge areas (such as Employee Relations). The other covers HRCI's seven main knowledge areas (such as Strategic Business Management and Workforce Planning and Employment. It includes about 91 specific HRCI "Knowledge of" subject areas within these seven main topic areas with which those taking the test should be familiar.

You'll find throughout this book special Knowledge Base icons starting in Chapter 2 to denote coverage of SHRM and/or HRCI knowledge topics.

HR and the Manager's Human Resource Philosophy

Technical expertise is important, but at the end of the day, people's actions are always based in part on the basic assumptions they make, and this is especially true in regard to human resource management. The basic assumptions you make about people—Can they be trusted? Do they dislike work? Why do they act as they do? How should they be treated?—together comprise your philosophy of human resource management. And every personnel decision you make—the people you hire, the training you provide, your leadership style, and the like—reflects (for better or worse) this basic philosophy.

How do you go about developing such a philosophy? To some extent, it's preordained. There's no doubt that you will bring to your job an initial philosophy based on your experiences, education, values, assumptions, and background. But your philosophy doesn't have to be set in stone. It should evolve as you accumulate knowledge and experiences. For example, after a worker uprising in China at the Hon Hai-owned Foxconn plant that assembles Apple iPhones, the personnel philosophy at the plant softened in response to the workers' (and Apple's) discontent.[110] In any case, no manager should manage others without first understanding the personnel philosophy that is driving his or her actions.

One of the things molding your own philosophy is that of your organization's top management. While it may or may not be stated, it is usually communicated by the managers' actions and permeates every level and department in the organization. For example, here is part of the personnel philosophy of the founder of the Polaroid Corp., stated many years ago:

> To give everyone working for the company a personal opportunity within the company for full exercise of his talents—to express his opinions, to share in the progress of the company as far as his capacity permits, and to earn enough money so that the need for earning more will not always be the first thing on his mind. The opportunity, in short, to make his work here a fully rewarding and important part of his or her life.[111]

Current "best companies to work for" lists include many organizations with similar philosophies. For example, the CEO of software giant SAS has said,

> We've worked hard to create a corporate culture that is based on trust between our employees and the company . . . a culture that rewards innovation, encourages employees to try new things and yet doesn't penalize them for taking chances, and a culture that cares about employees' personal and professional growth.[112]

Similarly, when Google founders Larry Page and Sergey Brin began building Google, they set out to make it a great place to work. Google doesn't just offer abundant benefits and stock options.[113] Google's team of social scientists run experiments, for instance, to determine successful middle managers' skills.[114] The aim is to keep "Googlers" happy (and Google successful and growing). We'll look closer at how managers maintain positive employee relations in Chapters 3 and 13.

MyLab Management Apply It!

How does a company actually go about putting its human resource philosophy into action? If your professor has assigned this activity, go to the Assignments section of **www.pearson.com/mylab/management** to complete the video exercise.

LEARNING OBJECTIVE 1-5
Outline the plan of this book.

The Plan of This Book

The Basic Themes and Features

In this book, we'll use four themes and features to highlight particularly important issues, and to provide continuity from chapter to chapter.

Practical Tools for Every Manager

First, human resource management is the *responsibility of every manager*—not just those in human resources. Throughout every page in this book, you'll therefore find an emphasis on practical material that you as a manager will need to perform your day-to-day management responsibilities, even if you never spend one day as an HR manager. Special *HR Tools for Line Managers and Small Businesses* discussions provide small business owners/managers in particular with techniques to better manage their small businesses. *Know Your Employment Law* discussions highlight the practical information all managers need to make better HR-related decisions at work. *Employee Engagement Guide for Managers* discussions show how managers improve employee engagement.

Second, managers use human resource management techniques to *improve performance, productivity, and profitability*. To highlight this, you will find special discussions titled:

Improving Performance: HR Tools for Line Managers and Small Businesses. These discussions highlight actual tools and practices any manager can use to improve performance at work.

Improving Performance: HR as a Profit Center. We've seen that employers want human resource management practices that add value. To illustrate this throughout the book, most chapters contains an illustrative Improving Performance: HR as a Profit Center discussion. These show actual examples of how human resource management practices add measurable value—by reducing costs or boosting revenues.

Improving Performance: HR Practices Around the Globe. These features highlight how actual companies around the globe use effective HR practices to improve their teams' and companies' performance.

Improving Performance Through HRIS. These discussions highlight how managers use human resource technology to improve performance.

Diversity Counts. These features provide insights and guidelines for managing a diverse workforce.

Third, the book emphasizes how digital and high-tech trends are shaping human resource management. You'll therefore find *Trends* discussions such as *Trends Shaping HR: Digital and Social Media* in most chapters.

Fourth, particularly with today's "distributed HR," every line and staff manager should understand how the employer's human resource management policies and practices produce the employee skills and performance the company needs *to achieve its strategic aims*. Special chapter-opener scenarios and *Improving Performance: The Strategic Context* features illustrate this in most chapters. And we'll use the Hotel Paris continuing case starting in Chapter 3 to apply that idea.

Chapter Contents Overview

Following is a brief overview of the chapters and their content.

PART 1: INTRODUCTION

Chapter 1: Introduction to Human Resource Management. The manager's human resource management jobs; crucial global and competitive trends; how managers use technology and modern HR measurement systems to improve HR management.

Chapter 2: Equal Opportunity and the Law. What you should know about equal opportunity laws; how these laws affect activities such as interviewing, selecting employees, and evaluating performance; *Know Your Employment Law* features highlight important laws in each chapter.

Chapter 3: Human Resource Management Strategy and Analysis. What is strategic planning; strategic human resource management; building high-performance HR practices; tools for evidence-based HR; employee engagement at Kia Motors.

PART 2: RECRUITMENT, PLACEMENT, AND TALENT MANAGEMENT

Chapter 4: Job Analysis and the Talent Management Process. How to analyze a job; how to determine the human resource requirements of the job, as well as its specific duties; and what is talent management.

Chapter 5: Personnel Planning and Recruiting. Human resource planning; determining what sorts of people need to be hired; recruiting them.

Chapter 6: Employee Testing and Selection. Techniques you can use to ensure that you're hiring the right people.

Chapter 7: Interviewing Candidates. How to interview candidates effectively.

PART 3: TRAINING AND DEVELOPMENT

Chapter 8: Training and Developing Employees. Providing the training and development to ensure that your employees have the knowledge and skills needed to accomplish their tasks.

Chapter 9: Performance Management and Appraisal. Techniques you can use for appraising employee performance.

Chapter 10: Managing Careers and Retention. Causes of and solutions for employee turnover, and how to help employees manage their careers.

PART 4: COMPENSATION

Chapter 11: Establishing Strategic Pay Plans. How to develop equitable pay plans for your employees.

Chapter 12: Pay for Performance and Financial Incentives. Pay-for-performance plans such as financial incentives, merit pay, and incentives that help tie performance to pay.

Chapter 13: Benefits and Services. Providing benefits that make it clear the firm views its employees as long-term investments and is concerned with their welfare.

PART 5: ENRICHMENT TOPICS IN HUMAN RESOURCE MANAGEMENT

Chapter 14: Building Positive Employee Relations. Developing employee relations programs and employee involvement strategies; ensuring ethical and fair treatment through discipline and grievance processes.

Chapter 15: Labor Relations and Collective Bargaining. How to deal with unions, including the union organizing campaign; negotiating and agreeing upon a collective bargaining agreement between unions and management; and managing the agreement via the grievance process.

Chapter 16: Safety, Health, and Risk Management. How to make the workplace safe, including the causes of accidents; laws governing your responsibilities for employee safety and health; risk management methods.

Chapter 17: Managing Global Human Resources. Special topics in managing the HR side of multinational operations.

Chapter 18: Managing Human Resources in Small and Entrepreneurial Firms. Special topics for managing human resources in smaller firms.

The Topics Are Interrelated

In practice, do not think of each of this book's topics as being unrelated to the others. Each topic interacts with and affects the others, and all should align with the employer's strategic plan. For example, hiring people who don't have the potential to learn the job will doom their performance, regardless of how much training they get. Similarly, we will see throughout this book that each human resource management function, from job analysis to recruiting, selecting, training, and rewarding employees, should aim to produce the employee behaviors and competencies that the company needs to achieve its strategic goals.

Chapter Review

Chapter Section Summaries

1-1. All managers should be able to answer, **What is human resource management, and why is it important?** Doing so helps managers avoid problems like hiring the wrong person for the job. And more important, it can help ensure that managers get results through people. Line managers' human resource duties include placing the right person on the job, and orienting and training new employees.

1-2. **The trends shaping human resource management** are influencing what human resource managers do and how they do it. Globalization means more competition, and more competition means more pressure to lower costs and to make employees more productive and quality conscious. Technology is requiring more employees to be technologically well informed and pressuring employers to improve their human resource processes by applying new distributive technological tools. There is more emphasis on "knowledge work" and therefore on building "human capital," the knowledge, education, training, skills, and expertise of a firm's employees. Workforce and demographic changes mean that the workforce is becoming older and more diverse.

1-3. In terms of the **components or pillars of human resource management today,** employers expect their human resource management teams to focus more on big-picture issues, including instituting human resource policies and practices that support the companies' strategic objectives, and to foster high performance through engaged employees.

1-4. To do so, **the human resource managers** need **new competencies.** They should be able to apply evidence-based human resource management, which means the use of data, facts, analytics, scientific rigor, critical evaluation, and critically evaluated research/case studies to support human resource management proposals, decisions, practices, and conclusions.

1-5. In understanding the overall **plan of this book,** keep several important themes in mind: that human resource management is the responsibility of every manager, that the workforce is increasingly diverse, that employers and their human resource managers face the need to manage in challenging economic times, and that human resource managers must be able to defend their plans and contributions in measurable terms—to use evidence-based management—to show they've added value.

Discussion Questions

1-1. Explain what HR management is and how it relates to the management process.

1-2. Give examples of how HR management concepts and techniques can be of use to all managers.

1-3. Illustrate the HR management responsibilities of line and staff managers.

1-4. Compare the authority of line and staff managers. Give examples of each.

Individual and Group Activities

1-5. Working individually or in groups, develop outlines showing how trends like workforce diversity, technological innovation, globalization, and changes in the nature of work have affected the college or university you are attending now. Present in class.

1-6. Working individually or in groups, contact the HR manager of a local bank. Ask the HR manager how he or she is working as a strategic partner to manage human resources, given the bank's strategic goals and objectives. Back in class, discuss the responses of the different HR managers.

1-7. Working individually or in groups, interview an HR manager. Based on that interview, write a short presentation regarding HR's role today in building competitive organizations.

1-8. Working individually or in groups, bring several business publications such as *Bloomberg Businessweek* and *The Wall Street Journal* to class, or access them in class via the Web. Based on their contents, compile a list titled "What HR Managers and Departments Do Today."

1-9. Based on your personal experiences, list 10 examples showing how you used (or could have used) human resource management techniques at work or school.

1-10. Laurie Siegel, former senior vice president of human resources for Tyco International, took over her job just after numerous charges forced the company's previous board of directors and top executives to leave the firm. Hired by new CEO Edward Breen, Siegel had to tackle numerous difficult problems starting the moment she assumed office. For example, she had to help hire a new management team. She had to do something about what the outside world viewed as a culture of questionable ethics at her company. And she had to do something about the company's top-management compensation plan, which many felt contributed to the allegations by some that some former company officers had used the company as a sort of private ATM.

Siegel came to Tyco after a very impressive career. For example, she had been head of executive compensation at Allied Signal, and was a graduate of the Harvard Business School. But, as strong as her background was, she obviously had her work cut out for her when she took the senior vice president of HR position at Tyco.

Working individually or in groups, conduct an Internet search and/or library research to answer the following questions: What human resource management–related steps did Siegel take to help get Tyco back on the right track? Do you think she took the appropriate steps? Why or why not? What, if anything, do you suggest she do now?

1-11. Appendices A and B at the end of this book (pages 614–634) list the knowledge someone studying for the HRCI (Appendix A) or SHRM (Appendix B) certification exam needs to have in each area of human resource management (such as in Strategic Management and Workforce Planning). In groups of several students, do four things: (1) review Appendix A and/or Appendix B; (2) identify the material in this chapter that relates to the Appendix A and/or Appendix B required knowledge lists; (3) write four multiple-choice exam questions on this material that you believe would be suitable for inclusion in the HRCI exam and/or the SHRM exam; and (4) if time permits, have someone from your team post your team's questions in front of the class, so that students in all teams can answer the exam questions created by the other teams.

KNOWLEDGE BASE

Experiential Exercise

HR and "The Profit"

Written and copyrighted by Gary Dessler, PhD.

Purpose: The purpose of this exercise is to provide practice in identifying and applying the basic concepts of human resource management by illustrating how managers use these techniques in their day-to-day jobs.

Required Understanding: Be thoroughly familiar with the material in this chapter, and with at least one or two episodes of CNBC's *The Profit* with Marcus Lemonis, www.tv.com/shows/the-profit/watch/. (Access a library of past episodes at URLs such as www.cnbc.com/live-tv/the-profit)

How to Set Up the Exercise/Instructions:

- Divide the class into teams of several students.
- Read this: As you may know by watching billionaire Marcus Lemonis as he works with actual small businesses in which he's taken an ownership share, human resource management often plays an important role in what he and the business owners and managers need to do to be successful. For example, at Grafton Furniture, a lack of clarity about who does what (a lack of up-to-date job descriptions) leads to inadequate supervision of some ongoing orders and to lower profit margins. Questions also arise at Grafton about, for instance, the effectiveness of the training that some managers (including the owner's son) have received.
- Watch several of these shows (or reruns of the shows), and then meet with your team and answer the following questions:

1-12. What specific HR functions (recruiting, interviewing, training, and so on) can you identify Mr. Lemonis addressing on this show? Make sure to give specific examples based on the show.

1-13. What specific HR functions can you identify as being problematical in this company? Again, please give specific answers.

1-14. In terms of HR functions (such as recruiting, selection, interviewing, compensating, appraising, and so on) what exactly would you recommend doing to improve this company's performance?

1-15. Present your team's conclusions to the class.

Application Case

Jack Nelson's Problem[115]

Written and copyrighted by Gary Dessler, PhD.

As a new member of the board of directors for a local bank, Jack Nelson was being introduced to all the employees in the home office. When he was introduced to Ruth Johnson, he was curious about her work and asked her what the machine she was using did. Johnson replied that she really did not know what the machine was called or what it did. She explained that she had only been working there for 2 months. However, she did know precisely how to operate the machine. According to her supervisor, she was an excellent employee.

At one of the branch offices, the supervisor in charge spoke to Nelson confidentially, telling him that "something was wrong," but she didn't know what. For one thing, she explained, employee turnover was too high, and no sooner had one employee been put on the job than another one resigned. With customers to see and loans to be made, she continued, she had little time to work with the new employees as they came and went.

All branch supervisors hired their own employees without communication with the home office or other branches. When an opening developed, the supervisor tried to find a suitable employee to replace the worker who had quit.

After touring the 22 branches and finding similar problems in many of them, Nelson wondered what the home office should do or what action he should take. The banking firm generally was regarded as being a well-run institution that had grown from 27 to 191 employees during the past 8 years. The more he thought about the matter, the more puzzled Nelson became. He couldn't quite put his finger on the problem, and he didn't know whether to report his findings to the president.

Questions

1-16. What do you think is causing some of the problems in the bank's home office and branches?

1-17. Do you think setting up an HR unit in the main office would help?

1-18. What specific functions should an HR unit carry out? What HR functions would then be carried out by supervisors and other line managers? What role should the Internet play in the new HR organization?

CHAPTER 1

Continuing Case

Carter Cleaning Company

Written and copyrighted by Gary Dessler, PhD.

Introduction

A main theme of this book is that human resource management activities like recruiting, selecting, training, and rewarding employees are not just the job of a central HR group but rather a job in which every manager must engage. Perhaps nowhere is this more apparent than in the typical small service business. Here the owner/manager usually has no HR staff to rely on. However, the success of his or her enterprise (not to mention his or her family's peace of mind) often depends largely on the effectiveness through which workers are recruited, hired, trained, evaluated, and rewarded. Therefore, to help illustrate and emphasize the front-line manager's HR role, throughout this book we will use a continuing case based on an actual small business in the southeastern United States. Each chapter's segment of the case will illustrate how the case's main player—owner/manager Jennifer Carter—confronts and solves personnel problems each day at work by applying the concepts and techniques of that particular chapter. Here is background information that you will need to answer questions that arise in subsequent chapters. (We also present a second, unrelated "application case" case incident in each chapter.)

Carter Cleaning Centers

Jennifer Carter graduated from State University in June 2011 and, after considering several job offers, decided to do what she always planned to do—go into business with her father, Jack Carter.

Jack Carter opened his first laundromat in 1991 and his second in 2001. The main attraction of these coin laundry businesses for him was that they were capital—rather than labor—intensive. Thus, once the investment in machinery was made, the stores could be run with just one unskilled attendant and none of the labor problems one normally expects from being in the retail service business.

The attractiveness of operating with virtually no skilled labor notwithstanding, Jack had decided by 2007 to expand the services in each of his stores to include the dry cleaning and pressing of clothes. He embarked, in other words, on a strategy of "related diversification" by adding new services that were related to and consistent with his existing coin laundry activities. He added these for several reasons. He wanted to better utilize the unused space in the rather large stores he currently had under lease. Furthermore, he was, as he put it, "tired of sending out the dry cleaning and pressing work that came in from our coin laundry clients to a dry cleaner 5 miles away, who then took most of what should have been our profits." To reflect the new, expanded line of services, he renamed each of his two stores Carter Cleaning Centers and was sufficiently satisfied with their performance to open four more of the same type of stores over the next 5 years. Each store had its own on-site manager and, on average, about seven employees and annual revenues of about $550,000. It was this six-store chain that Jennifer joined after graduating.

Her understanding with her father was that she would serve as a troubleshooter/consultant to the elder Carter with the aim of both learning the business and bringing to it modern management concepts and techniques for solving the business's problems and facilitating its growth.

Questions

1-19. Make a list of five specific HR problems you think Carter Cleaning will have to grapple with.

1-20. What would you do first if you were Jennifer?

Writing Assignments

1-21. From a practical point of view, why is it important for all managers and future managers to have a good command of human resource management concepts and techniques?

1-22. Think of some companies that you are familiar with or that you've read about where you think the human resource managers have been successful in "adding value." What do the HR managers do to lead you to your conclusion?

MyLab Management Try It!

How would you apply the concepts and skills you learned in this chapter? If your professor has assigned this activity, go to the Assignments section of **www.pearson.com/mylab/management** to complete the simulation.

PERSONAL INVENTORY ASSESSMENTS

Go to **www.pearson.com/mylab/management** to complete the Personal Inventory Assessment related to this chapter.

Key Terms

organization, 3
manager, 3
managing, 3
management process, 3
human resource management (HRM), 3
authority, 5
line authority, 5
staff authority, 5
line manager, 5
staff manager, 5
strategic human resource management, 16
employment engagement, 18
ethics, 18

Endnotes

1. https://www.upwork.com/, accessed March 9, 2018.
2. See, as just one example, Seongmin Ryu and Sunghoon Kim, "First-Line Managers' Involvement and HR Effectiveness: The Case of South Korea," *Human Resource Management* 52, no. 6 (November–December 2013), pp. 947–966.
3. Fred K. Foulkes, "The Expanding Role of the Personnel Function," *Harvard Business Review,* March–April 1975. See also www.bls.gov/oco/ocos021.htm, accessed October 3, 2011.
4. Steve Bates, "No Experience Necessary? Many Companies Are Putting Non-HR Executives in Charge of HR with Mixed Results," *HR Magazine* 46, no. 11 (November 2001), pp. 34–941. See also Adrienne Fox, "Do Assignments Outside HR Pay Off?" *HR Magazine,* November 2011, p. 32. One study concluded that the best path to the CEO's office involves getting experience in as many of the business's functions as possible. Neil Irwin, "A Winding Path to the Top," *The New York Times*, September 11, 2016, pp. B1, 4.
5. "Why Chief Human Resources Officers Make Great CEOs," *Harvard Business Review*, December 2014, p. 31. In general, CEOs of the largest companies tend to work their way up within the same industry and company, and to gain experience in a variety of business functions while building their general management skills. See Michael Koch et al., "The New Way to the Top: Career Patterns of *Fortune* 100 CEOS," *Human Resource Management* 56, no. 2 (March–April 2017), pp. 367–285.
6. "A Profile of Human Resource Executives," *BNA Bulletin to Management,* June 21, 2001, p. S5; "Today's HR Executives: How Career Paths Have Changed—and Stayed the Same," http://knowledge.wharton.upenn.edu/article/todays-hr-executives-how-career-paths-have-changed-and-stayed-the-same, accessed July 25, 2014; https://www.shrm.org/learningandcareer/career/pages/accelerate-your-career.aspx, accessed March 9, 2018.
7. https://www.shrm.org/learningandcareer/career/pages/accelerate-your-career.aspx, accessed March 9, 2018.
8. Historically, most U.S. employees worked for employers with fewer than 100 workers. However around 2005 that changed. Today more employees work for larger employers (2,500 or more) then for small ones. Theo Francis, "Why You Probably Work for a Giant Company," *The Wall Street Journal*, April 7, 2017, p. A-10.
9. See "Small Business: A Report of the President" (1998), www.SBA.gov/ADV/stats, accessed March 9, 2006; and www.census.gov/econ/smallbus.html, accessed May 13, 2015.
10. See, for example, Susan Mayson and Rowena Barrett, "The 'Science' and 'Practice' of HR in Small Firms," *Human Resource Management Review* 16 (2006), pp. 447–455; and "How Organizational Staff Size Influences HR Metrics," Society for Human Resource Management, 2015, p. 2.
11. "2014 HR Service Delivery and Technology Survey," www.towerswatson.com, accessed March 31, 2018.
12. For another perspective on this see, for example, Chris Brewster, Michael Brooks, and Paul Gollan, "The Institutional Antecedents of the Assignment of HRM Responsibilities to Line Managers," *Human Resource Management*, July–August 2015, 54, no. 4, pp. 57–597.
13. Some human resource management departments suffer from a dubious image. Employees often view them as somewhere to turn to for problems like sexual harassment, but many (or most) such departments view their first responsibility as protecting the employer. Erika Fry and Claire Zillman, "HR Is Not Your Friend," *Fortune*, March 1, 2018, pp. 99–106.
14. Some firms have worked on eliminating their traditional human resource departments, with generally mixed results. See, for example, Todd Henneman, "Is HR at Its Breaking Point?" *Workforce Management,* March 22, 2013, pp. 29–33.
15. See "2014 HR Service Delivery and Technology Survey," Towers Watson, www.towerswatson.com, accessed March 31, 2018.
16. "2016 Industry Trends in Human Resources Technology and Services Delivery Survey," http://www.isg-one.com/docs/default-source/default-document-library/hr-tech-report.pdf?sfvrsn=0, accessed March 31, 2018.
17. "Technology to Play Role in Updating HR Delivery Services, Report Finds," *Bloomberg BNA Bulletin to Management,* September 4, 2012, p. 281. See also Meg McSherry Breslin, "Strategic Move? Report Examines Future of HR," *Workforce Management,* November 2012, p. 14.
18. The HR consulting company Mercer found that companies whose HR departments used centers of expertise, HR business partners, and HR shared services performed better in terms of metrics such as attracting the necessary talent and innovation. "Only One in Three Organizations Deploy the Key Components of a High-Performing HR Service Delivery Model, Find Mercer," May 31, 2017, www.Mercer.com/newsroom/2017.
19. www.bls.gov/news.release/ecopro.t01.htm, accessed July 29, 2012.
20. "Talent Management Leads in Top HR Concerns," *Compensation & Benefits Review,* May/June 2007, p. 12; www.bls.gov/news.release/ecopro.t01.htm, accessed May 12, 2015.
21. https://insight.kellogg.northwestern.edu/article/how-to-revamp-the-visa-program-for-highly-skilled-workers, accessed April 16, 2017.
22. http://www.latimes.com/business/technology/la-fi-tn-silicon-valley-h1b-changes-20170404-story.html accessed April 16, 2017.
23. https://www.bls.gov/emp/ep_table_201.htm, accessed April 16, 2017.
24. Accenture, "Top Trends That Will Reshape the Future of HR: The Future of HR," www.accenture.com/us-en/Pages/insight-future-of-HR.aspx, accessed March 6, 2015.

25. Erika Fry, "Start Up: You," *Fortune* 171, no. 1 (January 1, 2015), pp. 84–87.
26. Farhad Manjoo, "Uber's Business Model Could Change Your Work," *The New York Times,* January 29, 2015, pp. B1, B8.
27. Genevieve Douglas, "What Gigs Offer Workers That You Don't: Entrepreneurship Maybe," *Bloomberg BNA Bulletin to Management*, August 29, 2017.
28. https://www.upwork.com/, accessed March 9, 2018.
29. https://www.upwork.com/, accessed March 9, 2018.
30. Lauren Weber and Rachel Silverman, "On-Demand Workers: 'We Are Not Robots,'" *The Wall Street Journal,* January 28, 2015, pp. B1, B7.
31. Genevieve Douglas, "HR Must Focus on Building Organizations for the Future," *Bloomberg BNA Bulletin to Management*, March 21, 2017.
32. Lauren Weber, "The End of Employees," *The Wall Street Journal*, February 3, 2017, pp. A1, A10.
33. See, for example, Genevieve Douglas, "Freelancers Can Solve Hiring Obstacles but Bring Risks," *Bloomberg BNA Bulletin to Management*, March 14, 2017.
34. Manjoo, "Uber's Business Model Could Change Your Work," p. B8.
35. Russell Crook et al., "Does Human Capital Matter? A Meta-Analysis of the Relationship between Human Capital and Firm Performance," *Journal of Applied Psychology* 96, no. 3 (2011), pp. 443–456.
36. This idea was probably first expounded years ago by Professor Peter Drucker; see Peter Drucker, "The Coming of the New Organization," *Harvard Business Review,* January–February 1988, p. 47.
37. Genevieve Douglas, "New Technology Is Worthless When Workers Lack the Skills to Use It," *Bloomberg BNA, Bulletin to Management*, February 6, 2018.
38. "Human Resources Wharton," www.knowledge.wharton.upe .edu, accessed January 8, 2006.
39. See, for example, Anthea Zacharatos et al., "High-Performance Work Systems and Occupational Safety," *Journal of Applied Psychology* 90, no. 1 (2005), pp. 77–93. See also Jennifer Schramm, "Effective HR Practices Drive Profit," *HR Magazine,* November 2012, p. 88.
40. www.census.gov/foreign-trade/statistics/historical/gands.pdf, accessed March 9, 2018.
41. Rich Miller et al., "Backlash to World Economic Order Clouds Outlook and IMF Talks," https://www.technocracy.news/backlash-world-economic-order-clouds-outlook-imf-talks/, accessed August 15, 2018.
42. "Study Predicts 4.1 Million Service Jobs Offshored by 2008," *BNA Bulletin to Management,* August 2, 2005, p. 247; and Patrick Thibodeau, "Offshoring Shrinks Number of IT Jobs, Study Says," *Computerworld,* March 21, 2012, www.computerworld .com/s/article/9225376/Offshoring_shrinks_number_of_IT_jobs_study_says_, accessed October 5, 2012.
43. Due to rising costs abroad and customer pushback, many firms today are bringing jobs back. See, for example, "Here, There and Everywhere," *The Economist,* January 19, 2013, pp. 1–20.
44. For a snapshot of the economy at that time, see www.bls.gov/opub/ted/2006/may/wk2/art01 .htm, accessed April 18, 2009.
45. www.census.gov/foreign-trade/statistics/historical/gands.pdf, accessed September 9, 2018.
46. Heather Long, "U.S. Economy to Grow 2.7 Percent in 2018, Boosted by Trump Tax Overhaul," *The Washington Post*, January 22, 2018, https://www.washingtonpost .com/news/wonk/wp/2018/01/22/u-s-economy-to-grow-nearly-3-percent-in-2018-because-of-trump-tax-cuts-imf-says/?utm_term=.b1fe2283f9fd, accessed March 9, 2018.
47. Peter Coy, "This Economist Foresees 15 Years of Labor Shortages," *Bloomberg Businessweek,* March 21, 2014, www.businessweek.com/printer/articles/191219-this-economist-foresees-15-years-of-labor-shortages, accessed April 30, 2014.
48. See, for example, Kevin Hamlin and Dexter Roberts, "The Asian Jobs Ladder Is Broken," *Bloomberg Businessweek*, June 26, 2017, pp. 58–59; Max Chafkin and Josh Eidelson, "Changing Lanes," *Bloomberg BusinessWeek*, June 28, 2017, pp. 60–69; and Mark Whitehouse and Dorothy Gambrell, "How Screwed Is Your Job?," *Bloomberg Businessweek*, June 26, 2017, pp. 50–53.
49. Bureau of Labor Statistics, Employment Projections: 2016–26 Summary, https://www.bls.gov/news.release/ecopro.nr0.htm, accessed March 9, 2018; www.cbo.gov/publication/54318, accessed September 9, 2018.
50. See, for example, "The Weight of Expectations," *The Economist*, December 16, 2017, pp. 63–65.
51. Bureau of Labor Statistics, Employment Projections: 2016–26 Summary, https://www .bls.gov/news.release/ecopro .nr0.htm, accessed March 9, 2018.
52. Shelly Hagan, "Prime-Age Men May Never Return to U.S. Workforce, Fed Paper Says," *Bloomberg BNA, Bulletin to Management*, February 27, 2018; Henry Curr, "Wanted: Jobs for the Boys," *The Economist*, www .theworldin.com/article/14413/edition2018wanted-jobs--boys, accessed March 8, 2018.
53. "Talent Management Leads in Top HR Concerns," *Compensation & Benefits Review,* May/June 2007, p. 12; "Talent Management, ACA among Top Issues Facing HR in 2013," *Bloomberg BNA Bulletin to Management,* January 15, 2013, p. 22. See also Douglas Ready, Linda Hill, and Robert Thomas, "Building a Game-Changing Talent Strategy," *Harvard Business Review,* January–February 2014, pp. 63–68.
54. Darrell West, "The Paradox of Worker Shortages at a Time of High National Unemployment," *Brookings,* April 10, 2013, www.brookings .edu/research/papers/2013/04/11-worker-shortage-immigration-west, accessed April 30, 2014.
55. Richard Vedder, Christopher Denhart, and Jonathan Robe, "Why Are Recent College Graduates Underemployed?" *The Center for College Affordability,* http://centerforcollegeaffordability .org/uploads/Underemployed%20 Report%202.pdf, accessed April 30, 2014; and https://www .bls.gov/opub/ted/2017/37-percent-of-may-2016-employment-in-occupations-typically-requiring-postsecondary-education.htm, accessed March 31, 2018.
56. Bureau of Labor Statistics, https://www.bls.gov/opub/ted/2017/37-percent-of-may-2016-employment-in-occupations-typically-requiring-postsecondary-education.htm, accessed March 31, 2018.
57. Ibid.
58. "Making It in America," *The Economist*, October 14, 2017, pp. 57–58.
59. See, for example, David Ferris, "X-Factor for Factories Is Factoring-In Recruiting," *Workforce Management,* December 2012, p. 8.
60. See "A Third Industrial Revolution," *The Economist,* April 21, 2012, pp. 1–20; and Jeffrey Immelt, "The CEO of General Electric on Sparking an American Manufacturing Renewal," *Harvard Business Review,* March 2012, pp. 43–46.
61. Timothy Appel, "Better Off a Blue-Collar," *The Wall Street Journal,* July 1, 2003, p. B1; Adrienne Fox, "At Work in 2020," *HR Magazine,* January 2010, pp. 18–23; Matthew Patane, "Alcoa Investing $190 Million into Davenport Plant," https://www.desmoinesregister .com/story/money/business/development/2014/11/03/alcoa-davenport-works-expansion/18409019/, accessed March 31, 2018.
62. Martin Berman-Gorvine, "HR Not Immune from Changes Automation Will Bring," *Bloomberg BNA Bulletin to Management*, March 14, 2017.
63. Accenture, "Top Trends That Will Reshape the Future of HR."
64. Ibid; Roy Maurer, "Looking through the Glassdoor," *HR Magazine* 62, no. 1 (February 2017), pp. 24–25.
65. Josh Bersin, "Transformative Tech: A Disruptive Year Ahead," *HR Magazine*, pp. 29–37, February 2017.
66. Josh Bersin, "Big Data in Human Resources: Talent Analytics (People Analytics) Comes of Age," www.forbes .com/sites/joshbersin/2013/02/17/bigdata-in-human-resources-talent-analytics-comes-of-age, accessed March 29, 2015.
67. Steven Prokesch, "Reinventing Talent management: How GE Uses Analytics to Guide a More Digital, Far-Flung Workforce," *Harvard Business Review*, September–October 2017, pp. 54–55.
68. Sam Schechner, "Algorithms Move into Management," *The Wall Street Journal,* December 11, 2017, pp. B1, B4.
69. Thomas Davenport and Rajiv Ronanki, "Artificial Intelligence for the Real World," *Harvard Business Review*, January–February 2018, pp. 108–116.
70. Ibid.
71. Michael Porter and James Heppelmann, "Why Every Organization Needs an Augmented Reality Strategy," *Harvard Business Review*, November–December 2017, pp. 46–57.
72. This is based on Bruce Kaufman, "The Historical Development of American HRM Broadly Viewed," *Human Resource Management Review* 24 (2014), pp. 196–218. See also D. Ulrich and J. H. Dulebohn,

"Are We There Yet? What's Next for HR?" *Human Resource Management Review* 25, no. 2 (June 2015), pp. 188–204; and D. J. Cohen, "HR Past, Present and Future: A Call for Consistent Practices and a Focus on Competencies," *Human Resource Management Review* 25, no. 2 (June 2015), pp. 205–215.

73. For a book describing the history of human resource management, see, for example, SHRM, *A History of Human Resources*, www.shrmstore .shrm.org/a-history-of-human- -resources.html, accessed October 4, 2012.
74. "Human Capital Critical to Success," *Management Review*, November 1998, p. 9. See also "HR 2018: Top Predictions," *Workforce Management* 87, no. 20 (December 15, 2008), pp. 20–21; and Edward Lawler III, "Celebrating 50 Years: HR: Time for a Reset?" *Human Resource Management* 50, no. 2 (March–April 2011), pp. 171–173.
75. See, for example, D. L. Stone, D. I. Deadrick, J. M. Lukaszewski, and R. Johnson, "The Influence of Technology on the Future of Human Resource Management," *Human Resource Management Review* 25, no. 2 (June 2015), pp. 216–231.
76. Anthony Abbatiello, "The Digital Override." *Workforce*, May 2014, pp. 36–39. See also Laime Vaitkus, "Technology Will Disrupt Jobs and Hiring but Reduce Bias," *Bloomberg BNA Bulletin to Management*, January 31, 2017.
77. Tim Good, Catherine Farley, Himanshu Tambe, and Susan Cantrell, "Trends Reshaping the Future of HR: Digital Radically Disrupts HR," Accenture 2015.
78. Ibid. Some companies today think they're better off without an HR department, but the results are decidedly mixed. Lauren Weber and Rachel Feintzeig, "Is It a Dream or a Drag? Companies without HR," *The Wall Street Journal*, April 9, 2014, pp. B1, B7.
79. This is based on "The Future of Business: Human Resources, How HR Leaders Are Reinventing Their Roles in Transforming Business," *The Economist Intelligence Unit*, 2014.
80. Ibid; Roy Maurer, "Looking through the Glassdoor," *HR Magazine* 62, no. 1 (February 2017), pp. 24–25.
81. Based on "Our Story," L.L.Bean, pp. 1–19, from www.llbean.com/ customerService/aboutLLBean/ images/110408_About-LLB .pdf; www.llbean.com/; Michael Arndt, "L.L.Bean Follows Its Shoppers to the Web," *Business Week*, March 1, 2010; http://www.llbean.com/llb/ shop/515428. www.llbean.com/ customerService/aboutLLBean/ images/110408_About-LLB. pdf, accessed June 1, 2011; www.llbean.com/llb/ shop/515428, accessed May 14, 2015.
82. http://llbeancareers.com/- culture.htm, accessed February 28, 2010; www .llbean.com/llb/shop/515428, accessed May 14, 2015; https:// llbeancareers.com/index.htm, accessed March 9, 2018; https:// llbeancareers.com/culture.htm, accessed March 9, 2018.
83. http://llbeancareers.com/- culture.htm, accessed February 28, 2010; www.llbean .com/llb/shop/515428, accessed May 14, 2015.
84. https://llbeancareers.com/ hiring_process.htm, accessed March 9, 2018.
85. https://www.llbean.com/llb/ shop/515428?nav=ftlink, accessed March 9, 2018
86. Arndt, "L.L.Bean Follows Its Shoppers to the Web."
87. See, for example, Rebecca Kehoe and Christopher Collins, "Human Resource Management and Unit Performance in Knowledge Intensive Work," *Journal of Applied Psychology* 102, no. 8 (2017), pp. 1222–1236. There seems to be room for improvement. One study found that only 5% of HR heads rated their employers' programs as "excellent" and 34% as "good." "Less Than Half of HR Leaders Rate Programs, Talent Excellent or Good, Deloitte Reports," *Bloomberg BNA Bulletin to Management*, March 17, 2015, p. 83.
88. Robert Grossman, "IBM's HR Takes a Risk," *HR Magazine*, April 1, 2007.
89. https://www.shrm.org/ ResourcesAndTools/business- solutions/Documents/ Organizational%20Staff%20Size. pdf, accessed March 31, 2018.
90. See, for example, www .personneltoday.com/blogs/ hcglobal-human-capital- management/2009/02/theres- no-such-thing-as-eviden.html, accessed April 18, 2009.
91. The evidence-based movement began in medicine. In 1996, in an editorial published by the *British Medical Journal*, David Sackett, MD, defined *evidence-based medicine* as "use of the best-available evidence in making decisions about patient care" and urged his colleagues to adopt its tenets. "Evidence-Based Training™: Turning Research into Results for Pharmaceutical Sales Training," an AXIOM White Paper © 2006 AXIOM Professional Health Learning LLC. All rights reserved.
92. Susan Wells, "From HR to the Top," *HR Magazine*, June 2003, p. 49. See also "HR Will Have More Opportunities to Demonstrate Value in 2012," *Bloomberg BNA Bulletin to Management*, January 17, 2012, p. 22.
93. "2016 Industry Trends in Human Resources Management Technology and Delivery," http://www.isg-one.com/ docs/default-source/default- document-library/hr-tech- report.pdf?sfvrsn=0, accessed March 31, 2018.
94. As an example, see also Rebecca Kehoe and Christopher Collins, "Human Resource Management and Unit Performance in Knowledge Intensive Work," *Journal of Applied Psychology* 102, no. 8 (August, 2017), pp. 1222–1236.
95. Sully Taylor, Joyce Osland, and Caroline Egri, "Guest Editors' Introduction: Introduction to HRM's Role in Sustainability: Systems, Strategies, and Practices," *Human Resource Management* 51, no. 6 (November–December 2012), p. 789.
96. Melanie Powers, "In the Green," *HR Magazine*, October 2017, pp. 26–34.
97. Cathy Dubois and David Dubois, "Strategic HRM as Social Design for Environmental Sustainability Organization," *Human Resource Management* 51, no. 6 (November–December 2012), p. 799.
98. Michael Christian, Adela Garza, and Jerel Slaughter, "Work Engagement: A Quantitative Review and Test of Its Relations with Task and Contextual Performance," *Personnel Psychology* 60, no. 4 (2011), pp. 89–136.
99. Adrienne Fox, "Raising Engagement," *HR Magazine*, May 2010, pp. 35–40.
100. Except as noted, this is based on Kathryn Tyler, "Prepare for Impact," *HR Magazine* 56, no. 3 (March 2011), pp. 53–56.
101. www.gallup.com/ strategicconsulting/163007/ state-american-workplace.aspx; Bruce Louis Rich et al., "Job Engagement: Antecedents and Effects on Job Performance," *Academy of Management Journal* 53, no. 3 (2010), pp. 617–635; "Special Report: Employee Engagement—Losing Lifeblood," *Workforce Management*, July 2011, pp. 24–27.
102. "Five Ways to Improve Employee Engagement Now," *Gallup Business Journal*. Gallup.com, accessed April 7, 2014.
103. Ibid. Some say engagement can backfire. To get their jobs done, some overloaded employees, at the pain of getting penalized, work long days and weekends and stay tethered to their jobs round-the-clock through their smart phones. One study found that workers react to situations like these in one of three ways. Some employees are accepting and do what the employer demands of them. Some are "passing" and appeared to be doing what they're supposed to do but are actually finding ways to reduce their loads by getting around the system. Other simply "reveal" that they have other commitments, and tell their employers that they're unwilling to abandon those commitments by working around the clock. Erin Reid and Lakshmi Ramarajan, "Managing the High-Intensity Workplace," *Harvard Business Review*, June 2016, pp. 85–90.
104. "Meatpacking Case Highlights HR's Liability," *Workforce Management*, September 20, 2008, p. 6.
105. Kevin Wooten, "Ethical Dilemmas in Human Resource Management," *Human Resource Management Review* 11 (2001), p. 161. See also Ann Pomeroy, "The Ethics Squeeze," *HR Magazine* 51, no. 3 (March 2006), pp. 48–55.
106. Richard Vosburgh, "The Evolution of HR: Developing HR as an Internal Consulting Organization," *Human Resource Planning* 30, no. 3 (September 2007), pp. 11–24; and the RBL Group, "2012 Human Resource Competency Study," www.rbl.net/index.php/ hrcs/index/overview, accessed October 4, 2012.
107. Dave Ulrich and Wayne Brockbank, *The HR Value Proposition* (Boston: Harvard Business School Publishing, 2005).
108. SHRM and HRCI provide sample practice questions. See, for example, https://www .hrci.org/how-to-get-certified/ preparation-overview/hrci- practice-exams, accessed April 16, 2017.
109. https://www.shrm.org/ certification/about/ aboutshrmcertification/ pages/shrm-cp.aspx, accessed April 16, 2017.
110. See, for example, "When the Jobs Inspector Calls," *The Economist*,

March 31, 2012, p. 73; and Paul Mozur, "Foxconn Workers: Keep Our Overtime," *The Wall Street Journal,* December 18, 2012, pp. B1–B2.
111. Fred Foulkes and Henry Morgan, "Organizing and Staffing the Personnel Function," *Harvard Business Review,* May–June 1977.
112. "Working at SAS: An Ideal Environment for New Ideas," SAS Web site, April 20, 2012. Copyright © 2011 by SAS Institute, Inc. Reprinted with permission. All rights reserved. For more on how SAS creates its outstanding work environment, see https://www.sas.com/en_us/careers/life-at-sas.html, accessed March 2018.
113. Farhad Manjoo, "The Happiness Machine," January 21, 2013, www.slate.com, accessed April 6, 2014.
114. Ibid.
115. From *Supervision in Action: The Art of Managing Others, 4th edition*, Pearson Education, Inc., Upper Saddle River, New Jersey.

Tony Tallec/Alamy Stock Photo

Equal Opportunity and the Law

LEARNING OBJECTIVES

When you finish studying this chapter, you should be able to:

2-1 **List** the basic features of Title VII of the 1964 Civil Rights Act and at least five other early equal employment laws.

2-2 **List** the basic features of at least five post-1990 employment laws, and explain with examples how to avoid accusations of sexual harassment at work.

2-3 **Illustrate** two defenses you can use in the event of discriminatory practice allegations, and list specific discriminatory personnel management practices in recruitment, selection, promotion, transfer, layoffs, and benefits.

2-4 **List** the steps in the EEOC enforcement process.

2-5 **Give examples** of attitudes that undermine diversity efforts, and explain how you would create a diversity management program.

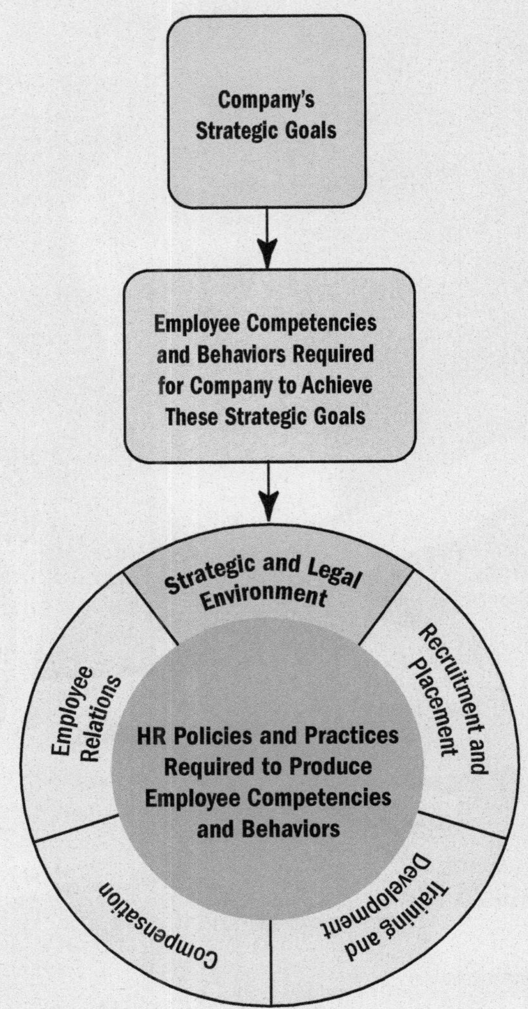

A few years ago lawyers filed a federal lawsuit against Uber Technologies. They said Uber's questionable performance appraisal system produced performance ratings that led to male Uber employees getting better raises than women.[1] We will see how to avoid such problems.

WHERE ARE WE NOW . . .

Every HR action you take as a manager, from interviewing applicants to training, appraising, and rewarding them, has equal employment implications. Therefore, the purpose of this chapter is to provide you with the knowledge to deal more effectively with equal employment questions on the job. The main topics we cover are equal opportunity **Laws Enacted from 1964 to 1991**, the **Laws Enacted from 1991** to the present, **Defenses Against Discrimination Allegations and Discriminatory Employment Practices**, the **EEOC Enforcement** process, and **Diversity Management**.

Equal Opportunity Laws Enacted from 1964 to 1991

LEARNING OBJECTIVE 2-1

List the basic features of Title VII of the 1964 Civil Rights Act and at least five other early equal employment laws.

Hardly a day goes by without equal opportunity lawsuits at work.[2] One survey of corporate counsels found that such lawsuits were their biggest litigation fears.[3] Performing day-to-day supervisory tasks like hiring employees without understanding these laws is fraught with peril.

Actually, laws barring discrimination against minorities in the United States are nothing new. The Fifth Amendment to the U.S. Constitution (ratified in 1791) states that "no person shall be deprived of life, liberty, or property, without due process of the law." The Thirteenth Amendment (1865) outlawed slavery, and courts have held that it bars racial discrimination. The Civil Rights Act of 1866 gives all persons the same right to make and enforce contracts and to benefit from U.S. laws.[4] But as a practical matter, Congress and presidents avoided dramatic action on implementing equal employment laws until the early 1960s. At that point, civil unrest among minorities and women and changing traditions prompted them to act. Congress passed a multitude of new civil rights laws.

Title VII of the 1964 Civil Rights Act

Title VII of the 1964 Civil Rights Act
The section of the act that says an employer cannot discriminate on the basis of race, color, religion, sex, or national origin with respect to employment.

Title VII of the 1964 Civil Rights Act was one of the first of these laws. As amended by the 1972 Equal Employment Opportunity Act, Title VII states that an employer cannot discriminate based on race, color, religion, sex, or national origin. Specifically, it states that it shall be an unlawful employment practice for an employer:

1. To fail or refuse to hire or to discharge an individual or otherwise to discriminate against any individual with respect to his or her compensation, terms, conditions, or privileges of employment, because of such individual's race, color, religion, sex, or national origin.
2. To limit, segregate, or classify employees or applicants for employment in any way that would deprive or tend to deprive any individual of employment opportunities or otherwise adversely affect his or her status as an employee, because of such individual's race, color, religion, sex, or national origin.

Title VII bars discrimination on the part of most employers, including all public or private employers of 15 or more persons and most labor unions. It also covers all private and public educational institutions, the federal government, and state and local governments. It bars public and private employment agencies from failing or refusing to refer for employment any individual because of race, color, religion, sex, or national origin.

Equal Employment Opportunity Commission (EEOC)
The commission, created by Title VII, empowered to investigate job discrimination complaints and sue on behalf of complainants.

Title VII established the **Equal Employment Opportunity Commission (EEOC)** to administer and enforce the Civil Rights Act at work. It consists of five members appointed by the president with the advice and consent of the Senate. Each member serves a 5-year term. In popular usage, the EEOC also includes the thousands of staff the EEOC has around the United States. They receive and investigate job discrimination complaints from aggrieved individuals. When the EEOC finds reasonable cause that the charges are justified, it attempts (through conciliation) to reach an agreement.[5] If this fails, it can go to court. The EEOC may file discrimination charges on behalf of aggrieved individuals, or the individuals may file on behalf of themselves.[6] We'll discuss the EEOC procedure later in this chapter.[7]

HR AND THE GIG ECONOMY: *DISCRIMINATION IN THE GIG ECONOMY?*

Most companies use recruiters, supervisors, and/or HR professionals to do their hiring, so if an applicant suffers discrimination it's usually pretty clear who did it.[8] But what do you do when you're a gig worker, doing work through a gig economy company like Uber, Task Rabbit, or Fiverr? Here the people doing the "hiring" are usually Task Rabbit, Uber, or Fiverr users, and they're hiring based on reviews compiled from previous users, or from photos in your profile. What stops customers from illegally discriminating?

Unfortunately, the answer may be, "not much." For example, in one study of labor markets like Task Rabbit and Fiverr, black service providers got more negative reviews than did white ones. Because the rating algorithms are then based partly on prior customers' reviews, the black service providers were usually less likely to get new gigs. It's therefore a problem that gig companies (and customers) need to address.

Executive Orders

Various U.S. presidents signed executive orders expanding equal employment in federal agencies. For example, the Johnson administration (1963–1969) issued Executive Orders 11246 and 11375. These required that government contractors with contracts of more than $50,000 and 50 or more employees take **affirmative action** to ensure employment opportunities for those who may have suffered past discrimination. They also established the **Office of Federal Contract Compliance Programs (OFCCP).** It implements the orders and ensures compliance.[9]

affirmative action
Steps that are taken for the purpose of eliminating the present effects of past discrimination.

Office of Federal Contract Compliance Programs (OFCCP)
This office is responsible for implementing the executive orders and ensuring compliance of federal contractors.

Equal Pay Act of 1963

Under the **Equal Pay Act of 1963** (amended in 1972), it is unlawful to discriminate in pay on the basis of sex when jobs involve equal work; require equivalent skills, effort, and responsibility; and are performed under similar working conditions. Pay differences derived from seniority systems, merit systems, and systems that measure earnings by production quantity or quality or from any factor other than sex do not violate the act. Unfortunately, this act notwithstanding, women still earn only about 70% as much as men in similar jobs; we'll address this inequity and how to deal with it in our chapter on establishing strategic pay plans.

Equal Pay Act of 1963
The act requiring equal pay for equal work, regardless of sex.

Age Discrimination in Employment Act of 1967

The **Age Discrimination in Employment Act of 1967 (ADEA)** made it unlawful to discriminate against employees or applicants who are between 40 and 65 years of age. Subsequent amendments effectively ended most mandatory retirement at age 65. Most states and local agencies, when acting as employers, must also adhere to the ADEA.[10]

Age Discrimination in Employment Act of 1967 (ADEA)
The act prohibiting arbitrary age discrimination and specifically protecting individuals over 40 years old.

You can't get around the ADEA by replacing employees who are, say, 60 with someone over 40. In one case the U.S. Supreme Court held that an employee who is over 40 years of age might sue for discrimination if a "significantly younger" employee replaces him or her, even if the replacement is also over 40. The Court didn't specify what "significantly younger" meant, but here the plaintiff was replaced by someone 16 years younger.[11]

Younger managers especially may have to guard against age prejudices. For example, Staples fired a 64-year-old man, saying he stole a bell pepper. He sued for age discrimination. It transpired that a Staples manager had told colleagues to "take a closer look at the older people" and "write them up and get rid of them." The fired employee won his case (for $16 million) and an appeal.[12]

Similarly, recruitment ads often use phrases like "applicants should have received their degrees 2014–2018," or "should have 4–6 years' experience." While not always illegal, such phrases sometimes mean, "if you're over 40, don't apply."[13] Age discrimination at large tech firms may exceed that for gender or race.[14]

Lawyers like the ADEA. It allows jury trials and double damages to those proving "willful" discrimination.[15] It's advisable to have antiharassment policies addressing older employees. For example ban derogatory use of words like "grandpa" to refer to older people.[16]

Vocational Rehabilitation Act of 1973

The **Vocational Rehabilitation Act of 1973** requires employers with federal contracts of more than $2,500 to take affirmative action in employing handicapped persons. It does not require hiring unqualified people. It does require an employer to take steps to accommodate a handicapped worker unless doing so imposes an undue hardship on the employer.

Vocational Rehabilitation Act of 1973
The act requiring certain federal contractors to take affirmative action for disabled persons.

Pregnancy Discrimination Act of 1978

The **Pregnancy Discrimination Act** of 1978 prohibits using pregnancy, childbirth, or related medical conditions to discriminate in hiring, promotion, suspension, or discharge, or in any term or condition of employment. Furthermore, under the act, if an employer offers its employees disability coverage, then it must treat pregnancy and childbirth like any other disability, and include it in the plan as a covered condition.[17]

Pregnancy Discrimination Act
An amendment to Title VII of the Civil Rights Act that prohibits sex discrimination based on "pregnancy, childbirth, or related medical conditions."

More women are suing under this act, and it's easy to see why.[18] As one example, a Chipotle restaurant let go a pregnant employee. She told the jury that despite a history of positive performance feedback, her manager allegedly began harassing her when she said she was pregnant. For example, she was made to announce bathroom breaks to coworkers and told she couldn't leave early for doctors' appointments.

The jury awarded her actual losses plus $500,000 in punitive damages.[19] The bottom line is that managers should base "any [such] decision on whether an employee can do the job and on medical documentation, not on a manager's interpretation."[20]

Federal Agency Guidelines

The federal agencies charged with ensuring compliance with these laws and executive orders have their own implementing guidelines. These spell out recommended procedures for complying with the law.[21]

The EEOC, Civil Service Commission, Department of Labor, and Department of Justice together issued **Uniform Guidelines.**[22] These set forth "highly recommended" procedures for things like employee selection and record keeping. As an example, they specify that employers must *validate* any employment selection devices (like tests) that screen out disproportionate numbers of women or minorities, and they explain how to do so. (We explain this procedure in Chapter 6.) The EEOC and other agencies also periodically issue updated guidelines clarifying and revising their positions on matters such as sexual harassment. The American Psychological Association has its own (non-legally binding) Standards for Educational and Psychological Testing.

Uniform Guidelines
Guidelines issued by federal agencies charged with ensuring compliance with equal employment federal legislation explaining recommended employer procedures in detail.

Early Court Decisions Regarding Equal Employment Opportunity

Several court decisions between 1964 and 1991 helped clarify courts' interpretations of equal employment opportunity (EEO) laws such as Title VII.

GRIGGS V. DUKE POWER COMPANY *Griggs* was a landmark case because the Supreme Court used it to define unfair discrimination. Lawyers sued the Duke Power Company on behalf of Willie Griggs, an applicant for a job as a coal handler. The company required its coal handlers to be high school graduates. Griggs claimed this requirement was illegally discriminatory. He said it wasn't related to success on the job, and it resulted in more blacks than whites being rejected for these jobs. Griggs won the case. The Court's decision was unanimous. In his written opinion, Chief Justice Burger laid out three crucial guidelines affecting equal employment legislation.

- First, the Court ruled that the *discrimination does not have to be overt to be illegal.* The plaintiff does not have to show that the employer intentionally discriminated against the employee or applicant. Instead, the plaintiff just has to show that discrimination took place.
- Second, the Court held that an employment practice (in this case, requiring the high school degree) *must be job related* if it has an unequal impact on members of a **protected class.** (For example, if arithmetic is not required to perform the job, don't test for arithmetic.)
- Third, Chief Justice Burger's opinion placed the *burden of proof on the employer* to show that the hiring practice is job related. Thus, the employer must show that the employment practice (in this case, requiring a high school degree) is necessary for satisfactory job performance if the practice discriminates against members of a protected class. Said Justice Burger:

protected class
Persons such as minorities and women protected by equal opportunity laws, including Title VII.

> The act proscribes not only overt discrimination, but also practices that are fair in form, but discriminatory in operation. The touchstone is business necessity. If an employment practice which operates to exclude Negroes cannot be shown to be related to job performance, the practice is prohibited.[23]

For employers, *Griggs* established these five principles:

1. A test or other selection practice must be job related, and the burden of proof is on the employer.
2. An employer's intent not to discriminate is irrelevant.[24]

3. If a practice is "fair in form but discriminatory in operation," the courts will not uphold it.
4. *Business necessity* is the defense for any existing program that has adverse impact. The court did not define business necessity.
5. Title VII does not forbid testing. However, the test must be job related (valid), in that performance on the test must relate to performance on the job.

ALBEMARLE PAPER COMPANY V. MOODY In the *Albemarle* case, the Court provided more details on how employers could prove that tests or other screening tools relate to job performance.[25] For example, the Court said that if an employer wants to test candidates for a job, then the employer should first clearly document and understand the job's duties and responsibilities. Furthermore, the job's performance standards should be clear and unambiguous. That way, the employer can identify which employees are performing better than others. The Court's ruling also established the EEOC (now Federal) Guidelines on validation as the procedures for validating employment practices.

The Laws Enacted from 1991 to the Present

The Civil Rights Act of 1991

LEARNING OBJECTIVE 2-2

List the basic features of at least five post-1990 employment laws, and explain with examples how to avoid accusations of sexual harassment at work.

Several subsequent Supreme Court rulings in the 1980s limited the protection of women and minority groups under equal employment laws. For example, they raised the plaintiff's burden of proving that the employer's acts were in fact discriminatory. This prompted Congress to pass a new Civil Rights Act. President George H. W. Bush signed the **Civil Rights Act of 1991 (CRA 1991)** into law in 1991. The effect of CRA 1991 was to roll back equal employment law to where it stood before the 1980s decisions and to place more responsibility on employers.

Civil Rights Act of 1991 (CRA 1991)
The act that places the burden of proof back on employers and permits compensatory and punitive damages.

BURDEN OF PROOF First, CRA 1991 addressed the issue of *burden of proof.* Burden of proof—what the plaintiff must show to establish possible illegal discrimination, and what the employer must show to defend its actions—plays a central role in equal employment cases.[26] Today, in brief, once an aggrieved applicant or employee demonstrates that an employment practice (such as "must lift 100 pounds") has an adverse impact on a particular group, then the burden of proof shifts to the employer, who must show that the challenged practice is job related.[27] For example, the employer has to show that lifting 100 pounds is required for performing the job in question, and that the business could not run efficiently without the requirement—that it is a business necessity.[28]

MONEY DAMAGES Before CRA 1991, victims of *intentional* discrimination (which lawyers call *disparate treatment*) who had not suffered financial loss and who sued under Title VII could not then sue for compensatory or punitive damages. All they could expect was to have their jobs reinstated (or to get a particular job). They were also eligible for back pay, attorneys' fees, and court costs.

CRA 1991 makes it easier to sue for *money damages* in such cases. It provides that an employee who is claiming intentional discrimination can ask for (1) compensatory damages, and (2) punitive damages, if he or she can show the employer engaged in discrimination "with malice or reckless indifference to the federally protected rights of an aggrieved individual."[29]

"mixed-motive" case
A discrimination allegation case in which the employer argues that the employment action taken was motivated not by discrimination, but by some nondiscriminatory reason such as ineffective performance.

MIXED MOTIVES Some employers in **"mixed-motive" cases** had taken the position that even though their actions were discriminatory, other factors like the employee's dubious behavior made the job action acceptable. Under CRA 1991, an employer cannot avoid liability by proving it would have taken the same action—such as terminating someone—even without the discriminatory motive.[30] *If there is any such motive, the practice may be unlawful.*[31]

The Americans with Disabilities Act

Americans with Disabilities Act (ADA)
The act requiring employers to make reasonable accommodations for disabled employees; it prohibits discrimination against disabled persons.

The **Americans with Disabilities Act (ADA)** of 1990 prohibits employment discrimination against qualified disabled individuals.[32] It prohibits employers with 15 or more workers from discriminating against qualified individuals with disabilities, with regard to applications, hiring, discharge, compensation, advancement, training, or other terms, conditions, or privileges of employment.[33] It also says employers must make "reasonable accommodations" for physical or mental limitations unless doing so imposes an "undue hardship" on the business.

The ADA does not list specific disabilities. Instead, EEOC guidelines say someone is disabled when he or she has a physical or mental impairment that "substantially limits" one or more major life activities. Initially, impairments included any physiological disorder or condition, cosmetic disfigurement, or anatomical loss affecting one or more of several body systems, or any mental or psychological disorder, but the list is growing.[34] (Recently, a Massachusetts court held that firing a qualified medical marijuana user may qualify for disability discrimination).[35]

The act specifies conditions that it does *not* regard as disabilities, including homosexuality, compulsive gambling, pyromania, and certain disorders resulting from the current illegal use of drugs.[36]

Mental disabilities account for the greatest number of ADA claims.[37] Under EEOC ADA guidelines, "mental impairment" includes "any mental or psychological disorder, such as . . . emotional or mental illness." Examples include major depression, anxiety disorders, and personality disorders. The ADA also protects employees with intellectual disabilities, including those with IQs below 70–75.[38] The guidelines say employers should be alert to the possibility that traits normally regarded as undesirable (such as chronic lateness, hostility, or poor judgment) may reflect mental impairments. Reasonable accommodation might then include providing barriers between work spaces.

qualified individuals
Under ADA, those who can carry out the essential functions of the job.

QUALIFIED INDIVIDUAL Just being disabled doesn't qualify someone for a job, of course. Instead, the act prohibits discrimination against **qualified individuals**—those who, with (or without) a reasonable accommodation, can carry out the *essential functions* of the job. The individual must have the requisite skills, educational background, and experience. A job function is essential when, for instance, it is the reason the position exists, or it is so highly specialized that the employer hires the person for his or her expertise or ability to perform that particular function. For example, when an Iowa county highway worker had an on-the-job seizure, his driver's license was suspended, and the court ruled he had no ADA claim because he couldn't perform the essential functions of the job.[39]

REASONABLE ACCOMMODATION If the individual can't perform the job as currently structured, the employer must make a "reasonable accommodation" unless doing so would present an "undue hardship."[40] Reasonable accommodation might include redesigning the job, modifying work schedules, or modifying or acquiring equipment or other devices; widening door openings or permitting telecommuting are examples.[41] For example, about 70% of working-age blind adults are unemployed or underemployed. Existing technologies such as screen-reading programs might enable most to work successfully.[42] Review the company's Web sites to ensure they don't hamper people with handicaps.[43]

Attorneys, employers, and the courts continue to work through what "reasonable accommodation" means.[44] In one classic case, a Walmart door greeter with a bad back asked if she could sit on a stool while on duty. The store said no. The federal court agreed door greeters must act in an "aggressively hospitable manner," which can't be done from a stool.[45] Standing was an essential job function. You can use technology and common sense to make reasonable accommodation (see Figure 2-1).

THE ADA AMENDMENTS ACT OF 2008 (ADAAA) Employers traditionally prevailed in almost all—96%—federal circuit court ADA decisions.[46] One case typifies what plaintiffs faced. An assembly worker sued Toyota, arguing that carpal tunnel syndrome

FIGURE 2-1 Examples of How to Provide Reasonable Accommodation

- Employees with *mobility or vision impairments* may benefit from voice-recognition software.
- Word-prediction software suggests words based on context with just one or two letters typed.
- Real-time translation captioning enables employees to participate in meetings.
- Vibrating text pagers notify employees when messages arrive.
- Arizona created a disability-friendly Web site to help link prospective employees and others to various agencies.

prevented her from doing her job.[47] The U.S. Supreme Court ruled that the ADA covers carpal tunnel syndrome only if her impairments affect not just her job performance, but also her daily living activities. The employee admitted that she could perform personal chores such as washing her face and fixing breakfast. The Court said the disability must be central to the employee's daily living (not just to his or her job).[48]

However, the ADA Amendments Act of 2008 (ADAAA) made it easier for employees to show that their disabilities are influencing one of their "major life activities," such as reading and thinking.[49] For example, sensitivity to perfume might be considered a disability.[50] Employers must therefore redouble their efforts to ensure they're complying with the ADA.[51]

Many employers simply take a progressive approach. Common employer concerns about people with disabilities (for instance, that they are less productive and have more accidents) are generally baseless.[52] For example, Walgreens tries to fill at least one-third of the jobs at its large distribution centers with people with disabilities.[53]

Figure 2-2 summarizes some important ADA guidelines for managers and employers.

Uniformed Services Employment and Reemployment Rights Act

Under the Uniformed Services Employment and Reemployment Rights Act (1994), employers are generally required, among other things, to reinstate employees returning from military leave to positions comparable to those they had before leaving.[54]

Genetic Information Nondiscrimination Act of 2008 (GINA)

The Genetic Information Nondiscrimination Act of 2008 (GINA) prohibits discrimination by health insurers and employers based on people's genetic information. Specifically, it prohibits the use of genetic information in employment, prohibits the intentional acquisition of genetic information about applicants and employees, and imposes strict confidentiality requirements.[55]

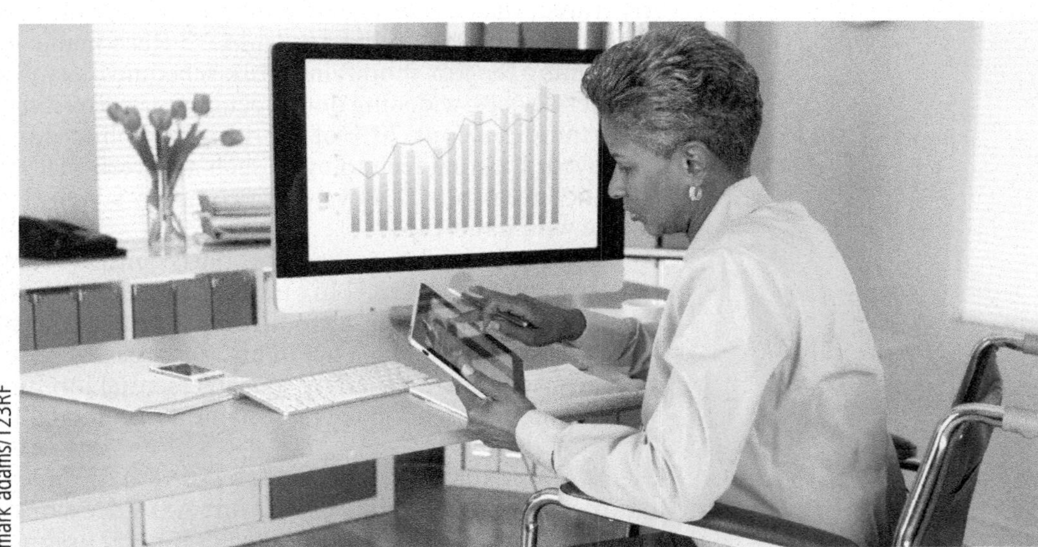

Technology enables employers to accommodate disabled employees.

FIGURE 2-2 ADA Guidelines for Managers and Employers

- *Do not* deny a job to a disabled individual if the person is qualified and able to perform the essential job functions.
- *Make* a reasonable accommodation unless doing so would result in undue hardship.
- *Know* what you can ask applicants. In general, you may *not* make preemployment inquiries about a person's disability before making an offer. However, you *may* ask questions about the person's ability to perform essential job functions.
- *Itemize* essential job functions on the job descriptions. In virtually any ADA legal action, a central question will be, what are the essential functions of the job?
- *Do not* allow misconduct or erratic performance (including absences and tardiness), even if that behavior is linked to the disability.

State and Local Equal Employment Opportunity Laws

In addition to federal laws, all states and many local governments prohibit employment discrimination. The state or local laws usually cover employers (like those with less than 15 employees) not covered by federal legislation.[56]

Employers ignore city and state EEO laws at their peril. In New York City, for instance, city law applies to employers with as few as 4 employees (not 15, as under Title VII).[57] Managers use manuals such as *HR Compliance Basics: Your State and Federal Employment Law Manual* (available from the SHRM) to understand local EEO requirements.

State and local equal employment opportunity agencies (often called *Human Resources Commissions* or *Fair Employment Commissions*) also play a role in equal employment compliance. When the EEOC receives a discrimination charge, it usually defers it for a limited time to the state and local agencies that have comparable jurisdiction. If that doesn't achieve satisfactory remedies, the charges go back to the EEOC for resolution.

Religious Discrimination[58]

The EEOC enforces laws prohibiting discrimination based on age, disability, equal pay/compensation, genetic information, national origin, pregnancy, race/color, religion, retaliation, sex, and sexual harassment.

Religious discrimination involves treating someone unfavorably because of his or her religious beliefs. The law protects not only people who belong to traditional, organized religions, such as Buddhism, Christianity, Hinduism, Islam, and Judaism, but also others who have sincerely held religious, ethical, or moral beliefs. Unless it would be an undue hardship on the employer, an employer must reasonably accommodate an employee's religious beliefs or practices. This applies to schedule changes or leave for religious observances, as well as to such things as religious dress or grooming practices. These might include, for example, wearing particular head coverings or other religious dress (such as a Jewish yarmulke or a Muslim headscarf), or wearing certain hairstyles or facial hair (such as Rastafarian dreadlocks or Sikh uncut hair and beard).

One question is how far employers must go to accommodate employees' religious practices. For example, the EEOC found reasonable cause that food giant Cargill violated Title VII by telling Muslim employees at one plant they couldn't have prayer breaks.[59] Here what is "reasonable" depends partly on how disruptive the accommodation would be. For example, such breaks might be too disruptive for high-speed continuous production lines.[60]

Trends in Discrimination Law

Some trends are expanding equal employment's impact, while others are forming new headwinds.

In terms of the former, the U.S. Supreme Court held that the Federal Defence of Marriage Act's exclusion of state-sanctioned, same-sex marriages was unconstitutional.[61] The Department of Labor (DOL) then held that under the Employee

Retirement Income Security Act (ERISA), "The term 'spouse' will be read to refer to any individuals who are lawfully married under any state law, including those . . . who are [now] domiciled in a state that doesn't recognize such marriages."[62] In 2014, then-President Obama signed an executive order barring federal contractors from discriminating against lesbian, gay, bisexual, and transgender employees, for instance in benefits.[63] In 2017, a federal appeals court ruled that the Title VII ban on sex discrimination means employers cannot discriminate against lesbian and gay workers.[64] Several states require that employers permit people who don't identify with either the male or female gender to check off a third, "non-binary" classification.[65] The DOL passed regulations requiring that federal contractors employ a minimum (7%) of disabled workers or face penalties, possibly including loss of their contracts.[66]

Recent decisions may produce headwinds. The U.S. Supreme Court upheld a Michigan constitutional amendment banning affirmative action in admissions to the state's public universities. This may allow voters in other states to eliminate affirmative action-based admissions to their public universities.[67] And in two other decisions, the Court made it more difficult for someone to bring a retaliation claim against an employer; it also more strictly defined "supervisor," reducing the likelihood someone could show that an employer was responsible for a "supervisor's" harassing behavior.[68] With its stated goal of reducing regulations, the Republican administration could be less supportive of EEO regulations (and regulations in general). In 2017, Attorney General Sessions said religious organizations could employ only people whose beliefs are consistent with the companies' religious principles.[69]

Table 2-1 summarizes selected equal employment opportunity laws, actions, executive orders, and agency guidelines.

Sexual Harassment

The past few years have witnessed a dramatic increase in accusations and admissions of sexual harassment.[70]

sexual harassment
Harassment on the basis of sex that has the purpose or effect of substantially interfering with a person's work performance or creating an intimidating, hostile, or offensive work environment.

Under Title VII, **sexual harassment** generally refers to harassment on the basis of sex when such conduct has the purpose or effect of substantially interfering with a person's work performance or creating an intimidating, hostile, or offensive work environment. In one recent year, the EEOC received 11,717 sexual harassment charges, about 15% of which were filed by men.[71] (The U.S. Supreme Court held, in *Oncale v. Sundowner Offshore Services Inc.,* that same-sex sexual harassment is also actionable under Title VII.[72]) One study found "women experienced more sexual harassment than men, minorities experienced more ethnic harassment than whites, and minority women experience more harassment overall than majority men, minority men, and majority women."[73] In late 2017 the EEOC updated its sexual harassment guidelines.[74]

Federal Violence Against Women Act of 1994
The act that provides that a person who commits a crime of violence motivated by gender shall be liable to the party injured.

Under EEOC guidelines, employers have an affirmative duty to maintain workplaces free of sexual harassment and intimidation. CRA 1991 permits victims of intentional discrimination, including sexual harassment, to have jury trials and to collect compensatory damages for pain and suffering and punitive damages, where the employer acted with "malice or reckless indifference" to the person's rights.[75] The **Federal Violence Against Women Act of 1994** further provides that a person "who commits a crime of violence motivated by gender and thus deprives another" of her rights shall be liable to the party injured.

WHAT IS SEXUAL HARASSMENT? EEOC guidelines define *sexual harassment* as unwelcome sexual advances, requests for sexual favors, and other verbal or physical conduct of a sexual nature that takes place under any of the following conditions:

1. Submission to such conduct is made either explicitly or implicitly a term or condition of an individual's employment.
2. Submission to or rejection of such conduct by an individual is used as the basis for employment decisions affecting such individual.
3. Such conduct has the purpose or effect of unreasonably interfering with an individual's work performance or creating an intimidating, hostile, or offensive work environment.

TABLE 2-1 Summary of Important Equal Employment Opportunity Laws*

Action	What It Does
Title VII of 1964 Civil Rights Act, as amended	Bars discrimination because of race, color, religion, sex, or national origin; instituted the EEOC.
Executive orders	Prohibit employment discrimination by employers with federal contracts of more than $10,000 (and their subcontractors); establish office of federal compliance; require affirmative action programs.
Federal agency guidelines	Guidelines cover discrimination based on sex, national origin, and religion, as well as on employee selection and other procedures such as test validation.
Supreme Court decisions: *Griggs v. Duke Power Co.*, *Albemarle v. Moody*	Ruled that job requirements must be related to job success; that discrimination need not be overt to be proved; that the burden of proof is on the employer to prove the qualification is valid.
Equal Pay Act of 1963	Requires equal pay for men and women for performing similar work.
Age Discrimination in Employment Act of 1967	Prohibits discriminating against a person age 40 or over in any area of employment because of age.
State and local laws	Often cover organizations too small to be covered by federal laws.
Vocational Rehabilitation Act of 1973	Requires affirmative action to employ and promote qualified handicapped persons and prohibits discrimination against handicapped persons.
Pregnancy Discrimination Act of 1978	Prohibits discrimination in employment against pregnant women, or those with related conditions.
Vietnam Era Veterans' Readjustment Assistance Act of 1974	Requires affirmative action in employment for veterans of the Vietnam War era.
Ward Cove v. Atonio	Made it more difficult to prove a case of unlawful discrimination against an employer.
Americans with Disabilities Act of 1990	Strengthens the need for most employers to make reasonable accommodations for disabled employees at work; prohibits discrimination.
Civil Rights Act of 1991	Reverses various U.S. Supreme Court decisions; places burden of proof back on employer and permits compensatory and punitive money damages for discrimination.
ADA Amendments Act of 2008	Makes it easier for employee to show that his or her disability "substantially limits" a major life function.
Genetic Information Non-discrimination Act	Signed into law in May 2008, prohibits discriminating against employees and applicants based on their genetic information.

* The actual laws (and others) can be accessed via a search at www.usa.gov/Topics/Reference-Shelf/Laws.shtml, accessed June 28, 2018.

PROVING SEXUAL HARASSMENT There are three main ways someone can prove sexual harassment:

1. ***Quid Pro Quo.*** The most direct is to prove that rejecting a supervisor's advances adversely affected what the EEOC calls a "tangible employment action," such as hiring, firing, promotion, demotion, and/or work assignment. In one case, the employee showed that continued job success and advancement were dependent on her agreeing to the sexual demands of her supervisors. "Sexual harassment" generally requires that the behavior be pervasive or severe. Thus, in one case, the court ruled that although the supervisor had touched the employee's shoulder twice as he drove her back from work and also mentioned that she "owed him" for hiring her, she did not have a trial-able sexual harassment claim.[76]
2. ***Hostile Environment Created by Supervisors.*** The harassment need not have tangible consequences such as demotion. For example, one court found that a male supervisor's behavior had substantially affected a female employee's emotional and psychological ability to the point that she felt she had to quit her job. Therefore, even though the supervisor made no direct threats or promises in exchange for sexual advances, his advances interfered with the woman's performance and created an offensive work environment. That was sufficient to prove sexual harassment. Courts generally do not interpret as sexual harassment sexual relationships that arise during the course of employment but that do not have a substantial effect on that employment.[77] The U.S. Supreme Court also held

that sexual harassment law doesn't cover ordinary "intersexual flirtation." In his ruling, Justice Antonin Scalia said courts must carefully distinguish between "simple teasing" and truly abusive behavior.[78]

3. ***Hostile Environment Created by Coworkers or Nonemployees.*** Coworkers or nonemployees can trigger such suits. One court held that a mandatory sexually provocative uniform led to lewd comments by customers. When the employee refused to wear the uniform, she was fired. The employer couldn't show there was a job-related necessity for the uniform, and only female employees wore it. The court ruled that the employer, in effect, was responsible for the sexually harassing behavior. Such abhorrent client behavior is more likely when the clients are in positions of power, and when they think no one will penalize them.[79] Employers are also liable for the sexually harassing acts of nonsupervisory employees if the employer knew or should have known of the conduct.

WHEN IS THE ENVIRONMENT "HOSTILE"? Hostile environment sexual harassment generally means the intimidation, insults, and ridicule were sufficiently severe to alter the employee's working conditions. Courts look at several things. These include whether the discriminatory conduct is *frequent or severe*; whether it is *physically threatening* or humiliating, or a mere offensive utterance; and whether it unreasonably *interferes* with an employee's work performance.[80] Courts also consider whether the employee subjectively *perceives* the work environment as being abusive. For example, did he or she welcome the conduct or immediately complain?[81]

SUPREME COURT DECISIONS The U.S. Supreme Court used a case called *Meritor Savings Bank, FSB v. Vinson* to endorse broadly the EEOC's guidelines on sexual harassment. Two other Supreme Court decisions further clarified sexual harassment law.

In the first, *Burlington Industries v. Ellerth*, the employee accused her supervisor of *quid pro quo* harassment. She said her boss propositioned and threatened her with demotion if she did not respond. He did not carry out the threats, and she was promoted. In the second case, *Faragher v. City of Boca Raton*, the employee accused the employer of condoning a hostile work environment. She said she quit her lifeguard job after repeated taunts from other lifeguards. The Court ruled in favor of the employees in both cases.

The Court's written decisions have two implications for employers and managers. First, in *quid pro quo* cases it is *not* necessary for the employee to suffer a tangible job action (such as a demotion) to win the case. Second, the Court laid out an important defense against harassment suits. It said the employer must show that it took "reasonable care" to prevent and promptly correct any sexually harassing behavior *and* that the employee unreasonably failed to take advantage of the employer's policy.

These decisions suggest an employer can defend itself against sexual harassment liability by showing two things:

- First, it must show "that the employer exercised reasonable care to *prevent* and *correct promptly* any sexually harassing behavior."[82]
- Second, it must demonstrate that the plaintiff "unreasonably *failed to take advantage* of any preventive or corrective opportunities provided by the employer." The employee's failure to use formal reporting systems would satisfy the second component.[83]

The following Tools feature provides guidelines for managers.

IMPROVING PERFORMANCE: *HR TOOLS FOR LINE MANAGERS AND SMALL BUSINESSES*

How to Address Sexual Harassment:[84]

- Take all complaints about harassment seriously.
- Issue a strong policy statement condemning such behavior. Describe the prohibited conduct, assure protection against retaliation, describe a confidential complaint process, and provide impartial investigation and corrective action.

- Take steps to prevent sexual harassment from occurring. For example, communicate to employees that the employer will not tolerate sexual harassment, and take immediate action when someone complains. After firing host Matt Lauer, NBC now requires any employees who know of inappropriate workplace relationships to report them to human resources.[85]
- Establish a management response system that includes an immediate reaction and investigation. Some organizations use an app from www.projectcallisto.org/ to facilitate recording and reporting sexual harassment.[86]
- Train supervisors and managers to increase their awareness of the issues, and discipline managers and employees involved in sexual harassment. ■

WHY THE LAW ISN'T ENOUGH Unfortunately, several problems can negate the legal requirements.

First, "Women perceive a broader range of socio-sexual behaviors (touching, for instance) as harassing."[87] In one study, about 58% of employees reported experiencing potentially harassment-type behaviors at work. About four times as many men as women found the behavior flattering or benign.[88] Sexual harassment training and policies can reduce this problem.[89]

Second, victims are often fearful (for instance, of not getting the job). In one study, the male interviewer asked female applicants improper questions such as "Do you have a boyfriend?" and "Do people findyou desirable?"[90] All the applicants answered all the questions. When asked why, they said they felt more fear than anger in the interview.

Third, victims often won't complain. For example, two Air Force generals appeared before the U.S. Congress' House Armed Services Committee to explain (among other things) how 23 instructors at an Air Force base could engage in unprofessional relationships or sexual assaults against 48 female trainees. The Air Force blamed both a climate of fear among female personnel (who believed that reporting the offenses to superior officers would be futile or counterproductive) and "a weak command structure."[91]

Finally, neither harassment training nor the HR department are always helpful. Many such training programs simply fulfill the employer's legal obligation to show that it educated employees about the firm's antiharassment policies. And when they do receive harassment reports, many HR departments do nothing.[92] As one extreme example, the Weinstein Company's HR department allegedly bounced harassment complaints back to Mr. Weinstein when people made allegations about him.[93]

WHAT THE EMPLOYEE CAN DO First, complain. Remember that courts generally look to whether *the harassed employee used the employer's reporting procedures to file a complaint promptly*. If the employer has an effectively communicated complaint procedure, use it and then cooperate in the investigation.[94] In that context, steps an employee can take include:

1. Speak with the harasser and his or her boss, stating that the unwanted overtures should cease.
2. Inform your own supervisor.
3. If the problem does not cease, file written reports regarding the unwelcome conduct and unsuccessful efforts to get it to stop with the harasser's manager and/or the human resource director.
4. If these do not suffice, the accuser may file a claim with the EEOC. In serious cases, the employee can also consult an attorney about suing the harasser for assault and battery, intentional infliction of emotional distress, injunctive relief, and to recover compensatory and punitive damages.[95]

MyLab Management Apply It!

What do you think of how one employer actually dealt with problems such as sexual harassment? If your professor has assigned this activity, go to the Assignments section of **www.pearson.com/mylab/management** to complete the video exercise.

TRENDS SHAPING HR: *DIGITAL AND SOCIAL MEDIA*

Some employees will use Facebook and other accounts to harass and bully coworkers (as with disparaging comments). Here, employers must distinguish between illegal online harassment (that applying to race, religion, national origin, age, sex/gender, genetic information, and disability discrimination) and common personality conflicts. However, at a minimum, employers should have a zero-tolerance policy on bullying.[96]

Of course, social media has also been a boon for staffing, for instance for finding candidates on LinkedIn. However, viewing an applicant's social media profile can be problematic, as it may reveal information on things like religion, race, and sexual orientation.[97] Some states forbid employers from requiring or even requesting employees' or applicants' passwords. It's therefore sensible to have policies restricting who can check out candidates online and how they can do it. Supervisors probably should not do such checking themselves. ■

LEARNING OBJECTIVE 2-3

Illustrate two defenses you can use in the event of discriminatory practice allegations, and list specific discriminatory personnel management practices in recruitment, selection, promotion, transfer, layoffs, and benefits.

Defenses Against Discrimination Allegations

To understand how employers defend themselves against employment discrimination claims, we should first briefly review some basic legal terminology.

Discrimination law distinguishes between disparate *treatment* and disparate *impact. Disparate treatment* means intentional discrimination. Disparate treatment "exists where an employer treats an individual differently because that individual is a member of a particular race, religion, gender, or ethnic group."[98] A rule that says "We don't hire drivers over 60 years of age" exemplifies this.

Disparate impact means that "an employer engages in an employment practice or policy that has a greater adverse impact (effect) on the members of a protected group under Title VII than on other employees, regardless of intent."[99] A rule that says "Employees must have college degrees to do this particular job" exemplifies this (because more white males than some minorities earn college degrees).

Disparate impact claims do not require proof of discriminatory intent. Instead, the plaintiff must show that the apparently neutral employment practice (such as requiring a college degree) creates an adverse impact—a significant disparity—between the proportion of (say) minorities in the available labor pool and the proportion you hire. Thus, disparate impact allegations require showing that the act produced an adverse impact. If it has, then the employer will probably have to defend itself (for instance, by arguing that there is a business necessity for the practice). Adverse impact "refers to the total employment process that results in a significantly higher percentage of a protected group in the candidate population being rejected for employment, placement, or promotion."[100] Then the burden of proof shifts to the employer.

The Central Role of Adverse Impact

adverse impact
The overall impact of employer practices that result in significantly higher percentages of members of minorities and other protected groups being rejected for employment, placement, or promotion.

Showing that one of the employer's employment practices or policies has an **adverse impact** therefore plays a central role in discriminatory practice allegations.[101] Under Title VII and CRA 1991, a person who believes that (1) he or she was a victim of unintentional discrimination because of an employer's practices need only, (2) establish a *prima facie* case of discrimination. This means showing, for instance, that the employer's selection procedures (like requiring a college degree for the job) did have an adverse impact on the protected minority group.

So, for example, if a minority applicant feels he or she was a victim of discrimination, the person need only show that the employer's selection process resulted in an adverse impact on his or her group. (For example, if 80% of the white applicants passed the test, but only 20% of the black applicants passed, a black applicant has a *prima facie* case proving adverse impact.) Then the burden of proof shifts to the employer. It becomes the employer's task to prove that its test (or application blank or the like) is a valid predictor of performance on the job (and that it applied its selection process fairly and equitably to both minorities and nonminorities).

Employees who believe they are victims of harassment should have a mechanism for filing a complaint.

Dmytro Zinkevych/123RF

In practice, an applicant or employee can use one of the following five methods to show that one of an employer's procedures (such as a selection test) has an adverse impact on a protected group.

disparate rejection rates
A test for adverse impact in which it can be demonstrated that there is a discrepancy between rates of rejection of members of a protected group and of others.

4/5ths rule
Federal agency rule that a minority selection rate less than 80% (4/5ths) of that for the group with the highest rate is evidence of adverse impact.

DISPARATE REJECTION RATES The **disparate rejection rate** method compares the rejection rates for a minority group and another group (usually the remaining nonminority applicants).[102]

Federal agencies use a **"4/5ths rule"** to assess disparate rejection rates: "A selection rate for any racial, ethnic, or sex group which is less than four-fifths or 80% of the rate for the group with the highest rate will generally be regarded as evidence of adverse impact, while a greater than four-fifths rate will generally not be regarded as evidence of adverse impact." For example, suppose the employer hires 60% of male applicants but only 30% of female applicants. Four-fifths of the 60% male hiring rate would be 48%. Because the actual female hiring rate of 30% is less than 48%, adverse impact exists as far as these federal agencies are concerned.[103]

THE STANDARD DEVIATION RULE Similarly, the courts have used the *standard deviation rule* to confirm adverse impact. (The standard deviation is a statistical measure of variability. It is a measure of the dispersion of a set of data from its mean. Suppose we calculate the average height of students in your management class. In simplest terms, the standard deviation helps to describe, among other things, how wide a range there is in height between the shortest and tallest students and the class's average student height.) In selection, the standard deviation rule holds that, as a rule of thumb, the difference between the numbers of minority candidates we *would have expected* to hire and whom *we actually hired* should be less than two standard deviations.

Consider this example. Suppose 300 applicants apply for 20 openings; 80 of the applicants are women, and the other 220 are men. We use our screening processes and hire 2 females and 18 males. Did our selection process have an adverse impact? To answer this, we can compute the standard deviation:

$$SD = \sqrt{\frac{\textit{(Number of minority applicants)}}{\textit{(Number of total applicants)}} \times \frac{\textit{(Number of nonminority applicants)}}{\textit{(Number of total applicants)}} \times \textit{(Number of applicants selected)}}$$

In our case:

$$SD = \sqrt{\left(\frac{80}{300} \times \frac{220}{300} \times 20\right)} = \sqrt{(0.2667 \times 0.7333 \times 20)}$$
$$= \sqrt{3.911} = SD = 1.977$$

In our example, women are 26% (80/300) of the applicant pool. We should therefore *expect* to hire 26% of the 20 people hired, or about 5 women. We *actually* hired 2 women. The difference between the numbers of women we would expect to hire and whom we actually hired is 5 − 2 = 3. We can use the standard deviation rule to gauge if there is adverse (disparate) impact. In our example, the standard deviation is 1.977. Again, the standard deviation rule holds that as a rule of thumb, the difference between the numbers of minority candidates we would have expected to hire and whom we actually hired should be less than two standard deviations. Two times 1.9777 is about 4. Since the difference between the number of women we would have expected to hire (5) and actually hired (2) is 3, the results suggest that our screening did not have adverse impact on women. (Put another way, in this case, hiring just 2 rather than 5 is not a highly improbable result.)[104]

restricted policy
Another test for adverse impact, involving demonstration that an employer's hiring practices exclude a protected group, whether intentionally or not.

RESTRICTED POLICY The **restricted policy** approach means demonstrating that the employer's policy intentionally or unintentionally excluded members of a protected group. Here the problem is usually obvious—such as policies against hiring guards less than 6 feet tall. Evidence of restricted policies such as these is enough to prove adverse impact and to expose an employer to litigation.

POPULATION COMPARISONS This approach compares (1) the percentage of minority/protected group and white workers in the organization with, (2) the percentage of the corresponding group in the labor market.

"Labor market," of course, varies with the job. For some jobs, such as secretary, it makes sense to compare the percentage of minority employees with the percentage of minorities in the surrounding community, since they will come from that community. But determining whether an employer has enough black engineers might involve determining the number available nationwide, not in the surrounding community.

Employers use *workforce analysis* to analyze the data regarding the firm's use of protected versus nonprotected employees in various job classifications. The process of comparing the percentage of minority employees in a job (or jobs) at the company with the number of similarly trained minority employees available in the relevant labor market is *utilization analysis*.

MCDONNELL DOUGLAS TEST Lawyers in disparate impact cases use the previous approaches (such as population comparisons) to test whether an employer's policies or actions have the effect of unintentionally screening out disproportionate numbers of women or minorities. Lawyers use the McDonnell Douglas test for showing (intentional) disparate treatment, rather than (unintentional) disparate impact.

This test grew out of a case at the former McDonnell Douglas Corporation. The applicant was qualified, but the employer rejected the person and continued seeking applicants. Did this show that the hiring company intentionally discriminated against the female or minority candidate? The U.S. Supreme Court set four rules for applying the McDonnell Douglas test:

1. That the person belongs to a protected class;
2. That he or she applied and was qualified for a job for which the employer was seeking applicants;
3. That, despite this qualification, he or she was rejected; and
4. That, after his or her rejection, the position remained open and the employer continued seeking applications from persons with the complainant's qualifications.

If the plaintiff meets all these conditions, then a *prima facie* case of disparate treatment is established. At that point, the employer must articulate a legitimate nondiscriminatory reason for its action, and produce evidence but not prove that it acted based on such a reason. If it meets this relatively easy standard, the plaintiff then has the burden of proving that the employer's articulated reason is merely a pretext for engaging in unlawful discrimination.

ADVERSE IMPACT EXAMPLE Assume you turn down a member of a protected group for a job with your firm. You do this based on a test score (although it could have been interview questions or something else). Further, assume that this person feels he or she was discriminated against due to being in a protected class, and decides to sue your company.

Basically, all he or she must do is show that your procedure (such as the selection test) had an adverse impact on members of his or her minority group. The plaintiff can apply five approaches here. These are disparate rejection rates, the standard deviation rule, restricted policy, population comparisons, and, for disparate *treatment* cases, the McDonnell Douglas test. Once the person proves adverse impact (to the court's satisfaction), the burden of proof shifts to the employer. The employer must defend against the discrimination charges.

There is nothing in the law that says that because your procedure has an adverse impact on a protected group, you can't use it. In fact, it may well happen that some tests screen out disproportionately higher numbers of, say, blacks than they do whites. What the law does say is that once your applicant has made his or her case (showing adverse impact), the burden of proof shifts to you. Now the employer must defend use of the procedure.

There are then two basic defenses employers use to justify an employment practice that has an adverse impact on members of a minority group: the bona fide occupational qualification (BFOQ) defense and the business necessity defense.

Bona Fide Occupational Qualification

bona fide occupational qualification (BFOQ)
Requirement that an employee be of a certain religion, sex, or national origin where that is reasonably necessary to the organization's normal operation. Specified by the 1964 Civil Rights Act.

An employer can claim that the employment practice is a **bona fide occupational qualification (BFOQ)** for performing the job. Title VII specifically permits this defense. Title VII provides that "it should not be an unlawful employment practice for an employer to hire an employee . . . on the basis of religion, sex, or national origin *in those certain instances where religion, sex, or national origin is a bona fide occupational qualification* reasonably necessary to the normal operation of that particular business or enterprise."

However, courts usually interpret the BFOQ exception narrowly. It is usually a defense to a disparate treatment case based upon direct evidence of *intentional* discrimination, rather than to disparate impact (unintentional) cases. As a practical matter, employers use it mostly as a defense against charges of intentional discrimination based on age.

AGE AS A BFOQ The Age Discrimination in Employment Act (ADEA) permits disparate treatment in those instances when age is a BFOQ.[105] For example, age is a BFOQ when the Federal Aviation Agency sets a compulsory retirement age of 65 for commercial pilots.[106] Actors required for youthful or elderly roles suggest other instances when age may be a BFOQ. However, courts set the bar high: The reason for the age limit must go to the essence of the business. A court said a bus line's maximum-age hiring policy for bus drivers was a BFOQ. The court said the essence of the business was safe transportation of passengers, and, given that, the employer could strive to employ the most qualified persons available.[107]

RELIGION AS A BFOQ Religion may be a BFOQ in religious organizations or societies that require employees to share their particular religion. For example, religion may be a BFOQ when hiring persons to teach in a religious school. But again, courts construe this defense very narrowly.

GENDER AS A BFOQ Gender may be a BFOQ for positions like actor, model, and restroom attendant requiring physical characteristics possessed by one sex. However, for most jobs today, it's difficult to claim that gender is a BFOQ. For example, gender is not a BFOQ just because the position requires lifting heavy objects. A Texas man filed a complaint against Hooters of America alleging that one of its franchisees would not hire him as a waiter because it "merely wishes to exploit female sexuality as a marketing tool to attract customers and ensure profitability" and so was limiting hiring to females.[108] Hooters argued a BFOQ defense before reaching a confidential settlement.

NATIONAL ORIGIN AS A BFOQ A person's country of national origin may be a BFOQ. For example, an employer who is running the Chinese pavilion at a fair might claim that Chinese heritage is a BFOQ for persons to deal with the public.

Business Necessity

"Business necessity" is a defense created by the courts. It requires showing that there is an overriding business purpose for the discriminatory practice and that the practice is therefore acceptable.

It's not easy to prove business necessity.[109] The Supreme Court made it clear that business necessity does not encompass such matters as avoiding an employer inconvenience, annoyance, or expense. For example, an employer can't generally discharge employees whose wages have been garnished merely because garnishment (requiring the employer to divert part of the person's wages to pay his or her debts) creates an inconvenience. The Second Circuit Court of Appeals held that business necessity "must not only directly foster safety and efficiency" but also be essential to these goals.[110] Furthermore, "the business purpose must be sufficiently compelling to override any racial impact. . . ."[111]

However, many employers use the business necessity defense successfully. In an early case, *Spurlock v. United Airlines*, a minority candidate sued United Airlines. He said that its requirements that pilot candidates have 500 flight hours and college degrees were unfairly discriminatory. The court agreed that the requirements did have an adverse impact on members of the person's minority group. But it held that in light of the cost of the training program and the huge human and economic risks in hiring unqualified candidates, the selection standards were a business necessity and were job related.[112]

In general, when a job requires a small amount of skill and training, the courts closely scrutinize any preemployment standards or criteria that discriminate against minorities. There is a correspondingly lighter burden when the job requires a high degree of skill, and when the economic and human risks of hiring an unqualified applicant are great.[113]

Attempts by employers to show that their selection tests or other employment practices are *valid* are examples of the business necessity defense. Here the employer must show that the test or other practice is job related—in other words, that it is a valid predictor of performance on the job. Where the employer can establish such validity, the courts have generally supported using the test or other employment practice as a business necessity. In this context, *validity* means the degree to which the test or other employment practice is related to or predicts performance on the job; Chapter 6 explains validation. The following Know Your Employment Law discussion sums up how to apply all this.

KNOW YOUR EMPLOYMENT LAW

Examples of What You Can and Cannot Do

Before proceeding, we should review what federal fair employment laws allow (and do not allow) you to say and do.

Federal laws like Title VII usually don't expressly ban preemployment questions about an applicant's race, color, religion, sex, or national origin. In other words, "with the exception of personnel policies calling for outright discrimination against the members of some protected group," it's not the questions but their impact.[114] Thus, illustrative inquiries and practices like those on the next few pages are not illegal per se. For example, it isn't illegal to ask a job candidate about her marital status (although such a question might seem discriminatory). You can ask. However, be prepared to show either that you do not discriminate or that you can defend the practice as a BFOQ or business necessity.

But, in practice, there are two reasons to avoid such questions. First, although federal law may not bar such questions, many state and local laws do.

Second, the EEOC has said that it will disapprove of such practices, so just asking the questions may draw its attention. Such questions become illegal if a complainant can show you use them to screen out a greater proportion of his or her protected group's applicants, and you can't prove the practice is required as a business necessity or BFOQ.

Let's look now at some of the potentially discriminatory practices to avoid.[115]

Recruitment

Word of Mouth You cannot rely upon word-of-mouth dissemination of information about job opportunities when your workforce is all (or mostly all) white or all members of some other class such as all female, all Hispanic, and so on. Doing so reduces the likelihood that others will become aware of the jobs.

Misleading Information It is unlawful to give false or misleading information to members of any group, or to fail or refuse to advise them of work opportunities and the procedures for obtaining them.

Help-Wanted Ads "Help wanted—male" and "help wanted—female" ads are violations unless gender is a bona fide occupational qualification for the job. The same applies to ads that suggest age discrimination. For example, you cannot advertise for a "young" man or woman.

Selection Standards

Educational Requirements Courts have found educational qualifications to be illegal when (1) minority groups are less likely to possess the educational qualifications (such as a high school degree), and (2) such qualifications are also not job related. However, there may be jobs for which educational requirements (such as college degrees for pilot candidates) are a necessity.

Tests Courts deem tests unlawful if they disproportionately screen out minorities or women *and* they are not job related. According to a former U.S. Supreme Court Chief Justice,

> Nothing in the [Title VII] act precludes the use of testing or measuring procedures; obviously they are useful. What Congress has forbidden is giving these devices and mechanisms controlling force unless they are demonstrating a reasonable measure of job performance.

The employer must be prepared to show that the test results are job related—for instance, that test scores relate to on-the-job performance.

Preference to Relatives Do not give preference to relatives of current employees with respect to employment opportunities if your current employees are substantially nonminority.

Height, Weight, and Physical Characteristics Physical requirements such as minimum height are unlawful unless the employer can show they're job related. For example, a U.S. Appeals Court upheld a $3.4 million jury verdict against Dial Corp. Dial rejected 52 women for entry-level jobs at a meat-processing plant because they failed strength tests, although strength was not a job requirement.[116] *Maximum* weight rules generally don't trigger adverse legal rulings. To qualify for reasonable accommodation, obese applicants must be at least 100 pounds above their ideal weight or there must be a physiological cause for their disability. However, legalities aside, managers should be vigilant.[117] Studies show that obese individuals are less likely to be hired, less likely to receive promotions, more likely to get undesirable sales assignments, and more likely to receive poor customer service.[118]

Arrest Records Unless the job requires security clearance, do not ask an applicant whether he or she has been arrested or spent time in jail, or use an arrest record to disqualify a person automatically. Due to racial and ethnic disparities in arrest and prison rates, both the EEOC and the Office of Federal Contract Compliance Programs (OFCCP) set forth new guidance discouraging employers from using blanket exclusions against individuals with criminal records.[119]

Application Forms Employment applications generally shouldn't contain questions about applicants' disabilities, workers' compensation history, age, arrest record, or U.S. citizenship. It's generally best to collect personal information required for legitimate reasons (such as emergency contact) after you hire the person.[120]

Discharge Due to Garnishment Disproportionate numbers of minorities suffer garnishment procedures (in which creditors make a claim to some of the person's wages). Therefore, firing a minority member whose salary is garnished is illegal, unless you can show some overriding business necessity.

Sample Discriminatory Promotion, Transfer, and Layoff Practices

Fair employment laws protect not just job applicants but also current employees. For example, the Equal Pay Act requires that equal wages be paid for substantially similar work performed by men and women. Therefore, courts may hold that any employment practices regarding pay, promotion, termination, discipline, or benefits that

1. Are applied differently to different classes of persons,
2. Adversely impact members of a protected group, and
3. Cannot be shown to be required as a BFOQ or business necessity are illegally discriminatory.

Personal Appearance Regulations and Title VII Employees sometimes file suits against employers' dress and appearance codes under Title VII. They usually claim sex discrimination, but sometimes claim racial or even religious discrimination. A sampling of court rulings follows:[121]

- ***Dress.*** In general, employers do not violate the Title VII ban on sex bias by requiring all employees to dress conservatively. For example, a supervisor's suggestion that a female attorney tone down her attire was permissible when the firm consistently sought to maintain a conservative dress style and counseled men to dress conservatively. However, Alamo Rent-A-Car lost a case when it tried to prevent a Muslim woman employee from wearing a headscarf.
- ***Hair.*** Courts usually favor employers here. For example, employer rules against facial hair do not constitute sex discrimination because they discriminate only between clean-shaven and bearded men, discrimination not qualified as sex bias under Title VII. Courts have also rejected arguments that prohibiting cornrow hairstyles infringed on black employees' expression of cultural identification.
- ***Uniforms.*** When it comes to discriminatory uniforms and/or suggestive attire, however, courts frequently side with employees. For example, requiring female employees (such as waitresses) to wear sexually suggestive attire as a condition of employment has been ruled as violating Title VII in many cases.[122]
- ***Tattoos and body piercings.*** About 38% of Millennials in one survey had tattoos as compared with 15% of baby boomers. About 23% of Millennials had body

piercings as compared with 1% of baby boomers. One case involved a waiter with religious tattoos on his wrists at Red Robin Gourmet Burgers. The company insisted he cover his tattoos at work; he refused. Red Robin settled the suit after the waiter claimed that covering the tattoos would be a sin based on his religion.[123] ■

> MyLab Management Talk About It 1
>
> If your professor has assigned this, go to the Assignments section of **www.pearson.com/mylab/management** to complete these discussion questions. Have you ever had an experience in which an employer apparently violated one or more of the preceding guidelines—for example, told you to change your hairstyle—or have you ever simply noticed a violation (such as a store posting a sign that said "delivery boy wanted")? What was your reaction? What did you do? Are there situations in which the employer may have been within the law to do what he or she did?

Finally, keep three other things in mind:

1. *Good intentions are no excuse.* As the Supreme Court held in the *Griggs* case, good intent or absence of discriminatory intent does not redeem procedures that operate as built-in headwinds for minority groups and are unrelated to measuring job capability.
2. One cannot claim that a *union agreement necessitates some discriminatory practice*. Equal employment opportunity laws prevail.[124]
3. A strong defense *is not your only recourse.* The employer can agree to eliminate the illegal practice and (when required) to compensate the people discriminated against.

The EEOC Enforcement Process

LEARNING OBJECTIVE 2-4

List the steps in the EEOC enforcement process.

Even careful employers eventually face employment discrimination claims and have to deal with the EEOC.[125] All managers (not just human resource managers) play roles in this process. Figure 2-3 provides an overview of this EEOC enforcement process.[126]

- ***File Charge.*** The process begins when someone files a claim with the EEOC. Either the aggrieved person or a member of the EEOC who has reasonable cause to believe that a violation occurred must file the claim in writing and under oath.[127] Under CRA 1991, the discrimination claim must be filed within 300 days (when there is a similar state law) or 180 days (where there is no similar state law) after the alleged incident took place (2 years for the Equal Pay Act).[128] The U.S. Supreme Court, in *Ledbetter v. Goodyear Tire & Rubber Company,* held that employees claiming Title VII pay discrimination must file their claims within 180 days of when they first receive the allegedly discriminatory pay. Congress then passed, and President Obama signed, the Lilly Ledbetter Fair Pay Act into law. Employees can now file such claims anytime, as long as they're still receiving an "infected" paycheck. (The EEOC recently received 91,503 private-sector discrimination charges in one fiscal year.[129]) One may obtain employment practices liability insurance against discrimination claims.[130]
- ***Charge Acceptance.*** The EEOC's common practice is to accept a charge and orally refer it to the state or local agency on behalf of the charging party. If the agency waives jurisdiction or cannot obtain a satisfactory solution, the EEOC processes it upon the expiration of the deferral period.[131]
- ***Serve Notice.*** After a charge is filed (or the state or local deferral period has ended), the EEOC has 10 days to serve notice on the employer. Attorneys advise against submitting lengthy statements in response to a charge. Instead, provide a concise explanation describing why the actions were lawful.[132] Figure 2-4 lists some questions to ask after receiving a bias complaint from the EEOC.

FIGURE 2-3 The EEOC Charge-Filing Process

Note: Parties may settle at any time.

Source: Based on www.eeoc.gov.

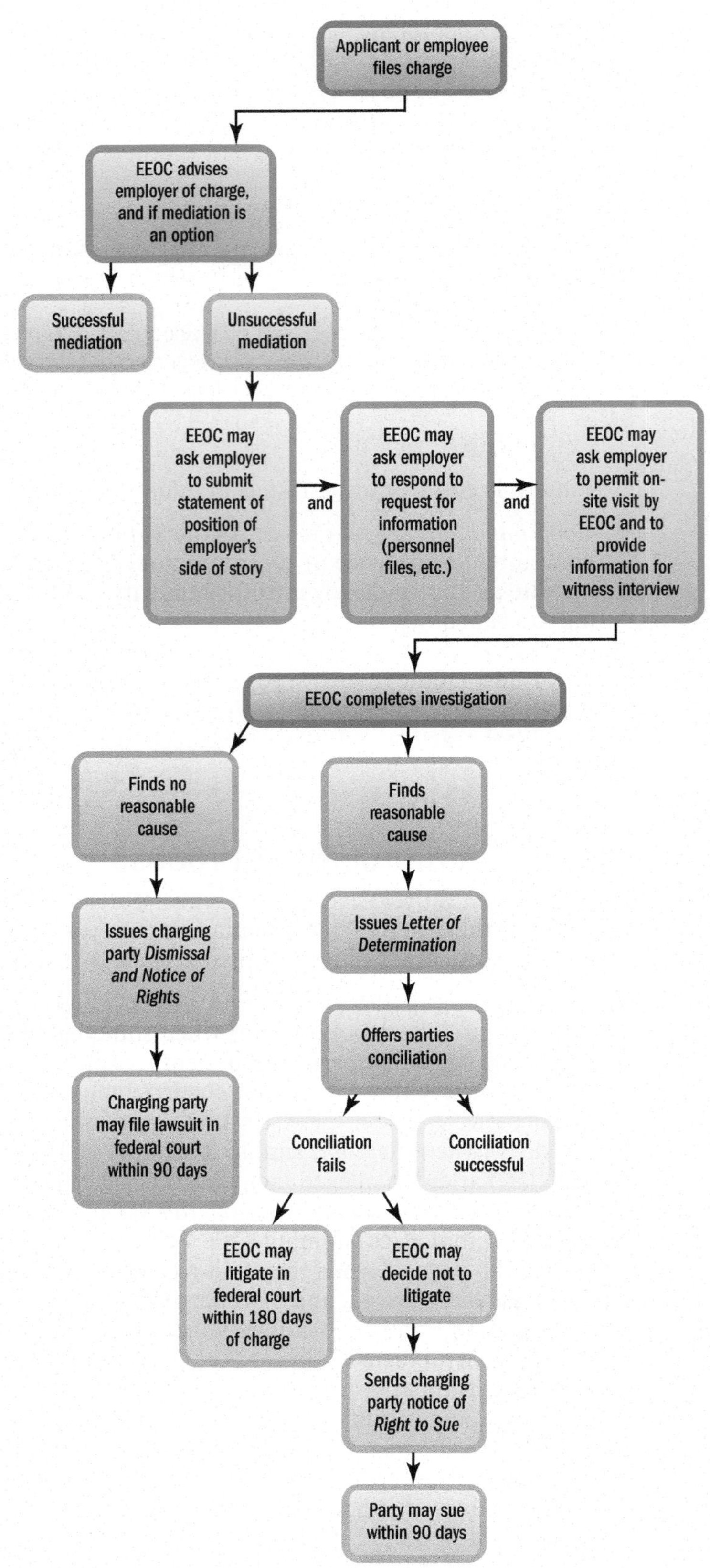

FIGURE 2-4 Questions to Ask When an Employer Receives Notice That the EEOC Has Filed a Bias Claim

Source: Based on Bureau of National Affairs, Inc., "Fair Employment Practices: Summary of Latest Developments," January 7, 1983, p. 3; Kenneth Sovereign, *Personnel Law* (Upper Saddle River, NJ: Prentice Hall, 1999), pp. 36–37; and Equal Employment Opportunity Commission, "What You Can Expect After a Charge Is Filed," www.eeoc.gov/employers/process.cfm, accessed June 28, 2018.

1. Exactly what is the charge, and is your company covered by the relevant statutes? (For example, Title VII and the Americans with Disabilities Act generally apply only to employees with 15 or more employees.) Did the employee file his or her charge on time, and was it processed in a timely manner by the EEOC?
2. What protected group does the employee belong to?
3. Is the EEOC claiming disparate impact or disparate treatment?
4. Are there any obvious bases upon which you can challenge and/or rebut the claim? For example, would the employer have taken the action if the person did not belong to a protected group?
5. If it is a sexual harassment claim, are there offensive comments, calendars, posters, screensavers, and so on, on display in the company?
6. In terms of the practicality of defending your company against this claim, who are the supervisors who actually took the allegedly discriminatory actions, and how effective will they be as potential witnesses? Have you received an opinion from legal counsel regarding the chances of prevailing?

- ***Investigation/Fact-Finding Conference.*** The EEOC then investigates the charge to determine whether there is reasonable cause to believe it is true; it has 120 days to decide.[133] Early in the investigation, the EEOC holds an initial *fact-finding conference.* The EEOC's focus here is often to find weak spots in each party's position. It uses these to push for a settlement.
- ***Cause/No Cause.*** If it finds no reasonable cause, the EEOC must dismiss the charge and issue the charging party a Notice of Right to Sue. The person then has 90 days to file a suit on his or her own behalf.
- ***Conciliation.*** If the EEOC does find cause, it has 30 days to work out a conciliation agreement. The EEOC conciliator meets with the employee to determine what remedy would be satisfactory. It then tries to negotiate a settlement with the employer.
- ***Notice to Sue.*** If this conciliation is not satisfactory, the EEOC may bring a civil suit in a federal district court, or issue a Notice of Right to Sue to the person who filed the charge.

Voluntary Mediation

The EEOC refers about 10% of its charges to a voluntary mediation mechanism, "an informal process in which a neutral third party assists the opposing parties to reach a voluntary, negotiated resolution of a charge of discrimination."[134] If the parties don't reach agreement (or one of the parties rejects participation), the EEOC processes the charge through its usual mechanisms.[135]

Faced with an offer to mediate, the employer has three options: Agree to mediate the charge; make a settlement offer without mediation; or prepare a "position statement" for the EEOC. If the employer does not mediate or make an offer, the position statement is required. It should include a robust defense, including information relating to the company's business and the charging party's position; a description of any rules or policies and procedures that are applicable; and the chronology of the offense that led to the adverse action.[136]

Mandatory Arbitration of Discrimination Claims

Many employers, to avoid EEOC litigation, require applicants and employees to agree to arbitrate such claims. The EEOC does not favor mandatory arbitration. However, the U.S. Supreme Court's decisions (in *Gilmer v. Interstate/Johnson Lane Corp.* and similar cases) make it clear that "employment discrimination plaintiffs [employees] may be compelled to arbitrate their claims under some circumstances."[137] Given this, employers "may wish to consider inserting a mandatory arbitration clause in their employment applications or employee handbooks."[138] To protect such a process against appeal, the employer should institute steps to protect against arbitrator bias, allow the arbitrator to offer a claimant broad relief (including reinstatement), and allow for a reasonable amount of prehearing fact finding.

alternative dispute resolution or ADR program
Grievance procedure that provides for binding arbitration as the last step.

Rockwell International has a grievance procedure that provides for binding arbitration as the last step. Called (as is traditional) an **alternative dispute resolution or ADR program,** Rockwell gradually extended the program to all nonunion employees at some locations. New hires at Rockwell must sign the agreement. Current employees must sign it prior to promotion or transfer. U.S. federal agencies must have ADR programs.[139] ADR plans are popular, although the EEOC generally prefers mediation for handling bias claims.[140]

The accompanying HR Tools feature provides some guidelines to follow in addressing EEOC claims.

IMPROVING PERFORMANCE: *HR TOOLS FOR LINE MANAGERS AND SMALL BUSINESSES*

Chances are the EEOC won't file a suit, but getting a notice saying it's investigating is still scary. Whether you are managing one team or your own small business, every manager should know in advance what the EEOC will be looking for and what to do. A checklist follows.[141]

During the EEOC Investigation:

- ✓ *Conduct your own investigation* to get the facts.
- ✓ Ensure that there is information in the EEOC's file *demonstrating lack of merit* of the charge.
- ✓ *Limit the information supplied* to only those issues raised in the charge itself.
- ✓ *Get as much information* as possible about the *charging party's claim.*
- ✓ *Meet with the employee* who made the complaint to clarify all the relevant issues. For example, what happened? Who was involved?
- ✓ Remember that *the EEOC can only ask (not compel) employers* to submit documents and ask for the testimony of witnesses under oath.
- ✓ Give the EEOC a *position statement.* It should contain words to the effect that "the company has a policy against discrimination and would not discriminate in the manner charged in the complaint."
- ✓ Support the statement with documentation.

During the Fact-Finding Conference:

- ✓ Because the only official record is the notes the EEOC investigator takes, *keep your own records.*
- ✓ Bring an *attorney.*
- ✓ Make sure you are *fully informed* of the charges and facts of the case.
- ✓ Before appearing, *witnesses (especially supervisors) need to be aware* of the legal significance of the facts they will present.

During the EEOC Determination and Attempted Conciliation:

- ✓ If there is a finding of cause, *review it carefully*, and point out inaccuracies in writing to the EEOC.
- ✓ Use this letter to try again to convince the parties that the charge is *without merit.*
- ✓ *Conciliate prudently.* If you have properly investigated the case, there may be no real advantage in settling at this stage.
- ✓ Remember: Odds are that *no suit will be filed* by the EEOC.

Two Mistakes to Avoid

Finally, keep two other things in mind.

- ✓ First, avoid *management malpractice,* which is aberrant managerial conduct that "exceeds all bounds usually tolerated by society."[142] In one outrageous example, the employer demoted a manager to janitor and humiliated him. The jury awarded the man millions. Supervisors who commit management malpractice may be personally liable for paying some of the judgment.

✓ Second, *do not retaliate*. Retaliation occurs when employers treat applicants, employees, former employees, or people closely associated with them, less favorably because, for instance, they threatened to file a discrimination charge.[143] Retaliation is the most common charge filed with the EEOC.[144] ■

> **MyLab Management Talk About It 2**
>
> If your professor has assigned this, go to the Assignments section of **www.pearson.com/mylab/management** to complete these discussion questions. Check with the EEOC's Web site and compile a list of the biggest financial settlements this past year for retaliation claims. About how much was the average claim? What you would do to *avoid* doing something that prompted the EEOC to become interested in your company?

LEARNING OBJECTIVE 2-5

Give examples of attitudes that undermine diversity efforts, and explain how you would create a diversity management program.

Diversity Management

Diversity means being diverse or varied and at work means having a workforce composed of two or more groups of employees with various racial, ethnic, gender, cultural, national origin, handicap, age, and religious backgrounds.[145] We introduce diversity and diversity management here, and then address them in features throughout the book.

diversity
The variety or multiplicity of demographic features that characterize a company's workforce, particularly in terms of race, sex, culture, national origin, handicap, age, and religion.

stereotyping
Ascribing specific behavioral traits to individuals based on their apparent membership in a group.

gender-role stereotypes
The tendency to associate women with certain (frequently nonmanagerial) jobs. On the other hand, diversity can be an engine of performance, as the following feature shows.

discrimination
Taking specific actions toward or against a person based on the person's group.

tokenism
When a company appoints a small group of women or minorities to high-profile positions, rather than more aggressively seeking full representation for that group.

ethnocentrism
The tendency to view members of other social groups less favorably than members of one's own group.

Potential Threats to Diversity

Workforce diversity produces both benefits and problems for employers. Unmanaged, it can produce behavioral barriers that reduce cooperation. Potential problems include:

- **Stereotyping.** Here someone ascribes specific behavioral traits to individuals based on their apparent membership in a group:[146] for example, "older people can't work hard." Cheryl Sandberg, Facebook's Chief Operating Officer, says many people hold such unconscious assumptions (stereotypes); one is that men are expected to be assertive while women should be collaborative. So, a woman who pushes for more for herself is viewed as "bossy," whereas a man is viewed as doing his job.[147] Put another way, women confront **gender-role stereotypes,** the tendency to associate women with certain (frequently nonmanagerial) jobs.[148]

  Prejudice is a bias toward prejudging someone based on that person's traits, as in "we won't hire him because he's old." Some people's biases are subconscious. To check, try asking questions like, "Do I typically hire the same type of person?" and "To whom do I generally assign the best projects?"[149]
- **Discrimination** is prejudice in action. It means taking specific actions toward or against the person based on the person's group.[150] Of course, it's generally illegal to discriminate at work based on someone's age, race, gender, disability, or national origin. But in practice, discrimination may be subtle. For example, many argue that a "glass ceiling," enforced by an "old boys' network" (friendships built in places like exclusive clubs), hinders women from reaching top management.
- **Tokenism** means a company appoints a small group of women or minorities to high-profile positions, rather than more aggressively seeking full representation for that group.[151]
- **Ethnocentrism** is the tendency to view members of other social groups less favorably than one's own. Thus, in one study, managers attributed the performance of some minorities less to their abilities and more to help they received from others. The same managers attributed the performance of *non*minorities to their own abilities.[152]

IMPROVING PERFORMANCE: *HR AS A PROFIT CENTER*

Diversity can actually drive higher profits. In one study, researchers examined the diversity climate in 654 stores of a large U.S. retail chain. They defined *diversity climate* as the extent to which employees in the stores said the firm promotes equal opportunity and inclusion. They found the highest sales growth in stores with the highest pro-diversity climate, and the lowest in stores where subordinates and managers reported less hospitable diversity climates.[153] Another study found racial discrimination to be related negatively to employee commitment, while organizational efforts to support diversity reduced such negative effects.[154] When Merck needed halal certification for one of its medicines, it turned to its Muslim employees. They helped Merck bring the product to market faster and helped ensure its acceptance among Muslims.[155]

More than 50 of the largest U.S. companies, including GE, Microsoft, and Walmart, filed briefs with the U.S. Supreme Court arguing that affirmative action produces increased sales and profits. ■

> MyLab Management Talk About It 3
>
> If your professor has assigned this, go to the Assignments section of **www.pearson.com/mylab/management** to complete these discussion questions. What do you think accounts for the fact that diversity apparently seems to produce higher profits? Do you think that would always be the case? Why or why not?

Managing Diversity

managing diversity
Maximizing diversity's potential benefits while minimizing its potential barriers.

The key to deriving such benefits is properly managing diversity's potential problems. **Managing diversity** means maximizing diversity's potential benefits while minimizing the potential problems—such as prejudice—that can undermine cooperation. In practice, diversity management requires both compulsory and voluntary actions. Compulsory actions (particularly EEO law compliance) can't guarantee cooperation. Managing diversity therefore also relies on taking voluntary steps to encourage employees to work together productively.[156]

TOP-DOWN DIVERSITY MANAGEMENT PROGRAMS The employer may institute a *diversity management program,* usually at the initiative of a top executive. The program's main aim is to make employees more sensitive to and better able to deal with cultural differences. First, make sure diversity training is the solution, or if some other approach is more advisable. Next, set measurable program goals, for instance, in terms of quantifiable attitudes toward diversity.[157] Then, five steps are typical:[158]

Provide strong leadership. Companies with exemplary reputations in managing diversity typically have CEOs who champion the cause of diversity. Leadership here means, for instance, becoming a role model for the behaviors required for the change. One study concluded that top managers who excelled at creating inclusive organizations were also those who were personally passionate about encouraging inclusion and diversity.[159]

Assess the situation. One study found that the most common tools for assessing a company's diversity include equal employment hiring and retention metrics, employee attitude surveys, management and employee evaluations, and focus groups.

Provide diversity training and education. The most common starting point for a diversity management effort is usually some type of employee education program.

Change culture and management systems. Combine education programs with other concrete steps aimed at changing the organization's culture and management systems. For example, change the performance appraisal procedure to appraise supervisors based partly on their success in reducing intergroup conflicts.

Evaluate the diversity management program. For example, do employee attitude surveys now indicate any improvement in employees' attitudes toward diversity?

The problem is that many diversity programs are ineffective. Some fail because even positively inclined employees may resist participating in mandatory programs.[160] Others fail by providing a false sense of security. For instance one study found that appointing diversity committees and chief diversity officers lulled managers into believing their workplace was inclusive when it was not.[161]

Some firms are therefore pursuing alternatives. The consulting firm Deloitte LLP concluded that gender-based diversity groups are no longer the best way to encourage diversity. Instead, it is creating what it calls inclusion councils. Rather than groups comprised of only women or minorities, the councils each include a diversity of inputs and points of view.[162]

DIVERSITY THROUGH ENGAGEMENT Others wisely design their diversity efforts to elicit their employees' engagement and active participation.[163] For example, at software company SAP, the Chief Learning Officer discovered that while participants rated SAP's diversity training program highly, the program seemed to produce only limited results. She therefore replaced it with a year-long leadership development program she called the "Leadership Excellence Acceleration Program" (LEAP). Every year LEAP gathers together high-performing female employees. For a year they then engage in exercises such as in-house team consulting assignments and listening to speakers.[164] SAP also offers female employees a global business network of 8,000 female employees, and SAP's board recently committed to boosting the leadership positions held by SAP women to 25% (from 23%).[165] SAP's efforts seem to be successful, in terms its female employees moving into management positions.[166]

Implementing the Affirmative Action Program

Equal employment opportunity aims to ensure that anyone, regardless of race, color, disability, sex, religion, national origin, or age, has an equal opportunity based on his or her qualifications. *Affirmative action* means taking actions (in recruitment, hiring, promotions, and compensation) to eliminate the current effects of past discrimination.

Affirmative action is still a significant workplace issue. The incidences of major court-mandated affirmative action programs are down, but courts still use them. Furthermore, many employers must still engage in voluntary programs. For example, Executive Order (EO) 11246 (issued in 1965) requires federal contractors to take affirmative action to improve employment opportunities for groups such as women and racial minorities. It covers about 22% of the U.S. workforce.[167] In discussing methods for increasing diversity, two researchers say that "few are as effective as affirmative action policies."[168]

good-faith effort strategy
An affirmative action strategy that emphasizes identifying and eliminating the obstacles to hiring and promoting women and minorities, and increasing the minority or female applicant flow.

Under guidelines such as EO 11246, the key aims of affirmative action programs are (1) to use numerical analysis to determine which (if any) target groups the firm is underutilizing relative to the relevant labor market, and (2) to eliminate the barriers to equal employment. Many employers pursue these aims with a **good-faith effort strategy;** this emphasizes identifying and eliminating the obstacles to hiring and promoting women and minorities, and increasing the minority or female applicant flow. Reasonable steps to take include those shown in Figure 2-5 (page 58).

For example, place recruiting ads on online minority-oriented job sites. Diversity candidate Web sites with job banks include the National Urban League, Hispanic Online, Latino Web, Society of Hispanic Engineers, Gay.com, Association for Women in Science, and Minorities Job Bank.

EMPLOYEE RESISTANCE Avoiding employee resistance to affirmative action programs is important. Here, studies suggest that current employees need to believe the program is fair. *Transparent selection procedures* (explaining clearly what selection tools and standards the company uses) help in this regard. *Communication* is also crucial. Show that the program doesn't involve preferential selection standards. Provide details on the qualifications of all new hires (both minority and nonminority). *Justifications* for the program should emphasize redressing past discrimination and the practical value of diversity, not underrepresentation.[169]

FIGURE 2-5 Steps in an Affirmative Action Program

1. Issue a written equal employment policy indicating that the firm is an equal employment opportunity employer and the employer's commitment to affirmative action.
2. Demonstrate top-management support for the equal employment policy—for instance, appoint a high-ranking EEO administrator.
3. Publicize internally and externally the equal employment policy and affirmative action commitment.
4. Survey current minority and female employment by department and job classification to determine where affirmative action programs are especially desirable.
5. Carefully analyze employer human resources practices to identify and eliminate hidden barriers.
6. Review, develop, and implement specific HR programs to improve female and minority utilization.
7. Use focused recruitment to find qualified applicants from the target group(s).
8. Establish an internal audit and reporting system to monitor and evaluate progress.
9. Develop support for the affirmative action program, inside the company and in the community.

PROGRAM EVALUATION Is the diversity program effective? Some commonsense questions to ask include:

- Are there women and minorities reporting directly to senior managers, and in senior manager positions?
- Do women and minorities have a fair share of the jobs that are the traditional stepping-stones to successful careers in the company?
- Do women and minorities have equal access to international assignments?
- Is the employer taking steps that ensure that female and minority candidates will be in the company's career development pipeline?
- Are turnover rates for female and minority managers the same or lower than those for white males?
- Do employees report that they perceive positive behavior changes as a result of the diversity efforts?[170]

reverse discrimination
Claim that due to affirmative action quota systems, white males are discriminated against.

Reverse Discrimination

Reverse discrimination means discriminating against *non*minority applicants and employees.[171] Many court cases have addressed these issues.

Rawpixel.com/Shutterstock

Diversity management can blend a diverse workforce into a close-knit and productive community.

In one of the first such cases, *Bakke v. Regents of the University of California* (1978), the University of California at Davis Medical School denied admission to white student Allen Bakke, allegedly because of the school's affirmative action quota system, which required that a specific number of openings go to minority applicants. In a 5-to-4 vote, the U.S. Supreme Court struck down the policy that made race the only factor in considering applications for a certain number of class openings and thus allowed Bakke's admission.

Bakke was followed by many other cases. In 2009, the U.S. Supreme Court ruled in an important reverse discrimination suit brought by Connecticut firefighters. In *Ricci v. DeStefano*, 19 white firefighters and one Hispanic firefighter said the city of New Haven should have promoted them based on their successful test scores. The city argued that certifying the tests would have left them vulnerable to lawsuits from minorities for violating Title VII.[172] The Court ruled in favor of the (predominantly white) plaintiffs. In New Haven's desire to avoid making promotions that might appear to adversely impact minorities, Justice Kennedy wrote that "the city rejected the test results solely because the higher scoring candidates were white." The consensus of observers was that the decision would make it harder for employers to ignore the results obtained by valid tests, even if the results disproportionately impact minorities.[173]

The bottom line seems to be that employers should emphasize the external recruitment and internal development of better-qualified minority and female employees, "while basing employment decisions on legitimate criteria."[174]

Chapter Review

Chapter Section Summaries

2-1. Several of the most important **equal employment opportunity laws became law in the period from 1964 to 1991.**

- Title VII of the 1964 Civil Rights Act states that an employer cannot discriminate based on race, color, religion, sex, or national origin. Title VII established the Equal Employment Opportunity Commission and covers most employees.
- Under the Equal Pay Act of 1963 (amended in 1972), it is unlawful to discriminate in pay on the basis of sex when jobs involve equal work, skills, effort, and responsibility and are performed under similar working conditions.
- The Age Discrimination in Employment Act of 1967 made it unlawful to discriminate against employees or applicants who are between 40 and 65 years of age.
- The Vocational Rehabilitation Act of 1973 requires most employers with federal contracts to take affirmative action when employing handicapped persons.
- The Pregnancy Discrimination Act of 1978 prohibits using pregnancy, childbirth, or related medical conditions to discriminate in hiring, promotion, suspension, or discharge or in any term or condition of employment.
- The EEOC, Civil Service Commission, Department of Labor, and Department of Justice together issued Uniform Guidelines. These set forth "highly recommended" procedures regarding HR activities like employee selection and record keeping.
- *Griggs v. Duke Power Company* was an important early case. Here, Chief Justice Burger held that in employment, discrimination does not have to be overt to be illegal, and an employment practice that discriminates must be job related.

2-2. Equal employment law continues to evolve, with important **new legislation enacted since 1990–1991.**

- The Civil Rights Act of 1991 reversed the effects of several Supreme Court rulings—for instance, underscoring that the burden of proof is the employer's once a plaintiff establishes possible illegal discrimination.
- The Americans with Disabilities Act prohibits employment discrimination against qualified disabled individuals. It also says

employers must make "reasonable accommodations" for physical or mental limitations unless doing so imposes an "undue hardship" on the business.

- The Federal Violence Against Women Act of 1994 provided women with another way to seek relief for (violent) sexual harassment. Basically, sexual harassment refers to unwelcome sexual advances, requests for sexual favors, and other verbal or physical conduct of a sexual nature that takes place, for instance, when such conduct is made either explicitly or implicitly a term or condition of an individual's employment. Three main ways to prove sexual harassment include *quid pro quo*, hostile environment created by supervisors, and hostile environment created by coworkers or those who are not employees.

2-3. Employers use various **defenses against discrimination allegations.** Here employers need to distinguish between disparate treatment (intentional discrimination) and disparate impact (a policy that has an adverse impact regardless of intent). Plaintiffs show adverse impact by the standard deviation rule or by showing disparate rejection rates, restricted policy, or population comparisons, or by applying the McDonnell Douglas test. Employers defend themselves by showing that the employment practice is a bona fide occupational qualification (for instance, gender is a BFOQ for a position such as model). Or they may defend themselves by using the business necessity defense, which requires showing that there is an overriding business purpose. Given all this, the manager needs a working knowledge of *discriminatory employment practices*. For example, in recruitment, employers no longer use "help wanted—male" ads.

2-4. All managers play an important role in **the EEOC enforcement process.** The basic steps in this process include filing the charge, charge acceptance by the EEOC, serving notice on the employer, the investigation/fact-finding conference, a finding of cause/no cause, conciliation efforts, and (if necessary) a notice to sue. The EEOC refers about 10% of its charges to voluntary mediation mechanisms.

2-5. **Managing diversity** means maximizing diversity's potential benefits while minimizing the potential barriers. General steps include providing strong leadership, assessing the situation, providing diversity training and education, changing the culture and management systems, and evaluating the diversity management program's results. Affirmative action generally means taking actions to eliminate the present effects of past discrimination. Many employers still pursue voluntary, good-faith effort strategies in identifying and eliminating the obstacles to hiring and promoting women and minorities. Other employers are under court-mandated requirement to do so.

Discussion Questions

2-1. What important precedents were set by the *Griggs v. Duke Power Company* case? The *Albemarle v. Moody* case?

2-2. Explain each of the four examples of a bona fide occupational qualification.

2-3. What is sexual harassment? How can an employee prove sexual harassment?

2-4. What is the difference between disparate treatment and disparate impact?

Individual and Group Activities

2-5. Working individually or in groups, respond to these three scenarios based on what you learned in this chapter. Under what conditions (if any) do you think the following constitute sexual harassment? (a) A female manager fires a male employee because he refuses her requests for sexual favors. (b) A male manager refers to female employees as "sweetie" or "baby." (c) A female employee overhears two male employees exchanging sexually oriented jokes.

2-6. Working individually or in groups, discuss how you would set up an affirmative action program.

2-7. Compare and contrast the issues presented in *Bakke* with more recent court rulings on affirmative action. Working individually or in groups, discuss the current direction of affirmative action.

2-8. Working individually or in groups, write a one-page paper titled "What the Manager Should

Know About How the EEOC Handles a Person's Discrimination Charge."

2-9. Explain the difference between affirmative action and equal employment opportunity.

2-10. Assume you are the manager in a small restaurant; you are responsible for hiring employees, supervising them, and recommending them for promotion. Working individually or in groups, compile a list of potentially discriminatory management practices you should avoid.

2-11. Appendices A and B at the end of this book (pages 614–634) list the knowledge someone studying for the HRCI (Appendix A) or SHRM (Appendix B) certification exam needs to have in each area of human resource management (such as in Strategic Management and Workforce Planning). In groups of several students, do four things: (1) review Appendix A and/or B; (2) identify the material in this chapter that relates to the Appendix A and/or B required knowledge lists; (3) write four multiple-choice exam questions on this material that you believe would be suitable for inclusion in the HRCI exam and/or the SHRM exam; and, (4) if time permits, have someone from your team post your team's questions in front of the class, so that students in all teams can answer the exam questions created by the other teams.

KNOWLEDGE BASE

Experiential Exercise

"Space Cadet" or Victim?[175]

Written and copyrighted by Gary Dessler, PhD.

Discrimination lawsuits are rarely simple because the employer will often argue that the person was fired due to poor performance rather than discrimination. So, there's often a "mixed-motive" element to such situations. The facts of a case illustrate this (*Burk v. California Association of Realtors*, California Court of Appeals, number 161513, unpublished, 12/12/03). The facts were as follows. The California Association of Realtors maintained a hotline service to provide legal advice to real estate agents. One of the 12 lawyers who answered this hotline was a 61-year-old California attorney who worked there from 1989 to 2000. Until 1996 he received mostly good reviews. At that time, association members began filing complaints about his advice. His supervisor told him to be more courteous.

Two years later, association members were still complaining about this individual. Among other things, association members who called in filed complaints referring to him as "a space cadet" and "incompetent." Subsequently, his supervisor contacted six association members whom the 61-year-old lawyer had recently counseled; five of the six said they had had bad experiences. The association fired him for mistreating association members and providing inadequate legal advice.

The 61-year-old lawyer sued the association, claiming that the firing was age related. To support his claim, he noted that one colleague had told him that he was "probably getting close to retirement" and that another colleague had told him he was "getting older." The appeals court had to decide whether the association fired the 61-year-old lawyer because of his age or because of his performance.

Purpose: The purpose of this exercise is to provide practice in analyzing and applying knowledge of equal opportunity legislation to a real problem.

Required Understanding: Be thoroughly familiar with the material presented in this chapter. In addition, read the preceding "space cadet" case on which this experiential exercise is based.

How to Set Up the Exercise/Instructions:

- Divide the class into groups.
- Each group should develop answers to the following questions:

  2-12. Based on what you read in this chapter, on what legal basis could the 61-year-old California attorney claim he was a victim of discrimination?

  2-13. On what laws and legal concepts did the employer apparently base its termination of this 61-year-old attorney?

  2-14. Based on what laws or legal concepts could you take the position that it is legal to fire someone for poor performance even though there may be a discriminatory aspect to the termination? (This is not to say that there necessarily was such a discriminatory aspect with this case.)

  2-15. If you were the judge called on to make a decision on this case, what would your decision be, and why?

- The court's decision follows, so please do not read this until you've completed the exercise.

In this case, the California State Appeals court held that "the only reasonable inference that can be drawn from the evidence is that [plaintiff] was terminated because he failed to competently perform his job of providing thorough, accurate, and courteous legal advice to hotline callers."

Application Case

Seeking Gender Equity at Starbucks

Written and copyrighted by Gary Dessler PhD.

Starbucks is progressive in terms of gender equity policies.[176] By the 1990s it was offering health insurance coverage to Starbucks partners (employees) who were in lesbian and gay relationships, and its health care insurance covers gender reassignment surgery. More recently it announced that it had eliminated its partners' gender wage gap: Starbucks male and female partners performing similar work are paid almost exactly the same—within 99.7% of each other (compared with about 70% nationwide).

However, several large Starbucks shareholders think its gender efforts still fall short. For example, Zevin Asset Management proposed that Starbucks report on whether its paid family leave policy was discriminatory. According to Starbucks, the policy is generous and competitive for a retail chain. For example, it gives Starbucks corporate office workers 16 weeks paid leave if they gave birth, and 12 weeks if they are new fathers or adoptive parents. Starbucks says its program is exceptional because even employees who work just 20 hours a week can use it. But Zevin says the problem is that the policy is discriminatory because retail store workers who give birth or adopt only get six weeks of paid leave and fathers get none. Some shareholders say this will harm Starbucks' reputation, because it is on record as saying that it tries to treat corporate and retail partners the same.

Although shareholders often reject proposals like these, employers may still implement the recommendations, particularly when they involve equitable treatment. Several years ago, for instance another investment firm proposed that several tech giants like Amazon and Apple pay male and female employees equitably. The proposal never came to a vote, because the tech firms soon closed their gender wage gaps.

So at the end of the day, such proposals present top managers with a dilemma. Starbucks, for instance, believed that its parental leave policy was already one of the best in the industry, and that was probably true. Yet it did seem somewhat inequitable to offer better benefits to corporate office workers then to those in the retail stores.

Questions

2-16. Do you agree that it is inequitable to offer the corporate workers better benefits then the store partners? Why? Is that what the law would seem to say?

2-17. What arguments would you make as Starbucks' CEO concerning why the current policy is fair?

2-18. How would you handle this situation if you were running a company that was confronted by a shareholder making these demands?

Continuing Case

Carter Cleaning Company

Written and copyrighted by Gary Dessler, PhD.

A Question of Discrimination

One of the first problems Jennifer faced at her father's Carter Cleaning Centers concerned the inadequacies of the firm's current HR management practices and procedures.

One problem that particularly concerned her was the lack of attention to equal employment matters. Each store manager independently handled virtually all hiring; the managers had received no training regarding such fundamental matters as the types of questions they should not ask of job applicants. It was therefore not unusual for female applicants to be asked questions such as "Who's going to take care of your children while you are at work?" and for minority applicants to be asked questions about arrest records and credit histories. Nonminority applicants—three store managers were white males and three were white females—were not asked these questions, as Jennifer discerned from her interviews with the managers. Based on discussions with her father, Jennifer deduced two reasons for the laid-back attitude toward equal employment: (1) her father's lack of insight about the legal requirements, and (2) the fact that, as Jack Carter put it, "Virtually all our workers are women or minority members anyway, so no one can come in here and accuse us of being discriminatory, can they?"

Jennifer decided to mull that question over, but before she could, she was faced with two serious equal rights problems. Two women in one store privately confided to her that their manager was making unwelcome sexual advances toward them. One claimed he had threatened to fire her unless she "socialized" with him after hours. And during a fact-finding trip to another store, an older gentleman—he was 73 years old—complained of the fact that although he had almost 50 years of experience, he was paid less than people half his age in the same job. Jennifer's review of the stores resulted in the following questions.

Questions

2-19. Is it true, as Jack Carter claims, that "virtually all our workers are women or minority members anyway, so no one can come in here and accuse us of being discriminatory"?

2-20. How should Jennifer and her company address the sexual harassment charges and problems?

2-21. How should she and her company address the possible problems of age discrimination?

2-22. Given the fact that each of its stores has only a handful of employees, is her company covered by equal rights legislation?

2-23. And finally, aside from the specific problems, what other personnel management matters (application forms, training, and so on) have to be reviewed given the need to bring them into compliance with equal rights laws?

Writing Assignments

2-24. Explain the main features of Title VII, the Equal Pay Act, the Pregnancy Discrimination Act, the Americans with Disabilities Act, and the Civil Rights Act of 1991.

2-25. What are the two main defenses you can use in the event of a discriminatory practice allegation, and what exactly do they involve?

MyLab Management Try It!

How would you apply the concepts and skills you learned in this chapter? If your professor has assigned this activity, go to the Assignments section of **www.pearson.com/mylab/management** to complete the simulation.

PERSONAL INVENTORY ASSESSMENTS

Go to **www.pearson.com/mylab/management** to complete the Personal Inventory Assessment related to this chapter.

Key Terms

Endnotes

1. Patrick Dorrian, "Uber Accused of Nationwide Sex-Based Pay and Promotional Bias," *Bloomberg BNA Bulletin to Management*, November 7, 2017.
2. For example, see http://eeoc.gov/eeoc/newsroom/index.cfm. As another example, see "Wells Fargo to Pay $3.5 Million to Resolve Black Brokers' Claims," *Bloomberg BNA Bulletin to Management*, January 10, 2017.
3. Betsy Morris, "How Corporate America Is Betraying Women," *Fortune*, January 10, 2005, pp. 64–70.
4. Based on or quoted from International Association of Official Human Rights Agencies, *Principles of Employment Discrimination Law* (Washington, DC). See also Bruce Feldacker, *Labor Guide to Labor Law* (Upper Saddle River, NJ: Prentice Hall, 2000); "EEOC Attorneys Highlight How Employers Can Better Their Nondiscrimination Practices," *Bloomberg BNA Bulletin to Management*, July 20, 2008, p. 233; and www.eeoc.gov, accessed August 4, 2013. Plaintiffs still bring equal employment claims under the Civil Rights Act of 1866. For example, in 2008 the U.S. Supreme Court held that the act prohibits retaliation against someone who complains of discrimination against others when contract rights (in this case, an employment agreement) are at stake. Charles Louderback, "U.S. Supreme Court Decisions Expand Employees' Ability to Bring Retaliation Claims," *Compensation & Benefits Review*, September/October 2008, p. 52. Employment discrimination law is a changing field, and the appropriateness of the rules, guidelines, and conclusions in this chapter may also be affected by factors unique to the employer's operation. They should be reviewed by the employer's attorney before implementation.
5. For a conciliation agreement, see "FedEx to Pay $3 Million, Amend Practices to Settle OFCCP Charges of Bias in Hiring," *Bloomberg BNA Bulletin to Management*, March 27, 2012, p. 97.
6. Individuals may file under the Equal Employment Act of 1972.
7. By 2018, for the first time in many years, the EEOC had a Republican majority; this will probably change the EEOC's enforcement policies. Josh Eidelson, "US Discrimination Watchdog Is Headed for Pro-Business Makeover," *Bloomberg BNA Bulletin to Management*, October 17, 2017.
8. This is based on Joshua Brustein "Studies Show Racial

and Gender Discrimination Throughout the Gig Economy," https://www.bloomberg.com/news/articles/2016-11-22/studies-show-racial-and-gender-discrimination-throughout-the-gig-economy November 22, 2016; Marta Moakley, "EEOC Targets Gig Economy, Workplace Discrimination in Strategic Enforcement Plan," *XpertHR Legal Editor*, October 25, 2016, http://www.xperthr.com/news/eeoc-targets-gig-economy-workplace-discrimination-in-strategic-enforcement-plan/23960/; Will Knight, "Is the Gig Economy Rigged?" *MIT Technology Review*, November 17, 2016, https://www.technologyreview.com/s/602832/is-the-gig-economy-rigged/. Such discrimination seems to work both ways. For example, one of these studies found that Boston Uber drivers cancelled trips more often when prospective riders had African-American sounding names.

9. "The Employer Should Validate Hiring Tests to Withstand EEOC Scrutiny, Officials Advise," *Bloomberg BNA Bulletin to Management*, April 1, 2008, p. 107. President Obama's administration directed more funds and staffing to the OFCCP. "Restructured, Beefed Up OFCCP May Shift Policy Emphasis, Attorney Says," *Bloomberg BNA Bulletin to Management*, August 18, 2009, p. 257. When the Labor Department demanded pay information back to Google's formation, as well as names and contacts for about 20,000 of its workers, Google sued; in 2017 an administrative law judge ruled that for now it didn't have to give the OFCCP that information. See Chris Opfer, "Google Faced the Labor Department, and Google Won," *Bloomberg BNA Bulletin to Management*, April 4, 2017.
10. See, for example, "Divided EEOC Approves Draft of Rule Amending Age Discrimination Regulations," *Bloomberg BNA Bulletin to Management*, November 22, 2011, p. 369.
11. "High Court: ADEA Does Not Protect Younger Workers Treated Worse Than Their Elders," *BNA Bulletin to Management* 55, no. 10 (March 4, 2004), pp. 73–80. See also D. Aaron Lacy, "You Are Not Quite as Old as You Think: Making the Case for Reverse Age Discrimination Under the ADEA," *Berkeley Journal of Employment and Labor Law* 26, no. 2 (2005), pp. 363–403; Nancy Ursel and Marjorie Armstrong-Stassen, "How Age Discrimination in Employment Affects Stockholders," *Journal of Labor Research* 17, no. 1 (Winter 2006), pp. 89–99; www.eeoc.gov/laws/statutes/adea.cfm, accessed October 3, 2011; and Patrick Dorrian, "Older Workers Can Sue for Age Bias Even if Comparators Are 40-Plus," *Bloomberg BNA Bulletin to Management*, January 17, 2017.
12. "Staples Must Pay Fired Older Workers $16M for Age Bias," *Bloomberg BNA Bulletin to Management*, June 7, 2016, p. 181.
13. Another lawsuit was filed against RJ Reynolds Tobacco Company. The plaintiff was 49 years old when he first applied, and the company never replied to him. His attorneys subsequently told him that the employer's resume screening guidelines allegedly bump out older candidates. "Applicant Can Use Disparate Impact Theory for Age Claim," *Bloomberg BNA Bulletin to Management*, December 8, 2015, p. 389.
14. Jeff Greene, "Men and Women in Tech Struggle to Land Work after 40," *Bloomberg BNA Bulletin to Management*, October 3, 2017.
15. www.eeoc.gov/laws/statutes/adea.cfm, accessed October 3, 2011.
16. Martin Berman-Gorvine, "Older Workers Need Reassurance against Age Bias," *Bloomberg BNA Bulletin to Management*, June 20, 2017.
17. The U.S. Supreme Court ruled in *California Federal Savings and Loan Association v. Guerra* that if an employer offers no disability leave to any of its employees, it can (but need not) grant pregnancy leave to a woman disabled for pregnancy, childbirth, or a related medical condition.
18. John Kohl, Milton Mayfield, and Jacqueline Mayfield, "Recent Trends in Pregnancy Discrimination Law," *Business Horizons* 48, no. 5 (September 2005), pp. 421–429; and www.eeoc.gov/eeoc/statistics/enforcement/pregnancy.cfm, accessed October 3, 2011.
19. Lisa Nagele-Piazza, "Pregnant Worker Awarded 550,000K in Discrimination Suit," *HR Magazine*, October 2016, p. 14.
20. "Pregnancy Claims Rising; Consistent Procedures Paramount," *Bloomberg BNA Bulletin to Management*, November 23, 2010, p. 375.
21. www.uniformguidelines.com/uniformguidelines.html, accessed November 23, 2007.
22. The EEOC and the OFCCP agreed to coordinate their efforts more closely and to share information on employers with federal contracts or subcontracts. "EEOC, OFCCP Issue Updated Agreement on Coordinated Enforcement, Data Sharing," *Bloomberg BNA Bulletin to Management*, November 22, 2011, p. 371.
23. *Griggs v. Duke Power Company*, 3FEP cases 175.
24. This is applicable only to Title VII and CRA 91; other statutes require intent.
25. James Ledvinka, *Federal Regulation of Personnel and Human Resources Management* (Boston: Kent, 1982), p. 41.
26. Bruce Feldacker, *Labor Guide to Labor Law* (Upper Saddle River, NJ: Prentice Hall, 2000), p. 513.
27. "The Eleventh Circuit Explains Disparate Impact, Disparate Treatment," *BNA Fair Employment Practices*, August 17, 2000, p. 102. See also Kenneth York, "Disparate Results in Adverse Impact Tests: The 4/5ths Rule and the Chi Square Test," *Public Personnel Management* 31, no. 2 (Summer 2002), pp. 253–262; and "Burden of Proof Under the Employment Non-Discrimination Act," www.civilrights.org/lgbt/enda/burden-of-proof.html, accessed August 8, 2011.
28. We'll see that the process of filing a discrimination charge goes something like this: The plaintiff (say, a rejected applicant) demonstrates that an employment practice (such as a test) has a disparate (or "adverse") impact on a particular group. *Disparate impact* means that an employer engages in an employment practice or policy that has a greater adverse impact (effect) on the members of a protected group under Title VII than on other employees, regardless of intent. (Requiring a college degree for a job would have an adverse impact on some minority groups, for instance.) Disparate impact claims do *not* require proof of discriminatory intent. Instead, the plaintiff's burden is to show two things. First, he or she must show that a significant disparity exists between the proportion of (say) women in the available labor pool and the proportion hired. Second, he or she must show that an apparently neutral employment practice, such as word-of-mouth advertising or a requirement that the jobholder "be able to lift 100 pounds," is causing the disparity. Then, once the plaintiff fulfills his or her burden of showing such disparate impact, the *employer* has the heavier burden of proving that the challenged practice is job related. For example, the employer has to show that lifting 100 pounds is actually required for effectively performing the position in question, and that the business could not run efficiently without the requirement—that it is a business necessity.
29. Commerce Clearing House, "House and Senate Pass Civil Rights Compromise by Wide Margin," *Ideas and Trends in Personnel*, November 13, 1991, p. 179.
30. Mark Kobata, "The Civil Rights Act of 1991," *Personnel Journal*, March 1992, p. 48.
31. Again, though, if the "employer shows that it would have taken the same action even absent the discriminatory motive, the complaining employee will not be entitled to reinstatement, back pay, or damages"; www.eeoc.gov/policy/docs/caregiving.html#mixed, accessed September 24, 2011.
32. Elliot H. Shaller and Dean Rosen, "A Guide to the EEOC's Final Regulations on the Americans with Disabilities Act," *Employee Relations Law Journal* 17, no. 3 (Winter 1991–1992), pp. 405–430; and www.eeoc.gov/ada, accessed November 20, 2007.
33. "ADA: Simple Common Sense Principles," *BNA Fair Employment Practices*, June 4, 1992, p. 63; and www.eeoc.gov/facts/ada17.html, accessed September 24, 2011.
34. Shaller and Rosen, "A Guide to the EEOC's Final Regulations," p. 408. Other specific examples include "epilepsy, diabetes, cancer, HIV infection, and bipolar disorder"; www.eeoc.gov/laws/regulations/adaaa_fact_sheet.cfm, accessed June 27, 2018.
35. Kevin McGowan, "Fired Medical Marijuana User Can Sue for Disability Bias," *Bloomberg BNA Bulletin to Management*, July 25, 2017.
36. Shaller and Rosen, "A Guide to the EEOC's Final Regulations," p. 409. Thus, one court held that a worker currently engaging in illegal use of drugs was "not a qualified individual with a disability" under the ADA. "Drug Addict Lacks ADA Protection, Quarter Firms," *Bloomberg BNA Bulletin to Management*, April 26, 2011, p. 133.
37. James McDonald Jr., "The Americans with Difficult Personalities Act," *Employee Relations Law Journal* 25, no. 4 (Spring 2000), pp. 93–107; and Betsy Bates, "Mental Health Problems Predominate in ADA Claims," *Clinical Psychiatry News*, May 2003, http://findarticles.com/p/articles/mi_hb4345/is_5_31/ai_n29006702, accessed September 24, 2011. For a detailed discussion of dealing with this issue, see www.eeoc.gov/facts/intellectual_disabilities.html, accessed September 2, 2011.
38. "EEOC Guidance on Dealing with Intellectual Disabilities,"

Workforce Management, March 2005, p. 16.
39. "Driver Fired After Seizure on Job Lacks ADA Claim," *Bloomberg BNA Bulletin to Management*, January 4, 2011, p. 6.
40. www.ada.gov/reg3a.html#Anchor-Appendix-52467, accessed January 23, 2009.
41. See "EEOC Guidance on Telecommuting as ADA Accommodation Discussed," *Bloomberg BNA Bulletin to Management*, October 16, 2012, p. 335.
42. Martha Frase, "An Underestimated Talent Pool," *HR Magazine*, April 2009, pp. 55–58; and Nicole LaPorte, "Hiring the Blind, While Making a Green Statement," *The New York Times*, March 25, 2012, p. b3; and http://www.freedomscientific.com/Products/Blindness/Jaws, accessed January 23, 2017.
43. Genevieve Douglas, "Websites Could Be Next Disability Law Litigation Hotspot," *Bloomberg BNA Bulletin to Management*, October 17, 2017.
44. M. P. McQueen, "Workplace Disabilities Are on the Rise," *The Wall Street Journal*, May 1, 2007, p. A1.
45. "No Sitting for Store Greeter," *BNA Fair Employment Practices*, December 14, 1995, p. 150. For more illustrative cases, see Tillinghast Licht, "Reasonable Accommodation and the ADA-Courts Draw the Line," at http://library.findlaw.com/2004/Sep/19/133574.html, accessed September 6, 2011.
46. For example, a U.S. circuit court found that a depressed former kidney dialysis technician could not claim ADA discrimination after the employer fired him for attendance problems. The court said he could not meet the essential job function of predictably coming to work. "Depressed Worker Lacks ADA Claim, Court Decides," *BNA Bulletin to Management*, December 18, 2007, p. 406. See also www.eeoc.gov/press/5-10-01-b.html, accessed January 8, 2008.
47. *Toyota Motor Manufacturing of Kentucky, Inc. v. Williams*. 534 U.S. 184 (2002).
48. "Supreme Court Says Manual Task Limitation Needs Both Daily Living, Workplace Impact," *BNA Fair Employment Practices*, January 17, 2002, p. 8.
49. "EEOC Issued Its Final Regulations for ADA Amendments Act," *Workforce Management*, June 2011, p. 12.
50. "Rise in ADA Cases Calls for Focus on Accommodations, Job Descriptions," *Bloomberg BNA Bulletin to Management*, September 25, 2012, p. 310.
51. Lawrence Postol, "ADAAA Will Result in Renewed Emphasis on Reasonable Accommodations," *Society for Human Resource Management Legal Report*, January 2009, pp. 1–3.
52. Mark Lengnick-Hall et al., "Overlooked and Underutilized: People with Disabilities Are an Untapped Human Resource," *Human Resource Management* 47, no. 2 (Summer 2008), pp. 255–273.
53. Susan Wells, "Counting on Workers with Disabilities," *HR Magazine*, April 2008, p. 45.
54. "Wachovia Violated USERRA by Failing to Reinstate Reservist to Comparable Job," *Bloomberg BNA Bulletin to Management*, September 20, 2011, p. 297.
55. www.eeoc.gov/press/2-25-09.html, accessed April 3, 2009; and Susan Hauser, "Sincerely Yours, Gina," *Workforce Management*, July 2011, pp. 16–18.
56. James Ledvinka and Robert Gatewood, "EEO Issues with Preemployment Inquiries," *Personnel Administrator* 22, no. 2 (February 1997), pp. 22–26.
57. "Employers More Vulnerable Under New York City Statute," *Bloomberg BNA Bulletin to Management*, July 31, 2012, p. 245.
58. Quoted or paraphrased from www.eeoc.gov/laws/types/index.cfm; www.eeoc.gov/laws/types/religion.cfm; www.eeoc.gov/eeoc/internal_eeo/index.cfm; and www.eeoc.gov/federal/otherprotections.cfm, all accessed May 9, 2013.
59. Madison Alder, "Disputes over Prayer Breaks Reflect Changing Workforce," *Bloomberg BNA Bulletin to Management*, August 22, 2017.
60. "More Muslim Workers Allege Bias to Prayer Breaks," *Bloomberg BNA Bulletin to Management*, May 10, 2016, p. 150.
61. "Employer Should Respond to DOMA with Steps That Offset Risks, Attorneys Say," *Bloomberg BNA Bulletin to Management*, July 2, 2013, pp. 209–210.
62. "DOL Says 'Spouse' and 'Marriage' in ERISA Include Same-Sex Legally Married Couples," *Bloomberg BNA Bulletin to Management*, September 24, 2013, p. 305.
63. "OFCCP Announces Final Rule Protecting LGBT Federal Contractor Workers from Bias," *Bloomberg BNA Bulletin to Management*, December 9, 2014.
64. Kevin McGowan, "Landmark Gay Bias Ruling May Move Issue Closer to High Court," *Bloomberg BNA Bulletin to Management*, April 11, 2017.
65. Jay-Ann Cataga, "When Workers Are Male or Female, EEOC Reporting Is Complex," *Bloomberg BNA Bulletin to Management*, October 3, 2017.
66. "OFCCP Announces 'Higher Historic' Final Rules on Contractor Hiring of Veterans, Disabled," *Bloomberg BNA Bulletin to Management*, September 3, 2013, p. 281; Lauren Weber, "Are You Disabled? Now Your Boss Wants to Know," *The Wall Street Journal*, March 19, 2014, p. B1.
67. Adam Liptak, "Justices Back Ban on Race as Factor in College Entry," *The New York Times*, April 23, 2014, pp. A1, A 12.
68. Melanie Trottman and Lauren Weber, "Bar Is Raised in Worker Bias Cases," *The Wall Street Journal*, June 25, 2013, p. B1, B8.
69. Chris Strohm and Arit John, "US Issues Religious Freedom Memo Giving Leeway in Hiring," *Bloomberg BNA Bulletin to Management*, October 10, 2017.
70. "Sexual Harassment Scandals Imperil Democrats More Than Republicans," *The Economist*, November 25, 2017, p. 24; "An Open Secret," *The Economist*, October 21, 2017, pp. 59–62; "Sex and Power," *The Economist*, October 21, 2017, p. 16. An abbreviated list of those accused of sexual harassment recently includes movie producer Harvey Weinstein, Sen. Al Franken, television host Charlie Rose, and Congressman John Conyers. One reportedly defended himself by saying that when he grew up in the '60s and '70s the "rules were different"; however, most would agree that all or most of the reported behaviors were never acceptable.
71. www.eeoc.gov/types/sexual_harassment.html, accessed April 24, 2009; and www.eeoc.gov/eeoc/statistics/enforcement/sexual_harassment.cfm, accessed October 3, 2011.
72. Richard Wiener et al., "The Fit and Implementation of Sexual Harassment Law to Workplace Evaluations," *Journal of Applied Psychology* 87, no. 4 (2002), pp. 747–764. For instance, a U.S. Court of Appeals told a male Walmart employee that he could proceed with his claim that a female supervisor had sexually harassed him. "Man's Harassment Claims Advanced," *Bloomberg BNA Bulletin to Management*, September 6, 2011, p. 285.
73. Jennifer Berdahl and Celia Moore, "Workplace Harassment: Double Jeopardy for Minority Women," *Journal of Applied Psychology* 91, no. 2 (2006), pp. 426–436.
74. Jacquie Lee, "Sexual Harassment Guidelines Get 'Timely' Update from EEOC," *Bloomberg BNA Bulletin to Management*, November 14, 2017.
75. Larry Drake and Rachel Moskowitz, "Your Rights in the Workplace," *Occupational Outlook Quarterly* (Summer 1997), pp. 19–29.
76. "EEOC: "Boss's Shoulder Touching Not Sexual Harassment," *Bloomberg BNA Bulletin to Management*, February 11, 2014, p. 45.
77. Patricia Linenberger and Timothy Keaveny, "Sexual Harassment: The Employer's Legal Obligations," *Personnel* 58 (November/December 1981), p. 64; and "Court Examines Workplace Flirtation," http://hr.blr.com/HR-news/Discrimination/Sexual-Harassment/Court-Examines-Workplace-Flirtation, accessed October 2, 2011.
78. Edward Felsenthal, "Justice's Ruling Further Defines Sexual Harassment," *The Wall Street Journal*, March 5, 1998, p. B5.
79. Hilary Gettman and Michele Gelfand, "When the Customer Shouldn't Be King: Antecedents and Consequences of Sexual Harassment by Clients and Customers," *Journal of Applied Psychology* 92, no. 3 (2007), pp. 757–770.
80. See the discussion in "Examining Unwelcome Conduct in a Sexual Harassment Claim," *BNA Fair Employment Practices*, October 19, 1995, p. 124. See also Michael Zugelder et al., "An Affirmative Defense to Sexual Harassment by Managers and Supervisors: Analyzing Employer Liability and Protecting Employee Rights in the U.S.," *Employee Responsibilities and Rights* 18, no. 2 (2006), pp. 111–122.
81. Ibid.; "Examining Unwelcome Conduct in a Sexual Harassment Claim," p. 124.
82. For example, a server/bartender filed a sexual harassment claim against Chili's Bar & Grill. She claimed that her former boyfriend, also a restaurant employee, had harassed her. The court ruled that the restaurant's prompt response warranted ruling in favor of it. "Ex-Boyfriend Harassed, but Employer Acted Promptly," *Bloomberg BNA Bulletin to Management*, January 8, 2008, p. 14.
83. See Mindy D. Bergman et al., "The (Un)reasonableness of Reporting: Antecedents and Consequences of Reporting Sexual Harassment," *Journal of Applied Psychology* 87, no. 2 (2002), pp. 230–242. See also www.eeoc.gov/policy/docs/harassment-facts.html, accessed October 2, 2011.
84. Adapted from *Sexual Harassment Manual for Managers and Supervisors* (Riverwood, IL: CCH Incorporated, a Wolters-Kluwer Company, 1991); www.eeoc.gov/types/sexual_harassment.html, accessed May 6, 2007; and www.eeoc.gov/

policy/docs/-harassment-facts .html, accessed October 2, 2011.
85. Emily Smith, "NBC Orders Staff to Rat Out Misbehaving Colleagues or Be Fired," at https://pagesix.com, accessed December 27, 2017.
86. Rebecca Greenfield, "Can Apps Get Victims to Report Workplace Harassment?" *Bloomberg BNA bulletin to Management*, June 20, 2017.
87. Maria Rotundo et al., "A Meta-Analytic Review of Gender Differences in Perceptions of Sexual Harassment," *Journal of Applied Psychology* 86, no. 5 (2001), pp. 914–922. See also Nathan Bowling and Terry Beehr, "Workplace Harassment from the Victim's Perspective: A Theoretical Model and Meta Analysis," *Journal of Applied Psychology* 91, no. 5 (2006), pp. 998–1012.
88. Jennifer Berdahl and Karl Aquino, "Sexual Behavior at Work: Fun or Folly?" *Journal of Applied Psychology* 94, no. 1 (2009), pp. 34–47.
89. Jathan Janov, "Sexual Harassment and the Three Big Surprises," *HR Magazine* 46, no. 11 (November 2001), p. 123ff. California mandates sexual harassment prevention training for supervisors: See "California Clarifies Training Law; Employers Take Note," *BNA Bulletin to Management*, November 20, 2007, p. 375.
90. "#YouToo?" *The Economist*, December 23, 2017, pp. 81–85.
91. Ana Campoy and Julian Barnes, "Air Force Combats Sex Misconduct," *The Wall Street Journal*, November 15, 2012, p. A-8; and James Risen, "Air Force Leaders Testify on Culture That Led to Sexual Assaults of Recruits," *The New York Times*, January 24, 2013, p. A-15.
92. Claire Miller, Noam Scheiber, and Julie Creswell, "If Training and HR Failed to Stop Harassers, Where Can Victims Turn?" *The New York Times*, December 13, 2017, pp. B1, B7.
93. Rebecca Greenfield, "Why Your HR Department Can't Stop Sexual Harassment," *Bloomberg BNA Bulletin to Management*, October 31, 2017.
94. Mary Rowe, "Dealing with Sexual Harassment," *Harvard Business Review*, May–June 1981, p. 43; the quoted material goes on to say that "the employer still bears the burden of proving that the employee's failure was unreasonable. If the employee had a justifiable fear of retaliation, his or her failure to utilize the complaint process may not be unreasonable" and is quoted from www.uiowa.edu/~eod/policies/sexual-harassment-guide/employer-liablity.htm, accessed October 3, 2011.
95. As of 2017 the EEOC was testing a new online system to let people submit EEOC inquiries and to schedule appointments, as a way to encourage people who believe they were discriminated against to reach out to the EEOC. Patrick Dorrian, "Federal Job Bias Tool Rolled Out in Five Cities," *Bloomberg BNA Bulletin to Management*, March 21, 2017.
96. "Employers Should Address Inappropriate Behavior on Social Sites," *Bloomberg BNA Bulletin to Management*, February 19, 2013, p. 62.
97. "Be Careful with Social Media When Vetting Potential Workers," *Bloomberg BNA Bulletin to Management*, June 25, 2013, p. 206.
98. John Moran, *Employment Law* (Upper Saddle River, NJ: Prentice Hall, 1997), p. 166.
99. "The Eleventh Circuit Explains Disparate Impact, Disparate Treatment," p. 102.
100. John Klinefelter and James Thompkins, "Adverse Impact in Employment Selection," *Public Personnel Management*, May/June 1976, pp. 199–204; and www.eeoc.gov/policy/docs/factemployment_procedures .html, accessed October 2, 2011.
101. Moran, *Employment Law*, p. 168.
102. Employers use several types of statistics in addressing adverse impact. (For a discussion, see Robert Gatewood and Hubert Feild, *Human Resource Selection* [Fort Worth, TX: The Dryden Press, 1994], pp. 40–42, and Jean Phillips and Stanley Gully, *Strategic Staffing* [Upper Saddle River, NJ: Pearson, 2012], pp. 68–69.) For example, *stock statistics* might compare *at a single point in time* (1) the percentage of female engineers the company has, as a percentage of its total number of engineers, with (2) the number of trained female engineers in the labor force as a percentage of the total number of trained engineers in the labor force. Here, the question of relevant labor market is important. For example, the relevant labor market if you're hiring unskilled assemblers might be the local labor market within, say, 20 miles from your plant, whereas the relevant labor market for highly skilled engineers might well be national and possibly international. *Flow statistics* measure proportions of employees, in particular, groups at two points in time: before selection and after selection takes place. For example, when comparing the percentage of minority applicants who applied with the percentage hired, the employer is using flow statistics. An employer's company-wide minority hiring statistics may be defensible company-wide but not departmentally. The employer therefore may employ *concentration statistics* to drill down and determine the concentration of minorities versus nonminorities in particular job categories.
103. One study found that using the 4/5ths rule often resulted in false-positive ratings of adverse impact, and that incorporating tests of statistical significance could improve the accuracy of applying the 4/5ths rule. See Philip Roth, Philip Bobko, and Fred Switzer, "Modeling the Behavior of the 4/5ths Rule for Determining Adverse Impact: Reasons for Caution," *Journal of Applied Psychology* 91, no. 3 (2006), pp. 507–522.
104. The results must be realistic. In this example, hiring 2 out of 5 women suggests there is no adverse impact. But suppose we had hired only 1 woman. Then the difference between those we would be expected to hire (5) and whom we actually hired (1) would rise to 4. Hiring just one less woman might then trigger adverse impact issues, because twice the standard deviation is also about 4. However, realistically, it probably would not trigger such concerns, because with such small numbers, one person makes such a difference. The point is that tools like the 4/5ths rule and the standard deviation rule are only rules of thumb. They do not themselves determine if the employer's screening process is discriminatory. This fact may work both for and against the employer. As the Uniform Guidelines (www .uniformguidelines.com/qandaprint.html) put it, "Regardless of the amount of difference in selection rates, unlawful discrimination may be present, and may be demonstrated through appropriate evidence. . . ."
105. The ADEA does not just protect against intentional discrimination (disparate treatment). Under a Supreme Court decision (*Smith v. Jackson*, Miss., 2005), it also covers employer practices that seem neutral but that actually bear more heavily on older workers (disparate impact). "Employees Need Not Show Intentional Bias to Bring Claims Under ADEA, High Court Says," *BNA Bulletin to Management* 56, no. 14 (April 5, 2005), p. 105.
106. The Fair Treatment for Experienced Pilots Act raised commercial pilots' mandatory retirement age from 60 to 65 in 2008. Allen Smith, "Congress Gives Older Pilots a Reprieve," *HR Magazine*, February 2008, p. 24.
107. *Usery v. Tamiami Trail Tours*, 12FEP cases 1233. Alternatively, an employer faced with an age discrimination claim may raise the factors other than age (FOA) defense. Here, it argues that its actions were "reasonable" based on some factor other than age, such as the terminated person's poor performance.
108. www.foxnews.com/story/0,2933,517334,00.html, accessed January 7, 2010.
109. Howard Anderson and Michael Levin-Epstein, *Primer of Equal Employment Opportunity* (Washington, DC: The Bureau of National Affairs, 1982), pp. 13–14.
110. *U.S. v. Bethlehem Steel Company*, 3FEP cases 589.
111. *Robinson v. Lorillard Corporation*, 3FEP cases 653.
112. *Spurlock v. United Airlines*, 5FEP cases 17.
113. Anderson and Levin-Epstein, *Primer of Equal Employment Opportunity*, p. 14.
114. Ledvinka and Gatewood, "EEO Issues with Preemployment Inquiries," pp. 22–26.
115. Ibid.; www.eeoc.gov/laws/practices/index.cfm, accessed August 2, 2013.
116. "Eighth Circuit OKs $3.4 Million EEOC Verdict Relating to Pre-Hire Strength Testing Rules," *BNA Bulletin to Management*, November 28, 2006, p. 377.
117. Svetlana Shkolnikova, "Weight Discrimination Could Be as Common as Racial Bias," www.usatoday.com/news/health/weightloss/2008-05-20-overweight-bias_N.htm, accessed January 21, 2009.
118. Jenessa Shapiro et al., "Expectations of Obese Trainees: How Stigmatized Trainee Characteristics Influence Training Effectiveness," *Journal of Applied Psychology* 92, no. 1 (2007), pp. 239–249. See also Lisa Finkelstein et al., "Bias Against Overweight Job Applicants: Further Explanations of When and Why," *Human Resource Management* 46, no. 2 (Summer 2007), pp. 203–222. For an interesting study, see T. A. Judge and D. M. Cable, "When It Comes to Pay, Do the Thin Win? The Effect of Weight on Pay for Men and Women," *Journal of Applied Psychology*, January 2011.
119. "OFCCP Issues Criminal Records Directive, Cautions Contractors on Blanket Exclusions," *Bloomberg BNA Bulletin to Management*, February 12, 2013, p. 49; and "EEOC to Focus on Hiring, Pay and Harassment," *HR Magazine*, February 2013, p. 11.
120. See, for example, www.eeoc.gov/policy/docs/guidance-inquiries .html, accessed June 28, 2009.

121. This is based on *BNA Fair Employment Practices*, April 13, 1989, pp. 45–47; and "Crossed: When Religion and Dress Code Policies Intersect," www.mcguire_woods.com/news-resources/item.asp?item=3108, accessed October 2, 2011.
122. Eric Matusewitch, "Tailor Your Dress Codes," *Personnel Journal* 68, no. 2 (February 1989), pp. 86–91; Matthew Miklave, "Sorting Out a Claim of Bias," *Workforce* 80, no. 6 (June 2001), pp. 102–103, and "Laws and Cases Affecting Appearance," www.boardmanlawfirm.com/perspectives_articles/appearance.php, accessed September 8, 2011.
123. Rita Pyrillis, "Body of Work," *Workforce Management*, November 7, 2010, pp. 20–26.
124. This isn't ironclad, however. For example, the U.S. Supreme Court, in *Stotts*, held that a court cannot require retention of black employees hired under a court's consent decree in preference to higher-seniority white employees who were protected by a bona fide seniority system. It's unclear whether this decision also extends to personnel decisions not governed by seniority systems. *Firefighters Local 1784 v. Stotts* (*BNA*, April 14, 1985).
125. In a more recent plan, the EEOC said it would focus on hiring, and particularly enforcing its guidance on indiscriminate use of criminal conduct in background screening; on gender-based pay discrepancies; and on enforcing its requirements against harassment based on race, ethnicity, religion, age, and disability. "EEOC to Focus on Hiring, Pay and Assessment," p. 11.
126. Prudent employers often purchase employment practices liability insurance to insure against some or all of the expenses involved with defending against discrimination, sexual harassment, and wrongful termination-type claims. Antone Melton-Meaux, "Maximizing Employment Practices Liability Insurance Coverage," *Compensation & Benefits Review*, May/June 2008, pp. 55–59.
127. Litigants must watch the clock. In an equal pay decision, the U.S. Supreme Court held (in *Ledbetter v. Goodyear Tire & Rubber Company*) that the employee must file a complaint within 180 (or 300) days of the employer's decision to pay the allegedly unfair wage. The clock starts with that first pay decision, not with the subsequent paychecks that the employee receives. "Justices Rule 5–4 Claim-Filing Period Applies to Pay Decision, Not Subsequent Paycheck," *BNA Bulletin to Management* 58, no. 23 (June 5, 2007), pp. 177–184; and www.eeoc.gov/eeoc/statistics/enforcement/charges.cfm, accessed May 1, 2012. A U.S. Supreme Court case will make it more difficult for plaintiffs to file class-action claims for discrimination. See "Supreme Court Hands Wal-Mart Big Victory: Reverses Approval of Class-Action Claim," *BNA Bulletin to Management*, June 21, 2011, p. 193.
128. In 2007, the U.S. Supreme Court, in *Ledbetter v. Goodyear Tire & Rubber Company*, held that employees claiming Title VII pay discrimination must file their claims within 180 days of when they first receive the allegedly discriminatory pay. As of 2009, Congress was working to formulate new legislation enabling an employee to file a claim at any time, as long as the person is still receiving an "infected" paycheck.
129. www.eeoc.gov/eeoc/statistics/enforcement/charges.cfm accessed January 24, 2017.
130. "EPLI Now Established Employer Litigation Strategy," *Bloomberg BNA Bulletin to Management*, November 29, 2011, p. 382.
131. If the charge was filed initially with a state or local agency within 180 days after the alleged unlawful practice occurred, the charge may then be filed with the EEOC within 30 days after the practice occurred or within 30 days after the person received notice that the state or local agency has ended its proceedings.
132. "Attorneys: Employer Should Handle EEOC Discharges Strategically," *Bloomberg BNA Bulletin to Management*, October 15, 2013, p. 334.
133. "EEOC Attorneys Stress the Importance of Cooperation During Investigations," *Bloomberg BNA Bulletin to Management*, March 8, 2011, p. 73.
134. www.eeoc.gov/mediate/facts.html, accessed June 29, 2009.
135. "EEOC's New Nationwide Mediation Plan Offers Option of Informal Settlements," *BNA Fair Employment Practices*, February 18, 1999, p. 21; and www.eeoc.gov/employees/mediation.cf, accessed October 2, 2011.
136. Timothy Bland, "Sealed Without a Kiss," *HR Magazine*, October 2000, pp. 85–92.
137. Stuart Bompey and Michael Pappas, "Is There a Better Way? Compulsory Arbitration of Employment Discrimination Claims After *Gilmer*," *Employee Relations Law Journal* 19, no. 3 (Winter 1993–1994), pp. 197–216, and www.eeoc.gov/policy/docs/mandarb.html, accessed September 5, 2011. The EEOC says here, for instance, that "the employer imposing mandatory arbitration is free to manipulate the arbitral mechanism to its benefit."
138. See Bompey and Pappas, pp. 210–211.
139. David Nye, "When the Fired Fight Back," *Across-the-Board*, June 1995, pp. 31–34; and www.eeoc.gov/federal/fed_employees/adr.cfm, accessed October 3, 2011.
140. "EEOC Opposes Mandatory Arbitration," *BNA Fair Employment Practices*, July 24, 1997, p. 85; and www.eeoc.gov/employees/mediation.cfm, accessed October 2, 2011.
141. "Tips for Employers on Dealing with EEOC Investigations," *BNA Fair Employment Practices*, October 31, 1996, p. 130; "Conducting Effective Investigations of Employee Bias Complaints," *BNA Fair Employment Practices*, July 13, 1995, p. 81; Commerce Clearing House, *Ideas and Trends*, January 23, 1987, pp. 14–15; http://eeoc.gov/employers/investigations.html, accessed October 4, 2009; and www.eeoc.gov/employers/process.cfm, accessed January 25, 2017.
142. Kenneth Sovereign, *Personnel Law*, 4th ed. (Upper Saddle River, NJ: Prentice Hall, 1999), p. 220. Perhaps surprisingly, more senior managers than nonmanagers report suffering retaliation when reporting workplace misconduct. *Bloomberg BNA Bulletin to Management*, September 11, 2012, p. 294. This includes what one report calls "traceable retaliation," such as demotions, physical harm, and online harassment.
143. www.eeoc.gov/employers/smallbusiness/faq/what_is_retaliation.cfm, accessed January 24, 2017.
144. https://www.eeoc.gov/eeoc/plan/upload/2016par.pdf, accessed January 24, 2017.
145. See, for example, Michael Carrell and Everett Mann, "Defining Work-Force Diversity in Public Sector Organizations," *Public Personnel Management* 24, no. 1 (Spring 1995), pp. 99–111; Richard Koonce, "Redefining Diversity," *Training and Development Journal*, December 2001, pp. 22–33; and Kathryn Canas and Harris Sondak, *Opportunities and Challenges of Workplace Diversity* (Upper Saddle River, NJ: Pearson, 2008), pp. 3–27. Others list race and ethnicity diversity, gender diversity, age diversity, disability diversity, sexual diversity, and cultural and national origin diversity as examples. Lynn Shore et al., "Diversity in Organizations: Where Are We Now and Where Are We Going?" *Human Resource Management Review* 19 (2009), pp. 117–133.
146. Taylor Cox Jr., *Cultural Diversity in Organizations* (San Francisco, CA: Berrett Kohler Publishers, Inc., 1993), p. 88; also see Stefanie Johnson et al., "The Strong, Sensitive Type: Effects of Gender Stereotypes and Leadership Prototypes on the Evaluation of Male and Female Leaders," *Organizational Behavior and Human Decision Processes* 106, no. 1 (May 2008), pp. 39–60.
147. Cheryl Sandberg, "Women Are Leaning In—But They Face Pushback," *The Wall Street Journal*, September 27, 2016, p. R2.
148. For example, see Zoe Kinias and Jessica Sim, "Facilitating Women's Success in Business: Interrupting the Process of Stereotype Threat Through Affirmation of Personal Values," *Journal of Applied Psychology*, 101, no. 11 (2016), pp. 1585–1597.
149. "Outsmarting Our Brains: Overcoming Hidden Biases to Harness Diversity's True Potential," Ernst & Young LLP, 2013; and Dana Wilkie, "Bringing Bias into the Light," *HR Magazine*, December 2014, pp. 32–27.
150. Cox, *Cultural Diversity in Organizations*, p. 64.
151. Cox, *Cultural Diversity in Organizations*, pp. 179–80.
152. J. H. Greenhaus and S. Parasuraman, "Job Performance Attributions and Career Advancement Prospects: An Examination of Gender and Race Affects," *Organizational Behavior and Human Decision Processes* 55 (July 1993), pp. 273–298. Much research here focuses on how ethnocentrism prompts consumers to avoid certain products based on their country of origin. See, for example, T. S. Chan et al., "How Consumer Ethnocentrism and Animosity Impair the Economic Recovery of Emerging Markets," *Journal of Global Marketing* 23, no. 3 (July/August 2010), pp. 208–225.
153. Patrick McKay et al., "A Tale of Two Climates: Diversity Climate from Subordinates' and Managers' Perspectives and Their Role in Store Unit Sales Performance," *Personnel Psychology* 62 (2009), pp. 767–791.
154. Maria del Carmen Triana, Maria Fernandez Garcia, and Adrian Colella, "Managing Diversity: How Organizational Efforts to Support Diversity Moderate the Effects of Perceived Racial Discrimination on Affective Commitment," *Personnel Psychology* 63 (2010), pp. 817–843.

155. "Selling the Supremes on Diversity," *Bloomberg Businessweek*, October 20–October 28, 2012, p. 38.
156. As an example, leaders who facilitated high levels of power sharing within their groups helped to reduce the frequently observed positive relationship between increased diversity and increased turnover. But leaders who were inclusive of only a select few followers "may actually exacerbate the relationship between diversity and turnover" (p. 1422). Lisa Nishii and David Mayer, "Do Inclusive Leaders Help to Reduce Turnover in Diverse Groups? The Moderating Role of Leader–Member Exchange in the Diversity to Turnover Relationship," *Journal of Applied Psychology* 94, no. 6 (2009), pp. 1412–1426.
157. Faye Cocchiara et al., "A Gem for Increasing the Effectiveness of Diversity Training," *Human Resource Management* 49, no. 6 (November–December 2010), pp. 1089–1106.
158. For diversity management steps, see Cox, *Cultural Diversity in Organizations*, p. 236. See also Patricia Digh, "Creating a New Balance Sheet: The Need for Better Diversity Metrics," *Mosaics*, Society for Human Resource Management, September/October 1999, p. 1; and Richard Bucher, *Diversity Consciousness* (Upper Saddle River, NJ: Pearson Prentice Hall, 2004), pp. 109–137.
159. Boris Groysberg and Katherine Connolly, "Great Leaders Who Make the Mix Work," *Harvard Business Review*, September 2013, pp. 68–76.
160. Frank Dobbin and Alexandra Kalev, "Why Diversity Programs Fail," *Harvard Business Review*, July–August 2016, p. 59.
161. Mark Phillis, "You Have a Chief Diversity Officer, But Is Your Workplace Inclusive?" *Workforce,* June 2016, pp. 20–21.
162. Jeff Greene, "Deloitte Thinks Diversity Groups Are Passé," *Bloomberg BNA Bulletin to Management*, July 25, 2017.
163. Ibid.
164. Nikki Waller, "How Men and Women See the Workplace Differently," *The Wall Street Journal*, September 27, 2016, pp. R1, R2.
165. Rita Pyrillis, "SAP Feted for Gender Diversity," *Workforce*, April 2016, p. 17.
166. Nikki Waller, "How Men and Women See the Workplace Differently," *The Wall Street Journal*, September 27, 2016, pp. R1, R2.
167. David Harrison et al., "Understanding Attitudes Toward Affirmative Action Programs in Employment: Summary and Meta-Analysis of 35 Years of Research," *Journal of Applied Psychology* 91, no. 5 (2006), pp. 1013–1036; and Margaret Fiester et al., "Affirmative Action, Stock Options, I-9 Documents," *HR Magazine*, November 2007, p. 31.
168. Ivona Hideg and D. Lance Ferris "Dialectical Thinking and Fairness-Based Perspectives of Affirmative Action," *Journal of Applied Psychology*, 102, no. 5 (2017), pp. 782–801.
169. David Harrison et al., "Understanding Attitudes Toward Affirmative Action Programs in Employment: Summary and Meta-Analysis of 35 Years of Research," *Journal of Applied Psychology* 91, no. 5 (2006), pp. 1013–1036.
170. Bill Leonard, "Ways to Tell If a Diversity Program Is Measuring Up," *HR Magazine*, July 2002, p. 21; and Ye Yang Zheng and Brenda White, "The Evaluation of a Diversity Program at an Academic Library," *Library Philosophy and Practice*, 2007, http://unllib.unl.edu/LPP/yang.pdf, accessed October 2, 2011.
171. In a recent variant to this, the immigrant and employee rights section of the Department of Justice recently launched a new "protecting US workers" program. It aims to identify employers who engage in unlawful discrimination against US workers, for example by abusing the H–1B specialty occupation visa. Laura Francis, "DOJ, State Focus on Immigration-Based Bias Against US Worker," *Bloomberg BNA Bulletin to Management*, October 17, 2017.
172. http://newsfeedresearcher.com/data/articles_n17/tests-city-court.html, accessed April 24, 2009.
173. Adam Liptak, "Supreme Court Finds Bias Against White Firefighters," *The New York Times*, June 30, 2009, pp. A1, A13.
174. Ibid., p. 560.
175. Based on "On Appeal, Hotheaded Hotline Lawyer Loses Age, Disability Discrimination Claims," *BNA Human Resources Report*, January 12, 2004, p. 17.
176. This case is based on Emily Chasan, "Starbucks, Google Assailed by Investors over Gender Policies," *Bloomberg BNA Bulletin to Management*, October 10, 2017; Molly Redden, "Starbucks Investors Press Coffee Chain for Change on Unequal Family Leave," October 2, 2017, www.guardian.com/business/; Joanna Fantozzi, "Starbucks Looks to Reduce Gender Wage Gap," April 28, 2017, www.thedailymail.com; "Starbucks Commitment to Inclusion," https://news.Starbucks.com; all accessed January 19, 2018.

Tang dewei - imaginechina/AP Images

Human Resource Management Strategy and Performance

LEARNING OBJECTIVES

When you finish studying this chapter, you should be able to:

3-1 **Give** examples of each of the seven steps in the strategic management process.

3-2 **List** with examples the main types of strategies.

3-3 **Define** *strategic human resource management*, and give an example of strategic human resource management in practice.

3-4 **Give** at least five examples of HR metrics.

3-5 **Give** five examples of what employers can do to have high-performance systems.

3-6 **Explain** how you would design a program to improve employee engagement.

When the Ritz-Carlton Company took over managing the Portman Hotel in Shanghai, China, the hotel already had a good reputation among business travelers. However, many luxury hotels were opening there. To stay competitive, the Portman's new managers decided to reposition the hotel with a new strategy, one that emphasized outstanding customer service. But they knew that improving the service would require new employee behaviors, and therefore new selection, training, and pay policies and practices. We will see what they did.

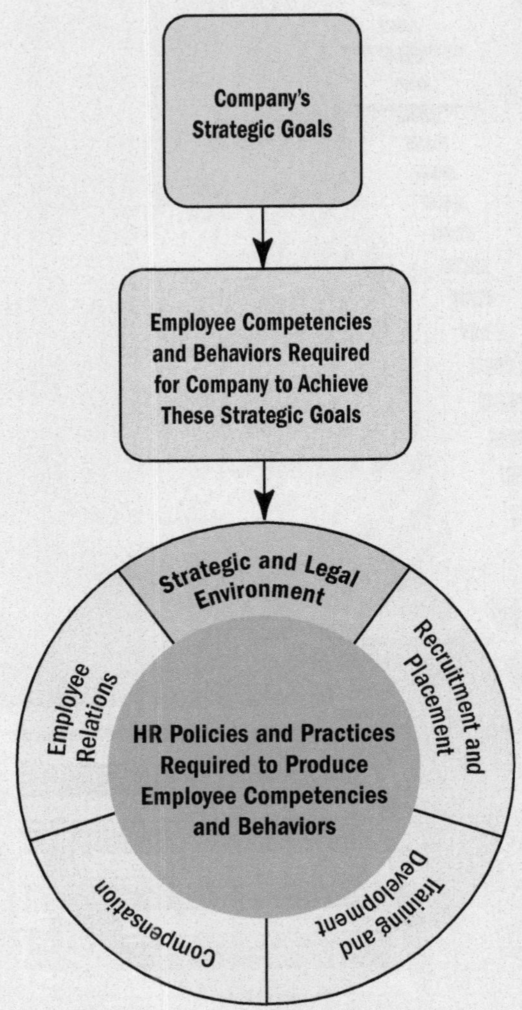

WHERE ARE WE NOW . . .

The next part of this book, Part 2, turns to the nuts and bolts of human resource management, including activities like analyzing jobs and recruiting and selecting employees. Ideally, activities like these should produce the employee behaviors and competencies the firm needs to achieve its strategic goals. Therefore, the main purpose of the present chapter is to explain how managers formulate human resource strategies for their companies. We'll address the **Strategic Management Process**, **Types of Strategies**, **Strategic Human Resource Management**, **HR Metrics and Benchmarking**, **High-Performance Work Systems**, and **Employee Engagement**. We'll turn in the following chapter to how to analyze jobs and recruit employees.

LEARNING OBJECTIVE 3-1

Give examples of each of the seven steps in the strategic management process.

The Strategic Management Process

Employers can't intelligently design their human resource policies and practices without understanding the role these policies and practices are to play in achieving their companies' strategic goals. In this chapter, we look at how managers design strategic and human resource plans, and how they evaluate the results of their plans. We start with an overview of the basic management planning process.

The Management Planning Process

The basic management planning process consists of five steps: setting objectives, making basic planning forecasts, reviewing alternative courses of action, evaluating which options are best, and then choosing and implementing your plan. A *plan* shows the course of action for getting from where you are to the goal. *Planning* is always "goal-directed" (such as, "double sales revenue to $16 million in fiscal year 2020").

In companies, it is traditional to view the goals from the top of the firm down to front-line employees as a chain or *hierarchy of goals*. Figure 3-1 illustrates this. At the top, the president sets long-term or "strategic" goals (such as "double sales revenue to $16 million in fiscal year 2020"). His or her vice presidents then set goals for their units that flow from, and make sense in terms of accomplishing, the president's goal (see Figure 3-1). Then their own subordinates set goals, and so on down the chain.[1]

KNOWLEDGE BASE

Policies and procedures provide day-to-day guidance employees need to do their jobs in a manner that is consistent with the company's plans and goals. Policies set broad guidelines delineating how employees should act. For example, "It is the policy of this company to comply with all laws, regulations, and principles of ethical conduct." *Procedures* spell out what to do if a specific situation arises. For example:

> Any employee who believes this policy has been violated must report this belief to the employee's immediate supervisor. If that is not practical, the employee should file a written report with the Director of Human Resources. There is to be no retaliation in any form.[2]

Employers write their own policies and procedures, or adapt ones from existing sources (or both). For example, most employers have employee manuals listing the

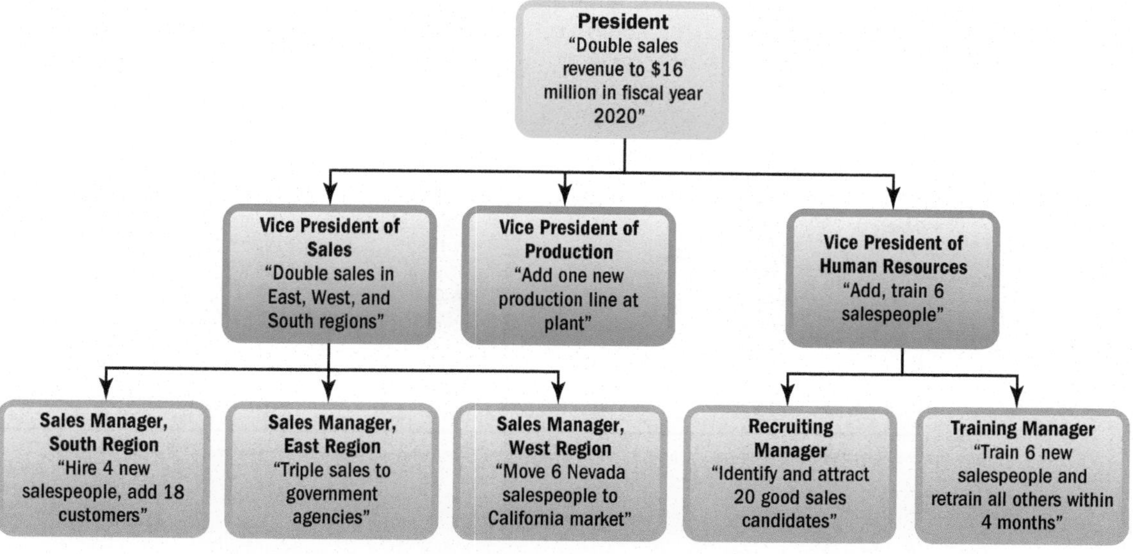

FIGURE 3-1 **Sample Hierarchy of Goals Diagram for a Company**

company's human resource policies and procedures. An online search for prepackaged HR policies manuals would produce choices (for instance go to www.bizmanualz.com/, and then click HR Policies and Procedures Manual).[3]

What Is Strategic Planning?

strategic plan
The company's plan for how it will match its internal strengths and weaknesses with external opportunities and threats in order to maintain a competitive advantage.

strategy
A course of action the company can pursue to achieve its strategic aims.

strategic management
The process of identifying and executing the organization's strategic plan by matching the company's capabilities with the demands of its environment.

Setting goals for the company usually starts at the top, by formulating an overall strategic plan for the company. A **strategic plan** is the company's overall plan for how it will match its internal strengths and weaknesses with its external opportunities and threats in order to maintain a competitive position. The strategic planner asks, "Where are we now as a business, and where do we want to be?" He or she then formulates a strategic plan to help guide the company to the desired end point.[4] When Walmart bought Jet.com to expand online, and WeWork branched out into renting entire facilities to companies like IBM, they were engaged in strategic planning.

A **strategy** is a course of action. Both PepsiCo and Coca-Cola face the same basic problem—people are drinking fewer sugared drinks. However, they each chose different strategies to deal with this. PepsiCo *diversified* by selling more food items like chips. Coca-Cola *concentrated* on sweet beverages, and on boosting advertising to (hopefully) boost Coke sales.[5]

Finally, **strategic management** is the process of identifying and executing the organization's strategic plan by matching the company's capabilities (strengths and weaknesses) with the demands of its environment (its competitors, customers, and suppliers, for instance).

The Strategic Management Process

Figure 3-2 summarizes the strategic management process. Its seven steps include (1) ask, "What business are we in now?"; (2) evaluate the firm's internal and external strengths, weaknesses, opportunities, and threats; (3) formulate a new business direction; (4) decide on strategic goals; and (5) choose specific strategies or courses of action. Steps (6) and (7) are to implement and then evaluate the strategic plan.

The strategic management process begins (step 1) by asking, "What business are we in?" Here the manager defines the company's current business. Specifically, "What products do we sell, where do we sell them, and how do our products or services differ from our competitors'?" For example, the Coca-Cola Company sells mostly sweetened beverages such as Coke and Sprite, while PepsiCo sells drinks but also foods such as Quaker Oats and Frito chips.

The second step is to ask, "*Are we in the right business* given our strengths and weaknesses and the challenges that we face?" To answer this, managers "audit" or study both the firm's environment and the firm's internal strengths and weaknesses. The *environmental scan worksheet* in Figure 3-3 is a guide for compiling information

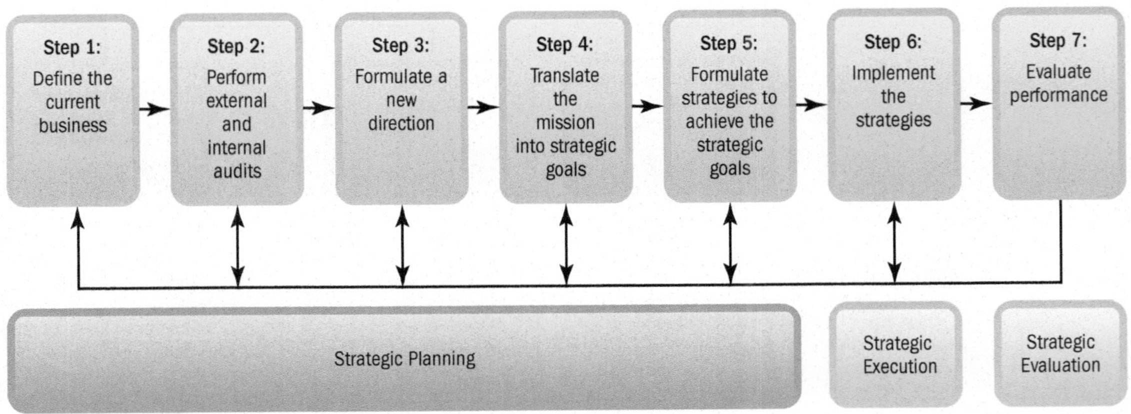

FIGURE 3-2 **The Strategic Management Process**

FIGURE 3-3 **Worksheet for Environmental Scanning**

Economic Trends
(such as recession, inflation, employment, monetary policies)

Competitive and Market Trends
(such as market/customer trends, entry/exit of competitors, new products from competitors)

Political Trends
(such as legislation and regulation/deregulation)

Technological Trends
(such as introduction of new production/distribution technologies, rate of product obsolescence, trends in availability of supplies and raw materials)

Social Trends
(such as demographic trends, mobility, education, evolving values)

Geographic Trends
(such as opening/closing of new markets, factors affecting current plant/office facilities location decisions)

about the company's environment. As you can see, this includes the economic, competitive, and political trends that may affect the company. The *SWOT chart* in Figure 3-4 is widely used. Managers use it to compile and organize the company's strengths, weaknesses, opportunities, and threats. This audit may also include analyzing the so-called PEST factors. These include Political factors such as government regulations and employment laws; Economic factors including unemployment and economic growth; Social factors such as changing demographics and health consciousness trends; and Technological factors such as social media, digitalization, and self-driving vehicles. In any case, the manager's aim is to create a strategic plan that makes sense in terms of the company's strengths, weaknesses, opportunities, and threats.

Next, based on this analysis (in other words, on the environmental scan, SWOT, and PEST analyses), the task in step 3 is to decide *what should our new business be*, in terms of what we sell, where we will sell it, and how our products or services differ from

FIGURE 3-4 SWOT Matrix, with Generic Examples

Potential Strengths	Potential Opportunities
• Market leadership • Strong research and development • High-quality products • Cost advantages • Patents	• New overseas markets • Failing trade barriers • Competitors failing • Diversification • Economy rebounding
Potential Weaknesses	**Potential Threats**
• Large inventories • Excess capacity for market • Management turnover • Weak market image • Lack of management depth	• Market saturation • Threat of takeover • Low-cost foreign competition • Slower market growth • Growing government regulation

competitors' products and services? Some managers express the essence of their new business with a *vision statement*. A **vision statement** is a general statement of the firm's intended direction; it shows, in broad terms, "what we want to become."[6] For example, PepsiCo's vision is to pursue performance within a framework of socially responsible purposes. Because of this, PepsiCo CEO Indra Nooyi and her executives choose which businesses to be in based on that vision's focus on human sustainability, environmental sustainability, and talent sustainability.[7] For example, that vision prompted PepsiCo to add the healthy Quaker Oats and Gatorade to its lineup of products.

vision statement
A general statement of the firm's intended direction; it shows, in broad terms, "what we want to become."

Whereas the vision statement describes in broad terms what the business should be, the company's **mission statement** summarizes what the company's main tasks are today. Several years ago, Ford adopted what was for several years a powerful Ford mission statement—making "Quality Job One."

mission statement
Summarizes the answer to the question, "What business are we in?"

In any case, the next step (step 4) is to translate the desired new direction into *strategic goals*. At Ford, for example, what exactly did making "Quality Job One" mean for each department in terms of how they would boost quality? The answer was laid out in goals such as "no more than 1 initial defect per 10,000 cars."

Next, (step 5) the manager *chooses strategies*—courses of action—that will enable the company to achieve its strategic goals. For example, how should Ford pursue its goal of no more than 1 initial defect per 10,000 cars? Perhaps open two new high-tech plants, and put in place new, rigorous employee selection, training, and performance-appraisal procedures.

Step 6, *strategy execution,* means translating the strategies into action. This means actually hiring (or firing) people, building (or closing) plants, and adding (or eliminating) products and product lines.

Finally, in step 7, the manager *evaluates* the results of his or her planning and execution. Things don't always turn out as planned. All managers should periodically assess the progress of their strategic decisions.

LEARNING OBJECTIVE 3-2
List with examples the main types of strategies.

Types of Strategies

In practice, managers engage in three types or levels of strategic planning, *corporate-level* strategic planning, *business unit* (or *competitive*) strategic planning, and *functional* (or *departmental*) strategic planning (see Figure 3-5).

Corporate Strategy

For any business, the corporate strategy answers the question, "What businesses will we be in?" Specifically, the **corporate-level strategy** identifies the portfolio of businesses that, in total, comprise the company and how these businesses relate to each other. For example, with a *concentration* (single-business) corporate strategy,

corporate-level strategy
Type of strategy that identifies the portfolio of businesses that, in total, comprise the company and the ways in which these businesses relate to each other.

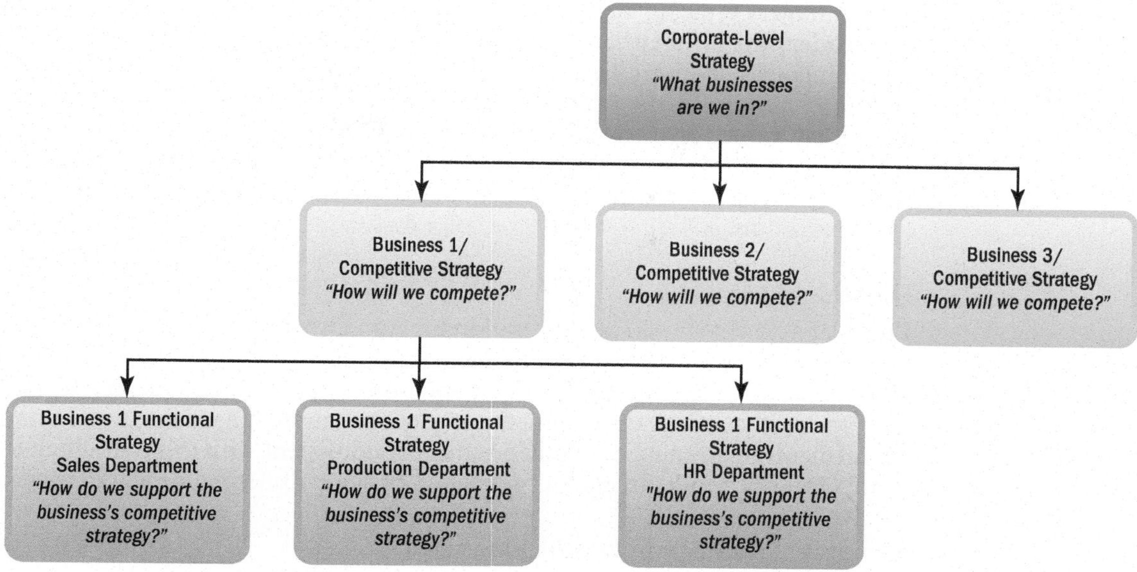

FIGURE 3-5 **Type of Strategy at Each Company Level**

the company offers one product or product line, usually in one market. WD-40 Company is one example. With one spray lubricant, its product scope is narrow. A *diversification* corporate strategy means the firm will expand by adding new product lines. Here product scope is wider. PepsiCo is diversified. Thus, PepsiCo added Frito-Lay chips and Quaker Oats to its drinks businesses, and both Google (with its Waymo division) and Apple are moving into the self-driving car business.[8]

A *vertical integration* strategy means the firm expands by, perhaps, producing its own raw materials, or selling its products directly. Thus, Apple opened its own Apple stores. With a *consolidation* strategy, the company reduces its size. With *geographic expansion*, the company grows by entering new territorial markets, for instance, by taking the business abroad.

Competitive Strategy

Once the manager decides what businesses to be in, each business needs a basis on which to compete. For example, within PepsiCo, each of its businesses (such as Pepsi and Frito-Lay) should have a *business-level/competitive strategy* (again, see Figure 3-5). The **competitive strategy** identifies how to build and strengthen the business's competitive position in the marketplace.[9] It answers the question, for instance, How should Pizza Hut compete with Papa John's? or How should Walmart compete with Target?

competitive strategy
A strategy that identifies how to build and strengthen the business's long-term competitive position in the marketplace.

competitive advantage
Any factors that allow an organization to differentiate its product or service from those of its competitors to increase market share.

Managers build their competitive strategies around their businesses' competitive advantages. **Competitive advantage** means any factors that allow a company to differentiate its product or service from those of its competitors to increase market share. Coca-Cola has a "secret formula" that shows how to create its famous beverage. However, competitive advantages needn't be tangible. For example, here is how a former vice president of human resources at the Toyota Motor Manufacturing facility in Georgetown, Kentucky, described the importance of human capital as a competitive advantage:

> People are behind our success. Machines don't have new ideas, solve problems, or grasp opportunities. Only people who are involved in thinking can make a difference. . . . Every auto plant in the United States has basically the same machinery. But how people are utilized and involved varies widely from one company to another. The workforce gives any company its true competitive edge.[10]

Managers typically adopt one or more of three standard competitive strategies—cost leadership, differentiation, or focus—to achieve competitive advantage. *Cost leadership* means becoming the low-cost leader in an industry; Walmart is an example. With *differentiation,* the firm seeks to be unique in its industry along dimensions that are widely valued by buyers.[11] Thus, Volvo stresses its cars' safety, and Artisan Pizza stresses fresh ingredients. *Focusers* carve out a market niche. Thus Jopwell.com is "The leading career advancement platform for Black, Latinx, and Native American students and professionals."[12]

Functional Strategy

functional strategy
A strategy that identifies the broad activities that each department will pursue in order to help the business accomplish its competitive goals.

Each department should operate within the framework of its business's competitive strategy. **Functional strategies** identify what each department must do to help the business accomplish its strategic goals. Thus, for, say, P&G to make its Olay skincare products a top-tier brand, its product development, production, marketing, sales, and human resource departments must engage in activities that are consistent with this unit's high-quality mission.[13] Inferior products, cheap packaging, or sloppy salespeople would not do.

Managers' Roles in Strategic Planning

Devising the company's overall strategic plan is top management's responsibility. However, few top executives formulate strategic plans without lower-level managers' input. No one knows more about the firm's competitive pressures, product and industry trends, and employee capabilities than do the company's department managers.

For example, the human resource manager is in a good position to supply "competitive intelligence"—information on competitors. Details regarding competitors' incentive plans, employee opinion surveys about customer complaints, and information about pending legislation such as labor laws are examples. Human resource managers should also be the masters of information about their own firms' employees' strengths and weaknesses.

In practice, devising the firm's overall strategic plan involves frequent discussions among and between top and lower-level managers. The top managers then use this information to hammer out their strategic plan.

KNOWLEDGE BASE

Strategic Human Resource Management

LEARNING OBJECTIVE 3-3
Define *strategic human resource management*, and give an example of strategic human resource management in practice.

The company's top managers choose overall corporate strategies, and then choose competitive strategies for each of the company's businesses. Then departmental managers within each of these businesses formulate functional strategies for their departments. Their aim should be to have functional strategies that will support the competitive strategy and the company-wide strategic aims. The marketing department would have marketing strategies. The production department would have production strategies. The human resource management ("HR") department would have *human resource management strategies*.

HR in Action at the Hotel Paris Starting as a single hotel in a Paris suburb in 1995, the Hotel Paris is now a chain of nine hotels, with two in France, one each in London and Rome, and others in New York, Miami, Washington, Chicago, and Los Angeles. To see how managers use strategic human resource management to improve performance, see the Hotel Paris Case on pages 92–93 and answer the questions.

What Is Strategic Human Resource Management?

strategic human resource management
Formulating and executing human resource policies and practices that produce the employee competencies and behaviors the company needs to achieve its strategic aims.

Every company's human resource management policies and activities should make sense in terms of the firm's strategic aims. For example, a high-end hotel like the Shanghai Portman will have different employee selection, training, and pay policies than will a small roadside motel because the Shanghai's customers expect exceptional service. **Strategic human resource management** means formulating and executing human resource policies and practices that produce the employee competencies and behaviors the company needs to achieve its strategic aims. The following Strategic Context feature illustrates this.

IMPROVING PERFORMANCE: *THE STRATEGIC CONTEXT*

The Shanghai Ritz-Carlton Portman Hotel

When the Ritz-Carlton Company took over managing the Portman Hotel in Shanghai, China, the new management reviewed the Portman's strengths and weaknesses and its fast-improving local competitors. They decided that to compete, they had to improve the hotel's level of service. Achieving that in turn meant formulating new human resource management plans for hiring, training, and rewarding hotel employees. It meant putting in place a new human resource strategy for the Portman Hotel, one aimed at improving customer service. Their HR strategy involved taking these steps:

- *Strategically*, they set the goal of making the Shanghai Portman outstanding by offering superior customer service.
- To achieve this, Shanghai Portman employees would have to exhibit new *skills and behaviors*, for instance, in terms of how they treated and responded to guests.
- To produce these employee skills and behaviors, management implemented new human resource management *plans, policies, and procedures*. For example, they introduced the Ritz-Carlton Company's *human resource system* to the Portman: "Our selection [now] focuses on talent and personal values because these are things that can't be taught . . . it's about caring for and respecting others."[14] In 2017 Ritz-Carlton became part of Marriott, but Ritz-Carlton's "Gold Standards" credo remains the same. It says, in part: "We pledge to provide the finest personal service and facilities for our guests who will always enjoy a warm, relaxed, yet refined ambience."[15]

Management's efforts paid off. Their new human resource plans and practices helped to produce the employee behaviors required to improve the Portman's level of service, thus attracting new guests. Travel publications were soon calling it the "best employer in Asia," "overall best business hotel in Asia," and "best business hotel in China," recognition that continues to this day.[16] Profits soared, in no small part due to effective strategic human resource management.

MyLab Management Talk About It 1

If your professor has assigned this, go to the Assignments section of **www.pearson.com/mylab/management** to complete this discussion question. Asian culture is different from that in the United States. For example, team incentives tend to be more attractive to people in Asia than are individual incentives. How do you think these cultural differences would have affected how the hotel's new management selected, trained, appraised, and compensated the Shanghai Portman's employees?

The basic idea of strategic human resource management is this: In formulating human resource management policies and activities, the manager should formulate policies that produce the employee skills and behaviors that the company needs to achieve its strategic goals.[17]

The HR strategy is dynamic, not static. In other words, the manager should determine where each HR activity (recruiting, and so on) is now, and where it should be in order to support the employer's strategic aims. The key to success is to think through how the manager is going to transform the various HR activities so that they align with and support the company's strategic priorities.[18] The bottom line is that the manager should not design any HR activities without understanding very clearly the business's strategic needs, and how to align the HR activities with those strategic needs.

Figure 3-6 outlines this idea. First, the manager formulates *strategic plans* and goals. Next, he or she asks, "What *employee skills and behaviors* will we need to achieve these plans and goals?" And finally, he or she asks, "Specifically what recruitment, selection, training, and other *HR policies and practices* should we put in place so as to produce the required employee skills and behaviors?" Managers often refer to their specific HR policies and practices as *human resource strategies*.[19] The accompanying HR as a Profit Center feature presents another strategic human resource management example.

FIGURE 3-6 The HR Strategy Model

Note: This figure opens each chapter of this book and says this: The company's HR policies and practices should produce the employee competencies and behaviors that the company needs to achieve its strategic goals.

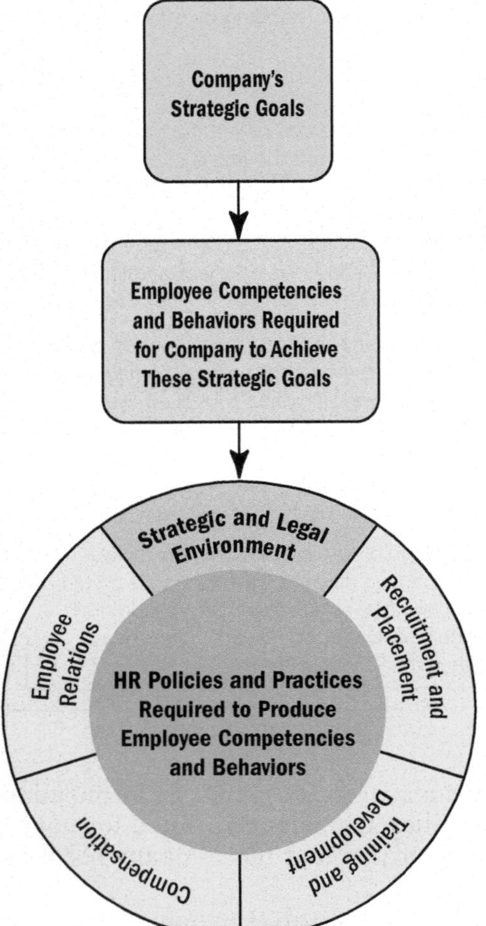

IMPROVING PERFORMANCE: *HR AS A PROFIT CENTER*

The Zappos "WOW" Way

When your strategy involves selling shoes and clothes online to people who can't try them on, you need employees who are energized and enjoy what they're doing—Zappos (part of Amazon) wants employees to deliver "WOW" through service.[20] That's why Zappos' founders knew they needed special methods for hiring, developing, and retaining employees, and that's just what they created. As their Web site says, "This ain't your mama's HR! Recruiting, benefits, and employee relations keep this cruise ship afloat with fun, inventive ways of getting employees motivated and educated about the Zappos Family of companies, their benefits, and the other fun stuff going on around here!"[21]

While they may not appeal to everyone, these "fun, inventive techniques" include interviewing job applicants in what looks like the set of a talk show, asking employees to submit their own designs for Steve Madden shoes, and (during Zappos' annual "Bald & Blue Day") having some employees volunteer to shave their heads or dye their hair blue.[22] And, if you're not happy working at Zappos, the company will pay you to leave—it wants no one there who doesn't truly want to be there. Zappos also believes in what it calls "Holacracy," namely encouraging every employee to be innovative.[23]

Again, that may not be for everyone, but it works for Zappos. It knows that selling online profitably requires energized employees who really enjoy what they're doing. Management uses these special HR practices to cultivate the energized and fun environment that Zappos needs to execute its strategy, and judging from Zappos' success they seem to be working. ■

> **MyLab Management Talk About It 2**
>
> If your professor has assigned this, go to the Assignments section of **www.pearson.com/mylab/management** to complete this discussion question. Why do you think Zappos' top managers believe it is so important for employees to provide a "WOW" factor in their business?

Sustainability and Strategic Human Resource Management

Today's emphasis on *sustainability* has important consequences for human resource management. *Strategic human resource management* means having human resource policies and practices that produce the employee skills and behaviors that are necessary to achieve the company's strategic goals, and these often include sustainability goals.

For example, PepsiCo wants to deliver "Performance with Purpose." This means achieving financial performance while also achieving human sustainability, environmental sustainability, and talent sustainability.[24] PepsiCo's human resource managers can help the company achieve these goals.[25] For example, they can work with top management to institute *flexible work arrangements* that help sustain the environment by reducing commuting. They can use *incentive systems* to motivate employees to achieve PepsiCo's sustainability goals.[26] The bottom line is that HR policies and practices can support a firm's sustainability strategy and goals.

> **MyLab Management Apply It!**
>
> How would you evaluate the process these managers used to formulate their strategic plan? If your professor has assigned this activity, go to the Assignments section of **www.pearson.com/mylab/management** to complete the video exercise.

Strategic Human Resource Management Tools

Managers use several tools to translate the company's strategic goals into human resource management policies and practices. These tools include the strategy map, the HR scorecard, and the digital dashboard.

strategy map
A strategic planning tool that shows the "big picture" of how each department's performance contributes to achieving the company's overall strategic goals.

STRATEGY MAP The **strategy map** summarizes how each department's performance contributes to achieving the company's overall strategic goals. It helps the manager and each employee visualize and understand the role his or her department plays in achieving the company's strategic plan. Management gurus sometimes say that the map clarifies employees' "line of sight." It does this by visually linking their efforts with the company's ultimate goals.[27]

Figure 3-7 presents a strategy-map example for Southwest Airlines. The top-level target is to achieve its profitability, costs, and revenue goals. Then the strategy map shows the chain of activities that help Southwest Airlines achieve these goals. Like Walmart, Southwest has a low-cost-leader strategy. So, for example, to boost revenues and profitability Southwest must fly fewer planes (to keep costs down), maintain low prices, and maintain on-time flights. In turn (further down the strategy map), on-time flights and low prices require fast turnaround. This, in turn, requires motivated ground and flight crews. The resulting strategy map helps each department understand what it needs to do to support Southwest's low-cost strategy.[28] For example, what steps must Southwest's human resource team take to boost the motivation and dedication of its ground crews?

HR scorecard
A process for assigning financial and nonfinancial goals or metrics to the human resource management–related chain of activities required for achieving the company's strategic aims and for monitoring results.

THE HR SCORECARD Many employers quantify and computerize the strategy map's activities. The HR scorecard helps them to do so. The **HR scorecard** is not a scorecard. It refers to a process for assigning financial and nonfinancial goals or metrics

FIGURE 3-7 Strategy Map for Southwest Airlines

Source: Based on TeamCHRYSALIS.com, accessed July 2006; http://mcknightkaney.com/Strategy_Maps_Primer.html; www.strategymap.com.au/home/StrategyMapOverview.html.

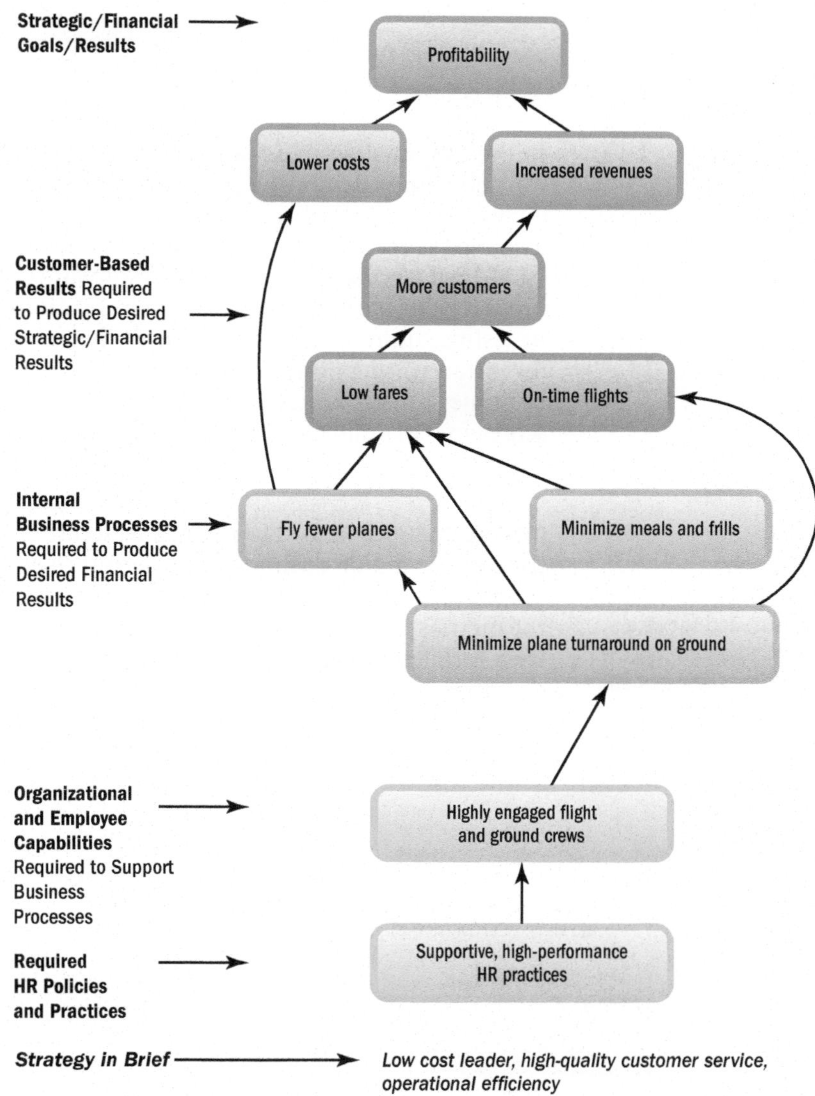

A digital dashboard presents the manager with desktop graphs and charts, showing a computerized picture of how the company is doing on all the metrics from the HR scorecard process.

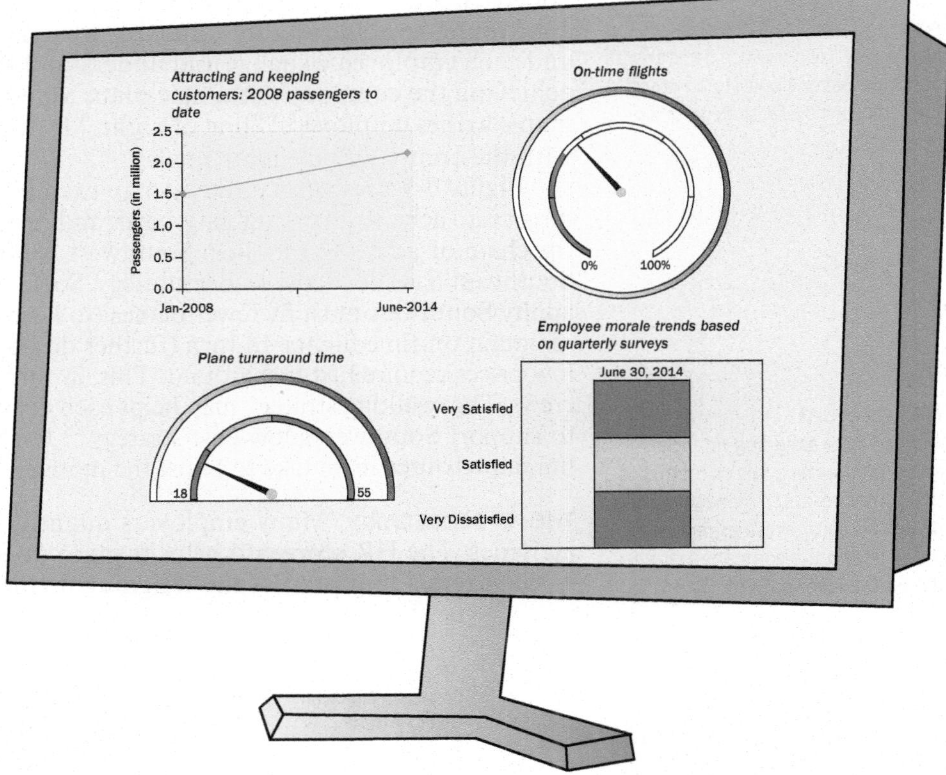

to the human resource management-related strategy-map chain of activities required for achieving the company's strategic aims.[29] (Metrics for Southwest might include airplane turnaround time, percent of on-time flights, and ground crew productivity.) The idea is to take the strategy map and to quantify it.

Managers use special scorecard software to facilitate this. The computerized scorecard process helps the manager quantify the relationships between (1) the HR activities (amount of testing, training, and so forth), (2) the resulting employee behaviors (customer service, for instance), and (3) the resulting firm-wide strategic outcomes and performance (such as customer satisfaction and profitability).[30] The HR scorecard derives from the "balanced scorecard" planning approach, which aims to balance hard data such as financial measures with soft data such as customer satisfaction in assessing a company's performance.

digital dashboard
Presents the manager with desktop graphs and charts, and shows a computerized picture of where the company stands on all those metrics from the HR scorecard process.

DIGITAL DASHBOARDS The saying "a picture is worth a thousand words" explains the purpose of the digital dashboard. A **digital dashboard** presents the manager with desktop graphs and charts, showing a computerized picture of how the company is doing on all the metrics from the HR scorecard process. As in the preceding illustration, a top Southwest Airlines manager's dashboard might display real-time trends for various strategy-map activities, such as fast turnarounds and on-time flights. This enables the manager to take corrective action. For example, if ground crews are turning planes around slower today, financial results tomorrow may decline unless the manager takes action.

Figure 3-8 summarizes the three strategic planning tools.

Strategy Map	HR Scorecard	Digital Dashboard
Graphical tool that summarizes the chain of activities that contribute to a company's success, and so shows employees the "big picture" of how their performance contributes to achieving the company's overall strategic goals.	A process for assigning financial and nonfinancial goals or metrics to the human resource management-related chain of activities required for achieving the company's strategic aims and for monitoring results.	Presents the manager with desktop graphs and charts, so he or she gets a picture of where the company has been and where it's going, in terms of each activity in the strategy map.

FIGURE 3-8 **Three Important Strategic HR Tools**

HR Metrics, Benchmarking, and Data Analytics

LEARNING OBJECTIVE 3-4

Give at least five examples of HR metrics.

We've seen that strategic human resource management means formulating HR policies and practices that produce the employee competencies and behaviors the company needs to achieve its strategic goals. Being able to measure results is essential to this process. For example, it would have been futile for the Ritz-Carlton Portman Shanghai's managers to set "better customer service" as a goal if they couldn't measure customer service.[31] Relevant measures might include, for instance, hours of training per employee, productivity per employee, and (via customer surveys) customer satisfaction.

human resource metrics
The quantitative gauge of a human resource management activity, such as employee turnover, hours of training per employee, or qualified applicants per position.

Human resource managers use many such measures (or **"human resource metrics"**). For example, there is (on average) one human resource employee per 100 company employees for firms with 100–249 employees. This HR employee-to-employee ratio drops to about 0.79 for firms with 1,000–2,499 employees and to 0.72 for firms with more than 7,500 employees.[32] Figure 3-9 illustrates other human resource management metrics. They include employee tenure, cost per hire, and annual overall turnover rate.[33]

Benchmarking

Just measuring how one is doing (for instance, in terms of employee productivity) is rarely enough for deciding what (if anything) to change. Instead, most managers want to know

Organizational Data

- Revenue
- Revenue per FTE
- Net Income Before Taxes
- Net Income Before Taxes per FTE
- Positions Included Within the Organization's Succession Plan

HR Department Data

- Total HR Staff
- HR-to-Employee Ratio
- Percentage of HR Staff in Supervisory Roles
- Percentage of HR Staff in Professional/Technical Roles
- Percentage of HR Staff in Administrative Support Roles
- Reporting Structure for the Head of HR
- Types of HR Positions Organizations Expect to Hire in this year

HR Expense Data

- HR Expenses
- HR Expense to Operating Expense Ratio
- HR Expense to FTE Ratio

Compensation Data

- Annual Salary Increase
- Salaries as a Percentage of Operating Expense
- Target Bonus for Non-Executives
- Target Bonus for Executives

Tuition/Education Data

- Maximum Reimbursement Allowed for Tuition/Education Expenses per Year
- Percentage of Employees Participating in Tuition/Education Reimbursement Programs

Employment Data

- Number of Positions Filled
- Time-to-Fill
- Cost-Per-Hire
- Employee Tenure
- Annual Overall Turnover Rate
- Annual Voluntary Turnover Rate
- Annual Involuntary Turnover Rate

Expectations for Revenue and Organizational Hiring

- Percentage of Organizations Expecting Changes in Revenue in Current Year Compared with Previous Year
- Percentage of Organizations Expecting Changes in Hiring in Current Year Compared with Previous Year

Metrics for More Profitable Organizations

- Total HR Staff
- HR-to-Employee Ratio
- HR Expenses
- HR Expense to Operating Expense Ratio
- HR Expense to FTE Ratio
- Annual Salary Increase
- Target Bonus for Non-Executives
- Target Bonus for Executives
- Maximum Reimbursement Allowed for Tuition/Education Expenses-Per-Year
- Percentage of Employees Participating in Tuition/Education Reimbursement Programs
- Time-to-Fill
- Cost-Per-Hire
- Annual Overall Turnover Rate

FIGURE 3-9 **Metrics for the SHRM® 2017 Customized Human Capital Benchmarking Report**

Source: Reprinted with permission from the Society for Human Resource Management.

"How are we doing?" *in relation to something*. For example, are our accident rates rising or falling? Similarly, the manager may want to *benchmark* the results—compare high-performing companies' results to your own, to understand what makes them better.[34]

The Society for Human Resource Management's (SHRM's) benchmarking service enables employers to compare their own HR metrics with those of other companies. The employer can request comparable (benchmark) figures not just by industry, but by employer size, company revenue, and geographic region. (See http://shrm.org/research/benchmarks/.)

Figure 3-10 illustrates one of the SHRM's many sets of comparable benchmark measures. It shows how much employers are spending for tuition reimbursement programs.

Strategy-Based Metrics

Benchmarking provides one perspective on how your company's human resource management system is performing.[35] It shows how your human resource management system's performance compares to the competition. However, it may *not* reveal the extent to which your firm's HR practices are supporting its strategic goals. Thus, if the strategy calls for doubling profits by improving customer service, to what extent are our new training practices helping to improve customer service?

strategy-based metrics
Metrics that specifically focus on measuring the activities that contribute to achieving a company's strategic aims.

Managers use *strategy-based metrics* to answer such questions. **Strategy-based metrics** measure the activities that contribute to achieving a company's strategic aims.[36] Thus, for the Portman Shanghai, the strategic HR metrics might include 100% employee testing, 80% guest returns, incentive pay as a percent of total salaries, and sales up 50%. If changes in HR practices such as increased training have their intended effects, then strategic metrics like guest returns should also rise.

What Are HR Audits?

HR audit
An HR audit is an analysis of the completeness, efficiency, and effectiveness of the organization's HR functions, including its HR policies, practices, processes, and relevant metrics.

Human resource managers often assess matters like employee turnover and safety via *human resource audits*. An **HR audit** is an analysis of the completeness, efficiency, and effectiveness of the organization's HR functions, including its HR policies, practices, processes, and relevant metrics.[37] This generally involves using a checklist to review the company's human resource functions (recruiting, testing, training, and so on), as well as ensuring that the firm is adhering to regulations, laws, and company policies. The HR auditor may first review payroll data, focusing on what and when each employee was paid. He or she will then turn to whether the human resource records are in order (for instance, are medical records kept separate from résumés?). He or she will also review the employer's handbooks and policies, for instance, checking for disability accommodation policies, social media policies, and family and medical leave policies.[38]

FIGURE 3-10 SHRM Customized Human Capital Benchmarking Report

Source: "HR Expense Data," from *SHRM Customized Human Capital Benchmarking Report*. Reprinted with permission from the Society for Human Resource Management. All rights reserved. www.shrm.org/Research/benchmarks/Documents/sample_humnba_capital_report.pdf.

Tuition/Education Data					
	n	25th Percentile	Median	75th Percentile	Average
Maximum reimbursement allowed for tuition/education expenses per year	32	$1,000	$5,000	$7,500	$6,000
Percentage of employees participating in tuition/education reimbursement programs	32	1.0%	3.0%	5.0%	4.0%

Beyond that, HR audits vary in scope. Typical areas audited include:[39]

1. Roles and headcount (including job descriptions, and employees categorized by exempt/nonexempt and full- or part-time)
2. Compliance with federal, state, and local employment-related legislation
3. Recruitment and selection (including use of selection tools, background checks, and so on)
4. Compensation (policies, incentives, survey procedures, and so on)
5. Employee relations (union agreements, performance management, disciplinary procedures, employee recognition)
6. Mandated benefits (Social Security, unemployment insurance, workers' compensation, and so on)
7. Group benefits (insurance, time off, flexible benefits, and so on)
8. Payroll (such as legal compliance)
9. Documentation and record keeping. For example, do our files include résumés and applications, offer letters, job descriptions, performance evaluations, benefit enrollment forms, payroll change notices, and documentation related to personnel actions such as employee handbook acknowledgments?[40]
10. Training and development (new employee orientation, development, technical and safety, career planning, and so on)
11. Employee communications (employee handbook, newsletter, recognition programs)
12. Termination and transition policies and practices

TRENDS SHAPING HR: *DIGITAL AND SOCIAL MEDIA*

Data like monthly payroll costs are interesting but relatively useless until converted to information. *Information* is data presented in a form that makes it useful for making decisions. For example, knowing your cost per hire is interesting. However, presenting cost-per-hire data that shows whether the cost is trending up or down provides information you can use to make decisions.[41]

Data analytics means using statistical and mathematical analysis to find relationships and make predictions. For example, when online bookstores use algorithms to predict which books you're most likely to buy based on things like what books you've already bought and similarities between you and other groups, they are using data analytics.[42] Data analytics relies on data mining. *Data mining* sifts through huge amounts of employee data to identify correlations that employers then use to improve their employee-selection and other practices. *Data mining* is "the set of activities used to find new, hidden, or unexpected patterns in data."[43]

Big data is basically data analytics on steroids. The basic idea (of scientifically analyzing data to find relationships and make predictions) is the same. However, with "big data" the volume, velocity, and variety of data that are analyzed are much greater. In terms of *volume,* for example, Walmart now collects about 2.5 petabytes of data—2.5 million gigabytes—*every hour* from its customer transactions.[44] Similarly, in terms of *velocity*, all these data are being created more or less instantaneously (as at Walmart); that means companies can use them to more quickly adapt in real time (for instance, to who's buying what products, and so how to adjust online promotions). Finally, big data capitalizes on the huge *variety* of data now available. For instance, data come not just from Walmart's transactions but from customers' mobile phones, GPS, and social networks too.

Talent Analytics

Data analytics tools like these enable employers to analyze together employee data (like employee demographics, training, and performance ratings) from traditional sources such as employee records, as well as data from new sources (like company internal social media sites, GPS tracking, and e-mail activity).[45] Employers then use *talent analytics* (data analytics applied to HR issues) to answer questions that in the past they couldn't answer, or couldn't answer as well. For example, human resource consultant Aon Hewitt has an "analytics engine" that analyzes its client's employee and performance data. Computer dashboards then enable its clients to answer questions such as "Are there potential turnover trends we should further analyze to head off potential problems?"[46] "What factors drive our high-performing salespeople?" And, "what sorts of people are most likely to have accidents and submit claims?"

Talent analytics can produce striking profitability results. For example, Best Buy used talent analytics to discover that a 0.1% increase in employee engagement led to a more than $100,000 rise in a Best Buy store's annual operating income.[47] Employers use talent analytics to answer several types of talent management questions:

- **Human Capital Facts** For example, "What are the key indicators of my organization's overall health?" JetBlue found that employee engagement correlated with financial performance.
- **Analytical HR** For example, "Which units, departments, or individuals need attention?" Lockheed Martin collects performance data in order to identify units needing improvement.
- **Human Capital Investment Analysis** For example, "Which actions have the greatest impact on my business?" By monitoring employee satisfaction levels, Cisco improved its employee retention rate from 65% to 85%, saving the company nearly $50 million in recruitment, selection, and training costs. A Google talent analytics team analyzed data on employee backgrounds, capabilities, and performance.[48] It identified factors (such as an employee feeling underutilized) likely to lead to the employee leaving—and thus helped it reduce turnover. Microsoft identified correlations among the schools and companies its employees arrived from and the employees' subsequent performance. This helped it improve its recruitment and selection practices.[49] ■

MyLab Management Talk About It 3

If your professor has assigned this, go to the Assignments section of **www.pearson.com/mylab/management** to complete this discussion question. Could Best Buy or some of these other companies have made the same discoveries without using talent analytics tools? How?

Digital tools like talent analytics enable HR managers to be more scientific and analytical. And, they often shift "who does HR" *from* the human resource department *to* other departments (such as finance), and sometimes to line managers like the heads of departments (for instance, Aon Hewitt's digital dashboard shows line managers when there's a turnover problem).

Digital tools like these show great promise. In one study, 82% of high-performing organizations gave human resource management leaders such analytical workforce data, compared with 33% of low-performing ones.[50]

TRENDS SHAPING HR: *SCIENCE IN TALENT MANAGEMENT*

Data analytics facilitates making decisions based on a measurable and objective review of the situation. Managers have a name for this. *Evidence-based human resource management* means using data, facts, analytics, scientific rigor, critical evaluation, and critically evaluated research/case studies to support human resource management proposals, decisions, practices, and conclusions.[51]

You may sense that being evidence-based is similar to being scientific, and if so, you are correct. A *Harvard Business Review* article even argues that managers must become more scientific and "think like scientists" when making business decisions.[52]

But how can managers think like scientists? Objectivity, experimentation, and prediction are the heart of science. In gathering evidence, scientists (or managers) first need to be *objective*, or there's no way to trust their conclusions. Recently, a medical school disciplined several professors. They had failed to reveal that they were on the payroll of the drug company that supplied the drugs, the results of which the doctors were studying. Who could trust their objectivity or conclusions?

Being scientific also requires *experimentation.* An experiment is a test one sets up in such a way as to ensure that he or she understands the reasons for the results obtained. For example, in their *Harvard Business Review* article, "A Step-by-Step Guide to Smart Business Experiments," the authors argue that if you want to judge a new incentive plan's impact on corporate profits, don't start by implementing the plan with all employees. Instead, implement it with an "experimental" group (which gets the incentive plan) *and* with a "control" group (a group that does *not* get the incentive plan). Doing so will help you gauge if any performance improvement stemmed from the incentive or from some other cause (such as a new company-wide training program).[53] And, it will enable you to *predict* how changing the incentive plan will affect performance.

For managers, the point of being "scientific" is to make better decisions by forcing you to gather the facts. "Is this sales incentive plan really boosting sales?" "We've spent \$40,000 in the past 5 years on our tuition-refund plan; what (if anything) did we get out of it?" What's the evidence?

Successful HR managers need to be scientific today. As an example, the chemical company BASF Corp. used talent analytics to analyze data on the relationship among stress, health, and productivity in its 15,000 U.S. headquarters staff. Based on that analysis, the company instituted health programs that it calculated would more than pay for themselves in increased productivity by reducing stress.[54]

Throughout this book we will show examples of how managers use evidence to make better human resource management decisions. For example: Which recruitment source produces our best candidates? Does it pay to use this testing program? And, does our safety program really lead to fewer accidents? ■

> MyLab Management Talk About It 4
>
> If your professor has assigned this, go to the Assignments section of **www.pearson.com/mylab/management** to complete this discussion question. If it is apparently so easy to do what BASF did to size up the potential benefits of health programs, why do more employers not do so?

LEARNING OBJECTIVE 3-5

Give five examples of what employers can do to have high-performance systems.

High-Performance Work Systems

high-performance work system (HPWS)
A set of human resource management policies and practices that promote organizational effectiveness.

One reason to measure, benchmark, and scientifically analyze HR practices is to promote high-performance work practices. A **high-performance work system (HPWS)** is a set of human resource management policies and practices that together produce superior employee performance.

What exactly are these high-performance work practices? In one study, researchers collected data from 359 firms before, during, and after the 2007–2009 recession. They found that firms that used more effective staffing and training outperformed competitors before, during, and after the recession.[55]

Another study looked at 17 manufacturing plants, some of which adopted high-performance work system practices. The high-performance plants paid more (median wages of \$16 per hour compared with \$13 per hour for all plants), trained more, used more sophisticated recruitment and hiring practices (tests and validated interviews, for instance), and used more self-managing work teams.[56] Those with the high-performance HR practices performed significantly better than did those without such practices. Service companies (such as hotels) particularly gain from such high-performance work systems and practices.[57]

Studies like these show that high-performance work systems' policies and practices do differ from less productive ones (Table 3-1). For example, high-performing companies recruit more job candidates, use more selection tests, and spend many more hours training employees. Table 3-1 illustrates three things.

First, it shows examples of *human resource metrics* such as hours of training per employee, or qualified applicants per position. (In Table 3-1, the metric for "Number of qualified applicants per position" is 37 in the high-performing companies.) Managers use these to assess their companies' performance and to compare one firm with another.[58]

Second, it illustrates *what employers must do* to have high-performance systems. For example, high-performing companies have more than four times the number of qualified applicants per job than do low performers. They also hire based on validated selection tests, and extensively train employees.

Third, Table 3-1 shows that high-performance work practices usually *aspire to encourage employee involvement and self-management.* In other words, an aim of the high-performance recruiting, screening, training, and other human resources practices is to nurture an engaged, involved, informed, empowered, and self-motivated workforce.[59]

TABLE 3-1 Examples Selected from Several Studies of How Recruitment, Selection, Training, Appraisal, Pay, and Other Practices Differ in High-Performance and Low-Performance Companies

	Lower-Performance Companies' HR Practice Averages (e.g., company performance in terms of sales/employee, innovation, and employee retention)*	Higher-Performance Companies' HR Practice Averages (e.g., company performance in terms of sales/employee, innovation, and employee retention)*
Recruitment: Average number of qualified applicants per position	8	37
Selection: Average percentage of employees hired based on a validated *selection* test	4%	30%
Training: Average number of hours of *training* for new employees	35 hours	117 hours
Appraisal: Average percentage of employees receiving a regular *performance appraisal*	41%	95%
Pay Practices: Average percentage of the workforce eligible for *incentive pay*	28%	84%
Use of Teams: Average percentage of the workforce routinely working in all teams: semiautonomous, cross-functional, or project teams	11%	42%
Self-Directed Teams: Percent of companies with *semiautonomous or autonomous* work teams	9%	70%
Operational Information Sharing: Employees receive relevant operating performance information	62%	82%
Financial Information Sharing: Employees receive relevant financial performance information	43%	66%

*Findings rounded.

Based on "Comparison of HR Practices in High-Performance and Low-Performance Companies," by B. E. Becker, et al., from *The HR Scorecard: Linking People, Strategy and Performance* (Boston: Harvard Business School Press, 2001); Barry Macy, Gerard Farias, Jean-Francois Rosa, and Curt Moore, "Built to Change: High-Performance Work Systems and Self-Directed Work Teams—A Longitudinal Field Study," *Research in Organizational Change and Development,* 16, pp. 339–418, 2007; James Gathrie, Wenchuan Liu, Patrick Flood, and Sarah MacCurtain, "High Performance Work Systems, Workforce Productivity, and Innovation: A Comparison of MNCs and Indigenous Firms," The Learning, Innovation and Knowledge (LINK) Research Centre Working Paper Series, WP 04-08, 2008. Michael C. Campion, and Malika Masimova, "A High Performance Work Practices Taxonomy: Integrating the Literature and Directing Future Research," *Journal of Management*, 39, no. 5, July 2013, pp. 1184–1220.

LEARNING OBJECTIVE 3-6

Explain how you would design a program to improve employee engagement.

Employee Engagement Guide for Managers: Employee Engagement and Performance

Employee engagement refers to being psychologically involved in, connected to, and committed to getting one's jobs done. Engaged employees "experience a high level of connectivity with their work tasks," and work hard to accomplish their task-related goals.[60]

Employee engagement is important because it drives performance and productivity. For example, based on a Gallup survey, business units with the highest levels of employee engagement have an 83% chance of performing above the company median; those with the lowest employee engagement have only a 17% chance.[61] According to one review of the evidence, employee engagement is correlated with employees' customer service productivity, and improvements in employee engagement were associated with significant increases in sales, product quality, productivity, safety incidents at work, retention and absenteeism, and revenue growth.[62] One consulting firm estimates that a 5% increase in employee engagement correlates to a 0.7% increase in operating margins.[63] Companies with highly engaged employees are also less likely to be unionized.[64] In one survey, highly engaged employees lost only about 7.5 days of productivity per year, compared to about 14 days for disengaged employees.[65] A survey by consultants Watson Wyatt Worldwide concluded that companies with highly engaged employees have 26% higher revenue per employee.[66]

The Employee Engagement Problem

The problem is that, depending on the study, only about 21–30% of employees nationally are engaged.[67] Gallup distinguishes among engaged employees "who work with passion and feel a profound connection to their company," not-engaged employees who are essentially "checked out," and actively disengaged employees. The latter "act out their unhappiness" by undermining what their engaged coworkers are accomplishing.[68] Gallup found that about 30% of employees were engaged, 50% were not engaged, and 20% were actively disengaged.

What Can Managers Do to Improve Employee Engagement?

Managers improve employee engagement by taking concrete steps to do so. We'll look more closely at how they do this in a moment, but one important activity is *providing supportive supervision.* For example, a Gallup survey found that managers who focus their support and coaching on their employees' strengths can "practically eliminate active disengagement"; conversely, "bosses from hell" kill employee engagement.[69] Other steps managers can take to foster engagement include making sure employees (1) *understand* how their departments contribute to the company's success, (2) *see how their efforts contribute* to achieving the company's goals, (3) get a *sense of accomplishment* from working at the firm,[70] and (4) are highly *involved*—as when working in self-managing teams.[71] Employers should also *hold managers responsible* for employee engagement. For example, WD-40 Company has its managers meet periodically with their employees to discuss how to improve employee engagement.[72]

How to Measure Employee Engagement

Firms like Gallup (www.gallup.com), and Towers Watson (go to www.towerswatson.com/en-US, then click Solutions, and then Surveys) offer comprehensive employee engagement survey services. However, monitoring employee engagement needn't be complicated. With about 180,000 employees worldwide, the consulting firm Accenture uses a three-part "shorthand" method it calls "say, stay, and strive." First, Accenture assesses how positively the employee speaks about the company and recommends it to others. Second, it looks at who stays with the company, and why. Third, it looks at "strive." For instance, "do employees take an active role in the overall success of the organization by moving beyond just doing tasks to going above and beyond?"[73]

The Employee Engagement Guide for Managers sections in this and the following chapters will show how managers use human resource activities to improve employee engagement.

How Kia Motors (UK) Improved Performance with an HR Strategy Aimed at Boosting Employee Engagement

Kia Motors is a successful automobile manufacturer employing tens of thousands of employees around the world, and one famous for its 10-year warranty and for the quality and value of its products. However, Kia was not always so successful. In July 1997, Kia was under bankruptcy protection and having difficulty servicing its $10.6 billion of debt.[74] In 1998, Hyundai Motorcar Company of Korea purchased 51% of Kia. That triggered a multiyear program aimed at improving Kia's operating performance. Today, Hyundai owns about one-third of Kia Motors, although Kia is still a close-knit part of Hyundai Motor Group.

THE CHALLENGES After several years of improving operating conditions under Hyundai Motor Group, Kia (as well as most auto manufacturers around the world) ran into strong headwinds as credit tightened and consumers cut spending around 2006. Looking at the situation in 2006–2007, Kia's chairman, writing in the company's annual report said,

> In today's automobile industry, competition is so severe that even the bold at heart, if well-informed, would be hesitant to confidently predict future victors in the car market. Japanese automobile companies are unrelenting in their measures against us, while latecomers, such as China, are speeding up to catch up with us as far as they can. Stagnation and the world economic growth, coupled with exchange-rate risks and other major threats, present unfavorable economic conditions for any global player.[75]

In the face of these challenges, the chairman went on to lay out what Kia's strategy for dealing with this intense global competition would be. As he said:

> We intend to base future growth on raising our competencies as a global maker in all areas including production, sales, marketing, branding, as well as before and after servicing. We will also concentrate on our global quality management we have driven so far. We will first strengthen our basic competitiveness in terms of production costs and final products. Second, we will exclude all the unnecessary elements from the management through advanced systems to groundwork the base of stable profit making. Third, we will efficiently invest in new future businesses with our specialized R&D and global production bases.[76]

Also in 2006–2007, Kia Motor's UK subsidiary (Kia UK), which employed about 2,500 people, faced particularly dire circumstances; these included rapidly falling sales, increased financial losses, and low levels of employee engagement. Employee turnover was 31%. The direct cost to the company from the 31% turnover alone was estimated at about 600,000 British pounds (about $1 million) in 2006 (due to higher than necessary recruitment, legal, and employee dismissal costs).[77]

THE NEW HUMAN RESOURCE MANAGEMENT STRATEGY Gary Tomlinson, Kia UK's newly appointed head of HR, believed that Kia UK's low employee engagement was probably both a cause and an effect of the unit's poor performance. In fact, a survey of Kia UK employees had identified numerous personnel issues including possibly poor morale and communications. He knew Kia UK needed a new HR strategy to address this. He also knew that this strategy should support the parent company's strategy of basing "future growth on raising our competencies as a global maker in all areas including production, sales, marketing, branding, as well as before and after servicing."

Tomlinson (with the support of Kia UK's top management) wisely decided to develop, as he put it, "an employee engagement strategy to improve employee morale and address the high levels of employee turnover."[78] In brief, the idea was that, by (1) putting in place new HR policies and practices aimed at improving employee engagement, he could (2) change Kia UK employees' behavior (improve performance and reduce turnover, for instance), and thereby (3) support the parent company's stated strategy of "raising our competencies as a global maker in all areas." The following shows what he actually did to boost employee engagement.

HOW TO EXECUTE AN EMPLOYEE ENGAGEMENT STRATEGY Actually executing Kia UK's employee engagement HR strategy involved six steps (and these provide a roadmap for any such endeavor). First, Kia UK set *measurable objectives* for the program. These objectives included improving by at least 10% survey feedback scores for line managers' behaviors in terms of communication, the quality of appraisal feedback they gave their direct reports, the recognition of work done, and the respect between manager and employee.[79] Other objectives included reducing employee turnover employment costs (e.g., recruitment costs) by at least 10% per year.

Second, Kia UK held an extensive *leadership development* program. For example, it sent all managers for training to improve their management skills. Kia then tested the new skills with "360-degree" assessment tools (having managers' bosses, peers, and subordinates rate the managers' new leadership skills).

Third, Kia UK instituted new *employee recognition programs.* These included, for instance, giving "Outstanding Awards" to selected employees quarterly, and "Kia thank you" cards for jobs well done.[80]

Fourth, Kia UK *improved internal communications.* For example, it instituted quarterly employee briefings and more extensive use of performance appraisals, and launched a new corporate intranet called Kia Vision (this provided key business information and other useful communiqués to all employees). Based on employee feedback, Kia UK also decided, as part of the enhanced communications, to institute an *employee forum.* This consisted of one representative from each department; the forum in effect empowered and involved employees by enabling them to express opinions, suggestions, and concerns about their jobs.

Fifth, Kia instituted a new *employee development program.* This involved using the company's appraisal process to identify employees' training needs. Kia then created training plans for each employee. It based these plans on Kia's needs and on the employee's stated career aspirations.

Sixth, Kia UK made a number of changes to its *compensation and other policies*. For instance, it eliminated bonuses and substituted fixed-rate percentage-based salary increases. It also rewrote the entire employee handbook and all HR policies and procedures "to ensure they were aligned with [Kia UK's new] cultural values."[81]

THE RESULTS The results of the new employee engagement program were impressive. Employee surveys of employee engagement and of line managers' communications and other behaviors improved markedly; employee turnover fell from 31% in 2006 to 15% in 2007, to 5% in 2008, and to below 2% by the end of 2009. Recruitment and turnover costs fell by more than 400,000 British pounds within two years, a 71% reduction.[82]

Earlier we said that *strategic human resource management* means having the HR policies and practices that will produce the employee competencies and behaviors that the company needs to achieve its strategic goals. Kia UK's employee engagement program illustrates how one company actually did this.

Chapter Review

Chapter Section Summaries

3-1. All managers' personnel and other decisions should be consistent with the goals that cascade down from the firm's overall strategic plan. Those goals form a hierarchy, starting with the president's overall strategic goals (such as double sales revenue to $16 million) and filtering down to what each individual manager needs to do in order to support that overall company goal.

The strategic planning process's seven steps include: (1) ask, "Where are we now as a business?"; (2) evaluate the firm's internal and external strengths, weaknesses, opportunities, and threats; (3) formulate a new business direction; (4) decide on strategic goals; and (5) choose specific strategies or courses of action; steps (6) and (7) are to implement and then evaluate the strategic plan.

3-2. We distinguished among **three types of strategies:** corporate, business/competitive, and functional/department strategies.

3-3. Each function or department in the business needs its own functional strategy, and **strategic human resource management** means formulating and executing human resource policies and practices that produce the employee competencies and behaviors the company needs to achieve its strategic aims. Human resource strategies are the specific human resource management policies and practices managers use to support their strategic aims. Important and popular **strategic human resource management** tools include the strategy map, the HR scorecard, and digital dashboards.

3-4. The manager will want to gather and analyze data prior to making decisions. **Human resource metrics** (quantitative measures of some human resource management activities such as employee turnover) are critical in creating high-performance human resource policies and practices.

3-5. A **high-performance work system** is a set of human resource management policies and practices that together produce superior employee performance.

3-6. Employee engagement is important because it drives performance and productivity. Actually **executing Kia UK's employee engagement HR strategy** involved six steps. These were: set *measurable objectives* for the program; provide *leadership development,* for example, send all managers for training to improve their management skills; institute new *employee recognition programs,* for instance, giving "Outstanding Awards" to selected employees quarterly; institute a new *employee development program,* for instance, using the company's appraisal process to identify employees' training needs and to create training plans for each employee; and change the *compensation* and *other policies* to ensure they are aligned with the new cultural values.

Discussion Questions

3-1. Give an example of hierarchical planning in an organization.

3-2. What is the difference between a corporate strategy and a competitive strategy? Give one example of each.

3-3. Explain why strategic planning is important to all managers.

3-4. Explain with examples each of the eight steps in the strategic management process.

3-5. Explain with examples how human resources management can be instrumental in helping a company create a competitive advantage.

3-6. Outline how you would implement an employee engagement program.

Individual and Group Activities

3-7. With three or four other students, form a strategic management group for your college or university. Your assignment is to develop the outline of a strategic plan for the college or university. This should include such things as strategic goals and corporate, competitive, and functional strategies. In preparing your plan, make sure to show the main strengths, weaknesses, opportunities, and threats the college faces, and which prompted you to develop your particular strategic plans.

3-8. Using the Internet or library resources, review the annual reports of five companies. Bring to class examples of how those companies say they are using their HR processes to help the company achieve its strategic goals.

3-9. Interview an HR manager and write a short report on "The Strategic Roles of the HR Manager at XYZ Company."

3-10. Using the Internet or library resources, bring to class and discuss at least two examples of how companies are using an HR scorecard to help create HR systems that support the company's strategic aims. Do all managers seem to mean the same thing when they refer to HR scorecards? If not, how do they differ?

3-11. In teams of several students, choose a company for which you will develop an outline of a strategic HR plan. What seem to be this company's main strategic aims? What is the firm's competitive strategy? What would the strategic map for this company look like? How would you summarize your recommended strategic HR policies for this company?

3-12. Appendices A and B at the end of this book (pages 614–634) list the knowledge someone studying for the HRCI (Appendix A) or SHRM (Appendix B) certification exam needs to have in each area of human resource management (such as in Strategic Management and Workforce Planning). In groups of several students, do four things: (1) review Appendix A and/or B; (2) identify the material in this chapter that relates to the Appendix A and/or B required knowledge lists; (3) write four multiple-choice exam questions on this material that you believe would be suitable for inclusion in the HRCI exam and/or the SHRM exam; and (4) if time permits, have someone from your team post your team's questions in front of the class, so that students in all teams can answer the exam questions created by the other teams.

KNOWLEDGE BASE

CHAPTER 3

Experiential Exercise

Developing an HR Strategy for Starbucks

Written and copyrighted by Gary Dessler, PhD.

A few years ago, Starbucks was facing serious challenges. Sales per store were stagnant or declining, and its growth rate and profitability were down. Many believed that its introduction of breakfast foods had diverted its "baristas" from their traditional jobs as coffee-preparation experts. McDonald's and Dunkin' Donuts were introducing lower-priced but still high-grade coffees. Starbucks' former CEO stepped back into the company's top job. You need to help him formulate a new direction for his company.

Purpose: The purpose of this exercise is to give you experience in developing an HR strategy, in this case, by developing one for Starbucks.

Required Understanding: You should be thoroughly familiar with the material in this chapter.

How to Set Up the Exercise/Instructions: Set up groups of several students for this exercise. You are probably already quite familiar with what it's like to have a cup of coffee or tea in a Starbucks coffee shop, but if not, spend some time in one prior to this exercise. Meet in groups and develop an outline for an HR strategy for Starbucks Corp. Assume that for a corporate strategy Starbucks will remain primarily an international chain of coffee shops. Your outline should include four basic elements: a business/competitive strategy for Starbucks, the workforce requirements (in terms of employee competencies and behaviors) this strategy requires, specific HR policies and the activities necessary to produce these workforce requirements, and suggestions for metrics to measure the success of the HR strategy.

Application Case

Tesla's Strategy

Written and copyrighted by Gary Dessler, PhD.

By 2017 Tesla Motors briefly had a market value higher than the much-larger General Motors. Tesla's strategic plan, formulated in 2006 by company founder Elon Musk, was to start by offering a high-performance energy-efficient electric roadster "without compromises" and then expand to offer less-expensive family cars, while eventually enabling battery recharging with solar power devices.[83]

By early 2017, it was clear that Tesla was not soon going to achieve its goal of producing 5,000 Model 3 family sedans per week, and the company also faced numerous human resource management–related challenges.[84]

For example, hundreds of workers stopped building Tesla's battery factory near Reno, Nevada, claiming that outside contract workers were lowering their pay. Workers at Tesla's car plant complained of high employee accident rates. Musk reportedly said that Tesla wasn't skimping on safety to make more profit, but rather to survive and continue to offer employment.

Tesla also laid off about 700 workers at its California manufacturing facility. Many union activists asked why, having to ramp up production of the new Tesla Model 3, the company would dismiss so many employees. Some felt it wasn't because of poor performance reviews, but because Tesla wanted to fire employees who wanted a union. Elon Musk defends dismissing the 700 workers. Basically, he said (1) most companies have performance reviews and use them to screen out employees, and (2) because it wants the highest-quality cars, Tesla needs to have higher performance standards than its competitors. As Musk says, if a little company wants to compete with a giant one, the little one must have a lot more skill, or it will get pummeled.

Some of Tesla's HR procedures are also somewhat unusual. For example, Tesla requires that new employees sign confidentiality agreements prohibiting them from discussing Tesla's business strategy and working conditions. The United Auto Workers filed unfair labor practice charges against Tesla, claiming that such agreements violate employees' rights.

Tesla does use some sophisticated HR tools to improve its HR processes. For example, they used talent analytics to determine if employee referral programs improve their recruitment and retention processes and distributed an employee engagement survey.

By May 2017, Tesla appointed a new HR head, Gaby Toledano, with the title Chief People Officer. In announcing the appointment, Tesla noted that she would help Tesla address its labor and harassment disputes. Ms. Toledano acknowledged that some disputes between workers weren't reaching the HR office fast enough, but she said she's working on the problem. Furthermore, Tesla employees receive antidiscrimination and antiharassment training.

Questions

3-13. Was Tesla's human resource strategy consistent with its overall strategy to produce "uncompromising" high-performance cars?

3-14. Given what Kia UK accomplished, should Tesla implement such an engagement program? Why?

3-15. What would you do now if you were Tesla's Chief People Officer?

3-16. Based on the case, provide examples for Tesla of at least four strategically required organizational outcomes, and four required workforce competencies and behaviors.

3-17. Provide a brief illustrative outline of a strategy map for Tesla.

CHAPTER 3

Continuing Case

Carter Cleaning Company

Written and copyrighted by Gary by Dessler, PhD.

The High-Performance Work System

As a person who keeps up with the business press, Jennifer Carter is familiar with the benefits of programs such as total quality management and high-performance work systems.

Jack, her father, actually installed a total quality program of sorts at Carter, and it has been in place for about 5 years. This program takes the form of employee meetings. Jack holds employee meetings periodically, but particularly when there is a serious problem in a store—such as poor-quality work or machine breakdowns. When problems like these arise, instead of trying to diagnose them himself or with Jennifer, he contacts all the employees in that store and meets with them when the store closes. Hourly employees get extra pay for these meetings. The meetings have been useful in helping Jack to identify and rectify several problems. For example, in one store all the fine white blouses were coming out looking dingy. It turned out that the cleaner/spotter had been ignoring the company rule that required cleaning ("boiling down") the perchloroethylene cleaning fluid before washing items like these. As a result, these fine white blouses were being washed in cleaning fluid that had residue from other, earlier washes.

Jennifer now wonders whether these employee meetings should be expanded to give the employees an even bigger role in managing the Carter stores' quality. "We can't be everywhere watching everything all the time," she said to her father. "Yes, but these people only earn about $8 to $15 per hour. Will they really want to act like mini-managers?" he replied.

Questions

3-18. Would you recommend that the Carters expand their quality program? If so, specifically what form should it take?

3-19. Assume the Carters want to institute a high-performance work system as a test program in one of their stores. Write a one-page outline summarizing important HR practices you think they should focus on.

Translating Strategy into HR Policies and Practices Case*,§

** The accompanying strategy map for this chapter is in MyLab Management; the overall map on the inside back cover of this text outlines the relationships involved.*

Improving Performance at the Hotel Paris

The Hotel Paris International

Starting as a single hotel in a Paris suburb in 1995, the Hotel Paris is now a chain of nine hotels, with two in France, one each in London and Rome, and others in New York, Miami, Washington, Chicago, and Los Angeles. As a corporate strategy, the Hotel Paris's management and owners want to continue to expand geographically. They believe doing so will let them capitalize on their reputation for good service, by providing multicity alternatives for their satisfied guests. The problem is, their reputation for good service has been deteriorating. If they cannot improve service, it would be unwise for them to expand, since their guests might prefer other hotels after trying the Hotel Paris.

Several things are complicating their problem. Tourists increasingly stay at short-term rental apartments (often through sites such as airbnb .com) for a fraction of what fine hotels cost. In 2018 Airbnb agreed to more stringently comply with the limits on the lengths of rentals in the heart of Paris, but not elsewhere. Marriott recently acquired the Starwood hotels chain (including many brands such as Ritz-Carlton) and will present increased competition. And the election as French president of Emmanuel Macron in 2017 prompted widespread optimism among many in France regarding the country's growth prospects, but also the possibility of some labor strife, at least in the short run.

The Strategy

Top management, with input from the HR and other managers, and with the board of directors' approval, chooses a new competitive

§ Written and copyrighted by Gary Dessler, PhD.

strategy and formulates new strategic goals. It decides: "The Hotel Paris International will use superior guest services to differentiate the Hotel Paris properties, and to thereby increase the length of stays and the return rate of guests, and thus boost revenues and profitability." All Hotel Paris managers—including the director of HR services—must now formulate strategies that support this competitive strategy.

The Strategically Required Organizational Outcomes

The Hotel Paris's basic strategy is to use superior guest services to expand geographically. For HR director Lisa Cruz, reviewing the hotel's activities makes it clear that achieving the hotel's strategic aims means achieving a number of required organizational outcomes. For example, Lisa and her management colleagues must take steps that produce fewer customer complaints and more written compliments, more frequent guest returns and longer stays, and higher guest expenditures per visit.

The Strategically Relevant Workforce Competencies and Behaviors

The question facing Lisa, then, is this: What competencies and behaviors must our hotel's employees exhibit, if we are to produce required organizational outcomes such as fewer customer complaints, more compliments, and more frequent guest returns? Thinking through this question helps Lisa come up with an answer. For example, the hotel's required employee competencies and behaviors would include, "high-quality front-desk customer service," "taking calls for reservations in a friendly manner," "greeting guests at the front door," and "processing guests' room service meals efficiently." All require motivated, high-morale employees.

The Strategically Relevant HR Policies and Activities

The HR manager's task now is to identify and specify the HR policies and activities that will enable the hotel to produce these crucial workforce competencies and behaviors. For example, "high-quality front-desk customer service" is one such required behavior. From this, the HR director identifies HR activities to produce such front-desk customer service efforts. For example, she decides to *institute practices to improve the disciplinary fairness and justice in the company*, with the aim of *improving employee morale*. Her assumption is that enhanced fairness will produce higher morale and that higher morale will produce improved front-desk service.

The Strategy Map

Next, Lisa, working with the hotel's chief financial officer (CFO), outlines a strategy map for the hotel. This outlines the cause-and-effect links among the HR activities, the workforce behaviors, and the organizational outcomes (the figure on this book's inside back cover shows the overall map; you'll find detailed maps for each HR function in each chapter's related MyLab Management page).

This map and its linkages reflect certain assumptions on Lisa's part. For example, based on experience and discussions with the firm's other managers, she formulates the following *hypothesis* about how HR affects hotel performance: Improved grievance procedures cause improved morale, which leads to improved front-desk service, which leads to increased guest returns, which leads to improved financial performance. The HR director then chooses metrics to measure each of these factors. For example, she decides to measure "improved disciplinary procedures" in terms of how many grievances employees submit each month. She measures "improved morale" in terms of "scores on our hotel's semiannual attitude survey," and measures "high-quality front-desk customer service" in terms of "customer complaints per month."

She moves on to quantifying the cause-and-effect links among these measures. For example: "Can we show top management that there is a measurable, sequential link between improved disciplinary procedures, high morale, improved front-desk service, number of guest return visits, and hotel financial performance (revenues and profits)?" If she can show such links, she has a persuasive case that shows HR's measurable contribution to the hotel's bottom-line financial performance.

In practice, the HR manager may well just rely on a largely subjective but logical argument to make the case for such cause-and-effect linkages. But ideally, she will use statistical methods such as correlation analysis to determine if measurable links exist, and (if so) what their magnitudes are. In this way, she might find, for instance, that a 10% improvement in grievance rates is associated with an almost 20% improvement in morale. Similarly, a 20% improvement in morale is associated with a 30% reduction in customer front-desk complaints. Furthermore, a 30% reduction in complaints is associated with a 20% increase in guest return visits, and a 20% increase in return rate is associated with a 6% rise in hotel revenues. It would appear that a relatively small HR effort in reducing grievances might have a big effect on this hotel's bottom-line performance!

Several things complicate this measurement process. For example, it's risky to draw cause–effect conclusions from correlation measures like these (do fewer grievances lead to higher morale, or vice versa?). Furthermore, it's rare that a single factor (such as grievance rates) will have such effects alone, so we may want to measure the effects of several HR policies and activities on morale simultaneously.

As explained in this chapter, computerization could enable Lisa to build a more comprehensive HR scorecard process, one that might handle links among dozens of cause-and-effect metrics. (Several vendors supply such scorecard software.) If not, then she will rely more on the logic and common sense underlying the strategy map to make her case.

How We Will Use the Hotel Paris Case

A Hotel Paris case in each chapter will show how Lisa, the Hotel Paris's HR director, uses that chapter's concepts and techniques to: (1) create HR policies and practices that help the Hotel Paris, (2) produce the employee competencies and behaviors the company needs, and (3) to produce the customer service the Hotel Paris requires to achieve its strategic goals.

For example, she will endeavor to improve workforce competencies and behaviors by instituting improved recruitment (processes Chapter 5), and measure improved recruitment in terms of "number of qualified applicants per position." Similarly, she will recommend to management that they change the company's pay policies, so that the "target percentile for total compensation is in the top 25%." She could argue, based on competitors' experience, that doing so will translate into improved customer service behavior, more satisfied customers, and improved hotel performance. In practice, all the human resource management functions we discuss in this book influence employee competencies and behaviors, and thereby organizational performance.

You will find the strategy map for each Dessler *Human Resource Management* chapter's topic in the chapter's MyLab Management; the summary map on the inside back cover of this book outlines the overall relationships involved for the Hotel Paris.

Questions

3-20. Draw a more simplified and abbreviated strategy map for the Hotel Paris. Specifically, summarize in your own words an example of the hierarchy of links among the hotel's *HR practices*, necessary *workforce competencies* and behaviors, and required *organizational outcomes*.

3-21. Using Table 3-1 and Figure 3-9, list at least 15 metrics the Hotel Paris could use to measure its HR practices.

Writing Assignments

3-22. Define and give at least two examples of the cost-leadership competitive strategy and the differentiation competitive strategy.

3-23. You own a small business, and your friend, over lunch, just mentioned that "it sounds like you have an employee engagement problem." What exactly would you do to improve employee engagement in your company now?

MyLab Management Try It!

How would you apply the concepts and skills you learned in this chapter? If your professor has assigned this activity, go to the Assignments section of **www.pearson.com/mylab/management** to complete the simulation.

PERSONAL INVENTORY ASSESSMENTS

Go to **www.pearson.com/mylab/management** to complete the Personal Inventory Assessment related to this chapter.

Key Terms

strategic plan, 72
strategy, 72
strategic management, 72
vision statement, 74
mission statement, 74
corporate-level strategy, 74
competitive strategy, 75
competitive advantage, 75
functional strategy, 76
strategic human resource management, 76
strategy map, 79
HR scorecard, 79
digital dashboard, 80
human resource metric, 81
strategy-based metrics, 82
HR audit, 82
high-performance work system (HPWS), 85

Endnotes

1. For a good discussion of aligning goals, see, for example, Eric Krell, "Change Within," *HR Magazine,* August 2011, pp. 43–50.
2. James Jenks, *The Hiring, Firing (And Everything in Between) Personnel Forms Book* (Ridgefield, CT: Round Lake Publishing Co., 1994).
3. https://www.bizmanualz.com/, accessed January 29, 2018.
4. For perspectives on strategic planning, see, for example, Donald Sull and Kathleen Eisenhardt, "Simple Rules for a Complex World," *Harvard Business Review*, September 2012, pp. 69–75; and Martin Reeves, Claire Love, and Philipp Tillmann, "Your Strategy Needs a Strategy," *Harvard Business Review*, September 2012, pp. 76–83.
5. For example see, http://www.coca-colacompany.com/brands/the-coca-cola-company#, and http://www.pepsico.com/brands, both accessed January 30, 2018.
6. See, for example, Fred David, *Strategic Management* (Upper Saddle River, NJ: Prentice Hall, 2007), p. 11.
7. Tony Bingham and Pat Galagan, "Doing Good While Doing Well," *TD*, June 2008, p. 33. See also www.pepsico.com/Purpose/Our-Mission-and-Values, accessed July 31, 2014; http://www.pepsico.com/sustainability/performance-with-purpose/our-goals, accessed January 31, 2018.
8. https://www.macrumors.com/2018/01/25/apple-self-driving-fleet/, accessed January 31, 2018.
9. Paul Nutt, "Making Strategic Choices," *Journal of Management Studies*, January 2002, pp. 67–96.
10. Commerce Clearing House, "HR Role: Maximize the Competitive Advantage of People," *Ideas and Trends in Personnel*, August 5, 1992, p. 121.
11. Michael Porter, *Competitive Strategy* (New York: The Free Press, 1980), p. 14. See also Chris Zook and James Allen, "The Great Repeatable Business Model," *Harvard Business Review,* November 2011, pp. 107–112.
12. https://www.jopwell.com/, accessed January 31, 2018.
13. https://www.olay.com/en-us#Search%20javascript:void(0), accessed January 30, 2018.
14. Arthur Yeung, "Setting People Up for Success: How the Portman Ritzcarlton Hotel Gets the Best from Its People," *Human Resource Management*, Summer 2006, 45, no. 2, pp. 267–275.
15. www.ritzcarlton.com/en/about/oldstandards, accessed January 31, 2018.
16. http://www.ritzcarlton.com/en/about/awards, accessed January 31, 2018.
17. Accenture, a major global consulting company, puts it this way: HR strategy involves "[C]reating an HR vision and roadmap that supports strategic business outcomes while delivering high-value talent and HR services that drive an improved employee and manager experience." https://www.accenture.com/us-en/service-human-resources-hr-service-offering, accessed January 26, 2017.
18. Arthur Mazer, "HR Transformation Strategy," 2018, https://www2.deloitte.com/us/en/pages/human-capital/solutions/hr-transformation-strategy-and-planning.html.
19. Brian Hults, "Integrate HR with Operating Strategy," *HR Magazine,* October 2011, pp. 54–56. One review of strategic human resource management research in the United States concluded that "strategic human resource management researchers as a

group deserve a D to F grade." Bruce Couchman, "Strategic Human Resource Management Research in the United States: A Failing Grade After 30 Years?" *Academy of Management Perspectives*, May 2012, pp. 12–34.

20. Michael Hargis and Don Bradley III, "Strategic Human Resource Management in Small and Growing Firms: Aligning Valuable Resources," *Academy of Strategic Management Journal* 10, no. 2, July 2011, pp. 105–126; http://about.-zappos.com/our-unique-culture/zappos-core-values, accessed March 16, 2015; http://jobs.jobvite.com/zappos/p/why#values, accessed January 31, 2018.
21. "Meet the Zappos Family: Human Resources" from Zappos website. Copyright © 1999–2012 by Zappos.com, Inc. http://about.zappos.com/meet-zappos-family/zapposcom-inc/human-resources. Reprinted with permission.
22. www.weknownext.com/workplace/delivering-hr-at-zappos-hr-magazine-june-2011, accessed August 23, 2012. See also, Richard Feloni, "Here's What Happened to Zappos' HR Boss When the Company Got Rid of Managers and Her Job Became Obsolete," February 12, 2016, http://www.businessinsider.com/zappos-hr-boss-hollie-delaney-talks-about-holacracy-2016-2, accessed January 29, 2017.
23. http://jobs.jobvite.com/zappos/p/how, accessed January 31, 2018.
24. www.pepsico.com/Purpose/Performance-with-Purpose/Goals, accessed May 5, 2014.
25. For an excellent discussion of how human resource management practices can support sustainability goals, see Dubois and Dubois, op. cit., pp. 816–818.
26. www.pepsico.com/Purpose/Performance-with-Purpose/Goals, accessed May 5, 2014.
27. Paul Buller and Glenn McEvoy, "Strategy, Human Resource Management and Performance: Sharpening Line of Sight," *Human Resource Management Review* 22 (2012), pp. 43–56.
28. Managers can use the Active-Strategy Company's *Active-Strategy Enterprise* to create and automate their strategy maps, and to access them through an iPhone or similar devices. See www.activestrategy.com/solutions/strategy_mapping.aspx, accessed March 24, 2009.
29. When focusing on HR activities, managers call this an *HR scorecard*. When applying the same process broadly to all of the company's activities, including, for example, sales, production, and finance, managers call it the "balanced scorecard process."
30. The "balanced" in *balanced scorecard* refers to a balance of goals—financial and nonfinancial.
31. See, for example, "Using HR Performance Metrics to Optimize Operations and Profits," *PR Newswire*, February 27, 2008; and "How to 'Make Over' Your HR Metrics," *HR Focus* 84, no. 9 (September 2007), p. 3.
32. SHRM Human Capital Benchmarking Study: 2007 Executive Summary.
33. For additional information on HR metrics, see, for example, Karen M. Kroll, "Repurposing Metrics for HR: HR Professionals Are Looking Through a People-Focused Lens at the CFO's Metrics on Revenue and Income per FTE," *HR Magazine* 51, no. 7 (July 2006), pp. 64–69; and http://shrm.org/metrics/library_publishedover/measurementsystemsTOC.asp, accessed February 2, 2008.
34. See, for example, "Benchmarking for Functional HR Metrics," *HR Focus* 83, no. 11 (November 2006), p. 1; and John Sullivan, "The Last Word," *Workforce Management*, November 19, 2007, p. 42. SHRM makes various metrics calculators available at https://www.shrm.org/resourcesandtools/tools-and-samples/pages/spreadsheets.aspx, accessed July 2, 2018.
35. See Brian Becker and Mark Huselid, "Measuring HR? Benchmarking Is Not the Answer!" *HR Magazine* 8, no. 12 (December 2003), www.charmed.org, accessed February 2, 2008.
36. Ibid.
37. As one example of many, see "Conducting Human Resource Audits," June 16, 2016, SHRM, https://www.shrm.org/resourcesandtools/tools-and-samples/toolkits/pages/humanresourceaudits.aspx, accessed July 2, 2018.
38. "Best Practices for a Human Resources Compliance Audit," *Bloomberg BNA Bulletin to Management*, January 21, 2014, pp. 22–24.
39. Grensing-Pophal, "HR Audits: Know the Market"; and Bill Coy, "Introduction to the Human Resources Audit," La Piana Associates, Inc., www.lapiana.org/consulting, accessed May 1, 2008.
40. Dana R. Scott, "Conducting a Human Resources Audit," *New Hampshire Business Review*, August 2007. See also Eric Krell, "Auditing Your HR Department," *HR Magazine*, September 2011, pp. 101–103.
41. "Executive Workplace Analytics," http://www.aon.com/hongkong/human-capital-consulting/hrbpo/executive_workforce_analytics.jsp, accessed July 2, 2018.
42. Andrew McAfee and Erik Brynjolfsson, "Big Data: The Management Revolution," *Harvard Business Review*, October 1, 2012, https://hbr.org/2012/10/big-data-the-management-revolution/ar, accessed April 4, 2015.
43. George Marakas, *Decision Support Systems* (Upper Saddle River, NJ: Prentice Hall, 2003), p. 326.
44. www.forbes.com/sites/bernardmarr/2017/01/23/really-big-data-at-walmart-real-time-insights-from-their-40-petabyte-data-cloud/#c36aa976c105; www.forbes.com/sites/brentdykes/2017/06/28/big-data-forget-volume-and-variety-focus-on-velocity/#2e74f3e66f7d; all accessed August 30, 2018.
45. Josh Bersin, "Big Data in Human Resources: Talent Analytics (People Analytics) Comes of Age," February 17, 2013, http://www.forbes.com/sites/joshbersin/2013/02/17/bigdata-in-human-resources-talent-analytics-comes-of-age/, accessed June 20, 2015.
46. Ibid., p. 54. See also Cliff Stevenson, "Five Ways High Performance Organizations Use HR Analytics," www.i4cp.com/print/trendwatchers/2012/12/12/five-ways-high-performance-organizations-use-hr-analytics, accessed July 14, 2013.
47. Thomas Davenport, Jeanne Harris, and Jeremy Shapiro, "Competing on Talent Analytics," *Harvard Business Review*, October 2010, pp. 52–58.
48. Ed Frauenheim, "Keeping Score with Analytics Software," *Workforce Management* 86, no. 10 (May 21, 2007), pp. 25–33. See also Andrew McAfee and Eric Brynjolfsson, "Big Data: The Management Revolution," *Harvard Business Review*, October 2012, pp. 61–68. Installing a talent analytics system can be expensive, perhaps $3.5 million, including the data warehouse and additional technology, licenses, and administrators. However, the payoff can be even larger. One study found that the stock prices of companies with effective talent analytics systems outperformed peers by 30%. See Laime Vaitkus, "Money Makes the Case for Workforce Analytics," *Bloomberg BNA Bulletin to Management*, February 14, 2017.
49. Steven Baker, "Data Mining Moves to Human Resources," *Bloomberg Businessweek*, March 12, 2009, www.BusinessWeek.com/magazine/, accessed April 13, 2011.
50. Cliff Stevenson, "Five Ways High Performance Organizations Use HR Analytics," www.i4cp.com/print/trendwatchers/2012/12/12/five-ways-high-performance-organizations-use-hr-analytics, accessed July 14, 2013.
51. See, for example, www.personneltoday.com/blogs/hcglobal-human-capital-management/2009/02/theres-no-such-thing-as-eviden.html, accessed October 2, 2012.
52. Eric Anderson and Duncan Simester, "A Step-by-Step Guide to Smart Business Experiments," *Harvard Business Review*, March 2011, pp. 98–105.
53. Ibid.
54. Bill Roberts, "How to Put Analytics on Your Side," *HR Magazine*, October 2009, pp. 43–46.
55. Youngsang Kim and Robert Ployhart, "The Effects of Staffing and Training on Firm Productivity and Profit Growth Before, During, and After the Great Recession," *Journal of Applied Psychology* 99, no. 3 (2014), p. 378.
56. www.bls.gov/opub/ted/2006/may/wk2/art01.htm, accessed April 18, 2009; and "Super Human Resources Practices Result in Better Overall Performance, Report Says," *BNA Bulletin to Management*, August 26, 2004, pp. 273–274. See also Wendy Boswell, "Aligning Employees with the Organization's Strategic Objectives: Out of Line of Sight, Out of Mind," *International Journal of Human Resource Management* 17, no. 9 (September 2006), pp. 1014–1041. A study found that some employers, which the researchers called *cost minimizers*, intentionally took a lower-cost approach to human resource practices, with mixed results. See Soo Min Toh et al., "Human Resource Configurations: Investigating Fit with the Organizational Context," *Journal of Applied Psychology* 93, no. 4 (2008), pp. 864–882.
57. Samuel Aryee et al., "Impact of High Performance Work Systems on Individual—and Branch—Level Performance: Test of a Multilevel Model of Intermediate Linkages," *Journal of Applied Psychology* 97, no. 2 (2012), pp. 287–300. See also Achim Krausert, "HRM Systems for Knowledge Workers: Differences Among Top Managers, Middle Managers, and Professional Employees," *Human Resource Management* 53, no. 1 (January–February 2014), pp. 67–87.
58. See, for example, www.halogensoftware.com/blog/are-you-using-hr-analytics-and-metrics-effectively, accessed August 27, 2014.

59. See, for example, J. G. Messersmith, "Unlocking the Black Box: Exploring the Link Between High-Performance Work Systems and Performance," *Human Resource Management International Digest* 20, no. 3 (2012), pp. 1118–1132.
60. Michael Christian, Adela Garza, and Jerel Slaughter, "Work Engagement: A Quantitative Review and Test of Its Relations with Task and Contextual Performance," *Personnel Psychology* 60, no. 4 (2011), pp. 89–136.
61. Adrienne Fox, "Raising Engagement," *HR Magazine*, May 2010, pp. 35–40. See also www.gallup.com/strategicconsulting/163007/state-american-workplace.aspx.
62. Kevin Kruse, "Why Employee Engagement? (These 28 Research Studies Prove the Benefits)," September 4, 2012, www.forbes.com.
63. Ibid.
64. "Employee Engagement and Labor Relations," *Gallup Business Journal*, www.businessjournal.gallup.com, accessed April 10, 2014.
65. "Fatter Bottom Line Results from Sustained Engagement," *Bloomberg BNA Bulletin to Management*, July 30, 2013, p. 243.
66. Except as noted, this is based on Kathryn Tyler, "Prepare for Impact," *HR Magazine*, 56, no. 3 (March 2011), pp. 53–56.
67. www.gallup.com/strategicconsulting/163007/state-american-workplace.aspx; Bruce Louis Rich et al., "Job Engagement: Antecedents and Effects on Job Performance," *Academy of Management Journal*, 53, no. 3 (2010), pp. 617–635; "Special Report: Employee Engagement—Losing Lifeblood," *Workforce Management*, July 2011, pp. 24–27.
68. "Five Ways to Improve Employee Engagement Now," *Gallup Business Journal:* www.businessjournal.gallup.com, accessed April 7, 2014.
69. www.gallup.com/strategicconsulting/163007/state-american-workplace.aspx and http://www.gallup.com/services/178514/state-american-workplace.aspx accessed June 20, 2015.
70. Rich et al., "Job Engagement."
71. Alison Konrad, "Engaging Employees through High-Involvement Work Practices," *Ivey Business Journal*, March/April 2006, p. 1.
72. Michael Tucker, "Make Managers Responsible," *HR Magazine*, March 2012, pp. 75–78. See also J. Anitha, "Determinants of Employee Engagement and Their Impact on Employee Performance," *International Journal of Productivity and Performance Management* 63, no. 3 (2014), pp. 308–323.
73. Paula Ketter, "What's the Big Deal About Employee Engagement?" *TD*, January 2008, pp. 47–48.
74. "Kia Motors in Big Trouble," *Business Career* 14, no. 8 (August 1997), pp. 12–13.
75. Kia Motors Corporation, 2006 annual report, page 6.
76. Ibid.
77. Gary Tomlinson, "Building a Culture of High Employee Engagement," *Strategic HR Review* 9, no. 3 (2010), pp. 25–31.
78. Ibid.
79. Ibid.
80. Ibid.
81. Ibid.
82. Ibid. Note that during these years economic activity in the UK was tumbling, which may account for at least some of the reduced turnover.
83. Elon Musk, Co-Founder & CEO of Tesla Motors, "The Secret Tesla Motors Master Plan (just between you and me)," August 2, 2006, https://www.tesla.com/blog/secret-tesla-motors-master-plan-just-between-you-and-me, accessed January 29, 2018.
84. This case is based on: Nathan Bomey, "Tesla's Make or Break Year? 2018 Will Test Elon Musk," *USA Today*, December 27, 2017, USA Today.com; Kate Conger, "Tesla's HR Hitters Out Amidst Complaints over Discrimination and Unsafe Working Conditions," May 24, 2017, https://Gizmodo.com; Gregory Lewis, "Three Ways Data Shapes the Talent Strategy at Tesla, Chevron, and LinkedIn," March 30, 2017, https://business.LinkedIn.com; David Dayen, "Why Would Tesla Lay Off Hundreds of Workers When It's Ramping Up Production?" October 19, 2017, www.fastcompany.com; Timothy Lee, "Tesla Fires Hundreds of Workers," October 14, 2017, https://arstechnica.com; Laura Kolodny, "Tesla Employees Detail How They Were Fired, Claim Dismissals Were Not Performance Related," https://www.CNBC.com; Kirsten Korosec, "Elon Musk: Why Tesla Fired 700 Employees," November 2, 2017, http://Fortune.com; Sarah Alexander, "How Tesla Engages Its Employees to Drive Business Results," September 11, 2015, https://www.geteverwise.com; Kirsten Korosec, "Union to Tesla: Giga Factory Worker Protest Is Just the Beginning," May 26, 2016, www.fortune.com; "UAW Hits Tesla with Charges," management report, November 2017, page 6; Alan Ohnsman, "Labor Group Says Tesla Plant's Worker Injury Rate Tops Industry Average," May 24, 2017, www.Forbes.com; Alyssa Perry, "Tesla Faces Complaints over Harassment and Racial Tensions," January 12, 2018, www.NPR.org; all accessed January 29, 2018.

PART TWO Recruitment, Placement, and Talent Management

Monty Rakusen/Cultura/Getty Images

Job Analysis and the Talent Management Process

LEARNING OBJECTIVES

When you finish studying this chapter, you should be able to:

4-1 **Define** talent management, and explain what talent management-oriented managers do.

4-2 **Discuss** the process of job analysis, including why it is important.

4-3 **Explain and use** at least three methods of collecting job analysis information.

4-4 **Explain** how you would write a job description, and what sources you would use.

4-5 **Explain** how to write a job specification.

4-6 **Give** examples of competency-based job analysis.

When Daimler opened its Mercedes-Benz assembly plant in Alabama, its managers had a dilemma. Their strategy was to create a high-performance plant that Daimler could then extend to other plants in America, South Africa, Brazil, and Germany. The dilemma was that while plant managers couldn't hire, train, or pay their employees without knowing what each employee was expected to do, in this plant self-managing teams assembled the vehicles, and so workers' tasks might change every day. How do you hire people whose job duties are always changing?[1] We'll see what they did.

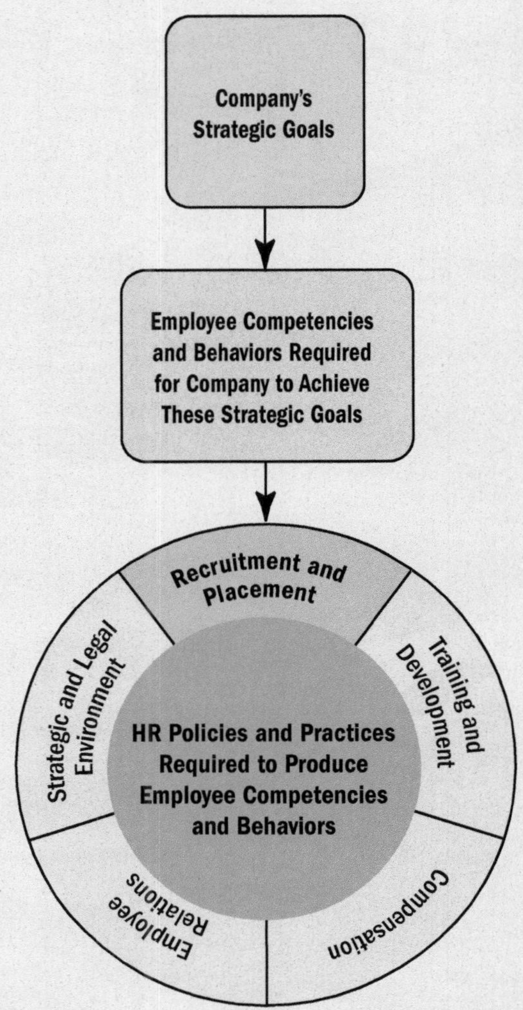

WHERE ARE WE NOW . . .

Managers should know what a job entails before deciding who to recruit and hire for it, so human resource management really starts with determining what the job entails. The main purpose of this chapter is to show you how to analyze jobs and write job descriptions. We discuss several techniques for analyzing jobs and explain how to write job descriptions and job specifications. The main topics we address include **The Talent Management Process**, **The Basics of Job Analysis**, **Methods for Collecting Job Analysis Information**, **Writing Job Descriptions**, **Writing Job Specifications**, and **Using Competencies Models**. Then, in Chapter 5 (Personnel Planning and Recruiting), we'll see how to actually find the employees you need.

LEARNING OBJECTIVE 4-1

Define talent management, and explain what talent management-oriented managers do.

Talent Management Process

For many people, Chapters 4–13 represent the heart of this book, specifically recruitment, selection, training, appraisal, career planning, and compensation. Managers traditionally view these activities as a series of steps:

1. Decide what positions to fill, through job analysis, personnel planning, and forecasting.
2. Build a pool of job applicants, by recruiting internal or external candidates.
3. Obtain application forms and perhaps have initial screening interviews.
4. Use selection tools like tests, interviews, background checks, and physical exams to identify viable candidates.
5. Decide to whom to make an offer.
6. Orient, train, and develop employees so they have the competencies to do their jobs.
7. Appraise employees to assess how they're doing.
8. Compensate employees to maintain their motivation.

This stepwise view makes sense. For example, the employer needs job candidates before selecting whom to hire.

The problem with the stepwise view is twofold. First, the process usually isn't really stepwise. For example, managers don't just train employees (step 6 above) and then appraise how they're doing (step 7). Instead (to use our example), the appraisal may well also loop back to shape the employee's subsequent training. So, first, rather than view these eight HR activities as stepwise, it is best to view them holistically—because the steps interactively affect each other and work together. The second problem is that focusing just on each step may cause the manager to miss the forest for the trees. It's not just each step but the *results you obtain* by applying them together that's important. So, second, it's important to remember that each and every step should be focused on achieving, in unison, some specific result (such as, say, improving customer service).

talent management
The goal-oriented and integrated process of planning, recruiting, developing, managing, and compensating employees.

Recognizing all this, the trend today is to view these eight activities not stepwise but as part of a coordinated *talent management* effort.[2] We will define **talent management** as *the holistic, integrated and results- and goal-oriented process of planning, recruiting, selecting, developing, managing, and compensating employees*.[3] What does this mean in practice? The manager who takes a talent management approach tends to take actions such as the following:

1. He or she starts with the results and asks, "What recruiting, testing, training, or pay action should I take to produce the employee competencies we need *to achieve our company's goals*?"
2. He or she treats activities such as recruiting and training as interrelated. For example, the manager knows that having employees with the right skills depends as much on recruiting and training as on applicant testing.
3. Because talent management is holistic and integrated, he or she will probably use the same "profile" of required human skills, knowledge, and behaviors ("competencies") for formulating a job's recruitment plans as for making selection, training, appraisal, and compensation decisions for it.
4. And, to ensure the activities are all focused on the same ends, the manager will take steps to coordinate the talent management functions (recruiting and training, for example). Doing so often involves using talent management software.

Talent Management Software

Employers use talent management software to help ensure that their talent management activities are aimed in a coordinated way to achieve the company's HR aims. For example, Oracle says its Talent Management suite helps the manager to hire the best talent, provide real-time evaluations of workforce performance, and "[a]lign and develop your workforce with your talent management goals."[4] SilkRoad Technology's Talent Management Solution includes applicant tracking, onboarding, performance management, and compensation support. It helps the manager to " . . . recruit, manage, and retain your best employees."[5]

The Basics of Job Analysis

Talent management starts with understanding what jobs need to be filled, and the human traits and competencies employees need to do those jobs effectively.

LEARNING OBJECTIVE 4-2

Discuss the process of job analysis, including why it is important.

What Is Job Analysis?

Organizations consist of positions that have to be staffed. The organization chart (see Figure 4-1) shows the title of each supervisor's position and, by means of connecting lines, who is accountable to whom, who has authority for each area, and who is expected to communicate with whom. **Job analysis** is the procedure through which you determine the duties of the company's positions and the characteristics of the people to hire for them.[6] Job analysis produces information for writing **job descriptions** (a list of what the job entails) and **job** (or "person") **specifications** (what kind of people to hire for the job). Virtually every personnel-related action—interviewing applicants, and training and appraising employees, for instance—requires knowing what the job entails and what human traits one needs to do the job well.[7] Just about every employer today—from Marriott to Airbnb—uses job analysis and the job descriptions that stem from it.[8]

job analysis
The procedure for determining the duties and skill requirements of a job and the kind of person who should be hired for it.

job descriptions
A list of a job's duties, responsibilities, reporting relationships, working conditions, and supervisory responsibilities—one product of a job analysis.

job specifications
A list of a job's "human requirements," that is, the requisite education, skills, personality, and so on—another product of a job analysis.

The supervisor or human resources specialist normally collects one or more of the following types of information via the job analysis:

- ***Work activities.*** Information about the job's actual work activities, such as cleaning, selling, teaching, or painting. This list may also include how, why, and when the worker performs each activity.
- ***Human behaviors.*** Information about human behaviors the job requires, like sensing, communicating, lifting weights, or walking long distances.
- ***Machines, tools, equipment, and work aids.*** Information regarding tools used, materials processed, knowledge dealt with or applied (such as finance or law), and services rendered (such as counseling or repairing).

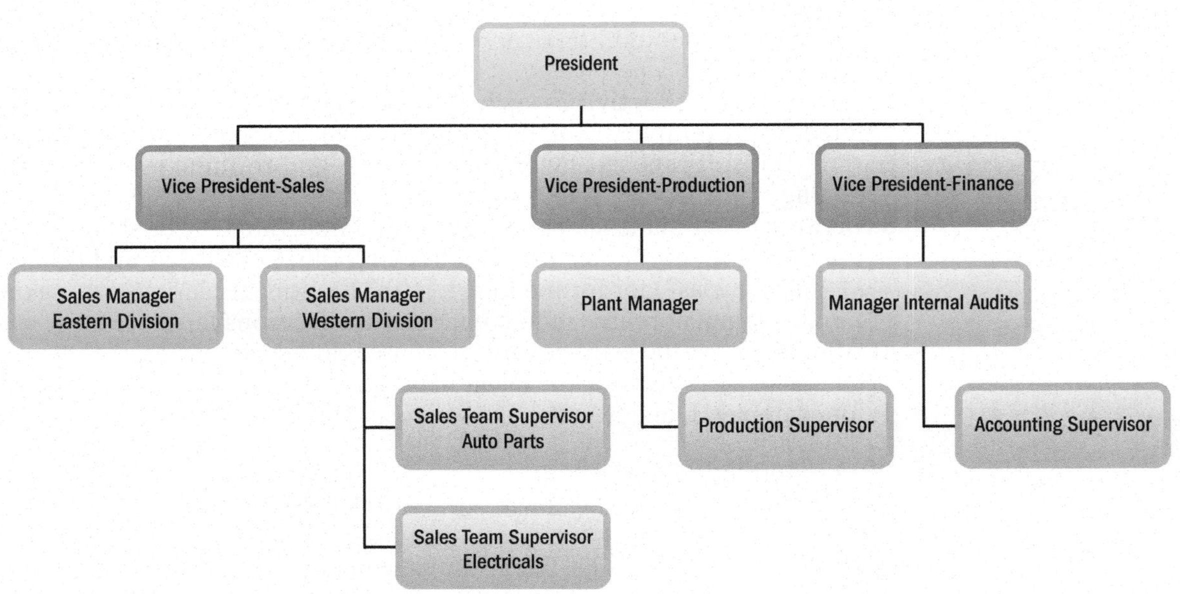

FIGURE 4-1 **Organization Chart**

- ***Performance standards.*** Information about the job's performance standards (in terms of quantity or quality levels for each job duty, for instance).
- ***Job context.*** Information about such matters as physical working conditions, work schedule, incentives, and, for instance, the number of people with whom the employee would normally interact.
- ***Human requirements.*** Information such as knowledge or skills (education, training, work experience) and required personal attributes (aptitudes, personality, interests).

Uses of Job Analysis Information

As Figure 4-2 summarizes, job analysis is important because it supports just about all human resource management activities.

RECRUITMENT AND SELECTION Information about what duties the job entails and what human characteristics are required to perform these duties helps managers decide what sort of people to recruit and hire.

EEO COMPLIANCE Knowing a job's duties is necessary for determining, for example, whether a selection test is a valid predictor of success on the job. Furthermore, to comply with the ADA, employers should know each job's *essential job functions—which requires a job analysis.*

PERFORMANCE APPRAISAL A performance appraisal compares an employee's actual performance of his or her duties with the job's performance standards. Managers use job analysis to learn what these duties and standards are.

COMPENSATION Compensation (such as salary and bonus) usually depends on the job's required skill and education level, safety hazards, degree of responsibility, and so on—all factors you assess through job analysis.

TRAINING The job description lists the job's specific duties and requisite skills—thus pinpointing what training the job requires.

Conducting a Job Analysis

There are six steps in doing a job analysis of a job, as follows.

STEP 1: **Identify the use** to which the information will be put because this will determine how you collect the information. Some data collection techniques—like interviewing the employee—are good for writing job descriptions. Other techniques, like the position

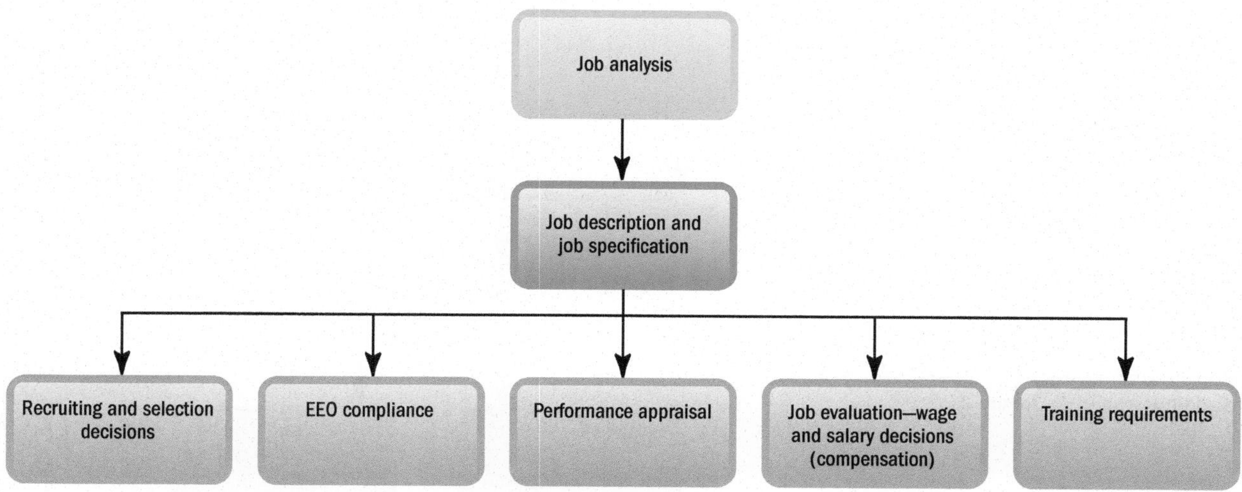

FIGURE 4-2 **Uses of Job Analysis Information**

analysis questionnaire we describe later, provide numerical ratings for each job; these can be used to compare jobs for compensation purposes.

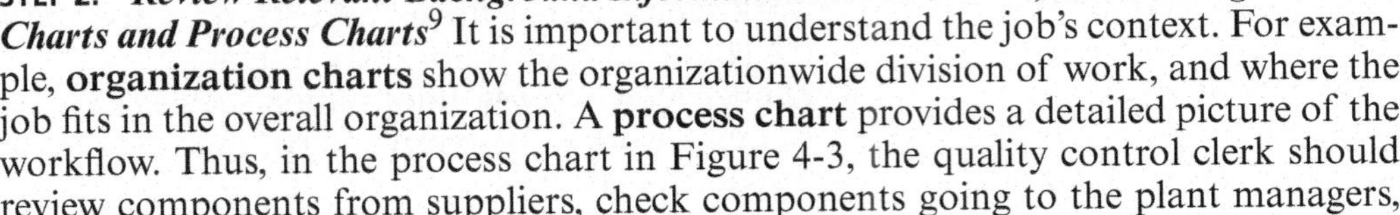

STEP 2: ***Review Relevant Background Information About the Job, Such as Organization Charts and Process Charts***[9] It is important to understand the job's context. For example, **organization charts** show the organizationwide division of work, and where the job fits in the overall organization. A **process chart** provides a detailed picture of the workflow. Thus, in the process chart in Figure 4-3, the quality control clerk should review components from suppliers, check components going to the plant managers, and give information regarding the components' quality to these managers. Finally, an existing job description may provide a starting point for revising the job description.

organization chart
A chart that shows the organization-wide distribution of work, with titles of each position and interconnecting lines that show who reports to and communicates with whom.

process chart
A workflow chart that shows the flow of inputs to and outputs from a particular job.

Workflow Analysis Reviewing the organization chart, process chart, and job description helps the manager identify what a job's duties and demands are now. However, it does *not* answer questions like "Does how this job relates to other jobs make sense?" or "Should this job even exist?" To answer such questions, the manager may conduct a *workflow analysis.* **Workflow analysis** is a detailed study of the flow of work from job to job in one identifiable work process (such as processing a mortgage application). In turn, this analysis may lead to changing or "reengineering" the job. The following HR as a Profit Center feature illustrates workflow analysis.

workflow analysis
A detailed study of the flow of work from job to job in a work process.

IMPROVING PEFORMANCE: *HR AS A PROFIT CENTER*

Boosting Productivity Through Work Redesign[10]

The Atlantic American insurance company conducted a workflow analysis to identify inefficiencies in how it processes insurance claims. As the firm's HR director said, "We followed the life of a claim to where it arrived in the mail and where it eventually ended up" in order to find ways to improve the process.[11]

The workflow analysis prompted several performance-boosting redesigns of the insurance claim jobs. The firm reduced from four to one the number of people opening mail, replacing three people with a machine that does it automatically. A new date stamping machine lets staff stamp 20 pages at a time rather than one. A new software program adds bar codes to each claim automatically, rather than manually. The new system lowered costs. ■

> **MyLab Management Talk About It 1**
>
> If your professor has assigned this, go to the Assignments section of **www.pearson.com/mylab/management** to complete these discussion questions. Based on your experience, what would the workflow look like for the process a dry-cleaning store uses to accept and chronicle a new order of clothes from a customer? How might this process be improved?

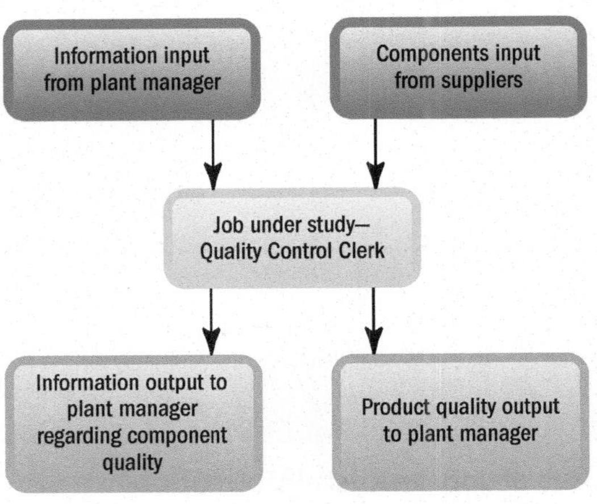

FIGURE 4-3 Process Chart for Analyzing a Job's Workflow

Source: Henderson, Richard I., *Compensation Management in a Knowledge Based World*, 9th Ed., © 2003, p.137. Reprinted and Electronically reproduced by permission of Pearson Education, Inc., Upper Saddle River, New Jersey.

In conducting a workflow analysis, the manager may use a *flow process chart*; this lists in order each step of the process. The manager may convert this step-by-step flow process chart into a diagrammatic process chart. This shows, with arrows and circles, each step in the process.

business process reengineering
Redesigning business processes, usually by combining steps, so that small multifunction process teams using information technology do the jobs formerly done by a sequence of departments.

Business Process Reengineering The workflow analysis at American Atlantic led to a *reengineering* of its claims processing operation. **Business process reengineering** means redesigning business processes, usually by combining steps so that small multifunction teams, often using information technology, do the jobs formerly done by a sequence of departments. The basic reengineering approach is to:

1. Identify a business process to be redesigned (such as processing an insurance claim)
2. Measure the performance of the existing processes
3. Identify opportunities to improve these processes
4. Redesign and implement a new way of doing the work
5. Assign ownership of sets of formerly separate tasks to an individual or a team who use new computerized systems to support the new arrangement

As at Atlantic American, reengineering usually requires redesigning individual jobs. For example, workers doing date stamping must now know how to use the new date-stamping machine.

job enlargement
Assigning workers additional same-level activities.

job rotation
Systematically moving workers from one job to another.

job enrichment
Redesigning jobs in a way that increases the opportunities for the worker to experience feelings of responsibility, achievement, growth, and recognition.

Job Redesign Early economists enthusiastically described why specialized jobs were more efficient (as in, "practice makes perfect"). Today, most agree that specialized jobs can backfire, for instance by sapping morale. Experts typically suggest three ways to redesign specialized jobs to make them more challenging. **Job enlargement** means assigning workers additional same-level activities. Thus, the worker who previously only bolted the seat to the legs might attach the back too. **Job rotation** means systematically moving workers from one job to another.

Psychologist Frederick Herzberg argued that the best way to motivate workers is through what he called job enrichment. **Job enrichment** means redesigning jobs in a way that increases the opportunities for the worker to experience feelings of responsibility, achievement, growth, and recognition—and therefore more motivation. It does this by *empowering* the worker—for instance, by giving the worker the skills and authority to inspect the work, instead of having supervisors do that. Herzberg said empowered employees would do their jobs well because they wanted to, and quality and productivity would rise. That philosophy, in one form or another, is the theoretical basis for the team-based self-managing jobs in many companies around the world today.

STEP 3: ***Select Representative Positions*** Next, with a job to analyze, the manager generally selects a sample of positions to focus on. For example, it is usually unnecessary to analyze the jobs of all the firm's 200 assembly workers; instead a sample of 10 jobs will do.

STEP 4: ***Actually Analyze the Job*** The actual job analysis involves greeting each job holder; briefly explaining the job analysis process and the participants' roles in this process; spending about 15 minutes interviewing the employee to get agreement on a basic summary of the job; identifying the job's broad areas of responsibility, such as "calling on potential clients"; and then interactively identifying specific duties/tasks within each area using one of the methods we describe just below.[12]

STEP 5: ***Verify the Job Analysis Information with the Worker Performing the Job and with His or Her Immediate Supervisor*** This will help confirm that the information (for instance, on the job's duties) is correct and complete and help to gain their acceptance.

STEP 6: ***Develop a Job Description and Job Specification*** The *job description* lists the duties, activities, and responsibilities of the job, as well as its important features, such as working conditions. The *job specification* summarizes the personal qualities, traits, skills, and background required for getting the job done.

LEARNING OBJECTIVE 4-3

Explain and use at least three methods of collecting job analysis information.

Methods for Collecting Job Analysis Information

There are many ways (interviews or questionnaires, for instance) to collect job information.[13] The basic rule is to use those that best fit your purpose. Thus an interview might be best for creating a list of job duties. The more quantitative "position analysis questionnaire" may be best for quantifying each job's value for pay purposes. Before actually analyzing the job, keep several things in mind.

- Make the job analysis a *joint effort by a human resources manager, the worker, and the supervisor.* The human resource manager might observe the worker doing the job, and have the supervisor and worker complete job questionnaires. The supervisor and worker then verify the HR manager's list of job duties.
- *Make sure the questions and the process are clear* to the employees.
- *Use several job analysis methods*. For example, a questionnaire might miss a task the worker performs just occasionally. Therefore it's prudent to follow up the questionnaire with a short interview.

The Interview

Job analysis interviews range from unstructured ("Tell me about your job") to highly structured ones with hundreds of specific items to check off.

Managers may conduct individual interviews with each employee, group interviews with groups of employees who have the same job, and/or supervisor interviews with one or more knowledgeable supervisors. Use group interviews when a large number of employees are performing similar or identical work, since this can be a quick and inexpensive way to gather information. As a rule, the workers' immediate supervisor attends the group session; if not, you can interview the supervisor separately.

The interviewee should understand the reason for the interview. There's a tendency for workers to view such interviews, rightly or wrongly, as "efficiency evaluations." If so, interviewees may hesitate to describe their jobs accurately.

TYPICAL QUESTIONS Typical interview questions include the following:

What is the job being performed?

What exactly are the major duties of your position?

Hero Images/Getty Images

It is helpful to spend several minutes prior to collecting job analysis information explaining the process that you will be following.

What physical locations do you work in?

What are the education, experience, skill, [and any certification and licensing] requirements?

In what activities do you participate?

What are the job's responsibilities and duties?

What are the basic accountabilities or performance standards that typify your work?

What are your responsibilities? What are the environmental and working conditions involved?

What are the job's physical, emotional, and mental demands?

What are the health and safety conditions?

Are you exposed to any hazards or unusual working conditions?

STRUCTURED INTERVIEWS Many managers use questionnaires to guide the interview. Figure 4-4 presents one example. It includes questions regarding matters like the general purpose of the job, supervisory responsibilities, job duties, and skills required.

PROS AND CONS The interview's wide use reflects its advantages. It's a simple and quick way to collect information. Skilled interviewers can also unearth important activities that occur occasionally, or informal contacts not on the organization chart. The employee can also vent frustrations that might otherwise go unnoticed.

Distortion of information is the main problem.[14] Job analysis often precedes changing a job's pay rate. Employees therefore often view it as pay-related, and exaggerate some responsibilities while minimizing others. In one study, researchers listed possible job duties either as simple task statements ("record phone messages and other routine information") or as ability statements ("ability to record phone messages and other routine information"). Respondents were more likely to report performing the ability-based versions of the statements. There may be a tendency for people to inflate their job's importance when abilities are involved, to impress the perceptions of others.[15]

INTERVIEWING GUIDELINES To get the best information possible:

- Establish rapport with the interviewee. Know the person's name, speak understandably, briefly review the interview's purpose, and explain how the person was chosen for the interview.
- Use a structured guide that lists questions. This ensures you'll identify crucial questions ahead of time and that all interviewers (if more than one) cover all the required questions. (However, also ask, "Was there anything we didn't cover with our questions?")
- Make sure you don't overlook crucial but infrequently performed activities—like a nurse's occasional emergency room duties. Ask the worker to list his or her duties in order of importance and frequency of occurrence.
- After completing the interview, review the information with the worker's supervisor and the worker.

Questionnaires

Having employees fill out questionnaires to describe their job duties and responsibilities is another popular job analysis approach.

Some questionnaires are structured checklists. Here each employee gets an inventory of perhaps hundreds of specific duties or tasks (such as "change and splice wire"). He or she must indicate if he or she performs each task and, if so, how much time is normally spent on each. At the other extreme, the questionnaire may simply ask, "describe the major duties of your job."

FIGURE 4-4 Job Analysis Questionnaire for Developing Job Descriptions

Source: Adapted from www.tsu.edu/PDFFiles/Human%20Resources/HR%20Forms/JAQ%20FORM_rev%20100809%20a.pdf; www.delawarepersonnel.com/class/forms/jaq/jaq.shtml; www.uh.edu/human-resources/forms/JAQ.doc; www.tnstate.edu/hr/documents/.../Job%20Analysis%20Questionnaire.doc (all accessed July 24, 2013).

JOB ANALYSIS QUESTIONNAIRE*

PURPOSE AND INSTRUCTIONS

Because no one knows the job as well as the person doing it, we are asking you to complete this form. The purpose is to obtain current information on your job based on a review of job duties and responsibilities. We are not asking you about your job performance; only what your job requires you to do.

EMPLOYEE DATA (PLEASE PRINT):

Your Name: ______________________ Today's date ______________

Employee ID: ______________________

Location/Department: ______________________

Your Job Title: ______________________ Job Code: ______________

How long have you been in your current position: __________

Work Telephone Number: ______________________

Supervisor's Name: ______________________ Supervisor's Title: ______________

SUMMARY OF DUTIES/RESPONSIBILITIES

Give a brief description of the main function/purpose of your job. This statement should be a brief summary of the responsibilities listed in the next section.

____

____

____

Listing of Job Duties

What do you do on your job? Please list your job's specific duties/responsibilities in the space below. In doing so:

Please list the most important duties/responsibilities first. Write a separate statement for each duty/responsibility.

At the end of each statement please indicate the approximate percent of your workday (25%, 7%, etc.) you spend on that duty.

Please place an asterisk (*) next to the duties that you consider to be absolutely essential to this job.

____

____

____

____

____

(Add additional duties as necessary)

Are there duties you are now performing that are not now in your job description? If so please list them on back of this page.

(Continued)

FIGURE 4-4 *Continued*

Minimum Level of Education (or Equivalent Experience) This Job Requires

What is the minimum level of education necessary to perform your job? Select only one please:

1. Elementary education.
2. Some high school.
3. A high school diploma or equivalent (G.E.D.).
4. A formal vocational training program (approximately one year), an apprenticeship, or some formal college education.
5. An associate's degree (AA, AS).
6. A bachelor's degree (BA, BS).
7. A master's degree (MA, MS, MBA, MPA).
8. A doctorate degree (Ph.D., MD, JD, EED).
9. Are you required to be licensed or certified to perform your work?

[ ] Yes [ ] No List type ______________________________

Required Training on Job

What is the level of on-the-job or classroom training someone requires to do your job? Please select one choice below:

1. No additional training required.
2. A day or two.
3. A week.
4. A month.
5. Several months.
6. One year.
7. Two years or more.

SUPERVISORY RESPONSIBILITIES

Do you supervise others as part of your job? If so please briefly describe the nature of your supervisory responsibilities.

PHYSICAL JOB DEMANDS

Please briefly describe this job's main physical demands. For example, does it involve Sitting? Walking? Standing? Lifting? Detailed repetitive motions? Climbing? Etc.

Working Conditions: Environmental and Safety Job Demands

Please list this job's working conditions, such as: air-conditioned office work; outdoor or indoor extreme heat or cold; wet; noise; job hazards; working in elevated conditions; etc.

EMPLOYEE COMMENTS

Is there any other information that would be important in understanding your job? If so, please give us your comments below.

SUPERVISOR'S REVIEW

Based on your understanding of the job as it currently exists, please review the employee's response and provide your own comments in the space below. **Please do not change the employee's responses.**

In practice, the questionnaire often falls between these two extremes. As illustrated in Figure 4-4, a typical job analysis questionnaire might include several open-ended questions (such as "Give a brief description of the main function/purpose of your job.") as well as structured questions (concerning, for instance, education required).

Questionnaires have pros and cons. This is a quick and efficient way to obtain information from a large number of employees; it's less costly than interviewing dozens of workers, for instance. However, developing and testing it (perhaps by making sure the workers understand the questions) can be time-consuming. And as with interviews, employees may distort their answers.

Observation

Direct observation is especially useful when jobs consist of observable physical activities—assembly-line worker and accounting clerk are examples. However, it's usually not appropriate when the job entails a lot of mental activity (lawyer, design engineer). Nor is it useful if the employee only occasionally engages in important activities, such as a nurse who handles emergencies. *Reactivity*—the worker's changing what he or she normally does because you are watching—is another problem.

Managers often use direct observation and interviewing together. One approach is to observe the worker on the job during a complete work cycle. (The *cycle* is the time it takes to complete the job; it could be a minute for an assembly-line worker or an hour, a day, or longer for complex jobs.) Here you take notes of all the job activities. Then, ask the person to clarify open points and to explain what other activities he or she performs that you didn't observe.

Participant Diary/Logs

diary/log
Daily listings made by workers of every activity in which they engage along with the time each activity takes.

Another method is to ask workers to keep a **diary/log;** here for every activity engaged in, the employee records the activity (along with the time) in a log.

Some firms give employees pocket dictating machines and pagers. Then randomly during the day, they page the workers, who dictate what they are doing at that time.

Quantitative Job Analysis Techniques

Qualitative methods like interviews and questionnaires are not always suitable. For example, if your aim is to compare jobs for pay purposes, a mere listing of duties may not suffice. You may need to say that, in effect, "Job A is twice as challenging as Job B, and so is worth twice the pay." To do this, it helps to have quantitative ratings for each job. The position analysis questionnaire and the Department of Labor approach are quantitative methods for doing this.

position analysis questionnaire (PAQ)
A questionnaire used to collect quantifiable data concerning the duties and responsibilities of various jobs.

POSITION ANALYSIS QUESTIONNAIRE The **position analysis questionnaire (PAQ)** is a very popular quantitative job analysis tool, consisting of a questionnaire containing 194 items.[16] The 194 items (such as "written materials") each represent a basic element that may play a role in the job.[17] The items each belong to one of five PAQ basic activities: (1) Having Decision-Making/Communication/Social Responsibilities, (2) Performing Skilled Activities, (3) Being Physically Active, (4) Operating Vehicles/Equipment, and (5) Processing Information. The final PAQ "score" reflects the job's rating on each of these five activities. To get those scores, the job analyst decides if each of the 194 items (such as one on using "written materials") applies to the job and, if so, to what extent. For example, within the "Processing Information" activity section, an item on the extent to which the job requires using "written materials" such as books and reports might get a rating of 4. Since the PAQ scale ranges from 1 to 5, a 4 suggests that written materials do play a significant role in this job. The analyst can use an online version of the PAQ (see www.paq.com) for each job he or she is analyzing.

One of the PAQ's strengths is in assigning jobs to job classes for pay purposes. With ratings for each job's decision-making, skilled activity, physical activity, vehicle/equipment operation, and information-processing characteristics, you can quantitatively compare jobs relative to one another,[18] and then classify jobs for pay purposes.[19]

DEPARTMENT OF LABOR (DOL) PROCEDURE Experts at the U.S. Department of Labor did much of the early work developing job analysis.[20] They used their results to compile what was for many years the bible of job descriptions, the *Dictionary of Occupational Titles*. This mammoth book contained detailed information on virtually every job in America. Internet-based tools have largely replaced the *Dictionary*.[21] However, the U.S. Department of Labor job analysis procedure remains a good example of how to quantitatively rate, classify, and compare jobs. As Table 4-1 shows, the DOL method uses a set of standard activities called *worker functions* to describe what a worker must do with respect to *data, people*, and *things*. With respect to data, for instance, the functions include synthesizing and copying. For people, they include mentoring and supervising. For things, basic functions include manipulating and handling.

Each worker function has an importance rating. Thus, "coordinating" is 1, whereas "copying" is 5. If you were analyzing the job of a receptionist/clerk, for example, you might label the job 5, 6, 7 to represent copying data, speaking/signaling people, and handling things. You might code a psychiatric aide in a hospital 1, 7, 5 in relation to data, people, and things. In practice, you would score each task that the worker performed as part of his or her job in terms of data, people, and things. Then you would use the highest combination (say 4, 6, 5) to rate the overall job, since this is the highest level that you would expect a successful job incumbent to attain. If you were selecting a worker for that 4, 6, 5 job, you'd expect him or her to be able to at least compute (4), speak/signal (6), and tend (5). If you were comparing jobs for pay purposes, a 4, 6, 5 job should rank higher (see Table 4-1) than a 6, 8, 6 job. The manager can then present a summary of the job along with its 3-digit rating on a form such as in Figure 4-5.[22]

Online Job Analysis Methods[23]

Employers also use online job analysis methods. Here the human resource department generally distributes standardized job analysis questionnaires to geographically disbursed employees online, with instructions to complete the forms and return them by a particular date. The job analyst may then convene, online, job experts to

TABLE 4-1 Basic Department of Labor Worker Functions

	Data	People	Things
Basic Activities	0 Synthesizing	0 Mentoring	0 Setting up
	1 Coordinating	1 Negotiating	1 Precision working
	2 Analyzing	2 Instructing	2 Operating/controlling
	3 Compiling	3 Supervising	3 Driving/operating
	4 Computing	4 Diverting	4 Manipulating
	5 Copying	5 Persuading	5 Tending
	6 Comparing	6 Speaking/signaling	6 Feeding/offbearing
		7 Serving	7 Handling
		8 Taking instructions/helping	

Note: Determine employee's job "score" on data, people, and things by observing his or her job and determining, for each of the three categories, which of the basic functions illustrates the person's job. "0" is high; "6," "8," and "7" are lows in each column.

FIGURE 4-5 **Sample Report Based on Department of Labor Job Analysis Technique**

Job Analysis Schedule

1. Established Job Title DOUGH MIXER
2. Ind. Assign (bake prod.)
3. SIC Code(s) and Title(s) 2051 Bread and other bakery products

4. JOB SUMMARY:

Operates mixing machine to mix ingredients for straight and sponge (yeast) doughs according to established formulas, directs other workers in fermentation of dough, and curls dough into pieces with hand cutter.

5. WORK PERFORMED RATINGS:

	D	P	(T)
Worker Functions	Data	People	Things
	5	6	2

Work Field Cooking, Food Preparing

6. WORKER TRAITS RATING (to be filled in by analyst):

Training time required
Aptitudes
Temperaments
Interests
Physical demands
Environment conditions

discuss and finalize the knowledge, skills, abilities, and other characteristics doing the job requires.[24]

Without a job analyst actually sitting there with the employee or supervisor, there's a chance they won't cover important points or that misunderstandings arise. Therefore, all instructions should be clear, and test the process first.

The U.S. Navy used Internet-based job analysis.[25] To keep ambiguities to a minimum, it had the employees complete structured online job analysis forms step by step and duty by duty, as follows:

- First, the online form lists *a set of work activities* (such as "Getting Information" and "Monitor Processes") from the Department of Labor O*NET work activities list (see Figure 4-6).[26]
- Next, the form directs employees to *select those work activities* that are important to their job.
- Then, the form asks them to *list actual duties* of their jobs that fit each of those selected work activities. For example, suppose an employee chose "Getting Information" as an important work activity. Now he or she would list next to "Getting Information" specific job duties, such as "bring new orders from our vendors to the boss's attention."

Again, the main caveat with online job analysis is to strip the process of ambiguities. The Navy's online method proved effective.[27]

FIGURE 4-6 O*NET Generalized Work Activities Categories

Note: The U.S. Navy employees were asked to indicate if their jobs required them to engage in work activities such as: Getting Information; Monitoring Processes; Identifying Objects; Inspecting Equipment; and Estimating Quantifiable Characteristics.
Source: From O*NET Web site, www.onetonline.org.

Print-friendly Version
(Outline View | **Description View)**

Generalized Work Activities — General types of job behaviors occurring on multiple jobs

- Information Input — Where and how are the information and data gained that are needed to perform this job?
  - Looking for and Receiving Job-Related Information — How is information obtained to perform this job?
    - **Getting Information** — Observing, receiving, and otherwise obtaining information from all relevant sources.
    - **Monitor Processes, Materials, or Surroundings** — Monitoring and reviewing information from materials, events, or the environment, to detect or assess problems.
  - Identify and Evaluating Job-Relevant Information — How is information interpreted to perform this job?
    - **Identifying Objects, Actions, and Events** — Identifying information by categorizing, estimating, recognizing differences or similarities, and detecting changes in circumstances or events.
    - **Inspecting Equipment, Structures, or Material** — Inspecting equipment, structures, or materials to identify the cause of errors or other problems or defects.
    - **Estimating the Quantifiable Characteristics of Products, Events, or Information** — Estimating sizes, distances, and quantities; or determining time, costs, resources, or materials needed to perform a work activity.

MyLab Management Apply It!

If your professor has assigned this activity, go to the Assignments section of **www.pearson.com/mylab/management** to complete the video exercise.

Writing Job Descriptions

LEARNING OBJECTIVE 4-4

Explain how you would write a job description, and what sources you would use.

The most important product of job analysis is the job description. A job description is a written statement of what the worker actually does, how he or she does it, and what the job's working conditions are. You use this information to write a job specification; this lists the knowledge, abilities, and skills required to perform the job satisfactorily.[28]

HR in Action at the Hotel Paris In reviewing the Hotel Paris's employment systems, the HR manager was concerned that virtually all the company's job descriptions were out of date, and that many jobs had no descriptions at all. She knew that without accurate job descriptions, all her improvement efforts would be in vain. To see how this was handled, see the case on page 127 of this chapter.

Diversity Counts

You might assume that job descriptions are only of use in business settings, but that's not the case. For example, for parents who want the best care for their kids, writing up a job description before hiring a child-care worker could be quite useful. For instance, because what children learn when they're very young predicts their future academic and career success, facilitating early-childhood learning is a crucial task for many caregivers.[29] And yet because few parents think through and write a job description before recruiting their child-care workers, many hire this important person not clearly crystallizing what they want this person to do—including, for instance, facilitating learning.

A well-thought-out job description might benefit everyone involved. The parent—knowing that supporting early-childhood learning is so important—might put more effort into finding and training the child's caregiver (95% of whom are women). The child might benefit from a more nurturing learning environment. And the caregiver would gain if, after recognizing how many challenging tasks she is responsible for, the parent would raise her salary from the current national average of about $19,000 per year—just about the poverty level for a family of three. ■

There is no standard format for writing a job description. However, most descriptions contain sections that cover:

1. Job identification
2. Job summary
3. Responsibilities and duties
4. Authority of incumbent
5. Standards of performance
6. Working conditions
7. Job specification

Figures 4-7 and 4-8 present two sample forms of job descriptions.

Job Identification

As in Figure 4-7, the job identification section (on top) contains several types of information.[30] The *job title* specifies the name of the job, such as *inventory control clerk*. The Fair Labor Standards Act (FLSA) status section identifies the job as exempt or nonexempt. (Under the FLSA, certain positions, primarily administrative and professional, are exempt from the act's overtime and minimum wage provisions.) *Date* is the date the job description was approved.

There may also be a space to indicate who approved the description and perhaps one showing the job's location in terms of facility/division and department. This section might also include the supervisor's title and information regarding salary and/or pay scale. There might also be space for the pay grade/level of the job, if there is one. For example, a firm may classify programmers as programmer II, programmer III, and so on.

WHAT'S IN A NAME (OR IN A JOB TITLE)? Some job titles are quite creative. For example, Pinterest calls its designers Pixel Pushers, and its interns Pinterns.[31] One study concluded that employees who participate in retitling their jobs and who have more descriptive job titles tend to be more satisfied and to feel more recognized.[32]

The U.S. Navy discovered that the hard way. From the Navy's earliest days, sailors traditionally had descriptive job titles such as "electrician's mate first class." In part to strip its job titles of gender-specific labels containing "man" or "men," the Navy decided to group all sailors with the same pay rate together, with the same (bland) job title such as "petty officer first class."[33] An uproar ensued. A petition with over 100,000 signatures got to the White House. The Navy returned to its traditional job titles.

Job Summary

The job summary should summarize the essence of the job, and should include only its major functions or activities. Thus (in Figure 4-7), the telesales rep " . . . is responsible for selling college textbooks. . . ." For the job of mailroom supervisor, "the mailroom supervisor receives, sorts, and delivers all incoming mail properly, and he or she handles all outgoing mail including the accurate and timely posting of such mail."[34]

Some experts state unequivocally that "one item frequently found that should never be included in a job description is a 'cop-out clause' like 'other duties, as assigned,'"[35] since this leaves open the nature of the job. Finally, state in the summary that the employee is expected to carry out his or her duties efficiently, attentively, and conscientiously.

JOB TITLE: Telesales Respresentative	**JOB CODE:** 100001
RECOMMENDED SALARY GRADE:	**EXEMPT/NONEXEMPT STATUS:** Nonexempt
JOB FAMILY: Sales	**EEOC:** Sales Workers
DIVISION: Higher Education	**REPORTS TO:** District Sales Manager
DEPARTMENT: In-House Sales	**LOCATION:** Boston
	DATE: April 2013

SUMMARY (Write a brief summary of job.)

The person in this position is responsible for selling college textbooks, software, and multimedia products to professors, via incoming and outgoing telephone calls, and to carry out selling strategies to meet sales goals in assigned territories of smaller colleges and universities. In addition, the individual in this position will be responsible for generating a designated amount of editorial leads and communicating to the publishing groups product feedback and market trends observed in the assigned territory.

SCOPE AND IMPACT OF JOB

Dollar responsibilities (budget and/or revenue)

The person in this position is responsible for generating approximately $2 million in revenue, for meeting operating expense budget of approximately $4000, and a sampling budget of approximately 10,000 units.

Supervisory responsibilities (direct and indirect)

None

Other

REQUIRED KNOWLEDGE AND EXPERIENCE (Knowledge and experience necessary to do job)

Related work experience

Prior sales or publishing experience preferred. One year of company experience in a customer service or marketing function with broad knowledge of company products and services is desirable.

Formal education or equivalent

Bachelor's degree with strong academic performance or work equivalent experience.

Skills

Must have strong organizational and persuasive skills. Must have excellent verbal and written communications skills and must be PC proficient.

Other

Limited travel required (approx 5%)

(Continued)

FIGURE 4-7 **Sample Job Description, Pearson Education**

Source: Reprinted and electronically reproduced by permission of Pearson Education, Inc., Upper Saddle River, New Jersey.

Relationships

There may be a "relationships" statement (not in Figure 4-7) that shows the jobholder's relationships with others inside and outside the organization. The following presents some illustrative relationships for a human resource manager.[36]

PRIMARY RESPONSIBILITIES (List in order of importance and list amount of time spent on task.)

Driving Sales (60%)

- Achieve quantitative sales goal for assigned territory of smaller colleges and universities.
- Determine sales priorities and strategies for territory and develop a plan for implementing those strategies.
- Conduct 15–20 professor interviews per day during the academic sales year that accomplishes those priorities.
- Conduct product presentations (including texts, software, and Web site); effectively articulate author's central vision of key titles; conduct sales interviews using the PSS model; conduct walk-through of books and technology.
- Employ telephone selling techniques and strategies.
- Sample products to appropriate faculty, making strategic use of assigned sampling budgets.
- Close class test adoptions for first edition products.
- Negotiate custom publishing and special packaging agreements within company guidelines.
- Initiate and conduct in-person faculty presentations and selling trips as appropriate to maximize sales with the strategic use of travel budget. Also use internal resources to support the territory sales goals.
- Plan and execute in-territory special selling events and book-fairs.
- Develop and implement in-territory promotional campaigns and targeted email campaigns.

Publishing (editorial/marketing) 25%

- Report, track, and sign editorial projects.
- Gather and communicate significant market feedback and information to publishing groups.

Territory Management 15%

- Track and report all pending and closed business in assigned database.
- Maintain records of customer sales interviews and adoption situations in assigned database.
- Manage operating budget strategically.
- Submit territory itineraries, sales plans, and sales forecasts as assigned.
- Provide superior customer service and maintain professional bookstore relations in assigned territory.

Decision-Making Responsibilities for This Position:

Determine the strategic use of assigned sampling budget to most effectively generate sales revenue to exceed sales goals.
Determine the priority of customer and account contacts to achieve maximum sales potential.
Determine where in-person presentations and special selling events would be most effective to generate the most sales.

Submitted By: Jim Smith, District Sales Manager	Date: April 10, 2013
Approval:	Date:
Human Resources:	Date:
Corporate Compensation:	Date:

FIGURE 4-7 ***Continued***

Reports to: Vice president of employee relations.

Supervises: Human resource clerk, test administrator, labor relations director, and one secretary.

Works with: All department managers and executive management.

Outside the company: Employment agencies, executive recruiting firms, union representatives, state and federal employment offices, and various vendors.[37]

FIGURE 4-8 **Marketing Manager Description from Standard Occupational Classification**

Source: U.S. Department of Labor, Bureau of Labor Statistics.

U.S. Department of Labor
Bureau of Labor Statistics
Standard Occupational Classification

www.bls.gov | Advanced Search | A-Z Index

BLS Home | Programs & Surveys | Get Detailed Statistics | Glossary | What's New | Find It! In DOL

11-2021 Marketing Managers

Determine the demand for products and services offered by a firm and its competitors and identify potential customers. Develop pricing strategies with the goal of maximizing the firm's profits or share of the market while ensuring the firm's customers are satisfied. Oversee product development or monitor trends that indicate the need for new products and services.

Responsibilities and Duties

This is the heart of the job description. It should present a list of the job's responsibilities and duties. As in Figure 4-7, list each of the job's major duties separately, and describe it in a few sentences. In the figure, for instance, the job's duties include "achieve quantitative sales goal . . . " and "determine sales priorities. . . ." Typical duties for other jobs might include making accurate postings to accounts payable, maintaining favorable purchase price variances, and repairing production-line tools and equipment. This section may also define the jobholder's authority limits. For example, the jobholder might have authority to approve purchase requests up to $5,000, grant time off or leaves of absence, discipline department personnel, recommend salary increases, and interview and hire new employees.

Usually, the manager's basic question here is, "How do I determine what the job's duties are and should be?" The answer first is, from the *job analysis*; this should reveal what the employees on each job are doing now.

Standard Occupational Classification (SOC)
Classifies all workers into one of 23 major groups of jobs that are subdivided into minor groups of jobs and detailed occupations.

Second, you can review various sources of standardized job description information. For example, the U.S. government's **Standard Occupational Classification (SOC)** (www.bls.gov/soc/socguide.htm) classifies all workers into one of 23 major groups of jobs, such as "Management Occupations" and "Healthcare Occupations." These in turn contain 96 minor groups of jobs, which in turn include 821 detailed occupations, such as the marketing manager description in Figure 4-8. The employer can use standard descriptions like these to identify a job's duties and responsibilities, such as "Determine the demand for products."

The employer may also use other popular sources of job description information, such as www.jobdescription.com. Another simple solution is just to *Google* the job description you want, by seeing online what others are doing. Thus, someone writing job descriptions for *marketing manager* would readily find relevant online descriptions using methods like these:

- Go to http://hiring.monster.com. Then click Resource Center, then Recruiting and Hiring Advice, then Job Descriptions. Then find the Marketing and Sales Manager Sample Job Description.[38]
- Go to www.careerplanner.com. Then click Job Descriptions, then scroll down to the job description you're interested in.[39]
- O*NET online, as noted, is another option for finding job duties. We present an example in the HR Tools for Line Managers and Small Businesses feature at the end of this section.

TRENDS SHAPING HR: *DIGITAL AND SOCIAL MEDIA*

Thanks to social media such as LinkedIn, line managers today can do things for which they formerly required HR managers. For example, (to paraphrase what someone posted on LinkedIn): *I hope some of you IT recruiters out there can help me to better understand what I need to put into the job descriptions that I'm writing for the O*NET developers and development managers I'm recruiting for*. The first of many replies listed 12 tasks including: (1) Do technical skills match the desired job?, (2) What technical problems were solved by the job seeker?, and (3) Did job seeker know about Cloud Deployment?[40] ■

Writing clear job duties is an art. For a teacher, for example, one duty might be:[41]

Incorrect: Ensures that students learn fifth-grade English with the aim of passing the required common exam.

Comment: What the teacher does is ambiguous, and the expected process and results of the teacher's actions aren't clear.

Correct: Studies past common English exams to understand what they typically involve; prepares yearly, weekly, and daily lesson plans; presents each day's lesson clearly with follow-up questions to ensure learning; administers weekly tests to confirm learning; and counsel students one-on-one in class lessons as necessary.

KNOW YOUR EMPLOYMENT LAW

Writing Job Descriptions That Comply with the ADA

The list of job duties is crucial to employers' efforts to comply with the Americans with Disabilities Act (ADA). Under the ADA, the individual must have the requisite skills, educational background, and experience to perform the job's essential functions. The EEOC says, "Essential functions are the basic job duties that an employee must be able to perform, with or without reasonable accommodation."[42] Factors to consider include:

- Whether the position exists to perform that function
- The number of other employees available to perform the function
- The degree of expertise or skill required to perform the function
- Whether employees in the position are actually required to perform the function[43]
- What the degree of expertise or skill required to perform the function is[44]

As an example, answering calls and directing visitors to the proper offices might be essential functions for a receptionist. The EEOC says it will consider both the employer's judgment about which functions are essential, and a written job description prepared before advertising or interviewing for a job as evidence of essential functions. Other evidence includes the actual work experience of present or past employees in the job, the time spent performing a function, and the consequences of not requiring that function.

If the disabled individual can't perform the job as currently structured, the employer is required to make a "reasonable accommodation," unless doing so would present an "undue hardship." The EEOC says reasonable accommodation may include:

- acquiring or modifying equipment or devices,
- part-time or modified work schedules,
- adjusting or modifying examinations, training materials, or policies,
- providing readers and interpreters, and
- making the workplace readily accessible to and usable by people with disabilities. ■

Standards of Performance and Working Conditions

A "standards of performance" section lists the standards the company expects the employee to achieve for each of the job description's main duties and responsibilities. One way to set standards is to finish the statement, "I will be completely satisfied with your work when . . . ." This sentence, completed for each duty, should produce a usable set of performance standards. For example:

***Duty:* Accurately Posting Accounts Payable**

1. Post all invoices received within the same working day.
2. Route all invoices to the proper department managers for approval no later than the day following receipt.
3. Commit an average of no more than three posting errors per month.

Finally, the job description may list the job's working conditions, such as noise level or hazardous conditions.

IMPROVING PERFORMANCE: *HR TOOLS FOR LINE MANAGERS AND SMALL BUSINESSES*

Using O*NET

Without their own job analysts or even HR managers, many small business owners face two hurdles when doing job analyses. First, most need a more streamlined approach than those provided by questionnaires like Figure 4-4. Second is the concern that, in writing their job descriptions, they'll overlook duties that should be assigned. What they need is an encyclopedia listing all the possible positions they might encounter, including a list of the duties normally assigned to these positions.

The small business owner has at least three options. The *Standard Occupational Classification*, mentioned earlier, provides detailed descriptions of thousands of jobs and their human requirements. Web sites like www.jobdescription.com provide customizable descriptions by title and industry. And the Department of Labor's O*NET is a third alternative. We'll focus here on how to write a job description using O*NET (http://online.onetcenter.org).[45] It is free to use.

O*NET

The U.S. Department of Labor's online occupational information network, called O*NET, enables anyone to see the most important characteristics of various occupations, as well as the experience, education, and knowledge required to do each job well. Both the Standard Occupational Classification and O*NET list the specific duties associated with numerous occupations. O*NET also lists skills, including *basic skills* such as reading and writing, *process skills* such as critical thinking, and *transferable skills* such as persuasion and negotiation.[46] An O*NET job listing also includes information on worker requirements (required knowledge, for instance), occupation requirements (such as compiling, coding, and categorizing data, for instance), and experience requirements (including education and job training). Employers and career planners also use O*NET to check the job's labor market characteristics, such as employment projections and earnings data.[47]

The steps in using O*NET to facilitate writing a job description follow.

STEP 1. ***Review Your Plan.*** Ideally, the jobs you need should flow from your departmental or company plans. Do you plan to enter or exit businesses? What do you expect your sales to be in the next few years? What departments will have to be expanded or reduced? What kinds of new positions will you need?

STEP 2. ***Develop an Organization Chart.*** Start with the organization as it is now. Then produce a chart showing how you want it to look in a year or two. Microsoft Office and others offer free tools.[48]

STEP 3. ***Use a Job Analysis Questionnaire.*** Next, gather information about each job's duties. (You can use job analysis questionnaires, such as those shown in Figures 4-4 and 4-9.)

STEP 4. ***Obtain Job Duties from O*NET.*** The list of job duties you uncovered through the job analysis in step 3 may or may not be complete. We'll therefore use O*NET to compile a more complete list. (Refer to the A, B, and C examples pictured.)

Source: Reprinted by permission of O*NET OnLine.

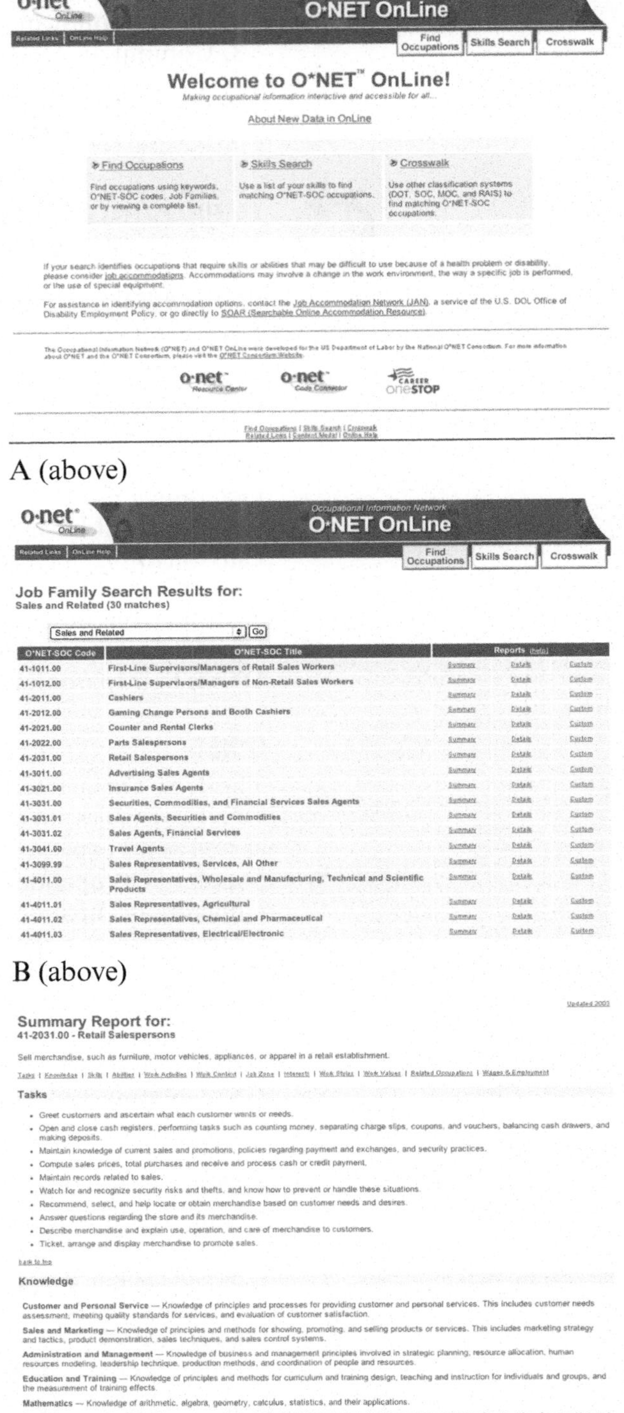

A (above)

O*NET-SOC Code	O*NET-SOC Title	Reports		
41-1011.00	First-Line Supervisors/Managers of Retail Sales Workers	Summary	Details	Custom
41-1012.00	First-Line Supervisors/Managers of Non-Retail Sales Workers	Summary	Details	Custom
41-2011.00	Cashiers	Summary	Details	Custom
41-2012.00	Gaming Change Persons and Booth Cashiers	Summary	Details	Custom
41-2021.00	Counter and Rental Clerks	Summary	Details	Custom
41-2022.00	Parts Salespersons	Summary	Details	Custom
41-2031.00	Retail Salespersons	Summary	Details	Custom
41-3011.00	Advertising Sales Agents	Summary	Details	Custom
41-3021.00	Insurance Sales Agents	Summary	Details	Custom
41-3031.00	Securities, Commodities, and Financial Services Sales Agents	Summary	Details	Custom
41-3031.01	Sales Agents, Securities and Commodities	Summary	Details	Custom
41-3031.02	Sales Agents, Financial Services	Summary	Details	Custom
41-3041.00	Travel Agents	Summary	Details	Custom
41-3099.99	Sales Representatives, Services, All Other	Summary	Details	Custom
41-4011.00	Sales Representatives, Wholesale and Manufacturing, Technical and Scientific Products	Summary	Details	Custom
41-4011.01	Sales Representatives, Agricultural	Summary	Details	Custom
41-4011.02	Sales Representatives, Chemical and Pharmaceutical	Summary	Details	Custom
41-4011.03	Sales Representatives, Electrical/Electronic	Summary	Details	Custom

B (above)

C (above)

Start by going to www.onetonline.org/[49] (A). Here, click on *Find Occupations*. Assume you want to create job descriptions for a retail salesperson. Key *Retail Sales* in the Industry Keyword drop-down box. This brings you to the Occupations matching "retail sales" page (B).[50]

Clicking on the *Retail Salespersons* summary produces the job summary and specific occupational duties for retail salespersons (C).[51] For a small store, you might want to combine the duties of the "retail salesperson" with those of "first-line supervisors/managers of retail sales workers."

STEP 5. ***List the Job's Human Requirements from O*NET.*** Next, return to the summary for *Retail salespersons* (C). Here, click, for example, Knowledge, Skills, and Abilities. Use this information to help develop a job specification for your job. Use this information for recruiting, selecting, and training your employees.

STEP 6. ***Finalize the Job Description.*** Finally, perhaps using Figure 4-9 as a guide, write an appropriate job summary for the job. Then use the information obtained previously in steps 4 and 5 to create a complete listing of the tasks, duties, and human requirements of each of the jobs you will need to fill. ■

FIGURE 4-9 **Simple Job Description Questionnaire**

Source: Copyright Gary Dessler, PhD.

Background Data for Job Description

Job Title ______________________ Department ______________________

Job Number ______________________ Written by ______________________

Today's Date ______________________ Applicable DOT Codes ______________________

I. Applicable DOT Definition(s):

II. Job Summary:
(List the more important or regularly performed tasks.)

III. Reports To:

IV. Supervises: ______________________

V. Job Duties: ______________________
(Briefly describe, for each duty, what employee does and, if possible, how employee does it. Show in parentheses at end of each duty the approximate percentage of time devoted to duty.)

A. Daily Duties:

B. Periodic Duties:
(Indicate whether weekly, monthly, quarterly, etc.)

C. Duties Performed at Irregular Intervals:

> **MyLab Management Talk About It 2**
>
> If your professor has assigned this, go to the Assignments section of **www.pearson.com/mylab/management** to complete these discussion questions. Pick a job that someone with whom you are familiar is doing, such as a bus driver, mechanic, and so on. Review the O*NET information for that job. To what extent does the person seem to have what it takes to do that job, based on the O*NET information? How does that correspond to how he or she is actually doing?

Writing Job Specifications

LEARNING OBJECTIVE 4-5
Explain how to write a job specification.

The job specification takes the job description and answers the question, "What human traits and experience are required to do this job effectively?" It shows what kind of person to recruit and for what qualities you should test that person. It may be a section of the job description, or a separate document. Often—as in Figure 4-7 ("REQUIRED KNOWLEDGE AND EXPERIENCE") on pages 113–114—it is part of the job description.[52]

Specifications for Trained versus Untrained Personnel

Writing job specifications for trained and experienced employees is relatively straightforward. Here job specifications tend to focus on factors such as length of previous service, quality of relevant training, and previous job performance.

The problems are more complex when you're filling jobs with untrained people (with the intention of training them on the job). Here you must specify qualities such as physical traits, personality, interests, or sensory skills that imply some potential for performing the job or for trainability. Thus, for a job that requires detailed manipulation, you might want someone who scores high on a test of finger dexterity. Employers identify the job's human requirements either through a subjective, judgmental approach or through statistical analysis (or both).

Filling jobs with untrained employees requires identifying the personal traits that predict performance.

Blend Images - Hill Street Studios/Brand X Pictures/Getty Images

Specifications Based on Judgment

Most job specifications simply reflect the educated guesses of people like supervisors and human resource managers. The basic procedure here is to ask, "What does it take in terms of education, intelligence, training, and the like to do this job well?"

How does one make such "educated guesses"? You could simply review the job's duties, and deduce from those what human traits and skills the job requires. You can also choose human traits and skills from those listed in Web-based job descriptions like those at www.jobdescription.com. (For example, one job description there lists "Generates creative solutions" and "Manages difficult or emotional customer situations.") O*NET online is another option. Job listings there include lists of required education, experience, and skills.

In any case, use common sense. Don't ignore behaviors that may apply to almost any job but that might not normally surface through a job analysis. Industriousness is an example. Who wants an employee who doesn't work hard? One researcher collected information from 18,000 employees in 42 different hourly entry-level jobs.[53] Generic work behaviors that he found to be important to all jobs included thoroughness, attendance, unruliness [lack of], and scheduling flexibility (for instance, offers to stay late when store is busy). Another study, of over 7,000 executives, found that crucial top-leader behaviors included: takes initiative, practices self-development, displays high integrity, drives for results, and develops others.[54]

HR AND THE GIG ECONOMY *DO GIG WORKERS NEED JOB SPECIFICATIONS?*

Hiring nonemployee gig workers doesn't mean the employer doesn't need job descriptions and job specifications. The employer must still ensure that the workers at least fit certain minimum requirements.

Therefore both Lyft and Uber list "driver requirements," which are essentially job specifications.[55] Driver requirements vary somewhat by location, but both Uber and Lyft require drivers to be at least 21, have a Social Security number and in-state driver's license (at least one year old), have in-state insurance, and undergo both DMV and national and county-wide background checks. For Uber the background check also requires no recent DUI or drug-related offenses, or incidents of driving without insurance or license, or fatal accidents, or history of reckless driving, and no criminal history. And your car must pass muster. For example, it must be a four-door sedan, seat four or more (excluding driver), be 2001 or newer, have in-state plates and be currently registered, and pass Uber's vehicle inspection.

MyLab Management Talk About It 3

If your professor has chosen to assign this, go to the Assignments section of **www.pearson.com/mylab/management** to complete these discussion questions. Based on your experience, what other human requirements would you say there are to be a good Uber or Lyft driver? Should the companies add these as requirements? Why?

Job Specifications Based on Statistical Analysis

Basing job specifications on statistical analysis (rather than only judgment) is more defensible, but it's also more difficult. The aim is to determine statistically the relationship between (1) some *predictor* (human trait such as height, intelligence, or finger dexterity), and (2) some indicator or *criterion* of job effectiveness, such as performance as rated by the supervisor. The basic procedure is predictive validation.

This procedure has five steps: (1) analyze the job and decide how to measure job performance, (2) select personal traits like finger dexterity that you believe should predict performance, (3) test candidates for these traits, (4) measure these candidates' subsequent job performance, and (5) statistically analyze the relationship between the human trait (finger dexterity) and job performance. Your aim is to determine whether the trait predicts performance.

Why is this more defensible than the judgmental approach? First, if the trait doesn't predict performance, why use it? Second, equal rights laws prohibit using traits that you can't prove distinguish between high and low job performers. But, in practice, most employers rely on judgmental approaches.

The Job-Requirements Matrix

Although most employers use job descriptions and specifications to summarize their jobs' duties and responsibilities, the **job-requirements matrix** is also popular.[56] A typical matrix lists the following information, in five columns:

job-requirements matrix
A more complete description of what the worker does and how and why he or she does it; it clarifies each task's purpose and each duty's required knowledge, skills, abilities, and other characteristics.

Column 1: Each of the job's four or five *main job duties* (such as *post accounts payable*)

Column 2: The *task statements* for the main tasks associated with each main job duty

Column 3: The relative *importance* of each main job duty

Column 4: The *time spent* on each main job duty

Column 5: The *knowledge, skills, ability*, and *other* human characteristics (KSAO) related to each main job duty[57]

task statement
Written item that shows *what* the worker does on one particular job task; *how* the worker does it; the *knowledge, skills, and aptitudes required* to do it; and the *purpose of the task.*

The main step in creating a job-requirements matrix involves writing the *task statements.* Each **task statement** describes *what* the worker does on each of a main job duty's separate job tasks and *how* the worker does it.

Employee Engagement Guide for Managers

As noted earlier, the manager should not ignore, while writing the job specification, desirable on-the-job behaviors that apply to almost any job but that might not normally surface through a job analysis. *Employee engagement* is an example.

The human resource consulting company Development Dimensions International conducted a study of 3,800 employees, and identified several personal characteristics that seemed to predict the likelihood someone would be engaged.[58] These traits included adaptability, passion for work, emotional maturity, positive disposition, self-advocacy, and achievement orientation.

A sensible suggestion is to seek out people who already have records of being engaged employees. Because past behavior is often the best predictor of future behavior, one suggestion is that if you want to hire people who are more likely to become engaged employees, "... look for examples of engagement in other areas of life."[59] For example, seek out candidates with a demonstrated commitment to serve others, such as nurses, veterans, and voluntary first responders.

LEARNING OBJECTIVE 4-6

Give examples of competency-based job analysis.

Using Competencies Models

Many people still think of a "job" as a set of specific duties someone carries out for pay, but the concept of job is changing. Companies today continue to flatten their hierarchies, squeezing out managers, and leaving the remaining workers with more jobs to do. Changes like these tend to blur where one job starts and another ends. In situations like these, relying on a list of job duties that itemizes specific things you expect the worker to do is often impractical.[60]

Many employers are therefore using a different job analysis approach. Instead of listing the job's duties, they list, in *competency models* (or profiles), the knowledge, skills, and experience someone needs to do the job. Such models or profiles (see Figure 4-10) list the competencies employees must be able to exhibit to get their jobs done.[61] In

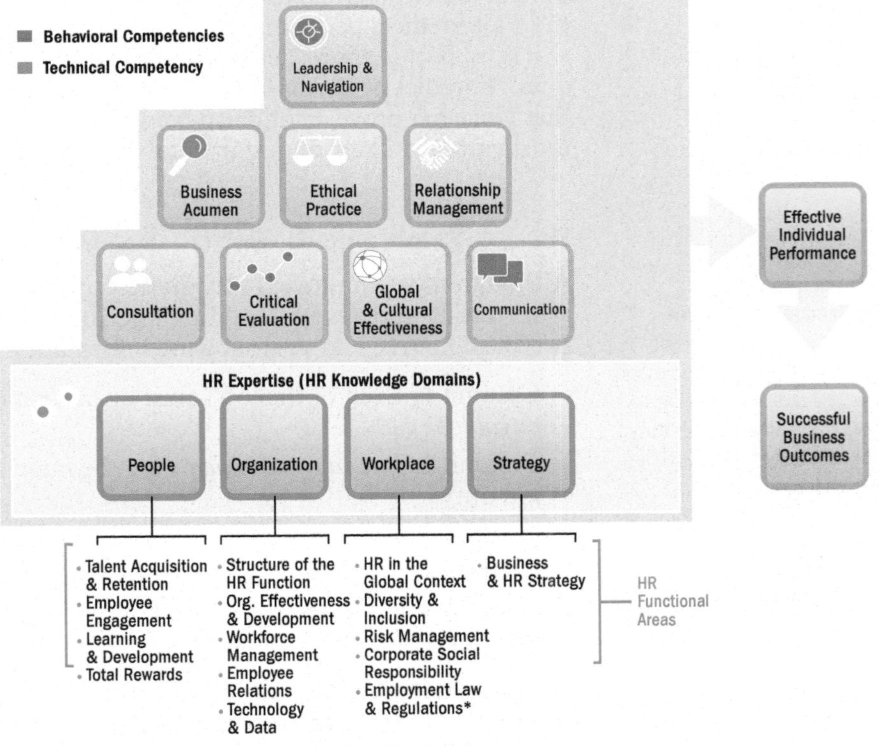

FIGURE 4-10 HR Manager Competency Model

Source: The SHRM Body of Competency and Knowledge. ©2014, Society for Human Resource Management, Alexandria, VA. Used with permission. All rights reserved.

creating a competency model for HR managers, the Society for Human Resource Management describes a competency as a "cluster of highly interrelated attributes" (such as research design knowledge, critical thinking skills, and deductive reasoning abilities) that give rise to the behaviors (such as *critical evaluation*) someone would need to perform a given job (in this case, HR manager) effectively.[62]

The competency model or profile then becomes the guidepost for recruiting, selecting, training, evaluating, and developing employees for each job.[63] In other words, the manager *hires* new employees using tests that measure the profile's list of competencies, *trains* employees with courses that develop these competencies, and *appraises* performance by assessing the worker's competencies. The accompanying Strategic Context feature illustrates.

IMPROVING PERFORMANCE: *THE STRATEGIC CONTEXT*

Daimler Alabama

By 2020, Daimler intends to use its expanded Tuscaloosa, Alabama factory complex to start building hybrid and (eventually) electric SUVs.[64] That's a step it could take because its original factory there, which came on line about 20 years before, has been so successful.

In planning its original Alabama Mercedes-Benz factory, Germany-based Daimler's strategy was to design a high-tech factory.[65] The plant emphasizes *just-in-time* inventory methods, so inventories stay negligible due to the arrival "just in time" of parts. It also organizes employees into *work teams*, and emphasizes that all employees must dedicate themselves to *continuous improvement* (seeking continuously to find better ways to do things).

Such a production strategy requires certain employee competencies (skills and behaviors). For example, it requires multiskilled and flexible employees who are eager to work cooperatively in teams.

Competency-based job analysis played an important role in this factory. Guidelines here regarding whom to hire and how to train them are based more on the competencies someone needs to do the job (such as "ability to work cooperatively on a team") than on lists of job duties. Because employees don't have to follow detailed job descriptions showing what "my job" is, it's easier for employees to move from job to job within their teams. Not being pigeonholed also encourages workers to look beyond their own jobs to find ways to improve things. For instance, one team found a $0.23 plastic prong that worked better than the one for $2.50 the plant was using to keep car doors open during painting. Building its modern "continuous improvement" plant meant Daimler needed employees who thought for themselves. Organizing its jobs around worker competencies and using **competency-based job analysis** helped Daimler achieve its strategic aims here.

competency-based job analysis
Describing the job in terms of measurable, observable, behavioral competencies (knowledge, skills, and/or behaviors) that an employee doing that job must exhibit to do the job well.

MyLab Management Talk About It 4

If your professor has assigned this, go to the Assignments section of **www.pearson.com/mylab/management** to complete these discussion questions. Specifically, what competencies would you look for in a prospective Alabama plant employee? Why?

How to Write Competencies Statements

The process for identifying a job's required competencies (competency-based job analysis—describing the job in terms of measurable, observable, behavioral competencies) is similar to a traditional job analysis. Thus, you might interview job incumbents and ask about job responsibilities and activities, and required skills and knowledge.

But instead of compiling lists of job duties, your aim is to finish the statement, "*In order to perform this job competently, the employee should be able to. . . .*" Use your knowledge of the job to answer this, or the worker's or supervisor's insights, or use information from a source such as O*NET, or from the Department of Labor's Office of Personnel Management (see www.opm.gov). Then, for each competency write a *competency statement*.

A good competency statement includes three elements.[66] One is the *name and a brief description* of the competency, such as "Project Management—creating accurate and effective project schedules." The second is a *description of the observable behaviors* that represent proficiency in the competency, such as "continuously manage project

FIGURE 4-11 Skills Matrix

Level 6	6	6	6	6	6
Level 5	5	5	5	5	5
Level 4	4	4	4	4	4
Level 3	3	3	3	3	3
Level 2	2	2	2	2	2
Level 1	1	1	1	1	1
	Technical Expertise/Skills	Decision-Making and Problem Solving Skills	Interpersonal Skills	Leadership Skills	Commercial Awareness Skills

Note: This is an example of a skills matrix for technical/engineering product development employees. The blue numbered boxes show the level required for each skill for these product development employees. An accompanying key would provide specific examples for each level of each skill, with difficulty increasing for each skill level starting at Level 1. For example, Level 1 for Technical Expertise/Skills might say "has or is in process of acquiring the basic knowledge necessary to do this type of job," while Level 6 might say, "Capable of conducting and supervising highly complex analytical tasks requiring advanced technical know-how and skills."
Source: Copyright Gary Dessler, PhD.

risks and dependencies by making timely decisions." Third are *proficiency levels.* For example (for project management from low to high):[67]

- ***Proficiency Level 1.*** *Identify* project risks and dependencies and communicate routinely to stakeholders
- ***Proficiency Level 2.*** *Develop systems to monitor* risks and dependencies and report changes
- ***Proficiency Level 3.*** *Anticipate* changing conditions and impact to risks and dependencies and take preventive action

BP EXAMPLE British Petroleum's (BP's) exploration division executives wanted to shift employees from a job duties–oriented "that's-not-my-job" attitude to one that motivated employees to obtain the skills required to accomplish broader responsibilities.[68]

Their solution was a skills matrix like that in Figure 4-11. They had skills matrices for each job or job family (such as drilling managers). As in Figure 4-11, each matrix listed (1) the types of skills required to do that job, such as technical expertise, and (2) the minimum skill required for proficiency at each level. The figure's note shows how to actually use the matrix.

BP's talent management efforts in this unit could now focus on recruiting, hiring, training, appraising, and rewarding employees based on the set of skills employees need to perform the job in question.

Chapter Review

Chapter Section Summaries

4-1. Employers today often view all the staff–train–reward activities as part of a single integrated talent management **process.** Talent management is *the holistic, integrated, and results and goal-oriented process of planning, recruiting, selecting, developing, managing, and compensating employees*. Taking a talent management perspective means: keep in mind that the talent management tasks are parts of a single interrelated talent management process; make sure talent management decisions such as staffing and pay are goal-directed; use the same "profile" for formulating recruitment plans for a job as you do for making selection, training, appraisal, and payment decisions for it; and integrate all the talent management functions.

4-2. Job analysis is the procedure through which you determine the duties of the department's positions and the characteristics of the people to hire for them. Job descriptions are a list of what the job entails, while job specifications identify what kind of people to hire for the job. The job analysis itself involves collecting information on matters such as work activities; required human behaviors; and machines, tools, and equipment used. The basic steps in job analysis include deciding on the use of the job analysis information, reviewing relevant background information, analyzing the job, verifying the information, and developing job descriptions and job specifications.

4-3. There are various **methods for collecting job analysis information.** These include interviews, questionnaires, observation, participant diary/logs, and quantitative techniques such as position analysis questionnaires. Employers increasingly collect information from employees via the Internet.

4-4. Managers should know how to **write job descriptions.** While there is no standard format, most descriptions contain sections that cover job identification, a job summary, a listing of responsibilities and duties, the job incumbent's authority, and performance standards. It may also contain information regarding the job's working conditions and the job specifications. Many employers use Internet sources such as www.jobdescription.com to facilitate writing job descriptions.

4-5. In **writing job specifications,** distinguish between specifications for trained versus untrained personnel. For trained employees, you're looking primarily for traits like experience. For untrained personnel, you should identify traits that might predict success on the job. Most job specifications come from the educated guesses of people like supervisors, and are based mostly on judgment. Some employers use statistical analyses to identify predictors or human traits that relate to success on the job. Human traits that may predict the job candidates' likelihood to be *engaged* and that the manager might therefore want to include in the job specification include adaptability, passion for work, emotional maturity, positive disposition, self-advocacy, achievement orientation, and a work history that includes a demonstrated commitment to serve others.

4-6. With **competencies models** and profiles, the aim is to create descriptions of what is required for exceptional performance in a given role or job, in terms of required competencies, knowledge, and experience. Each job's profile then becomes the benchmark for creating recruitment, selection, training, and evaluation and development plans for each job. *Competency-based job analysis* means describing the job in terms of measurable, observable, behavioral competencies (such as skills).

Discussion Questions

4-1. Why, in summary, should managers think of staffing, training, appraising, and paying employees as a talent management process?

4-2. What items are typically included in the job description?

4-3. We discussed several methods for collecting job analysis data—questionnaires, the position analysis questionnaire, and so on. Compare and contrast these methods, explaining what each is useful for and listing the pros and cons of each.

4-4. Describe the types of information typically found in a job specification.

4-5. Explain how you would conduct a job analysis.

4-6. Do you think all companies can really do without detailed job descriptions? Why or why not?

4-7. Explain how you would create a job-requirements matrix for a job.

4-8. In a company with only 25 employees, is there less need for job descriptions? Why or why not?

Individual and Group Activities

4-9. Working individually or in groups, obtain copies of job descriptions for clerical positions at the college or university where you study, or the firm where you work. What types of information do they contain? Do they give you enough information to explain what the job involves and how to do it? How would you improve on the description?

4-10. Working individually or in groups, use O*NET to develop a job description for your professor in this class. Based on that, use your judgment to develop a job specification. Compare your conclusions with those of other students or groups. Were there any significant differences? What do you think accounted for the differences?

4-11. Appendices A and B at the end of this book (pages 614–634) list the knowledge someone studying for the HRCI (Appendix A) or SHRM (Appendix B) certification exam needs to have in each area of human resource management

(such as in Strategic Management and Workforce Planning). In groups of several students, do four things: (1) review Appendix A and/or B; (2) identify the material in this chapter that relates to the Appendix A and/or Appendix B required knowledge lists; (3) write four multiple-choice exam questions on this material that you believe would be suitable for inclusion in the HRCI exam and/or the SHRM exam; and (4) if time permits, have someone from your team post your team's questions in front of the class, so that students in all teams can answer the exam questions created by the other teams.

Experiential Exercise

The Instructor's Job Description

Written and copyrighted by Gary Dessler, PhD.

Purpose: The purpose of this exercise is to give you experience in developing a job description, by developing one for your instructor.

Required Understanding: You should understand the mechanics of job analysis and be thoroughly familiar with the job analysis questionnaires. (See Figures 4-4 and 4-9.)

How to Set Up the Exercise/Instructions: Set up groups of several students for this exercise. As in all exercises in this book, the groups should be separated and should not converse with each other. Half of the groups in the class will develop the job description using the job analysis questionnaire (Figure 4-4), and the other half of the groups will develop it using the job description questionnaire (Figure 4-9). Each student should review his or her questionnaire (as appropriate) before joining his or her group.

4-12. Each group should do a job analysis of the instructor's job: Half of the groups will use the Figure 4-4 job analysis questionnaire for this purpose, and half will use the Figure 4-9 job description questionnaire.

4-13. Based on this information, each group will develop its own job description and job specification for the instructor.

4-14. Next, each group should choose a partner group, one that developed the job description and job specification using the alternate method. (A group that used the job analysis questionnaire should be paired with a group that used the job description questionnaire.)

4-15. Finally, within each of these new combined groups, compare and critique each of the two sets of job descriptions and job specifications. Did each job analysis method provide different types of information? Which seems superior? Does one seem more advantageous for some types of jobs than others?

CHAPTER 4

Application Case

The Flood

Written and copyrighted by Gary Dessler, PhD.

In August 2017, hurricane Maria hit Miami, Florida, and the Optima Air Filter Company. Many employees' homes were devastated. Optima found that it had to hire almost three completely new crews, one for each shift. The problem was that the "old-timers" had known their jobs so well that no one had ever bothered to draw up job descriptions for them. When about 30 new employees began taking their places, there was general confusion about what they should do and how they should do it.

The flood quickly became old news to the firm's out-of-state customers, who wanted filters, not excuses. Phil Mann, the firm's president, was at his wits' end. He had about 30 new employees, 10 old-timers, and his original factory supervisor, Maybelline. He decided to meet with Linda Lowe, a consultant from the local university's business school. She immediately had the old-timers fill out a job questionnaire that listed all their duties. Arguments ensued almost at once: Both Phil and Maybelline thought the old-timers were exaggerating to make themselves look more important, and the old-timers insisted that the lists faithfully reflected their duties. Meanwhile, the customers clamored for their filters.

Questions

4-16. Should Phil and Linda ignore the old-timers' protests and write the job descriptions as they see fit? Why? Why not? How would you go about resolving the differences?

4-17. How would you have conducted the job analysis? What should Phil do now?

Continuing Case

Carter Cleaning Company

Written and copyrighted by Gary Dessler, PhD.

The Job Description

Based on her review of the stores, Jennifer concluded that one of the first matters she had to attend to involved developing job descriptions for her store managers.

As Jennifer tells it, her lessons regarding job descriptions in her basic management and HR management courses were insufficient to convince her of the pivotal role job descriptions actually play in the smooth functioning of an enterprise. Many times during her first few weeks on the job, Jennifer found herself asking one of her store managers why he was violating what she knew to be recommended company policies and procedures. Repeatedly, the answers were either "Because I didn't know it was my job" or "Because I didn't know that was the way we were supposed to do it." Jennifer knew that a job description, along with a set of standards and procedures that specified what was to be done and how to do it would go a long way toward alleviating this problem.

In general, the store manager is responsible for directing all store activities in such a way that quality work is produced, customer relations and sales are maximized, and profitability is maintained through effective control of labor, supply, and energy costs. In accomplishing that general aim, a specific store manager's duties and responsibilities include quality control, store appearance and cleanliness, customer relations, bookkeeping and cash management, cost control and productivity, damage control, pricing, inventory control, spotting and cleaning, machine maintenance, purchasing, employee safety, hazardous waste removal, human resource administration, and pest control.

The questions that Jennifer had to address follow.

Questions

4-18. What should be the format and final form of the store manager's job description?

4-19. Is it practical to specify standards and procedures in the body of the job description, or should these be kept separate?

4-20. How should Jennifer go about collecting the information required for the standards, procedures, and job description?

4-21. What, in your opinion, should the store manager's job description look like and contain?

Translating Strategy into HR Policies and Practices Case*,§

**The accompanying strategy map for this chapter is in MyLab Management; the overall map on the inside back cover of this text outlines the relationships involved.*

Improving Performance at the Hotel Paris

The New Job Descriptions

The Hotel Paris's competitive strategy is "To use superior guest service to differentiate the Hotel Paris properties, and to thereby increase the length of stay and return rate of guests, and thus boost revenues and profitability." HR manager Lisa Cruz must now formulate functional policies and activities that support this competitive strategy and boost performance by eliciting the required employee behaviors and competencies.

As an experienced human resource director, the Hotel Paris's Lisa Cruz knew that recruitment and selection processes invariably influenced employee competencies and behavior and, through them, the company's bottom line. Everything about the workforce—its collective skills, morale, experience, and motivation—depended on attracting and then selecting the right employees.

In reviewing the Hotel Paris's employment systems, she was therefore concerned that virtually all the company's job descriptions were out of date, and that many jobs had no descriptions at all. She knew that without accurate job descriptions, all her improvement efforts would be in vain. After all, if you don't know a job's duties, responsibilities, and human requirements, how can you decide whom to hire or how to train them? To create human resource policies and practices that would produce employee competencies and behaviors needed to achieve the hotel's strategic aims, Lisa's team first had to produce a set of usable job descriptions.

A brief analysis, conducted with her company's CFO, reinforced that observation. They chose departments across the hotel chain that did and did not have updated job descriptions. While they understood that many other factors might be influencing the results, they believed that the statistical relationships they observed did suggest that having job descriptions had a positive influence on various employee behaviors and competencies. Perhaps having the descriptions facilitated the employee selection process, or perhaps the departments with the descriptions just had better managers. In any case, Lisa received the go-ahead to design new job descriptions for the chain.

While the resulting job descriptions included numerous traditional duties and responsibilities, most also included several competencies unique to each job. For example, job descriptions for the front-desk clerks included competencies such as "able to check a guest in or out in five minutes or less." Most service employees' descriptions included the competency, "able to exhibit patience and guest supportiveness even when busy with other activities." Lisa knew that including these competencies would make it easier for her team to devise useful employee selection, training, and evaluation processes.

Questions

In teams or individually:

4-22. Based on the hotel's stated strategy and on what you learned here in Chapter 4 of Dessler *Human Resource Management*, list at least four more important employee behaviors important for the Hotel Paris's staff to exhibit.

4-23. If time permits, spend some time prior to class observing the front-desk clerk at a local hotel. In any case, create a job description for a Hotel Paris front-desk clerk.

§ Written and copyrighted by Gary Dessler, PhD.

Writing Assignments

4-24. What is job analysis? How can you make use of the information it provides?

4-25. Explain what a competencies model is and what the model would look like for the job of university professor.

MyLab Management Try It!

How would you apply the concepts and skills you learned in this chapter? If your professor has assigned this activity, go to the Assignments section of **www.pearson.com/mylab/management** to complete the simulation.

PERSONAL INVENTORY ASSESSMENTS

Go to **www.pearson.com/mylab/management** to complete the Personal Inventory Assessment related to this chapter.

Key Terms

talent management, 99
job analysis, 100
job description, 100
job specifications, 100
organization chart, 102
process chart, 102
workflow analysis, 102
business process reengineering, 103
job enlargement, 103
job rotation, 103
job enrichment, 103
diary/log, 108
position analysis questionnaire (PAQ), 108
Standard Occupational Classification (SOC), 115
job-requirements matrix, 121
task statement, 121
competency-based job analysis, 123

CHAPTER 4

Endnotes

1. Daimler is expanding this plant; see Gail Kalinoski, "Daimler AG to Invest $1B in AL Mercedes-Benz Facility," October 20, 2017, *Commercial Property Executive*, https://www.cpexecutive.com/post/daimler-ag-to-invest-1b-in-al-mercedes-benz-facilities/, February 2, 2018.
2. See, for example, Toni Hodges DeTuncq and Lynn Schmidt, "Examining Integrated Talent Management," *TD*, September 2013, pp. 31–35; and T. N. Krisãan and Hugh Scullion, "Talent Management and Dynamic View of Talent in Small and Medium Enterprises," *Human Resource Management Review*, 27 (2017), pp. 431–441.
3. www.talent_management101.com, accessed December 10, 2007; and www.astd.org/Publications/Blogs/ASTD-Blog/2009/05/How-DoYou-Define-Talent-Management, accessed June 16, 2014. See also Nikki Dries, "Talent Management, from Phenomenon to Theory: Introduction to the Special Issue," *Human Resource Management Review*, 23 (2013), pp. 267–271.
4. https://go.oracle.com/LP=36875?elqCampaignId=48547&src1=ad:pas:bi:dg:hcm&src2=wwmk160606p00037c0002&SC=sckw=WWMK160606P00037C0002, accessed February 2, 2017.
5. www.silkRoadTech.com, accessed December 10, 2007; http://www.silkroad.com/, accessed February 2, 2017.
6. For a good discussion of job analysis, see James Clifford, "Job Analysis: Why Do It, and How Should It Be Done?" *Public Personnel Management* 23, no. 2 (Summer 1994), pp. 321–340; and "Job Analysis," www.paq.com/index.cfm?FuseAction=bulletins.job-analysis, accessed February 3, 2009.
7. One writer calls job analysis "the hub of virtually all human resource management activities necessary for the successful functioning organizations." See Parbudyal Singh, "Job Analysis for a Changing Workplace," *Human Resource Management Review* 18 (2008), p. 87.
8. https://www.ere.net/how-to-write-a-rocking-job-description-for-recruitment/ accessed February 2, 2018.
9. Richard Henderson, *Compensation Management: Rewarding Performance* (Upper Saddle River, NJ: Prentice Hall, 1994), pp. 139–150. See also T. A. Stetz et al., "New Tricks for an Old Dog: Visualizing Job Analysis Results," *Public Personnel Management* 38, no. 1 (Spring 2009), pp. 91–100.
10. Based on Ron Miller, "Streamlining Claims Processing," *eWeek* 23, no. 25 (June 19, 2006), pp. 33, 35.
11. Ron Miller, "Streamlining Claims Processing," *eWeek* 23, no. 25 (June 19, 2006), pp. 33, 35.
12. Darin Hartley, "Job Analysis at the Speed of Reality," *TD*, September 2004, pp. 20–22.
13. For a recent example, see, for example, Frederick P. Morgeson, Edited by Steven G. Rogelberg *The SAGE Encyclopedia of Industrial and Organizational Psychology*, 2nd ed., https://msu.edu/~morgeson/morgeson_2017b.pdf, accessed February 2, 2018.
14. Wayne Cascio, *Applied Psychology in Human Resource Management* (Upper Saddle River, NJ: Prentice Hall, 1998), p. 142. Distortion of information is a potential problem with all self-report methods of gathering information. See, for example, http://apps.opm.gov/ADT/ContentFiles/AssessmentDecisionGuide071807.pdf, accessed October 1, 2011.
15. Frederick Morgeson et al., "Self Presentation Processes in Job Analysis: A Field Experiment Investigating Inflation in Abilities, Tasks, and Competencies," *Journal of Applied Psychology* 89, no. 4 (November 4, 2004), pp. 674–686; and Frederick Morgeson and Stephen

Humphrey, "The Work Design Questionnaire (WDQ): Developing and Validating a Comprehensive Measure for Assessing Job Design and the Nature of Work," *Journal of Applied Psychology* 91, no. 6 (2006), pp. 1321–1339.

16. Note that the PAQ (and other quantitative techniques) can also be used for job evaluation, which is explained in Chapter 11.
17. http://www.paq.com/, accessed February 2, 2017.
18. We will see that job evaluation is the process through which jobs are compared to one another and their values determined for pay purposes. Some use the PAQ for job evaluation.
19. Jack Smith and Milton Hakel, "Convergence Among Data Sources, Response Bias, and Reliability and Validity of a Structured Job Analysis Questionnaire," *Personnel Psychology* 32 (Winter 1979), pp. 677–692. See also Frederick Morgeson and Stephen Humphrey, "The Work Design Questionnaire (WDQ): Developing and Validating a Comprehensive Measure for Assessing Job Design and the Nature of Work," *Journal of Applied Psychology* 91, no. 6 (2006), pp. 1321–1339; www.paq.com/index.cfm?FuseAction=bulletins.job-analysis, accessed February 3, 2009.
20. www.paq.com/index.cfm?FuseAction=bulletins.job-analysis, accessed February 3, 2009.
21. For an online version see https://occupationalinfo.org/, accessed February 2, 2018.
22. Another technique, *functional job analysis*, is similar to the DOL method. However, it rates the job not just on data, people, and things, but also on the extent to which performing the task requires four other things—specific instructions, reasoning and judgment, mathematical ability, and verbal and language facilities.
23. This is based on Dianna Stone et al., "Factors Affecting the Effectiveness and Acceptance of Electronic Selection Systems," *Human Resource Management Review* 23 (2013), pp. 53–54.
24. Ibid.
25. Ibid., p. 295.
26. You can access the site at www.onetcenter.org/content.html/4.A#cm_4.A, accessed June 20, 2015.
27. Digitizing the information also enables the employer to quantify, tag, and electronically store and access it more readily. Lauren McEntire et al., "Innovations in Job Analysis: Development and Application of Metrics to Analyze Job Data," *Human Resource Management Review* 16 (2006), pp. 310–323.
28. See, for example, Kathryn Tyler, "Job Worth Doing: Update Descriptions," *HR Magazine*, January 2013, pp. 47–49.
29. This feature is based on Rebecca Ruiz, "Care for the Caregivers: Child-Care Providers Have Long Been Thought of as Full-Time Baby Sitters. The Government Can Help Them Become Well-Paid Professionals." *The American Prospect* 21.8 (2010), A17+. *Academic OneFile.* Web. 26 Mar. 2013.
30. Regarding this discussion, see Henderson, *Compensation Management*, pp. 175–184. See also Louisa Wah, "The Alphabet Soup of Job Titles," *Management Review* 87, no. 6 (June 1, 1998), pp. 40–43.
31. Ashley Ross, "Job Titles Retailored to Fit," *The New York Times*, September 1, 2013, p. 11.
32. "Creative Job Titles Can Energize Workers," *Harvard Business Review*, May 2016, pp. 24, 25.
33. Ben Kesling and Gordon Lubold, "Navy Restores Traditional Job Titles," *The Wall Street Journal*, December 22, 2016, p. 87.
34. For discussions of writing job descriptions, see James Evered, "How to Write a Good Job Description," *Supervisory Management*, April 1981, pp. 14–19; Roger J. Plachy, "Writing Job Descriptions That Get Results," *Personnel*, October 1987, pp. 56–58; and Jean Phillips and Stanley Gulley, *Strategic Staffing* (Upper Saddle River, NJ: Pearson Education, 2012), pp. 89–95.
35. Evered, "How to Write a Good Job Description," p. 16.
36. Ibid.
37. Ibid.
38. http://hiring.monster.com/hr/hr-best-practices/recruiting-hiring-advice/job-descriptions/marketing-director-job-description-sample.aspx, accessed February 3, 2017.
39. https://www.careerplanner.com/JobDescSearchTool.cfm, accessed February 3, 2017.
40. www.linkedin.com/groups/Best-job-descriptions-40949.S.201279941, accessed March 26, 2013.
41. http://academicaffairs.ucsd.edu/staffhr/classification/task--statements.html, accessed March 27, 2013.
42. www.eeoc.gov/facts/ada17.html, accessed July 17, 2013.
43. Deborah Kearney, *Reasonable Accommodations: Job Descriptions in the Age of ADA, OSHA, and Workers Comp* (New York: Van Nostrand Reinhold, 1994), p. 9. See also Paul Starkman, "The ADA's Essential Job Function Requirements: Just How Essential Does an Essential Job Function Have to Be?" *Employee Relations Law Journal* 26, no. 4 (Spring 2001), pp. 43–102; and Benjamin Wolkinson and Sarah Wolkinson, "The Pregnant Police Officer's Overtime Duties and Forced Leave Policies under Title VII, the ADA, and FMLA," *Employee Relations Law Journal* 36, no. 1 (Summer 2010), pp. 3–20.
44. Kearney, *Reasonable Accommodations.*
45. O*Net™ is a trademark of the U.S. Department of Labor, Employment, and Training Administration. https://www.onetonline.org/, accessed February 3, 2017.
46. See, for example, Christelle Lapolice et al., "Linking O*NET Descriptors to Occupational Literacy Requirements Using Job Component Validation," *Personnel Psychology* 61 (2008), pp. 405–441.
47. Mariani, "Replace with a Database."
48. https://support.office.com/en-us/article/Create-an-organization-chart-21ADA00D-82E6-4340-9033-439AC2843C37, accessed February 3, 2017.
49. https://www.onetonline.org/, accessed February 3, 2017.
50. https://www.onetonline.org/find/quick?s=retail+sales, accessed February 3, 2018.
51. https://www.onetonline.org/link/summary/41-2031.00, accessed February 3, 2018.
52. Based on Ernest J. McCormick and Joseph Tiffin, *Industrial Psychology* (Upper Saddle River, NJ: Prentice Hall, 1974), pp. 56–61.
53. Steven Hunt, "Generic Work Behavior: An Investigation into the Dimensions of Entry-Level, Hourly Job Performance," *Personnel Psychology* 49 (1996), pp. 51–83.
54. "Are the Best People Being Promoted?" *Harvard Business Review*, September 2013, p. 89.
55. https://www.lyft.com/drive-with-lyft?1v=jb_apply&utm_source=perengo&ref=DRIVER500BONUS&utm_jobtitle=Lyft%20Driver&adgroup=SJC&var3=68543f9f6da1825c-1485814525700&adname=68543f9f6da1825c-1485814525700&scid=2&_sp=68543f9f6da1825c.1485814525700; http://www.idrivewithuber.com/uber-driver-requirements/, both accessed January 30, 2017.
56. Jean Phillips and Stanley Gully, *Strategic Staffing* (Upper Saddle River, NJ: Pearson Education, 2012), pp. 96–102.
57. Ibid., p. 102.
58. "Hiring Engaged and Self-Motivated New Employees Is Often the Intangible Ingredient That Eludes Managers in the Selection Process," http://www.HR.com, February 21, 2006, accessed January 21, 2014.
59. Paul Marciano, "How to Hire Engaged Employees," http://www.monster.com/about/b/how-to-hire-engaged-employees, accessed June 20, 2015.
60. Jeffrey Shippmann et al., "The Practice of Competency Modeling," *Personnel Psychology* 53, no. 3 (2000), p. 703.
61. Michael Campion et al., "Doing Competencies Well: Best Practices in Competency Modeling," *Personnel Psychology* 64 (2011), pp. 225–262.
62. www.shrm.org/certification/Documents/SHRM-BoCK-FINAL4.pdf, p. 4, accessed March 20, 2015.
63. Richard S. Wellins et al., "Nine Best Practices for Effective Talent Management," DDI Development Dimensions International, Inc. www.ddiworld.com/DDIWorld/media/white-papers/ninebestpracticetalentmanagement_wp_ddi.pdf?extpdf, accessed August 20, 2011. For a discussion of competency modelling, see Campion et al., "Doing Competencies Well."
64. https://www.cpexecutive.com/post/daimler-ag-to-invest-1b-in-al-mercedes-benz-facilities/, accessed February 2, 2018.
65. Based on Lindsay Chappell, "Mercedes Factories Embrace a New Order," *Automotive News*, May 28, 2001. See also www.autoblog.com/2009/03/23/rumormillmercedes-benz-expected-to-expandalabama-plant, accessed March 25, 2009, http://mbusi.com, accessed August 20, 2011.
66. This is adapted from Campion et al., "Doing Competencies Well."
67. Ibid.
68. See, for example, Carol Spicer, "Building a Competency Model," *HR Magazine*, April 2009, pp. 34–36.

Sorbis/Shutterstock

Personnel Planning and Recruiting

LEARNING OBJECTIVES

When you finish studying this chapter, you should be able to:

5-1 **Define** workforce planning, and explain how to develop a workforce plan.

5-2 **Explain** the need for effective recruiting and how to make recruiting more effective.

5-3 **Discuss** the main internal sources of candidates.

5-4 **Describe** how to use recruiting to improve employee engagement.

5-5 **Discuss** the main outside sources of candidates, and create an employment ad.

5-6 **Explain** how to recruit a more diverse workforce.

5-7 **Discuss** practical guidelines for obtaining application information.

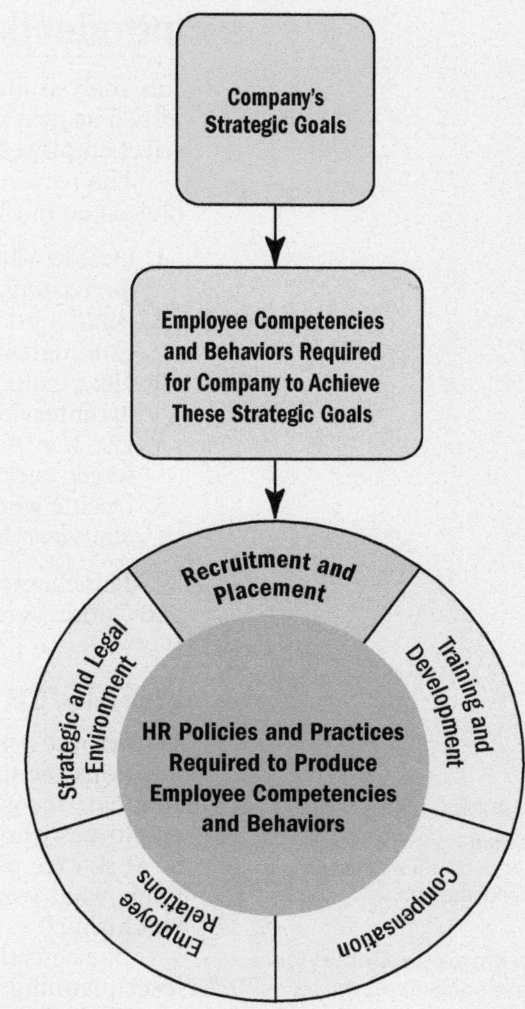

Like most luxury hotel chains, Four Seasons builds its strategy around offering superior customer service, and doing that requires highly motivated and high-morale employees.[1] Therefore, in thinking through how to recruit employees, Four Seasons managers decided to use recruitment to help increase the employee motivation and morale that they believed would lead to improved customer service. We will see what they did.

WHERE ARE WE NOW . . .

In Chapter 4, we discussed job analysis and the methods managers use to create job descriptions, job specifications, and competency profiles or models.The purpose of this chapter is to improve your effectiveness in recruiting candidates. The topics we discuss include include **Workforce Planning and Forecasting, Why Effective Recruiting is Important, Internal Sources of Recruits, Employee Engagement Guide, Outside Sources of Recruits, Recruiting a More Diverse Workforce,** and **Developing and Using Application Forms.** Then, in Chapter 6, we'll turn to the methods managers use to select the best employees from this applicant pool.

Introduction

Job analysis identifies the duties and human requirements of each of the company's jobs. The next step is to decide which of these jobs you need to fill, and to recruit and select employees for them.

The recruiting and selecting process can be envisioned as a series of hurdles, as illustrated in Figure 5-1: [2]

1. Decide what positions to fill, through *workforce/personnel planning and forecasting*.
2. Build a pool of candidates for these jobs, by *recruiting* internal or external candidates.
3. Have candidates complete *application forms* and perhaps undergo initial screening interviews.
4. Use *selection tools* like tests, background investigations, and physical exams to screen candidates.
5. Decide who to make an offer to, by having the supervisor and perhaps others *interview* the candidates.

This chapter focuses on personnel planning and on recruiting employees. Chapters 6 and 7 address tests, background checks, physical exams, and interviews.

Workforce Planning and Forecasting

LEARNING OBJECTIVE 5-1
Define workforce planning, and explain how to develop a workforce plan.

workforce (or employment or personnel) planning
The process of deciding what positions the firm will have to fill, and how to fill them.

Workforce (or employment or personnel) planning is the process of deciding what positions the firm will have to fill, and how to fill them. Its aim is to identify and to eliminate the gaps between the employer's projected workforce needs and the current employees who might be suitable for filling those needs. The manager should engage in workforce planning before recruiting and hiring employees. After all, if you don't know what your employment needs will be in the next few months or years, why are you hiring?

One consulting firm's workforce planning methodology illustrates the basic workforce planning process.[3]

First, Towers Watson *reviews the client's business plan and workforce data* (for instance, on how revenue influences staffing levels). This helps them understand how projected business changes may influence the client's headcount and skills requirements.

Second, they *forecast and identify what positions the firm will have to fill and potential workforce gaps*; this helps them understand what new future positions they'll have to fill, and what current employees may be promotable into them.

Third, they develop a *workforce strategic plan*; here they prioritize key workforce gaps (such as, what positions will have to be filled, and who do we have who can fill them?) and identify specific (recruitment, training, and other) plans for filling any gaps.

FIGURE 5-1 Steps in Recruitment and Selection Process

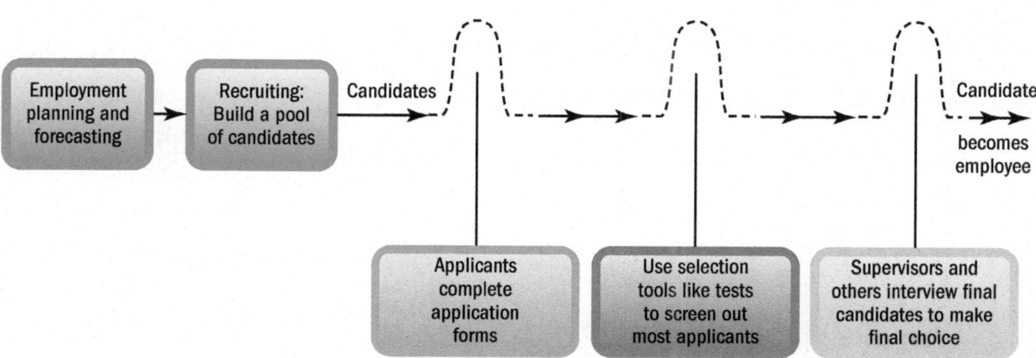

The recruitment and selection process is a series of hurdles aimed at selecting the best candidate for the job.

Workforce scan

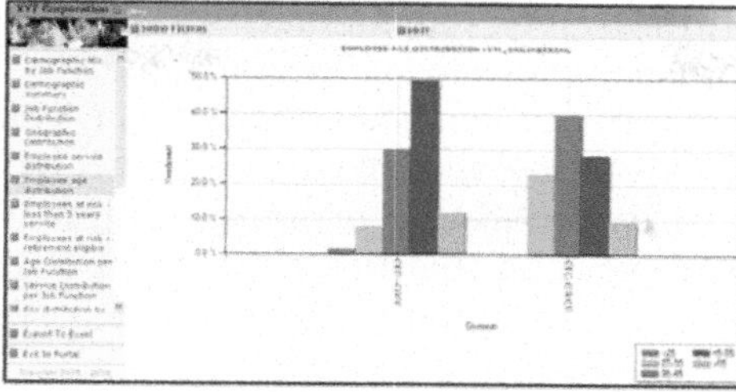

Dashboards

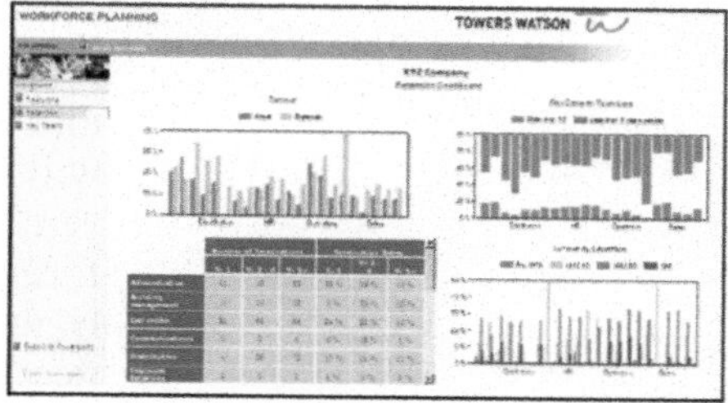

Workforce projection model

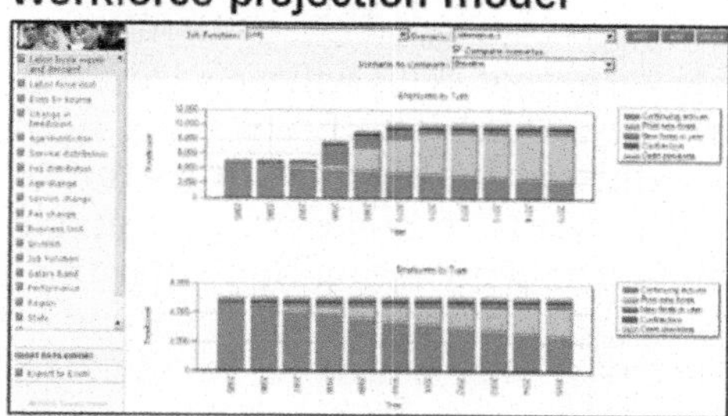

External labour scan

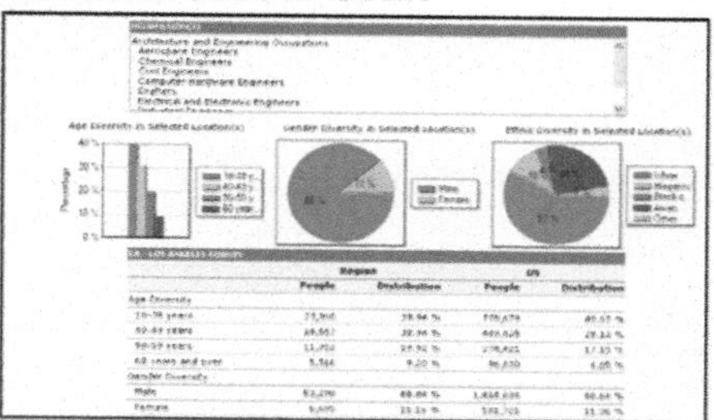

The dashboards, which are part of Towers Watson's workforce planning Internet software, help clients manage the workforce planning process.

Source: © Towers Watson 2012. Used with permission.

Finally, they implement the plans (for instance, new recruiting and training programs), and use various metrics to monitor the process.

Towers Watson clients can use its special "MAPS" software to facilitate this workforce planning process. MAPS contains dashboards (see the preceding four exhibits). The manager uses these, for instance, to monitor key recruitment metrics and for a detailed analysis of the current workforce and historical workforce trends.

Workforce planning embraces all future positions, from maintenance clerk to CEO. However, we'll see that most firms call the process of deciding how to fill executive jobs *succession planning*.[4]

Strategy and Workforce Planning

Workforce planning should be an integral part of the firm's strategic planning process. For example, plans to enter new businesses, to build new plants, or to reduce activities will all influence the personnel skills the employer needs and the positions to be filled. At the same time, decisions regarding *how* to fill these positions will require other HR plans, such as training and recruiting plans. The Strategic Context feature illustrates.

IMPROVING PERFORMANCE: *THE STRATEGIC CONTEXT*

Four Seasons[5]

As noted, Four Seasons builds its strategy around offering superior customer service, and that requires highly motivated and high-morale employees.[6] Four Seasons uses its recruitment practices to inspire such motivation and morale. One way Four Seasons does this is by filling hotel positions around the world with internal transfers. In one year, for instance, about 280 employees relocated from hotels from one country to another within the Four Seasons chain. Employees love it. It gives them a chance to see the world, while building a career with a great hotel chain.[7] And it's great for Four Seasons too, because the resulting high morale and motivation supports Four Seasons' strategic goal of superior customer service. In other words, Four Seasons uses recruitment practices that produce the excellent service the chain needs to achieve its strategic goals.

MyLab Management Talk About It 1

If your professor has assigned this, go to the Assignments section of **www.pearson.com/mylab/management** to complete these discussion questions. Can you think of any other benefits Four Seasons may derive from its policy of transferring employees among its hotels? What are they?

Like any good plans, employment plans are built on forecasts—basic assumptions about the future. Here, the manager will usually need three sets of employment forecasts: one for *personnel needs* (demand), one for the supply of *inside candidates*, and one for the supply of *outside candidates*. (As at Four Seasons, the employer will usually have to decide whether to fill projected openings internally with current employees or externally by bringing in new people). Then with these three forecasts, the manager can identify needs-supply gaps, and develop training and other plans to fill the anticipated gaps. We will start with forecasting personnel needs/demand.

Forecasting Personnel Needs (Labor Demand)

How many people with what skills will we need? Managers consider several factors.[8]

Most importantly, a firm's future staffing needs reflect demand for its products or services, adjusted for changes in its turnover rate and productivity, and for changes the firm plans to make in its strategic goals. Forecasting workforce demand therefore starts with estimating what the demand will be for your products or services. Short term, management should be concerned with daily, weekly, and seasonal forecasts.[9] For example, retailers track daily sales trends because they know, for instance, that Mother's Day produces a jump in business and a need for additional store staff. Seasonal forecasts are critical for retailers contemplating end-of-year holiday sales, and for many firms such as landscaping and air-conditioning vendors. Longer term, managers will try to get a sense for future demand by speaking with customers and by following industry publications and economic forecasts. Such future predictions won't be precise, but should help you address the potential changes in demand.

The basic process for forecasting personnel needs is to forecast revenues first. Then estimate the size of the staff required to support this sales volume. However, managers must also consider other factors. These include projected turnover, decisions to upgrade (or downgrade) products or services, productivity changes, financial resources, and decisions to enter or leave businesses. The basic tools for projecting personnel needs include trend analysis, ratio analysis, and the scatter plot.

trend analysis
Study of a firm's past employment needs over a period of years to predict future needs.

TREND ANALYSIS **Trend analysis** means studying variations in the firm's employment levels over the past few years. For example, compute the number of employees at the end of each of the last 5 years in each subgroup (like sales, production, secretarial, and administrative) to identify trends.

Trend analysis can provide an initial rough estimate of future staffing needs. However, employment levels rarely depend just on the passage of time. Other factors (like productivity and retirements, for instance), and changing skill needs will influence impending workforce needs.

ratio analysis
A forecasting technique for determining future staff needs by using ratios between, for example, sales volume and number of employees needed.

RATIO ANALYSIS Another simple approach, **ratio analysis,** means making forecasts based on the historical ratio between (1) some causal factor (like sales volume), and (2) the number of employees required (such as number of salespeople). For example, suppose a salesperson traditionally generates $500,000 in sales. If the sales revenue to salespeople ratio remains the same, you would require six new salespeople next year (each of whom produces an extra $500,000) to produce a hoped-for extra $3 million in sales.

Like trend analysis, ratio analysis assumes that things like productivity remain about the same. If sales productivity were to rise or fall, the ratio of sales to salespeople would change.

scatter plot
A graphical method used to help identify the relationship between two variables.

THE SCATTER PLOT **A scatter plot** shows graphically how two variables—such as sales and your firm's staffing levels—are related. If they are, then if you can forecast the business activity (like sales), you should also be able to estimate your personnel needs.

For example, suppose a 500-bed hospital expects to expand to 1,200 beds over the next 5 years. The human resource director wants to forecast how many registered nurses the hospital will need. The human resource director realizes she must determine the relationship between hospital size (in number of beds) and number of nurses required. She calls eight hospitals of various sizes and finds this:

Size of Hospital (Number of Beds)	Number of Registered Nurses
200	240
300	260
400	470
500	500
600	620
700	660
800	820
900	860

Figure 5-2's graph compares hospital size and number of nurses. If the two are related, then the points you plot (from the data in the table above) will tend to fall on a straight line, as here. If you carefully draw in a line to minimize the distances between the line and each one of the plotted points, you will be able to estimate the number of nurses needed for each hospital size. Thus, for a 1,200-bed hospital, the human resource director would assume she needs about 1,210 nurses.

While simple, tools like scatter plots have drawbacks.[10]

1. Historical sales/personnel relationships assume that the firm's existing activities and skill needs will continue as is.
2. They tend to reward managers for adding employees, irrespective of the company's needs.
3. They tend to institutionalize existing ways of doing things, even in the face of change.

Computerized systems (like Towers Watson's) and Excel spreadsheets help managers translate estimates of projected productivity and sales levels into forecastable personnel requirements. *Computerized forecasts* enable managers to build more variables into their personnel projections. Thus, at Chelan County Public Utility District, the development manager built a statistical model encompassing such things as age, tenure,

FIGURE 5-2 Determining the Relationship between Hospital Size and Number of Nurses

Note: After fitting the line, you can project how many employees you'll need, given your projected volume.

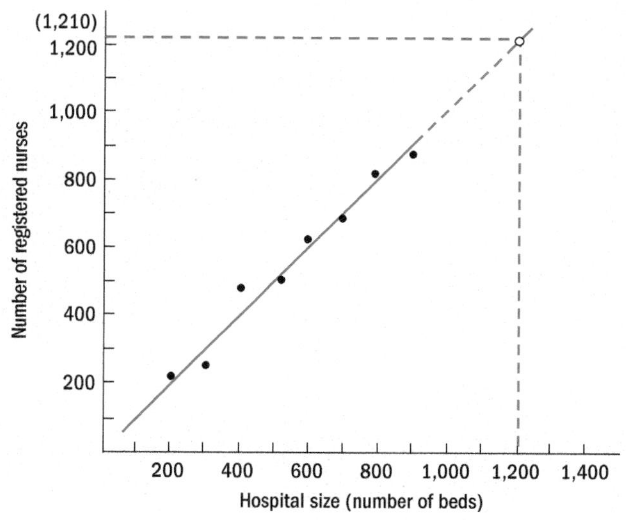

turnover rate, and time to train new employees.[11] This model helped quickly identify five occupational "hotspots" among 33 occupational groups at the company. This in turn prompted Chelan to focus more closely on creating plans to retain and hire, for instance, more systems operators.[12]

MANAGERIAL JUDGMENT Few historical trends, ratios, or relationships will continue unchanged into the future. Judgment is thus needed to adjust the forecast. Important factors that may modify your initial forecast of personnel requirements include decisions to upgrade quality or enter into new markets; technological and administrative changes resulting in increased productivity; and financial resources available, for instance, a projected budget crunch.

Forecasting the Supply of Inside Candidates

The personnel demand forecast provides only half the staffing equation, by answering the question: "How many employees in what positions will we *need*?" Next, the manager must forecast the *supply* (availability) of inside and outside candidates.

Most firms start with possible inside candidates. The main task here is determining which current employees are qualified or trainable for the projected openings. Department managers or owners of smaller firms can use manual devices to track employee qualifications (or will simply know who can do what). For example, you can create your own *personnel skills inventory and development record form.*[13] For each current employee, list the person's skills, education, company-sponsored courses taken, career and development interests, languages, desired assignments, and other relevant experiences. Computerized versions of skills inventory systems are also available.[14]

personnel replacement charts
Company records showing present performance and promotability of inside candidates for the most important positions.

position replacement card
A card prepared for each position in a company to show possible replacement candidates and their qualifications.

Personnel replacement charts (Figure 5-3) are another option, particularly for the firm's top positions. They show the present performance and promotability for each position's potential replacement. As an alternative, with a **position replacement card** you create a card for each position, showing possible replacements as well as their present performance, promotion potential, and training.

Larger firms obviously can't track the qualifications of hundreds or thousands of employees manually. They therefore computerize this information, using various packaged software systems such as Survey Analytics's Skills Inventory Software.

FIGURE 5-3 Personnel or Management Replacement Chart Showing Development Needs of Potential Future Division Vice Presidents

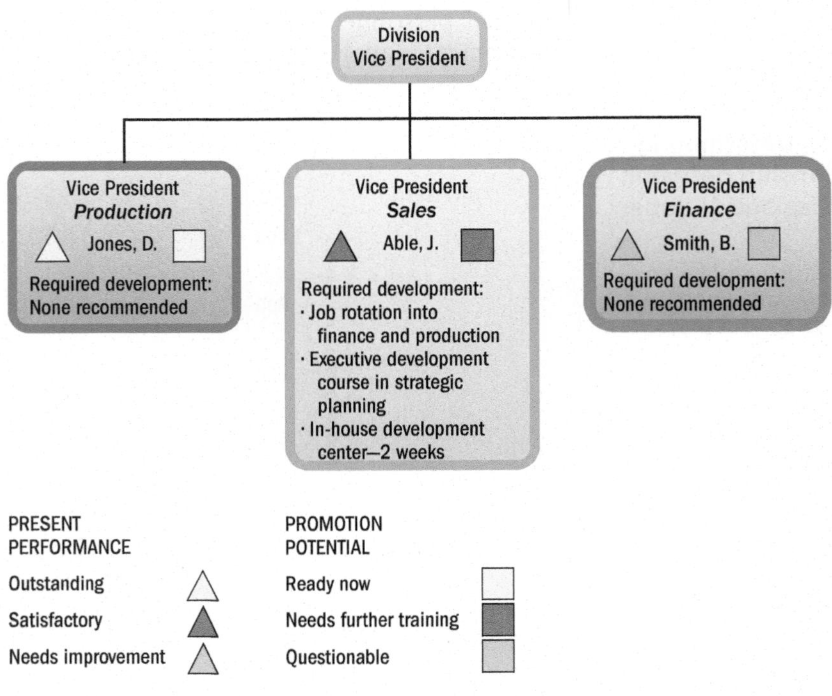

Skills inventory systems such as one from Perceptyx (www.perceptyx.com) enables employers to collect and compile employee skills information in real time via online employee surveys. Skills inventory programs help management anticipate staffing and skills shortages, and also facilitate workforce planning, recruitment, and training.[15] They typically include items like *work experience codes, product knowledge*, the employee's *level of familiarity* with the employer's product lines or services, the person's *industry experience, formal education*, industry *experiences*, foreign *language* skills, *relocation* limitations, *career* interests, and *performance* appraisals.

The usual skills inventory process is for the employee, the supervisor, and human resource manager to enter information about the employee's background, experience, and skills via the system. Then, when a manager needs someone for a position, he or she uses key words to describe the position's specifications (for instance, in terms of education and skills). The computerized system then produces a list of qualified candidates. As the user of one such system said, "The [SumTotal] platform allows us to track and assess the talent pool and promote people within the company. . . . The succession module helps us to identify who the next senior managers could be and build development plans to help them achieve their potential."[16]

The employer must secure all its employee data.[17] Employees have legal rights regarding who has access to information about them.[18] Internet access makes it relatively easy for more people to access the firm's computerized files.[19] The U.S. Office of Personnel Management lost data on as many as 14 million current and former employees this way.[20] Figure 5-4 summarizes some guidelines for keeping employee data safe.

MARKOV ANALYSIS Employers also use a mathematical process known as *Markov analysis* (or "transition analysis") to forecast availability of internal job candidates. Markov analysis involves creating a matrix that shows the probabilities that employees in the chain of feeder positions for a key job (such as from junior engineer, to engineer, to senior engineer, to engineering supervisor, to director of engineering) will move from position to position and therefore be available to fill the key position.

Forecasting the Supply of Outside Candidates

If there won't be enough skilled inside candidates to fill the anticipated openings (or you want to go outside for another reason), you will turn to outside candidates.

Forecasting workforce availability depends first on the manager's own sense of what's happening in his or her industry and locale. For example, unemployment rates above 7% a few years ago signaled to HR managers that finding good candidates might be easier.[21] The manager then supplements such observations with formal labor market analyses. For example, look for economic projections online from the U.S. Congressional Budget Office (www.cbo.gov) and the Bureau of Labor Statistics (www.bls.gov/emp/ep_pub_occ_projections.htm). You may also want to forecast specific occupations. O*NET (discussed in Chapter 4) reports

FIGURE 5-4 Keeping Data Safe

Source: Reprinted with permission from *HR Magazine*, November 2005. © SHRM.

Since intruders can strike from outside an organization or from within, HR departments can help screen out potential identity thieves by following four basic rules:

- Perform background checks on anyone who is going to have access to personal information.
- If someone with access to personal information is out sick or on leave, don't hire a temporary employee to replace him or her. Instead, bring in a trusted worker from another department.
- Perform random background checks such as random drug tests. Just because someone passed 5 years ago doesn't mean their current situation is the same.
- Limit access to information such as SSNs, health information, and other sensitive data to HR managers who require it to do their jobs.

projections for most occupations. The U.S. Bureau of Labor Statistics publishes annual occupational projections both online and in the *Monthly Labor Review* and in *Occupational Outlook Quarterly*.

Today's emphasis on technology means many applicants may lack basic skills such as math, communication, creativity, and teamwork.[22] Such needs, too, get factored into the employer's workforce and training plans.

Predictive Workforce Monitoring

When a new executive took over staffing at Valero Energy, he reviewed Valero's projected retirements, growth plans, and turnover history. He discovered that projected employment shortfalls were four times what Valero could fill with its current recruitment plans. He formulated new personnel plans for boosting employee retention and for recruiting and screening more candidates.[23]

Most employers review their workforce plans every year or so, but this isn't always sufficient For instance, Valero almost lacked sufficient time to implement a plan to address replacing employees who would soon retire.

Some employers therefore plan continuously: they do *predictive workforce monitoring*. For example, Intel conducts semiannual "Organization Capability Assessments." The staffing department works with the firm's business heads twice a year to assess workforce needs—both immediate and up to 2 years off.[24] Boeing considers various factors when predicting talent gaps as part of its periodic "workforce modeling" process. These include workforce characteristics such as age, retirement eligibility for job groups, economic trends, anticipated increases or decreases in staffing levels, and internal transfers/promotions.[25]

Matching Projected Labor Supply and Demand with a Plan

Workforce planning should culminate in a workforce plan. This plan should identify the positions to be filled; potential internal and external candidates or sources (such as temp agencies) for these positions; the training and promotions moving people into the positions will entail; and the resources that implementing the plan will require, for instance, in recruiter fees, estimated training costs, and interview expenses.[26]

Succession Planning

In 2018, Apple CEO Tim Cook announced that Apple's board had a succession plan for who could become CEO should Cook step down.[27]

succession planning
The ongoing process of systematically identifying, assessing, and developing organizational leadership to enhance performance.

Succession planning involves developing workforce plans for the company's top positions. **Succession planning** is the ongoing process of systematically identifying, assessing, and developing organizational leadership to enhance performance.[28] It entails three main steps: identify key position needs, develop inside candidates, and assess and choose inside (or outside) candidates who will fill the key positions.[29]

First, based on the company's strategic and business plans, top management and the human resource director identify what the company's future key position needs will be. Matters to address include defining key positions and "high potentials," reviewing the company's current talent, and creating (based on the company's strategy) skills profiles for the key positions.[30]

After identifying future key positions, management turns to creating candidates for these jobs. "Creating" means identifying inside (or bringing in outside) candidates and providing them with the developmental experiences they require to be viable candidates. Employers develop high-potential employees through internal training and cross-functional experiences, job rotation, external training, and global/regional assignments.[31]

Finally, succession planning requires assessing these candidates and selecting those who will actually fill the key positions.[32]

As at Apple, the firm's board of directors should ensure that top management succession plans are in place. In fact, monitoring plans for and approving top management appointments is one of a corporate board's essential roles. (The others are overseeing strategy, performance, governance, and integrity.)[33]

EXAMPLE Several years ago, Dole Foods' strategy involved improving financial performance by reducing redundancies and centralizing certain activities, including succession planning.[34] For succession planning, Dole chose software from Pilat. (Several vendors supply succession planning software.[35]) The Pilat system keeps the data on its own servers for a fee. Dole's managers access the program via the Web using a password. They fill out online résumés for themselves, including career interests, and note special considerations such as geographic restrictions.

The managers also assess themselves on several competencies. Then, once the manager provides his or her input, the program notifies that manager's boss, who assesses his or her subordinate and indicates whether the person is promotable. This assessment and the online résumés then go automatically to the division head and the divisional HR director. Dole's senior vice president for human resources then uses the information to create career development plans for each manager, including seminars and other programs.

MyLab Management Apply It!

How does a company actually do workforce planning? If your professor has assigned this activity, go to the Assignments section of **www.pearson.com/mylab/management** to complete the video exercise.

LEARNING OBJECTIVE 5-2

Explain the need for effective recruiting and how to make recruiting more effective.

Why Effective Recruiting Is Important

Assuming the company authorizes you to fill a position, the next step is to build up, through recruiting, an applicant pool.[36] **Employee recruiting** means finding and/or attracting applicants for the employer's open positions.

employee recruiting
Finding and/or attracting applicants for the employer's open positions.

Recruiting is important. If only two candidates apply for two openings, you may have little choice but to hire them. But if 10 or 20 applicants appear, you can use interviews and tests to screen out all but the best.

Improving Recruitment Effectiveness: Recruiters, Sources, and Branding

Of course, it's not just recruiting but effective recruiting that you want. Recruiters, sources, and employer "brand" are important.

In one early study of recruiter effectiveness, subjects were 41 graduating college students who'd been on several job interviews.[37] When asked afterwards why they thought a particular company might be a good fit, 39 mentioned the nature of the job, but 23 said they'd been turned off by the recruiters. For example, some were dressed sloppily; others were rude. Therefore, the employer should carefully select and train recruiters. Training should include interpersonal skills (such as in communicating), and basic knowledge about how to recruit and how EEO laws affect recruiters.

Recruitment sourcing involves determining what your recruitment options (referrals, online ads, and so on) are, and then assessing which are best for the job in question. For assessing which source is best, most employers look at how many applicants the source generates. However quantity doesn't necessarily mean quality. Other effectiveness metrics should include, for each source, how many of its applicants were hired, how well its applicants performed on the job, how many failed and had to be replaced, and applicants' performance in terms of training, absence, and turnover.[38]

Similarly, the employer's *brand* or reputation affects recruiting success. Most obviously, it is futile to recruit if the employer's reputation is that it's an awful place to work.

How does the employer want others to see it as a place to work? The branding often focuses on what it's like to work at the company, including company values and the work environment.[39] GE, for instance, stresses innovation (hiring "bright, interesting people working together on new and exciting projects").[40] Others stress being environmentally responsible.[41]

Job applicants' employer reviews are widely available on sites like glassdoor.com, so employers must be diligent. Ensure that all applicants are treated courteously and that no reviews go unanswered.[42]

The Recruiting Yield Pyramid

recruiting yield pyramid
The historical arithmetic relationships between recruitment leads and invitees, invitees and interviews, interviews and offers made, and offers made and offers accepted.

Filling a handful of positions might require recruiting dozens or hundreds of candidates. Managers therefore use a staffing or **recruiting yield pyramid,** as shown in Figure 5-5, to gauge the staffing issues it needs to address. In Figure 5-5, the company knows it needs 50 new entry-level accountants next year. From experience, the firm also knows the following:

- The ratio of offers made to actual new hires is 2 to 1.
- The ratio of candidates interviewed to offers made is 3 to 2.
- The ratio of candidates invited for interviews to candidates interviewed is about 4 to 3.
- Finally, the firm knows that of six leads that come in from all its recruiting sources, it typically invites only one applicant for an interview—a 6-to-1 ratio.

Therefore, the firm must generate about 1,200 leads to be able to invite in 200 viable candidates of which it interviews about 150, and so on.

KNOW YOUR EMPLOYMENT LAW

Recruiting Employees

As we explained in Chapter 2, numerous federal, state, and local laws and court decisions restrict what employers can and cannot do when recruiting job applicants. In practice, "the key question in all recruitment procedures is whether the method limits qualified applicants from applying."[43] So, for example, gender-specific ads that call for "busboy" or "fireman" would obviously raise red flags. Similarly, courts will often question word-of-mouth recruiting because workers tend to nominate candidates of the same nationality, race, and religion.[44]

Other laws are relevant. For example, it is illegal for employers to conspire not to hire each other's employees. Yet Apple and Google paid over $400 million to settle a claim alleging that they did just that.[45] ■

THE SUPERVISOR'S ROLE Line and staff cooperation in recruitment is essential. The human resource manager charged with filling an open position is seldom very familiar with the job itself. So, for example, the recruiter will want to know from the supervisor what the job really entails and its job specifications, as well as informal things like the supervisor's leadership style and how the team gets along.

HR in Action at the Hotel Paris As they reviewed the details of the Hotel Paris's current recruitment practices, Lisa Cruz and the firm's CFO became increasingly concerned. They found that the recruitment function was totally unmanaged. To see how they handled this, see the case on pages 163–164 of this chapter.

FIGURE 5-5 Recruiting Yield Pyramid

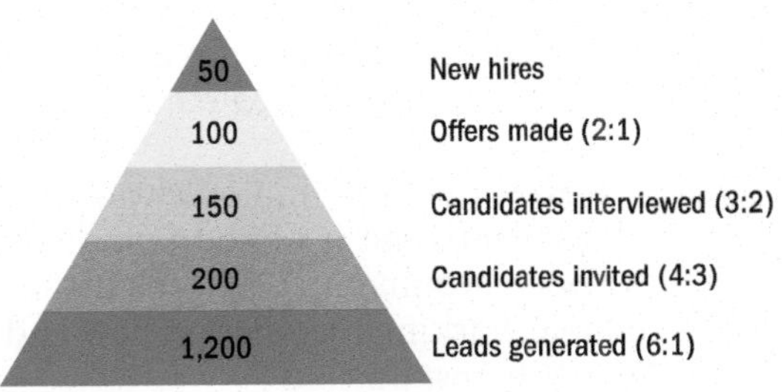

Internal Sources of Candidates

LEARNING OBJECTIVE 5-3

Discuss the main internal sources of candidates.

Recruiting typically brings to mind LinkedIn, employment agencies, and classified ads, but internal sources—in other words, current employees or "hiring from within"—are often the best sources of candidates.

Filling open positions with inside candidates has advantages. There is really no substitute for knowing a candidate's strengths and weaknesses, as you should after working with them for some time. Current employees may also be more committed to the company. Morale and engagement may rise if employees see promotions as rewards for loyalty and competence. And inside candidates should require less orientation and (perhaps) training than outsiders.

There are other advantages. External hires tend to come in at higher salaries than do those promoted internally, and some apparent "stars" hired from outside may still disappoint. On the other hand, some firms—particularly those facing challenges, such as McDonald's—have done very well by bringing in outsiders.[46]

One executive recruiter argues that internal candidates are always better than external ones unless the internal candidates simply can't pass muster. One study concluded that firms that hired their CEOs from inside rather than outside performed better.[47]

Hiring from within can also backfire. Inbreeding is a potential drawback, if new perspectives are required. The process of posting openings and getting inside applicants can also be a waste of time, when the department manager already knows whom he or she wants to hire. Rejected inside applicants may become discontented; telling them why you rejected them and what remedial actions they might take is crucial.

There are some practical rules to use in determining whether to go outside or promote from within. For example, if you need specific skills that aren't currently available in your company, or have to embark on a tough turnaround, or your current succession planning or skills inventory systems are inadequate, it may be best to look outside. On the other hand, if your company is thriving and you have effective succession planning and skills inventories, have the skills you need internally, and have a unique and strong company culture, then look within.[48]

Finding Internal Candidates

job posting
Publicizing an open job to employees (often by literally posting it on bulletin boards) and listing its attributes, like qualifications, supervisor, working schedule, and pay rate.

In a perfect world, the employer will adhere to formal internal-recruitment policies and procedures. These typically rely heavily on job posting and on the firm's skills inventories. **Job posting** means publicizing the open job to employees (usually by literally posting it on company intranets or bulletin boards). These postings list the job's attributes, like qualifications, supervisor, work schedule, and pay rate. *Qualifications skills inventories* may reveal to the company's recruiters those employees who have the right background for the open job. Ideally, the employer's internal-recruitment system therefore matches the best inside candidate with the job. In practice, this doesn't always happen. For better or worse, internal politics and having the right connections may well lead to placements that seem (and indeed may be) unfair and suboptimal.

Rehiring someone who left your employ has pros and cons. Former employees are known quantities (more or less) and are already familiar with how you do things. On the other hand, employees who you let go may return with negative attitudes.[49] Inquire (before rehiring) about what they did during the layoff and how they feel about returning. After a probationary period, credit them with the years of service they had accumulated before they left.[50]

Employee Engagement Guide for Managers

LEARNING OBJECTIVE 5-4

Describe how to use recruiting to improve employee engagement.

Promotion from Within

Many employers encourage internal recruiting, on the reasonable assumption that doing so improves employee engagement. Thus, as IBM shifted from supplying mostly hardware to consulting, it assessed its skills gaps and instituted workforce plans to train current employees for new jobs; this assumedly fostered employee engagement.

Similarly, International Paper appointed a single person "to provide support to all [business units], Staff Groups and Regions for Workforce Planning and Engagement."[51] Conversely, other employers, faced with strategic shifts, simply dismiss employees who don't "fit."

FedEx has had strong internal recruiting and promotion-from-within policies almost from its inception. FedEx's commitment to promotion from within grew out of founder Frederick Smith's belief that "when people are placed first they will provide the highest possible service, and profits will follow."[52] FedEx weaves together promotion from within with other policies—including annual employee attitude surveys, employee recognition and reward programs, a leadership evaluation process, extensive employee communication, and an employee appeals process—to foster employee commitment and engagement. FedEx's approach underscores the need to take an integrated approach to fostering employee engagement. For example, promotion-from-within is futile without effective performance appraisal and training practices.

Also, as at FedEx, effective promotion from within requires a system for accessing career records and *posting job openings*, one that guarantees eligible employees are informed of openings and considered for them. FedEx calls its job posting system JCATS (Job Change Applicant Tracking System). Announcements of new job openings via this online system usually take place each Friday. All employees applying for the position get numerical scores based on job performance and length of service. They are then advised as to whether they were chosen as candidates.

A manager interested in fostering his or her employees' engagement can draw several useful guidelines from FedEx's system: show a genuine interest in your employees' career aspirations; provide career-oriented appraisals; have a formal job-posting system; see that your employees have access to the training they need; and balance your desire to keep good employees with the benefits of helping them learn of and apply for other positions in your company.

Outside Sources of Candidates

LEARNING OBJECTIVE 5-5

Discuss the main outside sources of candidates, and create an employment ad.

Employers can't always get all the employees they need from their current staff, and sometimes they just don't want to. We look at the sources firms use to find outside candidates next.

Informal Recruiting and the Hidden Job Market

Many job openings aren't publicized at all; jobs are created and become available when employers serendipitously encounter the right candidates. The author of *Unlock the Hidden Job Market* estimates that perhaps half of all positions are filled without formal recruiting.[53] Similarly, one survey found that 28% of those surveyed found their most recent job through word of mouth. Nineteen percent used online job boards, 16% direct approaches from employers and employment services, 7% print ads, and only 1% social media sites (although 22% used sites like LinkedIn to *search* for jobs).[54]

Recruiting via the Internet[55]

Most employers post ads on their own Web sites, as well as on job boards such as Indeed.com, Monster, and CareerBuilder. For example, by using Indeed's smartphone app, job hunters can search for jobs by key word, read job descriptions and salaries, save jobs to a list of favorites, e-mail job links, search for jobs nearby, and often directly apply for the job. Employers should also make their job listings easily recognizable by Google's job search tool. When a job seeker types a specific job search term (such as, "social media marketing director jobs for law firms in Cleveland Ohio") into Google's search box, its search algorithms unearth relevant listings from both employers and from job listings services like LinkedIn and CareerBuilder.[56]

Employers use various methods to facilitate online recruiting. In Hungary, the local office of accountants PriceWaterhouseCoopers (PWC) lets prospective applicants use a online simulation it calls Multipoly, to let applicants better understand what working for PWC is like. The firm attributes a significant increase in applicants to use of the game.[57] McDonald's posted employee testimonials on social networking sites to attract applicants.[58] Other employers simply scan through job boards' résumé listings. The *dot-jobs* domain gives job seekers a one-click conduit for finding jobs at the employers who register at www.[employer's name].jobs. For example, applicants seeking a job at Disneyland can go to www.Disneyland.jobs. *Hire Vue* "lets candidates create video interviews and send them to employers to review, share, and compare with other applicants."[59]

Virtual (fully online) job fairs are another option. Here online visitors see a similar setup to a regular job fair. They can listen to presentations, visit booths, leave résumés and business cards, participate in live chats, and get contact information from recruiters and hiring managers.[60] Fairs last about 5 hours.

ONLINE RECRUITMENT AROUND THE GLOBE Just about every country has its own recruitment sites, such as Zhaopin.com in China. The popularity of baitoru.com in Japan shows how culture is changing there. After decades in which most workers there had lifetime job security, that system recently has broken down. Today large numbers of Japanese workers are part-time or temporary. They use baitoru.com to find jobs.[61]

PROS AND CONS Online recruiting generates more responses quicker and for a longer time at less cost than just about any other method. And, because they are more comprehensive in describing the jobs, Web-based ads have a stronger effect on applicant attraction than do printed ads.[62] But, online recruiting has two potential problems.

First is bias.[63] Older people and some minorities are less likely to be online, so such recruiting may exclude some older applicants (and certain minorities). Similarly, some ads reportedly have dropdown boxes that won't allow (older applicants) adding data prior to 1980, and some media, such as Facebook, enable recruiters to specify that ads target particular (usually younger) age groups.

The second problem is Internet overload: Employers end up deluged with résumés. Self-screening helps: The Cheesecake Factory posts detailed job duties listings, so those not interested needn't apply. Another approach is to have job seekers complete a short online prescreening questionnaire, then use these to identify those who may proceed in the hiring process.[64] Most employers also use applicant tracking systems, to which we now turn.

Using Recruitment Software and Artificial Intelligence

applicant tracking systems (ATS)
Online systems that help employers attract, gather, screen, compile, and manage applicants.

Internet overload means that most employers use applicant tracking software to screen applications.[65] **Applicant tracking systems (ATS)** are online systems that help employers attract, gather, screen, compile, and manage applicants.[66] They also provide other services, including requisitions management (for monitoring the firm's open jobs), applicant data collection (for scanning applicants' data into the system), and reporting (to create various reports such as cost per hire and hire by source).[67] Most systems are from *application service providers* (ASPs). These basically redirect applicants from the employer's to the ASP's site. Thus, applicants who log on to take a test at the employer are actually taking the test at the ASP's site.[68] As one example, a bank uses its ATS to bump applicants who don't meet the job's basic requirements; it then e-mails them suggesting they review the bank's site for more appropriate positions. This bank then uses either phone or video interviews to reduce the applicant pool to a few candidates. Then its recruiters interview those at headquarters and send them through the final selection process.[69]

Similarly, software like that from Breezy HR (https://breezy.hr/) offers what it calls "end-to-end" recruitment solutions. For example, the recruitment manager can use Breezy HR's software application to create the position title and position description for the ad, and to automatically post the ad to more than 40 job boards such as Indeed and ZipRecruiter. The recruiter then uses the Breezy HR application to schedule interviews, conduct video interviews, keep track of applicants in tabular form, discuss each applicant within the app with members of the recruiter's team, and compile and report statistics, for instance to the EEOC. Similar systems are available from Automatic Data Processing (ADP.com), HRsmart (hrsmart.com), SilkRoad Technology (silkroad.com), and Monster (monster.com).

ARTIFICIAL INTELLIGENCE SYSTEMS Employers also use artificial intelligence–based systems to improve recruitment.[70]

Here the main focus is on automating the résumé analysis. To paraphrase one expert, why read through 10,000 résumés if a machine can instantaneously find the top 20?

For example, Textkernel (www.textkernel.com/) can quickly scan thousands of résumés and find viable candidates. It uses AI to identify alternative words. Thus if a recruiter wants a candidate with experience in autonomous driving technology, Textkernel would scan the résumés not just for "autonomous driving" but also for similar words (like "self-driving") that its algorithms have found people use in place of "autonomous driving." SAP's Resume Matcher takes the employer's position description and scans Wikipedia entries to better understand the human traits, skills, and experience the job requires.[71] That helps it quickly read through résumés to rank those that are best.

Even with AI, beware of bias. How the bots define "good candidate" depends on what the employer did in the past. So, if the employer usually chose young white candidates from top universities to hire from its applicant pool, then the AI system will tend to favor such candidates.

TRENDS SHAPING HR: *SCIENCE IN TALENT MANAGEMENT*

When research from Google's "People Operations" (HR) group found that job boards weren't cost-effective for them, they created their own in-house recruiting team. This in-house team uses a proprietary candidate database called gHire. Google's recruiters continually expand and winnow this candidate list, by searching social networking and other sites, by searching who's working where, and by reaching out to prospective hires and maintaining dialogues with them, sometimes for years. These in-house recruiters produce handpicked candidates and account for about half of Google's yearly hires.[72]

Google also actively solicits employee referrals. Because inside referrals turned out to be great candidates, Google analyzed how to boost employee referrals. It found that higher referral fees weren't the answer (because Googlers already loved recommending great candidates). Instead, Google streamlined the selection process, so more referrals got hired.

Google uses outside recruiters sparingly for special assignments and dropped job boards years ago.[73] ■

IMPROVING ONLINE ADS The ad you post requires thought. The best Web ads don't just transfer newspaper ads to the Web. As one specialist put it, "Getting recruiters out of the 'shrunken want ad mentality' is a big problem." Figure 5-6 is an example of recycling a print ad to the Web. The ineffective Web ad has needless abbreviations and doesn't say much about why the job seeker should want that job.[74]

Now look at the effective Web ad in Figure 5-6. It provides good reasons to work for this company. It starts with an attention-grabbing heading and uses the extra space to provide more specific job information. Many employers include the entire job description.[75] Ideally, an ad also should provide a way (such as a checklist of the job's human requirements) for potential applicants to gauge if the job is a good fit.[76]

Furthermore, it's best to place employment information one click away from the home page. Applicants can submit their résumés online at most larger firms' Web sites.

Finally, online recruiting requires caution for *applicants*. Some job boards don't check the legitimacy of the "recruiters" who place ads. Applicants may submit personal details, not realizing who is getting them.[77]

FIGURE 5-6 **Ineffective and Effective Web Ads**

Ineffective Ad, Recycled from Magazine to the Web	Effective Web Ad (Space Not an Issue)
Process Engineer Pay: $65k–$85k/year Immediate Need in Florida for a Wastewater Treatment Process Engineer. Must have a min. 4–7 years Industrial Wastewater exp. Reply KimGD@WatersCleanX.com	Do you want to help us make this a better world? We are one of the top wastewater treatment companies in the world, with installations from Miami to London to Beijing. We are growing fast and looking for an experienced process engineer to join our team. If you have at least 4–7 years' experience designing processes for wastewater treatment facilities and a dedication to make this a better world, we would like to hear from you. Pay range depending on experience is $65,000–$85,000. Please reply in confidence to KimGD@WatersCleanX.com

TRENDS SHAPING HR: *DIGITAL AND SOCIAL MEDIA*

LinkedIn and Beyond

Accenture predicts that about 80% of new recruits will soon come through prospective employees' social media connections.[78]

Recruiters use social media recruiting in several ways. They dig through social Web sites and competitors' publications to find applicants who may not even be looking for jobs. They seek passive candidates (people not actively looking for jobs) by using social networking sites such as *LinkedIn Recruiter Lite* (a premium service) to browse members' résumés and to find such candidates.[79] Many firms use Twitter to announce job openings to job seekers who subscribe to their Twitter feeds.[80] Theladders.com's Pipeline™ networking tool lets recruiters maintain a dialogue with prospective job seekers even before they're interested in seeking a job. Others use Facebook's friend-finding search function, and Twitter, to learn more about prospective and actual candidates. TalentBin searches sites such as Pinterest to find qualified tech workers.[81] Many employers have social media strategies and career pages that establish an online presence highlighting the benefits of working for them.[82] At one diversity conference, consultants Hewitt Associates displayed posters asking attendees to text message *hewdiversity* to a specific 5-digit number. Each person texting then became part of Hewitt's "mobile recruiting network," periodically receiving text messages regarding Hewitt openings.[83] (The employer should retain the text messages, in case it is audited, for instance by the EEOC.)[84]

LinkedIn Recruiter Lite lets employers post jobs on LinkedIn. The employer can also conduct its own LinkedIn search for talent, by using Recruiter Lite's search filters to search through LinkedIn's database. Recruiters then use LinkedIn's InMail to send short personalized messages to people they're interested in. And by joining relevant LinkedIn groups the recruiter can discover other LinkedIn group members who might be potential hires.[85] This not only helps them generate more relevant applicants, but also lets the recruiter mine the applicants' sites for feedback from the person's blog comments and his or her likes/dislikes. Recruiters also post job openings on professional associations and other social networks.[86] (Note that in one scam, hackers created LinkedIn profiles and then engaged in online chats with recruiters, to obtain access to employees' e-mails and profiles within the company.)[87]

The Oracle Taleo Social Sourcing Cloud Service is integrated with social sites like LinkedIn, Twitter, and Facebook. It notifies the company's current employees about open positions, and then scans their social connections for referral suggestions that they may want to make. With the My Staffing Pro applicant tracking system, applicants can apply on Facebook, share job openings, and connect with hiring managers.[88] ■

Advertising

While Web-based recruiting is replacing traditional help wanted ads, print ads are still popular. To use such help wanted ads successfully, employers should address two issues: the advertising medium and the ad's construction.

THE MEDIA The best medium—the local paper, *The Wall Street Journal*, *The Economist*, for instance—depends on the positions for which you're recruiting. For example, the local newspaper is often a good source for local blue-collar help, clerical employees, and lower-level administrative employees. On the other hand, if recruiting for workers with special skills, such as furniture finishers, you'd probably want to advertise in places with furniture manufacturers, such as the Carolinas, even if your plant is in Tennessee. The point is to target your ads where they'll reach your prospective employees.

For specialized employees, advertise in trade and professional journals like *American Psychologist*, *Sales Management*, *Chemical Engineering*, and *Women's Wear Daily*. Help wanted ads in papers like *The Wall Street Journal* can be good sources of middle- or senior-management personnel. Most of these print outlets include online ads with the purchase of print help wanted ads. Electronic Arts included information about its internship program on its video game manuals.

CONSTRUCTING (WRITING) THE AD Experienced advertisers use the guide AIDA (attention, interest, desire, action) to construct ads. First, you must grab attention to the ad. Why does the ad in Figure 5-7 attract attention? The phrase "next key player" helps.

Next, develop interest in the job. For instance, "Are you looking to make an impact?"

Create desire by spotlighting words such as *travel* or *challenge*. As an example, having a graduate school nearby may appeal to engineers and professional people.

Finally, the ad should prompt action with a statement like "call today."

Job applicants view ads with more specific job information as more attractive and more credible.[89] If the job has big drawbacks, consider a realistic ad. When the New York City Administration for Children's Services was having problems with employee

FIGURE 5-7 Help Wanted Ad That Draws Attention

Source: "Help Wanted Ad That Draws Attention," in Giombetti Associates, Hampden, MA. Reprinted with permission.

Are You Our Next Key Player?

PLANT CONTROLLER **Northern New Jersey**

Are you looking to make an impact? Can you be a strategic business partner and team player, versus a classic, "bean counter"? Our client, a growing **Northern New Jersey** manufacturer with two locations, needs a high-energy, self-initiating, technically competent Plant Controller. Your organizational skills and strong understanding of general, cost, and manufacturing accounting are a must. We are not looking for a delegator, this is a hands-on position. If you have a positive can-do attitude and have what it takes to drive our accounting function, read oh!

Responsibilities and Qualifications:

- Monthly closings, management reporting, product costing, and annual budget.
- Accurate inventory valuations, year-end physical inventory, and internal controls.
- 4-year Accounting degree, with 5–8 years experience in a manufacturing environment.
- Must be proficient in Microsoft Excel and have general computer skills and aptitude.
- Must be analytical and technically competent, with the leadership ability to influence people, situations, and circumstances.

If you have what it takes to be our next key player, tell us in your cover letter, *"Beyond the beans, what is the role of a Plant Controller?"* **Only cover letters addressing that question will be considered. Please indicate your general salary requirements in your cover letter and email or fax your resume and cover letter to:**

Ross Giombetti
Giombetti Associates
2 Allen Street, P.O. Box 720
Hampden, MA 01036
Email: Rossgiombetti@giombettiassoc.com
Fax: (413) 566-2009

retention, it began using these ads: "Wanted: men and women willing to walk into strange buildings in dangerous neighborhoods, [and] be screamed at by unhinged individuals. . . ."[90]

Employment Agencies

There are three main types of employment agencies: (1) public agencies operated by federal, state, or local governments; (2) agencies associated with nonprofit organizations; and (3) privately owned agencies.

PUBLIC AND NONPROFIT AGENCIES Every state has a public, state-run employment service agency. The U.S. Department of Labor supports these agencies, through grants and through other assistance such as a nationwide computerized job bank. Similarly the DOL's CareerOneStop enables agency counselors to advise applicants about available jobs in other states as well.

Some employers have mixed experiences with public agencies. For one thing, applicants for unemployment insurance are required to register and to make themselves available for job interviews. Some of these people are not interested in returning to work, so employers can end up with applicants who have little desire for immediate employment. And fairly or not, employers probably view some of these local agencies as lethargic in their efforts to fill area employers' jobs.

Yet these agencies are useful. Beyond just filling jobs, counselors will visit an employer's work site, review the employer's job requirements, and even assist the employer in writing job descriptions. Most states have turned their local state employment service agencies into "one-stop" shops—neighborhood training/employment/career assessment centers.[91] At Oregon State's centers, job seekers can use "iMatch" skills assessment software, while employers can get up-to-date local economic news and use the center's online recruitment tools.[92] More employers should be taking advantage of these centers (formerly the "unemployment offices" in many cities).

Most (nonprofit) professional and technical societies, such as the Institute for Electrical and Electronic Engineers (IEEE), have units that help members find jobs. Many special public agencies place people who are in special categories, such as those who are disabled.

PRIVATE AGENCIES Private employment agencies are important sources of clerical, white-collar, and managerial personnel. They charge fees (set by state law and posted in their offices) for each applicant they place. Most are "fee-paid" jobs, in which the employer pays the fee. Use one if:

1. Your firm doesn't have its own human resources department and feels it can't do a good job recruiting and screening.
2. You must fill a job quickly.
3. There is a perceived need to attract more minority or female applicants.
4. You want to reach currently employed individuals, who might feel more comfortable dealing with agencies than with competing companies.
5. You want to reduce the time you're devoting to recruiting.[93]

Yet using employment agencies requires avoiding the potential pitfalls. For example, the employment agency's screening may let poor applicants go directly to the supervisors responsible for hiring, who may in turn naively hire them. Conversely, improper screening at the agency could block potentially successful applicants.

To help avoid problems:

1. Give the agency an accurate and complete job description.
2. Make sure tests, application blanks, and interviews are part of the agency's selection process.
3. Periodically review equal employment data on candidates accepted or rejected by your firm, and by the agency.

4. Screen the agency. Check with other managers to find out which agencies have been the most effective at filling the sorts of positions you need filled. Review the Internet and classified ads to discover the agencies that handle the positions you seek to fill.
5. Supplement the agency's reference checking by checking at least the final candidate's references yourself.

Recruitment Process Outsourcers

Recruitment process outsourcers (RPOs) are special vendors that handle all or most of an employer's recruiting needs. They usually sign short-term contracts with the employer, and receive a monthly fee that varies with the amount of actual recruiting the employer needs done. This makes it easier for an employer to ramp up or ramp down its recruiting expenses, as compared with paying the relatively fixed costs of an in-house recruitment office.[94] Large RPOs include Manpower Group Solutions, Allegis Global Solutions, and IBM Recruitment Services.[95]

On-Demand Recruiting Services

on-demand recruiting services (ODRS)
Services that provide short-term specialized recruiting to support specific projects without the expense of retaining traditional search firms.

On-demand recruiting services (ODRS) are recruiters who are paid by the hour or project, instead of a percentage fee, to support a specific project. For example, when the human resource manager for a biotech firm had to hire several dozen people with scientific degrees and experience in pharmaceuticals, she used an ODRS firm. A traditional recruiting firm might charge 20% to 30% of each hire's salary. The ODRS firm charged by time, rather than per hire. It handled recruiting and prescreening, and left the client with a short list of qualified candidates.[96]

HR AND THE GIG ECONOMY: *TEMPORARY WORKERS AND ALTERNATIVE STAFFING*

Vast numbers of workers today work in the gig (also called the sharing, 1099, and on-demand) economy.[97] From Uber drivers to temp employees, they typically work in freelance, contract, temporary, or consultant capacities.

For example, many employers build their staff wholly or in part around freelance programmers, designers, or marketers. Freelancer community Web sites enable such employers to recruit based on the freelancer's reputation and work product. For example, upwork.com (see www.upwork.com) reports its members' skills assessments, and lists detailed project work experience, making it easier for prospective employers to decide who to hire. The TopCoder.com (see www.topcoder.com/how-it-works/) programming community site enables employers to identify top programmers based on their reputations.

Temporary Workers

Employers also increasingly supplement their permanent workforces by hiring contingent or temporary workers, often through temporary help employment agencies. Also known as *part-time* or *just-in-time workers*, the contingent workforce is big and growing, and it isn't limited to clerical or maintenance staff. It includes thousands of engineering, science, and management support occupations, such as temporary chief financial officers, human resource managers, and chief executive officers.[98]

Employers use temps for many reasons. One is the trend toward organizing around short-term projects. For example, Makino, which manufactures machine tools, now outsources the installation of large machines to contract firms, who in turn hire temps to do the installations. Flexibility is another concern, with more employers wanting to quickly reduce employment levels if the economic turnaround proves short-lived.[99] Other employers use temp agency–supplied workers to "try out" prospective employees. Employers have also long used "temps" to fill in for employees who were out sick or on vacation.

The employer should compare costs of temps versus permanent employees. Productivity in output per hour paid can be higher, since temps often only get paid when they're working—not for days off. However, temps often cost employers more per hour because the agency gets a fee. But the agency also does the recruiting, whereas for permanent employees the employer should include costs such as for placing ads and interviewers' time.[100]

alternative staffing
The use of nontraditional recruitment sources.

Temporary employees are examples of **alternative staffing**—basically, the use of nontraditional recruitment sources. Other alternative staffing arrangements include "in-house temporary employees" (people employed directly by the company, but on an explicit short-term basis) and "contract technical employees" (highly skilled workers like engineers, who are supplied for long-term projects under contract from outside technical services firms).

THE TEMP AGENCY Employers hire temp workers either through direct hires or through temporary staff agencies. Direct hiring involves simply hiring workers and placing them on the job. The employer usually pays these people directly, as it does all its employees, but classifies them separately, as casual, seasonal, or temporary employees, and often pays few if any benefits.[101] The other approach is to use a temp agency. Here the agency handles all the recruiting, screening, and payroll administration for the temps. Thus, Nike hired Kelly Services to manage Nike's temp needs.

When working with temporary agencies, understand their policies. For example, with temps, the time sheet is not just a verification of hours worked. Once the worker's supervisor signs it, it's usually an agreement to pay the agency's fees. What is the policy if the client wants to hire one of the agency's temps as a permanent employee? How does the agency plan to recruit employees? And finally, check their references.[102]

TEMP EMPLOYEES' CONCERNS To make temporary relationships successful, those supervising temps should understand their concerns. In one survey, temporary workers said they were:

1. Treated by employers in a dehumanizing and ultimately discouraging way.
2. Insecure about their employment and pessimistic about the future.
3. Worried about their lack of insurance and pension benefits.
4. Misled about their job assignments and in particular about whether temporary assignments were likely to become full-time.
5. "Underemployed" (particularly those trying to return to the full-time labor market).[103]

MyLab Management Talk About It 2

If your professor has assigned this, go to the Assignments section of **www.pearson.com/mylab/management** to complete these discussion questions. Go to one or more sites like elance.com. If you were a programming manager for a company, could you use the site to find and hire a new employee directly? If not, what else might you need?

KNOW YOUR EMPLOYMENT LAW

Contract Employees

For purposes of most employment laws, with certain limited exceptions, employees of temporary staffing firms working in an employer's workplace will be considered to be employees both of the agency and of the employer.[104] The employer's liability depends on the degree to which its supervisors control the temp employee's activities. Therefore, the more the agency does, the better. For example, have the agency handle training. Let it negotiate and set the pay rates and vacation/time-off policies.

Employers can take other steps. Require the agency to follow the employer's background checking process, and to assume the legal risks if the employer and agency are found to be jointly responsible. Carefully track how many temporary employees your company actually has. Screen and supervise temporary employees with care if they may have access to your intellectual property and computer systems.[105] Don't treat temporary workers as "employees," for instance, in terms of business cards, employee handbooks, or employee ID badges.[106] ■

POACHING In 2018 Uber agreed to pay Google about $245 million to settle claims that an employee of Google's Waymo driverless car division took Waymo secrets with him when he joined Uber.

"Poaching" employees from competitors can produce good recruits but can be problematical. For example, the employee almost always has a fiduciary responsibility to the current employer, for instance, regarding proprietary information. Therefore, keep the possibility of litigation in mind. Don't ask for or accept proprietary information about your competitor.

There is no way for a target firm to become "poaching proof." However, steps such as having employees sign noncompete agreements and antisolicitation clauses prohibiting them from soliciting current customers may help protect the employer for a time.[107] Both Apple and Google allegedly took a more dubious approach: According to several lawsuits, they simply agreed between themselves not to poach each other's employees, but then agreed to a $415 million legal settlement.[108]

Offshoring and Outsourcing Jobs

Rather than bringing people in to do the company's jobs, outsourcing and offshoring send the jobs out. *Outsourcing* means having outside vendors supply services (such as benefits management, market research, or manufacturing) that the company's own employees previously did in-house. *Offshoring* means having outside vendors or employees *abroad* supply services that the company's own employees previously did in-house.

Employees, unions, legislators, and even many business owners feel that "shipping jobs out" (particularly overseas) is ill-advised. That notwithstanding, employers are sending jobs out, and not just blue-collar jobs. For example, U.S. employers shipped about 135,000 IT jobs recently to countries like India.[109]

Sending out jobs, particularly overseas, presents employers with special personnel challenges. One is the likelihood of cultural misunderstandings (such as between your home-based customers and the employees abroad). Others are security and information privacy concerns; the need to deal with foreign contract, liability, and legal systems issues; and the fact that the offshore employees need special training (for instance, in using pseudonyms like "Jim" without discomfort).

Rising wages in Asia, coupled with reputational issues, a desire to invest more in local communities, and political pressures are prompting employers to bring jobs back. Several U.S. employers including Apple and Microsoft are shifting jobs back to America.[110]

America's H-1B visa program originally aimed to help U.S. employers temporarily hire workers from abroad in specialty occupations. Today, newspaper accounts of employers bringing in foreign workers to be trained by their American counterparts before taking over their jobs has prompted legislators (and others) to argue that the program is misused.[111] For example, they want to limit use of H-1B visas to skilled foreign workers.[112] With the program under scrutiny, the number of evidence requests (required to confirm the need for the visa) recently rose from about 17% of

The numbers of temporary and freelance workers are increasing all over the world.

Hero Images/Getty Images

applications to over 46%.[113] Giant outsourcers, such as India's Infosys Ltd, reacted with plans to hire thousands of U.S. workers, and by opening technology centers in the United States.[114]

Executive Recruiters

Executive recruiters (also known as *headhunters*) are special employment agencies employers retain to seek out top-management talent for their clients. The percentage of your firm's positions filled by these services might be small. However, these jobs include key executive and technical positions. For executive positions, headhunters may be your only source of candidates. The employer always pays the fees.

There are contingent and retained executive recruiters. Members of the Association of Executive Search Consultants usually focus on executive positions paying $150,000 or more and on "*retained* executive search." They are paid regardless of whether the employer hires the executive through the search firm's efforts. *Contingency-based recruiters* tend to handle junior- to middle-level management job searches in the $80,000 to $160,000 range. Recruiter fees are around 15% to 25% of the executive's total first-year pay (salary plus bonus).[115] Top recruiters (all retained) include Heidrick and Struggles, Egon Zehnder International, Russell Reynolds, and Spencer Stuart.

The challenging part of recruiting has always been finding potential candidates. Not surprisingly, Internet-based databases now dramatically speed up such searches. Executive recruiters are also creating specialized units aimed at specialized functions (such as sales) or industries (such as oil products).

Recruiters bring a lot to the table. They have many contacts and are relatively adept at finding qualified candidates who aren't actively looking to change jobs. They can keep your firm's name confidential, and can save top management's time by building an applicant pool. The recruiter's fee might actually turn out to be small when you compare it to the executive time saved.

The big issue is ensuring that the recruiter really understands your needs and then delivers properly vetted candidates. It is essential that the employer explain completely what sort of candidate is required. Some recruiters also may be more interested in persuading you to hire a candidate than in finding one who will really do the job. And one or two of the "final candidates" may actually just be fillers to make the recruiter's one "real" candidate look better.

WORKING WITH RECRUITERS Retaining and working with executive recruiters require some caution. In choosing and working with one, guidelines include[116]

1. Make sure the firm can conduct a thorough search. Under their ethics code, a recruiter can't approach the executive talent of a former client for a period of 2 years after completing a search for that client. Since former clients are off limits for 2 years, the recruiter must search from a constantly diminishing pool.[117]
2. Meet the individual who will actually handle your assignment.
3. Make sure to ask how much the search firm charges. Get the agreement in writing.[118]
4. Make sure the recruiter and you agree on what sort of individual to hire for the position.
5. Ask if the recruiter has vetted the final candidates. Do not be surprised if the answer is, "No, I just get candidates—we don't really screen them."
6. *Never* rely solely on any recruiter to do all the reference checking. Let them check the candidates' references, but get notes of these references in writing from the recruiter (if possible). Recheck at least the final candidates' references yourself.
7. Consider using a recruiter who has a special expertise in your specific industry—he or she may have the best grasp of who is available.

INTERNAL RECRUITING More employers are bringing management recruiting in-house. They still use executive recruiters such as Heidrick and Struggles to conduct top officer (CEO and president) and board member placements, and to conduct confidential searches. But employers such as General Electric and Google now have their own internal recruiting offices doing much of their own management recruiting. Time Warner reported saving millions of dollars per year using internal recruiting teams.[119]

With employers increasingly finding new ways of recruiting top management talent, executive search firms are diversifying. For example, the head of Korn/Ferry says his firm is increasingly being asked to investigate prospective candidates' backgrounds, and his firm is also expanding into areas such as employee development.[120] The accompanying HR Tools feature explains what small businesses can do.

IMPROVING PERFORMANCE: *HR TOOLS FOR LINE MANAGERS AND SMALL BUSINESSES*

Recruiting 101

There comes a time in the life of most small businesses when it dawns on the owner that new blood is needed to take the company to the next level. Should the owner personally recruit this person?

While most large firms don't think twice about hiring executive search firms, small-firm owners will understandably hesitate before committing to a fee that could reach $60,000 or more for a $120,000 marketing manager.

However, engaging in a search like this is not like seeking supervisors or data entry clerks. Chances are, you won't find a top manager by placing ads. He or she is probably not reading the want ads. You'll end up with résumés of people who are, for one reason or another, out of work, unhappy with their work, or unsuited for your job. Many may be capable. But you will have to ferret out the gem by interviewing and assessing them.

You won't know where to place or how to write the ads; or where to search, who to contact, or how to screen out the laggards who may appear to be viable candidates. Even if you do, this process will be time-consuming and will divert your attention from other duties.

If you do decide to do the job yourself, consider retaining an industrial psychologist to spend 4 or 5 hours assessing the problem-solving ability, personality, interests, and energy level of the two or three candidates in which you are most interested. The input can provide a valuable perspective on the candidates.

Exercise special care with applicants from competing companies. Some of the issues at 2018's Uber versus Google Waymo autonomous driving technology trial included, for instance, "Is information 'stolen' if you simply remember it?", and "Even if the engineer developed the solution him or herself, the person cannot tell new employers about specific engineering solutions." Always ascertain if applicants are bound by noncompete or nondisclosure agreements. And perhaps check with an attorney before asking certain questions—regarding patents or potential antitrust issues, for instance.[121]

If you're a manager with an open position to fill in a *Fortune* 500 company, even you may find you have a dilemma. You may find that your firm's HR office will do little recruiting, other than, perhaps, placing an ad on CareerBuilder. On the other hand, your firm almost surely will not let you place your own help wanted ads. What to do? Use word of mouth to "advertise" your open position within and outside your company. And contact your colleagues in other firms to let them know you are recruiting. ■

MyLab Management Talk About It 3

If your professor has assigned this, go to the Assignments section of **www.pearson.com/mylab/management** to complete these discussion questions. You own a small chemical engineering company and want to hire a new president. Based on what you read in this chapter, how would you go about doing so, and why?

Referrals and Walk-Ins

Employee referral campaigns are a very important recruiting option. Here the employer posts announcements of openings and requests for referrals on its Web site, bulletin boards, and/or wallboards. It often offers prizes or cash awards for referrals that lead to hiring. For example, at health-care giant Kaiser Permanente, referring someone for one of its "award-eligible positions" can produce bonuses of $3,000 or more.[122] The Container Store trains employees to recruit candidates from among the firm's customers. Many employers use tools like Jobvite Refer to make it easier for their employees to publicize the firm's open positions via their own social media sites.[123]

Referral's big advantage is that it tends to generate "more applicants, more hires, and a higher yield ratio (hires/applicants)."[124] Current employees tend to provide accurate information about their referrals because they're putting their own reputations on the line. And the new employees may come with a more realistic picture of what the firm is like. A SHRM survey found that of 586 employer respondents, 69% said employee referral programs are more cost-effective than other recruiting practices, and 80% specifically said they are more cost-effective than employment agencies. On average, referral programs cost around $400–$900 per hire in incentives and rewards.[125]

If morale is low, address that prior to asking for referrals. And if you don't hire someone's referral, explain to your employee/referrer why you did not hire his or her candidate. In addition, remember that relying on referrals might be discriminatory where a workforce is already homogeneous. Employee referral programs can also backfire when most of a firm's employees are nonminority. Here one suggestion is to offer bigger bonuses for diversity hires.[126]

WALK-INS Particularly for hourly workers, walk-ins—direct applications made at your office—are a big source of applicants. Sometimes, posting a "Help Wanted" sign outside the door may be the most cost-effective way of attracting good local applicants. Treat walk-ins courteously, for both the employer's community reputation and the applicant's self-esteem. Many employers give every walk-in a brief interview, even if it is only to get information on the applicant "in case a position should be open in the future." Employers also typically receive unsolicited applications from professional and white-collar applicants. Good business practice requires answering all applicants' letters of inquiry promptly.

College Recruiting

college recruiting
Sending an employer's representatives to college campuses to prescreen applicants and create an applicant pool from the graduating class.

College recruiting—sending an employer's representatives to college campuses to prescreen applicants and create an applicant pool from the graduating class—is important. Recently, the entry-level job market has been the strongest it's been in years, and historically, almost 40% of such jobs have gone to recent college graduates.[127]

One problem is that such recruiting is expensive. Schedules must be set well in advance, company brochures printed, interview records kept, and much time spent on campus. And recruiters are sometimes ineffective. Some are unprepared, show little interest in the candidate, and act superior. Many don't screen candidates effectively. Employers need to train recruiters in how to interview candidates, how to explain what the company has to offer, and how to put candidates at ease. The recruiter should be personable and have a record of attracting good candidates.[128]

The campus recruiter has two main goals. One is to determine if a candidate is worthy of further consideration. Traits to assess include communication skills, education, experience, and technical and interpersonal skills. The other aim is to make the employer attractive to candidates. A sincere and informal attitude, respect for the applicant, and prompt follow-up emails/letters can help sell the employer to the interviewee.

Employers who build relationships with opinion leaders such as career counselors and professors have better recruiting results.[129] Building close ties with a college's career center provides recruiters with useful feedback regarding things like labor market conditions and the effectiveness of one's online and offline recruiting ads.[130]

Employers should narrow the list of schools its recruiters visit, using criteria such as quality of academic program, number of students enrolled, curriculum, distance to campus, competitive environment (students salary expectations, and so forth), and student body diversity.[131]

Employers generally invite good candidates for an on-site visit. The invitation should be warm but businesslike, and provide a choice of dates. Have a host meet the applicant, preferably at the airport or at his or her hotel. A package containing the applicant's schedule as well as other information—such as annual reports and employee benefits—should be waiting for the applicant at the hotel.

Plan the interviews and adhere to the schedule. Avoid interruptions; give the candidate the undivided attention of each person with whom he or she interviews. Have another recently hired graduate host the candidate's lunch. Make any offer as soon as possible, preferably at the time of the visit. Frequent follow-ups to "find out how the decision process is going" may help to tilt the applicant in your favor.

What else to do? A study of 96 graduating students provides some insights. Fifty-three percent said "on-site visit opportunities to meet with people in positions similar to those applied for, or with higher-ranking persons" had a positive effect. Fifty-one percent mentioned, "impressive hotel/dinner arrangements and having well-organized site arrangements." "Disorganized, unprepared interviewer behavior, or uninformed, useless answers" turned off 41%. Schools such as the University of Virginia provide job-seeking students with guidelines about what to expect at the employer's on-site visit.[132]

INTERNSHIPS Internships can be win–win situations. For students, they can mean honing business skills, learning more about potential employers, and discovering one's career likes (and dislikes). Employers can use the interns to make useful contributions while evaluating them as possible full-time employees. A study found that about 60% of internships turned into job offers.[133]

Unfortunately, some internships turn into nightmares. Many interns, particularly in industries like fashion and media, report long unpaid days of menial work.[134] Courts have laid out several criteria for determining whether someone is actually an "intern." Criteria include: whether both the intern and employer understand that no compensation is expected; whether the internship provides training similar to an educational environment; and whether the internship is tied to the person's formal education program.[135]

Military Personnel

Returning and discharged U.S. military personnel provide an excellent source of trained and disciplined recruits.[136] Yet all too often they have trouble getting placed. To help remedy this, the federal government offers tax credits to employers who hire veterans, and many employers including Walmart have special programs to recruit veterans.[137] The military also has programs to facilitate soldiers finding jobs. Thus the U.S. Army's Partnership for Youth Success enables someone entering the Army to select a post-Army corporate partner as a way to help soldiers find a job after leaving the Army.[138]

Misconceptions about veterans (for instance, that posttraumatic stress disorders influence job performance) are generally not valid.[139] Walmart has a program offering jobs to honorably discharged veterans who left the service in the past year.[140] The Web site www.helmetstohardhats.org puts vets together with building trades employers.[141]

The accompanying Profit Center feature describes how one employer reduced recruiting costs.

IMPROVING PERFORMANCE: *HR AS A PROFIT CENTER*

Cutting Recruitment Costs[142]

GE Medical hires about 500 technical workers a year to design sophisticated medical devices such as CT scanners. It has cut its hiring costs by 17%, reduced time to fill the positions by 20% to 30%, and cut in half the percentage of new hires who don't work out.[143]

GE Medical's HR team accomplished this in part by applying its purchasing techniques to its dealings with recruiters. For example, it called a meeting and told 20 recruiters that it would work with only the 10 best. To measure "best," the company created measures inspired by manufacturing techniques, such as "percentage of résumés that result in interviews" and "percentage of interviews that lead to offers." Similarly, GE Medical discovered that current employees are very effective as references. For instance, GE Medical interviews just 1% of applicants whose résumés it receives, while 10% of employee referrals result in actual hires. So GE Medical took steps to double the number of employee referrals. It simplified the referral forms, eliminated bureaucratic submission procedures, and added a small reward like a gift certificate for referring a qualified candidate. GE also upped the incentive—$2,000 if someone referred is hired, and $3,000 if he or she is a software engineer. (In 2018, GE spun off ownership of its Medical/Healthcare unit to GE shareholders.) ■

> **MyLab Management Talk About It 4**
>
> If your professor has assigned this, go to the Assignments section of **www.pearson.com/mylab/management** to complete this discussion question. What other tools described in this chapter could GE Medical use to improve recruiting efficiency?

LEARNING OBJECTIVE 5-6
Explain how to recruit a more diverse workforce.

Recruiting a More Diverse Workforce

The recruiting tools we described to this point are certainly useful for recruiting minority applicants, too. However, diversity recruiting requires several special steps. For example, Facebook is said to award its recruiters more points for hiring black, Hispanic, or female engineers.[144] Facebook also has its hiring managers interview at least one person from an underrepresented group for each open position.[145] Pinterest recently set aggressive diversity goals, such as to hire women for 30% of open engineer jobs. Although it missed that goal, women still represented 22% of the engineers it hired. Microsoft ties manager bonuses to hiring diverse employees.[146]

Recruiting Women

Given the progress women have made in getting and excelling in a wide range of professional, managerial, and military occupations, one might assume that employers need no special recruitment efforts to recruit women, but that's not the case. For example, women still face headwinds in certain male-dominated occupations such as engineering. Women also carry the heavier burden of child-rearing, fill proportionately fewer high-level managerial posts, and still earn only about 70% of what men earn for similar jobs. Many employers therefore focus particular efforts on recruiting qualified women.[147]

The most effective strategy is top management driven.[148] Here the employer emphasizes the importance of recruiting women, identifies gaps in the recruitment and retention of women, and implements a comprehensive plan to attract female applicants. The overall aim is to show that the employer is somewhere women want to work, and the details of any such plan needn't be complicated. For example, particularly for "nontraditional" jobs (like engineering), use the company Web site to highlight women now doing those jobs. Emphasize the employer's mentoring program for moving women up. Offer real workplace flexibility; for example, not just flexible hours but the option of staying on a partner track even while working part-time. Focus some of the recruiting effort on women's organizations, women's employment Web sites, and women's colleges. Make sure benefits cover matters such as prenatal care. Maintain a zero-tolerance sexual harassment policy.

Recruiting Single Parents

Recently, there were about 15 million single-parent families with children under 18 maintained by the mother and about 5 million maintained by the father.[149] (And keep in mind that many of these issues also apply to families in which both parents are struggling to make ends meet.) In one survey:

> Many described falling into bed exhausted at midnight without even minimal time for themselves. . . . They often needed personal sick time or excused days off to care for sick children. As one mother noted, "I don't have enough sick days to get sick."[150]

Given such concerns, the first step in attracting and keeping single parents is making the workplace user friendly.[151] A supportive attitude on the supervisor's part can go far toward making the single parent's work–home balancing act more bearable.[152] Many firms have *flextime* programs that provide employees some schedule flexibility (such as 1-hour windows at the beginning or end of the day). Unfortunately, for many single parents this may not be enough. CNN even offered a "Work/Life Balance Calculator" to assess how far out of balance one's life may be.[153] We'll discuss other options in Chapter 13, Benefits and Services.

Older Workers

About 32% of Americans age 65 to 69 were employed recently, as were 19% of all those over 65.[154] It therefore makes sense for employers to encourage older workers to stay (or to come to work at the company). The big draw is to provide opportunities for flexible (and often shorter) work schedules.[155] At one company, workers over 65 can progressively shorten their work schedules; another company uses "mini shifts" to accommodate those interested in working less than full-time. Other suggestions include the following: phased retirement that allows workers to ease out of the workforce,[156] portable jobs for "snowbirds" who wish to live in warmer climates in the winter, part-time projects for retirees, and full benefits for part-timers.[157]

As always in recruiting, project the right image. The most effective ads emphasize schedule flexibility, and accentuate the firm's equal opportunity employment statement, *not* "giving retirees opportunities to transfer their knowledge."[158]

Not just single parents, but also their children may occasionally need some extra support.

Stewart Cohen/Agefotostock

Diversity Counts: Older Workers

Older workers are good workers. A study focused on the validity of six common stereotypes about older workers: that they are less motivated, less willing to participate in training and career development, more resistant to change, less trusting, less healthy, and more vulnerable to work–family imbalance.[159] They actually found not a negative but a weakly positive relationship between age and motivation and job involvement (suggesting that as age goes up motivation rises). They did find a weak negative relationship between age and trainability. Age was weakly but positively related to willingness to change, and to being more trusting. Older workers were no more likely than younger ones to have psychological problems or day-to-day physical health problems, but were more likely to have heightened blood pressure and cholesterol. Older workers did not experience more work–family imbalance. So there was little support for the common age stereotypes.

What should employers do? First, raise employees', managers', and recruiters' awareness about incorrect age stereotypes. And provide opportunities for more contacts with older people and for information flows between younger and older workers.[160] ■

Recruiting Minorities

Similar prescriptions apply to recruiting minorities.[161] First, *understand* the barriers that prevent minorities from applying. For example, some minority applicants won't meet the educational or experience standards for the job; many employers therefore offer remedial training. In one retail chain, a lack of role models stopped women from applying. Other times schedule flexibility is crucial.

After recognizing the impediments, one turns to formulating plans for remedying them and for attracting and retaining minorities and women. This may include, for instance, basic skills training, flexible work options, role models, and redesigned jobs.

Next, implement these plans. For example, many job seekers check with friends when job hunting, so encouraging your minority employees to assist in your recruiting makes sense. Diversity recruitment specialists include www.diversity.com and www.2trabajo.com.[162] Others collaborate with specialist professional organizations, such as the National Black MBA Association (http://careersuccess.nbmbaa.org/).

Some employers experience difficulty in assimilating people previously on welfare. Applicants sometimes lack basic work skills, such as reporting for work on time, or working in teams. The key to welfare-to-work seems to be a pretraining program, consisting of counseling and basic skills training over several weeks, offered by the employer and/or many states.[163]

The Disabled

Bias against disabled applicants may or may not be intentional but surely occurs. In one study, researchers replied to accounting job openings by sending résumés and cover letters from fictitious candidates; all "candidates" were qualified, but some letters revealed a disability. The candidates with expressed disabilities were chosen by recruiters 26% less frequently for follow-up than were those with no revealed disability.[164]

The research is quite persuasive regarding the fact that in terms of virtually all work criteria, employees with disabilities are capable workers. Thousands of employers in the United States and elsewhere have found that disabled employees provide an excellent and largely untapped source of competent, efficient labor for jobs ranging from information technology to creative advertising to receptionist.[165]

Employers can do several things to tap this huge potential workforce. The U.S. Department of Labor's Office of Disability Employment Policy offers several programs, including one that helps link disabled college undergraduates who are looking for summer internships with potential employers.[166] All states have local agencies (such as "Corporate Connections" in Tennessee) that provide placement services and other recruitment and training tools and information for employers seeking to hire the disabled. Employers also must use common sense. For example, employers who post job openings only in newspapers may miss potential employees who are visually impaired.[167]

LEARNING OBJECTIVE 5-7

Discuss practical guidelines for obtaining application information.

Developing and Using Application Forms

Purpose of Application Forms

application form
The form that provides information on education, prior work record, and skills.

With a pool of applicants, the prescreening process can begin. The **application form** is usually the first step in this process (some firms first require a brief, prescreening interview or online test).

A filled-in application provides four types of information. First, you can make judgments on *substantive matters*, such as whether the applicant has the education and experience to do the job. Second, you can draw conclusions about the applicant's *previous progress* and growth, especially important for management candidates. Third, you can draw tentative conclusions about the applicant's *stability* based on previous work record (although years of downsizing suggest the need for caution here). Fourth, you may be able to use the data in the application to *predict* which candidates will succeed on the job.

Application Guidelines

Ineffective use of the application can cost the employer dearly. Managers should keep several practical guidelines in mind. In the "Employment History" section, request detailed information on each prior employer, including the name of the supervisor and his or her e-mail address and telephone number; this is essential for reference checking. In signing the application, the applicant should certify that falsified statements may be cause for dismissal, that investigation of credit and employment and driving record is authorized, that a medical examination and drug screening tests may be required, and that employment is for no definite period.

Estimates of how many applicants exaggerate their qualifications range from 40% to 70%.[168] The most common problems concern education and job experience. A majority of graduating seniors reportedly believe that employers expect a degree of exaggeration on résumés. Much of this exaggeration occurs on résumés, but may occur on application forms too. Therefore, make sure applicants complete the form and sign a statement on it indicating that the information is true. The court will almost always support a discharge for falsifying information when applying for work.[169]

Finally, doing a less-than-complete job of filling in the form may reflect poor work habits. Some applicants scribble "see résumé attached" on the application. This is not acceptable. You need the signed, completed form. Some firms no longer ask applicants for résumés at all, but instead request (where permitted) and then peruse Web presence links, such as Twitter or LinkedIn accounts.[170]

Most employers need several application forms. For technical and managerial personnel, the form may require detailed answers to questions about education and training. The form for hourly factory workers might focus on tools and equipment. Figure 5-8 illustrates one employment application.

KNOW YOUR EMPLOYMENT LAW

Application Forms and EEO Law[171]

Application forms must comply with equal employment laws. Problematical items include

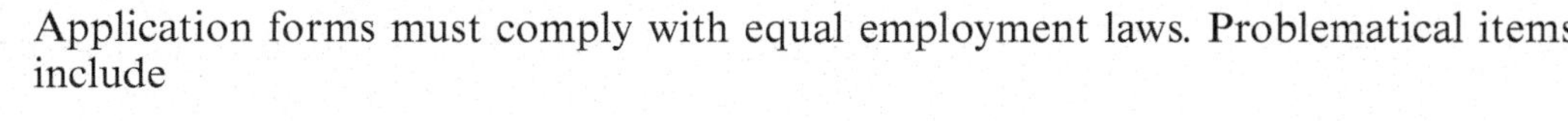

Education. A question on dates of attendance and graduation is a potential violation, since it may reveal the applicant's age.

FIGURE 5-8 FBI Employment Application

Source: From FBI Preliminary Application for Honors Internship Program, Federal Bureau of Investigation.

FIELD OFFICE USE ONLY

HP

Div: Program:

FEDERAL BUREAU OF INVESTIGATION

Preliminary Application for Honors Internship Program (Please Type or Print in Ink)

Date: ______________

I. PERSONAL HISTORY

Name in Full (Last, First, Middle, Maiden)	List College(s) attended, Major, Degree (if applicable), Grade Point Average
Birth Date (Month, Day, Year) Birth Place:	Social Security Number: (Optional)

Current Address

Street ______ Apt. No. ______ Home Phone ______ Area Code ______ Number

City ______ State ______ Zip Code ______ Work Phone ______ Area Code ______ Number

Are you: Licensed Driver ☐ Yes ☐ No U. S. Citizen ☐ Yes ☐ No

Have you served on active duty in the Armed Forces of the United States? ☐ Yes ☐ No	Branch of military service and dates of active duty:	Type of Discharge

How did you learn or become interested in the FBI Honors Internship Program?

Do you have a foreign language background? ☐ Yes ☐ No List proficiency for each language on reverse side.

Have you ever been arrested or charged with any violation including traffic, but excluding parking tickets? ☐ Yes ☐ No If so, list all such matters even if found not guilty, not formally charged, no court appearance, or matter settled by payment of fine or forfeiture of collateral. Include date, place, charge, disposition, details, and police agency on reverse side.

II. EMPLOYMENT HISTORY

Identify your most recent three years FULL-TIME work experience, after high school (excluding summer, part-time and temporary employment).

From	To	Description of Work	Name/Location of Employer

III. PERSONAL DECLARATIONS

Persons with a disability who require an accommodation to complete the application process are required to notify the FBI of their need for the accommodation.

Have you used marijuana during the last three years or more than 15 times? ☐ Yes ☐ No

Have you used any illegal drug(s) or combination of illegal drugs, other than marijuana, more than 5 times or during the last 10 years? ☐ Yes ☐ No

All Information provided by applicants concerning their drug history will be subject to verification by a preemployment polygraph examination.

Do you understand all prospective FBI employees will be required to submit to an urinalysis for drug abuse prior to employment? ☐ Yes ☐ No

I am aware that willfully withholding information or making false statements on this application constitutes a violation of Section 1001, Title 18, U.S. Code and if appointed, will be the basis for dismissal from the Federal Bureau of Investigation. I agree to these conditions and I hereby certify that all statements made by me on this application are true and complete, to the best of my knowledge.

____

Signature of Applicant as usually written. **(Do Not Use Nickname)**

The Federal Bureau of Investigation is an equal opportunity employer.

Arrest record. The courts have usually held that employers violate Title VII by disqualifying applicants from employment because of an arrest. This item has an adverse impact on minorities, and employers usually can't show it's required as a business necessity.

Notify in case of emergency. It is generally legal to require the name, address, and phone number of a person to notify in case of emergency. However, asking the relationship of this person could indicate the applicant's marital status or lineage.

Membership in organizations. Some forms ask to list memberships in clubs, organizations, or societies. Employers should include instructions not to include organizations that would reveal race, religion, physical handicaps, marital status, or ancestry.

Physical handicaps. It is usually illegal to require the listing of an applicant's physical handicaps or past illnesses unless the application blank specifically asks only for those that "may interfere with your job performance." Similarly, it is generally illegal to ask if the applicant has received workers' compensation.

Marital status. In general, the application should not ask whether an applicant is single, married, divorced, separated, or living with anyone, or the names, occupations, and ages of the applicant's spouse or children.

Housing. Asking whether an applicant *owns, rents*, or *leases* a house may be discriminatory. It can adversely affect minority groups and is difficult to justify on business necessity.

Video résumés. More candidates are submitting video résumés, a practice replete with benefits and threats. To facilitate using video résumés, several Web sites compile multimedia résumés for applicants.[172] The danger is that a video makes it more likely that rejected candidates may claim discrimination.[173] ■

Using Application Forms to Predict Job Performance

Some employers analyze application information ("biodata") to *predict* employee tenure and performance. In one study, the researchers found that applicants who had longer tenure with previous employers were less likely to quit, and also had higher performance within 6 months after hire.[174] Examples of predictive biodata items might include "quit a job without giving notice," "graduated from college," and "traveled considerably growing up."[175]

Choose biodata items with three things in mind. First, equal employment law limits the items you'll want to use (avoid age, race, or gender, for instance). And, noninvasive items are best. In one study, subjects perceived items such as "dollar sales achieved" and "grade point average in math" as not invasive. Items such as "birth order" and "frequent dates in high school" were more invasive. Finally, some applicants will successfully fake biodata answers ("quit my job") to impress the employer.[176]

Mandatory Arbitration

Many employers, aware of the high costs of litigation, require applicants to agree on their applications to mandatory arbitration should a dispute arise.

Different federal courts have taken different positions on the enforceability of such "mandatory alternative dispute resolution" clauses. They are generally enforceable, with two caveats. First, it must be a fair process. For example, the agreement should be a signed and dated separate agreement. Use simple wording. Provide for reconsideration and judicial appeal if there is an error of law. The employer must absorb most of the cost of the arbitration process. The process should be reasonably swift. Employees should be eligible to receive the full remedies they would have had if they had access to the courts.[177]

Second, mandatory arbitration clauses turn some candidates off. In one study, 389 MBA students read simulated employment brochures. Mandatory employment arbitration had a significantly negative impact on the attractiveness of the company as a place to work.[178]

Building Your Management Skills: The Human Side of Recruiting

In one survey, almost 60% of job seekers said they had a poor applicant experience; the worst feedback came from those who never even heard back from the companies they applied to.[179] In another study, recruiter incivility hurt job seekers' "self-efficacy"—basically, the person's confidence in his or her ability to get a job. What comments qualified as "uncivil"? Comments or action that were *dismissive* of the applicant's qualifications (" the recruiter looked at my résumé and said they'd never hire someone like me"); *unresponsive* or untimely communication ("they said they'd get back to me and they never did"); *rude* interactions ("after waiting for my interview for 15 minutes, the interviewer just kept checking her watch while I was talking"); *belittling* ("the interviewer talked down to me in a demeaning tone"); and *rushing* through the interview.[180] Most employers can and should do better.

Chapter Review

Chapter Section Summaries

5-1. Recruitment and selection start with **workforce planning and forecasting.** Workforce planning is the process of deciding what positions the firm will have to fill, and how to fill them. This often starts by forecasting personnel needs, perhaps using trend analysis, ratio analysis, scatter plots, or computerized software packages. Next forecast the supply of inside candidates. Here employers use manual systems and replacement charts and computerized skills inventories. Forecasting the supply of outside candidates is important, particularly when good candidates are more difficult to come by.

5-2. Managers need to understand why **effective recruiting is important.** Without enough candidates, employers cannot effectively screen the candidates or hire the best. Some employers use a recruiting yield pyramid to estimate how many applicants they need to generate in order to fill predicted job openings.

5-3. Filling open positions with **internal sources of candidates** has several advantages. You are familiar with their strengths and weaknesses, and they require less orientation. Finding internal candidates often utilizes job posting. For filling the company's projected top-level positions, succession planning—the ongoing process of systematically identifying, assessing, and developing organizational leadership to enhance performance—is the process of choice.

5-4. Workforce plans influence **employee engagement.** For example, plans to develop and retain employees and promote from within tend to foster engagement, while contrary policies may erode it. Recognizing this, at some companies such as FedEx, internal recruiting and promotion from within both play central roles in employee engagement. The promotion-from-within policy includes helping employees identify and develop their promotion potential. It also requires a coordinated system for accessing career records and posting job openings.

5-5. Employers use a variety of **outside sources of candidates** when recruiting applicants. These include recruiting via the Internet, advertising and employment agencies (including public and nonprofit agencies, and private agencies), temporary agencies and other alternative staffing methods, executive recruiters, college recruiting, referrals and walk-ins, and military personnel.

5-6. Understanding how to **recruit a more diverse workforce** is important. Whether the target is the single parent, older workers, or minorities, the basic rule is to understand their special needs and to create a set of policies and practices that create a more hospitable environment in which they can work.

5-7. **Employers develop and use application forms** to collect essential background information about the applicant. The application should enable you to make judgments on substantial matters such as the person's education and to identify the person's job references and supervisors. Of course, it's important to make sure the application complies with equal employment laws, for instance, with respect to questions regarding physical handicaps.

Discussion Questions

5-1. Briefly outline the workforce planning process.

5-2. Briefly explain each step in the recruitment and selection process.

5-3. What are the four main types of information that application forms provide?

5-4. How, specifically, do equal employment laws apply to personnel recruiting activities?

5-5. What are the five main things you would do to recruit and retain a more diverse workforce?

Individual and Group Activities

5-6. Bring to class several classified and display ads from the Web or the Sunday help wanted ads. Analyze the effectiveness of these ads using the guidelines discussed in this chapter.

5-7. Working individually or in groups, develop a 5-year forecast of occupational market conditions for five occupations such as accountant, nurse, and engineer.

5-8. Working individually or in groups, visit the local office of your state employment agency (or check out its site online). Come back to class prepared to discuss the following questions: What types of jobs seem to be available through this agency, predominantly? To what extent do you think this particular agency would be a good source of professional, technical, and/or managerial applicants? What sorts of paperwork are applicants to the state agency required to complete before their applications are processed by the agency? What other services does the office provide? What other opinions did you form about the state agency?

5-9. Working individually or in groups, find at least five employment ads, either on the Internet or in a local newspaper, that suggest that the company is family friendly and should appeal to women, minorities, older workers, and single parents. Discuss what the firm is doing to be family friendly.

5-10. Working individually or in groups, interview a manager between the ages of 25 and 35 at a local business who manages employees age 40 or older. Ask the manager to describe three or four of his or her most challenging experiences managing older employees.

5-11. Appendices A and B at the end of this book (pages 614–634) list the knowledge someone studying for the HRCI (Appendix A) or SHRM (Appendix B) certification exam needs to have in each area of human resource management (such as in Strategic Management and Workforce Planning). In groups of several students, do four things: (1) review Appendix A and/or B; (2) identify the material in this chapter that relates to the Appendix A and/or B required knowledge lists; (3) write four multiple-choice exam questions on this material that you believe would be suitable for inclusion in the HRCI exam and/or the SHRM exam; and, (4) if time permits, have someone from your team post your team's questions in front of the class, so that students in all teams can answer the exam questions created by the other teams.

KNOWLEDGE BASE

Experiential Exercise

The Nursing Shortage

Written and copyrighted by Gary Dessler, PhD.

As of February 2018, U.S. unemployment was quite low, and that was doubly the case for nurse professionals. Virtually every hospital was aggressively recruiting nurses. Many were turning to foreign-trained nurses, for example, by recruiting nurses in the Philippines. Experts expect nurses to be in very short supply for years to come.

Purpose: The purpose of this exercise is to give you experience in creating a recruitment program.

Required Understanding: You should be thoroughly familiar with the contents of this chapter, and with the nurse recruitment program of a hospital such as Mt. Sinai Hospital in New York (see https://careers.mountsinai.org/).[181]

How to Set Up the Exercise/Instructions: Set up groups of four to five students for this exercise. The groups should work separately and should not converse with each other. Each group should address the following tasks:

5-12. Based on information available on the hospital's Web site, create a hard-copy ad for the hospital to place in the Sunday edition of *The New York Times*. Which (geographic) editions of the *Times* would you use, and why?

5-13. Analyze the hospital's current online nurses' ad. How would you improve on it?

5-14. Prepare in outline form a complete nurses' recruiting program for this hospital, including all recruiting sources your group would use.

CHAPTER 5

Application Case

Techtonic Group

Written and copyrighted by Gary Dessler, PhD.

It's been estimated that there are more than 600,000 unfilled technical jobs (systems engineers, programmers, and so on) in the United States.[182] Therefore, IT companies like Techtonic Group are continually battling for good applicants.

For many years, Techtonic outsourced app software development to Armenia; CEO Heather Terenzio flew twice a year to work with the people there. However, programmers' salaries in Eastern Europe were rising, and the distances involved and the language differences complicated managing the projects. Therefore, the CEO decided there had to be a better way. Since the programmers abroad required more and more detailed instructions, she decided she could hire junior people closer to home. Then with about the same effort and instructions Techtonic could do its programming locally.

The problem was, how do you recruit talent when the unemployment rate for tech workers is close to zero? Ms. Terenzio had a novel solution. Rather than looking for college graduates with technical degrees, Techtonic set up a training/apprenticeship program. The aim was to attract people who didn't necessarily have college degrees but who expressed a strong desire for doing programming. People apply for the five-week program at "Techtonic Academy," where they learn basic computer coding skills. Some of the graduates than qualify for an eight-month paid apprenticeship at Techtonic, where they learn software development.

The program is successful. They usually get about 400 applicants for each of the 15 spots in each five-week Academy program. The city of Boulder helps subsidize the program, and the applicants don't pay for classes. The company is now expanding its academy/apprenticeship programs to other U.S. cities.

Questions

5-15. Specifically what recruiting sources would you use to attract participants to the Techtonic Academy, and apprenticeship programs?

5-16. What other recruitment sources (other than the academy and apprenticeship programs) would you recommend Techtonic use, and why?

5-17. What suggestions would you make to Techtonic for improving its recruiting processes?

Continuing Case

Carter Cleaning Company

Written and copyrighted by Gary Dessler, PhD.

Getting Better Applicants

If you were to ask Jennifer and her father what the main problem was in running their firm, their answer would be quick and short: hiring good people. Originally begun as a string of coin-operated laundromats requiring virtually no skilled help, the chain grew to six stores, each heavily dependent on skilled managers, cleaner/spotters, and pressers. Employees generally have no more than a high school education, and the market for them is very competitive. Over a typical weekend, literally dozens of want ads for experienced pressers or cleaner/spotters can be found in area newspapers. All these people usually are paid around $15 per hour, and they change jobs frequently. Jennifer and her father thus face the continuing task of recruiting and hiring qualified workers out of a pool of individuals they feel are almost nomadic in their propensity to move from area to area and job to job. Turnover in their stores (as in the stores of many of their competitors) often approaches 400%. "Don't talk to me about human resources planning and trend analysis," says Jennifer. "We're fighting an economic war, and I'm happy just to be able to round up enough live applicants to be able to keep my trenches fully manned."

In light of this problem, Jennifer's father asked her to answer the following questions:

Questions

5-18. First, how would you recommend we go about reducing the turnover in our stores?

5-19. Provide a detailed list of recommendations concerning how we should go about increasing our pool of acceptable job applicants so we no longer face the need to hire almost anyone who walks in the door. (Your recommendations regarding the latter should include completely worded online and hard-copy advertisements and recommendations regarding any other recruiting strategies you would suggest we use.)

Translating Strategy into HR Policies and Practices Case*,§

The accompanying strategy map for this chapter is in MyLab Management; the overall map on the inside back cover of this text outlines the relationships involved.

Improving Performance at the Hotel Paris

The New Recruitment Process

The Hotel Paris's competitive strategy is "to use superior guest service to differentiate the Hotel Paris properties, and to thereby increase the length of stay and return rate of guests, and thus boost revenues and profitability." HR manager Lisa Cruz must now formulate functional policies and activities that support this competitive strategy and boost performance, by eliciting the required employee behaviors and competencies.

As a longtime HR professional, Lisa Cruz was well aware of the importance of effective employee recruitment. If the Hotel Paris didn't get enough applicants, it could not be selective about who to hire. And, if it could not be selective about who to hire, it wasn't likely that the hotels would enjoy the customer-oriented employee behaviors that the company's strategy relied on. She was therefore disappointed to discover that the Hotel Paris was paying virtually no attention to the job of recruiting prospective employees. Individual hotel managers slapped together help wanted ads when they had positions to fill, and no one in the chain had any measurable idea of how many recruits these ads were producing or which recruiting approaches worked the best (or worked at all). Lisa knew that it was time to step back and get control of the Hotel Paris's recruitment function.

As they reviewed the details of the Hotel Paris's current recruitment practices, Lisa Cruz and the firm's CFO became increasingly concerned. What they found, basically, was that the recruitment function was totally unmanaged. The previous HR director had simply allowed the responsibility for recruiting to remain with each separate hotel, and the hotel managers, not being HR professionals, usually just took the path of least resistance when a job became available by placing help wanted ads in their local papers. There was no sense of direction from the Hotel Paris's headquarters regarding what sorts of applicants the company preferred, what media and alternative sources of recruits its managers should use, no online recruiting, and, of course, no measurement at all of effectiveness of the recruitment process. The company totally ignored recruitment-source metrics that other firms used effectively, such as number of qualified applicants per position, percentage of jobs filled from within, the offer-to-acceptance ratio, acceptance by recruiting source, turnover by recruiting source, and selection test results by recruiting source. This despite the fact, as the CFO put it, "that high-performance companies consistently score much higher

CHAPTER 5

§ Written and copyrighted by Gary Dessler, PhD.

than low-performing firms on HR practices such as number of qualified applicants per position, and percentage of jobs filled from within."

It was safe to say that achieving the Hotel Paris's strategic aims depended largely on the quality of the people that it attracted to, and then selected for, employment at the firm. "What we want are employees who will put our guests first, who will use initiative to see that our guests are satisfied, and who will work tirelessly to provide our guests with services that exceed their expectations," said the CFO. Lisa and the CFO both knew this process had to start with better recruiting. The CFO gave her the green light to design a new recruitment process.

Lisa and her team had the firm's IT department create a central recruiting link for the Hotel Paris's Web site, with geographical links that each local hotel could use to publicize its openings. The HR team created a series of standard ads the managers could use for each job title. These standard ads emphasized the company's service-oriented values, and basically said (without actually saying it) that if you were not people oriented you should not apply. They emphasized what it was like to work for the Hotel Paris, and the excellent benefits (which the HR team was about to get started on) the firm provided. It created a new intranet-based job posting system and encouraged employees to use it to apply for open positions. For several jobs, including housekeeping crew and front-desk clerk, applicants must now first pass a short prescreening test to apply. The HR team analyzed the performance (for instance, in terms of applicants/source and applicants hired/source) of the various local newspapers and recruiting firms the hotels had used in the past, and chose the best to be the approved recruiting sources in their local areas.

After 6 months with these and other recruitment function changes, the number of applicants was up on average 40%. Lisa and her team were now set to institute new screening procedures that would help them select the high-commitment, service-oriented, motivated employees they were looking for.

Questions

5-20. Given the hotel's required personnel skills, what recruiting sources would you have suggested it use, and why?

5-21. What would a Hotel Paris help wanted ad look like?

5-22. Based on what you know and on what you learned here in Chapter 5 of Dessler *Human Resource Management*, how would you suggest Hotel Paris measure the effectiveness of its recruiting efforts?

Writing Assignments

5-23. What are the pros and cons of five sources of job candidates?

5-24. As explained in this chapter, tecãology is in many ways revolutionizing how employers recruit for employees. You manage a small women's clothing store and need to hire an assistant manager. How would you use social media to recruit candidates?

MyLab Management Try It!

How would you apply the concepts and skills you learned in this chapter? If your professor has assigned this activity, go to the Assignments section of **www.pearson.com/mylab/management** to complete the simulation.

Key Terms

workforce (or employment or personnel) planning, 132
trend analysis, 134
ratio analysis, 134
scatter plot, 134
personnel replacement charts, 136
position replacement card, 136
succession planning, 138
employee recruiting, 139
recruiting yield pyramid, 140
job posting, 141
applicant tracking systems (ATS), 143
on-demand recruiting services (ODRS), 148
alternative staffing, 148
college recruiting, 153
application form, 158

Endnotes

1. Robert Hackett, "A Global Opportunity," *Fortune* 171, no. 2 (February 1, 2015), p. 22.
2. How long should the total process take? A recent study concluded (somewhat counterintuitively) that applicant assessment length does *not* increase applicant attrition. Jay Hardy III, Carter Gibson, Matthew Sloan, and Allison Carr, "Are Applicants More Likely to Quit Longer Assessments? Examining the Effect of Assessment Length on Applicant Attrition Behavior," *Journal of Applied Psychology* 102, no. 7 (2017), pp. 1148–1158.
3. This section is quoted or paraphrased from, "Workforce Planning: Translating the Business Plan into the People Plan," Towers Watson, www.towerswatson.com/en-GB/

Insights/IC-Types/Survey-Research-Results/2012/11/workforce-planning-translating-the-business-plan-into-the-people-plan?page=0, accessed February 18, 2018.

4. "Transforming Talent Management: Pursuing New Perspectives," 2013 Talent Management Conference & Exposition, Society for Human Resource Management, "Preparing for Tomorrow's Talent Gap: Five Strategies to Start Today" Workshop, p. 4. See also "Succession Planning Orientation Guide," *Workforce*, February 2014, pp. 32–34.
5. Based on Robert Hackett, "A Global Opportunity," *Fortune* 171, no. 2 (February 1, 2015), p. 22. For a full list of Four Seasons Hotels employee benefits see, http://jobs.fourseasons.com/home/working-at-fs/benefits/, accessed February 19, 2018.
6. Hackett, "A Global Opportunity." As noted, for a full list of Four Seasons Hotels employee benefits, see http://jobs.fourseasons.com/home/working-at-fs/benefits/, accessed February 19, 2018.
7. Ibid.
8. Jones Shannon, "Does HR Planning Improve Business Performance?" *Industrial Management*, January/February 2003, p. 20. See also Michelle Harrison et al., "Effective Succession Planning," *TD*, October 2006, pp. 22–23, and Jean Phillips and Stanley Gully, *Strategic Staffing* (Upper Saddle River, NJ: Pearson Education, 2012), pp. 116–181.
9. Phillips and Gully, *Strategic Staffing*, pp. 116–181.
10. Shannon, "Does HR Planning Improve Business Performance?" p. 16.
11. See, for example, Fay Hansen, "The Long View," *Workforce Management*, April 20, 2008, pp. 1, 14.
12. Bill Roberts, "Can They Keep Our Lights On?" *HR Magazine*, June 2010, pp. 62–68. For an example of a computerized personnel planning system, see www.kronos.com/scheduling-software/scheduling.aspx, accessed October 2, 2011.
13. See, for example, www.shrm.org/TemplatesTools/hrqa/Pages/Howcanaskillsinventorybeused for strategicHRplanning.aspx, accessed February 6, 2014.
14. http://skillsdbpro.com/SkillsDBPROWeb.html; http://skillsdbpro.com/client-list/; and www.surveyanalytics.com/skills-inventory.html, accessed June 22, 2015.
15. www.surveyanalytics.com/skills-inventory-software.html, accessed June 1, 2011.
16. Debbie Hancock, Vice President of Human Resources. SumTotal Talent Platform: Succession Planning. www.sumtotalsystem.com.
17. For a discussion, see, for example, "Pitfalls Abound for Employers Lacking Electronic Information Retention Policies," *Bloomberg BNA Bulletin to Management*, January 1, 2008, pp. 1–2.
18. The legislation includes the Federal Privacy Act of 1974 (applies to federal workers), the New York Personal Privacy Act of 1985, HIPAA (regulates use of medical records), and the Americans with Disabilities Act.
19. Ibid. See also Bill Roberts, "Risky Business," *HR Magazine*, October 2006, pp. 69–72.
20. www.wired.com/2015/06/opm-breach-security-privacy-debacle/, accessed August 25, 2015.
21. See, for example, Society for Human Resource Management, "HR's Insight into the Economy," *Workplace Visions* 4 (2008), p. 5.
22. www.astd.org/NR/rdonlyres/CBAB6F0D-97FA-4B1F-920C-6EBAF98906D1/0/BridgingtheSkillsGap.pdf, accessed June 1, 2011.
23. Carolyn Hirschman, "Putting Forecasting in Focus," *HR Magazine*, March 2007, pp. 44–49.
24. "Next Generation Talent Management," www.hewittassociates.com/_MetaBasicCMAssetCache_/Assets/Articles/next_generation.pdf, accessed November 9, 2010.
25. "Boeing Soars Over Potential Talent Gaps with Its Workforce Planning Strategies," *Bloomberg BNA Bulletin to Management*, February 19, 2013, p. 57.
26. Phillips and Gully, *Strategic Staffing*, pp. 116–181.
27. Mark Gurman, "Apple Has a Deep Bench of Potential Tim Cook Successors," https://www.bloomberg.com/news/articles/2018-02-13/apple-executive-bench-is-deep-as-ceo-succession-question-raised, accessed February 18, 2018.
28. See, for example, Soonhee Kim, "Linking Employee Assessments to Succession Planning," *Public Personnel Management* 32, no. 4 (Winter 2003), pp. 533–547; Michael Laff, "Talent Management: From Hire to Retire," *TD*, November 2006, pp. 42–48; and "CEO Succession Planning and Talent Considerations," http://deloitte.wsj.com/riskandcompliance/2013/05/28/ceo-succession-planning-and-talent-considerations/, accessed February 18, 2018.
29. See, for example, David Day, "Developing Leadership Talent," SHRM Foundation, www.shrm.org/about/foundation/research/Documents/Developing%20Lead%20Talent-%20FINAL.pdf, accessed October 4, 2011.
30. Quoted in Susan Wells, "Who's Next," *HR Magazine*, November 2003, p. 43. See also Christee Atwood, "Implementing Your Succession Plan," *TD*, November 2007, pp. 54–57; and Day, "Developing Leadership Talent."
31. See "Succession Management: Identifying and Developing Leaders," *BNA Bulletin to Management* 21, no. 12 (December 2003), p. 15; and Day, "Developing Leadership Talent."
32. Kim, "Linking Employee Assessments to Succession Planning."
33. "CEO Succession Planning and Talent Considerations."
34. Bill Roberts, "Matching Talent with Tasks," *HR Magazine*, November 2002, pp. 91–96; https://www.shrm.org/hr-today/news/hr-magazine/pages/1102hrtech.aspx, accessed February 17, 2018.
35. https://www.saba.com/us/apps/succession-work/; https://www.adp.com/solutions/large-business/services/talent-management/succession-management.aspx, accessed February 17, 2018.
36. On the other hand, Facebook and Intuit are doing "program hiring"; here they hire particularly promising candidates, although they don't have specific jobs for them. Lindsay Gellman, "When a Job Offer Comes without a Job," *The Wall Street Journal*, December 2, 2015, pp. B1, B7.
37. Sara Rynes, Robert Bretz Jr., and Barry Gerhart, "The Importance of Recruitment and Job Choice: A Different Way of Looking," *Personnel Psychology* 44, no. 3 (September 1991), pp. 487–521. For other insights about what makes recruiters effective, see, for example, Bezon Karter, "The 5 Clumsy Mistakes Most Recruiters Make," *Social Talent*, October 11, 2016, https://www.socialtalent.com/blog/recruitment/5-clumsy-mistakes-most-recruiters-make, accessed February 18, 2018.
38. Phillips and Gully, *Strategic Staffing.*
39. "Recruitment Marketing," www.recruiter.com/recruitment_marketing/, accessed May 1, 2012.
40. www.ge.com/careers/why_ge.html, accessed May 1, 2012.
41. Stanley Gully, Jean Phillips, William Castellano, Khongji Han, and Andrea Kim, "A Mediated Moderation Model of Recruiting Socially and Environmentally Responsible Job Applicants," *Personnel Psychology* 66 (2013), p. 966.
42. Genevieve Douglas, "Panicked by Online Company Reviews? Here's What to Do," *Bloomberg BNA Bulletin to Management*, September 26, 2017.
43. Kenneth Sovereign, *Personnel Law* (Upper Saddle River, NJ: Prentice Hall, 1999), pp. 47–49.
44. Ibid., p. 48.
45. "Apple, Google Agree to Pay $415 Million in Settlement of Antitrust Hiring Charges," *Bloomberg BNA Bulletin to Management*, January 27, 2015, p. 27.
46. Todd Henneman, "The Insiders or the Outsiders?" *Workforce*, March 2014, pp. 29–31, 48.
47. Ibid.
48. Eric Krell, "Look Outside or Seek Within?" *HR Magazine*, January/February 2015, pp. 61–64.
49. "Hiring Works the Second Time Around," *BNA Bulletin to Management*, January 30, 1997, p. 40; and Issie Lapowsky, "How to Rehire Former Employees," *INC.*, May 18, 2010, www.inc.com/guides/2010/05/rehiring-former-employees.html, accessed October 3, 2011.
50. Ibid.
51. See www.linkedin.com/jobs2/view/10696437, accessed June 22, 2015.
52. www.fedex.com/ma/about/overview/philosophy.html, accessed February 18, 2018.
53. Lauren Weber and Leslie Kwoh, "Beware the Phantom Job Listing," *The Wall Street Journal*, January 9, 2013, p. B1.
54. "Many Workers Use Social Networking Sites in Job Hunt, Edit Own Content, Survey Finds," *Bloomberg BNA Bulletin to Management*, May 10, 2011, p. 147.
55. See, for example, J. De Avila, "Beyond Job Boards: Targeting the Source," *The Wall Street Journal* (Eastern Edition), July 2, 2009, pp. D1, D5; and C. Fernandez-Araoz et al., "The Definitive Guide to Recruiting in Good Times and Bad" [Financial crisis spotlight], *Harvard Business Review*, 87, no. 5 (May 2009), pp. 74–84.
56. Kris Dunn, "The New Sheriff in Town: Google Jobs," *Workforce*, September/October 2017, p. 14.
57. Dave Zielinski, "The Gamification of Recruitment," *HR Magazine*, November 2015, pp. 59–61.
58. "Innovative HR Programs Cultivate Successful Employees," *Nation's Restaurant News* 41, no. 50 (December 17, 2007), p. 74.
59. Sarah Fister Gale, "Social Media Transforms a Recruiting Source Software Industry," *Workforce Management*, workforce.com, June 2013, p. 26. See also Thomas Cottereau, "The Future of Live Video Interviews for Recruitment," *HR Magazine*, November 2014, pp. 48–50. Similarly, Main Line Health, a healthcare network with 10,000 employees, uses

Web-based video for prescreening applicants, allowing them to respond on their own schedule to prerecorded questions; Main Line recruiters then view these videos and invite selected applicants for in-person interviews. Drew Robb, "For HR, Video Is a Star," *HR Magazine*, February 2016, p. 65.

60. Elizabeth Agnvall, "Job Fairs Go Virtual," *HR Magazine*, July 2007, p. 85; Gary Stern, "Virtual Job Fairs Becoming More of a Reality," *Workforce Management*, February 2011, p. 11.
61. Yuko Takeo and Nao Sano, "A Job Website Thrives in the New Japan," *Bloomberg Businessweek*, pp. 41–42.
62. Matthias Baum and Rudiger Kabst, "The Effectiveness of Recruitment Advertisements and Recruitment Websites: Indirect and Interactive Effects on Applicant Attraction," *Human Resource Management* 53, no. 3 (May–June 2014), pp. 353–378.
63. "EEOC Issues Much Delayed Definition of 'Applicant,'" *HR Magazine*, April 2004, p. 29; Valerie Hoffman and Greg Davis, "OFCCP's Internet Applicant Definition Requires Overhaul of Recruitment and Hiring Policies," *Society for Human Resources Management Legal Report*, January/February 2006, p. 2; "Online Hiring Faces Scrutiny for Age Bias," *Business Management Daily*, January 10, 2018, accessed February 18, 2018.
64. This carries legal risks, particularly if the device disproportionately screens out minority or female applicants. Lisa Harpe, "Designing an Effective Employment Prescreening Program," *Employment Relations Today* 32, no. 3 (Fall 2005), pp. 43–51.
65. Lauren Weber, "Your Résumé versus Oblivion," *The Wall Street Journal*, January 24, 2012, pp. B1, B6.
66. William Dickmeyer, "Applicant Tracking Reports Make Data Meaningful," *Workforce*, February 2001, pp. 65–67; and, as an example, www.icims.com/prelude/1101/3009?_vsrefdom=google_ppc&gclid=CPHki_nx1KsCFcPt7QodmkjLDA, accessed October 4, 2011.
67. Paul Gilster, "Channel the Resume Flood with Applicant Tracking Systems," *Workforce*, January 2001, pp. 32–34; Dickmeyer, "Applicant Tracking Reports Make Data Meaningful"; and, as an example, www.icims.com/prelude/1101/3009?_vsrefdom=google_ppc&gclid=CPHki_nx1KsCFcPt7QodmkjLDA, accessed October 4, 2011.
68. Note also that for EEO purposes, "Feds Want a Look at Online Job Sites," *HR Magazine*, November 2008, p. 12.
69. Weber, "Your Resume versus Oblivion."
70. Pamela Babcock, "Intelligent Technology Is Changing Recruiting," *HR News*, February 24, 2017; Ted Greenwald, "Workplace Technology (A Special Report)—How AI Is Transforming the Workplace . . .," *The Wall Street Journal*, March 13, 2017, p. R1; Emma Boyde, "Robo-Recruiters Are Quick to Replicate Human Bias," FT.com, December 7, 2017.
71. https://www.sap.com/documents/2017/08/fea3fccf-cd7c-0010-82c7-eda71af511fa.html, accessed February 15, 2018.
72. Laszlo Bock, *Work Rules!* (New York: Twelve: 2015), pp. 81, 82.
73. Ibid., pp. 79–86.
74. Sarah Gale, "Internet Recruiting: Better, Cheaper, Faster," *Workforce*, December 2001, p. 75.
75. "Help Wanted—and Found," *Fortune*, October 2, 2006, p. 40.
76. James Breaugh, "Employee Recruitment: Current Knowledge and Important Areas for Future Research," *Human Resource Management Review* 18 (2008), p. 114.
77. "Job Seekers' Privacy Has Been Eroded with Online Job Searchers, Report Says," *BNA Bulletin to Management*, November 20, 2003, p. 369. The jobseeker can first review each job board's privacy policy, as at https://www.jobvite.com/privacy-policy/, accessed February 18, 2018, but the best approach may be to use caution.
78. Anthony Abbatiello, "The Digital Override," *Workforce*, May 2014, pp. 36–39; "Social Recruiting in 2012, the Ladders.com," Special Advertising Supplement to *Workforce Management*, 2012; and http://cdn.theladders.net/static/recruit-ladder/pdf/WP%20Social%20Recruiting%20in%202012.pdf, accessed July 2, 2014.
79. Aliah Wright, "Your Social Media Is Showing," *HR Magazine*, March 2012, p. 16. However, one survey by Glassdoor concluded that about half of those making hiring decisions say their passive recruiting efforts are less effective than they used to be: fewer passive candidates respond to unsolicited e-mails and phone calls than in the past. Sarah Fister Gale, "The New Recruits in the Recruiting," *Workforce*, May 2015, p. 44. Google, Facebook, and Glassdoor recently introduced their own recruiting services: Martin Berman-Gorvine, "Move Over LinkedIn: Facebook Is Entering Job Recruiting Market," *Bloomberg BNA Bulletin to Management*, March 13, 2018; and Genevieve Douglas, "Glassdoor Shifts Focus as Employers Push Hunt for Star Workers," *Bloomberg BNA Bulletin to Management*, March 13, 2018.
80. Jennifer Arnold, "Twittering at Face Booking While They Were," *HR Magazine*, December 2009, p. 54.
81. Ibid.
82. *Bloomberg BNA Bulletin to Management*, "Certain Social Media Tools Are Helping HR Connect Swiftly with the Right Job Candidates," July 24, 2012, p. 233.
83. Jennifer Taylor Arnold, "Recruiting on the Run," February 2010, *HR Magazine*, pp. 65–67.
84. Sarah Fister Gale, "OMG UR Hired!" *Workforce*, September/October 2017, p. 10.
85. https://premium.linkedin.com/premiumhiring/features, accessed April 6, 2015.
86. Jim Lundy, "Research Note," *Aragon Research* 3 (January 31, 2014).
87. Martin Berman-Gorvine, "Real Online Profile or Dangerous Scam? HR Beware," *Bloomberg BNA Bulletin to Management*, August 22, 2017.
88. http://mystaffingpro.com/, accessed February 12, 2017.
89. Breaugh, "Employee Recruitment," p. 111.
90. Ibid., p. 113.
91. Find your nearest one-stop center at www.servicelocator.org.
92. Lynn Doherty and E. Norman Sims, "Quick, Easy Recruitment Help: From a State?" *Workforce*, May 1998, p. 36.
93. Ibid.
94. Robert Grossman, "How to Recruit a Recruitment Outsourcer," *HR Magazine*, July 2012, pp. 51–54; and Susan Ladika, "A Lot to Process," *Workforce Management*, July 2012, pp. 16–18. See also Max Mihelich, "RPO Is on the Go," *Workforce*, February 2014, pp. 44–47.
95. Sarah Fister Gale, "RPO Customers: We Want More of Everything," *Workforce*, January/February 2017, pp. 44–45.
96. Martha Frase-Blunt, "A Recruiting Spigot," *HR Magazine*, April 2003, pp. 71–79.
97. Taryn Barnes, "Real Gig-Getters," *Workforce*, October 2015, p. 50.
98. One "Wharton MBA and GE alum" manages short-term projects for major companies and served as interim CEO for one firm. See Jodi Greenstone Miller and Matt Miller, "The Best Executive and Professional Jobs May No Longer Be Full-Time Gigs," *Harvard Business Review*, May 2012, p. 51.
99. "As Hiring Falters, More Workers Are Temporary," *The New York Times*, December 20, 2010, pp. A1, A4.
100. Shari Cauldron, "Contingent Workforce Spurs HR Planning," *Personnel Journal*, July 1994, p. 60; "Cost of Temporary Staffing vs. Cost of Full-time Employee," https://www.snelling.com/2015/06/11/cost-of-temporary-staffing-vs-cost-of-full-time-employee/, accessed February 18, 2018.
101. Robert Bohner Jr. and Elizabeth Salasko, "Beware the Legal Risks of Hiring Temps," *Workforce*, October 2002, pp. 50–57. See also Fay Hansen, "A Permanent Strategy for Temporary Hires," *Workforce Management*, February 26, 2007, p. 27; and Robert Grossman, "Strategic Temp–tations," *HR Magazine*, March 2012, pp. 24–34.
102. This is based on or quoted from Nancy Howe, "Match Temp Services to Your Needs," *Personnel Journal*, March 1989, pp. 45–51. See also Stephen Miller, "Collaboration Is Key to Effective Outsourcing," *HR Magazine* 58 (2008), pp. 60–61; and, as an example, www.bbb.org/shreveport/accredited-business-directory/employment-contractors-temporary-help/plain-dealing-la, accessed September 23, 2011.
103. Daniel Feldman, Helen Doerpinghaus, and William Turnley, "Managing Temporary Workers: A Permanent HRM Challenge," *Organizational Dynamics* 23, no. 2 (Fall 1994), p. 49. See also Kathryn Tyler, "Treat Contingent Workers with Care," *HR Magazine*, March 2008, p. 75; and www.employment.oregon.gov/EMPLOY/ES/BUS/index.shtml, accessed October 4, 2011.
104. Carolyn Hirschman, "Are Your Contractors Legal?" *HR Magazine*, March 2004, pp. 59–63. See also Dori Meinert, "Modern-Day Slavery," *HR Magazine*, May 2012, pp. 22–24.
105. Margaret Steen, "More Employers Take on Temps, but Planning Is Paramount," *Workforce Management*, May 2011, p. 14.
106. Heather Jackson and Cary Donham, "Five Things to Know about Working with Staffing Firms," *Workforce Management*, October 2013, p. 47.
107. Harry Davis and Christopher Giampapa, "How to Protect Your Firm from Employee Raiding," *Bloomberg BNA Bulletin to Management* 66, no. 18 (May 5, 2015), pp. 51–52.
108. "Apple and Google Will Pay $415 Million; Intuit and eBay Settle in Separate No Poach Case," *Bloomberg BNA*

Bulletin to Management, September 15, 2015, p. 201.

109. Patrick Thibodeau, "Offshoring Shrinks Number of IT Jobs, Study Says," http://www.computerworld.com/article/2502949/it-outsourcing/offshoring-shrinks-number-of-it-jobs—study-says.html, accessed February 13, 2017.
110. Ed Frauenheim, "Homeward Bound," *Workforce Management*, February 2013, pp. 26–31.
111. See, for example, Esther Lander and Andrew Turnbull, "Defending and Avoiding Citizenship Discrimination Claims When Using Staffing Firms with H1-B Visa Holders," *Bloomberg BNA Bulletin to Management*, 67, no. 11 (March 15, 2016), pp. 51–54.
112. Eli Stocols and Laura Meckler, "Trump Unveils H-1B Order," *The Wall Street Journal,* April 19, 2017, p. A4; and Vindu Goel, "How 'Hire American' Could Affect the World of Tech Workers," *The New York Times*, April 19, 2017, p. A16 See also Laura Francis, "More Uncertainty for Businesses Now That Travel Ban Allowed," *Bloomberg BNA Bulletin to Management*, December 12, 2017, and Joshua Brustein, "Trump H-1B Reform as Companies Rethinking Use of Visa Program," *Bloomberg BNA Bulletin to Management*, November 14, 2017.
113. Laura Francis, "High Skilled Visas Getting More Government Scrutiny," *Bloomberg BNA Bulletin to Management*, January 2, 2018.
114. Michelle Rafter, "Hiring and the H-1B," *Workforce*, September/October 2017, pp. 44–46.
115. See for example, Susan Wells, "Slow Times for Executive Recruiting," *HR Magazine*, April 2003, pp. 61–67; Barbara Ashton, "Crazy High Recruiter Fees? What You Need to Know to Make Your Investment Pay Off," published on June 5, 2015, https://www.linkedin.com/pulse/crazy-high-recruiter-fees-take-look-unfilled-vacancy-costs-ashton, accessed February 18, 2018; Ken Sundheim, "A Guide to Hiring Recruitment Firms," https://www.forbes.com/sites/kensundheim/2013/09/19/331/#2220bf3ccaa5, accessed February 18, 2018.
116. Michelle Martinez, "Working with an Outside Recruiter? Get It in Writing," *HR Magazine*, January 2001, pp. 98–105; Elizabeth Wasserman, "How to Work with an Executive Search Firm," https://www.inc.com/guides/use-an-executive-search-firm.html, accessed February 18, 2018.
117. See, for example, Stephenie Overman, "Searching for the Top," *HR Magazine*, January 2008, p. 49.
118. Bill Leonard, "Recruiting from the Competition," *HR Magazine*, February 2001, pp. 78–86. See also G. Anders, "Secrets of the Talent Scouts," *The New York Times* (Late New York Edition), March 15, 2009, pp. 1, 7 (Sec. 3).
119. Carol Hymowitz and Jeff Green, "These Days, Anybody Can Headhunt," *Bloomberg Businessweek*, January 27, 2013, pp. 19–20; Joann Lublin, "More Executive Recruiting Ships in House," *The Wall Street Journal*, October 10, 2012, p. B8.
120. Lauren Weber, "Here's What Boards Want in Executives," *The Wall Street Journal*, December 10, 2014, p. B5.
121. Based on John Wareham, *Secrets of a Corporate Headhunter* (New York: Playboy Press, 1981), pp. 213–225; Aarian Marshall, "Greed, Ambition, and Trade Secrets: Welcome to Waymo v. Uber," February 1, 2018, https://www.wired.com/story/waymo-uber-self-driving-car-trial-preview/, accessed February 18, 2018; Kirsten Korosec, "Waymo v. Uber: What You Need To Know About the High-Stakes Self-Driving Tech Trial," http://fortune.com/2018/02/05/waymo-v-uber-what-you-need-to-know-about-the-high-stakes-self-driving-tech-trial/, accessed February 18, 2018.
122. www.kaiserpermanentejobs.org/employee-referral-program.aspx, accessed August 20, 2011.
123. Mark Feffer, "New Connections," *HR Magazine*, April 2015, pp. 46–50.
124. Breaugh, "Employee Recruitment," p. 109.
125. "Tell a Friend: Employee Referral Programs Earn High Marks for Low Recruiting Costs," *BNA Bulletin to Management*, June 28, 2001, p. 201.
126. Rebecca Greenfield, "Hiring an Employee's Buddy Is Fueling a Major Workplace Crisis," *Bloomberg BNA Bulletin to Management*, January 10, 2017.
127. Sara Rynes, Marc Orlitzky, and Robert Bretz Jr., "Experienced Hiring versus College Recruiting: Practices and Emerging Trends," *Personnel Psychology* 50 (1997), pp. 309–339. See also Lisa Munniksma, "Career Matchmakers: Partnering with Collegiate Career Centers Offers Recruiters Access to Rich Source of Applicants," *HR Magazine* 50, no. 2 (February 2005), p. 93, and Brian Weed, "The Entry-Level Job Market Is the Strongest It's Been in Years," http://college.usatoday.com/2017/05/17/did-you-just-graduate-the-entry-level-job-market-is-the-strongest-its-been-in-years/, accessed February 17, 2018.
128. See, for example, Breaugh, "Employee Recruitment," p. 111; "Recruiters Look to Be Big Man on Campus," *Workforce Management*, September 2010, p. 12.
129. Greet Van Hoye and Filip Lievens, "Tapping the Grapevine: A Closer Look at Word-of-Mouth as a Recruitment Source," *Journal of Applied Psychology* 94, no. 2 (2009), pp. 341–352.
130. Munniksma, "Career Matchmakers."
131. Joe Mullich, "Finding the Schools That Yield the Best Job Applicant ROI," *Workforce Management*, March 2004, pp. 67–68; "Selecting Target Schools: Ensuring Your URR Program Is Hitting the Mark," https://www.naceweb.org/talent-acquisition/candidate-selection/selecting-target-schools-ensuring-your-urr-program-is-hitting-the-mark/, accessed February 18, 2018.
132. Wendy Boswell et al., "Individual Job Choice Decisions and the Impact of Job Attributes and Recruitment Practices: A Longitudinal Field Study," *Human Resource Management* 42, no. 1 (Spring 2003), pp. 23–37; James Breaugh, "Employee Recruitment: Current Knowledge and Important Areas for Future Research"; https://career.virginia.edu/interviewing/day-prep/site-visits-employers, accessed February 18, 2018.
133. Hao Zhao Oh and Robert Liden, "Internship: A Recruitment and Selected Perspective," *Journal of Applied Psychology* 96, no. 1 (2011), pp. 221–229.
134. Teddy Wayne, "The No-Limits Job," *The New York Times*, March 3, 2013, Sunday Styles p. 1. Over the past few years, unpaid interns have increasingly sued their employers, and won. See Max Mihelich, "Free Advice on Unpaid Internships," *Workforce*, August 2014, pp. 40–43.
135. Lawrence Peikes and Christine Salmon Wachter, "Court Adopts New Test for Determining Interns Status," *HR Magazine*, October 2015, p. 73.
136. Dori Meinert, "The Value of Veterans," *HR Magazine*, November 2016, pp. 53–55.
137. Christopher Stone and Dianna Stone, "Factors Affecting Hiring Decisions about Veterans," *Human Resource Management Review* 25, no. 1 (2015), pp. 68–79.
138. Theresa Minton-Eversole, "Mission: Recruitment," *HR Magazine*, January 2009, pp. 43–45; https://www.goarmy.com/benefits/additional-incentives/partnership-for-youth-success.html, accessed February 17, 2018.
139. See, for example, Stephanie Castellano, "The Value of Veterans," *TD*, February 2013, p. 16.
140. Wal-Mart to Hire Projected 100,000 Vets over Five Years," *Bloomberg BNA Bulletin to Management*, January 22, 2013, p. 26; https://walmartcareerswithamission.com/, accessed February 17, 2018.
141. http://www.helmetstohardhats.org/, accessed February 17, 2018.
142. Based on Thomas Stewart, "In Search of Elusive Tech Workers," *Fortune*, February 16, 1998, pp. 171–172; and Beth Rosenthal, "GE Looks to Recruitment Process Outsourcer to Find 'Meat And Potatoes' Candidates as Well as 'The Purple Squirrel,'" http://www.outsourcing-center.com/2006-10-ge-looks-to-recruitment-process-outsourcer-to-find-meat-and-potatoes-candidates-as-well-as-the-purple-squirrel-article-37479.html, accessed February 17, 2018.
143. Thomas Stewart, "In Search of Elusive Tech Workers," *Fortune*, February 16, 1998, pp. 171–172; and www.outsourcing-center.com/2006-10-ge-looks-to-recruitment-process-outsourcer-to-find-meat-and-potatoes-candidates-as-well-as-the-purple-squirrel-article-37479.html, accessed October 5, 2011.
144. Ellen McGirt, "Google Searches Its Soul," *Fortune*, February 1, 2017, p. 55.
145. Ibid.
146. Ellen Huet, "In the Land of the Blind Hire," *Bloomberg Businessweek*, January 23–29, 2017, pp. 27–28.
147. Furthermore, much of the recent increase in the proportion of people participating in the workforce came about because women, and particularly unskilled women, are coming back to work. "All the Working Ladies," *The Economist*, August 19, 2017, p. 25.
148. www.recruitingtrends.com/recruiting-women/; http://online.wsj.com/article/SB10001424127887323764804578314450063914388.html; www.theresumator.com/blog/how-to-recruit-women-for-your-workforce/; http://blogs.-kenan-flagler.unc.edu/2012/06/12/the-new-business-imperative-recruiting-and-retaining-women-in-the-workplace/. All accessed May 9, 2013.
149. https://www.census.gov/prod/2013pubs/p20-570.pdf, accessed February 13, 2017.
150. Judith Casey and Marcie Pitt-Catsouphes, "Employed Single Mothers: Balancing Job and Home Life," *Employee Assistance Quarterly* 9, no. 324 (1994), p. 42.

151. "Barclaycard Helps Single Parents to Find Employment," *Personnel Today*, November 7, 2006.
152. Caroline Straub, "Antecedents and Organizational Consequences of Family Supportive Supervisor Behavior: A Multilevel Conceptual Framework for Research," *Human Resource Management Review* 22 (2012), pp. 15–26.
153. Susan Glairon, "Single Parents Need More Flexibility at Work, Advocate in Denver Says," *Daily Camera*, February 8, 2002; www.cnn.com/2008/LIVING/worklife/06/04/balance.calculator, accessed February 17, 2018.
154. Ben Steverman, "Working Past 70: Americans Can't Seem to Retire," *Bloomberg BNA Bulletin to Management*, July 18, 2017.
155. Alison Wellner, "Tapping a Silver Mine," *HR Magazine*, March 2002, p. 29.
156. Phased retirements are increasingly popular, with various employers, letting employees close to retirement reduce their schedules to between 16 and 30 hours weekly. Carol Hymowitz, "American Firms Want to Keep Older Workers a Bit Longer," *Bloomberg BNA Bulletin to Management*, January 3, 2017.
157. Sue Shellenbarger, "Gray Is Good: Employers Make Efforts to Retain Older, Experienced Workers," *The Wall Street Journal*, December 1, 2005. See also Robert Grossman, "Keep Pace with Older Workers," *HR Magazine*, May 2008, pp. 39–46.
158. Gary Adams and Barbara Rau, "Attracting Retirees to Apply: Desired Organizational Characteristics of Bridge Employment," *Journal of Organizational Behavior* 26, no. 6 (September 2005), pp. 649–660.
159. Thomas Ng and Daniel Feldman, "Evaluating Six Common Stereotypes About Older Workers with Meta-analytical Data," *Personnel Psychology* 60, no. 6 (2012), pp. 821–858.
160. Ibid.
161. Abby Ellin, "Supervising the Graybeards," *The New York Times*, January 16, 2000, p. B16; Derek Avery and Patrick McKay, "Target Practice: An Organizational Impression Management Approach to Attracting Minority and Female Job Applicants," *Personnel Psychology* 59 (2006), pp. 157–189.
162. A list of minority job boards can be found at https://workology.com/18-job-boards-perfect-for-diversity-recruiting-compliance-efforts/, accessed February 18, 2018.
163. Herbert Greenberg, "A Hidden Source of Talent," *HR Magazine*, March 1997, pp. 88–91; "CalWORKs Welfare-to-Work Program," http://ehsd.org/benefits/calworks-welfare-to-work-program/, accessed February 18, 2018.
164. Noam Scheiber, "Study Using Fake Job Letters Exposes Bias against Disabled," *The New York Times*, November 2, 2015, pp. B1, B2.
165. Linda Moore, "Firms Need to Improve Recruitment, Hiring of Disabled Workers, EEO Chief Says," *Knight Ridder/Tribune Business News*, November 5, 2003. See also "Recruiting Disabled More Than Good Deed, Experts Say," *BNA Bulletin to Management*, February 27, 2007, p. 71.
166. "Students with Disabilities Available," *HR Briefing*, June 15, 2002, p. 5; the program can be found at https://www.dol.gov/odep/wrp/PathwaysGuide.htm, accessed February 18, 2018.
167. Moore, "Firms Need to Improve Recruitment."
168. This paragraph is based on Jennifer L. Wood, James M. Schmidtke, and Diane L. Decker, "Lying on Job Applications: The Effects of Job Relevance, Commission, and Human Resource Management Experience," *Journal of Business and Psychology* 22 (2007), pp. 1–9.
169. Kenneth Sovereign, *Personnel Law* (Upper Saddle River, NJ: Pearson, 1999), pp. 51, 132.
170. Rachel Emma Silverman, "No More Resumes, Say Some Firms," *The Wall Street Journal*, January 24, 2012, p. B6.
171. Recruitment bias remains a problem. Recently, the Bass Pro Outdoor World chain tentatively agreed to pay over $10 million to settle EEOC charges that its recruitment processes may have discriminated against black and Hispanic job-seekers. Patrick Dorrian, "Bass Pro Agrees to Pay $10.5 Million to Black, Hispanic Jobseekers," *Bloomberg BNA Bulletin to Management*, August 1, 2017.
172. Alina Dizik, "Wooing Job Recruiters with Video Resumes," *The Wall Street Journal*, May 20, 2010, p. D4. As of August 20, 2014, these companies included resumebook.tv and optimalresume.com.
173. Kathy Gurchiek, "Video Resumes Spark Curiosity, Questions," *HR Magazine*, May 2007, pp. 28–30; "Video Resumes Can Illuminate Applicants' Abilities, but Pose Discrimination Concerns," *BNA Bulletin to Management*, May 20, 2007, pp. 169–170.
174. Murray Barrick and Ryan Zimmerman, "Hiring for Retention and Performance," *Human Resource Management* 48, no. 2 (March/April 2009), pp 183–206.
175. James Breaugh, "The Use of Biodata for Employee Selection: Test Research and Future Directions," *Human Resource Management Review* 19 (2009), pp. 219–231. Utilizing biodata items presumes that the employer can show that the items predict performance. Biodata items such as "graduated from college" may have an adverse impact on minorities, but studies suggest that employers can avoid that problem through judicious choice of biodata items (p. 229).
176. Fred Mael, Mary Connerley, and Ray Morath, "None of Your Business: Parameters of Biodata Invasiveness," *Personnel Psychology* 49 (1996), pp. 613–650; Kenneth Law et al., "Impression Management and Faking in Biodata Scores among Chinese Job-Seekers," *Asia Pacific Journal of Management* 19, no. 4 (December 2002), pp. 541–556; Thomas E. Becker and Alan Colquitt, "Potential versus Actual Faking of a Biodata Form: An Analysis along Several Dimensions of Item Type," *Personnel Psychology* 45, no. 2 (December 2006), pp. 389–406.
177. "Supreme Court Denies Circuit City's Bid for Review of Mandatory Arbitration," *BNA Bulletin to Management*, June 6, 2002, p. 177; "Supreme Court Gives the Employers Green Light to Hold Most Employees to Arbitration Pacts," *BNA Bulletin to Management*, March 29, 2001, pp. 97–98; Megan Leonhardt, "Getting Screwed at Work? The Sneaky Way You May Have Given Up Your Right to Sue," September 27, 2017, http://time.com/money/4958168/big-companies-mandatory-arbitration-cant-sue/, accessed February 18, 2018.
178. Douglas Mahony et al., "The Effects of Mandatory Employment Arbitration Systems on Applicants Attraction to Organizations," *Human Resource Management* 44, no. 4 (Winter 2005), pp. 449–470; See also H. John Bernardin et al., "Mandatory and Binding Arbitration: Effects on Employee Attitudes and Recruiting Results," *Human Resource Management* 50, no. 2 (March–April 2011), pp. 175–200.
179. Sarah Fister Gale, "Candidate Experience Tech Is Ticking Them Off," *Workforce*, September/October 2016, p. 10.
180. Abdifatah A. Ali, Ann Marie Ryan, Brent J. Lyons, Mark J. Ehrhart, and Jennifer L. Wessel, "The Long Road to Employment: Incivility Experienced by Job Seekers," *Journal of Applied Psychology*, 101, no. 3 (2016), pp. 333–349.
181. https://careers.mountsinai.org/, accessed February 17, 2018.
182. Tony Bingham and Pat Galagan, "Offshore No More," *TD*, December 2017, pp. 27–36.

Globe/Newswire/AP Images

Employee Testing and Selection

LEARNING OBJECTIVES

When you finish studying this chapter, you should be able to:

6-1 **Answer** the question: Why is it important to test and select employees?

6-2 **Explain** what is meant by reliability and validity.

6-3 **List** and briefly describe the basic categories of selection tests, with examples.

6-4 **Explain** how to use two work simulations for selection.

6-5 **Describe** four ways to improve an employer's background checking process.

Zulily offers fashions, shoes, and other items through its online e-commerce site. Because it's competing with Amazon and other such sites, Zulily has to differentiate itself. Part of how it does this is by running new sales daily, offering up to 70% off, and offering "big brands you love."[1] Another way is by ensuring that employees adhere to its basic values, namely: "we work for mom" (meaning "we do everything for our customers"); "make the impossible happen"; "embrace change"; "color outside the lines" (don't imitate); "take ownership"; and "work as a team." But with strategic values like those, how do you select employees who you're sure will fit in?[2] We'll see what they did.

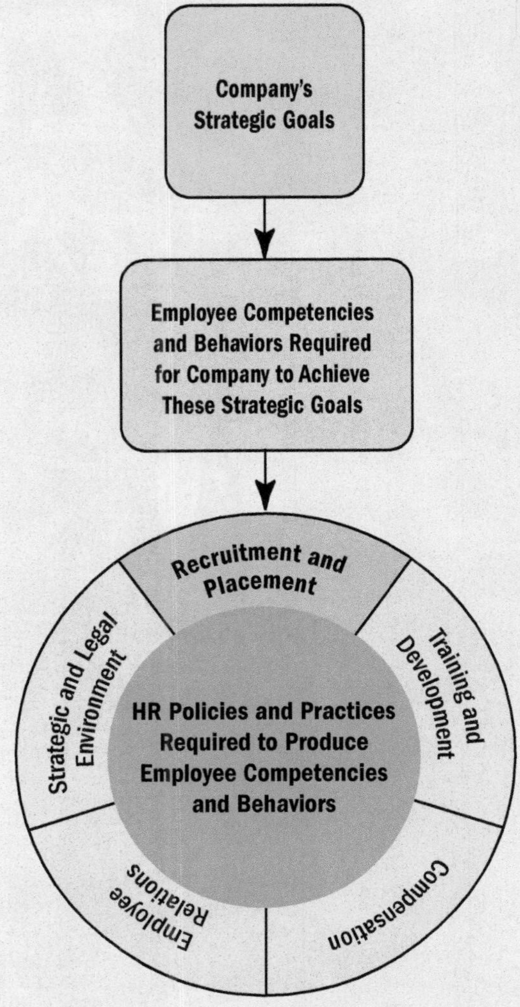

WHERE ARE WE NOW . . .

Chapter 5 focused on how to build an applicant pool. The purpose of Chapter 6 is to explain how to use various tools to select the best candidate for the job. The main topics we'll cover include the **Selection Process, Basic Testing Techniques, Types of Tests, Work Samples and Simulations,** and **Making Background and Reference Checks.** In Chapter 7, we will turn to the techniques you can use to improve your skills at what is probably the most widely used screening tool, the selection interview.

LEARNING OBJECTIVE 6-1

Answer the question: Why is it important to test and select employees?

Why Employee Selection Is Important

After reviewing the applicants' résumés, the manager turns to selecting the best candidate for the job. This usually means using the screening tools we discuss in this and the following chapter: tests, assessment centers, interviews, and background and reference checks.[3] (Applicants may first be prescreened to reduce the applicant pool to a manageable number, as discussed in Chapter 5.) The aim of employee selection is to achieve *person–job fit*. This means matching the knowledge, skills, abilities, and other competencies (KSACs) that are required for performing the job (based on job analysis) with the applicant's KSACs.

Of course, a candidate might be "right" for a job, but wrong for the organization.[4] For example, an experienced airline pilot might excel at American Airlines but perhaps not at Southwest, where the organizational values require that all employees help out, even with baggage handling. Therefore, while person–job fit is usually the main consideration, *person–organization fit* is important too.

In any case, selecting the right person is crucial for several reasons. First, employees with the right skills will perform better for you and the company. Those without these skills or who are abrasive or obstructionist won't perform effectively, and your own performance and the firm's will suffer. The bad apple on a team will diminish its morale and engagement, along with its efforts.[5] The time to screen out undesirables is before they are in the door.

Second, effective selection is important because it is costly to recruit and hire employees. One survey found that the average cost of hiring an employee who doesn't work out is about $50,000.[6] Testing can help: in one call center, the 90-day employee attrition rate fell from 41% to 12% after testing began.[7]

negligent hiring
Hiring workers with questionable backgrounds without proper safeguards.

Third, inept hiring has legal consequences. Equal employment laws require nondiscriminatory selection procedures.[8] And **negligent hiring** means hiring employees with criminal records or other problems who then use access to customers' homes (or similar opportunities) to commit crimes.[9] In one case, an apartment manager entered a woman's apartment and assaulted her.[10] The court found the apartment complex's owner negligent for not checking the manager's background properly.[11] Such suits are rising.[12]

The Basics of Testing and Selecting Employees

LEARNING OBJECTIVE 6-2

Explain what is meant by reliability and validity.

As with most personnel functions, technology (including *machine learning*) is changing how employers select employees. In this chapter, we'll discuss these and other popular selection tools, starting with tests. A *test* is basically a sample of a person's behavior. Any test or screening tool has two important characteristics, *reliability* and *validity*. We'll start with the former.

Reliability

reliability
The consistency of scores obtained by the same person when retested with the identical tests or with alternate forms of the same test.

Reliability is a selection tool's first requirement and refers to its consistency: "A reliable test is one that yields consistent scores when a person takes two alternate forms of the test or when he or she takes the same test on two or more different occasions."[13] If a person scores 90 on an intelligence test on a Monday and 130 when retested on Tuesday, you probably wouldn't have much faith in the test.

You can measure reliability in several ways. One is to administer a test to a group one day, re-administer the same test several days later to the same group, and then correlate the first set of scores with the second (called *test-retest reliability estimates*).[14] Or you could administer a test and then administer what experts believe to be an equivalent test later; this would be an *equivalent or alternate form estimate*. (The Scholastic Assessment Test [SAT] is one example.) Or, compare the test taker's answers to certain questions on the test with his or her answers to a separate set of questions on the same test aimed at measuring the same thing. This is an *internal comparison estimate*. For example, a psychologist includes 10 items on a test believing that they all measure interest in working outdoors, and then determines the degree to which responses to these 10 items vary together.

FIGURE 6-1 Test Score Correlation Examples

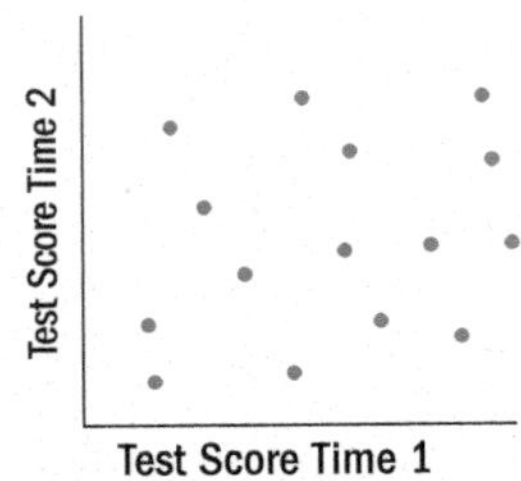

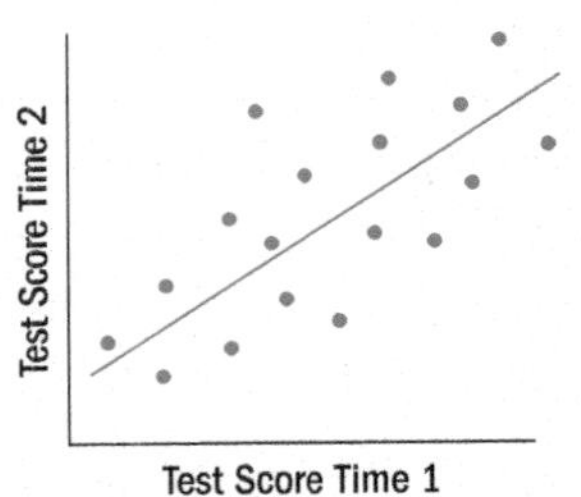

Many things cause a test to be unreliable. These include physical conditions (quiet one day, noisy the next), differences in the test taker (healthy one day, sick the next), and differences in test administration (courteous one day, curt the next). Or the questions may do a poor job of sampling the material; for example, test one focuses more on Chapters 1 and 3, while test two focuses more on Chapters 2 and 4.

Because measuring reliability generally involves comparing two measures that assess the same thing, it is typical to judge a test's reliability in terms of a *reliability coefficient*. This basically shows the degree to which the two measures (say, test score one day and test score the next day) are correlated.

Figure 6-1 illustrates correlation. In both the left and the right scatter plots, the psychologist compared each applicant's time 1 test score (on the *x*-axis) with his or her subsequent (time 2) test score (on the *y*-axis). On the left, the scatter plot points (each point showing one applicant's test score and subsequent test performance) are dispersed. There seems to be no correlation between test scores obtained at Time 1 and at Time 2. On the right, the psychologist tried a new test. Here the resulting points fall in a predictable pattern. This suggests that the applicants' test scores correlate closely with their previous scores.

Validity

test validity
The accuracy with which a test, interview, and so on, measures what it purports to measure or fulfills the function it was designed to fill.

Reliability, while indispensable, tells you only that the test is measuring something consistently. *Validity* tells you whether the test is measuring what you think it's supposed to be measuring.[15] **Test validity** answers the question "Does this test measure what it's supposed to measure?" Put another way, it refers to the correctness of the inferences that we can make based on the test.[16] For example, if Jane's scores on mechanical comprehension tests are higher than Jim's, can we be sure that Jane possesses more mechanical comprehension than Jim?[17] With employee selection tests, *validity* often refers to evidence that the test is job related—in other words, that performance on the test accurately predicts job performance. A selection test must be valid because, without proof of validity, there is no logical or (under EEO law) legally permissible reason to use it to screen job applicants.

A test, as we said, is a sample of a person's behavior, but some tests are more clearly representative of the behavior being sampled than others. A swimming test clearly corresponds to a lifeguard's on-the-job behavior. On the other hand, there may be no apparent relationship between the test and the behavior. Thus, in Figure 6-2, the psychologist asks the person to interpret the picture, and then draws conclusions about the person's personality and behavior. Here it is more difficult to prove that the tests are measuring what they are said to measure, in this case, some aspect of the person's personality—in other words, prove that they're valid.

criterion validity
A type of validity based on showing that scores on the test (predictors) are related to job performance (criterion).

There are several ways to demonstrate a test's validity.[18] **Criterion validity** involves demonstrating statistically a relationship between scores on a selection procedure and job performance of a sample of workers. For example, it means demonstrating that those who do well on the test also do well on the job, and that those who do poorly on the test do poorly on the job. The test has validity to the extent that the people with higher test scores perform better on the job. In psychological measurement, a *predictor* is the measurement (in this case, the test score) that you are trying to relate to a *criterion*, such as performance on the job. The term *criterion validity* reflects that terminology.

FIGURE 6-2 A Slide from the Rorschach Test

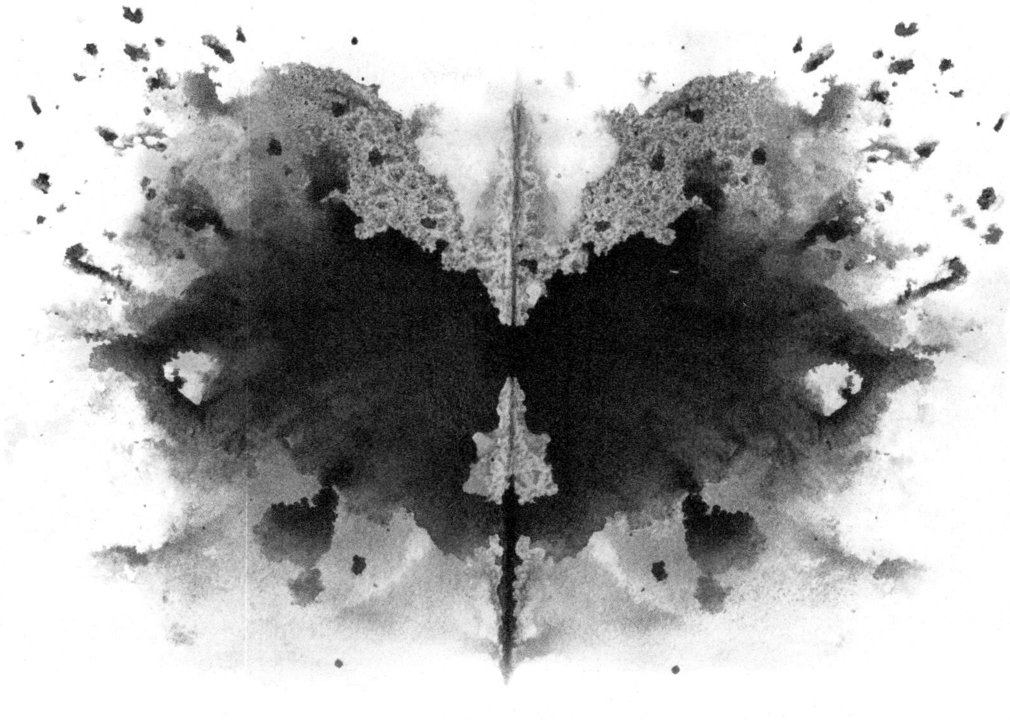

Fotografie/123RF

content validity
A test that is content valid is one that contains a fair sample of the tasks and skills actually needed for the job in question.

Content validity is a demonstration that the content of a selection procedure is representative of important aspects of performance on the job. For example, employers may demonstrate the *content validity* of a test by showing that the test constitutes a fair sample of the job's content. The basic procedure here is to identify job tasks that are critical to performance, and then randomly select a sample of those tasks to test. In selecting students for dental school, one might give applicants chunks of chalk, and ask them to carve something like a tooth. If the content you choose for the test is a representative sample of the job, then the test is probably content valid. Clumsy dental students need not apply. Subject matter experts (SMEs, such as practicing dentists) help choose the tasks.

construct validity
A test that is construct valid is one that demonstrates that a selection procedure measures a construct and that construct is important for successful job performance.

Construct validity means demonstrating that (1) a selection procedure measures a construct (an abstract idea such as morale or honesty) and (2) that the construct is important for successful job performance.

At best, invalid tests are a waste of time; at worst, they are discriminatory. Tests you buy "off the shelf" should include information on their validity.[19] But ideally, you should revalidate the tests for the job(s) at hand. In any case, tests rarely predict performance with 100% accuracy (or anywhere near it). Therefore, don't make tests your only selection tool; also use other tools like interviews and background checks.

Evidence-Based HR: How to Validate a Test

Employers often opt to demonstrate evidence of a test's validity using criterion validity. Here, in order for a selection test to be useful, you need evidence that scores on the test relate in a predictable way to performance on the job. Thus, other things being equal, students who score high on the graduate admissions tests also do better in graduate school. Applicants who score high on mechanical comprehension tests perform better as engineers. In other words, you validate the test before using it by ensuring that scores on the test are a good predictor of some *criterion* like job performance—thus demonstrating the test's *criterion validity*.[20]

An industrial psychologist usually conducts the validation study. The human resource department coordinates the effort. Strictly speaking, the supervisor's role is just to make sure that the job's human requirements and performance standards are clear to the psychologist. But in practice, anyone using tests (or test results) should know something about validation. Then you can better understand how to use tests and interpret their results. The validation process consists of five steps.

STEP 1: ANALYZE THE JOB The first step is to analyze the job and write job descriptions and job specifications. The aim here is to specify the human traits and skills you believe are required for job performance. These requirements become the *predictors,* the human traits and skills you believe predict success on the job. For an assembler's job, *predictors* might include manual dexterity and patience.[21]

In this first step, also define "success on the job," since it's this success for which you want predictors. The standards of success are *criteria*. You could use production-related criteria (quantity, quality, and so on), personnel data (absenteeism, length of service, and so on), or worker performance (reported by supervisors).

STEP 2: CHOOSE THE TESTS Once you know the predictors (such as manual dexterity) the next step is to decide how to test for them. Employers usually base this choice on experience, previous research, and "best guesses." They usually don't start with just one test. Instead, they choose several tests and combine them into a test battery. The test battery aims to measure an array of possible predictors, such as aggressiveness, extroversion, and numerical ability.

What tests are available and where do you get them? Ideally, use a professional, such as an industrial psychologist. However, many firms publish tests.[22] Some tests are available to virtually any purchaser, others only to qualified buyers (such as with advanced degrees in psychology). Figure 6-3 lists some Web sites that provide information about tests or testing programs. Firms such as HRdirect of Pompano Beach, Florida, offers employment testing materials including a clerical skills test, telemarketing ability test, and sales abilities test.

STEP 3: ADMINISTER THE TEST Next, administer the selected test(s). One option is to administer the tests to employees currently on the job. You then compare their test scores with their current performance; this is *concurrent (at the same time) validation.* Its advantage is that data on performance are readily available. The disadvantage is that current employees may not be representative of new applicants (who, of course, are really the ones for whom you are interested in developing a screening test). Current employees have already had on-the-job training and screening by your existing selection techniques.

Predictive validation is the second and more dependable way to validate a test. Here you administer the test to applicants before you hire them, then hire these applicants using only existing selection techniques, not the results of the new tests. After they've been on the job for some time, measure their performance and compare it to their earlier test scores. You can then determine whether you could have used their performance on the new test to predict their subsequent job performance.

FIGURE 6-3 Examples of Web Sites Offering Information on Tests or Testing Programs

- www.hr-guide.com/data/G371.htm
  Provides general information and sources for all types of employment tests.
- http://ericae.net
  Provides technical information on all types of employment and nonemployment tests.
- www.ets.org/testcoll
  Provides information on more than 20,000 tests.
- www.kaplan.com
  Information from Kaplan test preparation on how various admissions tests work.
- www.assessments.biz
  One of many firms offering employment tests.

STEP 4: RELATE YOUR TEST SCORES AND CRITERIA Here, ascertain if there is a significant relationship between test scores (the predictor) and performance (the criterion). The usual method is to determine the statistical relationship between (1) scores on the test and (2) job performance using correlation analysis, which shows the degree of statistical relationship.

expectancy chart
A graph showing the relationship between test scores and job performance for a group of people.

If there is a correlation between test and job performance, you can develop an **expectancy chart.** This presents the relationship between test scores and job performance graphically. To do this, split the employees into, say, five groups according to test scores, with those scoring the highest fifth on the test, the second highest fifth, and so on. Then compute the percentage of high job performers in each of these five test score groups, and present the data in an expectancy chart like that in Figure 6-4.

In this case, someone scoring in the top fifth of the test has a 97% chance of being a high performer, while one scoring in the lowest fifth has only a 29% chance of being a high performer.[23]

STEP 5: CROSS-VALIDATE AND REVALIDATE Before using the test, you may want to check it by "cross-validating"—in other words, by again performing steps 3 and 4 on a new sample of employees. At a minimum, revalidate the test periodically.

Psychologists easily score many psychological tests online or using interpretive Windows-based software. However, managers can easily score many tests, like the Wonderlic Personnel Test, themselves.

Bias

Most employers know they shouldn't use biased tests in the selection process.[24] For example, a particular IQ test may provide a valid measure of cognitive ability for middle-class whites but not for some minorities, if the score depends on familiarity with certain aspects of middle-class culture.[25] For many years many industrial psychologists believed they were adequately controlling test bias, but experts have questioned that.[26] Employers should therefore redouble their efforts to ensure that the tests they're using aren't producing biased decisions.

Utility Analysis

Knowing that a test predicts performance isn't always useful. For example, if it's going to cost the employer $1,000 per applicant for the test, and hundreds of applicants must be tested, the cost of the test may exceed the benefits.

Answering the question, "Does it pay to use the test?" requires *utility analysis.* Two selection experts say, "Using dollar and cents terms, [utility analysis] shows the degree to which use of a selection measure improves the quality of individuals selected

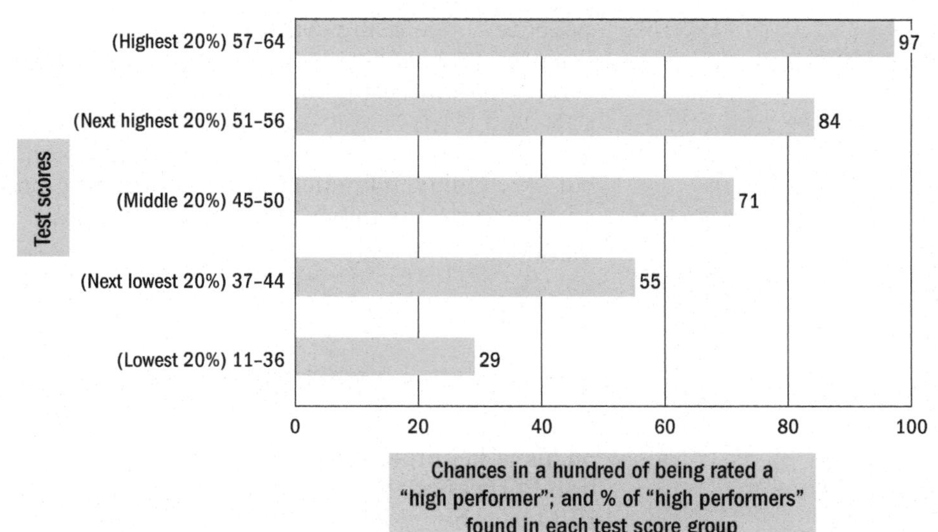

FIGURE 6-4 **Expectancy Chart**

Note: This expectancy chart shows the relation between scores made on the Minnesota Paper Form Board and rated success of junior draftspersons. *Example:* Those who score between 37 and 44 have a 55% chance of being rated high performer and those scoring between 57 and 64 have a 97% chance.

over what would have happened if the measure had not been used."[27] The information required for utility analysis generally includes, for instance, the validity of the selection measure, a measure of job performance in dollars, applicants' average test scores, cost of testing an applicant, and the number of applicants tested and selected. The accompanying HR as a Profit Center discussion shows how employers use tests to improve performance.

IMPROVING PERFORMANCE: *HR AS A PROFIT CENTER*

Using Tests to Cut Costs and Boost Profits

Financial services firm Key Bank wanted a better way to screen and select tellers and call-center employees.[28] The company calculated it cost about $10,000 to select and train an employee, but it was losing 13% of new tellers and call-center employees within the first 90 days. That turnover number dropped to 4% after Key Bank implemented a computerized *virtual job tryout candidate assessment screening tool.* It requires candidates to respond to realistic situations, such as impatient customers. "We calculated a $1.7 million cost savings in teller turnover in one year, simply by making better hiring decisions, reducing training costs, and increasing quality of hires," said the firm's human resources director. ■

MyLab Management Talk About It 1

If your professor has assigned this, go to the Assignments section of **www.pearson.com/mylab/management** to complete this discussion. Choose a position with which you are familiar, such as a counterperson at a McDonald's restaurant, and describe how you would create a selection process for it similar to those in this feature.

MyLab Management Apply It!

How does a company actually do testing? If your professor has assigned this activity, go to the Assignments section of **www.pearson.com/mylab/management** to complete the video exercise.

Validity Generalization

Many employers won't find it cost-effective to conduct validity studies for the selection tools they use. These employers must find tests and other screening tools that have been shown to be valid in other settings (companies), and then bring them in-house in the hopes that they'll be valid there, too.[29]

If the test is valid in one company, to what extent can we generalize those validity findings to our own company? *Validity generalization* "refers to the degree to which evidence of a measure's validity obtained in one situation can be generalized to another situation without further study."[30] Factors to consider include existing validation evidence regarding using the test for various specific purposes, the similarity of the subjects with those in your organization, and the similarity of the jobs.[31]

Under the Uniform Guidelines, validation of selection procedures is desirable, but "the Uniform Guidelines require users to produce evidence of validity only when adverse impact is shown to exist. If there is no adverse impact, there is no validation requirement under the Guidelines."[32]

KNOW YOUR EMPLOYMENT LAW

Testing and Equal Employment Opportunity

Suppose a plaintiff shows that one of your selection procedures has an adverse impact on his or her protected class. If so, you may have to demonstrate the validity and selection fairness of the allegedly discriminatory test or item. With respect to testing, the EEO laws boil down to two things: (1) You must be able to prove that your tests are related to success or failure on the job, and (2) you must prove that your tests don't

Many employers administer online employment tests to job candidates.

Image Source/Alamy Stock Photo

unfairly discriminate against either minority or nonminority subgroups.[33] (Note that the same burden of proving job relatedness falls on interviews and other techniques, including performance appraisals, that falls on tests.) ■

Test Takers' Individual Rights and Test Security

Test takers have rights to privacy and feedback under the American Psychological Association's (APA) standard for educational and psychological tests. These guide psychologists but are *not* legally enforceable. Test takers have rights such as:

- To the confidentiality of test results.
- To informed consent regarding use of these results.
- To expect that only people qualified to interpret the scores will have access to them, or that sufficient information will accompany the scores to ensure their appropriate interpretation.
- To expect the test is fair. For example, no test taker should have prior access to the questions or answers.[34]

The Federal Privacy Act gives federal employees the right to inspect their personnel files and limits the disclosure of personnel information without the employee's consent, among other things.[35] Common law provides employees some protection against disclosing information about them to people outside the company. The main application here involves defamation (either libel or slander), but there are privacy issues, too.[36] The bottom line is this:

1. Make sure you appreciate the need to keep employees' information confidential.
2. Adopt a "need to know" policy. For example, if an employee has been rehabilitated after a period of drug use, the new supervisor may not "need to know."

Diversity Counts: Gender Issues in Testing

Employers using selection tests should know that gender issues may distort results. Some parents and others socialize girls into traditionally female roles and boys into traditionally male roles. For example, they may encourage young boys but not girls to make things with tools, or young girls but not boys to take care of their siblings. Such encouragement may translate into differences in how males and females answer items on and score on, say, tests of vocational interests. And these test score differences may

FIGURE 6-5 Sample Test

Source: Based on a sample selection test from *The New York Times*.

CHECK YES OR NO	YES	NO
1. You like a lot of excitement in your life.		
2. An employee who takes it easy at work is cheating on the employer.		
3. You are a cautious person.		
4. In the past three years you have found yourself in a shouting match at school or work.		
5. You like to drive fast just for fun.		

Analysis: According to John Kamp, an industrial psychologist, applicants who answered no, yes, yes, no, no to questions 1, 2, 3, 4, and 5 are statistically likely to be absent less often, to have fewer on-the-job injuries, and, if the job involves driving, to have fewer on-the-job driving accidents. Actual scores on the test are based on answers to 130 questions.

cause counselors and others to nudge men and women into what tend to be largely gender-segregated occupations, for instance, male engineers and female nurses.

The bottom line is that employers and others need to interpret the results of various tests (including of interests and aptitudes) with care. Such results may sometimes say more about how the person was brought up and socialized than about the person's inherent ability to do some task. ■

How Do Employers Use Tests at Work?

About 80% of the biggest U.S. employers now use testing.[37] To see what such tests are like, try the short test in Figure 6-5.

Tests are not just for lower-level workers. In general, as work demands increase (in terms of skill requirements, training, and pay), employers tend to rely more on selection testing.[38] And, employers don't use tests just to find good employees, but to screen out bad ones.[39] For good reason: In retail, employers apprehended about one out of every 28 workers for stealing.[40]

HR in Action at the Hotel Paris As she considered what to do next to improve the employees' performance in a way that would support the Hotel Paris's strategy, Lisa Cruz, the Hotel Paris's HR director, knew that employee selection had to play a role. The Hotel Paris currently had an informal screening process in which local hotel managers obtained application forms, interviewed applicants, and checked their references. To see how she improved their system, see the case on page 199.

LEARNING OBJECTIVE 6-3

List and briefly describe the basic categories of selection tests, with examples.

Types of Tests

We can conveniently classify tests according to whether they measure cognitive (mental) abilities, motor and physical abilities, personality and interests, or achievement.[41] We'll look at each.

Tests of Cognitive Abilities

Cognitive tests include tests of general reasoning ability (intelligence) and tests of specific mental abilities like memory and inductive reasoning.

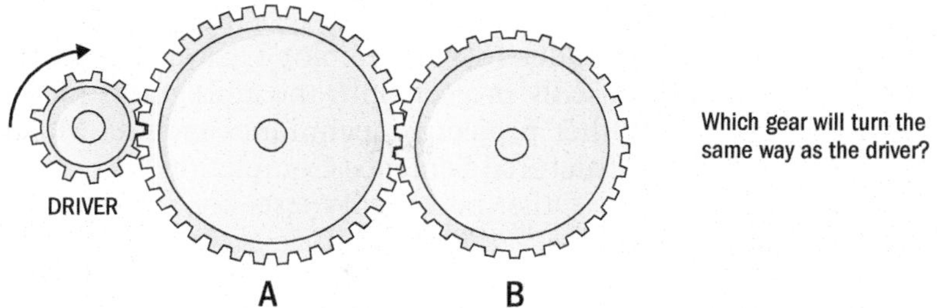

FIGURE 6-6 Type of Question Applicant Might Expect on a Test of Mechanical Comprehension

INTELLIGENCE TESTS Intelligence (IQ) tests are tests of general intellectual abilities. They measure not a single trait but rather a range of abilities, including memory, vocabulary, verbal fluency, and numerical ability. An adult's IQ score is a "derived" score; it reflects the extent to which the person is above or below the "average" adult's intelligence score.

Intelligence is often measured with individually administered tests like the Wechsler Adult Intelligence Scale. Employers can administer other IQ tests such as the Wonderlic individually or to groups of people.[42] In one illustrative study of firefighter trainees' performance over 23 years, the researchers found that a measure of general intellectual ability and a physical ability assessment were highly predictive of trainee performance.[43]

SPECIFIC COGNITIVE ABILITIES There are also measures of specific mental abilities, such as deductive reasoning, verbal comprehension, memory, and numerical ability.

Psychologists often call such tests *aptitude tests*, since they purport to measure aptitude for the job in question. Consider the Test of Mechanical Comprehension illustrated in Figure 6-6, which tests applicants' understanding of basic mechanical principles. This may reflect a person's aptitude for jobs—like that of machinist or engineer—that require mechanical comprehension. Other tests of mechanical aptitude include the Mechanical Reasoning Test and the SRA Test of Mechanical Aptitude.

Tests of Motor and Physical Abilities

You might also want to measure motor abilities, such as finger dexterity, manual dexterity, and (if hiring pilots) reaction time. Thus, the Crawford Small Parts Dexterity Test measures the speed and accuracy of simple judgment as well as the speed of finger, hand, and arm movements.

Tests of *physical* abilities may also be required. These include static strength (such as lifting weights), dynamic strength (pull-ups), body coordination (jumping rope), and stamina.[44] Applicants for the U.S. Marines must pass its Initial Strength Test (2 pull-ups, 35 sit-ups, and a 1.5-mile run).

Measuring Personality and Interests

A person's cognitive and physical abilities alone seldom explain his or her job performance. As one consultant put it, most people are hired based on qualifications, but are fired because of attitude, motivation, and temperament.[45]

Personality tests measure basic aspects of an applicant's personality. Industrial psychologists often focus on the "big five" personality dimensions: extraversion, emotional stability/neuroticism, agreeableness, conscientiousness, and openness to experience.[46]

> Neuroticism represents a tendency to exhibit poor emotional adjustment and experience negative effects, such as anxiety, insecurity, and hostility. Extraversion represents a tendency to be sociable, assertive, active, and to experience positive effects, such as energy and zeal. Openness to experience is the disposition to be imaginative, nonconforming, unconventional, and autonomous. Agreeableness is the tendency to be trusting, compliant, caring, and gentle. Conscientiousness is comprised of two related facets: achievement and dependability.[47]

Some personality tests are *projective*. The psychologist presents an ambiguous stimulus (like an inkblot or clouded picture), and the person reacts. The person supposedly projects into the ambiguous picture his or her attitudes, such as insecurity. Other projective techniques include Make a Picture Story (MAPS) and the Forer Structured Sentence Completion Test.

Other personality tests are *self-reported*: applicants fill them out. Thus, available online,[48] the Myers-Briggs test provides a personality type classification useful for decisions such as career selection and planning. Similarly the DISC Profile learning instrument enables the user to gain insight into his or her behavioral style.[49]

Personality test results do often correlate with job performance. For example, "in personality research, conscientiousness has been the most consistent and universal predictor of job performance."[50] Neuroticism is negatively related to motivation and to job engagement.[51] Extroversion correlates with success in sales, management, and expatriate jobs.[52] Emotional stability, extroversion, and agreeableness predicted whether expatriates would leave their overseas assignments early.[53] The HR Practices feature presents an example.

IMPROVING PERFORMANCE: *HR PRACTICES AROUND THE GLOBE*

Testing for Assignments Abroad[54]

Living and working abroad require some special talents. Not everyone can easily adapt to having one's family far away, and to dealing with colleagues with different cultural values. Doing so requires high levels of adaptability and interpersonal skills.[55]

Employers often use special inventories such as the Global Competencies Inventory (GCI) here. It focuses on three aspects of adaptability.

- ✓ The Perception Management Factor assesses people's tendency to be rigid in their view of cultural differences, to be judgmental about those differences, and to deal with complexity and uncertainty.
- ✓ The Relationship Management Factor assesses a person's awareness of the impact he or she is having on others.
- ✓ The Self-Management Factor assesses one's mental and emotional health.

MyLab Management Talk About It 2

If your professor has assigned this, go to the Assignments section of **www.pearson.com/mylab/management** to complete this discussion. You are trying to decide if you would be a good candidate for a job abroad, but you don't want to take any formal tests. Discuss another indicator you would use to answer the question, "Would I be a good candidate for a job abroad?"

There are several personality test caveats. *First,* projective personality tests are difficult to interpret and score; it usually requires an expert to analyze test takers' responses and infer their personalities. *Second,* for this and other reasons, personality tests can trigger legal challenges.[56] *Third,* experts debate whether self-report personality tests suffer from low validity.[57] *Fourth*, people can and will fake responses to personality and integrity tests.[58] The bottom line: make sure the personality tests you use predict performance for the jobs you are testing for.

interest inventory
A personal development and selection device that compares the person's current interests with those of others now in various occupations so as to determine the preferred occupation for the individual.

INTEREST INVENTORIES **Interest inventories** compare one's interests with those of people in various occupations. Thus, the Strong Career Interests Test provides a report comparing one's interests to those of people already in occupations like accounting or engineering. Someone taking the Self-Directed Search (SDS) (www.self-directed-search.com) uses it to identify likely high-fit occupations. The assumption is that someone will do better in occupations in which he or she is interested, and indeed such inventories can predict employee performance and turnover.[59] Poor fit frustrates workers.[60]

Achievement Tests

Achievement tests measure what someone has learned. Most of the tests you take in school are achievement tests. They measure your "job knowledge" in areas like economics, marketing, or human resources. Achievement tests are also popular at work. For example, the Purdue Test for Machinists and Machine Operators tests the job knowledge of experienced machinists with questions like "What is meant by 'tolerance'?" Some achievement tests measure the applicant's abilities; a swimming test is one example.

IMPROVING PERFORMANCE THROUGH HRIS: *COMPUTERIZATION AND ONLINE TESTING*

Computerized and/or online testing is increasingly replacing paper-and-pencil tests. For example, Timken Company uses online assessment of math skills for hourly position applicants.[61] The applicant tracking systems we discussed in Chapter 5 often include online prescreening tests.[62] (Here ATS users should particularly ensure that rejection standards are valid, and inform applicants quickly regarding their status.)[63] Vendors (as in www.iphonetypingtest.com) make tests available for applicants to take via smart phones.[64] Development Dimensions International developed a computerized multimedia skill test that Ford uses for hiring assembly workers. "The company can test everything from how people tighten the bolt, to whether they followed a certain procedure correctly. . . ."[65]

In addition to being quicker and less expensive to administer, computerized tests have other benefits. For example, vendors such as PreVisor (www.previsor.com) offer adaptive personality tests. These adapt the next question to each test taker's answers to the previous question. This improves validity and makes it less likely candidates can share test questions (because each candidate gets what amounts to a customized test).[66] For essay tests, a computer program trained to read applicants' essays recently produced scores as reliable as those of a human rater.[67] Most tests described in this chapter are available in computerized form. ■

TRENDS SHAPING HR: *USING ANALYTICS, MACHINE LEARNING, AND ARTIFICIAL INTELLIGENCE IN EMPLOYEE SELECTION*

The Holy Grail of employee selection is to identify predictors that characterize top-notch candidates and to do so quickly and effectively. Employers increasingly use several related analytical and technical tools to improve and expedite the employee selection process.

analytics
Using tools like statistical techniques to examine data, in order to draw cause–effect conclusions from that data.

Analytics refers to using tools like statistical techniques to examine data, in order to draw cause–effect conclusions from that data.[68] *Talent analytics* means using such techniques to let employers search through their employee data to identify patterns and correlations that show what types of people or processes succeed or fail.[69]

For example, a financial services company hired people on the assumption that what mattered for job performance were things like where they went to school and their grades.[70] However, a statistical analysis found that school and grades didn't matter at all. What did matter were things like whether the applicant had demonstrated success in prior jobs, had shown an ability to succeed with vague instructions, and had "no typos, errors, or grammatical mistakes on résumés."

As another example, department store chain Bon-Ton Stores Inc. had high turnover among its cosmetics sales associates. Bon-Ton chose 450 current cosmetics associates who filled out anonymous surveys aimed at identifying employee traits. By using talent analytics to analyze these and other data, the company identified cosmetics associates' traits that correlated with performance and tenure. Bon-Ton had assumed that the best associates were friendly and enthusiastic about cosmetics. However, the best were actually problem solvers. They take information about what the customer wants and needs, and solve the problem.[71] Talent analysis thereby helped Bon-Ton formulate better selection criteria.

machine learning
Software that can improve its own performance and learn on its own.

Machine learning basically refers to software that can improve its own performance and learn on its own. For example, the newsfeeds you subscribe to are often designed to identify the types of articles you prefer, and to feed you more of those articles: The software is "learning" without human intervention.[72]

Machine learning software "learns" to associate the (1) characteristics of an input (like loan applications) with (2) responses (like who defaults on loans). For example, a bank might use machine learning to review the data in its thousands of loan applications (the input) to determine the characteristics of the people who are most likely to repay their loans (the response).[73] Then, going forward, it could use what the machine learning software learned, to scrutinize future loan applicants who do not meet those characteristics.[74]

Machine learning doesn't just rely on tests, although tests may be one component. Instead, it can identify how factors like word use (does the person often say "tired"?), comments in social media postings, and tiny video interview facial gestures, were related to employee performance in particular companies in the past, and therefore how they may do so in the future.[75] For example, HireVue's software analyzes its clients' past video employment interviews for signs like facial expressions and voice modulation to determine which predict applicant's suitability for jobs. It can then analyze each new candidate's interview for tell-tale signs that predict performance. For checking references, Skillsurvey's tools help employers anticipate the candidate's prospective performance based on words his or her references use when responding to job specific behavioral questions.[76] Koru has an employer's current employees complete short surveys. Then its software identifies the traits and behaviors (such as persistence) for which applicant should be assessed, and provides a graphic profile.[77]

Many such tools use *algorithms*. These programs quickly crunch through thousands of "if–then" branches (sequentially checking experience, traits, word usage, facial gestures, and so on), to find the best matching candidates for the job. They do this based on what the systems previously learned about what traits historically correlated with high performance on that particular job.[78]

artificial intelligence
Using technology (particularly computers) to carry out tasks in a way that we would consider "human" or "smart."

Finally, these and other tools are building blocks for artificial intelligence systems. **Artificial intelligence** basically means using technology (particularly computers) to carry out tasks in a way that we would consider "human" or "smart."[79] ■

LEARNING OBJECTIVE 6-4
Explain how to use two work simulations for selection.

Work Samples and Simulations

work samples
Actual job tasks used in testing applicants' performance.

With **work samples**, you present examinees with situations representative of the job for which they're applying, and evaluate their responses.[80] Experts consider these (and *simulations,* like the assessment centers we also discuss in this section) to be tests. But they differ from most tests because they directly measure job performance.

Using Work Sampling for Employee Selection

work sampling technique
A testing method based on measuring performance on actual basic job tasks.

The **work sampling technique** tries to predict job performance by requiring job candidates to perform one or more samples of the job's tasks. For example, work samples for a cashier may include counting money.[81]

Work sampling has advantages. It measures actual job tasks, so it's harder to fake answers. The work sample's content—the actual tasks the person must perform—is not as likely to be unfair to minorities (as might a personnel test that possibly emphasizes middle-class concepts and values).[82] Work sampling doesn't delve into the applicant's personality, so there's little chance of applicants viewing it as an invasion of privacy. Designed properly, work samples also exhibit better validity than do other tests designed to predict performance.

The basic procedure is to select a sample of several tasks crucial to performing the job, and then to test applicants on them.[83] An observer monitors performance on each task, and indicates on a checklist how well the applicant performs. For example, in creating a work sampling test for maintenance mechanics, experts first listed all crucial job tasks (like "install pulleys and belts"). Four crucial tasks were installing pulleys and belts, disassembling and installing a gearbox, installing and

FIGURE 6-7 Example of a Work Sampling Question

Note: This is one step in installing pulleys and belts.

Checks key before installing against:	
—shaft	score 3
—pulley	score 2
—neither	score 1

Note: This is one step in installing pulleys and belts.

aligning a motor, and pressing a bushing into a sprocket. Since mechanics could perform each task in a slightly different way, the experts gave different weights to different approaches.

Figure 6-7 shows one of the steps required for the task *installing pulleys and belts*—"checks key before installing . . ." Here the examinee might choose to check the key against (1) the shaft, (2) the pulley, or (3) neither. The applicant performs the task, and the observer checks off the score for the approach used.

Situational Judgment Tests

Situational judgment tests are personnel tests "designed to assess an applicant's judgment regarding a situation encountered in the workplace."[84] For example:

> You are a sales associate at Best Buy in Miami, Florida. The store sells electronics, including smart phones. Competition comes from other neighborhood retailers, and from online firms. Many customers who come to your store check the product with you, and then buy it on Amazon. As a sales associate, you are responsible for providing exceptional customer service, demonstrating product knowledge, and maximizing sales. You get a weekly salary, with no sales incentive. How would you respond to this situation?
>
> **Situation:**
>
> A customer comes to you with a printout for a Samsung Galaxy phone from Amazon.com, and proceeds to ask detailed questions about battery life and how to work the phone, while mentioning that "Amazon's price is $50 less than yours." You have been with this customer for almost 30 minutes, and there are other customers waiting. You would:
>
> 1. Tell the customer to go buy the phone on Amazon.
> 2. Tell the customer to wait 20 minutes while you take care of another customer.
> 3. Tell the customer that the local Sprint Mobility dealer has the phone for even less than Amazon.
> 4. Explain the advantages of similar phones you have that may better fulfill the buyer's requirements.
> 5. Ask your supervisor to come over and try to sell the customer on buying the Galaxy from you.

HR AND THE GIG ECONOMY: *FREELANCE WORKERS*

Many employers today build their staff wholly or in part around freelance workers like short-term self-employed programmers, designers, or marketers. One Web site design company owner says that if he needs designers for short projects he "just posts" the job online and gets multiple applications within minutes.[85]

Freelancer community Web sites enable such employers to recruit and select the right freelance team, based on each freelancer's reputation and work product. For example, Upwork.com (see www.upwork.com/) reports its members' skills assessments and lists detailed project work experience, making it easier for prospective employers to decide who to hire. Similarly, the TopCoder.com (see www.topcoder.com/) programmer community site helps employers identify top programmers based on the reputations they earned within the community.

MyLab Management Talk About It 3

If your professor has assigned this, go to the Assignments section of **www.pearson.com/mylab/management** to complete these discussion questions. Go to one or more sites like these. If you were a programming manager for a company, could you use the site to find and hire a new employee directly? If not, what else might you need?

Management Assessment Centers

management assessment center
A simulation in which management candidates are asked to perform realistic tasks in hypothetical situations and are scored on their performance. It usually also involves testing and the use of management games.

A **management assessment center** is a 2- to 3-day simulation in which 10 to 12 candidates perform realistic management tasks (like making presentations) under the observation of experts who appraise each candidate's leadership potential. For example, The Cheesecake Factory created its Professional Assessment and Development Center to help select promotable managers. Candidates undergo 2 days of exercises, simulations, and classroom learning to see if they have the skills for key management positions.[86]

Typical simulated tasks include

- ***The in-basket.*** The candidate gets reports, memos, notes of incoming phone calls, e-mails, and other materials collected in the actual or computerized in-basket of the simulated job he or she is about to start. The candidate must take appropriate action on each item. Trained evaluators review the candidate's efforts.
- ***Leaderless group discussion.*** Trainers give a leaderless group a discussion question and tell members to arrive at a group decision. They then evaluate each group member's interpersonal skills, acceptance by the group, leadership ability, and individual influence.
- ***Management games.*** Participants solve realistic problems as members of simulated companies competing in a marketplace.
- ***Individual oral presentations.*** Here trainers evaluate each participant's communication skills and persuasiveness.
- ***Testing.*** These may include tests of personality, mental ability, interests, and achievements.
- ***The interview.*** Most require an interview with a trainer to assess interests, past performance, and motivation.

Supervisor recommendations usually play a big role in choosing center participants. Line managers usually act as assessors and arrive at their ratings through consensus.[87] Assessment centers are expensive to develop, take longer than conventional tests, require managers acting as assessors, and often require psychologists. However, studies suggest they are worth it.[88] For many years, studies suggested that cognitive ability tests did a better job of predicting job performance then did assessment centers. A recent study found assessment centers were superior.[89]

Situational Testing and Video-Based Situational Testing

situational test
A test that requires examinees to respond to situations representative of the job.

video-based simulation
A situational test in which examinees respond to video simulations of realistic job situations.

Situational tests require examinees to respond to situations representative of the job. Work sampling (discussed earlier) and some assessment center tasks (such as in-baskets) are "situational," as are miniature job training (described next) and the situational interviews we address in Chapter 7.[90]

The **video-based simulation** presents the candidate with several online or computer video situations, each followed by one or more multiple-choice questions. For example, the scenario might depict an employee handling a situation on the job. At a critical moment, the scenario ends, and the video asks the candidate to choose from several courses of action. For example:

(*A manager is upset about the condition of the department and takes it out on one of the department's employees.*)

MANAGER: Well, I'm glad you're here.

ASSOCIATE: Why?

MANAGER: I take a day off and come back to find the department in a mess. You should know better.

ASSOCIATE: But I didn't work late last night.

MANAGER: But there have been plenty of times before when you've left this department in a mess.

(*The scenario stops here.*)

If you were this associate, what would you do?

a. Let the other associates responsible for the mess know that you took the heat.
b. Straighten up the department, and try to reason with the manager later.
c. Suggest to the manager that he talk to the other associates who made the mess.
d. Take it up with the manager's boss.[91]

The Miniature Job Training and Evaluation Approach

miniature job training and evaluation
Training candidates to perform several of the job's tasks, and then evaluating the candidates' performance prior to hire.

Miniature job training and evaluation involves training candidates to perform several of the job's tasks, and then evaluating their performance prior to hire. Like work sampling, *miniature job training and evaluation* tests applicants with actual samples of the job, so it is inherently content relevant and valid.

For example, when Honda built an auto plant in Lincoln, Alabama, it had to hire thousands of new employees. Working with an Alabama industrial development training agency, Honda began running help wanted ads.

Honda and the agency first eliminated those applicants who lacked the education or experience, and then gave preference to applicants near the plant. About 340 applicants per 6-week session received special training at a new facility about 15 miles south of the plant. It included classroom instruction, watching videos of current Honda employees in action, and actually practicing particular jobs. Some candidates who watched the videos simply dropped out when they saw the work's pace and repetitiveness.

The training sessions served two purposes. First, job candidates learned the actual skills they'll need to do the Honda jobs. Second, the training sessions enabled special assessors from the Alabama state agency to scrutinize the trainees' work and to rate them. They then invited those who graduated to apply for jobs at the plants. Honda teams, consisting of employees from HR and departmental representatives, did the final screening.[92]

Realistic Job Previews

Sometimes, a dose of realism makes the best screening tool. For example, when Walmart began explicitly explaining and asking about work schedules and work preferences, turnover improved.[93] In general, applicants who receive realistic job previews are more likely to turn down job offers, but their employers are more likely to have less turnover and be more resilient.[94] The Strategic Context feature illustrates this principle.

IMPROVING PERFORMANCE: *THE STRATEGIC CONTEXT*

"Speed Dating" Employee Selection at Zulily

With guiding values like "we work for mom," and "take ownership," Zulily must carefully select employees who fit its culture and adhere to its values. How does Zulily do that?[95] By ensuring that candidates actually experience what it's like to work there. For example, Zulily holds periodic online candidate screening events. At these events, prospective candidates meet the teammates they might be working with at the company, and participate in speed dating–type interviews; some candidates then may get job offers right there.

The speed dating format might seem a bit impersonal, but it's effective for Zulily. To paraphrase a manager there, the speed dating interviews give candidates a chance to experience the fast-paced way we do business, and to see firsthand our employees' commitment to customers, and to embracing change, and working in teams. For Zulily, a realistic exposure to what it's like to work there has proven to be an effective way to select candidates who fit, and therefore to executing its strategy.[96]

MyLab Management Talk About It 4

If your professor has assigned this, go to the Assignments section of **www.pearson.com/mylab/management** to complete these discussion questions. Do you think it would really go counter to the sort of culture Zulily is trying to nurture to have a central HR department simply test candidates and assign them to work teams with just an interview with the team supervisor? Why?

Choosing a Selection Method

The employer should consider several things before choosing a particular selection tool (or tools). These include the tool's reliability and validity, its practicality (in terms of utility analysis), applicant reactions, adverse impact, cost, and the tool's *selection ratio* (does it screen out, as it should, a high percentage of applicants or admit virtually all?).[97] Table 6-1 summarizes the validity, potential adverse impact, and cost of several assessment methods. The HR Tools discussion shows how line managers may devise their own tests.

IMPROVING PERFORMANCE: *HR TOOLS FOR LINE MANAGERS AND SMALL BUSINESSES*

Employee Testing and Selection

One of the ironies of being a line manager in even the largest of companies is that, when it comes to screening employees, you're often on your own. Some large firms' HR departments may work with the hiring manager to design and administer the sorts of screening tools we discussed in this chapter. But in many of these firms, the HR departments do little more than some preliminary prescreening (for instance, arithmetic tests for clerical applicants), and then follow up with background checks and drug and physical exams.

Employers such as Honda first train and then have applicants perform several of the job tasks, and then evaluate the candidates before hiring them.

Anday Sacks/Getty Images

What should you do if you are, say, a marketing manager, and want to screen some of your job applicants more formally? It is possible to devise your own test battery, but caution is required. Purchasing and then using packaged intelligence tests or psychological tests or even tests of marketing ability could be problematical. Doing so may violate company policy, raise validity questions, and expose your employer to EEO liability if problems arise.

A preferred approach is to devise and use screening tools, the face validity of which is obvious. The work sampling test we discussed is one example. It's not unreasonable, for instance, for the marketing manager to ask an advertising applicant to spend half an hour designing an ad, or to ask a marketing research applicant to quickly outline a marketing research program for a hypothetical product. Similarly, a production manager might reasonably ask an inventory control applicant to spend a few minutes using a standard inventory control model to solve an inventory problem.

For small business owners, some tests' ease of use makes them particularly good for small firms. One is the *Wonderlic Personnel Test*; it measures general mental ability in about 15 minutes. The tester reads the instructions, and then keeps time as the candidate works through the 50 short problems on two pages. The tester scores the test by totaling the number of correct answers. Comparing the person's score with the minimum scores recommended for various occupations

TABLE 6-1 Evaluation of Selected Assessment Methods

Assessment Method	Validity	Adverse Impact	Costs (Develop/Administer)
Cognitive ability tests	High	High (against minorities)	Low/low
Job knowledge test	High	High (against minorities)	Low/low
Personality tests	Low to moderate	Low	Low/low
Integrity tests	Moderate to high	Low	Low/low
Structured interviews	High	Low	High/high
Situational judgment tests	Moderate	Moderate (against minorities)	High/low
Work samples	High	Low	High/high
Assessment centers	Moderate to high	Low to moderate, depending on exercise	High/high
Physical ability tests	Moderate to high	High (against females and older workers)	High/high

Source: From Selection Assessment Methods, SHRM Foundation, 2005. Reprinted by permission from SHRM Foundation.

shows whether the person achieved the minimally acceptable score for the type of job in question. The *Predictive Index* measures work-related personality traits on a two-sided sheet. For example, there is the "social interest" pattern for a person who is generally unselfish, congenial, and unassuming. This person would be a good personnel interviewer, for instance. A template makes scoring simple.

Finally, for some jobs past performance is a more useful predictor of performance than are formal selection tests. For example, one study of prospective NFL players concluded that collegiate performance was a significantly better predictor of NFL performance than were physical ability tests.[98] ■

MyLab Management Talk About It 5

If your professor has assigned this, go to the Assignments section of **www.pearson.com/mylab/management** to complete this discussion. You own a small ladies' dress shop in a mall and want to hire a salesperson. Create a test for doing so.

Background Investigations and Other Selection Methods

Testing is only part of an employer's selection process. Other tools may include background investigations and reference checks, preemployment information services, honesty testing, and substance abuse screening.

LEARNING OBJECTIVE 6-5

Describe four ways to improve an employer's background checking process.

Why Perform Background Investigations and Reference Checks?

One major company was about to announce a new CEO until they discovered he had a wife and two children in one state as well as a wife and two children in another state.[99] More mundanely, the recruiter HireRight found that of the over 600,000 educational verifications they did in one 12-month period, 32% had discrepancies.[100]

One of the easiest ways to avoid hiring mistakes is to check the candidate's background thoroughly. Doing so is inexpensive and (if done right) useful. There's usually no reason why even supervisors in large companies can't check the references of someone they're about to hire, as long as they know the rules.

Most employers check and verify the job applicant's background information and references. In one survey of about 700 human resource managers, 87% said they conduct reference checks, 69% conduct background employment checks, 61% check employee criminal records, 56% check employees' driving records, and 35% sometimes or always check credit.[101] Commonly verified data include legal eligibility for employment (in compliance with immigration laws), dates of prior employment, military service (including discharge status), education, identification (including date of birth and address to confirm identity), county criminal records (current residence, last residence), motor vehicle record, credit, licensing verification, Social Security number, and reference checks.[102] Some employers check executive candidates' civil litigation records, with the candidate's prior approval.[103] Some states prohibit private employers from asking about criminal records on initial written applications.[104] Some employers also do ongoing due diligence background checks for current employees.[105]

There are two main reasons to check backgrounds—to verify the applicant's information (name and so forth) and to uncover damaging information.[106] Lying on one's application isn't unusual. A survey found that 23% of 7,000 executive résumés contained exaggerated or false information.[107]

How deeply you search depends on the position. For example, a credit check is more important for hiring an accountant than a groundskeeper. In any case, also periodically check the credit ratings of employees (like cashiers) who have easy access to company assets, and the driving records of employees who use company cars.

Yet most managers don't view references as very useful. Few employers will talk freely about former employees. For example, in one poll, the Society for Human Resource Management found that 98% of 433 responding members said their organizations would verify dates of employment for current or former employees. However, 68% said they wouldn't discuss work performance; 82% said they wouldn't discuss character or personality; and 87% said they wouldn't disclose a disciplinary action.[108]

Many supervisors don't want to damage a former employee's chances for a job; others might prefer giving an incompetent employee good reviews to get rid of him or her.

Another reason is legal. Employers providing references generally can't be successfully sued for defamation unless the employee can show "malice"—that is, ill will, culpable recklessness, or disregard of the employee's rights.[109] But many managers and companies understandably still don't want the grief.

KNOW YOUR EMPLOYMENT LAW

Giving References

Federal laws that affect references include the Privacy Act of 1974, the Fair Credit Reporting Act of 1970, the Family Education Rights and Privacy Act of 1974 (and Buckley Amendment of 1974), and the Freedom of Information Act of 1966. They give people the right to know the nature and substance of information in their credit files and files with government agencies, and (Privacy Act) to review records pertaining to them from any private business that contracts with a federal agency. The person may thus see your comments.[110] The employer must also adhere to the Fair Credit Reporting Act's requirements. For instance, make sure applicants consent to having their credit checked.[111]

Beyond that, common law (and in particular the tort of defamation) applies to any information you supply. Communication is defamatory if it is false and tends to harm the reputation of another by lowering the person in the estimation of the community or by deterring other persons from dealing with him or her.

Truth is not always a defense. In some states, employees can sue employers for disclosing to a large number of people true but embarrassing private facts about the employee. One older case involved a supervisor shouting that the employee's wife had been having sexual relations with certain people. The jury found the employer liable for invasion of the couple's privacy and for intentional infliction of emotional distress.[112]

Although the risk of suit may be low,[113] the net result is that most employers and managers restrict who can give references and what they can say. (One study found a "culture of silence" among hospitals regarding sharing such information.)[114] As a rule, only authorized managers should provide information. Other suggestions include "Don't volunteer information," "Avoid vague statements," and "Do not answer trap questions such as, 'Would you rehire this person?'" In practice, many firms have a policy of not providing any information about former employees except for their dates of employment, last salary, and position titles.[115]

(However, *not* disclosing relevant information can be dangerous, too. In one case, a company fired an employee for allegedly bringing a handgun to work. After his next employer fired him for absenteeism, he returned to that company and shot several employees. The injured parties and their relatives sued the previous employer, who had provided the employee with a clean letter of recommendation.)

The person alleging defamation has various legal remedies, including suing the source of the reference for defamation, invasion of privacy, interference with contract, and discrimination.[116] In one case, a court awarded a man $56,000 after a company turned him down for a job after the former employer called him a "character." Many firms will check references for a small fee (Google *reference checking service*).[117] One supervisor hired such a firm. It found that someone at the supervisor's previous company suggested that the employee was ". . . not comfortable with taking risks, or making big decisions." The former employee sued, demanding an end to defamation and $45,000 in compensation.[118]

There are several things managers and employers can do to get better information.

Most employers still at least try to verify an applicant's current (or former) position and salary with his or her current (or former) employer by phone (assuming you cleared doing so with the candidate). Others call the applicant's current and previous supervisors to try to discover more about the person's motivation, technical competence, and ability to work with others (although, again, many employers have policies against providing such information). Figure 6-8 shows one form for phone references. ■

Automated online reference checking can improve the results. With a system such as Skill Survey's Pre-Hire 360 (www.skillsurvey.com/reference-checking-solution/), the hiring employer inputs the applicant's name and e-mail address. Then the person's preselected references rate the applicant's skills anonymously, using a survey. The system then compiles these references into a report for the employer.[119]

TRENDS SHAPING HR: *DIGITAL AND SOCIAL MEDIA*

Digital tools are changing the background-checking process. Employers are Googling applicants or checking Facebook and LinkedIn, and what they're finding isn't always pretty. One candidate described his interests on Facebook as smoking pot and shooting people. The student may have been kidding, but didn't get the job.[120] An article called "Funny, They Don't Look Like My References" notes that the LinkedIn premium service "Reference Search" lets employers identify people in their own networks who worked for the same company when a job candidate did, and to thus use them to get references on the candidate.[121] According to LinkedIn, you just select Reference Search, then enter a company name, candidate's name, and the timeframe, and click search. Employers are integrating such tools with software solutions such as Oracle's Taleo system, to facilitate obtaining such information and then integrating it into the candidate's dashboard-accessible profile.

Web and social media background searches can be problematical. Although applicants usually don't list race, age, disability or ethnic origin on their résumés, their Facebook pages may reveal such information, setting the stage for possible EEOC claims. Or, an overeager supervisor might conduct his or her own Facebook page "background check."[122]

In any case, it's probably best to get the candidate's prior approval for a social networking search.[123] And do not use a pretext or fabricate an identity.[124] Maryland law restricts employer demands for applicant usernames and passwords.[125] Other states will undoubtedly follow.

The solution isn't necessarily to prohibit the legitimate use of social media–based information (unless perusing such information is illegal under the law, as in Maryland). Instead, follow intelligent social media staffing policies and procedures. For example, inform employees and prospective employees ahead of time regarding what information the employer plans to review. Assign one or two specially trained human resource professionals to search social media sites. And warn unauthorized employees (such as prospective supervisors) about accessing such information.[126] ■

MyLab Management Talk About It 6

If your professor has assigned this, go to the Assignments section of **www.pearson.com/mylab/management** to complete this discussion question. Review your Facebook or other social media site. How do you think a prospective employer would react to what you've posted there?

FIGURE 6-8 Reference Checking Form

Source: Reprinted with permission of the Society for Human Resource Management (www.shrm.org), Alexandria, VA 22314.

(Verify that the applicant has provided permission before conducting reference checks.)

Candidate Name ______________________________

Reference Name ______________________________

Company Name ______________________________

Dates of Employment
From: ______________ To: ______________

Position(s) Held ______________________________

Salary History ______________________________

Reason for Leaving ______________________________

Explain the reason for your call and verify the above information with the supervisor (including the reason for leaving)

1. Please describe the type of work for which the candidate was responsible.
2. How would you describe the applicant's relationships with coworkers, subordinates (if applicable), and with superiors?
3. Did the candidate have a positive or negative work attitude? Please elaborate.
4. How would you describe the quantity and quality of output generated by the former employee?
5. What were his/her strengths on the job?
6. What were his/her weaknesses on the job?
7. What is your overall assessment of the candidate?
8. Would you recommend him/her for this position? Why or why not?
9. Would this individual be eligible for rehire? Why or why not?

Other comments?

Using Preemployment Information Services

It is easy to have employment screening services check out applicants. Big providers include Accurate Background (accuratebackground.com), First Advantage (FADV.com), HireRight LLC (hireright.com), and Sterling Talent Solutions (https://www.sterlingtalentsolutions.com/).[127] They use databases to access information about matters such as workers' compensation, credit histories, and conviction and driving records. For example, retail employers use First Advantage Corporation's Esteem Database to see if their job candidates have previously been involved in suspected retail thefts.[128] Another firm advertises that for less than $50 it will do a criminal history report, motor vehicle/driver's record report, and (after the person is hired) a workers' compensation claims report history, plus confirm identity, name, and Social Security number. There are thousands of databases, including sex offender registries and criminal and educational histories. Blockchain technology expedites checking applicants' credentials. For example, when a university issues a digital diploma, the *blockcerts* mobile app creates a unique "fingerprint" of it. This facilitates quickly confirming the degree's legitimacy.[129]

There are three reasons to use caution with background checking services.[130] First, EEO laws apply. For example, many states have "Ban the Box" laws prohibiting prospective employers from questioning applicants about convictions until late in the hiring process.[131] So be careful not to use the product of an unreasonable investigation.

Second, various federal and state laws govern how employers acquire and use applicants' and employees' background information. At the federal level, the Fair Credit Reporting Act is the main directive. In addition, at least 21 states impose their own requirements. Authorizing background reports while complying with these laws requires four steps, as follows:

Step 1: ***Disclosure and authorization.*** Before requesting reports, the employer must disclose to the applicant or employee that a report will be requested and that the employee/applicant may receive a copy. (Do this on the application form.)

Step 2: ***Certification.*** The employer must certify to the background checking firm that the employer will comply with the federal and state legal requirements—for example, that the employer obtained written consent from the employee/applicant.

Step 3: ***Providing copies of reports.*** Under federal law, the employer must provide copies of the report to the applicant or employee if adverse action (such as withdrawing a job offer) is contemplated.[132]

Step 4: ***Notice after adverse action.*** If the employer anticipates taking an adverse action, the employee/applicant must get an *adverse action notice*. The employee/applicant then has various remedies under the law.[133]

Finally, the criminal background information may be flawed. Many return "possible matches" for the wrong person (who happens to be a criminal).[134] One such firm paid a $2.6 million penalty after the Federal Trade Commission sued it for such erroneous reporting.[135]

Steps for Making the Background Check More Valuable

There are steps one can take to improve the usefulness of the background information being sought. Specifically:

- Include on the application form a statement for applicants to sign explicitly authorizing a background check, such as:

  I hereby certify that the facts set forth in the above employment application are true and complete to the best of my knowledge. I understand that falsified statements or misrepresentation of information on this application or omission of any information sought may be cause for dismissal, if employed, or may lead to refusal to make an offer and/or to withdrawal of an offer. I also authorize investigation of credit, employment record, driving record, and, once a job offer is made or during employment, workers' compensation background if required.

- Phone references tend to produce more candid assessments. Use a form, such as Figure 6-8. Remember that you can get relatively accurate information regarding dates of employment, eligibility for rehire, and job qualifications. It's more difficult to get other background information (such as reasons for leaving a previous job).[136]
- Persistence and attentiveness to possible red flags improve results. For example, if the former employer hesitates or seems to qualify his or her answer, don't go on to the next question. Try to unearth what the applicant did to make the former employer pause. If he says, "Joe requires some special care," say, "Special care?"
- Compare the application to the résumé; people tend to be more creative on their résumés than on their application forms, where they must certify the information.
- Try to ask open-ended questions (such as, "How much structure does the applicant need in his/her work?") to get the references to talk more about the candidate. But keep in mind:[137] Stick to information that you're going to use; using arrest information is highly problematical; use information that is specific and job related; many states and municipalities prohibit asking about salary history; and keep information confidential.
- Ask the references supplied by the applicant to suggest other references. You might ask each of the applicant's references, "Could you give me the name of another person who might be familiar with the applicant's performance?" Then you begin getting information from references that may be more objective, because they did not come directly from the applicant (or use LinkedIn's Reference Search service).
- Aim for "360" reference checking: A full picture requires contacting the person's former supervisors, colleagues, and subordinates.[138]

The Polygraph and Honesty Testing

polygraph
A device that measures physiological changes like increased perspiration, on the assumption that such changes reflect lying.

The **polygraph** is a device that measures physiological changes like increased perspiration. The assumption is that such changes reflect changes in emotional state that accompany lying.

Complaints about offensiveness plus grave doubts about the polygraph's accuracy culminated in the Employee Polygraph Protection Act of 1988.[139] With a few exceptions, the law prohibits employers from conducting polygraph examinations of all job applicants and most employees.[140] Federal laws don't prohibit paper-and-pencil honesty tests or chemical testing, as for drugs.

Local, state, and federal government employers (including the FBI) can use polygraphs for selection screening and other purposes, but state laws restrict many local and state governments. Private employers can use polygraph testing, but only under strictly limited circumstances.[141] These include firms with national defense or security contracts, and private businesses (1) hiring private security personnel, (2) hiring persons with access to drugs, or (3) some doing ongoing investigations, such as a theft.

WRITTEN HONESTY TESTS Paper-and-pencil (or computerized or online) honesty tests are special types of personality tests designed to predict job applicants' proneness to dishonesty and other forms of counterproductivity.[142] Most measure attitudes regarding things like tolerance of others who steal and admission of theft-related activities. They include the MINT test of integrity, published by Assessio (www.assessio.com/).[143]

Studies support such tests' validity.[144] One study involved 111 employees hired by a convenience store chain to work at store or gas station counters.[145] The firm estimated that "shrinkage" equaled 3% of sales, and believed that internal theft accounted for much of this. Scores on an honesty test successfully predicted theft here (as measured by termination for theft).

graphology
The use of handwriting analysis to determine the writer's personality characteristics and moods, and even illnesses, such as depression.

Graphology is the use of handwriting analysis to determine the writer's personality characteristics and moods, and even illnesses, such as depression.[146] It thus bears some resemblance to projective personality tests, although graphology's validity is highly suspect. The handwriting analyst studies an applicant's handwriting and signature to discover the person's needs, desires, and psychological makeup. In one typical example, the graphologist notes that a writing sample has small handwriting, a vertical stance, and narrow letters (among other things) and so is indicative of someone with uptight tendencies. One recent study reports successfully identifying writers' genders through graphology.[147] There are computerized systems for expediting graphology analyses.[148]

Most scientific studies suggest graphology has little or no validity, or that when graphologists do accurately size up candidates, it's because they were also privy to other background information. Yet some firms have embraced it.[149] Given the practical need to validate selection tools, most experts shun it.

"HUMAN LIE DETECTORS" Some employers use so-called human lie detectors, experts who may (or may not) be able to identify lying just by watching candidates.[150] One Wall Street firm uses a former FBI agent. He sits in on interviews and watches for signs of candidate deceptiveness. Signs include pupils changing size (fear), irregular breathing (nervousness), crossing legs ("liars distance themselves from an untruth"), and quick verbal responses (scripted statements).

TESTING FOR HONESTY: PRACTICAL GUIDELINES With or without testing, there's a lot a manager can do to screen out dishonest applicants or employees. Specifically:

- Ask blunt questions.[151] Says one expert, there is nothing wrong with asking the applicant direct questions, such as, "Have you ever stolen anything from an employer?" "Have you recently held jobs other than those listed on your application?" "Is any information on your application misrepresented or falsified?"
- Listen carefully. Thus liars may try to answer direct questions somewhat evasively. For example, ask them if they've ever used drugs, and they might say, "I don't take drugs."[152]
- Watch for telltale body signals. For example, someone who is not telling the truth may move his or her body slightly away from you.[153] Establish a baseline by seeing how the person's body is positioned when he or she is undoubtedly telling the truth. Know that it is *not* true that adult liars won't look you in the eye when they're lying; polished liars may actually do so excessively.[154]
- Do a credit check. Include a clause in your application giving you the right to conduct background checks, including credit checks and motor vehicle reports.
- Check all employment and personal references.
- Use written honesty tests and psychological tests.
- Test for drugs. Devise a drug-testing program and give each applicant a copy of the policy.
- Establish a search-and-seizure policy, and conduct searches. Give each applicant a copy of the policy and require each to return a signed copy. The policy should state, "All lockers, desks, and similar property remain the property of the company and may be inspected routinely."

Honesty testing requires caution. Having just taken and "failed" what is fairly obviously an "honesty test," the candidate may leave the premises feeling mistreated. Some "honesty" questions also pose invasion-of-privacy issues. And some states such as Massachusetts and Rhode Island limit paper-and-pencil honesty testing.

Physical Exams

Once the employer extends the person a job offer, a medical exam is often the next step in selection (although it may also occur after the new employee starts work).

There are several reasons for preemployment medical exams: to verify that the applicant meets the job's physical requirements, to discover any medical limitations you should consider in placement, and to establish a baseline for future workers' compensation claims. Exams can also reduce absenteeism and accidents and detect communicable diseases.

Under the Americans with Disabilities Act, an employer cannot reject someone with a disability if he or she is otherwise qualified and can perform the essential job functions with reasonable accommodation. Recall that the ADA permits a medical exam during the period between the job offer and commencement of work if such exams are standard practice for all applicants for that job category.[155]

Substance Abuse Screening

Most employers conduct drug screenings, and many applicants are flunking the tests.[156] The most common practice is to test candidates just before they're formally hired. Many also test current employees when there is reason to believe they've been using drugs—after a work accident, or with obvious behavioral symptoms such as chronic lateness. Some firms routinely administer drug tests on a random or periodic basis, while others require drug tests when they transfer or promote employees to new positions. Most employers that conduct such tests use urine sampling. Numerous vendors provide workplace drug-testing services.[157] Employers may use urine testing to test for illicit drugs, breath alcohol tests to determine amount of alcohol in the blood, blood tests to measure alcohol or drugs in the blood at the time of the test, hair analyses to reveal drug history, saliva tests for substances such as marijuana and cocaine, and skin patches to determine drug use.[158] It is more difficult recently to find applicants who can pass a drug test.[159] As a result, more employers today are relaxing their standards about hiring those who fail tests, particularly for marijuana.[160]

Drug testing, while ubiquitous, is neither as simple nor as effective as it might appear. First, no drug test is foolproof. Some urine sample tests can't distinguish between legal and illegal substances; for example, Advil can produce positive results for marijuana. Furthermore, there's a cottage industry offering products that purportedly help applicants pass drug tests (Google *products for beating drug tests*).[161] (Employers should view the presence of adulterants in a sample as a positive test.) One alternative, hair follicle testing, requires a small sample of hair, which the lab analyzes.[162] But here, too, classified ads advertise chemicals to rub on the scalp to fool the test. Employers should choose the lab they engage for testing with care.

There's also the question of what is the point. Unlike roadside breathalyzers for DUI drivers, tests for drugs show only whether drug residues are present; they do not indicate impairment (or, for that matter, habituation or addiction). To paraphrase one pundit, "Do you really want to fire someone for using marijuana at home?"[163] Some therefore argue that testing is not justifiable on the grounds of boosting workplace safety.[164] Many feel the testing procedures themselves are degrading and intrusive. Many employers reasonably counter that they don't want drug-prone employees on their premises.

Drug Testing Legal Issues

Drug testing raises numerous legal issues. Employees may claim drug tests violate their rights to privacy. Hair follicle testing is less intrusive than urinalysis but can actually produce more personal information: A short hair segment could record months of drug use.[165] The National Labor Relations Board upheld a union member's right to have representation after failing a drug test; this may "severely disrupt and limit" unionized employers' ability to test and deal with employees who are under the influence.[166] Courts require that employers who administer drug tests to employees who have accidents focus on recent drug use.[167]

Several federal laws affect workplace drug testing, and multistate employers must ensure they also comply with state laws (some states permit medical marijuana use, for instance).[168] Under the Americans with Disabilities Act, a court would probably consider a former drug user (who no longer uses illegal drugs and has successfully completed or is participating in a rehabilitation program) as a qualified applicant with a disability.[169] Under the Drug Free Workplace Act of 1988, federal contractors must maintain a workplace free from illegal drugs. While this doesn't require contractors to conduct drug testing or rehabilitate affected employees, many do. Under the U.S. Department of Transportation workplace regulations, firms with over 50 eligible employees in transportation industries must conduct alcohol testing on workers with sensitive or safety-related jobs. These include mass transit workers, air traffic controllers, train crews, and school bus drivers.[170] Other laws, including the Federal Rehabilitation Act of 1973 and various state laws, protect rehabilitating drug users or those who have a physical or mental addiction.

What should an employer do when a job candidate tests positive? As a rule, most companies won't hire such candidates, but current employees have more legal recourse. Most must be told the reason for dismissal if the reason is a positive drug test. And again, there are industry-specific and state-specific requirements. For example, certain transportation companies and federal contractors must comply with federal drug-testing rules for their industries. Similarly, state laws vary. For example, in several states you cannot fire someone for a first failed drug test if he or she agrees to rehabilitation.[171]

Particularly where sensitive jobs are concerned, courts tend to side with employers. In one classic case, a U.S. Court of Appeals ruled that Exxon acted properly in firing a truck driver who failed a drug test. Exxon requires random testing of employees in safety-sensitive jobs. The employee drove a tractor-trailer carrying 12,000 gallons of flammable motor fuel and tested positive for cocaine. The union representing the employee challenged the firing. An arbitrator reduced the penalty to a 2-month suspension, but the appeals court ruled that the employer acted properly in firing the truck driver.[172]

Complying with Immigration Law

Employees hired in the United States must prove they are eligible to work here. The requirement to verify eligibility does not provide any basis to reject an applicant just because he or she is a foreigner, not a U.S. citizen, or an alien residing in the United States, as long as that person can prove his or her identity and employment eligibility. To comply with this law, employers should follow procedures outlined in the so-called I-9 Employment Eligibility Verification form. Recently the federal government has been tightening its oversight.[173] Many employers are using the federal government's voluntary electronic employment verification program, E-Verify.[174] Federal contractors must use it.[175] There is no charge to use E-Verify.[176] Many employers now use automated I-9 verification systems with drop-down menus to electronically compile and submit applicants' I-9 data.[177] The I-9 forms contain a prominent "antidiscrimination notice."[178]

Applicants can prove their eligibility for employment in two ways. One is to show a document (such as a U.S. passport or alien registration card with photograph) that proves both identity and employment eligibility. The other is to show a document that proves the person's identity, along with a second document showing his or her employment eligibility, such as a work permit.[179] In any case, it's always advisable to get two forms of proof of identity.

Identity theft—undocumented workers stealing and using an authorized worker's identity—is a problem even with E-Verify.[180] The federal government is tightening restrictions on hiring undocumented workers. Realizing that many documents are fakes, the government is putting the onus on employers to make sure whom they're hiring.

You can verify Social Security numbers by calling the Social Security Administration. Employers can avoid accusations of discrimination by verifying the documents of all applicants, not just those they may think are suspicious.[181]

Chapter Review

Chapter Section Summaries

6-1. Careful **employee selection is important** for several reasons. Your own performance always depends on your subordinates; it is costly to recruit and hire employees; and mismanaging the hiring process has various legal implications including equal employment, negligent hiring, and defamation.

6-2. Whether you are administering tests or making decisions based on test results, managers need to understand several **basic testing concepts.** Reliability refers to a test's consistency, while validity tells you whether the test is measuring what you think it's supposed to be measuring. Criterion validity means demonstrating that those who do well on the test also do well on the job while content validity means showing that the test constitutes a fair sample of the job's content. Validating a test involves analyzing the job, choosing the tests, administering the test, relating your test scores and criteria, and cross-validating and revalidating. Test takers have rights to privacy and feedback as well as to confidentiality.

6-3. Whether they are administered via paper and pencil, by computer, or online, we discussed several main **types of tests.** Tests of cognitive abilities measure things like reasoning ability and include intelligence tests and tests of specific cognitive abilities such as mechanical comprehension. There are also tests of motor and physical abilities, and measures of personality and interests. With respect to personality, psychologists often focus on the "big five" personality dimensions: extroversion, emotional stability/neuroticism, agreeableness, conscientiousness, and openness to experience. Achievement tests measure what someone has learned.

6-4. With **work samples and simulations,** you present examinees with situations representative of the jobs for which they are applying. One example is the management assessment center, a 2- to 3-day simulation in which 10 to 12 candidates perform realistic management tasks under the observation of experts who appraise each candidate's leadership potential. Video-based situational testing and the miniature job training and evaluation approach are two other examples.

6-5. Testing is only part of an employer's selection process; you also want to conduct **background investigations and other selection procedures.**

- The main point of doing a background check is to verify the applicant's information and to uncover potentially damaging information. However, care must be taken, particularly when giving a reference, that the employee not be defamed and that his or her privacy rights are maintained.
- Given former employers' reluctance to provide a comprehensive report, those checking references need to do several things. Make sure the applicant explicitly authorizes a background check, use a checklist or form for obtaining telephone references, and be persistent and attentive to potential red flags.
- Given the growing popularity of computerized employment background databases, many or most employers use preemployment information services to obtain background information.
- For many types of jobs, honesty testing is essential, and paper-and-pencil tests have proven useful.
- Most employers also require that new hires, before actually coming on board, take physical exams and substance abuse screening. It's essential to comply with immigration law, in particular by having the candidate complete an I-9 Employment Eligibility Verification Form and submit proof of eligibility.

Discussion Questions

6-1. What is the difference between reliability and validity?

6-2. Explain why you think a certified psychologist who is specifically trained in test construction should (or should not) be used by a small business that needs an employment test.

6-3. Why is it important to conduct preemployment background investigations? How would you do so?

6-4. Explain how you would get around the problem of former employers being unwilling to give bad references on their former employees.

6-5. How can employers protect themselves against negligent hiring claims?

Individual and Group Activities

6-6. Write a short essay discussing some of the ethical and legal considerations in testing.

6-7. Working individually or in groups, develop a list of specific selection techniques that you would suggest your dean use to hire the next HR professor at your school. Explain why you chose each selection technique.

6-8. Working individually or in groups, contact the publisher of a standardized test such as the Scholastic Assessment Test, and obtain from it written information regarding the test's validity and reliability. Present a short report in class discussing what the test is supposed to measure and the degree to which you think the test does what it is supposed to do, based on the reported validity and reliability scores.

6-9. Appendices A and B at the end of this book (pages 614–634) list the knowledge someone

studying for the HRCI (Appendix A) or SHRM (Appendix B) certification exam needs to have in each area of human resource management (such as in Strategic Management and Workforce Planning). In groups of several students, do four things: (1) review Appendix A and/or B; (2) identify the material in this chapter that relates to the Appendix A and/or B required knowledge lists; (3) write four multiple-choice exam questions on this material that you believe would be suitable for inclusion in the HRCI exam and/or the SHRM exam; and (4) if time permits, have someone from your team post your team's questions in front of the class, so that students in all teams can answer the exam questions created by the other teams.

Experiential Exercise

A Test for a Reservation Clerk

Written and copyrighted by Gary Dessler, PhD.

Purpose: The purpose of this exercise is to give you practice in developing a test to measure *one specific ability* for the job of airline reservation clerk for a major airline. If time permits, you'll be able to combine your tests into a test battery.

Required Understanding: Your airline has decided to outsource its reservation jobs to Asia. You should be fully acquainted with the procedure for developing a personnel test and should read the following description of an airline reservation clerk's duties:

> Customers contact our airline reservation clerks to obtain flight schedules, prices, and itineraries. The reservation clerks look up the requested information on our airline's online flight schedule systems, which are updated continuously. The reservation clerk must speak clearly, deal courteously and expeditiously with the customer, and be able to find quickly alternative flight arrangements in order to provide the customer with the itinerary that fits his or her needs. Alternative flights and prices must be found quickly, so that the customer is not kept waiting, and so that our reservations operations group maintains its efficiency standards. There may be a dozen or more alternative routes between the customer's starting point and destination.

You may assume that we will hire about one-third of the applicants as airline reservation clerks. Therefore, your objective is to create a test that is useful in selecting a third of those available.

How to Set Up the Exercise/Instructions: Divide the class into teams of five or six students. The ideal candidate will need to have a number of skills to perform this job well. Your job is to select a single skill and to develop a test to measure that skill. Please use only the materials available in the room. The test should permit quantitative scoring and may be an individual or a group test.

Please go to your assigned groups. As per our discussion of test development in this chapter, each group should make a list of the skills relevant to success in the airline reservation clerk's job. Each group should then rate the importance of these skills on a 5-point scale. Then, develop a test to measure what you believe to be the top-ranked skill. If time permits, the groups should combine the various tests from each group into a test battery. If possible, leave time for a group of students to take the test battery.

Application Case

The Insider

Written and copyrighted by Gary Dessler, PhD.

A federal jury convicted a stock trader who worked for a well-known investment firm, along with two alleged accomplices, of insider trading. According to the indictment, the trader got inside information about pending mergers from lawyers. The lawyers allegedly browsed around their law firm picking up information about corporate deals others in the firm were working on. The lawyers would then allegedly pass their information on to a friend, who in turn passed it on to the trader. Such "inside" information reportedly helped the trader (and his investment firm) earn millions of dollars. The trader would then allegedly thank the lawyers, for instance, with envelopes filled with cash.

Things like that are not supposed to happen. Federal and state laws prohibit them. And investment firms have their own compliance procedures to identify and head off shady trades. The problem is that controlling such behavior once the firm has someone working for it who may be prone to engage in inside trading isn't easy. "Better to avoid hiring such people in the first place," said one pundit.

Over lunch at Bouley restaurant in Manhattan's TriBeCa area, the heads of several investment firms were discussing the conviction, and what they could do to make sure something like that didn't occur in their firms. "It's not just compliance," said one. "We've got to keep out the bad apples." They ask you for your advice.

Questions

6-10. We want you to design an employee selection program for hiring stock traders. We already know what to look for as far as technical skills are concerned—accounting courses, economics, and so on. What we want is a program for screening out potential bad apples. To that end, please let us know the following: What screening test(s) would you suggest, and why? What questions should we add to our application form? Specifically how should we check candidates' backgrounds, and what questions should we ask previous employers and references?

6-11. What else (if anything) would you suggest?

Continuing Case

Carter Cleaning Company

Written and copyrighted by Gary Dessler, PhD.

Honesty Testing

Jennifer Carter, of the Carter Cleaning Centers, and her father have what the latter describes as an easy but hard job when it comes to screening job applicants. It is easy because for two important jobs—the people who actually do the pressing and those who do the cleaning/spotting—the applicants are easily screened with about 20 minutes of on-the-job testing. As with typists, Jennifer points out, "Applicants either know how to press clothes fast or how to use cleaning chemicals and machines, or they don't, and we find out very quickly by just trying them out on the job." On the other hand, applicant screening for the stores can also be frustratingly hard because of the nature of some of the other qualities that Jennifer would like to screen for. Two of the most critical problems facing her company are employee turnover and employee honesty. Jennifer and her father sorely need to implement practices that will reduce the rate of employee turnover. If there is a way to do this through employee testing and screening techniques, Jennifer would like to know about it because of the management time and money that are now being wasted by the never-ending need to recruit and hire new employees. Of even greater concern to Jennifer and her father is the need to institute new practices to screen out those employees who may be predisposed to steal from the company.

Employee theft is an enormous problem for the Carter Cleaning Centers, and not just cash. For example, the cleaner/spotter often opens the store without a manager present, to get the day's work started, and it is not unusual for that person to "run a route." Running a route means that an employee canvasses his or her neighborhood to pick up people's clothes for cleaning and then secretly cleans and presses them in the Carter store, using the company's supplies, gas, and power. It would also not be unusual for an unsupervised person (or his or her supervisor, for that matter) to accept a 1-hour rush order for cleaning or laundering, quickly clean and press the item, and return it to the customer for payment without making out a proper ticket for the item posting the sale. The money, of course, goes into the worker's pocket instead of into the cash register.

The more serious problem concerns the store manager and the counter workers who actually handle the cash. According to Jack Carter, "You would not believe the creativity employees use to get around the management controls we set up to cut down on employee theft." As one extreme example of this felonious creativity, Jack tells the following story: "To cut down on the amount of money my employees were stealing, I had a small sign painted and placed in front of all our cash registers. The sign said: YOUR ENTIRE ORDER FREE IF WE DON'T GIVE YOU A CASH REGISTER RECEIPT WHEN YOU PAY. CALL 552–0235. It was my intention with this sign to force all our cash-handling employees to give receipts so the cash register would record them for my accountants. After all, if all the cash that comes in is recorded in the cash register, then we should have a much better handle on stealing in our stores. Well, one of our managers found a way around this. I came into the store one night and noticed that the cash register this particular manager was using just didn't look right, although the sign was placed in front of it. It turned out that every afternoon at about 5:00 p.m. when the other employees left, this character would pull his own cash register out of a box that he hid underneath our supplies. Customers coming in would notice the sign and, of course, the fact that he was meticulous in ringing up every sale. But unknown to them, for about 5 months the sales that came in for about an hour every day went into his cash register, not mine. It took us that long to figure out where our cash for that store was going."

Here is what Jennifer would like you to answer:

Questions

6-12. What would be the advantages and disadvantages to Jennifer's company of routinely administering honesty tests to all its employees?

6-13. Specifically, what other screening techniques could the company use to screen out theft-prone and turnover-prone employees, and how exactly could these be used?

6-14. How should her company terminate employees caught stealing, and what kind of procedure should be set up for handling reference calls about these employees when they go to other companies looking for jobs?

Translating Strategy into HR Policies and Practices Case*,§

**The accompanying strategy map for this chapter is in MyLab Management; the overall map on the inside back cover of this text outlines the relationships involved.*

Improving Performance at the Hotel Paris

The New Employee Testing Program

The Hotel Paris's competitive strategy is "To use superior guest service to differentiate the Hotel Paris properties, and to thereby increase the length of stay and return rate of guests, and thus boost revenues and profitability." HR manager Lisa Cruz must now formulate functional policies and activities that support this competitive strategy and boost performance, by eliciting the required employee behaviors and competencies.

As she considered what to do next, Lisa Cruz, the Hotel Paris's HR director, knew that employee selection had to play a role. The Hotel Paris currently had an informal screening process in which local hotel managers obtained application forms, interviewed applicants, and checked their references. However, a pilot project using an employment test for service people at the Chicago hotel had produced startling results. Lisa found consistent, significant relationships between test performance and a range of employee competencies and behaviors such as speed of check-in/out, employee turnover, and percentage of calls answered with the required greeting. She knew that such employee capabilities and behaviors translated into the improved guest service performance the Hotel Paris needed to execute its strategy. She therefore had to decide what selection procedures would be best.

Lisa's team, working with an industrial psychologist, designs a test battery that they believe will produce the sorts of high-morale, patient, people-oriented employees they are looking for. It includes a preliminary, computerized test in which applicants for the positions of front-desk clerk, door person, assistant manager, and security guard must deal with an apparently irate guest; a work sample in which front-desk clerk candidates spend 10 minutes processing an incoming "guest"; a personality test aimed at weeding out applicants who lack emotional stability; the Wonderlic test of mental ability; and the Phase II Profile for assessing candidate honesty. Their subsequent validity analysis shows that scores on the test batteries predict scores on the hotel's employee capabilities and behavior metrics. A second analysis confirmed that, as the percentage of employees hired after testing rose, so too did the hotel's employee capabilities and behaviors scores, for instance (see the strategy map), in terms of speed of check-in/out, and the percent of guests receiving the Hotel Paris required greeting.

Lisa and the CFO also found other measurable improvements apparently resulting from the new testing process. For example, it took less time to fill an open position, and cost per hire diminished, so the HR department became more efficient. The new testing program thus did not only contribute to the hotel's performance by improving employee capabilities and behaviors. It also did so by directly improving profit margins and profits.

Questions

6-15. Provide a detailed example of a security guard work "sampletest."

6-16. Provide a detailed example of two personality test items you would suggest they use, and why you would suggest using them.

6-17. Based on what you read here in this Dessler *Human Resource Management* chapter, what other tests would you suggest to Lisa, and why would you suggest them?

6-18. How would you suggest Lisa try to confirm that it is indeed the testing and not some other change that accounts for the improved performance.

§Written and copyrighted by Gary Dessler, PhD.

Writing Assignments

6-19. Explain how you would go about validating a test. How can this information be useful to a manager?

6-20. Explain how digital and social media have changed the employee selection process, and the advice you would give an employer about avoiding problems with using such tools for selection.

MyLab Management Try It!

How would you apply the concepts and skills you learned in this chapter? If your professor has assigned this activity, go to the Assignments section of **www.pearson.com/mylab/management** to complete the simulation.

PERSONAL INVENTORY ASSESSMENTS

Go to **www.pearson.com/mylab/management** to complete the Personal Inventory Assessment related to this chapter.

Key Terms

negligent hiring, 171
reliability, 171
test validity, 172
criterion validity, 172
content validity, 173
construct validity, 173
expectancy chart, 175
interest inventory, 180
analytics, 181
machine learning, 182
artificial intelligence, 182
work samples, 182
work sampling technique, 182
management assessment center, 184
situational test, 184
video-based simulation, 184
miniature job training and evaluation, 185
polygraph, 192
graphology, 193

Endnotes

1. https://a248.e.akamai.net/media.zulily.com/images/careers/landing/zulily_values_update_03.20.2017_150dpi.pdf, accessed February 23, 2018.
2. https://a248.e.akamai.net/media.zulily.com/images/careers/landing/zulily_values_update_03.20.2017_150dpi.pdf, accessed February 23, 2018.
3. Psychologists have called selection and recruitment the "supreme problem." Robert Ployhart et al., "Solving the Supreme Problem: 100 Years of Selection and Recruitment at the Journal of Applied Psychology," *Journal of Applied Psychology* 102, no. 3 (2017), pp. 291–304.
4. See, for example, Jean Phillips and Stanley Gully, *Strategic Staffing* (Upper Saddle River, NJ: Pearson Education, 2012), pp. 234–235.
5. www.pwc.com/us/en/hr, accessed February 24, 2018.
6. "Regret That Bad Hire? It's an Expensive Global Problem," *Bloomberg BNA Bulletin to Management*, June 4, 2013, p. 179. Note that in one survey, about 16% of HR professionals said their firms were less rigorous about checking the backgrounds of executive candidates then nonexecutives. This is a dubious practice, given the high cost of hiring the wrong executive. Genevieve Douglas, "Employers Beware Potential Skeletons in Executives' Closets," *Bloomberg BNA Bulletin to Management*, May 9, 2017.
7. Lauren Weber, "To Get a Job, New Hires Are Put to the Test," *The Wall Street Journal*, April 15, 2015, pp. A1, A10.
8. Even if they use a third party to prepare an employment test, contractors are "ultimately responsible" for ensuring the tests' job relatedness and EEO compliance. "DOL Officials Discuss Contractors' Duties on Validating Tests," *BNA Bulletin to Management*, September 4, 2007, p. 287. Furthermore, enforcement units are increasing their scrutiny of employers who rely on tests and screening. See "Litigation Increasing with Employer Reliance on Tests, Screening," *Bloomberg BNA Bulletin to Management*, April 8, 2008, p. 119. However, see also C. Tuna et al., "Job-Test Ruling Cheers Employers," *The Wall Street Journal*, July 1, 2009, p. B1–B2.
9. See, for example, Ann Marie Ryan and Marja Lasek, "Negligent Hiring and Defamation: Areas of Liability Related to Pre-Employment Inquiries," *Personnel Psychology* 44, no. 2 (Summer 1991), pp. 293–319. See also Jay Stuller, "Fatal Attraction," *Across the Board* 42, no. 6 (November–December 2005), pp. 18–23.
10. For example, Ryan Zimmerman, "Wal-Mart to Toughen Job Screening," *The Wall Street Journal*, July 12, 2004, pp. B1–B8. See also Michael Tucker, "Show and Tell," *HR Magazine*, January 2012, pp. 51–52.
11. Negligent hiring highlights the need to think through what the job's human requirements really are. For example, "nonrapist" isn't likely to appear as a required knowledge, skill, or ability in a job analysis of an apartment manager, but in situations like this, screening for such tendencies is obviously required. To avoid negligent hiring claims, "make a systematic effort to gain relevant information about the applicant, verify documentation, follow up on missing records or gaps in employment, and keep a detailed log of all attempts to obtain information, including the names and dates for phone calls or other requests." Fay Hansen, "Taking 'Reasonable' Action to Avoid Negligent Hiring Claims," *Workforce Management*, September 11, 2006, p. 31. Similarly, the Employers Liability Act of 1969 holds employers responsible for their employees' health and safety at work. Because personality traits may predict problems such as unsafe behaviors and bullying, this act makes careful employee selection even more advisable.
12. Martin Berman-Gorvine, "Employee Background Checks Have Companies Caught in the Middle," *Bloomberg BNA Bulletin to Management*, June 27, 2017.
13. Kevin Murphy and Charles Davidshofer, *Psychological Testing: Principles and Applications* (Upper Saddle River, NJ: Prentice Hall, 2001), p. 73.
14. Ibid., pp. 116–119.
15. W. Bruce Walsh and Nancy Betz, *Tests and Assessment* (Upper Saddle River, NJ: Prentice Hall, 2001); see also, https://www.eeoc.gov/policy/docs/qanda_clarify_procedures.html, accessed February 26, 2018.
16. Murphy and Davidshofer, *Psychological Testing*, p. 74.
17. Ibid.
18. See James Ledvinka, *Federal Regulation of Personnel and Human Resource Management* (Boston: Kent, 1982), p. 113; and Murphy and Davidshofer, *Psychological Testing*, pp. 154–165.
19. www.siop.org/workplace/employment%20testing/information_to_consider_when_cre.aspx, accessed March 22, 2009.
20. The procedure you would use to demonstrate content validity differs from that used to demonstrate criterion validity (as described in steps 1 through 5). Content validity tends to emphasize judgment. Here, you first do a careful job analysis to identify the work behaviors required. Then combine several samples of those behaviors into a test. A typing and computer skills test for a clerk would be an example. The fact that the test is a comprehensive sample of actual, observable, on-the-job behaviors is what lends the test its content validity.
21. Murphy and Davidshofer, *Psychological Testing*, p. 73. See also Chad Van Iddekinge and Robert Ployhart, "Developments in the Criterion-Related Validation of Selection Procedures: A Critical Review and Recommendations for Practice," *Personnel Psychology* 60, no. 1 (2008), pp. 871–925.
22. Psychological Assessment Resources, Inc., in Odessa, Florida, is typical.
23. Experts sometimes have to develop separate expectancy charts and cutting points for minorities and nonminorities if the validation studies indicate that high performers from either group (minority or nonminority) score lower (or higher) on the test.
24. In employment testing, bias has a precise meaning. Specifically, "bias is said to exist when a test makes systematic errors in measurement or prediction." Murphy and Davidshofer, *Psychological Testing*, p. 303.
25. Ibid., p. 305.
26. Herman Aguinis, Steven Culpepper, and Charles Pierce, "Revival of Test Bias Research in Preemployment Testing," *Journal of Applied Psychology* 95, no. 4 (2010), p. 648.
27. Robert Gatewood and Hubert Feild, *Human Resource Selection* (Mason, OH: South-Western, Cengage Learning, 2008), p. 243.
28. This is based on Dave Zielinski, "Effective Assessments," *HR Magazine*, January 2011, pp. 61–64.

29. The Uniform Guidelines say, "Employers should ensure that tests and selection procedures are not adopted casually by managers who know little about these processes . . . no test or selection procedure should be implemented without an understanding of its effectiveness and limitations for the organization, its appropriateness for a specific job, and whether it can be appropriately administered and scored."
30. Phillips and Gully, *Strategic Staffing*, p. 220.
31. Ibid., p. 220.
32. www.uniformguidelines.com/qandaprint.html, accessed July 19, 2013. Conversely, validating a test that suffers from adverse impact may not be enough. Under the Uniform Guidelines, the employer should also find an equally valid *but less adversely impacting* alternative.
33. For a recent discussion, see, for example, Jonathan Cottrell, Daniel Newman, and Glenn Roisman, "Explaining the Black–White Gap in Cognitive Test Scores: Toward a Theory of Adverse Impact," *Journal of Applied Psychology* 100, no. 6 (2015), pp. 1713–1736.
34. A complete discussion of the APA's "Ethical Principles of Psychologists and Code of Conduct" is beyond this text's scope. But points it addresses include competence, integrity, respect for people's dignity, nondiscrimination, and sexual harassment. From "Ethical Principles of Psychologists and Code of Conduct," *American Psychologist* 47 (1992), pp. 1597–1611; and www.apa.org/ethics/code/index.aspx, accessed September 9, 2011.
35. Susan R. Mendelsohn and Kathryn K. Morrison, "The Right to Privacy in the Work Place," *Personnel* 65, no. 7 (July 1998), p. 22.
36. Kenneth Sovereign, *Personnel Law* (Upper Saddle River, NJ: Prentice Hall, 1999), pp. 204–206.
37. Weber, "To Get a Job, New Hires Are Put to the Test."
38. Steffanie Wilk and Peter Capelli, "Understanding the Determinants of Employer Use of Selection Methods," *Personnel Psychology* 56 (2003), p. 117. For an example of tests for top managers, see, for example, https://www.criteriacorp.com/solution/pre_employment_testing_for_general_and_operations_managers.php, accessed February 26, 2018.
39. Kevin Hart, "Not Wanted: Thieves," *HR Magazine*, April 2008, p. 119.
40. Sarah Needleman, "Businesses Say Theft by Their Workers Is Up," *The Wall Street Journal*, December 11, 2008, p. B8.
41. Except as noted, this is based on Laurence Siegel and Irving Lane, *Personnel and Organizational Psychology* (Burr Ridge, IL: McGraw-Hill, 1982), pp. 170–185. See also Cabot Jaffee, "Measurement of Human Potential," *Employment Relations Today* 17, no. 2 (Summer 2000), pp. 15–27; Maureen Patterson, "Overcoming the Hiring Crunch; Tests Deliver Informed Choices," *Employment Relations Today* 27, no. 3 (Fall 2000), pp. 77–88; Kathryn Tyler, "Put Applicants' Skills to the Test," *HR Magazine*, January 2000, p. 74; Murphy and Davidshofer, *Psychological Testing*, pp. 215–403; Elizabeth Schoenfelt and Leslie Pedigo, "A Review of Court Decisions on Cognitive Ability Testing, 1992–2004," *Review of Public Personnel Administration* 25, no. 3 (2005), pp. 271–287.
42. See, for example, Paul Agnello, Rachel Ryan, and Kenneth Yusko, "Implications of Modern Intelligence Research for Assessing Intelligence in the Workplace," *Human Resource Management Review* 25, no. 1 (2015), pp. 47–55; and C. A. Scherbaum and H. W. Goldstein, "Intelligence and the Modern World of Work," *Human Resource Management Review* 25, no. 1, March 2015, pp. 1–3.
43. Norman Henderson, "Predicting Long-Term Firefighter Performance from Cognitive and Physical Ability Measures," *Personnel Psychology* 60, no. 3 (2010), pp. 999–1039. Things are not always straightforward. For example, for a mid-management job, the peak IQ for leadership behavior was about 120–124 in one study after which leader behavior dropped off. John Antonakis, Robert J. House, and Dean Simonton, "Can Supersmart Leaders Suffer from Too Much of a Good Thing? The Curvilinear Effect of Intelligence on Perceived Leadership Behavior," *Journal of Applied Psychology* 102, no. 7 (2017), pp. 1003–1021.
44. As an example, results of meta-analyses in one study indicated that isometric strength tests were valid predictors of both supervisory ratings of physical performance and performance on work simulations. See Barry R. Blakley, Miguel Quinones, Marnie Swerdlin Crawford, and I. Ann Jago, "The Validity of Isometric Strength Tests," *Personnel Psychology* 47 (1994), pp. 247–274; and www.military.com/military-fitness/marine-corps-fitness-requirements/marine-corps-fitness-test, accessed October 4, 2011.
45. William Wagner, "All Skill, No Finesse," *Workforce*, June 2000, pp. 108–116. See also, for example, James Diefendorff and Kajal Mehta, "The Relations of Motivational Traits with Workplace Deviance," *Journal of Applied Psychology* 92, no. 4 (2007), pp. 967–977. The relationship between personality and job performance isn't necessarily one way. One study found that success on the job looped back and influenced workers' personalities. Bart Wille and Filip De Fruyt, "Vocations as a Source of Identity: Reciprocal Relations between Big Five Personality Traits and RIASEC Characteristics over 15 Years," *Journal of Applied Psychology* 99, no. 2 (2014), pp. 262–281.
46. See, for example, Joyce Hogan et al., "Personality Measurement, Faking, and Employee Selection," *Journal of Applied Psychology* 92, no. 5 (2007), pp. 1270–1285; Colin Gill and Gerard Hodgkinson, "Development and Validation of the Five Factor Model Questionnaire (FFMQ): An Adjectival-Based Personality Inventory for Use in Occupational Settings," *Personnel Psychology* 60 (2007), pp. 731–766; and Lisa Penney and Emily Witt, "A Review of Personality and Performance: Identifying Boundaries, Contingencies, and Future Research Directions," *Human Resource Management Review* 20, no. 1 (2011), pp. 297–310.
47. Timothy Judge et al., "Personality and Leadership: A Qualitative and Quantitative Review," *Journal of Applied Psychology* 87, no. 4 (2002), p. 765.
48. www.myersbriggs.org/my-mbti-personality-type/, accessed July 10, 2018.
49. www.discprofileusa.com/the-difference-between-myers-briggs-and-disc/, accessed July 10, 2018.
50. L. A. Witt et al., "The Interactive Effects of Conscientiousness and Agreeableness on Job Performance," *Journal of Applied Psychology* 87, no. 1 (2002), pp. 164–169. There are many other examples, for instance, Nailah Ayub et al., "Personality Traits and Conflict Management Styles in Predicting Job Performance and Conflict," *International Journal of Conflict Management* 28, no. 5 (2017), pp. 671–694.
51. Timothy Judge and Remus Ilies, "Relationship of Personality to Performance Motivation: A Meta Analytic Review," *Journal of Applied Psychology* 87, no. 4 (2002), pp. 797–807; Gil Sharoni et al., "Job Engagement: Antecedents and Outcomes," *Journal of Organizational Psychology* 15, no. 1 (May 2015), pp. 34–48.
52. Murray Barrick et al., "Personality and Job Performance: Test of the Immediate Effects of Motivation Among Sales Representatives," *Journal of Applied Psychology* 87, no. 1 (2002), p. 43; Awais Bhatti Muhammad and Sharan Kaur, "Effects of Individual Characteristics on Expatriates' Adjustment and Job Performance," *European Journal of Training and Development* 37, no. 6 (2013), pp. 544–563.
53. Paula Caligiuri, "The Big Five Personality Characteristics as Predictors of Expatriate Desire to Terminate the Assignment and Supervisor Rated Performance," *Personnel Psychology* 53 (2000), pp. 67–68. For some other examples, see Ryan Zimmerman, "Understanding the Impact of Personality Traits on Individuals' Turnover Decisions: A Meta-Analytic Path Model," *Personnel Psychology* 60, no. 1 (2008), pp. 309–348.
54. Adapted from www.kozaigroup.com/-inventories.php, accessed March 3, 2008; and https://www.kozaigroup.com/global-competencies-inventory-gci/, accessed February 26, 2018.
55. Adapted from www.kozaigroup.com/-inventories.php, accessed March 3, 2008; and https://www.kozaigroup.com/global-competencies-inventory-gci/, accessed February 26, 2018.
56. For example, one court held that the Minnesota Multiphasic Personality Inventory (MMPI) is a medical test (because it can screen out applicants with psychological impairments) and so might violate the ADA. Diane Cadrain, "Reassess Personality Tests after Court Case," *HR Magazine* 50, no. 9 (September 2005), p. 30.
57. Frederick Morgeson et al., "Reconsidering the Use of Personality Tests in Personnel Selection Contexts," *Personnel Psychology* 60 (2007), p. 683; and Frederick Morgeson et al., "Are We Getting Fooled Again? Coming to Terms with Limitations in the Use of Personality Tests for Personnel Selection," *Personnel Psychology* 60 (2007), p. 1046; Robert Tett and Neil Christiansen, "Personality Tests at the Crossroads: A Response to Morgeson, Campion, Dipboye, Hollenbeck, Murphy, and Schmitt," *Personnel Psychology* 60 (2007), p. 967. See also Deniz Ones et al., "In Support of Personality Assessment in Organizational Settings," *Personnel Psychology* 60 (2007), pp. 995–1027.
58. See also Edwin A. J. van Hoot and Marise Ph. Born, "Intentional Response Distortion on Personality Tests: Using Eye Tracking to Understand Response Processes When

Thinking," *Journal of Applied Psychology* 97, no. 2 (2012), pp. 301–316.

59. Chad H. Van Iddeking et al., "Are You Interested? A Meta-Analysis of Relations between Vocational Interests and Employee Performance and Turnover," *Journal of Applied Psychology* 96, no 6 (2011), pp. 1167–1194.
60. Dracos Iliescu et al., "Vocational Fit and Counterproductive Work Behaviors: A Self-Regulation Perspective," *Journal of Applied Psychology* 100, no. 1 (2015), pp. 21–39.
61. Ed Frauenheim, "More Companies Go with Online Test to Fill in the Blanks," *Workforce Management*, May 2011, p. 12. See also, John Bateson et al., "When Hiring, First Test, and Then Interview," *Harvard Business Review*, November 2013, p. 34.
62. Requiring job seekers to complete prescreening questionnaires and screening selected applicants out on this basis carries legal and business consequences. See, for example, Lisa Harpe, "Designing an Effective Employment Prescreening Program," *Employment Relations Today* 32, no. 3 (Fall 2005), pp. 41–43.
63. See, for example, Meg Breslin, "Can You Handle Rejection?" *Workforce Management*, October 2012, pp. 32–36.
64. www.iphonetypingtest.com, accessed March 23, 2009.
65. Except as noted, this is based on Dave Zielinski, "Effective Assessments," *HR Magazine*, January 2011, pp. 61–64.
66. Ed Frauenheim, "Personality Tests Adapt to the Times," *Workforce Management*, February 2010, p. 4.
67. Michael C. Campion, Michael A. Campion, Emily D. Campion, and Matthew Reider, "Initial Investigation into Computer Scoring of Candidate Essays for Personnel Selection," *Journal of Applied Psychology* 101, no. 7 (2016), pp. 958–975.
68. Jackei Wong, "Data Analytics versus Artificial Intelligence," February 6, 2017, www.linkedin.com/pulse/data-analytics-vs-artificial-intelligence-jackei-wong/, accessed February 24, 2018.
69. Based on Joseph Walker, "Meet the New Boss: Big Data," *The Wall Street Journal*, September 20, 2012, p. B1. Also see Josh Bersin, "Big Data in Human Resources: Talent Analytics (People Analytics) Comes of Age," www.forbes.com/sites/joshbersin/2013/02/17/bigdata-in-human-resources-talent-analytics-comes-of-age, accessed March 29, 2015.
70. Josh Bersin, "Big Data in Human Resources: Talent Analytics (People Analytics) Comes of Age" February 17, 2013, www.Forbes.com/sites/Joshbersin/2013/02/17/, accessed February 24, 2018.
71. Bill Roberts, "Hire Intelligence," *HR Magazine*, May 2011, p. 64.
72. Scott Steinberg, "What Is the Difference between Machine Learning and AI?" https://mobilebusinessinsights.com, accessed February 24, 2018.
73. Andrew Ng, "What Artificial Intelligence Can and Can't Do Right Now," November 9, 2016, https://hbr.org/2016/11/, accessed February 24, 2018.
74. The machine learning software "learns" what it is about employees that make some high performers and can then translate that knowledge into screening job candidates. "How to Leverage AI for Talent Management," *HR*, April 28, 2017, www.HRtechnologist.com/articles, accessed February 24, 2018.
75. Jennifer Alsever, "Where Does the Algorithm See You in 10 Years?" *Fortune*, June 1, 2017, pp. 74–79.
76. http://www.skillsurvey.com/reference-checking-scientific-approach/, accessed February 24, 2018.
77. https://www.joinkoru.com/, accessed February 24, 2018.
78. Ji-A Min, "How Artificial Intelligence Is Changing Talent Acquisition," www.tlnt.com, accessed February 24, 2018.
79. Bernard Marr, "What Is the Difference between Artificial Intelligence and Machine Learning?" December 6, 2016, www.forbes.com/sites/bernardmarr/2016/12/06/what-is-the-difference-between-artificial-intelligence-and-machine-learning/#483645472742, accessed July 10, 2018.
80. Jeff Weekley and Casey Jones, "Video-Based Situational Testing," *Personnel Psychology* 50 (1997), p. 25.
81. Elaine Pulakos, *Selection Assessment Methods*, SHRM Foundation, 2005, p. 14.
82. However, studies suggest that blacks may be somewhat less likely to do well on work sample tests than are whites. See, for example, Philip Roth, Philip Bobko, and Lynn McFarland, "A Meta-Analysis of Work Sample Test Validity: Updating and Integrating Some Classic Literature," *Personnel Psychology* 58, no. 4 (Winter 2005), pp. 1009–1037; and Philip Roth et al., "Work Sample Tests in Personnel Selection: A Meta-Analysis of Black–White Differences in Overall and Exercise Scores," *Personnel Psychology* 60, no. 1 (2008), pp. 637–662.
83. Siegel and Lane, *Personnel and Organizational Psychology*, pp. 182–183.
84. Quoted from Deborah Whetzel and Michael McDaniel, "Situational Judgment Tests: An Overview of Current Research," *Human Resource Management Review* 19 (2009), pp. 188–202.
85. Steve Bates, "Freelance Nation," *HR Magazine*, July/August 2015, p. 47.
86. "Help Wanted—and Found," *Fortune*, October 2, 2006, p. 40. See also Brian Hoffman et al., "Exercises and Dimensions Are the Currency of Assessment Centers," *Personnel Psychology* 60, no. 4 (2011), pp. 351–395.
87. Annette Spychalski, Miguel Quinones, Barbara Gaugler, and Katja Pohley, "A Survey of Assessment Center Practices in Organizations in the United States," *Personnel Psychology* 50, no. 1 (Spring 1997), pp. 71–90. See also Winfred Arthur Jr. et al., "A Meta Analysis of the Criterion Related Validity of Assessment Center Data Dimensions," *Personnel Psychology* 56 (2003), pp. 124–154; and Brian Hoffman et al., "Exercises and Dimensions Are the Currency of Assessment Centers," *Personnel Psychology* 60, no. 4 (2011), pp. 351–395.
88. See, for example, John Meriac et al., "Further Evidence for the Validity of Assessment Center Dimensions: A Meta-Analysis of the Incremental Criterion-Related Validity of Dimension Ratings," *Journal of Applied Psychology* 93, no. 5 (2008), pp. 1042–1052.
89. Earlier conclusions may have been clouded by the fact that participants in assessment centers had already been previously screened for cognitive ability. Paul Sackett, Lauren Shawach, and Heidi Keiser, "Assessment Centers versus Cognitive Ability Test: Challenging the Conventional Wisdom on Criterion Related Validity," *Journal of Applied Psychology* 102, no. 10 (2017), pp. 1435–1447.
90. Weekley and Jones, "Video-Based Situational Testing," p. 26. Some employers, such as Knack, use video games to determine candidates' creativity and ability to multitask. Catherine Rampell, "Your Next Job Application Could Involve a Video Game," *The New York Times*, January 25, 2014.
91. Rampell, "Your Next Job Application Could Involve a Video Game."
92. Robert Grossman, "Made from Scratch," *HR Magazine*, April 2002, pp. 44–53.
93. Coleman Peterson, "Employee Retention, the Secrets behind Wal-Mart's Successful Hiring Policies," *Human Resource Management* 44, no. 1 (Spring 2005), pp. 85–88. See also Murray Barrick and Ryan Zimmerman, "Reducing Voluntary, Avoidable Turnover through Selection," *Journal of Applied Psychology* 90, no. 1 (2005), pp. 159–166.
94. James Breaugh, "Employee Recruitment: Current Knowledge and Important Areas for Future Research," *Human Resource Management Review* 18 (2008), pp. 106–107; J Kevin Eschleman and W. Chris Wright, "(Mis)Steps for Attracting High Resilience Workers," *Industrial and Organizational Psychology* 9, no. 2 (June 2016), pp. 429–435.
95. Geri Coleman, "HR in the Age of Disruption," *HR Magazine* 61, no. 7 (September 2016), pp. 68–73.
96. Op. cit.
97. Phillips and Gully, *Strategic Staffing*, p. 223.
98. Brian J. Hoffman, John W. Michel, and Kevin J. Williams, "On the Predictive Efficiency of Past Performance and Physical Ability: The Case of the National Football League," *Human Performance* 24, no. 2 (2011), pp. 158–172.
99. Lara Walsh, "To Tell the Truth: Catching Tall Tales on Résumés," *Workforce*, December 2014, p. 10.
100. "Resume Fakery Is Rampant, Global; Employer Caution Needed, *Bloomberg BNA Bulletin to Management*, November 4, 2014, p. 351.
101. "Internet, E-Mail Monitoring Common at Most Workplaces," *BNA Bulletin to Management*, February 1, 2001, p. 34. See also "Are Your Background Checks Balanced? Experts Identify Concerns over Verifications," *BNA Bulletin to Management*, May 13, 2004, p. 153; Julia Levashina et al., "Don't Select until You Check: Expected Background Checking Practices," *Employee Responsibilities and Rights Journal* 29, no. 3 (September 2017), pp. 127–148; "Background Checking—The Use of Credit Background Checks in Hiring Decisions," July 19, 2012, www.shrm.org/hr-today/trends-and-forecasting/research-and-surveys/pages/creditbackgroundchecks.aspx, accessed July 10, 2018.
102. Merry Mayer, "Background Checks in Focus," *HR Magazine*, January 2002, pp. 59–62; and Carroll Lachnit, "Protecting People and Profits with Background Checks," *Workforce*, February 2002, p. 52; SHRM, "Background Checks: Background Check Policy and Procedure," September 22, 2016, https://www.shrm.org/ResourcesAndTools/tools-and-samples/policies/Pages/backgroundcheck.aspx, accessed February 26, 2018.

103. Matthew Heller, "Special Report: Background Checking," *Workforce Management*, March 3, 2008, pp. 35–54.
104. Bill Roberts, "Close-up on Screening," *HR Magazine*, February 2011, pp. 23–29.
105. Roy Maurer, "Making Every Check Count," *HR Magazine*, October 2016, p. 69.
106. Seymour Adler, "Verifying a Job Candidate's Background: The State of Practice in a Vital Human Resources Activity," *Review of Business* 15, no. 2 (Winter 1993), p. 6; Michael G. Aamodt, "Conducting Background Checks for Employee Selection," http://www.siop.org/SIOP-SHRM/SHRM-SIOP_Background_Checks.pdf, accessed February 26, 2018.
107. Heller, "Special Report: Background Checking," p. 35.
108. Dori Meinert, "Seeing behind the Mask," *HR Magazine* 56, no. 2 (February 2011), www.shrm.org/Publications/ hrmagazine/Editorial Content/2011/0211/Pages/0211meinert.aspx, accessed August 20, 2011.
109. Ibid., p. 55.
110. For example, one U.S. Court of Appeals found that bad references might be grounds for a suit when they are retaliations for the employee having previously filed an EEOC claim. "Negative Reference Leads to Charge of Retaliation," *BNA Bulletin to Management*, October 21, 2004, p. 344.
111. Martin Berman-Gorvine, "Employee Background Checks Have Companies Caught in the Middle."
112. *Kehr v. Consolidated Freightways of Delaware*, Docket No. 86–2126, July 15, 1987, U.S. Seventh Circuit Court of Appeals. Discussed in *Commerce Clearing House, Ideas and Trends*, October 16, 1987, p. 165.
113. For example, Todd Humber, "Open Season on References . . . Finally," *Canadian HR Reporter* 30, no. 10 (May 29, 2017), p. 18.
114. Donna Malvey et al., "The Fear Factor in Healthcare: Employee Information Sharing," *Journal of Healthcare Management* 58, no. 3 (May/Jun 2013), pp. 225–237.
115. James Bell, James Castagnera, and Jane Patterson Young, "Employment References: Do You Know the Law?" *Personnel Journal* 63, no. 2 (February 1984), pp. 32–36. In order to demonstrate defamation, several elements must be present: (a) the defamatory statement must have been communicated to another party; (b) the statement must be a false statement of fact; (c) injury to reputation must have occurred; and (d) the employer must not be protected under qualified or absolute privilege. For a discussion, see Ryan and Lasek, "Negligent Hiring and Defamation," p. 307. See also James Burns Jr., "Employment References: Is There a Better Way?" *Employee Relations Law Journal* 23, no. 2 (Fall 1997), pp. 157–168; Humber, "Open Season on References."
116. For additional information, see Lawrence E. Dube Jr., "Employment References and the Law," *Personnel Journal* 65, no. 2 (February 1986), pp. 87–91. See also Mickey Veich, "Uncover the Resume Ruse," *Security Management*, October 1994, pp. 75–76; and "Avoiding Defamation in the Workplace, Giving References and Disciplining Employees While Avoiding Liability," http://corporate.findlaw.com/litigation-disputes/avoiding-defamation-in-the-workplace-giving-references-and.html, accessed February 26, 2018.
117. "Undercover Callers Tip Off Job Seekers to Former Employers' Negative References," *BNA Bulletin to Management*, May 27, 1999, p. 161, https://www.google.com/search?client=firefox-b-1&source=hp&ei=526UWu3KJqaC5wKbx5bgAg&q=reference+checking+service&oq=reference+checking+&gs_l=psy-ab.1.0.0l10.2284.9425.0.13218.19.19.0.0.0.0.275.2318.7j6j4.17.0....0...1.1.64.psy-ab..2.17.2306...0i131k1.0.b9ngHHAu_aM, accessed February 26, 2018.
118. Eileen Zimmerman, "A Subtle Reference Trap for Unwary Employers," *Workforce*, April 2003, p. 22.
119. Michelle Goodman, "Reference Checks Go Tech," *Workforce Management*, May 2012, pp. 26–28; www.skillsurvey.com/reference-checking-solution/, accessed September 2, 2018.
120. Alan Finder, "When a Risqué Online Persona Undermines a Chance for a Job," *The New York Times*, June 11, 2006, p. 1.
121. Natasha Singer, "Funny, They Don't Look Like My References," *The New York Times*, November 9, 2014, p. 4.
122. "Practitioners Discuss Various Pitfalls of Using Social Media to Vet Job Applicants," *Bloomberg BNA Bulletin to Management*, November 1, 2011, pp. 345–346.
123. Rita Zeidner, "How Deep Can You Probe?" *HR Magazine*, October 1, 2007, pp. 57–62.
124. "Web Searches on Applicants Are Potentially Perilous for Employers," *Bloomberg BNA Bulletin to Management*, October 14, 2008, p. 335.
125. "Maryland Is First State to Restrict Employer Demands for Employee, Applicant Passwords," *Bloomberg BNA Bulletin to Management*, May 8, 2012, p. 145.
126. "Practitioners Discuss Various Pitfalls of Using Social Media to Vet Job Applicants," www.bna.com/practitioners-discuss-various-n12884904116/, accessed July 4, 2014.
127. "Background checking providers," *Workforce*, July/August 2017, p. 47.
128. Stephanie Clifford and Jessica Silver-Greenberg, "Retailers Track Employee Thefts in Vast Databases," *The New York Times*, April 4, 2013, pp. A1, A16.
129. Jasmine Ye Han, "Blockchain Verified Credentials Could Change the Game of Hiring," *Bloomberg BNA Bulletin to Management*, November 7, 2017.
130. Jeffrey M. Hahn,"Pre-Employment Information Services: Employers Beware?" *Employee Relations Law Journal* 17, no. 1 (Summer 1991), pp. 45–69. See also "Pre-Employment Background Screenings Have Evolved, but So Have Liability Risks," *BNA Bulletin to Management*, November 1, 2005, p. 345.
131. "Employer Concerns about Liability Loom as Push for Ban the Box Policies Spread," *Bloomberg BNA Bulletin to Management*, August 19, 2014, pp. 257–258.
132. Under California law, applicants or employees must have the option of requesting a copy of the report regardless of action.
133. Teresa Butler Stivarius, "Background Checks: Steps to Basic Compliance in a Multistate Environment," *Society for Human Resource Management Legal Report*, March–April 2003, pp. 1–8.
134. See, for example, Dori Meinert, "Search and Verify," *HR Magazine*, December 2012, pp. 37–41.
135. "Background Check Firm Pays $2.6 Million Penalty," *Workforce Management*, October 2012, p. 12.
136. See Paul Taylor et al., "Dimensionality and the Validity of a Structured Telephone Reference Check Procedure," *Personnel Psychology* 57 (2004), pp. 745–772, for a discussion of checking other work habits and traits.
137. "Getting Applicant Information Difficult but Still Necessary," *BNA Bulletin to Management*, February 5, 1999, p. 63. See also Robert Howie and Laurence Shapiro, "Pre-Employment Criminal Background Checks: Why Employers Should Look Before They Leap," *Employee Relations Law Journal*, Summer 2002, pp. 63–77; Joyce Cutler, "Cities, States Lead Sway to Barring Salary History Queries," *Bloomberg BNA Bulletin to Management*, August 4, 2017; Martin Berman-Gorvine, "Tech Giants Stop Asking for Salary History, Everywhere in the US," *Bloomberg BNA Bulletin to Management*, January 2, 2018.
138. Michael Wier, "Dishonest References Test Recruitment," *Canadian HR Reporter* 31, no. 1 (January 2018), p. 7.
139. Polygraphs are still widely used in law enforcement and reportedly are quite useful. See, for example, Laurie Cohen, "The Polygraph Paradox," *The Wall Street Journal*, March 22, 2008, p. A1.
140. Also prohibited are other mechanical or electrical devices that attempt to measure honesty or dishonesty, including voice stress analyzers.
141. After a tragedy in Manhattan several years ago, more parents began turning to private investigators and industrial psychologists to conduct checks, including polygraph tests, on prospective nannies. Gabrielle Birkner, "Nanny Interviews Get More Aggressive," *The Wall Street Journal*, December 15–16, 2012, pp. A19, A21.
142. See, for example, "Assessment & Selection: Other Assessment Methods," https://www.opm.gov/policy-data-oversight/assessment-and-selection/other-assessment-methods/integrityhonesty-tests/, accessed February 26, 2018.
143. Norma Fritz, "In Focus: Honest Answers—Post Polygraph," *Personnel*, April 1989, p. 8. See also Richard White Jr., "Ask Me No Questions, Tell Me No Lies: Examining the Uses and Misuses of the Polygraph," *Public Personnel Management* 30, no. 4 (Winter 2001), pp. 483–493; http://www.assessio.com/, accessed February 26, 2018.
144. A meta-analysis concluded that "relations between integrity tests and measures of job performance tend to be rather weak." Chad H. Van Iddeking et al., "The Criterion Related Validity of Integrity Tests: An Updated Meta-Analysis," *Journal of Applied Psychology* 97, no. 3 (2012), pp. 499–530, a point disputed by a panel of test publishers. William G. Harris et al., "Test Publishers' Perspective on 'An Updated Meta-Analysis': Comment on Van Iddeking, Ross, Raymark, and Odle-Dusseau (2012)," *Journal of Applied Psychology* 97, no. 3 (2012), pp. 531–536.
145. John Bernardin and Donna Cooke, "Validity of an Honesty Test in Predicting Theft Among Convenience Store Employees," *Academy of Management Journal* 36, no. 5 (1993), pp. 1097–1108. There are many

such examples. See, for example, Bill Roberts, "Your Cheating Heart," *HR Magazine*, June 2011, pp. 55–57.

146. Murat Topaloglu and Sehar Ekmekci, "Gender Detection and Identifying One's Handwriting with Handwriting Analysis," *Expert Systems with Applications* 79 (August 15, 2017), p. 236; Marco Giannini et al., "Is Graphology Useful in Assessing Major Depression?" *National Library of Medicine. Psychological Reports* (January 1, 2018): 33294118759667.
147. Topaloglu and Ekmekci, "Gender Detection and Identifying One's Handwriting."
148. Afnan Garoot et al., "A Comprehensive Survey on Handwriting and Computerized Graphology," The Institute of Electrical and Electronics Engineers, Inc. (IEEE) Conference Proceedings, Vol. 01, (2017).
149. Bill Leonard, "Reading Employees," *HR Magazine*, April 1999, pp. 67–73. On the other hand some recent studies suggest graphology may be of use: Anupam Varshney and ShaliniPuri, "A Survey on Human Personality Identification on the Basis of Handwriting Using ANN," The Institute of Electrical and Electronics Engineers, Inc. (IEEE) Conference Proceedings; Piscataway (2017).
150. This is based on Kyle Stock, "Wary Investors Turn to Lie Pros," *The Wall Street Journal*, December 29, 2010, p. C3.
151. These are based on "Divining Integrity through Interviews," *BNA Bulletin to Management*, June 4, 1987, p. 184; and *Commerce Clearing House*, Ideas and Trends, December 29, 1998, pp. 222–223. See also Bridget A. Styers and Kenneth S. Shultz, "Perceived Reasonableness of Employment Testing Accommodations for Persons with Disabilities," *Public Personnel Management* 38, no. 3 (Fall 2009), pp. 71–91.
152. Ibid.
153. www.clearfit.com/resource-center/hiring-process/how-to-spot-someone-lying-in-an-interview/, accessed February 19, 2014.
154. www.forbes.com/sites/carolkinseygoman/2013/05/20/7-tips-for-spotting-liars-at-work/, accessed February 19, 2014.
155. Mick Haus, "Pre-Employment Physicals and the ADA," *Safety and Health*, February 1992, pp. 64–65. See also Styers and Shultz, "Perceived Reasonableness of Employment Testing Accommodations."
156. Lisa Nagele-Piazza, "Failed Workplace Drug Tests Reach 12-Year High," May 24, 2017, https://www.shrm.org/resourcesandtools/legal-and-compliance/employment-law/pages/positive-drug-test-rates-climb.aspx, accessed February 26, 2018.
157. For example, www.questdiagnostics.com/home/companies/employer/drug-screening/testing-reasons/pre-employment.html, accessed August 22, 2014.
158. Rita Zeidner, "Putting Drug Screening to the Test," *HR Magazine*, November 2010, p. 26.
159. Jackie Calmes, "One Step Short of Hired," *The New York Times*, May 18, 2016, pp. B1, B3; Lauren Weber, "Tests Show More American Workers Using Drugs," *The Wall Street Journal*, May 17, 2017.
160. Steve Bates, "Rethinking Zero Tolerance on Drugs in the Workplace: Some Employers Relax Pre-employment Drug Standards in Order to Fill Jobs," December 5, 2017, https://www.shrm.org/resourcesandtools/hr-topics/talent-acquisition/pages/rethinking-zero-tolerance-drugs-workplace.aspx, accessed February 26, 2018.
161. https://www.google.com/search?client=firefox-b-1&ei=7pGUWqu4GoPJ5gKbgIXADg&q=products+for+beating+drug+tests&oq=products+for+beating+drug+tests&gs_l=psy-ab.12..0i22i30k1.2256.10183.0.13610.31.31.0.0.0.0.293.3793.3j17j6.26.0..2..0...1.1.64.psy-ab..5.26.3775...0j0i131k1j0i67k1j0i22i10i30k1j0i13k1j0i13i30k1j0i13i5i30k1j33i22i29i30k1j0i8i13i30k1.0.Ed8lZTAYYek, accessed February 26, 2018.
162. Chris Berka and Courtney Poignand, "Hair Follicle Testing—An Alternative to Urinalysis for Drug Abuse Screening," *Employee Relations Today*, Winter 1991–1992, pp. 405–409; for an example, see www.americanscreeningcorp.com/default.aspx, accessed October 8, 2011.
163. R. J. McCunney, "Drug Testing: Technical Complications of a Complex Social Issue," *American Journal of Industrial Medicine* 15, no. 5 (1989), pp. 589–600; discussed in Scott Macdonald, Samantha Wells, and Richard Fry "The Limitations of Drug Screening in the Workplace," *International Labour Review* 132, no. 1 (1993), p. 102; and, "United States: Should a Worker Be Fired for Using Medical Marijuana at Home?" *Asia News Monitor*, October 15, 2015.
164. MacDonald et al., "The Limitations of Drug Screening," p. 103.
165. Ann M. O'Neill, "Legal Issues Presented by Hair Follicle Testing," *Employee Relations Today*, Winter 1991–1992, pp. 411–415; R. M. White, "Drugs in Hair. Part I. Metabolisms of Major Drug Classes," *Forensic Science Review* 29, no. 1 (Jan 2017), pp. 23–55.
166. Daniel Johns, "The National Labor Relations Board's Misapplication of Weingarten Rights to Employer Substance Abuse Testing Programs," *Labor Law Journal* 67, no. 1 (Spring 2016), pp. 285–297.
167. Lee Dryden, "OSHA Will Require Employers to Report Injuries, Illnesses," *Michigan Lawyers Weekly*, August 2016.
168. Lisa Nagele-Piazza, "How Can Multistate Employers Develop Solid Drug-Testing Policies?" July 10, 2017, https://www.shrm.org/resourcesandtools/legal-and-compliance/state-and-local-updates/pages/multistate-employer-drug-testing-policies.aspx, accessed February 26, 2018.
169. "The Americans with Disabilities Act and 'Current' Illegal Drug Use," http://corporate.findlaw.com/litigation-disputes/the-americans-with-disabilities-act-and-current-illegal-drug.html, accessed February 26, 2018.
170. Richard Lisko, "A Manager's Guide to Drug Testing," *Security Management* 38, no. 8 (August 1994), p. 92. See also "Office of Drug & Alcohol Policy & Compliance," https://www.transportation.gov/odapc, accessed February 26, 2018; "Overview of Drug and Alcohol Rules," https://www.fmcsa.dot.gov/regulations/drug-alcohol-testing/overview-drug-and-alcohol-rules, accessed February 26, 2018.
171. Lisa Nagele-Piazza, "Workplace Drug-Testing Rules Vary from State to State," August 21, 2017, https://www.shrm.org/resourcesandtools/legal-and-compliance/state-and-local-updates/pages/an-employee-failed-a-drug-test-.aspx, accessed February 26, 2018.
172. *Exxon Corp. v. Esso Workers Union, Inc.*, CA1#96–2241, 7/8/97; discussed in *BNA Bulletin to Management*, August 7, 1997, p. 249.
173. For the form, see www.uscis.gov/files/form/i-9.pdf, accessed October 4, 2011. California recently advised local employers that the federal government's ICE officers could not enter facilities without a warrant. Laura Mahoney, "California to Employers: ICE Needs a Warrant to Enter," *Bloomberg BNA Bulletin to Management*, February 20, 2018.
174. "More Than 500,000 Employers Are Now Enrolled in E-Verify Program," *Bloomberg BNA Bulletin to Management*, January 28, 2014, p. 27.
175. "President Bush Signs Executive Order: Federal Contractors Must Use E-Verify," *Bloomberg BNA Bulletin to Management*, June 17, 2008, p. 193.
176. www.dhs.gov/files/programs/gc_1185221678150.shtm, accessed February 21, 2010. Many small business owners in particular find that the new E-Verify system makes it more difficult to fill open positions. Angus Loten, Sarah Needleman, and Adam Janofsky, "Small Business Has a Beef with E-Verify," *The Wall Street Journal*, July 25, 2013, p. B6.
177. Davis Zielinski, "Automating I-9 Verification," *HR Magazine*, May 2011, pp. 57–60. Employees themselves can use E-Verify to confirm their U.S. work authorization status. "New Tools Will Aid Employers during Verification Process," *Bloomberg BNA Bulletin to Management*, March 15, 2011, and Matthew Orso and Susan Rodriguez, "The Compliance Risks of I-9 Software," *HR Magazine*, September 2016, pp. 83–84.
178. "As E-Verify, No Match Rules, I-9 Evolve, Employers Need to Stay on Top of Issues," *Bloomberg BNA Bulletin Management*, April 15, 2008, p. 121. For the latest I-9 form see www.uscis.gov/files/form/i-9.pdf, accessed September 7, 2013. In 2017, the Republican administration said it was moving toward requiring use of E-verify by all employers. Laura Francis, "Mandatory E-Verify, More Enforcement Spending in Trump Budget," *Bloomberg BNA Bulletin to Management*, March 21, 2017.
179. Note that the acceptable documents on page 3 of the previous I-9 form did not reflect the most current list of acceptable documents for confirming identity and eligibility. For the latest I-9 form see www.uscis.gov/files/form/i-9.pdf, accessed September 7, 2013.
180. "Identity Theft Remains Top Challenge for E-Verify," *Bloomberg BNA Bulletin to Management*, April 19, 2011, p. 121.
181. Russell Gerbman, "License to Work," *HR Magazine*, June 2000, pp. 151–160; the I-9 form clearly states that the employer may not discriminate. See www.uscis.gov/i-9, accessed September 2, 2018.

BravoKiloVideo/Shutterstock

Interviewing Candidates

LEARNING OBJECTIVES

When you finish studying this chapter, you should be able to:

7-1 **Give** examples of the main types of selection interviews.

7-2 **Give** examples of the main errors that can undermine an interview's usefulness.

7-3 **Define** a structured situational interview and explain how to conduct effective selection interviews.

7-4 **Give** examples of how to use employee selection to improve employee engagement.

7-5 **List** the main points in developing and extending the actual job offer.

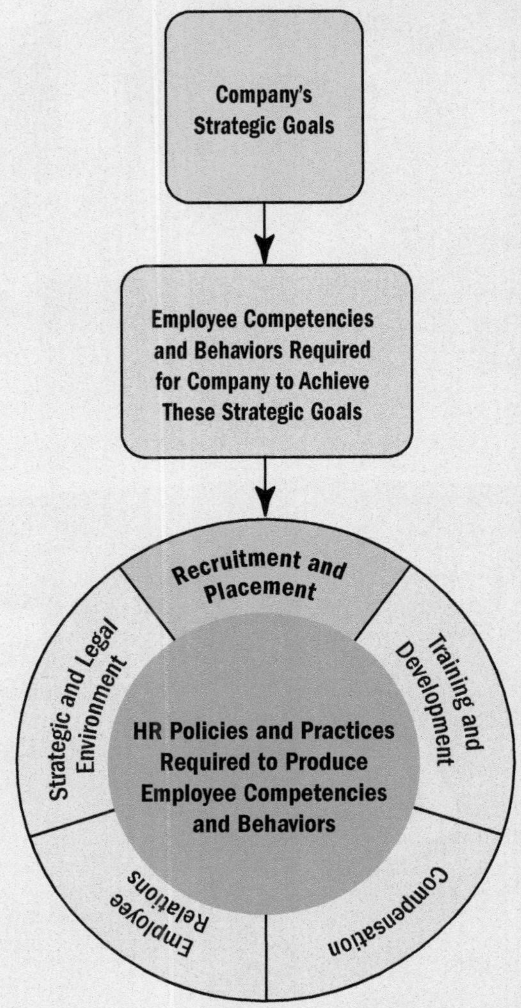

When it comes to hiring, Urban Outfitters knows just what it's looking for.[2] The lifestyle retailer, with over 200 stores in the United States, Canada, and Europe, built its strategy around fostering a culture of creativity and individuality within its stores. Its managers know that maintaining this unique store environment requires employees that match its core values of community, pride, creativity, and respect. The question is, how do you find and attract such applicants, while controlling hiring costs in the competitive retail industry?

WHERE ARE WE NOW . . .

Chapter 6 discussed important tools managers use to select employees. Now we'll turn to one of these tools—the employment interview. The main topics we'll cover include **Types of Interviews**, **Things That Undermine Interviewing's Usefulness**, **Designing and Conducting Effective Selection Interviews**, **Using a Total Selection Process to Improve Employee Engagement**, and **Making the Offer**. In Chapter 8, we'll turn to training the new employee.

If the interview is just one of several selection tools, why devote a whole chapter to it? Because interviews are the most widely used selection procedure, and most people aren't nearly as good at interviewing as they think they are.[1]

LEARNING OBJECTIVE 7-1

Give examples of the main types of selection interviews.

Basic Types of Interviews

Managers use several interviews at work, such as performance appraisal interviews and exit interviews. A *selection interview* (the focus of this chapter) is a selection procedure designed to predict future job performance based on applicants' oral responses to oral inquiries.[3] Many techniques in this chapter also apply to appraisal and exit interviews. However, we'll postpone discussions of those two interviews until later chapters.

There are several ways to conduct selection interviews. For example, we can classify selection interviews according to

1. How *structured* they are
2. Their "content"—the *types of questions* they contain
3. How the firm *administers* the interviews (for instance, one-on-one or via a committee)

Each has pros and cons. We'll look at each.

Structured versus Unstructured Interviews

unstructured (or nondirective) interview
An unstructured conversational-style interview in which the interviewer pursues points of interest as they come up in response to questions.

structured (or directive) interview
An interview following a set sequence of questions.

First, most interviews vary in the degree to which the interviewer structures the interview process.[4] In **unstructured (or nondirective) interviews**, the manager follows no set format. A few questions might be specified in advance, but they're usually not, and there is seldom a formal guide for scoring "right" or "wrong" answers. Typical questions here might include, for instance, "Tell me about yourself," "Why do you think you'd do a good job here?" and "What would you say are your main strengths and weaknesses?" Some describe this as little more than a general conversation.[5]

At the other extreme, in **structured (or directive) interviews**, the employer lists questions ahead of time, and may even weight possible alternative answers for appropriateness.[6] McMurray's Patterned Interview was one early example. The interviewer followed a printed form to ask a series of questions, such as "How was the person's present job obtained?" Comments printed beneath the questions (such as "Has he/she shown self-reliance in getting his/her jobs?") then guide the interviewer in evaluating the answers. Some experts still restrict the term "structured interview" to interviews like these, which are based on carefully selected job-related questions with predetermined answers.

But in practice, interview structure is a matter of degree. Sometimes the manager may just want to ensure he or she has a list of questions to ask so as to avoid skipping any questions. Here, he or she might choose questions from a list like that in Figure 7-3 (page 219). The structured interview guide in Figure 7A-1 (pages 231–233) illustrates a more structured approach. As another example, the Department of Homeland Security uses the structured guide in Figure 7-1 (pages 208–209) to help screen Coast Guard officer candidates. It contains a formal candidate rating procedure, and enables geographically dispersed interviewers to complete the form via the Web.[7]

Structured interviews are generally best.[8] In such interviews, all interviewers generally ask all applicants the same questions. Partly because of this, these interviews tend to be more consistent, reliable, and valid. Having a standardized list of questions can also help less talented interviewers conduct better interviews. Standardizing the interview also enhances job relatedness (the questions chosen tend to provide insights into how the person will actually do the job), reduces overall subjectivity and thus the potential for bias, and may "enhance the ability to withstand legal challenge."[9] However, blindly following a structured format may not provide enough opportunity to pursue points of interest. The interviewer should always be able to ask follow-up questions and pursue points of interest as they develop. We'll see how to create a structured interview later in this chapter.

Interview Content (What Types of Questions to Ask)

We can also classify interviews based on the "content" or the types of questions interviewers ask. Many interviewers ask relatively unfocused questions, such as "What do you want to be doing in 5 years?" Questions like these usually don't provide much insight into how the person will do on the job. That is why *situational, behavioral*, and *job-related* questions are best.

situational interview
A series of job-related questions that focus on how the candidate would behave in a given situation.

behavioral interview
A series of job-related questions that focus on how the candidate reacted to actual situations in the past.

In a **situational interview,** you ask the candidate what his or her behavior *would be* in a given situation.[10] For example, ask a supervisory candidate how he or she would act in response to a subordinate coming to work late 3 days in a row.

Whereas situational interviews ask applicants to describe how they *would* react to a hypothetical situation today or tomorrow, **behavioral interviews** ask applicants to describe *how they reacted* to actual situations in the past.[11] *Situational* questions start with phrases such as, "Suppose you were faced with the following situation. . . . What would you do?" *Behavioral* questions start with phrases like, "Can you think of a time when. . . . What did you do?"[12] In one variant, Vanguard uses an interviewing

FIGURE 7-1 Officer Programs Applicant Interview Form

Source: From Officer Programs Applicant Interview Form CG_5527, http://www.uscg.mil/forms/cg/CG_5527.pdf accessed August 29, 2015.

U.S. Department of Homeland Security CG-5527 (06-04)	**Officer Programs Applicant Interview Form**	1. Date:

2. Name of Applicant (Last, First, MI)

3. **Overall Impression:** Compare this applicant to others you have interviewed or known. (Note: Scores of 4 through 7 constitute a recommendation for selection.)

NOT RECOMMENDED			RECOMMENDED			
Unsatisfactory 1☐	Limited Potential 2☐	Fair Performer 3☐	Good Performer 4☐	Excellent Performer 5☐	Exceptional Performer 6☐	Distinguished Performer 7☐

Comments:

4. **Performance of Duties:** Measures an applicant's ability to manage and to get things done.

Unsatisfactory	Limited Potential	Fair Performer	Good Performer	Excellent Performer	Exceptional Performer	Distinguished Performer
1☐	2☐	3☐	4☐	5☐	6☐	7☐

Comments:

5. **Communication Skills:** Measures an applicant's ability to communicate in a positive, clear, and convincing manner.

Unsatisfactory	Limited Potential	Fair Performer	Good Performer	Excellent Performer	Exceptional Performer	Distinguished Performer
1☐	2☐	3☐	4☐	5☐	6☐	7☐

Comments:

6. **Names of Board Members**	7. **Rank**	8. **Command/Unit**	9. **Signature**	10. **Career Total of Interviews Conducted**

PREVIOUS EDITIONS ARE OBSOLETE *CONTINUED ON REVERSE*

Reset

FIGURE 7-1 *Continued*

Page 2 - CG-5527 (06-04)

11. **Leadership Skills:** Measures an applicant's ability to support, develop, direct, and influence others in performing work.

Unsatisfactory	Limited Potential	Fair Performer	Good Performer	Excellent Performer	Exceptional Performer	Distinguished Performer
1☐	2☐	3☐	4☐	5☐	6☐	7☐

Comments:

12. **Personal and Professional Qualities:** Measures qualities which illustrate the applicant's character.

Unsatisfactory	Limited Potential	Fair Performer	Good Performer	Excellent Performer	Exceptional Performer	Distinguished Performer
1☐	2☐	3☐	4☐	5☐	6☐	7☐

Comments:

Reset

technique it calls STAR. Vanguard managers ask interviewees about a particular situation (S) or task (T) they faced to uncover the actions (A) the candidates took, and the results (R) of their actions.[13]

Behavioral interviews are increasingly popular.[14] When Citizen's Banking Corporation in Flint, Michigan, found that 31 of the 50 people in its call center quit in one year, the center's head switched to behavioral interviews. Many who left did so because they didn't enjoy irate questions from clients. So she no longer tries to predict how candidates will act based on asking them if they want to work with angry clients. Instead, she asks behavioral questions like, "Tell me about a time you were speaking with an irate person, and how you turned the situation around." This makes it harder to fool the interviewer; only four people left in the following year.[15]

Bain & Company uses case interviews as part of its candidate selection process. By having candidates explain how they would address the case "client's" problems, the case interview combines elements of behavioral and situational questioning to provide a more realistic assessment of the candidate's consulting skills.

job-related interview
A series of job-related questions that focus on relevant past job-related behaviors.

stress interview
An interview in which the applicant is made uncomfortable by a series of often rude questions. This technique helps identify hypersensitive applicants and those with low or high stress tolerance.

OTHER TYPES OF QUESTIONS In a **job-related interview,** the interviewer asks applicants questions about job-relevant past experiences. The questions here don't revolve around hypothetical or actual situations or scenarios. Instead, the interviewer asks questions such as, "Which courses did you like best in business school?" The aim is to draw conclusions about, say, the candidate's ability to handle the job's financial aspects.

There are other, lesser-used types of questions. In a **stress interview,** the interviewer seeks to make the applicant uncomfortable with occasionally rude questions. The aim is supposedly to spot sensitive applicants and those with low (or high) stress tolerance. Thus, a candidate for a customer relations manager position who obligingly mentions having had four jobs in the past 2 years might be told that frequent job changes reflect irresponsible and immature behavior. If the applicant then responds with a reasonable explanation of why the job changes were necessary, the interviewer might pursue another topic. On the other hand, if the formerly tranquil applicant reacts explosively, the interviewer might deduce that the person has a low tolerance for stress.

The stress interview's invasive and ethically dubious nature demands that the interviewer be both skilled in its use and sure the job really requires handling stress. This is definitely not an approach for amateur interrogators or for those without the skills to keep the interview under control.

Puzzle questions are popular. Recruiters see how candidates think under pressure. For example, an interviewer at Microsoft asked a tech service applicant this: "Mike and Todd have $21 between them. Mike has $20 more than Todd does. How much money has Mike, and how much money has Todd?"[16] (The answer is two paragraphs below.)

HR in Action at the Hotel Paris As an experienced HR professional, Lisa knew that the company's new testing program would go only so far. To see how the Hotel Paris created a new interview process, see the case on page 226.

How Should We Conduct the Interview?

Employers also administer interviews in various ways: *one-on-one or by a panel of interviewers, sequentially or all at once, computerized or personally,* or *online.*

Most selection interviews are probably still *one-on-one* and *sequential.* In a one-on-one interview, two people meet alone, and one interviews the other by seeking oral responses to oral inquiries. Employers tend to schedule these interviews *sequentially.* In a *sequential (or serial) interview*, several persons interview the applicant, in sequence, one-on-one, and then make their hiring decision. In an **unstructured sequential interview,** each interviewer generally just asks questions as they come to mind. In a **structured sequential interview,** each interviewer rates the candidates on a standard evaluation form, using standardized questions. The hiring manager then reviews these ratings before deciding whom to hire.[17] (Answer: Mike had $20.50, Todd $0.50.)

unstructured sequential interview
An interview in which each interviewer forms an independent opinion after asking different questions.

structured sequential interview
An interview in which the applicant is interviewed sequentially by several persons; each rates the applicant on a standard form.

panel interview
An interview in which a group of interviewers questions the applicant.

mass interview
A panel interviews several candidates simultaneously.

A **panel interview,** also known as a board interview, is an interview conducted by a team of interviewers (usually two to three), who together question each candidate and then combine their ratings of each candidate's answers into a final panel score. This contrasts with the *one-on-one interview* (in which one interviewer meets one candidate) and a *serial interview* (where several interviewers assess a single candidate one-on-one, sequentially).[18]

The panel format enables interviewers to ask follow-up questions, much as reporters do in press conferences. This may elicit more meaningful responses than a series of one-on-one interviews. On the other hand, some candidates find panel interviews more stressful, so they may actually inhibit responses. (An even more stressful variant is the **mass interview.** Here a panel interviews several candidates simultaneously. The panel might pose a problem, and then watches to see which candidate takes the lead in formulating an answer.)

Whether panel interviews are more or less reliable and valid than sequential interviews depends on how the employer actually does the panel interview. For example, *structured* panel interviews in which members use scoring sheets with descriptive scoring examples for "good" and "bad" sample answers are more reliable and valid than those that don't. Training panel interviewers may boost interview reliability.[19]

For better or worse, some employers use "speed dating" interviewing. One sent e-mails to all applicants for an advertised position. Four hundred (of 800 applicants) showed up. Over several hours, applicants first mingled with employees, and then (in a so-called speed dating area) had one-on-one contacts with employees for a few minutes each. Based on this, the recruiting team chose 68 candidates for follow-up interviews.[20]

PHONE INTERVIEWS Employers also conduct interviews via phone. Somewhat counterintuitively, these can actually be more useful than face-to-face interviews for judging one's conscientiousness, intelligence, and interpersonal skills. Because they needn't worry about appearance or handshakes, each party can focus on answers. And perhaps candidates—somewhat surprised by an unplanned call from the recruiter—give more spontaneous answers.[21] In one study, interviewers tended to evaluate applicants more favorably in telephone versus face-to-face interviews, particularly where interviewees were less physically attractive. The applicants preferred the face-to-face interviews.[22]

COMPUTER-BASED JOB INTERVIEWS A *computerized selection interview* is one in which a job candidate's oral and/or keyed replies are obtained in response to computerized oral, visual, or written questions and/or situations. Most such interviews present a series of multiple-choice questions regarding background, experience, education, skills, knowledge, and work attitudes. Some confront candidates with realistic scenarios (such as irate customers) to which they must respond.[23]

ONLINE VIDEO INTERVIEWS With phone and tablet video functionalities like FaceTime™ and Skype™, Web-based "in-person" interview use is widespread; about 18% of candidates took such interviews in one study.[24] College career centers and outplacement firms use the InterviewStream 360 Video Practice Interview System, to have students or job seekers record interviews for their own development and for prospective employers.[25] InterviewStream, Inc. (www.InterviewStream.com) offers employer clients prerecorded and live video interview management systems for prescreening candidates and interviewing remote talent. Or, the client and candidate can use InterviewStream's live video conference platform for a live interview.[26] Employers including Microsoft use the virtual community Second Life to conduct job interviews. Job seekers create avatars to represent themselves.[27] And as explained in Chapter 6, HireVue's software analyzes its clients' past video employment interviews for signs like facial expressions and voice modulation to determine which predict applicants' suitability for jobs.

Hilton Worldwide recruits in 94 countries, so distances often make in-person interviews impractical. Now, online video interviews make it easy for Hilton to do initial screening interviews.[28] Another firm's CEO conducts initial screening interviews via text-only chats or instant messaging because, he says, it reduces potential distractions like gender, ethnicity, and body language.[29]

An online video interview requires little special preparation for employers, but Career FAQs (www.careerfaqs.com.au) lists things that *interviewees* should keep in mind. It's often the obvious things people overlook (for more on how to take interviews, see Appendix 2 to this chapter, page 234):[30]

- ***Look presentable.*** It might seem strange sitting at home in a suit, but it could make a difference.
- ***Clean up the room.*** Do not let the interviewer see clutter.
- ***Test first.*** As Career FAQs says, "Five minutes before the video interview is not a good time to realize that your Internet is down . . ."
- ***Do a dry run.*** Record yourself before the interview to see how you're "coming across."
- ***Relax.*** The golden rule with such interviews is to treat them like face-to-face meetings. Smile, look confident and enthusiastic, make eye contact, and don't shout, but do speak clearly.

IMPROVING PERFORMANCE: *THE STRATEGIC CONTEXT*

Asynchronous Interviews at Urban Outfitters

Asynchronous mobile device–based interviews let interviewees "do" the interview at their leisure from wherever they are, and the hiring managers to review the interviews at their leisure.[31]

For example, Urban Outfitters wants store employees who share its core values of Community, Pride, Creativity, and Respect.[32] The question is, how does it find and attract such applicants, while controlling hiring costs in the competitive retail industry? Because it receives so many applications, the company first used group interviews for selecting sales associates. Retail managers would interview six to eight candidates at once, in a group interview. Store managers didn't think this was a good fit for Urban Outfitter's culture, though.

Urban Outfitters switched to HireVue on-demand interviews in its 200 retail stores. The HireVue system enabled applicants to watch videos about Urban Outfitters and the job, and then to respond in writing and by video to Urban's interview questions and instructions, at their leisure, "on demand." The hiring managers then reviewed the recorded interviews, usually outside of peak business hours when the stores weren't as busy.

The new system reportedly has been a boon to Urban Outfitters. It reduced screening time by 80%, lets store managers process many more applicants, and is preferred by applicants, 90% of whom can do their interviews after hours. The HireVue system also supports Urban Outfitters' strategy. As it says:

> Moving to digital interviewing has transformed our hiring process into a true reflection of the Urban Outfitters culture. Our value in creativity and community and our nonconformist approach now begins with our candidate experience. No other initiative has impacted our hiring teams like digital recruiting has.[33]

MyLab Management Talk About It 1

If your professor has assigned this, go to the Assignments section of **www.pearson.com/mylab/management** to complete this discussion. You have to hire dozens of waitstaff every year for a new restaurant on Miami Beach. Explain how you would use a HireVue interview, including questions and tasks for candidates.

LEARNING OBJECTIVE 7-2

Give examples of the main errors that can undermine an interview's usefulness.

Avoiding Errors That Can Undermine an Interview's Usefulness

Interviews hold an ironic place in the hiring process: Everyone uses them, but they're generally not particularly valid. The key is to do them properly. If you do, then the interview is generally a good predictor of performance and is comparable with many other selection techniques.[34] Keep three things in mind—use structured interviews, know what to ask, and avoid the common interviewing errors.

First, *structure the interview.*[35] Structured interviews (particularly structured interviews using situational questions) are more valid than unstructured interviews for predicting job performance. They are more valid partly because they are more reliable—for example, the same interviewer administers the interview more consistently from candidate to candidate.[36] Situational structured interviews yield a higher mean validity than do job-related (or behavioral) interviews, which in turn yield a higher mean validity than do "psychological" interviews (which focus more on motives and interests).[37]

Second, interviews are better at revealing some things than others, so know what to focus on. In one study, interviewers were able to size up the interviewee's extroversion and agreeableness. What they could *not* assess accurately were important traits like conscientiousness and emotional stability.[38] Interview questions such as "Describe the work environment or culture in which you are most productive and happy" may help unearth cultural fit.[39] One implication seems to be, focus more on situational and job knowledge questions that help you assess how the candidate will actually respond to typical situations on that job.

Third, whether the interview is in person or online, effective employment interviewers understand and avoid the following common interview errors.[40]

First Impressions (Snap Judgments)

Interviewers tend to jump to conclusions—make snap judgments—about candidates during the first few minutes of the interview (or even before it starts, based on test scores or résumés). One researcher estimates that in 85% of the cases, interviewers had made up their minds before the interview even began, based on first impressions gleaned from candidates' applications and personal appearance.[41] In one study, giving interviewers the candidates' test scores biased the candidates' ultimate assessments. In another study, interviewers judged candidates who they were told once suffered from depression more negatively.[42] Even structured interviews are usually preceded by a brief discussion, and the impressions one makes here can contaminate even a structured interview's results.[43]

First impressions are especially damaging when the prior information is negative. In one study, interviewers who previously received unfavorable reference letters about applicants gave those applicants less credit for past successes and held them more responsible for past failures after the interview. And the interviewers' final decisions (to accept or reject those applicants) *always* reflected what they expected of the applicants based on the references, quite aside from the applicants' actual interview performance.[44]

Add to this two more interviewing facts. First, interviewers are more influenced by unfavorable than favorable information about the candidate. Second, their impressions are much more likely to change from favorable to unfavorable than from unfavorable to favorable. Indeed, many interviewers mostly search for negative information, often without realizing it.

The bottom line is that most interviews are loaded against applicants. One who starts well could easily end up with a low rating because unfavorable information predominates. And for the interviewee who starts out poorly, it's almost impossible to overcome that first bad impression.[45] One psychologist interviewed CEOs of 80 top companies. She concluded that you "don't even get to open your mouth."[46] Instead, the interviewer will size up your posture, handshake, smile, and "captivating aura." It's difficult to overcome that first impression.

Not Clarifying What the Job Requires

Interviewers who don't have an accurate picture of what the job entails and the sort of candidate that's best for it usually make their decisions based on incorrect stereotypes of what a good applicant is. They then erroneously match interviewees with their incorrect stereotypes. You should clarify what sorts of traits you're looking for, and why, before starting the interview.

One classic study involved 30 professional interviewers.[47] Half got just this brief job description: "the eight applicants here represented by their application blanks are applying for the position of secretary." The other interviewers got much more explicit job information, including bilingual ability, for instance.

More job knowledge translated into better interviews. The 15 interviewers with more job information generally all agreed about each candidate's potential; those without it did not. The latter also didn't discriminate as well among applicants—they tended to give them all high ratings. (What screeners actually look for is another matter. A researcher spoke with 120 hiring decision makers. She found that most of them were actually looking for "personal chemistry," in terms of having things like backgrounds and hobbies that matched their own.)[48]

Candidate-Order (Contrast) Error and Pressure to Hire

candidate-order (or contrast) error
An error of judgment on the part of the interviewer due to interviewing one or more very good or very bad candidates just before the interview in question.

Candidate-order (or contrast) error means that the order in which you see applicants affects how you rate them. In one study, managers had to evaluate a sample candidate who was "just average" after first evaluating several "unfavorable" candidates. They scored the average candidate more favorably than they might otherwise because, in contrast to the unfavorable candidates, the average one looked better than he actually was. This contrast effect can be huge: In some early studies, evaluators based only a small part of the applicant's rating on his or her actual potential.[49]

Pressure to hire accentuates this problem. Researchers told one group of managers to assume they were behind in their recruiting quota. They told a second group they were ahead. Those "behind" rated the same recruits more highly.[50]

Nonverbal Behavior and Impression Management

The applicant's nonverbal behavior (smiling, avoiding your gaze, and so on) can affect his or her rating. In one study, 52 human resource specialists watched videotaped job interviews in which *the applicants' verbal content was identical*, but their nonverbal behavior differed markedly. Researchers told applicants in one group to exhibit minimal eye contact, a low energy level, and low voice modulation. Those in a second group demonstrated the opposite behavior. Twenty-three of the 26 personnel specialists who saw the high-eye-contact, high-energy candidate would have invited him or her for a second interview. None who saw the low-eye-contact, low-energy candidate would have recommended a second interview.[51] So, it pays interviewees to "look alive."

Nonverbal behaviors are probably so important because interviewers infer your personality from how you behave in the interview. In one study, 99 graduating college seniors completed questionnaires that included measures of personality, among other things. The students then reported their success in generating follow-up interviews and job offers. The interviewee's personality, particularly his or her level of extroversion, had a pronounced influence on whether he or she received follow-up interviews and job offers.[52] In turn, extroverted applicants seem particularly prone to self-promotion, and self-promotion is strongly related to the interviewer's perceptions of candidate–job fit.[53] Even structuring the interview doesn't cancel out such effects;[54] as one study concludes, "No matter how much an interview is structured, nonverbal cues cause interviewers to make attributions about candidates."[55]

IMPRESSION MANAGEMENT Clever candidates capitalize on that fact. One study found that some used ingratiation to persuade interviewers to like them. For instance, the candidates praised the interviewers or appeared to agree with their opinions, thus signaling they shared similar beliefs. Sensing that a perceived similarity in attitudes may influence how the interviewer rates them, some interviewees try to emphasize (or fabricate) such similarities.[56] Others make self-promoting comments about their accomplishments.[57] Self-promotion means promoting one's own skills and abilities to create the impression of competence.[58] Psychologists call using techniques like ingratiation and self-promotion "impression management." Most interviewers aren't likely to know they're being misled.[59] Self-promotion can be an effective tactic, but faking or lying generally backfires.[60]

Effect of Personal Characteristics: Attractiveness, Gender, Race

Unfortunately, physical attributes also distort assessments.[61] For example, people usually ascribe more favorable traits and more successful life outcomes to attractive people.[62] Similarly, race can play a role, depending on how you conduct the interview. In one study, the white members of a racially balanced interview panel rated white candidates higher, while the black interviewers rated black candidates higher. But in all cases, *structured* interviews produced less of a difference between minority and white interviewees than did unstructured ones.[63] One study concludes, ". . . structured interviews can minimize or eliminate potential bias with respect to demographic similarity between applicants and interviewers."[64]

The use of employment discrimination "testers" makes nondiscriminatory interviewing even more important. The EEOC says testers are "individuals who apply for employment which they do not intend to accept, for the sole purpose of uncovering unlawful discriminatory hiring practices."[65] Although not really seeking employment, testers have legal standing with the courts and EEOC.[66]

One civil rights group sent four university students—two white, two black—to an employment agency, supposedly in pursuit of a job. The civil rights group gave the four "testers" backgrounds and training to make their qualifications appear almost identical. The white tester/applicants got interviews and job offers. The black tester/applicants got neither interviews nor offers.[67] The HR Practices feature (page 215) shows why care is required abroad too.

Diversity Counts: Applicant Disability and the Employment Interview

In general, candidates evidencing various attributes and disabilities (such as child-care demands, HIV-positive status, or being wheelchair-bound) have less chance of obtaining a positive decision, even when they perform well in a structured interview.[68] In one study, the researchers manipulated the candidates' appearance, for instance "by placing scar-like marks on the cheeks of some of the applicants for some interviews, but not for others." Results revealed that managers who interviewed a facially stigmatized applicant (versus a nonstigmatized applicant) "rated the applicant lower [and] recalled less information about the interview" (in part, apparently, because staring at the "scars" distracted the interviewers).[69] One study found interviewers to be more lenient toward those with disabilities, however.[70]

Another study surveyed 40 disabled people from various occupations. The disabled people felt that interviewers tend to avoid directly addressing the disability, and therefore make their decisions without all the facts.[71]

What the disabled people prefer is a discussion that lets the employer address his or her concerns and reach a knowledgeable conclusion. Among the questions they said they would like interviewers to ask were these: Is there any kind of setting or special equipment that will facilitate the interview process for you? Is there any specific technology that you currently use or have used that assists the way you work? What other kind of support did you have in previous jobs? Is there anything that would benefit you? Discuss a barrier or obstacle, if any, that you have encountered in any of your previous jobs. How was that addressed? And, do you anticipate any transportation or scheduling issues with the position's work schedule? ■

IMPROVING PERFORMANCE: *HR PRACTICES AROUND THE GLOBE*

Selection Practices Abroad[72]

In choosing selection criteria abroad, the manager walks a thin line between using the parent company's selection process and adapting it to local cultural differences. One study focused on Bangladesh.[73] Traditional selection practices there are different from the United States. For example, "age is considered synonymous to wisdom." Therefore, job advertisements for mid- and senior-level positions often set a *minimum* age as a selection criteria. But managers of multinational subsidiaries there are slowly implementing their corporate headquarters' prescribed HRM practices. As a result, the multinationals are influencing local recruitment and selection practices. That said, the manager should still factor in a country's unique cultural needs before holding an interview there.

MyLab Management Talk About It 2

If your professor has assigned this, go to the Assignments section of **www.pearson.com/mylab/management** to complete this discussion. You are interviewing candidates in Bangladesh, and you have a great candidate who unfortunately is 25 years old, when the job calls for someone at least 40. List three interview questions you would ask to see if the person is still qualified.

Interviewer Behavior

Finally, the list of ways in which *interviewers* themselves wreck interviews is boundless. For example, some interviewers inadvertently telegraph the expected answers, as in: "This job involves a lot of stress. You can handle that, can't you?" Even subtle cues (like a smile or nod) can telegraph the desired answer.[74] Some interviewers talk so much that applicants can't answer questions. At the other extreme, some interviewers let the applicant dominate the interview. When interviewers have favorable preinterview impressions of the applicant, they tend to act more positively toward that person (smiling more, for instance).[75] Other interviewers play interrogator, gleefully pouncing on inconsistencies. Some interviewers play amateur psychologist, unprofessionally probing for hidden meanings in what the applicant says. Others ask discriminatory questions."[76]

In summary, interviewing errors to avoid include:

- First impressions (snap judgments)
- Not clarifying what the job involves and requires
- Candidate-order error and pressure to hire
- Nonverbal behavior and impression management
- The effects of interviewees' personal characteristics
- The interviewer's inadvertent behaviors

We'll address what *interviewees* can do to apply these findings and to excel in the interview in Appendix 2 to this chapter.

LEARNING OBJECTIVE 7-3

Define a structured situational interview and explain how to conduct effective selection interviews.

structured situational interview
A series of job-relevant questions with predetermined answers that interviewers ask of all applicants for the job.

How to Design and Conduct an Effective Interview

There is little doubt that the **structured situational interview**—a series of job-relevant questions with predetermined answers that interviewers ask of all applicants for the job—produces superior results.[77] The basic idea is to (1) write situational (what would you do), behavioral (what did you do), or job knowledge questions, *and* (2) have job experts (like those supervising the job) write several answers for each of these questions, rating the answers from good to poor. (A knowledge question for a social media marketing job would be: "How would you measure the success of your social campaigns?" A situational question would be, "There's a crisis on one of our social media channels. How do you handle it?" A behavioral question is, "Tell me about a successful social campaign you've run.")[78] The people (usually a panel of two to three) who interview the applicants then use rating sheets anchored with examples of good or bad answers to rate interviewees' answers.

Designing a Structured Situational Interview

The procedure is as follows.[79]

Step 1. **Analyze the job.** Write a job description including: a list of job duties; required knowledge, skills, and abilities; and other worker qualifications.

Step 2. **Rate the job's main duties.** Rate each job duty, say from 1 to 5, based on how important it is to the job.

Step 3. **Create interview questions.** Create situational, behavioral, and job knowledge interview questions for each job duty, with more questions for the important duties. The people who create the questions usually write them as critical incidents. For example, to probe for conscientiousness, the interviewer might ask this situational question:

> Your spouse and two teenage children are sick in bed with colds. There are no relatives or friends available to look in on them. Your shift starts in 3 hours. What would you do?

Step 4. **Create benchmark answers.** Next, *for each question*, develop ideal (benchmark) answers for good (a 5 rating), marginal (a 3 rating), and poor (a 1 rating) answers. The structured interview guide (pages 231–233) presents an example. Three benchmark answers (from low to high) for the example question in step 3 might be, "I'd stay home—my spouse and family come first" (1); "I'd phone my supervisor and explain my situation" (3); and "Because they only have colds, I'd come to work" (5).

Step 5. **Appoint the interview panel and conduct interviews.** Employers generally conduct structured situational interviews using a panel, rather than one-on-one. Panels usually consist of two or three members, preferably those who wrote the questions and answers. They may also include the job's supervisor and/or incumbent, and an HR representative. The same panel interviews all candidates for the job.[80]

The panel members review the job description, questions, and benchmark answers before the interview. One panel member introduces the applicant, and asks all questions of all applicants in this and succeeding candidates' interviews (to ensure consistency). However, all panel members record and rate the applicant's answers on the rating sheet (as on pages 232–233), by indicating where the candidate's answer to each question falls relative to the benchmark poor, marginal, or good answers. At the end of the interview, someone answers any questions the applicant has.[81]

Web-based programs help interviewers design and organize behaviorally based selection interviews. For example, SelectPro (www.selectpro.net) enables interviewers to create behavior-based selection interviews, custom interview guides, and automated online interviews. The following summarizes how to conduct an effective interview.

IMPROVING PERFORMANCE: *HR TOOLS FOR LINE MANAGERS AND SMALL BUSINESSES*

In Summary: How to Conduct an Effective Interview

You may not have the time or inclination to create a structured situational interview. However, there is still much you can do to make your interviews systematic.

Step 1: First, know the job. Don't start the interview unless you understand the job's duties and what human skills you're looking for. Study the job description.

Step 2: Structure the interview. *Any* structuring is better than none. If pressed for time, you can still do several things to ask more consistent and job-relevant questions, without developing a full-blown structured interview.[82] For example:[83]

- Base questions on *actual job duties.* This will minimize irrelevant questions.
- Use *job knowledge, situational, or behavioral questions*. Questions that simply ask for opinions and attitudes, goals and aspirations, and self-evaluations allow candidates to present themselves in an overly favorable manner or avoid revealing weaknesses.[84] Figure 7-2 illustrates structured questions.
- *Use the same questions* with all candidates. This improves reliability. It also reduces bias by giving all candidates the same opportunity.
- For each question, if possible, *have several ideal answers* and a score for each. Then rate each candidate's answers against this scale.
- If possible, use an *interview form.* Interviews based on structured guides like the ones in Figure 7-1 (pages 208–209) or Figure 7A-1, the "structured interview guide" on pages 232–233, usually result in better interviews.[85] At least list your questions before the interview.

Step 3: Get organized. Hold the interview in a private place to minimize interruptions. Prior to the interview, review the candidate's application and résumé. Note any areas that are vague or that may indicate strengths or weaknesses.

Step 4: Establish rapport. The main reason for the interview is to find out about the applicant. Start by putting the person at ease. Greet the candidate, and start the interview by asking a noncontroversial question, perhaps about the weather that day.

Step 5: Ask questions. Try to follow the situational, behavioral, and job knowledge questions you wrote out ahead of time. (That notwithstanding,

FIGURE 7-2 Examples of Questions That Provide Interview Structure

Job Knowledge Questions

1. What steps would you follow in changing the fan belt on a Toyota Camry?
2. What factors would you consider in choosing a computer to use for work?

Experience Questions

3. What experience have you had actually repairing automobile engines?
4. What experience have you had creating marketing programs for consumer products?

Behavioral (Past Behavior) Questions

5. Tell me about a time when you had to deal with a particularly obnoxious person. What was the situation, and how did you handle it?
6. Tell me about a time when you were under a great deal of stress. What was the situation, and how did you handle it?

Situational (What Would You Do) Questions

7. Suppose your boss insisted that a presentation had to be finished by tonight, but your subordinate said she has to get home early to attend an online class, so she is unable to help you. What would you do?
8. The CEO just told you that he's planning on firing your boss, with whom you are very close, and replacing him with you. What would you do?

glassdoor.com says that "What are your strengths" is still the top [of 50] job interview questions asked.)[86] Figure 7-3 contains the list of 50 questions glassdoor.com found were most popular (such as "Why do you want to leave your current company?"). And remember that many states and municipalities now ban asking about job applicant pay history.[87] Also, in asking your questions:

Don't telegraph the desired answer.
Don't interrogate the applicant as if the person is on trial.
Don't monopolize the interview, nor let the applicant do so.
Do ask open-ended questions.
Do encourage the applicant to express thoughts fully.
Do draw out the applicant's opinions and feelings by repeating the person's last comment as a question (e.g., "You didn't like your last job?").
Do ask for examples.[88]
Do ask, "If I were to arrange for an interview with your boss, what would he or she say are your strengths, weaker points, and overall performance?"[89]

Step 6: Take brief, unobtrusive notes during the interview. This helps avoid making a snap decision early in the interview, and may help jog your memory once the interview is over. Jot down the key points of what the interviewee says.[90]

Step 7: Close the interview. Leave time to answer any questions the candidate may have and, if appropriate, to advocate your firm to the candidate.

Try to end the interview on a positive note. Tell the applicant whether there's any interest and, if so, what the next step will be. Make rejections diplomatically—"Although your background is impressive, there are other candidates whose experience is closer to our requirements." Remember, as one recruiter says, "An interview experience should leave a lasting, positive impression of the company, whether the candidate receives and accepts an offer or not."[91] If the applicant is still under consideration but you can't reach a decision now, say so.

Step 8: Review the interview. Once the candidate leaves, review your interview notes, score the interview answers (if you used a guide), and make a decision.

Chris Ryan/Caiaimage/Gettyimage

Go into the interview with an accurate picture of the traits of an ideal candidate, know what you're going to ask, and be prepared to keep an open mind about the candidate.

1. What are your strengths?
2. What are your weaknesses?
3. Why are you interested in working for *[insert company name here]*?
4. Where do you see yourself in five years? Ten years?
5. Why do you want to leave your current company?
6. Why was there a gap in your employment between *[insert date]* and *[insert date]*?
7. What can you offer us that someone else can not?
8. What are three things your former manager would like you to improve on?
9. Are you willing to relocate?
10. Are you willing to travel?
11. Tell me about an accomplishment you are most proud of.
12. Tell me about a time you made a mistake.
13. What is your dream job?
14. How did you hear about this position?
15. What would you look to accomplish in the first 30 days/60 days/90 days on the job?
16. Discuss your résumé.
17. Discuss your educational background.
18. Describe yourself.
19. Tell me how you handled a difficult situation.
20. Why should we hire you?
21. Why are you looking for a new job?
22. Would you work holidays/weekends?
23. How would you deal with an angry or irate customer?
24. What are your salary requirements? *(Hint: If you're not sure what's a fair salary range and compensation package, research the job title and/or company on Glassdoor.)*
25. Give a time when you went above and beyond the requirements for a project.
26. Who are our competitors?
27. What was your biggest failure?
28. What motivates you?
29. What's your availability?
30. Who's your mentor?
31. Tell me about a time when you disagreed with your boss.
32. How do you handle pressure?
33. What is the name of our CEO?
34. What are your career goals?
35. What gets you up in the morning?
36. What would your direct reports say about you?
37. What were your bosses' strengths/weaknesses?
38. If I called your boss right now and asked him/her what is an area that you could improve on, what would he/she say?
39. Are you a leader or a follower?
40. What was the last book you've read for fun?
41. What are your co-worker pet peeves?
42. What are your hobbies?
43. What is your favorite Web site?
44. What makes you uncomfortable?
45. What are some of your leadership experiences?
46. How would you fire someone?
47. What do you like the most and least about working in this industry?
48. Would you work 40+ hours a week?
49. What questions haven't I asked you?
50. What questions do you have for me?

FIGURE 7-3 **Suggested Supplementary Questions for Interviewing Applicants**
Source: www.glassdoor.com/blog/common-interview-questions.

In rejecting a candidate, one perennial question is, should you provide an explanation or not? In one study, rejected candidates who received an explanation felt that the rejection process was fairer. Unfortunately, doing so may not be practical. Most employers say little, to avoid pushback and legal problems.[92] Templates for rejections letters are available from SHRM and others.[93] ■

MyLab Management Talk About It 3

If your professor has assigned this, go to the Assignments section of **www.pearson.com/mylab/management** to complete this discussion. Write a one-paragraph (single-spaced) memo to the people who do your company's recruiting on the topic, "The five most important things an interviewer can do to have a useful selection interview."

Competency Profiles and Employee Interviews

We've seen that many companies use competency models or profiles for recruiting, selecting, training, appraising, and compensating employees. Employers can use such a profile for formulating job-related situational, behavioral, and knowledge interview questions. Table 7-1 summarizes this, for chemical engineer candidates, with sample interview questions.

MyLab Management Apply It!

What do you think of how Zipcar conducts its interviewing candidates program? If your professor has assigned this activity, go to the Assignments section of **www.pearson.com/mylab/management** to complete the video exercise.

LEARNING OBJECTIVE 7-4

Give examples of how to use employee selection to improve employee engagement.

Employee Engagement Guide for Managers

Building Engagement: A Total Selection Program

Many employers create a *total selection program* aimed at selecting candidates whose totality of attributes best fits the employer's total requirements. The program Toyota Motor uses to select employees for auto assembly team jobs illustrates this.

Toyota looks for several things. It wants employees with good interpersonal skills, due to the job's emphasis on teamwork. Toyota's emphasis on *kaizen*—on having the workers improve job processes through worker commitment to top quality—helps explain its emphasis on reasoning and problem-solving skills and on hiring intelligent, educated, and engaged workers.[94] Quality is a Toyota core value, so Toyota wants a history of quality commitment in those it hires. Toyota holds group interviews. By asking candidates about what they are proudest of, Toyota gets a better insight into the person's values regarding quality and doing things right. Toyota also wants employees with an eagerness to learn, and who are willing to try things Toyota's way or the team's way. Toyota's production system relies on consensus decision making, job rotation, and flexible career paths, which in turn require open-minded, flexible team players, not dogmatists.

TABLE 7-1 Asking Competency Profile-Oriented Interview Questions

Profile Competency	Example of Competency	Sample Interview Question
Skill	Able to use computer drafting software	Tell me about a time you used CAD Pro computerized design software.
Knowledge	How extreme heat affects hydrochloric acid (HCl)	Suppose you have an application where HCl is heated to 400 degrees Fahrenheit at 2 atmospheres of pressure; what happens to the HCl?
Trait	Willing to travel abroad at least 4 months per year visiting facilities	Suppose you had a family meeting to attend next week and we informed you that you had to leave for a job abroad immediately. How would you handle that?
Experience	Designed pollution filter for acid-cleaning facility	Tell me about a time when you designed a pollution filter for an acid-cleaning facility. How did it work? What particular problems did you encounter?

The Toyota Way

Toyota's hiring process aims to identify such assembler candidates. The process takes about 20 hours and six phases over several days:[95]

- **Step 1:** an in-depth online application (20–30 minutes)
- **Step 2:** a 2- to 5-hour computer-based assessment
- **Step 3:** a 6- to 8-hour work simulation assessment
- **Step 4:** a face-to-face interview
- **Step 5:** a background check, drug screen, and medical check
- **Step 6:** job offer

For example, in step 1, applicants complete applications summarizing their experience and skills, and often view a video describing Toyota's work environment and selection system. This provides a realistic preview of the work and of the hiring process's extensiveness. Many applicants drop out here.

Step 2 assesses the applicant's technical knowledge and potential. Here applicants take tests that help identify problem-solving skills, learning potential, and occupational preferences. Skilled trade applicants (experienced mechanics, for instance) also take tool and die or general maintenance tests. Vendors offer practice Toyota tests.[96]

In step 3, applicants engage in simulated realistic production activities in Toyota's assessment center, under the observation of Toyota screening experts. The production (work sample) test assesses how well each candidate does on an actual assembler task. Also here, group discussion exercises help show how each applicant interacts with others in their group and solves problems.

In one simulation, candidates play the roles of the management and the workers of a firm making electrical circuits. During one scenario, the team must decide which circuit should be manufactured and how to effectively assign people, materials, and money to produce them. In another, participants role-play a team responsible for choosing new features for next year's car. Team members first individually rank 12 features based upon market appeal and then suggest one feature not included on the list. They must then come to a consensus on the best rank ordering. As one candidate who went through this process said, "There are three workstations in which you will be required to spend 2 hours at each one. You then have to get in a group and problem-solve a special project with them for another hour or so. I left my house at 5 A.M. and did not return until 6:30 P.M.; it was a very long day."[97]

The time and effort applicants must invest in their Toyota visits are no accident. Toyota seeks engaged, flexible, quality-oriented team players, and those who lack these traits tend not to make it through the screening process. The rigorousness of the process tends to screen out the less engaged.

In summary, Toyota uses a total hiring process to identify and select engaged employees. Four common themes are apparent from Toyota's process. First, *value-based hiring* means it clarifies its own values before it embarks on an employee selection program. Whether based on excellence, kaizen/continuous improvement, integrity, or some other, value-based hiring begins with clarifying what your firm's values are and what you're looking for in employees.

Second, high-engagement firms such as Toyota commit the time and effort for an *exhaustive screening process*. Eight to ten hours of interviewing even for entry-level employees is not unusual, and firms like this will often spend 20 hours or more with someone before deciding to hire. Many are rejected.

Third, the screening process doesn't just identify knowledge and technical skills. Instead, it seeks candidates whose *values and skills match* the needs of the firm. Teamwork, kaizen, problem solving, engagement, and flexibility are essential values at Toyota, so problem-solving skills, interpersonal skills, and engagement with the firm's commitment to quality are crucial human requirements.

Fourth, *self-selection* is important. In some firms this just means realistic previews. At others, practices such as long probationary periods in entry-level jobs help screen out those who don't fit. At Toyota, the long screening process itself demands a sacrifice in terms of time and effort.

TRENDS SHAPING HR: *SCIENCE IN TALENT MANAGEMENT*

As another example, Google takes a scientific, evidence-based approach to its selection (and other HR) practices.

In its hiring process, Google starts (as explained in Chapter 4) with strong candidates. For example, its internal recruiting group proactively identifies candidates, rather than using job boards to attract unscreened résumés.

The main elements in Google's selection process include work samples, testing, and interviewing. Virtually all of Google's technical hires take work sample tests, such as actually writing algorithms. Work samples are combined with testing of cognitive ability (similar to IQ tests), and of conscientiousness. Early in its evolution Google put candidates through a dozen or more interviews. However, Google's analysis showed that after the first four interviews the amount of useful information it got was small. It therefore now generally makes hiring decisions after the fourth interview.

The interviews emphasize situational and behavioral questions. For specific questions, Google provides its interviewers with its QDroid system; this e-mails each interviewer specific questions to ask the candidate for the specific job. Google interviewers were once known for trick questions, but the emphasis now is on using validated questions (from the QDroid system). The questions aim to assess the candidate's cognitive ability, leadership (particularly willingness to lead projects), "Googleyness" (values such as fun-loving and conscientious), and role-related knowledge (such as in computer science).

Who actually does the interviewing? Here Google believes in the "wisdom of crowds": the interviewing "crowd" includes not just the prospective boss but also prospective subordinates and representatives of other unrelated departments. Google then averages all the interviewers' interview ratings on a candidate to get a score. Finally, the hiring committee reviews the file, as does a Google senior manager, and then the CEO, before an offer is made.[98]

Google is continually analyzing and improving its selection process. For example, it periodically runs experiments that identify common keywords so as to analyze résumés of successful Google employees in particular jobs. Google then looks for these keywords in applicants who it *rejected* over the past year, and reevaluates these rejected applicants for these keywords, hiring many of these former "rejects" as a result. Similarly, interviewers get printouts showing how effective they've been as interviewers in terms of candidates hired or not hired. The process is thus analytical, evidence-based, and scientific. ■

Developing and Extending the Job Offer

LEARNING OBJECTIVE 7-5

List the main points in developing and extending the actual job offer.

After all the interviews, background checks, and tests, the employer decides to whom to make an offer, using one or more approaches. The *judgmental* approach subjectively weighs all the evidence about the candidate. The *statistical* approach quantifies all the evidence and perhaps uses a formula to predict job success. The *hybrid* approach combines statistical results with judgment. Statistical and hybrid are more defensible; judgmental is better than nothing.

The employer will base the details of the actual offer on, for instance, the candidate's apparent attractiveness as a prospective employee, the level of the position, and pay rates for similar positions. Next the employer extends an actual job offer to the candidate verbally. Here, the employer's point person (who might be the person to whom the new employee will report, or the human resource director, for instance) discusses the offer's main parameters. These include, for instance, pay rates, benefits, and actual job duties. There may be some negotiations. Then, once agreement is reached, the employer will extend a written job offer to the candidate.

There are several issues to consider with the written offer. Perhaps most important, understand the difference between a job offer letter and a contract. In a job offer letter, the employer lists the offer's basic information. This typically starts with a welcome sentence. It then includes job-specific information (such as details on salary and pay), benefits information, paid leave information, and terms of employment (including, for instance, successful completion of physical exams). There should be a strong statement that the employment relationship is "at will." There is then a closing statement. This again welcomes the employee, mentions who the employer's point person is if any questions arise, and instructs the candidate to sign the letter of offer if it is acceptable. It is prudent to have an attorney review the offer before extending it.[99]

For many positions (such as executive) a contract is in order. Unlike a letter of offer (which should always be "at will"), an employment contract may have a duration (such as 3 years). Therefore, the contract will also describe grounds for termination or resignation, and severance provisions. The contract will almost always also include terms regarding confidentiality, nondisclosure requirements, and covenants not to compete (some *job offer letters* for positions such as engineer may include such provisions as well). See www.shrm.org/template-tools/toolkits for more information.

Depending upon the position, the employment contract (and, occasionally, the offer letter) may include a relocation provision. This lays out what the employer is willing to pay the new employee to relocate, for instance, in terms of moving expenses. State law generally governs enforcement of individual employment contracts. Letter of offer and employment contract samples are available online.[100]

Chapter Review

Chapter Section Summaries

7-1. A selection interview is a selection procedure designed to predict future job performance based on applicants' oral responses to oral inquiries; we discussed several **basic types of interviews.** There are structured versus unstructured interviews. We also distinguished between interviews based on the types of questions and on how you administer the interview.

7-2. One reason selection interviews are often less useful than they should be is that managers make predictable **errors that undermine an interview's usefulness.** They jump to conclusions or make snap judgments based on preliminary information, they don't clarify what the job really requires, they succumb to candidate-order error and pressure to hire, and they let a variety of nonverbal behaviors and personal characteristics undermine the validity of the interview.

7-3. The manager should know how to **design and conduct an effective interview.** The structured situational interview is a series of job-related questions with predetermined answers that interviewers ask of all applicants for the job. Steps in creating a structured situational interview include analyzing the job, rating the job's main duties, creating interview questions, creating benchmark answers, and appointing the interview panel and conducting interviews.

7-4. **High-engagement firms** like Toyota use total hiring programs to select employees. Activities include clarifying the firm's values, committing the time and effort, matching the applicant's values with the firm's, having realistic previews, and encouraging self-selection.

7-5. Finally the employer turns to **developing and extending the job offer.** Distinguish between a job offer letter and a contract. The former lists the offer's basic information, including details on salary and pay, benefits information, paid leave information, and terms of employment. There should be a strong statement specifying that the employment relationship is "at will." In contrast to a letter of offer, it is not unusual for an employment contract to have a duration (such as 3 years).

Discussion Questions

7-1. There are several ways to conduct a selection interview. Explain and illustrate the basic ways in which you can classify selection interviews.

7-2. Briefly describe each of the following types of interviews: unstructured panel interviews, structured sequential interviews, job-related structured interviews.

7-3. For what sorts of jobs do you think unstructured interviews might be most appropriate? Why?

7-4. How would you explain the fact that structured interviews, regardless of content, are generally more valid than unstructured interviews for predicting job performance?

7-5. Briefly discuss what an interviewer can do to improve his or her interviewing performance.

7-6. What items should a letter of offer definitely contain?

7-7. What parallels do you see between the Toyota and Google total selection processes? What differences?

Individual and Group Activities

7-8. Prepare and give a short presentation titled "How to Be Effective as a Selection Interviewer."

7-9. Use the Internet to find employers who now do preliminary selection interviews via the Web. Do you think these interviews are useful? Why? How would you improve them?

7-10. In groups, discuss and compile examples of "the worst interview I ever had." What was it about these interviews that made them so bad? If time permits, discuss as a class.

7-11. In groups, prepare an interview (including a sequence of at least 20 questions) you'll use to interview candidates for the job of teaching a course in human resource management. Each group should present its interview questions in class.

7-12. Several years ago, Lockheed Martin Corp. sued the Boeing Corp., accusing it of using Lockheed's trade secrets to help win a multibillion-dollar government contract. Among other things, Lockheed claimed that Boeing had obtained those trade secrets from a former Lockheed employee who switched to Boeing.[101] But of the methods companies use to commit corporate espionage, one writer says that hiring away the competitor's employees is just the most obvious method companies use. One writer says, "One of the more unusual scams—sometimes referred to as 'help wanted'—uses a person posing as a corporate headhunter who approaches an employee of the target company with a potentially lucrative job offer. During the interview, the employee is quizzed about his responsibilities, accomplishments, and current projects. The goal is to extract information without the employee realizing there is no job."[102]

Assume you own a small high-tech company. What would you do (in terms of employee training, or a letter from you, for instance) to try to minimize the chance that one of your employees will fall into that kind of a trap? Also, compile a list of 10 questions that you think such a corporate spy might ask one of your employees.

7-13. Appendices A and B at the end of this book (pages 614–634) list the knowledge someone studying for the HRCI (Appendix A) or SHRM (Appendix B) certification exam needs to have in each area of human resource management (such as in Strategic Management and Workforce Planning). In groups of several students, do four things: (1) review Appendix A and/or B; (2) identify the material in this chapter that relates to the Appendix A and/or B required knowledge lists; (3) write four multiple-choice exam questions on this material that you believe would be suitable for inclusion in the HRCI exam and/or the SHRM exam; and (4) if time permits, have someone from your team post your team's questions in front of the class, so that students in all teams can answer the exam questions created by the other teams.

KNOWLEDGE BASE

Experiential Exercise

The Most Important Person You'll Ever Hire

Written and copyrighted by Gary Dessler, PhD.

Purpose: The purpose of this exercise is to give you practice using some of the interview techniques you learned from this chapter.

Required Understanding: You should be familiar with the information presented in this chapter, and read this: For parents, children are precious. It's therefore interesting that parents who hire "nannies" to take care of their children usually do little more than ask several interview questions and conduct what is often, at best, a perfunctory reference check. Given the often questionable validity of interviews, and the (often) relative inexperience of the father or mother doing the interviewing, it's not surprising that many of these arrangements end in disappointment. You know from this chapter that it is difficult to conduct a valid interview unless you know exactly what you're looking for and, preferably, structure the interview. Most parents simply aren't trained to do this.

How to Set Up the Exercise/Instructions: Set up groups of five or six students. Two students will be the interviewees, while the other students in the group will serve as panel interviewers. The interviewees will develop an interviewer assessment form, and the panel interviewers will develop a structured situational interview for a "nanny."

7-14. Instructions for the interviewees: The interviewees should leave the room for about 20 minutes. While out of the room, the interviewees should develop an "interviewer assessment form" based on the information presented in this chapter regarding factors that can undermine the usefulness of an interview. During the panel interview, the interviewees should assess the interviewers using the interviewer assessment form. After the panel interviewers have conducted the interview, the interviewees should leave the room to discuss their notes. Did the interviewers exhibit any of the factors that can undermine the usefulness of an interview? If so, which ones? What suggestions would you (the interviewees) make to the interviewers on how to improve the usefulness of the interview?

7-15. Instructions for the interviewers: While the interviewees are out of the room, the panel interviewers will have 20 minutes to develop a short structured situational interview form for a "nanny." The panel interview team will interview two candidates for the position. During the panel interview, each interviewer should be taking notes on a copy of the structured situational interview form. After the panel interview, the panel interviewers should discuss their notes. What were your first impressions of each interviewee? Were your impressions similar? Which candidate would you all select for the position, and why?

CHAPTER 7

Application Case

The Out-of-Control Interview

Written and copyrighted by Gary Dessler, PhD.

Maria Fernandez is a bright, popular, and well-informed mechanical engineer who graduated with an engineering degree from State University in June 2018. During the spring preceding her graduation, she went out on many job interviews, most of which she thought were conducted courteously and were reasonably useful in giving both her and the prospective employer a good impression of where each of them stood on matters of importance to both of them. It was, therefore, with great anticipation that she looked forward to an interview with the one firm in which she most wanted to work: Apex Environmental. She had always had a strong interest in the environment and believed that the best use of her training and skills lay in working for a firm like Apex, where she thought she could have a successful career while making the world a better place.

The interview, however, was a disaster. Maria walked into a room where five men—the president of the company, two vice presidents, the marketing director, and another engineer—began throwing questions at her that she felt were aimed primarily at tripping her up rather than finding out what she could offer through her engineering skills. The questions ranged from being unnecessarily discourteous ("Why would you take a job as a waitress in college if you're such an intelligent person?") to being irrelevant and sexist ("Are you planning on starting a family anytime soon?"). Then, after the interview, she met with two of the gentlemen individually (including the president), and the discussions focused on her technical expertise. She thought that these later discussions went fairly well. However, given the apparent aimlessness and even mean-spiritedness of the panel interview, she was astonished when several days later the firm made her a job offer.

The offer forced her to consider several matters. From her point of view, the job itself was perfect. She liked what she would be doing, the industry, and the firm's location. And in fact, the president had been quite courteous in subsequent discussions. She was left wondering whether the panel interview had been intentionally tense to see how she'd stand up under pressure, and, if so, why they would do such a thing.

Questions

7-16. How would you explain the nature of the panel interview Maria had to endure? Specifically, do you think it reflected a well-thought-out interviewing strategy on the part of the firm or carelessness on the part of the firm's management? If it were carelessness, what would you do to improve the interview process at Apex Environmental?

7-17. Would you take the job offer if you were Maria? If you're not sure, what additional information would help you make your decision?

7-18. The job of applications engineer for which Maria was applying requires (a) excellent technical skills with respect to mechanical engineering, (b) a commitment to working in the area of pollution control, (c) the ability to deal well and confidently with customers who have engineering problems, (d) a willingness to travel worldwide, and (e) a very intelligent and well-balanced personality. List 10 questions you would ask when interviewing applicants for the job.

Continuing Case

Carter Cleaning Company

Written and copyrighted by Gary Dessler, PhD.

The Better Interview

Like virtually all the other HR-related activities at Carter Cleaning Centers, the company currently has no organized approach to interviewing job candidates. Store managers, who do almost all the hiring, have a few of their own favorite questions that they ask. But in the absence of any guidance from management, they all admit their interview performance leaves something to be desired. Similarly, Jack Carter himself is admittedly most comfortable dealing with what he calls the "nuts and bolts" machinery aspect of his business and has never felt particularly comfortable having to interview management or other job applicants. Jennifer is sure that this lack of formal interviewing practices, procedures, and training account for some of the employee turnover and theft problems. Therefore, she wants to do something to improve her company's performance in this important area.

Questions

7-19. In general, what can Jennifer do to improve her employee interviewing practices? Should she develop interview forms that list questions for management and nonmanagement jobs? If so, how should these look, and what questions should be included? Should she initiate a computer-based interview approach? If so, why and how?

7-20. Should she implement an interview training program for her managers, and if so, specifically what should be the content of such a training program? In other words, if she did decide to start training her management people to be better interviewers, what should she tell them, and how should she tell it to them?

Translating Strategy into HR Policies and Practices Case*,§

** The accompanying strategy map for this chapter is in MyLab Management; the overall map on the inside back cover of this text outlines the relationships involved.*

Improving Performance at the Hotel Paris

The New Interviewing Program

The Hotel Paris's competitive strategy is "To use superior guest service to differentiate the Hotel Paris properties, and to thereby increase the length of stay and return rate of guests, and thus boost revenues and profitability." HR manager Lisa Cruz must now formulate functional policies and activities that support this competitive strategy, by eliciting the required employee behaviors and competencies.

As an experienced HR professional, Lisa knew that the company's new testing program would go only so far. She knew that, at best, employment tests accounted for perhaps 30% of employee performance. It was essential that she and her team design a package of interviews that her hotel managers could use to assess—on an interactive and personal basis—candidates for various positions. It was only in that way that the hotel could hire the sorts of employees whose competencies and behaviors would translate into the kinds of outcomes—such as improved guest services—that the hotel required to achieve its strategic goals.

Lisa received budgetary approval to design a new employee interview system. She and her team started by reviewing the job descriptions and job specifications for the positions of front-desk clerk, assistant manager, security guard, valet, door person, and housekeeper. Focusing on developing structured interviews for each position, the team set about devising interview questions. For example, for the front-desk clerk and assistant manager, they formulated several *behavioral questions*, including, "Tell me about a time when you had to deal with an irate person, and what you did," and "Tell me about a time when you had to deal with several conflicting demands at once, such as having to study for several final exams at the same time, while working. How did you handle the situation?" They also developed a number of *situational questions*, including "Suppose you have a very pushy incoming guest who insists on being checked in at once, while at the same time you're trying to process the check-out for another guest who must be at the airport in 10 minutes. How would you handle the situation?" For these and other positions, they also developed several *job knowledge* questions. For example, for security guard applicants, one question her team created was, "What are the local legal restrictions, if any, regarding using products like Mace if confronted by an unruly person on the hotel grounds?" The team combined the questions into structured interviews for each job, and turned to testing, fine-tuning, and finally using the new system.

Questions

7-21. For the jobs of security guard and valet, develop five additional situational, five behavioral, and five job knowledge questions, with descriptive good/average/poor answers.

7-22. Combine, (based on what you read in this Dessler, *Human Resource Management* chapter) your questions into a complete interview that you would give to someone who must interview candidates for these jobs.

§ Written and copyrighted by Gary Dessler, PhD.

Writing Assignments

7-23. Briefly discuss and give examples of at least five common interviewing mistakes. What recommendations would you give for avoiding these interviewing mistakes?

7-24. What parallels do you see between the Toyota and Google total selection processes? What differences?

PERSONAL INVENTORY ASSESSMENTS

Go to **www.pearson.com/mylab/management** to complete the Personal Inventory Assessment related to this chapter.

Key Terms

unstructured (or nondirective) interview, 207
structured (or directive) interview, 207
situational interview, 208
behavioral interview, 208
job-related interview, 209
stress interview, 209
unstructured sequential interview, 210
structured sequential interview, 210
panel interview, 210
mass interview, 210
candidate-order (or contrast) error, 213
structured situational interview, 216

Endnotes

1. Derek Chapman and David Zweig, "Developing a Nomological Network for Interview Structure: Antecedents and Consequences of the Structured Selection Interview," *Personnel Psychology* 58 (2005), pp. 673– 702; Jason Dana, "The Utter Uselessness of Job Interviews," *The New York Times*, April 8, 2017, https://www.nytimes.com/2017/04/08/opinion/sunday/the-utter-uselessness-of-job-interviews.html, accessed February 5, 2018.
2. This is adapted from http://learn.hirevue.com/urbanoutfitters-casestudy, accessed February 4, 2018.
3. Michael McDaniel et al., "The Validity of Employment Interviews: A Comprehensive Review and Meta-Analysis," *Journal of Applied Psychology* 79, no. 4 (1994), p. 599. See also Laura Graves and Ronald Karren, "The Employee Selection Interview: A Fresh Look at an Old Problem," *Human Resource Management* 35, no. 2 (Summer 1996), pp. 163–180. For an argument against holding selection interviews, see D. Heath et al., "Hold the Interview," *Fast Company*, no. 136 (June 2009), pp. 51–52.
4. Therese Macan, "The Employment Interview: A Review of Current Studies and Directions for Future Research," *Human Resource Management Review* 19 (2009), pp. 203–218. See also, Rebecca Knight, "How to Conduct an Effective Job Interview," *Harvard Business Review*, January 23, 2015, https://hbr.org/2015/01/how-to-conduct-an-effective-job-interview, accessed February 2, 2018.
5. Duane Schultz and Sydney Schultz, *Psychology and Work Today* (Upper Saddle River, NJ: Prentice Hall, 1998), p. 830. A study found that interview structure "was best described by four dimensions: questioning consistency, evaluation standardization, question sophistication, and rapport building." Chapman and Zweig, "Developing a Nomological Network."
6. McDaniel et al., "The Validity of Employment Interviews," p. 602.
7. We'll see later in this chapter that there are other ways to "structure" selection interviews. Many of them have nothing to do with using structured guides like these.
8. See also Julia Levashina, Christopher Hartwell, Frederick Morageson, and Michael Campion, "The Structured Employment Interview: Narrative and Quantitative Review of the Research Literature," *Personnel Psychology* 67 (2014), pp. 241–293.
9. Laura Gollub Williamson et al., "Employment Interview on Trial: Linking Interview Structure with Litigation Outcomes," *Journal of Applied Psychology* 82, no. 6 (1996), p. 908. As an example, the findings of one study "demonstrate the value of using highly structured interviews to minimize the potential influence of applicant demographic characteristics on selection decisions." Julie McCarthy, Chad Van Iddekinge, and Michael Campion, "Are Highly Structured Job Interviews Resistant to Demographic Similarity Effects?" *Personnel Psychology* 60, no. 3 (2010), pp. 325–359.
10. Williamson et al., "Employment Interview on Trial."
11. McDaniel et al., "The Validity of Employment Interviews," p. 602.
12. Paul Taylor and Bruce Small, "Asking Applicants What They Would Do versus What They Did: A Meta-Analytic Comparison of Situational and Past Behavior Employment Interview Questions," *Journal of Occupational and Organizational Psychology* 75, no. 3 (September 2002), pp. 277–295.
13. Margery Weinstein, "You're Hired!" *Training* 48, no. 4, pp. 34–37; www.trainingmag.com/article/you%E2%80%99re-hired, accessed July 19, 2013.
14. Aparna Nancherla, "Anticipated Growth in Behavioral Interviewing," *TD*, April 2008, p. 20.
15. Bill Stoneman, "Matching Personalities with Jobs Made Easier with Behavioral Interviews," *American Banker*, November 30, 2000, p. 8a. For suggestions on improving behavioral interviewing see, for example, "4 Tips for Conducting an Effective Behavioral Interview." Glassdoor.com, November 10, 2016, https://www.glassdoor.com/employers/blog/4-tips-for-conducting-an-effective-behavioral-interview/, accessed February 4, 2018.
16. Martha Frase-Blunt, "Games Interviewers Play," *HR Magazine*, January 2001, pp. 104–114. For a selection of more actual puzzle questions, see, for example, https://www.glassdoor.com/Interview/puzzle-interview-questions-SRCH_KT0,6.htm, accessed February 5, 2018.
17. Kevin Murphy and Charles Davidshofer, *Psychological Testing* (Upper Saddle River, NJ: Prentice Hall, 2001), pp. 430–431.
18. Marlene Dixon et al., "The Panel Interview: A Review of Empirical Research and Guidelines for Practice," *Public Personnel Management* 31, no. 3 (Fall 2002), pp. 397–429. For detailed instructions for conducting panel interviews see, for example, "Structured Interviews: A Practical Guide," Office of Personnel Management, 2008, pp. 25–26, https://www.opm.gov/policy-data-oversight/assessment-and-selection/structured-interviews/guide.pdf, accessed February 5, 2018.
19. Ibid. See also M. Ronald Buckley, Katherine A. Jackson, and Mark C. Bolino, "The Influence of Relational Demography on Panel Interview Ratings: A Field Experiment," *Personnel Psychology* 60, no. 3 (Autumn 2007), pp. 627–646.
20. Emily Maltby, "To Find the Best Hires, Firms Become Creative," *The Wall Street Journal*, November 17, 2009, p. B6.
21. "Phone Interviews Might Be the Most Telling, Study Finds," *BNA Bulletin to Management*, September 1998, p. 273; and Lisa M. Moynihan et al., "A Longitudinal Study of the Relationships Among Job Search Self-Efficacy, Job Interviews, and Employment Outcomes," *Journal of Business and Psychology* 18, no. 2 (Winter 2003), pp. 207–233. For phone interview job search suggestions, see, for example, Janet Wagner, "Can You Succeed in a Phone Interview?" *Strategic*

Finance 91, no. 10 (April 2010), pp. 22, 61.

22. Susan Strauss et al., "The Effects of Videoconference, Telephone, and Face-to-Face Media on Interviewer and Applicant Judgments in Employment Interviews," *Journal of Management* 27, no. 3 (2001), pp. 363–381. If the employer records a video interview with the intention of sharing it with hiring managers who don't participate in the interview, it's advisable to first obtain the candidate's written permission. Matt Bolch, "Lights, Camera . . . Interview!" *HR Magazine,* March 2007, pp. 99–102.
23. Douglas Rodgers, "Computer-Aided Interviewing Overcomes First Impressions," *Personnel Journal*, April 1987, pp. 148–152; see also Linda Thornburg, "Computer-Assisted Interviewing Shortens Hiring Cycle," *HR Magazine*, February 1998, p. 73ff; and http://interviewstream.com/demorequest?gclid=COyxjOqd36sCFUbs7QodMziuOw, accessed August 22, 2014.
24. "LinkedIn Isn't Just for Hiring Anymore; Useful for Branding, Career Growth as Well," *Bloomberg BNA Bulletin to Management*, August 27, 2013, p. 275.
25. http://interviewstream.com/About, accessed August 22, 2014.
26. Job interviewing apps are also available through Apple's App Store. One is from *Martin's iPhone Apps*. For people seeking technical jobs, this app includes hundreds of potential interview questions, such as brain teasers and algorithms. www.martinreddy.net/iphone/interview, accessed August 21, 2014.
27. Anjali Athavaley, "A Job Interview You Don't Have to Show Up For," *The Wall Street Journal*, June 20, 2007, http://online.wsj.com/article/SB118229876637841321.html, accessed April 8, 2011.
28. "Video Interviews Used to Connect with Candidates, Reduce Cost," *Bloomberg BNA Bulletin to Management*, March 11, 2014, p. 78.
29. Matt Mullenweg, "The CEO of Automattic on Holding 'Auditions' to Build a Strong Team," *Harvard Business Review*, April 2014, pp. 39–42.
30. These are quoted or adapted from www.careerfaqs.com.au/getthatjob_video_interview.asp, accessed March 2, 2009.
31. Similarly, Goldman Sachs used to conduct first-round on-campus interviews, but recently changed its process. Now undergraduates seeking summer internships or jobs first take a HireVue online interview using standardized questions. ("Goldman Sachs Is Making a Change to the Way It Hires," http://www.cnbc.com/2016/06/23/goldman-sachs-is-making-a-change-to-the-way-it-hires.html; see also Dahlia Bazzaz, "Job Seekers Face Virtual Interviews," *The Wall Street Journal*, August 17, 2016, p. B6.
32. Urban Outfitters faces a challenging retail environment. In 2017 it filed for bankruptcy protection and closed several stores, while planning new store openings for 2018. Tonya Garcia, "Urban Outfitters' Problem Isn't Too Many Stores—It's That Women Don't Want the Clothes It's Selling," *Market Watch*, March 11, 2017, https://www.marketwatch.com/story/urban-outfitters-problem-isnt-too-many-stores-its-that-women-dont-want-their-clothes-2017-03-08, accessed February 4, 2018.
33. http://learn.hirevue.com/urbanoutfitters-casestudy, accessed February 4, 2018. Similarly, a recruitment system from Breezy HR (https://breezy.hr/features/candidate-management) includes an asynchronous video assessment interview tool. The candidate video-records his or her answers to a set of questions at the person's convenience; then the recruiter watches and assesses the video answers when time permits. https://breezy.hr/features/candidate-management, accessed February 4, 2018.
34. For example, structured employment interviews using either situational questions or behavioral questions tend to yield high criterion-related validities (.63 versus .47). This is particularly so where the raters can use descriptively anchored rating scale answer sheets; these use short descriptors to illustrate good, average, or poor performance. Taylor and Small, "Asking Applicants What They Would Do Versus What They Did." See also McCarthy et al., "Are Highly Structured Job Interviews Resistant to Demographic Similarity Effects?" Some suggest using construct validity to validate employment interviews. Doing so involves showing which constructs (such as conscientiousness) explain interview ratings variations, explaining how these items may relate to job performance, and then testing the statistical relationships. Maria Ambani, Sorin Valcea, and M. Ronald Buckley, "The Relentless Pursuit of Construct Validity in the Design of Employment Interviews," *Human Resource Management Review* 24 (2014), pp. 160–175.
35. Williamson et al., "Employment Interview on Trial," p. 900.
36. Frank Schmidt and Ryan Zimmerman, "A Counter-intuitive Hypothesis about Employment Interview Validity and Some Supporting Evidence," *Journal of Applied Psychology* 89, no. 3 (2004), pp. 553–561. See also, "Structured Interviews: A Practical Guide," Office of Personnel Management, op. cit.
37. This validity discussion and these findings are based on McDaniel et al., "The Validity of Employment Interviews," pp. 607–610; the validities for situational, job-related, and psychological interviews were (.50), (.39), and (.29), respectively.
38. Murray Barrick et al., "Accuracy of Interviewer Judgments of Job Applicant Personality Traits," *Personnel Psychology* 53 (2000), pp. 925–951.
39. Susan Heathfield, "Applicant Answers to Interview Questions about Cultural Fit," *The Balance*, September 9, 2016, https://www.thebalance.com/interview-questions-cultural-fit-1918480, accessed February 5, 2018.
40. Christopher Hartwell and Michael A. Campion, "Getting on the Same Page: The Effect of Normative Feedback Interventions on Structured Interview Ratings," *Journal of Applied Psychology* 101, no. 6 (2016), pp. 757–778.
41. McDaniel et al., "The Validity of Employment Interviews," p. 608.
42. Anthony Dalessio and Todd Silverhart, "Combining Biodata Test and Interview Information: Predicting Decisions and Performance Criteria," *Personnel Psychology* 47 (1994), p. 313; and Nora Reilly et al., "Benchmarks Affect Perceptions of Prior Disability in a Structured Interview," *Journal of Business & Psychology* 20, no. 4 (Summer 2006), pp. 489–500.
43. Brian Swider, Murray Barrick, and T. Brad Harris, "Initial Impressions: What They Are, What They Are Not, and How They Influence Structured Interview Outcomes," *Journal of Applied Psychology* 101, no. 5 (2016), pp. 625–638.
44. S. W. Constantin, "An Investigation of Information Favorability in the Employment Interview," *Journal of Applied Psychology* 61 (1976), pp. 743–749. It should be noted that a number of the studies discussed in this chapter involve having interviewers evaluate interviews based on written transcripts (rather than face-to-face) and that a study suggests that this procedure may not be equivalent to having interviewers interview applicants directly. See Charles Gorman, William Glover, and Michael Doherty, "Can We Learn Anything about Interviewing Real People from 'Interviews' of Paper People? A Study of the External Validity Paradigm," *Organizational Behavior and Human Performance* 22, no. 2 (October 1978), pp. 165–192; and Frederick P. Morgeson, Matthew H. Reider, Michael A. Campion, and Rebecca A. Bull, "Review of Research on Age Discrimination in the Employment Interview," *Journal of Business Psychology* 22 (2008), pp. 223–232.
45. David Tucker and Patricia Rowe, "Relationship between Expectancy, Causal Attribution, and Final Hiring Decisions in the Employment Interview," *Journal of Applied Psychology* 64, no. 1 (February 1979), pp. 27–34. See also Robert Dipboye, Gail Fontenelle, and Kathleen Garner, "Effect of Previewing the Application on Interview Process and Outcomes," *Journal of Applied Psychology* 69, no. 1 (February 1984), pp. 118–128; Reilly et al., "Benchmarks Affect Perceptions of Prior Disability in a Structured Interview"; and Che-jen Su, Nicolas Lorgnier, Jin-hsing Yang, and Seung HeeHow Oh, "Does the Interview Change the Importance of Résumé Information in Acceptance Decisions? An Experimental Study in the Hotel Industry," *Service Business* 9, no. 4 (December 2015), pp. 711–732.
46. Anita Chaudhuri, "Beat the Clock: Applying for Job? A New Study Shows That Interviewers Will Make Up Their Minds About You Within a Minute," *The Guardian*, June 14, 2000, pp. 2–6. Further illustrating the problem here, another study concluded that it's more difficult to make a good impression on a pessimist than on an optimist: Leilani Goodmon et al., "Jumping to Negative Impressions Again: The Role of Pessimism, Information Valence, and Need for Cognitive Closure in Impression Formation," *North American Journal of Psychology* 19, no. 3 (December 2017), pp. 745–768.
47. John Langdale and Joseph Weitz, "Estimating the Influence of Job Information on Interviewer Agreement," *Journal of Applied Psychology* 57 (1973), pp. 23–27. See also, Brian Kleiner, "How to Hire Employees Effectively," *Management Research News* 22, no. 4 (1999), pp. 10–13. There have been roughly related studies more recently, although not focusing on the same design, predictors, and criteria: See, for example, Pia Ingold et al., "Why Do Situational Interviews

Predict Job Performance? The Role of Interviewees' Ability to Identify Criteria," *Journal of Business and Psychology* 30, no. 2 (June 2015), pp. 387–398.

48. Lauren Rivera, "Guess Who Doesn't Fit in at Work," *The New York Times*, May 31, 2015, p. SR 5.
49. R. E. Carlson, "Effect of Applicant Sample on Ratings of Valid Information in an Employment Setting," *Journal of Applied Psychology* 54 (1970), pp. 217–222. See also, Richard Posthuma, Frederick Morgeson, and Michael Campion, "Beyond Employment Interview Validity: A Comprehensive Narrative Review of Recent Research and Trends Over Time," *Personnel Psychology* 55 (2002), pp. 1–87.
50. R. E. Carlson, "Selection Interview Decisions: The Effect of Interviewer Experience, Relative Quota Situation, and Applicant Sample on Interview Decisions," *Personnel Psychology* 20 (1967), pp. 259–280. See also, Posthuma et al., "Beyond Employment Interview Validity."
51. See, for example, Scott T. Fleischmann, "The Messages of Body Language in Job Interviews," *Employee Relations* 18, no. 2 (Summer 1991), pp. 161–166; James Westphal and Ithai Stern, "Flattery Will Get You Everywhere (Especially If You're a Male Caucasian): How Ingratiation, Board Room Behavior, and a Demographic Minority Status Affect Additional Board Appointments at U.S. Companies," *Academy of Management Journal* 50, no. 2 (2007), pp. 267–288.
52. David Caldwell and Jerry Burger, "Personality Characteristics of Job Applicants and Success in Screening Interviews," *Personnel Psychology* 51 (1998), pp. 119–136. See also, Timothy DeGroot and Janaki Gooty, "Can Nonverbal Cues Be Used to Make Meaningful Personality Attributions in Employment Interviews?" *Journal of Business Psychology* 24 (2009), p. 179.
53. Amy Kristof-Brown et al., "Applicant Impression Management: Dispositional Influences and Consequences for Recruiter Perceptions of Fit and Similarity," *Journal of Management* 28, no. 1 (2002), pp. 27–46. See also Lynn McFarland et al., "Impression Management Use and Effectiveness across Assessment Methods," *Journal of Management* 29, no. 5 (2003), pp. 641–661.
54. Timothy DeGroot and Janaki Gooty, "Can Nonverbal Cues Be Used to Make Meaningful Personality Attributions in Employment Interviews?" Tattoos and/or piercings result in lower hireability ratings for applicants, particularly for customer facing jobs. Andrew Timming, Dennis Nickson, Daniel Re, and David Perett, "What Do You Think of My Ink? Assessing the Effects of Body Art on Employment Chances," *Human Resource Management* 56, no. 1 (January–February 2017), pp. 133–149.
55. Timothy Degroot and Janaki Gooty "Can Nonverbal Cues Be Used to Make Meaningful Personality Attributions in Employment Interviews?" *Journal of Business and Psychology* 24, no. 2 (June 2009), pp. 179–192.
56. Richard Posthuma, Frederick Morgeson, and Michael Campion, "Beyond Employment Interview Validity: A Comprehensive Narrative Review of Recent Research and Trends Over Time," *Personnel Psychology* 55 (2002), pp. 1–87.
57. C. K. Stevens and A. L. Kristof, "Making the Right Impression: A Field Study of Applicant Impression Management during Interviews," *Journal of Applied Psychology* 80 (1995), pp. 587– 606; Schultz and Schultz, *Psychology and Work Today*, p. 82. See also Jay Stuller, "Fatal Attraction," *Across the Board* 42, no. 6 (November/December 2005), pp. 18–23. See also Allen Huffcutt et al., "Understanding Applicant Behavior in Employment Interviews: A Theoretical Model of Interviewee Performance," *Human Resource Management Review* 20, no. 1 (2011), pp. 350–367.
58. Chad Higgins and Timothy Judge, "The Effect of Applicant Influence Tactics on Recruiter Perceptions of Fit and Hiring Recommendations: A Field Study," *Journal of Applied Psychology* 89, no. 4 (2004), pp. 622–632. Some researchers in this area question results like these. The problem is that much of the interviewing research uses students as raters and hypothetical jobs, so it's not clear that we can apply the findings to the real world. For example, see Frederick P. Morgeson, Matthew H. Reider, Michael A. Campion, and Rebecca A. Bull, "Review of Research on Age Discrimination in the Employment Interview," *Journal of Business Psychology* 22 (2008), pp. 223–232.
59. Nicolas Roulin, et al., "Interviewers' Perceptions of Impression Management in Employment Interviews," *Journal of Managerial Psychology* 29, no. 2 (2014), pp. 141–163.
60. Brian Swider et al., "Managing and Creating an Image in the Interview: The Role of Interviewee Initial Impressions," *Journal of Applied Psychology* 96, no. 6 (2011), pp. 1275–1288.
61. See, for example, Madeline Heilmann and Lois Saruwatari, "When Beauty Is Beastly: The Effects of Appearance and Sex on Evaluations of Job Applicants for Managerial and Nonmanagerial Jobs," *Organizational Behavior and Human Performance* 23 (June 1979), pp. 360–372; Cynthia Marlowe, Sandra Schneider, and Carnot Nelson, "Gender and Attractiveness Biases in Hiring Decisions: Are More Experienced Managers Less Biased?" *Journal of Applied Psychology* 81, no. 1 (1996), pp. 11–21; and Timothy DeGroot and Janaki Gooty, "Can Nonverbal Cues Be Used to Make Meaningful Personality Attributions in Employment Interviews?"
62. Marlowe et al., "Gender and Attractiveness Biases," p. 11. Another study came to similar results in China: Margaret Maurer-Fazio and Lei Lei, "As Rare as a Panda: How Facial Attractiveness, Gender, and Occupation Affect Interview Callbacks at Chinese Firms," *International Journal of Manpower* 36, no. 1 (2015), pp. 68–85.
63. Allen Huffcutt and Philip Roth, "Racial Group Differences in Employment Interview Evaluations," *Journal of Applied Psychology* 83, no. 2 (1998), pp. 179–189.
64. Julie M. McCarthy et al., "Are Highly Structured Job Interviews Resistant to Demographic Similarity Effects?" *Personnel Psychology* 63, no. 2 (Summer 2010), pp. 325–359.
65. This is based on John F. Wymer III and Deborah A. Sudbury, "Employment Discrimination: 'Testers'—Will Your Hiring Practices 'Pass'?" *Employee Relations Law Journal* 17, no. 4 (Spring 1992), pp. 623–633. Similar conclusions have been obtained, for example: Devah Pager et al., "Discrimination in a Low-Wage Labor Market: A Field Experiment," *American Sociological Review* 74, no. 5 (October 2009), pp. 777–799.
66. See for example, https://www.eeoc.gov/eeoc/meetings/6-22-11/bendick.cfm, accessed February 5, 2018.
67. Wymer and Sudbury, "Employment Discrimination," p. 629.
68. N. S. Miceli et al., "Potential Discrimination in Structured Employment Interviews," *Employee Responsibilities and Rights* 13, no. 1 (March 2001), pp. 15–38.
69. Juan Madera and Michele Hebl, "Discrimination against Facially Stigmatized Applicants in Interviews: An Eye Tracking and Face-to-Face Investigation," *Journal of Applied Psychology* 97, no. 2 (2012), pp. 317–330.
70. Ellyn Brecher et al., "The Structured Interview: Reducing Biases Toward Job Applicants with Physical Disabilities," *Employee Responsibilities and Rights Journal* 18 (2006), pp. 155–170.
71. Andrea Rodriguez and Fran Prezant, "Better Interviews for People with Disabilities," *Workforce*, www.workforce. com, accessed November 14, 2003. Remember that under the Americans with Disabilities Act, the interviewer must limit his or her questions to whether the applicant has any physical or mental impairment that may interfere with his or her ability to perform the job's essential tasks.
72. Based on Monowar Mahmood, "National Culture vs Corporate Culture: Employee Recruitment and Selection Practices of Multinationals in a Developing Country Context," *Journal of International Management Studies* 11, no.1 (Jan. 2011), p. 110. Published by International Academy of Business and Economics, from www. iabe. org/domains/iabe/journal.aspx?journalid.
73. Monowar Mahmood, "National Culture versus Corporate Culture: Employee Recruitment and Selection Practices of Multinationals in a Developing Country Context," *Journal of International Management Studies* 11, no. 1 (January 2011), p. 110. Published by International Academy of Business and Economics, www. iabe.org/domains/iabeX/journal.aspx?journalid=16, accessed July 19, 2013.
74. Thomas Dougherty, Daniel Turban, and John Callender, "Confirming First Impressions in the Employment Interview: A Field Study of Interviewer Behavior," *Journal of Applied Psychology* 79, no. 5 (1994), p. 663. See also, Nikoletta Bika, "9 Common Interviewer Mistakes That Put Off Candidates," https://resources.workable.com/tutorial/common-interviewer-mistakes, accessed February 5, 2018.
75. Posthuma, Morgeson, and Campion, "Beyond Employment Interview Validity," pp. 1–87.
76. Arthur Pell, "Nine Interviewing Pitfalls," *Managers Magazine*, January 1994, p. 20; quote from Alan M. Saks and Julie M. McCarthy, "Effects of Discriminatory Interview

Questions and Gender on Applicant Reactions," *Journal of Business and Psychology* 21, no. 2 (Winter 2006), p. 175.

77. This section is based on Elliot Pursell et al., "Structured Interviewing," *Personnel Journal* 59 (November 1980), pp. 907–912; and G. Latham et al., "The Situational Interview," *Journal of Applied Psychology* 65 (1980), pp. 422–427. See also Michael Campion, Elliott Pursell, and Barbara Brown, "Structured Interviewing: Raising the Psychometric Properties of the Employment Interview," *Personnel Psychology* 41 (1988), pp. 25–42; and Paul R. Bernthal, "Recruitment and Selection," www.ddiworld.com/DDIWorld/media/trend-research/recruitment-and-selection_ere_es_ddi. pdf?ext=. pdf, accessed October 10, 2011. See also K. G. Melchers et al., "Is More Structure Really Better? A Comparison of Frame-of-Reference Training and Descriptively Anchored Rating Scales to Improve Interviewers' Rating Quality," *Personnel Psychology* 64, no. 1 (2011), pp. 53–87.
78. "10 Social Media Marketing Interview Questions and Answers," https://www.upwork.com/i/interview-questions/social-media-marketing/, accessed February 1, 2018.
79. See Phillip Lowry, "The Structured Interview: An Alternative to the Assessment Center?" *Public Personnel Management* 23, no. 2 (Summer 1994), pp. 201–215. See also Todd Maurer and Jerry Solamon, "The Science and Practice of a Structured Employment Interview Coaching Program," *Personnel Psychology* 59, no. 2 (Summer 2006), pp. 433–456.
80. Pursell et al., "Structured Interviewing," p. 910.
81. From a speech by industrial psychologist Paul Green and contained in *BNA Bulletin to Management*, June 20, 1985, pp. 2–3. For additional practical guidance see, for example, www. state.gov/documents/organization/107843.pdf, accessed October 10, 2012.
82. Williamson et al., "Employment Interview on Trial," p. 901; Michael Campion, David Palmer, and James Campion, "A Review of Structure in the Selection Interview," *Personnel Psychology* 50 (1997), pp. 655–702. See also Maurer and Solamon, "The Science and Practice of a Structured Employment Interview," and, Posthuma, Morgeson, and Campion, "Beyond Employment Interview Validity," pp. 1–87.
83. Unless otherwise specified, the following are based on Williamson et al., "Employment Interview on Trial," pp. 901–902.
84. Campion, Palmer, and Campion, "A Review of Structure," p. 668.
85. Carlson, "Selection Interview Decisions."
86. https://www.glassdoor.com/blog/common-interview-questions/ accessed February 4, 2018.
87. Genevieve Douglas, "Pay Inquiry Bans Give some Employers Compliance Headaches," *Bloomberg BNA Bulletin to Management*, February 20, 2018.
88. Pamela Kaul, "Interviewing Is Your Business," *Association Management*, November 1992, p. 29. See also Rebecca Knight, "How to Conduct an Effective Job Interview," *Harvard Business Review*.
89. Edwin Walley, "Successful Interviewing Techniques," *The CPA Journal* 63 (September 1993), p. 70; and Randy Myers, "Interviewing Techniques: Tips from the Pros," *Journal of Accountancy* 202, no. 2 (August 2006), pp. 53–55.
90. Catherine Middendorf and Therese Macan, "Note Taking in the Employment Interview: Effects on Recall and Judgment," *Journal of Applied Psychology* 87, no. 2 (2002), pp. 293–303.
91. Kristen Weirick, "The Perfect Interview," *HR Magazine*, April 1, 2008, p. 85.
92. Stephen Gilliland et al., "Improving Applicants' Reactions to Rejection Letters: An Application of Fairness Theory," *Personnel Psychology* 54 (2001), pp. 669–703.
93. https://www.shrm.org/resourcesandtools/tools-and-samples/hr-forms/pages/interview_rejectionletter-positionfilled.aspx, accessed February 5, 2018.
94. See, for example, Gary Dessler, *Winning Commitment* (New York: McGraw-Hill, 1993).
95. "Toyota Looking for 1,500 Outstanding Mississippians from All Backgrounds," www.Mississippi.org/press-room/Toyota-looking-for-1500, accessed February 17, 2014.
96. See, for example, https://www.practiceaptitudetests.com/top-employer-profiles/toyota-assessments/, https://www.jobtestprep.com/toyota-test-prep, and https://www.graduatesfirst.com/portfolio-items/toyota/, accessed February 4, 2018.
97. "Toyota Hiring Process," www. indeed.com/forum/cmp/Toyota/Toyota-Hiring-Process/t31886, accessed August 22, 2014; https://www.indeed.com/forum/cmp/Toyota/Toyota-Hiring-Process/t31886, accessed February 4, 2018.
98. Bock, *Work Rules!* pp. 87–127.
99. www.Shrm.org/template-tools/how-to-guides, accessed March 3, 2012.
100. See, for example, http://jobsearchtech.about.com/od/jobofferletters/a/jobofferletter.htm, https://templates.office.com/en-us/Search/results?query=letter+of+offer, https://www.rocketlawyer.com/document/employment-contract.rl#/, and https://www.pandadoc.com/free-employment-contract-template/, all accessed February 4, 2018.
101. Tim Barker, "Corporate Espionage Takes Center Stage with Boeing Revelation," *Knight Ridder/Tribune Business News*, June 15, 2003.
102. Ibid.
103. See particularly the classic but still excellent discussion of job hunting and interviewing in Richard Payne, *How to Get a Better Job Quickly* (New York: New American Library, 1979). For a sampling of other advice, see, for example, Alison Doyle, "Job Interview Do's and Don'ts," *The Balance*, https://www. thebalance.com/job-interview-do-s-and-don-ts-2061313, and Bernard Marr, "Job Interview: The All Time Classic Do's And Don'ts," https://www.linkedin.com/pulse/job-interview-all-time-classic-dos-donts-bernard-marr, both accessed February 5, 2018.
104. Tony Lee, "10 Classic Interview Questions to Ask . . . And the Responses You Want to Hear," *HR Magazine*, December 2017/January 2018, pp. 57–61.
105. Celia Moore, Sun Young Lee, Kawon Kim, and Daniel Cable, "The Advantage of Being Oneself: The Role of Applicant Self-Verification in Organizational Hiring Decisions," *Journal of Applied Psychology* 102, no. 11 (2017), pp. 1493–1513.

Appendix 1 for Chapter 7

Structured Interview Guide

STEP 1—Create a Structured Interview Guide

Instructions:
First, here in step 1, create a structured interview guide like this one (including a competency definition, a lead question, and benchmark examples and answers, for instance) ***for each of the job's required competencies***:

Competency: Interpersonal Skills

Definition:
Shows understanding, courtesy, tact, empathy, concern; develops and maintains relationships; may deal with people who are difficult, hostile, distressed; relates well to people from varied backgrounds and situations; is sensitive to individual differences.

Lead Questions:
Describe a situation in which you had to deal with people who were upset about a problem. What specific actions did you take? What was the outcome or result?

Benchmark Level	Level Definition	Level Examples
5	Establishes and maintains ongoing working relationships with management, other employees, internal or external stakeholders, or customers. Remains courteous when discussing information or eliciting highly sensitive or controversial information from people who are reluctant to give it. Effectively handles situations involving a high degree of tension or discomfort involving people who are demonstrating a high degree of hostility or distress.	Presents controversial findings tactfully to irate organization senior management officials regarding shortcomings of a newly installed computer system, software programs, and associated equipment.
4		Mediates disputes concerning system design/architecture, the nature and capacity of data management systems, system resources allocations, or other equally controversial/sensitive matters.
3	Cooperates and works well with management, other employees, or customers, on short-term assignments. Remains courteous when discussing information or eliciting moderately sensitive or controversial information from people who are hesitant to give it. Effectively handles situations involving a moderate degree of tension or discomfort involving people who are demonstrating a moderate degree of hostility or distress.	Courteously and tactfully delivers effective instruction to frustrated customers. Provides technical advice to customers and the public on various types of IT such as communication or security systems, data management procedures or analysis.
2		Familiarizes new employees with administrative procedures and office systems.
1	Cooperates and works well with management, other employees, or customers during brief interactions. Remains courteous when discussing information or eliciting non-sensitive or non-controversial information from people who are willing to give it. Effectively handles situations involving little or no tension, discomfort, hostility, or distress.	Responds courteously to customers' general inquiries. Greets and assists visitors attending a meeting within own organization.

FIGURE 7A-1 **Structured Interview Guide**

Source: From Conducting Effective Structured Interviews Resource Guide for Hiring Managers and Supervisors, 2005, United States Department of State Bureau of Human Resources.

STEP 2—INDIVIDUAL EVALUATION FORM

Instructions:
Next, in step 2, create a form for evaluating each job candidate on each of the job's competencies:

Candidate to be assessed: ______________________________

Date of Interview: ______________________________

Competency: Problem Solving

Definition:
Identifies problems; determines accuracy and relevance of information; uses sound judgment to generate and evaluate alternatives, and to make the recommendations.

Question:
Describe a situation in which you identified a problem and evaluated the alternatives to make a recommendation or decision. What was the problem and who was affected?

Probes:
How did you generate and evaluate your alternatives? What was the outcome?

Describe specific behaviors observed: (Use back of sheet, if necessary)

1-Low	2	3-Average	4	5-Outstanding
Uses logic to identify alternatives to solve routine problems. Reacts to and solves problems by gathering and applying information from standard materials or sources that provide a limited number of alternatives.		Uses logic to identify alternatives to solve moderately difficult problems. Identifies and solves problems by gathering and applying information from a variety of materials or sources that provide several alternatives.		Uses logic to identify alternatives to solve complex or sensitive problems. Anticipates problems and identifies and evaluates potential sources of information and generates alternatives to solve problems where standards do not exist.

Final Evaluation:	Printed Name:	Signature:

FIGURE 7A-1 *Continued*

STEP 3—PANEL CONSENSUS EVALUATION FORM

Instructions:
Finally, in step 3, create a panel consensus evaluation form like this one, which the members of the panel who interviewed the candidate will use to evaluate his or her interview performance.

Candidate: ______________________________

Date: ______________________________

Panel Consensus Evaluation Form

Instructions:
Translate each individual evaluation for each competency onto this form. If all of the individual competency evaluations are within one rating scale point, enter the average of the evaluations in the column labeled Group Evaluation. If more than one point separates any two raters, a consensus discussion must occur with each party justifying his/her evaluation. The lead interviewer or his/her designee should take notes on the consensus discussion in the space provided. Any changes in evaluation should be initialed and a final evaluation entered for each competency.

Competency	Final Individual Evaluations			Group Evaluation
	(1)	(2)	(3)	
Interpersonal Skills				
Self-Management				
Reasoning				
Decision Making				
Problem Solving				
Oral Communication				
Total Score				

Consensus Discussion Notes:

Signature Panel Member 1: ______________________________

Signature Panel Member 2: ______________________________

Signature Panel Member 3: ______________________________

FIGURE 7A-1 *Continued*

Appendix 2 for Chapter 7

Interview Guide for Interviewees

Before managers move into positions where they have to interview others, they usually must navigate some interviews themselves. It's therefore useful to apply some of what we discussed in this chapter to navigating one's own interviews.

Beyond trying to determine how you would perform the technical parts of the job, interviewers will try to discover what you are like as a person. In other words, how you get along with other people and your desire to work. They will look here at how you behave. For example, they will note whether you respond concisely, cooperate fully in answering questions, state personal opinions when relevant, and keep to the subject at hand; these are very important elements in influencing the interviewer's decision.

Getting an Extra Edge

There are six things to do to get an extra edge in the interview.[103]

1. ***Preparation is essential.*** Before the interview, learn all you can about the employer, the job, and the people doing the recruiting. On the Web, using social media, or looking through business periodicals, find out what is happening in the employer's field. Try to unearth the employer's problems. Be ready to explain why you think you would be able to solve such problems, citing some of your *specific accomplishments* to make your case.
2. ***Uncover the interviewer's real needs.*** Spend as little time as possible briefly answering your interviewer's first questions and as much time as possible getting him or her to describe his or her needs. Determine what the person is expecting to accomplish, and the type of person he or she feels is needed. Use open-ended questions such as, "Could you tell me more about that?"
3. ***Relate yourself to the interviewer's needs.*** Once you know the type of person your interviewer is looking for and the sorts of problems he or she wants solved, you are in a good position to describe your own accomplishments *in terms of the interviewer's needs.* Start by saying something like, "One of the problem areas you've said is important to you is similar to a problem I once faced." Then state the problem, describe your solution, and reveal the results.
4. ***Think before answering.*** Answering a question should be a three-step process: Pause—Think—Speak. *Pause* to make sure you understand what the interviewer is driving at, *think* about how to structure your answer, and then *speak.* In your answer, try to emphasize how hiring you will help the interviewer solve his or her problem.
5. ***Remember that appearance and enthusiasm are important.*** Appropriate clothing, good grooming, a firm handshake, and energy are important. Maintain eye contact. In addition, speak with enthusiasm, nod agreement, and remember to take a moment to frame your answer (pause, think, speak) so that you sound articulate and fluent. Remember that many interviewers seek "chemistry" in terms of similarity of experiences when they're interviewing.
6. ***Make a good first impression.*** Remember that in most cases interviewers make up their minds about the applicant early in the interview. A good first impression may turn to bad during the interview, but it's unlikely. Bad first impressions are almost impossible to overcome. Experts suggest paying attention to the following key interviewing considerations:
   - Appropriate clothing
   - Good grooming
   - A firm handshake
   - The appearance of controlled energy
   - Pertinent humor and readiness to smile
   - A genuine interest in the employer's operation and alert attention when the interviewer speaks
   - Pride in past performance
   - An understanding of the employer's needs and a desire to serve them

Tackling the "Standard" Questions

Be vigilant in answering familiar, standard questions such as "tell me about yourself."[104] For example, know that asking "tell me about yourself" helps recruiters size up your poise and communication skills. A good answer to "What are your greatest strengths?" should focus on the strengths related to the job you're interviewing for. Good answers to "What are your weaknesses?" include what you're doing to improve yourself. Interviewees who can't answer "What can you tell me about our company and industry?" may lack conscientiousness. Answering "What you like most and least about your most recent job?" should touch on liking the same values, activities, and culture that the job at hand involves. And someone who says "no" when asked "Do you have any questions?" may have thought too little about the job.

Should You Be Forthright?

Imagine a job candidate who by experience and education is highly qualified for a job, but who lacks some important trait(s): for example, he or she doesn't dress stylishly for an interview with an upscale department store. How forthright should you be if asked why you didn't dress up more?

Based on a recent study, otherwise top-notch candidates should be forthright.[105] This study found that a strong drive to "self-verify"—to "present oneself accurately so that others understand you as you understand yourself"—may help differentiate you from the other top candidates. The researchers measured self-verification with items such as "I like to be myself rather than trying to act like someone I'm not."

So, if you like being authentic and presenting yourself accurately to others, do so, as long as for the job at hand you're an otherwise top-notch candidate. (Doing this backfired for inferior candidates.)

Jonathan Weiss/Shutterstock

Training and Developing Employees

LEARNING OBJECTIVES

When you finish studying this chapter, you should be able to:

8-1 **Summarize** the purpose and process of employee orientation.

8-2 **Give** an example of how to design onboarding to improve employee engagement.

8-3 **List and briefly explain** each of the steps in the training process.

8-4 **Explain** how to use five training techniques.

8-5 **List and briefly discuss** four management development methods.

8-6 **List and briefly discuss** the importance of the steps in leading organizational change.

8-7 **Explain** why a controlled study may be superior for evaluating the training program's effects.

For a century AT&T was America's "phone company," but it has changed dramatically in the past few years. In 2000, its wireless network data traffic was negligible.[1] The part of its business depending on software was similarly negligible, but by 2020 it will have risen to 75%. Like competitors such as Comcast, AT&T's strategy is to drive the company toward a new digital future, one in which telecommunications, media, and entertainment converge, and customers can get the information, access, and entertainment they need, anywhere, on whatever digital device they choose to use. That's exciting for AT&T's customers and shareholders. But what do you do with the 150,000 or so AT&T employees who were hired by a phone company years ago to do very different, nondigital, nonsoftware jobs? We'll see what AT&T did.

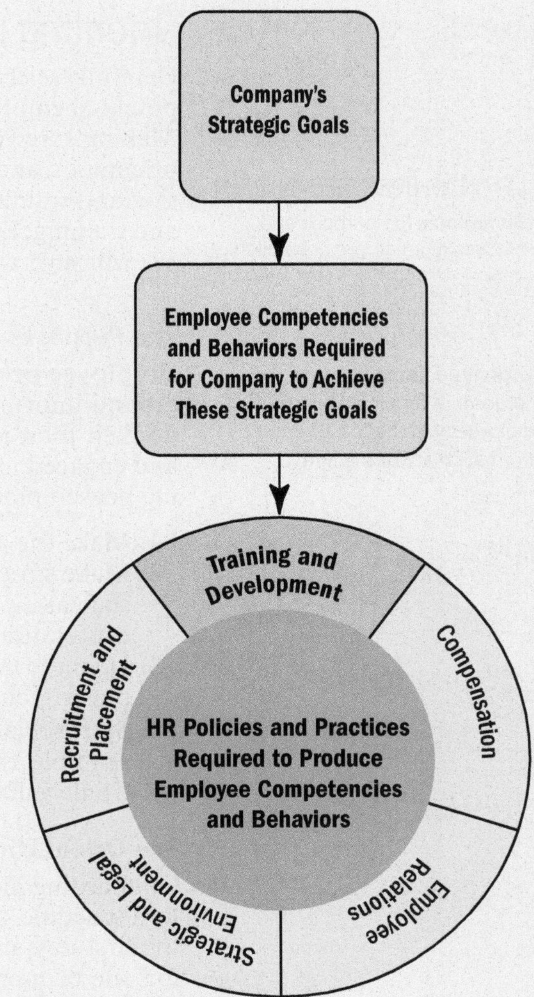

WHERE ARE WE NOW . . .

Chapters 6 and 7 focused on the methods managers use to interview and select employees. Once employees are on board, the employer must train them. The purpose of this chapter is to increase your effectiveness in training employees. The main topics we'll cover include **Orienting and Onboarding New Employees**, **Designing Onboarding to Improve Employee Engagement**, **The Training Process**, **Implementing Training Programs**, **Management Development Methods**, **Leading Organizational Change**, and **Evaluating the Training Effort**. Then, in Chapter 9, we'll turn to appraising employees.

Orienting and Onboarding New Employees

LEARNING OBJECTIVE 8-1
Summarize the purpose and process of employee orientation.

Carefully selecting employees doesn't guarantee they'll perform effectively. Even high-potential employees can't do their jobs if they don't know what to do or how to do it. Making sure your employees do know what to do and how to do it is the purpose of orientation and training. The human resources department usually designs the orientation and training programs, but the supervisor does most of the day-to-day orienting and training. Every manager therefore should know how to orient and train employees. We will start with orientation.

The Purposes of Employee Orientation/Onboarding

employee orientation
A procedure for providing new employees with basic background information about the firm.

Employee orientation (or *onboarding*) provides new employees with the basic background information (such as computer passwords and company rules) they need to do their jobs; ideally it should also help them start becoming emotionally attached to and engaged in the firm.[2] The manager wants to accomplish four things when orienting new employees:

1. Make the new employee feel welcome and at home and part of the team.
2. Make sure the new employee has the basic information to function effectively, such as e-mail access, personnel policies and benefits, and work behavior expectations.
3. Help the new employee understand the organization in a broad sense (its past, present, culture, and strategies and vision of the future).
4. Start socializing the person into the firm's culture and ways of doing things.[3] For example, the Mayo Clinic's "heritage and culture" program emphasizes Mayo Clinic values such as teamwork, integrity, customer service, and mutual respect.[4]

The Orientation Process

Onboarding ideally begins before the person's first day, with a welcome note, orientation schedule, and list of documents (such as tax documents) needed the first day. On the first day, make sure colleagues know the new employee is starting, and arrange for one or more of them to take the person to lunch. On subsequent days, the new employee should meet colleagues in other departments. After about two weeks, speak with the employee to identify any concerns.[5]

The length of the onboarding program depends on what you cover. Some take several hours. The human resource specialist (or, in smaller firms, the office manager) performs the first part of the orientation by explaining basic matters like working hours and benefits. Then the supervisor continues by explaining the department's organization, introducing the person to his or her new colleagues, familiarizing him or her with the workplace, and reducing first-day jitters. At a minimum, the orientation should provide information on matters such as employee benefits, personnel policies, safety measures and regulations, and a facilities tour; making the new employee feel special and proud about working for the company is advisable;[6] new employees should receive (and sign for) print or Internet-based employee handbooks covering such matters. You'll find a variety of orientation checklists online.[7]

At the other extreme, L'Oréal's onboarding program extends about 2 years. It includes roundtable discussions, meetings with key insiders, on-the-job learning, individual mentoring, and experiences such as site visits.[8]

Supervisors should be vigilant. Follow up on and encourage new employees to engage in activities (such as taking breaks with colleagues) that will enable them to "learn the ropes." Especially for new employees with disabilities, integration and socialization are highly influenced by coworkers' and supervisors' behavior.[9]

Those *being* oriented should show they're involved. Two things seem to show managers that the people they're orienting are engaged. First, show you're trying to master and perform the tasks at hand (such as learning about the new job and company). Second, show you're trying to assimilate socially, for instance by interacting with new colleagues.[10]

Employers should onboard new executives too. In one survey "poor grasp of how the organization works" was a problem for 69% of new senior executives. This onboarding should include the firm's operational plans and key business areas, key team members' career histories, key external stakeholders, and briefings on the firm's culture and how it "gets things done."[11]

THE EMPLOYEE HANDBOOK Employers should assume that their employee handbook's contents are legally binding commitments. Even apparently sensible handbook policies (such as "the company will not retaliate against employees who raise concerns about important issues in the workplace") can backfire without proper disclaimers. The handbook should include a disclaimer stating "nothing in this handbook should be taken as creating a binding contract between employer and employees, and all employment is on an at will basis."[12] Say that statements of company policies, benefits, and regulations do not constitute the terms and conditions of an employment contract, either expressed or implied. Do not insert statements such as "No employee will be fired without just cause" or statements that imply or state that employees have tenure. The firm's handbook policies may then evolve, as the prevailing political climate—for instance in terms of EEOC and union–management relations guidelines—change.[13]

ORIENTATION TECHNOLOGY Employers use technology to support orientation. For example, at the University of Cincinnati, new employees spend about 45 minutes online learning about their new employer's mission, organization, and policies and procedures. ION Geophysical uses an online onboarding portal solution called RedCarpet. It includes a streaming video welcome message, and photos and profiles of new colleagues.[14] With Workday's iPhone app, users can search their company's directory for names, images, and contact information; call or e-mail coworkers directly; and view physical addresses on Google Maps.[15] Some employers place scannable QR codes along the orientation tour's stops, to provide information about each department and its role.[16] Employers use team activities and gamification (awarding points for completing parts of the program, for instance) to energize their onboarding programs.[17]

LEARNING OBJECTIVE 8-2

Give an example of how to design onboarding to improve employee engagement.

Employee Engagement Guide for Managers: Onboarding at Toyota

In many firms today, orientation goes well beyond providing basic information about things like work hours.[18] Onboarding at Toyota Motor Manufacturing USA illustrates this. While it does cover routine topics such as company benefits, its main aim is to engage Toyota's new employees in the firm's ideology of quality, teamwork, personal development, open communication, and mutual respect.[19] The initial program takes about 4 days:[20]

Day 1: The first day begins early and includes an overview of the program, a welcome to the company, and a discussion of the firm's organizational structure and human resource department by the firm's human resources vice president. He or she devotes about an hour and a half to discussing Toyota history and culture, and about 2 hours to employee benefits. Managers then spend several hours discussing Toyota's commitment to quality and teamwork.

Day 2: A typical second day focuses first on the importance of mutual respect, teamwork, and open communication at Toyota. The rest of the day covers topics such as safety, environmental affairs, and the Toyota production system.

Day 3: Given the importance of working in teams at Toyota, this day begins with 2½ to 3 hours devoted to communication training, such as "making requests and giving feedback." The rest of the day covers matters such as

Toyota's problem-solving methods, quality assurance, hazard communications, and safety.

Day 4: Topics today include teamwork training and the Toyota suggestion system. This session also covers what work teams are responsible for and how to work together as a team. The afternoon session covers fire prevention and fire extinguisher training. By the end of day 4, new employees should be well on their way to being engaged in Toyota's ideology, in particular its mission of quality and its values of teamwork, continuous improvement, and problem solving.[21]

The bottom line is that there's more to orienting employees than introducing them to new coworkers. Even without a program like Toyota's, use the onboarding opportunity to start instilling in the new employee the company values and traditions in which you expect the person to become engaged.

LEARNING OBJECTIVE 8-3
List and briefly explain each of the steps in the training process.

Overview of the Training Process

training
The process of teaching new or current employees the basic skills they need to perform their jobs.

Directly after orientation, training should begin. **Training** means giving new or current employees the skills that they need to perform their jobs, such as showing new salespeople how to sell your product. Training might involve having the current jobholder explain the job to the new hire, or multiweek classroom or Internet classes. In one recent year, employers spent about $1,300 per employee on training.[22]

Training is important.[23] If even high-potential employees don't know what to do and how to do it, they will improvise or do nothing useful at all. Furthermore, high achievers often begin looking for new positions due to dissatisfaction with inadequate training.[24] Employers also know that training fosters engagement. For example, Coca-Cola UK uses employee development plans, training, and leadership development to attract and retain the best employees and inspire their engagement.[25]

KNOW YOUR EMPLOYMENT LAW

Training and the Law

Managers should understand training's legal implications. With respect to *discrimination*, Title VII of the Civil Rights Act of 1964 and related legislation requires that the employer avoid discriminatory actions in all aspects of its human resource management process, and that applies to selecting which employees to train. Employers face much the same consequences for discriminating against protected individuals when selecting candidates for training as they would in selecting candidates for jobs or for promotion.

negligent training
A situation where an employer fails to train adequately, and the employee subsequently harms a third party.

Inadequate training can also expose the employer to liability for **negligent training.** As one expert puts it, "It's clear from the case law that where an employer fails to train adequately and an employee subsequently does harm to third parties, the court will find the employer liable." Among other things, the employer should confirm the applicant/employee's claims of skill and experience, provide adequate training (particularly where employees work with dangerous equipment), and evaluate the training to ensure that it is actually reducing risks.[26] ■

Aligning Strategy and Training

The employer's strategic plans should guide its long-range training goals.[27] In essence, the task is to identify the employee behaviors the firm will need in order to execute its strategy, and then to deduce what skills and knowledge employees will need. Then, put in place training goals and programs to instill these competencies. For example, with the health-care landscape changing, the Walgreens chain had to reformulate its strategy. It broadened its offerings, and today is the second-largest dispenser of flu shots in the United States. Its in-store health clinics provide medical care. It purchased drugstore.com.

The strategic changes affected the skills that Walgreens employees required, and therefore its training and other staffing policies. For example, Walgreens established Walgreens University. It offers more than 400 programs Walgreens employees can take to build their skills (and even get college credit in pharmacy-related topics). For example, some programs develop assistant store manager skills, and Walgreens in-store health clinic nurse practitioners can take courses to expand their medical care expertise. Thus, Walgreens reformulated its training (and other) HR policies to produce the employee skills the company needed to support its new strategy.[28] The accompanying Strategic Context feature provides another example.

IMPROVING PERFORMANCE: *THE STRATEGIC CONTEXT*

Supporting AT&T's Strategy for a Digital Future

AT&T's strategy is to drive the company toward a new digital future ("from cables to the cloud," to paraphrase a top manager). But what do you do with the employees hired years ago to do very different jobs?[29]

AT&T embarked on a massive retraining program, called Workforce 2020. It had three main pillars: *Skill needs identification, training and development,* and *evaluation.*

First, AT&T's managers *identified the skills* its employees would need for its new digital future, along with the current skills gaps, and what it called "future role profiles." These individual profiles itemized the skills the company and therefore each of its employees would need.

Second, AT&T helped employees identify and obtain the required *training and development*. For example, it created an online employee career platform. This contains tools such as for assessing one's aptitudes against the jobs AT&T would need. It also contains online courses, ultra-short "nanodegree" training programs (on coding, for instance), and access to special online graduate and undergraduate degree programs.

Third, AT&T *evaluates the effectiveness* of its Workforce 2020 program in terms of *Activity, Hydraulics, Business Outcomes,* and *Sentiment*. *Activity* means measuring things such as skills gaps. *Hydraulics* means people actually moving into new roles throughout AT&T. *Business outcomes* means tangible organizational improvements, for instance in efficiency. And, *sentiment* refers to measuring attitudes such as employees' inclination to recommend AT&T as a place to work.

AT&T's Worforce 2020 program enabled its current employees to develop the skills AT&T's digital convergence strategy required. Over 140,000 employees were recently pursuing the learning they need to fill AT&T's new jobs and roles.

MyLab Management Talk About It 1

If your professor has assigned this, go to the Assignments section of **www.pearson.com/mylab/management** to complete this discussion question. What other human resource management steps should AT&T take in order to help it achieve its digital futures strategy?

The ADDIE Five-Step Training Process

The employer should use a rational training process. The gold standard here is still the basic analysis-design-develop-implement-evaluate (ADDIE) training process model that training experts have used for years.[30] As an example, one training vendor describes its training process as follows:[31]

- *Analyze* the training need.
- *Design* the overall training program.
- *Develop* the course (actually assembling/creating the training materials).
- *Implement* training, by actually training the targeted employee group using methods such as on-the-job or online training.
- *Evaluate* the course's effectiveness.

We'll look at each step next.

Analyzing the Training Needs

The training needs analysis may address the employer's *strategic/longer-term* training needs and/or its *current* training needs.

STRATEGIC TRAINING NEEDS ANALYSIS Strategic goals (perhaps to enter new lines of business or to expand abroad) often mean the firm will have to fill new jobs. *Strategic training needs analysis* identifies the training employees will need to fill these future jobs. For example, when Wisconsin-based Signicast Corp. decided to build a new high-tech plant, its top managers knew the plant's employees would need new skills to run the computerized machines. They worked closely with their HR team to formulate hiring and training programs to ensure the firm would have the people required to populate the new plant.

CURRENT EMLPLOYEES' TRAINING NEEDS ANALYSIS Most training efforts aim to improve current performance—specifically training new employees, and those whose performance is deficient.

How you analyze current training needs depends on whether you're training new or current employees. The main task for *new* employees is to determine what the job entails and to break it down into subtasks, each of which you then teach to the new employee.

Analyzing *current* employees' training needs is more complex, because you must also ascertain whether training is the solution. For example, performance may be down due to poor motivation. Managers use *task analysis* to identify new employees' training needs, and *performance analysis* to identify current employees' training needs.

***NEW* EMPLOYEES: TASK ANALYSIS FOR ANALYZING TRAINING NEEDS** Particularly with lower-level workers, it's customary to hire inexperienced personnel and train them. The aim here is to give these new employees the skills and knowledge they need to do the job. **Task analysis** is a detailed study of the job to determine what specific skills (like reading spreadsheets) the job requires. Here job descriptions and job specifications are essential. They list the job's specific duties and skills, which are the basic reference points in determining the training required. Managers also uncover training needs by reviewing performance standards, performing the job, and questioning current jobholders and supervisors.[32]

task analysis
A detailed study of a job to identify the specific skills required.

Some managers supplement the job description and specification with a *task analysis record form*. This form (see Table 8-1) consolidates information regarding required tasks and skills. As it illustrates, the form contains six columns of information, such as "Skills or knowledge required."

***CURRENT* EMPLOYEES: PERFORMANCE ANALYSIS OF TRAINING NEEDS** For underperforming current employees, you can't assume that training is the solution. In other words, is it lack of training, or something else? **Performance analysis** is the process of verifying that there is a performance deficiency and determining whether the employer should correct such deficiencies through training or some other means (like transferring the employee).

performance analysis
Verifying that there is a performance deficiency and determining whether that deficiency should be corrected through training or through some other means (such as transferring the employee).

Performance analysis begins with comparing the person's actual performance to what it should be. Doing so helps to confirm that there is a performance deficiency, and (hopefully) helps the manager to identify its cause. Examples of performance deficiencies might be:

I expect each salesperson to make 10 new contracts per week, but John averages only six.

Other plants our size average no more than two serious accidents per month; we're averaging five.

TABLE 8-1 Sample Task Analysis Record Form

	Task List	When and How Often Performed	Quantity and Quality of Performance	Conditions Under Which Performed	Skills or Knowledge Required	Where Best Learned
1.	Operate paper cutter	4 times per day		Noisy pressroom: distractions		
1.1	Start motor	4 times per day				On the job
1.2	Set cutting distance		±tolerance of 0.007 in.		Read gauge	On the job
1.3	Place paper on cutting table		Must be completely even to prevent uneven cut		Lift paper correctly	On the job
1.4	Push paper up to cutter				Must be even	On the job
1.5	Grasp safety release with left hand		100% of time, for safety		Essential for safety	On the job but practice first with no distractions
1.6	Grasp cutter release with right hand				Must keep both hands on releases	On the job but practice first with no distractions
1.7	Simultaneously pull safety release with left hand and cutter release with right hand				Must keep both hands on releases	On the job but practice first with no distractions
1.8	Wait for cutter to retract		100% of time, for safety		Must keep both hands on releases	On the job but practice first with no distractions
1.9	Retract paper				Wait until cutter retracts	On the job but practice first with no distractions
1.10	Shut off		100% of time, for safety			On the job but practice first with no distractions
2.	Operate printing press					
2.1	Start motor					

Note: Task analysis record form showing some of the tasks and subtasks performed by a printing press operator.

Ways to identify how a current employee is doing include

- Performance appraisals
- Job-related performance data (including productivity, absenteeism and tardiness, grievances, waste, late deliveries, product quality, repairs, and customer complaints)
- Observations by supervisors or other specialists
- Interviews with the employee or his or her supervisor
- Tests of things like job knowledge, skills, and attendance
- Attitude surveys
- Individual employee daily diaries
- Assessment center results
- Special performance gap analytical software, such as from Saba Software, Inc.

CAN'T DO/WON'T DO Uncovering *why* performance is down is the heart of performance analysis. The aim here is to distinguish between can't-do and won't-do problems. First, determine whether it is a *can't-do* problem and, if so, its specific causes.

For example: The employees don't know what to do or what your standards are; there are obstacles such as lack of tools or supplies; there are no job aids (such as color-coded wires that show assemblers which wire goes where); you've hired people who haven't the required skills; or training is inadequate.

Or, it might be a *won't-do* problem. Here employees could do a good job if they wanted to. One expert says, "Perhaps the biggest trap that trainers fall into is [developing] training for problems that training just won't fix."[33] For instance, the better solution might be to change the incentives.

competency model
A graphic model that consolidates, usually in one diagram, a precise overview of the competencies (the knowledge, skills, and behaviors) someone would need to do a job well.

COMPETENCY PROFILES AND MODELS IN TRAINING AND DEVELOPMENT Employers often focus on building work-related competencies or skills.[34] The **competency model** consolidates, usually in one diagram, a precise overview of the competencies someone would need to do the job well. Figure 4-10 (on page 122) was one example. For example, the Association for Talent Development (ATD) built a competencies model for the job of training and development professional. It includes 10 core trainer competencies, including *being able to achieve performance improvement, instructional design*, and *training delivery*. As one competency example, the model describes *instructional design* as "designing, creating, and developing formal learning solutions to meet organizational needs; analyzing and selecting the most appropriate strategy, methodologies, and technologies to maximize the learning experience and impact."[35] Training a trainer would thus require, for instance, making sure he or she could, once training is complete, exhibit these skills and knowledge (competencies).[36]

Competencies-oriented training is similar to other training. Trainees often learn through a mix of real-world exercises, teamwork, classes, and online resources, under a learning coach; the aim is to show mastery of particular competencies.[37] This often involves starting with a list of competencies to be learned, criteria for assessing competencies mastery, and examples of the competencies (such as using a spreadsheet). Students then complete their projects and assessors evaluate their competencies.

Designing the Training Program

Armed with the needs analysis results, the manager next designs the training program. *Design* means planning the overall training program including training objectives, delivery methods, and program evaluation. Substeps include setting performance objectives, creating a detailed training outline (all training program steps from start to finish), choosing a program delivery method (such as lectures or Web), and verifying the overall program design with management.

Most employers can build training programs based on existing online and offline content offered by training content providers.

Tinpixels/Getty Images

The design should include summaries of how you plan to set a training environment that motivates your trainees both to learn and to transfer what they learn to the job. It is also here that the manager reviews possible training program content (including workbooks, exercises, and activities), and estimates a training program budget.[38] If the program will use technology, the manager should include a review of the technology as part of the analysis.[39] We'll look more closely next at several specific design issues.

SETTING LEARNING OBJECTIVES[40] At the outset, the trainer should clearly define the program's desired learning outcomes.[41] "Clients" will usually phrase their training requests in broad terms, such as "we need sales training." It's the trainer's job to unearth the reasons behind the request, so as to formulate tangible program outcomes (such as "improved product knowledge").

Training, development, learning, or (more generally) *instructional objectives* should specify in measurable terms what the trainee should be able to do after successfully completing the training program.[42] For example:

> *The technical service representative will be able to adjust the color guidelines on this HP Officejet All-in-One printer copier within 10 minutes according to the device's specifications.*

The learning objectives should first address any performance deficiencies that you identified. Thus, if the sales team's sales are 40% too low, the objectives should focus on ensuring that the team members get the product knowledge they need to boost sales. But at the same time, the learning objectives must be practical, given the constraints.

One constraint is financial. The employer will generally want to see and approve a *training budget* for the program. Typical costs include the development costs (of having, say, a human resource specialist working on the program for a week or two), the direct and indirect (overhead) costs of the trainers' time, participant compensation (for the time they're actually being trained), and the cost of evaluating the program. There are algorithms for estimating training program costs, for instance, in terms of labor hours and direct costs.[43] The question, of course, isn't just "Can we afford this program?" but "Does it pay to spend this much, given the benefits we'll receive—will it improve performance, and if so by how much?" Therefore, prepare to defend the program on a benefits-versus-costs basis.

There are also other constraints to consider. For example, time constraints may require reducing three or four desirable learning objectives to one or two.

CREATING A MOTIVATIONAL LEARNING ENVIRONMENT Municipalities running programs for traffic violators know there's often no better way to get someone's attention than to present a terrifying video accident. They know the best training starts not with a lecture but by making the material meaningful.

The same is true at work. Learning requires both ability and motivation, and the training program's design should accommodate both. In terms of *ability*, the learner–trainee needs (among other things) the required reading, writing, and mathematics skills. Trainees are rarely homogeneous, for instance, in terms of intellectual capacity. In setting the learning environment, the manager therefore should address several trainee-ability issues. For example, how will our program accommodate differences in trainee abilities? Do we need to provide remedial training?

Second, the learner must also be motivated. No manager should waste his or her time showing a disinterested employee how to do something (even if he or she has the requisite ability).

Many books exist on how to motivate employees, but several specific observations are pertinent here.[44] The training program's effects will be diminished if trainees return to their jobs to snide comments such as, "I hope you liked your little vacation" from colleagues. Therefore, the low-hanging fruit in motivating trainees is to make sure the trainee's peers and supervisor support the training effort. Ideally, particularly for larger programs, top management should visibly support the program. Beyond that, various motivation theories provide useful guidance. From behavior modification, we know that the training should provide opportunities for positive reinforcement. "Expectancy theory" shows us that the trainees need to know they have the ability to succeed in the program, and that the value to them of completing the program is high. Self-efficacy is crucial—trainees must believe they have the capacity to succeed. We can summarize such motivational points as follows.

MAKE THE LEARNING MEANINGFUL Learners are more motivated to learn something that has meaning for them. Therefore:

1. Provide a bird's-eye view of the material that you are going to present. For example, show why it's important, and provide an overview.[45]
2. Use familiar examples.
3. Organize the information so you can present it logically.
4. Use familiar terms and concepts.
5. Use visual aids.
6. Create a perceived training need in trainees' minds.[46] In one study, pilots who experienced pretraining accident-related events subsequently learned more from an accident-reduction training program than did those experiencing fewer such events.[47] Similarly, "before the training, managers need to sit down and talk with the trainee about why they are enrolled in the class, what they are expected to learn, and how they can use it on the job." Creating "a desire to learn is crucial."[48]
7. Goal setting is important. In one study, some trainees set goals at the start of the program for the skills they were being taught. After training, they were rated more highly on these skills than were those who hadn't set goals.[49]

MAKE SKILLS TRANSFER OBVIOUS AND EASY Make it easy to transfer new skills and behaviors from the training site to the job site:

1. Maximize the similarity between the training situation and the work situation.
2. Provide adequate practice.
3. Label or identify each feature of the machine and/or step in the process.
4. Direct the trainees' attention to important aspects of the job. For example, if you're training a customer service rep to handle calls, explain the different types of calls he or she will encounter.[50]
5. Provide "heads-up" information. For example, supervisors often face stressful conditions. You can reduce the negative impact by letting supervisory trainees know they might occur.[51]
6. Trainees learn best at their own pace. If possible, let them pace themselves.
7. Intermingle opportunities for trainees to use their new skills or knowledge throughout the training.[52]

REINFORCE THE LEARNING Make sure the learner gets plenty of feedback. In particular:

1. Trainees learn best when the trainers immediately reinforce correct responses, perhaps with a quick "well done."
2. Learning diminishes late in the day. Partial-day training is generally superior to full-day training.
3. Provide follow-up assignments at the close of training, so trainees are reinforced by applying back on the job what they've learned.[53]
4. Incentivize. For example, Hudson Trail Outfitters offers trainees incentives of outdoor gear for completing training program segments.[54]

ENSURE TRANSFER OF LEARNING TO THE JOB Less than 35% of trainees seem to be transferring what they learned to their jobs a year after training. Improving on that requires steps at each training stage. *Prior to training*, get trainee and supervisor input in designing the program, institute a training attendance policy, and encourage employees to participate.

During training, provide trainees with training experiences and conditions (surroundings, equipment) that resemble the actual work environment.

After training, reinforce what trainees learned, for instance, reward employees for using new skills.[55]

TRENDS SHAPING HR: *DIGITAL AND SOCIAL MEDIA*

the cloud
Refers to placing software programs and services on vendors' remote servers, from which they can then deliver these programs and services seamlessly to employees' digital devices.

When designing the program, a key question is how to deliver it. Increasingly, this occurs via "the cloud." Basically, **the cloud** refers to placing software programs and services on vendors' remote servers, from which they can then deliver these programs and services seamlessly to employees' digital devices.

Cloud-based training revolutionized training, by enabling employers to outsource much or all of their training activities. Because the vendor hosts both the courses and the overall learning management system, the employer need not concern itself with setting up or updating the programs on its own computers; the vendor manages the software. Furthermore, the more advanced cloud-based learning management systems let trainees access the training software and courses from wherever they are, using a variety of mobile devices. This not only improves convenience, but also facilitates collaboration among employees when, for instance, they're working together on a training project. ■

Developing the Program

Program development means actually assembling the program's training content and materials. It means choosing the specific content the program will present, as well as designing/choosing the specific instructional methods (lectures, cases, Web-based, and so on) you will use. Training equipment and materials include (for example) iPads, workbooks, lectures, PowerPoint slides, Web- and computer-based activities, course activities, and trainer resources (manuals, for instance).

Some employers create their own training content, but there's also a vast selection of online and offline content. The Association for Talent Development's Web site (www.td.org) illustrates the many off-the-shelf training and development offerings available. It includes certificate programs on topics such as coaching, consulting skills, and presentation skills, as well as online workshops on hundreds of topics such as game design, survey design, and developing a mentoring program. (Trainers Warehouse and HRdirect are among many other suppliers.)[56]

MyLab Management Apply It!
What do you think of how Wilson Learning conducts its training programs? If your professor has assigned this activity, go to the Assignments section of **www.pearson.com/mylab/management** to complete the video exercise.

HR in Action at the Hotel Paris As Lisa and the CFO reviewed measures of the Hotel Paris's current training efforts, it was clear that some changes were in order. Most other service companies provided at least 40 hours of training per employee per year, while the Hotel Paris offered, on average, no more than five or six. To see how they handled this, see the case on pages 271–272.

LEARNING OBJECTIVE 8-4
Explain how to use five training techniques.

Implementing the Training Program

Once you design and develop the training program, management can implement and then evaluate it. *Implement* means actually provide the training, using one or more of the instructional methods we discuss next.

Note first that there are several practical steps one can take before, during, and after the actual training to improve trainees' learning and engagement:

Before the actual training, send announcements far in advance, provide directions, provide a contact, and make sure participants have pretraining materials.

During training, make sure all participants have a point of contact in case they have questions or need guidance.

After training, remember training does *not* end when the program ends. Instead, periodically ascertain that trainees are transferring their learning to the job.[57]

On-the-Job Training

We'll see that much training today takes place online or uses other digital tools such as iPhones or iPads. However, much training is still in-person and interpersonal, as on-the-job training notably illustrates.

on-the-job training (OJT)
Training a person to learn a job while working on it.

On-the-job training (OJT) means having a person learn a job by actually doing it. Every employee, from mailroom clerk to CEO, should get on-the-job training when he or she joins a firm. In many firms, OJT is the only training available.[58]

TYPES OF ON-THE-JOB TRAINING The most familiar on-the-job training is the *coaching or understudy method.* Here, an experienced worker or the trainee's supervisor trains the employee. This may involve simply observing the supervisor, or (preferably) having the supervisor or job expert show the new employee the ropes, step-by-step. On-the-job training was part of multifaceted training at Men's Wearhouse, which combined on-the-job training with comprehensive initiation programs and continuing-education seminars. Every manager was accountable for developing his or her subordinates.[59] *Job rotation*, in which an employee (usually a management trainee) moves from job to job at planned intervals, is another OJT technique. *Special assignments* similarly give lower-level executives firsthand experience in working on actual problems.

Do not take the on-the-job training effort for granted. Instead, plan out and structure the OJT experience. Train the trainers themselves (often the employees' supervisors), and provide training materials. (They should know, for instance, how to motivate learners). Because low expectations may translate into poor trainee performance, supervisor/trainers should emphasize their high expectations. Effective coaching is essential. In one study of pharmaceuticals sales representatives, supervisors' coaching skills were associated with significant differences in goal attainment between sales districts.[60]

Many firms use *peer training* for OJT.[61] For example, some adopt "peer-to-peer development." The employer selects several employees who spend several days per week over several months learning what the technology or change will entail, and then spread the new skills and values to their colleagues back on the job.[62] Others use employee teams to analyze jobs and prepare training materials. Some teams reportedly conduct task analyses more quickly and effectively than did training experts. Figure 8-1 presents steps to help ensure OJT success.[63]

Apprenticeship Training

apprenticeship training
A structured process by which people become skilled workers through a combination of classroom instruction and on-the-job training.

Apprenticeship training is a process by which people become skilled workers, usually through a combination of formal learning and long-term on-the-job training, often under a master craftsperson's tutelage. When steelmaker Dofasco (now part of ArcelorMittal) discovered that many of its employees would be retiring within 5 to 10 years, it revived its apprenticeship program. New recruits spent about 32 months learning various jobs under the tutelage of experienced employees.[64]

Many apprenticeships pay well. For example, at the Tennessee Valley Authority, starting apprentices earn about $40,000 a year and can earn up to $65,000, before moving onto $75,000 jobs as linemen.[65] The Manufacturing Institute provides a step-by-step manual for creating apprenticeship programs.[66]

The U.S. Department of Labor promotes apprenticeship programs. More than 460,000 apprentices participate in 28,000 programs, and registered programs can receive federal and state contracts and other assistance.[67] The Trump administration recently proposed boosting government spending on its Apprenticeship USA program, to encourage more employers to offer apprenticeships.[68]

Figure 8-2 lists popular apprenticeships.

FIGURE 8-1 Steps in On-the-Job Training

Step 1: Prepare the learner

1. Put the learner at ease.
2. Explain why he or she is being taught.
3. Create interest and find out what the learner already knows about the job.
4. Explain the whole job and relate it to some job the worker already knows.
5. Place the learner as close to the normal working position as possible.
6. Familiarize the worker with equipment, materials, tools, and trade terms.

Step 2: Present the operation

1. Explain quantity and quality requirements.
2. Go through the job at the normal work pace.
3. Go through the job at a slow pace several times, explaining each step. Between operations, explain the difficult parts, or those in which errors are likely to be made.
4. Again, go through the job at a slow pace several times; explain the key points.
5. Have the learner explain the steps as you go through the job at a slow pace.

Step 3: Do a tryout

1. Have the learner go through the job several times, slowly, explaining each step to you. Correct mistakes and, if necessary, do some of the complicated steps the first few times.
2. Run the job at the normal pace.
3. Have the learner do the job, gradually building up skill and speed.
4. Once the learner can do the job, let the work begin, but don't abandon him or her.

Step 4: Follow-up

1. Designate to whom the learner should go for help.
2. Gradually decrease supervision, checking work from time to time.
3. Correct faulty work patterns before they become a habit. Show why the method you suggest is superior.
4. Compliment good work.

Informal Learning

Training experts use the notation "70/20/10" to show that as a rule, 70% of job learning occurs informally on or off the job, 20% reflects social interactions (for instance, among employees on the job), and only 10% is actual formal training.[69] A sampling of what would constitute informal training would include participating in meetings, coaching other people, attending conferences, searching the Internet for information, working with customers, job rotation, reading books and journals, playing video games, and watching TV.[70]

FIGURE 8-2 Some Popular Apprenticeships

Source: From Available Occupations, www.doleta.gov/OA/occupations.cfm, accessed March 4, 2018. This lists apprenticeships by city and state.

The U.S. Department of Labor's Registered Apprenticeship program offers access to more than 1,000 occupations, such as the following:

- Able seaman
- Carpenter
- Chef
- Child care development specialist
- Construction craft laborer
- Dental assistant
- Electrician
- Elevator constructor
- Fire medic
- Law enforcement agent
- Over-the-road truck driver
- Pipefitter

Employers facilitate informal learning. For example, one Siemens plant places tools in cafeteria areas to take advantage of the work-related discussions taking place. Even installing whiteboards with markers can facilitate informal learning.[71] Google supports on-site cafeterias, with free or subsidized food. Employees eat together, and through their interactions learn new ideas and build stronger relationships.[72]

Job Instruction Training

job instruction training (JIT)
Listing each job's basic tasks, along with key points, in order to provide step-by-step training for employees.

Many jobs consist of a sequence of steps best learned step-by-step. Such step-by-step training is called **job instruction training (JIT).** First, list the job's required steps (let's say for using a mechanical paper cutter) each in its proper sequence. Then list a corresponding "key point" (if any) beside each step. The steps in such a *job instruction training sheet* show trainees what to do, and the key points show how it's to be done—and why, as follows:

Steps	Key Points
1. Start motor	None
2. Set cutting distance	Carefully read scale—to prevent wrong-sized cut
3. Place paper on cutting table	Make sure paper is even—to prevent uneven cut
4. Push paper up to cutter	Make sure paper is tight—to prevent uneven cut
5. Grasp safety release with left hand	Do not release left hand—to prevent hand from being caught in cutter
6. Grasp cutter release with right hand	Do not release right hand—to prevent hand from being caught in cutter
7. Simultaneously pull cutter and safety releases	Keep both hands on corresponding releases—avoid hands being on cutting table
8. Wait for cutter to retract	Keep both hands on releases—to avoid having hands on cutting table
9. Retract paper	Make sure cutter is retracted; keep both hands away from releases
10. Shut off motor	None

As another example, the "van exit" steps UPS teaches drivers include: Shift into the lowest gear or into park; turn off the ignition; apply the parking brake; release the seatbelt with left hand; open the door; place the key on your ring finger.[73]

Lectures

Lecturing is a quick and simple way to present knowledge to large groups of trainees, as when the sales force needs to learn a new product's features.[74] Here are some guidelines for presenting a lecture:[75]

- Don't start out on the wrong foot, for instance, with an irrelevant joke.
- Speak only about what you know well.
- Remember that clarity is king: make sure your audience is clear about what you're saying.
- Give your listeners signals. For instance, if you have a list of items, start by saying something like, "There are four reasons why the sales reports are necessary. . . . The first. . . ."
- Use anecdotes and stories to show rather than tell.
- Be alert to your audience. Watch body language for negative signals like fidgeting or boredom.
- Maintain eye contact with the audience.
- Make sure everyone can hear. Repeat questions that you get from trainees.
- Leave hands hanging naturally at your sides.
- Talk from notes or PowerPoint slides, rather than from a script.

- Break a long talk into a series of short talks. Don't give a short overview and then spend a 1-hour presentation going point by point through the material. Break the long talk into a series of 10-minute talks, each with its own introduction. Write brief PowerPoint slides, and spend about a minute on each. Each introduction highlights what you'll discuss, why it's important to the audience members, and why they should listen to you.[76]
- Practice. If possible, rehearse under conditions similar to those under which you will actually give your presentation.

Programmed Learning

programmed learning
A systematic method for teaching job skills, involving presenting questions or facts, allowing the person to respond, and giving the learner immediate feedback on the accuracy of his or her answers.

Whether the medium is a textbook, iPad, or the Internet, **programmed learning** is a step-by-step, self-learning method that consists of three parts:

1. Presenting questions, facts, or problems to the learner
2. Allowing the person to respond
3. Providing feedback on the accuracy of answers, with instructions on what to do next

Generally, programmed learning presents facts and follow-up questions frame by frame. What the next question is often depends on how the learner answers the previous question. The built-in feedback from the answers provides reinforcement.

Programmed learning reduces training time. It also facilitates learning by letting trainees learn at their own pace, get immediate feedback, and reduce their risk of error. Some argue that trainees do not learn much more from programmed learning than from a textbook. Yet studies generally support programmed learning's effectiveness.[77] In addition to the usual programmed learning, computerized *intelligent tutoring systems* learn what questions and approaches worked and did not work for the learner, and then adjust the instructional sequence to the trainee's unique needs.

Behavior Modeling

behavior modeling
A training technique in which trainees are first shown good management techniques in a film, are asked to play roles in a simulated situation, and are then given feedback and praise by their supervisor.

Behavior modeling involves (1) showing trainees the right (or "model") way of doing something, (2) letting trainees practice that way, and then (3) giving feedback on the trainees' performance. Behavior modeling is one of the most widely used, well-researched, and highly regarded psychologically based training interventions.[78] The basic procedure is as follows:

1. ***Modeling.*** First, trainees watch live or video examples showing models behaving effectively in a problem situation. Thus, the video might show a supervisor effectively disciplining a subordinate, if teaching "how to discipline" is the aim of the training program.
2. ***Role-playing.*** Next, the trainees get roles to play in a simulated situation; here they are to practice the effective behaviors demonstrated by the models.
3. ***Social reinforcement.*** The trainer provides reinforcement in the form of praise and constructive feedback.
4. ***Transfer of training.*** Finally, trainees are encouraged to apply their new skills when they are back on their jobs.

Audiovisual-Based Training

Although increasingly replaced by Web-based methods, audiovisual-based training techniques like DVDs, films, PowerPoint, and audiotapes are still used.[79] The Ford Motor Company uses videos in its dealer training sessions to simulate problems and reactions to various customer complaints, for example.

Vestibule Training

With vestibule training, trainees learn on the actual or simulated equipment but are trained off the job (perhaps in a separate room or *vestibule*). Vestibule training is necessary when it's too costly or dangerous to train employees on the job. Putting new assembly-line workers right to work could slow production, for instance, and when safety is a concern—as with pilots—simulated training may be the only practical alternative. As an example, UPS uses a life-size learning lab to provide a 40-hour, 5-day realistic training program for driver candidates.[80]

Electronic Performance Support Systems (EPSS)

electronic performance support systems (EPSS)
Sets of computerized tools and displays that automate training, documentation, and phone support; integrate this automation into applications; and provide support that's faster, cheaper, and more effective than traditional methods.

job aid
A set of instructions, diagrams, or similar methods available at the job site to guide the worker.

Electronic performance support systems (EPSS) are computerized tools and displays that automate training, documentation, and phone support.[81] When you call a Dell service rep, he or she is probably asking questions prompted by an EPSS; it takes you both, step-by-step, through an analytical sequence. Without the EPSS, Dell would have to train its service reps to memorize an unrealistically large number of solutions. Clients such as Oracle, HP, and L'Oréal use customized EPSS solutions from Whatfix (https://whatfix.com/reviews/).[82]

Performance support systems are modern job aids. **Job aids** are sets of instructions, diagrams, or similar methods available at the job site to guide the worker.[83] Job aids work particularly well on complex jobs that require multiple steps, or where it's dangerous to forget a step. For example, airline pilots use job aids (a checklist of things to do prior to takeoff).

Videoconferencing

Videoconferencing involves delivering programs over broadband lines, the Internet, or satellite. Vendors such as Cisco offer videoconference products such as Webex and TelePresence.[84] Cisco's Unified Video Conferencing (CUVC) product line combines Cisco group collaboration and decision-making software with videoconferencing, video telephony, and realistic "TelePresence" capabilities.[85]

Computer-Based Training

Computer-based training (CBT) uses interactive computer-based systems to increase knowledge or skills. For example, employers use CBT to teach employees safe methods for avoiding falls. The system lets trainees replay the lessons and answer questions and is especially effective when paired with actual practice under a trainer.[86]

Computer-based training is increasingly realistic. For example, *interactive multimedia training* integrates text, video, graphics, photos, animation, and sound to create a complex training environment with which the trainee interacts.[87] In training a physician, for instance, such systems let medical students take a hypothetical patient's medical history, conduct an examination, and analyze lab tests. The students can then interpret the data and make a diagnosis.

SIMULATED LEARNING AND GAMING "Simulated learning" means different things to different people. A survey asked training professionals what experiences qualified as simulated learning experiences. Answers included "virtual reality-type games," "step-by-step animated guide," "scenarios with questions and decision trees overlaying animation," and "online role-play with photos and videos."[88]

The U.S. Armed Forces use simulation-based training programs. For example, the army developed video game–type training programs called Full-Spectrum Command and Full-Spectrum Warrior for training troops in urban warfare. They offer realistic "you are there" features and cultivate real-time leadership and decision-making skills.[89]

Many employers use computerized simulations (sometimes called *interactive learning*) to inject realism into their training. Orlando-based Environmental Tectonics Corporation created an Advanced Disaster Management simulation for emergency medical response trainees. One simulated scenario involves a plane crash. So realistic that it's "unsettling," trainees including firefighters and airport officials respond to the simulated crash's sights and sounds via pointing devices and radios.[90] The Cheesecake Factory uses a simulation that shows employees how to build the "perfect hamburger."[91]

Specialist multimedia companies such as Simulation Development Group (www.simstudios.com) produce programs like these. They produce custom titles as well as generic programs, for instance for leadership development.

Virtual reality puts the trainee in an artificial three-dimensional environment that simulates events and situations experienced on the job.

Egor Kotenko/123RF

Virtual reality (VR) puts the trainee in an artificial three-dimensional environment that simulates events and situations experienced on the job.[92] Sensory devices transmit how the trainee is responding to the computer, and the trainee "sees, feels, and hears" what is going on, assisted by special goggles and sensory devices.[93] Several National Football League teams use VR to train their quarterbacks in going through plays, and thousands of students have taken virtual field trips via Google's VR pioneer expeditions program.[94] Facebook's purchase of virtual reality glasses maker Oculus VR Inc. highlights virtual reality's growing potential.[95]

Training games needn't be complicated. For example, the trainers at Korea Ginseng Corporation (a leader in health-foods) wrote games accessible through app interfaces. Each round of each game is comprised of five multiple-choice quizzes. The more answers the employees get right and the quicker they give their answers, the more points they earn. The trainee/players compete against each other, with the top trainees profiled publicly with their names and pictures.[96]

Online/Internet-Based Training

Most employers are moving from classroom-based to online-based learning because of the efficiencies involved. For example, until recently, Utah-based Clearlink's employee training was classroom based. Sales agents often returned to the field without being tested on what they learned, and in general the training was less than effective. Clearlink switched to online learning. Its trainers turned from classroom training to creating new online e-learning courses and monitoring training results. The agents were relieved to be able to get their training on demand without interfering with their daily duties. The company estimates it saved almost $800,000 in one recent year by digitizing its training.[97]

Employers use online learning to deliver almost all the types of training we've discussed to this point. For example, China's state-owned postal service, China Post, created a center to manage its online training college, which now delivers about 9,000 hours of training annually, offering over 600 programs.[98] ADP trains new salespeople online, using a Blackboard learning management system similar to one used by college students.[99]

Learning management systems (LMS) are special software tools that support online training by helping employers identify training needs and to schedule, deliver, assess, and manage the online training itself. GM uses an LMS to help dealers deliver training. The LMS includes a course catalog, supervisor-approved self-enrollment, and pre- and postcourse tests.[100] Other typical LMS features include a course library, quizzes, reports and dashboards (for monitoring training performance), gamification elements (such as points and badges), messaging and notification systems, and a facility for scheduling and delivering both virtual and classroom training.[101]

Online learning doesn't necessarily teach individuals faster or better.[102] But, of course, the need to teach large numbers of students remotely, or to enable trainees to study at their leisure, often makes e-learning attractive.[103] Some employers opt for *blended learning*. Here, trainees use multiple delivery methods (such as manuals, in-class lectures, and Web-based seminars or "webinars") to learn the material.[104] Thus, the tool manufacturer Stihl offers prospective tool and die makers online learning combined with hands-on technical training classes.[105] We'll look closer at some online learning elements.

KNOWLEDGE BASE

LEARNING PORTALS A learning portal offers employees online access to training courses. Many employers arrange to have an online training vendor make its courses available via the employer's portal. Most often, the employer contracts with application service providers (ASPs). When employees go to their firm's learning portal, they actually link to the menu of training courses that the ASP offers for the employer.

Suppliers of learning portals include Pathgather (www.pathgather.com), and PwC's L&D app.[106] Skillsoft (www.skillsoft.com) offers access to thousands of cases, courses, webinars, and other education content. Grovo (www.grovo.com/content) offers short, micro learning content. Open Sesame (www.opensesame.com) combines and curates thousands of online courses from various sources, in Business Skills, Safety, Compliance, Technology, Industry, and Specific Certifications.[107] Employers such as L'Oréal, Marks & Spencer, and AT&T help their employees enroll in moocs (massive open online courses), widely available through platforms such as Coursera and EDX.

virtual classroom
Teaching method that uses special collaboration software to enable multiple remote learners, using their PCs or laptops, to participate in live audio and visual discussions, communicate via written text, and learn via content such as PowerPoint slides.

THE VIRTUAL CLASSROOM A **virtual classroom** uses collaboration software to enable multiple remote learners, using their PCs, tablets, or laptops, to participate remotely in live audio and visual discussions, communicate via written text, and learn via content such as PowerPoint slides.

The virtual classroom combines the best of online learning offered by systems like Blackboard with live video and audio.[108] Thus, Elluminate Live! lets learners view video, collaborate with colleagues, and learn with shared PowerPoint slides.[109]

MOBILE AND MICRO LEARNING More and more learning and development is being "microsized" and delivered through mobile devices.[110]

Mobile learning (or "on-demand learning") means delivering learning content on the learner's demand, via mobile devices like smart phones, laptops, and tablets, wherever and whenever the learner has the time and desire to access it.[111] For example, trainees can take full online courses using dominKnow's (www.dominknow.com) iPhone-optimized Touch Learning Center Portal.[112]

Most large employers distribute internal communications and training via mobile devices.[113] Employees at CompuCom Systems Inc. access instruction manuals through mobile devices; the company subsidizes employee purchases of smart phones or tablets to facilitate this. J. P. Morgan encourages employees to use instant messaging, for instance, to update colleagues about new products quickly. Natural user interfaces such as Apple's Siri facilitate such training.[114]

The essential requirement here is to link desired outcomes (such as quickly brushing up on "how to close a sale") with concise and targeted micro lessons.[115] IBM uses mobile learning to deliver just-in-time information (for instance, about new product features) to its sales force. To facilitate this, its training department often breaks up, say, an hour program into "micro" 10-minute pieces. Such "micro learning" training requires "stripping down" the message to its essentials.[116] Graphics and videos improve the learning experience.

Employers also use social media such as LinkedIn, Facebook, and Twitter, and virtual worlds like Second Life to communicate company news and messages and to provide training.[117] For example, British Petroleum (BP) uses Second Life to train new gas station employees. The aim here is to show new gas station employees how to use the safety features of gasoline storage tanks. BP built three-dimensional renderings of the tank

Web 2.0 learning
Training that uses online technologies such as social networks, virtual worlds (such as Second Life), and systems that blend synchronous and asynchronous delivery with blogs, chat rooms, bookmark sharing, and tools such as 3-D simulations.

systems in Second Life. Trainees use these to "see" underground and observe the effects of using the safety devices.[118]

Web 2.0 learning is learning that utilizes online technologies such as social networks, virtual worlds (such as Second Life), and systems blending synchronous and asynchronous delivery with blogs, chat rooms, bookmark sharing, and tools like 3-D simulations.[119] *Collaborative peer forums* require trainee teams to virtually "sell" their sales solution to an executive.[120] *Scenario-based e-learning* involves inserting realistic problems ("work scenarios") into trainees' e-learning lessons.[121]

Diversity Counts: Online Accessibility

Various laws and initiatives require that individuals with handicaps have full access to online training courses and content.[122] For example, the Web Content Accessibility Guidelines 2.0[123] requires that educational and training content be *perceivable*, *operable*, *understandable*, and *robust* for people with handicaps. *Perceivable* means, for instance, that the program provides captions for multimedia and enables them to see and hear content. *Operable* means, for instance, that users have enough time to use the content. *Understandable* means the text is readable and understandable. *Robust* means the program is compatible with browsers and user tools. ■

HR AND THE GIG ECONOMY: *ON-DEMAND MICRO LEARNING AT UBER*[124]

If you think all those Uber drivers simply go on the road with no formal training, you're wrong. There are hundreds of things those drivers must know about driving for Uber—from how to use the Uber app and driving systems, to how to greet and deal with customers—and Uber needs to train more than 30,000 new drivers every week. How do they do it?

Uber's training challenge is similar to that of most firms that rely on gig workers. The main problems are (1) the trainees aren't permanent employees but largely just "passing through," so you must carefully control what you invest in their training; and (2) the workers are all working on their own schedules, so training must be available when each worker wants it, on demand.

So, the short answer to "How does Uber do it?" is that driver training is online, on-demand, and delivered in microparcels. Uber uses a learning management system called MindFlash, which offers its clients around the globe thousands of courses, often focused on training gig workers like Uber's.[125] Among other benefits, the MindFlash system provides real-time reporting of trainees' results, so Uber knows if a driver is ready to go to work.

Gig-friendly training programs like Uber's have several characteristics. First, everyone involved—management, HR, and especially the gig workers—submit detailed "blueprints" of the workers' daily activities, from which workers' (in this case drivers') duties, skills and knowledge, and required training can be ascertained. Then, the courses are split into short digestible microcourses, stored on the vendor's cloud, and delivered on demand to each worker's mobile device when he or she wants it.

Lifelong and Literacy Training Techniques

lifelong learning
Provides employees with continuing learning experiences over their tenure with the firm, with the aims of ensuring they have the opportunity to learn the skills they need to do their jobs and to expand their occupational horizons.

Lifelong learning means providing employees with continuing learning experiences over their time with the firm, with the aim of ensuring they have the opportunity to learn the skills they need to do their jobs and to expand their horizons. Lifelong learning may thus range from basic remedial skills (for instance, English as a second language) to college degrees. So, for example, a restaurant server might work during the day and pursue a college degree at night, through an employer-subsidized lifelong learning program. Some states support lifelong learning with tax credits. For example, Washington State's Workforce Board offers state employers a lifelong learning account (LiLA) program. Somewhat similar to 401(k) plans, LiLA plans accept employer and employee contributions (without the tax advantages of 401(k) plans), and the employee can use these funds to better himself or herself.[126]

LITERACY TRAINING By one estimate, about one in seven workers can't read their employers' manuals.[127]

Employers often turn to private firms like Education Management Corporation to provide the requisite education.[128] Another simple approach is to have supervisors teach basic skills by giving employees writing and speaking exercises.[129] For example, if an employee needs to use a manual to find out how to change a part, teach that person how to use the index to locate the relevant section. Some call in teachers from a local high school. The National Center for Literacy Education provides source material and suggestions for literacy training.[130]

DIVERSITY TRAINING Diversity training aims to improve cross-cultural sensitivity, so as to foster more harmonious working relationships among a firm's employees. It typically includes improving interpersonal skills, understanding and valuing cultural differences, improving technical skills, socializing employees into the corporate culture, indoctrinating new workers into the U.S. work ethic, improving English proficiency and basic math skills, and improving bilingual skills for English-speaking employees.[131]

Most employers opt for an off-the-shelf diversity training program such as Just Be F.A.I.R. from Sollah Interactive. It includes full video, audible narration, user interactions, and pre- and postassessments. Vignettes illustrate such things as the potential pitfalls of stereotyping people.[132] Prism (www.prismdiversity.com/) offers employers diversity and inclusion courses such as "Choosing Respectful Behaviors for All Employees" and "Inclusion and Diversity Training for Executives."[133]

Team Training

Teamwork doesn't always come naturally. Companies devote many hours to training new employees to listen to each other and to cooperate. For example, a plant suffered from high turnover and absenteeism.[134] The plant manager addressed these in part through team training to improve team functioning. Team training focused on technical, interpersonal, and team management issues. In terms of *technical training*, for instance, management encouraged team employees to learn each other's jobs, to encourage flexible team assignments. **Cross training** means training employees to do different tasks or jobs than their own; doing so facilitates job rotation, as when you expect team members to occasionally share jobs or parts of jobs. Thus, some auto dealerships cross train sales and finance employees, so they each learn more about the challenges and details of selling and financing cars.[135]

cross training
Training employees to do different tasks or jobs than their own; doing so facilitates flexibility and job rotation.

Interpersonal problems often undermine teamwork. Team training therefore typically includes *interpersonal skills* training such as in listening, communicating, handling conflict, and negotiating. Effective teams also require *team management* skills, for instance, in problem solving, meetings management, consensus decision making, and team leadership.

Many employers use team training to build more cohesive management teams. Some use outdoor "adventure" training for this. This involves taking the management team out into rugged terrain, perhaps to learn "survival" skills and thereby foster trust and cooperation. App builder RealScout used the California Survival School for one program. Coders, marketing executives, and others spent several days in the mountains surviving—building their own shelters and learning to forage for food and start fires without matches. The reasonable assumption is that the teamwork learned surviving in the field will carry over once the team is back in the office.[136]

The accompanying HR Tools discussion shows how managers can create their own training programs.

IMPROVING PERFORMANCE: *HR TOOLS FOR LINE MANAGERS AND SMALL BUSINESSES*

Creating Your Own Training Program

While it would be nice if supervisors in even the largest firms could expect their firms to provide packaged training programs to train the new people they hire, many times they cannot. However, you still have many options.

Create Your Own Five-Step Training Program

Remember ADDIE—analyze (is training the problem?), design (including learning objectives, and motivating the trainee), develop (what specific materials and methods will we use?), implement (train the person), and evaluate. For many types of jobs, start by *setting training objectives*—be specific about what your employee should be able to do after training. Write a job description—list of the job's duties—if not already available. Write (see Table 8-1, page 243) a *task analysis record form* showing the steps in each of the employee's tasks. Write a *job instruction training form*; here list a key point (such as "carefully read scale") for each step (such as "set cutting distance"). Finally, compile the objectives, job description, task analysis form, and job instruction form in a *training manual.* Also, include an introduction to the job and an explanation of how the job relates to other jobs in the company.

Use Private Vendors

The small business owner can tap hundreds of suppliers of prepackaged training solutions. These range from self-study programs from the American Management Association (www.amanet.org) and SHRM (www.shrm.org), to specialized programs. For example, the employer might arrange with PureSafety to have its employees take occupational safety courses from www.puresafety.com.

SkillSoft.com is another example.[137] Its courses include software development, business strategy and operations, professional effectiveness, and desktop computer skills. The buyer's guide from the Association for Talent Development (www.td.org) is a good place to start to find a vendor (check under "Resources and Tools").[138]

Check the SBA

The government's Small Business Administration (see www.SBA.gov/training) provides a virtual campus that offers online courses, workshops, publications, and learning tools aimed at supporting small businesses.[139] For example, the small business owner can link under "Small Business Planner" to "Writing Effective Job Descriptions," and "The Interview Process: How to Select the Right Person." See the site map at www.sba.gov/sitemap for examples of what it offers.

Check NAM

The National Association of Manufacturers (NAM) is the largest industrial trade organization in the United States. It represents about 14,000 member manufacturers, including 10,000 small and midsized companies.

NAM helps employees maintain and upgrade their work skills and continue their professional development. It offers courses and a skills certification process.[140] There are no long-term contracts to sign. Employers simply pay about \$10–\$30 per course taken by each employee. The catalog includes OSHA, quality, and technical training as well as courses in areas like customer service. ■

> MyLab Management Talk About It 2
>
> If your professor has assigned this, go to the Assignments section of **www.pearson.com/mylab/management** to complete this discussion question. What would you tell the owner of a small restaurant whose employees haven't been trained properly to do?

Implementing Management Development Programs

LEARNING OBJECTIVE 8-5
List and briefly discuss four management development methods.

Management development is any attempt to improve managerial performance by imparting knowledge, changing attitudes, or increasing skills. It thus includes in-house programs like courses, coaching, and rotational assignments; professional programs like those given by SHRM; online programs from various sources; and university programs like MBAs.

Management development is important for several reasons. For one thing, promotion from within is a major source of management talent, and virtually all promoted managers require development to prepare them for their new jobs. Furthermore, management development facilitates organizational continuity, by preparing employees and current managers to smoothly assume higher-level positions.

management development
Any attempt to improve current or future management performance by imparting knowledge, changing attitudes, or increasing skills.

Strategy's Role in Management Development

Management development programs should reflect the firm's strategic plans. For example, strategies to enter new businesses or expand overseas imply that the employer will need succession plans to obtain and/or develop managers who have the skills to manage these new businesses. Management development programs then impart the knowledge, attitudes, and skills these managers will need to excel at their jobs.[141]

Some management development programs are company-wide and involve all or most new (or potential) managers. Thus, new MBAs may join GE's management development program and rotate through various assignments and educational experiences. The firm may then slot superior candidates onto a "fast track," a development program that prepares them more quickly for senior-level commands. Other development programs aim to fill specific top positions, such as CEO.

Management development supports the employer's *succession planning process.*[142] *Succession planning*, as explained in Chapter 5 (page 138), involves developing workforce plans for the company's top positions; it is the ongoing process of systematically identifying, assessing, and developing organizational leadership to enhance performance.

Candidate Assessment and the 9-Box Grid

Some high-potential managers fail in their jobs, while some low-potential managers excel. How then does an employer choose who to send through an expensive development program?

The 9-Box Grid is one tool. It shows *Potential* from low to medium to high on the vertical axis, and *Performance* from low to medium to high across the bottom—a total of nine possible boxes.

The grid can simplify, somewhat, the task of choosing development candidates. At the extremes, for instance, low potentials/low performers would not move on. The high-potential/high-performance stars most assuredly would. Most employers focus their development resources on high-performance/high-potential stars, and secondarily on those rated high-potential/moderate-performance, or high-performance/moderate-potential.[143] Other employers focus development resources on the company's "mission-critical employees"—those central to the firm's success and survival. We'll see how later in this section.

In any case, individual assessment should always precede development. At frozen foods manufacturer Schwan, senior executives first whittle 40 or more development candidates down to about 10. Then their program begins with a 1-day assessment by outside consultants of each manager's leadership strengths and weaknesses. This assessment becomes the basis for each manager's individual development plan. Action-learning (practical) projects then supplement individual and group training activities.[144]

We'll look at some popular development activities next.

Managerial On-the-Job Training and Rotation

job rotation
A management training technique that involves moving a trainee from department to department to broaden his or her experience and identify strong and weak points.

Managerial on-the-job training methods include job rotation, the coaching/understudy approach, and action learning. **Job rotation** means moving managers from department to department to broaden their understanding of the business and to test their abilities. The trainee may be a recent college graduate, or a senior manager being groomed for further promotion. In addition to providing a well-rounded experience, job rotation helps avoid stagnation, through the constant introduction of new points of view in each department. It also helps identify each trainee's strong and weak points. Periodic job changing can also improve interdepartmental cooperation: managers become more understanding of each other's problems; and rotation widens one's acquaintances among management. At LVMH (which owns Louis Vuitton), rotating employees among luxury brands gives employees what two experts call "extraordinarily rich learning opportunities."[145]

The accompanying HR Practices feature illustrates this.

IMPROVING PERFORMANCE: *HR PRACTICES AROUND THE GLOBE*

Global Job Rotation

As firms expand globally, job rotation takes on a new meaning. At firms like Shell and BP, rotating managers globally is a primary means through which the firms maintain their flexibility and responsiveness even as they grow to an enormous size.

An advantage of global job rotation (rotating managers from, say, Sweden to New York) is that it builds a network of informal ties that ensures superior cross-border communication and mutual understanding as well as tight interunit coordination and control.

Improved communication and understanding stem from the personal relationships forged as managers work in the firm's various locations. These activities can also enhance organizational control. When employees from the firm's global locations are rotated or brought together at, say, the Harvard Business School or Europe's INSEAD for a management-training program, the aim is more than just teaching basic skills. It is also to build a stronger identification with the company's culture and values. By creating shared experiences and values and a consistent view of the firm and its goals, such activities can facilitate communication. Similarly the sense of shared values (such as "the customer is always right") can facilitate self control, by helping keep managers' behavior in line with the firm's policies and procedures. Finally, cross-border assignments can be magnets for attracting and retaining the best management talent.[146]

MyLab Management Talk About It 3

If your professor has assigned this, go to the Assignments section of **www.pearson.com/mylab/management** to complete this discussion. Using Web sites such as www.sony.net (click "Careers") and www.mckinsey.com (insert *how multinationals can attract the talent they need* into their search box), discuss examples of how multinational companies use job rotation and other means to develop their managers.

COACHING/UNDERSTUDY APPROACH In this on-the-job method, the trainee works directly with a senior manager or with the person he or she is to replace; the latter is responsible for the trainee's coaching. Normally, the understudy relieves the executive of certain responsibilities, giving the trainee a chance to learn the job.

action learning
A training technique by which management trainees are allowed to work full-time analyzing and solving problems in other departments.

ACTION LEARNING **Action learning** programs give managers released time to work analyzing and solving problems in departments other than their own. It is one of the fastest-growing leadership development techniques, used by companies ranging from Wells Fargo to Boeing.[147] Basics include carefully selecting teams of 5 to 25 members, assigning them real-world business problems that extend beyond their usual areas of expertise, and structured learning through coaching and feedback. The employer's senior managers usually choose the projects and decide whether to accept the teams' recommendations.[148]

For example, one Pacific Gas & Electric Company (PG&E) program had three phases:

1. A 6- to 8-week *framework* phase, where the team defines and collects data on an issue;
2. The *action forum*—2 to 3 days at PG&E's learning center discussing the issue and developing recommendations; and
3. *Accountability sessions*, where the teams meet with management to review progress.[149]

STRETCH ASSIGNMENTS Stretch assignments are assignments that "push employees beyond their comfort zone," placing them in jobs and assignments different from and more demanding than those to which they are accustomed.[150] The critical issue here is to understand the employee's capabilities: The assignment should be challenging but not overwhelming.

Off-the-Job Management Training and Development Techniques

There are also many off-the-job methods for training and developing managers.

case study method
A development method in which the manager is presented with a written description of an organizational problem to diagnose and solve.

As most everyone knows, the **case study method** has trainees solve realistic problems after studying written or video case descriptions. The person then analyzes the case, diagnoses the problem, and presents his or her findings and solutions in a discussion with other trainees. *Integrated case scenarios* create long-term, comprehensive case situations. One FBI Academy scenario starts with "a concerned citizen's telephone call and ends 14 weeks later with a simulated trial. In between is the stuff of a genuine investigation. . . ." The scripts include background stories, detailed personnel histories, and role-playing instructions; their aim is to develop specific skills, such as interviewing witnesses.[151]

management game
A development technique in which teams of managers compete by making computerized decisions regarding realistic but simulated situations.

Computerized **management games** enable trainees to learn by making realistic decisions in simulated situations. For example, *Interpret* is a team exercise that "explores team communication, the management of information and the planning and implementation of a strategy. It raises management trainees' communication skills, helps them to better manage the information flow between individuals and the team, and improves planning and problem-solving skills."[152] In other games each team might have to decide how much to spend on advertising, how much to produce, and how much inventory to maintain.

People learn best by being involved, and games gain such involvement. They also help trainees develop problem-solving skills, and focus attention on planning rather than just putting out fires. They can develop leadership skills and foster cooperation and teamwork.

"Gamification" of training in general also reportedly improves learning, engagement, and morale and is fairly easy to achieve. For instance, use point systems, badges, and leaderboards in the training.[153]

OUTSIDE SEMINARS Numerous companies and universities offer Web-based and traditional classroom management development seminars and conferences. The selection of 1- to 3-day training programs offered by the American Management Association illustrates what's available. For instance, its offerings range from "developing your emotional intelligence" to "assertiveness training," "assertiveness training for managers," "assertiveness training for women in business," "dynamic listening skills for successful communication," and "fundamentals of cost accounting."[154] Specialized groups, such as SHRM, provide specialized seminars for their professions' members.[155]

UNIVERSITY-RELATED PROGRAMS Many universities provide executive education in leadership, supervision, and the like. These can range from 1- to 4-day programs to executive development programs lasting 1 to 4 months. The Advanced Management Program of Harvard's Graduate School of Business Administration is one of many such programs.[156]

Many employers want customized programs. In one, Hasbro sought to improve its executives' creativity skills. Dartmouth's Amos Tuck Business School provided a "custom approach to designing a program that would be built from the ground up to suit Hasbro's specific needs."[157] Technology giant Philips sought to accelerate innovation and leadership excellence. It entered a 6-year collaboration with the University of Pennsylvania's Wharton School and the Center for Creative Leadership (CCL). Their customized "Octagon" leader development program emphasized both strategic business skills, and behavioral leadership skills.[158]

role-playing
A training technique in which trainees act out parts in a realistic management situation.

ROLE-PLAYING The aim of **role-playing** is to create a realistic situation and then have the trainees assume the parts (or roles) of specific persons in that situation. Each trainee gets a role, such as:

> You are the head of a crew of telephone maintenance workers, each of whom drives a small service truck to and from the various jobs. Every so often you get a new truck to exchange for an old one, and you have the problem of deciding

to which of your crew members you should give the new truck. Often there are hard feelings, so you have a tough time being fair.[159]

When combined with the general instructions and other roles, role-playing can trigger spirited discussions among the trainees. The aim is to develop trainees' skills in areas like leadership and delegating. For example, a supervisor could experiment with both a considerate and an autocratic leadership style, whereas in the real world this isn't so easy. Role-playing may also help someone to be more sensitive to others' feelings.

in-house development center
A company-based method for exposing prospective managers to realistic exercises to develop improved management skills.

CORPORATE UNIVERSITIES Many firms establish **in-house development centers** (often called *corporate universities*). GE's Crotonville, New York, management training center was one of the first; it provides GE management employees with a very extensive range of courses and seminars, such as one 2-week program for selected middle managers where they receive coaching on topics ranging from finance to presentation skills.[160] As with management development in general, the best corporate universities (1) actively align offerings with corporate goals, (2) focus on developing skills that support business needs, (3) evaluate learning and performance, (4) use technology to support learning, and (5) partner with academia.[161]

Increasingly employers offer virtual—rather than brick-and-mortar—corporate university services. For example, Cerner Health offers its employees "Cerner KnowledgeWorks." This provides three types of knowledge. *Dynamic knowledge* "is real-time content . . . such as e-mails, instant messages, or conference calls." *Moderated content* "includes best practices, such as case studies or wikis that capture information about situations where we did well and how we did it." *Codified content* "is more formal documentation of official company practices, and includes installation guides, help files, and formal training or courses."[162]

executive coach
An outside consultant who questions the executive's associates in order to identify the executive's strengths and weaknesses, and then counsels the executive so he or she can capitalize on those strengths and overcome the weaknesses.

EXECUTIVE COACHES Many firms retain executive coaches to help develop their top managers' effectiveness. An **executive coach** is an outside consultant who questions the executive's boss, peers, subordinates, and (sometimes) family in order to identify the executive's strengths and weaknesses, and to counsel the executive so he or she can capitalize on those strengths and overcome the weaknesses.[163] Executive coaching can cost $50,000 per executive or more, so a careful evaluation is needed before retaining one. In particular, ask, how valuable is the manager's performance to the company, how willing is he or she to participate, what is the challenge the manager is facing, and what if any are the alternatives to executive coaching? Experts recommend using formal assessments prior to coaching, to uncover strengths and weaknesses and to provide more focused coaching.[164]

The coaching field is unregulated, so managers should do their due diligence. Check references, and consult the International Coach Federation, a trade group.[165]

THE SHRM LEARNING SYSTEM The Society for Human Resource Management (SHRM) encourages HR professionals to qualify for certification by taking examinations. The society offers several preparatory training programs.[166] These include self-study, and a college/university option that includes classroom interaction with instructors and other learners.[167]

Leadership Development at Cigna

As a leadership development example, Cigna offers various leadership development programs by specialty, for example, an Actuarial Executive Development Program, a Financial Development Program, and a HealthService Leadership Program.[168] According to Cigna, its HealthService Leadership Program (HLP) "focuses on building general leadership talent through executive coaching, dynamic rotational roles, and personalized development to create a pipeline for future executive positions at Cigna." The program entails functional rotations each lasting 12 to 24 months, during which trainees improve their general management and leadership skills. They do this, for instance, through leadership assessments, mentorships, and experiential learning. The functions the trainees are exposed to include, for example, Marketing, Product, Finance, Service Operations, and Strategy and Business Development.

TRENDS SHAPING HR: *CUSTOMIZED TALENT MANAGEMENT-DIFFERENTIAL DEVELOPMENT ASSIGNMENTS*

In today's competitive environment, the usual HR practice of allocating development opportunities and other scarce resources across the board or based solely on performance makes less sense. It often makes more sense to focus more of the employer's resources on the "mission-critical employees" who the employer deems most crucial to the company's future growth.

We'll look closer at how employers do this in the following chapter, but several examples follow:

- High-potential trainees in Johnson & Johnson's "LeAD" leadership development program receive advice and regular assessments from coaches brought in from outside the company.[169]
- Some companies share future strategies on a privileged basis with rising leaders. For example, they invite them to quarterly meetings with high-level executives, and they let them access an online portal where the rising leaders can review the company's strategy and critical metrics.[170] ■

Characteristics of Effective Leadership Development Programs

What are the characteristics of effective leadership training programs?[171] One major study's findings suggest this: The best programs begin with *a thorough needs analysis* to determine tangible program goals; *mandatory participation* in the program is as effective as voluntary participation; self-administered programs are *less* effective than *trainer-based programs; practice-based programs* are more effective than information-based programs; providing *feedback* to trainees boosts the program's effectiveness; *on-site programs* (at the company's facilities) are generally more effective than off-site training programs; *face-to-face* leadership training programs are more effective than virtually based programs; and leadership training is as effective for *senior-level leaders* as for lower-level ones.

Managing Organizational Change Programs

LEARNING OBJECTIVE 8-6

List and briefly discuss the importance of the steps in leading organizational change.

With firms from AT&T and Comcast to Barnes & Noble and Macy's being disrupted by digital competitors, reorganizations are increasingly familiar, but often fail. McKinsey and Company surveyed 1,800 executives to identify why reorganizations fail. Top reasons included *employees resisting the changes*, *insufficient resources devoted to the effort*, *individual productivity declining as employees become distracted*, *leaders resisting the changes*, and *the organization chart changes but the people are still working the same*.[172]

In addition, *clarity of purpose* is essential. For example, two change experts say that most major change programs (or "transformations") aim to achieve one of five basic purposes or "quests": *customer focus, nimbleness, innovation, sustainability,* or *boosting global presence*.[173] They found that when transformations fail, it's generally because those running them either neglect to clarify up front the program's purpose/quest, or pursue the wrong quest, or focus on multiple quests.

In any case, companies often have little choice but to change how they do things. For example, Microsoft changed its CEO a few years ago, then reorganized, changed its strategy to include supplying hardware (tablets, etc.), and made other personnel changes. As here, organizational change may impact a company's strategy, culture, structure, technologies, or the attitudes and skills of its employees.

Again, the hardest part is often overcoming employee resistance. Individuals, groups, and even entire organizations tend to resist change. They do this because they're accustomed to the usual way of doing things or because of perceived threats to their influence, for instance.[174]

Lewin's Change Process

Psychologist Kurt Lewin formulated a model to summarize the basic process for implementing a change with minimal resistance. To Lewin, all behavior in organizations was a product of two kinds of forces: those striving to maintain the status quo and those pushing for change. Implementing change thus means reducing the forces for the status quo or building up the forces for change. Lewin's process consists of three steps:

1. ***Unfreezing*** means reducing the forces that are striving to maintain the status quo, usually by presenting a provocative problem or event to get people to recognize the need for change and to search for new solutions.
2. ***Moving*** means developing new behaviors, values, and attitudes. The manager may accomplish this through organizational structure changes, through conventional training and development activities, and sometimes through the other organizational development techniques (such as team building) we'll discuss later.
3. ***Refreezing*** means building in the reinforcement to make sure the organization doesn't slide back into its former ways of doing things—for instance, change the incentive system.

In practice, to deal with employee intransigence, some experts suggest that the manager use a process such as the following to implement the change.[175] To bring about a desired organizational change at work:

1. ***Establish a sense of urgency.*** For example, present employees with a (fictitious) analyst's report describing the firm's imminent demise.
2. ***Mobilize commitment*** through joint diagnoses of problems. Create a task force to diagnose the problems facing the department or the company. This can help to produce a shared understanding of what can and must be improved.
3. ***Create a guiding coalition.*** It's never easy to implement big changes alone. Therefore, create a "guiding coalition" of influential people. They'll act as missionaries and implementers.
4. ***Develop and communicate a shared vision*** of what you see coming from the change. Keep the vision simple (for example, "We will be faster than anyone at satisfying customer needs.").[176]

Create a sense of urgency, for example, by presenting employees with a report describing the firm's imminent demise—if corrective actions aren't taken.

Rawpixel.com/Shutterstock

5. ***Help employees make the change.*** Eliminate impediments. For example, do current policies or procedures make it difficult to act? Do intransigent managers discourage employees from acting?
6. ***Aim first for attainable short-term accomplishments.*** Use the credibility from these to make additional changes.[177]
7. ***Reinforce the new ways of doing things*** with changes to the company's systems and procedures. For example, use new appraisal systems and incentives to reinforce the desired new behaviors.
8. ***Monitor and assess progress.*** In brief, this involves comparing the company's progress with where it should be.

Using Organizational Development

Beyond this process, there are many other ways to reduce resistance. Among the many suggestions here are that managers impose rewards or sanctions that guide employee behaviors, explain why the change is needed, negotiate with employees, give inspirational speeches, or ask employees to help design the change.[178]

organizational development
A special approach to organizational change in which employees themselves formulate and implement the change that's required.

Organizational development (OD) taps into the latter. **Organizational development** is a change process through which employees formulate the change that's required and implement it, often with the assistance of trained consultants. OD has several distinguishing characteristics:

1. It usually involves *action research*, which means collecting data about a group, department, or organization, and feeding the information back to the employees so they can analyze it and develop hypotheses about what the problems might be.
2. It applies behavioral science knowledge to improve the organization's effectiveness.
3. It changes the organization in a particular direction—toward empowerment, improved problem solving, responsiveness, quality of work, and effectiveness.

For example, according to experts French and Bell, one OD method, *team-building meetings*, begins with the consultant interviewing each of the group members and the leader before the meeting.[179] They are asked what their problems are, how they think the group functions, and what obstacles are keeping the group from performing better. The consultant then categorizes the interview data into themes (such as "inadequate communications") and presents the themes to the group at the start of the meeting. The group ranks the themes in terms of importance, and the most important ones become the agenda for the meeting. The group then explores and discusses the issues, examines the underlying causes of the problems, and begins devising solutions.

Survey research is another of many OD options (see Table 8-2). It requires having employees, usually throughout the organization, complete attitude surveys. The

TABLE 8-2 Categories of OD Interventions

Human Process	Human Resource Management
T-groups	Goal setting
Process consultation	Performance appraisal
Third-party intervention	Reward systems
Team building	Career planning and development
Organizational confrontation meeting	Managing workforce diversity
Survey research	Employee wellness
Technostructural	**Strategic**
Formal structural change	Integrated strategic management
Differentiation and integration	Culture change
Cooperative union–management projects	Strategic change
Quality circles	Self-designing organizations
Total quality management	
Work design	

facilitator then uses those data as a basis for problem analysis and action planning. Surveys are a convenient way to unfreeze a company's management and employees. They provide a comparative, graphic illustration of the fact that the organization does have problems to solve.

Evaluating the Training Effort

LEARNING OBJECTIVE 8-7

Explain why a controlled study may be superior for evaluating the training program's effects.

Two experts contend that after spending $560 billion on training in one recent year, employers are getting a poor return on their investment, because it "doesn't lead to better organizational performance. . . ."[180] Particularly with today's emphasis on measuring results, the manager should therefore evaluate the training program.

There are several things you can measure: participants' *reactions* to the program, what (if anything) the trainees *learned* from the program, and to what extent their on-the-job *behavior* or *results* changed as a result of the program. In one older survey of about 500 U.S. organizations, 77% evaluated their training programs by eliciting reactions, 36% evaluated learning, and about 10% to 15% assessed the program's behavior and/or results; recent evidence suggests these figures probably haven't changed much.[181]

There are two basic issues to address when evaluating training programs. One is the design of the evaluation study and, in particular, whether to use controlled experimentation. The second is, "What should we measure?"

Designing the Study

In deciding how to design the evaluation study, the basic concern is this: How can we be sure that the training (rather than, say, a company-wide wage increase) caused the results that we're seeing? The *time series design* is one option. Here, as in Figure 8-3, you take a series of performance measures before and after the training program. This can provide some insight into the program's effectiveness.[182]

FIGURE 8-3 Using a Time Series Graph to Assess a Training Program's Effects

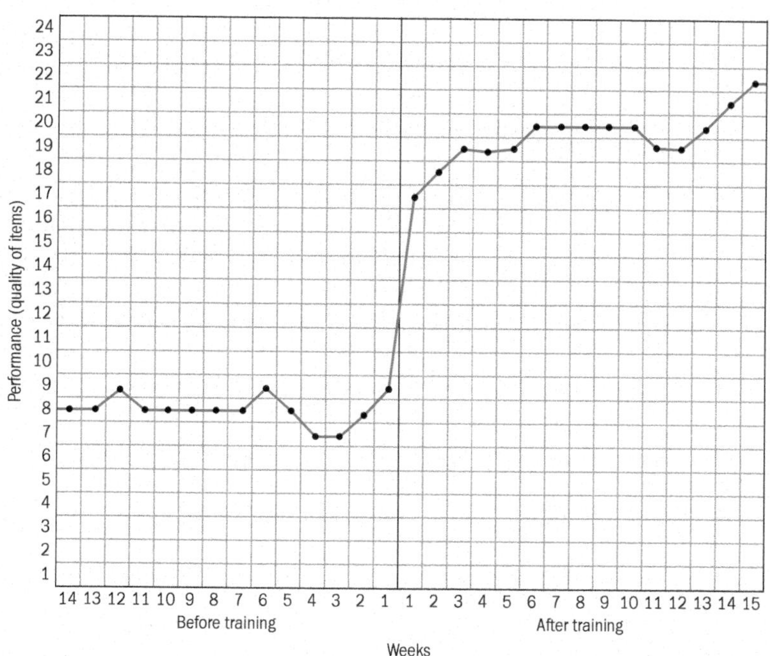

However, you can't be absolutely sure that the training (rather than, say, the raise) caused any change.

controlled experimentation
Formal methods for testing the effectiveness of a training program, preferably with before-and-after tests and a control group.

Controlled experimentation is therefore the gold standard. A controlled experiment uses a training group and a control group that receives no training. Data (for instance, on quantity of sales or quality of service) are obtained both before and after one group is exposed to training and before and after a corresponding period in the control group. This makes it easier to determine the extent to which any change in the training group's performance resulted from the training, rather than from some organizationwide change like a raise in pay. (The pay raise should have affected employees in both groups.)[183]

Training Effects to Measure

The widely used Kirkpatrick Model of training evaluation (named for its developer) lists four training effects employers can measure:[184]

1. ***Reaction.*** Evaluate trainees' reactions to the program. Did they like the program? Did they think it worthwhile?
2. ***Learning.*** Test whether they learned the principles, skills, and facts they were supposed to learn.
3. ***Behavior.*** Ask whether the trainees' on-the-job behavior changed because of the training program. For example, are employees in the store's complaint department more courteous toward disgruntled customers?
4. ***Results.*** Most important, ask, "What results did we achieve, in terms of the training objectives previously set?" For example, did the number of customer complaints diminish? Reactions, learning, and behavior are important. But if the training program doesn't produce measurable performance-related results, then it probably hasn't achieved its goals.[185]

Evaluating each of these is straightforward. Figure 8-4 presents one page from a sample evaluation questionnaire for assessing *reactions*. Or, you might assess trainees' *learning* by testing their new knowledge. For *behavioral change,* perhaps assess the effectiveness of a supervisory performance appraisal training program by asking that person's subordinates, "Did your supervisor provide you with examples of good and bad performance when he or she appraised your performance most recently?" Finally, directly assess a training program's *results* by measuring, say, the percentage of phone caller questions that call center trainees subsequently answered correctly. Similarly, a careful comparison of the training program's costs and benefits can enable the human resource team to compute the program's return on investment. Online calculators are available to facilitate such analyses.[186]

A program at MGM Resorts illustrates training evaluation.[187] In the hospitality industry, how likely guests are to return is a crucial metric, and is measured at MGM by "Net Promoter Scores" (NPS). With MGM's NPS scores not up to par, its training team concluded "guest facing" employees weren't sufficiently engaged. It created an Essentials of Hotel Management Program for front desk and assistant managers. The program emphasized skills like collaboration and communications. At the end of the approximately 1-year program, NPS scores had risen about 2% (which is considered a notable accomplishment).[188]

OPM **INSTRUCTOR HANDOUTS** ***United States Office of Personnel Management***

TRAINING EVALUATION FORM

TITLE OF COURSE: **"Work and Family Issues — A Module for Supervisors and Managers"**
NAME OF INSTRUCTOR:

DATE OF TRAINING
Started:__________
Ended:__________

NAME: (Optional)	**POSITION TITLE/GRADE:**	
AGENCY:	**OFFICE PHONE:** (Optional)	**OFFICE ADDRESS:** (Optional)

Rate Your Knowledge and Skill Level (Circle your rating)	**Overall, how would you rate this course?**
Before this course Low ------------------------------------High 1 2 3 4 5 After this course Low ------------------------------------High 1 2 3 4 5	_ Excellent _Very Good _ Good _ Fair _ Poor

EVALUATION OF COURSE
(Check appropriate box)

ITEMS OF EVALUATION How did the course sharpen your knowledge or skills in:	Excellent	Very Good	Good	Fair	Poor	Not Applicable
1. What work and family programs are	◦	◦	◦	◦	◦	◦
2. Who uses work and family programs	◦	◦	◦	◦	◦	◦
3. How to recognize/solve work/family issues	◦	◦	◦	◦	◦	◦
4. Helping you take practical steps on the job	◦	◦	◦	◦	◦	◦

RATING OF INSTRUCTOR

1. Presentation, organization, delivery	◦	◦	◦	◦	◦	◦
2. Knowledge and command of the subject	◦	◦	◦	◦	◦	◦
3. Use of audio-visuals or other training aids	◦	◦	◦	◦	◦	◦
4. Stimulation of an open exchange of ideas, participation, & group interaction	◦	◦	◦	◦	◦	◦

STRONG POINTS OF THE COURSE
◦
◦
◦

WEAK POINTS OF THE COURSE
◦
◦
◦

ADDITIONAL DATA YOU WOULD LIKE TO HAVE COVERED IN COURSE
◦
◦
◦

ADDITIONAL COMMENTS/OR RECOMMENDATIONS

FIGURE 8-4 A Training Evaluation Form

Source: From Instructor Handouts: Training Evaluation Form, United States Office of Personnel Management.

Chapter Review

Chapter Section Summaries

8-1. Getting your new employee up to speed begins with **orienting and training** him or her. Employee orientation means providing new employees with the information they need to function, and helping them start being emotionally attached to the firm.

8-2. There is more to orienting employees than introducing them to their coworkers. Even without a company-wide program like Toyota's, use the onboarding opportunity to begin instilling in the new employee the company values and traditions in which you expect the person to become **engaged.**

8-3. We used the acronym **ADDIE** to outline the **training process:** analyze, develop, design, implement, and evaluate. Before training employees, it's necessary to analyze their training needs and design the training program. In training new employees, employers use task analysis—basically, a detailed study of the job—to determine what skills the job requires. For current employees, performance analysis is required, specifically to verify that there is performance efficiency and to determine if training is the solution. Distinguishing between can't-do and won't-do problems is the main issue here. Once you understand the issues, you can design a training program, which means identifying specific training objectives, clarifying a training budget, and then actually designing the program in terms of the actual content.

8-4. With this in place, you can turn to **implementing the training program.** Specific training methods include on-the-job training, apprenticeship training, informal learning, job instruction training, lectures, programmed learning, audiovisual-based training, vestibule training, videoconferencing, electronic performance support systems, and computer-based training. Frequently, programs are Internet-based, with employees accessing packaged online programs, backed up by learning management systems, through their company's learning portals. Employers also increasingly use mobile learning, for instance, delivering short courses and explanations to employees' smart phones. Lifelong learning can help ensure employees have the basic educational backgrounds they need to succeed on their jobs. Diversity training aims to create better cross-cultural sensitivity with the goal of fostering more harmonious working relationships.

8-5. Most training methods are useful for all employees, but some are particularly appropriate for **management development programs.** Like all employees, new managers often get on-the-job training, for instance, via job rotation and coaching. In addition, it's usual to supply various off-the-job training and development opportunities—for instance, using the case study method, management games, outside seminars, university-related programs, corporate universities, executive coaches, and (for human resource managers) the SHRM learning system.

8-6. When facing challenges, managers have to execute **organizational change programs.** These may aim at changing the company's strategy, culture, structure, technologies, or the attitudes and skills of the employees. Often, the trickiest part of organizational change is overcoming employees' resistance to it. With that in mind, steps in an effective organizational change program include establishing a sense of urgency, mobilizing commitment, creating a guiding coalition, developing and communicating a shared vision, helping employees make the change, consolidating gains, reinforcing new ways of doing things, and monitoring and assessing progress. Organizational development involves action research, which means collecting data about a group and feeding the information back to the employees so they can analyze it and develop hypotheses about what the problems might be.

8-7. Whatever the training program, it's important to **evaluate the training effort.** You can measure reaction, learning, behavior, or results, ideally using a control group that is not exposed to training, in parallel with the group that you're training.

Discussion Questions

8-1. "A well-thought-out orientation program is essential for all new employees, whether they have experience or not." Explain why you agree or disagree with this statement.

8-2. Explain how you would apply our "motivation points" (pages 246–247) in developing a lecture, say, on orientation and training.

8-3. What are some typical on-the-job training techniques? What do you think are some of the main drawbacks of relying on informal on-the-job training? What are some advantages to using cloud-based training?

8-4. Describe the pros and cons of five management development methods.

8-5. Do you think job rotation is a good method to use for developing management trainees? Why or why not?

8-6. What is organizational development, and how does it differ from traditional approaches to organizational change?

8-7. List and briefly explain each of the steps in the training process.

Individual and Group Activities

8-8. You're the supervisor of a group of employees whose task is to assemble disk drives that go into computers. You find that quality is not what it should be and that many of your group's devices have to be brought back and reworked. Your boss says, "You'd better start doing a better job of training your workers."

a. What are some of the staffing factors that could be contributing to this problem?

b. Explain how you would go about assessing whether it is in fact a training problem.

8-9. Choose a task with which you are familiar—mowing the lawn, making a salad, or studying for a test—and develop a job instruction sheet for it.

8-10. Working individually or in groups, develop a short, programmed learning program on the subject "Guidelines for Giving a More Effective Lecture."

8-11. Find three or four actual examples of employers using social media for training purposes. At what levels of managers are the offerings aimed? What seem to be the most popular types of programs? Why do you think that's the case?

8-12. Working individually or in groups, develop several specific examples to illustrate how a professor teaching human resource management could use at least four of the techniques described in this chapter in teaching his or her HR course.

8-13. Working individually or in groups, develop an orientation program for high school graduates entering your university as freshmen.

8-14. Appendices A and B at the end of this book (pages 614–634) list the knowledge someone studying for the HRCI (Appendix A) or SHRM (Appendix B) certification exam needs to have in each area of human resource management (such as in Strategic Management and Workforce Planning). In groups of several students, do four things: (1) review Appendix A and/or B; (2) identify the material in this chapter that relates to the Appendix A and/or B required knowledge lists; (3) write four multiple-choice exam questions on this material that you believe would be suitable for inclusion in the HRCI exam and/or the SHRM exam; and (4) if time permits, have someone from your team post your team's questions in front of the class, so that students in all teams can answer the exam questions created by the other teams.

KNOWLEDGE BASE

8-15. Perhaps no training task in Afghanistan was more pressing than creating the country's new army in the early 2000s, which is an ongoing task. These were the people who were to help the coalition bring security to Afghanistan. However, many new soldiers and even officers had no experience. There were language barriers between trainers and trainees. And some trainees found themselves quickly under fire from insurgents when they went as trainees out into the field. Based on what you learned about training from this chapter, list the five most important things you would tell the U.S. officer in charge of training to keep in mind as he designs the training program.

Experiential Exercise

Flying the Friendlier Skies

Written and copyrighted by Gary Dessler, PhD.

Purpose: The purpose of this exercise is to give you practice in developing a training program for the job of airline reservation clerk for a major airline.

Required Understanding: You should be fully acquainted with the material in this chapter and should read the following description of an airline reservation clerk's duties:

> Customers contact our airline reservation clerks to obtain flight schedules, prices, and itineraries. The

reservation clerks look up the requested information on our airline's online flight schedule systems, which are updated continuously. The reservation clerk must deal courteously and expeditiously with the customer, and be able to quickly find alternative flight arrangements in order to provide the customer with the itinerary that fits his or her needs. Alternative flights and prices must be found quickly, so that the customer is not kept waiting, and so that our reservations operations group maintains its efficiency standards. It is often necessary to look under various routings, since there may be a dozen or more alternative routes between the customer's starting point and destination.

You may assume that we just hired 30 new clerks, and that you must create a 3-day training program.

How to Set Up the Exercise/Instructions: Divide the class into teams of five or six students.

Airline reservation clerks obviously need numerous skills to perform their jobs. This airline has asked you to quickly design the outline of a training program for its new reservation clerks.

8-16. You may want to start by listing the job's main duties and by reviewing any work you may have done for the exercise at the end of Chapter 6.

8-17. In any case, please produce the requested outline, making sure to be very specific about what you want to teach the new clerks, and what methods and aids you suggest using to train them.

Application Case

Reinventing the Wheel at Apex Door Company

Written and copyrighted by Gary Dessler, PhD.

Jim Delaney, president of Apex Door, has a problem. No matter how often he tells his employees how to do their jobs, they invariably "decide to do it their way," as he puts it, and arguments ensue between Jim, the employee, and the employee's supervisor. One example is the door-design department, where the designers are expected to work with the architects to design doors that meet the specifications. While it's not "rocket science," as Jim puts it, the designers invariably make mistakes—such as designing in too much steel, a problem that can cost Apex tens of thousands of wasted dollars, once you consider the number of doors in, say, a 30-story office tower.

The order processing department is another example. Jim has a very specific and detailed way he wants the order written up, but most of the order clerks don't understand how to use the multipage order form. They simply improvise when it comes to a detailed question such as whether to classify the customer as "industrial" or "commercial."

The current training process is as follows. None of the jobs has a training manual per se, although several have somewhat out-of-date job descriptions. The training for new people is all on the job. Usually, the person leaving the company trains the new person during the 1- or 2-week overlap period, but if there's no overlap, the new person is trained as well as possible by other employees who have filled in occasionally on the job in the past. The training is the same throughout the company—for machinists, secretaries, assemblers, engineers, and accounting clerks, for example.

Questions

8-18. What do you think of Apex's training process? Could it help to explain why employees "do things their way"? If so, how?

8-19. What role should job descriptions play in training at Apex?

8-20. Explain in detail what you would do to improve the training process at Apex. Make sure to provide specific suggestions, please.

Continuing Case

Carter Cleaning Company

Written and copyrighted by Gary Dessler, PhD.

The New Training Program

The Carter Cleaning Centers currently have no formal orientation or training policies or procedures, and Jennifer believes this is one reason why the standards to which she and her father would like employees to adhere to are generally not followed.

The Carters would prefer that certain practices and procedures be used in dealing with the customers at the front counters. For example, all customers should be greeted with what Jack refers to as a "big hello." Garments they drop off should immediately be inspected for any damage or unusual stains so these can be brought to the customer's attention, lest the customer later return to pick up the garment and erroneously blame the store. The garments are then supposed to be placed together in a nylon sack immediately to separate them from other customers' garments. The ticket also has to be carefully written, with the customer's name and telephone number and the date clearly noted on all copies. The counter person is also supposed to take the opportunity to try to sell the customer additional services such as waterproofing, or simply notify the customer that "Now that people are doing their spring cleaning, we're having a special on drapery cleaning all this month." Finally, as the customer leaves, the counter person is supposed to make a courteous comment like "Have a nice day." Each of the other jobs in the stores—pressing, cleaning and spotting, and so forth—similarly contain certain steps, procedures, and, most important, standards the Carters would prefer to see upheld.

The company has had problems, Jennifer feels, because of a lack of adequate employee training and orientation. For example, two new employees became very upset last month when they discovered that they were not paid at the end of the week, on Friday, but instead were paid (as are all Carter employees) on the following Tuesday. The Carters use the extra two days in part to give them time to obtain everyone's hours and compute their pay. The other reason they do it, according to Jack, is that "frankly, when we stay a few days behind in paying employees it helps to ensure that they at least give us a few days' notice before quitting on us. While we are certainly obligated to pay them anything they earn, we find that psychologically they seem to be less likely to just walk out on us Friday evening and not show up Monday morning if they still haven't gotten their pay from the previous week. This way they at least give us a few days' notice so we can find a replacement."

There are other matters that could be covered during orientation and training, says Jennifer. These include company policy regarding paid holidays, lateness and absences, health benefits (there are none, other than workers' compensation), substance abuse, eating or smoking on the job (both forbidden), and general matters like the maintenance of a clean and safe work area, personal appearance and cleanliness, time sheets, personal telephone calls, and personal e-mail.

Jennifer believes that implementing orientation and training programs would help to ensure that employees know how to do their jobs the right way. And she and her father further believe that it is only when employees understand the right way to do their jobs that there is any hope their jobs will be accomplished the way the Carters want them to be accomplished.

Questions

8-21. Specifically, what should the Carters cover in their new employee orientation program, and how should they convey this information?

8-22. In the HR management course Jennifer took, the book suggested using a job instruction sheet to identify tasks performed by an employee. Should the Carter Cleaning Centers use a form like this for the counter person's job? If so, what should the form look like, say, for a counter person?

8-23. Which specific training techniques should Jennifer use to train her pressers, her cleaner/spotters, her managers, and her counter people? Why should these training techniques be used?

Translating Strategy into HR Policies and Practices Case*,§

The accompanying strategy map for this chapter is in MyLab Management; the overall map on the inside back cover of this text outlines the relationships involved.

Improving Performance at the Hotel Paris

The New Training Program

The Hotel Paris's competitive strategy is "To use superior guest service to differentiate the Hotel Paris properties, and to thereby increase the length of stay and return rate of guests, and thus boost revenues and profitability." HR manager Lisa Cruz must now formulate functional policies and activities that support this competitive strategy, by eliciting the required employee behaviors and competencies.

As she reviewed her company's training processes, Lisa had many reasons to be concerned. For one thing, the Hotel Paris relied almost exclusively on informal on-the-job training. New security guards attended a 1-week program offered by a law enforcement agency, but all other new hires, from assistant manager to housekeeping crew, learned the rudiments of their jobs from their colleagues and their supervisors, on the job. Lisa noted that the drawbacks of this informality were evident when she compared the Hotel Paris's performance on various training metrics with those of other hotels and service firms. For example, in terms of number of hours training per employee per year, number of hours training for new employees, cost per trainee hour, and percent of payroll spent on training, the Hotel Paris was far from the norm when benchmarked against similar firms.

As Lisa and the CFO reviewed measures of the Hotel Paris's current training efforts, it was clear that (when compared to similar companies) some changes were in order. Most other service companies provided at least 40 hours of training per employee per year, while the Hotel Paris offered, on average, no more than 5 or 6. Similar firms offered at least 40 hours of training per *new* employee, while the Hotel Paris offered, at most, 10. Even the apparently "good" metrics comparisons simply masked poor results. For example, whereas most service firms spend about 8% of their payrolls on training, the Hotel Paris spent less than 1%. The problem, of course, was that the Hotel Paris's training wasn't more efficient, it was simply nonexistent.

Given this and the commonsense links between (1) employee training and (2) employee performance, the CFO gave his go-ahead for Lisa and her team to design a comprehensive package of training programs for all Hotel Paris employees. They retained a training supplier to design a 1-day training program composed of lectures and audiovisual material for all new employees. This program covered the Hotel Paris's history, its competitive strategy, and its critical employee capabilities and behaviors, including the need to be customer oriented. With a combination of lectures and video examples of correct and incorrect behaviors, the behavior-modeling part of this program aimed to cultivate in new employees the company's essential values, including, "we endeavor to do everything we can to make the guests' stay 100% pleasant."

The team developed separate training programs for each of the hotel's other individual job categories. For example, it retained a special vendor to create computer-based training programs, complete with interactive scenarios, for both the front-desk clerks and telephone operators. As with all the new training programs, they had these translated into the languages of the countries in which the Hotel Paris did business. The team chose to stay with on-the-job training for both the housekeeping and valet/door person job categories, but formalized this training with special handbooks for each job category's supervisory staff. For assistant managers, the team developed a new videoconference-based online training and development program. In this way, the new managers could interact with other assistant managers around the chain, even as they were learning the basics of their new jobs. Lisa and the CFO were not at all surprised to find that within a year of instituting the new training programs, scores on numerous employee capabilities and behavior metrics (including speed of check-in/out, percent of employees scoring at least 90% on Hotel Paris's values quiz, and percent room cleaning infractions) improved markedly. They knew from previous analyses that these improvements would, in turn, drive improvements in customer and organizational outcomes, and strategic performance.

§ Written and copyrighted by Gary Dessler, PhD.

Questions

8-24. Based on what you read in this chapter, what would you have suggested Lisa and her team do first with respect to training, particularly in terms of the company's strategy? Why?

8-25. Have Lisa and the CFO sufficiently investigated whether training is really called for? Why? What would you suggest?

8-26. Based on what you read in this Dessler *Human Resource Management* chapter and what you may access via the Web, develop a detailed training program for one of these hotel positions: security guard, housekeeper, or door person.

Writing Assignments

8-27. John Santos is an undergraduate business student majoring in accounting. He just failed the first accounting course, Accounting 101. He is understandably upset. How would you use performance analysis to identify what, if any, are John's training needs?

8-28. Knowing that you are taking an HR management course, a friend asks you this: I just hired a nanny for my child, and I want to make sure she knows what to do; in outline form, what should I cover in the training program I give her?

MyLab Management Try It!

How would you apply the concepts and skills you learned in this chapter? If your professor has assigned this activity, go to the Assignments section of **www.pearson.com/mylab/management** to complete the simulation.

PERSONAL INVENTORY ASSESSMENTS

Go to **www.pearson.com/mylab/management** to complete the Personal Inventory Assessment related to this chapter.

Key Terms

employee orientation, 238
training, 240
negligent training, 240
task analysis, 242
performance analysis, 242
competency model, 244
the cloud, 247
on-the-job training (OJT), 248
apprenticeship training, 248
job instruction training (JIT), 250
programmed learning, 251
behavior modeling, 251
electronic performance support systems (EPSS), 252
job aid, 252
virtual classroom, 254
Web 2.0 learning, 255
lifelong learning, 255
cross training, 256
management development, 258
job rotation, 258
action learning, 259
case study method, 260
management game, 260
role-playing, 260
in-house development center, 261
executive coach, 261
organizational development, 264
controlled experimentation, 266

Endnotes

1. This case is based on John Donovan and Cathy Benko, "AT&T's Talent Overhaul: Can the Firm Really Retrain Hundreds of Thousands of Employees?" *Harvard Business Review*, October 2016, pp. 69–73.
2. Marjorie Derven, "Management Onboarding," *TD*, April 2008, pp. 49–52. See also www.roberthalf.com/onboarding, accessed August 23, 2014; and Alex Moore, "Learning Meets the Internet of Things," *TD*, December 2017, pp. 18–20.

3. Sabrina Hicks, "Successful Orientation Programs," *TD*, April 2000, p. 59. See also Howard Klein and Natasha Weaver, "The Effectiveness of an Organizational Level Orientation Program in the Socialization of New Hires," *Personnel Psychology* 53 (2000), pp. 47–66; Laurie Friedman, "Are You Losing Potential New Hires at Hello?" *TD*, November 2006, pp. 25–27; and Talya N. Bauer, "Onboarding New Employees: Maximizing Success," *SHRM Foundation*, www.right.com/thought-leadership/research/shrm-foundations-effective-practice-guidelines-series-onboarding-new-employees-maximizing-success-sponsored-by-right-management.pdf, accessed March 2, 2014; Jon Wolper, "Get on Board with Onboarding," *TD*, January 2017, pp. 18–20
4. Sheila Hicks et al., "Orientation Redesign," *TD*, July 2006, pp. 43–46.
5. "The First 90 Days: Help New Employees Start out on the Right Foot," *HR Magazine*, December 2015/January 2016, p. 27.
6. See, for example, John Kammeyer-Mueller and Connie Wanberg, "Unwrapping the Organizational Entry Process: Disentangling Multiple Antecedents and Their Pathways to Adjustments," *Journal of Applied Psychology* 88, no. 5 (2003), pp. 779–794; "First Minutes Are Critical in New-Employee Orientation," https://www.forbes.com/sites/hbsworkingknowledge/2013/04/01/first-minutes-of-new-employee-orientation-are-critical/#bf1024e48308, accessed March 5, 2018.
7. www.shrm.org/templatestools/samples/hrforms/articles/pages/1cms_002153.aspx, http://hrweb.berkeley.edu/guides/managing-hr/recruiting-staff/new-employee/checklist, and www.go2hr.ca/articles/new-hire-orientation-checklist, all accessed March 30, 2015.
8. www.right.com/thought-leadership/research/shrm-foundations-effective-practice-guidelines-series-onboardingnew-employees-maximizing-success-sponsored-by-right-management.pdf, accessed August 23, 2014.
9. Mukta Kulkarni and Mark Lengnick-Hall, "Socialization of People with Disabilities in the Workplace," *Human Resource Management* 60, no. 4 (July–August 2011), pp. 521–540.
10. Allison Ellis, et al., "Newcomer Adjustment: Examining the Role of Managers' Perception of Newcomer Proactive Behavior during Organizational Socialization," *Journal of Applied Psychology* 102, no. 7 (2017), pp. 993–1001.
11. Martin Byford et al., "Onboarding Isn't Enough," *Harvard Business Review*, May–June 2017, pp. 78–86.
12. "Drug Rep Claims Handbook Protection from Retaliation," *Bloomberg BNA Bulletin to Management*, December 18, 2012, p. 8.
13. To some extent, the policies employers put in manuals reflect the prevailing political environment. For example, President Obama's National Labor Relations Board (NLRB) took legal steps to stop employers from using policies—such as requiring confidentiality agreements—that restricted employees from discussing the terms and conditions of their employment. The Republican administration may be more open to such policies. Robert Brody and Alexander Friedman, "As We Transition from the Obama to the Trump Era, Employers Must Walk the Employee Handbook Tightrope," *Bloomberg BNA Bulletin to Management*, January 2, 2018.
14. Jennifer Taylor Arnold, "Ramping Up Onboarding," *HR Magazine*, May 2010, pp. 75–78.
15. www.workday.com/company/news/workdaymobility.php, accessed March 24, 2009.
16. "Four Ways to Use QR Codes to Enliven Your Learning Event," *TD*, January 2013, p. 19.
17. Daniel Bortz, "All on Board," *HR Magazine*, December 2017/January 2018, pp. 45–47.
18. For example, IBM's "assimilation process" has three main steps: *affirming* (welcoming the new employee and assigning a coach); *beginning* (he or she is met in person, meets the team, is introduced on the intranet onboarding platform, and learns his or her roles and responsibilities); and *connecting* (which includes having an "ask coach" make sure the employee is on track). www.right.com/thought-leadership/research/shrm-foundations-effective-practice-guidelines-series-onboarding-new-employees-maximizing-success-sponsored-by-right-management.pdf.
19. See, Gary Dessler, *Winning Commitment: How to Build and Keep a Competitive Workforce* (New York: McGraw-Hill, 1993); Gary Dessler, "How to Earn Your Employees' Commitment," *Academy of Management Executive* 13, no. 2 (1999). For some recent insights see, for example, Jennifer Statham, "New Toyota President Drives Workforce in Alabama," April 9, 2017, http://www.al.com/business/index.ssf/2017/04/new_toyota_president_drives_wo.html, accessed March 5, 2018.
20. Ibid., and see www.autonews.com/article/20050718/SUB/507180713/toyota-seeks-efficiency-training-for-all; http://thetoyotaway.org/excerpts.html; www.toyotageorgetown.com/tps1.asp; http://sloanreview.mit.edu/article/what-really-happened-to-toyota; and www.glassdoor.com/Reviews/Employee-Review-Toyota-Tsusho-America-RVW3553588.htm, all accessed February 28, 2014.
21. Ibid.
22. Maria Ho, "Learning Investment and Hours Are on the Rise," *TD*, December 2017, p. 38.
23. For a discussion of the evolution of training and development, see Bradford Bell et al., "100 Years of Training and Development Research: What We Know and Where We Should Go," *Journal of Applied Psychology* 102, no. 3 (2017), pp. 305–323.
24. "Lack of Training Fuels Desire to Job Search," *TD*, January 2013, p. 23.
25. Go to www.coca-cola.co.uk, then click "About Us" and "Employment—Our People."
26. Ibid., p. 33.
27. Rita Smith, "Aligning Learning with Business Strategy," *TD*, November 2008, pp. 41–43.
28. Paul Harris, "The Value Add of Learning," *TD*, October 2014, pp. 53–55.
29. This case is based on John Donovan and Cathy Benko, "AT&T's Talent Overhaul: Can the Firm Really Retrain Hundreds of Thousands of Employees?" *Harvard Business Review*, October 2016, pp. 69–73.
30. W. Clayton Allen, "Overview and Evolution of the ADDIE Training System," *Advances in Developing Human Resources* 8, no. 4 (November 2006), pp. 430–441.
31. www.intulogy.com/process, accessed April 20, 2011.
32. P. Nick Blanchard and James Thacker, *Effective Training: Systems, Strategies, and Practices* (Upper Saddle River, NJ: Prentice Hall, 1999), pp. 138–139. See also Matthew Casey and Dennis Doverspike, "Training Needs Analysis and Evaluation for New Technologies Through the Use of Problem Based Inquiry," *Performance Improvement Quarterly* 18, no. 1 (2005), pp. 110–124; and Judy Murray, "Get to the Root of the Problem," *TD*, February 2017, pages 26–29.
33. Tom Barron, "When Things Go Haywire," *TD*, February 1999, pp. 25–27; see also, for example, Bill Stetar, "Training: It's Not Always the Answer," *Quality Progress*, March 2005, pp. 44–49, http://performancetechnology.com/ptg_pdfs/qp0305stetar.pdf, accessed October 11, 2012.
34. "Retooling Vocational Education," *The Economist*, August 23, 2014, p. 66.
35. Justin Arneson et al., "Training and Development Competencies: We Define to Create Competitive Advantage," *TD*, January 2013, p. 45.
36. See also, for example, Jennifer Salopek, "The Power of the Pyramid," *TD*, May 2009, pp. 70–73.
37. Pat Galagan, "It's the Competency That Matters, Not the Course," *TD*, January 2015, pp. 24–27.
38. Employers increasingly utilize learning content management systems (LCMS) to compile author training content. See, for example, Bill Perry, "Customized Content at Your Fingertips," *TD*, June 2009, pp. 29–30.
39. P. Nick Blanchard and James Thacker, *Effective Training* (Upper Saddle River, NJ: Pearson, 2010), pp. 26–94, 153–199, 285–316; see also Bruno Neal, "e-ADDIE!," *TD* 65, no. 3 (March 2011), pp. 76–77.
40. Jay Bahlis, "Blueprint for Planning Learning," *TD*, March 2008, pp. 64–67.
41. Gillian Douglas and Shannon McKenzie, "Writing Choice–Based Learning Objectives," *TD*, August 2017, pp. 24–26.
42. P. Nick Blanchard and James Thacker, *Effective Training: Systems, Strategies, and Practices* (Upper Saddle River, NJ: Prentice Hall, 2007), p. 8; and G. Sadri, "Boosting Performance Through Self-Efficacy," *TD* 65 no. 6 (June 2011), pp. 30–31.
43. Emily Baumann and Greta Ballentine, "Estimate Training Resources with Precision," *TD*, February 2014, pp. 20–22.
44. Ibid.
45. Ibid., p. 90.
46. Kenneth Wexley and Gary Latham, *Developing and Training Human Resources in Organizations* (Upper Saddle River, NJ: Prentice Hall, 2002), p. 305.
47. Ibid.
48. Kathryn Tyler, "Focus on Training," *HR Magazine*, May 2000, pp. 94–102; Murray Goldberg, "How to Motivate and Engage Your Trainees," Marine Learning Systems, March 23, 2016, https://www.marinels.com/how-to-motivate-and-engage-your-trainees/, accessed March 5, 2018.

49. Stefanie Johnson, "Go for the Goal (as): Relationship between Goal Setting and Transfer of Training Following Leadership Development," *Academy of Management Learning & Education* 11, no. 4 (2012), pp. 555–569.
50. Janice A. Cannon-Bowers et al., "Framework for Understanding Pre-Practice Conditions and Their Impact on Learning," *Personnel Psychology* 51 (1998), pp. 291–320; see also J. S. Goodman et al., "Feedback Specificity, Information Processing, and Transfer of Training," *Organizational Behavior and Human Decision Processes* 115 no. 2 (July 2011), pp. 253–267.
51. Ibid., p. 305.
52. Sebastian Bailey, "Seven Tricks to Make Learning Stick," *TD*, April 2016, pp. 63–66.
53. Ibid., and see Kendra Lee, "Reinforce Training," *Training* 48 no. 3 (May/June 2011), p. 24.
54. Eric Krell, "Get Sold on Training Incentives," *HR Magazine*, February 2013, p. 57.
55. Alan Saks and Monica Belcourt, "An Investigation of Training Activities and Transfer of Training in Organizations," *Human Resource Management* 45, no. 4 (Winter 2006), pp. 629– 648. The percentage of managers transferring behaviors from training to the job may be as low as 10% to 20%. See George Vellios, "On the Level," *TD*, December 2008, pp. 26–29. See also K. Lee, "Implement Training Successfully," *Training* 46, no. 5 (June 2009), p. 16.
56. Large training providers include Element K, Geo Learning, learn.com, Outsmart, Plateau, Saba People Systems, and Sum-Total Systems. "Training Providers," *Workforce Management*, January 2011, p. 8. See also Jean Barbazette, "Take the Pain out of Writing Training Materials," *TD*, April 2013, pp. 108–110.
57. ASTD Infoline, "Planning and Organizing Training Events," August 2013; and Robert Hewes, "Step-by-Step," *TD*, February 2014, pp. 56–61.
58. Wexley and Latham, *Developing and Training Human Resources in Organizations*, pp. 78–79.
59. Donna Goldwasser, "Me a Trainer?" *Training*, April 2001, pp. 60–66; http://employment.menswearhouse.com/ats/advantageSelector.action;jsessionid=C6EA17158451F5A2902F7195B678CF6A?type=training, accessed June 1, 2011.
60. Jason Dahling, Samantha Taylor, Samantha Chau, and Stephen Dwight, "Does Coaching Matter? A Multilevel Model Linking Managerial Coaching Skill and Frequency to Sales Goal Attainment," *Personnel Psychology*, 69 (2016), pp. 863–894.
61. See, for example, www.aps-online.net/consulting/structured_ojt.htm, accessed June 1, 2011; and Kathryn Tyler, "15 Ways to Train on the Job," *HR Magazine* 53 no. 9 (September 2008), pp. 105–108.
62. Valerie Davis-Howard, "Unleash Change through a Peer-to-Peer Approach," *TD*, July 2014, pp. 76–77.
63. The following four steps in on-the-job training based on William Berliner and William McLarney, *Management Practice and Training* (Burr Ridge, IL: McGraw-Hill, 1974), pp. 442–443. For the discussion of employee task analysis, see "Eight Steps to Better On-the-Job Training," *HR Focus* 80, no. 7 (July 2003), pp. 11, 13–14.
64. Cindy Waxer, "Steelmaker Revives Apprentice Program to Address Graying Workforce, Forge Next Leaders," *Workforce Management*, January 30, 2006, p. 40.
65. Lance Lambert, "You're Hired, Trump Tells 5 Million Future Apprentices," *Bloomberg BNA Bulletin to Management*, June 27, 2017.
66. "Employer's Playbook for Building an Apprenticeship Program," http://www.themanufacturinginstitute.org/~/media/14B36E1969704C3BADF11A1BE0F21B3D.ashx, accessed March 5, 2018.
67. Kermit Kaleba, "New Changes to Apprenticeship Program Could Be Forthcoming," *TD*, February 2008, p. 14.
68. Lambert, "You're Hired, Trump Tells 5 Million Future Apprentices."
69. Ibraiz Tarique, *Seven Trends in Corporate Training and Development* (Upper Saddle River, NJ: Pearson, 2014, p. 67. See also Elaine-Biech, "The 90% Solution," *TD*, December 2016, pp. 58–63.
70. Tarique, *Seven Trends in Corporate Training and Development*, p. 71.
71. Aparna Nancherla, "Knowledge Delivered in Any Other Form Is . . . Perhaps Sweeter," *TD*, May 2009, pp. 54–60.
72. "Collaboration Teambuilding in the Cafeteria," *Harvard Business Review*, December 2015, pp. 24–25.
73. Nadira Hira, "The Making of a UPS Driver," *Fortune*, November 12, 2007, p. 120.
74. Arthur Winfred Jr. et al., "Effectiveness of Training in Organizations: A Meta Analysis of Design and Evaluation Features," *Journal of Applied Psychology* 88, no. 2 (2003), pp. 234–245.
75. Donald Michalak and Edwin G. Yager, *Making the Training Process Work* (New York: Harper & Row, 1979), pp. 108–111. See also Richard Wiegand, "Can All Your Trainees Hear You?" *TD* 41, no. 8 (August 1987), pp. 38–43; "Do's and Don'ts at the Podium," *Journal of Accountancy* 200, no. 3 (September 2005); and "Preparing a Lecture," Yale Center for Teaching and Learning, https://ctl.yale.edu/teaching/ideas-teaching/preparing-lecture, accessed March 5, 2018.
76. Jacqueline Schmidt and Joseph Miller, "The Five-Minute Rule for Presentations," *TD*, March 2000, pp. 16–17; and "Dos and Don'ts at the Podium," op cit.
77. G. N. Nash, J. P. Muczyk, and F. L. Vettori, "The Role and Practical Effectiveness of Programmed Instruction," *Personnel Psychology* 24 (1971), pp. 397–418; Duane Schultz and Sydney Ellen Schultz, *Psychology and Work Today* (Upper Saddle River, NJ: Prentice Hall, 1998), pp. 181–183; chemistry study based on N. Izzet Kurbanoglu, Yavuz Taskesenligil, and Mustafa Sozbilir, "Programmed Instruction Revisited: A Study on Teaching Stereochemistry," *Chemistry Education Research and Practice* 7, no. 1 (2006), pp. 13–21.
78. Paul Taylor et al., "A Meta-Analytic Review of Behavior Modeling Training," *Journal of Applied Psychology* 90, no. 4 (2005), pp. 692–719.
79. Wexley and Latham, Developing and Training *Human Resources in Organizations*, pp. 131–133. See also Teri O. Grady and Mike Matthews, "Video . . . Through the Eyes of the Trainee," *Training* 24, no. 7 (July 1987), pp. 57–62; "New ARTBA PPE Video and Laborers' Night Work Suggestions Highlight Construction Safety Advances," *EHS Today* 2, no. 7 (July 2009), p. 51.
80. Paula Ketter, "What Can Training Do for Brown?" *TD*, May 2008, pp. 30–36.
81. Craig Marion, "What Is the EPSS Movement and What Does It Mean to Information Designers?" http://www.smnweb.com/e-hr/letture/perform/EPSS%20Movement.htm, August 20, 1999, accessed June 28, 2015.
82. https://whatfix.com/reviews/, accessed March 5, 2018.
83. Blanchard and Thacker, *Effective Training*, 2010, p. 163.
84. www.cisco.com/en/US/products/ps10352/index.html, accessed June 28, 2015.
85. www.radvision.com/Support/cisco.htm, accessed June 1, 2011.
86. Dina Berta, "Computer-Based Training Clicks with Both Franchisees and Their Employees," *Nation's Restaurant News*, July 9, 2001, pp. 1, 18; and "Is Online Fall Protection Training Effective?" *EHS Today* 3, no. 7 (July 2010).
87. Blanchard and Thacker, *Effective Training*, p. 247; see also Michael Laff, "Simulations: Slowly Proving Their Worth," *TD*, June 2007, pp. 30–34.
88. Laff, "Simulations." See also Fatimah Lateef, "Simulation-Based Learning: Just Like the Real Thing," *Journal of Emergencies, Trauma, and Shock* 3, no. 4 (October–December 2010), pp. 348–352.
89. Paul Harris, "Simulation: The Game Is On," *TD*, October 2003, p. 49. See also Jenni Jarventaus, "Virtual Threat, Real Sweat," *TD*, May 2007, pp. 72–78. More employers are extending simulations to creating training games for employees. As in well-known entertainment games like Angry Birds, the advantages from a learning standpoint of using games include constant feedback on how you're doing, "accrued grading" in which you move ahead challenge by challenge, competition and cooperation, and the "freedom to fail," particularly to learn from one's own mistakes. Sebastian Deterding, "Gameful Design for Learning," *TD*, July 2013, pp. 61–63. See also Karl Kapp and Sharon Boller, "Gametime," *TD*, January 2017, pp. 37–41.
90. Jarventaus, "Virtual Threat, Real Sweat."
91. Drew Robb, "Let the Games Begin," *HR Magazine*, September 2012, p. 96.
92. Blanchard and Thacker, *Effective Training*, p. 248.
93. Ibid., p. 249. See also Kim Kleps, "Virtual Sales Training Scores a Hit," *TD*, December 2006, pp. 63–64, and "What Is Virtual Reality Training?" Virtual Reality Society, https://www.vrs.org.uk/virtual-reality-education/what-is-virtual-reality-training.html, accessed March 5, 2018.
94. Anders Gronstedt, "From Immersion to Presence," *TD*, June 2016, pp. 55–56.
95. www.reuters.com/article/2014/03/26/us-facebook-acquisition-idUSBREA2O1WX20140326, accessed June 28, 2015. See also Jennifer Hofmann, "Are You Virtually Competent?" *TD*, April 2015, pp. 54–59.
96. Gi Hun Yang and Jae Young Lee, "Learning While Playing," *TD*, May 2016, pp. 46–52.

97. Cammie Cable, "Sales Up, Costs Down," *TD*, June 2016, pp. 68–69.
98. Pat Galagan, "Made Fast in China," *TD*, January 2013, p. 30.
99. Kevin Alansky, "Blackboard Pays Off for ADP," *TD* 65, no. 6 (June 2011), pp. 68–69; see also Barbara Carnes, "The Ties That Bind," *TD*, January 2013, pp. 38–40.
100. John Zonneveld, "GM Dealer Training Goes Global," *TD*, December 2006, pp. 47–51. See also "What's Next for the LMS?" *TD*, September 2011, p. 16.
101. www.litmos.com/learning-management-system; www.talentlms.com; http://money.CNN.com/2014/09/03/technology/enterprise/what-is-the-cloud, both accessed March 31, 2015.
102. Zonneveld, op cit.
103. For a list of guidelines for using e-learning, see, for example, Mark Simon, "E-Learning No How," *TD*, January 2009, pp. 34–39. See also Sarah Gilbert, "E-Learning Design with Ease," *TD*, July 2014, pp. 70–71.
104. "The Next Generation of Corporate Learning," *TD*, June 2004, p. 47; Jennifer Hofmann and Nanatte Miner, "Real Blended Learning Stands Up," *TD*, September 2008, pp. 28–31; J. Hofmann, "Top 10 Challenges of Blended Learning," *Training* (Minneapolis, Minn.) 48, no. 2 (March/April 2011), pp. 12–13; and Lee Salz, "Use Webinars for Training and Revenue," *Training* 48, no. 2 (March/ April 2011), p. 14.
105. Tony Bingham and Pat Galagan, "Training Powers Up That Steele," *TD*, January 2014, p. 31.
106. https://itunes.apple.com/app/pwc-l-d-portal/id1080257670?mt=8&ign-mpt=uo%3D4; Josh Bersin, "Employee Learning Enters the Digital Age," *HR Magazine*, August 2017, pp. 59–60.
107. Amanda Reed, "Transforming a 95-Year-Old Organization through e-Learning," *TD*, August 2017, pp. 70–71.
108. See, for example, http://www.blackboard.com/online-collaborative-learning/virtual-classroom.html, accessed March 5, 2018.
109. Traci Sitzmann et al., "The Comparative Effectiveness of Web-Based and Classroom Instruction: A Meta-Analysis," *Personnel Psychology* 59 (2006), pp. 623–664. See also https://sas.elluminate.com/site/internal/home, accessed March 7, 2017.
110. Sarah Foster Gale, "L & D Today: Microsized, Personalized, and Really, Really Short," *Workforce*, July/August 2017, p. 44.
111. Jennifer Taylor Arnold, "Learning on-the-Fly," *HR Magazine*, September 2007, p. 137; see also M. Donahue, "Mobile Learning Is the Next Generation in Training." *Hotel Management* 226, no. 4 (April 4, 2011), p. 17; and Geoff Holle, "Using Mobile Technology to Support Talent Development," *TD*, January 2017, pp. 22–24.
112. www.dominknow.com, accessed March 9, 2017.
113. Bill Roberts, "From IT Learning to Mobile Learning," *HR Magazine*, August 2012, pp. 61–65.
114. Chris Pirie, "Technology Plus Learning Equals Inspiration," *TD*, December 2012, pp. 39–46.
115. Christopher Pappas, "8 Best Practices for Just-in-Time Online Training," November 3, 2016, https://elearningindustry.com/best-practices-just-in-time-online-training, accessed March 5, 2018.
116. Ann Paul, "Micro Learning 101." *HR Magazine*, May 2016, pp. 37–41. See also, Megan Cole, "Talent Development Pros Predict Spike In Micro-Learning," *TD*, May 2017, p. 9.
117. Catherine Skrzypinski, "Social Media Changes Employee Expectations Regarding Communication," *HR Magazine*, January 2013, p. 14; see also Dan Steer, "Improve Formal Learning with Social Media," *TD*, December 2012, pp. 31–33.
118. Pat Galagan, "Second That," *TD*, February 2008, pp. 34–37.
119. Paraphrased from Manuel London and M. J. Hall, "Unlocking the Value of Web 2.0 Technologies for Training and Development: The Shift from Instructor-Controlled, Adaptive Learning to Learner-Driven, Generative Learning," *Human Resource Management* 50, no. 6 (November–December 2011), p. 761.
120. This is based on ibid., pp. 763–765.
121. Ruth Clark, "Accelerate Expertise with Scenario-Based e-Learning," *TD*, August 2016, pp. 51–55.
122. Among other things, the Rehabilitation Act of 1973 aims to extend grants to states for vocational rehabilitation services, with special emphasis on services to those with the most severe handicaps, https://www.eeoc.gov/eeoc/history/ada25th/rehab_act-1973.cfm, accessed March 5, 2018.
123. https://www.w3.org/TR/WCAG20/, accessed March 2, 2018.
124. Karen McCandless, "How to Train Your Staff in the Gig Economy," May 19, 2016, https://lab.getapp.com/how-to-train-your-staff-in-the-gig-economy/; Margery Weinstein, "Training Challenges in Today's 'Gig Economy,'" July 24, 2015, https://trainingmag.com/training-challenges-today%E2%80%99s-%E2%80%9Cgig-economy%E2%80%9D; "How the Gig Economy Is Revolutionizing Restaurant Training Programs," https://www.hotschedules.com/blog/how-the-gig-economy-is-revolutionizing-restaurant-training-programs/, all accessed March 7, 2017.
125. https://www.mindflash.com/, accessed March 9, 2017.
126. Susan Ladika, "When Learning Lasts a Lifetime," *HR Magazine*, May 2008, p. 57; http://www.wtb.wa.gov/LifelongLearningAccount.asp, accessed March 4, 2018.
127. https://www.panopto.com/blog/1-in-7-workers-cant-read-your-manual-whats-a-trainer-to-do/, accessed March 7, 2017.
128. Jennifer Salopek, "The Growth of Succession Management," *TD*, June 2007, pp. 22–24; and Kermit Kaleba, "Businesses Continue to Push for Lifelong Learning," *TD*, June 2007, p. 14.
129. Rita Zeidner, "One Workforce—Many Languages," *HR Magazine*, January 2009, pp. 33–37.
130. http://www.ncte.org/ncle, accessed March 5, 2018.
131. Matthew Reis, "Do-It-Yourself Diversity," *TD*, March 2004, pp. 80–81. See also, Alex Lindsey, Eden King, Ashley Membere, and Ho Kwan Cheung, "Two Types of Diversity Training That Really Work," *Harvard Business Review*, July 28, 2017, https://hbr.org/2017/07/two-types-of-diversity-training-that-really-work, accessed March 4, 2018.
132. https://sollah.com/training-solutions/just-be-fair-basic-diversity-training/, accessed March 4, 2018. Jennifer Salopek, "Trends: Lost in Translation," *TD*, December 2003, p. 15; www.visionpoint.com/training-solutions/title/just-be-fair-basic-diversity-training, accessed June 17, 2011; http://sollah.com/training-solutions/just-be-fair-basic-diversity-training/, accessed March 7, 2017.
133. http://www.prismdiversity.com/products/inclusion_diversity-training.html?Nav=DiversityBtn, accessed March 5, 2018.
134. Blanchard and Thacker, *Effective Training*, 2003, pp. 403–405.
135. Hannah Lutz, "Cross Training Boosts Resources and Teamwork," *Automotive News*, January 30, 2017, p. 40.
136. Rebecca Greenfield, "Startup vs. Wild," *Bloomberg Businessweek*, December 7, 2015, pp. 99-101.
137. http://www.skillsoft.com/business-solutions/, accessed March 7, 2017.
138. https://www.td.org/Professional-Resources, accessed March 7, 2017.
139. Ibid; https://www.sba.gov/tools/sba-learning-center/search/training, accessed March 7, 2017.
140. www.themanufacturinginstitute.org/Skills-Certification/Right-Skills-Now/Right-Skills-Now.aspx, accessed August 24, 2014.
141. Paula Caligiuri, "Developing Global Leaders," *Human Resource Management Review* 16 (2006), pp. 219–228.
142. Ibid.
143. Gail Johnson Morris and Kim Rogers, "High Potentials Are Still Your Best Bet," *TD*, February 2013, pp. 58–62.
144. Ann Pomeroy, "Head of the Class," *HR Magazine*, January 2005, p. 57. Of course, traits like cognitive ability and personality also mold job success, not just training. See, for example, Lisa Dragoni et al., "Developing Executive Leaders: The Relative Contribution of Cognitive Ability, Personality, and the Accumulation of Work Experience in Predicting Strategic Thinking Competency," *Personnel Psychology* 60, no. 4 (2011), pp. 829–861.
145. Andrew Shipilov and Frederic Godart, "Luxury's Talent Factories," *Harvard Business Review*, June 2015, p. 101.
146. See Paul Evans, Yves Doz, and Andre Laurent, *Human Resource Management in International Firms* (New York: St. Martin's Press, 1990), pp. 122– 124; www.sony.net/SonyInfo/csr_report/employees/training/index3.html; accessed March 4, 2014; and www.mckinsey.com/insights/organization/how_multinationals_can_attract_the_talent_they_need, accessed March 5, 2018.
147. Michael Marquardt, "Action Learning around the World," *TD*, February 2015, pp. 45–49.
148. "Thrown into Deep End, Workers Surface as Leaders," *BNA Bulletin to Management*, July 11, 2002, p. 223. See also Michelle Peters, "Accomplish Two for One with Action Learning," *TD*, February 2013, pp. 52–54; Hyeon-Cheol Bong and Yonjoo Cho, "Defining Success in Action Learning: An International Comparison," *European Journal of Training and Development* 41, no. 2 (February 2017), pp. 160+.
149. For another example, this in the public sector, see, for example, Andrew Rahaman, "Questions, Answers, and Problem Solving in the Public Sector: Action

Learning Can Transform the Way Decisions Are Made within an Agency, and Improve the Processes by Which an Agency Operates," *TD* 70, no. 3 (March 2016), pp. 48+.

150. Tarique, *Seven Trends in Corporate Training and Development*, p. 114.

151. Chris Whitcomb, "Scenario-Based Training at the FBI," *TD*, June 1999, pp. 42–46. See also Michael Laff, "Serious Gaming: The Trainer's New Best Friend," *TD*, January 2007, pp. 52–57. Some schools use such case scenarios to train professionals such as accountants: Aini Aman, Ruhanita Maelah, and Sofiah Md Auzair, "Implementation of Integrated Case Studies Course for Accounting Students," *Procedia—Social and Behavioral Sciences* 59, no. 17 (October 2012), pp. 9–17.

152. http://teamcommunication.blogspot.com, accessed July 6, 2014.

153. Carol Leaman, "Boost Basic Job Skills Training," *TD*, August 2014, pp. 34–39.

154. American Management Association, www.amanet.org, accessed July 6, 2014.

155. For information on the SHRM learning system, see www.shrm.org/Education/educationalproducts/learning/Pages/default.aspx?utm_campaign=LearningSystem_All_2012&utm_medium=mailing&utm_source=brochure, accessed July 21, 2013.

156. For a list of Harvard programs, see https://www.exed.hbs.edu/Pages/default.aspx, accessed May 18, 2017.

157. Ann Pomeroy, "Head of the Class," *HR Magazine*, January 2005, p. 57. See also Michael Laff, "Centralized Training Leads to Nontraditional Universities," *TD*, January 2007, pp. 27–29; Chris Musselwhite, "University Executive Education Gets Real," *TD*, May 2006, p. 57; and Ralph Miller and David Abdow, "Executive Education That Works," *TD*, December 2012, pp. 28–30.

158. https://executiveeducation.wharton.upenn.edu/thought-leadership/wharton-at-work/2011/10/custom-leadership, accessed March 5, 2018.

159. Norman Maier, Allen Solem, and Ayesha Maier, *The Role Play Technique* (San Diego, CA: University Associates, 1975), pp. 2–3. See also Karen Griggs, "A Role Play for Revising Style and Applying Management Theories," *Business Communication Quarterly* 68, no. 1 (March 2005), pp. 60–65.

160. Seth Stevenson, "How Do You Make Better Managers?" http://www.slate.com/articles/business/psychology_of_management/2014/06/ge_s_crotonville_management_campus_where_future_company_leaders_are_trained.html, accessed March 5, 2018.

161. Martha Peak, "Go Corporate U!" *Management Review* 86, no. 2 (February 1997), pp. 33–37; and Jessica Li and Amy Lui Abel, "Prioritizing and Maximizing the Impact of Corporate Universities," *TD* 65, no. 5 (May 2011), pp. 54–57.

162. Russell Gerbman, "Corporate Universities 101," *HR Magazine*, February 2000, pp. 101–106; Holly Dolezalek, "University 2.0," *Training* 44, no. 8 (September 2007), pp. 22–23. As another example, see Paul Harris, "A New Era Dawns for TD," *TD* 71, no. 10 (October 2017), pp. 38+.

163. "Executive Coaching: Corporate Therapy," *The Economist*, November 15, 2003, p. 61. See also Steve Gladis, "Executive Coaching Builds Steam in Organizations," *TD*, December 2007, pp. 59–61.

164. "As Corporate Coaching Goes Mainstream, Key Prerequisite Overlooked: Assessment," *BNA Bulletin to Management*, May 16, 2006, p. 153; Dougless McKenna, "Who Needs an Executive Coach?" *Forbes*, Aug 4, 2009, https://www.forbes.com/2009/08/04/need-executive-consultant-ceonetwork-leadership-coach.html#283888be5134, accessed March 5, 2018.

165. https://coachfederation.org/, accessed March 5, 2018.

166. www.shrm.org/Education/educationalproducts/learning/Pages/default.aspx.

167. For information on the SHRM learning system, see www.shrm.org/Education/educationalproducts/learning/Pages/default.aspx?utm_campaign=LearningSystem_All_2012&utm_medium=mailing&utm_source=brochure, accessed July 21, 2013.

168. https://www.cigna.com/careers/early-career-hiring/leadership-development/, accessed March 4, 2018.

169. Quoted and abstracted from "Five Rules for Talent Management in the New Economy," May 2010, www.towerswatson.com/viewpoints/1988, accessed August 22, 2011.

170. Ibid.

171. Christina Lacerenza, et al., "Leadership Training Design, Delivery, and Implementation: A Meta-Analysis," *Journal of Applied Psychology* 102, no. 13 (2017), pp. 1686–1718.

172. Stephen Heidari-Robinson and Suzanne Heywood, "Getting Reorgs Right," *Harvard Business Review*, November 2016, pp. 85–89.

173. N. Amand and Jean Lewis Barsoux, "What Everyone Gets Wrong about Change Management," *Harvard Business Review*, November–December 2017, pp. 79–84.

174. See, for example, John Austin, "Mapping out a Game Plan for Change," *HR Magazine*, April 2009, pp. 39–42.

175. The steps are based on Michael Beer, Russell Eisenstat, and Bert Spector, "Why Change Programs Don't Produce Change," *Harvard Business Review*, November–December 1990, pp. 158–166; Thomas Cummings and Christopher Worley, *Organization Development and Change* (Minneapolis, MN: West Publishing Company, 1993); John P. Kotter, "Leading Change: Why Transformation Efforts Fail," *Harvard Business Review*, March–April 1995, pp. 59–66; and John P. Kotter, *Leading Change* (Boston: Harvard Business School Press, 1996). See also Eric Abrahamson, "Change without Pain," *Harvard Business Review*, July–August 2000, pp. 75–79; and David Herold et al., "Beyond Change Management: A Multilevel Investigation of Contextual and Personal Influences on Employees' Commitment to Change," *Journal of Applied Psychology* 92, no. 4 (2007), p. 949.

176. Kotter, "Leading Change," p. 85.

177. Beer, Eisenstat, and Spector, "Why Change Programs Don't Produce Change," p. 164.

178. Stacie Furst and Daniel Cable, "Employee Resistance to Organizational Change: Managerial Influence Tactics and Leader Member Exchange," *Journal of Applied Psychology* 3, no. 2 (2008), p. 453.

179. Wendell French and Cecil Bell Jr., *Organization Development* (Upper Saddle River, NJ: Prentice Hall, 1995), pp. 171–193. For examples of actual team-building programs, see, for example, www.teambuildinginc.com and www.teamcraft.com, both accessed August 24, 2014.

180. Michael Beer, Magnus Finnstrom, and Derek Schrader, "Why Leadership Training Fails—and What to Do about It," *Harvard Business Review*, October 2016, pp. 49–56.

181. Wexley and Latham, *Developing and Training Human Resources in Organizations*, p. 128; Gary M. Stern, "Company Training Programs: What Are They Really Worth?" *Forbes*, May 27, 2011, http://fortune.com/2011/05/27/company-training-programs-what-are-they-really-worth/, accessed March 5, 2018; M. Srimannarayana, "From Reactions to Return on Investment: A Study on Training Evaluation Practices," *Indian Journal of Industrial Relations* 53, no. 1 (July 2017), pp. 1+.

182. Wexley and Latham, *Developing and Training Human Resources in Organizations*, p. 153.

183. See, for example, Jack Phillips and Patti Phillips, "Moving from Evidence to Proof," *TD* 65, no. 8 (August 2011), pp. 34–39, for a discussion of a process for gathering training assessment data.

184. James Kirkpatrick and Wendy Kirkpatrick, "Evaluation Blunders and Missteps to Avoid," *Training and Development*, November 2016, p. 39.

185. However, see Phyllis Tharenou et al., "A Review and Critique of Research on Training and Organizational Level Outcomes," *Human Resource Management Review* 17 (2007), pp. 251–273.

186. For some examples, see, for instance, http://exceltemplates.net/images/2009/trainingcost.jpg, www.tjtaylor.net/resources-tools2.htm, www.redhat.com/resourcelibrary/onlinetools/training-roi-calculator, and www.fastrak-consulting.co.uk/tactix/Features/tngroi/tngroi.htm. See also Tamar Elkeles, Patty Phillips, and Jack Phillips, "ROI Calculations for Technology-Based Learning," *TD*, January 2015, pp. 42–47.

187. Jennifer Salopek, "Showstopping Learning," *TD*, October 2014, pp. 56–59.

188. Ibid.

Andriy Popov/123RF

Performance Management and Appraisal

LEARNING OBJECTIVES

When you finish studying this chapter, you should be able to:

9-1 **Describe** the performance appraisal process.

9-2 **Discuss** the pros and cons of at least eight traditional performance appraisal methods.

9-3 **Give examples** of how to deal with potential appraisal error problems.

9-4 **List** steps to take in the appraisal interview.

9-5 **Explain** key points in how to use the appraisal interview to boost employee engagement.

9-6 **Explain** how you would take a performance management approach to appraisal.

"Deloitte" is the name under which thousands of professionals in independent firms around the world provide audit, consulting, tax, and related services to clients.[1] These dispersed Deloitte firms, while all under the Deloitte umbrella, are independent firms not responsible for each other's obligations. In the United States, Deloitte USA LLP strives to deliver to its many clients results that are quantifiable and enduring. As a company that offers complex audit and consulting services to America's top companies, consistently delivering such results depends on having a human resource strategy dedicated to getting the best from its employees. Particularly with an increasingly Millennial workforce, that requires an effective performance management system. We'll see what they did.

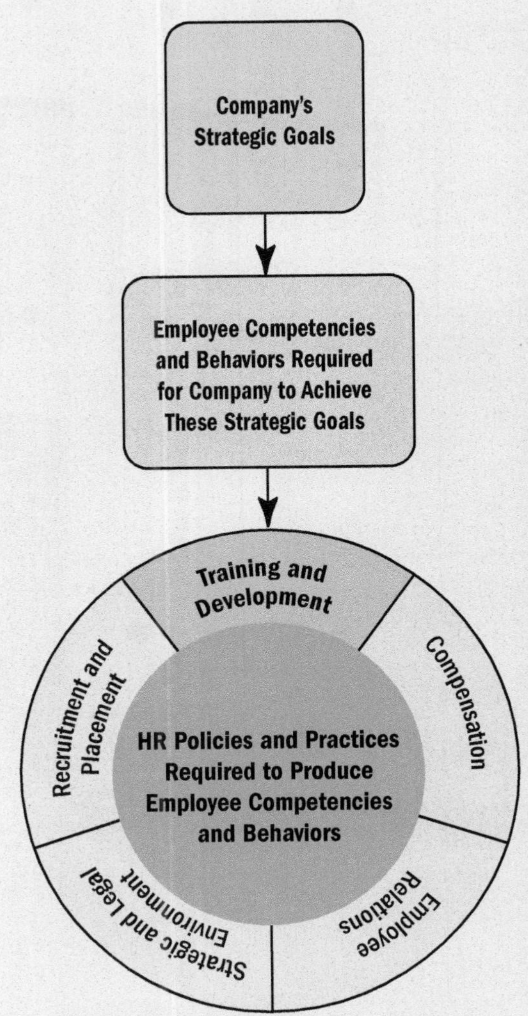

WHERE ARE WE NOW ...

Chapters 6–8 explained selecting, training, and developing employees. After employees have been on the job for some time, you should appraise their performance. The purpose of this chapter is to show you how to do that. The main topics we cover include the **Basics of Performance Appraisal**, **Tools for Appraising Performance, Dealing with Rater Error Appraisal Problems, The Appraisal Interview**, **Employee Engagement Guide for Managers**, and **Performance Management**. Career planning is a logical consequence of appraisal: We'll turn to career planning in Chapter 10.

Basics of Performance Appraisal

LEARNING OBJECTIVE 9-1

Describe the performance appraisal process.

Few things supervisors do are fraught with more peril than appraising subordinates' performance. Employees tend to be overly optimistic about their ratings. And they know their raises, careers, and peace of mind may hinge on how you rate them. As if that's not enough, few appraisal processes are as fair as employers think they are. Many obvious and not-so-obvious problems (such as the tendency to rate everyone "average") distort the process.[2] However, the perils notwithstanding, performance appraisal plays a big role in managing people.

The Performance Appraisal Process

performance appraisal
Evaluating an employee's current and/or past performance relative to his or her performance standards.

performance appraisal process
A three-step appraisal process involving (1) setting work standards, (2) assessing the employee's actual performance relative to those standards, and (3) providing feedback to the employee with the aim of helping him or her to eliminate performance deficiencies or to continue to perform above par.

Performance appraisal means evaluating an employee's current and/or past performance relative to his or her performance standards. You may equate appraisal forms like Figure 9-1 with "performance appraisal," but appraisal involves more than forms. It also requires setting performance standards, and assumes that the employee receives the training, feedback, and incentives required to eliminate performance deficiencies. Stripped to its essentials, performance appraisal always involves the three-step **performance appraisal process:** (1) setting work standards; (2) assessing the employee's actual performance relative to those standards (this often involves some rating form); and (3) providing feedback to the employee with the aim of helping him or her to eliminate performance deficiencies or to continue to perform above par.

Effective appraisals actually begin before the actual appraisal, with the manager defining the employee's job and performance criteria. *Defining the job* means making sure that you and your subordinate agree on his or her duties and job standards and on the appraisal method you will use.

Why Appraise Performance?

There are five reasons to appraise subordinates' performance.

- First we'll see that although many employers are replacing or complementing annual reviews with frequent, informal discussions between managers and employees,[3] most employers base pay, promotion, and retention decisions in large part on the employee's appraisal.
- Appraisals play a central role in the employer's *performance management* process. Performance management means continuously ensuring that each employee's performance makes sense in terms of the company's overall goals.
- The appraisal lets the manager and subordinate develop plans for correcting deficiencies, and to reinforce strengths.
- Appraisals provide an opportunity to review the employee's career plans in light of his or her strengths and weaknesses. We address career planning in Chapter 10.
- Appraisals enable the supervisor to identify if there is a training need, and the training required.

FIGURE 9-1 **Sample Faculty Evaluation Survey**

Source: Copyright Gary Dessler, PhD.

Instructions: Thoughtful evaluations help the faculty member better understand and improve his or her teaching practices. For each of the following eight items, please assign a score, giving your highest score of 7 for Outstanding, a score of 4 for Average, your lowest score of 1 for Needs Improvement, and an NA if the question is not applicable:

Evaluation Items

____ 1. The instructor was prepared for his/her lectures.
____ 2. The course was consistent with the course objectives.
____ 3. The instructor was fair in how he/she graded me.
____ 4. The instructor carefully planned and organized this course.
____ 5. The instructor was available during his/her posted office hours.
____ 6. The instructor responded to online inquiries in a timely manner.
____ 7. In terms of knowledge and/or experience, the instructor was competent to teach this course.
____ 8. Overall how would you rate this course?

Defining the Employee's Goals and Performance Standards

The performance appraisal should compare "what should be" with "what is." Managers use one or more of three bases—*goals*, *job dimensions* or traits, and behaviors or *competencies*—to establish ahead of time what the person's performance standards should be.

First, the manager can assess to what extent *the employee is attaining his or her numerical goals*. Such goals should derive from the company's overall profitability, cost reduction, or efficiency goals. For example, a company-wide goal of reducing costs by 10% should translate into goals for how individual employees and/or teams will cut costs. The HR as a Profit Center discussion shows an example.

IMPROVING PERFORMANCE: *HR AS A PROFIT CENTER*

Setting Performance Goals at Ball Corporation

Ball Corporation supplies metal packaging to customers such as food processors and paint manufacturers worldwide.[4] The management team at one Ball plant concluded that it could improve plant performance by instituting an improved process for setting goals and for ensuring that the plant employees' behaviors were in synch with these goals.[5] The new program began by training plant leaders on how to improve performance, and on communicating daily performance goals. They in turn communicated and tracked daily goal attainment by distributing team scorecards to the plant's work teams. Plant employees received special coaching and training to ensure they had the skills required for achieving the goals. Within 12 months the plant increased production by 84 million cans, reduced customer complaints by 50%, and obtained a return on investment of more than $3 million.[6] ■

> MyLab Management Talk About It 1
>
> If your professor has assigned this, go to the Assignments section of **www.pearson.com/mylab/management** to complete this discussion. Explain what performance appraisal process behaviors the Ball program included.

Managers often say that effective goals are "SMART." They are *specific*, and clearly state the desired results. They are *measurable*, and answer the question, "How much?" They are *attainable*. They are *relevant*, and clearly reflect what the company wants to achieve. And they are *timely*, with deadlines and milestones.[7] Research provides insights into setting motivational goals. The accompanying HR Tools discussion summarizes these.

IMPROVING PERFORMANCE: *HR TOOLS FOR LINE MANAGERS AND SMALL BUSINESSES*

How to Set Effective Goals

Behavioral science research studies suggest four guidelines for setting performance goals:

1. Assign specific goals. Employees who receive specific goals usually perform better than those who do not. Don't just say, "do your best."
2. Assign measurable goals. Put goals in quantitative terms, and include target dates/deadlines. If measurable results will not be available, then "satisfactory completion"—such as "satisfactorily attended workshop"—is ok.
3. Assign challenging but doable goals. Goals should be challenging, but not so difficult that they appear unrealistic.
4. Encourage participation. Managers often face this question: Should I tell my employees what their goals are, or let them participate with me in setting their goals? The evidence suggests that participatively set goals do not consistently result in higher performance than assigned goals, nor do assigned goals

consistently result in higher performance than participative ones. It is only when the participatively set goals are set higher than the assigned ones that the participatively set goals produce higher performance. Because it tends to be easier to set higher standards when your employees participate, participation tends to improve performance.[8] ■

MyLab Management Talk About It 2

If your professor has assigned this, go to the Assignments section of **www.pearson.com/mylab/management** to complete this discussion question. "Why is it not a good idea to simply tell employees to 'do their best' when assigning a task?"

A *second* basis upon which to appraise someone is with a form with *basic job dimensions* or *traits* such as "communication" or "teamwork." The assumption is that "good teamwork" is a useful standard for "what should be."

A third option is to appraise employees based *on their mastery of the competencies* (the skills, knowledge, and/or personal behaviors) the job requires. For example, we saw in Chapter 4 that BP's exploration division appraises employees' skills using a skills matrix (see Figure 4-11, page 124). This matrix shows the basic skills to be assessed (such as "technical expertise"), and the minimum level of each skill the job requires. Employees with the requisite level of each skill are qualified to fill the position.

Who Should Do the Appraising?

Appraisal by the immediate supervisor is still the heart of most appraisals. This makes sense. The supervisor is usually in the best position to observe and evaluate the subordinate's performance, and is responsible for that person's performance.

The human resources department is advisory. Generally, they provide the advice on what appraisal tool to use, but leave final decisions on procedures to operating managers. The human resource team should also train supervisors to improve their appraisal skills, monitor the appraisal system's effectiveness, and ensure that it complies with EEO laws.

Relying only on supervisors' appraisals isn't advisable. For example, the supervisor may not appreciate how customers and colleagues see the employee's performance. There is also always some danger of bias. If so, managers have several options.

PEER APPRAISALS Peer appraisals—appraisals by one's peers—are popular. The American military requires generals and admirals to be evaluated by their peers (and subordinates).[9] Facebook has employees compile peer reviews every 6 months.[10] Google employees receive annual feedback from their supervisor and their peers.[11] At one software firm, employees recognize each other with "wins" and "project completions" during monthly video meetings.[12]

Typically, an employee due for a peer appraisal chooses an appraisal chairperson. The latter (perhaps with the employee's input) then selects a supervisor and several peers to evaluate the employee's work.

Peer appraisals are useful. Peers see aspects of the person that the boss may never see, so peers' opinions can be useful. Knowing your colleagues will appraise you can also change behavior. In one study, instituting peer appraisals had "an immediate positive impact on [improving] perception of open communication, task motivation, social loafing, group viability, cohesion, and satisfaction."[13]

Crowd Appraisals Social media tools allow almost everyone in the company (the "crowd," as in "crowd appraisals") to continuously appraise their peers' work. Rypple (owned by salesforce.com) illustrates one such "social performance management platform."[14] Employees and managers use it to provide feedback and recognition.[15] For example, Washington-based LivingSocial employees use Rypple to comment on each other's work. LivingSocial then uses these comments as input to its formal employee appraisals.[16] Employers often combine such reviews with Globoforce (www.globoforce.com)–type rewards sites, to automate the rewarding and recognizing of colleagues.[17]

Virtual Games Many employers conduct peer appraisals by using virtual appraisal games. For example, one company created a virtual game that helps employees evaluate and reward each other. Each employee has an avatar. They use these to give real-time feedback to each other, along with virtual gifts and points.[18]

RATING COMMITTEES A rating committee typically consists of the employee's immediate supervisor and three or four other supervisors.[19]

Using multiple raters is advantageous. It helps cancel out problems such as bias on the part of individual raters.[20] It can also help pick up the different facets of an employee's performance observed by different appraisers.[21] It's thus advantageous to obtain ratings from the supervisor, his or her boss, and at least one other manager who is familiar with the employee's work. At a minimum, require that the supervisor's boss sign off on any appraisals the supervisor does.

SELF-RATINGS Some employers obtain employees' self-ratings, usually along with supervisors' ratings. The problem, of course, is that employees usually rate themselves higher than do their supervisors or peers.[22] One older study found that, when asked to rate their own job performances, 40% of employees in jobs of all types placed themselves in the top 10%, and virtually all remaining employees rated themselves in the top 50%; some believe incompetent performers aren't capable of objectively assessing themselves.[23] It's probably best to just ask subordinates to list their accomplishments for the period, before the manager does the appraisal.[24]

APPRAISAL BY SUBORDINATES Many employers have subordinates rate their managers, usually for developmental rather than for pay purposes. Google, for example, has subordinates assess their managers twice a year with questions such as "my manager shows consideration for me as a person."[25] Not surprisingly, anonymity affects the feedback. Managers who receive feedback from subordinates who identify themselves view the upward feedback process more positively. However, subordinates who identify themselves tend to give inflated ratings.[26]

The evidence suggests that upward feedback does improve managers' performance. One study focused on 252 managers during five annual administrations of an upward

Many employers use rating committees to appraise employees.

Dave and Les Jacobs/Blend Images/Getty Images

feedback program. Managers who were initially rated poor or moderate "showed significant improvements in [their] upward feedback ratings over the five-year period."[27]

Of course, employees no longer need their employers in order to appraise their boss—sites like Glassdoor and apps like Memo let employees post anonymous comments.[28]

360-DEGREE FEEDBACK With 360-degree feedback, the employer collects performance information all around an employee—from supervisors, subordinates, peers, and internal or external customers—generally for developmental rather than pay purposes.[29] The usual process is to have all raters complete online appraisal surveys. Computerized systems then compile this into individualized reports to ratees.

Results are mixed. An older study found that multisource feedback led to "generally small" improvements in subsequent ratings by supervisors, peers, and subordinates.[30] On the other hand, such feedback can wake someone up. One manager, surprised that peers and others called him "Attila the Hun," ratcheted down his disagreeable behaviors.[31] In any case, make sure the feedback the person receives is productive, unbiased, and development oriented.[32] And, collect multisource feedback by using an online system such as Sumtotal's 360 Degree Feedback.[33]

Traditional Tools for Appraising Performance

LEARNING OBJECTIVE 9-2

Discuss the pros and cons of at least eight traditional performance appraisal methods.

We'll see that many employers use online tools such as Oracle's TBE Performance Management Cloud Service to automate the performance appraisal/management process. With their digital dashboards, these tools monitor, report, and correct performance deviations in real time. Yet many employers still use traditional performance appraisal tools like those described next, often supplementing them with frequent coaching and/or continuous feedback via mobile platforms.[34]

Graphic Rating Scale Method

The **graphic rating scale** is the simplest and most popular method for appraising performance. You'll find several varieties. As in the one in Figure 9-2, the scale may list several *job dimensions or traits* (such as "communication" or "teamwork") and a range of performance values (from "below expectations" to "role model" or "unsatisfactory" to "outstanding") for each trait. The supervisor rates each subordinate by circling or checking the score that best describes the subordinate's performance for each trait, and totals the ratings.

graphic rating scale
A scale that lists a number of traits and a range of performance for each. The employee is then rated by identifying the score that best describes his or her level of performance for each trait.

A *competency- (or skill- or behavior-)* based graphic rating scale is another option.[35] Figure 9-3 (page 285) shows a partial form for a pizza chef. This rating form assesses the person's competencies and skills. Here the employer wants to appraise a pizza chef's job-related skills, one of which is: "Be able to maintain adequate inventory of pizza dough." As another example, Section I of Figure 9-4 (page 286) focuses on behavioral competencies. Here "Effectively leads and motivates nurses" is a required behavioral competency for a nurse supervisor. Some employers use competency-based self-appraisals, which the employee then discusses with his or her supervisor.[36]

Finally, the scale might rate (as in Section II of Figure 9-4) how well the employee did with respect to achieving specific profit, cost, or efficiency *goals*. "Nursing unit experienced zero patient medication errors in period" is one example.

Alternation Ranking Method

alternation ranking method
Ranking employees from best to worst on a particular trait, choosing highest, then lowest, until all are ranked.

Ranking employees from best to worst on a trait or traits is another option. Since it's usually easier to distinguish between the worst and best employees, an **alternation ranking method** is most popular. First, list all subordinates to be rated, and then cross out the names of any not known well enough to rank. Then, on a form like that in Figure 9-5 (page 287), indicate the employee who is the highest on the performance dimension being measured and the one who is the lowest. Then choose the next highest and the next lowest, alternating between highest and lowest until all employees have been ranked.

Sample Performance Rating Form

Employee's Name ______________________ Level: Entry-level employee

Manager's Name ______________________

Key Work Responsibilities	Results/Goals to Be Achieved
1. ________	1. ________
2. ________	2. ________
3. ________	3. ________
4. ________	4. ________

Communication

1	2	3	4	5
Below Expectations Even with guidance, fails to prepare straight-forward communications, including forms, paperwork, and records, in a timely and accurate manner; products require considerable corrections. Even with guidance, fails to adapt style and materials to communicate straightforward information.		**Meets Expectations** With guidance, prepares straightforward communications, including forms, paperwork, and records, in a timely and accurate manner; products require minimal corrections. With guidance, adapts style and materials to communicate straightforward information.		**Role Model** Independently prepares communications, such as forms, paperwork, and records, in a timely, clear, and accurate manner; products require few, if any, corrections. Independently adapts style and materials to communicate information.

Organizational Know-How

1	2	3	4	5
Below Expectations <performance standards appear here>		**Meets Expectations** <performance standards appear here>		**Role Model** <performance standards appear here>

Personal Effectiveness

1	2	3	4	5
Below Expectations <performance standards appear here>		**Meets Expectations** <performance standards appear here>		**Role Model** <performance standards appear here>

Teamwork

1	2	3	4	5
Below Expectations <performance standards appear here>		**Meets Expectations** <performance standards appear here>		**Role Model** <performance standards appear here>

Achieving Business Results

1	2	3	4	5
Below Expectations <performance standards appear here>		**Meets Expectations** <performance standards appear here>		**Role Model** <performance standards appear here>

FIGURE 9-2 **Sample Graphic Performance Rating Form with Behavioral Examples**

Source: Reproduced with permission of the SHRM Foundation.

FIGURE 9-3 **One Item from an Appraisal Form Assessing Employee Performance on Specific Job-Related Skills**

Position: Pizza Chef			
Competency/Skill 1: Be able to maintain adequate inventory of pizza dough		Rating	
Each round pizza dough must be between 12 and 14 ounces each, kneaded at least 2 minutes before being placed in the temperature- and humidity-controlled cooler, and kept there for at least 5 hours prior to use. There should be enough, but no more, for each day's demand.	Needs improvement	Satisfactory	Excellent

Paired Comparison Method

paired comparison method
Ranking employees by making a chart of all possible pairs of the employees for each trait and indicating which is the better employee of the pair.

The **paired comparison method** makes the ranking method more precise. For every trait (quantity of work, quality of work, and so on), you compare every employee with every other employee. With, say, five employees to rate, you use a chart as in Figure 9-6 (page 287) of all possible pairs of employees for each trait. Then choose who the better employee of the pair is. In Figure 9-6, Maria ranked highest (has the most + marks) for quality of work, whereas Art was ranked highest for creativity.

Forced Distribution Method

forced distribution method
Similar to grading on a curve; predetermined percentages of ratees are placed in various performance categories.

The **forced distribution method** is similar to grading on a curve. Here, the manager places predetermined percentages of ratees into performance categories. At Lending Tree, the top 15% ratees are "1's," the middle 75% are "2's," and the bottom 10% are "3's" and the "first to go." GE used top 20%, middle 70%, and bottom 10% for its managers, and most of the bottom 10% lost their jobs.[37] (GE no longer strictly adheres to its 20/70/10 split. Their current system is reportedly more informal and less stressful.)[38]

Forced distribution's big advantage is in preventing supervisors from simply rating all or most employees "satisfactory" or "high." But as students know, with this method you're either in the top 5% or 10% (and get that "A"), or you're not. Forced distribution systems may also increase the risk of discriminatory adverse impact.[39] One survey found that 77% of employers were at least "somewhat satisfied" with forced ranking, while the remaining 23% were dissatisfied. The biggest complaint: 44% said it damages morale.[40] Forced distribution motivates effort and perhaps performance, but leaves many employees feeling that their appraisals were dysfunctional.[41] Some writers call it "Rank and Yank."[42] Furthermore, distinguishing between top and bottom performers is usually not even the problem: "The challenge is to differentiate meaningfully between the other 80%."[43] Therefore, a committee should review any employee's low ranking.

For many years, Microsoft graded employees against each other in what employees called the "stack."[44] It now uses frequent qualitative appraisals.

Critical Incident Method

critical incident method
Keeping a record of uncommonly good or undesirable examples of an employee's work-related behavior and reviewing it with the employee at predetermined times.

With the **critical incident method,** the supervisor keeps a log of positive and negative examples (critical incidents) of a subordinate's work-related behaviors. Every 6 months or so, supervisor and subordinate meet to discuss the latter's performance, using the incidents as examples. One study involved 112 first-line supervisors. The conclusion of this and similar studies is that compiling critical incidents as they occur anchors the eventual appraisal in reality and thus improves appraisal outcomes.[45]

It's thus advisable to keep a diary of such incidents.[46] This provides examples the supervisor can use to explain the person's rating. It makes the supervisor think about the subordinate's appraisal all during the year (so the rating doesn't just reflect the employee's most recent performance). The downside is that such incidents don't produce relative ratings for pay raise purposes.

Section I: Competencies: Does this employee exhibit the core competencies the job requires?

Exhibits Leadership Competency

Effectively leads and motivates nurses: Builds a culture that is open and receptive to improved clinical care; sets clear goals for nurses; is supportive of nurses; motivates nurses to achieve their goals.

Generally exceeds expectations	Generally meets expectations	Generally fails to meet expectations
_______	_______	_______

Exhibits Technical Supervisory Competency

Effectively supervises nurses' technical activities: Exhibits the command of technical nursing knowledge and skills required to supervise nurses effectively, such as, assuring that nurses accurately administer medications, treat patients, intervene effectively to patients' expressions of symptoms, and accurately carry out physicians' instructions.

Generally exceeds expectations	Generally meets expectations	Generally fails to meet expectations
_______	_______	_______

Exhibits Managerial Supervisory Competency

Effectively manages unit: Develops annual, monthly, weekly, and daily plans within context of hospital's plans; effectively organizes and assigns nurses' work; maintains required nursing staffing levels and trains nurses; effectively monitors and controls nursing unit performance using hospital-approved metrics.

Generally exceeds expectations	Generally meets expectations	Generally fails to meet expectations
_______	_______	_______

Exhibits Communications Competency

Effectively communicates: Actively listens to and understands what others say; effectively conveys facts and ideas in writing and orally.

Generally exceeds expectations	Generally meets expectations	Generally fails to meet expectations
_______	_______	_______

Exhibits Decision-Making Competency

Effectively recognizes and solves problems and makes decisions: uses data to analyze alternatives and support conclusions; able to solve problems even of moderate to high complexity.

Generally exceeds expectations	Generally meets expectations	Generally fails to meet expectations
_______	_______	_______

Section II: Goals: Did this employee achieve his or her goals for the period you are appraising?

Primary goals employee was to achieve for this period *(Note: list specific goals)*	Rating 5 Exceeded goal 3 Met goal 1 Did not achieve goal	Explanations and/or examples
Goal 1 Zero patient medication errors	5 4 ③ 2 1	Nursing unit experienced zero patient medication errors.
Goal 2	5 4 3 2 1	
Goal 3	5 4 3 2 1	
Goal 4	5 4 3 2 1	
Goal 5	5 4 3 2 1	

Employee name and signature	Person doing appraisal	Date of appraisal

Source: Copyright Gary Dessler, PhD.

FIGURE 9-4 Pearson Pennsylvania Hospital Competencies and Goals-Based Appraisal Form for a Nurse-Supervisor

Source: Copyright Gary Dessler, PhD.

FIGURE 9-5 **Alternation Ranking Method**

ALTERNATION RANKING SCALE

Trait: ______________________

For the trait you are measuring, list all the employees you want to rank. Put the highest-ranking employee's name on line 1. Put the lowest-ranking employee's name on line 20. Then list the next highest ranking on line 2, the next lowest ranking on line 19, and so on. Continue until all names are on the scale.

Highest-ranking employee

1. ______	11. ______
2. ______	12. ______
3. ______	13. ______
4. ______	14. ______
5. ______	15. ______
6. ______	16. ______
7. ______	17. ______
8. ______	18. ______
9. ______	19. ______
10. ______	20. ______

Lowest-ranking employee

In Table 9-1, one of the assistant plant manager's duties was to supervise procurement and minimize inventory costs. The critical incident log shows that he or she let inventory storage costs rise 15%; this provides an example of what performance to improve.

Narrative Forms

All or part of the written appraisal may be in narrative form, as in Figure 9-7. Here the person's supervisor assesses the employee's past performance and required areas of improvement. The supervisor's narrative assessment helps the employee understand where his or her performance was good or bad, and how to improve that performance.

FIGURE 9-6 **Paired Comparison Method**

Note: + means "better than." − means "worse than." For each chart, add up the number of +'s in each column to get the highest-ranked employee.

FOR THE TRAIT "QUALITY OF WORK"

	Employee rated:				
As Compared to:	A Art	B Maria	C Chuck	D Diane	E José
A Art		+	+	−	−
B Maria	−		−	−	−
C Chuck	−	+		+	−
D Diane	+	+	−		+
E José	+	+	+	−	

Maria ranks highest here

FOR THE TRAIT "CREATIVITY"

	Employee rated:				
As Compared to:	A Art	B Maria	C Chuck	D Diane	E José
A Art		−	−	−	−
B Maria	+		−	+	+
C Chuck	+	+		−	+
D Diane	+	−	+		−
E José	+	−	−	+	

Art ranks highest here

TABLE 9-1 Examples of Critical Incidents for Assistant Plant Manager

Continuing Duties	Targets	Critical Incidents
Schedule production for plant	90% utilization of personnel and machinery in plant; orders delivered on time	Instituted new production scheduling system; decreased late orders by 10% last month; increased machine utilization in plant by 20% last month
Supervise procurement of raw materials and inventory control	Minimize inventory costs while keeping adequate supplies on hand	Let inventory storage costs rise 15% last month; overordered parts "A" and "B" by 20%; underordered part "C" by 30%
Supervise machinery maintenance	No shutdowns due to faulty machinery	Instituted new preventative maintenance system for plant; prevented a machine breakdown by discovering faulty part

behaviorally anchored rating scale (BARS)
An appraisal method that aims at combining the benefits of narrative critical incidents and quantified ratings by anchoring a quantified scale with specific narrative examples of good and poor performance.

Behaviorally Anchored Rating Scales

A **behaviorally anchored rating scale (BARS)** is an appraisal tool that anchors a numerical rating scale with specific illustrative examples of good or poor performance. Developing a BARS typically involves five steps:

1. ***Write critical incidents.*** Ask the job's jobholders and/or supervisors to write specific illustrations (critical incidents) of effective and ineffective performance on the job.

FIGURE 9-7 Sample Narrative Appraisal Form
Source: Copyright Gary Dessler, PhD.

Supervisory Appraisal of Employee: Narrative Form

Employee's Name	Department	Present Position
Appraisal Date	Supervisor Name/Title	Performance Period

Supervisor-Appraiser: First, briefly describe results for each of this employee's goals this year. Then, preferably using specific examples, describe the level of the employee's job knowledge, skills, and abilities. Then, jointly set goals for the coming period and describe required employee training and development in each area. Finally, describe your overall assessment of this employee's work this period.

Appraisal Criteria	**Narrative Appraisal**	**Goals, Training, & Development**
Job-Related Goals 1. ________ 2. ________ 3. ________	 ________ ________ ________	 ________ ________ ________
Employee Job Knowledge	Sam's knowledge of chemical engineering is exceptional; her colleagues use her as a resource when they have questions.	Help prepare her for more responsibility by enrolling in a chemical engineering masters degree program.
Employee Job Skills		
Employee Job Abilities		
Overall Assessment		

2. ***Develop performance dimensions.*** Have these people cluster the incidents into five or ten performance dimensions, such as "salesmanship skills."
3. ***Reallocate incidents.*** To verify these groupings, have another team who also knows the job reallocate the original critical incidents to the cluster they think it fits best. Retain a critical incident if most of this second team assigns it to the same cluster as did the first.
4. ***Scale the incidents.*** This second group then rates the behavior described by the incident as to how effectively or ineffectively it represents performance on the dimension.
5. ***Develop a final instrument.*** Choose about six or seven of the incidents as the performance dimension's behavioral anchors.[47] Figure 9-8 illustrates a BARS, for a car salesperson.

Three researchers developed a BARS for grocery checkout clerks.[48] They collected many checkout clerk critical incidents, and then grouped these into eight performance dimensions: Knowledge and Judgment; Conscientiousness; Skill in Human Relations;

FIGURE 9-8 **Behaviorally Anchored Rating Scale**

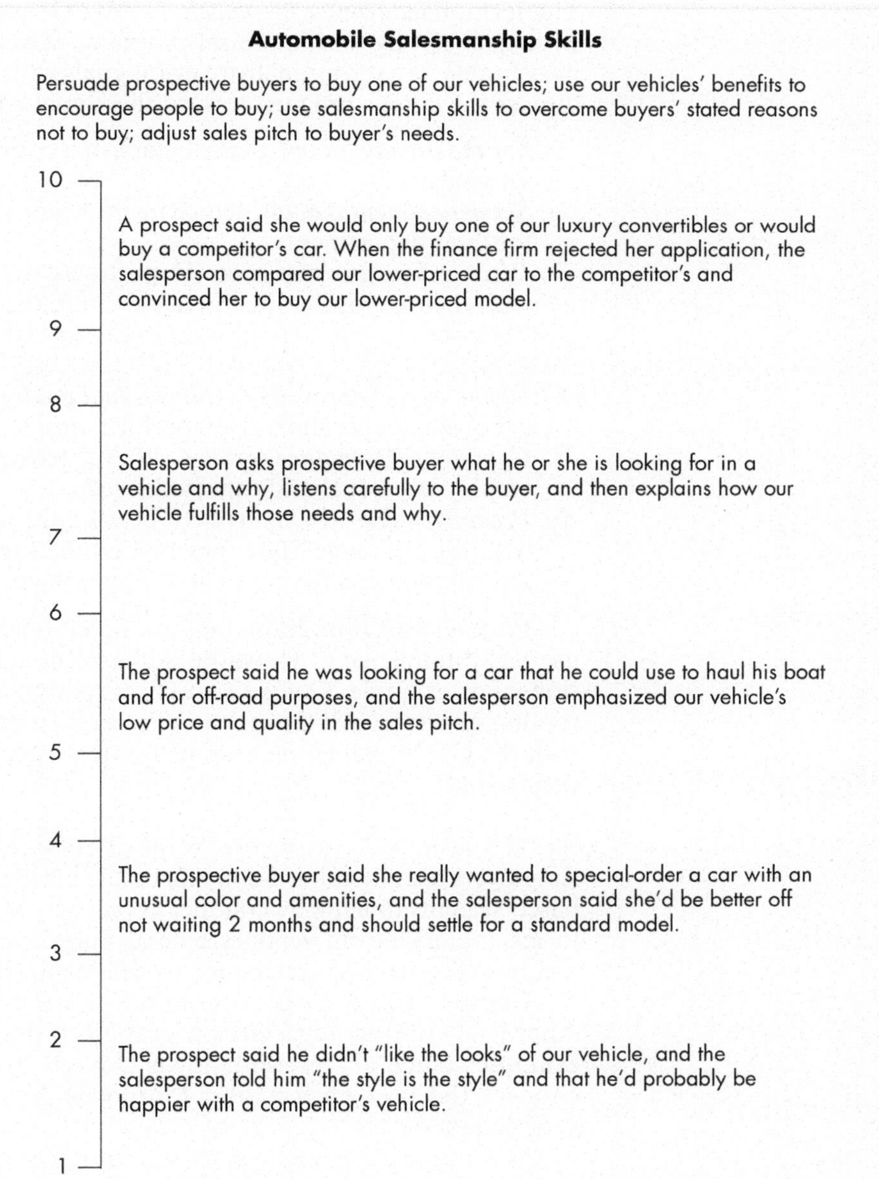

Skill in Operation of Register; Skill in Bagging; Organizational Ability of Checkstand Work; Skill in Monetary Transactions; and Observational Ability.

They then developed behaviorally anchored rating scales *for each of these eight dimensions*. Each contained a vertical scale (ranging from 1 to 9) for rating performance from "extremely poor" to "extremely good." Then they inserted specific critical incidents (such as "by knowing the price of items, this checker would be expected to look for mismarked and unmarked items") to anchor or illustrate each level of performance.

The BARS method has several advantages. Most notably, the critical incidents along the scale illustrate what to look for in terms of superior, average, and poor performance. They also make it easier to explain the ratings to appraisees. And, the clustering of similar critical incidents into several performance dimensions (such as "salesmanship skills") helps make the performance dimensions more independent of one another. (For example, a rater should be less likely to rate an employee high on all dimensions simply because he or she was rated high in "salesmanship skills.")[49]

Management by Objectives

The term *management by objectives (MBO)* usually refers to a multistep company-wide goal-setting and appraisal program. MBO requires the manager to set specific measurable, organizationally relevant goals with each employee, and then periodically discuss the latter's progress toward these goals. The steps are

1. ***Set the organization's goals.*** Establish a company-wide plan for next year and set goals.
2. ***Set departmental goals.*** Department heads and their superiors jointly set goals for their departments.
3. ***Discuss departmental goals.*** Department heads discuss the department's goals with their subordinates and ask them to develop their own individual goals. They should ask, "How could each employee help the department attain its goals?"
4. ***Define expected results (set individual goals).*** Department heads and their subordinates set short-term performance targets for each employee.
5. ***Conduct performance reviews.*** After a period, department heads compare each employee's actual and expected results.
6. ***Provide feedback.*** Department heads hold periodic performance review meetings with subordinates. Here they discuss the subordinates' performance and make any plans for rectifying or continuing the person's performance.

Formal MBO programs require numerous time-consuming meetings, and their use has diminished.[50] However, some companies successfully use streamlined versions. For example, Google's CEO sets company-wide "OKRs" (objectives and key results) quarterly. All Google employees then make sure their own goals are in synch with the CEO's. All employees' goals are posted on Google's internal website next to their names.[51]

Appraisal in Practice: Using Forms, Installed Software, or Cloud-Based Systems

Employers use either hard-copy forms, installed appraisal software packages, or cloud-based systems to actually conduct appraisals. Many smaller employers use hard-copy forms, available from vendors such as Staples and HR Direct.[52] Forms are simple to use, but become time-consuming as headcount rises.

Computerization expedites appraisals. Thus with one early package, Employee Appraiser, the manager sees a graphic rating scale with behaviorally anchored examples (such as "presents ideas clearly" and "lacks structure"). The manager chooses the best phrase, and Employee Appraiser generates an appraisal with sample text.[53]

Most computerized appraisal packages today (whether installed locally or cloud-based) are *modules*—components of talent management systems that also

Hero Images/Getty Images

Many employers today make use of computerized or online appraisals for evaluating employee performance.

include, for instance, applicant tracking systems. For example, with Bamboo HR (see www.bamboohr.com) the employer can adopt the full bamboo HR system or just the appraisal module. The module is available as both a cloud service, or installed on Mac or Windows systems.[54]

Electronic Performance Monitoring

electronic performance monitoring (EPM)
Having supervisors electronically monitor the amount of computerized data an employee is processing per day, and thereby his or her performance.

Electronic performance monitoring (EPM) systems allow managers to monitor the employees' rate, accuracy, and time spent working online.[55]

EPM can improve productivity, but also seems to raise employee stress. However, one researcher concludes that electronic performance monitoring "represents the future of performance feedback where supervisors can electronically monitor the amount and quality of work an employee is producing and have objective indicators of employee performance immediately available and visible."[56]

Similarly, some employers track workers' performance through wearables. For example, the British retailer Tesco has warehouse workers wear armbands. These track which specific goods each worker is moving and how long the task is taking to complete, and quantify and report things like how long it takes each worker to fulfill each order.[57]

Conversation Days

When employees at Juniper Networks Inc. expressed concerns about their annual performance reviews and the lack of positive feedback, Juniper changed the process. Instead of once-a-year performance reviews, there are now semiannual "conversation days." The stress in these manager–employee conversations is on areas for improvement and growth, and on setting stretch goals that align with the employee's career interests. There are no explicit performance ratings. GE is similarly experimenting with substituting frequent conversations for traditional appraisals.

Using Multiple Methods

Which appraisal tool to use? In practice, most use a rating form that merges several approaches. For example, Figure 9-2 (page 284) has a numerical graphic rating scale anchored with behavioral incidents such as "Even with guidance, fails to…." The Strategic Context feature (page 302) shows how one employer created a new appraisal system.

TRENDS SHAPING HR: *CUSTOMIZED TALENT MANAGEMENT*

There is usually some customizing of appraisals. For example, rating a salesperson based on whether she attained her sales goals assumes she had her own goals to meet.

Today, some employers are customizing their appraisal in other ways. For example, some companies adapt their appraisals and rewards to how critical the employees are to the company's strategic success—their "mission-critical" employees. Thus, GE prioritizes jobs and focuses on what it calls its employee "game changers."[58] Unilever includes 15% of employees per management level in its high-potential list each year.[59] Shell China appoints "career stewards" to meet regularly with "emerging leaders."[60] McKinsey & Co. recommends limiting the "high potential group in whom the company invests heavily to no more than 10 to 20% of managerial and professional staff."[61]

Figure 9-9 illustrates one way to customize appraisals. One company might use a 3 × 3 matrix to plot employees by *Performance* (high, average, low) and *Value to the Organization* (critical, important, non-critical). Consider a chemical engineering company. Here the firm's experienced engineers may be "critical," engineer-trainees, sales, accounting, and HR "important," and outsourceable employees such as maintenance "non-critical."

This company would then tie each employee's pay, development, dismissal, and other personnel decisions to each employee's position in the matrix, in other words to both their performance rating and their criticalness to the company (so, not unreasonably, someone with more critical skills might get more development than would someone who is "non-critical"). This employer might also design its incentives, promotions, and raises to support rather than turn off the mission-critical engineers.[62] ■

The Gig Economy feature shows how Uber assesses its drivers.

HR AND THE GIG ECONOMY: *RATING UBER DRIVERS*[63]

Uber's driver rating system rates drivers on three metrics—on how passengers rate the driver, on what percentage of rides the driver accepts, and on how many he or she cancels. Uber reportedly wants drivers to maintain at least an 80–90% acceptance rate and no more than a 5% trip cancellation rate.

As most Uber users know, after every ride Uber prompts the passenger to rate the driver on a 1–5 star scale. A new driver begins with a 5-star rating. Then, as more passengers rate the driver, the driver's average rating tends to change. The driver's rating is generally an average of his or her last 500 trips. For drivers, an average below 4.6 reportedly puts the driver in the "danger zone" for possible deactivation. Only about 2–3% of drivers fall here. One or two star ratings often reflect arguments or harassment. Drivers get weekly emails with notices if their activation is in danger.

Potential Rating Problems

As with most ratings systems, the driver ratings may say more about the passenger than about the driver. For example, people may view a 4-star rating as a "B," when in fact at Uber it's a failing grade. Furthermore, most employers try to minimize biased appraisals by supervisors: that's harder to guard against when the rater isn't an employee (and is probably a stranger). Furthermore, extraneous factors (such as surge pricing) can trigger lower ratings.

How to Get a Better Driver Rating

In any case, Uber and Uber drivers list some of the things drivers can do to get better ratings. Some things to avoid include having an attitude, not knowing your way around, reckless driving, and texting while driving. Some "Do's" for drivers include offer passengers bottled water, open the door, offer to carry bags, keep the car clean—and don't ask for five-star ratings.

MyLab Management Talk About It 3

If your professor has assigned this, go to the Assignments section of **www.pearson.com/mylab/management** to discuss the following. Write a paragraph that addresses the question: "What (based on what I read in this chapter) is good about the Uber driver rating system, and what could Uber do to improve it?"

HOW CRITICAL? How Critical Is This Person's Position to Our Company?	EMPLOYEE PERFORMANCE High	Average	Low
This person is in a position that is critical to our company's survival and growth	Provide additional development experiences and rewards	Provide additional development experiences and rewards	Consider additional training to improve performance
This person's position serves an important role but is not critical to our company's survival and growth	Provide additional development experiences to move to more important role	Consider additional training	Consider additional training, or replacement
This person is in a position that is non-critical and (for example) is outsourceable	Consider providing additional training and development to move to more important role	Consider additional training	Consider dismissal or outsourcing

FIGURE 9-9 **One Way to Customize Appraisals**

LEARNING OBJECTIVE 9-3
Give examples of how to deal with potential appraisal error problems.

Dealing with Rater Error Appraisal Problems

In a perfect world, all employers would use performance appraisal systems with clear goals, fair appraisals, swift feedback, and useful coaching. Alas, that is rarely the case.[64] Graphic-type rating forms in particular are susceptible to several "rater error" problems. These are systematic errors in judgment that occur when people evaluate each other: unclear standards, halo effect, central tendency, leniency or strictness, and bias.

Potential Rating Problems

unclear standards
An appraisal that is too open to interpretation.

UNCLEAR STANDARDS Table 9-2 illustrates the **unclear standards** problem. This rating scale seems objective. However, it might well result in unfair appraisals, because the traits and degrees of merit are ambiguous. For example, different supervisors might define "good" performance, "fair" performance, and so on, differently. The same is true of traits such as "quality of work."[65]

The way to fix this problem is to include descriptive phrases that define or illustrate each trait, as in Figure 9-2. That form spells out what measures like "Role Model" or "Below Expectations" actually mean. This specificity leads to more consistent and more easily explained appraisals.

halo effect
In performance appraisal, the problem that occurs when a supervisor's rating of a subordinate on one trait biases the rating of that person on other traits.

HALO EFFECT Experts define **halo effect** as "the influence of a rater's general impression on ratings of specific ratee qualities."[66] For example, supervisors often rate unfriendly employees lower on all traits, rather than just on "gets along well with others." Being aware of this problem is a step toward avoiding it. Supervisory training can also alleviate the problem, as can using a BARS (on which, recall, the performance dimensions are usually more independent of each other).

TABLE 9-2 **A Graphic Rating Scale with Unclear Standards**

	Excellent	Good	Fair	Poor
Quantity of work				
Quality of work				
Creativity				
Integrity				

Note: For example, what exactly is meant by "good," "quantity of work," and so forth?

Supervisors must be familiar with appraisal techniques, understand and avoid problems that can cripple appraisals, and know how to conduct appraisals fairly.

Issa Bin Saleh AlKindy/arabianEye/Getty Images

central tendency
A tendency to rate all employees the same way, such as rating them all average.

CENTRAL TENDENCY **Central tendency** means rating all employees average. For example, if the rating scale ranges from 1 to 7, raters tend to avoid the highs (6 and 7) and lows (1 and 2) and rate most of their people between 3 and 5. Doing so distorts the evaluations, making them less useful for promotion, salary, or counseling purposes. Ranking employees instead of using graphic rating scales can reduce this problem, since ranking means you can't rate them all average.

strictness/leniency
The problem that occurs when a supervisor has a tendency to rate all subordinates either high or low.

LENIENCY OR STRICTNESS Other supervisors tend to rate all their subordinates high (or low), just as some instructors are notoriously high or low graders. This **strictness/leniency** problem is especially severe with graphic rating scales. *Ranking* forces supervisors to distinguish between high and low performers.

There are other solutions. The employer can recommend that supervisors avoid giving all their employees high (or low) ratings. A second is to require a distribution—that, say, about 10% of the people should be rated "excellent," 20% "good," and so forth. (But remember it may not be an error at all, as when all subordinates really are superior.)[67]

RECENCY EFFECTS Recency means letting what the employee has done recently blind you to what his or her performance has been over the year. The main solution is to accumulate critical incidents all year long.

Diversity Counts: The Problem of Bias

bias
The tendency to allow individual differences such as age, race, and sex to affect the appraisal ratings employees receive.

Biased appraisals (**bias** means the tendency to allow individual differences such as age, race, and sex to affect the appraisal ratings employees receive) have various causes. One is rater personality. For example, raters who score higher on "conscientiousness" tend to give their peers lower ratings—they were stricter, in other words; those more "agreeable" gave higher ratings—they were more lenient.[68] Furthermore, "performance ratings amplify the quality of the personal relationship between boss and employee. Good relationships tend to create good [appraisal] experiences, bad relationships bad ones."[69]

Unfortunately, subordinates' demographic traits (age, race, gender, and so on) also affect ratings. For example, it's often argued that a "glass ceiling" largely explains the few women in top management jobs. A study suggests something more troubling.

The study concluded that "all else being equal, an evaluator will provide a lower performance evaluation to a female subordinate with stronger competence signals compared to a female subordinate with weaker competent signals."[70] In other words, the better a female employee is, in terms of her actual performance and her educational and work experience, the more likely it is that she'll be rated lower.

Is that possible? Unfortunately, based on this study, yes. Not all evaluators were prone to this negative bias. Only "male evaluators who are high on SDO [those inclined to be socially dominant] and evaluating a high-performing female subordinate appear to be prone."[71] But unless employers guard against such bias, they could be condoning biased promotion and pay decisions against some of their highest-performing and highest-potential employees.

Bias is one reason to use multiple raters, to have the supervisor's boss review ratings, and/or to have "calibration" meetings where supervisors explain among themselves the appraisals they gave.[72] ■

The Need for Fairness

So, due to either the supervisor's ineptness or the appraisal method's inherent unfairness, many appraisals are unfair. The employees' standards should be clear, employees should understand the basis on which you're going to appraise them, and the appraisal should be objective.[73] Give the employee an opportunity to express his or her opinions.

In practice, the quality of the interpersonal relationship between the supervisor and employee will shape the appraisal's impact. Supervisors should be trained in both the technical and interpersonal aspects of appraising employees and giving feedback.[74] They should understand how to build trust, engage in continuous performance conversations, diagnose and productively address performance issues, and deliver and react to feedback constructively.[75] To facilitate this, the employer should evaluate supervisors partly based on their effectiveness in managing performance.[76]

Figure 9-10 lists best practices for ensuring fair appraisals. Table 9-3 summarizes each appraisal method's pros and cons.

KNOW YOUR EMPLOYMENT LAW

Appraising Performance

The performance appraisal often plays a role in employment lawsuits, such as when employees claim that they were fired for poor performance in violation of an implied contract, or claim they were defamed during or in an appraisal.[77] Similarly, courts often find that inadequate appraisal systems lie at the root of illegal discriminatory

FIGURE 9-10 Checklist of Best Practices for Administering Fair Performance Appraisals

- Base the performance review on duties and standards from a job analysis.
- Try to base the performance review on observable job behaviors or objective performance data.
- Make it clear ahead of time what your performance expectations are.
- Use a standardized performance review procedure for all employees.
- Make sure whoever conducts the reviews has frequent opportunities to observe the employee's job performance.
- Either use multiple raters or have the rater's supervisor evaluate the appraisal results.
- Include an appeals mechanism.
- Document the appraisal review process and results.
- Discuss the appraisal results with the employee.
- Let the employees know ahead of time how you're going to conduct the reviews.
- Let the employee provide input regarding your assessment of him or her.
- Indicate what the employee needs to do to improve.
- Train the supervisors who will be doing the appraisals. Make sure they understand the procedure to use, how problems (like leniency and strictness) arise, and how to deal with them.

TABLE 9-3 Important Advantages and Disadvantages of Appraisal Tools

Tool	Advantages	Disadvantages
Graphic rating scale	Simple to use; provides a quantitative rating for each employee.	Standards may be unclear; halo effect, central tendency, leniency, bias can also be problems.
BARS	Provides behavioral "anchors." BARS is very accurate.	Difficult to develop.
Alternation ranking	Simple to use (but not as simple as graphic rating scales). Avoids central tendency and other problems of rating scales.	Can cause disagreements among employees and may be unfair if all employees are, in fact, excellent.
Forced distribution method	End up with a predetermined number or % of people in each group.	Employees' appraisal results depend on your choice of cutoff points.
Critical incident method	Helps specify what is "right" and "wrong" about the employee's performance; forces supervisor to evaluate subordinates on an ongoing basis.	Difficult to rate or rank employees relative to one another.
MBO	Tied to jointly agreed-upon performance objectives.	Time-consuming.

actions, such as in cases concerning layoffs, discharges, or merit pay.[78] For example, in one classic case the court held that the employer violated Title VII when it laid off several Hispanic-surnamed employees based on poor performance ratings. The court said the practice was illegal because: the firm based the appraisals on subjective supervisory observations; it did not administer and score the appraisals in a standardized fashion; and two of the three supervisory evaluators did not have daily contact with the employees they appraised. Personal bias, unreasonably rating everyone high or low, and relying just on recent events are some other reasons courts have used to declare appraisal processes as unfair.[79]

Steps to ensure your appraisals are legally defensible include the following:

- Base the appraised duties and criteria on a job analysis.
- Give performance standards to employees in writing.
- Don't just give a single overall rating; appraise several dimensions (quality, quantity, etc.) and have a system to combine these.
- One appraiser should never have absolute authority to determine a personnel action.
- Document everything.[80]
- Train supervisors. At least provide raters with written instructions on how to use the rating scale.
- In reviews of U.S. court decisions, actions reflecting *fairness* and *due process* were most important.[81]
- Finally, to help minimize the discriminatory effects of performance appraisal, "treat everyone in exactly the same way."[82] ■

LEARNING OBJECTIVE 9-4

List steps to take in the appraisal interview.

Managing the Appraisal Interview

Periodic appraisals typically culminate in an **appraisal interview.** Here the manager and the subordinate review the appraisal and make plans to remedy deficiencies and reinforce strengths. These interviews are often uncomfortable. Few people like to receive—or give—negative feedback. Adequate preparation and effective

appraisal interview
An interview in which the supervisor and subordinate review the appraisal and make plans to remedy deficiencies and reinforce strengths.

implementation are essential. Supervisors face four types of appraisal situations, each with its unique objectives:[83]

- *Satisfactory—Promotable* is the easiest interview: The person's performance is satisfactory and promotion looms. Your objective is to develop specific development plans.
- *Satisfactory—Not promotable* is for employees whose performance is satisfactory but for whom promotion is not possible. The objective here is to maintain satisfactory performance. The best option is usually to find incentives that maintain performance, such as extra time off, a small bonus, or recognition.
- When the person's performance is *unsatisfactory but correctable*, the interview objective is to lay out an action/development plan for correcting the unsatisfactory performance.
- Finally, the interview where the employee is *unsatisfactory* and the situation is *uncorrectable* may be particularly tense. Dismissal is often the usual option.

How to Conduct the Appraisal Interview

Useful interviews begin before the interview. Beforehand, review the person's job description, compare performance to the standards, and review previous appraisals. Give the employee a week's notice to review his or her work. Set a time for the interview. Interviews with lower-level personnel like clerical workers should take less than an hour. Interviews with management employees often take 1 or 2 hours. Conduct the interview privately with no interruptions.

An effective interview requires effective coaching skills. Coaching doesn't mean telling someone what to do. Instead, it is a process.[84] *Preparation* means understanding the problem and the employee. Here the manager will watch the employee at work to see what he or she is doing, review productivity data, and observe the workflow.

Planning the solution is next. This requires reaching agreement on the problem, and laying out a change plan in the form of *steps to take, measures of success,* and *date to complete.*

With agreement on a plan, the manager can start the *actual coaching*. One writer says, "An effective coach offers ideas and advice in such a way that the subordinate can hear them, respond to them, and appreciate their value."[85] Useful guidelines include the following:

1. ***Talk in terms of objective work data.*** Use examples such as absences, tardiness, and productivity.
2. ***Don't get personal.*** Don't say, "You're too slow producing those reports." Instead, compare the person's performance to a standard. ("These reports should normally be done within 10 days.") Similarly, don't compare the person's performance to that of other people. ("He's quicker than you are.")
3. ***Encourage the person to talk.*** Stop and listen to what the person is saying; ask open-ended questions (such as, "What do you think we can do to improve the situation?"). Use a command such as "Go on." Restate the person's last point as a question, as in, "You don't think you can get the job done?"
4. ***Get agreement.*** Make sure the person leaves knowing specifically what he or she is doing right and doing wrong, and with agreement on how things will be improved, and has an action plan with targets and dates.

MAKE IT A DIALOGUE Whether subordinates express satisfaction with the appraisal interview depends on their not feeling threatened, having an opportunity to present their feelings, and being able to influence the course of the interview.

For example, researchers audiotaped 48 actual annual appraisal interviews.[86] They analyzed these based on the communications that occurred between the supervisors and the employees. Some supervisors used more relation-oriented behaviors in the interviews, making comments like "I agree with that," and "that's a good idea." Other supervisors did not. The researchers found that such relation-oriented comments elicited positive employee responses, such as "I see what you mean, could we do this?"

The results showed that the best appraisal interviews weren't monologues in which supervisors simply stuck to a script about what employees did right or wrong. Instead, to paraphrase the researchers, *the best appraisal interviews are dialogues between equal partners*.[87]

How to Handle a Defensive Subordinate

When a supervisor tells someone his or her performance is poor, the first reaction is often denial. Denial is a defense mechanism. By denying the fault, the person avoids having to question his or her own competence.

Therefore, dealing with defensiveness is an important appraisal skill. In his book *Effective Psychology for Managers*, psychologist Mortimer Feinberg suggests the following:

1. Recognize that defensive behavior is normal.
2. Never attack a person's defenses. Don't try to "explain someone to themselves" (as in, "You know the reason you're using that excuse is that you can't bear to be blamed."). Instead, concentrate on the fact ("sales are down").
3. Postpone action. Sometimes it's best to do nothing. Employees may react to sudden threats by hiding behind their defenses. Given sufficient time, a more rational reaction takes over.
4. Recognize your limitations. The supervisor is (probably) not a psychologist. Offering understanding is one thing; trying to deal with psychological problems is another.

How to Criticize a Subordinate

When necessary, criticize in a manner that lets the person maintain his or her dignity—in private, and constructively. Provide examples of critical incidents and specific suggestions. Avoid once-a-year "critical broadsides" by giving feedback periodically, so that the formal review contains no surprises. Never say the person is "always" wrong. Criticism should be objective and free of personal bias.

When the employee is not doing well, the manager will have to decide how candid to be. Former GE CEO Jack Welch once said it's cruel to tell someone who's mediocre that their work is satisfactory.[88] Someone who might have changed course may instead waste years in a dead-end job, only to be dismissed when a more demanding boss arrives.

Some managers do take a hard line. Not all employees are salvageable, and not all managers will spend time trying to overcome an employee's faults. For example, when one Netflix manager requested a performance improvement plan for a worker, the then-head of HR said basically, "Don't waste your time." Her position was, why waste time coaching this person if she'll probably never do the job right anyway?[89]

On the other hand, many employers are now emphasizing praise over criticism. One tells its managers not to touch on more than two areas that need improvement but instead to emphasize subordinates' strengths. Most *Fortune* 500 companies use the Gallup StrengthsFinder tool (www.gallupstrengthscenter.com) to help employees identify and build on their strengths. Facebook has used StrengthsFinder to help train supervisors in a style that better fits its mostly Millennial-aged staff. It would seem that to attract, motivate, and retain today's new employees, a less critical appraisal approach may be advisable.[90]

GET AGREEMENT ON A PLAN The aim of the appraisal should be to improve unsatisfactory performance (and/or to reinforce exemplary performance). The appraisal should therefore result in a plan (Figure 9-11) for what the employee must do to improve his or her efforts.

How to Handle a Written Warning

The employee's performance may be so weak that it requires a written warning. Such warnings serve two purposes: (1) to shake your employee out of his or her bad habits, and (2) to help you defend your rating to your own boss and (if needed) to the courts.

FIGURE 9-11 **Sample Employee Development Plan**

SAMPLE EMPLOYEE DEVELOPMENT PLAN: Employee's Name			
Employee's main objectives for this period:	Did employee fully achieve objective (include rating from appraisal form, from Poor to Outstanding)?	What training or other actions are required for improved performance on this objective?	Completion dates:
1.			
2.			
3.			
4.			
5.			
Employee Signature		Manager Signature	

Copyright Gary dessler, PhD

Written warnings should list the employee's standards, make it clear that the employee was aware of the standard, specify any deficiencies relative to the standard, and show that the employee had an opportunity to correct his or her performance.

Figure 9-12 provides an appraisal interview checklist.

Appraisal Interview Checklist

Interview Item: Did you	Yes	No
1. Review the employee's job description, previous appraisals, goals, and current job standards prior to the interview?		
2. Provide adequate time and a private, cordial, non-threatening environment for the interview?		
3. Focus your discussion and comments on objective work data?		
4. Encourage the appraisee to talk (restate last comment as a question, etc.), and make it clear you are listening (nod, etc.)?		
5. Give the appraisee an opportunity to fully present his or her ideas and feelings?		
6. Consciously avoid attacking the appraisee's defenses?		
7. Criticize in a way that allowed the appraisee to maintain his or her dignity?		
8. Discuss your evaluation of each of the appraisee's job duties and/or goals?		
9. Reach agreement on the training and development required to improve the appraisee's performance?		
10. Discuss, as appropriate, the steps the employer may take if improvement goals are not met?		
11. Discuss the appraisee's performance in light of his or her career aspirations?		

FIGURE 9-12 **Appraisal Interview Checklist**

Source: Copyright Gary Dessler, PhD.

LEARNING OBJECTIVE 9-5

Explain key points in how to use the appraisal interview to boost employee engagement.

Employee Engagement Guide for Managers

Use the Appraisal Interview to Build Engagement

Managers can use the appraisal interview to improve their employees' engagement. Here are relevant findings and implications.

1. Employees who understand how they and their departments contribute to the company's success are more engaged.[91] Therefore, *take the opportunity to show the employee how his or her efforts contribute to the "big picture"—to his or her team's and the company's success.*
2. Another study found that employees' engagement rose when they experienced what the researchers called "psychological meaningfulness" (namely, the perception that one's role in the organization is worthwhile and valuable).[92] *Use the interview to emphasize the meaningfulness to the company of what the employee is doing.*
3. Employees who experience "psychological safety" (the perception that it's safe to bring oneself to a role without fear of damage to self-image, status, or career) were more engaged.[93] Therefore, *be candid and objective but do so supportively and without unnecessarily undermining the employee's self-image.*[94]
4. Efficacy drives engagement, so use the interview to make sure your employee *has what he or she needs* to do a good job.[95]
5. Managers should be candid and honest, but don't unnecessarily emphasize the negatives. Doing so undermines employee engagement. In one survey, Gallup asked about 1,000 U.S. employees to respond to two statements: "My supervisor focuses on my strengths or positive characteristics" and "My supervisor focuses on my weaknesses or negative characteristics." It found that about three times more employees whose *managers focused on strengths* were engaged, compared with those who focused on weaknesses.[96]
6. Involvement in decision making and letting employees voice their opinions improve employee engagement.[97] Use the interview as an opportunity to *show your employees that you listen to their ideas and value their contributions.*
7. Engagement rises when employees have an opportunity to improve their careers.[98] During the interview discuss the person's evaluation *in the context of where he or she sees himself or herself heading career-wise.*[99]
8. Research shows "a significant positive association between (1) distributive [what rewards people get] and informational [what information they get] justice dimensions, and (2) employee engagement."[100] Bottom line: *Make sure that the interviewee views the appraisal and the rewards or remedial actions as fair.*

KNOWLEDGE BASE

Performance Management

LEARNING OBJECTIVE 9-6

Explain how you would take a performance management approach to appraisal.

Performance appraisal is fine in theory, but in practice appraisals don't always go smoothly. Goals aren't set, the "appraisal" is a form from an office supply store, and the yearly feedback, if any, may be agonizing, with both participants fleeing before any coaching takes place. This runs counter to common sense. Employees should know what their goals are, performance feedback should be useful, and if there is a problem, the time to take action is right away, not 6 months later.

Total Quality Management and Performance Appraisal

Management experts have long argued that most performance appraisals neither motivate employees nor guide their development.[101] Some proponents of the total quality management (TQM) movement even argued for eliminating performance appraisals altogether.[102] *Total quality management* (TQM) programs are organizationwide programs that integrate all functions and processes of the business such that all aspects of the business including design, planning, production, distribution, and field service are aimed at maximizing customer satisfaction through continuous improvements.[103] TQM programs are built on a philosophy encapsulated by several principles, such as: cease dependence on inspection to achieve quality; aim for continuous improvement; institute extensive training; drive out fear so that everyone may work effectively; remove barriers that rob employees of their pride of workmanship (in particular, the annual merit rating); and institute a vigorous program of self-improvement.[104] Basically, TQM advocates argue that the organization is a system of interrelated parts, and that employees' performance is more a function of things like training, communication, tools, and supervision than of their motivation.

What would performance appraisal look like in such a company? Visitors to Toyota Motor's Lexington, Kentucky, Camry plant would find such a system. Teams of employees monitor their own results, generally without managers' interventions. In frequent meetings, the team members continuously align those results with the work team's standards and with the plant's overall quality and productivity goals. Team members who need coaching and training receive it. Procedures that need changing are changed.

What Is Performance Management?

That is performance management in action. In comparing performance management and performance appraisal, "the distinction is the contrast between (1) a year-end event (the completion of the appraisal form) and (2) a process that starts the year with performance planning and is integral to the way people are managed throughout the year."[105] **Performance management** is the *continuous* process of identifying, measuring, and developing the performance of individuals and teams and *aligning* their performance with the organization's *goals*.[106] We can summarize performance management's six basic elements as follows:[107]

performance management
The *continuous* process of identifying, measuring, and developing the performance of individuals and teams and *aligning* their performance with the organization's *goals*.

- ***Direction sharing*** means communicating the company's goals to all employees and then translating these into departmental, team, and individual goals.
- ***Goal alignment*** means having a method that enables managers and employees to *see the link* between the employees' goals and those of their department and company.
- ***Ongoing performance monitoring*** usually means computerized systems to continuously measure the team's and/or employee's progress toward meeting performance goals.
- ***Ongoing feedback*** means providing face-to-face and computerized continuous feedback regarding progress toward goals.
- ***Coaching and developmental support*** should be part of the feedback process.
- ***Recognition and rewards*** should provide incentives to keep the employee's goal-directed performance on track.

TRENDS SHAPING HR: *DIGITAL AND SOCIAL MEDIA*

Employers often use technology to support performance management. For example, with Oracle's TBE Performance Management Cloud Service, performance management involves:

- First, *assign financial and nonfinancial goals* (goals that support the company's overall strategic goals) to each team's activities. For example, an airline might measure ground crew aircraft turnaround time in terms of "improve turnaround time to 26 minutes per plane this year."
- Second, *inform all teams and employees* of their goals.
- Next, *use technology* (cloud-based performance management software, HR scorecards, and digital dashboards) to continuously display, monitor, and assess each team's and employee's performance (see Figure 9-13). Oracle TBE Performance Management Cloud Service illustrates this.[108] Because the goals are "in the cloud" rather than printed in documents, managers needn't wait until the annual or semiannual reviews to revise them. And the system's portable dashboards enable managers to continuously monitor each team or employee's performance, let employees update progress toward goal achievement, and let employees and managers log comments so the process is real-time and interactive. For more details, see www.oracle.com/taleo-tbe.
- Finally, if exceptions are noted, *take corrective action* before things swing out of control. ■

PERFORMANCE GOAL MANAGEMENT

Report Card | Link | Edit | Options | Copy

Details - 2018 Performance Goal Scorecard — In Progress (01/01/2018 - 12/31/2018)

Goals for Brown, Lisa — Score 4.5

Employee's Individual Performance Goals

Goal	Target	Weight	Score	Date
Achieve 10% Sales Increase	8	45	7.0	June 2018
Improved Customer Satisfaction Rating	4.2	25	4.0	June 2018
Meet Budgetary Constraints	5	15	2.5	June 2018
Improved Leadership Ratings	4.8	15	4.5	June 2018

Departmental Performance Goals

Goal	Target	Weight	Score	Date
Achieve 15% Sales Increase	5	50	3.5	June 2018
Increase Online sales 10%	3.5	25	2.8	June 2018
Meet Budgetary Constraints	5	10	4.2	June 2018
All Employees Cross-Trained on All Products	4.5	15	3.5	June 2018

FIGURE 9-13 **Summary of Performance Management Report**

Source: Based on "Personal Goal Management" from the Active Strategy Website. Copyright © 2012 by ActiveStrategy, Inc.

MyLab Management Apply It!

Who does this company have doing its appraisals? If your professor has assigned this activity, go to the Assignments section of **www.pearson.com/mylab/management** to complete the video exercise.

Performance Management in Action

The trend today is to provide real-time feedback on performance.[109] For example, GE began using a smart phone app it calls PD@GE to let supervisors assess employees continuously rather than once a year.[110] IBM Corp. introduced a new app-based performance review it calls Checkpoint.[111] It allows for more continuous monitoring of performance and feedback.

Goldman Sachs still uses annual reviews, but added a new system through which employees also get continuous feedback. Goldman also compiles 360-degree feedback on its employees. Morgan Stanley no longer uses numerical appraisal ratings, instead emphasizing qualitative feedback.[112]

"Performance management" doesn't mean a company can't be tough. For many years, Kimberly-Clark Corp. was reportedly known for lifetime employment and for retaining even underperforming employees. Then it instituted a new performance management system, including continuous online performance reviews to carefully track employees' performance relative to their goals. Turnover is up dramatically.[113]

The Strategic Context feature shows how one company developed a performance management system to support its strategy.

IMPROVING PERFORMANCE: *THE STRATEGIC CONTEXT*

Deloitte's New Performance Management Process[114]

The mission of Deloitte LLP and Deloitte USA LLP is to deliver results that are quantifiable and enduring. For a company that provides complex audit and consulting services to many of America's largest companies, delivering "enduring results" requires an effective performance management system.

Yet while the frequent subjective feedback at the heart of performance management is laudable, many performance management systems suffer from one calamitous weakness: at the end of the day, the employer needs a way to differentiate among employees and to make hard-nosed pay raise and promotional decisions; Any performance management process that can't do that isn't very practical.

THE PROBLEM Deloitte's managers knew they could improve their performance management system. Many questioned whether the system improved performance. They knew traditional performance ratings often said more about the manager's personality than about the employee's performance. Furthermore, with 65,000 employees, Deloitte was devoting two *million* hours per year to appraisals. And the appraisals focused more on history than on how to improve employees' performance. Management decided to change the process.

THE NEW GOALS The team creating the new performance management process set three goals: first, it should *recognize employee performance*, particularly in terms of bonuses; second, the new process should *clearly reflect employee performance*. Third, the new process should *energize performance*, by monitoring performance often enough so that employees could improve their performance during their assignments. (In any year, a Deloitte employee may be assigned to one or more teams working on assignments [such as an audit], for a particular client project.)

THE NEW PERFORMANCE MANAGEMENT PROCESS Deloitte's new performance management process has several features. First, each team member *interacts with his or her team leader periodically* during the assignment, to get frequent feedback on how the employee is doing and how to improve.

Second, at the end of the assignment, rather than the team leaders just presenting their opinions about how the employee performed, the team leader provides an "employee performance snapshot" by reporting on how the team leader *plans to act* regarding the employee, specifically: (1) From what I know about this person's performance, if it were my money, here is how I would compensate this person; (2) based on what you know about this person's performance, would you want this person on your team again; (3) do you think this person's performance is such that it might harm the customer or the team; and (4) would you say this person is ready for promotion today?

Then, at the end of the year, Deloitte compiles all these assignment "snapshots" *in a year-end evaluation*. That evaluation, plus input from a team leader who knows the employee's performance personally, determines the employee's compensation.

MyLab Management Talk About It 4

If your professor has assigned this, go to the Assignments section of **www.pearson.com/mylab/management** to complete this discussion. Deloitte is a global company. Discuss two cultural differences between the United States and any one other country that you might have thought would make having a single system challenging.

The Manager's Role in Performance Management

Technology isn't mandatory for managers who want to take a performance management approach. What is mandatory is having the right managerial philosophy and on-the-job behaviors. As a philosophy, performance management reflects nonthreatening TQM principles such as cease dependence on inspection to achieve quality, aim for continuous improvement, institute extensive training, and drive out fear so that everyone may work effectively. The manager's behaviors should therefore include linking employees' goals to the company's goals, giving employees continuous feedback, providing required resources and coaching, rewarding good performance, and remembering that employees' performance reflects more than just whether they're "motivated."[115]

HR in Action at the Hotel Paris Both Lisa and the firm's CFO were concerned by the current disconnect between (1) what their current appraisal process was focusing on and (2) what the company wanted to accomplish in terms of its strategic goals. They wanted the firm's new performance management system to help breathe life into the firm's strategic performance. To see what they did, read the case pages 306–307 of this chapter.

Chapter Review

Chapter Section Summaries

9-1. **Performance appraisal** means evaluating an employee's current or past performance relative to his or her performance standards. Managers appraise their subordinates' performance to obtain input on which promotion and salary raise decisions can be made, to develop plans for correcting performance deficiencies, and for career-planning purposes. Supervisory ratings are still at the heart of most appraisal processes.

9-2. The appraisal is generally conducted using one or more popular **appraisal methods or tools.** These include graphic rating scales, alternation ranking, paired comparison, forced distribution, critical incidents, behaviorally anchored rating scales, MBO, computerized performance appraisals, and electronic performance monitoring.

9-3. The appraisal process can be improved by eliminating chronic **problems** that often undermine appraisals and graphic rating scales in particular. These problems include unclear standards, halo effect, central tendency, leniency or strictness, and bias.

9-4. An appraisal typically culminates in an **appraisal interview.** Adequate preparation (including giving the subordinate notice, reviewing his or her job description and past performance, choosing the right place for the interview, and leaving enough time for it) is essential.

9-5. The manager can use the appraisal interview to improve the employees' level of **engagement.** For example, show the employee how his or her efforts contribute to the team's and the company's success; use the interview to emphasize the meaningfulness to the company of what the employee is doing; and emphasize support rather than threats.

9-6. **Performance management** is the *continuous* process of identifying, measuring, and developing the performance of individuals and teams and *aligning* their performance with the organization's *goals*. It means continuous interactions and feedback to ensure continuous improvement in the employee's and team's capacity and performance. Most important, it requires remembering that your employee's performance usually reflects more than just whether he or she is "motivated."

CHAPTER 9

Discussion Questions

9-1. What is the purpose of a performance appraisal?

9-2. Answer the question, "Who should do the appraising?"

9-3. Discuss the pros and cons of four performance appraisal tools.

9-4. Explain how you would use the alternation ranking method, the paired comparison method, and the forced distribution method.

9-5. Explain in your own words how you would go about developing a behaviorally anchored rating scale.

9-6. Explain the problems to be avoided in appraising performance.

9-7. Compare and contrast performance management and performance appraisal.

Individual and Group Activities

9-8. Working individually or in groups, develop a graphic rating scale for the following jobs: secretary, professor, bus driver.

9-9. Working individually or in groups, describe the advantages and disadvantages of using the forced distribution appraisal method for college professors.

9-10. Working individually or in groups, develop, over the period of a week, a set of critical incidents covering the classroom performance of one of your instructors.

9-11. Appendices A and B at the end of this book (pages 614–634) list the knowledge someone studying for the HRCI (Appendix A) or SHRM (Appendix B) certification exam needs to have in each area of human resource management (such as in Strategic Management and Workforce Planning). In groups of several students, do four things: (1) review Appendix A and/or B; (2) identify the material in this chapter that relates to the Appendix A and/or B required knowledge lists; (3) write four

KNOWLEDGE BASE

multiple-choice exam questions on this material that you believe would be suitable for inclusion in the HRCI exam and/or the SHRM exam; and (4) if time permits, have someone from your team post your team's questions in front of the class, so that students in all teams can answer the exam questions created by the other teams.

9-12. When he was doing his show *The Apprentice*, Donald Trump often told apprentices "You're fired!" Review recent (or archived) episodes of Donald Trump's *The Apprentice* and answer this: What performance appraisal system did Mr. Trump use, and do you think it resulted in valid appraisals? What techniques discussed in this chapter did he seem to apply? How would you suggest he might change his appraisal system to make it more effective?

Experiential Exercise

Grading the Professor

Written and copyrighted by Gary Dessler, PhD.

Purpose: The purpose of this exercise is to give you practice in developing and using a performance appraisal form.

Required Understanding: You are going to develop a performance appraisal form for an instructor and should therefore be thoroughly familiar with the discussion of performance appraisals in this chapter.

How to Set Up the Exercise/Instructions: Divide the class into groups of four or five students.

9-13. First, based on what you now know about performance appraisal, do you think Figure 9-1 is an effective scale for appraising instructors? Why or why not?

9-14. Next, your group should develop its own tool for appraising the performance of an instructor. Decide which of the appraisal tools (graphic rating scales, alternation ranking, and so on) you are going to use, and then design the instrument itself.

9-15. Next, have a spokesperson from each group post his or her group's appraisal tool on the board. How similar are the tools? Do they all measure the same factors? Which factor appears most often? Which do you think is the most effective tool on the board?

9-16. The class should select the top ten factors from all of the appraisal tools presented to create what the class perceives to be the most effective tool for appraising the performance of the instructor.

Application Case

Appraising the Secretaries at Sweetwater U

Written and copyrighted by Gary Dessler, PhD.

Rob Winchester, newly appointed vice president for administrative affairs at Sweetwater State University, faced a tough problem shortly after his university career began. Three weeks after he came on board in September, Sweetwater's president, Rob's boss, told Rob that one of his first tasks was to improve the appraisal system used to evaluate secretarial and clerical performance at Sweetwater U. The main difficulty was that the performance appraisal was traditionally tied directly to salary increases given at the end of the year. Therefore, most administrators were less than accurate when they used the graphic rating forms that were the basis of the clerical staff evaluation. In fact, what usually happened was that each administrator simply rated his or her clerk or secretary as "excellent." This cleared the way for them to receive a maximum pay raise every year.

But the current university budget simply did not include enough money to fund another "maximum" annual raise for every staffer. Furthermore, Sweetwater's president felt that the custom of providing invalid feedback to each secretary on his or her year's performance was not productive, so he had asked the new vice president to revise the system. In October, Rob sent a memo to all administrators, telling them that in the future no more than half the secretaries reporting to any particular administrator could be appraised as "excellent." This move, in effect, forced each supervisor to begin ranking his or her secretaries for quality of performance. The vice president's memo met widespread resistance immediately—from administrators, who were afraid that many of their secretaries would begin leaving for more lucrative jobs, and from secretaries, who felt that the new system was unfair and reduced each secretary's chance of receiving a maximum salary increase. A handful of secretaries had begun picketing outside the president's home on the university campus. The picketing, caustic remarks by disgruntled administrators, and rumors of an impending slowdown by the secretaries (there were about 250 on campus) made Rob Winchester wonder whether he had made the right decision by setting up forced ranking. He knew, however, that there were a few performance appraisal experts in the School of Business, so he decided to set up an appointment with them to discuss the matter.

He met with them the next morning. He explained the situation as he had found it: The current appraisal system had been set up when the university first opened 10 years earlier. A committee of secretaries had developed it. Under that system, Sweetwater's administrators filled out forms similar to the one shown in Table 9-2. This once-a-year appraisal (in March) had run into problems almost immediately because it was apparent from the start that administrators varied widely in their interpretations of job standards, as well as in how conscientiously they filled out the forms and supervised their secretaries. Moreover, at the end of the first year it became obvious to everyone that each secretary's salary increase was tied directly to the March appraisal. For example, those rated "excellent" received the maximum increases, those rated "good" received smaller increases, and those given neither rating received only the standard across-the-board cost-of-living increase. Because universities in general—and Sweetwater, in particular—have paid secretaries somewhat lower salaries than those prevailing in private industry, some secretaries left in a huff that first year. From that time on, most administrators simply rated all secretaries excellent in order to reduce staff turnover, thus ensuring each a maximum increase. In the process, they also avoided the hard feelings aroused by the significant performance differences otherwise highlighted by administrators.

Two Sweetwater experts agreed to consider the problem, and in 2 weeks they came back to the vice president with the following recommendations. First, the form used to rate the secretaries was grossly insufficient. It was unclear what "excellent" or "quality of work" meant, for example. They recommended instead a form like that in Figure 9-2. In addition, they recommended that the vice president rescind his earlier memo and no longer attempt to force university administrators to arbitrarily rate at least half their secretaries as something less than excellent. The two consultants pointed out that this was unfair, since it was quite possible that any particular administrator might have staffers who were all or virtually all excellent—or conceivably, although less likely, all below standard. The experts said that the way to get all the administrators to take the appraisal process more seriously was to stop tying it to salary increases. In other words, they recommended that every administrator fill out a form as in Figure 9-2 for each secretary at least once a year and then use this form as the basis of a counseling session. Salary increases would have to be made on some basis other than the performance appraisal, so that administrators would no longer hesitate to fill out the rating forms honestly.

Rob thanked the two experts and went back to his office to ponder their recommendations. Some of the recommendations (such as substituting the new rating form for the old) seemed to make sense. Nevertheless, he still had serious doubts as to the efficacy of any graphic rating form, particularly compared with his original, preferred forced ranking approach. The experts' second recommendation—to stop tying the appraisals to automatic salary increases—made sense but raised at least one very practical problem: If salary increases were not to be based on performance appraisals, on what were they to be based? He began wondering whether the experts' recommendations weren't simply based on ivory tower theorizing.

Questions

9-17. Do you think that the experts' recommendations will be sufficient to get most of the administrators to fill out the rating forms properly? Why or why not? What additional actions (if any) do you think will be necessary?

9-18. Do you think that Vice President Winchester would be better off dropping graphic rating forms, substituting instead one of the other techniques we discussed in this chapter, such as a ranking method? Why or why not?

9-19. What performance appraisal system would you develop for the secretaries if you were Rob Winchester? Defend your answer.

CHAPTER 9

Continuing Case

Carter Cleaning Company

Written and copyrighted by Gary Dessler, PhD.

The Performance Appraisal

After spending several weeks on the job, Jennifer was surprised to discover that her father had not formally evaluated any employee's performance for all the years that he had owned the business. Jack's position was that he had "a hundred higher-priority things to attend to," such as boosting sales and lowering costs, and, in any case, many employees didn't stick around long enough to be appraisable anyway. Furthermore, contended Jack, manual workers such as those doing the pressing and the cleaning did periodically get positive feedback in terms of praise from Jack for a job well done, or criticism, also from Jack, if things did not look right during one of his swings through the stores. Similarly, Jack was never shy about telling his managers about store problems so that they, too, got some feedback on where they stood.

This informal feedback notwithstanding, Jennifer believes that a more formal appraisal approach is required. She believes that there are criteria such as quality, quantity, attendance, and punctuality that should be evaluated periodically even if a worker is paid on piece rate. Furthermore, she feels quite strongly that the managers need to have a list of quality standards for matters such as store cleanliness, efficiency, safety, and adherence to budget on which they know they are to be formally evaluated.

Questions

9-20. Is Jennifer right about the need to evaluate the workers formally? The managers? Why or why not?

9-21. Develop a performance appraisal method for the workers and managers in each store.

Translating Strategy into HR Policies and Practices Case*,§

** The accompanying strategy map for this chapter is in the MyLab Management; the overall map on the inside back cover of this text outlines the relationships involved.*

Improving Performance at the Hotel Paris

The New Performance Management System

The Hotel Paris's competitive strategy is "To use superior guest service to differentiate the Hotel Paris properties, and to thereby increase the length of stay and return rate of guests, and thus boost revenues and profitability." HR manager Lisa Cruz must now formulate appraisal policies and activities that support this competitive strategy, by eliciting the required employee behaviors and competencies.

Lisa knew that the Hotel Paris's performance appraisal system was inadequate. When the founders opened their first hotel, they went to an office-supply store and purchased a pad of performance appraisal forms. The hotel chain used these. Each form was a two-sided page. Supervisors indicated whether the employee's performance in terms of various standard traits including quantity of work, quality of work, and dependability was excellent, good, fair, or poor. Lisa knew that, among other flaws, this appraisal tool did not force either the employee or the supervisor to focus the appraisal on the extent to which the employee was helping the Hotel Paris to achieve its strategic goals. She wanted a system that focused the employee's attention on taking those actions that would contribute to helping the company achieve its goals, for instance, in terms of improved customer service.

§ Written and copyrighted by Gary Dessler, PhD.

Both Lisa and the firm's CFO were concerned by the current disconnect between (1) what the current appraisal process was focusing on and (2) what the company wanted to accomplish in terms of its strategic goals. They wanted the firm's new performance management system to help breathe life into the firm's strategic performance, by focusing employees' behavior specifically on the performances that would help the Hotel Paris achieve its strategic goals.

Lisa and her team created a performance management system that focused on both competencies and objectives. In designing the new system, their starting point was the job descriptions they had created for the hotel's employees. These descriptions each included required competencies. Consequently, using a form similar to Figure 9-3, the front-desk clerks' appraisals now focus on competencies such as "able to check a guest in or out in 5 minutes or less." Most service employees' appraisals include the competency, "able to exhibit patience and guest support of this even when busy with other activities." There were other required competencies. For example, the Hotel Paris wanted all service employees to show initiative in helping guests, to be customer oriented, and to be team players (in terms of sharing information and best practices). Each of these competencies derives from the hotel's aim of becoming more service oriented. Each employee now also receives one or more strategically relevant objectives for the coming year. (One, for a housecleaning crewmember, said, "Martha will have no more than three room cleaning infractions in the coming year," for instance.)

In addition to the goals- and competencies-based appraisals, other Hotel Paris performance management forms laid out the development efforts that the employee would undertake in the coming year. Instructions also reminded the supervisors that, in addition to the annual and semiannual appraisals, they should continuously interact with and update their employees. The result was a comprehensive performance management system: The supervisor appraised the employee based on goals and competencies that were driven by the company's strategic needs. And, the actual appraisal resulted in new goals for the coming year, as well as in specific development plans that made sense in terms of the company's and the employees' needs and preferences.

Questions

9-22. Choose one job, such as front-desk clerk. Based on any information you have (including job descriptions you may have created in other chapters), write a list of duties, competencies, and performance standards for that chosen job.

9-23. Based on that, and on what you read in this Dessler *Human Resource Management* chapter, create a performance appraisal form for appraising that job.

CHAPTER 9

Writing Assignments

9-24. Discuss the pros and cons of using different potential raters to appraise a person's performance.

9-25. As a new supervisor, you're about to hold your first-ever appraisal interview with one of your subordinates, someone who has not been performing very well for the past 6 months. What should you keep in mind about managing the appraisal interview as you begin the conversation?

PERSONAL INVENTORY ASSESSMENTS

Go to **www.pearson.com/mylab/management** to complete the Personal Inventory Assessment related to this chapter.

Key Terms

performance appraisal, 279
performance appraisal process, 279
graphic rating scale, 283
alternation ranking method, 283
paired comparison method, 285
forced distribution method, 285
critical incident method, 285
behaviorally anchored rating scale (BARS), 288
electronic performance monitoring (EPM), 291
unclear standards, 293
halo effect, 293
central tendency, 294
strictness/leniency, 294
bias, 294
appraisal interview, 297
performance management, 301

Endnotes

1. https://www2.deloitte.com/us/en/pages/about-deloitte/articles/about-deloitte. html?icid=bottom_about-deloitte, accessed March 12, 2018.
2. See, for example, Howard Risher, "Performance Management Needs to Be Fixed," *Compensation & Benefits Review* 44, no. 4 (2014), pp. 191–194.
3. Peter Cappelli and Anna Tavis, "The Performance Management Revolution," *Harvard Business Review*,

October 2016, https://hbr.org/2016/10/the-performance-management-revolution, accessed March 31, 2018.
4. www.ball.com, accessed September 9, 2018.
5. "Aligning People and Processes for Performance Improvement," *TD* 65, no. 3 (March 2011), p. 80.
6. Ibid.
7. "Get SMART about Setting Goals," *Asia Africa Intelligence Wire,* May 22, 2005; For examples of setting smart goals, see http://hrweb.mit.edu/performance-development/goal-setting-developmental-planning/smart-goals, accessed March 31, 2018.
8. See, for example, E. A. Locke and G. P. Latham, "Building a Practically Useful Theory of Goal Setting and Task Motivation. A 35-Year Odyssey," *American Psychologist* 57, no. 9 (2002), pp. 705–717. Letting employees help set their performance measures (in terms of what is measured, and how it's measured when they're appraised) is associated with improved job performance. Bianca Groen et al., "High Job Performance through Codeveloping Performance Measures with Employees," *Human Resource Management*, 56, no. 1 (January–February 2017), pp. 111–132.
9. Thom Shanker, "Conduct at Issue as Subordinates Review Officers," *The New York Times*, April 14, 2013, pp. A1, A4.
10. www.quora.com/What-does-Facebooks-performance-review-process-look-like, accessed April 2, 2015.
11. Bock, *Work Rules!* (New York: 12, 2015), p. 171.
12. Martin Berman-Gorvine, "Coworker Recognition Programs Yield Employers Great Returns," *Bloomberg BNA Bulletin to Management*, January 10, 2017.
13. Vanessa Druskat and Steven Wolf, "Effects and Timing of Developmental Peer Appraisals in Self-Managing Work-Groups," *Journal of Applied Psychology* 84, no. 1 (1999), pp. 58–74. For a review, see Erich Dierdorff and Eric Surface, "Placing Peer Ratings in Context: Systematic Influences beyond Ratee Performance," *Personnel Psychology* 60, no. 1 (Spring 2007), pp. 93–126.
14. Leena Rao, "Salesforce Debuts 'Rypple-Powered Work.com' to Help Companies Manage Talent, Partners with Facebook," September 19, 2012, http://techcrunch.com/2012/09/19/salesforce-debuts-rypple-powered-work-com-to-help-companies-manage-talent/, accessed April 5, 2013; Eric Mosley, "The Power of the Crowd Sourced Performance Review," *Compensation & Benefits Review* 45, no. 6 (2013), pp. 320–323.
15. Rao, "Salesforce Debuts 'Rypple-Powered Work.com.'"
16. Rachel Silverman and Leslie Kwoh, "Performance Reviews Facebook Style," *The Wall Street Journal*, August 1, 2012, p. B6.
17. Toni Veranges, "Held in High Regard," *HR Magazine*, November 2014, pp. 54–56. See also, https://www.persistent.com/media/press-releases/persistent-systems-emee-helps-tcabs-launch-exclusive-cab-miles-program/, accessed April 23, 2018.
18. "Game Changing Performance Management: A Software Company Makes a Game Out of Yearly Performance Appraisals," *TD* 68, no. 1 (January 2014), p. 80.
19. See, for example, Brian Hoffman and David Woehr, "Disentangling the Meaning of Multisource Performance Rating Source and Dimension Factors," *Personnel Psychology* 62 (2009), pp. 735–765.
20. As one study concluded, "Far from being a source of non-meaningful error variance, the discrepancies among ratings from multiple perspectives can in fact capture meaningful variance in multilevel managerial performance." In-Sue Oh and Christopher Berry, "The Five Factor Model of Personality and Managerial Performance: Validity Gains Through the Use of 360° Performance Ratings," *Journal of Applied Psychology* 94, no. 6 (2009), p. 1510.
21. See, for example, Kevin Murphy et al., "Raters Who Pursue Different Goals Give Different Ratings," *Journal of Applied Psychology* 89, no. 1 (2004), pp. 158–164.
22. Such findings may be culturally related. One study compared self and supervisor ratings in "other-oriented" cultures (as in sia, where values tend to emphasize teams). It found that self and supervisor ratings were related. M. Audrey Korsgaard et al., "The Effect of Other Orientation on Self: Supervisor Rating Agreement," *Journal of Organizational Behavior* 25, no. 7 (November 2004), pp. 873–891. See also Heike Heidemeier and Klaus Mosar, "Self-Other Agreement in Job Performance Ratings: A Meta-Analytic Test of a Process Model," *Journal of Applied Psychology* 94, no. 2 (2009), pp. 353–370.
23. Forest Jourden and Chip Heath, "The Evaluation Gap in Performance Perceptions: Illusory Perceptions of Groups and Individuals," *Journal of Applied Psychology* 81, no. 4 (August 1996), pp. 369–379; Sheri Ostroff, "Understanding Self-Other Agreement: A Look at Rater and Ratee Characteristics, Context, and Outcomes," *Personnel Psychology* 57, no. 2 (Summer 2004), pp. 333–375; Dick Grote, "Let's Abolish Self-Appraisal," *Harvard Business Review*, July 11, 2011, https://hbr.org/2011/07/lets-abolish-self-appraisal.html, accessed March 13, 2018.
24. Dick Grote, op. cit.
25. Leah Fessler, Quartz, August 21, 2017, https://qz.com/1058760/manager-feedback-at-google-employees-are-asked-13-questions-about-their-bosses-as-part-of-a-semi-annual-review-goog-googl/, accessed March 13, 2018.
26. David Antonioni, "The Effects of Feedback Accountability on Upward Appraisal Ratings," *Personnel Psychology* 47 (1994), pp. 349–355. Similarly, raters who are also periodically assessed by their ratees tend to give their ratees higher performance ratings. Michael Harari and Cort Rudolph, "The Effect of Greater Accountability on Performance Ratings: A Meta-Analytic Review," *Human Resource Management Review*, 27 (2017), pp. 121–133.
27. Alan Walker and James Smither, "A Five-Year Study of Upward Feedback: What Managers Do with Their Results Matters," *Personnel Psychology* 52 (1999), pp. 393–423; and Austin F. R. Smith and Vincent J. Fortunato, "Factors Influencing Employee Intentions to Provide Honest Upward Feedback Ratings," *Journal of Business Psychology* 22 (2008), pp. 191–207.
28. Lindsay Gellman, "Memo Lets Workers Vent Anonymously about the Boss," *The Wall Street Journal,* January 21, 2015, p. B7.
29. See, for example, "360-Degree Feedback on the Rise Survey Finds," *BNA Bulletin to Management,* January 23, 1997, p. 31; Leanne Atwater et al., "Multisource Feedback: Lessons Learned and Implications for Practice," *Human Resource Management* 46, no. 2 (Summer 2007), p. 285. However, a small number of employers are beginning to use 360-degree feedback for performance appraisals, rather than just development. See, for example, Tracy Maylett, "360° Feedback Revisited: The Transition from Development to Appraisal," *Compensation & Benefits,* September/October 2009, pp. 52–59.
30. James Smither et al., "Does Performance Improve Following Multi-Score Feedback? A Theoretical Model, Meta Analysis, and Review of Empirical Findings," *Personnel Psychology* 58 (2005), pp. 33–36.
31. Harriet Edleson, "Do 360 Evaluations Work?" http://www.apa.org/monitor/2012/11/360-evaluations.aspx, accessed March 13, 2018.
32. Jim Meade, "Visual 360: A Performance Appraisal System That's 'Fun,'" *HR Magazine,* July 1999, pp. 118–119, www.halogensoftware.com/landing/free-trial/360-multiraterfeedback?source=msn&c=Search-e360&kw=360%2520evaluations, accessed August 28, 2014.
33. http://www.sumtotalsystems.com/solutions/talent/360-degree-feedback/, accessed March 13, 2018.
34. Martin Berman-Gorvine, "Annual Review Plus Frequent Coaching Boost Job Performance," *Bloomberg BNA Bulletin to Management*, October 10, 2017.
35. See for example, Howard Risher, "Getting Serious about Performance Management," *Compensation & Benefits Review*, November/December 2005, pp. 18–26; "Understanding Competency Based Performance Self Appraisal Reviews," https://docs.oracle.com/cd/E16582_01/doc.91/e15117/wrk_wi_emp_self_src_apprs.htm#EOAHR00194, accessed March 31, 2018.
36. "Understanding Competency Based Performance Self Appraisal Reviews," https://docs.oracle.com/cd/E16582_01/doc.91/e15117/wrk_wi_emp_self_src_apprs.htm#EOAHR00194, accessed March 31, 2018.
37. Leslie Kwoh, "Rank and Yank Retains Vocal Fans," *The Wall Street Journal*, January 31, 2012, p. B12.
38. https://qz.com/428813/ge-performance-review-strategy-shift/, accessed March 31, 2018.
39. Gary Giumetti, Amber Schroeder, and Fred Switzer III, "Forced Distribution Rating Systems: When Does 'Rank and Yank' Lead to Adverse Impact?" *Journal of Applied Psychology* 100, no. 1 (2015), pp. 180–193.
40. "Survey Says Problems with Forced Ranking Include Lower Morale and Costly Turnover," *BNA Bulletin to Management*, September 16, 2004, p. 297; Martha C. White, "Amazon's Use of 'Stack' Ranking for Workers May Backfire, Experts Say," https://www.nbcnews.com/business/business-news/trump-blocks-broadcom-takeover-bid-qualcomm-n856021, accessed March 13, 2018.
41. Sue Moon, Steven Scullen, and Gary Latham, "Precarious Curve Ahead: The Effects of Forced Distribution Rating

Systems on Job Performance," *Human Resource Management Review*, 26 (2016), pp. 166–179.

42. Steve Bates, "Forced Ranking: Why Grading Employees on a Scale Relative to Each Other Forces a Hard Look at Finding Keepers, Losers May Become Weepers," *HR Magazine* 48, no. 6 (June 2003), p. 62. See also D. J. Schleicher et al., "Rater Reactions to Forced Distribution Rating Systems," *Journal of Management* 35, no. 4 (August 2009), pp. 899–927.
43. Clinton Wingrove, "Developing an Effective Blend of Process and Technology in the New Era of Performance Management," *Compensation & Benefits Review*, January/February 2003, p. 26.
44. Shira Ovide and Rachel Feintzeig, "Microsoft Abandons Dreaded 'Stack,'" *The Wall Street Journal*, November 13, 2013, p. B1.
45. Juan Sanchez and Phillip De La Torre, "A Second Look at the Relationship between Rating and Behavioral Accuracy in Performance Appraisal," *Journal of Applied Psychology* 81, no. 1 (1996), p. 7. See also "How to … Improve Appraisals," *People Management* 15, no. 3 (January 29, 2009), p. 57.
46. Angelo DeNisi and Lawrence Peters, "Organization of Information in Memory and the Performance Appraisal Process: Evidence from the Field," *Journal of Applied Psychology* 81, no. 6 (1996), pp. 717–737. See also A. Fox, "Curing What Ails Performance Reviews," *HR Magazine* 54, no. 1 (January 2009), pp. 52–56.
47. Based on Donald Schwab, Herbert Heneman III, and Thomas DeCotiis, "Behaviorally Anchored Scales: A Review of the Literature," *Personnel Psychology* 28 (1975), pp. 549–562. For a discussion, see also Uco Wiersma and Gary Latham, "The Practicality of Behavioral Observation Scales, Behavioral Expectation Scales, and Trait Scales," *Personnel Psychology* 30, no. 3 (Autumn 1986), pp. 619–689; and Neil M. A. Hauenstein, Reagan D. Brown, and Andrea L. Sinclair, "BARS and Those Mysterious, Missing Middle Anchors," *Journal of Business and Psychology*, 25, no.4, (2010), pp. 663–672.
48. Lawrence Fogli, Charles Hulin, and Milton Blood, "Development of First Level Behavioral Job Criteria," *Journal of Applied Psychology* 55 (1971), pp. 3–8. See also Joseph Maiorca, "How to Construct Behaviorally Anchored Rating Scales (BARS) for Employee Evaluations," *Supervision*, August 1997, pp. 15–19; and Hauenstein et al., "BARS and Those Mysterious, Missing Middle Anchors."
49. Kevin R. Murphy and Joseph Constans, "Behavioral Anchors as a Source of Bias in Rating," *Journal of Applied Psychology* 72, no. 4 (November 1987), pp. 573–577; Aharon Tziner, "A Comparison of Three Methods of Performance Appraisal with Regard to Goal Properties, Goal Perception, and Ratee Satisfaction," *Group & Organization Management* 25, no. 2 (June 2000), pp. 175–191. BARS is similar to another appraisal method, Behavioral Observation Scales (BOS), but the latter involves rating how frequently the ratees exhibit the illustrative behaviors.
50. Many managers say goal setting is no panacea, and some jobs, for instance in R&D, may not be well measured by goals. Howard Risher, "Individual Performance Goals Can Be Problematic," *Compensation & Benefits Review* 45, no. 2 (2013), pp. 63–66.
51. Laszlo Bock, *Work Rules!* p. 155.
52. https://www.staples.com/performance+appraisal+form/directory_performance+appraisal+form; https://www.hrdirect.com/forms-and-recordkeeping/performance-management-forms/evaluation-forms/employee-appraisal-form-downloadable, accessed August 4, 2018
53. See for example, http://www.cnet.com/products/success-factors-employee-appraiser-5-0-deluxe/, accessed August 4, 2018.
54. https://www.capterra.com/p/141446/BambooHR/, accessed August 4, 2018.
55. See, for example, Stoney Alder and Maureen Ambrose, "Towards Understanding Fairness Judgments Associated with Computer Performance Monitoring: An Integration of the Feedback, Justice, and Monitoring Research," *Human Resource Management Review* 15, no. 1 (March 2005), pp. 43–67. For an analysis of EPM, see Katherine J. S. Rogers, Michael J. Smith, and Pascale C. Sainfort, "Electronic Performance Monitoring, Job Design and Psychological Stress," paper available at www.igi-global.com/chapter/electronic-performance-monitoring-job-design/45284, accessed October 12, 2012.
56. Alder and Ambrose, "Towards Understanding Fairness Judgments"; and David T. Goomas, "Electronic Performance Self Monitoring and Engineered Labor Standards for 'Man-Up' Drivers in a Distribution Center," *Journal of Business and Psychology* 21 no. 4 (Summer 2007), pp. 541–558. Reprinted by permission from Springer Publishing. Cleared via Copyright Clearance Center.
57. H. James Wilson, "Wearables in the Workplace," *Harvard Business Review*, September 2013, pp. 23–25.
58. Adapted or quoted from "Next Generation Talent Management," Hewitt.com, accessed June 2010.
59. Ibid.
60. Ibid.
61. Adapted or quoted from Gunter Stahl et al., "Global Talent Management: How Leading Multinationals Build and Sustain Their Talent Pipelines," Faculty and Research Working Paper, INSEAD, 2007.
62. Herman Aguinis and Ernest O'Boyle Jr., "Star Performers in 21st-Century Organizations," *Personnel Psychology* 67 (2014), pp. 313–315.
63. Based on Jon Younger and Norm Smallwood, "Performance Management in the Gig Economy," *Harvard Business Review*, January 11, 2016, https://hbr.org/2016/01/performance-management-in-the-gig-economy; Cath Everett, "What Does the Gig Economy Mean for HR?" *Personnel Today*, February 15, 2016, http://www.personneltoday.com/hr/gig-economy-what-it-means-for-hr/; Philip McCabe, "The 'Gig Economy': How Does HR Need to Adapt to This New Breed of Employee?" *HR Zone*, July 28, 2016, http://www.hrzone.com/engage/employees/the-gig-economy-how-does-hr-need-to-adapt-to-this-new-breed-of-employee, all accessed March 11, 2017.
64. See, for example, Jonathan Segal, "Performance Management Blunders," *HR Magazine*, November 2010, pp. 75–77.
65. See, for example, Adrienne Fox, "Curing What Ails Performance Reviews," *HR Magazine*, January 2009, pp. 52–55.
66. Andrew Solomonson and Charles Lance, "Examination of the Relationship between True Halo and Halo Effect in Performance Ratings," *Journal of Applied Psychology* 82, no. 5 (1997), pp. 665–674; see also, Herman Aguinis, *Performance Management* (Boston: Pearson, 2013), p. 178.
67. Manuel London, Edward Mone, and John C. Scott, "Performance Management and Assessment: Methods for Improved Rater Accuracy and Employee Goal Setting," *Human Resource Management* 43, no. 4 (Winter 2004), pp. 319–336; Herman Aguinis, *Performance Management*, p. 178.
68. Ted Turnasella, "Dagwood Bumstead, Will You Ever Get That Raise?" *Compensation & Benefits Review*, September–October 1995, pp. 25–27. See also Solomonson and Lance, "Examination of the Relationship Between True Halo and Halo Effect," pp. 665–674, and Herman Aguinis, *Performance Management*, p. 178.
69. Annette Simmons, "When Performance Reviews Fail," *Training & Development* 57, no. 9 (September 2003), pp. 47–53.
70. M. Ena Inesi, and Daniel M. Cable, "When Accomplishments Come Back to Haunt You: The Negative Effect of Competence Signals on Women's Performance Evaluations," *Personnel Psychology*, 68 (2015), pp. 615–657.
71. Ibid., p. 647
72. Joanne Sammer, "Calibrating Consistency," *HR Magazine*, January 2008, pp. 73–74. As one study concludes, "Far from being a source of non-meaningful error variance, the discrepancies among ratings from multiple perspectives can in fact capture meaningful variance in multilevel managerial performance." In-Sue Oh and Christopher Berry, "The Five Factor Model of Personality and Managerial Performance: Validity Gains Through the Use of 360° Performance Ratings," *Journal of Applied Psychology* 94, no. 6 (2009), p. 1510.
73. G. R Weaver and L. K. Treviño, "The Role of Human Resources in Ethics/Compliance Management: A Fairness Perspective," *Human Resource Management Review*, 2001, pp. 113–134. Also see, Julie McCarthy et al., "Progression through the Ranks: Assessing Employee Reactions to High Stakes Employment Testing," *Personnel Psychology* 62 (2009), p. 826.
74. This is based on Howard Risher, "Getting Performance Management on Track," *Compensation & Benefits Review* 43, no. 5 (2011), pp. 273–281.
75. E. Pulakos and R. O'Leary, "Why Is Performance Management Broken? *Industrial and Organizational Psychology* 4 (2011), pp. 146–164.
76. Ibid.
77. Herman Aguinis, *Performance Management*, pp. 280–285.
78. David Martin et al., "The Legal Ramifications of Performance Appraisal: The Growing Significance," *Public Personnel Management* 29, no. 3 (Fall 2000), pp. 381–383; Herman Aguinis, *Performance Management*, pp. 280–285.

79. This is based on Kenneth L. Sovereign, *Personnel Law* (Upper Saddle River, NJ: Prentice Hall, 1994), pp. 113–114; Herman Aguinis, *Performance Management*, pp. 280–285.
80. Austin et al., "Legal Requirements and Technical Guidelines," p. 282.
81. Wayne Cascio and H. John Bernardin, "Implications of Performance Appraisal Litigation for Personnel Decisions," *Personnel Psychology*, Summer 1981, pp. 211–212; J. M. Werner and M. C. Bolino, "Explaining U.S. Courts of Appeals Decisions Involving Performance Appraisals: Accuracy, Fairness, and Validation," *Personnel Psychology*, 50 (1997), pp 1–24; and see Elaine Pulakos, *Performance Management*, SHRM Foundation, 2004.
82. Herman Aguinis, *Performance Management*, p. 280.
83. Based on Robert Johnson, *The Appraisal Interview Guide* (New York: AMACOM, 1979), pp. 5–50; Judy Block, *Performance Appraisal on the Job: Making It Work for You* (New York: Executive Enterprises Publications, 1981), pp. 58–62.
84. This is based on Richard Luecke, *Coaching and Mentoring* (Boston: Harvard Business School Press, 2004), pp. 8–9.
85. Ibid., p. 9.
86. Annika Meinecke, Simone Kauffeld, and Nale Lehman-Willenbrock, "What Happens during Annual Appraisal Interviews? How Leader–Follower Interactions Unfold and Impact Interview Outcomes," *Journal of Applied Psychology*, 102, no. 7 (2017), pp. 1054–1074.
87. Ibid., p. 1069.
88. Jack Welch, broadcast interview at Fairfield University, C-SPAN, May 5, 2001.
89. Patty McCord, "How Netflix Reinvented HR," *Harvard Business Review,* January–February 2014, pp. 71–76.
90. Rachel Feintzeig, "You're Awesome! Firms Scrap Negative Feedback," *The Wall Street Journal*, February 11, 2015, pp. B1, B5.
91. "Working Today: Understanding What Drives Employee Engagement," from the 2003 TowersPerrin Talent Report. Copyright TowersPerrin.
92. Jamie Gruman and Alan Saks, "Performance Management and Employee Engagement," *Human Resource Management Review* 21, no. 2 (2011), p. 123.
93. Ibid.
94. Ibid.
95. "Sustainable Employee Engagement," *Training & Development* 67, no. 2 (February 2013), p. 20.
96. "Driving Engagement by Focusing on Strengths," *Gallup Business Journal*: http://BusinessJournal.Gallup.com/content/124214/driving-engagement, accessed March 8, 2014.
97. Dilys Robinson, Sarah Perryman, and Sue Hayday, "The Drivers of Employee Engagement," Institute for Employment Studies, April 2004. See also, Kenneth Le Van, "Exploring the Relationships between Performance Appraisal and Employee Engagement," University of Texas at Tyler, April 25, 2017, https://scholarworks.uttyler.edu/cgi/viewcontent.cgi?article=1018&context=hrd_grad, accessed March 31, 2018.
98. Dilys Robinson, Sarah Perryman, and Sue Hayday, "The Drivers of Employee Engagement," Institute for Employment Studies, April 2004.
99. Ibid.
100. Vishal Gupta and Sushil Kumar, "Impact of Performance Appraisal Justice on Employee Engagement: A Study of Indian Professionals," *Employee Relations* 35, no. 1 (2013), pp. 61–78.
101. See, for example, Edward Lawler, "Performance Management: The Next Generation," *Compensation & Benefits Review*, May–June 1994, p. 16.
102. See, for example, Greg Boudreau, "Response: What TQM Says about Performance Appraisal," *Compensation & Benefits Review*, June 1994, pp. 20–24.
103. Based in part on Joel D. Ross, *Total Quality Management: Text, Cases, and Readings* (Delray Beach, FL: St. Lucie Press, 1993), p. 1.
104. Ibid., pp. 2–3, 35–36.
105. Howard Risher, "Getting Serious about Performance Management," *Compensation & Benefits Review*, November/December 2005, p. 19. See also Marie-Helene Budworth, "Performance Management: Where Do We Go from Here?" *Human Resource Management Review* 20, no. 1 (2011), pp. 81–84.
106. Peter Glendinning, "Performance Management: Pariah or Messiah," *Public Personnel Management* 31, no. 2 (Summer 2002), pp. 161–178. See also Herman Aguinis, *Performance Management*, p. 2; "Performance Management Orientation Guide," *Workforce Management*, July 2012, pp. 20–22; and Angelo Kinicki, Kathryn Jacobson, Suzanne Peterson, and Gregory Prussia, "Development and Validation of the Performance Management Behavior Questionnaire," *Personnel Psychology* 60, no. 6 (2013), p. 4.
107. These are quoted or paraphrased from Risher, "Getting Serious about Performance Management," p. 19.
108. https://go.oracle.com/LP=3174?elqCampaignId=6310&src1=ad:pas:go:dg:tal&src2=wwmk14054343mpp012&SC=sckw=WWMK14054343MPP012, accessed April 4, 2015.
109. Peter Cappelli and Anna Tavis, "The Performance Management Revolution," *Harvard Business Review*, October 2016, p. 61; see also "Performance Feedback Getting More Frequent," *Bloomberg BNA Bulletin to Management*, August 2, 2016, p. 246.
110. "GE Scraps Employee Rating Scale as It Rethinks Annual Reviews," *Bloomberg BNA Bulletin to Management*, August 9, 2016, p. 251.
111. Bravetta Hassell, "IBM's New Checkpoint Reflects Employee Preferences," *Workforce*, April 2016, p. 12.
112. Liz Hoffman, "Goldman Makes Feedback Shift," *The Wall Street Journal*, April 22–23, 2017, pp. B1, B2.
113. Lauren Weber, "Nowhere to Hide for Deadwood Workers," *The Wall Street Journal*, August 22, 2016, pp. A1, A10.
114. Based on Martin Buckingham and Ashley Goodall, "Reinventing Performance Management," *Harvard Business Review*, April 2015, pp. 40–50.
115. Howard Risher, "Getting Serious about Performance Management," *Compensation & Benefits Review*, November/December 2005, p. 45.

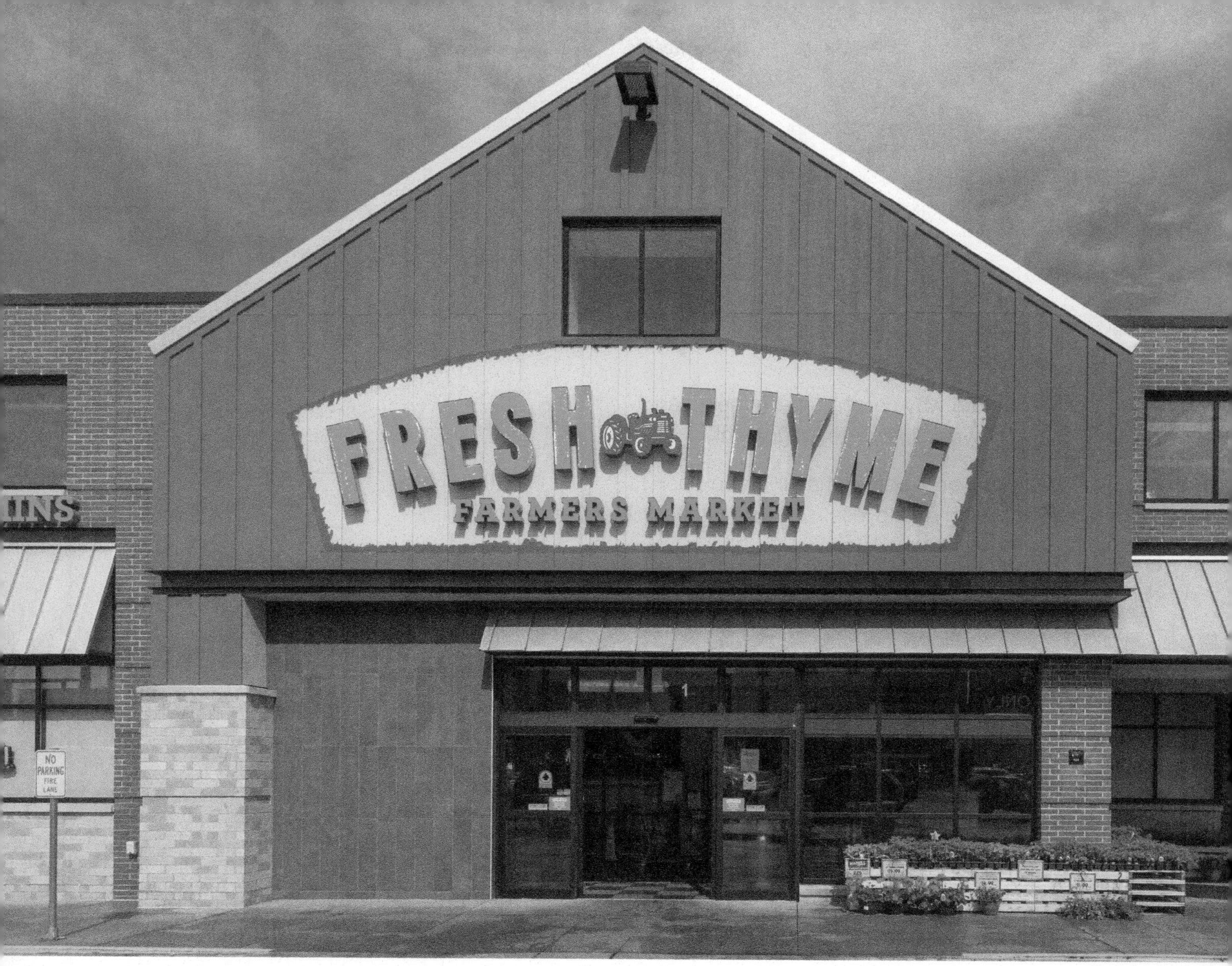

Ken Wolter/Shutterstock

10 Managing Careers and Retention

LEARNING OBJECTIVES

When you finish studying this chapter, you should be able to:

10-1 **Discuss** what employers and supervisors can do to support employees' career development needs.

10-2 **Explain** why career development can improve employee engagement.

10-3 **Describe** a comprehensive approach to retaining employees.

10-4 **List and briefly explain** the main decisions employers should address in reaching promotion and other employee life-cycle career decisions.

10-5 **Explain** each of the main grounds for dismissal.

With national grocery chains like Kroger's, local chains like Publix, and giants like Walmart and Amazon, it's not easy finding a grocery niche but Fresh Thyme Farmers Market did so.[1] They've only been in business since 2014, but already have more than 50 stores in 10 states, with plans to open 20 more stores soon. Their strategy is to offer fresh local organic foods, with about half of each store devoted to fresh produce. Its stores have dietitians on staff, and employees pride themselves on getting customers to eat healthy. The question is, how do you attract and retain employees like those. We'll see what they did.

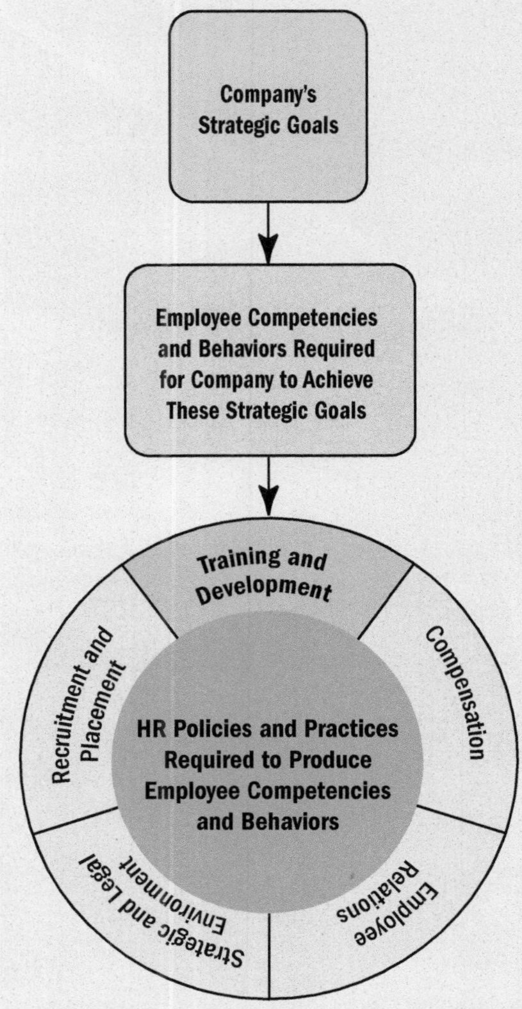

WHERE ARE WE NOW . . .

Having invested in selecting, training, and appraising employees, the employer of course wants them to want to stay with the firm. The main purpose of this chapter is to explain how to support your employees' career development needs and improve employee retention. The main topics we'll address are **Career Management**, **Improving Employee Engagement Through Career Management**, **Managing Employee Turnover and Retention**, **Employee Life-Cycle Management**, and **Managing Dismissals**.

Career Management

LEARNING OBJECTIVE 10-1

Discuss what employers and supervisors can do to support employees' career development needs.

After appraising performance, it's often necessary to address career-related issues and to discuss these issues with subordinates.

The traditional role of personnel activities like screening, training, and appraising is to staff the company with employees who have the requisite interests, abilities, and skills. Often, however, many employers also use human resource management activities to help their employees realize their full career potential.[2] They do this not just because they think that it's the right thing to do, but because hopefully everyone gains—the employees with more fulfilling careers, and the employer with improved employee relations, engagement, and retention. We'll address career planning and related topics in this chapter.

Before proceeding, we should define important terms we will be using throughout this chapter. We may define **career** as the occupational positions a person holds over the years. **Career management** is the process for enabling employees to better understand and develop their career skills and interests and to use these skills and interests most effectively both within the company and after they leave the firm. **Career development** is the lifelong series of activities (such as workshops) that contribute to a person's career exploration, establishment, success, and fulfillment. **Career planning** is the deliberate process through which someone becomes aware of personal skills, interests, knowledge, motivations, and other characteristics; acquires information about opportunities and choices; identifies career-related goals; and establishes action plans to attain specific goals.

career
The occupational positions a person has had over many years.

career management
The process for enabling employees to better understand and develop their career skills and interests, and to use these skills and interests more effectively.

career development
The lifelong series of activities that contribute to a person's career exploration, establishment, success, and fulfillment.

career planning
The deliberate process through which someone becomes aware of personal skills, interests, knowledge, motivations, and other characteristics and establishes action plans to attain specific goals.

HR in Action at the Hotel Paris If the Hotel Paris wanted satisfied guests, they had to have engaged employees who did their jobs as if they owned the company, even when the supervisor was nowhere in sight. But for the employees to be engaged, Lisa knew the Hotel Paris had to make it clear that the company was also committed to its employees. To see what they did, see the case on pages 336–337 of this chapter.

Careers Today

People once viewed careers as a sort of upward stairway from job to job, more often than not with one or a few firms. Today, many people do still move up, but many (or most) find themselves having to reinvent themselves. For example, the sales rep, laid off by a publishing firm that's just merged, may reinvent her career as an account executive at a media-oriented advertising firm.[3]

Careers today differ in other ways from a few years ago. With many more women pursuing professional and managerial careers, families must balance the challenges associated with dual-career pressures. What people want from their careers is changing too. Baby boomers—those retiring in the next few years—tended to be job- and employer-focused. People entering the job market now often covet opportunities for more balanced work–family lives.

The Psychological Contract

One implication is that what employers and employees expect from each other is changing. What the employer and employee expect of each other is part of what psychologists call a *psychological contract.* This is "an unwritten agreement that exists between employers and employees."[4] The psychological contract identifies each party's mutual expectations. For example, the unstated agreement is that management will treat employees fairly and provide satisfactory work conditions, hopefully in a long-term relationship. Employees are expected to respond "by demonstrating a good attitude, following directions, and showing loyalty to the organization."[5]

The problem is that with today's labor markets, neither the employer nor the employee can count on long-term commitments from each other. That changes the psychological contract, and makes career management more critical for the employee, who may have to prepare for the time that he or she must move on.

The Employee's Role in Career Management

The employee, the manager, and the employer all have roles in the employee's career development. For example, the manager should provide timely and objective performance feedback, offer developmental assignments and support, and have career development discussions with the employee. He or she should act as a coach, appraiser, advisor, and mentor, listening to and clarifying the employee's career plans, giving feedback, generating career options, and linking the employee to organizational resources and career options. For its part, the employer should provide career-oriented training, development, and promotional opportunities, offer career information and career programs, and give employees a variety of career options.

Ultimately, however, the employee is responsible for his or her own career. He or she must assess interests, skills, and values; seek out career information resources; and take steps to ensure a happy and fulfilling career. For the employee, career planning means matching individual strengths and weaknesses with occupational opportunities and threats. In other words, the person wants to pursue occupations, jobs, and a career that capitalize on his or her interests, aptitudes, values, and skills. The person also wants to choose occupations, jobs, and a career that make sense in terms of projected future demand for occupations. Ideally, he or she should think through an ideal future "self" to strive for.[6]

As one example, career-counseling expert John Holland says that personality (including values, motives, and needs) is an important career choice determinant. For example, a person with a strong social orientation might be attracted to careers that entail interpersonal rather than intellectual or physical activities and to occupations such as social work. Holland found six basic personality types or orientations. For a nominal fee, individuals can use his Self-Directed Search (SDS) test (available online at www.self-directed-search.com) to assess their occupational orientations and preferred occupations. The SDS has an excellent reputation, but one study of 24 no-cost online career assessment websites concluded that they were easy to use but suffered from insufficient validation and confidentiality. However, a number of online career assessment instruments such as Career Key (www.careerkey.org) do reportedly provide validated information.[7] O*NET offers a free online "My Next Move" occupations and career assessment system (www.onetcenter.org/mynextmove.html). You will find other useful career tools in the following two exercises, and in this chapter's appendix.

EXERCISE 1 One useful exercise for identifying occupational skills is to head a page "The School or Occupational Tasks I Most Enjoyed Doing." Then write a short essay describing the tasks. Provide as much detail as you can about your duties and responsibilities, and what you found enjoyable about each task. (It's not necessarily the most enjoyable *job* you've had, but the most enjoyable *task* you've had to perform within your jobs.) Next, on other pages, do the same thing for two other tasks. Now scrutinize the three essays. Underline the skills that you mentioned the most often. For example, did you especially enjoy the hours you spent on the Internet doing research when you worked one summer as an intern?[8]

EXERCISE 2 Another exercise can prove enlightening. On a page, answer the question: "If you could have any kind of job, what would it be?" Invent your own job if need be, and don't worry about what you *can* do—just what you want to do.[9]

HR AND THE GIG ECONOMY: *THE PORTFOLIO CAREER*

portfolio careers
Careers based on using one's skills to create a livelihood from multiple income sources, often from several jobs paying different rates.

More people today—especially Millennials and Generation X-ers—are embracing **portfolio careers,** careers based on using one's skills to create a livelihood from multiple income sources, often from several jobs paying different rates.[10] For example, someone might use her marketing skills for temporary marketing manager gigs, her writing and marketing skills to write a column and blog, and her coaching skills to teach online courses.

Are Portfolio Careers for you?

Millions of people support themselves through portfolio careers today, and each is probably doing so for his or her own reasons—from just wanting to be independent, to not finding a full-time job, or needing flexibility for family matters.

DO YOU HAVE WHAT IT TAKES TO DO THIS? There are some questions to ask yourself. For example, are you comfortable not having the same job to go to every day; are you good at juggling several different big tasks; and do you have the social and salesmanship skills to get out and line up a continually changing cast of clients? And of course, what saleable skills do you have for which someone will pay you?

IS IT PRACTICAL? Think it through first. Ask yourself who your potential clients are, how much you might earn, and what the odds are you'll be able to put it all together. Bounce your ideas off friends, and talk with them about which ideas seem more likely to succeed. (On the other hand, "nothing ventured, nothing gained," so don't be too practical! One benefit of portfolio careers is that you can make adjustments as you learn.)

The Employer's Role in Career Management

Along with the employee, the person's manager and employer have career management responsibilities. These depend partly on how long the employee has been with the firm.

For example, *before hiring*, realistic job interviews can help prospective employees more accurately gauge whether the job is a good fit for them. Especially for recent college graduates, *the first job* can be crucial for building confidence and a more realistic picture of what he or she can and cannot do: providing challenging first jobs and having an experienced mentor who can help the person learn the ropes are important. Some refer to this as preventing **reality shock,** a phenomenon that occurs when a new employee's high expectations and enthusiasm confront the reality of a boring, unchallenging job. Periodic *job rotation* can help the person develop a more realistic picture of what he or she is good at, and thus the career moves that might be best. Thus, Intuit offers new graduates entrée into its Rotational Development Programs.[11] These are 2-year programs in which employees first learn about Intuit's products, customers, employees, strategies, and values. Next the employees complete four 6-month rotations, getting experience in a range of Intuit business units and a variety of functions, for instance, product management, marketing, and human resources. All Rotational Development Program participants are paired with an executive advisor, who provides career coaching and mentoring.

reality shock
Results of a period that may occur at the initial career entry when the new employee's high job expectations confront the reality of a boring or otherwise unattractive work situation.

Finally, we will see that once the person has been *on the job* for a while, career-oriented appraisals are important. Here the manager not only appraises the employee but also uses the results to help the person to match his or her strengths and weaknesses with a feasible career path.

Employer Career Management Methods

Employers including AFLAC, American Express, and Accenture recognize that it pays to help employees improve their careers. For example, American Express opened several career counseling centers for its call-center workers, and both Genentech and AFLAC hired career counselors, and are better preparing their line managers to give career advice.[12] Google has employees who volunteer to act as career coaches and mentors for other employees, and who Google officially designates "career gurus." In one year, over 1,000 Google employees (Googlers) used the gurus' services.[13]

Self-help e-learning tools appear to be the most popular employer-provided career services, followed by career assessment and feedback, and on-site training.[14] Such tools—which help users work through career information and instructional resources themselves—are especially useful when users want to improve their careers, and where guidance counseling is available if questions arise.[15]

A *career planning workshop* is "a planned learning event in which participants are expected to be actively involved, completing career planning exercises and inventories and participating in career skills practice sessions."[16] A typical workshop includes self-assessment exercises (skills, interests, values, and so on), an assessment of important occupational trends, and goal-setting and action-planning segments.

Career coaches generally help employees create 1- to 5-year plans showing where their careers with the firm may lead. Then, the employer and employee base the latter's development plans on what he or she needs to move up.[17] The coaches help individual employees identify their development needs and to obtain the training, professional development, and networking opportunities that they require to satisfy those needs.

Career development systems needn't be complicated. Even just receiving performance feedback from supervisors, having individual development plans, and having access to training is enough for many employees. Beyond that, job postings, formal career-oriented performance appraisals, formal counseling and mentoring with managers, and individual succession planning for high-potential employees are valuable.[18] Figure 10-1 illustrates a simple employee career planning form.

IMPROVING PERFORMANCE: *THROUGH HRIS*

Integrating Talent Management and Career and Succession Planning

The employer should endeavor to integrate its career planning with its other HR activities efforts. As one example, an employee's career planning and development plans should reflect his or her performance appraisal ratings and training plans. Similarly, as explained in Chapter 5 (pages 138–139), succession plans should reflect employees' career interests.

Integrated talent management software helps to achieve such coordination. For example, Halogen Succession enables the employer to "identify the skills and competencies required to support your 3- to 5-year strategic plans and cultivate these in your high-potential employees with career and development planning."[19] ■

Diversity Counts: Toward Career Success

People with disabilities tend to have less career success than do those without disabilities.[20] Some barriers may be self-imposed. For instance, some with disabilities may have lower career expectations, or may not proactively seek the accommodations they are due under EEO law.

However, the problem more often reflects unfortunate assumptions and actions by managers and coworkers. Though well meaning, they may view those with disabilities as unable to perform various jobs, negatively evaluate them as being poor occupational fits, and assume that jobs designed for those without disabilities are inappropriate for those with disabilities. Figure 10-2 (page 318) presents some positive strategies for people with disabilities. ■

The Manager as Mentor and Coach

Do not underestimate the impact that a supervisor can have on his or her employee's career development. With little or no additional effort than realistic performance reviews and candid career advice, a competent supervisor can help the employee get on and stay on the right career track. At the other extreme, an unsupportive supervisor may look back on years of having inhibited his or her employees' career development. In a study of world-class leaders, one researcher says that his big surprise was the extent to which they engaged in "ongoing, intensive one-on-one tutoring" of their subordinates.[21]

The manager can do several things to support subordinates' career development needs. When the subordinate first starts, help the person develop the skills required to do the job well. Schedule regular performance appraisals, and address whether the person's skills and performance are consistent with his or her career aspirations. Ask questions such as "In terms of career, what are you interested in doing, in both the

Employee's Name	Employee's Current Position	Today's Date

I Performance Summary: *Briefly discuss this employee's performance over the past year (or other period), in terms of his or her achievement of assigned goals, effectiveness at interacting with colleagues, and any other criteria you believe are relevant here:*

II Strengths: *Based on your evaluation and experience with and discussions with employee, what would you say are his or her main strengths?*

III Career Aspirations and Goals: *Based on your experience with and discussions with employee, what would the two of you agree should be this person's career goals over the next 1-3 years and beyond?*

IV Areas for Development: *Based on what you know about this employee, what would the two of you agree are the main areas for development he or she should concentrate on over the next year or two?*

Development Objectives and Activities: *Planned to achieve this person's career goals.*

Development Activities	Specific Action Plans	Milestones/Dates
1		
2		
3		
4		
5		

Signatures: Supervisor_____________ Employee_____________

FIGURE 10-1 **Employee Career Development Plan**

Source: Copyright Gary Dessler, PhD.

short- and long-term?"[22] Provide the employee with at least an informal development plan like that in Figure 10-1. Keep subordinates informed about the firm's current career-related benefits, and encourage them to use them.[23]

mentoring
Advising, counseling, and guiding.

Here the manager may act as mentor. **Mentoring** means having experienced senior people advising, counseling, and guiding employees' longer-term career development.

FIGURE 10-2 Career Guideline Suggestions for Those with Disabilities

Source: Career management strategies of people with disabilities. *Human Resource Management*, May–June 2014 *(53)*3, pp. 455–456. Reprinted by permission from John Wiley & Sons, Inc. Cleared via Copyright Clearance Center.

Strategy	Key Import of Strategy
Espousing a positive mind-set and demonstrating extreme persistence	Overcome worries and focus on tasks at hand
Sensitizing people to ability over disability: • Signaling ability by learning new skills • Signaling ability by helping coworkers through newly gained skills • Signaling ability by trying to enhance performance through feedback seeking	Trounce stereotypes regarding competence
Engaging in disability advocacy: • Awareness building • Influencing organizational policymaking with regard to accommodation	Sensitize others to performance potential of all PWD and help all PWD perform
Building, leveraging, and contributing to relevant networks: • Forming networks comprising PWD • Seeking mentors who have a disability • Serving as role models or mentors to other PWD	Aid general adjustment and career growth of self and other PWD

An employee who agonizes over which career to pursue or how to navigate office politics may need mentoring.

Mentoring may be formal or informal. Informally, mid- and senior-level managers may voluntarily help less-experienced employees—for instance, by giving them career advice and helping them to navigate office politics. Many employers also have formal mentoring programs. For instance, the employer may pair protégés with potential mentors, and provide training to help mentor and protégé better understand their respective responsibilities. Studies show that having a mentor give career-related guidance and act as a sounding board can enhance one's career satisfaction and success.[24]

For the supervisor, mentoring is both valuable and risky. It is valuable insofar as you can influence in a positive way the careers of your less-experienced subordinates and colleagues. The danger is that it can backfire. **Coaching** focuses on teaching daily tasks that you can easily relearn, so coaching's downside is usually limited. *Mentoring* focuses on relatively hard-to-reverse longer-term career issues, and often touches on the person's psychology (motives, and how one gets along with others, for instance). Because the supervisor is usually not a psychologist or trained career advisor, he or she must be cautious in the mentoring advice he or she gives.

coaching
Educating, instructing, and training subordinates.

Research on what supervisors can do to be better mentors reveals few surprises. Effective mentors *set high standards*, are willing to *invest the time* and effort the mentoring relationship requires, and actively *steer protégés* into important projects, teams, and jobs. They *model* the right behaviors, and *motivate and inspire* those they're mentoring.[25] Effective mentoring requires *trust*, and the level of trust reflects the mentor's *professional competence, consistency, ability to communicate*, and readiness to *share control*.[26]

However, studies suggest that traditional mentoring is less effective for women than it is for men. For example, in one survey of employees who had "active mentoring relationships" in one year, 72% of the men received one or more promotions in the ensuing 2 years, compared with 65% of the women. A CEO or other senior executive mentored 78% of the men, compared with 69% of the women.[27]

Some employers therefore assign female employees to mentors who have more organizational clout. For example, when Deutsche Bank discovered that several female managing directors had left the firm for better jobs at competitors, it began pairing them with mentor/sponsors from the bank's executive committee. The latter were in a position to advocate the women for promotion.

LEARNING OBJECTIVE 10-2
Explain why career development can improve employee engagement.

Employee Engagement Guide for Managers

Career Management

As mentioned earlier in this chapter, labor market turbulence has understandably prompted many people to ask why they should be loyal to their employers. "Why," they might ask, "should I be loyal to you if you're just going to dump me when you decide to cut costs again?" Employers today therefore have to think through how they're going to maintain employee engagement, and thereby minimize voluntary departures, and maximize employee effort.

Commitment-Oriented Career Development Efforts

Given the importance to most people of a fulfilling and successful career, career planning and development can play an important role in employee engagement. Managed effectively, the employer's career development process should send the signal that the employer cares about the employee's career success. As mentioned earlier, this doesn't necessarily have to be complicated. For example, performance appraisals provide an easy opportunity to link the employee's performance, career interests, and developmental needs into a coherent career plan. With *career-oriented appraisals*, the supervisor and employee jointly merge the latter's past performance, career preferences, and developmental needs into a formal career plan.

Such appraisals needn't be automated but online systems are available. For example, Halogen eAppraisal™ helps the manager to identify employee development activities that are appropriate given the employee's developmental needs and career preferences. The employer then organizes development activities around the person's needs.

The JCPenney Management Career-Grid approach provides another good example of what is possible (although tumultuous management changes several years ago sidelined much of this effort). Prior to the annual appraisal, the associate and his or her manager reviewed Penney's career grid. The grid listed all supervisory positions at Penney (grouped by operation jobs, merchandise jobs, personnel jobs, and general management jobs); it also included specific job titles such as "regional catalog sales manager." The firm also provided thumbnail job descriptions for all the grid's jobs.

The grid also identified typical promotional routes. For example, when considering the next assignment for a management associate, the supervisor could consider not only merchandise positions but also operations and personnel positions. Promotional projections could cross all four groups, as well as one or two job levels. For example, a senior merchandising manager might be projected for promotion to either assistant buyer or general merchandise manager. In sum, Penney's grid approach shows how employers can use a career-oriented appraisal process to guide the employee and manager to focus on the former's strengths, weaknesses, and career prospects and plans.[28]

Other employers use special training and development programs to facilitate their employees' career development. The accompanying HR Practices Around the Globe feature provides an example.

IMPROVING PERFORMANCE: *HR PRACTICES AROUND THE GLOBE*

Career Development at Medtronic[29]

Medtronic is a global medical technology company with more than 85,000 employees around the world. The company offers a wide range of career planning and development support tools aimed at helping employees understand their occupational strengths and weaknesses and reach their potential. These tools include customized development plans, self-assessment and feedback tools, mentoring programs, comprehensive on-site classes covering business, engineering, and science topics, tuition reimbursement scholarships, and online job listings so the employee can seek out new career opportunities within the company.

In addition, new MBA employees can participate in Medtronic's corporate Leadership Development Rotation Program. This is a 2- to 3-year program. It includes 12- to 18-month assignments in two different geographic locations, thus providing participants with both a broad understanding of Medtronics, and in-depth functional experiences. Functional tracks include clinical, corporate development, finance, and human resources, for instance.

In addition to their job assignments, participants engage in other developmental experiences including peer mentoring programs, functional training, and leadership workshops. Among other things, candidates for this program are required to have 3 to 5 years of professional and relevant work experience and an MBA (or other masters-level degree as appropriate) and to be mobile and willing to pursue opportunities abroad.

MyLab Management Talk About It 1

If your professor has assigned this, go to the Assignments section of **www.pearson.com/mylab/management** to complete this discussion. Look more closely at this program (go to www.Medtronic.com; then click "Careers" and "Career Growth") or a similar program and discuss why it should positively affect employee engagement.

Managing Employee Turnover and Retention

LEARNING OBJECTIVE 10-3

Describe a comprehensive approach to retaining employees.

Not all employees' career plans will coincide with the company's needs. *Turnover*—the rate at which employees leave the firm—varies markedly among industries. For example, turnover in the accommodation and food services industry is very high, with over half the industry's employees voluntarily leaving each year. In contrast, voluntary turnover in educational services is about 12%.[30]

Furthermore, such figures only reflect employees who leave voluntarily. They don't include involuntary separations, such as for poor performance.[31] Combining voluntary and involuntary turnover produces some astounding statistics. For example, the turnover in many food service firms is around 100% per year. In other words, many restaurants need to replace just about all their employees every year! Turnover is expensive, as the HR as a Profit Center discussion shows.

IMPROVING PERFORMANCE: *HR AS A PROFIT CENTER*

Turnover and Performance

What is the link between turnover and organizational performance? One study analyzed the costs of turnover in a call center with 31 agents and 4 supervisors.[32] Tangible costs associated with an agent's leaving included the costs of recruiting, screening, interviewing, and testing applicants, as well as the cost of wages while the new agent was oriented and trained. Intangible costs included the cost of lost productivity for the new agent (who is less productive at first), the cost of rework for the new agent's errors, and the supervisory cost for coaching the new agent. The researchers estimated the cost of an agent leaving at about $21,551. This call center averaged 18.6 vacancies per year (about a 60% turnover rate). Therefore, the researchers estimated the total annual cost of agent turnover at $400,853. Taking steps to cut this turnover rate in, say, half could save this firm about $200,000 per year. The bottom line is that HR practices can have a big influence on employee turnover, and thereby on the company's profitability. ■

MyLab Management Talk About It 2

If your professor has assigned this, go to the Assignments section of **www.pearson.com/mylab/management** to complete this discussion. Discuss three steps you would take to reduce the need to dismiss employees.

Reducing turnover requires identifying and managing the reasons for both voluntary and involuntary turnover.[33] We address managing voluntary turnover here, and managing involuntary turnover later in the chapter.

Managing Voluntary Turnover

In reducing turnover, the logical place to start is by measuring the number of employees (particularly top performers and high potentials) who leave the company.[34] SHRM recommends computing turnover as follows: "First calculate turnover for each month by dividing the number of [voluntary] separations during the month by the average number of employees during that month and multiplying by 100. Then calculate the annual turnover rate by adding the 12 months of turnover percentages together."[35]

However, identifying *why* employees voluntarily leave isn't so easy. People dissatisfied with their jobs are more likely to leave, but the sources of dissatisfaction are many. In one survey, the five top reasons that top-performing employees gave for leaving (ranked from high to low) were pay, promotional opportunities, work–life balance, career development, and health-care benefits.[36] Another survey of employees based on exit interviews found the top five reasons employees left were, career development (22%), work–life balance (12%), management behavior (11%), compensation and benefits (9%), and well-being (9%).[37] Of those who left due to "career development," most said they didn't like the work they were doing, while others blamed lack of growth and development.[38] In another study job motivation, social support, and burnout correlated with turnover intentions.[39] Other reasons employees leave include unfairness, not having their voices heard, and lack of recognition.[40]

Practical considerations also affect turnover. For example, high unemployment reduces voluntary turnover, and some locales have fewer job opportunities (and thus turnover). Furthermore, losing low-performing employees isn't as problematic as losing high-performing ones. The restaurant chain Applebee's gives managers incentives for reducing turnover of top-performing employees.[41]

In any case, given the many things prompting employees to leave, what can one do to reduce voluntary turnover? We'll discuss some tactics, but there is no silver bullet. The manager should understand that retaining employees is a talent management issue, and that the best retention strategies are therefore multifunctional. For example, employees who aren't interested in their jobs, sense that they're not suited for their jobs, or feel undercompensated are more likely to leave. Employers can address such issues only by instituting effective and coordinated talent management (recruitment, selection, training, appraisal, and compensation) practices. Put another way, turnovers (both voluntary and involuntary) often start with poor selection decisions, compounded by inadequate training, insensitive appraisals, and inequitable pay. Trying to formulate a "retention strategy" without considering all HR practices is futile.

A Comprehensive Approach to Retaining Employees

However, identifying problems is an important first step. Effectively conducted *exit interviews* provide useful insights into turnover problem areas. Many employers routinely administer *attitude surveys* to monitor employees about matters such as supervision and pay. Sometimes simply asking, "All things considered, how satisfied are you with your job?" can be as effective as soliciting employees' attitudes toward various facets of the job (such as supervision and pay).[42] Open-door policies and anonymous "*hotlines*" help management identify and remedy morale problems. Usually conducted by the employee's manager, the aim of a *stay interview* is to head off retention problems by finding out "how the employee is doing." Typical questions include, "When you travel to work each day, what are you looking forward to?" and "How can I best support you?" Unlike anonymous group surveys, stay interviews are one on one, and reportedly provide useful information for reducing turnover and improving engagement.[43] Sometimes, analyzing the situation leads to simple solutions. Walmart discovered it could significantly reduce voluntary turnover by providing aggressively *realistic previews* about the job's demands and work hours.[44] Then, having identified potential problems, the employer can take steps like the following to boost employee retention.

RAISE PAY The most obvious explanation for why employees quit is often also the correct one: low pay. Particularly for high performers and key employees, enhanced pay has been the retention tool of choice for many employers.[45]

HIRE SMART "Retention starts up front, with the selection and hiring of the right employees."[46] This refers not just to the worker but also to hiring the right supervisors. For example, FedEx conducts periodic employee attitude surveys. The supervisor then meets to review the results with his or her employees to address any leadership problems the surveys raise.

DISCUSS CAREERS One expert says, "Professionals who feel their company cares about their development and progress are much more likely to stay."[47] Periodically discuss with employees their career preferences and prospects, and help them lay out career plans.[48]

PROVIDE DIRECTION People can't do their jobs if they don't know what to do or what their goals are. Therefore, retaining employees requires making it clear what your expectations are regarding their performance and what their responsibilities are.

OFFER FLEXIBILITY In one survey, workers identified "flexible work arrangements" and "telecommuting" as the two top benefits that would encourage them to choose one job over another.

USE HIGH-PERFORMANCE HR PRACTICES In one study, call centers that made more use of high-involvement work practices (for instance, employee empowerment, problem-solving groups, and self-directed teams) had lower rates of quits, dismissals, and total turnover. So did those that "invested" more in employees (for instance, in terms of promotion opportunities, high relative pay, pensions, and full-time jobs).[49]

COUNTEROFFER? If a valued employee says he or she is leaving, should you make a counteroffer? Many argue against doing so, calling it a "Band-Aid for a head wound."[50] Employers who do allow counteroffers need a policy that specifies what people and positions are eligible for counteroffers, allowable compensation enhancements, and how to determine the offer.[51]

TRENDS SHAPING HR: *DIGITAL AND SOCIAL MEDIA*

Digital and social media tools can improve the employee retention process. Software company SAS's employee-retention program sifts through employee data on traits like skills, tenure, performance, education, and friendships. It can predict which high-value employees are more likely to quit in the near future (allowing SAS to try to head that off).[52] Alliant Techsystems created a "flight risk model" to calculate the probability an employee would leave and to take corrective action.[53] Based on its analysis of previous survey results, Google's "Googlegeist" survey contains five questions aimed at identifying Googlers who are more likely to leave; if a team's responses fall below 70% favorable, Google knows to take corrective action.[54] Websites such as Globoforce (www.globoforce.com) enable each employee's colleagues to comment on and to recognize and reward the person's contributions. Vendors assert this leads to "dramatic improvements in employee engagement, retention and measurable adoption of corporate culture."[55] ■

■ IMPROVING PERFORMANCE: *THE STRATEGIC CONTEXT*

Fresh Thyme Farmers Market

Strategic human resource management means formulating HR policies and practices that produce the employee skills and behaviors the company needs to achieve its strategic aims. Fresh Thyme's strategy is to offer fresh, local, organic foods, with about half of each store devoted to fresh produce.[56] Its employees are evangelists about getting customers to eat healthy. What sorts of people does Fresh Thyme want to recruit and hire, and what do they do to retain them?

A company that sells "health and awareness" needs employees who enjoy engaging with customers, particularly about fresh and healthy foods. It helps that fast growth means big opportunities for employees. Fresh Thyme also works hard to develop its employees' careers. For example, it offers extensive training, from "bagging 101," to finance courses for managers. The point is Fresh Thyme has an integrated set of recruitment, selection, training, and career development practices that support its "fresh and healthy" strategy while also supporting employee retention.

MyLab Management Talk About It 3

If your professor has assigned this, go to the Assignments section of **www.pearson.com/mylab/management** to complete this discussion question. Do you think Fresh Thyme should work out a career development plan for each of its employees? Why?

Job Withdrawal

Unfortunately, voluntary turnover is just one way that employees withdraw. Withdrawal in general means separating oneself from one's current situation—it's a means of escape for someone who is dissatisfied or fearful. At work, *job withdrawal* has been defined as "actions intended to place physical or psychological distance between employees and their work environments."[57]

Absences and voluntary turnover are two obvious types of job withdrawal. Others can be less obvious if no less corrosive. Some examples include "taking undeserved work breaks, spending time in idle conversation and neglecting aspects of the job one is obligated to perform."[58] Other employees stop "showing up" mentally ("psychological withdrawal"), perhaps daydreaming at their desks while productivity suffers.[59] The employee is there, but mentally absent. In fact, the *job withdrawal process* tends to be incremental, often evolving from daydreaming to absences to quitting: "When an employee perceives that temporary withdrawal will not resolve his/her problems, then the employee is apt to choose a more permanent form of withdrawal (i.e., turnover, assuming that alternative work opportunities are available)."[60]

Studies confirm the high costs of job withdrawal, so understanding its causes is important.[61] Many people have experienced the desire to withdraw—to "get away" from some situation—so it's perhaps not difficult to empathize with those who feel they must escape. Some think of it in terms of pain versus pleasure. People tend to move toward situations that make them feel good, and away from those that make them feel bad.[62] People are repelled by situations that produce unpleasant, uncomfortable emotions, and are attracted to those that produce pleasant, comfortable ones.[63]

The manager can therefore think of withdrawal-reducing strategies in terms of reducing the job's negative effects, and/or of raising its positive effects. Because potential negatives and positives are virtually limitless, addressing withdrawal problems again requires a comprehensive human resource management approach.[64] Illustrative potential negatives include, for instance, boring jobs, poor supervision, low pay, bullying, lack of career prospects, and poor working conditions. Potential positives include job enrichment, supportive supervision, equitable pay/family-friendly benefits, disciplinary/appeals processes, career development opportunities, safe working conditions, and high-morale colleagues.[65] Interviews, surveys, and observation can help identify issues to address.

With more employees taking their jobs home via smart phones and iPads, employee "detachment" (not withdrawal) isn't always a bad thing. Two researchers found detaching oneself from work improves family life. They advise working out a system for ensuring some quality family time. For example, the employee and his or her partner might "agree on certain rules such as keeping the weekend free of work, or switching off the mobile phone after dinner."[66]

LEARNING OBJECTIVE 10-4

List and briefly explain the main decisions employers should address in reaching promotion and other employee life-cycle career decisions.

Employee Life-Cycle Career Management

An employee's tenure with a firm tends to follow a life cycle, from employment interview to first job, promotion, transfer, and perhaps retirement. We'll look here at the latter three.

promotion
Advancement to a position of increased responsibility.

Making Promotion Decisions

Promotions traditionally mean advancements to positions of increased responsibility.

Promotions are important. They're obviously a good way to reward performance. Furthermore, hiring outsiders has become more expensive. By one estimate, it now costs about 36% more to hire new employees than it did a few years ago. (This is partly due to more job openings, and partly because the gig economy diverts many potential hires to working on their own). The bottom line is that employers need well thought-out promotion practices and policies. For example, unfairness or secrecy about why people get promoted can devalue the promotion process. An effective promotion strategy therefore includes effective promotion from within systems and practices, making more promotions available, and ensuring that your employees are as aware of their own company's job openings as they are of other companies'.[67]

Also address how to handle those *not* promoted.[68] In one study, military officer training candidates *not* promoted were more likely to engage in counterproductive work behaviors (such as verbal and physical aggression, property theft, and sleeping on duty) than were those who were promoted.

KNOW YOUR EMPLOYMENT LAW

Establish Clear Guidelines for Managing Promotions

In general, promotion processes must comply with all the same antidiscrimination laws as do procedures for recruiting and selecting employees or any other HR actions. For example, Title VII of the 1964 Civil Rights Act covers any "terms, conditions, or privileges of employment." Similarly, under the Age Discrimination in Employment Act of 1967, "covered employers may not select individuals for hiring, promotion, or reductions in force in a way that unlawfully discriminates on the basis of age."[69]

The employer should establish safeguards to ensure that promotion decisions don't prompt discrimination claims, or claims of retaliation, as many do. For example, the Fifth U.S. Circuit Court of Appeals allowed a woman's claim of retaliation to proceed when she showed that she was turned down for promotion because a supervisor she had previously accused of sexual harassment persuaded her current supervisor not to promote her.[70]

One way to defend against such claims is to make sure promotion procedures are clear and objective. For example, the Eighth U.S. Circuit Court of Appeals held that a company's failure to set objective guidelines and procedures for promoting employees may suggest employment discrimination.[71] (In this case, the court found that the organization, a community college, did not consistently use the same procedures for hiring and promotions, and did not clarify when and under what conditions vacant positions were announced.) In another case, the employer turned down a 61-year-old employee for a promotion because the person who interviewed him said he did not "get a real feeling of confidence" from the candidate.[72] In this case, "the court made it clear that while subjective reasons can justify adverse employment decisions, an employer must articulate any clear and reasonably specific factual bases upon which it based its decision." In other words, have objective evidence supporting your subjective assessment for promotion. ■

Crucial promotion-related decisions include the following.

DECISION 1: IS SENIORITY OR COMPETENCE THE RULE? In setting promotion policies, one decision is whether to base promotion on seniority or competence, or some combination of the two.

Today's focus on performance favors competence. However, this depends on several things. Union agreements sometimes contain clauses emphasizing seniority. Civil service regulations that stress seniority often govern promotions in many public-sector organizations.

DECISION 2: HOW SHOULD WE MEASURE COMPETENCE? If the firm opts for competence, it must define and measure competence. Defining and measuring *past* performance is relatively straightforward. But promotions should also rest on procedures for predicting the candidate's future performance.

For better or worse, most employers use prior performance as a guide, and assume that (based on exemplary prior performance) the person will do well on the new job. Many use tests or assessment centers, or tools such as the 9-Box Grid (Chapter 8, page 258), to evaluate promotable employees and identify those with executive potential.

For example, given the public safety issues involved, police departments tend to be very systematic when evaluating candidates for promotion to command positions. For the police, traditional promotion reviews include a written knowledge test, an assessment center, time-in-grade (for example, candidates for police captain in Little Rock, Arkansas, need a minimum 5 years as police officer, 2 years as sergeant, and 2 years as lieutenant before applying for promotion to captain),[73] a score based on recent performance appraisal ratings, and a personnel records review. The latter includes evaluation of supervisory-related education and experience, ratings from multiple sources, and systematic evaluation of behavioral evidence.[74]

DECISION 3: IS THE PROCESS FORMAL OR INFORMAL? Many firms have informal promotion processes. They may or may not post open positions, and key managers may use their own unpublished promotion criteria. Here employees (and courts) may conclude that factors like "who you know" are more important than performance, and that working hard to get ahead—at least in this firm—is futile.

Other employers set formal promotion policies and procedures. Employees receive a *formal promotion policy* describing the criteria by which the firm awards promotions. A *job posting policy* states the firm will post open positions and their requirements, and circulate these to all employees. As explained in Chapter 5 (Personnel Planning and Recruiting), many employers also maintain *employee qualification databanks* and use replacement charts and computerized employee information systems to assist in such planning.

DECISION 4: VERTICAL, HORIZONTAL, OR OTHER? Promotions aren't necessarily upward. Thus, some employees, such as engineers, may have little or no interest in promotion to managerial roles.

Several options are available. Some firms, such as the exploration division of British Petroleum (BP), create two parallel career paths, one for managers and another for "individual contributors" such as high-performing engineers. At BP, individual contributors can move up to nonsupervisory senior positions, such as "senior engineer." These jobs have most of the financial rewards attached to management-track positions at that level.

Another option is to move the person horizontally. For instance, a production employee may move to human resources to develop his or her skills and to test and challenge his or her aptitudes. In a sense, "promotions" are possible even when leaving the person in the same job. For example, you might enrich the job and provide training to enhance the opportunity for assuming more responsibility.

In any case, there are practical steps to take in formulating promotion policies.[75] Establish eligibility requirements, for instance, in terms of minimum tenure and performance ratings. Require the hiring manager to review the job description, and revise if necessary. Vigorously review all candidates' performance and history. Preferably promote only those who meet the job's requirements. And reach out to employees who may have aspired to a promotion but who were not yet ready to be promoted. To paraphrase Google's chief HR officer, doing so is far better than having them quit or withdraw.[76]

Diversity Counts: The Gender Gap

Women constitute more than 45% of the workforce, but hold less than 2% of top management positions. Blatant or subtle discrimination may account for much of this. In one study, promoted women had to receive higher performance ratings than promoted men to get promoted, "suggesting that women were held to stricter standards for promotion."[77] Women report greater barriers (such as being excluded from informal networks) than do men, and have more difficulty getting developmental assignments. Many employers obstruct women's promotional prospects from the beginning. For example, women make up almost half of entry-level hires, but are 18% less likely than men to be promoted to manager.[78]

Although there are notable exceptions (for instance, Ursula M. Burns was CEO of Xerox, and Indra Nooyi was Pepsico's CEO), minority women seem particularly at risk. An older survey asked minority women what they saw as the career barriers. They said not having an influential mentor (47%), lack of informal networking with influential colleagues (40%), lack of company role models for members of the same racial or ethnic group (29%), and a lack of high-visibility assignments (28%).[79] Yet a more recent survey from McKinsey & Company and LeanIn.org came to about the same conclusions: Managers don't advocate for them, help them manage company politics, provide advice, nor give them stretch assignments.[80]

What to do about this? Here are suggestions, aimed at addressing the key findings of the McKinsey & Company/Lean In survey *Women in the Workplace 2017*:[81]

"Women hit the glass ceiling early." Women are 18% less likely to be promoted to manager. *Recognize this as a potential problem, and ensure training and appraisal processes are proactively nondiscriminatory.*

"Men are more likely to say they get what they want without having to ask." Men are more likely to have gotten promotions and raises, and to thus already be satisfied without asking for more. *Make sure you execute promotion and compensation decisions equitably.*

"Women get less of the support that advances careers." Women are less likely to receive advice from managers on how to advance. *Improve mentoring and networking practices.* For example, Marriott instituted leadership conferences for women. Speakers offered practical tips for career advancement, and shared their experiences. The conferences also provided informal opportunities for Marriott women to meet and forge business relationships.

"Women are less optimistic they can reach the top." Women are less likely than men to aspire to top management. *Have mentors encourage, as appropriate, stretch assignments for female employees and encourage them to apply for promotions as appropriate, and have female top management role models.* Also, *eliminate barriers*. For example, some practices (such as required late-night meetings) may seem gender neutral but in fact disproportionately affect women.

"Men are less committed to gender diversity efforts." Men are less likely to consider gender diversity a priority; some even see it as impeding their own advancement. *The top manager should make it clear that he or she is fully committed to gender diversity.*

"Many women still work a double shift." About 54% of women do all or most of the household work, compared to 22% of men. *Institute career tracks (including reduced hours and flexible work schedules) that allow women to periodically reduce their time at work, but remain on a partner track.* When the accounting firm Deloitte saw it was losing female auditors, it instituted a new flexible/reduced work schedule. This enabled many working mothers to stay with the firm.[82] ■

Managing Transfers

transfers
Reassignments to similar positions in other parts of the firm.

A **transfer** is a move from one job to another, usually with no change in salary or grade. Employers may transfer a worker to vacate a position where he or she is no longer needed, to fill one where he or she is needed, or more generally to find a better fit for the employee within the firm. Many firms today boost productivity by consolidating positions. Transfers are a way to give displaced employees a chance for another assignment or, perhaps, some personal growth. Employees seek transfers for many reasons, including personal enrichment, more interesting jobs, greater convenience—better hours, location of work, and so on—or to jobs offering greater advancement possibilities. Transfers for the firm's convenience—once widely used—are used less of late.

Managing Retirements

Retirement planning is a significant issue for employers.[83] In the United States, the number of 25- to 34-year-olds is growing relatively slowly, and the number of 35- to 44-year-olds is declining. So, with many employees in their 60s approaching retirement age, employers face a problem: either retain and attract potential retirees, or face the possibility of not filling all their open positions.

Many have wisely chosen to fill their staffing gaps in part with current or soon-to-be retirees. Fortuitously, 78% of employees in one survey said they expect to continue working in some capacity after normal retirement age (64% said they want to do so part-time). Only about a third plan to continue work for financial reasons; about 43% just want to stay active.[84]

The bottom line is that "retirement planning" is no longer just about helping current employees slip into retirement.[85] It should also help the employer to retain, in some capacity, the skills and brainpower of those who would normally retire and leave the firm. HR managers, employees, and supervisors should all have input into the employer's retirement processes.[86]

RETIREMENT PROGRAM STEPS A reasonable first step is to conduct numerical analyses of pending retirements. This should include a demographic analysis (including a census of the company's employees), determining the current average retirement age for the company's employees, and assessing how retirements will affect the employer's health-care and pension benefits. The employer can then determine the extent of the "retirement problem," and take fact-based steps to address it.[87]

Employers seeking to attract and/or retain retirees should take several steps. The general idea is to institute human resource policies that encourage and support older workers. Not surprisingly, studies show that loyal employees are more likely to stay beyond their normal retirement age.[88] It therefore helps to create a culture that honors

Cathy Yeulet/123RF

Employers are transferring employees less often, partly because of family resistance.

experience. For example, CVS knows that traditional recruiting media might not attract older workers; CVS thus works through the National Council on Aging, city agencies, and community organizations to find new employees. They also welcome older workers: "I'm too young to retire. [CVS] is willing to hire older people. They don't look at your age but your experience," said one dedicated older worker.[89] Others modify selection procedures. For example, one British bank stopped using psychometric tests, replacing them with role-playing exercises to gauge how candidates deal with customers.

Other techniques employers use to keep older workers include offering them part-time positions, hiring them as consultants or temporary workers, offering them flexible work arrangements, encouraging them to work past traditional retirement age, providing training to upgrade skills, and instituting phased retirement programs (gradually reduced work schedules).[90]

MyLab Management Apply It!

If your professor has assigned this activity, go to the Assignments section of **www.pearson.com/mylab/management** to complete the video exercise.

Managing Dismissals

LEARNING OBJECTIVE 10-5

Explain each of the main grounds for dismissal.

dismissal
Involuntary termination of an employee's employment with the firm.

Not all employee separations are voluntary. Some career plans and appraisals end not in promotion or graceful retirement but in **dismissal**—involuntary termination of an employee's employment with the firm. Many dismissals are avoidable. For example, many dismissals flow from bad hiring decisions. Using assessment tests, background checks, drug testing, and clearly defined jobs can reduce such dismissals.[91]

Grounds for Dismissal

There are four bases for dismissal: unsatisfactory performance, misconduct, lack of qualifications for the job, and changed requirements of (or elimination of) the job.

Unsatisfactory performance refers to a persistent failure to perform assigned duties or to meet prescribed standards on the job.[92] Specific reasons include lack of productivity or poor-quality work, excessive absenteeism, tardiness, or an adverse attitude.

Misconduct is deliberate and willful violation of the employer's rules and may include stealing, rowdy behavior, sexual harassment, and physical violence or threats at work.

Lack of qualifications for the job is an employee's inability to do the assigned work, although he or she wants to. Because this employee may be trying to do the job, it is reasonable to try to salvage him or her—perhaps through further training or by assigning the employee to another job.

Changed requirements of the job is an employee's incapability of doing the job after the nature of the job has changed. Similarly, you may have to dismiss an employee when his or her job is eliminated. Again, the employee may be industrious, so it is reasonable to retrain or transfer this person, if possible.

insubordination
Willful disregard or disobedience of the boss's authority or legitimate orders; criticizing the boss in public.

Insubordination, a form of misconduct, is sometimes the grounds for dismissal. The two basic categories of insubordination are *unwillingness* to carry out the manager's orders, and *disrespectful behavior* toward the manager. (This assumes that the orders were legitimate, and that the manager did not incite the reaction through his or her own extreme behavior.) Examples of insubordination include the following:[93]

1. Direct disregard of the boss's authority
2. Direct disobedience of, or refusal to obey, the boss's orders, particularly in front of others
3. Deliberate defiance of clearly stated company policies, rules, regulations, and procedures
4. Public criticism of the boss
5. Blatant disregard of reasonable instructions
6. Contemptuous display of disrespect

7. Disregard for the chain of command
8. Participation in (or leadership of) an effort to undermine and remove the boss from power

FAIRNESS SAFEGUARDS Dismissals are never easy. However, the manager can take steps to make them fair.[94] First, allow the employee to explain why he (or she) did what he did. It could turn out, for instance, that the employee "disobeyed" the order because he or she did not understand it. Second, people who get *full explanations* of why and how termination decisions were made "were more likely to perceive their layoff as fair . . . and indicate that they did not wish to take the past employer to court."

Third, have a formal *multistep procedure* (including warning) and an appeal process.

Fourth, *the person who actually does the dismissing* is important. Employees in one study whose managers informed them of an impending layoff viewed the dismissal fairer than did those told by, say, a human resource manager. Some employers take a less diplomatic approach. About 10% of respondents in one survey said they've used e-mail to fire employees.[95] When JCPenney dismissed thousands of employees in 2012, many were fired in groups of a few dozen to over 100 in an auditorium.[96] Use the right person, and dismiss humanely.

Fifth, dismissed employees who feel they've been treated unfairly financially are more likely to sue. Many employers use severance pay to blunt that (Figure 10-3). Most provide severance based on position level, salary, and tenure, but only about half have formal severance policies.[97]

KNOW YOUR EMPLOYMENT LAW

Termination at Will

terminate at will
In the absence of a contract, either the employer or the employee can terminate at will the employment relationship.

For more than 100 years, the prevailing rule in the United States has been that without an employment contract, either the employer or the employee can **terminate at will** the employment relationship. In other words, the employee could resign for any reason, at will, and the employer could similarly dismiss an employee for any reason, at will. Today, however, dismissed employees increasingly take their cases to court, and employers are finding that they no longer have a blanket right to fire.

Three main protections against wrongful discharge eroded the termination-at-will doctrine—*statutory exceptions, common law exceptions,* and *public policy exceptions.*

First, *statutory exceptions* include federal and state equal employment and workplace laws that prohibit certain dismissals. For example, Title VII of the Civil Rights Act of 1964 prohibits discharging employees based on race, color, religion, sex, or national origin.[98] Eighteen states and the District of Columbia have laws protecting LGBT workers from termination for sexual orientation. However, in 29 states someone can still be terminated based on sexual orientation.[99] For federal employees, the EEOC held that Title VII of the Civil Rights Act of 1964 applies to LGBT individuals.[100]

Second, numerous *common law exceptions* exist. Courts create these exceptions based on precedents. For example, courts have held that employee handbooks

FIGURE 10-3 Average Minimum and Maximum Weeks of Severance Pay by Position Level

Source: "Severance & Separation Benefits", 2017–2018 Seventh Edition, Lee Hecht Harrison, https://www.lhh.com/us/en/our-knowledge/2018/severance-and-separation-benefits, accessed March 17, 2018. Copyright 2018 by Lee Hecht Harrison. Reprinted with permission

AVERAGE MINIMUM AND MAXIMUM WEEKS BY POSITION LEVEL

Position Level (Employee Group)	Average Minimum # Weeks	Average Maximum # Weeks
C-Suite	22.9	44.7
Senior Management	16.1	39.0
Directors	8.9	32.2
Managers	6.0	29.3
Supervisors	5.2	27.4
Professional/Technical	4.9	27.3
Exempt	5.0	27.1
Non-Exempt	4.2	25.3

promising termination only "for just cause" may create an exception to the at-will rule.[101]

Finally, under the *public policy exception,* courts have held a discharge to be wrongful when it was against a well-established public policy. Thus, a public policy exception might prohibit an employer from firing an employee for refusing to break the law. ■

Avoiding Wrongful Discharge Suits

Wrongful discharge (or *wrongful termination*) occurs when an employee's dismissal does not comply with the law or with the contractual arrangement stated or implied by the employer. (In a wrongful *constructive discharge* claim, the plaintiff argues that he or she was forced to quit because the employer made the working conditions intolerable.)[102]

Avoiding wrongful discharge suits requires several things.[103] *First,* have employment policies including grievance procedures that help show that you treat employees fairly. Also use severance pay to blunt a dismissal's sting.[104] No termination is pleasant, but the first line of defense is to handle it justly.[105]

Second, review and refine all employment-related policies, procedures, and documents to limit challenges. Procedural steps include the following:[106]

- Have applicants sign the employment application. Make sure it contains a statement that "the employer can terminate at any time."
- Review your employee manual to delete statements that could undermine your defense in a wrongful discharge case. For example, delete "employees can be terminated only for just cause."
- Have written rules listing infractions that may require discipline and discharge.
- If a rule is broken, get the worker's side of the story in front of witnesses, and preferably get it signed. Then check out the story.
- Be sure employees get a written appraisal at least annually. If an employee shows evidence of incompetence, give that person a warning. Provide an opportunity to improve.
- Keep careful confidential records of all actions such as employee appraisals, warnings or notices, and so on.
- Finally, ask the questions in Figure 10-4.

FIGURE 10-4 Avoiding Wrongful Discharge Claims

Source: Sovereign, K. L. (1999). *Personal law (4th ed.).* Copyright © 1999 Pearson Education, Inc. Reprinted by permission of Pearson Education, Inc., Upper Saddle River, NJ; Pack, A., & Capito, K. (2012, September 11). 8 questions an employer should ask before taking an adverse employment action. www.dinsmore.com/adverse_employment_action_steps, accessed May 31, 2017; Wrongful termination checklist. http://employment.findlaw.com/losing-a-job/wrongful-termination-checklist.html, accessed May 1, 2017.

Avoiding Wrongful Discharge Claims: Some Questions to Ask Before Making the Dismissal Final

Avoiding wrongful discharge claims is a complicated matter that involves, for instance, ensuring that the dismissal is fair and that it does not involve issues of discrimination, harassment, retaliation, or breach of contract. Illustrative questions to ask would include:

- Is the employee covered by any type of written agreement, including a collective bargaining agreement?
- Is there any workers' compensation involvement?
- Have reasonable rules and regulations been communicated and enforced?
- Has the employee been given an opportunity to explain any rule violations or to correct poor performance?
- Is there any direct or circumstantial evidence (such as statements) that the employee is being terminated for discriminatory reasons?
- Are similar employees treated differently on the basis of age, gender, race or other protected group category?
- Did an employer make unwelcome sexual advances, request sexual favors, or seek to establish a romantic or sexual relationship?
- Before being fired, did the employee report potential violations in the company to a supervisor, colleagues, your human resources department, or an enforcement agency such as OSHA?
- Is the employee working under a written contract and if so, did it establish permissible reasons for termination or a termination procedure?
- Did the employer, supervisor, or superior make any verbal promises, such as saying the person's job was "guaranteed" or ensuring "tenure" at work?
- How long has the employee been working here and is this his or her first discipline issue?
- Are you sure there have been past warnings?
- Has anyone else committed this offense and been treated differently?

Supervisor Liability

Courts *may* hold managers personally liable for their supervisory actions, including for dismissals.[107] For example, the Fair Labor Standards Act defines *employer* to include "any person acting directly or indirectly in the interest of an employer in relation to any employee."[108] This can mean the individual supervisor.

There are several ways to reduce the likelihood of having personal liability become an issue.

- *Follow company policies and procedures.* An employee may initiate a claim against a supervisor who he or she alleges did not follow policies and procedures.
- *Carefully consider and fully document* the basis for any termination decision.
- Administer the dismissal in a manner that does not add to the employee's *emotional hardship* (as would having the employee publicly collect his or her belongings and leave the office).
- *Do not act in anger,* since doing so undermines the appearance of objectivity.
- Finally, *use the HR department* for advice regarding how to handle difficult dismissal situations.

Security Measures

The employer should use a checklist to ensure (for instance) that dismissed employees return all keys and company property, and (often) that they're accompanied out of the building.[109] For example, the employer should disable Internet-related accounts of former employees, plug holes that could allow them to gain illegal online access, and have rules for return of company laptops and handhelds. As a matter of policy, the employer should immediately inform the IT department of an impending employee separation, to enable IT to take the necessary actions. These actions should include, for instance, disabling access and passwords and changing IP addresses.[110]

The Termination Interview and Exit Process

termination interview
The interview in which an employee is informed of the fact that he or she has been dismissed.

Dismissing an employee is one of the most difficult tasks you can face at work. The dismissed employee, even if warned many times, may react with disbelief or even violence. (Review the impending interview with an attorney, if you believe protected characteristics such as gender or age may become issues during or after the interview.)[111] Guidelines for the **termination interview** are as follows:[112]

1. ***Plan the interview.***
   - Make sure the employee keeps the appointment time.
   - Have employee agreements, the human resource file, and a release announcement prepared in advance.
   - Have phone numbers ready for medical or security emergencies.
2. ***Get to the point.*** When the employee enters, give the person a moment to get comfortable and then tell him or her the purpose of the meeting and of your decision.
3. ***Describe the situation.*** Briefly, in three or four sentences, explain why the person is being let go. For instance, "Production in your area is down 4%, and we are continuing to have quality problems. We have talked about these problems several times in the past 3 months, and the solutions are not being followed through on. We have to make a change." Don't personalize the situation as in, "Your production is just not up to par." Emphasize the decision is irrevocable. State the effective date of the termination. Preserving the employee's dignity is important. Point out that the situation was carefully reviewed, but do not provide a detailed analysis of the documents supporting the discharge.[113]
4. ***Listen.*** Continue the interview for several minutes until the person appears to be talking freely and reasonably calmly.
5. ***Review the severance package.*** Describe severance payments, benefits, access to office support people, and the way references will be handled. Make no promises of benefits beyond those already in the support package.

6. ***Identify the next step.*** The terminated employee may be disoriented and unsure what to do next. Explain where the employee should go next, upon leaving the interview.

outplacement counseling
A formal process by which a terminated person is trained and counseled in the techniques of self-appraisal and securing a new position.

OUTPLACEMENT COUNSELING With **outplacement counseling** the employer arranges for an outside firm to provide terminated employees with career planning and job search skills. *Outplacement firms* usually provide such outplacement services. Employees (usually managers or professionals) who are let go typically have office space and secretarial services they can use at local offices of such firms, plus the counseling services. The outplacement counseling is part of the terminated employee's support or severance package. Why not just give the person the outplacement fee as additional severance? In general, providing outplacement services seems to have positive effects for both the terminated employee and the employer.[114]

exit interviews
Interviews with employees who are leaving the firm, conducted for obtaining information about the job or related matters, to give the employer insight about the company.

EXIT INTERVIEW Many employers conduct **exit interviews,** just prior to the employee leaving. These aim to give employers insights into their companies' strengths and weaknesses so as to improve employee retention.[115] Questions include: What made you start looking for a new job? How would you describe our company's culture? How would you describe your supervisor's management style? What did you like most/least about the company?[116] Other questions relate to HR (such as promotion processes), the work itself (including working conditions), and to competitive benchmarks (such as salaries compared to competitors'). Try to make sure the exiting employee leaves as a supporter of the employer.[117]

The assumption is that because the employee is leaving he or she will be candid, but this is debatable.[118] One older study found that at separation, 38% of those leaving blamed salary and benefits, and 4% blamed supervision. Followed up 18 months later, 24% blamed supervision and 12% blamed salary and benefits. That apparently hasn't changed. To paraphrase one top executive, someone's not going to blame his supervisor if he wants to get that person's recommendation.[119] Questioning should therefore be incisive.

THE EXIT PROCESS The exit interview is one part of a rational exit process. The employer should have a checklist.[120] As noted earlier, ensure that the employee returns all keys and company equipment, that all computer and database password access is terminated, that proper communications are sent internally (for instance, to other employees if appropriate, and to payroll) and externally, that the employee leaves the premises in a timely fashion, and that if necessary security precautions are followed.

More employees today quit without giving notice. Sometimes that's justified. For example, those taking jobs with competitors should no longer have access to the employer's information. But more often, quitting without notice reflects unfamiliarity with the traditional 2-week notice standard, or of seeing one's colleagues summarily dismissed.[121] Similarly, about 40% of workers laid off in one study placed negative social media reviews about the employer. The point is to make the separation as civil as possible.[122]

FOR THE EMPLOYEE What should you do if you get fired or passed over for a position?[123] Most people surrender to the usual stages of shock, denial, and anger. However, the better first step is usually to think through why you lost the job. Doing so isn't easy. Actively explore what (if anything) you did to contribute to the problem. Then objectively consider what you might do differently in the future, keeping in mind that you should view the loss (difficult though this may be) as an opportunity. Then evaluate your new options and be ready to seize the right opportunity.

Layoffs and the Plant Closing Law

layoff
An employer sending employees home due to a lack of work; this is typically a temporary situation.

A **layoff,** in which the employer sends workers home for a time for lack of work, is usually not a permanent dismissal (although it may turn out to be). Rather, it is a temporary one, which the employer expects will be short term. However, some employers use the term *layoff* as a euphemism for discharge or termination. In the deep recession years of 2008 and 2009 combined, employers carried out a total of about 51,000 mass layoffs, idling over 5 million workers.[124]

A study illustrates one firm's layoff process. Senior management first met to make strategic decisions about the size and timing of the layoffs. They also debated the relative importance of the skills the firm needed going forward. Supervisors then assessed their subordinates, rating their nonunion employees either A, B, or C (union employees were covered by a union agreement making layoffs dependent on seniority). The supervisors then informed each of their subordinates about his or her A, B, or C rating, and told each that those with C grades were most likely to be laid off.[125]

LAYOFF'S EFFECTS It's not surprising that layoffs often result in "deleterious psychological and physical health outcomes" for those losing their jobs, as well as for survivors.[126]

But not just the "victims" and "survivors" suffer. In one study, researchers "found that the more managers were personally responsible for handing out WARN notices to employees . . . the more likely they were to report physical health problems, to seek treatment for these problems, and to complain of disturbed sleep."[127]

Given all this, many employers try to minimize layoffs and dismissals during downturns. Reducing everyone's work hours and mandating vacations are two options. Others reduce layoffs by offering financial bonuses for improved productivity.[128]

Ironically, when some employees most need employee assistance programs (such as counseling)—after they're laid off—they lose them. More firms are therefore extending these program benefits for a month or two to former employees. For example, Florida's Sarasota County extended employee assistance program benefits for 2 months after it laid off some employees.[129]

The Worker Adjustment and Retraining Notification Act (WARN Act, or the plant closing law) requires employers of 100 or more employees to give 60 days' notice before closing a facility or starting a layoff of 50 or more people.[130]

Adjusting to Downsizings and Mergers

downsizing
The process of reducing, usually dramatically, the number of people employed by a firm.

Downsizing means reducing, usually dramatically, the number of people employed by a firm. The basic idea is to cut costs and raise profitability. Downsizings (some call them "productivity transformation programs")[131] require careful consideration of several matters.

1. First is making sure *the right people* are let go; this requires having an effective appraisal system in place.
2. Second is *compliance with all applicable laws,* including WARN.
3. Third is executing the dismissals in a manner that is *just and fair*.
4. Fourth is *security,* for instance, retrieving keys and ensuring that those leaving don't take prohibited items with them.
5. Fifth is reducing the remaining employees' uncertainty and addressing their concerns. This typically involves a postdownsizing announcement and program, including meetings where senior managers field questions from the remaining employees.

Providing advanced notice regarding the layoff can help cushion the otherwise negative effects. So can interpersonal sensitivity (in terms of the manager's demeanor during layoffs).[132] Layoffs can be more challenging abroad due to special legal obligations, such as requirements for a year's notice in some countries.

Supportiveness and creativity are especially important in companies that rely heavily on employee engagement and teamwork.[133] Here, turnover is especially disruptive, so it may be particularly important to avoid layoffs. Options here include: implement pay freezes or cuts; introduce a hiring freeze before reducing the workforce; provide candid communications about the need for the downsizing; give employees an opportunity to express their opinions about the downsizing; and be fair and compassionate in implementing the downsizing.[134]

Chapter Review

Chapter Section Summaries

10-1. Employees are ultimately responsible for their own careers, but employers and managers also have roles in **career management.** These include establishing company-based career centers, offering career planning workshops, providing employee development budgets, and offering online career development programs. Perhaps the simplest is to make the appraisal itself career-oriented, by linking the appraisal feedback to the employee's aspirations and plans.

10-2. The employer's career planning and development process and practices (including career-oriented appraisal) help to foster **employee engagement.** Managed effectively, the employer's career development process should send the signal that the employer cares about the employee's career success.

10-3. Managing voluntary turnover requires identifying its causes and then addressing them. A comprehensive approach to **retaining employees** should be multifaceted, and include improved selection, a well-thought-out training and career development program, assistance in helping employees lay out potential career plans, providing employees with meaningful work and recognition and rewards, promoting work–life balance, acknowledging employees' achievements, and providing all this within a supportive company culture.

10-4. Employers need to address employee **life-cycle career management** issues. Most notably, promotions can provide opportunities to reward exceptional performance, and to fill open positions with tested and loyal employees. Several decisions loom large in any firm's promotion process: Is seniority or competence the rule? How should we measure competence? Is the process formal or informal? Vertical, horizontal, or other? Women and people of color still experience relatively less career progress in organizations, and bias and more subtle barriers are often the cause. In general, the employer's promotion processes must comply with all the same antidiscrimination laws as do procedures for recruiting and selecting employees or any other HR actions. Transfers and retirements are other important career life-cycle issues.

10-5. **Managing dismissals** is an important part of any supervisor's job. Among the reasons for dismissal are unsatisfactory performance, misconduct, lack of qualifications, changed job requirements, and insubordination. In dismissing one or more employees, however, remember that termination at will as a policy has been weakened by exceptions in many states. Furthermore, care should be taken to avoid wrongful discharge suits.

CHAPTER 10

Discussion Questions

10-1. Why is it advisable for an employee retention effort to be comprehensive? What activities would you say are involved in such a program?

10-2. What is the employee's role in the career development process? The manager's role? The employer's role?

10-3. What are the main decisions employers should address in reaching promotion decisions?

10-4. Discuss at least four procedural suggestions for managing dismissals effectively.

10-5. What would you as a supervisor do to avoid someone accusing you of wrongful dismissal?

Individual and Group Activities

10-6. Many rightfully offer IBM as an example of an employer that works hard to improve employee retention and engagement. Browse through the employment pages of IBM's website (such as http://www-03.ibm.com/employment/index.shtml). In this chapter, we discussed actions employers can take to improve employee retention and engagement. From the information on IBM's Web pages, what is IBM doing to support retention and engagement?

10-7. In groups of four or five students, meet with one or two administrators and faculty members in your college or university and, based on this, write a two-page paper on the topic "the faculty promotion process at our college." What do you think of the process? Based on our discussion in this chapter, could you make any suggestions for improving it?

10-8. Working individually or in groups, choose two occupations (such as management consultant, HR manager, or salesperson) and use sources such as O*NET to size up the future demand for this occupation in the next 10 years or so. Does this seem like a good occupation to pursue? Why or why not?

10-9. In groups of four or five students, interview a small business owner or an HR manager with the aim of writing a two-page paper addressing the topic "steps our company is taking to reduce voluntary employee turnover." What is this employer's turnover rate now? How would you suggest it improve its turnover rate?

10-10. Appendices A and B at the end of this book (pages 614–634) list the knowledge someone studying for the HRCI (Appendix A) or SHRM (Appendix B) certification exam needs to have in each area of human resource management (such as in Strategic Management and Workforce Planning). In groups of several students, do four things: (1) review Appendix A and/or B; (2) identify the material in this chapter that relates to the Appendix A and/or B required knowledge lists; (3) write four multiple-choice exam questions on this material that you believe would be suitable for inclusion in the HRCI exam and/or the SHRM exam; and (4) if time permits, have someone from your team post your team's questions in front of the class, so that students in all teams can answer the exam questions created by the other teams.

10-11. Several years ago, a survey of college graduates in the United Kingdom found that although many hadn't found their first jobs, most were already planning "career breaks" and to keep up their hobbies and interests outside work. As one report of the findings put it, "the next generation of workers is determined not to wind up on the hamster wheel of long hours with no play."[135] Part of the problem seems to be that many already see their friends "putting in more than 48 hours a week" at work. Career experts reviewing the results concluded that many of these recent college grads "are not looking for high-pay, high-profile jobs anymore."[136] Instead, they seem to be looking to "compartmentalize" their lives. They want to keep the number of hours they spend at work down, so they can maintain their hobbies and outside interests. If you were mentoring one of these people at work, what three bits of career advice would you give him or her? Why? What (if anything) would you suggest their employers do to accommodate these graduates' stated career wishes?

10-12. Websites such as Sporting News occasionally run a story listing what they call the greatest coaches (for example, key "greatest coaches" into Google search).[137] Look at this list, and pick out two of the names. Then research these people online to determine what behaviors they exhibited that seem to account for why they were great coaches. How do these behaviors compare with what this chapter had to say about effective coaching?

Experiential Exercise

Where Am I Going . . . and Why?

Written and copyrighted by Gary Dessler, PhD.

Purpose: The purpose of this exercise is to provide you with experience in analyzing your career preferences.

Required Understanding: Students should be thoroughly familiar with the "Employee's Role in Career Management" section in this chapter, as well as using O*NET (which we discussed in Chapter 4).

How to Set Up the Exercise/Instructions: Using O*NET and the "Employee's Role in Career Management" section in this chapter, analyze your career-related inclinations (you can also take the Self-Directed Search for about $10 at www.self-directed-search.com). Based on this analysis, answer the following questions (if you wish, you may do this analysis in teams of three or four students).

10-13. What does your research suggest to you about what would be your preferable occupational options?

10-14. What are the prospects for these occupations?

10-15. Given these prospects and your own occupational inclinations, outline a brief, one-page career plan for yourself, including current occupational inclinations, career goals, and an action plan listing four or five development steps you will need to take in order to get from where you are now career-wise to where you want to be, based on your career goals.

Application Case

Uber Technologies Inc.

Written and copyrighted by Gary Dessler, PhD.

The year 2017 was a tough one for Uber Technologies Inc.[138] An Uber engineer posted a blog called "Reflecting on One Very, Very Strange Year in Uber," in which she detailed, among other things, a culture of harassment at Uber. Almost at once, Uber values that symbolized its "win at any cost" way of doing things (values like "builders build, always be hustlin'," and "meritocracy and toe stepping") were called into question. So in 2017, not only was Uber's core employee turnover too high, but six top executives stepped down, including the president, finance head, senior vice president of engineering, and CEO Travis Kalanick.

Uber's Board of Directors retained former attorney general Eric Holder, Jr. to conduct an analysis of Uber's culture. Holder's recommendations provide insight into the problems Uber needed to address. The lawyers recommended, for instance, that Uber: prohibit romantic relationships among employees where one person reports to the other; institute guidelines on using alcohol and controlled substances at work; adopt a zero tolerance policy with respect to harassment, discrimination, and retaliation; broaden its recruitment practices to include sources of minority job candidates; and that the Board of Directors create a special ethics and culture committee.

Questions

10-16. Without doing any more research beyond what you learned in this chapter, what steps would you suggest Uber take to improve employee retention?

10-17. Was there any information in previous chapters of this book that would help to illustrate other steps Uber could take to improve retention?

10-18. Use other Internet sources, including Uber.com, to finalize an answer to the question: What other steps should Uber take to improve employee retention?

Continuing Case

Carter Cleaning Company

Written and copyrighted by Gary Dessler, PhD.

The Career Planning Program

Career planning has always been a pretty low-priority item for Carter Cleaning, since "just getting workers to come to work and then keeping them honest is enough of a problem," as Jack likes to say. Yet Jennifer thought it might not be a bad idea to give some thought to what a career planning program might involve for Carter. Many of their employees had been with them for years in dead-end jobs, and she frankly felt a little bad for them: "Perhaps we could help them gain a better perspective on what they want to do," she thought. And she definitely believed that career support would have an effect on improving Carter's employee retention.

Questions

10-19. What would be the advantages to Carter Cleaning of setting up a career planning program?

10-20. Who should participate in the program? All employees? Selected employees?

10-21. Outline and describe the career development program you would propose for the cleaners, pressers, counter people, and managers at the Carter Cleaning Centers.

CHAPTER 10

Translating Strategy into HR Policies and Practices Case*,§

**The accompanying strategy map for this chapter is in MyLab Management; overall map on the inside back cover of this text outlines the relationships involved.*

Improving Performance at the Hotel Paris

The New Career Management System

The Hotel Paris's competitive strategy is "To use superior guest service to differentiate the Hotel Paris properties, and to thereby increase the length of stay and return rate of guests, and thus boost revenues and profitability." HR manager Lisa Cruz must now formulate functional policies and activities that support this competitive strategy, by eliciting the required employee behaviors and competencies.

Lisa Cruz knew that, as a hospitality business, the Hotel Paris was uniquely dependent upon having engaged, high-morale employees. In a factory or small retail shop, the employer might be able to rely on direct supervision to make sure that the employees were doing their jobs. But in a hotel, just about every employee is "on the front line." There is usually no one there to supervise the limousine driver when he or she picks up a guest at the airport, or when the valet takes the guest's car, or the front-desk clerk signs the guest in, or the housekeeping clerk needs to handle a guest's special request. If the hotel wanted satisfied guests, they had to have engaged employees who did their jobs as if they owned the company, even when the supervisor was nowhere in sight. But for the employees to be engaged, Lisa knew, the Hotel Paris had to make it clear that the company was also committed to its employees.

From her experience, she knew that one way to do this was to help her employees have successful and satisfying careers, and she was therefore concerned to find that the Hotel Paris had no career management process at all. Supervisors weren't trained to discuss employees' developmental needs or promotional options during the performance appraisal interviews. Promotional processes were informal. And the firm made no attempt to provide any career development services that might help its employees to develop a better understanding of what their career options were, or should be. Lisa was sure that engaged employees were key to improving the experiences of the hotel's guests, and that she couldn't boost employee engagement without doing a better job of attending to her employees' career needs. In two hotels she began encouraging supervisors to at least engage in career-oriented appraisals with their subordinates, on a pilot project basis.

§ Written and copyrighted by Gary Dessler, PhD.

For Lisa and the CFO, their preliminary research left little doubt about the advisability of instituting a new career management system at the Hotel Paris. Based on their pilot project, employees in those Hotel Paris hotels who had been working under the new career management directive were more engaged, received more complimentary letters from guests, and received higher performance appraisal ratings than did employees who did not have career plans. The CFO therefore gave the go-ahead to design and institute a new Hotel Paris career management program.

Lisa and her team knew that they already had most of the building blocks in place, thanks to the new performance management system they had instituted just a few weeks earlier. For example, the new performance management system already required that the supervisor appraise the employee based on goals and competencies that were driven by the company's strategic needs; and the appraisal itself produced new goals for the coming year and specific development plans for the employee. These development plans had to make sense in terms of both the company's and the employee's needs and preferences.

In addition to the new performance management elements already in place, Lisa and her team created an online "Hotel Paris Career Center." With links to a choice of career assessment tools such as the Self-Directed Search (www.self-directed-search.com) and wizard-based templates for developing one's own career plan, the site went far toward providing the Hotel Paris's employees with the career assistance that they required. Also on the site, a new "International Job Openings" link made it easier for Hotel Paris employees to identify positions for which they might be qualified. The results exceeded Lisa and the CFO's expectations. Virtually every employee produced a career plan within the first 6 months. The appraisal interviews often turned into animated, career-oriented development sessions, and soon the various measures of employee commitment and guest service were trending up.

Questions

10-22. "Many hotel jobs are inherently 'dead end'; for example, maids, laundry workers, and valets either have no great aspirations to move up, or are just using these jobs temporarily, for instance, to help out with household expenses." First, do you agree with this statement? Why, or why not? Second, list three more specific career activities you would recommend Lisa implement for these employees.

10-23. Using what you learned in this chapter of Dessler *Human Resource Management*, build on the company's new system by recommending two more specific career development activities the hotel should implement.

10-24. What other specific career development activities would you recommend in light of the fact that the Hotel Paris's hotels and employees are dispersed around the world?

Writing Assignments

10-25. You manage a small restaurant in Columbus, Ohio and keeping good employees is one of your biggest challenges. Most waitstaff and kitchen staff last no more than 8–9 months. Explain what you would do to improve employee retention.

10-26. Explain what you as a supervisor can do to support your employees' career management needs.

MyLab Management Try It!

How would you apply the concepts and skills you learned in this chapter? If your professor has assigned this activity, go to the Assignments section of **www.pearson.com/mylab/management** to complete the simulation.

PERSONAL INVENTORY ASSESSMENTS

Go to **www.pearson.com/mylab/management** to complete the Personal Inventory Assessment related to this chapter.

Key Terms

career, 313
career management, 313
career development, 313
career planning, 313
portfolio careers, 314
reality shock, 315
mentoring, 317
coaching, 318
promotion, 324
transfers, 326
dismissal, 328
insubordination, 328
terminate at will, 329
termination interview, 331
outplacement counseling, 332
exit interviews, 332
layoff, 332
downsizing, 333

Endnotes

1. "Fresh ideas: Fresh Thyme Farmers Market: Fresh Thyme Has Opened 56 Stores in Less Than Three Years and Plans to Open up to 17 More by the End of 2017," *Retail Merchandiser* 57, no. 2(March 2017), p. 56.
2. See, for example, Ans de Vos and Bart Cambre, "Career Management and High-Performing Organizations: A Set Theoretic Approach," *Human Resource Management* 56, no. 3 (May–June 2017), pp. 501–518.
3. For example, see Phyllis Moen and Patricia Roehling, *The Career Mystique* (Boulder, CO: Rowman & Littlefield Publishers, 2005); and Geoff Williams, "3 Steps to Reinventing Your Career," *U.S. News & World Report*, June 5, 2013, http://money.usnews.com/money/personal-finance/articles/2013/06/05/3-steps-to-reinventing-your-career, accessed September 2, 2014.
4. Stephen Robbins and Timothy Judge, *Organizational Behavior* (Upper Saddle River, NJ: Pearson Education, 2011), p. 285.
5. Ibid., p. 284.
6. Karoline Strauss et al., "Future Work Selves: How Salient Hoped-For Identities Motivate Proactive Career Behaviors," *Journal of Applied Psychology* 97, no. 3, pp. 580–598.
7. Edward Levinson et al., "A Critical Evaluation of the Web-Based Version of the Career Key," *Career Development Quarterly* 50, no. 1 (September 1, 2002), pp. 26–36; https://www.careerkey.org/choose-a-career/hollands-theory-of-career-choice.html, accessed March 5, 2017.
8. Richard Bolles, *What Color Is Your Parachute?* (Berkeley, CA: Ten Speed Press, 2003), pp. 5–6.
9. This example is based on Richard Bolles, *The Three Boxes of Life* (Berkeley, CA: Ten Speed Press, 1976). Richard Bolles updates his famous career book *What Color Is Your Parachute?* annually. It contains this and many other career exercises. The 2015 edition is published by Ten Speed Press in Berkeley, California.
10. Steven Lindner, "New Government Rule This Year Making Millions of Part-Timers Eligible for Overtime May Boost Opportunities for Portfolio Careerists," June 13, 2016, http://www.nydailynews.com/life-style/millennials-portfolio-careers-multiple-jobs-increasing-article-1.2671919; "Portfolio Careers: Is the Latest Work Trend Right For You?" https://www.forbes.com/sites/learnvest/2013/02/27/portfolio-careers-is-the-latest-work-trend-right-for-you/#640b029a7688; Ian Christie, "Pursue a Portfolio Career," www.monster.com; all accessed March 23, 2017.
11. http://careers.intuit.com/university/new-grads, accessed March 12, 2013.
12. Rachel Silverman, "Workers Get Help Climbing the Career Ladder," *The Wall Street Journal*, January 14, 2015, p. B6.
13. Laszlo Bock, *Work Rules!* (New York: Twelve, 2015), pp. 217–218.
14. Patty Gaul, "e-Learning Is Increasing as a Career Development Tool," *TD*, September 2017, p. 20.
15. Julia Kronholz, "Self-Help Career Services: A Case Report," *The Career Development Quarterly* 63, no. 3 (September 2015), pp. 282–288.
16. Fred Otte and Peggy Hutcheson, *Helping Employees Manage Careers* (Upper Saddle River, NJ: Prentice Hall, 1992), p. 143. Numerous vendors supply such workshops, such as http://www.centerforworklife.com/services-2/the-healthy-physician/work-life-balance-training/career-planning-workshops/, accessed March 16, 2018.
17. David Foote, "Wanna Keep Your Staff Happy? Think Career," *Computerworld*, October 9, 2000, p. 38. For an example, the U.S. Homeland Security Department's TSA has a career coaching/planning program. See http://tsacareercoaching.tsa.dhs.gov/index.php/faq-tsa-career-plan, accessed September 2, 2014.
18. Yehuda Baruch, "Career Development in Organizations and Beyond: Balancing Traditional and Contemporary Viewpoints," *Human Resource Management Review* 16 (2006), p. 131.
19. www.halogensoftware.com, accessed March 23, 2017. Also see, https://www.saba.com/resources/product-information/datasheet-hs-succession, accessed August 8, 2018.
20. Mukta Kulkarni and K. V. Gopakumar, "Career Management Strategies of People with Disabilities," *Human Resource Management* 53, no. 3 (May–June 2014), pp. 445–466.
21. Sydney Finkelstein, "The Best Leaders Are Great Teachers," *Harvard Business Review*, January–February 2018, p. 142.
22. https://www.right.com/wps/wcm/connect/right-us-en/home/thoughtwire/categories/talent-work/manager-as-career-coach-really, accessed March 16, 2018.
23. Bill Hayes, "Helping Workers with Career Goals Boosts Retention Efforts," *Boston Business Journal* 21, no. 11 (April 20, 2001), p. 38; https://www.right.com/wps/wcm/connect/right-us-en/home/thoughtwire/categories/talent-work/manager-as-career-coach-really, accessed March 16, 2018.
24. Michael Doody, "A Mentor Is a Key to Career Success," *Health-Care Financial Management* 57, no. 2 (February 2003), pp. 92–94.
25. Richard Luecke, *Coaching and Mentoring* (Boston: Harvard Business School Press, 2004), pp. 100–101; E. Wayne Hart, "Seven Ways to Be an Effective Mentor," *Fortune*, June 30, 2010, https://www.forbes.com/2010/06/30/mentor-coach-executive-training-leadership-managing-ccl.html#4e6519823fd3, accessed March 16, 2018.
26. Ferda Erdem and Janset Özen Aytemur, "Mentoring—A Relationship Based on Trust: Qualitative Research," *Public Personnel Management* 37, no. 1 (Spring 2008), pp. 55–65.
27. Herminia Ibarra, Nancy Carter, and Christine Silva, "Why Men Still Get More Promotions Than Women," *Harvard Business Review*, September 2010, pp. 80–85.
28. This is based on Gary Dessler, *Winning Commitment* (New York: McGraw-Hill, 1993), Chapter 10. See also www.glassdoor.com/Reviews/J-CPenney-Reviews-E361.htm, http://jobs.jcp.com/viewalljobs, and www.glassdoor.com/Reviews/Employee-Review-J-CPenney-RVW479729.htm, all accessed July 7, 2014.
29. www.Medtronic.com/careers/develop-your-potential, accessed March 12, 2013; www.medtronic.com/us-en/about-3/medtronic-plc-facts.html?cmpid=mdt_plc_2015_US_about_3_story_panel_featured_company_facts_cta_text_link_learn_more, accessed April 10, 2015.
30. See, for example, www.nobscot.com/survey/index.cfm and www.bls.gov/jlt, accessed April 27, 2011. For computing turnover, see SHRM, "Executive Brief: Differences in Employee Turnover across Key Industries," www.shrm.org, accessed August 30, 2012.
31. Jean Phillips and Stanley Gully, *Strategic Staffing* (Upper Saddle River, NJ: Pearson Education, 2012).
32. The following example is based on Barbara Hillmer, Steve Hillmer, and Gale McRoberts, "The Real Costs of Turnover: Lessons from a Call Center," *Human Resource Planning* 27, no. 3 (2004), pp. 34–41. Another study focused on turnover intentions among government technology workers. It concluded that human resource managers could influence turnover through practices such as promotion opportunities, training and development, pay and reward satisfaction, and family-friendly policies. Kim Soonhee, "The Impact of Human Resource Management on State Government IT Employee Turnover Intentions," *Public Personnel Management* 41, no. 2 (Summer 2012), p.257.
33. Park and Shaw, "Turnover Rates and Organizational Performance."
34. Adrienne Fox, "Drive Turnover Down," *HR Magazine*, July 2012, pp. 23–27.
35. SHRM, "Executive Brief."
36. www.worldatwork.org/waw/adimLink?id=17180, accessed April 27, 2011.
37. "Employees Reveal Top Reasons for Leaving in Scientific Study from Work Institute," http://work Institute.com, April 26, 2017.
38. Clara Von Ins, "Career Development Proved Key to Addressing Retention," *TD* 71, no. 7 (July 1, 2017), p. 10.
39. Jungin Kim, "What Increases Public Employees Turnover Intentions?" *Public Personnel Management* 44, no. 4 (December 2015), pp. 496+.
40. Phillips and Gully, *Strategic Staffing*, p. 329.
41. Phillips and Gully, *Strategic Staffing*, p. 328.
42. Stephen Robbins and Timothy Judge, *Organizational Behavior* (Upper Saddle River, NJ: Pearson Education, 2011), p. 81.
43. Katherine Tyler, "Who Will Stay and Who Will Go?" *HR Magazine*, December 2011, pp. 101–103.
44. See also David Ernest, David Allen, and Ronald Landis, "Mechanisms Linking Realistic Job Previews with Turnover: A Meta-analytic Path Analysis," *Personnel Psychology* 60, no. 4 (2011), pp. 865–897.
45. "Employers Using Cash to Retain Key Talent," *Bloomberg BNA Bulletin to Management*, June 26, 2012, p. 202.
46. Max Messmer, "Employee Retention: Why It Matters Now," *CPA Magazine*, June/July 2009, p. 28; and "The Employee Retention Challenge," Development Dimensions International, 2009.
47. Messmer, "Employee Retention."
48. Ibid. See also Eric Krell, "Five Ways to Manage High Turnover," *HR Magazine*, April 2012, pp. 63–65.
49. Rosemary Batt and Alexander Colvin, "An Employment

Systems Approach to Turnover: Human Resources Practices, Quits, Dismissals, and Performance," *Academy of Management Journal* 54, no. 4 (2011), pp. 695–717.
50. "Counteroffers: Smart Move to Keep a Star or Waste of Time?" *Bloomberg BNA Bulletin to Management*, November 6, 2012, p. 358.
51. Ibid.
52. Baker, op cit. Stephen Baker, "Data Mining Moves to Human Resources" *Bloomberg Business*, March 11, 2009. See also "HR Analytics," *Workforce Management*, August 2012, p. 24.
53. Ed Frauenheim, "Numbers Game," *Workforce Management* 90, no. 3 (March 2011), p. 21.
54. Bock, *Work Rules!* p. 142.
55. From www.globoforce.com, accessed April 7, 2013. Used by permission from Globoforce.
56. "Fresh Ideas: Fresh Thyme Farmers Market."
57. David Wilson, "Comparative Effects of Race/Ethnicity and Employee Engagement on Withdrawal Behavior," *Journal of Managerial Issues* 21, no. 2 (Summer 2009), pp. 165–166, 195–215.
58. Paul Eder and Robert Eisenberger, "Perceived Organizational Support: Reducing the Negative Influence of Coworker Withdrawal Behavior," *Journal of Management* 34, no. 1 (February 2008), pp. 55–68.
59. Wilson, "Comparative Effects of Race/Ethnicity and Employee Engagement."
60. Lisa Hope Pelled and Katherine R. Xin, "Down and Out: An Investigation of the Relationship between Mood and Employee Withdrawal Behavior," *Journal of Management* 25, no. 6 (1999), pp. 875–895.
61. Ibid.
62. Ibid.
63. Ibid.
64. Nor is the process simple. For example, in one study people who were not particularly guilt prone were more likely to be absent when they were dissatisfied at work than were those who assumedly did feel guiltier about staying out of work. Rebecca Schaumburg and Francis Flynn, "Clarifying the Link between Job Satisfaction and Absenteeism: The Role of Guilt Proneness," *Journal of Applied Psychology* 102, no. 6 (2017), pp. 982–992.
65. See, for example, Margaret Shaffer and David Harrison, "Expatriates' Psychological Withdrawal from International Assignments: Work, Nonwork, and Family Influences," *Personnel Psychology* 51, no. 1 (Spring 1998), pp. 87–118; Karl Pajo, Alan Coetzer, and Nigel Guenole, "Formal Development Opportunities and Withdrawal Behaviors by Employees in Small and Medium-Sized Enterprises," *Journal of Small Business Management* 48, no. 3 (July 2010), pp. 281–301; and P. Eder et al., "Perceived Organizational Support: Reducing the Negative Influence of Coworker Withdrawal Behavior," *Journal of Management* 34 no. 1 (February 2008), pp. 55–68.
66. Verena Hahn and Christian Dormann, "The Role of Partners and Children for Employees' Psychological Detachment from Work and Well-Being," *Journal of Applied Psychology* 98, no. 1 (2013), pp. 26–36.
67. Genevieve Douglas, "Rising Hiring Costs Shift Focus to Promotions, Other Strategies," *Bloomberg HR Blog*, November 7, 2017.
68. Saul Fine, Judith Goldenberg, and Yair Noam, "Beware of Those Left Behind: Counterproductive Work Behaviors among Non-promoted Employees and the Moderating Effect of Integrity," *Journal of Applied Psychology* 101, no. 12 (2016), pp. 1721–1729.
69. https://www.eeoc.gov/policy/docs/factemployment_procedures.html, accessed March 16, 2018.
70. *Gee v. Pincipi*, 5th Cir., number 01-50159, April 18, 2002, "Alleged Harasser's Comments Tainted Promotion Decision," www.shrm.org, accessed March 2, 2004.
71. Maria Danaher, "Unclear Promotion Procedures Smack of Discrimination," www.shrm.org, accessed March 2, 2004.
72. Elaine Herskowitz, "The Perils of Subjective Hiring and Promotion Criteria," www.shrm.org, accessed January 1, 2009.
73. https://www.littlerock.gov/!userfiles/editor/docs/hr/Police_Promotion_Procedure_Guidelines.pdf, accessed March 16, 2018.
74. George Thornton III and David Morris, "The Application of Assessment Center Technology to the Evaluation of Personnel Records," *Public Personnel Management* 30, no. 1 (Spring 2001), p. 55. See also, for example, https://www.littlerock.gov/!userfiles/editor/docs/hr/Police_Promotion_Procedure_Guidelines.pdf, accessed March 16, 2018.
75. Pamela Babcock, quoting Terry Henley, SPHR, in "Promotions: Is There a 'New Normal'?" www.shrm.org/hrdisciplines/employeereltions/articles/Pages/PromotionsIsThereaNewNormal.aspx, accessed June 1, 2011.
76. Bock, *Work Rules!* p. 358.
77. Karen Lyness and Madeline Heilman, "When Fit Is Fundamental: Performance Evaluations and Promotions of Upper-Level Female and Male Managers," *Journal of Applied Psychology* 91, no. 4 (2006), pp. 777–785.
78. Genevieve Douglas, "No Women in the C Suite? Look at Initial Promotions." *Bloomberg BNA Bulletin toManagement*, October 24, 2017.
79. "Minority Women Surveyed on Career Growth Factors," *Community Banker* 9, no. 3 (March 2000), p. 44.
80. Georgene Huang, "Minority Women Really Are Least Likely to Be Promoted in Corporate America," *Forbes*, October 12, 2017, https://www.forbes.com/sites/georgenehuang/2017/10/12/minority-women-really-are-least-likely-to-be-promoted-in-corporate-america/#3437adce3088, accessed March 16, 2018; https://womenintheworkplace.com/, accessed March 16, 2018.
81. https://womenintheworkplace.com/, accessed March 16, 2018.
82. Robin Shay, "Don't Get Caught in the Legal Wringer When Dealing with Difficult to Manage Employees," www.shrm.org, http://moss07.shrm.org/Publications/hrmagazine/EditorialContent/Pages/0702toc.aspx, accessed July 28, 2009.
83. See, for example, Carol Hyman, "Me, Retire?" *Bloomberg Businessweek*, October 2, 2017, pp. 47–48.
84. "Employees Plan to Work Past Retirement, but Not Necessarily for Financial Reasons," *BNA Bulletin to Management*, February 19, 2004, pp. 57–58. See also Mo Wang, "Profiling Retirees in the Retirement Transition and Adjustment Process: Examining the Longitudinal Change Patterns of Retirees' Psychological Well-Being," *Journal of Applied Psychology* 92, \no. 2 (2007), pp. 455–474.
85. See, for example, Matt Bolch, "Bidding Adieu," *HR Magazine*, June 2006, pp. 123–127; and Claudia Deutsch, "A Longer Goodbye," *The New York Times*, April 20, 2008, pp. H1, H10.
86. Mary Dean Lee et al., "Human Resource Approaches to Retirement: Gatekeeping, Improvising, Orchestrating, and Partnering," *Human Resource Management* 56, no. 3 (June 2017), pp. 455–477.
87. Luis Fleites and Lou Valentino, "The Case for Phased Retirement," *Compensation & Benefits Review*, March/April 2007, pp. 42–46.
88. Andrew Luchak et al., "When Do Committed Employees Retire? The Effects of Organizational Commitment on Retirement Plans under a Defined Benefit Pension Plan," *Human Resource Management* 47, no. 3 (Fall 2008), pp. 581–599.
89. Dychtwald et al., "It's Time to Retire Retirement," p. 52.
90. Eric Krell, "Ways to Phased Retirement," *HR Magazine*, October 2010, p. 90.
91. Andrea Poe, "Make Foresight 20/20," *HR Magazine*, February 20, 2000, pp. 74–80. See also Nancy Hatch Woodward, "Smoother Separations," *HR Magazine*, June 2007, pp. 94–97.
92. Joseph Famularo, *Handbook of Modern Personnel Administration* (New York: McGraw Hill, 1982), pp. 65.3–65.5. See also Carolyn Hirschman, "Off Duty, Out of Work," *HR Magazine*, www.shrm.org/hrmagazine/articles/0203/0203hirschman.asp, accessed January 10, 2008; Michael Sheldon, "Acceptable Reasons for Termination," https://www.thehartford.com/business-playbook/in-depth/valid-reasons-fire-employee-termination, accessed March 16, 2018.
93. Kenneth Sovereign, *Personnel Law* (Upper Saddle River, NJ: Prentice Hall, 1999), p. 148; "Disciplinary Issues: What Constitutes Insubordination?" www.shrm.org/TemplatesTools/hrqa/Pages/CMS_020144.aspx, accessed September 11, 2013.
94. C. R. Wanberg, L. W. Bunce, & M. B. Gavin, "Perceived Fairness of Layoffs among Individuals Who Have Been Laid Off: A Longitudinal Study" *Personnel Psychology*, 52, 1999, 59-84; Brian Klaas and Gregory Dell'omo, "Managerial Use of Dismissal: Organizational Level Determinants," *Personnel Psychology* 50 (1997), pp. 927–953; Nancy Hatch Woodward, "Smoother Separations," *HR Magazine*, June 2007, pp. 94–97.
95. "E-Mail Used for Layoffs, Humiliation," *BNA Bulletin to Management*, October 2, 2007, p. 315.
96. Donna Mattioli et al., "Penney Wounded by Deep Staff Cuts," *The Wall Street Journal*, April 15, 2013.
97. "Severance & Separation Benefits," 2017–2018 Seventh Edition, Lee Hecht Harrison, https://www.lhh.com/us/en/our-knowledge/2018/severance-and-separation-benefits, accessed March 17, 2018.
98. Robert Lanza and Morton Warren, "United States: Employment at Will Prevails Despite Exceptions to the Rule," *Society for Human Resource Management Legal Report*, October/November 2005, pp. 1–8.
99. Max Mihelich, "The Changing Landscape of LGBT Discrimination Laws," *Workforce*, October 2014, pp. 22–24.
100. "Facts about Discrimination in Federal Government Employment Based on Marital Status, Political Affiliation, Status as a

Parent, Sexual Orientation, or Transgender (Gender Identity) Status," www.eeoc.gov/federal/otherprotections.cfm, accessed July 9, 2015. See also, http://employment.findlaw.com/employment-discrimination/sexual-orientation-discrimination-in-the-workplace.html, accessed July 9, 2015.

101. Mihelich, op. cit.
102. http://employment.findlaw.com/losing-a-job/constructive-dismissal-and-wrongful-termination.html, accessed March 16, 2018.
103. James Coil III and Charles Rice, "Three Steps to Creating Effective Employee Releases," *Employment Relations Today*, Spring 1994, pp. 91–94; Richard Bayer, "Termination with Dignity," *Business Horizons* 43, no. 5 (September 2000), pp. 4–10; Betty Sosnin, "Orderly Departures," *HR Magazine* 50, no. 11 (November 2005), pp. 74–78; "Severance Pay: Not Always the Norm," *HR Magazine*, May 2008, p. 28; "Preventing Lawsuits for Wrongful Termination." http://corporate.findlaw.com/litigation-disputes/preventing-lawsuits-for-wrongful-termination.html, accessed March 31, 2018.
104. See, for example, Richard Hannah, "The Attraction of Severance," *Compensation & Benefits Review*, November/December 2008, pp. 37–44.
105. Jonathan Segal, "Severance Strategies," *HR Magazine*, July 2008, pp. 95–96.
106. Coil and Rice, "Three Steps to Creating Effective Employee Releases," "Fairness to Employees Can Stave Off Litigation"; Bayer, "Termination with Dignity"; Sosnin, "Orderly Departures"; "Severance Pay: Not Always the Norm."
107. Edward Isler et al., "Personal Liability and Employee Discipline," *Society for Human Resource Management Legal Report*, September/October 2000, pp. 1–4. How the courts will decide depends on among other things (for example, courts may more likely decide in favor of the plaintiff where there are public policy violations such as a supervisor demanding clearly improper actions by the employee). For example, some states such as Ohio and New Jersey have allowed plaintiffs to proceed against supervisors in such cases while others such as Utah and Texas have not: George L. Washington, Jr., "Assessing Individual Liability Claims against Supervisors and Managers in Cases of Wrongful Termination of Employment in Violation of Public Policy," ABA Section of Labor and Employment Law Employment Rights and Responsibilities Committee, March 2017, https://www.americanbar.org/content/dam/aba/events/labor_law/2017/03/err/papers/george_washington_paper_err.authcheckdam.pdf, accessed March 17, 2018; Jonathan Mook, "Can Individual Managers Be Held Liable for Wrongful Discharge? The Answer May Surprise You," April 10, 2013, https://hrdailyadvisor.blr.com/2013/04/10/5145/, accessed March 17, 2018.
108. https://www.americanbar.org/content/dam/aba/events/labor_law/basics_papers/flsa/kearns.authcheckdam.pdf, accessed March 17, 2018.
109. For an example of such as checklist, see https://www.delcor.com/resources/blog/a-hr-and-it-checklist-for-termination-of-employment, accessed March 17, 2018.
110. Jaikumar Vijayan, "Downsizings Leave Firms Vulnerable to Digital Attacks," *Computerworld* 25 (2001), pp. 6–7; "Employee Termination from an IT Perspective," https://www.thebalance.com/employee-termination-from-an-it-perspective-1919342, accessed March 17, 2018.
111. Dana Wilkie, "Right and Wrong Ways to Terminate: Avoiding Common Mistakes When Letting a Worker Go," Society for Human Resource Management, September 12, 2013, https://shrm.org/ResourcesAndTools/hr-topics/employee-relations/Pages/Right-Wrong-Ways-to-Terminate.aspx, accessed April 1, 2018.
112. Based on Coil and Rice, "Three Steps to Creating Effective Employee Releases." See also Martha Frase-Blunt, "Making Exit Interviews Work," *HR Magazine*, August 2004, pp. 9–11.
113. William J. Morin and Lyle York, *Outplacement Techniques* (New York: AMACOM, 1982), pp. 101–131; F. Leigh Branham, "How to Evaluate Executive Outplacement Services," *Personnel Journal* 62 (April 1983), pp. 323–326; Sylvia Milne, "The Termination Interview," *Canadian Manager*, Spring 1994, pp. 15–16; Matthew S. Wood and Steven J. Karau, "Preserving Employee Dignity during the Termination Interview: An Empirical Examination," *Journal of Business Ethics* 86, no. 4 (2009), pp. 519–534; "Employee Termination Checklist and Exit Interview Questionnaire," Updated on January 13, 2017, https://www.bizfilings.com/toolkit/tools/tools-forms/employee-termination-checklist-and-exit-interview-questionnaire, accessed March 17, 2018.
114. Bram Lowsky, "Inside Outplacement," *Workforce*, June 2014, pp. 36–39, 48.
115. Everett Spain and Boris Groysberg, "Making Exit Interviews Count," *Harvard Business Review*, April 2016, https://hbr.org/2016/04/making-exit-interviews-count, accessed March 17, 2018.
116. Marlene Piturro, "Alternatives to Downsizing," *Management Review*, October 1999, pp. 37–42; "How Safe Is Your Job?" *Money*, December 1, 2001, p. 130; https://www.glassdoor.com/employers/blog/7-must-ask-exit-interview-questions/, accessed March 17, 2018.
117. Everett Spain and Boris Groysberg, "Making Exit Interviews Count," *Harvard Business Review*, April 2016, pp. 88–94.
118. Joseph Zarandona and Michael Camuso, "A Study of Exit Interviews: Does the Last Word Count," *Personnel* 62, no. 3 (March 1981), pp. 47–48. For another point of view, see "Firms Can Profit from Data Obtained from Exit Interviews," *Knight-Ridder/Tribune Business News*, February 13, 2001, Item 0104 4446; and Everett Spain and Boris Groysberg, "Making Exit Interviews Count," *Harvard Business Review*, April 2016, pp. 88–94.
119. Everett Spain and Boris Groysberg, "Making Exit Interviews Count."
120. See, for example, https://www.hr360.com/Termination/Checklist.aspx, accessed March 15, 2018.
121. Sue Shellenbarger, "Two Weeks Notice? More Say, 'I'm Quitting Today,'" *The Wall Street Journal*, June 22, 2016, pp. B1, D2.
122. "Careful How You Fire Employees; You May Be Damaging Your Brand," *Bloomberg BNA Bulletin to Management*, August 7, 2015, p. 211.
123. Mitchell Lee Marks et al., "Rebounding from Career Setbacks," *Harvard Business Review*, October 2014, pp. 105–108.
124. "Mass Layoffs at Lowest Level since July 2008, BLS Says," *Bloomberg BNA Bulletin to Management*, January 12, 2010, p. 13.
125. Leon Grunberg, Sarah Moore, and Edward Greenberg, "Managers' Reactions to Implementing Layoffs: Relationship to Health Problems and Withdrawal Behaviors," *Human Resource Management* 45, no. 2 (Summer 2006), pp. 159–178.
126. Ibid.
127. Ibid.
128. "Adopting Laid-Off Alternatives Could Help Employers Survive, Even Thrive, Analysts Say," *Bloomberg BNA Bulletin to Management*, February 24, 2009, p. 57.
129. Joann Lublin, "Employers See Value in Helping Those Laid Off," *The Wall Street Journal*, September 24, 2007, p. B3.
130. See Rodney Sorensen and Stephen Robinson, "What Employers Can Do to Stay Out of Legal Trouble When Forced to Implement Layoffs," *Compensation & Benefits Review*, January/February 2009, pp. 25–32.
131. "Calling a Layoff a Layoff," *Workforce Management*, April 21, 2008, p. 41.
132. "Communication Can Reduce Problems, Litigation after Layoffs, Attorneys Say," *BNA Bulletin to Management*, April 14, 2003, p. 129. See also, "There Are Kinder Ways to Lay People Off—So Why Don't We Use Them?" http://knowledge.wharton.upenn.edu/article/is-there-are-kinder-ways-to-lay-people-off/, accessed March 17, 2018.
133. Roderick Iversen and Christopher Zatzick, "The Effects of Downsizing of Labor Productivity: The Value of Showing Consideration for Employees' Morale and Welfare and High Performance Work Systems," *Human Resource Management* 50, no. 1 (January/February 2011), pp. 29–44.
134. Ibid., p. 40.
135. "New Trend in Career Hunt," *Europe Intelligence Wire*, February 10, 2004.
136. Ibid.
137. See, for example, http://aol.sportingnews.com/ncaabasketball/story/2009-07-29/sporting-news-50-greatest-coaches-all-time, accessed July 7, 2014.
138. "Uber Report: Eric Holder's Recommendation for Change," *The New York Times*, June 14, 2017; Curtis Verschoor, "Uber Culture Causes Big Losses: Harassment and Mismanagement Have Led to Steep Losses for This Highflying Company," *Strategic Finance* 99, no. 3 (September 2017), p. 23.
139. Brett Arends, "How Summer Can Change Your Future," *The Wall Street Journal*, May 17–18, 2014, p. B8.
140. John Holland, *Making Vocational Choices: A Theory of Careers* (Upper Saddle River, NJ: Prentice Hall, 1973).
141. Bart Wille and Filip De Fruyt, "Vocations as a Source of Identity: Reciprocal Relations between Big Five Personality Traits and RIASEC Characteristics over 15 Years," *Journal of Applied Psychology* 99, no. 2 (2014), pp. 262–281.
142. Ibid., p. 5.
143. https://www.onetonline.org/help/onet/mynextmove, accessed August 5, 2018.
144. Ibid.
145. This is based on Edgar Schein, *Career Dynamics* (Reading,

MA; Addison Wesley, 1978), pp. 128–129; and Edgar Schein, "Career Anchors Revisited: Implications for Career Development in the 21st Century," *Academy of Management Executive* 10, no. 4 (1996), pp. 80–88.
146. Ibid., pp. 257–262. For a test of Schein's career anchor concept, see Yvon Martineau et al., "Multiple Career Anchors of Québec Engineers: Impact on Career Path and Success," *Relations Industrielles/Industrial Relations* 60, no. 3 (Summer 2005), pp. 45, 455–482.
147. https://www.bls.gov/ooh/, accessed March 16, 2018.
148. Deb Koen, "Revitalize Your Career," *TD*, January 2003, pp. 59–60; Kerry Hannon, "How To Love Your Job Even If You Don't Like It," https://www.forbes.com/sites/nextavenue/2014/11/17/how-to-love-your-job-even-if-you-dont-like-it/#50cd924c2cb3, accessed March 17, 2018.
149. Christopher Boyce, Alex Wood, Michael Daly, and Constantine Sedikides, "Personality Change Following Unemployment," *Journal of Applied Psychology* 100, no. 4 (2015), pp. 991–1011.
150. Jon Wolper, "The Power of Referrals," *TD*, July 2016, p. 10.
151. See John Wareham, "How to Make a Headhunter Call You," *Across-the-Board* 32, no. 1 (January 1995), pp. 49–50; and Deborah Wright Brown and Alison Konrad, "Job Seeking in a Turbulent Environment: Social Networks and the Importance of Cross-Industry Ties to an Industry Change," *Human Relations* 54, no. 8 (August 2001), p. 1018. This is also the recommendation of Richard Bolles, whose *What Color Is Your Parachute?* has long been a number-one selling career management guide: http://www.jobhuntersbible.com/, accessed March 25, 2017.
152. Jennifer Schramm, "Are You on #Social Media?" *HR Magazine*, December 2015/January 2016, p. 57.
153. Based on Phyllis Korkke, "How to Say 'Look at Me!' to an Online Recruiter," *New York Times*, January 20, 2013, p. 8; and Eilene Zimmerman, "Recruiting a Recruiter for Your Next Job," *The New York Times*, April 7, 2013, p. 10.
154. Sheryl Jean, "Say Goodbye to Paper, Hello to Social Resume," *Miami Herald*, March 4, 2013, p. 19.
155. Susan Adams, "The 10 Best Websites for Your Career," *Forbes*, www.forbes.com/sites/susanadams/2012/09/14/the-10-best-websites-for-your-career, accessed April 10, 2015.
156. A classic but still very useful job search guides available: Richard Payne, *How to Get a Better Job Quicker* (New York: Mentor, 1987), pp. 54–87.
157. "Read This Before You Put a Resume Online," *Fortune*, May 24, 1999, pp. 290–291; "Securing Your Resume for Online Job Hunting," https://www.scambusters.org/onlinejobhunting.html, accessed March 17, 2018; "Use Caution When Seeking Employment Online," https://www.bbb.org/new-york-city/get-consumer-help/articles/use-caution-when-seeking-employment-online/, accessed March 17, 2018.
158. Sara Needleman, "Posting a Job Profile Online? Keep It Polished," August 29, 2006, *The Wall Street Journal*, p. B7.
159. Rachel Silverman, Lauren Weber, Lindsay Gelman, and Rachel Feintzeig, "New Year, New Job? Read This First," *The Wall Street Journal*, January 2, 2015, p. B1.
160. Payne, *How to Get a Better Job Quicker*.
161. Sue Shellenbarger, "The Six-Month Job Interview," *The Wall Street Journal*, January 20, 2016, pp. B1, B3.

Appendix for Chapter 10

Managing Your Career and Finding a Job

The individual must be responsible for creating and managing his or her own career. And, in today's job marketplace, knowing how to find and get a job is crucial.

Making Career Choices

Many people don't put much thought into their careers. Some choose majors based on class scheduling preferences, favorite professors, or unstated psychological motives. Others stumble into jobs because "that's all that was available." If there was ever anything that demanded fact-based decisions, it is choosing your career.

The first and essential step is to learn as much as possible about your interests, aptitudes, and skills. The most direct way to do this is through experience, preferably a roster of jobs, internships, and experiences that will help you crystallize what it is you like to do and are great at. Getting experience doesn't just help career planning: In one study, the researchers sent out 9,400 fictitious resumes for "applicants" that differed in things like grade point average, major, and university. On-the-job experience—for instance, via internships—seemed to be the single most important factor in getting a job interview.[139] Beyond that, there are career tests and exercises you can use.

IDENTIFY YOUR OCCUPATIONAL ORIENTATION Career-counseling expert John Holland says that personality (including values, motives, and needs) is one career choice determinant. For example, a person with a strong social orientation on Holland's Self-Directed Search (SDS) might be attracted to careers that entail interpersonal rather than intellectual or physical activities and to occupations such as social work. Based on research with his earlier Vocational Preference Test (VPT), Holland found six basic personality types or orientations (see www.self-directed-search.com).[140]

1. ***Realistic orientation.*** These people are attracted to occupations that involve physical activities requiring skill, strength, and coordination. Examples include forestry, farming, and agriculture.
2. ***Investigative orientation.*** Investigative people are attracted to careers that involve cognitive activities (thinking, organizing, understanding) rather than affective activities (feeling, acting, or interpersonal and emotional tasks). Examples include biologist, chemist, and college professor.
3. ***Artistic orientation.*** People here are attracted to careers that involve self-expression, artistic creation, expression of emotions, and individualistic activities. Examples include artists, advertising executives, and musicians.
4. ***Social orientation.*** These people are attracted to careers that involve interpersonal rather than intellectual or physical activities. Examples include clinical psychology, foreign service, and social work.
5. ***Enterprising orientation.*** Verbal activities aimed at influencing others characterize enterprising personalities. Examples include managers, lawyers, and public relations executives.

6. ***Conventional orientation.*** A conventional orientation favors careers that involve structured, rule-regulated activities, as well as careers in which it is expected that the employee subordinate his or her personal needs to those of the organization. Examples include accountants and bankers.

Most people have more than one "RIASEC" occupational orientation (they might be social, realistic, and investigative, for example), and Holland believed that the more similar or compatible these orientations are, the less internal conflict or indecision a person will face in making a career choice. You can take Holland's SDS online for a small fee (see www.self-directed-search.com). Of course, as someone gains experience, it is possible (or likely) that his or her RIASEC scores will change over time.[141]

IDENTIFY YOUR SKILLS You may have a "conventional" orientation, but whether you have *the skills* to be an accountant, banker, or credit manager will affect which occupation you ultimately choose. Therefore, you have to identify your skills. We presented some exercises for this earlier in this chapter, on page 314.

APTITUDES AND SPECIAL TALENTS For career planning purposes, a person's aptitudes are usually measured with a test battery such as the general aptitude test battery (GATB), which most state one-stop career centers make available. This instrument measures various aptitudes including intelligence and mathematical ability. You can also use specialized tests, such as for mechanical comprehension. Holland's Self-Directed Search will also provide some insights into your aptitudes, as will O*NET.[142]

O*NET O*NET offers a free online "My Next Move" career assessment system (https://www.onetonline.org/help/onet/mynextmove).[143] It includes *O*NET Interest Profiler*, a tool that offers customized career suggestions on over 900 different careers based on a person's interests and level of education and work experience. Users obtain important information including skills, tasks, salaries, and employment outlook for occupations.[144]

IDENTIFY YOUR CAREER ANCHORS Professor Edgar Schein says that career planning is a continuing process of discovery—one in which a person slowly develops a clearer occupational self-concept in terms of what his or her talents, abilities, motives, needs, attitudes, and values are. Schein also says that as you learn more about yourself, it becomes apparent that you have a dominant *career anchor*, a concern or value that you will not give up if a [career] choice has to be made.

Career anchors, as their name implies, are the pivots around which a person's career swings; a person becomes conscious of them because of learning, through experience, about his or her talents and abilities, motives and needs, and attitudes and values. Based on his research at the Massachusetts Institute of Technology, Schein believes that career anchors are difficult to predict because they are evolutionary and a product of

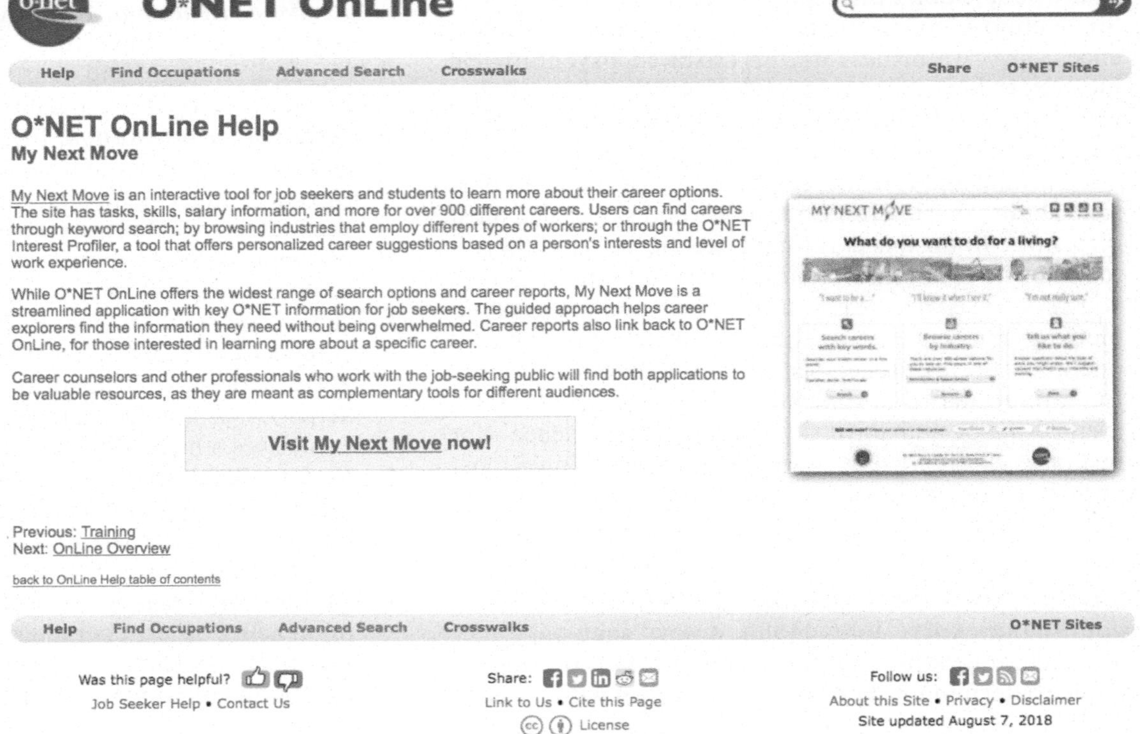

As noted in the accompanying text, O*NET offers a free comprehensive online "My Next Move" occupation and career assessment system for building your future career (https://www.onetonline.org/help/onet/mynextmove).

Source: https://www.onetonline.org/help/onet/mynextmove, accessed August 6, 2018.

a process of discovery. Some people may never find out what their career anchors are until they have to make a major choice—such as whether to take the promotion to the headquarters staff or strike out on their own by starting a business. It is at this point that all the person's past work experiences, interests, aptitudes, and orientations converge into a meaningful pattern that helps show what (career anchor) is the most important factor in driving the person's career choices. Based on his study of MIT graduates, Schein identified five career anchors.[145]

TECHNICAL/FUNCTIONAL COMPETENCE People who had a strong technical/functional career anchor tended to avoid decisions that would drive them toward general management. Instead, they made decisions that would enable them to remain and grow in their chosen technical or functional fields.

MANAGERIAL COMPETENCE Other people showed a strong motivation to become managers, and their career experience enabled them to believe they had the skills and values required. A management position of high responsibility is their ultimate goal. When pressed to explain why they believed they had the skills necessary to gain such positions, many in Schein's research sample answered that they were qualified because of what they saw as their competencies in a combination of three areas: (1) *analytical competence* (ability to identify, analyze, and solve problems under conditions of incomplete information and uncertainty); (2) *interpersonal competence* (ability to influence, supervise, lead, manipulate, and control people at all levels); and (3) *emotional competence* (the capacity to be stimulated by emotional and interpersonal crises rather than exhausted or debilitated by them, and the capacity to bear high levels of responsibility without becoming paralyzed).

CREATIVITY Some of the graduates had become successful entrepreneurs. To Schein these people seemed to have a need "to build or create something that was entirely their own product—a product or process that bears their name, a company of their own, or a personal fortune that reflects their accomplishments." For example, one graduate had become a successful purchaser, restorer, and renter of townhouses in a large city; another had built a successful consulting firm.

AUTONOMY AND INDEPENDENCE Some seemed driven by the need to be on their own, free of the dependence that can arise when a person elects to work in a large organization where promotions, transfers, and salary decisions make them subordinate to others. Many of these graduates also had a strong technical/functional orientation. Instead of pursuing this orientation in an organization, they had decided to become consultants, working either alone or as part of a relatively small firm. Others had become professors of business, freelance writers, and proprietors of a small retail business.

SECURITY A few of the graduates were mostly concerned with long-run career stability and job security. They seemed willing to do what was required to maintain job security, a decent income, and a stable future in the form of a good retirement program and benefits. For those interested in *geographic security*, maintaining a stable, secure career in familiar surroundings was generally more important than pursuing superior career choices, if choosing the latter meant injecting instability or insecurity into their lives by forcing them to pull up roots and move to another city. For others, security meant *organizational security*. They might today opt for government jobs, where tenure still tends to be a way of life. They were much more willing to let their employers decide what their careers should be.

ASSESSING CAREER ANCHORS To help you identify career anchors, take a few sheets of blank paper and write out your answers to the following questions:[146]

1. What was your major area of concentration (if any) in high school? Why did you choose that area? How did you feel about it?
2. What is (or was) your major area of concentration in college? Why did you choose that area? How did you feel about it?
3. What was your first job after school? (Include military if relevant.) What were you looking for in your first job?
4. What were your ambitions or long-range goals when you started your career? Have they changed? When? Why?
5. What was your first major change of job or company? What were you looking for in your next job?
6. What was your next major change of job, company, or career? Why did you initiate or accept it? What were you looking for? (Do this for each of your major changes of job, company, or career.)
7. As you look back over your career, identify some times you have especially enjoyed. What was it about those times that you enjoyed?
8. As you look back, identify some times you have not especially enjoyed. What was it about those times you did not enjoy?
9. Have you ever refused a job move or promotion? Why?
10. Now review all your answers carefully, as well as the descriptions for the five career anchors (technical/functional competence, managerial competence, creativity and independence, autonomy, security). Based on your answers to the questions, rate, for yourself, each of the anchors from 1 to 5. 1 equals low importance, 5 equals high importance.

Technical/functional competence ______________
Managerial competence ______________
Creativity and independence ______________
Autonomy ______________
Security ______________

What Do You Want to Do?

IDENTIFY HIGH-POTENTIAL OCCUPATIONS Learning about your skills and interests is only step one in choosing an occupation. You also have to identify those occupations that fit your occupational orientations, skills, career anchors, and occupational preferences, and that are (preferably) in high demand in the years to come.

Here, use the Internet. The U.S. Department of Labor's online *Occupational Outlook Handbook* (https://www.bls.gov/ooh/) is updated each year, and provides detailed descriptions and information on hundreds of occupations.[147] O*NET (https://www.onetonline.org/) provides occupational demand projections. Another site here is https://www.ncda.org/aws/NCDA/pt/sp/resources.

Finding the Right Job

Your next step is to find a job that you want in the company and locale where you want to work.

Before leaving a current job, make sure leaving is what you want. Many people, dissatisfied at work, assume it must be the job or the occupation. But why switch from being a lawyer to a teacher, when it's not the profession but your law firm's 80-hour weeks that are the problem?

One must use a process of elimination. For example, you may like your occupation and employer, but not how your specific job is structured. Others may find their employers' ways of doing things are the problem. Or, it may in fact be the occupation.

In any case, the solution should fit the cause. For example, if, after thinking it through, you are satisfied with your occupation and where you work, but not with your job as it's organized now, try reconfiguring it. For example, seek to delegate or eliminate job functions you least prefer; volunteer for new duties; seek out a challenging "stretch assignment"; even "decluttering" your office may help.[148] If it's the specific employer, look elsewhere.

If you're involuntarily out of work for more than a few years, perhaps take extra care. One study followed a group of workers, some of whom became and stayed unemployed. These unemployed workers' personalities changed. In before-and-after testing, the long-term unemployed showed reduced levels of agreeableness, conscientiousness, and openness. Don't hesitate to get some supportive counselling if need be.[149]

JOB SEARCH TECHNIQUES Many people send out hundreds of resumes and get few replies. As we saw in Chapters 4 (Recruiting) and 5 (Selection) modern digital tools attract huge numbers of applicants and use software to screen out almost all of them.

As a result, most people seek jobs in a manner that's almost exactly opposite to the approach most experts deem best. For example, in surveys of human resource professionals, about 70% say the best way to get a job is through referrals, but less than 10% of job seekers see referrals as their best option. Instead they rely on job boards, which HR professionals rank much lower. Use sites such as LinkedIn and Facebook to help build your network, and to publicize your availability to potential job referrers.[150]

PERSONAL CONTACTS *The best way to get job leads is usually through personal contacts (networking)*, such as friends, former colleagues, and relatives.[151] Let as many responsible people as possible know that you're looking for a job and the kind of job you want. (Beware, though, if you don't want your job search getting back to your current boss. If that's the case, then just choose two or three close friends and ask them to be discreet checking around for you.)

No matter how close your friends are to you, by the way, you do not want to impose on them—they're not an employment agency, remember. It's usually best to just ask them for the name of someone they think you should talk to. Then you do the heavy lifting.

SOCIAL MEDIA In one survey, about 90% of HR professionals surveyed said it was "very important" or "somewhat important" for job seekers to be on LinkedIn, about 83% said the same for being on the job hunter's professional or association site, and about 60% cited Facebook.[152]

Employers scour social media for recruits, so job seekers should make sure their names stand out. For example, create a Twitter presence. Those "Liking" a company on Facebook may receive early notice of job openings. Spend a few minutes each day on LinkedIn making new connections, and share links and advice with your LinkedIn network.[153] Join LinkedIn industry groups to build visibility. Make sure your résumé is in PDF format and readable on a phone screen. To bring yourself to recruiters' attention, follow up on comments they make on their blogs or on industry websites. *Social résumés* provide snapshots of who the job searcher is by combining text material, photos, and samples of a person's work in infographic résumés posted on social media such as Twitter, LinkedIn, and blogs.[154]

Finally, remember that prospective employers may Google you before extending the offer, and ask for access to your Facebook and LinkedIn pages. Be careful what's on them.

ONLINE JOB BOARDS AND EMPLOYER WEBSITES Most large job search sites such as Monster.com have local-area search capabilities. Useful open-job aggregator sites include Indeed.com and SimplyHired.com. Idealist.com is good for nonprofit jobs, and there's USAJobs for federal jobs.[155] Use *The Wall Street Journal's* career Web site (www.careerjournal.com) for career advice and insights. Most big-city newspapers also have their own (or links to) online local job listings. In addition to job boards like Monster and specialized ones (like https://www.efinancialcareers.com/), virtually all large companies, industries, and crafts have their own specialized sites. For example, the American Marketing Association (https://jobs.ama.org/) and Financial Executives International (www.fei.org) have active job sites.

ANSWERING ADVERTISEMENTS Answering ads is a low-probability way to get a job, and this is particularly so as the level of jobs increases. Furthermore, applicant tracking services crunch through thousands of résumés in seconds, making it even harder to stand out by answering ads. Nevertheless, good sources of classified ads for professionals and managers include *The New York Times*, *The Wall Street Journal*, and specialized journals in your field that list job openings. All these sources also post the positions online, of course.

For application letters or résumés, be sure to create the right impression with the materials you submit; check the style, grammar, and neatness, and adapt your résumé to the job for which you are applying. In your cover letter or email, specifically address why your background and accomplishments fit the advertised position.

Be careful in replying to blind ads. Some recruiters and employers run ads even when no position exists just to gauge the market, and there is also some risk of blundering into responding to your own firm.

EMPLOYMENT AGENCIES Agencies are especially good at placing people in jobs paying up to about $80,000, but they can be useful for higher-paying jobs as well. The employer usually pays the fees for professional and management jobs. Assuming you know the job you want, review a few back issues of your paper's Sunday classified ads and sites like LinkedIn to identify agencies that handle the positions you want. Approach three or four initially, preferably in response to specific ads, and avoid signing any contract that gives an agency the exclusive right to place you.

States' one-stop career centers can be helpful. In them, job seekers can not only apply for unemployment benefits, but also register with the state job service, talk to career counselors, use computers to write résumés and access the Internet, take tests, and use career libraries offering books and videos on various employment topics. In some centers job hunters can make use of free computers and photocopiers to facilitate job searches.

EXECUTIVE RECRUITERS Employers retain executive recruiters to seek out top talent for their clients; employers always pay any fees. Recruiters do not do career counseling, but if you know the job you want, it pays to contact a few (but they usually use contacts, and LinkedIn to find passive candidates). Send/email your résumé and a cover note summarizing your objective in precise terms, including job title and the size of company desired, work-related accomplishments, current salary, and salary requirements. (Beware, because some firms call themselves executive search or career consultants but do no searches: In return for an (often hefty) fee they help you manage your search. Remember that with a search firm you never pay a fee.)

CAREER COUNSELORS Career counselors will not help you find a job per se; rather, they specialize in aptitude testing, career counseling, and resume preparation. Search under "Career Counseling" or "Vocational Guidance." Their services usually cost $500 or so and may include some psychological testing and interviews with an experienced career counselor. Check the firm's services, prices, and history as well as the credentials of the person you will be dealing with.

EXECUTIVE SEARCH CONSULTANTS Executive marketing consultants manage your job-hunting campaign. They generally are not recruiters and do not have jobs to fill. Depending on the services you choose, your cost will range from $600 to $5,000 or more. The process may involve months of weekly meetings. Services include résumé and letter writing, interview skill building, and developing a full job-hunting campaign. Before approaching a consultant, it's advisable to do your own self-appraisal (as explained in this appendix) and read books like Richard Bolles's *What Color Is Your Parachute?*

Also do your due diligence, and remember these consultants are *not* recruiters and will not get you a job—you must do the legwork. Then check the Better Business Bureau, and decide which of these firms (if any) is for you.

WRITING YOUR RÉSUMÉ Your résumé usually still plays a big role in determining whether you get the interview. Of course, don't produce a slipshod résumé: Avoid overcrowded pages, hard-to-read copies, typographical errors, and other problems of this sort. And do not use a make-do résumé. Produce a new résumé for each job you are applying for, gearing your job objective and accomplishments to the job you want. Here are some résumé pointers, as offered by employment counselor Richard Payne and other experts.[156]

Start your résumé with your name, home and e-mail and website (if any) addresses, and home or cell phone number. Next, state your *job objective*. Gear this to the job you're applying for. It should summarize in one sentence the specific position you want, where you want to do it (type and size of company), and a special reason an employer might have for wanting you to fill the job.

For example, "Marketing manager in a medium-size e-commerce company in a situation in which strong creative skills would be valuable."

For each of your previous jobs, write a paragraph that shows job title, whom (job title) you reported to, who reported to you, how many people reported to you, the operational and human resource budgets you controlled, and what your job entailed (in one sentence).

Your accomplishments should be the heart of your résumé. These show for each of your previous jobs: (1) a concrete action you took and why you took it and (2) the specific result of your action—the "payoff." For example, "As production supervisor, I introduced a new process to replace costly hand soldering of component parts. The new process reduced assembly time per unit from 30 to 10 minutes and reduced labor costs by over 60%." Use several of these statements for each job.

Keep your résumé to two pages or less, and list education, military service (if any), and personal background (hobbies, interests, associations) on the last page. For most job applications today, it's important that the résumé is electronically readable. Applicant tracking systems scan through résumés, screening out those that don't seem to match (often based on the absence of certain key words). Therefore, present your qualifications using powerful key words appropriate to the job or jobs for which you are applying. For example, a trainer might use key words and phrases such as: *computer-based training, interactive video*, and *group facilitator*.

If you post your résumé online, experts suggest taking precautions. At a minimum, date your résumé (in case it lands on your boss's desk 2 years from now). Also insert a disclaimer forbidding unauthorized transmission by headhunters; consider posting a "confidential" resume on a job board listing your capabilities but not your name or employer—you can be reached via the job board. Scammers will use someone's online resume to pretend to be an employer, and then request bank account information "to facilitate salary direct deposits".[157]

CHAPTER 10

ONLINE BIOS Employers often encourage or require their professionals and managers to post brief biographies on corporate intranets or websites. These bios let other employees know about their colleagues' expertise; they can also attract recruiters' inquiries. Tips for writing such bios include:[158]

Fill it with details. "The more information you enter, the more likely a person seeking someone with your background will find you."

Avoid touchy subjects. For example, avoid religion and politics.

Look the part. Your profile may require posting photos. If so, dress in professional attire.

Make it search friendly. Make sure your profile contains the key words you think someone searching for someone with your background and expertise would be looking for, such as *manager, supervisor*, or *engineer*.

Use abbreviations. Abbreviations are important. For example, someone searching the site might more readily punch in "MBA" than "Masters in Business Administration."

Say it with numbers. Describe specifically how your work has contributed to your current employer's and past employer's bottom lines.

Proofread. Carefully proofread your online profile, as you would your résumé.

Handling the Interview

You have done all your homework, and now you have a job interview scheduled. What must you do to excel in the interview? First review our "Interview Guide for Interviewees" on page 234. Then, here are other suggestions.

PREPARE Before the interview, learn about the employer, the job, and the people doing the recruiting. Search the Internet to find out what's happening in the industry. Know that you may have a "job tryout," in which you'll have to show how well you can do aspects of the job.[159] Many locales prohibit employers from asking applicants about their salary histories, but realistically be prepared to answer when the interviewer asks for your salary requirements.

FIRST IMPRESSIONS Interviewers usually jump to conclusions about candidates during the first few seconds of the interview. Therefore, you really do have just one chance to make a good first impression. Appropriate clothing, good grooming and posture, eye contact, a firm handshake, and energy are important.

UNCOVER THE INTERVIEWER'S NEEDS Spend as little time as possible answering your interviewer's first questions and as much time as possible getting the person to describe his or her needs—what the person is looking to get accomplished and the type of person needed. Use open-ended questions, such as "Could you tell me more about that?"

RELATE YOURSELF TO THE PERSON'S NEEDS Once you understand the person your interviewer is looking for and the sorts of problems he or she needs solved, you are in a good position to describe your own accomplishments in terms of the interviewer's needs.[160] Start by saying something like, "One of the problem areas you've indicated is important to you is similar to a problem I once faced." Then state the problem, describe your solution, and reveal the results.

MAKE A GOOD APPEARANCE AND SHOW ENTHUSIASM Appearance, a firm handshake, and visual cues such as looking the interviewer in the eyes are crucial. Remember that studies of interviews show that in almost 80% of the cases, interviewers make up their minds about the applicant during the first few moments of the interview. A good first impression may turn bad during the interview, but it is unlikely. Bad first impressions, however, are almost impossible to overcome.

NONVERBAL BEHAVIOR AND IMPRESSION MANAGEMENT Remember (Chapter 7) that your *non*verbal behavior will have a big impact on your interview rating. In one study, 23 of the 26 human resources specialists who saw the high-eye-contact, high-energy-level candidate would have invited him or her for a second interview. *None* who saw the low-eye-contact, low-energy-level candidate would have done so.

Similarly, **self-promotion (promoting one's own skills and competence)** is strongly related to the interviewer's perceptions of candidate–job fit. Some interviewees use "ingratiation" to persuade interviewers to like them: For instance, they praised the interviewers or agreed with their opinions, thus signaling they shared similar beliefs.

Some candidates check with recruiters to determine their status, which can be a turnoff. Something more subtle, like sending a link to an article touching on something you discussed with the recruiter, is usually better.[161]

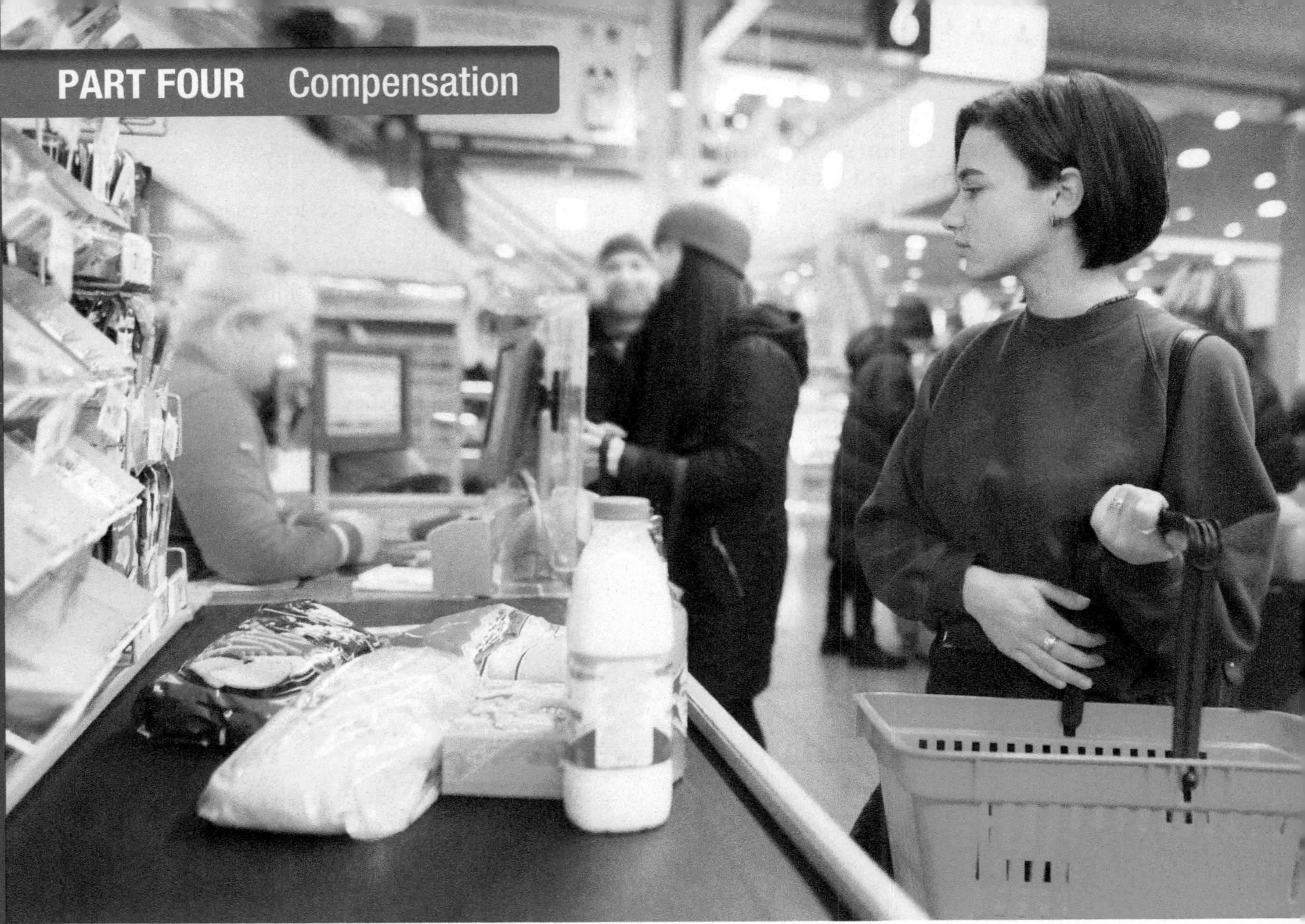
Bodnar Taras/Shutterstock

11 Establishing Strategic Pay Plans

LEARNING OBJECTIVES

When you finish studying this chapter, you should be able to:

11-1 **List** the basic factors determining pay rates.

11-2 **Define and give** an example of how to conduct a job evaluation.

11-3 **Explain** in detail how to establish a market-competitive pay plan.

11-4 **Explain** how to price managerial and professional jobs.

11-5 **Explain** the difference between competency-based and traditional pay plans.

11-6 **Describe** the importance of total rewards for improving employee engagement.

In the grocery business, when Walmart opens a store, the nearby stores' usual reaction is to cut costs, particularly wages and benefits. So as Wegmans Food Markets, Inc., adds more stores and increasingly competes with Walmart, its management needs to decide this: Should we cut pay to better compete based on cost, or pursue a different compensation strategy?[1] We'll see how Wegmans boosted profits by raising pay.

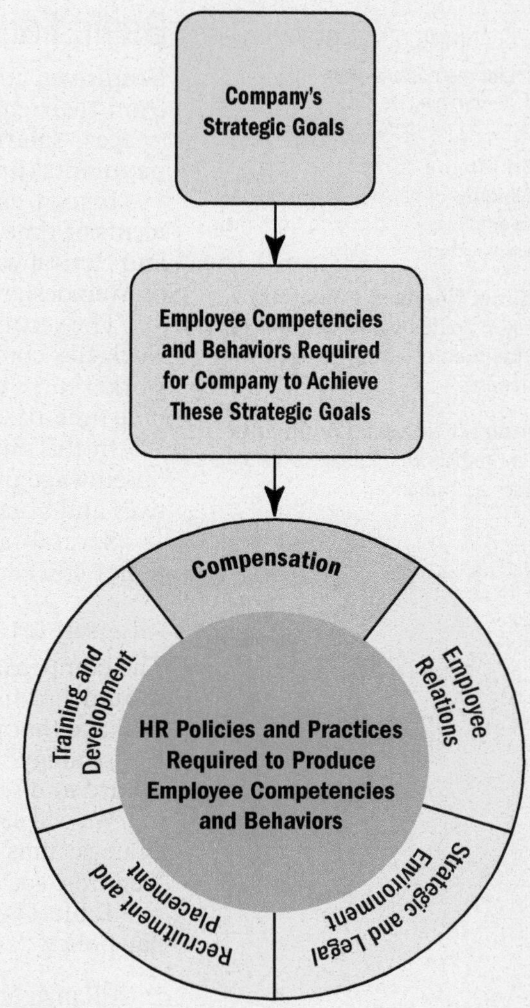

WHERE ARE WE NOW . . .

Once you've appraised and coached your employees, they of course expect to be paid. Prudent employers don't set pay rates arbitrarily. Each employee's pay should make sense in terms of what other employees earn, and this requires a pay plan. The main purpose of this chapter is to show you how to establish a pay plan. The main topics we cover are **Basic Factors in Determining Pay Rates**, **Job Evaluation Methods**, **How to Create a Market-Competitive Pay Plan**, **Pricing Managerial and Professional Jobs**, **Contemporary Topics in Compensation**, and **Total Rewards for Employee Engagement**. The next chapter focuses specifically on pay-for-performance and incentive plans.

LEARNING OBJECTIVE 11-1

List the basic factors determining pay rates.

employee compensation
All forms of pay or rewards going to employees and arising from their employment.

direct financial payments
Pay in the form of wages, salaries, incentives, commissions, and bonuses.

indirect financial payments
Pay in the form of financial benefits such as insurance.

Basic Factors in Determining Pay Rates

Employee compensation includes all forms of pay going to employees and arising from their employment. It has two main components, **direct financial payments** (wages, salaries, incentives, commissions, and bonuses) and **indirect financial payments** (financial benefits like employer-paid insurance and vacations).

In turn, employers can make direct financial payments to employees based on increments of time or based on performance. Time-based pay still predominates. Blue-collar and clerical workers receive hourly or daily wages, for instance. Others, like managers or Web designers, tend to be salaried and paid weekly, monthly, or yearly.

The second direct payment option is to pay for performance. For example, piecework ties compensation to the amount of production (or number of "pieces") the worker turns out. Sales commissions tie pay to sales. Many employers' pay plans combine time-based pay and incentives.

In this chapter, we explain how to formulate plans for paying employees a time-based wage or salary. Subsequent chapters cover performance-based financial incentives and bonuses (Chapter 12) and employee benefits (Chapter 13).

Several factors should influence any pay plan's design. These include strategic policy considerations, as well as equity, legal, and union considerations.

Aligning Total Rewards with Strategy

The compensation plan should first advance the firm's strategic aims—management should produce an *aligned reward strategy.* This means creating a compensation package that produces the employee behaviors the firm needs to achieve its competitive strategy.[2] Put another way, there should be a clear "line of sight" between each reward and specific business goals.

We will see that many employers formulate a total rewards strategy to support their strategic aims. *Total rewards* encompass traditional pay, incentives, and benefits, but also "rewards" such as more challenging jobs (job design), career development, and recognition.

Table 11-1 lists illustrative questions to ask when crafting a strategy-oriented pay policy.

HR in Action at the Hotel Paris Even a casual review by Lisa Cruz and the CFO made it clear that the Hotel Paris's compensation plan wasn't designed to support the firm's new strategic goals. To see how they handled this, see the case on page 384 of this chapter.

Equity and Its Impact on Pay Rates

In studies at Emory University, researchers investigated how capuchin monkeys reacted to inequitable pay. Some monkeys got sweet grapes in return for trading pebbles; others got cucumber slices. If a monkey receiving a cucumber slice saw a neighbor get grapes, it slammed down the pebble or refused to eat.[3] It seems even lower primates may demand fair treatment in pay.

Among humans, too, *the equity theory of motivation* postulates that people are motivated to maintain a balance between what they perceive as their contributions and their rewards. Equity theory states that if a person perceives an inequity, a tension or drive will develop that motivates him or her to reduce the tension and perceived inequity. Research tends to support equity theory, particularly as it applies to those underpaid.[4] For example, in one study turnover of retail buyers was significantly lower when the buyers perceived fair treatment in rewards and in how employers allocated

TABLE 11-1 Do Our Compensation Policies Support Our Strategic Aims?

- What are our strategic aims?
- What employee behaviors and skills do we need to achieve our strategic aims?
- What compensation policies and practices—salary, incentive plans, and benefits—will help to produce the employee behaviors we need to achieve our strategic aims?

rewards.[5] Overpaying can sometimes backfire, too, perhaps "due to feelings of guilt or discomfort."[6]

In compensation, one can address *external, internal, individual*, and *procedural* equity.[7]

- ***External equity*** refers to how a job's pay rate in one company compares to the job's pay rate in other companies.
- ***Internal equity*** refers to how fair the job's pay rate is when compared to other jobs within the same company (for instance, is the sales manager's pay fair, when compared to what the production manager earns?).
- ***Individual equity*** refers to the fairness of an individual's pay as compared with what his or her coworkers are earning for the same or very similar jobs within the company, based on each person's performance.
- ***Procedural equity*** refers to the "perceived fairness of the processes and procedures used to make decisions regarding the allocation of pay."[8]

Managers address equity issues in various ways. They use salary surveys (surveys of what other employers are paying) to monitor and maintain external equity. They use job analysis and comparisons of each job ("job evaluation") to maintain internal equity. They use performance appraisal and incentive pay to maintain individual equity. And they use communications, grievance mechanisms, and employees' participation to help ensure that employees view the pay process as procedurally fair. Some firms administer attitude surveys to monitor employees' pay satisfaction. Questions typically include, "How satisfied are you with your pay?" and "What factors do you believe we used to determine your pay?"[9]

Davis-Bacon Act (1931)
A 1931 law that sets wage rates for laborers employed by contractors working for the federal government.

Walsh-Healey Public Contract Act (1936)
A 1936 law that requires minimum wage and working conditions for employees working on any government contract amounting to more than $10,000.

"Open pay" policies—listing what everyone earns—may help reduce inequities (such as the gender pay gap), but can obviously cause other disagreements.[10] Some firms therefore maintain pay rate secrecy.[11] The research concerning pay secrecy is inconclusive, and most employers don't have open pay policies.[12] However, the federal government mandated pay transparency for all businesses having contracts with it.[13] And of course for external equity, online pay sites like Salary.com preclude secrecy. Short of "open pay," some experts advise at least explaining how the company computes compensation.[14]

Legal Considerations in Compensation

Employers do not have free rein in designing pay plans. Various laws specify things like minimum wages, overtime rates, and benefits.[15] For example, the **1931 Davis-Bacon Act** lets the secretary of labor set wage rates for laborers and mechanics employed by contractors working for the federal government. The **1936 Walsh-Healey Public Contract Act** sets basic labor standards for employees working on any government contract that amounts to more than $10,000. It contains minimum wage, maximum hour, and safety and health provisions, and requires time-and-a-half pay for work over 40 hours a week. **Title VII of the 1964 Civil Rights Act** makes it unlawful for employers to discriminate against any individual with respect to hiring, compensation, terms, conditions, or privileges of employment because of race, color, religion, sex, or national origin.[16] We'll look next at other important compensation-related laws.

Title VII of the 1964 Civil Rights Act
This act makes it unlawful for employers to discriminate against any individual with respect to hiring, compensation, terms, conditions, or privileges of employment because of race, color, religion, sex, or national origin.

Fair Labor Standards Act (1938)
This 1938 act provides for minimum wages, maximum hours, overtime pay, and child labor protection. The law, amended many times, covers most employees.

THE 1938 FAIR LABOR STANDARDS ACT The **Fair Labor Standards Act,** originally passed in 1938 and since amended many times, contains minimum wage, maximum hours, overtime pay, equal pay, record-keeping, and child labor provisions that are familiar to most working people.[17] It covers virtually all U.S. workers engaged in the production and/or sale of goods for interstate and foreign commerce. In addition, agricultural workers and those employed by certain larger retail and service companies are included. State fair labor standards laws cover most employers not covered by the Fair Labor Standards Act (FLSA).[18]

One familiar provision governs *overtime pay.* It says employers must pay overtime at a rate of at least one-and-a-half times normal pay for any hours worked over 40 in a workweek. Thus, if a worker covered by the act works 44 hours in one week, he or she must be paid for 4 of those hours at a rate equal to one-and-a-half times the hourly or weekly base rate the person would have earned for 40 hours.[19] For example, if the person earns $12 an hour (or $480 for a 40-hour week), he or she would be paid at the rate of $18 per hour ($12 times 1.5) for each of the 4 overtime hours worked, or $72 ($18 times 4) for the extra 4 hours. If the employee instead receives time off for the overtime hours, the employer must compute the number of hours granted off at the one-and-a-half-times rate (6 hours off for the 4 hours of overtime in our case), in lieu of overtime pay. The FLSA mandates special damages against employers who pressure workers to work extra hours unpaid.[20]

KNOW YOUR EMPLOYMENT LAW

The Workday

Employers should be vigilant for employees who arrive early or leave late, lest the extra time spent on the property obligate it to compensate the employee for that time. For example, a diligent employee may get dropped off at work early and spend, say, 20 minutes before his or her day actually starts doing work-related chores, like compiling a list of clients to call that day. Tyson Foods recently paid over $12 million to resolve suits by workers who said they should have been paid for time spent putting on and removing their protective work gear.[21] While there is no hard and fast rule, some courts follow the rule that employees who arrive 15 or more minutes early are presumed to be working unless the employer can prove otherwise.[22] If using time clocks, employers should instruct employees not to clock in more than 5–10 minutes early (or out 5–10 minutes late).

Smart phones give employers further reason to meticulously record workers' hours. A Department of Labor app lets employees track their work hours.[23] The Chicago Police Department distributed smart phones to its officers. One officer subsequently sued, claiming he wasn't paid overtime for the hours he spent using his smart phone off the clock. Vendors such as Pacific Timesheet (www.pacifictimesheet.com) provide mobile payroll time sheets.[24] Outside the office, employees can fill these in via their iPhones or similar devices.[25] New time clocks reduce "buddy punching" with instant photos and biometric sensors.[26] ■

The FLSA also sets a *minimum wage*. This sets a floor for employees covered by the act (and usually bumps up wages for practically all workers when Congress raises the minimum). The minimum wage was $7.25 in 2018. Many states have their own minimum wage. For example, the minimum wage as of 2018 was $10.50 in California and $11.00 Massachusetts.[27] New York State is debating raising its minimum wage to $15 per hour. Various cities have set their own (higher) minimum wages.[28] Under new federal rules, workers on federal contracts earn a minimum of $10.10 per hour.[29]

FLSA *child labor provisions* prohibit employing minors between 16 and 18 years old in hazardous occupations, and carefully restrict employment of those under 16.

A great many employers today pay people as "independent contractors" rather than as employees. The Know Your Employment Law feature (page 354) explains about paying this type of worker.

EXEMPT/NONEXEMPT Specific categories of employees are *exempt* from the FLSA or certain provisions of the act, and particularly from the act's overtime provisions. They are "exempt employees." A person's exemption depends on his or her responsibilities, duties, and salary. Bona fide executive, administrative (like office managers), and professional employees (like architects) are generally exempt from the minimum wage and overtime requirements of the act.[30] A white-collar worker earning more than $100,000 and performing any one exempt administrative, executive, or professional duty is automatically ineligible for overtime pay. Other employees can generally earn up to $23,660 per year and still automatically get overtime pay (so most employees earning less than $455 per week are nonexempt and earn overtime).[31] Figure 11-1 lists some examples of typically exempt and nonexempt jobs.

FIGURE 11-1 **Some Typical Exempt, Nonexempt Job Titles**

EXEMPT	NONEXEMPT
Lawyers	Paralegals
Medical doctors	Accounting clerks
Dentists	Bookkeepers
Engineers (with degrees)	Licensed practical nurses
Teachers	Clerical employees
Scientists	Most secretaries (although some, such as the CEO's secretary, might be exempt)
Registered nurses	Lab technicians
General managers	
Pharmacists	
Administrative employees*	

* The administrative exemption is designed for relatively high-level employees whose main job is to "keep the business running." Examples of administrative functions, whose high-level employees may typically be exempt, include labor relations and personnel (human resources employees), payroll and finance (including budgeting and benefits management), records maintenance, accounting and tax, marketing and advertising (as differentiated from direct sales), quality control, public relations (including shareholder or investment relations, and government relations), legal and regulatory compliance, and some computer-related jobs (such as network, Internet, and database administration).

In 2016, the Obama administration mandated new overtime rule exemptions.[32] Instead of the salary threshold of $23,660 per year (below which basically any person working was eligible for overtime pay) the new threshold was $47,476; basically *anyone* earning under $47,476 had to be paid overtime.

A federal judge blocked the new overtime rule, and for now the change is on hold. It appears that the current secretary of labor may agree that $23,660 is too low, but that jumping to more than $47,476 is excessive, so any increase may be less.[33] But to some extent the debate is moot. Many employers, including Walmart, seem to have accepted the new rule. Walmart, for instance, raised managers' salary to over the $47,476 threshold.[34]

If an employee is exempt from the FLSA's minimum wage provisions, then he or she is also exempt from its overtime pay provisions. However, certain employees are *always* exempt from overtime pay provisions. They include, among others, agricultural employees, live-in household employees, taxi drivers, and motion picture theater employees.[35]

Identifying exemptions is tricky. As noted, some jobs—for example, top managers and lawyers—are clearly exempt, while others—such as office workers earning less than $23,660 (as of 2018) per year—are clearly nonexempt. But beyond that, one should review the job before classifying it as exempt or nonexempt. Figure 11-2 presents a procedure for making this decision. Make sure, for instance, that the job currently does in fact require, say, an exempt-type supervisory duty.[36]

FLSA exemption lawsuits are on the rise. "Supervisors" are saying they're not exempt because they don't really supervise two or more employees.[37] And the U.S. Supreme Court held that drug company sales reps that call on doctors are FLSA-exempt outside salespersons.[38]

INEQUITY AND THE MINIMUM WAGE[39] Jamie Dimon, Chairman and CEO of JP Morgan Chase & Company wrote an article for *The New York Times*; he argued that years of wage stagnation had led to income inequality, with some people earning vastly more than others. Several 2016 presidential candidates made similar arguments.[40]

Many municipalities and employers are in fact moving to raise the local minimum wage. The San José, California, City Council voted to raise the local minimum to $15.

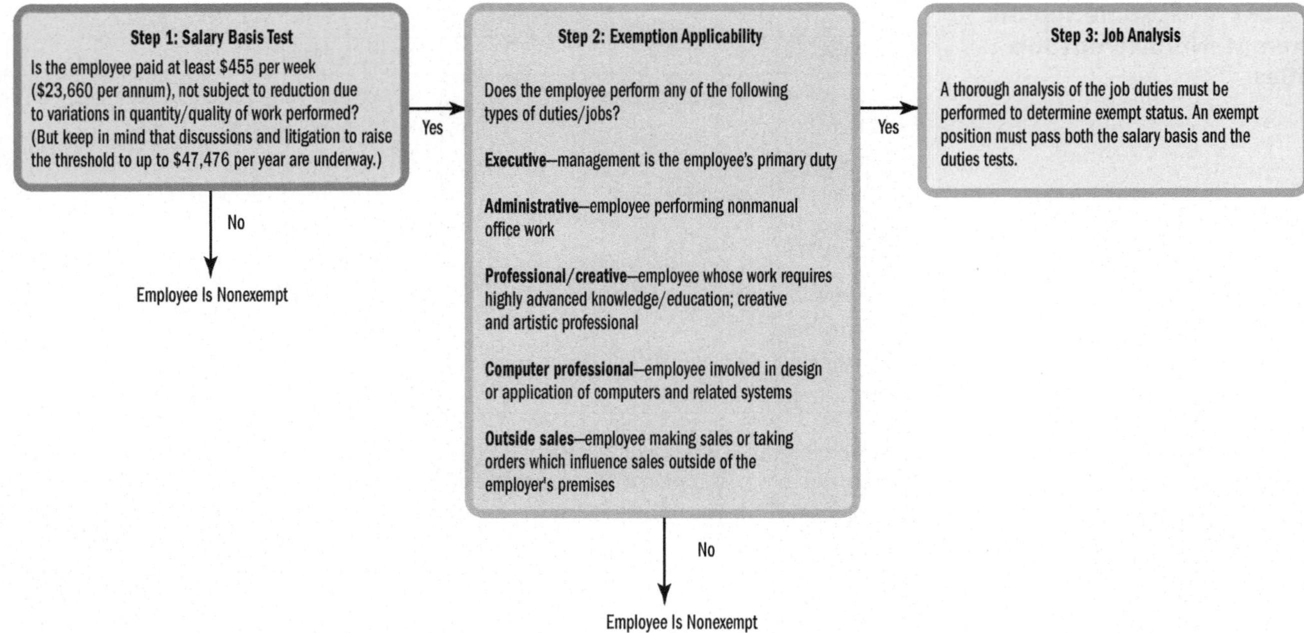

FIGURE 11-2 **Who Is Exempt?; Who Is Not Exempt?**

Source: Based on www.flsa.com/coverage.html, accessed August 5, 2011; https://webapps.dol.gov/elaws/whd/flsa/screen75.asp; www.dol.gov/whd/overtime/fs17a_overview.pdf, both accessed August 9, 2018.

Walmart said it would unilaterally pay all its U.S. hourly workers at least $10 per hour. McDonald's said it would raise its minimum wage to at least one dollar more than the local municipalities' minimum wage in all company-owned stores. MetLife recently set a $15 minimum wage for its employees.[41]

Some economists argue that higher minimum wages reduce the chances that traditionally low-wage workers (like younger people) will get hired. But an increasing number of employers —including Walmart—seem to agree that income inequality needs to be addressed.

KNOW YOUR EMPLOYMENT LAW

The Independent Contractor

Whether someone is an employee or an *independent contractor* is a continuing concern for employers.[42] For example, a federal court ruled that most of FedEx's roughly 15,000 owner–operator delivery people were independent contractors, not employees.[43]

Why claim that someone is an independent contractor? Because the FLSA's overtime and most other requirements do not apply, and the employer need not pay unemployment compensation, payroll taxes, Social Security taxes, or city, state, and federal income taxes or compulsory workers' compensation for that worker.

The problem is that many so-called independent contractor relationships aren't independent contractor relationships. In general, an individual is an independent contractor if the payer has the right to control or direct only the result of the work and not what will be done and how it will be done.[44] However, there is no single rule or test. Instead, courts look at the total situation. The major consideration is this: The more the employer controls what the worker does and how he or she does it, the more likely it is that the courts will find the worker to be an employee. Figure 11-3 lists some factors courts will consider. The IRS lists rules at its Web site.[45] Uber faces lawsuits that its drivers are employees, not independent contractors.

FIGURE 11-3 Independent Contractor or Employee Checklist

Source: Adapted from information in IRS, Employer's Supplemental Tax Guide, https://www.irs.gov/pub/irspdf/p15a.pdf accessed June 6, 2017.

The main question is, how much control does the employer exert over the person at work? Facts that provide evidence of the degree of control/independence fall into three categories: behavioral control, financial control, and relationship of the parties. Affirmative answers below generally suggest "independent contractor."

Behavioral control: Does the business direct and control how the worker does the task, such as:	Independent Contractor	Employee
1. When and where to do the work.		
2. What tools or equipment to use.		
3. What workers to hire or to assist with the work.		
4. Where to purchase supplies and services.		
5. Whether the business has retained the right to control the details of a worker's performance or instead has given up that right.		
Financial control: Does the business control the business/financial aspects of the worker's job, such as:		
6. The extent to which the worker has unreimbursed business expenses.		
7. The extent of the worker's investment.		
8. The extent to which the worker makes his or her services available to other businesses in the relevant market.		
9. Whether the worker is not generally guaranteed a regular wage amount for an hourly, weekly, or other period of time.		
10. The extent to which the worker can realize a profit or loss.		
Questions regarding the parties' relationship include:		
11. Whether the business does not provide the worker with employee-type benefits, such as insurance, a pension plan, vacation pay, or sick pay.		
12. Whether there's no expectation that the relationship will continue indefinitely, rather than for a specific project or period.		

To minimize the risks of independent contractor misclassification, employers should execute written agreements with all independent contractors; you'll find samples online.[46] Furthermore, employers should not impose work rules on or attempt to prohibit independent contractors from working for others. They should require independent contractors to provide their own tools and to be separately incorporated business entities.[47]

Because the Affordable Care Act covers employers with 50 or more employees, government agencies have been looking more closely at employers' independent contractors. To minimize problems, some employers are having staffing companies supply more of their workforce, thus staying below the 50-employee limit.[48] ■

HR AND THE GIG ECONOMY: *ARE GIG WORKERS EMPLOYEES OR INDEPENDENT CONTRACTORS?*

A few years ago, Uber and Lyft drivers filed suit in California, demanding to be treated as employees rather than independent contractors. The companies contend they're independent contractors who can work (or not) as much as they want, start and stop when they want, and use their own cars.

Yet the answer is not clear-cut. Although it's true that there's a lot "independent" about what the drivers do, the drivers' lawyers say that Lyft and Uber control what the drivers do at work. For example, algorithms and systems control what rides the drivers can accept or decline, the routes they take, how much they can earn, and even how they're evaluated (below an average rating of about 4.5 stars, a driver was in danger of deactivation.) The cases settled out of court. Uber agreed to pay about $100 million to drivers in certain states and to let them solicit tips; however, the settlement left the drivers as independent contractors.

Similar litigation continues.[49] Two federal appellate courts recently held that some FedEx drivers were employees, not independent contractors. In another case, an arbitrator ruled Uber drivers were independent contractors. A recent California decision may make it easier for drivers to press for employee status.[50]

Even in traditional workplaces there was some ambiguity about how to distinguish between independent contractors and employees. Today, gig workers are often free to come and go as they please and to quit any time, but at work computer algorithms tightly control their efforts. It's therefore even more difficult to distinguish between employees and independent contractors. Congress seems less inclined to curtail independent contractor use.[51] It is considering new gig economy laws but recently had not taken action.[52] Expect more lawsuits.

MyLab Management Talk About It 1

If your professor assigned this, go to the Assignments section of **www.pearson.com/mylab/management** to complete this discussion question. How would you itemize the arguments for and arguments against making Lyft and Uber drivers independent contractors?

Equal Pay Act
A 1963 amendment to the Fair Labor Standards Act designed to require equal pay for women doing the same work as men.

1963 EQUAL PAY ACT The **Equal Pay Act,** an amendment to the Fair Labor Standards Act, states that employees of one sex may not be paid wages at a rate lower than that paid to employees of the opposite sex for doing roughly equivalent work. Specifically, if the work requires equal skills, effort, and responsibility and involves similar working conditions, employees of both sexes must receive equal pay, unless the differences in pay stem from a seniority system, a merit system, the quantity or quality of production, or "any factor other than sex."

Employee Retirement Income Security Act (ERISA)
The 1974 law that provides government protection of pensions for all employees with company pension plans. It also regulates vesting rights (employees who leave before retirement may claim compensation from the pension plan).

1974 EMPLOYEE RETIREMENT INCOME SECURITY ACT Aimed at protecting employees' pensions, the **Employee Retirement Income Security Act (ERISA)** provides for the creation of government-run, employer-financed corporations to protect employees against the failure of their employers' pension plans. It also sets regulations regarding vesting rights (*vesting* refers to the equity or ownership the employees build up in their pension plans should their employment terminate before retirement). ERISA also regulates *portability rights* (the transfer of an employee's vested rights from one organization to another). It also contains fiduciary standards to prevent dishonesty in pension plan funding.

OTHER LEGISLATION AFFECTING COMPENSATION Various other laws influence compensation decisions. For example, the *Age Discrimination in Employment Act* prohibits age discrimination against employees who are 40 years of age and older in all aspects of employment, including compensation.[53] The *Americans with Disabilities Act* prohibits discrimination against qualified persons with disabilities in all aspects of employment. The *Family and Medical Leave Act* aims to entitle eligible employees, both men and women, to take up to 12 weeks of unpaid, job-protected leave for the birth of a child or for the care of a child, spouse, or parent. And various executive orders require employers that are federal government contractors or subcontractors to not discriminate in certain employment areas, including compensation.

Each state has its own *workers' compensation laws.* Among other things, these aim to provide prompt, sure, and reasonable income to victims of work-related accidents. The *Social Security Act of 1935* (as amended) provides for unemployment compensation for workers unemployed through no fault of their own for up to 26 weeks, and for retirement benefits. (We'll discuss Social Security benefits in a later chapter.) The federal wage garnishment law limits the amount of an employee's earnings that employers can withhold (garnish) per week, and protects the worker from discharge due to garnishment.

Union Influences on Compensation Decisions

Unions and labor relations laws also influence pay plan design. The National Labor Relations Act of 1935 (Wagner Act) granted employees the right to unionize and to bargain collectively. Historically, the wage rate has been the main issue in collective bargaining. However, unions also negotiate other pay-related issues, including time off with pay, income security (for those in industries with periodic layoffs), cost-of-living adjustments, and health care benefits.

The Wagner Act created the National Labor Relations Board (NLRB) to oversee employer practices and ensure that employees receive their rights. To do this, employers must furnish the union with "information that is relevant and necessary" to the union performing its duties.[54] This would include giving the union a written explanation of the employer's "wage curves"—the graph that relates job to pay rate. The union is also entitled to know members' salaries.

Pay Policies

The employer's compensation strategy will manifest itself in *pay policies.* For example, it might be the policy of a top hospital like Johns Hopkins to pay nurses 20% above the market wage.

Four managers discuss a print layout; one happens to be in a wheelchair. Federal law prohibits discrimination against qualified persons with disabilities in all aspects of employment, including compensation.

auremar/123RF

Employers need policies on a variety of compensation-related matters. These would include, for instance, how to set base salary (below, at, or above market rates); what employees (if any) can get stock options; how to award salary increases; how to handle leaves for military service, jury duty, and holidays; and whether to emphasize seniority or performance through annual raises (for example, it takes 18 years for a U.S. federal employee to progress from step 1 to step 9 of the government's pay scale). The accompanying Wegmans Food Markets feature illustrates how pay policies impact a company's performance.

IMPROVING PERFORMANCE: *THE STRATEGIC CONTEXT*

Wegmans Food Markets

Strategic compensation management means formulating a total rewards package that produces the employee skills and behaviors that the company needs to achieve its strategic goals.

Wegmans exemplifies this. It competes in the retail food sector, where profit margins are thin and where online competitors and giants like Walmart drive costs and prices down. The usual competitor's reaction is to cut employee benefits and costs.[55] Wegmans takes a different approach. Number 2 on Fortune's 100 Best Companies to Work For,[56] Wegmans views its workforce as an integral part of achieving Wegmans's strategic aims of *optimizing service while controlling costs by improving systems and productivity*. For example, one dairy department employee designed a new way to organize the cooler, thus improving ordering and inventory control.[57] The firm offers above-market pay rates, affordable health insurance, and a full range of employee benefits.[58] Wegmans's pay policies thus aim to produce exactly the sorts of high-productivity employee behaviors the company needs to achieve its strategic aims.

It's likely that its pay policies are one reason for Wegmans's exceptional profitability. For example, its employee turnover (about 6% for full-timers) is well below the industry's overall average of about 47%.[59] Its stores (which at about 120,000 square feet are much larger than competitors') average about $950,000 a week in sales (compared to a national average of $361,564), or about $49 million in sales annually, compared with a typical Walmart store's grocery sales of $23.5 million in sales.[60] As Wegmans's human resource head has said, good employees assure higher productivity, and that translates into better bottom-line results.[61]

MyLab Management Talk About It 2

If your professor has assigned this, go to the Assignments section of **www.pearson.com/mylab/management** to complete this discussion question. If Wegmans does so well with a high-pay policy, why don't more employers do this as well?

GEOGRAPHY How to account for geographic differences in cost of living is another big pay policy issue. For example, the average base pay for an office supervisor ranges from about $49,980 in Florida to $60,980 in New York.[62]

Employers handle cost-of-living differentials for transferees in several ways. One is to pay a differential for ongoing costs in addition to a one-time allocation. For example, one employer pays a differential of $6,000 per year to people earning $35,000 to $45,000 whom it transfers from Atlanta to Minneapolis. Others simply raise the employee's base salary. The accompanying feature on compensating expatriate employees expands on this.

IMPROVING PERFORMANCE: *HR PRACTICES AROUND THE GLOBE*

Compensating Expatriate Employees

The question of cost-of-living differentials has particular significance to multinational firms, where costs range widely from, say, France to Zambia. The challenge is in maintaining the expatriate's standard of living abroad.[63]

How should multinationals compensate expatriate employees—those it sends overseas? Two basic international compensation policies are popular: *the balance sheet or home-based* plan, and the *host-based plan*.[64]

With a *home-based salary plan*, an international transferee's base salary reflects his or her home country's salary. The employer then adds allowances for cost-of-living differences—housing and schooling costs, for instance, to "make the employee whole." Among other advantages, this approach avoids having to change the employee's home-based salary.

In the *host-based plan*, the firm ties the international transferee's base salary to the host country's salary structure. In other words, the manager from New York who is sent to France would have his or her base salary changed to the prevailing base salary for that position in France, rather than keep the New York base salary. The firm often tacks on cost-of-living, housing, schooling, and other allowances here as well.

Most multinational enterprises set expatriates' salaries according to the *home-based salary plan*. (Thus, a French manager assigned to Kiev by a U.S. multinational will generally have a base salary that reflects the salary structure in the manager's home country, in this case France.) In addition, the person typically gets allowances including cost-of-living, relocation, housing, education, and hardship allowances (for more challenging countries). The employer also usually pays any extra tax burdens resulting from taxes the manager is liable for over and above those he or she would have to pay in the home country.

MyLab Management Talk About It 3

If your professor has assigned this, go to the Assignments section of **www.pearson.com/mylab/management** to complete this discussion question. Why do you think most employers opt for the home-based salary plan?

LEARNING OBJECTIVE 11-2

Define and give an example of how to conduct a job evaluation.

Job Evaluation Methods

Employers use two basic approaches to setting pay rates: *market-based approaches* and *job evaluation methods*. Many firms, particularly smaller ones, simply use a *market-based* approach. Doing so involves conducting formal or informal salary surveys to determine what others in the relevant labor markets are paying for particular jobs. They then use these figures to price their own jobs. *Job evaluation methods* involve assigning values to each of the company's jobs. This process helps produce a pay plan in which each job's pay is equitable based on what other employers are paying for these jobs *and* based on each job's value to the employer.[65]

job evaluation
A systematic comparison done in order to determine the worth of one job relative to another.

Job evaluation is a formal and systematic comparison of jobs to determine the worth of one job relative to another. Job evaluation aims to determine a job's relative worth. Job evaluation eventually results in a *wage* or *salary structure* or hierarchy (this shows the pay rate for various jobs or groups of jobs). The basic principle of job evaluation is this: Jobs that require greater qualifications, more responsibilities, and more complex job duties should receive more pay than jobs with lesser requirements.[66] The basic job evaluation procedure is to compare jobs in relation to one another—for example, in terms of required effort, job complexity, and skills. Suppose you know (based on your job evaluation) the relative worth of the key jobs in your firm. You then conduct a salary survey to see what others are paying for similar jobs. By combining the information from the job evaluation and from the salary survey, you are on your way to being able to create a **market-competitive pay plan**—one where your pay rates are equitable both internally (based on each job's relative value) and externally (in other words, when compared with what other employers are paying).

market-competitive pay plan
Pay plan where pay rates are equitable both internally (based on each job's relative value) and externally (in other words when compared with what other employers are paying).

Compensable Factors

You can use two basic approaches to compare the worth of several jobs. First, you might decide that one job is more important than another is, and not dig any deeper. As an alternative, you could compare the jobs by focusing on certain basic factors the jobs have in common. Compensation management specialists call these **compensable factors**. They are the factors that establish how the jobs compare to one another, and that determine the pay for each job.

compensable factor
A fundamental, compensable element of a job, such as skills, effort, responsibility, and working conditions.

Some employers develop their own compensable factors. However, most use factors popularized by packaged job evaluation systems or by federal legislation. For

The job evaluation committee typically includes at least several employees, and has the important task of evaluating the worth of each job using compensable factors.

Ryan Lees/Agefotostock

example, the Equal Pay Act uses four compensable factors—skills, effort, responsibility, and working conditions. The method popularized by the Hay consulting firm emphasizes three factors: know-how, problem solving, and accountability. Walmart uses knowledge, problem-solving skills, and accountability requirements.

Choosing compensable factors plays a big role in job evaluation. You usually compare each job with all comparable jobs using the same compensable factors. However, the compensable factors you use depend on the job and the job evaluation method. For example, "decision making" might make sense for a manager's job, but not for a cleaner's job.[67]

Preparing for the Job Evaluation

Job evaluation is a judgmental process and demands close cooperation among supervisors, HR specialists, and employees and union representatives. The initial steps include identifying the need for the program, getting cooperation, and then choosing an evaluation committee. The committee then performs the actual evaluation.

Identifying the need for job evaluation shouldn't be difficult. For example, dissatisfaction reflected in high turnover, work stoppages, or arguments may result from paying employees different rates for similar jobs. Managers may express uneasiness with an informal way of assigning pay rates.

Employees may fear that a systematic evaluation of their jobs may reduce their pay rates, so *getting employees to cooperate* in the evaluation is important. For example, you can tell employees that because of the impending job evaluation program, pay rate decisions will no longer be made just by management whim, and that no current employee's rate will be adversely affected because of the job evaluation.

Finally, *choose a job evaluation committee.* The committee usually consists of about five members, most of whom are employees. Management has the right to serve on such committees, but employees may view this with suspicion. However, a human resource specialist can usually be justified to provide expert assistance. Union representation is possible. In most cases, though, the union's position is that it is accepting the results of the job evaluation only as an initial decision and is reserving the right to appeal actual job pricing decisions through grievance or bargaining channels.[68] Once appointed, each committee member should receive a manual explaining both the job evaluation process and how to conduct the job evaluation.

benchmark job
A job that is used to anchor the employer's pay scale and around which other jobs are arranged in order of relative worth.

The evaluation committee then performs three main functions. First, it usually identifies 10 or 15 key **benchmark jobs.** These will be the first jobs they'll evaluate and will serve as the anchors or benchmarks against which the relative importance or value of all other jobs is compared. Next, the committee may select *compensable factors* (although the human resources department will usually choose these). Finally, the committee performs its most important function—actually *evaluating the worth of each job.* For this, the committee will probably use one of the following methods: ranking, job classification, or point method.

Job Evaluation Methods: Ranking

ranking method
The simplest method of job evaluation that involves ranking each job relative to all other jobs, usually based on overall difficulty.

The simplest job evaluation method ranks each job relative to all other jobs, usually based on some overall factor like "job difficulty." There are several steps in the job **ranking method.**

1. ***Obtain job information.*** Job analysis is the first step. Here job descriptions for each job are prepared, and the information they contain about the job's duties is usually the basis for ranking jobs. (Sometimes job specifications are also prepared. However, the ranking method usually ranks jobs based on the whole job, rather than on several compensable factors. Therefore, job specifications, which tend to list job demands in terms of compensable factors such as problem solving, decision making, and skills, are not as important with ranking as they are for other job evaluation methods.)
2. ***Select and group jobs.*** It is usually not practical to make a single ranking for all jobs in an organization. The usual procedure is to rank jobs by department or in clusters (such as factory workers or clerical workers). This removes the need for direct comparison of, say, factory jobs and clerical jobs.
3. ***Select compensable factors.*** In the ranking method, it is common to use just one factor (such as job difficulty) and to rank jobs based on the whole job. However, regardless of the number of factors you choose, explain the definition of the factor(s) to the evaluators carefully so that they all evaluate the jobs consistently.
4. ***Rank jobs.*** For example, each rater gets a set of index cards, each of which contains a brief description of a job. Then they arrange these cards from lowest to highest. Some managers use an "alternation ranking method" to make this procedure more accurate. Here you take the cards, first choosing the highest and the lowest, then the next highest and next lowest, and so forth, until you've ranked all the cards. Table 11-2 illustrates such a job ranking. Jobs in this small health facility rank from orderly up to office manager. The corresponding current pay scales are shown in the column following the job titles. (After ranking, it is possible to slot additional jobs based on their difficulty between those already ranked and to assign each an appropriate wage rate.) The ranked listing of jobs enables us to compare each job's rank with its current pay, and decide if what we are currently paying is internally equitable; we may adjust a job's pay up or down, based on this. Online programs (for example, go to www.hr-guide.com, click under "Job Evaluation, Ranking," and then click "Interactive Ranking Program") can help you rank (and check the rankings of) your positions.[69]
5. ***Combine ratings.*** Usually, several raters rank the jobs independently. Then the rating committee (or the employer) can simply average the raters' rankings.
6. ***Compare current pay with what others are paying based on salary survey.*** Next, we show on the same table (in the middle column) what others in the community are paying for similar jobs, based on a salary survey that we conduct. This helps us ensure that our pay will be *externally* equitable.
7. ***Assign a new pay scale.*** Finally, we compare what we are currently paying for each job with what others are paying, and decide (in this case) to adjust our pay scale by raising what we pay for each job. The last column therefore shows our new pay scale.

This is the simplest job evaluation method, as well as the easiest to explain. And it usually takes less time than other methods.

TABLE 11-2 Job Ranking at Jackson Hospital

Ranking Order	Our Current Annual Pay Scale	What Others Pay: Salary Survey Pay	Our Final Assigned Pay
1. Office manager	$43,000	$45,000	$44,000
2. Chief nurse	42,500	43,000	42,750
3. Bookkeeper	34,000	36,000	35,000
4. Nurse	32,500	33,000	32,750
5. Cook	31,000	32,000	31,500
6. Nurse's aide	28,500	30,500	29,500
7. Orderly	25,500	27,000	27,000

Note: After ranking, it becomes possible to slot additional jobs (based on overall job difficulty, for instance) between those already ranked and to assign each an appropriate wage rate.

Drawbacks derive more from how managers use ranking than from the method itself. For example, there's a tendency to rely too heavily on "guesstimates" (of things like overall difficulty), since ranking usually does not use compensable factors. Similarly, ranking provides no yardstick for quantifying the value of one job relative to another. For example, job number 4 may in fact be five times "more valuable" than job number 5, but with the ranking method all you know is that one job ranks higher than the other. Ranking is usually more appropriate for small employers that can't afford the time or expense of a more elaborate method.

The *factor comparison method* is a special ranking method. It requires ranking each of a job's "factors" (such as education required, experience, and complexity), and then adding up the points representing the number of "degrees" of each factor each job has. Employers seldom use it today.

Job Evaluation Methods: Job Classification

job classification (or job grading)
A method for categorizing jobs into groups.

classes
Grouping jobs based on a set of rules for each group or class, such as amount of independent judgment, skill, physical effort, and so forth, required. Classes usually contain similar jobs.

grades
A job classification system like the class system, although grades often contain dissimilar jobs, such as secretaries, mechanics, and firefighters. Grade descriptions are written based on compensable factors listed in classification systems.

grade definition
Written descriptions of the level of, say, responsibility and knowledge required by jobs in each grade. Similar jobs can then be combined into grades or classes.

Job classification (or job grading) is a simple, widely used job evaluation method in which raters categorize jobs into groups; all the jobs in each group are of roughly the same value for pay purposes. We call these groups **classes** if they contain similar jobs, or **grades** if they contain jobs that are similar in difficulty but otherwise different. Thus, in the federal government's pay grade system, a "press secretary" and a "fire chief" might both be graded "GS-10" (GS stands for "General Schedule"). On the other hand, in its job class system, the state of Florida might classify all "secretary IIs" in one class, all "maintenance engineers" in another, and so forth.

In practice, there are several ways to categorize jobs. One is to write class or grade summaries or descriptions (similar to job descriptions); you then place jobs into the classes or grades based on how well they fit these descriptions. Another is to write a set of compensable factor–based rules for each class (for instance, how much independent judgment, skill, and physical effort does the class of jobs require?). Then categorize each job according to these rules.

The usual procedure blends these two: the analysts choose compensable factors and then develop short class or grade descriptions that describe each class (or grade) in terms of the amount or level of the factors in those jobs. For example, the U.S. government's classification system uses eight compensable factors: (1) difficulty and variety of work, (2) supervision received and exercised, (3) judgment exercised, (4) originality required, (5) nature and purpose of interpersonal work relationships, (6) responsibility, (7) experience, and (8) knowledge required. Based on these compensable factors, raters write a **grade definition** like that in Figure 11-4. This one shows one grade description (for grade GS-7) for the federal government's pay grade system. Then the evaluation committee reviews all job descriptions and slots each job into its appropriate grade, by comparing each job description to the rules in each grade description. Thus, the federal government system classifies the positions *automotive mechanic, welder, electrician,* and *machinist* in grade GS-10.

FIGURE 11-4 Example of a Grade Definition

Source: From "Grade Level Guide for Clerical and Assistance Work" from www.opm.gov/policy-data-oversight/classification-qualifications/classifying-general-schedule-positions/functional-guides/gscler.pdf, accessed September 12, 2018.

Grade	Nature of Assignment	Level of Responsibility
GS-7	Performs specialized duties in a defined functional or program area involving a wide variety of problems or situations; develops information, identifies interrelationships, and takes actions consistent with objectives of the function or program served.	Work is assigned in terms of objectives, priorities, and deadlines; the employee works independently in resolving most conflicts; completed work is evaluated for conformance to policy; guidelines, such as regulations, precedent cases, and policy statements require considerable interpretation and adaptation.

The classification method has several advantages. The main one is that most employers usually end up grouping jobs into classes or grades anyway, regardless of the evaluation method they use. They do this to avoid having to price separately dozens or hundreds of jobs. Of course, the job classification automatically groups the employer's jobs into classes. The disadvantages are that it isn't easy to write the class or grade descriptions, and considerable judgment is required to apply them. Yet many employers use this method with success.

Job Evaluation Methods: Point Method

point method
The job evaluation method in which a number of compensable factors are identified and then the degree to which each of these factors is present on the job is determined.

The **point method's** overall aim is to determine the degree to which the jobs you're evaluating contain selected compensable factors. It involves identifying several compensable factors for the jobs, as well as the degree to which each factor is present in each job. Assume there are five degrees of the compensable factor "responsibility" a job could contain. Further, assume you assign a different number of points to each degree of each compensable factor. Once the evaluation committee determines the degree to which each compensable factor (like "responsibility" and "effort") is present in a job, it can calculate a total point value for the job by adding up the corresponding degree points for each factor. The result is a quantitative point rating for each job. The point method of job evaluation is the most popular job evaluation method today.[70]

"PACKAGED" POINT PLANS A number of groups (such as the Hay Group, the National Electrical Manufacturer's Association, and the National Trade Association) have developed standardized point plans. Many thousands of employers use these systems. They contain ready-made factor and degree definitions and point assessments for a wide range of jobs. Employers can often use them with little or no modification.

Computerized Job Evaluations

Using job evaluation methods such as the point method can be time-consuming. Accumulating the information about "how much" of each compensable factor the job contains is a tedious process. The evaluation committees must debate the level of each compensable factor in each job. They then write down their consensus judgments and compute each job's point values or rankings. Many employers therefore turn to computerized systems (see example on page 364.)

Most such computerized systems have two main components.[71] There is, first, a structured questionnaire. This contains items such as "enter total number of employees who report to this position." Second, such systems may use statistical models. These allow the computer program to price jobs more or less automatically, by assigning points based on the questionnaire responses.

LEARNING OBJECTIVE 11-3
Explain in detail how to establish a market-competitive pay plan.

How to Create a Market-Competitive Pay Plan

As we said, many firms simply price their jobs based on what other employers are paying—they just use a market-based approach. However, most employers also base their pay plans on job evaluation methods like those just described. These evaluations assign

Computer-aided job evaluation can streamline the job evaluation process

Source: Reprinted by permission from Computer-aided job evaluation can streamline the job evaluation process, in Screen capture: www.hrsoftware.netcgi/JobEvaluation.cgi.

values (such as point values) to each job. This helps to produce a pay plan in which each job's pay is internally equitable, based, as it is, on the job's value to the employer (as measured, for instance, by how many points it warrants). However, even with the job evaluation approach, managers must adjust pay rates to fit the market.[72] After all, you want employees' pay to be equitable internally—relative to what their colleagues in the firm are earning—but also competitive externally—relative to what *other employers* are paying. In a *market-competitive pay plan* a job's compensation reflects the job's value in the company, as well as what other employers are paying for similar jobs in the marketplace. Because the point method (or "point-factor method") is so popular, we'll use it as the centerpiece of our step-by-step example for creating a market-competitive pay plan.[73] The 16 steps in creating a market-competitive pay plan begin with choosing benchmark jobs.

1. Choose Benchmark Jobs

Particularly when an employer has dozens or hundreds of different jobs, it's impractical and unnecessary to evaluate each of them separately. Therefore, the first step in the point method is to select benchmark jobs. Benchmark jobs are representative of the jobs the employer needs to evaluate. Like "accounting clerk" they should be common among employers (thus making it easier to survey what competitors are paying for similar jobs).[74]

2. Select Compensable Factors

The choice of compensable factors depends on tradition (as noted, the Equal Pay Act of 1963 uses four compensable factors: skill, effort, responsibility, and working conditions), and on strategic and practical considerations. For example, if your firm's competitive advantage is quality, you might substitute "responsibility for quality" for working conditions, or simply add it as a fifth factor.[75] Similarly, using "working conditions" makes little practical sense for evaluating executive jobs.

The employer should carefully define each factor. This is to ensure that the evaluation committee members will each apply the factors with consistency. Figure 11-5 shows (on

FIGURE 11-5 Illustrative Point Values and Degree Definitions for the Factor Job Complexity

Source: Copyright Gary Dessler, PhD.

Factor Definition: What Is Job Complexity? Job complexity generally refers to the amount of judgment, initiative, ingenuity, and complex data analysis that doing the job requires. To what extent does the person doing this job confront unfamiliar problems, deal with complex decisions, and have to exercise discretion?

Degree	Points	Job Complexity Degree Definitions: What to Look for in the Job
First	120	Here the job is routine and consists of repetitive operations requiring little or no choice of action and the automatic application of easily understood rules and procedures. For example, a filing clerk.
Second	240	Here the employee follows detailed instructions but may have to make limited decisions based on previously prescribed instructions which lay our prescribed alternatives. For example, a billing clerk or a receptionist.
Third	360	Here the employee again follows detailed instructions but because the number of matters to consider is more varied, the employee needs to exhibit initiative and independent judgment, under direct supervision. For example, a nurse's aide.
Fourth	480	Here the employee can generally follow standard practices but the presence of nonroutine problems requires that the employee be able to use initiative and judgment to analyze and evaluate situations, possibly modifying the standard procedures to adjust to the new situations. For example, a nurse.
Fifth	600	On this job, the employee needs to use independent judgment and plan and perform complex work under only general supervision, often working independently toward achieving overall results. For example, medical intern.

top) one such definition, in this case for the factor job complexity. The human resource specialist often draws up the definitions.

3. Assign Weights to Compensable Factors

Having selected compensable factors, the next step is to determine the relative importance (or weighting) of each factor (for instance, how much more important is "skill" than "effort"?). This is important because for each cluster of jobs some factors are bound to be more important than others are. Thus, for executive jobs the "mental requirements" factor would carry far more weight than would "physical requirements." To assign weights, we assume we have a total 100 percentage points to allocate for each job. Then (as an illustration), assign percentage weights of 60% for the factor job complexity, 30% for effort, and 10% for working conditions.[76]

4. Convert Percentages to Points for Each Factor

Next, we want to convert the percentage weights assigned to each compensable factor into point values for each factor (this is, after all, the point method). It is traditional to assume we are working with a total of 1,000 points (although one could use some other figure). To convert percentages to points for each compensable factor, *multiply the percentage weight for each compensable factor (from the previous step) by 1,000.*[77] This will tell you the *maximum number of points* for each compensable factor. Doing so in this case would translate into $1,000 \times 0.60 = 600$ possible points for job complexity, $1,000 \times 0.30 = 300$ points for effort, and $1,000 \times 0.10 = 100$ points for working conditions.

5. Define Each Factor's Degrees

Next, split each factor into degrees, and define (write degree definitions for) each degree so that raters may judge the amount or degree of a factor existing in a job.

Thus, for a compensable factor such as "job complexity" you might choose to have five degrees, ranging from "here the job is routine" to "uses independent judgment." (Our definitions for each degree are shown in Figure 11-5 under "Job Complexity Degree Definitions: What to Look for in the Job.") The number of degrees usually does not exceed five or six, and the actual number depends mostly on judgment. Thus, if all employees work either in a quiet, air-conditioned office or in a noisy, hot factory, then two degrees would probably suffice for the factor "working conditions." You need not have the same number of degrees for each factor, and you should limit degrees to the number necessary to distinguish among jobs.

6. Determine for Each Factor Its Factor Degrees' Points

The evaluation committee must be able to determine the number of points each job is worth. To do this, the committee must be able to examine each job and (from each factor's degree definitions) *determine what degree of each compensable factor* that job has. For them to do this, we must first assign points to *each degree of each compensable factor*. For example, in our illustration, we have five possible degrees of job complexity, and the job complexity compensable factor is worth up to 600 points maximum. In our case, we simply decide that the first degree level of job complexity is worth 120 (or one-fifth of 600) points, the second degree level is worth 240 points, the third degree level is worth 360 points, the fourth degree level is worth 480 points, and the fifth degree is worth the maximum 600 points (see Figure 11-5).[78] Do this for each factor (as in Table 11-3).

7. Review Job Descriptions and Job Specifications

The heart of job *evaluation* involves determining the amount or degree to which the job contains the selected compensable factors such as effort, job complexity, and working conditions. The team conducting the job evaluation will frequently do so by first reviewing each job's job description and job specification. As we explained in Chapter 4 (Job Analysis), it is through the job analysis that the manager identifies the job's duties and responsibilities and writes the job description and job specification. Ideally, therefore, the job analyst included, in the job description and specification, information about the compensable factors (such as job complexity) around which the employer plans to build its compensation plan.[79]

8. Evaluate the Jobs

Steps 1–7 provide us with the information (for instance, on points and degrees) based on which we can evaluate the jobs. The committee has also gathered the job descriptions and job specifications for the benchmark jobs they will focus on.

Then, from their review of each job description and job specification, the committee *determines the degree to which each compensable factor is present in each job*. Thus for, say, a job of master mechanic, the team might conclude (after studying the job description and job specification) that the master mechanic's job deserves the third-degree level of *job complexity* points, the first-degree level of *effort*, and the first-degree level of *working conditions*.

Knowing the job complexity, effort, and working conditions degrees for each job, *and knowing the number of points we previously assigned to each degree* of each

TABLE 11-3 Points Assigned to Factors and to Their Degrees (Revised)

Factors	First-Degree Points	Second-Degree Points	Third-Degree Points	Fourth-Degree Points	Fifth-Degree Points
Job complexity (Total maximum points equal 600)	120	240	360	480	600
Effort (Total maximum points equal 300)	60	120	180	240	300
Working conditions (Total maximum points equal 100 points)	20	40	60	80	100

compensable factor, we can now determine how many job complexity, effort, and working conditions points each benchmark job should contain. (We know the degree level for each factor for each job, so we merely check the corresponding points [see Table 11-3] that we previously assigned to each of these degrees.)

Finally, we add up these degree points for each job to determine each job's total number of points.[80] The master mechanic job gets 360 + 60 + 20 = 440 points from Table 11-3. This enables us to list a hierarchy of jobs, based upon each job's points. We can soon turn to assigning wage rates to each job (step 9). But first, we should define market-competitive pay plan and wage curve.

What should the pay rate be for each job? Of course, jobs with more points should command higher pay. The question is what pay rate to use. Our company's current, "internal" pay rates? Or pay rates based on what the "external" market is paying?[81]

market-competitive pay system
A pay system in which the employer's actual pay rates are competitive with those in the relevant labor market.

With a **market-competitive pay system,** the employer's actual pay rates are competitive with those in the relevant labor market, as well as equitable internally.[82] Put simply, the basic approach is to compare what the employer is *currently* paying for each job ("internal pay") with what the market is paying for the same or similar job ("external pay"), and then to combine this information to produce a market-competitive pay system.

wage curve
Shows the relationship between the value of the job and the average wage paid for this job.

WAGE CURVES **Wage curves** play a central role in assigning wage rates to jobs. The wage curve typically shows the pay rates paid for jobs, relative to the points or rankings assigned to each job by the job evaluation. Figure 11-6 presents an example. Note that it shows pay rates for jobs on the vertical axis, and point values for these jobs along the horizontal axis. The purpose of the wage curve is to show the relationships between (1) the value of the job (expressed in points) as determined by one of the job evaluation methods and (2) the pay rates for the job. (We'll see that many employers may combine jobs into classes or grades. Here the wage curve would show the relationship between average pay rates for each grade, and each grade's average point value.) The pay rates on the wage curve are traditionally those now paid by the employer. However, if there is reason to believe the current pay rates are out of step with the market rates for these jobs, the employer will have to adjust them. One way to do this is to compare a wage curve that shows the jobs' *current* wage rates relative to the jobs' points, with a second curve that shows *market* wage rates relative to points. We do this as follows.

9. Draw the Current (Internal) Wage Curve

First, to study how each job's points relates to its current pay rate, we start by drawing an *internal wage curve.* Plotting each job's points and the wage rate the employer is now paying for each job (or wage rates, if there are several for each job) produces a scatter plot as in Figure 11-7 (left). We now draw a wage curve (on the right) through these

FIGURE 11-6 Plotting a Wage Curve

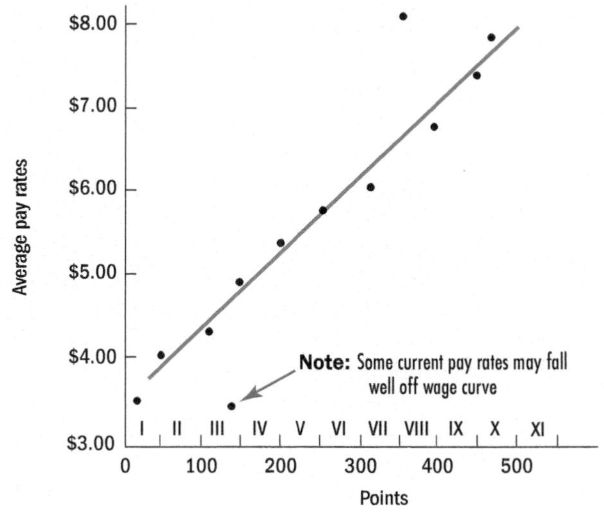

FIGURE 11-7 **The Current/ Internal Wage Curve**

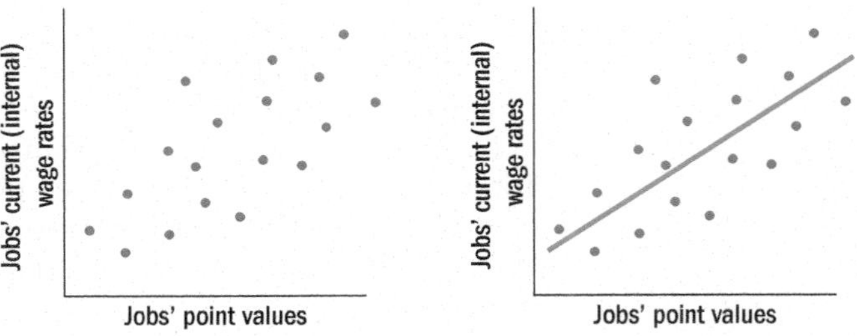

plots that shows how point values relate to current wage rates. We can draw this wage line by just estimating a line that best fits the plotted points (by minimizing the distances between the plots and the curve). Or we can use regression, a statistical technique. Using the latter will produce a current/internal wage curve that best fits the plotted points. In any case, we show the results in Figure 11-7 (right).[83]

10. Conduct a Market Analysis: Salary Surveys

salary survey
A survey aimed at determining prevailing wage rates. A good salary survey provides specific wage rates for specific jobs. Formal written questionnaire surveys are the most comprehensive, but telephone surveys and newspaper ads are also sources of information.

Next, we must compile the information needed to draw an *external wage curve* for our jobs, based on what other employers are paying for similar jobs. **Salary surveys**—surveys of what others are paying—play a big role in pricing jobs.[84] Employers use salary surveys in three ways. First, they use survey data to price benchmark jobs. Benchmark jobs are the anchor jobs around which they slot their other jobs, based on each job's relative worth to the firm. Second, employers typically price 20% or more of their positions directly in the marketplace (rather than relative to the firm's benchmark jobs), based on a survey of what comparable firms are paying for comparable jobs. (Google might do this for jobs like systems engineer, whose salaries fluctuate widely and often.) Third, surveys also collect data on benefits like insurance, sick leave, and vacations for decisions regarding employee benefits.

Salary surveys can be formal or informal. *Informal* phone or Internet surveys are good for checking specific issues, such as when a bank wants to confirm the salary at which to advertise a newly open teller's job, or whether some banks are really paying tellers an incentive. Some large employers can afford to send out their own *formal* surveys to collect compensation information from other employers. These ask about things like number of employees, overtime policies, starting salaries, and paid vacations.

Many employers use surveys published by consulting firms, professional associations, or government agencies. For example, the U.S. Department of Labor's Bureau of Labor Statistics' (BLS) *National Compensation Survey (NCS)* provides comprehensive reports of occupational earnings, compensation cost trends, and benefits (www.bls.gov/bls/wages.htm). A consultant might charge $12,000 for its salary survey—a lot of money, but a tiny fraction of the millions a client with 5,000 or so employees pays in compensation.[85]

Detailed occupational earnings are available from the *National Compensation Survey* for over 800 occupations in the United States, calculated with data from employers in all industry sectors in every state and the District of Columbia (http://stats.bls.gov/oes/current/oes_nat.htm). The *Current Employment Statistics Survey* is a monthly survey of the payroll records of business establishments that provides data on earnings of production and nonsupervisory workers at the national level. This provides information about earnings as well as production bonuses, commissions, and cost-of-living increases. The *National Compensation Survey—Benefits* provides information on the share of workers who participate in specified benefits, such as health care, retirement plans, and paid vacations. These data also show the details of those benefits, such as amounts of paid leave. Internationally, the BLS reports comparative hourly compensation costs in local currencies and U.S. dollars for production workers and all employees in manufacturing in its international labor comparisons tables.

Private consulting and/or executive recruiting companies like Hay Group, Towers Watson Global Data Services, and Aon/Hewitt (www.aon.com) publish data covering compensation for top and middle management and members of boards of directors. Professional organizations like the Society for Human Resource Management and

TABLE 11-4 Some Pay Data Web Sites

Sponsor	Internet Address	What It Provides	Downside
Salary.com	www.salary.com	Salary by job and ZIP code, plus job and description, for hundreds of jobs	Adapts national averages by applying local cost-of-living differences
U.S. Office of Personnel Management	www.opm.gov/oca/09Tables/index.asp	Salaries and wages for U.S. government jobs, by location	Limited to U.S. government jobs
Job Star	http://jobstar.org/tools/salary/sal-prof.php	Profession-specific salary surveys	Necessary to review numerous salary surveys for each profession
CNN Money	http://money.cnn.com	Input your current salary and city; for comparable salary in destination city	Based on national averages adapted to cost-of-living differences

the Financial Executives Institute publish surveys of compensation practices among members of their associations.[86]

USING THE INTERNET TO DO COMPENSATION SURVEYS Internet-based options make it easy for anyone to access published compensation survey information. Table 11-4 shows some popular salary survey Web sites.

Many of these sites, such as Salary.com, provide national salary levels for jobs that the site then arithmetically adjusts to each locale based on cost-of-living formulas. To get a real-time picture of what employers in your area are actually paying for, say, accounting clerks, it's useful to access the online Internet sites of one or two of your local newspapers. For example, the *South Florida Sun-Sentinel* (and many papers) uses a site called Careerbuilder.com. It lists just about all the job opportunities listed in the newspaper by category and, in many instances, their wage rates (www.careerbuilder.com).

11. Draw the Market (External) Wage Curve

The current/internal wage curve from step 9 is helpful. For example, showing, as it does, how a job's current pay rate compares with its points helps the employer identify jobs for which pay rates are currently too high or too low, relative to other jobs in the company. (For example, if a job's current wage rate is well above the internal wage curve, it suggests that the present wage rate for that job is inequitably high, given the number of points we've assigned to that job.)

What the current (internal) wage curve does *not* reveal is whether our pay rates are too high, too low, or just right relative to what other firms are paying. For this, we need to draw a *market* or *external wage* curve.

To draw the market/external wage curve, we produce a scatter plot and wage curve as in Figure 11-8 (left and right). However, instead of using our firm's current wage rates, we use market wage rates (obtained from salary surveys). The market/external wage curve thereby compares our jobs' points with market pay rates for our jobs.

FIGURE 11-8 The Market/ External Wage Curve

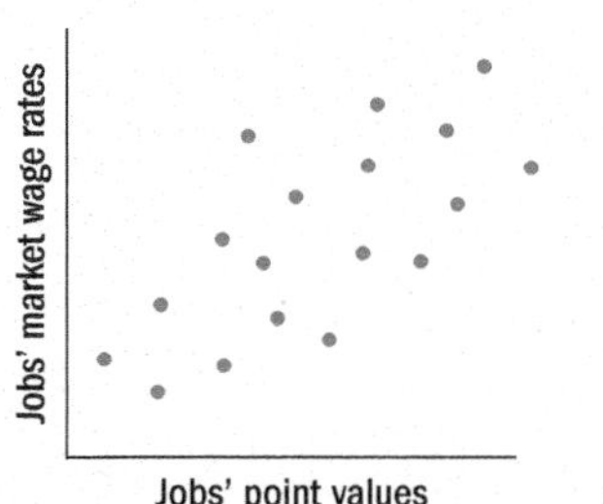

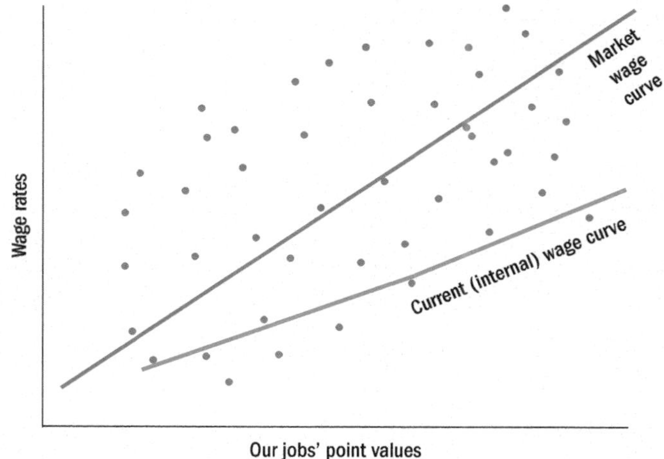

FIGURE 11-9 **Plotting Both the Market and Internal Wage Curves**

12. Compare and Adjust Current and Market Wage Rates for Jobs

How different are the market rates other employers are paying for our jobs and the current rates we are now paying for our jobs? To determine this, we combine both the current/internal and market/external wage curves on one graph, as in Figure 11-9. The market wage curve might be higher than our current wage curve (suggesting that our current pay rates may be too low), or below our current wage curve (suggesting that our current wage rates might be too high). Or perhaps market wage rates are higher for some of our jobs and lower for others.[87]

Based on comparing the current/internal wage curve and market/external wage curve in Figure 11-9, we must decide whether to adjust the current pay rates for our jobs, and if so how. This calls for a policy decision by management. Strategic considerations influence this decision. Do our strategic aspirations suggest we should pay more, the same, or less than competitors? For example, we might decide to move our current internal wage curve up (and thereby give everyone a raise), or down (and thereby perhaps withhold pay increases for some time), or adjust the slope of the internal wage curve to increase what we pay for some jobs and decrease what we pay for others. In any case, the wage curve we end up with (the orange line in Figure 11-10) should now be equitable internally (in terms of the point value of each job) and equitable externally (in terms of what other firms are paying).[88]

13. Develop Pay Grades

Employers typically group similar jobs (in terms of points) into grades for pay purposes. Then, instead of having to deal with hundreds of job rates, you might only have to focus on, say, pay rates for 10 or 12 pay grades. For example, Serco, a services firm that operates a London, England, light railway system, set up pay grades after ranking jobs using a system based on knowledge, management complexity, and the job's magnitude and impact on the organization.[89]

pay (or wage) grade
A pay grade is composed of jobs of approximately equal difficulty.

A **pay (or wage) grade** is composed of jobs of approximately equal difficulty or importance as determined by job evaluation. If you used the point method of job evaluation, the pay grade consists of jobs falling within a range of points. If the ranking method was used, the grade consists of a specific number of ranks. If you use the classification system, then your jobs are already categorized into classes (or grades).

DETERMINING THE NUMBER OF PAY GRADES It is standard to establish grades of equal point spread. (In other words, each grade might include all those jobs falling between 50 and 100 points, 100 and 150 points, 150 and 200 points, etc.) Since each grade is the same width, the main issue involves determining how many grades to have. There doesn't seem to be any optimal number, although 10 to 16 grades for a given job cluster

FIGURE 11-10 **Wage Structure**

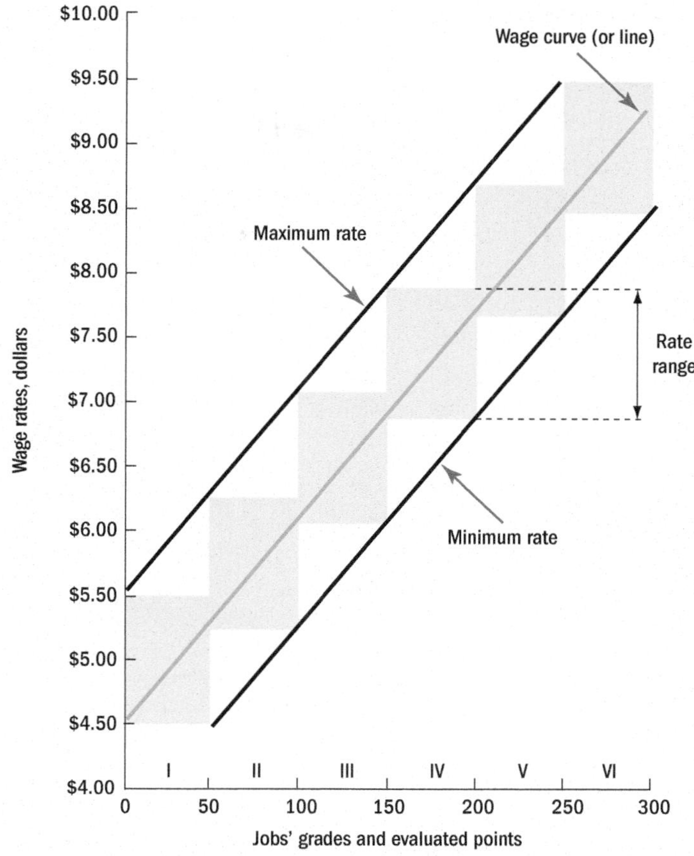

(shop jobs, clerical jobs, etc.) seems to be common. You need more pay grades if there are, say, 1,000 jobs to be graded than if there are only 100.

14. Establish Rate Ranges

Most employers do not pay just one rate for all jobs in a particular pay grade. For example, GE Medical won't want to pay all its accounting clerks, from beginners to long tenure, at the same rate, even though they may all be in the same pay grade. Instead, employers develop vertical pay (or "rate") ranges for each of the horizontal pay grades (or pay classes). These **pay (or rate) ranges** often appear as vertical boxes within each grade, showing minimum, maximum, and midpoint pay rates for that grade, as in Figure 11-10. (Specialists call this graph a *wage structure.* Figure 11-10 graphically depicts the range of pay rates—in this case, per hour—paid for each pay grade.) Alternatively, you may depict the pay range for each class or grade as steps in a table, as in Table 11-5. Here you will have specific corresponding pay rates for each step within each grade in tabular form. Thus, Table 11-5 shows the pay rates and steps for most federal government grades. As of the time of this pay schedule, for instance, employees in positions classified in grade GS-10 could be paid annual salaries between $47,630 and $61,922, depending on the level or step at which they were hired into the grade, the amount of time they were in the grade, and any merit increases they've received.

pay (or rate) ranges
A series of steps or levels within a pay grade, usually based upon years of service.

DEVELOPING RATE RANGES As in Figure 11-10, the wage curve usually anchors the average pay rate for each vertical pay range. The firm might then arbitrarily decide on a maximum and minimum rate for each grade, such as 15% above and below the wage curve. As an alternative, some employers allow the pay range for each grade to become taller (they include more pay rates) for the higher pay ranges, reflecting the greater demands

TABLE 11-5 U.S. Government Annual Rates by Grade and Step

Grade	Step 1	Step 2	Step 3	Step 4	Step 5	Step 6	Step 7	Step 8	Step 9	Step 10	Within Grade Amounts
1	$ 18,526	$ 19,146	$ 19,762	$ 20,375	$ 20,991	$ 21,351	$ 21,960	$ 22,575	$ 22,599	$ 23,171	VARIES
2	20,829	21,325	22,015	22,599	22,853	23,525	24,197	24,869	25,541	26,213	VARIES
3	22,727	23,485	23,243	25,001	25,759	26,517	27,275	28,033	28,791	29,549	758
4	25,514	26,364	27,214	28,064	28,914	29,764	30,614	31,464	32,314	33,164	850
5	28,545	29,497	30,449	31,401	32,353	33,305	34,257	34,209	36,161	37,113	952
6	31,819	32,880	33,941	35,002	36,063	37,124	38,185	39,246	40,307	41,368	1,061
7	35,359	36,538	37,717	38,896	40,075	41,254	42,433	43,612	44,791	45,970	1,179
8	39,159	40,464	41,769	43,074	44,379	45,684	46,989	48,294	49,599	50,904	1,305
9	43,251	44,693	46,135	47,577	49,019	50,461	51,903	53,345	54,787	56,229	1,442
10	47,630	49,218	50,806	52,394	53,982	55,570	57,158	58,746	60,334	61,922	1,588
11	52,329	54,073	55,817	57,561	59,305	61,049	62,793	64,537	66,281	68,025	1,744
12	62,722	64,813	66,904	68,995	71,086	73,177	75,268	77,359	79,450	81,541	2,091
13	74,584	77,070	79,556	82,042	84,528	87,014	89,500	91,986	94,472	96,958	2,486
14	88,136	91,074	94,012	96,950	99,888	102,826	105,764	108,702	111,640	114,578	2,938
15	103,672	107,128	110,584	114,040	117,496	120,952	124,408	127,864	131,320	134,776	3,456

Source: From salary table 2015-gs incorporating the 1% general schedule increase effective January 2015, from https://www.opm.gov/policy-data-oversight/pay-leave/salaries-wages/salary-tables/pdf/2017/GS.pdf.

and performance variability inherent in more complex jobs. As in Figure 11-10, most employers structure their rate ranges to overlap a bit, so an employee in one grade who has more experience or seniority may earn more than would someone in an entry-level position in the next higher pay grade.[90]

There are several reasons to use pay ranges for each pay grade. First, it lets the employer take a more flexible stance in the labor market. For example, it makes it easier to attract experienced, higher-paid employees into a pay grade at the top of the range, since the starting salary for the pay grade's lowest step may be too low to attract them. Pay ranges also let companies provide for performance differences between employees within the same grade or between those with different seniorities.

compa ratio
Equals an employee's pay rate divided by the pay range midpoint for his or her pay grade.

Compensation experts sometimes use *compa ratios.* The **compa ratio** equals an employee's pay rate divided by the pay range midpoint for his or her pay grade. A compa ratio of 1 means the employee is being paid exactly at the pay range midpoint. If the compa ratio is above 1 then the person's pay rate exceeds the midpoint pay for the job. If it is below, then the pay rate is less than the midpoint. The compa ratio can help reveal how many jobs in each pay grade are paid above and below competitive market pay rates.[91]

15. Address Remaining Jobs

To this point, we have focused our job evaluation on a limited number of benchmark jobs, as is traditional. We now want to add our remaining jobs to the wage structure. We can do this in two ways. We can evaluate each of the remaining jobs using the same process we just went through. Or we can simply slot the remaining jobs into the wage structure where we feel they belong, without formally evaluating and assigning points to these jobs. Jobs similar enough to our benchmark jobs we can easily slot into the wage structure. Jobs we're not sure about should undergo the same job evaluation process; we assign points to them and precisely slot them into the wage structure.[92]

16. Correct Out-of-Line Rates

Finally, the wage rate the firm is now paying for a particular job may fall well off the wage curve or well outside the rate range for its grade, as illustrated in Figure 11-6 (page 367). This means that the average pay for that job is currently too high or too low, relative to other jobs in the firm. For underpaid jobs, the solution is clear: Raise the wages of underpaid employees to the minimum of the rate range for their pay grade.

Current pay rates falling above the rate range are a different story. These are "red circle," "flagged," or "overrates." There are several ways to cope with this problem. One is to freeze the rate paid to these employees until general salary increases bring the other jobs into line. A second option is to transfer or promote the employees involved to jobs for which you can legitimately pay them their current pay rates. The third option is to freeze the rate for 6 months, during which time you try to transfer or promote the overpaid employees. If you cannot, then cut the rate you pay these employees to the maximum in the pay range for their pay grade. The accompanying HR Tools discussion explains a streamlined pay plan procedure for small businesses.

IMPROVING PERFORMANCE: *HR TOOLS FOR LINE MANAGERS AND SMALL BUSINESSES*

Developing a Workable Pay Plan

Pay plans are as important for small firms as large ones. Pay that is too high wastes money; too low triggers turnover; and internally inequitable causes endless demands for raises. The owner who wants to concentrate on major issues like sales needs a rational pay plan.

Surveying market rates come first. Sites like LinkedIn and Salary.com will show localized average pay rates for jobs in your geographic area. The Sunday newspaper classified ads (online and offline) will contain information on wages offered for jobs similar to those you're trying to price. Local job service "one-stop" offices can provide a wealth of information, as they compile extensive information on pay ranges and averages for many jobs. Employment agencies, always anxious to form ties with employers, will provide good data. Local college and university career centers will reveal prevailing pay rates for many jobs. Professional associations (such as the careers link for civil engineers at www.asce.org) are good sources of professionals' pay rates.

Smaller firms are making use of the Internet in other ways. StockHouse Media Corp (www.stockhouse.com) uses the Web for determining salaries for all the firm's personnel. For example, the HR manager surfs the Web to monitor rates and trends by periodically checking job boards, company Web sites, LinkedIn, and industry associations.[93]

If you employ more than 20 employees or so, conduct at least a rudimentary job evaluation (probably using the ranking method we covered on pages 361–362). For this you will need job descriptions (from, for example, O*NET and jobdescription.com), since these will be the source of data regarding the nature and worth of each job.

You may find it easier to split your employees into three clusters—say, managerial/professional, office/clerical, and plant personnel. For each of the three groups, choose one or more compensable factors. Then rank (or assign points to) each job in that cluster based on, say, a ranking job evaluation. For each job you will then want to create a pay range. In general, you might choose as the midpoint of that range the average market salary for that job, or an average of the market rate and what you are currently paying. Then produce a total range of about 30% around this average, broken into five steps. (Thus, assemblers, one of the plant personnel jobs, might earn from $8.00 to $12.60 per hour, in five steps.)

Required compensation policies will include amount of holiday and vacation pay (as we explain in Chapter 13), overtime pay policy, method of pay (weekly, biweekly, monthly), garnishments, and time card or sign-in sheet procedures. Many pay policy examples are available online.[94] ■

MyLab Management Talk About It 4

If your professor has assigned this, go to the Assignments section of **www.pearson.com/mylab/management** to complete these discussion questions. What type of job evaluation method would you use in a company with 15 employees? Why?

LEARNING OBJECTIVE 11-4

Explain how to price managerial and professional jobs.

Pricing Managerial and Professional Jobs

Developing compensation plans for managers or professionals is similar in many respects to developing plans for any employee. The basic aim is the same: to attract, motivate, and retain good employees. And job evaluation is about as applicable to managerial and professional jobs (below the top executive levels) as to production and clerical ones.

There are some big differences though. Managerial jobs tend to stress harder-to-quantify factors like judgment and problem solving more than do production and clerical jobs. There is also more emphasis on paying managers and professionals based on their performance or on what they can do, rather than on static job demands like working conditions. And one must compete in a marketplace for executives who often have rock star pay. So, job evaluation, although still important for management jobs, usually plays a secondary role to issues like bonuses, incentives, market rates, and benefits.

What Determines Executive Pay?

Because average CEO pay has leaped relative to the average worker's, executive pay has become a contentious topic today.

Whatever it is that accounts for CEO pay, it's apparently not always company performance. In one survey, the best-performing CEOs received the lowest average compensation, while those in low-performing companies were paid relatively well.[95] Conversely, one expert says CEOs with the highest 20% of compensation produced stock returns 60% greater than those of other firms in their industries.[96] Another study concluded that three main factors, *job complexity* (span of control, the number of functional divisions over which the executive has direct responsibility, and management level), the employer's *ability to pay* (total profit and rate of return), and the executive's *human capital* (educational level, field of study, work experience), accounted for about two-thirds of executive compensation variance.[97]

In practice, external equity plays a big role in setting a top manager's compensation plan. The board of director's compensation committee may retain a compensation consultant, and together they will choose and analyze top executives' pay in what they consider to be "peer companies"—companies that may (or may not) be in the same industry as theirs. Critics argue that this process creates upward pressures on CEO compensation, because the peer companies often are ones with higher-paid CEOs.[98] Alternatively, companies such as Berkshire Hathaway and Amazon tend to pay their founder/CEOs (Warren Buffet, Jeff Bezos) far less than do comparably sized firms; however, the CEOs have of course become very wealthy (as have many stockholders) through their stockholdings.[99]

Below the CEO, many employers do use job evaluation for pricing managerial jobs (at least, below the top jobs). The basic approach is to classify executive and management positions into grades, each with a salary range. As with nonmanagerial jobs, one alternative is to rank the executive and management positions in relation to each other, then group into classes those of similar value. However, firms also use the job classification and point methods, with compensable factors like position scope, complexity, and difficulty. As with any jobs, job analysis, salary surveys, and fine-tuning salary levels around wage curves play roles.

Shareholder activism and government oversight have tightened the restrictions on what companies pay top executives. For example, Walt Disney shareholders recently rejected (in a nonbinding vote) a plan to pay Disney CEO Robert Iger a total of almost $300 million over four years.[100]

Compensating Executives

Compensation for a company's top executives usually consist of several main elements.[101] *Base pay* includes the person's fixed salary. *Bonuses* are single payments generally to reward the manager for achieving a specific goal such as "total company profit over $18 million." *Short-term incentives* are usually cash or stock bonuses for achieving progress toward strategic goals, such as "reducing reliance on domestic sales from 80% to 50%." *Long-term incentives* aim to encourage the executive to take actions that drive up the value of the company's stock and include things like stock options. Finally, *executive benefits and perks* include things such as supplemental executive retirement pension plans. As an example, one CEO's total compensation was about $24 million in one year. Long-term stock awards and stock options of about $15 million were the largest component. About $1.5 million was base salary. About $3.5 million was annual incentive plan, just over $4 million was increased pensions and deferred compensation, and most of the rest went to "all other compensation."[102]

Salary is traditionally the cornerstone of executive compensation. On it, employers layer benefits, incentives, and perquisites. Top executive compensation packages can be whoppers. The CEOs of Charter Communications and of CBS recently earned a total of about $98 million and $68 million, respectively.[103]

Executive compensation emphasizes performance (discussed in Chapter 12) more than do other employees' pay plans, since organizational results reflect executives' contributions more than those of lower-echelon employees. Indeed, boards are boosting the emphasis on performance-based pay (in part due to shareholder activism). The big issue here is identifying the appropriate performance measures. Typical short-term measures include revenue growth and operating profit margin. Long-term measures include rate of return above some predetermined base. With so many complicated elements, employers must also be alert to the tax and securities law implications of their executive compensation decisions.

Compensating Professional Employees

In compensating professionals, employers should first ensure that the person is actually a "professional" under the law. The Fair Labor Standards Act "provides an exemption from both minimum wage and overtime pay for employees employed as bona fide executive, administrative, professional and outside sales employees."[104]

However, calling someone a professional doesn't make them one. In addition to earning at least $455 per week, the person's main duty must "be the performance of work requiring advanced knowledge," and "the advanced knowledge must be customarily acquired by a prolonged course of specialized intellectual instruction."[105] One company hired a high school graduate as an exempt "product design specialist II," earning $62,000 per year. The job required 12 years of relevant experience, but no particular education. The court ruled the job was *non*exempt.[106]

Beyond that, compensating professionals such as engineers and attorneys presents unique challenges.[107] Analytical jobs like these emphasize compensable factors such as creativity and problem solving that are not easily measured. Furthermore, how to measure performance? For example, the success of an engineer's idea depends on how the firm develops and markets it. And such jobs can be highly sensitive to market conditions and industry demand. For example, Facebook, Google (Alphabet), and Amazon reportedly hire about 30% of American computer science graduates, which creates highly competitive pricing conditions.[108] Wages for other jobs—such as for engineers in the heating and air conditioning industry—face less pressure.[109]

Employers can and do use job evaluation for professional jobs. Compensable factors here tend to focus on problem solving, creativity, job scope, and technical knowledge and expertise. Firms use the point method and job classification.

Yet, in practice, firms rarely rely on just job evaluation for pricing professional jobs. Factors like creativity (as noted) are hard to measure, and nonpay issues often influence professionals' job decisions. Tech firms in particular also take dramatic steps to keep their best engineers from leaving. A few years ago Google raised its employees' salaries by 10% in the face of defections by even their highest-paid professionals, such as the head of its Chrome OS team, to Facebook.[110] Many of them, well paid by most standards, still felt underpaid. Tech firms like Facebook also award far more stock options (or stock shares) than do most other industries, and many give large signing bonuses that they can claw back if someone leaves the company prematurely.[111]

Most employers therefore emphasize a market-pricing approach for these jobs. They price professional jobs in the marketplace as best they can, to establish the values for benchmark jobs. Then they slot these benchmark jobs and their other professional jobs into a salary structure. Each professional discipline (such as engineer) usually ends up having four to six grade levels, each with a broad salary range. This helps employers remain competitive when bidding for professionals who literally have global employment possibilities.[112] That way, even outside Silicon Valley, engineers' pay stays competitive: In one (non-high-tech) study a few years ago, the engineers earned a base salary of $89,000, and a bonus of about $9,000 based on personal performance, product profitability, and safety metrics.[113]

IMPROVING PERFORMANCE: *THROUGH HRIS*

Payroll Administration

Payroll administration is one of the first functions most employers computerize or outsource, and for good reason. Administering the payroll system—keeping track of each employee's FLSA worker status, wage rate, dependents, benefits, overtime, tax status, and so on; computing each paycheck; and then directing the actual printing of checks or direct deposits is a time-consuming task, one complicated by the need to comply with many federal, state, and local wage, hour, and other laws.

Many employers do perform this function in-house, usually with a payroll processing software package. Intuit's *Basic Payroll* lets the employer "enter hours worked and get instant paycheck calculations, including earnings, payroll taxes, and deductions. Then print paychecks yourself. *Basic Payroll* calculates federal and state payroll taxes for you, so you can easily e-pay federal taxes and write a check for state taxes."[114] Kronos's *Workforce Payroll* automates the payroll process, and offers self-service features. For example (see www.kronos.com/products/payroll), *Workforce Payroll* will "let your employees see pay stubs and earning histories, make changes to direct deposit and W-4 forms, print W-2s, and even check out how changes to their deductions will affect their paychecks."

On the other hand, many employers do outsource payroll administration to vendors such as ADP. In deciding which vendor to use, the employer should consider its goals and the potential economic benefits, as well as factors such as the vendor's reputation. SHRM recommends evaluating the initial list of prospective vendors based on the employer's goals for the relationship. Don't just consider the relative economic benefits of outsourcing the function (rather than doing it in-house), but also the desirability of integrating the employer's internal systems with the vendor's, streamlining tax compliance and filings, and increasing employee self-service.[115] ■

LEARNING OBJECTIVE 11-5
Explain the difference between competency-based and traditional pay plans.

Contemporary Topics in Compensation

In this section, we'll look at five important contemporary compensation topics: competency-based pay, broadbanding, comparable worth, board oversight of executive pay, and total rewards.

Competency-Based Pay

Some managers question whether job evaluations that slot jobs into narrow cubbyholes ("Machinist I," "Machinist II," and so on) might not actually be counterproductive. For example, high-performance work systems depend on flexible multiskilled job assignments and on teamwork, and there's no place here for employees to say, "That's not my job."

competency-based pay
Where the company pays for the employee's range, depth, and types of skills and knowledge, rather than for the job title he or she holds.

Competency-based pay aims to avoid that problem.[116] With competency (generally skill or knowledge-based) pay, you pay the employee for the skills and knowledge he or she is capable of using rather than for the responsibilities or title of the job

Many employers pay certain workers based on attained skill levels.

Monty Rakusen/Cultura/Getty Images

currently held.[117] Experts variously call this competence-, knowledge-, or skill-based pay. With competency-based pay, an employee in a class I job who could (but may not have to at the moment) do class II work gets paid as a class II worker, not a class I. *Competencies* are demonstrable personal characteristics such as knowledge, skills, and personal behaviors such as leadership. Why pay employees based on the skill levels they achieve, rather than based on the jobs they're assigned to? Because, for example, a company that organizes a facility around teams may want to encourage employees to get and to use the skills required to rotate among jobs.

As an example, review Chapter 4's Figure 4-11 on page 124. For this job, BP lists the minimum level of each skill (Technical Expertise, Problem Solving, and so on) someone holding this job must attain. As an employee achieves and is tested on each level of each skill, he or she would receive a bump in pay.

Broadbanding

Most firms end up with pay plans that slot jobs into classes or grades, each with its own vertical pay rate range. For example, the U.S. government's pay plan consists of 15 main grades (GS-1 to GS-15), each with its own pay range. For an employee whose job falls into one of these grades, the pay range for that grade dictates his or her minimum and maximum salary.

The question is, "How wide should the salary grades be, in terms of the number of job evaluation points they include?" (For example, should the U.S. government collapse its 15 salary grades into 5 or 6 broader bands?) There is a downside to having (say, 15) narrow grades. For instance, if you want someone whose job is in grade 2 to fill in for a time in a job that happens to be in grade 1, it's difficult to reassign that person without lowering his or her salary. Similarly, if you want the person to learn about a job that happens to be in grade 3, the employee might first want a corresponding raise to grade 3 pay. Traditional grade pay plans could thus breed inflexibility.

broadbanding
Consolidating salary grades and ranges into just a few wide levels or "bands," each of which contains a relatively wide range of jobs and salary levels.

That is why some firms broadband their pay plans.[118] **Broadbanding** means collapsing salary grades into just a few wide levels or bands, each of which contains a relatively wide range of jobs and pay levels. Figure 11-11 illustrates this. Here,

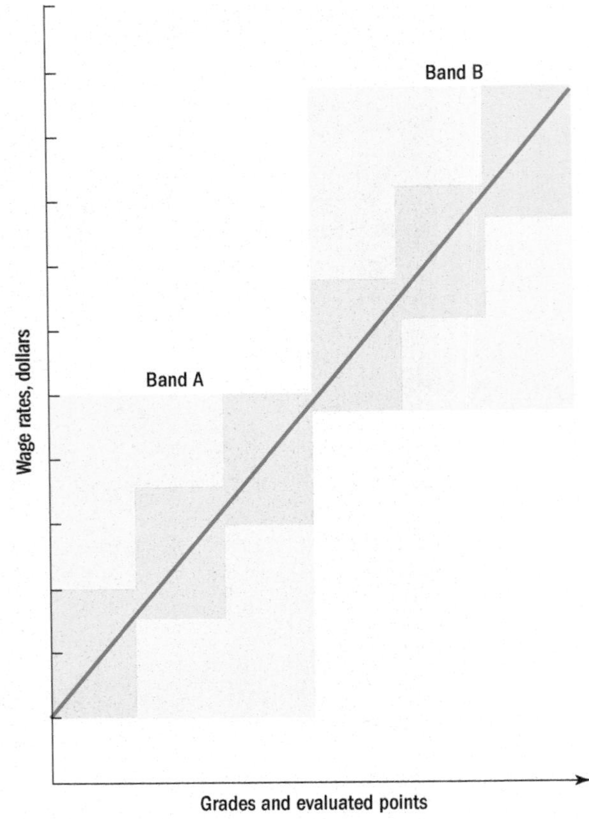

FIGURE 11-11 Broadbanded Structure and How It Relates to Traditional Pay Grades and Ranges

the company's previous six pay grades are consolidated into two broad grades or "broadbands."

A company may create broadbands for all its jobs, or for specific groups such as managers or professionals. The (vertical) pay rate range of each broadband is relatively large, since it ranges from the minimum pay of the lowest grade the firm merged into the broadband up to the maximum pay *of the highest merged grade.* Thus, for example, instead of having 10 salary grades, each of which contains a salary range of $15,000, the firm might collapse the 10 grades into three broadbands, each with a set of jobs such that the difference between the lowest- and highest-paid jobs might be $40,000 or more. (Again, see Figure 11-11). For the jobs that fall in this broadband, there is therefore a much wider range of pay rates. You can move an employee from job to job within the broadband more easily, without worrying about the employee's moving outside the (relatively) narrow rate range associated with a traditional narrow pay grade. This can make it easier to train someone on a higher level job, or to have them fill in for a time on a lower level job without worrying about pay levels.

Comparable Worth

comparable worth
The concept by which women who are usually paid less than men can claim that men in comparable rather than in strictly equal jobs are paid more.

Comparable worth refers to the requirement to pay men and women equal wages for jobs that are dissimilar but of comparable value (for instance measured in points) to the employer. This may mean comparing dissimilar jobs, such as nurses to mechanics. The question "comparable worth" seeks to address is this: Should you pay women who are performing jobs *equal* to men's or just *comparable* to men's the same as men?

County of Washington v. Gunther (1981) was a pivotal case. It involved Washington County, Oregon, prison matrons, who claimed sex discrimination. The county had evaluated roughly comparable (but different) men's jobs as having 5% more "job content" (based on a point evaluation system) than the women's jobs, but paid the men 35% more.[119] Why should there be such a pay discrepancy for roughly comparable jobs? After moving through the courts to the U.S. Supreme Court, Washington County finally agreed to pay 35,000 employees in female-dominated jobs almost $500 million in pay raises over 7 years to settle.

Comparable worth has implications for job evaluation. Virtually every comparable worth case that reached court involved the point method of job evaluation. By assigning points to dissimilar jobs, point plans facilitate comparability ratings among different jobs. Should employers still use point plans? Perhaps the wisest approach is for employers to price their jobs as they see fit (with or without point plans), but to also ensure that women have equal access to all jobs. In other words, eliminate sex-segregated jobs.

Diversity Counts: The Pay Gap

All this notwithstanding, women in the United States earn only about 81% as much as men.[120] This seems true even among the most highly trained. For example, new female medical doctors earn about $17,000 per year less than their male counterparts.[121] Reasons put forward for the gap include what one writer calls a "Motherhood Penalty" (women take more time off to care for the family, and are penalized career-wise for this), employer discrimination, the outdated notion that employers view women as having less leverage, the fact that professional men change jobs more often (gaining more raises in the process), and that women tend to end up in departments that pay less.[122] In any case, it's a problem employers have to recognize and address. Some, like Alphabet are already doing so. Pressures from investor groups, some states, and the national #MeToo movement are forcing others to do so.[123] ■

MyLab Management Apply It!

How do companies actually adjust salaries and raises? If your professor has assigned this activity, go to the Assignments section of **www.pearson.com/mylab/management** to complete the video exercise.

Board Oversight of Executive Pay

The company's board of directors is responsible for setting and approving top executives' pay, and boards today are scrutinizing that pay for two reasons: governmental regulation/legal, and shareholder activism/inequity.

First, legislation gives various governmental agencies oversight over executive pay. To ensure adequate disclosure, the Securities and Exchange Commission (SEC) requires detailed compensation-related information for the CEO, chief financial officer, and next three highest paid executives. The company usually summarizes this in a Summary Compensation Table in the company's annual proxy statement filed with the SEC.[124] The Dodd–Frank Law of 2010 requires that American companies give shareholders a (nonbinding) "say on pay." The Sarbanes–Oxley Act makes executives personally liable, under certain conditions, for corporate financial oversight lapses. Similarly, tax treatment and disclosure are overseen by the Departments of the Treasury and of Labor, and the Internal Revenue Service.[125]

Second, CEO pay compared with an average worker's pay has mushroomed in the past 20 or so years—the gap is about six times larger than it was then.[126] Boards therefore face shareholder activism on executive pay. Law firms file class-action suits demanding information from companies about their senior executive pay decisions.[127] As of 2018, public corporations in the United States must compute the ratio of CEO to median company employee pay.[128] The net result is that lawyers specializing in executive pay suggest that boards of directors ask themselves these questions:[129]

- Has our compensation committee identified its duties and processes?
- Is our compensation committee using the appropriate compensation advisors?
- Are there particular executive compensation issues that our committee should address?

- Do our procedures demonstrate diligence and independence (including careful deliberations and records)?
- Is our committee appropriately communicating its decisions? How will shareholders react?[130]

LEARNING OBJECTIVE 11-6

Describe the importance of total rewards for improving employee engagement.

Employee Engagement Guide for Managers

Total Rewards Programs

Total rewards is an important concept in compensation management. People bring to their jobs many needs—for challenging work and for respect and appreciation, for instance—not all of which are satisfied by pay or bonuses. "'Total rewards' encompass not only compensation and benefits but also personal and professional growth opportunities and a motivating work environment."[131] It includes not just traditional financial rewards (wages and incentives plus benefits and perks), but also nonfinancial and intangible rewards such as recognition, the nature of the job/quality of work, career development opportunities,[132] good relationships with colleagues, organizational justice, trust in employees, feeling of being valued and involved, opportunities for promotion,[133] and a great work climate.[134] Specific total rewards also include recognition programs and redesigned jobs (discussed in Chapter 4), telecommuting programs, health and well-being programs, and training and career development.

TRENDS SHAPING HR: *DIGITAL AND SOCIAL MEDIA*

Noncash recognition/appreciation rewards such as gift cards, merchandise, and recognition are parts of such total compensation.[135]

New digital and social media tools enable employees to recognize and reward each other. For example, a West Virginia DuPont plant installed an online system that enabled employees to give each other recognition; 95% were soon using it.[136] International Fitness Holdings lets employees use a Facebook-type app to recognize peers by posting messages and sending private e-mails.[137] Employers contract with sites like Globoforce.com to provide online recognition systems. ■

Total Rewards and Employee Engagement

When it comes to employee engagement, both material and nonmaterial rewards—total rewards—seem essential.[138] For example, one study found that base pay and benefits alone were weakly related to engagement.[139] However, intangible rewards (such as the nature of the job/quality of work and career development opportunities) had high or very high impacts on engagement and performance, when combined with base salary and short-term incentives or bonuses.[140]

It's therefore not surprising that many high-engagement employers emphasize total rewards. For example, the values laid out in Toyota's famous "The Toyota Way" include mutual trust and respect, stable employment, helping employees to develop their technical skills, and providing extensive benefits such as childcare. Disney emphasizes providing employees with a total rewards package that includes pay plus various benefits and career development opportunities.[141] Similarly, many "Best Companies to Work For" emphasize intangible rewards. For example, one top executive at NetApp takes an opportunity to call and thank several employees each day for their efforts; Whole Foods emphasizes employee involvement, for instance letting employees vote on new hires and see what all Whole Foods employees earn.[142] At SAS there is stimulating work, an empowering management philosophy, flexible work, and an emphasis on being happy at work.[143]

In addition to offering such rewards, the employer should issue total reward statements periodically. List all the rewards—financial and nonfinancial—the company offers, and note their importance to the employees' overall well-being.[144] This increases their impact.

Chapter Review

Chapter Section Summaries

11-1. In establishing strategic pay plans, managers first need to understand some **basic factors in determining pay rates.** Employee compensation includes both direct financial payments and indirect financial statements. The factors determining the design of any pay plan include legal, union, company strategy/policy, and equity. Legal considerations include, most importantly, the Fair Labor Standards Act, which governs matters such as minimum wages and overtime pay. Specific categories of employees are exempt from the act or certain provisions of the act, particularly its overtime provisions. The Equal Pay Act of 1963 and the Employee Retirement Income Security Act are other important laws.

11-2. Employers use two basic approaches to setting pay rates: *market-based approaches* and **job evaluation methods.** Many firms, particularly smaller ones, simply use a *market-based* approach. Job evaluation methods involve assigning values to each of the company's jobs. This helps to produce a pay plan in which each job's pay is equitable based on its value to the employer. Popular job evaluation methods include ranking, job classification, and the point method.

11-3. We said the process of **creating a market-competitive pay plan** while ensuring external, internal, and procedural equity consists of 16 steps as follows: (1) Choose benchmark jobs; (2) Select compensable factors; (3) Assign weights to compensable factors; (4) Convert percentages to points for each factor; (5) Define each factor's degrees; (6) Determine for each factor its factor degrees' points; (7) Review job descriptions and job specifications; (8) Evaluate the jobs; (9) Draw the current (internal) wage curve; (10) Conduct a market analysis: Salary surveys; (11) Draw the market (external) wage curve; (12) Compare and adjust current and market wage rates for jobs; (13) Develop pay grades; (14) Establish rate ranges; (15) Address remaining jobs; and (16) Correct out-of-line rates.

11-4. **Pricing managerial and professional jobs** involves some special issues. Managerial pay typically consists of base pay, short-term incentives, long-term incentives, and executive benefits and, particularly at the top levels, doesn't lend itself to job evaluation but rather to understanding the job's complexity, the employer's ability to pay, and the need to be competitive in attracting top talent.

11-5. We addressed five important **special topics in compensation.** More employers are moving from paying jobs based on their intrinsic duties toward paying jobs based on the competencies the job requires. Broadbanding means consolidating several rates and ranges into a few wide levels or "bands," each of which contains a relatively wide range of jobs in salary levels. Comparable worth refers to the requirement to pay men and women equal pay for jobs that are of comparable rather than strictly equal value to the employee. With many stockholders concerned with excessive executive remuneration, board oversight of executive pay has become an important issue, and boards of directors should use qualified advisors and exercise diligence and independence in formulating executive pay plans.

11-6. Research shows that if **employee engagement** is the aim, it makes sense to emphasize total rewards, not just financial rewards. For example, one study found that base pay and benefits alone had a weak relationship with employee engagement. However, total rewards including intangible rewards such as the nature of the job/quality of work, and career development opportunities had a high or very high impact on engagement and performance, when combined with base salary and short-term incentives or bonuses.

Discussion Questions

11-1. What is the difference between exempt and non-exempt jobs?

11-2. Should the job evaluation depend on an appraisal of the jobholder's performance? Why? Why not?

11-3. What is the relationship between compensable factors and job specifications?

11-4. Define and give an example of how to conduct a job evaluation.

11-5. The average pay for most university presidents is around $300,000 per year, but many earn much more. For example, the president of NYU received about $1 million in 1 year. Discuss why you would (or would not) pay university presidents as much as or more than many corporate CEOs.

11-6. Do small companies need to develop a pay plan? Why or why not?

11-7. After Walmart raised its minimum starting pay to $10 an hour, some longer-term employees (like one earning $12 per hour) complained that the strictly entry-level increase was unfair to them. And when the head of a company called Gravity Payments decided to pay all his employees at least $70,000 a year, some longer-tenure employees complained that it was unfair to raise new peoples' salaries and not theirs.[145] How should Walmart and Gravity address these complaints?

Individual and Group Activities

11-8. Working individually or in groups, conduct salary surveys for the following positions: entry-level accountant and entry-level chemical engineer. What sources did you use, and what conclusions did you reach? If you were the HR manager for a local engineering firm, what would you recommend that you pay for each job?

11-9. Working individually or in groups, develop compensation policies for the teller position at a local bank. Assume that there are four tellers: two were hired in May and the other two were hired in December. The compensation policies should address the following: appraisals, raises, holidays, vacation pay, overtime pay, method of pay, garnishments, and time cards.

11-10. Working individually or in groups, access relevant Web sites to determine what equitable pay ranges are for these jobs: chemical engineer, marketing manager, and HR manager, all with a bachelor's degree and 5 years' experience. Do so for the following cities: New York, New York; San Francisco, California; Houston, Texas; Denver, Colorado; Miami, Florida; Atlanta, Georgia; Chicago, Illinois; Birmingham, Alabama; Detroit, Michigan; and Washington, D.C. For each position in each city, what are the pay ranges and the average pay? Does geographical location impact the salaries of the different positions? If so, how?

11-11. Appendices A and B at the end of this book (pages 614–634) list the knowledge someone studying for the HRCI (Appendix A) or SHRM (Appendix B) certification exam needs to have in each area of human resource management (such as in Strategic Management and Workforce Planning). In groups of several students, do four things: (1) review Appendix A and/or B; (2) identify the material in this chapter that relates to the Appendix A and/or B required knowledge lists; (3) write four multiple-choice exam questions on this material that you believe would be suitable for inclusion in the HRCI exam and/or the SHRM exam; and (4) if time permits, have someone from your team post your team's questions in front of the class, so that students in all teams can answer the exam questions created by the other teams.

KNOWLEDGE BASE

11-12. Working individually or in groups, use the point system described in steps 1 to 16 in this chapter. Do so for a job description that you find online—a list like that at http://hiring.monster.com/hr/hr-best-practices/recruiting-hiring-advice/job-descriptions/sample-job-descriptions.aspx is useful. To simplify things, assume there is only one compensable factor you have to use, and that it is job complexity, so that you can use Figure 11-5.

11-13. How do you think politicians in the United States should address the problem of income inequality?

Experiential Exercise

Ranking the College's Administrators

Written and copyrighted by Gary Dessler, PhD.

Purpose: The purpose of this exercise is to give you experience in performing a job evaluation using the ranking method.

Required Understanding: You should be thoroughly familiar with the ranking method of job evaluation and obtain job descriptions for your college's dean, department chairperson, director of admissions, library director, registrar, and your professor.

How to Set Up the Exercise/Instructions: Divide the class into groups of four or five students. The groups will perform a job evaluation of the positions of dean, department chairperson, and professor using the ranking method.

Perform a job evaluation by ranking the jobs. You may use one or more compensable factors.

11-14. If time permits, a spokesperson from each group can put his or her group's rankings on the board. Did the groups end up with about the same results? How did they differ? Why do you think they differed?

Application Case

Salary Inequities at AstraZeneca

Written and copyrighted by Gary Dessler, PhD.

More than 50 years after passage of the Equal Pay Act, women in America still earn about 80 cents for every dollar earned by a man. That adds up to a loss for the average female worker of about $380,000 over a lifetime.

The U.S. Department of Labor's Office of Federal Contract Compliance Programs (OFCCP) entered into an agreement with AstraZeneca, a large international pharmaceuticals firm, for the company to pay some of its female sales associates a total of $250,000.[146] AstraZeneca had a contract valued at over $2 billion with the U.S. Department of Veterans Affairs to provide drugs to hospitals around the country. That made it subject to Executive Order 11246, which aims to ensure that employees of U.S. contractors and subcontractors with federal contracts pay their employees fairly without regard to sex, race, color, religion, and national origin.

After conducting a compliance review, the OFCCP concluded that AstraZeneca violated Executive Order 11246 by failing to ensure certain women employees were paid fairly. According to the OFCCP lawsuit, an AstraZeneca Business Center had routinely paid some of its female "primary care" and "specialty care" level III pharmaceutical sales specialists an average of $1,700 less than men with the same positions. Because of the company's pay secrecy policies, many of the women didn't know they were being paid less. In addition to the financial settlement, AstraZeneca and OFCCP will review records of the firm's female employees in 14 states. If they find additional statistical evidence of wage discrimination, the company must remedy it.

Questions

AstraZeneca has brought you in as a compensation consultant. Here are the questions they would like you to answer for them:

11-15. Although the case with OFCCP is closed, we wonder if there are any less-discriminatory explanations possible for why our women sales reps on average earned less than men. If so, what are they?

11-16. Our own company now uses a point method to evaluate jobs for pay purposes, and each resulting job class also has a rate range associated with it. Sales associates are now paid a salary that is not based on incentive pay. List three specific things we can do to ensure that a similar problem (inequitable pay based on gender) does not arise again, assuming they continue using the point plan.

11-17. What sort of compensation plan would you recommend for us, and why?

Continuing Case

Carter Cleaning Company

Written and copyrighted by Gary Dessler, PhD.

The New Pay Plan

Carter Cleaning Centers does not have a formal wage structure nor does it have rate ranges or use compensable factors. Wage rates are based mostly on those prevailing in the surrounding community and are tempered with an attempt on the part of Jack Carter to maintain some semblance of equity between what workers with different responsibilities in the stores are paid.

Carter does not make any formal surveys when determining what his company should pay. He peruses the want ads almost every day and conducts informal surveys among his friends in the local chapter of the laundry and cleaners trade association. While Jack has taken a "seat-of-the-pants" approach to paying employees, his salary schedule has been guided by several basic pay policies. Although many of his colleagues adhere to a policy of paying minimum rates, Jack has always followed a policy of paying his employees about 10% above what he feels are the prevailing rates, a policy that he believes reduces turnover while fostering employee loyalty. Of somewhat more concern to Jennifer is her father's informal policy of paying men about 20% more than women for the same job. Her father's explanation is, "They're stronger and can work harder for longer hours, and besides they all have families to support."

Questions

11-18. Is the company at the point where it should be setting up a formal salary structure based on a complete job evaluation? Why?

11-19. Is Jack Carter's policy of paying 10% more than the prevailing rates a sound one, and how could that be determined?

11-20. Similarly, is Carter's male–female differential wise? If not, why not?

11-21. Specifically, what would you suggest Jennifer do now with respect to her company's pay plan?

Translating Strategy into HR Policies and Practices Case*,§

* *The accompanying strategy map for this chapter is in MyLab Management; the overall map on the inside back cover of this text outlines the relationships involved.*

Improving Performance at the Hotel Paris

The New Compensation Plan

The Hotel Paris's competitive strategy is "To use superior guest service to differentiate the Hotel Paris properties, and to thereby increase the length of stay and return rate of guests, and thus boost revenues and profitability." HR manager Lisa Cruz must now formulate functional policies and activities that support this competitive strategy by eliciting the required employee behaviors and competencies.

Like several other HR systems at the Hotel Paris, the compensation program was unplanned and unsophisticated. The company has a narrow target range for what it will pay employees in each job category (front-desk clerk, security guard, and so forth). Each hotel manager decides where to start a new employee within that narrow pay range. The company has given little thought to tying general pay levels or individual employees' pay to the company's strategic goals. For example, the firm's policy is simply to pay its employees a "competitive salary," by which it means about average for what other hotels in the city are paying for similar jobs. Lisa knows that pay policies like these may actually run counter to what the company wants to achieve strategically, in terms of creating an extraordinarily service-oriented workforce. How can you hire and retain a top workforce, and channel its behaviors toward high-quality guest services, if you don't somehow link performance and pay? She and her team therefore turn to the task of assessing and redesigning the company's compensation plan.

Even the most casual review by Lisa Cruz and the CFO made it clear that the company's compensation plan wasn't designed to support the firm's new strategic goals. For one thing, they knew that they should pay somewhat more on average than did their competitors if they expected employees to exceed expectations when it came to serving guests. Yet their review of a variety of metrics (including the Hotel Paris's salary/competitive salary ratios, the total compensation expense per employee, and the target percentile for total compensation) suggested that in virtually all job categories the Hotel Paris paid no more than average and, occasionally, paid somewhat less.

The current compensation policies had also bred what one hotel manager called an "I don't care" attitude on the part of most employees. What she meant was that most Hotel Paris employees quickly learned that regardless of what their performance was, they always ended up getting paid about the same as employees who performed better and worse than they did. So, the firm's compensation plan actually created a disconnect between pay and performance: It was not channeling employees' behaviors toward those required to achieve the company's goals. In some ways, it was doing the opposite.

Lisa and the CFO knew they had to institute a new, strategic compensation plan. They wanted a plan that improved employee morale, contributed to employee engagement, reduced employee turnover, and rewarded (and thus encouraged) the sorts of service-oriented behaviors that boosted guest satisfaction. After meeting with the company's CEO and the board, the CFO gave Lisa the go-ahead to redesign the company's compensation plan, with the overall aim of creating a new plan that would support the company's strategic aims.

Lisa and her team (which included a consulting compensation expert) set numerous new measurable compensation policies for the Hotel Paris, and these new policies formed the heart of the new compensation plan. A new job evaluation study provided a more rational and fair basis upon which the company could assign pay rates. A formal compensation survey by the consultant established, for the first time at the Hotel Paris, a clear picture of what competitive hotels and similar businesses were paying in each geographic area, and enabled the Hotel Paris team to more accurately set targets for what each position at the hotel should be paying. Rather than just paying at the industry average, or slightly below, the new policy called for the Hotel Paris to move all its salaries into the 75th percentile over the next 3 years.

As they instituted the new compensation policies, Lisa and the CFO were pleased to learn from feedback from the hotel managers that they were already noting several positive changes. The number of applicants for each position had increased by over 50% on average, turnover dropped by 80%, and surveys of morale and commitment were producing higher results. Lisa and her team now began to consider how to inject more of a "pay for performance" element into the company's compensation plan, perhaps by instituting new bonuses and incentives.We will see what she did in Chapter 12.

Questions

11-22. Lisa knew little about setting up a new compensation plan. Based on what you learned here in Dessler *Human Resource Management*, what would you tell her if she asked, "How do I set up a new compensation plan for the Hotel Paris?"

11-23. Would you suggest that Hotel Paris implement a competency-based pay plan for its nonmanagerial staff? Why or why not? Outline what they need to do for one.

11-24. Devise a ranking job evaluation system for the Hotel Paris's nonmanagerial employees (housekeepers, valets, front-desk clerks, phone operators, waitstaff, groundskeepers, and security guards), and use it to show the worth of these jobs relative to one another.

§ Written and copyrighted by Gary Dessler, PhD.

Writing Assignments

11-25. You want to hire a new salesperson for the small dress shop you own in Columbus, Ohio, but first need to decide what sort of pay package to offer whomever you eventually hire. How would you conduct a salary survey to determine what the pay should be?

11-26. Compare and contrast the following methods of job evaluation: ranking, classification, factor comparison, and point method.

MyLab Management Try It!

How would you use pay or other components of a total rewards program to solve a "motivation problem" in a company? If your professor has assigned this activity, go to the Assignments section of **www.pearson.com/mylab/management** to complete the simulation.

Key Terms

employee compensation, 350
direct financial payments, 350
indirect financial payments, 350
Davis-Bacon Act (1931), 351
Walsh-Healey Public Contract Act (1936), 351
Title VII of the 1964 Civil Rights Act, 351
Fair Labor Standards Act (1938), 351
Equal Pay Act, 356
Employee Retirement Income Security Act (ERISA), 356
job evaluation, 359
market-competitive pay plan, 359
compensable factor, 359
benchmark job, 361
ranking method, 361
job classification (or job grading), 362
classes, 362
grades, 362
grade definition, 362
point method, 363
market-competitive pay system, 367
wage curve, 367
salary survey, 368
pay (or wage) grade, 370
pay (or rate) ranges, 371
compa ratio, 372
competency-based pay, 376
broadbanding, 377
comparable worth, 378

Endnotes

1. Elayne Robertson Demby, "Two Stores Refused to Join the Race to the Bottom for Benefits and Wages," *Workforce Management*, February 2004, pp. 57–59; Roberto A. Ferdman, "Why Wegmans Really Is the Best Supermarket in the U.S.," May 13, 2015, https://www.washingtonpost.com/news/wonk/wp/2015/05/13/why-wegmans-really-is-the-best-supermarket-in-the-u-s/?utm_term=.10d15a673968, accessed March 19, 2018.
2. Richard Henderson, *Compensation Management* (Reston, VA: Reston Publishing, 1980), pp. 101–127; Stacey L. Kaplan, "Total Rewards in Action: Developing a Total Rewards Strategy," *Benefits & Compensation Digest* 42, no. 8 (August 2005), pp. 32–37; "Few Organizations' Total Rewards and Business Strategies Fully Align, According to Mercer Survey," May 19, 2014, https://www.mercer.com/newsroom/few-reward-and-business-strategies-align-say-mercer-survey.html, accessed March 19, 2018.
3. Nicholas Wade, "Play Fair: Your Life May Depend on It," *The New York Times*, September 12, 2003, p. 12.
4. Robert Bretz and Stephen Thomas, "Perceived Inequity, Motivation, and Final Offer Arbitration in Major League Baseball," *Journal of Applied Psychology*, June 1992, pp. 280–282; Reginald Ell, "Addressing Employees' Feelings of Inequity: Capitalizing on Equity Theory in Modern Management," *Supervision* 72, no. 5 (May 2011), pp. 3–6.
5. James DeConinck and Duane Bachmann, "An Analysis of Turnover among Retail Buyers," *Journal of Business Research* 58, no. 7 (July 2005), pp. 874–882.
6. Michael Harris et al., "Keeping Up with the Joneses: A Field Study of the Relationships among Upward, Lateral, and Downward Comparisons and Pay Level Satisfaction," *Journal of Applied Psychology* 93, no. 3 (2008), pp. 665–673.
7. David Terpstra and Andre Honoree, "The Relative Importance of External, Internal, Individual, and Procedural Equity to Pay Satisfaction," *Compensation & Benefits Review*, November/December 2003, pp. 67–74.
8. Ibid., p. 68.
9. Millicent Nelson et al., "Pay Me More: What Companies Need to Know about Employee Pay Satisfaction," *Compensation & Benefits Review*, March/April 2008, pp. 35–42.
10. Rachel Emma Silverman, "Psst . . . . This Is What Your Coworker Is Paid," *The Wall Street Journal*, January 30, 2013, p. B6. Pay confidentiality may also violate the National Labor Relations Act, which permits workers to engage in concerted activities for collective bargaining "or other mutual aid or protection." Howard Risher, "Pay Transparency Is Coming," *Compensation & Benefits Review* 46, no. 1 (2014), pp. 3–5.
11. Pay inequities manifest in unexpected ways. In one study, the researchers studied the impact of keeping pay rates secret, rather than publicizing them. They found that individuals with lower levels of tolerance for inequity reacted particularly harshly to pay secrecy in terms of weaker individual test performance. Peter Bamberger and Elena Belogolovsky, "The Impact of Pay Secrecy on Individual Test Performance," *Personnel Psychology* 60, no. 3 (2010), pp. 965–996.
12. Frank Giancola, "What the Research Says about the Effects of Open Pay Policies on Employees' Pay Satisfaction and Job Performance," *Compensation & Benefits Review* 46, no. 3 (May/June 2014), pp. 161–168.
13. Debra Friedman, "Pay Transparency: The New Way of Doing Business," *Compensation & Benefits Review*, 46 (2014), pp. 292–294); Google, which has a contract with the interior department for cloud computing services was asked by the Department of Labor to provide pay information on its employees. Chris Opfer, "Google Faces Labor Department Lawsuit over Pay Data," *Bloomberg BNA Bulletin to Management*, January 10, 2017.
14. Martin Berman-Gorvine, "Want Employees to Be Happy with Their Pay? Try Talking to Them,"*Bloomberg BNA Bulletin to Management*, November 14, 2017.
15. Henderson, *Compensation Management*; see also Barry Gerhart and Sara Rynes, *Compensation: Theory, Evidence, and Strategic Implications* (Thousand Oaks, CA: Sage Publications, 2003); and Joseph Martocchio, *Strategic Compensation* (Upper Saddle River, NJ: Prentice Hall, 2006), pp. 67–94.
16. In *Ledbetter v. Goodyear Tire & Rubber Co.*, the U.S. Supreme Court notably restricted the amount of time (to 180 or 300 days) after each allegedly discriminatory pay decision under Title VII to file or forever lose the claim. Congress subsequently passed and President Obama signed a new law significantly expanding the amount of time to file such claims.
17. The Genetic Information Nondiscrimination Act amended the Fair Labor Standards Act to increase penalties for the death or serious injury of employees under age 18. Allen Smith, "Penalties for Child Labor Violations Increase," *HR Magazine*, July 2008, p. 19.
18. States including Alaska, Arkansas, California, Colorado, Connecticut, Hawaii, Illinois, Kentucky, Maryland, Minnesota, Montana, New Jersey, North Dakota, Oregon, Pennsylvania, Washington, West Virginia, and Wisconsin have their own overtime laws.
19. We'll see that the federal government is pressing to expand employment overtime eligibility. See, for example, "Obama Signs Memo Telling Labor Department to Expand

Employee Overtime Eligibility," *Bloomberg BNA Bulletin to Management*, March 18, 2014, pp. 81–82. Technology is changing what "the workday" means, and how to pay overtime. Recently, for instance, about 45% of workers said they already do work outside of office hours, and about 49% say they handle work e-mails after work. "Technology, Flexible Work Options Are Retiring the Traditional 9-to-5 Job," *Bloomberg BNA Bulletin to Management*, August 2, 2016, p. 243.

20. Martin Berman-Gorvine, "Informal Pressure to Work Overtime Is Risky for Everyone," *Bloomberg BNA Bulletin to Management*, November 21, 2017.
21. Jon Steingart, "Tyson Foods Agrees to Pay $12.6 Million after Visit to Supreme Court," *Bloomberg BNA Bulletin to Management*, August 8, 2017.
22. "LinkedIn to Pay $5.8 Million in Overtime Damages to 359 Employees in Four States, *Bloomberg BNA Bulletin to Management*, August 13, 2014.
23. James Coleman, "App Provides Reminder to Ensure Recordkeeping Is in Order," *Bloomberg BNA Bulletin to Management*, June 14, 2011, p. 191.
24. www.pacifictimesheet.com/timesheet_products/pacific_timesheet_handheld_pda_field_data_entry_software.htm, accessed March 23, 2009.
25. Coleman, "App Provides Reminder."
26. Dave Zielinski, "On the Clock," *HR Magazine*, April 2012, pp. 67–68. "Time stealing" is a serious problem. One study concluded that about 21% of hourly employees may be stealing company time, mostly by punching in and out earlier or later than scheduled. To deal with this problem, employers are increasingly utilizing biometric technology to track attendance. For example, one company uses a facial recognition device to identify who is punching in or out. Sarah Fister Gale, "Employers Punching in Biometric Technology to Track Attendance," *Workforce Management*, May 2013, p. 14.
27. www.ncsl.org/research/labor-and-employment/state-minimum-wage-chart.aspx, accessed April 12, 2015.
28. www.nbcnews.com/feature/in-plain-sight/minimum-wage-hikes-where-voters-gave-themselves-raise-n241616, accessed April 12, 2015.
29. *Gayle Cinquegrani,* "The DOL Releases Proposed Rule Setting $10.10 as Minimum Wage for Federal Contractors," *Bloomberg BNA Bulletin to Management*, June 17, 2014, pp. 185–186.
30. For a description of exemption requirements, see Jeffrey Friedman, "The Fair Labor Standards Act Today: A Primer," *Compensation*, January/February 2002, pp. 51–54; and "Fact Sheet #17A: Exemption for Executive, Administrative, Professional, Computer & Outside Sales Employees under the Fair Labor Standards Act (FLSA)," https://www.dol.gov/whd/overtime/fs17a_overview.pdf, accessed April 1, 2018.
31. https://www.dol.gov/whd/regs/compliance/overtime/modelPolicy_PF.htm, accessed March 19, 2018.
32. "DOL Issues Final Overtime Rule Doubling Exemption Threshold to $47,476," *Bloomberg BNA Bulletin to Management*, May 24, 2016, pp. 161–168; Noam Scheiber, "White House Moves to Make Millions Eligible for Overtime," *The New York Times*, May 18, 2016, pp. A1, B6; Rachel Silverman and Rachel Feintzeig, "Workers May Need to Clock Back In," *The Wall Street Journal*, October 7, 2015, p. B8; Ben Penn, "Employers Wrestle with Whether to Cancel Overtime Rule Plans," *Bloomberg BNABulletin to Management*, November 29, 2016.
33. Ben Penn, "Labor Department to Appeal, Seek Freeze of Overtime Rule Case," *Bloomberg BNA Bulletin to Management*, October 31, 2017.
34. See, for example, Marina Krakovsky, "Above the Bare Minimum," *HR Magazine*, September 2017, pp. 30–36.
35. How to apply these rules is not an exact science. If there's doubt about exemption eligibility, it's probably best to check with the local Department of Labor Wage and Hour office. See, for example, "Attorneys Say FLSA Draws aFine Line between Exempt/Nonexempt Employees," *BNA Bulletin to Management*, July 5, 2005, p. 219; Tim Watson and Barry Miller, "Tightening a White Collar Exemption," *HR Magazine*, December 2010, p. 95.
36. See, for example, Friedman, "The Fair Labor Standards Act Today"; Andre Honoree, "The New Fair Labor Standards Act Regulations and the Sales Force: Who Is Entitled to Overtime Pay?" *Compensation & Benefits Review*, January/February 2006, p. 31; www.shrm.org/issues/FLSA, accessed August 12, 2007; www.dol.gov/esa/whd/flsa, accessed August 12, 2007; and www.dol.gov/whd/flsa, accessed April 1, 2018.
37. Diane Cadrain, "Guard against FLSA Claims," *HR Magazine*, April 2008, pp. 97–100.
38. "Justices 5–4 Reject Labor Department View, Find Pharmaceutical Sales Reps FLSA-Exempt," *Bloomberg BNA Bulletin to Management*, June 19, 2012, p. 193.
39. For discussions of this topic, see for example, Peter Coy, "Is a $15 Minimum Wage Too High?" *Bloomberg Businessweek*, August 10–August 23, 2015, pp. 14–16; Jacob Bunge, "Tyson to Raise Wages for Chicken Plant Staff," *The Wall Street Journal*, October 24, 2015, p. B4; "Walmart to Raise Hourly Workers' Pay to $9.00 per Hour, Increasing to $10 in 2016," *Bloomberg BNA Bulletin to Management*, February 24, 2015, p. 57; "McDonald's Plans to Boost Pay, Offer Vacation to Non-franchise Workers," *Bloomberg BNA Bulletin to Management*, April 7, 2015, p. 107; and Joyce Cutler, "San Jose Is Latest Silicon Valley City to Okay $15 Minimum Wage," *Bloomberg BNA Bulletin to Management*, November 22, 2016.
40. Jamie Dimon, "Why We're Giving Our Employees a Raise," *The New York Times*, July 12, 2016, www.nytimes.com/2016/07/12/opinion/jamie-dimon-why-were-giving-our-employees-a-raise.html, accessed May 3, 2018.
41. Kristen Knebel, "MetLIfe Sets $15 Minimum Wage, Increases Retirement Benefits," *Bloomberg BNA Bulletin to Management*, February 20, 2018.
42. Several state legislatures have moved to tighten regulations regarding misclassifying workers as independent contractors, some going so far as adding criminal penalties for violations. "Misclassification Cases Draw More Attention, Attorneys Say," *Bloomberg BNA Bulletin to Management*, December 15, 2009, p. 399. The U.S. Department ofLabor is working with state agencies to challenge independent contractor worker misclassifications. "DOL, State Agencies, and Litigants Proceed with Challenges to Worker Misclassification," *Bloomberg BNA Bulletin to Management*, August 14, 2012, p. 257.
43. "Federal Court Mostly Rules for FedEx Ground in Driver Lawsuits Alleging Misclassification," *Bloomberg BNA Bulletin to Management*, December 21, 2010, p. 403. Different countries classify independent contractors in different ways, which requires knowledge of the specific local requirements. Eric Krell, "Status Check," *HR Magazine*, November 2011, pp. 63–66.
44. www.irs.gov/Businesses/Small-Businesses-&-Self-Employed/Independent-Contractor-Defined, accessed March 19, 2014.
45. http://www.irs.gov/Businesses/Small-Businesses-&-Self-Employed/Independent-Contractor-Self-Employed-or-Employee, accessed July 13, 2015.
46. See, for instance, www.uschambersmallbusinessnation.com/toolkits/tool/indcon_m.
47. This is based on Matthew Simpson, "Five Steps to Reduce the Risks of Miscalculation," *Bloomberg BNA Bulletin to Management*, February 21, 2012, p. 63.
48. Conrad De Aenlle, "Employee or Contractor? Healthcare Law Raises Stakes," *The New York Times,* February 15, 2015, p. BU 11. Under the Obama administration, the DOL became more aggressive against employers who misclassified employees as independent contractors. Keith Covington and John Rodgers, "The DOL Weighs in on Worker Misclassification," *Bloomberg BNA Bulletin to Management*, September 15, 2015, pp. S1–S4.
49. Richard Reibestein and Janet Barsky, "Five Key Independent Contractor Legal Developments in 2017—And What to Expect in 2018," *Bloomberg BNA Bulletin to Management*, January 9, 2018.
50. http://www.courts.ca.gov/opinions/documents/S222732.PDF, accessed May 3, 2018.
51. Ibid.
52. Tyrone Richardson, "Would Laws against Gig Workers Kill Growth?" *Bloomberg BNA Bulletin to Management*, September 12, 2017.
53. Robert Nobile, "How Discrimination Laws Affect Compensation," *Compensation & Benefits Review*, July/August 1996, pp. 38–42. Also see, for example, Joseph Martocchio, *Strategic Compensation* (Boston: Pearson, 2017), pp. 32–38.
54. See, for example, www.bls.gov/opub/cwc/cm20030124ar01p1.htm, accessed October 9, 2011; Barry Hirsch and Edward Schumacher, "Unions, Wages, and Skills," *Journal of Human Resources* 33, no. 1 (Winter 1998), p. 115; Daniel V. Johns, "NLRB Expands Employers' Duty to Respond to Union Requests for 'Presumptively Relevant' Information," November 12, 2012, http://www.ballardspahr.com/alertspublications/legalalerts/2012-11-12-nlrb-expands-employers-duty-to-respond-to-union-requests.aspx, accessed April 1, 2018.
55. Demby, "Two Stores Refused to Join the Race"; Roberto

A. Ferdman, "Why Wegmans Really Is the Best Supermarket in the U.S.," May 13, 2015, https://www.washingtonpost.com/news/wonk/wp/2015/05/13/why-wegmans-really-is-the-best-supermarket-in-the-u-s/?utm_term=.10d15a673968, accessed March 19, 2018.
56. http://fortune.com/best-companies/wegmans-food-markets/, accessed March 19, 2018.
57. Ibid.
58. https://jobs.wegmans.com/benefits, accessed March 19, 2019.
59. Demby, "Two Stores Refuse to Join the Race"; http://www.hoovers.com/company-information/cs/company-profile.wegmans_food_markets_inc.b9c57fce1a26e491.html, accessed March 19, 2918; http://fortune.com/best-companies/wegmans-food-markets/, accessed March 19, 2018.
60. Demby, "Two Stores Refuse to Join the Race."
61. Ibid.
62. www.bls.gov/oes/current/oes431011.htm, accessed July 27, 2013. Salaries in some specialties (such as engineering) and in some geographic areas (such as Silicon Valley) have become astronomical; firms like Amazon, Google, and Facebook compete to hire more engineers, and most are supplementing those big salaries with stock options grants. "Money Honeys: Tech Firms' Pay Wars," *TheEconomist*, November 5, 2016, p. 53.
63. Helen Deresky, *International Management* (Boston: Pearson, 2017), pp. 304–306.
64. Ibid.
65. See, for example, Joseph Martocchio, *Strategic Compensation* (Upper Saddle River, NJ: Pearson Education, 2011), p. 140; John Kilgour, "Job Evaluation Revisited: The Point-Factor Method," *Compensation & Benefits Review*, July/August 2008, pp. 37–46; and www.shrm.org/TemplatesTools/Toolkits/Pages/PerformingJobEvaluations.aspx, accessed April 5, 2014.
66. Martocchio, *Strategic Compensation*, 2006, p. 138. See also Nona Tobin, "Can Technology Ease the Pain of Salary Surveys?" *Public Personnel Management* 31, no. 1 (Spring 2002), pp. 65–78.
67. Job analysis (Chapter 4) can be a useful source of information on compensable factors, as well as on job descriptions and job specifications. For example, the position analysis questionnaire generates quantitative information on the degree to which the following five basic factors are present in each job: having decision-making/communication/social responsibilities, performing skilled activities, being physically active, operating vehicles or equipment, and processing information. As a result, a job analysis techniqueit is actually as (or some say, more) appropriate as a job evaluation technique (than for job analysis) because jobs can be quantitatively compared to one another on those five dimensions and their relative worth thus ascertained.
68. Michael Carrell and Christina Heavrin, *Labor Relations and Collective Bargaining* (Upper Saddle River, NJ: Prentice Hall, 2004), pp. 300–303.
69. www.hr-guide.com/data/G909.htm, accessed July 10, 2014.
70. Kilgour, "Job Evaluation Revisited," p. 40.
71. See, for example, http://pristina.usembassy.gov/uploads/images/TPAyt1xR9zbj_JQ2iG1tpw/caje1.pdf.
72. Martocchio, *Strategic Compensation*, 2011, p. 140.
73. For a discussion, see Roger Plachy, "The Point Factor Job Evaluation System: A Step-by-Step Guide, Part I," *Compensation & Benefits Review*, July/ August 1987, pp. 12–27; Roger Plachy, "The Case for Effective Point-Factor Job Evaluation, Viewpoint I," *Compensation & Benefits Review*, March/April 1987, pp. 45–48; Roger Plachy, "The Point-Factor Job Evaluation System: A Step-by-Step Guide, Part II," *Compensation & Benefits Review*, September/October 1987, pp. 9–24; and particularly Kilgour, "JobEvaluation Revisited," pp. 37–46.
74. Martocchio, *Strategic Compensation*, 2011, p. 141.
75. Kilgour, "Job Evaluation Revisited," pp. 37–46.
76. Ibid.
77. Ibid.
78. Ibid.
79. Ibid.
80. Ibid.
81. Ibid. Of course, the level of economic activity influences compensation expectations. Fay Hansen, "Currents in Compensation and Benefits," *Compensation & Benefits Review* 42, no. 6 (2010), p. 435.
82. Martocchio, *Strategic Compensation*, 2011, p. 151.
83. Kilgour, "Job Evaluation Revisited," pp. 37–46.
84. Henderson, *Compensation Management*, pp. 260–269. See also "Web Access Transforms Compensation Surveys," *Workforce Management*, April 24, 2006, p. 34; https://www.salary.com/compensation-surveys/, accessed March 19, 2018.
85. https://www.salary.com/compensation-surveys/, accessed March 19, 2018.
86. See Judy Canavan, "Compensation Surveys: The Good, the Bad, and the Ugly," *Compensation & Benefits Review* 46, no. 2 (2014), pp. 74–79.
87. Kilgour, "Job Evaluation Revisited," pp. 37–46. See also William Liccione, "Linking the Market and Internal Values of Jobs: Rethinking the Market Line," *Compensation & Benefits Review* 46, no. 2 (2014), pp. 80–88.
88. Kilgour, "Job Evaluation Revisited," pp. 37–46.
89. David W. Belcher, *Compensation Administration* (Englewood Cliffs, NJ: Prentice Hall, 1974), pp. 257–276; and Nicola Sullivan, "Serco Introduces Pay Grade Structure for Senior Staff," *Employee Benefits*, July 2010, p. 5.
90. Martocchio, *Strategic Compensation*, 2011, p. 185.
91. Ibid., p. 189.
92. Kilgour, "Job Evaluation Revisited," pp. 37–46.
93. Susan Marks, "Can the Internet Help You Hit the Salary Mark?" *Workforce*, January 2001, pp. 86–93.
94. For sources of sample policies see, for example, sites such as http://hr.blr.com/timesavers?type=54 and the HR systems discussion in Chapter 18.
95. Theo Francis and Joann Lublin, "Divide Persists between Pay, Performance," *The Wall Street Journal*, June 3, 2016, pp. B1, B5.
96. "American Chief Executives Are Not Overpaid," *The Economist*, September 8, 2012, p. 67.
97. Syed Tahir Hijazi, "Determinants of Executive Compensation and Its Impact on Organizational Performance," *Compensation & Benefits Review* 39, no. 2 (March–April 2007), p. 58(9).
98. Steven Clifford, "How Companies Actually Decide What to Pay CEOs," *The Atlantic*, June 14, 2017, www.theatlantic.com, accessed March 19, 2018.
99. Roger Lowenstein, "CEO Pay Is Out of Control. Here's How to Rein It In," *Fortune*, April 19, 2017, http://fortune.com/2017/04/19/, accessed March 19, 2018.
100. "Disney Shareholders Vote against CEO Iger's Pay Package," https://www.cnbc.com/2018/03/09/disney-shareholders-vote-against-ceo-igers-pay-package.html, accessed March 19, 2018.
101. Martocchio, *Strategic Compensation*, 2017, pp. 252–257; https://chiefexecutive.net/components-of-an-executive-compensation-plan/, accessed March 19, 2018.
102. Robert Pozen and S. P. Kothari, "Decoding CEO Pay," *Harvard Business Review*, July–August 2017, pp. 78–84.
103. https://www.usatoday.com/story/money/2017/05/23/ceo-pay-highest-paid-chief-executive-officers-2016/339079001/, accessed March 19, 2018.
104. www.dol.gov/whd/regs/compliance/fairpay/fs17d_professional.pdf, accessed June 1, 2011.
105. Ibid.
106. Roger S. Achille, "FLSA Requires Education for Professional Exemption," www.shrm.org/LegalIssues/FederalResources/Pages/2ndFLSAProfessionalExemption.Aspx, accessed August 28, 2011.
107. See, for example, Martocchio, *Strategic Compensation,* 2006; and Patricia Zingheim and Jay Schuster, "Designing Pay and Rewards in Professional Services Companies," *Compensation & Benefits Review*, January/February 2007, pp. 55–62.
108. "Money Honeys," p. 53.
109. See, for example, Kate Allen, "Engineers' Pay and Financial Performance," *ASHRAE Journal* 57, no. 2 (February 2015), pp. 44+.
110. Farhad Manjoo, "Engineers to the Valley: Pay Up," *Fast Company* 153, no. 38 (March 2011).
111. "Money Honeys," p. 53.
112. Dimitris Manolopoulos, "What Motivates Research and Development Professionals? Evidence from Decentralized Laboratories in Greece," *International Journal of Human Resource Management* 17, no. 4 (April 2006), pp. 616–647.
113. Amanda Pelliccione, "2016 Salary and Career Study: Engineering Salary Trends," *Control Engineering* 63, no. 9 (September 2016), p.12.
114. https://payroll.intuit.com/online-payroll/#pricingNav, accessed April 1, 2018.
115. www.shrm.org/HRdisciplines/pages/CMS_012013.aspx, accessed May 20, 2012.
116. See, for example, Robert Heneman and Peter LeBlanc, "Development of and Approach for Valuing Knowledge Work," *Compensation & Benefits Review*, July/August 2002, p. 47. About 12% of employers use skill-based pay, and 13% use competency-based pay. Frank Giancola, "Skill-Based Pay: Fad or Classic?" *Compensation & Benefits Review* 43, no. 4 (2011), pp. 220–226.
117. Gerald Ledford Jr., "Paying for the Skills, Knowledge, and Competencies of Knowledge Workers," *Compensation & Benefits Review*, July/August 1995, p. 56; see also P. K. Zingheim et al., "Competencies and Rewards: Substance or Just Style?" *Compensation & Benefits Review* 35, no. 5 (September/October 2003), pp. 40–44; Frank Giancola, "Skill-Based Pay: Fad or Classic?" *Compensation & Benefits*

Review 43, no. 4 (July 2011), pp. 220–226.

118. See, for example, www.shrm.org/hrdisciplines/compensation/articles/pages/salarystructures.aspx, accessed September 27, 2013.
119. *County of Washington v. Gunther*, U.S. Supreme Court, no. 80–426, June 8, 1981.
120. Laura Fitzpatrick, "Why Do Women Still Earn Less Than Men?" www.time.com/time/nation/article/0,8599,1983185,00.html, accessed September 4, 2014; Claire Suddath, "Why Can't Your Company Just Fix The Gender Wage Gap?" *Bloomberg BNA Bulletin to Management*, June 27, 2017.
121. Rachel Silverman, "Women Doctors Face Pay Disparity," *The Wall Street Journal*, February 8, 2011, p. D4.
122. Suddath, "Why Can't Your Company Just Fix The Gender Wage Gap; E. Frazier, "Raises for Women Executives Match Those for Men, but Pay Gap Persists," *The Chronicle of Philanthropy* 20, no. 24 (October 2, 2008), p. 33; Madeline Farber, Three Reasons the Pay Gap Still Exists," April 3, 2017, http://fortune.com/2017/04/03/equal-pay-day-2017-wage-gap/, accessed March 19, 2018; Martin Berman-Gorvine, "Pay Equity Movement Pushing Employers to Self-Audit," *Bloomberg BNA Bulletin to Management*, March 3, 2018; Genevieve Douglas, "#MeToo Movement Shines Spotlight on Pay Equity," *Bloomberg BNA Bulletin to Management*, January 30, 2018.
123. The California Fair Pay Act went into effect January 1, 2016, and aims to minimize the gender pay gap. Michelle Rafter, "Wagering on Equal Wages," *Workforce*, February 2016, pp. 33–35, 48.
124. "Executive Compensation," www.sec.gov/fast-answers/answers-execomphtm.html, accessed March 20, 2018.
125. See, for example, "Government Regulation of Executive Compensation," www.execomp.org, accessed March 20, 2018.
126. Anders Melin, "Executive Pay," www.bloomberg.com/quicktake/executive-pay/, accessed March 20, 2018.
127. "The Say on Pay Payday," *The Economist*, February 16, 2013, p. 65.
128. Melin, "Executive Pay," op cit.
129. Society for Human Resource Management, "Changing Leadership Strategies," *Workplace Visions*, no. 1 (2008), p. 3.
130. Ibid. See also Brent Longnecker and James Krueger, "The Next Wave of Compensation Disclosure," *Compensation & Benefits Review*, January/February 2007, pp. 50–54.
131. Robert L. Heneman, "Implementing Total Rewards Strategies," www.shrm.org/hrdisciplines/benefits/Documents/07RewardsStratReport.pdf, accessed March 24, 2014.
132. Dow Scott and Tom McMullen, "The Impact of Rewards Programs on Employee Engagement," *WorldatWork: Survey of Rewards and Employee Engagement*, June 2010, www.worldatwork.org.
133. Duncan Brown and Peter Reilly, "Reward and Engagement: The New Realities," *Compensation & Benefits Review*, 45, no. 3 (2013), pp. 145–157.
134. Tom McMullen, "Eight Recommendations to Improve Employee Engagement," *Journal of Compensation and Benefits*, July/August 2013, p. 23.
135. Melissa Van Dyke and Mike Ryan, "Changing the Compensation Conversation on the Growing Utility of Non-Cash Rewards and Recognition," *Compensation & Benefits Review* 44, no. 5 (2013), pp. 276–279.
136. Meg Breslin, "Solid Rewards Program Can Be Rewarding for Businesses," *Workforce Management*, January 2013, p. 8.
137. Dave Zielinski, "Giving Praise," *HR Magazine*, October 2012, p. 77.
138. Scott and McMullen, "The Impact Rewards Programs on Employee Engagement."
139. Ibid.
140. While some total rewards elements contribute to engagement and performance, it is not clear that others do. For example, it's not clear that "programs such as pet insurance and working at home add anything to the business success of our organization." See Jay Schuster and Patricia Zingheim, "Recalibrating Best Practice," *Compensation & Benefits Review* 45, no. 3 (2013), pp. 134–135.
141. http://disneycareers.com/en/working-here/total-rewards, accessed March 24, 2014.
142. This is based on George Bradt, "How the Best Big Companies to Work for Drive Appreciation, Access and Rewards," www.forbes.com/sites/georgebradt/2014/03/12/how-the-best-fortune-500--companies-to-work-for-drive-appreciation-access-rewards-2, accessed March 24, 2014.
143. www.sas.com/en_us/careers.html, accessed March 24, 2014.
144. McMullen, "Eight Recommendations to Improve Employee Engagement."
145. Sharon Pettypiece, "Unintended Consequences of Walmart's Raise: Unhappy Workers," *Bloomberg Businessweek*, August 6, 2015; Patricia Cohen, "The Raise That Roared," *The New York Times*, August 2, 2015, pp. 1, 4.
146. This case based on www.nature.com/scitable/forums/women-in-science/astrozeneca-settles-women-s-pay-inequality-20334719; www.dol.gov/opa/media/press/ofccp/OFCCP20110829.htm; and http://social.dol.gov/blog/astrazeneca-what-we-learned/, all accessed August 31, 2012.

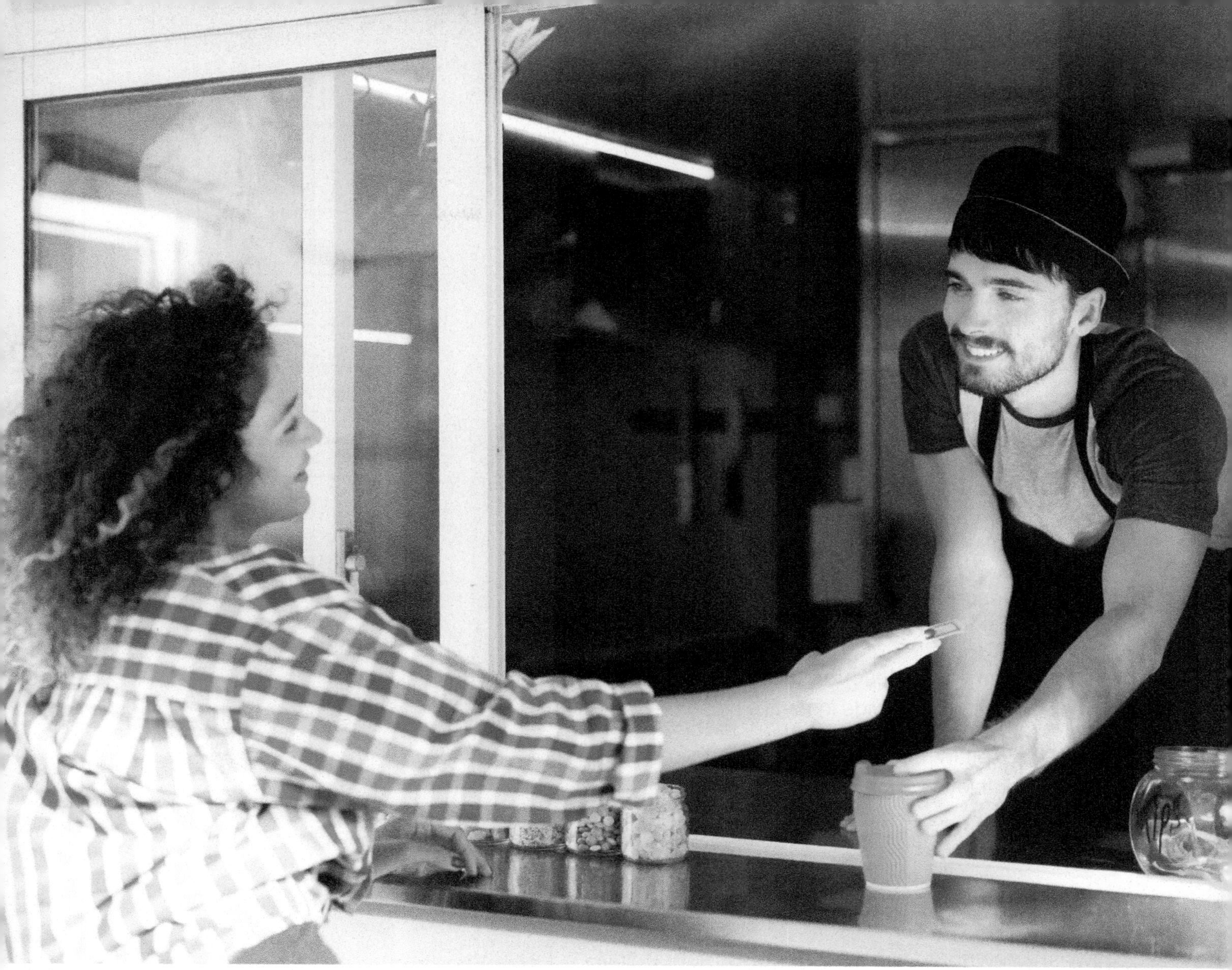
Vadim Guzhva/123RF

12 Pay for Performance and Financial Incentives

LEARNING OBJECTIVES

When you finish studying this chapter, you should be able to:

12-1 **Explain** how you would apply four motivation theories in formulating an incentive plan.

12-2 **Discuss** the main incentives for individual employees.

12-3 **Discuss** the pros and cons of commissions versus straight pay for salespeople.

12-4 **Describe** the main incentives for managers and executives.

12-5 **Name and describe** the most popular organization-wide incentive plans.

12-6 **Explain** how to use incentives to improve employee engagement.

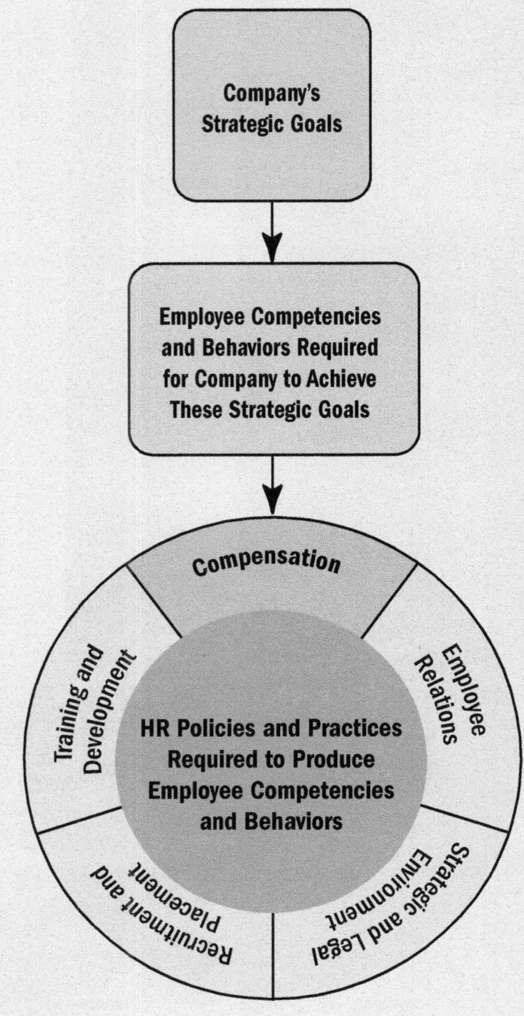

The owners of a 21-store fast-food franchise in the Midwest knew that their stores' performance and profits depended on their employees' performance. They hoped a new employee incentive program could boost their employees' and their stores' performance. We'll see what they did.

WHERE ARE WE NOW . . .

Chapter 11 focused on developing pay plans and on salaries and wages. Incentives are important in any pay plan. The main purpose of this chapter is to explain how managers use incentives to motivate employees. The main topics we'll discuss are **Money's Role in Motivation**, **Individual Employee Incentive and Recognition Programs**, **Incentives for Salespeople**, **Incentives for Managers and Executives**, **Team and Organization-Wide Incentive Plans**, and **Incentives and Employee Engagement**. In Chapter 13, we'll turn to the financial and nonfinancial benefits that comprise the third component of employee compensation packages.

LEARNING OBJECTIVE 12-1

Explain how you would apply four motivation theories in formulating an incentive plan.

financial incentives
Financial rewards paid to workers whose production exceeds some predetemined standard.

productivity
The ratio of outputs (goods and services) divided by the inputs (resources such as labor and capital).

fair day's work
Output standards devised based on careful, scientific analysis.

scientific management movement
Management approach based on improving work methods through observation and analysis.

pay-for-performance
Any plan that ties pay to some measure of performance, such as productivity or profitability.

variable pay
Any plan that ties pay to productivity or profitability, usually as one-time lump payments.

Money's Role in Motivation

Frederick Taylor popularized using **financial incentives**—financial rewards paid to workers whose production exceeds some predetermined standard—in the late 1800s. As a supervisor at the Midvale Steel Company, Taylor was concerned with what he called "systematic soldiering"—the tendency of employees to produce at the minimum acceptable level. Some workers had the energy to run home and work on their houses after a 12-hour day. Taylor knew that if he could harness this energy at work, Midvale could achieve huge productivity gains. **Productivity** "is the ratio of outputs (goods and services) divided by the inputs (resources such as labor and capital)."[1]

In pursuing his aim, Taylor turned to financial incentives. At the time, primitive incentive plans were in use, but were generally ineffective (because employers arbitrarily changed incentive rates).

Taylor made three contributions. He saw the need for formulating a **"fair day's work,"** namely precise output standards for each job. He spearheaded the **scientific management movement,** which emphasized improving work through observation and analysis. And he popularized using incentive pay to reward employees who produced over standard.

Incentive Pay Terminology

Managers often use two terms synonymously with incentive plans.[2] All incentive plans are **pay-for-performance** plans. They all tie employees' pay to the employees' performance. Some limit the term **variable pay** to group or team incentive plans,[3] but most use *variable pay* to include any performance-based incentive plan.

Linking Strategy, Performance, and Incentive Pay

Incentive pay—tying worker pay to performance—is popular.[4] The problem is that doing so is easier said than done. United Airlines tried replacing its quarterly bonus with a lottery. Instead of getting quarterly bonuses when United attained its performance goals, qualified employees would instead be eligible to win, say, $100,000 prizes. Employees revolted, and United returned to its bonus plan.[5] Another incentive plan, at Levi Strauss, is widely assumed to have been the last nail in the coffin of Levi's U.S.-based production.

Research on incentive plans is sketchy, but one older study found that just 28% of 2,600 U.S. workers said their companies' incentive plans motivated them. "Employees don't see a strong connection between pay and performance, and their performance is not particularly influenced by the company's incentive plan," said one expert.[6]

One problem is that many incentive plans incentivize the wrong behavior. For example, a Wells Fargo Bank incentive plan pushed bank employees to hit high sales goals, such as selling eight bank products per customer.[7] Bank employees opened accounts for thousands of customers without the customer's permission.[8] At ethics workshops, managers told employees not to create fake bank accounts. But employees knew they had to meet their sales goals, so they opened fake accounts.[9] Fines, lawsuits, and the CEO's exit came next.

Another big reason for incentive plans' often-dismal results is that incentives that may motivate some people won't motivate others. We'll review some motivation background next, and then go on to explain various incentive plans.

Motivation and Incentives

Several motivation theories have particular relevance to designing incentive plans.

MOTIVATORS AND FREDERICK HERZBERG Frederick Herzberg said the best way to motivate someone is to organize the job so that doing it provides the challenge and recognition we all need to help satisfy "higher-level" needs for things like accomplishment and recognition. These needs are relatively insatiable, says Herzberg, so challenging work provides a sort of built-in motivation generator. Doing things to satisfy a worker's "lower-level" needs for things like better pay and working conditions just keeps the person from becoming dissatisfied.

Herzberg says the factors ("hygienes") that satisfy lower-level needs are different from those ("motivators") that satisfy or partially satisfy higher-level needs. If *hygiene* factors (factors outside the job itself, such as working conditions, salary, and incentive pay) are inadequate, employees become dissatisfied. However, adding more of these hygienes (like incentives) to the job (supplying what Herzberg calls "extrinsic motivation") is an inferior way to try to motivate someone, because lower-level needs are quickly satisfied. Inevitably the person says, in effect, "I want another raise."

Instead of relying on hygienes, says Herzberg, managers interested in creating a self-motivated workforce should emphasize "job content" or *motivator* factors. Managers do this by enriching workers' jobs so that the jobs are more challenging, and by providing feedback and recognition—by making doing the job intrinsically motivating, in other words. In organizational psychology, **intrinsic motivation** is motivation that derives from the pleasure someone gets from doing the job or task. It comes from "within" the person, rather than from externally, such as from a financial incentive plan. Intrinsic motivation means that just doing the task provides the motivation. Herzberg makes the point that relying exclusively on financial incentives is risky. The employer should also provide the recognition and challenging work that most people crave.

intrinsic motivation
Motivation that derives from the pleasure someone gets from doing the job or task.

DEMOTIVATORS AND EDWARD DECI Psychologist Edward Deci's work highlights another potential downside to relying too heavily on extrinsic rewards: They may backfire. Deci found that extrinsic rewards could at times actually detract from the person's intrinsic motivation.[10] The point may be stated thusly: Be cautious in devising incentive pay for highly motivated employees, lest you inadvertently demean and detract from the desire they have to do the job out of a sense of responsibility.

EXPECTANCY THEORY AND VICTOR VROOM In general, people won't pursue rewards they find unattractive, or where the odds of success are very low. Psychologist Victor Vroom's expectancy motivation theory echoes these commonsense observations. He says a person's motivation to exert some level of effort depends on three things: the person's **expectancy** (in terms of probability) that his or her effort will lead to performance;[11] **instrumentality**, or the perceived connection (if any) between successful performance and actually obtaining the rewards; and **valence,** which represents the perceived value the person attaches to the reward.[12] In Vroom's theory:

expectancy
A person's expectation that his or her effort will lead to performance.

instrumentality
The perceived relationship between successful performance and obtaining the reward.

valence
The perceived value a person attaches to the reward.

$$\text{Motivation} = (\text{E} \times \text{I} \times \text{V}),$$

where E represents expectancy, I instrumentality, and V valence. If E or I or V is zero or inconsequential, there will be no motivation.

Vroom's theory has three implications for how managers design incentive plans.

- First, if employees don't *expect* that effort will produce performance, no motivation will occur. So, managers must ensure that their employees have the skills to do the job, and believe they can do the job. Thus, training, job descriptions, and confidence building and support are important in using incentives.
- Second, Vroom's theory suggests that employees must see the *instrumentality* of their efforts—they must believe that successful performance will in fact lead to getting the reward. Managers can accomplish this, for instance, by creating easy-to-understand incentive plans.
- Third, the reward itself must be of *value* to the employee. The manager should take into account individual employee preferences.

BEHAVIOR MODIFICATION/REINFORCEMENT AND B. F. SKINNER Using incentives also assumes the manager understands how consequences affect behavior.[13] Psychologist B.F. Skinner's findings are useful here. Managers apply Skinner's principles by using *behavior modification*. **Behavior modification** means changing behavior through rewards or punishments that are contingent on performance. For managers, behavior modification boils down to two main principles. First, that behavior that appears to lead to a positive consequence (reward) tends to be repeated, whereas behavior that

behavior modification
Using contingent rewards or punishment to change behavior.

appears to lead to a negative consequence (punishment) tends not to be repeated; and second, that managers can therefore get someone to change his or her behavior by providing the properly scheduled rewards (or punishment).

To arrange our discussion, we will organize the following sections around individual employee incentive and recognition programs, sales compensation programs, management and executive incentive compensation programs, and team- and organization-wide incentive programs. First, however, we look at some legal aspects of incentive plan design.

KNOW YOUR EMPLOYMENT LAW

Employee Incentives and the Law

Various laws affect incentive pay. Under the Fair Labor Standards Act, if the incentive the worker receives is in the form of a prize or cash award, the employer generally must *include the value of that award* when calculating the worker's overtime pay for that pay period.[14] So, unless you structure the incentive bonuses properly, the bonus itself becomes part of the week's wages. For example, suppose someone who earns $10 per hour for a 40-hour week also earns, in one week, performance incentive pay (a performance bonus) of $80 for the week, or $480 total pay for the week. Further, assume she *also* works 2 hours overtime that week. The overtime rate for each of the 2 hours she works overtime is not simply 1.5 times her regular $10-per-hour pay. Instead, it is 1.5 times $12 per hour. Why? Because with her performance bonus she earned $480 for the 40-hour week, and $480 divided by 40 hours is $12 per hour. Therefore, she will actually earn in total that week $480 plus the overtime pay of $12 per hour for the two extra hours, or $480 + $24 = $504 total for the week.

Certain bonuses are excludable from overtime pay calculations. For example, Christmas and gift bonuses that are not based on hours worked, or are so substantial that employees don't consider them a part of their wages, do not have to be included in overtime pay calculations. Similarly, purely discretionary bonuses in which the employer retains discretion over how much if anything to pay are excludable.

However, other types of incentive pay *must* be included. Under the Fair Labor Standards Act (FLSA), bonuses to include in overtime pay computations include those promised to newly hired employees; those provided for in union contracts or other agreements; and those announced to induce employees to work more productively or efficiently or to induce them to remain with the company. Such bonuses would include many of those we turn to next, such as individual and group production bonuses. ■

Individual Employee Incentive and Recognition Programs

Several incentive plans are particularly suited for use with individual employees.

LEARNING OBJECTIVE 12-2
Discuss the main incentives for individual employees.

piecework
A system of pay based on the number of items processed by each individual worker in a unit of time, such as items per hour or items per day.

Piecework

Piecework is the oldest incentive plan and still the most commonly used. Earnings are tied directly to what the worker produces. The person is paid a piece rate for each unit he or she produces. Thus, if Tom Smith gets $0.40 apiece for stamping out doorjambs, then he would get, say, $80 for stamping out 200.

Developing a workable piece rate plan requires job evaluation and (ideally) industrial engineering. Job evaluation enables you to assign an hourly wage rate to the job in question. But the crucial issue is the production standard, and this is often developed by industrial engineers. The engineers state production standards in terms of a standard number of minutes per unit or a standard number of units per hour. In Tom Smith's case, the job evaluation indicated that his doorjamb stamping job was worth $8.00 an hour. The industrial engineer determined that 20 jambs per hour was the standard production rate. Therefore, the engineered piece rate (for each doorjamb) was $8.00 divided by 20, which equals $0.40 per doorjamb.

straight piecework
An incentive plan in which a person is paid a sum for each item he or she makes or sells, with a strict proportionality between results and rewards.

With a **straight piecework** plan, Tom Smith would be paid based on the number of doorjambs he produced; there would be no guaranteed minimum wage. However, today most employers must guarantee their workers a minimum wage. With a guaranteed piecework plan, Tom Smith would be paid $7.25 per hour (the 2018 minimum wage) whether or not he stamped out 18 doorjambs per hour (at $0.40 each). But he would also get $0.40 for each unit over 18.

Piecework generally implies "straight piecework," a strict proportionality between results and rewards regardless of level of output. Thus, in Smith's case, he continues to get $0.40 apiece for stamping out doorjambs, even if he stamps out more than the planned, say, 500 per day. However, some piecework plans share productivity gains between worker and employer. For example, the employee might only get $0.35 per piece over 400 units per day, instead of $0.40. Other plans *boost* the employee's share once a threshold is met—such as paying Tom $0.45 each once he reached 400 units per day.

standard hour plan
A plan by which a worker is paid a basic hourly rate but is paid an extra percentage of his or her rate for production exceeding the standard per hour or per day. Similar to piecework payment but based on a percent premium.

The **standard hour plan** is like the piecework plan, with one difference. Instead of getting a rate per piece, the worker gets a pay premium equal to the percent by which his or her performance exceeds the standard. So if Tom's standard is 160 doorjambs per day ($64 per eight hour day), and he actually makes 200 jambs, he'd get an extra 25% (40/160), or $80. Using this approach may reduce workers' tendency to link their production standard (18 jambs per hour) to pay. This makes it easier to change the standard.

ADVANTAGES AND DISADVANTAGES Piecework incentive plans have several advantages. They are simple to calculate and easily understood by employees. Piecework plans appear equitable in principle, and their incentive value can be powerful since they tie pay directly to performance.

Piecework also has disadvantages. One is an unsavory reputation, based on employers' habit of arbitrarily raising production standards whenever workers earned "excessive" wages. A more subtle drawback is that because piece rates are quoted on a per piece basis, in worker's minds the production standard (in pieces per hour) becomes tied inseparably to what they earn. Piecework plans can thus engender rigidity. When the employer tries to raise production standards, resistance ensues. Employees may similarly focus less on quality, and may resist switching jobs (since doing so could reduce productivity). Even equipment maintenance may suffer as employees push to hit quotas.

Merit Pay as an Incentive

merit pay (merit raise)
Any salary increase awarded to an employee based on his or her individual performance.

Merit pay or a **merit raise** is a salary increase the firm awards to an individual employee based on individual performance. It is different from a bonus in that it usually becomes part of the employee's base salary, whereas bonuses are generally one-time payments. Although the term *merit pay* can apply to the incentive raises given to any employee, the term is more often used for professional, office, and clerical employees.

Merit pay has pros and cons. Advocates say granting pay raises across the board (*without* regard to merit) reduces performance by rewarding employees regardless of how they perform. Detractors argue, most notably, that since most appraisals are unfair, so too are the merit decisions based on them.

The evidence is mixed. For example, one study in a nuclear waste facility found a "very modest relationship between merit pay increase and performance rating."[15] Studies of merit pay for teachers found that merit pay was more linked to research productivity than to teaching effectiveness.[16] A recent survey found that only 20% of employers in North America said merit pay drives higher levels of performance.[17] (This survey also concluded that awarding raises for demonstrating job-critical knowledge and skills was the better option.)[18]

If a merit pay plan isn't working, one sensible reaction is to improve it. This starts with establishing effective appraisal procedures, to ensure that managers actually do tie merit awards to performance. Similarly, merit plan effectiveness requires really differentiating among employees. In one survey, the highest-paid office clerical employees got short-term incentive payouts of about 13%, the lowest-rated got 3%, and mid-rated employees got 8%.[19]

HR in Action at the Hotel Paris Based on their analysis, Lisa Cruz and the CFO concluded that, by any measure, their company's incentive plan was inadequate. The percentage of the workforce whose merit increase was tied to performance was effectively zero, because managers awarded merit pay across the board. To see how they handled this, see the case on pages 414–415.

MERIT PAY OPTIONS Two merit pay adaptations are popular. One awards merit raises in a lump sum once a year (making them, in effect, short-term bonuses for lower-level workers). Traditional merit increases become part of the employee's salary, but these *lump-sum merit raises* do not. This has two benefits. First, the merit raise is not baked into the employee's salary, so you need not pay it year after year. Lump-sum merit increases are also more dramatic. For example, a 5% lump-sum merit payment to a $30,000 employee is $1,500 cash, as opposed to a weekly merit payout of about $29.

The other adaptation ties merit awards to both individual and organizational performance. Table 12-1 shows an example. In this example, you measure company performance by profits. Here, company performance and the employee's performance (using his or her performance appraisal) receive equal weight in computing merit pay. In Table 12-1 an outstanding performer would receive 70% of his or her maximum lump-sum award even when the company's performance is marginal. However, employees with marginal or unacceptable performance get no lump-sum awards even when the firm's performance was outstanding. Alternatively, you might decide to award, say, 60% of someone's bonus based on the supervisor's appraisal, 30% based on department performance, and 10% based on company performance.

Incentives for Professional Employees

Professional employees are those whose work involves the application of learned knowledge to the solution of the employer's problems, such as lawyers and engineers.

Making incentive pay decisions for professional employees is challenging. For one thing, firms usually pay professionals well anyway. For another, they're already driven by the desire to produce high-caliber work.

However, it is unrealistic to assume that people like Google engineers work only for professional gratification. Few firms, therefore, work harder than Google to maintain competitive incentives for professionals. For example, Google reportedly pays higher incentives to engineers working on important projects. Those who choose the intrinsic motivation of working on more theoretical long-term projects are rewarded if their research pays off.[20] As at most Silicon Valley firms, Google's professionals also bask in the light of potentially millionaire-making stock option grants.

Dual-career ladders are another way to manage professionals' pay. At many employers, higher pay requires rerouting from, say, engineering into management.

TABLE 12-1 Merit Award Determination Matrix (an Example)

The Employee's Performance Rating (Weight = 0.50)	*The Company's Performance (Weight = 0.50)*				
	Outstanding	Excellent	Good	Marginal	Unacceptable
Outstanding	1.00	0.90	0.80	0.70	0.00
Excellent	0.90	0.80	0.70	0.60	0.00
Good	0.80	0.70	0.60	0.50	0.00
Marginal	—	—	—	—	—
Unacceptable	—	—	—	—	—

Note: To determine the dollar value of each employee's award: (1) multiply the employee's annual, straight-time wage or salary as of June 30 times his or her maximum incentive award (as determined by management or the board—such as, "10% of each employee's pay") and (2) multiply the resultant product by the appropriate percentage figure from this table. For example, if an employee had an annual salary of $40,000 on June 30 and a maximum incentive award of 7% and if her performance and the organization's performance were both "excellent," the employee's award would be $2,240: ($40,000 × 0.07 × 0.80 = $2,240).

However, not all professionals want management. Therefore, many employers institute one career path for managers, and another for technical experts, allowing the latter to earn higher pay without switching to management.[21]

Nonfinancial and Recognition-Based Awards

Employers often supplement financial incentives with various nonfinancial and recognition-based awards. The term *recognition program* usually refers to formal programs, such as employee-of-the-month programs. *Social recognition program* generally refers to informal manager–employee exchanges such as praise, approval, or expressions of appreciation for a job well done. *Performance feedback* means providing quantitative or qualitative information on task performance so as to change or maintain performance; showing workers a graph of how their performance is trending is an example.[22]

TRENDS SHAPING HR: *DIGITAL AND SOCIAL MEDIA*[23]

Employers are bulking up their recognition programs with digital support. For example, Baudville offers a workplace recognition e-card service called ePraise. Employers use this to tell employees they're appreciated. Intuit shifted its employee recognition, years of service, patent awards, and wellness awards programs to Globoforce.com, an online awards vendor. This "allowed us to build efficiencies and improved effectiveness" into the programs, says Intuit.[24]

Various new apps let employees showcase their awards, contributions, and praise from coworkers, and enable employees to praise each other.[25] For example, one lets employees "give recognition by picking out a badge and typing in a quick note to thank the people who matter most. . . ." Others let users post the positive feedback they receive to their LinkedIn profiles.

Mobile technology is also changing how employers incentivize front-line service people. For example, pay for a $5.00 espresso in many coffeehouses with a credit card and the iPad screen will ask how big a tip you want to leave—from $1.00 to $3.00.[26] ■

Most employers offer both financial and nonfinancial awards. At one company, customer service reps who exceed standards receive a plaque, a $500 check, their photo and story on the firm's intranet, and a dinner for themselves and their teams.[27] One survey of 235 managers found the most-used financial and nonfinancial rewards (from most used to least) were:[28] employee recognition, gift certificates, special events, cash rewards, merchandise incentives, e-mail/print communications, training programs, work/life benefits, variable pay, group travel, individual travel, and sweepstakes. The HR Tools feature elaborates.

IMPROVING PERFORMANCE: *HR TOOLS FOR LINE MANAGERS AND SMALL BUSINESSES*

The supervisor should not rely only on the employer's financial incentive plans for motivating subordinates. There are simply too many opportunities to motivate employees every day to let those opportunities pass. What to do?

First, the best option for motivating an employee is also the simplest—*make sure the employee has a doable goal* and that he or she agrees with it. It makes little sense to try to motivate employees with incentives if they don't know their goals or don't agree with them. Psychologist Edwin Locke and his colleagues have consistently found that specific, challenging goals lead to higher task performance than do specific unchallenging goals; vague goals ("do your best"); or no goals.

Second, *recognizing an employee's contribution* is a powerful motivation tool. Studies show that recognition has a positive impact on performance, either alone or combined with financial rewards. For example, in one study, combining financial rewards with recognition produced a 30% performance improvement in service firms, almost twice the effect of using each reward alone. Figure 12-1 presents a list.

FIGURE 12-1 Social Recognition and Related Positive Reinforcement Managers Can Use

- Challenging work assignments
- Freedom to choose own work activity
- Having fun built into work
- More of preferred task
- Role as boss's stand-in when he or she is away
- Role in presentations to top management
- Job rotation
- Encouragement of learning and continuous improvement
- Being provided with ample encouragement
- Being allowed to set own goals
- Compliments
- Expression of appreciation in front of others
- Note of thanks
- Employee-of-the-month award
- Special commendation
- Bigger desk
- Bigger office or cubicle

Source: Based on Bob Nelson, *1001 Ways to Reward Employees* (New York: Workman Publishing, 1994), p. 19; Sunny C. L. Fong and Margaret A. Shaffer, "The Dimensionality and Determinants of Pay Satisfaction: A Cross-Cultural Investigation of a Group Incentive Plan," *International Journal of Human Resource Management* 14, no. 4 (June 2003), p. 559 (22).

Third, use *social recognition* apps for positive reinforcement. As noted earlier, online tools such as Globoforce (www.globoforce.com/how-it-works/superior-innovation/social-recognition/) enable employees to recognize each other's contributions in real time, and encourage them to emulate outstanding behaviors.[29] One pitfall to avoid: awarding points for recognizing colleagues can lead to excessive compliments.[30] ■

MyLab Management Talk About It 1

If your professor has assigned this, go to the Assignments section of **www.pearson.com/mylab/management** to complete this discussion question.You have decided to verify that recognition does in fact improve performance. To that end, you will use an honest observation to praise someone's performance today. What was the effect of your experiment?

HR AND THE GIG ECONOMY: *RECOGNITION, NONFINANCIAL REWARDS, AND GIG WORKERS*

Some assume that pay is all that matters to gig workers, but that's not the case. One study found that gig workers will exhibit intrinsic motivation (motivation that comes from "inside" the person, driving him or her to do a good job), if the workers identify with the organization.[31] How to accomplish that? According to Mercer, a human resource management consultant, employers can do at least three things.[32]

Provide Meaning and Structure

Everyone wants to feel they're contributing in a meaningful way.Use company communications to provide gig workers with a context within which to understand how they're contributing to the company's success.

Create a Sense of Belonging and Connection

At work most people want to feel that they're part of a community. Take steps to make gig workers feel they're part of something, such as through online communities where they share stories and ideas.

Value and Respect Your Workforce

Treat your gig workers (and all workers) respectfully, and consider rewarding their progress with things like badges based on customer ratings.

Job Design

Although not usually considered an "incentive," job design (discussed in Chapter 4) can affect employee motivation. A study by Harvard Business School researchers concluded that job design is a primary driver of employee engagement. Another by Sibson Consulting concluded that job responsibility and feedback were the fifth- and seventh-most important drivers of employee engagement. Another study concluded that challenging work ranked as the seventh-most important driver for attracting employees.[33] Job design can thus be a useful part of a total rewards program.

The Strategic Context feature illustrates how employers combine incentives to boost profits.

IMPROVING PERFORMANCE: *THE STRATEGIC CONTEXT*

The Fast-Food Chain

The heart of just about any fast-food chain's strategy is to control performance: One asked, "Can financial and nonfinancial incentives boost performance in our fast-food chain?"

Two researchers studied the impact of financial and nonfinancial incentives on business performance in 21 stores of a Midwest fast-food franchise.[34] The researchers compared performance over time in stores that did and did not use financial and nonfinancial incentives. Each store had about 25 workers and two managers. The researchers trained the managers to identify measurable employee behaviors that were currently deficient but that could influence store performance. Example behaviors included "keeping both hands moving at the drive-through window" and "repeating the customer's order back to him or her."[35] Then the researchers instituted financial and nonfinancial incentive plans. They measured store performance in terms of gross profitability (revenue minus expenses), drive-through time, and employee turnover.

Financial Incentives

Some employees in some of the stores received financial incentives for exhibiting the desired behaviors. The financial incentives consisted of lump-sum bonuses in the workers' paychecks. For example, if the manager observed a work team exhibiting up to 50 behaviors (such as "working during idle time") during the observation period, he or she added $25 to the paychecks of all store employees that period; 50 to 100 behaviors added $50 per paycheck, and more than 100 behaviors added $75 per paycheck. Payouts eventually rose over time as the employees learned to enact the behaviors they were to exhibit.

Nonfinancial Incentives

The researchers trained the managers in some stores to use nonfinancial incentives such as feedback and recognition. For example, for *performance feedback* managers maintained charts showing the drive-through times at the end of each day. They placed the charts by the time clocks. Thus, these store employees could keep track of their store's performance on measures like drive-through times. The researchers also trained managers to administer *recognition* to employees. For instance, "I noticed that today the drive-through times were really good."[36]

Results

Both the financial and nonfinancial incentives improved employee and store performance.[37] For example, store profits rose 30% for those units where managers used financial rewards. Store profits rose 36% for those units where managers used nonfinancial rewards. During the same 9-month period, drive-through times decreased 19% for the financial incentives group, and 25% for the nonfinancial incentives groups. Turnover improved 13% for the financial incentives group, and 10% for the nonfinancial incentives group.

Implications for Managers

Here is what these findings mean for managers designing incentive plans:[38]

1. Link the incentive to behavior that is crucial for achieving strategic goals.[39] For example, this chain wanted to boost store performance and profits. Incentivizing employees to work faster and smarter accomplished that.
2. The point of an incentive is to motivate the person to work better. Therefore, it makes more sense to use an incentive plan when (1) motivation (not ability) is the problem; (2) when the employee's effort and results are directly related; and (3) when the employee can actually control the results you plan to incentivize. Put another way, make sure there is a clear link between the person's *effort and performance* and between the *performance and reward*, that the incentive is *attractive* to the employee, and that the employee *has the skills* to do the job.

3. Don't just rely on material rewards. Support the incentive plan with performance feedback (like the performance graphs) and with recognition.[40]
4. Set complete standards. For example, don't just pay for "repeating the customer's order" if speed is important too.
5. Be scientific. As in this study, *gather evidence*, and analyze the effects of the incentive plan over time.[41]

MyLab Management Talk About It 2

If your professor has assigned this, go to the Assignments section of **www.pearson.com/mylab/management** to complete this discussion question. The dean has asked you to design an incentive plan for your professor. How would you apply what you learned in this feature to do so?

LEARNING OBJECTIVE 12-3

Discuss the pros and cons of commissions versus straight pay for salespeople.

Incentives for Salespeople

As one survey said, "the performance metrics given to the sales team must drive behaviors that will help the company's . . . strategy to be successful."[42] Unfortunately, that survey also found that "30% of respondents believe their sales compensation program rewarded the right behaviors 'not well' or 'very poorly.'"[43] Employers are therefore moving to align how they measure and reward their salespeople, with their firms' strategic goals.[44]

Salary Plan

Sales compensation plans focus on salary, commissions, or some combination of the two.[45] Some firms pay salespeople fixed salaries (perhaps with occasional incentives such as bonuses, sales contest prizes, and the like).[46] Straight salary makes sense when the main aim is prospecting (finding new clients) or account servicing. Recruiting is another reason. Faced with difficulty attracting good salespeople, a car dealership in Lincolnton, North Carolina, offers straight salary as an option to salespeople who sell an average of at least eight vehicles a month (plus a small "retention bonus" per car sold).[47] Straight salary also makes it easier to switch salespersons' territories. The main disadvantage, of course, is that straight salary lacks commissions' motivation potential.

Commission Plan

Straight commission plans pay salespeople only for results. Commission plans tend to attract high-performing salespeople because they see that effort produces rewards. Sales costs are proportionate to sales rather than fixed, and the company's fixed sales costs are thus lower. Such plans are easy to understand and compute. Commission plan alternatives include straight commissions, quota bonuses (for meeting particular quotas), management by objectives programs (pay is based on specific metrics), and ranking programs (which reward high achievers but pay little or no bonuses to the lowest-performing salespeople).[48] About half of companies surveyed use "top-line" measures like revenue, while the others use bottom-line criteria like profits; some also use nonsales measures.[49]

However, in poorly designed plans, salespeople may focus on making the sale, and neglect nonselling duties such as servicing small accounts and pushing hard-to-sell items. Wide variations in pay can make some feel the plan is inequitable. Misjudging sales potential can lead to excessive commissions and to having to cut commission rates. Salespersons' pay may be excessive in boom times and low in recessions. Furthermore, sales performance—like any performance—reflects not just motivation, but also ability. If the person can't sell, commissions won't help.[50]

Combination Plan

Most companies pay salespeople a combination of salary and commissions. The combination varies by industry and by what the company hopes to achieve, but a split of about 60%–70% base salary and 40%–30% incentive seems typical.[51]

Combination plans have pros and cons.[52] They give salespeople a floor to their earnings, let the company specify what services the salary component is for (such as servicing current accounts), and still provide a performance incentive. But the salary isn't tied to performance, so the employer trades away some incentive value.

Combination plans also tend to be complicated, so misunderstandings can ensue. This isn't a problem with a simple salary-plus-commission plan, but most plans aren't so simple. For example, in a "commission-plus-drawing-account" plan, the salesperson is paid based on commissions. However, he or she can draw on future earnings during low sales periods. In the "commission-plus-bonus" plan, the firm pays its salespeople mostly based on commissions. However, they also get a small bonus for directed activities like selling slow-moving items.

Maximizing Sales Results

In setting sales quotas and commission rates, one wants to motivate sales activity but avoid excessive commissions. Unfortunately, the tendency to set commission rates informally often reduces such plans' effectiveness.[53]

Setting effective quotas is an art. Questions to ask include: Are quotas communicated to the sales force within 1 month of the start of the period? Does the sales force know how their quotas are set? Do you combine bottom-up information (like account forecasts) with top-down requirements (like the company business goals)? Are returns and de-bookings reasonably low?[54]

One expert suggests this rule as to whether the sales incentive plan is effective: 75% or more of the sales force achieving quota or better, 10% of the sales force achieving higher performance level (than previously), and 5% to 10% of the sales force achieving below-quota performance and receiving coaching.[55] Also consider the effect of sales carryover: In most firms, a significant portion of the sales in one year reflects a "carryover" (sales that would repeat even without any efforts by the sales force) of sales from the prior year. Paying the sales force a commission on all the current year's sales means the employer pays a commission on last year's carryover sales, which the salesperson had little or no role in bringing in this year.[56]

A survey of sales effectiveness reveals that salespeople at high-performing companies:

- Receive 38% of their total cash compensation in the form of *sales incentive pay* (compared with 27% for salespeople at low-performing companies)
- Are twice as likely to receive stock, *stock options*, or other equity pay as their counterparts at low-performing companies (36% versus 18%)
- Spend 264 more hours per year on *high-value sales activities* (e.g., prospecting, making sales presentations, and closing) than salespeople at low-performing companies
- Spend 40% more time each year with their *best potential customers*—qualified leads and prospects they know—than salespeople at low-performing companies
- Spend nearly 25% *less time on administration*, allowing them to allocate more time to core sales activities, such as prospecting leads and closing sales[57]

Distinguishing among performers is also important. For example, some companies distinguish among stars, laggards, and core sales performers. Companies that limit commission earnings can perversely encourage stars to stop selling when they reach their quotas. Laggards do better with more frequent, quarterly bonuses and social pressure to improve. Core performers—the midrange of the sales force—need multitier targets. The first tier target is what sales agents historically attain. The second tier is what a small percentage of the sales force attains. The third tier target is usually only attained by the company's star salespeople.[58] One expert advocates "acceleration": here the commission rate rises for those who meet their sales targets.[59] Finally, track cost of sales—for instance, a salesperson's *salary* plus *commissions* (assuming 100% of quota) plus *bonus* opportunities—divided by that person's sales revenues.[60]

ENTERPRISE INCENTIVE MANAGEMENT Many employers use Enterprise Incentive Management (EIM) software to track and control sales commissions.[61] For example, Oracle Sales Cloud enables management to easily create scorecard metrics such as number of prospecting calls and sales contracts, and to monitor these in real time on the system's dashboards.[62] It also helps users gamify the sales incentive process, by awarding points or badges based on each salesperson's performance.

Sales Incentives in Action

Traditionally, a car salesperson's commission is based on a percentage of the difference between the dealer's invoice cost and the amount the car is sold for, minus an amount to cover the "pack" or dealer overhead (the pack being perhaps $300 for a new car to $800 for a used car, and rising for pricier cars).[63]

This approach encourages the salesperson to hold firm on the retail price, and to push "after-sale products" like floor mats and side moldings. There may also be extra incentives to sell packages such as rustproofing. For selling slow-moving vehicles, the salesperson may get a "spiff"—an extra incentive bonus over commission. And there are bonuses, such as Salesperson of the Month (perhaps $300 for most cars sold).[64]

Incentives for Managers and Executives

LEARNING OBJECTIVE 12-4
Describe the main incentives for managers and executives.

Managers play a crucial role in divisional and company-wide profitability, and most employers therefore think through how to reward them. Most managers get short-term and long-term incentives in addition to salary. Short-term incentives might include, for instance, annual incentive plans (which reward achieving preset results and are usually paid in cash), discretionary bonuses (based on performance), retention bonuses, and the manager's share of any profit-sharing plan.[65] To link shareholders' and managers' interests, long-term incentives are often paid in stock or stock options.

Strategy and the Executive's Long-Term and Total Rewards Package

Whether consolidating operations or pursuing growth, firms can't fully implement most strategies in just 1 or 2 years. Therefore, the long-term signals you send managers via long-term incentives can determine whether the firm's strategy succeeds.

The executives' reward components—base salary, short-and long-term incentives, and benefits—must align with each other and with the company's strategic aims. Compensation experts suggest first specifying the strategic aims—"What is our strategy, and what are our strategic goals?"—and then deciding what long-term behaviors (boosting sales, cutting costs, and so on) are important for achieving these strategic aims. Next shape each component of the executive total compensation package (base salary, short-and long-term incentives, and benefits) to encourage these required behaviors; then combine the components into a plan. The point is this: Each pay component should help focus the manager's attention on the behaviors required to achieve the company's strategic goals.[66]

Using multiple, strategy-based performance criteria for incentivizing executives is best. Criteria include financial performance, number of strategic goals met, employee productivity measures, customer satisfaction surveys, and employee morale surveys.[67]

One expert estimates that the typical CEO's salary accounts for about one-fifth of his or her pay. A bonus based on explicit short-term performance standards accounts for another fifth, and long-term incentive awards such as stock options and long-term performance plans account for the remaining three-fifths.[68] Ideally, the performance standards should include a combination of market benchmarks (such as performance against competitors) as well as business performance standards (such as earnings per share growth).

SARBANES–OXLEY The Sarbanes–Oxley Act of 2002 affects how employers formulate their executive incentive programs. Congress passed Sarbanes–Oxley to inject a higher level of responsibility into executives' and board members' decisions. It makes them personally liable for violating their fiduciary responsibilities to their shareholders. The act also requires CEOs and CFOs of a public company to repay any bonuses, incentives, or equity-based compensation received from the company during the 12-month period following the issuance of a financial statement that the company must restate due to material noncompliance with a financial reporting requirement stemming from misconduct.[69]

annual bonus
Plans that are designed to motivate short-term performance of managers and that are tied to company profitability.

Short-Term Incentives and the Annual Bonus

For better or worse, employers are shifting away from long-term incentives to put more emphasis on short-term performance and incentives.[70] Most firms have **annual bonus** plans for motivating managers' short-term performance. Such short-term incentives can easily produce plus-or-minus adjustments of 25% or more to total pay. Three factors influence one's bonus: eligibility, fund size, and individual performance.

ELIGIBILITY Employers first decide eligibility. Traditionally, most based annual bonus eligibility on job level/title, base salary, and/or officer status. Some simply based eligibility on job level or job title, or salary.[71] Recently, more employers were offering a broader range of employee annual incentive plans ". . . in which both executives and other employees participate."[72]

The trend is evident from surveys of what determines bonus plan eligibility. Rather than job title or officer status, s*alary grade or band* was the most common eligibility determinant, reported by 42% of employers in one survey. This was followed by *title/reporting relationship* (24%), *officer status* (13%), *compensation committee approval* (11%), *discretionary* (6%), and *base salary* (2%).[73]

The percentage size of any bonus is typically greater for top executives. Thus, an executive earning $250,000 in salary may be able to earn another 80% of his or her salary as a bonus, while a manager in the same firm earning $100,000 can earn only another 30%. In one year, Microsoft's CEO was eligible for an annual bonus of up to 100% of his salary (but collected only half). A typical bonus percentage might be executives, 45% of base salary; managers, 25%; and supervisory personnel, 12%.

FUND SIZE Second, one must determine how big the annual bonus fund should be. Most employers (33% in one survey) use the sum of targets approach.[74] This means they estimate the likely bonus for each eligible ("target") employee, and total these to arrive at the bonus pool's size.

However, more employers are funding the short-term bonus based on financial results. Here there are no fixed rules about how much of the profits to pay out. One alternative is to reserve a minimal amount of the profits, say, 10%, for safeguarding stockholders' investments. Then establish a fund for bonuses equal to, say, 20% of the operating profit (profit from the company's core business) before taxes in excess of this safeguard amount. Suppose the operating profits were $200,000 (after putting away 10% to safeguard stockholders). Then the management bonus fund might be 20% of $200,000, or $40,000.

Most employers use more than one financial measure on which to base the bonus fund; sales, earnings per share, and cash flow are the most popular.[75] Other illustrative formulas include:

- Twelve percent of net earnings after deducting 6% of net capital
- Ten percent of the amount by which net income exceeds 5% of stockholders' equity

Employers also use formulas to set their bonus pools based on other measures they wish to emphasize. For example, Transocean Ltd., the firm that managed the Deepwater Horizon Gulf oil rig that sank in 2010, uses a formula that includes "safety" as 25% of the formula. After the Gulf explosion, senior Transocean executives donated safety bonuses to the victims' families.[76] Other firms decide bonuses on a discretionary basis.

THE INDIVIDUAL AWARDS Finally, one must decide the actual individual awards. Typically, the employer sets a target bonus (as well as maximum bonus, perhaps double the target bonus) for each eligible position. The actual bonus then reflects the manager's performance. For example, having previously decided which financial performance

Even in retail stores, it's not unusual to compensate managers partly based on short-term sales and profits.

Monkey Business Images/Shutterstock

measures (return on assets, revenue growth, and so on) to use to measure each manager's performance, the employer computes preliminary total company bonus estimates, and compares the total amount of money required with the bonus fund available.[77] If necessary, it then adjusts the individual bonus estimates. In any case, outstanding managers should receive at least their target bonuses, and marginal ones should receive at best below-average awards. Use what you save on the marginal employees to supplement the outstanding employees. A study of CEOs of Standard & Poor's 1500 companies for one 3-year period found that 57% of the CEOs received pay increases, although company performance (in terms of total shareholder return) did not improve.[78]

One question is whether to give managers bonuses based on individual performance, corporate performance, or both. Firms usually tie top-level executive bonuses mostly to overall corporate results (or divisional results if the executive heads a major division). But as one moves farther down, corporate profits become a less-accurate gauge of a manager's contribution. For supervisors or the heads of functional departments, it often makes more sense to base the bonus more on individual performance.

Many firms end up tying short-term bonuses to both organizational and individual performance. Perhaps the simplest method is the *split-award plan*. This makes the manager eligible for two bonuses, one based on his or her individual effort and one based on the organization's overall performance. Thus, a manager might be eligible for an individual performance bonus of up to $10,000, but receive only $2,000 at the end of the year, based on his or her individual performance evaluation. But the person might also receive a second bonus of $3,000, based on the firm's profits for the year.

One drawback to this approach is that it may give marginal performers too much—for instance, someone could get a company-based bonus, even if his or her own performance is mediocre. One way to avoid this is to use the *multiplier method*. As Table 12-2 illustrates, multiply the person's target bonus by 1.00, 0.80, or zero (if the firm's performance is excellent, and the person's performance is excellent, good, fair, or poor). A manager whose own performance is poor does not even receive the company-based bonus.

LONG TERM INCENTIVES Employers use *long-term incentives* to inject a long-term perspective into their executives' decisions. With only short-term (generally one year) criteria to shoot for, a manager could conceivably boost profitability by reducing plant maintenance, for instance; this tactic might catch up with the company 3 or 4 years

TABLE 12-2 Multiplier Approach to Determining Annual Bonus

Individual Performance (Based on Appraisal, Weight = 0.50)	*Company Performance (Based on Sales Targets, Weight = 0.50)*			
	Excellent	Good	Fair	Poor
Excellent	1.00	0.90	0.80	0.70
Good	0.80	0.70	0.60	0.50
Fair	0.00	0.00	0.00	0.00
Poor	0.00	0.00	0.00	0.00

Note: To determine the dollar amount of a manager's award, multiply the maximum possible (target) bonus by the appropriate factor in the matrix.

later. Popular long-term incentives include cash, stock options, stock, stock appreciation rights, and phantom stock.[79] PepsiCo's CEO was paid $26.4 million for one year, including a base salary of $1.6 million, stock awards of $6.25 million and a performance-based cash bonus of $13.9 million, a $4.26 million adjustment to her pension, plus perks such as air travel.[80]

Long-term incentives such as stock options, if well-designed, should only pay off if the firm achieves its strategic goals (such as "double our rate of return"), because the owners and investors should also benefit from the executives' efforts. Long-term incentives may also be "golden handcuffs," motivating executives to stay by letting them accumulate capital (usually options to buy company stock) that they can cash in only after a certain period. Again, popular long-term incentives include cash, stock, stock options, stock appreciation rights, and phantom stock.[81] We'll look at each.

stock option
The right to purchase a stated number of shares of a company stock at today's price at some time in the future.

STOCK OPTIONS A **stock option** is the right to purchase a specific number of shares of company stock at a specific price during a specific period. The executive thus hopes to profit by exercising his or her option to buy the shares in the future but at today's price. This assumes the stock will go up. Unfortunately, this depends partly on considerations outside the manager's control.[82] When stock markets dropped a while ago, many employers including Intel and Google adjusted their option plans to boost the likely payout.[83] The HR Practices Around the Globe feature addresses one aspect of this.

IMPROVING PERFORMANCE: *HR PRACTICES AROUND THE GLOBE*

Until January 2006, China basically prohibited publicly listed companies from offering stock incentive plans to their managers.[84] At that point better economic conditions and an evolving political philosophy led to new regulations. Soon 42 Chinese-listed companies were permitting such plans.

A study focused on those 42 companies. It sought to determine how the new incentive plans affected company performance. To understand the findings it's important to know that managing in China still has unique characteristics. For example, prior to becoming publicly listed firms, the big firms were usually owned by the government. Furthermore, the government may well continue to retain certain ownership control rights even after the firms go on the stock market. In such cases, the goals of the owners and the management may diverge. For example, government owners might want to maximize employment, rather than profitability. The question is, given such cultural and political realities, do management stock option plans in China translate into improved company performance, as they often do in the United States?

The researchers compared the performance of the 42 Chinese companies that did adopt management stock option plans with a control group of firms without such plans. One thing they found was that the stock option plans did improve firm performance in companies controlled by private shareholders, but not in companies controlled by the government. In the latter, goals such as maximizing employment may have outweighed boosting profits, thus limiting managers' profit-boosting efforts.

The findings highlight why managing globally is challenging. In this case, a stock option plan that might improve financial performance in the United States might fail in China, where the government owners' goals may well differ from the desire of managers to boost profits.

MyLab Management Talk About It 3

If your professor has assigned this, go to the Assignments section of **www.pearson.com/mylab/management** to complete these discussion questions.Given these findings, would it make sense for managers in government-controlled companies to receive stock options tied to something other than profitability, such as "no employees lose their jobs in this company"? Why?

The chronic problem with stock option plans is that many reward even managers who have lackluster performance, but there are also other problems. Several years ago some executives allegedly lied about the dates they received their options to boost their returns. Options may also encourage executives to take perilous risks in pursuit of higher profits.[85] One alternative may be to force recipients to convert their options into stock sooner. One paper argues that it's probably cheaper just to pay cash awards than stock options.[86]

OTHER STOCK PLANS Beyond that, the trend is toward tying rewards more explicitly to performance goals. Instead of stock options, more firms are granting various types of performance-based shares. With *performance-contingent restricted stock* the executive receives his or her shares only if he or she meets the preset performance targets.[87] With (time-based) *restricted stock plans*, the firm usually awards rights to the shares without cost to the executive but the employee is restricted from acquiring (and selling) the shares for, say, five years, and the award may be subject to forfeiture if the recipient ceases to be employed by the company for a set period. Unlike options, the recipient usually pays nothing for the stock. The employer's aim is to retain the employee's services during that time.[88] With *indexed options*, the option's exercise price fluctuates with the performance of, say, a market index. If the company's stock does no better than the index, the manager's options are worthless. With *premium priced options*, the exercise price is higher than the stock's closing price on the date of the grant, so the executive can't profit from them until the stock makes significant gains;[89] IBM has used these for years.[90]

Stock appreciation rights (SARs) let the recipient exercise the stock option (by buying the stock) or to take any appreciation in the stock price in cash, stock, or some combination of these. Under *phantom stock plans*, executives receive not shares but "units" that are similar to shares of company stock. Then at some future time, they receive value (usually in cash) equal to the appreciation of the "phantom" stock they own. Both SARs and phantom stock essentially "are bonus plans that grant not stock but rather the right to receive an award based on the value of the company's stock."[91] A *performance achievement plan* awards shares of stock for the achievement of predetermined financial targets, such as profit or growth in earnings per share. Most employees seem to prefer cash bonuses to either stock options or restricted stocks. Due to differences in employee preferences, when possible, enable each employee to choose whether to receive stock options or restricted stock.[92]

POTENTIAL PROBLEMS Two problems plague executive incentives: short termism, and lack of range. Many plans encourage short-term thinking. For example, the manager boosts earnings per share (and his or her short-term bonus) by cutting R&D, which in turn hurts earnings three or four years down the road. Relatedly, tying the incentive to one metric rather than to several can encourage counterproductive behavior. For example, incentivize the manager just for earnings, and he or she could boost earnings by cutting advertising and other costs, which in turn cause future revenues (unmeasured by the bonus plan) to fall.[93]

Three experts suggest several solutions. First, use *multiple metrics*, for instance earnings, and revenue growth, and R&D spending.[94]

Second, reward performance *relative to competitors*. For example, increasing a company's earnings when its industry grew 10%, isn't as impressive as increasing them 2% when industry sales and earnings fell. Rewarding performance relative to competitors also forces top managers to analyze what their competitors are doing, and how to improve their firm's relative position.

Third, include *nonfinancial targets*. Nonfinancial targets (such as employee engagement, and customer satisfaction) are harder to "game" than financial targets (such as boosting earnings by cutting R&D). Furthermore, nonfinancial measures can and do affect a company's long-term performance.

ETHICS AND INCENTIVES Recently, a truck stop company arranged to pay some managers commissions and bonuses based on how many dollars of diesel fuel trucking firms purchased each month. Federal prosecutors allege that doing so encouraged the managers to withhold the volume rebates the trucking firms were supposed to get. In one year, for instance, one officer with a base salary of about $400,000 earned about $14 million in bonuses and pay.[95]

Anyone designing a long-term incentive plan should remember the management truism: "People put their efforts where they know they'll be rewarded." The point is that simplistic incentives that focus on just one factor (such as cost-cutting) may encourage managers to ignore other important factors (such as long-term investment). Similarly, in the absence of strong ethical standards, incentives may breed unethical behavior.[96] Examples are depressingly familiar. For example, to paraphrase *Forbes*, one firm's culture now incentivizes aggressiveness at the expense of doing what's best for the client. For stock option plan designers, the solution is to include a sufficient array of bonus-able criteria in the incentive plan, while fostering an ethical culture.

Some Other Executive Incentives

golden parachute
A payment companies make in connection with a change in ownership or control of a company.

Companies offer other executive incentives. Some incentivize executives to stay with the firm. This is especially important when executives might flee because another company is stalking the firm with intentions to buy it. **Golden parachutes** are extraordinary payments (usually a combination of severance pay, accelerated vesting, and other benefits) made to executives in connection with a change in company ownership or control. Former Yahoo CEO Marissa Mayer reportedly received more than $54 million when Verizon bought Yahoo, and Oracle's co-presidents would each receive over $139 million, for instance.[97]

Some firms use loans as incentives, for example by guaranteeing large loans to directors and officers to buy company stock.

MyLab Management Apply It!

How does a company actually go about creating an incentive plan? If your professor has assigned this activity, go to the Assignments section of **www.pearson.com/mylab/management** to complete the video exercise.

LEARNING OBJECTIVE 12-5
Name and describe the most popular organization-wide incentive plans.

Team and Organization-Wide Incentive Plans

We've focused so far on individual employee incentives (such as piecework, commissions, and executive bonuses). Let's look now at incentives for teams, and for employees company-wide.

How to Design Team Incentives

team (or group) incentive plan
A plan in which a production standard is set for a specific work group, and its members are paid incentives if the group exceeds the production standard.

Firms increasingly rely on teams to manage their work. They therefore need incentive plans that focus teams on performance and encourage teamwork. **Team (or group) incentive plans** pay incentives to the team based on team performance.

The main question here is how to reward the team's performance, and the wrong choice can be lethal. Levi Strauss switched from an individual to a team incentive plan, one that rewarded the team as a whole for its output. Unfortunately, they ignored the fact that some employees worked harder than others. The slower ones (economists sometimes call them "free riders" because they take a free ride on others' efforts) were paid the same as the faster ones. The faster ones, no longer individually incentivized, slowed down, production declined, and Levi's closed its U.S. factories.

Given the potential free rider problem, companies usually incentivize teams in one of three ways: they pay the same incentives to each team member based on some overall standard, or pay different rates to each member based on performance, or pay different rates to each in some proportion to each team member's base pay.[98]

Free riders notwithstanding, the usual approach is probably still to tie rewards to some overall standard of group performance, such as "10 labor hours per car." One company established such an overall standard for its work teams. If the firm reached 100% of its goal, the employees would share in about 5% of the improvement (in labor costs saved). The firm divided the resulting bonus pool by the number of employees to compute the value of a "share." If the firm achieved less than 100% of its goal, the bonus pool was less. The results of this plan in terms of focusing teams on the firm's strategic goals were reportedly "extraordinary."[99] Firms such as Toyota that use team plans rely on employee selection, training, and peer pressure to minimize free riding.

While most employers just use their experience to estimate what the team goal or standard should be ("10 total labor hours per car"), others carefully engineer their production standards. If so, the employer typically bases the team incentive on either the piece rate or standard hour plan. All team members then typically receive the same share of the team's incentive pay. Thus, the team might receive, say, $5 for each wheel installed above the industrially engineered "standard" of 10 wheels per hour.

Occasionally, the employer may want to pay team members according to some other formula. For instance, instead of paying each team member based on how well the team as a whole does, pay everyone based on how well the *best* team member does. This counterintuitive option may make sense when an employer has reason to believe the new team incentive plan might demotivate high-performing team members. That's what happened at Levi's.

Team incentives often make sense. They reinforce team problem solving, and can help ensure cooperation. Team incentives also facilitate training, since each member has an interest in getting new members up to speed fast. The main disadvantage is the demotivating effects of free rider workers who share in the team-based pay but who don't put their hearts into it.

Team incentives can foster a sense of cooperation and unanimity.

GaudiLab/Shutterstock

Evidence-Based HR: Inequities That Undercut Team Incentives

Although about 85% of large employers reportedly use some type of group- or team-based incentives, studies suggest that team incentives are often counterproductive. Why?

A researcher studied business students enrolled in a graduate online MBA program.[100] She devised a method for categorizing how they said they reacted to the team incentives they'd experienced in the past.

Inequity was the big problem.[101] Sometimes all team members' financial compensation was the same, although one or two people "did the lion's share of the work." In other cases, the employer chose one or two team members for promotion, leaving others to feel they'd worked hard to support someone else's career. The bottom line is that unless you take steps to minimize interpersonal inequities, it may be best to pay employees based on their individual contributions, rather than on collective team performance.

Many employers take the team incentive idea to the next level and institute incentive plans in which all or most employees participate. **Organization-wide incentive plans** are plans in which all or most employees can participate, and which generally tie the reward to some measure of company-wide performance. Also called *variable pay plans*, we'll look at them next.

organization-wide incentive plan
Incentive plan in which all or most employees can participate.

Profit-Sharing Plans

profit-sharing plan
A plan whereby employees share in the company's profits.

Profit-sharing plans are plans in which all or most employees receive a share of the firm's annual profits. While that sounds good in theory, free riders may again be a problem: Some may ask, "If everyone gets paid the same whether they work hard or not, why bother?"[102]

Research is sketchy. Older studies found evidence that profit-sharing plans boost productivity and morale, but that their effect on profits is insignificant, once you factor in the costs of the plans' payouts.[103] Another study, in Spain, concluded that profit-sharing plans improve employee commitment.[104] A more recent study found that employee earnings rose faster in firms with profit-sharing plans.[105]

There are several profit-sharing plans. With *current profit-sharing* or cash plans, employees share in a portion of the employer's profits quarterly or annually. Here the firm simply distributes a percentage of profits (usually 15% to 20%) as profit shares to employees at regular intervals. For example, Southwest Airlines offers a broad-based (almost everyone is eligible) profit-sharing plan for employees. Several years ago it distributed a $228 million profit-sharing payout to employees.[106]

With *deferred profit-sharing* plans, the employer puts cash awards into trust accounts for the employees' retirement.[107] Employees' income taxes on the distributions are deferred until the employee retires or withdraws funds from the plan (thus "deferred profit-sharing plans"). Such plans are essentially pension plans that give the employer the option of deciding each year how much to contribute to the plan.

Scanlon Plans

Few would argue with the idea that one of the best ways of ensuring that employees are engaged and motivated is to ensure that by pursuing his or her goals, the worker pursues the employer's goals as well. Experts have proposed many ways to achieve this. However, few have been as successful as the **Scanlon plan,** developed in 1937 by Joseph Scanlon, a United Steel Workers Union official.[108] It is still popular today.

Scanlon plan
An incentive plan developed in 1937 by Joseph Scanlon and designed to encourage cooperation, involvement, and sharing of benefits.

The Scanlon plan is remarkably progressive, considering that it is now more than 80 years old. Scanlon plans have five basic features.[109] The first is Scanlon's *philosophy of cooperation*. This philosophy assumes that managers and workers must rid themselves of the "us" and "them" attitudes that normally inhibit employees from developing a sense of ownership in the company.

A second feature is what its practitioners call *identity*. This means that in order to focus employee involvement, the company must articulate its mission or purpose, and employees must understand how the business operates in terms of customers, prices, and costs. *Competence* is a third basic feature. The program, say three experts, "explicitly recognizes that a Scanlon plan demands a high level of competence from employees at all levels."[110] This suggests careful selection and training.

The fourth feature of the plan is the *involvement system*. Employees present improvement suggestions to the appropriate departmental-level committees, which transmit the valuable ones to the executive-level committee. It then decides whether to implement the suggestion.

The fifth element of the plan is the *sharing of benefits formula*. If a suggestion is implemented and successful, all employees usually share in 75% of the savings. For example, assume that the normal monthly ratio of payroll costs to sales is 50%. (Thus, if sales are $600,000, payroll costs should be $300,000.) Assume the firm implements suggestions that result in payroll costs of $250,000 in a month when sales were $550,000 and payroll costs therefore should have been $275,000 (50% of sales). The savings attributable to these suggestions is $25,000 ($275,000 minus $250,000). Workers would typically split 75% of this ($18,750), while $6,250 would go to the firm. In practice, the firm sets aside about one-quarter of the $18,750, for months when payroll costs exceed the standard.

Other Gainsharing Plans

gainsharing plan
An incentive plan that engages employees in a common effort to achieve productivity objectives and share the gains.

The Scanlon plan is one early version of today's **gainsharing plans.** Gainsharing is an incentive plan that engages many or all employees in a common effort to achieve a company's productivity objectives, with any resulting cost-savings gains shared among employees and the company.[111] In addition to the Scanlon plan, other popular gainsharing plans include the Lincoln, Rucker, and Improshare plans.

The basic difference among these plans is how employers determine employee bonuses. The Scanlon formula divides payroll expenses by total sales (or, sometimes, by total sales plus increases in inventory). In one version of the *Lincoln incentive system*, first instituted at the Lincoln Electric Company of Ohio, employees work on a guaranteed piecework basis. The company then distributes total annual profits (less taxes, 6% dividends to stockholders, and a reserve) each year among employees based on their merit rating. Most firms customize their gainsharing plans.

Results support gainsharing's effectiveness in settings ranging from automotive parts manufacturers, to hospitals. For example, in one study cost savings achieved by hospital physicians translated into cash payments to the physicians.[112] The U.S. Department of Health and Human Services approved certain hospital gainsharing plans.

At-Risk Pay Plans

earnings-at-risk pay plan
Plan that puts some portion of employees' normal pay at risk if they don't meet their goals, in return for possibly obtaining a much larger bonus if they exceed their goals.

Pay-for-performance plans can support an employer's cost control efforts. Base pay and benefits represent the lion's share of labor costs, and normally neither varies much even when sales plummet.[113] (Pay cuts adversely affect morale, and if sales fall one year, it's generally hard to cut labor costs without downsizing.) In an **earnings-at-risk pay plan,** employees agree to put some portion (say, 10%) of their normal pay at risk (forego it) if they don't meet their goals, in return for possibly obtaining a much larger bonus if they exceed their goals. For example, put part of the employees' pay "at risk" by replacing (1) 10% of each worker's wages with (2) a 10% bonus if the company meets its goals plus an additional 3% bonus if it exceeds these goals.

Employee Stock Ownership Plans

employee stock ownership plan (ESOP)
A corporation contributes shares of its own stock to a trust in which additional contributions are made annually. The trust distributes the stock to employees on retirement or separation from service.

Employee stock ownership plans (ESOPs) are company-wide retirement/incentive plans, in which the employer contributes shares of its stock (or cash to be used to purchase such stock) to a trust set up to purchase shares of the firm's stock for employees. The firm generally makes these contributions to the trust annually, in proportion to total employee compensation, up to a limit of 15% of compensation. The trust holds the stock in individual employee accounts. It then distributes the stock to employees upon retirement (or other separation from service), assuming the person has worked long enough to earn ownership of the stock.

ESOPs are popular. The company receives a tax deduction equal to the fair market value of the shares it transfers to the trustee; it can also claim an income tax deduction for dividends paid on ESOP-owned stock.[114] Employees, as noted, aren't taxed until they receive a distribution from the trust, usually at retirement. The Employee

Retirement Income Security Act (ERISA) allows a firm to borrow against employee stock held in trust and then repay the loan in pretax rather than after-tax dollars, another tax incentive.[115]

ESOPs can also help shareholders of closely held corporations (for instance, a family owns all the shares of a small regional bank and wants to sell all or some of its shares). They place some of their shares of the bank's stock into the ESOP trust. The banking company compensates them (perhaps by borrowing the money) for the shares they put in the trust, and the family then uses those funds to buy other assets.[116]

Studies suggest that ESOPs correlate with performance, but that it's probably "the cooperative culture that can be fostered by employee ownership that drives better workplace performance in ESOP firms."[117] In any case, the company's board and management have legal and fiduciary responsibilities for the ESOP fund, and must manage the fund prudently.

BROAD-BASED STOCK OPTIONS Some companies offer "broad-based stock option plans" in which all or most employees can participate. (Definitions of what is "broad-based" range from at least 20% of a company's employees, to a majority of full-time employees, to a plan "which includes most non-management employees.")[118] Perhaps because such plans foster a sense of cooperation and ownership (as do ESOPs), at least one study concluded that firms with broad-based stock option plans had higher productivity and annual growth rates than peers.[119]

However, in the early 2000s, many companies cut back on these. For example, Time Warner, Microsoft, Aetna, and Charles Schwab discontinued distributing stock options to most employees. Some of them, including Microsoft, instead award stock. With current tax laws, companies must show the options as an expense when awarded, reducing their attractiveness as a "costless" reward. Microsoft and others apparently feel awarding stock instead of stock options is a more direct and immediate way to link pay to performance.[120]

Incentive Plans in Practice: Nucor

Nucor Corp. is the largest steel producer in the United States. It also has the highest productivity and lowest labor cost per ton, consistently ranks as a "Best Places to Work," and hasn't had layoffs in decades.[121] Employees can earn bonuses of 100% or more of base salary, and all participate in one of four performance-based incentive plans. With the *production incentive plan*, operating and maintenance employees and supervisors get weekly bonuses based on their work groups' productivity. The *department manager incentive plan* pays department managers annual incentive bonuses based mostly on the ratio of net income to dollars of assets employed for their division. With the *professional and clerical bonus plan*, employees not in one of the two previous plans get bonuses based on their divisions' net income return on assets.[122] Finally, under the *senior officer incentive plan*, Nucor senior managers (whose base salaries are lower than those comparable firms) get bonuses based on Nucor's annual overall percentage of net income to stockholders equity.[123] In one recent year Nucor's CEO earned a total of $10.6 million, including $2.9 million in stock awards, $4 million in stock options, and $2.4 million in incentive plan awards tied to return on equity and Nucor's position in its sales comparison group.[124]

Nucor also divides 10% of its operating profits yearly among all employees (except senior officers). Depending on company performance, this may be from 1% to over 20% of an employee's pay.

LEARNING OBJECTIVE 12-6

Explain how to use incentives to improve employee engagement.

Employee Engagement Guide for Managers

Incentives and Engagement

A survey provides some insights into the role of incentive pay in fostering employee engagement. Of approximately 6,300 compensation professionals the researchers solicited, 736 responded to the survey.[125] Here's what the researchers found.

First, although the compensation professionals believed that total rewards programs can influence employee engagement, many of these professionals did *not* specifically include employee engagement as one of the goals of their compensation plans. About 60% agreed or strongly agreed that "employee engagement and performance metrics are incorporated into variable pay programs in our organization." But only 37% agreed or strongly agreed that "in the organization, engagement levels fostered by line managers are important factor in evaluating performance."

Second, they concluded that the most direct ways to encourage employee engagement with incentives are (1) to measure the extent to which *supervisors are encouraging their subordinates to be engaged*, and (2) to *use incentives to reward supervisors for improving employee engagement.*

Third, even more important than the rewards themselves, getting employees involved in developing the rewards programs was the "gold standard" for building employee cooperation and commitment.

So, in brief: Make improving employee engagement a formal target of your compensation plan; appraise and incentivize your supervisors partly based on whether they take steps to improve their subordinates' engagement; and if possible get employee input in devising the incentive plan.

Chapter Review

Chapter Section Summaries

12-1. In designing an effective financial incentive plan, it's important to understand the relationship between **money and motivation.** Hertzberg said the best way to motivate someone is to organize the job so that it provides the feedback and challenge that help satisfy the person's higher-level needs. Deci found that extrinsic rewards may actually detract from a person's intrinsic motivation. Vroom's expectancy motivation theory says a person's motivation depends on expectancy, instrumentality, and valence. Skinner's behavior modification–based approach means changing behavior through rewards or punishments that are contingent on performance.

12-2. Piecework is an **individual employee incentives and recognition program** incentive plan in which a person is paid a sum for each item he or she makes. Merit pay is a salary increase awarded based on individual performance. Nonfinancial and recognition-based awards include awards in the form of employee recognition, gift certificates, and individual travel. Many employers use enterprise incentive management systems to automate the planning, analysis, and management of their incentive plans.

12-3. **Incentives for salespeople** are typically sales commissions. Although the percentage of pay in the form of sales commission may vary, a survey found that salespeople at high-performing companies receive about 38% of their total cash compensation in sales-related variable pay.

12-4. Managers take many things into consideration when formulating **incentives for managers and executives.** Most firms have annual bonus plans aimed at motivating managers' short-term performance. The actual award often depends on some combination of individual performance and organizational performance, so that, for instance, high-performing managers get a bonus even if the company itself underperforms. Long-term incentives include stock options, "golden parachutes," and stock appreciation rights.

12-5. With more employers organizing their efforts around teams, **team and organization-wide incentive plans are more important.** With team incentives, the main question is whether to reward members based on individual or team performance; both have pros and cons. Organization-wide incentive plans are plans in which all or most employees can participate. These include profit-sharing plans in which employees share in the company's profits; gainsharing plans, including the Scanlon plan, engage employees in a common effort to achieve productivity objectives and thereby share the gains. With employee stock ownership plans the employer contributes shares of its own stock to a trust established to purchase shares of the firm's stock for employees.

12-6. Consciously make **employee engagement** a goal of your compensation plan; appraise and incentivize supervisors partly based on their effectiveness in improving their subordinates' engagement; and if possible enable employees to participate in devising the compensation plan.

Discussion Questions

12-1. Compare and contrast six types of incentive plans.

12-2. Explain five reasons why incentive plans fail.

12-3. Describe the nature of some important management incentives.

12-4. You are applying for a job as a manager and are at the point of negotiating salary and incentives. What questions would you ask your prospective employer concerning incentives? Describe the incentives package you would try to negotiate for yourself.

12-5. In this chapter, we listed a number of guidelines for instituting a pay-for-performance plan. Do you think these points make sense in terms of motivation theory? Why or why not?

12-6. What is merit pay? Do you think it's a good idea to award employees merit raises? Why or why not?

12-7. Give four examples of when you would suggest using team or group incentive programs rather than individual incentive programs.

Individual and Group Activities

12-8. Working individually or in groups, create an incentive plan for the following positions: chemical engineer, plant manager, used-car salesperson. What factors did you have to consider in reaching your conclusions?

12-9. A state university system in the Southeast instituted a "Teacher Incentive Program" (TIP) for its faculty. Faculty committees within each of the university's colleges were told to award $5,000 raises (not bonuses) to about 40% of their faculty members based on how good a job they did teaching undergraduates, and how many courses they taught per year. What are the potential advantages and pitfalls of such an incentive program? How well do you think it was accepted by the faculty? Do you think it had the desired effect?

12-10. Appendices A and B at the end of this book (pages 614–634) list the knowledge someone studying for the HRCI (Appendix A) or SHRM (Appendix B) certification exam needs to have in each area of human resource management (such as in Strategic Management and Workforce Planning). In groups of several students, do four things: (1) review Appendix A and/or B; (2) identify the material in this chapter that relates to the Appendix A and/or B required knowledge lists; (3) write four multiple-choice exam questions on this material that you believe would be suitable for inclusion in the HRCI exam and/or the SHRM exam; and (4) if time permits, have someone from your team post your team's questions in front of the class, so that students in all teams can answer the exam questions created by the other teams.

KNOWLEDGE BASE

12-11. Several years ago, the pension plan of the Utility Workers Union of America proposed that shareholders change the corporate bylaws of Dominion Resources, Inc., so that in the future management had to get shareholder approval of executive pay exceeding $1 million, as well as detailed information about the firm's executive incentive plans. The union pointed out that, usually, under IRS regulations, corporations can't deduct more than $1 million in pay for any of a company's top five paid executives. Under the new rules the Utility Workers Union is pushing, boards of directors will no longer be able to approve executive pay above $1 million; instead, shareholders would have to vote on it. In terms of effectively running a company, what do you think are the pros and cons of the union's recommendations? Would you vote for or against the union's recommendation? Why?

Experiential Exercise

Motivating the Employees at Pearson Urgent Care

Written and copyrighted by Gary Dessler, PhD.

Purpose: The purpose of this exercise is to give you practice developing an incentive plan.

Required Understanding: Be thoroughly familiar with this chapter, and read the following:

Pearson Urgent Care is a chain of walk in medical urgent care centers in New York City. Each walk in center has about 12 full time employees; Pearson's total number of employees is therefore about 75, including the walk in center employees and central office accountants, clerks, and managers. Pearson is run by Taylor Pearson MD. Her main business problem now is that online Yelp-type walk in center reviews are abysmal. Common customer complaints include:

- Front desk clerks who greet patients and obtain their medical history forms seem unfriendly and unhelpful.
- Nurses who take the patients to the examining rooms and review their medical histories seem uncaring.
- Doctors seem rushed and unwilling to explain in detail what the patient's problem is or how to deal with it.
- X-ray technicians seem rushed.

Table 12-3 summarizes Pearson's walk in center compensation plan. As you can see, Pearson currently pays all its walk in center team members based on wages or salaries.

How to Set Up the Exercise/Instructions: Divide the class into groups of several students. One or more groups should analyze each of the four teams in Table 12-3's first column. Each student group should analyze the compensation package for its Pearson team, and answer these questions:

12-12. In what ways might the current compensation method contribute to the customer service problems?

12-13. What recommendations would you make to improve the compensation system in a way that would likely improve customer satisfaction?

TABLE 12-3 Pearson Urgent Care Teams and Pay

Pearson Urgent Care Team	Main Responsibility of Team	Main Current Compensation Method
1. Front desk	Greet patients, process health forms.	Hourly wage.
2. Nurses	Complete patients' medical history.	Annual salary.
3. Doctors	Diagnose patients, provide prescriptions.	Annual salary.
4. X-ray technicians	Take prescribed x-rays.	Hourly wage.

Application Case

The HubSpot.com Sales Incentive Plan

Written and copyrighted by Gary Dessler, PhD.

Two graduates of MIT's Sloan School of Management founded HubSpot.com about 12 years ago.[126] HubSpot provides special customer relationship management (and other) software and systems aimed at helping clients use online content to attract potential customers to their Web sites, something known as "inbound" marketing.[127]

When the founders started HubSpot, their sales challenge was straightforward. At that point, the company only had about 100 customers, so they had to acquire as many customers as they could, as quickly as possible. Therefore, they focused their first sales compensation plan on what that plan's architect refers to as "hunting" for new customers. That first plan gave HubSpot salespeople a base salary, plus $2 dollars up front for every $1 of monthly recurring revenue they brought in from clients. Knowing that some clients might well leave, the sales compensation plan included a four-month claw back clause. In other words, if a client left for any reason within the first four months, HubSpot took back that entire commission from the salesperson. It was a straightforward sales compensation plan, and in less than six months HubSpot zoomed from 100 to 1000 customers, and its revenues jumped from $300,000 to $3 million. So far so good.

However, a problem soon became apparent. HubSpot had a big client retention problem. Way too many clients were dropping the service (mostly after four months). HubSpot's usual procedure was to assign each new client to a postsale consultant. That consultant was responsible for setting up the new client's service, and training its staff in how to use HubSpot software and services. Management first assumed that some postsale consultants were doing something to turn their clients off, and that that accounted for the client churn. But after analyzing client retention rates, it was apparent that the postsale consultants were not the problem: client churn for all postsale consultants was about the same.

Management therefore turned to analyzing client churn among salespeople, and there they found the problem. Some salespeople had more than 10 times the client churn than others! For some reason, some salespeople's clients remained long-term customers, while others left in droves. Some salespeople were doing a better job than others, in terms of the types of customers they focused on and what they told their clients HubSpot could accomplish for them.

Management believed that modifying the sales compensation plan was the way to solve the problem. The question was, what exactly should the new sales compensation plan look like?

Questions

12-14. How exactly would you change the HubSpot sales compensation plan to solve this client retention problem? Please be specific about what your new plan would consist of.

12-15. Management defined the client churn problem as a sales problem, to be solved with a modified sales compensation plan. What else could have caused the client churn problem, and how would you have solved that?

Continuing Case

Carter Cleaning Company

Written and copyrighted by Gary Dessler, PhD.

The Incentive Plan

The question of whether to pay Carter Cleaning Center employees an hourly wage or an incentive of some kind has always intrigued Jack Carter.

His basic policy has been to pay employees an hourly wage, except that his managers do receive an end-of-year bonus depending, as Jack puts it, "on whether their stores do well or not that year."

However, he is considering using an incentive plan in one store. Jack knows that a presser should press about 25 "tops" (jackets, dresses, blouses) per hour. Most of his pressers do not attain this ideal standard, though. In one instance, a presser named Walt was paid $8 per hour, and Jack noticed that regardless of the amount of work he had to do, Walt always ended up going home at about 3:00 P.M., so he earned about $300 at the end of the week. If it was a holiday week, for instance, and there were a lot of clothes to press, he might average 22 to 23 tops per hour (someone else did pants) and so he'd earn perhaps $300 and still finish each day in time to leave by 3:00 P.M. so he could pick up his children at school. But when things were very slow in the store, his productivity would drop to perhaps 12 to 15 pieces an hour, so that at the end of the week he'd end up earning perhaps $280, and in fact not go home much earlier than he did when it was busy.

Jack spoke with Walt several times, and while Walt always promised to try to do better, it gradually became apparent to Jack that Walt was simply going to earn his $300 per week no matter what. Though Walt never told him so directly, it dawned on Jack that Walt had a family to support and was not about to earn less than his "target" wage, regardless of how busy or slow the store was. The problem was that the longer Walt kept pressing each day, the longer the steam boilers and compressors had to be kept on to power his machines, and the fuel charges alone ran close to $6 per hour. Jack clearly needed some way short of firing Walt to solve the problem, because the fuel bills were eating up his profits.

His solution was to tell Walt that, instead of an hourly $8 wage, he would henceforth pay him $0.33 per item pressed. That way, said Jack to himself, if Walt presses 25 items per hour at $0.33 he will in effect get a small raise. He'll get more items pressed per hour and will therefore be able to shut the machines down earlier.

On the whole, the experiment worked well. Walt generally presses 25 to 35 pieces per hour now. He gets to leave earlier and, with the small increase in pay, he generally earns his target wage. Two problems have arisen, though. The quality of Walt's work has dipped a bit, plus his manager has to spend a minute or two each hour counting the number of pieces Walt pressed that hour. Otherwise, Jack is fairly pleased with the results of his incentive plan, and he's wondering whether to extend it to other employees and other stores.

Questions

12-16. Should this plan be extended to pressers in the other stores?

12-17. Should other employees (cleaner/spotters, counter people) be put on a similar plan? Why or why not? If so, how, exactly?

12-18. Is there another incentive plan you think would work better for the pressers? Describe it.

12-19. A store manager's job is to keep total wages to no more than 30% of sales and to maintain the fuel bill and the supply bill at about 9% of sales each. Managers can also directly affect sales by ensuring courteous customer service and by ensuring that the work is done properly. What suggestions would you make to Jennifer and her father for an incentive plan for store managers or front-desk clerks?

Translating Strategy into HR Policies and Practices Case*,§

**The accompanying strategy map for this chapter is in MyLab Management; the overall map in the inside back cover of this text outlines the relationships involved.*

Improving Performance at the Hotel Paris

The New Incentive Plan

The Hotel Paris's competitive strategy is "To use superior guest service to differentiate the Hotel Paris properties, and to thereby increase the length of stay and return rate of guests, and thus boost revenues and profitability." HR manager Lisa Cruz must now formulate functional policies and activities that support this competitive strategy by eliciting the required employee behaviors and competencies.

One of Lisa Cruz's biggest pay-related concerns is that the Hotel Paris compensation plan does not link pay to performance in any effective way. Because salaries were historically barely competitive, supervisors tended to award merit raises across the board. So, employees who performed well got only about the same raises as did those who performed poorly. Similarly, there was no bonus or incentive plan of any kind aimed at linking employee performance to strategically relevant employee capabilities and behaviors such as greeting guests in a friendly manner or providing expeditious check-ins and check-outs. The bottom line for Lisa and the CFO was that the company's financial rewards system—potentially, the single-biggest tool they had for channeling employee performance toward accomplishing the Hotel Paris's goals—was totally inadequate. She and her team thus turned to the job of deciding what sort of incentive-based reward systems to install.

Based on their analysis, Lisa Cruz and the CFO concluded that, by any metric, their company's incentive plan had to be changed. The percentage of the workforce whose merit increase or incentive pay was tied to performance was effectively zero, because managers awarded merit pay across the board. No more than 5% of the workforce (just the managers) was eligible for incentive pay. And, the percentage difference in incentive pay between a low-performing and a high-performing employee was less than 2%. Lisa knew from industry studies that in top firms, over 80% of the workforce had merit pay or incentive pay tied to performance. She also knew that in high-performing firms, there was at least a 5% or 6% difference in incentive pay between a low-performing and a high-performing employee. The CFO authorized Lisa to design a new strategy-oriented incentive plan for the Hotel Paris's employees. Their overall aim was to incentivize the pay plans of just about all the company's employees.

Lisa and the company's CFO laid out three measurable criteria that the new incentive plan had to meet. First, at least 90% (and preferably all) of the Hotel Paris's employees must be eligible for a merit increase or incentive pay that is tied to performance. Second, there must be at least a 10% difference in incentive pay between a low-performing and high-performing employee. Third, the new incentive plan had to include specific bonuses and evaluative mechanisms that linked employee behaviors in each job category with strategically relevant

§ Written and copyrighted by Gary Dessler, PhD.

employee capabilities and behaviors. For example, front-desk clerks were to be rewarded in part based on the friendliness and speed of their check-ins and check-outs, and the housecleaning crew was to be evaluated and rewarded in part based on the percentage of room cleaning infractions.

With these criteria in mind, Lisa and her team turned to designing the new merit and incentive pay plan. They created a larger merit pay pool, and instructed supervisors that employees scoring in the lower 10% of performance were to receive no merit pay, while the difference in merit pay between the top category and medium category employees was to be 10%. They contracted with an online employee recognition firm and instituted a new "Hotel Paris instantaneous thank-you award program." Under this program, any guest or any supervisor could recommend any hotel employee for an instantaneous recognition award; if approved by the department manager, the employee could choose the recognition award by going to the company's Web site. The incentive structure for all the company's managers, including hotel managers, assistant managers, and departmental managers, now ties at least 10% of each manager's annual pay to the degree to which his or her hotel achieves its strategic aims. The plan measures this in terms of ratings on the guest satisfaction index, average length of guest stay, and frequency of guest returns. Ratings on all these metrics soon began to rise.

Questions

12-20. Discuss what you think of the measurable criteria that Lisa and the CFO set for their new incentive plan.

12-21. Given what you know about the Hotel Paris's strategic goals, list three or four specific behaviors you would incentivize for each of the following groups of employees: front-desk clerks, hotel managers, valets, housekeepers.

12-22. Based on what you learned in this chapter of Dessler *Human Resource Management*, lay out a complete incentive plan (including all long- and short-term incentives) for the Hotel Paris's hotel managers.

Writing Assignments

12-23. When and why would you pay a salesperson based solely on commission? Based on a combined salary and commission?

12-24. Explain the role recognition and other nonmaterial incentives play in an effective incentive plan.

PERSONAL INVENTORY ASSESSMENTS

Go to **www.pearson.com/mylab/management** to complete the Personal Inventory Assessment related to this chapter.

Key Terms

financial incentives, 391
productivity, 391
fair day's work, 391
scientific management movement, 391
pay-for-performance, 391
variable pay, 391
intrinsic motivation, 392
expectancy, 392
instrumentality, 392
valence, 392
behavior modification, 392
piecework, 393
straight piecework, 394
standard hour plan, 394
merit pay (merit raise), 394
annual bonus, 402
stock option, 404
golden parachute, 406
team (or group) incentive plan, 406
organization-wide incentive plan, 408
profit-sharing plan, 408
Scanlon plan, 408
gainsharing plan, 409
earnings-at-risk pay plan, 409
employee stock ownership plan (ESOP), 409

Endnotes

1. Jay Heizer and Barry Render, *Operations Management* (Upper Saddle River, NJ: Pearson, 2001), p. 15.
2. See, for example, Mary Ducharme and Mark Podolsky, "Variable Pay: Its Impact on Motivation and Organisation Performance," *International Journal of Human Resources Development and Management* 6 (May 9, 2006), p. 68.
3. "Employers Use Pay to Lever Performance," *BNA Bulletin to Management*, August 21, 1997, p. 272; and "Variable Pay Is Superior to Bonus," *People Management*, February 24, 2011, p. 14.
4. Even the traditional holiday bonus is being replaced by performance-based pay. "Cash Bonuses Are Ghosts of Holidays Past, Survey Says," *BNA Bulletin to Management*, December 13, 2005, p. 396.

5. https://www.cnbc .com/2018/03/05/united-airlines-swaps-quarterly-bonuses-with-a-lottery-angering-some.html; https://www.washingtonpost.com/news/dr-gridlock/wp/2018/03/05/united-airlines-issues-ground-stop-on-plan-to-dole-out-employee-bonuses-by-lottery/?utm_term=.540ba9ad36e8, accessed March 22, 2018.
6. "Few Employees See the Pay for Performance Connection," *Compensation & Benefits Review* 17, no. 2 (June 2003); "Most Workers Not Motivated by Cash," *Incentive Today*, July–August 2004, p. 19; and "Pay-for-Performance Plans' Impact Uncertain: Study," *Modern Healthcare*, May 24, 2004, p. 34.
7. Emily Glazer, "Wells Revamps Pay after Scandal," *The Wall Street Journal*, January 7–8, 2017, pp. B1, B2.
8. Emily Glazer, "Wells Fargo: Tripped by Its Sales Culture," *The Wall Street Journal*, September 17–18, 2016, pp. A1, 88.
9. Michael Corkery and Stacy Cowley, "Warned about Excesses, Then Prodded to Sell," *The New York Times*, September 17, 2016, pp. A1, B3. BankAmerica subsidiary Merrill Lynch recently implemented a new incentive plan for its brokers. Each broker must now refer at least two customers to other parts of BankAmerica, such as its retail bank, or suffer pay cuts. Michael Wursthorn, "Merrill to Brokers: More Referrals or Pay Cut," *The Wall Street Journal*, December 8, 2016, p. B1. Incentive plans can have other dark consequences. One study found "a positive association between the proportion of managers eligible for bonuses in the organization and voluntary turnover among nonmanagement employees. . . ." Apparently, earning their bonuses caused the managers to pressure and stress out their subordinates. Dionne Poehler and Joseph Schmidt, "Does Pay-for-Performance Drain the Employment Relationship? The Effects of Manager Bonus Eligibility on Nonmanagement Employee Turnover," *Personnel Psychology* 69 (2016), pp. 395–429.
10. See, for example, Edward Deci, *Intrinsic Motivation* (New York: Plenum, 1975).
11. Ruth Kanfer, "Motivation Theory," in Harry C. Triandis, Marvin D. Dunnette, and Leaetta M. Hough, *Handbook of Industrial and Organizational Psychology* (Palo Alto, CA: Consulting Psychologists Press, 1994), p. 113. For a discussion about applying Vroom's principles, see B. Schaffer, "Leadership and Motivation." *Supervision* 69, no. 2 (February 2008), pp. 6–9.
12. For a discussion, see John P. Campbell and Robert Prichard, "Motivation Theory in Industrial and Organizational Psychology," in Marvin Dunnette (ed.), *Industrial and Organizational Psychology* (Chicago: Rand McNally, 1976), pp. 74–75; Kanfer, "Motivation Theory," pp. 115–116; and B. Schaffer, "Leadership and Motivation," op cit.
13. See, for example, Aubrey Daniels et al., "The Leader's Role in Pay Systems and Organizational Performance," *Compensation & Benefits Review*, May/June 2006, pp. 58–60; and Suzanne Peterson and Fred Luthans, "The Impact of Financial and Nonfinancial Incentives on Business Unit Outcomes over Time," *Journal of Applied Psychology* 91, no. 1 (2006), pp. 156–165.
14. See, for example, Diane Cadrain, "Cash versus Non-Cash Rewards," *HR Magazine*, April 2003, pp. 81–87.
15. Michael Harris et al., "A Longitudinal Examination of a Merit Pay System: Relationships among Performance Ratings, Merit Increases, and Total Pay Increases," *Journal of Applied Psychology* 83, no. 5 (1998), pp. 825–831. See also H. Risher, "Add Merit Pay for Performance," *Compensation and Benefits Review* 40, no. 6 (November/December 2008), pp. 22–29.
16. Eric R. Schulz and Denise Marie Tanguay, "Merit Pay in a Public Higher Education Institution: Questions of Impact and Attitudes," *Public Personnel Management* 35, no. 1 (Spring 2006), p. 71(18); Thomas S. Dee and Benjamin J. Keys, "Does Merit Pay Reward Good Teachers? Evidence from a Randomized Experiment," *Journal of Policy Analysis & Management* 23, no. 3 (Summer 2004), pp. 471–488. See also Sanghee Park and Michael Sturman, "How and What You Pay Matters: The Relative Effectiveness of Merit Pay, Bonuses and Long-Term Incentives on Future Job Performance," *Compensation & Benefits Review* 44, no. 2 (2012), pp. 80–85. One study concluded that merit raises are effective and have larger incentive effects than either bonuses or long-term incentives in companies that provide these pay-for-performance plans. Sanghee Park and Michael Sturman, "Evaluating Form and Functionality of Pay-for-Performance Plans: The Relative Incentive and Sword Effects of Merit Pay, Bonuses, and Long-Term Incentives," *Human Resource Management* 55, no. 4 (July–August 2016), pp. 697–719.
17. https://www.willistowerswatson.com/en/insights/2016/02/pay-for-performance-time-to-challenge-conventional-thinking?utm_source=email&utm_medium=C, accessed March 23, 2018.
18. Ibid.
19. Fay Hansen, "Wage and Salary Trends," *Compensation & Benefits Review* 40, no. 5 (November/December 2008), p. 5.
20. Steve Yegge, quoted in http://glinden.blogspot.com/2006/09/management-and-incentives-at-google.html, accessed June 1, 2011. See also Franck Giancola, "Should HR Professionals Devote More Time to Intrinsic Rewards?" *Compensation & Benefits Review* 46, no. 1 (2014), pp. 25–31.
21. Brian Skelton, "Dual-Career Tracks: Rewarding and Maintaining Technical Expertise," www.todaysengineer.org/2003/May/dual-ladder.asp, accessed September 8, 2014.
22. Peterson and Luthans, "The Impact of Financial and Nonfinancial Incentives."
23. "WorkSimple 'Praise' App Boosts Employee Recognition," *TD* (January 2012), p. 21, *Academic OneFile*, accessed March 17, 2013, also see http://blog.intuit.com/employees/6-mobile-apps-for-recognizing-and-rewarding-employees, accessed April 23, 2017; "Growing Your Employee Engagement Program," Employee Benefits, March 30, 2017.
24. Michelle V. Rafter, "Back in a Giving Mood," *Workforce Management* 88, no. 10 (September 14, 2009), pp. 25–29.
25. Like those at http://blog.intuit.com/employees/6-mobile-apps-for-recognizing-and-rewarding-employees.
26. Hilary Stout, "3 Dollar Tip on a 4-Dollar Cup of Coffee? Gratuities Grow, Automatically," *The New York Times*, February 1, 2015, pp. 1, 4.
27. See, for example, Leslie Yerkes, *Fun Works: Creating Places Where People Love to Work* (San Francisco, CA: Berrett-Koehler Publishers, 2007).
28. Charlotte Huff, "Recognition That Resonates," *Workforce Management*, September 11, 2006, pp. 25–29. A survey of executives concluded that three nonfinancial incentives—praise and commendation from immediate managers, attention from leaders, and opportunities to lead project or task forces—all ranked higher in motivational effectiveness than did financial incentives including stock options. Daniel Morrell, "Employee Perceptions and the Motivation of Non-Monetary Incentives," *Compensation & Benefits Review* 43, no. 5 (September/October 2011), pp. 318–323.
29. http://www.globoforce.com/how-it-works/superior-innovation/social-recognition/, accessed March 23, 2018.
30. Dave Zielinski, "Why Social Recognition Matters," February 20, 2015, https://www.shrm.org/ResourcesAndTools/hr-topics/technology/Pages/Why-Social-Recognition-Matters.aspx, accessed March 23, 2018.
31. Kevin Rockmann and Gary Ballinger, "Intrinsic Motivation and Organizational Identification among On-Demand Workers," *Journal of Applied Psychology* 100, no. 9, 2017, pp. 1305–1316.
32. "Three Keys to Engage and Motivate Your Gig Workers," February 5, 2018, https://www.mercer.com/search.html?q=gig+workers, accessed March 22, 2018.
33. www.deloitte.com/assets/DcomUnitedStates/Local%20Assets/Documents/us_consulting_2010StrategicSalesCompensationSurvey_072910.pdf, accessed September 8, 2014.
34. Peterson and Luthans, "The Impact of Financial and Nonfinancial Incentives," pp. 156–165.
35. Ibid., p. 159.
36. Ibid., p. 159.
37. Ibid., p. 162. See also "Delivering Incentive Compensation Plans That Work," *Financial Executive* 25, no. 7 (September 2009), pp. 52–54, and "Survey Finds Many Employers Not Satisfied with Their Pay-for-Performance Programs," *Bloomberg BNA Bulletin to Management*, January 7, 2014, p. 3.
38. For a checklist for determining when pay for performance is advisable, see Myron Glassman et al., "Evaluating Pay for Performance Systems: Critical Issues for Implementation," *Compensation & Benefits Review* 42, no. 4 (2010), p. 236.
39. "Two Frameworks for a More ROI-Minded Rewards Plan," *Pay for Performance Report*, February 2003, p. 1, www.ioma.com/issues/PFP/2003_02/518132-1.html, accessed November 3, 2009; and Alan Robinson and Dean Schroeder, "Rewards That Really Work," *Security Management*, July 2004, pp. 30–34. See also Patricia Zingheim and Jay Schuster, "What Are Key Pay Issues Right Now?" *Compensation & Benefits Review*, May/June 2007, pp. 51–55.
40. Reed Taussig, "Managing Cash Based Incentives," *Compensation & Benefits Review*, March/April 2002, pp. 65–68. See also Nigel Nicholson, "How to Motivate Your Problem People," *Harvard Business Review*, January 2003, pp. 57–65; and "Incentives, Motivation and Workplace

Performance," Incentive Research Foundation, www.incentivescentral.org/employees/whitepapers, accessed May 19, 2007.
41. Theodore Weinberger, "Evaluating the Effectiveness of an Incentive Plan Design within Company Constraints," *Compensation & Benefits Review*, November/December 2005, pp. 27–33; and Howard Risher, "Adding Merit to Pay for Performance," *Compensation & Benefits Review*, November/December 2008, pp. 22–29.
42. Deloitte. "2010 Strategic Sales Compensation Survey," accessed from http://woodscreek.com/files/SXPEG/Archive%202010/Deloitte%202010%20Strategic%20Sales%20Compensation%20Survey.pdf.
43. Ibid.
44. Deloitte Varicent, 2010 Strategic Sales Compensation Survey, p. 6, at www.deloitte.com/assets/Dcom-UnitedStates/Local%20Assets/Documents/us_consulting_2010StrategicSalesCompensationSurvey_072910.pdf, accessed August 29, 2011.
45. www.deloitte.com/assets/DcomUnitedStates/Local%20Assets/Documents/us_consulting_2010StrategicSalesCompensationSurvey_072910.pdf, accessed September 8, 2014. See also Pankaj Madhani, "Managing Salesforce Compensation: A Lifecycle Perspective," *Compensation & Benefits Review* 44, no. 6, pp. 315–326.
46. Straight salary by itself is not, of course, an incentive compensation plan as we use the term in this chapter.
47. Donna Harris, "Dealers Rethink How They Pay Salespeople," *Automotive News*, June 14, 2010, www.autonews.com/article/20100614/RETAIL07/306149932?C-SAuthResp=1%3A37354836 3270147%3A423310%3A412 9%3A24%3Aapproved%3A0 6E323F6579E1FCB5665B3 CC4B7C6C0B&=, accessed September 8, 2014.
48. Scott Ladd, "May the Sales Force Be with You," *HR Magazine*, September 2010, p. 105.
49. "More U.S. Companies Making Significant Changes to Sales Compensation Plans, Willis Towers Watson Survey Finds," www.willistowerwatson.com/en/press/2017, accessed March 23, 2018.
50. Sonjun Luo, "Does Your Sales Incentive Plan Pay for Performance," *Compensation & Benefits Review*, January/February 2003, pp. 331–345. See also James M. Pappas and Karen E. Flaherty, "The Moderating Role of Individual-Difference Variables in Compensation Research," *Journal of Managerial Psychology* 21, no. 1 (January 2006), pp. 19–35; and T. B. Lopez, C. D. Hopkins, and M. A. Raymond, "Reward Preferences of Salespeople: How Do Commissions Rate?" *Journal of Personal Selling & Sales Management* 26, no. 4 (Fall 2006), p. 381(10).
51. Bill O'Connell, "Dead Solid Perfect: Achieving Sales Compensation Alignment," *Compensation & Benefits Review*, March/April 1996, pp. 46–47. C. Albrech, "Moving to a Global Sales Incentive Compensation Plan," *Compensation & Benefits Review* 41, no. 4 (July/August 2009), p. 52; Elizabeth Wasserman, "How to Set Up a Sales Compensation Plan,"https://www.inc.com/guides/sales-compensation-plan.html, accessed March 23, 2018.
52. See, for example, Pankaj Madhani, "Realigning Fixed and Variable Pay in Sales Organizations: An Organizational Lifestyle Approach," *Compensation & Benefits Review* 42, no. 6, pp. 488–498.
53. Leslie Stretch, "From Strategy to Profitability: How Sales Compensation Management Drives Business Performance," *Compensation & Benefits Review*, May/June 2008, pp. 32–37.
54. S. Scott Sands, "Ineffective Quotas: The Hidden Threat to Sales Compensation Plans," *Compensation & Benefits Review* (March/April 2000), pp. 35–42. See also "Driving Profitable Sales Growth: 2006/2007 Report on Sales Effectiveness," www.watsonwyatt.com/research/resrender.asp?id=2006-US-0060&page=1, accessed May 20, 2007.
55. Peter Gundy, "Sales Compensation Programs: Built to Last," *Compensation & Benefits Review* (September/October 2002), pp. 21–28. See also T. B. Lopez, C. D. Hopkins, and M. A. Raymond, "Reward Preferences of Salespeople: How Do Commissions Rate?" *Journal of Personal Selling & Sales Management* 26, no. 4 (Fall 2006), p. 381(10).
56. Pankaj Madhani, "Reallocating Fixed and Variable Pay in Sales Organizations: a Sales Carryover Perspective," *Compensation & Benefits Review* 43, no. 6, (2011) pp. 346–360.
57. "Driving Profitable Sales Growth: 2006/2007 Report on Sales Effectiveness," www.watsonwyatt.com/research/resrender.asp?id=2006-US-0060&page=1, accessed May 20, 2007.
58. Thomas Steenburgh and Michael Ahearne, "Motivating Salespeople: What Really Works," *Harvard Business Review*, July–August 2012, pp. 71–75.
59. Ken Thoreson, "How to Create an Effective Sales Compensation Plan," October 31, 2014, www.salesforce.com, accessed March 23, 2018.
60. Ibid.
61. www.vuesoftware.com/Product/Compensation_Management.aspx, accessed September 8, 2014.
62. http://www.oracle.com/us/products/applications/057074.pdf, accessed March 23, 2018.
63. "Car Salesman Commission the Way It Works," http://carsalesprofessional.com/car-salesman-commission/, accessed June 26, 2011.
64. Ibid.
65. "Designing and Managing Incentive Compensation Programs," SHRM, January 12, 2018, www.shrm.com, accessed March 23, 2018.
66. Mark Meltzer and Howard Goldsmith, "Executive Compensation for Growth Companies," *Compensation & Benefits Review*, November/December 1997, pp. 41–50. See also Patricia Zingheim and Jay Schuster, "Designing Pay and Rewards in Professional Companies," *Compensation & Benefits Review*, January/February 2007, pp. 55–62; and Ronald Bottano and Russell Miller, "Making Executive Compensation Count: Tapping into the New Long-Term Incentive Portfolio," *Compensation & Benefits Review*, July/August 2007, pp. 43–47.
67. George Yancey, "Aligning the CEO's Incentive Plan with Criteria That Drive Organizational Performance," *Compensation & Benefits Review* 42, no. 3 (2010), pp. 190–196.
68. Richard Ericson, "Benchmarking for Executive Incentive Pay: The Importance of Performance Standards," *Compensation & Benefits Review* 43, no. 2, (2011), pp. 92–99. See also Robert J Greene, "Reward Performance? What Else?" *Compensation & Benefits Review* 47, no. 3 (2015), pp. 103–106.
69. See "The Impact of Sarbanes-Oxley on Executive Compensation," www.thelenreid.com, accessed December 11, 2003. See also Brent Longnecker and James Krueger, "The Next Wave of Compensation Disclosure," *Compensation & Benefits Review*, January/February 2007, pp. 50–54.
70. James Reda, "Executive Compensation: Balancing Risk, Performance and Pay," *Financial Executive* 25, no. 9 (November 2009), pp. 46–50. See also Bruce Ellig, "Short-Term Incentives: Top-Down or Bottom-Up?" *Compensation & Benefits Review* 43, no 3 (May/June 2011), pp. 179–183; "Compensation: The Case against Long-Term Incentive Plans," *Harvard Business Review*, October 2016, pp. 22–23.
71. Meltzer and Goldsmith, "Executive Compensation for Growth Companies," pp. 44–45; See also Jennifer Wynter-Palmer, "Is the Use of Short-Term Incentives Good Organization Strategy?" *Compensation & Benefits Review* 44, no. 5, 2013, pp. 254–265.
72. Max Smith and Ben Stradley, "New Research Tracks the Evolution of Annual Incentive Plans," *Executive Compensation*, Towers Watson, 2010, Towerswatson.com, accessed August 28, 2011.
73. Ibid.
74. Ibid.
75. Ibid.
76. Dionne Searcey, "Transocean Executives to Donate Bonuses," *The Wall Street Journal*, April 6, 2011, p. B1.
77. Bruce Ellig, "Executive Pay Financial Measurements," *Compensation & Benefits Review*, September/October 2008, pp. 42–49.
78. "Study: CEO Compensation Not Tied to Company Performance," *Bloomberg BNA Bulletin to Management*, March 22, 2011, p. 92.
79. See, for example, Bruce Ellig, "Long-Term Incentive Plan Combinations," *Compensation & Benefits Review* 46, no. 1 (2014), pp. 10–15.
80. https://www.bloomberg.com/news/articles/2016-03-18/pepsico-ceo-nooyi-s-pay-package-increases-18-to-26-4-million, accessed April 22, 2017.
81. See, for example, Bruce Ellig, "Stock Awards Can Be a Powerful Executive Pay Element," *Compensation & Benefits Review* 45, no. 6 (2013), pp. 309–319.
82. Benjamin Dunford et al., "Underwater Stock Options and Voluntary Executive Turnover: A Multidisciplinary Perspective Integrating Behavioral and Economic Theories," *Personnel Psychology* 61 (2008), pp. 687–726.
83. Phred Dvorak, "Slump Yields Employee Rewards," *The Wall Street Journal*, October 10, 2008, p. B2; Don Clark and Jerry DiColo, "Intel to Let Workers Exchange Options," *The Wall Street Journal*, March 24, 2009, p. B3.
84. Based on Robert Boylan, Maggie Foley, and Yu-Jun Lian, "Are Equity Incentives Effective in Chinese Listed Firms? New Evidence from Propensity Score Matching (PSN)," *International Journal of Business Strategy* 10, no. 3 (September 2010).
85. Wm. Gerard Sanders and Donald Hambrick, "Swinging for the Fences: The Effects of CEO Stock Options on Company Risk-Taking and Performance," *Academy of Management Journal* 50, no. 5 (2007), pp. 1055–1078.
86. "The Trouble with Stock Options," National Bureau of Economic Research,

http://www.nber.org/digest/mar04/w9784.html, accessed March 2, 2018.

87. www.mercer.com/pressrelease/details.jhtml/dynamic/idContent/1263210, accessed January 2, 2007.
88. www.nceo.org/main/article.php/id/43/, accessed June 1, 2011; John Leonard, "A Practical Guide to Equity Incentive Plans," January 1, 2010, Fairfield & Woods, P.C., http://www.fwlaw.com/news/8-a-practical-guide-equity-incentive-plans, accessed March 23, 2018.
89. Louis Lavelle, "How to Halt the Options Express," *BusinessWeek*, September 9, 2002; "Stock Options, Restricted Stock, Phantom Stock, Stock Appreciation Rights (SARs), and Employee Stock Purchase Plans (ESPPs)," National Center for Employee Ownership, https://www.nceo.org/articles/stock-options-restricted-phantom-sars-espps, accessed March 28, 2018.
90. Barbara Baksa, "IBM's Premium Priced Options," April 25, 2017, https://www.naspp.com/Blog/April-2017/IBM-s-Premium-Priced-Options, accessed March 23, 2018.
91. www.nceo.org/main/article.php/id/43/, accessed June 1, 2011.
92. Menahchem Abudy and Efrat Shust, "Employee's Attitudes toward Equity-Based Compensation," *Compensation & Benefits Review* 44, no. 5 (2013), pp. 246–253.
93. Radhakrishnan Gopalm, John Horn, and Todd Milbourne, "Comp Targets That Work," *Harvard Business Review*, September–October 2017, pp. 103–107.
94. Ibid., p. 104.
95. John Conigliaro, "Commissions, Bonuses Drove the Pilot Flying J Scandal, Prosecutors Say," *The Plain Dealer*, January 11, 2018, www.Cleveland.com/metro/index.SSF/2018/01/commissions_bonuses_drove_the.HTM, accessed March 2, 2018.
96. Christine Bevilacqua and Parbudyal Singh, "Pay for Performance—Panacea or Pandora's Box? Revisiting an Old Debate in the Current Economic Environment," *Compensation & Benefits Review*, September/October 2009, pp. 21–26.
97. Laurie Meisler and Jenn Zhao, "The Top 20 CEOs with Even Bigger Golden Parachutes than Marissa Mayer's," *Bloomberg*, August 17, 2016, https://www.bloomberg.com/graphics/2016-golden-parachutes/, accessed March 23, 2018.
98. Joseph Martocchio, *Strategic Compensation* (Boston: Pearson, 2017), p. 86.
99. Richard Seaman, "The Case Study: Rejuvenating an Organization with Team Pay," *Compensation & Benefits Review*, September/October 1997, pp. 25–30.
100. K. Merriman, "On the Folly of Rewarding Team Performance, While Hoping for Teamwork," *Compensation & Benefits Review*, January/February 2009, pp. 61–66.
101. As another example, see Bernd Irlenbusch and Gabriele K. Lünser, "Relative Rewards within Team-Based Compensation," November 2006. IZA Discussion Paper No. 2423. Available at SSRN: http://ssrn.com/abstract=947075, accessed May 21, 2011.
102. Thomas Cornelissen, John Heywood, Uwe Jirjahn, "Reciprocity and Profit Sharing: Is There an Inverse U-Shaped Relationship?" *Journal of Labor Research* 35, no. 2 (June 2014), pp. 205–225.
103. Seongsu Kim, "Does Profit Sharing Increase Firms' Profits?" *Journal of Labor Research*, Spring 1998, pp. 351–371. See also Jacqueline Coyle-Shapiro et al., "Using Profit-Sharing to Enhance Employee Attitudes: A Longitudinal Examination of the Effects on Trust and Commitment," *Human Resource Management* 41, no. 4 (Winter 2002), pp. 423–449.
104. Alberto Bayo-Moriones and Martin Larraza-Kintana, "Profit Sharing Plans and Effective Commitment: Does the Context Matter?" *Human Resource Management* 48, no. 2 (March–April 2009), pp. 207–226. Rather than simply using revenue or profits, some plans as at steelmaker Nucor use "economic profit" (or EP). We can define EP as "share of profits above a threshold level of profitability." Paul Farris et al., "Executive Compensation: Do Economic Profits Matter?" *Compensation & Benefits Review* 46, no. 5–6 (2014), pp. 276–286.
105. Richard Long and Tony Fang, "Do Employees Profit from Profit Sharing? Evidence from Canadian Panel Data," *ILR Review* 65, no. 4 (October 2012), pp. 899–927.
106. Joseph Blasi and Richard Freeman, "Southwest Airlines' Profit-Sharing Payout: What Capitalism Should Be," *Fortune*, April 17, 2014, http://fortune.com/2014/04/17/southwest-airlines-profit-sharing-payout-what-capitalism-should-be/, accessed March 23, 2018.
107. Under the U.S. tax code, "any arrangement that provides for the deferral of compensation in a year later than the year in which the compensation was earned may be considered a deferred compensation arrangement." Steven Friedman, "2008 Compliance Strategies for Employers in Light of Final 409A Regulations," *Compensation & Benefits Review*, March/April 2008, p. 27.
108. Brian Graham-Moore and Timothy Ross, *The Scanlon Way to Improved Productivity: A Practical Guide* (New York: Wiley, 1978), p. 2. For a review of potential problems, see Denis Collins, "Death of a Gainsharing Plan: Power Politics and Participatory Management," *Organizational Dynamics* 24 (Summer 1995), pp. 23–37. For an historical perspective on gainsharing's effectiveness, see Alexander Gardner, "Goal Setting and Gainsharing: The Evidence of Effectiveness," *Compensation & Benefits Review* 43, no 4 (July/August 2011), pp. 236–244.
109. These are based in part on Steven Markham, K. Dow Scott, and Walter Cox Jr. "The Evolutionary Development of a Scanlon Plan," *Compensation & Benefits Review*, March/April 1992, pp. 50–56. See also Woodruff Imberman, "Are You Ready to Boost Productivity with a Gainsharing Plan? To Survive and Prosper in Our Hyper-competitive Environment, Board Converters Must Motivate Employees at All Levels," *Official Board Markets* 82, no. 47 (November 25, 2006), p. 5(2); and James Reynolds and Daniel Roble, "Combining Pay for Performance with Gainsharing," *Healthcare Financial Management* 60, no. 11 (November 2006), p. 50(6).
110. Markham et al., "The Evolutionary Development of a Scanlon Plan," p. 51.
111. Barry W. Thomas and Madeline Hess Olson, "Gainsharing: The Design Guarantees Success," *Personnel Journal*, May 1998, pp. 73–79; and A. C. Gardner, "Goal Setting and Gainsharing: The Evidence on Effectiveness," *Compensation & Benefits Review* 43, no. 4 (July/August 2011), pp. 236–244.
112. Robert Coates, "The New Jersey Gainsharing Experience," *Physician Executive* 40, no. 10 (January/February 2014), pp. 46–51; Robert Zondo, "Evaluating the Effectiveness of a Gainsharing Programme for Labour Productivity Improvement," *Acta Commercii* 17, no. 1 (2017), pp. 1–10.
113. Robert Greene, "Variable Compensation: Good Fit to Turbulent Environments," *Compensation & Benefits Review* 44, no. 6, November/December 2012, p. 308.
114. See, for example, Teri Saylor, "ESOPs Help Some CPA Firms with Retention, Succession," *Journal of Accountancy*, May 2017, pp. 54–59.
115. See, for example, www.dol.gov/dol/topic/health-plans/erisa.htm, accessed March 23. 2018.
116. See, for example, David O'Leary, Norman Antin, and Jeffrey Haas, "ESOPs: A Powerful Tool for Closely Held Banks," Holland & Knight, March 13, 2017, https://www.hklaw.com/Publications/ESOPs-A-Powerful-Tool-for-Closely-Held-Banks-03-13-2017/, accessed March 23, 2018.
117. "Motivating Employees with Stock and Involvement," National Bureau of Economic Research, http://www.nber.org/digest/may04/w10177.html, accessed March 23, 2018.
118. Joseph Blasi, Douglas Kruse, James Sesil, and Maya Kroumova, "Broad-Based Stock Options and Company Performance: What the Research Tells Us," Working Paper Series in Human Resource Management, Department of Human Resource Management, Center for HR Strategy, Rutgers University, https://smlr.rutgers.edu/sites/default/files/documents/faculty_staff_docs/broad%20based%20stock%20options%20and%20compan%20performance%20what%20the%20research%20tells%20US.pdf, accessed March 23, 2018.
119. Ibid.
120. Eric Dash, "Time Warner Stops Granting Stock Options to Most of Staff," *The New York Times*, February 19, 2005, item 128921996.
121. Janet Wiscombe, "Can Pay for Performance Really Work?" *Workforce*, August 2001, p. 30; http://www.nucor.com/governance/incentive/, accessed March 24, 2018.
122. Susan Marks, "Incentives That Really Reward and Motivate," *Workforce*, June 2001, pp. 108–114.
123. Although not an issue at Nucor, the employer needs to beware of instituting so many incentive plans (cash bonuses, stock options, recognition programs, and so on) that employees don't have a clear priority of the employer's priorities. See, for example, Stephen Rubenfeld and Jannifer David, "Multiple Employee Incentive Plans: Too Much of a Good Thing?" *Compensation & Benefits Review*, March/April 2006, pp. 35–43.
124. John Downey, "Nucor CEO Gets Record Pay Package in 2016," *Charlotte Business Journal*, March 23, 2017, https://www.bizjournals.com/charlotte/news/2017/03/23/nucor-ceo-gets-record-pay-package-in-2016.html, accessed March 24, 2018.
125. This is based on Dow Scott and Tom McMullen, "The Impact of Rewards Programs on Employee Engagement," *WorldatWork*, June 2010.
126. www.hubspot.com, accessed March 24, 2018.
127. This is based on Mark Roberge, "The Right Way to Use Compensation," *Harvard Business Review*, April 2015, https://hbr.org, accessed March 23, 2018.

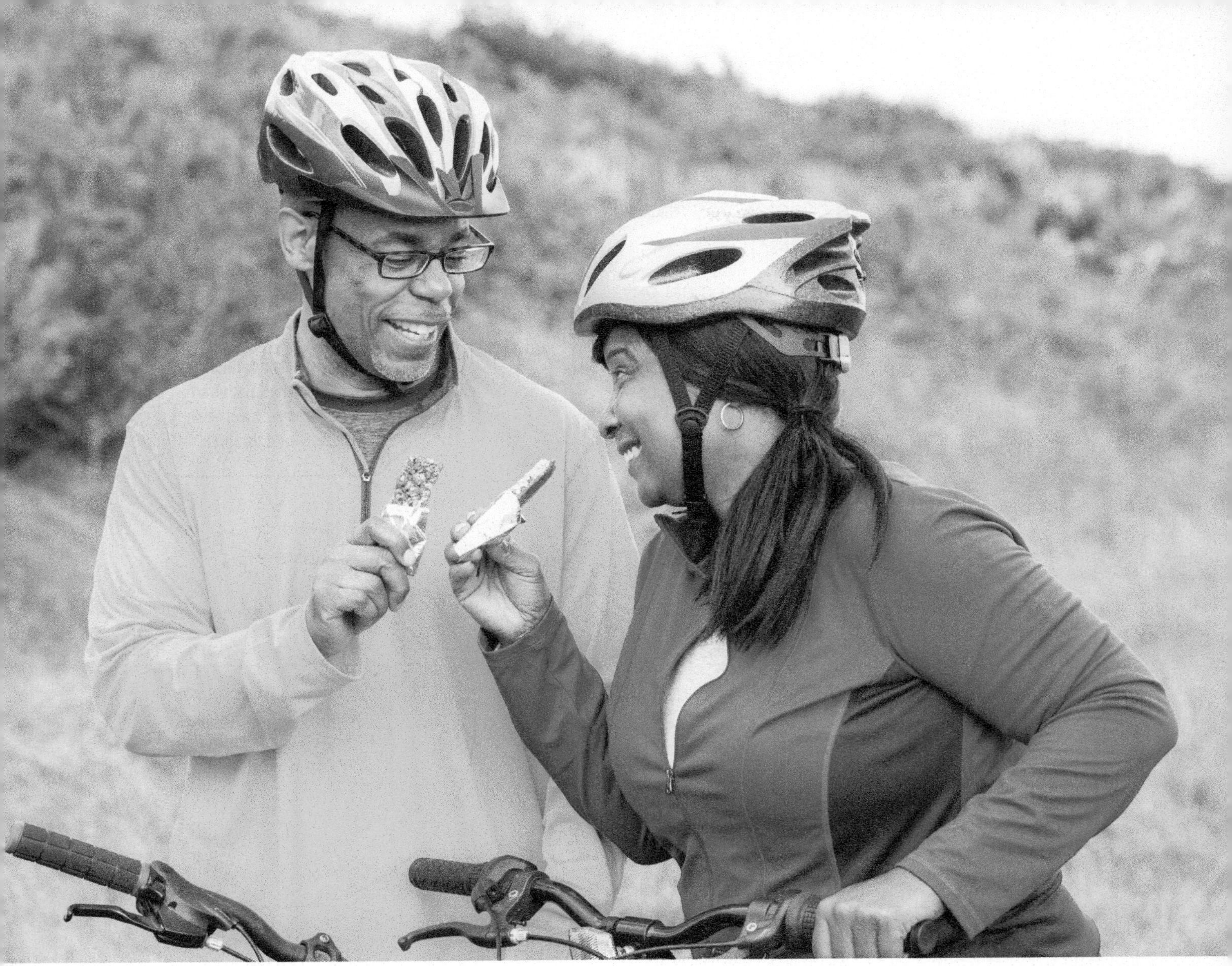
kali9/Getty Images

13 Benefits and Services

LEARNING OBJECTIVES

When you finish studying this chapter, you should be able to:

13-1 **Name and define** each of the main pay for time not worked benefits.

13-2 **Describe** each of the main insurance benefits.

13-3 **Discuss** the main retirement benefits.

13-4 **Outline** the main employees' services benefits.

13-5 **Explain** the main flexible benefit programs.

13-6 **Explain** how to use benefits to improve engagement, productivity, and performance.

About 30 years ago, Gary Erickson was biking through California and got an idea that changed his life—to create tastier and healthier health bars than those then available.[1] That was the beginning of Clif Bar, a company Erickson started as a small bakery and then grew into one with hundreds of employees selling healthy foods and drinks. He wanted an employee benefits plan for his employees that highlighted Clif Bar's healthy/sustainable focus; we'll see what he did.

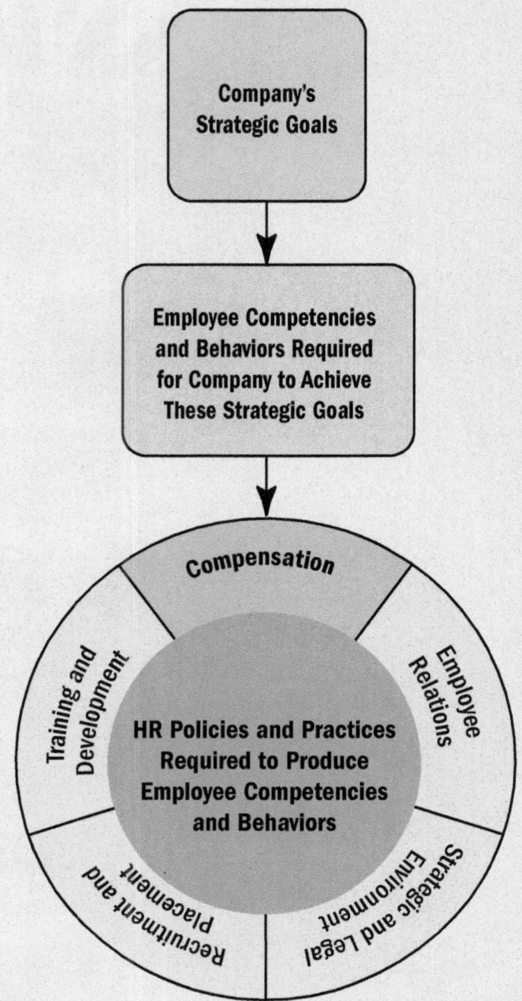

WHERE ARE WE NOW . . .

Chapters 11 and 12 addressed salaries (and wages) and incentives. The main purpose of this chapter is to explain the third major pay component: employee benefits. The main topics we discuss are **Pay for Time Not Worked Benefits**, **Insurance Benefits**, **Retirement Benefits**, **Employees' Services Benefits**, **Flexible Benefits**, and **Employee Engagement Guide for Managers**. This chapter completes our discussion of employee compensation.

The next chapter starts a new part of this book, and focuses on managing employee relations.

Introduction: The Benefits Picture Today

benefits
Indirect financial and nonfinancial payments employees receive for continuing their employment with the company.

"What are your benefits?" is the first thing many applicants ask. **Benefits**—indirect financial and nonfinancial payments employees receive for their employment with the company and which employers use to attract, recognize, and retain workers—are an important part of just about everyone's compensation.[2] They include things like health and life insurance, pensions, paid time off, and child-care assistance. Employee benefits account for about 31% of total compensation. Figure 13-1 summarizes the breakdown of benefits as a percentage of compensation.

For most employees, *health benefits* are the 800-pound gorilla of the benefits package. In one recent survey, benefits that people said they coveted most were health, dental, and vision benefits (88%), more flexible hours (88%), more vacation time (80%), and more work from home options (80%).[3] Even human resource managers can underestimate benefits' attractiveness. One survey concluded that many human resource managers erroneously assume that things like job security and autonomy are more important than benefits.[4] They aren't.

Policy Issues

Employers therefore should design benefits packages carefully, and there are many policy decisions to make. These include what benefits to offer, who receives coverage, whether to include retirees in the plan, whether to deny benefits to employees during initial "probationary" periods, how to finance benefits, cost-containment procedures, and how to communicate benefits options to employees.[5]

Legal issues loom large. Federal and state laws *mandate* some benefits (such as Social Security), while other benefits are *voluntary* (at the employer's discretion); see Table 13-1 (page 422). However, we'll see that federal law still affects even voluntary/discretionary benefits such as vacation leave. And employers must adhere to the laws of the states in which they do business. For example, California requires most state contractors to provide domestic partner benefits for employees.

There are many benefits and ways to classify them. We will classify them as (1) pay for time not worked (such as vacations), (2) insurance benefits, (3) retirement benefits, (4) personal services benefits, and (5) flexible benefits. We will start our discussion with pay for time not worked.

HR in Action at the Hotel Paris As they reviewed the benefits figures, Lisa Cruz and the CFO became increasingly concerned. They computed several benefits-related metrics for their firm, including *benefits costs as a percentage of payroll* and *sick days per full-time equivalent employee per year*. The results were not what they should have been. They had to change their benefits plan. To see how they handled this, read the case on pages 447–448.

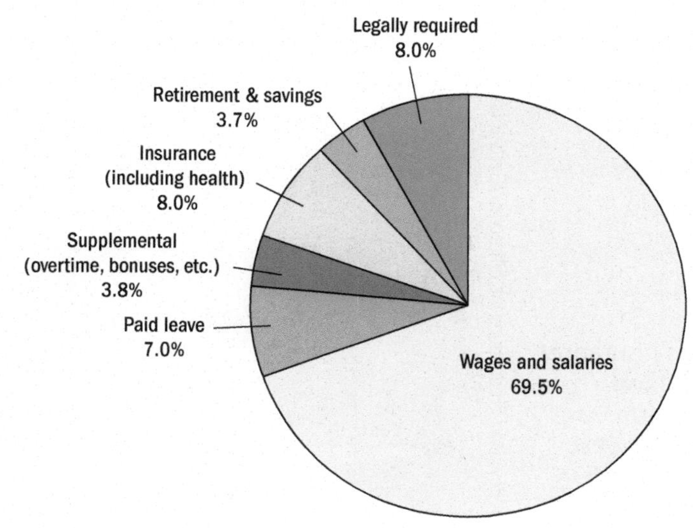

FIGURE 13-1 Relative Importance of Employer Costs for Employee Compensation (Private Industry), December 2017

Source: Based on Employer Costs for Employee Compensation—December 2017. http://www.bls.gov/news.release/pdf/ecec.pdf accessed March 30, 2018.

TABLE 13-1 Some Required and Discretionary Benefits

Benefits Required by Federal or Most State Laws	Benefits Discretionary on Part of Employer*
Social Security	Disability, health, and life insurance
Unemployment insurance	Pensions
Workers' compensation	Paid time off for vacations, holidays, sick leave, personal leave, jury duty, etc.
Leaves under Family and Medical Leave Act	Employee assistance and counseling programs; "family-friendly" benefits for child care, elder care, flexible work schedules, etc.; executive perquisites

Note: *Although not required under federal law, all these benefits are regulated in some way by federal law, as explained in this chapter.

Pay for Time Not Worked

LEARNING OBJECTIVE 13-1
Name and define each of the main pay for time not worked benefits.

Pay for time not worked—also called **supplemental pay benefits**—is very costly, because of how much time off most employees receive. Common time-off-with-pay benefits include holidays, vacations, jury duty, funeral leave, military duty, personal days, sick leave, sabbatical leave, maternity leave, and unemployment insurance payments for laid-off or terminated employees.

supplemental pay benefits
Benefits for time not worked such as unemployment insurance, vacation and holiday pay, and sick pay.

Unemployment Insurance

All states have their own **unemployment insurance (or compensation)** laws. These provide benefits to eligible workers who become unemployed through no fault of their own. The benefits derive from a tax on employers that can range from 0.1% to 5% of taxable payroll in most states. An employer's unemployment tax rate reflects its rate of employee terminations. Unemployment tax rates are rising in many states.

unemployment insurance (or compensation)
Provides benefits if a person is unable to work through some fault other than his or her own.

Yellow Dog Productions Inc./Photodisc/Getty Images

Unemployment insurance/compensation laws provide short-term benefits to people who lose their jobs through no fault of their own.

For example, prior to the 2007–2008 recession, Maryland's unemployment insurance tax rate was 0.3% or lower, but now ranges from 0.6% to 9.0% per employee.[6] All states follow federal unemployment insurance guidelines.

Not everyone dismissed by an employer is entitled to unemployment benefits—only those released through no fault of their own. Thus, strictly speaking, a worker fired for chronic lateness can't legitimately claim benefits. But many managers are lackadaisical in protecting their employers. Employers therefore spend thousands of dollars on unemployment taxes unnecessarily.

The main rule is to keep a list of written warnings to demonstrate that poor performance caused the dismissal. The checklist in Table 13-2 can help. (Those fired during their initial "90-day probation" *are* eligible for unemployment, so follow that checklist for them, too.)

Vacations and Holidays

Most firms offer vacation and holiday benefits. About 90% of full-time workers and 40% of part-timers get paid holidays, an average of eight paid holidays off.[7] Common U.S. paid holidays include New Year's Day, Memorial Day, Independence Day, Labor Day, Thanksgiving Day, and Christmas Day.[8] On average, American workers get about 9 days of vacation leave after 1 year's employment, 14 days after 5 years, and 17 after 10 years.[9]

Firms should address several holiday-and vacation-related policy issues, such as how many vacation days employees get, and which days (if any) are paid holidays. Other vacation policy decisions include: Are employees paid for accrued vacation time if they quit before taking their vacations? Will you pay employees for a holiday if they don't come to work the day before and the day after the holiday? And, should we pay some premium—such as time and a half—when employees must work on holidays?

In practice, vacation policies range from highly flexible, to traditional, to restrictive. Some employers have "unlimited vacation policies." One motive here is that with many workers answering e-mails 24/7, going home doesn't mean leaving work, so they deserve flexible vacations.[10] Such plans also aid recruiting. Of course, unlimited

TABLE 13-2 An Unemployment Insurance Cost-Control Checklist

Do You:

✓ Keep documented history of lateness, absence, and warning notices
✓ Warn chronically late employees before discharging them
✓ Have a rule that 3 days' absence without calling in is reason for automatic discharge
✓ Request doctor's note on return to work after absence
✓ Make written approval for personal leave mandatory
✓ Stipulate date for return to work from leave
✓ Obtain a signed resignation statement
✓ Mail job abandonment letter if employee fails to return on time
✓ Document all instances of poor performance
✓ Require supervisors to document the steps taken to remedy the situation
✓ Document employee's refusal of advice and direction
✓ Require all employees to sign a statement acknowledging acceptance of firm's policies and rules
✓ File the protest against a former employee's unemployment claim on time (usually within 10 days)
✓ Use proper terminology on claim form, and attach documented evidence regarding separation
✓ Attend hearings, and appeal unwarranted claims
✓ Check every claim against the individual's personnel file
✓ Routinely conduct exit interviews to produce information for protesting unemployment claims

Source: Copyright Gary Dessler, PhD.

vacation plans aren't really unlimited. While theoretically there's no limit on how many days off employees can take, in practice they must plan their schedules with their supervisors. When one company switched to such a plan, the average vacation days rose from 14 to 16.6, year-over-year. As a rule, very few employees actually take more time off.[11] Blackrock recently became the first big financial firm to introduce such a plan.[12]

Other employers take a traditional approach: employees are eligible for a certain number of annual vacation days (for instance all IBM employees get at least 3 weeks, and after 10 years get 4 weeks),[13] and place requests for vacations with their supervisors and perhaps their HR departments. Wage surveys provide typical vacation policies, which employers then usually describe in their employee manuals.

Some employers, concerned with excessive absence, emphasize restrictive, centralized absence oversight (called "integrated absence management"). This starts with collecting data. For instance, how many people are on leave; how many days of work is the employer losing; how much is the employer spending to replace absent workers; and what units have the attendance problems?[14] These employers then closely monitor all aspects of their employees' leaves and absences.

KNOW YOUR EMPLOYMENT LAW

Some Legal Aspects of Vacations and Holidays

Although federal law doesn't require vacation benefits, the employer must still formulate its vacation policy with care. As an example, with many employers' vacation policies, vacation pay accrues, say, on a biweekly basis. This means that these employers obligate themselves to pay new employees pro rata vacation pay if they leave the firm during their first year. But if the employer's vacation policy requires that a new employee pass his or her first employment anniversary *before becoming entitled* to a vacation, the employee gets no vacation pay if he or she leaves during that first year.

Another question is whether the employer can cancel an employee's scheduled vacation, for instance, due to a rush of orders. Here it's important that it formulate its vacation policy so it's clear that the employer reserves the right to require vacation cancellation and rescheduling if production so demands. ■

Sick Leave

sick leave
Provides pay to an employee when he or she is out of work because of illness.

Sick leave provides pay to employees when they're out of work due to illness. Most policies grant full pay for a specified number of sick days—perhaps 12 per year, usually accumulating at the rate of, say, 1 day per month of service. Six states and several cities now have mandatory paid leave sick laws.[15]

The problem with sick days is that many employees use them whether they're sick or not. In one survey, personal illnesses accounted for about 45% of unscheduled sick leave absences. Family issues (27%), personal needs (13%), and "entitlement" (9%) were other reasons cited.[16] Absenteeism costs U.S. employers about 20% of their total payrolls.[17]

COST-REDUCTION TACTICS Employers use several tactics to reduce excessive sick leave absence. About 87% use *pooled paid leave plans* (or *"banks"*). These lump together sick leave, vacation, and personal days into a single leave pool. In one SHRM survey, the average days awarded depended on the employee's time with the employer, and ranged from 13 to 26.[18] (Special absences like serious short-term illnesses and bereavement leave are usually handled separately.) Most firms don't include federal holidays in their paid time off "banks."[19]

Another tactic is to repurchase unused sick leave at the end of the year by paying their employees for each unused sick day. The problem is that legitimately sick employees may come to work. Others hold monthly lotteries in which only employees with perfect monthly attendance are eligible for a cash prize. At Marriott, employees can trade the value of some sick days for other benefits. Others aggressively investigate all absences, calling absent employees at home.[20] The accompanying Profit Center feature shows how one employer cut costs.

IMPROVING PERFORMANCE: *HR AS A PROFIT CENTER*

Controlling Sick Leave

Sick leave often gets out of control because employers don't measure it. In one survey, only 57% of employers formally tracked sick days for their exempt employees.[21] Three-fourths of the employers couldn't provide an estimate of what sick pay was costing them. Therefore, the employer should first have a system for monitoring sick leaves and for measuring their financial impact.[22]

As an example, when she became director of the United Kingdom's Driver and Vehicle Licensing Agency, the new director knew steps were needed to address its absence rate.[23] The rate had peaked at 14 days out per employee in 2005, at a cost of about $20 million per year (then £10.3 million).

The new director organized a human resource absence initiative.[24] The agency set a goal of reducing absences by 30% by 2010. Agency directors received absence-reduction goals, and their progress was tracked. The agency introduced new policies on special leave, rehabilitation support, and monitoring absentees. They made it easier for employees to swap work shifts, and introduced a guaranteed leave day policy.

By 2010, the sickness absence rate was down to 7.5 days per employee and productivity was up, for multiyear savings of about $48 million dollars (£24.4 million). ■

> **MyLab Management Talk About It 1**
>
> If your professor has assigned this, go to the Assignments section of **www.pearson.com/mylab/management** to complete this discussion question. A note on this agency in Wikipedia refers to "amazingly high" levels of sick leave among staff at the DVLA [around 2007], with employees having an average of three weeks a year sick leave."[25] What sorts of inaction on the part of previous managers could help explain such poor attendance?

KNOW YOUR EMPLOYMENT LAW

Leaves and the Family and Medical Leave Act and Other Laws

Parental leave is an important benefit. About half of workers are women; about 80% of them will become pregnant during their work lives. Furthermore, many workers are single parents. Several laws apply here. Under the Pregnancy Discrimination Act, employers must treat women applying for pregnancy leave as they would any other employee requesting a leave under the employer's sick leave policies. The Family and Medical Leave Act of 1993 (FMLA)[26] stipulates that:[27]

1. Private employers of 50 or more employees must provide eligible employees (women or men) up to 12 weeks of unpaid leave for their own serious illness, the birth or adoption of a child, or the care of a seriously ill child, spouse, or parent.
2. Employers may require employees to take their paid sick leave or annual leave as part of the 12-week leave provided in the law.
3. Employees taking leave are entitled to receive health benefits while they are on unpaid leave, under the same terms and conditions as when they were on the job.
4. Employers must guarantee most employees the right to return to their previous or equivalent position with no loss of benefits at the end of the leave.

Under the Americans with Disabilities Act (ADA), a qualified employee with a disability may be eligible for a leave if it's necessary to accommodate the employee.[28]

FMLA Guidelines

Managers who want to avoid granting nonrequired FMLA leaves must understand the law. For example, to be eligible for leave under the FMLA, the employee must have worked for the employer for at least a total of 12 months and have worked for 1,250 or more hours in the past 12 consecutive months.[29] If these conditions don't apply, no leave is required.

Employers should have procedures for all leaves of absence (including those under the FMLA). In particular:

- Give no employee a leave until the reason for the leave is clear.
- Confirm the legitimacy of any FMLA request. Employers can request sufficient medical facts and symptoms to confirm the eligible condition, prescriptions, appointments, and the treatment regimen.[30]
- Use a standard form to record both the employee's expected return date and the fact that, without an authorized extension, the firm may terminate his or her employment (see Figure 13-2). ■

Many employers enrich their parental leave plans to make them more attractive for mothers to return from maternity leave. For example, keep in touch during maternity leave, offer flexible jobs with reduced travel and hours, and offer longer leaves.[31]

FIGURE 13-2 Online Request for Leave Form

Source: From Request for Leave or Approved Absence, http://www.opm.gov/FORMS/PDF_FILL/opm71.pdf.

Request for Leave or Approved Absence

1. **Name** *(Last, first, middle)*

2. **Employee or Social Security Number (Enter only the last 4 digits of the Social Security Number (SSN))**

3. **Organization**

4. **Type of Leave/Absence** *(Check appropriate box(es) below)*	Date From	Date To	Time From	Time To	Total Hours
☐ Accrued Annual Leave					
☐ Restored Annual Leave					
☐ Advanced Annual Leave					
☐ Accrued Sick Leave					
☐ Advanced Sick Leave					

Purpose:
- ☐ Illness/injury/incapacitation of requesting employee
- ☐ Medical/dental/optical examination of requesting employee
- ☐ Care of family member, including medical/dental/optical examination of family member, or bereavement
- ☐ Care of family member with a serious health condition
- ☐ Other

	Date From	Date To	Time From	Time To	Total Hours
☐ Compensatory Time Off					
☐ Other Paid Absence *(Specify in Remarks)*					
☐ Leave Without Pay					

5. **Family and Medical Leave**

If annual leave, sick leave, or leave without pay will be used under the Family and Medical Leave Act of 1993, please provide the following information:

☐ **I hereby invoke my entitlement to Family and Medical Leave for:**
- ☐ Birth/Adoption/Foster Care
- ☐ Serious health condition of spouse, son, daughter, or parent
- ☐ Serious health condition of self

Contact your supervisor and/or your personnel office to obtain additional information about your entitlements and responsibilities under the Family and Medical Leave Act. Medical certification of a serious health condition may be required by your agency.

6. **Remarks:**

7. **Certification:** I hereby request leave/approved absence from duty as indicated above and certify that such leave/absence is requested for the purpose(s) indicated. I understand that I must comply with my employing agency's procedures for requesting leave/approved absence (and provide additional documentation, including medical certification, if required) and that falsification on this form may be grounds for disciplinary action, including removal.

7a. **Employee Signature** | 7b. **Date**

8a. **Official Action on Request:** ☐ Approved ☐ Disapproved *(If disapproved, give reason. If annual leave, initiate action to reschedule.)*

8b. **Reason for Disapproval:**

8c. **Supervisor Signature** | 8d. **Date**

PRIVACY ACT STATEMENT
Section 6311 of Title 5, United States Code, authorizes collection of this information. The primary use of this information is by management and your payroll office to approve and record your use of leave. Additional disclosures of the information may be: to the Department of Labor when processing a claim for compensation regarding a job connected injury or illness; to a State unemployment compensation office regarding a claim; to Federal Life Insurance or Health Benefits carriers regarding a claim; to a Federal, State, or local law enforcement agency when your agency becomes aware of a violation or possible violation of civil or criminal law; to a Federal agency when conducting an investigation for employment or security reasons; to the Office of Personnel Management or the General Accounting Office when the information is required for evaluation of leave administration; or the General Services Administration in connection with its responsibilities for records management.

Public Law 104-134 (April 26, 1996) requires that any person doing business with the Federal Government furnish a social security number or tax identification number. This is an amendment to Title 31, Section 7701. Furnishing the social security number, as well as other data, is voluntary, but failure to do so may delay or prevent action on the application. If your agency uses the information furnished on this form for purposes other than those indicated above, it may provide you with an additional statement reflecting those purposes.

Office of Personnel Management
5 CFR 630

Local Reproduction Authorized

OPM Form 71
Rev. September 2009
Formerly Standard Form (SF) 71
Previous editions usable

Print Form | Clear Form | Save Form

The FMLA mandates only unpaid leave. Therefore, several states implemented paid family leave laws.[32] Recently, there's been discussion of the need for federal parental paid leave legislation.[33]

Severance Pay

severance pay
A one-time payment some employers provide when terminating an employee.

Many employers provide **severance pay,** a one-time separation payment when terminating an employee. Most managers expect employees to give them 1 or 2 weeks' notice if they plan to quit, so severance pay seems appropriate when dismissing an employee. Reducing litigation from disgruntled former employees is another reason.[34] Severance pay also helps reassure employees that they'll receive some financial help if let go, too. If the employer obligates itself (for instance, in its employee handbook) to pay severance, then its "voluntary" plan must comply with additional ERISA rules.[35]

The reason for the dismissal usually affects the severance pay. About 95% of employees dismissed due to downsizings get severance pay, but only about a third of employers offer severance when dismissing for poor performance. It is uncommon to pay when employees quit.

The maximum weeks of severance pay tends to vary by position. In one survey about 45% of officers and senior executives got 52 weeks or more, 42% of professionals got 14–26 weeks, and 39% of administrative staff got 14–26 weeks. Few lower-level employees got no severance, but 13%–19% of officers and senior executives got no severance.[36]

GUIDELINES In any event, keep several things in mind when designing severance plans:

- List the situations for which the firm will pay severance, such as layoffs resulting from reorganizations.
- Require signing of a knowing and voluntary waiver/general release prior to remittance of any severance pay, absolving the employer from employment-related liability.
- Reserve the right to terminate or alter the severance policy.
- Make it clear that any continuing severance payments continue until only the stated deadline or until the employee gets a new job, whichever occurs first.
- Remember that, as with all personnel actions, employers must make severance payments, if any, equitably.[37]

IMPROVING PERFORMANCE: *HR PRACTICES AROUND THE GLOBE*

Severance Pay in France

Although President Emmanuel Macron is working to change it, French labor law is still complex and restrictive, and aimed mostly at protecting employees' rights.[38]

For example, when one employer refused two employees' requests to be fired, they stopped coming to work. He dismissed them, after which a labor tribunal held they'd been wrongfully terminated. The two former employees ended up getting about $60,000 each. Proceedings in these tribunals can go on for years.

Understandably, many employers take the easy way out and don't hire employees. Instead, they outsource work or use temps. President Macron wants to put a ceiling on the labor tribunal awards. He hopes that lifting that threat will make employers more willing to hire again. But unions are resisting capping awards, and striking. In any case, managers from other countries should understand French labor law before opening new facilities there.

supplemental unemployment benefits
Provide for a "guaranteed annual income" in certain industries where employers must shut down to change machinery or due to reduced work. These benefits are paid by the company and supplement unemployment benefits.

Supplemental Unemployment Benefits

In some industries such as automaking, shutdowns to reduce inventories or change machines are common. **Supplemental unemployment benefits** are cash payments that supplement the employee's unemployment compensation, to help the person maintain his or her standard of living while out of work.

Insurance Benefits

Most employers also provide various required or voluntary insurance benefits, such as workers' compensation and health insurance.

LEARNING OBJECTIVE 13-2
Describe each of the main insurance benefits.

Workers' Compensation

workers' compensation
Provides income and medical benefits to work-related accident victims or their dependents regardless of fault.

Workers' compensation laws aim to provide sure, prompt income and medical benefits to work-related accident victims or their dependents, regardless of fault. Every state has its own workers' compensation law and commission, and some run their own insurance programs. However, most require employers to carry workers' compensation insurance with private, state-approved insurance companies. Neither the state nor the federal government contributes any funds for workers' compensation.

HOW BENEFITS ARE DETERMINED Workers' compensation can be monetary or medical. In the event of a worker's death or disablement, the person's dependents receive a cash benefit based on prior earnings—usually one-half to two-thirds the worker's average weekly wage, per week of employment. Most states have a time limit—such as 500 weeks—for which benefits can be paid. If the injury causes a specific loss (such as an arm), the employee may receive additional benefits based on a statutory list of losses, even though he or she may return to work. In addition to these cash benefits, employers must furnish medical, surgical, and hospital services as required for the employee.

For workers' compensation to cover an injury or work-related illness, one must only prove that it arose while the worker was on the job. It doesn't matter that he or she may have been at fault.[39] Suppose you instruct employees to wear safety goggles at their machines. One worker doesn't and has an eye injury on the job. The company must still provide workers' compensation benefits.

Americans with Disabilities Act provisions generally prohibit employers from inquiring about an applicant's workers' compensation history. Furthermore, failing to let an employee who was on injury-related workers' compensation return to work, or not accommodating him or her, could trigger ADA lawsuits.

CONTROLLING WORKERS' COMPENSATION COSTS It is important to control workers' compensation claims (and therefore costs). The employer's insurance company usually pays the claim, but the employer's premiums may rise with more claims.

There are ways to reduce workers' compensation claims. First, new employees are most at risk: inexperienced (less than one year) workers have two to four times the loss costs, for instance.[40] Competent selection—background checks, testing, and drug testing—plus training are therefore crucial.[41] Also reduce accident-causing conditions, such as slippery floors or sloppy work habits. Check and comply with safety standards laws. Furthermore, some workers' compensation claims are not legitimate. Red flags include vague accident details, minor accidents resulting in major injuries, lack of witnesses, injuries occurring late Friday, and late reporting.[42]

Case management is popular for cost control. It is "the treatment of injured workers on a case-by-case basis by an assigned manager, usually a [specially trained] registered nurse, who coordinates with the physician and health plan to determine which care settings are the most effective for quality care and cost."[43]

Moving aggressively to support the injured employee and to get him or her back to work is important too. The involvement of an attorney and the duration of the claim both influence the worker's claim cost.[44] Many firms have programs such as physical therapy assistance to help reintegrate claim recipients.

Hospitalization, Health, and Disability Insurance

Health insurance looms large in many people's choice of employer, because it's so expensive.[45] Hospitalization, health, and disability insurance helps protect employees against hospitalization costs and from the income loss arising from off-the-job accidents or illness. Many employers purchase insurance from life insurance companies, casualty insurance companies, or Blue Cross (for hospital expenses) and Blue Shield

TABLE 13-3 Percentage of Employers Offering Some Popular Health Benefits

2015 Health Care and Welfare Benefits	
Dental insurance	96%
Prescription drug coverage	96%
Mental health coverage	91%
Mail-order prescription program	87%
Vision insurance	87%
Accidental death and dismemberment insurance (AD&D)	85%
Preferred provider organization (PPO)	85%
Contraceptive coverage	83%
Chiropractic coverage	81%
Long-term disability insurance	80%
Employee assistance program (EAP)	79%
Short-term disability insurance	74%
Medical flexible spending accounts	69%

Source: 2015 Employee Benefits, SHRM, https://www.shrm.org/hr-today/trends-and-forecasting/research-and-surveys/Documents/2015-Employee-Benefits.pdf, accessed April 23, 2017.

(for physician expenses) organizations. Others contract with health maintenance organizations or preferred provider organizations. The employer and employee usually both contribute to the plan. Experts forecasted the total cost of medical and pharmacy benefits to rise by 5% in 2018, to about $14,000 per employee.[46] And of course employers are dealing with implementing the Patient Protection and Affordable Care ("Obamacare") Act, as we will see.[47]

Table 13-3 illustrates the prevalence of health-related benefits.

COVERAGE Most employer health plans provide at least basic hospitalization and surgical and medical insurance for all eligible employees at group rates. Insurance is generally available to all employees—including new nonprobationary ones—regardless of health or physical condition. Most basic plans pay for hospital room and board, surgery charges, and medical expenses (such as doctors' visits to the hospital). Some also provide "major medical" coverage to meet the medical expenses resulting from serious illnesses.

Most employers' health plans also cover health-related expenses like doctors' visits, eye care, and dental services. Other plans pay for general and diagnostic visits to the doctor's office, vision care, hearing aids, and prescription drugs. *Disability insurance* provides income protection for salary loss due to illness or accident, and may continue until age 65 or beyond. Disability benefits usually range from 50% to 75% of the employee's base pay if he or she is disabled.

Under the Patient Protection and Affordable Care Act, employers with at least 50 full-time-equivalent employees are to offer minimum levels of affordable health-care coverage or pay a penalty.

health maintenance organization (HMO)
A prepaid health-care system that generally provides routine round-the-clock medical services as well as preventive medicine in a clinic-type arrangement for employees, who pay a nominal fee in addition to the fixed annual fee the employer pays.

HMOS Many employers offer membership in a **health maintenance organization (HMO),** a medical organization consisting of specialists (surgeons, psychiatrists, and so on), often operating out of a health-care center. HMOs provide routine medical services to employees who pay a nominal fee. Employees often have "gatekeeper" doctors who must approve appointments with specialist doctors. The HMO receives a fixed annual fee per employee from the employer (or employer and employee), regardless of whether it provides that person service.

PPOS Preferred provider organizations (PPOs) are a cross between HMOs and the traditional doctor–patient arrangement: They are "groups of health-care providers that contract with employers, insurance companies, or third-party payers to provide medical care services at a reduced fee."[48] Unlike HMOs, PPOs let employees select providers (such as doctors) from a relatively wide list, and see them in their offices, often without gatekeeper doctor approval. Providers agree to discounts and to certain controls, for example, on testing.[49]

MENTAL HEALTH BENEFITS The World Health Organization estimated that more than 34 million people in the United States between the ages of 18 and 64 suffer from mental illness.[50] Mental illnesses represent about 24% of all reported disabilities, more than disabling injuries, cardiovascular diseases, and cancer combined. For some reason Millennials are more likely to report being depressed.[51]

Mental health costs are rising. Reasons include widespread drug and alcohol problems, more states requiring employers to offer minimum mental health benefits, and the fact that mental health claims tend to trigger other health-care claims. The Mental Health Parity Act of 1996 (amended in 2008) sets minimum mental health-care benefits; it also prohibits employer group health plans from adopting mental health benefits limitations without comparable limitations on medical and surgical benefits.[52]

KNOW YOUR EMPLOYMENT LAW

Patient Protection and Affordable Care Act of 2010 and Other Laws

Under the Patient Protection and Affordable Care Act, employers with at least 50 full-time-equivalent employees are to offer minimum levels of affordable health-care coverage or pay a penalty of $167 per employee per month. To be eligible, an employee must work at least 30 hours per week or a total of 130 hours in a calendar month.[53] The bill was signed into law by President Obama in 2010, and employers faced a number of deadlines under the act.[54] By 2018, employers with health-care plans that cost more than the threshold the law sets (for instance, $27,500 for family coverage) had to pay a 40% tax on the amount of coverage over $27,500. Individual and group health plans that already provide dependent coverage must expand eligibility up to age 26.[55]

Under the law, each state (or, when necessary, the federal government) may run health insurance exchanges—in effect, marketplaces for buying and selling insurance. In part to discourage employers from dropping their health-care plans and sending employees to the health exchanges, the law imposes those fines of $2,000 ($167 per month) per worker on any employer with more than 50 workers who doesn't offer a health insurance plan. "Obamacare" health-care exchanges cover less than 10% of the health insurance market; employers' programs cover almost half the U.S. population.[56]

Because employers had to pay a 40% surcharge beginning in 2018 on health insurance plans exceeding $27,500 for a family (or $10,200 for an individual), many employers are moving to reduce their health-care benefits, for instance by increasing employee co-pays and deductibles.[57] To avoid penalties that could reach $2,000 per employee, some employers are directing employees who qualify for Medicaid to sign up for it, instead of employer-supplied insurance.[58] Some employers are eliminating their health plans, or turning more full-time workers into part-timers working less than 30 hours per week.[59] About 43% of employers surveyed say their workers will have to pay more for their health-care plans.[60] Others are reducing their coverage.[61] Other employers calculate that it may be cheaper to pay the penalty than supply the insurance.[62]

The Evolving Law

The Affordable Care Act did not please everyone, and many legislators in particular objected to it. For example, some say it entangles the federal government excessively in citizen's personal health matters, and that it provides excessive monetary subsidies to support the act's provisions. (Indeed, without a change, Obamacare premiums were projected to rise quickly).[63]

An early proposal would have changed or eliminated many of the Affordable Care Act's core provisions, by allowing individual states to waive compliance with them.[64] Congress's initial attempts to replace Obamacare failed to obtain sufficient support.

With uncertainty surrounding the Affordable Care Act, many insurers were uncertain they could continue providing coverage.[65] At least for 2018, employers were proceeding with most of the Obamacare rules in place.[66]

COBRA

COBRA—the Consolidated Omnibus Budget Reconciliation Act—requires most private employers to continue to make health benefits available to separated employees and their families for a time, generally 18 months after separation.[67] The former employee must pay for the coverage.

Employers ignore COBRA's rules at their peril. The employer does not want separated employees to leave and be injured, and then claim they were never told they could have continued their insurance coverage. Therefore, when a new employee first becomes eligible for the company's insurance plan, the person *must* receive (and acknowledge receiving) an explanation of his or her COBRA rights. And all employees separated from the company should sign a form acknowledging that they received and understand those rights. (See Figure 13-3 for a checklist.)

Other Laws

Other federal laws are pertinent. For example, the *Employee Retirement Income Security Act of 1974* (ERISA) sets minimum standards for most voluntarily established pension and health plans in private industry.[68] *The Newborn Mother's Protection Act of 1996* prohibits employers' health plans from using incentives to encourage employees to leave the hospital after childbirth after less than the legislatively determined

FIGURE 13-3 Illustrative COBRA Compliance Checklist

Source: Adapted from: www.cobraplus.com/wp-content/themes/cobra-plus/images/constant/COBRAetup.pdf; COBRA Checklist, www.shrm.org/resourcesandtools/; COBRA record keeping checklist, BLRBusiness and Legal Resources; and COBRA compliance checklist, http://brscobra.com/cobra-checklist, all accessed August 1, 2017. Copyright Gary Dessler, PhD.

Cobra to do list would include, for example:	✓ If Done
Complete COBRA services agreement with vendor.	☐
Complete COBRA census: who is covered, with their ages.	☐
Maintain records of those covered by group health plan.	☐
Notify all employees of their rights under COBRA.	☐
Document notification to qualified individuals if they are not eligible to continue coverage.	☐
Monitor COBRA election periods.	☐
Document all notifications (7 years).	☐
Receive signed COBRA election form.	☐
Maintain log of all inquiries received re COBRA.	☐
Track eligible individuals' COBRA payments.	☐
Notify insurers of cancellation of coverage.	☐
Notify qualified beneficiaries if they are not eligible for continued COBRA coverage.	☐
Mail COBRA qualifying event notice and election form to former employee.	☐
Maintain current addresses of those on COBRA.	☐
Maintain records of qualified COBRA beneficiaries.	☐
Terminate COBRA coverage.	☐

minimum stay. Employers who provide health-care services must follow the privacy rules of the *Health Insurance Portability and Accountability Act of 1996* (HIPAA).[69] Employers must provide the same health-care benefits to employees over the age of 65 that they do to younger workers, even though the older ones are eligible for federal Medicare health insurance. Under the *Americans with Disabilities Act*, the health plan generally shouldn't make distinctions based on disability. Under the *Genetic Information Nondiscrimination Act of 2008* (GINA), even innocent actions can be problems. For example, if a health plan administrator writes down that a member's mother passed away from breast cancer, making the note could conceivably violate the act.[70] States such as California have their own FMLAs.[71] ■

Trends in Employer Health-Care Cost Control

It can cost a business with 50 employees $1 million or more for insurance coverage. Health-care cost control is therefore one big way the HR department can improve profits.[72]

Cost control should start by measuring and auditing health-care costs.[73] One survey several years ago found that while the *standard* for claims errors was 3%, the *actual* percentage of claims with errors was about 6.3%. The standard for claims dollars paid in error was 1%; the *actual* percentage of claims dollars paid in error was 3.4%. Consultants who audit employers' health-care payments estimate up to *8%* overpayments. The bottom line is that auditing claims is essential.[74]

Beyond that, for many employers, deductibles and co-pays are the low-hanging fruit in health-care cost control. For example, at least 20% of employees were enrolled in high-deductible plans in one survey.[75]

OTHER COST-CONTROL TOOLS Employers take other cost-control steps. For example, employees use tax-sheltered health savings accounts (HSAs) to pay for "low dollar" (not catastrophic) medical expenses.[76] About 19% of employers surveyed had some form of health-care plan *spousal exclusion policies*, such as excluding a spouse when similar coverage was available from the spouse's employer.[77] Some employers offer *defined contribution health insurance plans*. Like 401(k) plans, defined contribution health insurance plans tie each employee's health-care benefits to what he or she and the employer contributes, rather than providing health-care benefits that are defined in advance.[78]

Many employers move Medicare-eligible retirees from their company health insurance plans into private individual exchanges. That reduces their own administrative obligations while offering retirees more choices for less money.[79] The exchanges are run by companies that include Mercer, and Aon Hewitt.

Other employers hire "patient advocates," such as nurses who review employees' medications and (with the consultation of independent physicians) recommend reduced medication regimens.[80] The U.S. Labor Department recently proposed rules making it easier for small businesses to band together to offer *minimal health benefits plans* (although some worry that such plans don't cover big health issues like childbirth).[81] Some employers have *on-site medical centers*; here patient confidentiality rules, and state laws regarding medical waste disposal are just two issues to consider.[82] Employers require that insurers use *accountable care organizations* (ACO), special vendors who help insurers, health-care providers, and others improve costs and outcomes.[83] Amazon recently was considering establishing its own health clinics for Amazon employees.

Also, *make sure employees know the costs* of their medical benefits.[84] For example, periodically send a statement to each employee listing the employer's costs for each health benefit. *Online selection* lets employees choose the best of the employer's health-care offerings, based on input from other employees concerning matters like doctor visits and specialists.

WELLNESS PROGRAMS The top two health-care employer priorities in one survey were, "Offer incentives or disincentives to motivate sustained health-care behavior change"; and "Promote a culture of health in the workplace [such as healthy cafeteria foods]"[85] Because various illnesses are preventable, many employers offer wellness/preventive programs. For example, in one 15-year period, the percentage of Johnson & Johnson employees who smoke dropped by two-thirds, in part assumedly due to its various wellness programs. J&J managers estimate the company earns about $2.75 for every $1.00 it spends on wellness.[86]

Employers offer various wellness/preventive services and incentives.[87] *Clinical prevention* programs include things like mammograms and checkups. Walgreens provides *on-site health-care services* such as mammograms.[88] Insurer USAA offers options like these: employees pay $300 a year to use company fitness centers, but those who go three or more times a week get 75% off; they have running and walking trails at many campuses, and mileage markers in company hallways; healthy foods are at eye level in the cafeterias, and pricing encourages workers to buy them; and employees have weight loss and other health incentives, and employees who meet the goals can earn up to $550. Other wellness programs include obesity management, stress management, and smoking cessation.

Incentives can boost wellness program participation, but may backfire.[89] (Whirlpool gave nonsmoker discounts worth about $500 on health-care premiums. It suspended 39 workers caught smoking outside the plant after claiming on their enrollment forms that they were nonsmokers.) Some employers offer standing desks. The desks may boost wellness; however, a recent study concluded that six hours a day of standing burned only about 54 calories—about the same as in a piece of fruit.[90]

Wellness program research is mixed. J&J, as noted, has had positive results but in another study, wellness programs (including with incentives) did not change employees' behavior much.[91] The key seems to be to motivate the employee to take steps to stay well. Two experts say this entails:

Leadership commitment and support For example, at Lincoln Industries, promoting health is embedded in the company's mission statement.[92]

Build a culture of health Good health emerges from a culture evidenced by elements such as health-promoting policies, healthy food offerings, staircases rather than elevators, and treadmills.

Employee involvement Wellness requires employee engagement—they have to want it. Employees should "own" the wellness program, and should have a big role in its creation and operation.

Spread the word For example, USAA continually communicates in multiple ways to employees that the wellness program is there to serve them.

The accompanying Profit Center feature shows how one employer cut costs.

IMPROVING PERFORMANCE: *HR AS A PROFIT CENTER*

The Doctor Is on the Phone

With more than 12,000 employees in its health plan, Rent-A-Center was looking for a better way to get its employees the medical advice they required, while also reducing health plan costs. The company signed an agreement with Teladoc, Inc. Teladoc's doctors provide medical consultations over the phone. In the first 16 months the new telemedicine program was in effect, Rent-A-Center saved more than $770,000 in doctor and hospital visits and in employee productivity that would have been lost.

The program seems to be win–win. The Teladoc consultation is free to employees, compared to a $20 office co-payment, and the doctors are available 24 hours per day, usually within 30 minutes. If necessary, they call in antibiotics prescriptions. And for Rent-A-Center, there's that extra $770,000 in their bottom line.[93] ■

MyLab Management Talk About It 2

If your professor has assigned this, go to the Assignments section of **www.pearson.com/mylab/management** to complete these discussion questions. Would you recommend this program to your employer? Why or why not?

Long-Term Care

Long-term care insurance—for things like nursing assistance for former employees in their old age—is a key employee benefit. The Health Insurance Portability and Accountability Act of 1996 lets employers and employees deduct long-term care insurance premiums from their income taxes, making this benefit more attractive.[94] Employers can also provide insurance benefits for related matters such as adult day care, assisted living, and custodial care.

Life Insurance

group life insurance
Provides lower rates for the employer or employee and includes all employees, including new employees, regardless of health or physical condition.

In addition to hospitalization and medical benefits, most employers provide **group life insurance** plans. Such plans generally offer lower rates than individual plans, and usually accept all employees regardless of health or physical condition.

In general, there are three key personnel policies to address: the benefits-paid schedule (the amount of life insurance is usually tied to the employee's annual earnings), supplemental benefits (continued life insurance coverage after retirement, for instance), and financing (the amount and percent the employee contributes).

Accidental death and dismemberment coverage provides a lump-sum benefit in addition to life insurance benefits when death is accidental. It also provides benefits in case of accidental loss of limbs or sight.

Benefits for Part-Time and Contingent Workers

About 19 million people work part-time (less than 35 hours a week).[95] More gig work, more phased retirements, and a desire to better balance work and family life help explain this phenomenon. In any case, many firms provide holiday, sick leave, and vacation benefits to part-timers, and more than 70% offer some form of health-care benefits to them.[96]

HR AND THE GIG ECONOMY: *GIG WORKER BENEFITS*

Employers that want to offer gig workers benefits are often reluctant to do so. The problem is providing gig workers with benefits, while maintaining their status as independent contractors not also entitled to things like payroll tax contributions.[97]

The head of one company, Handy (whose independent contractors go to people's homes to clean or make repairs), is trying to do something about it.[98] He's working with New York legislators to create legislation that would make it easier for employers to fund things like sick leave and portable benefits for their independent contractors, while keeping them as independent contractors.[99] Uber partners with Stride Health, a health-care insurance marketplace that helps Uber drivers arrange for insurance they (not Uber) pay for themselves.[100]

Retirement Benefits

LEARNING OBJECTIVE 13-3
Discuss the main retirement benefits.

Retirement benefits such as Social Security and pension plans are big HR issues, in no small part because the huge contingent of baby boomers (born 1946–1964) turns 65 between roughly now and 2029.

Social Security

Most people assume that **Social Security** provides income only when they are older than 62, but it actually provides three types of benefits. *Retirement benefits* provide an income if you retire at age 62 or thereafter and are insured under the Social Security Act. Second are *survivor's* or *death benefits*. These provide monthly payments to your dependents regardless of your age at death (assuming you're insured under Social Security). Finally, *disability payments* provide monthly payments to employees who become disabled totally (and to their dependents) if they meet certain requirements. The Social Security system also administers the Medicare program, which provides health services to people age 65 or older.

Social Security
Federal program that provides three types of benefits: retirement income at the age of 62 and thereafter, survivor's or death benefits payable to the employee's dependents regardless of age at time of death, and disability benefits payable to disabled employees and their dependents. These benefits are payable only if the employee is insured under the Social Security Act.

A tax on the employee's wages funds Social Security (technically, "Federal Old Age and Survivor's Insurance"). Recently, the maximum amount of earnings subject to Social Security tax was $128,400; the employer pays 7.65% and the employee 7.65%.[101] "Full retirement age" for nondiscounted Social Security benefits traditionally was 65—the usual age for retirement. It is now 67 for those born in 1960 or later.[102]

Pension Plans

pension plans
Plans that provide a fixed sum when employees reach a predetermined retirement age or when they can no longer work due to disability.

Pension plans provide income to individuals in their retirement, and just over half of full-time workers participate in some type of pension plan at work. Pension planners classify pension plans as *contributory versus noncontributory* plans, and as *defined contribution versus defined benefit* plans.[103] The employee contributes to contributory pension plans, while the employer makes all contributions to noncontributory plans. Defined benefits plans "define" how much the pension will be, while with defined contribution plans the benefits (if any) will depend on the contributions to the plan and on how the assets performed. Note that some plans are also "qualified" (or not), insofar as they receive favorable treatment under the tax code.

defined benefit pension plan
A plan that contains a formula for determining retirement benefits.

Again, with **defined benefit pension plans,** the employee's pension is specified ("defined"), in that the person knows in advance his or her pension benefits. A formula usually ties the pension to a percentage of the person's preretirement pay (for example, to an average of his or her last 5 years of employment), multiplied by the years he or she worked for the company). Due to tax law changes and other reasons, defined benefit plans now are a minority of pension benefit plans. However, even younger employees express a strong preference for defined benefit plans.[104] Some companies, such as Union Pacific, offer them as employee retention tools.[105]

defined contribution pension plan
A plan in which the employer's contribution to employees' retirement savings funds is specified.

portability
Instituting policies that enable employees to easily take their accumulated pension funds when they leave an employer.

Defined contribution pension plans specify ("define") what *contribution* the employee and employer will make to the employee's retirement or savings fund. Here the contribution is defined, not the pension. With a *defined benefit* plan, the employee can compute what his or her retirement *benefits* will be upon retirement. With a *defined contribution* plan, the actual pension will depend on the amounts contributed to the fund *and* on the success of the fund's investment earnings. Defined contribution plans are popular among employers due to their relative ease of administration, favorable tax treatment, and other factors. **Portability**—the ability of employees who leave the firm prior to retirement to take their accumulated pension funds with them—is easier with defined contribution plans.

In any case, CEO retirement packages tend to dwarf the average employee's.[106] For example, when Target's CEO stepped down after a huge credit card breach, he walked away with retirement plans worth more than $47 million, plus a $7.2 million severance payment and $4.1 million from vested stock awards.

401(k) plan
A defined contribution plan based on section 401(k) of the Internal Revenue Code.

401(K) PLANS The most popular defined contribution plans are based on section 401(k) of the Internal Revenue Code, and are called **401(k) plans.** The employee authorizes the employer to deduct a sum from his or her paycheck before taxes, and to invest it in the bundle of investments in his or her 401(k) account. The deduction is pretax, so the employee pays no tax on those dollars until after he or she retires (or removes the money from the 401(k) plan). The person can deduct annually an amount up to the IRS maximum (about $15,000). Employers often match employees' 401(k) contributions dollar for dollar up to a set percentage. The employer arranges, usually with an investment company such as Fidelity Investments, to administer the 401(k) plan and to make investment options (typically mutual stock funds and bond funds) available to the plan.

Employers must choose 401(k) providers with care. The employer has a fiduciary responsibility to its employees and must monitor the fund and its administration.[107] In addition to trustworthiness, the 401(k) plan provider should make it easy to enroll and participate in the plan.[108] Firms such as Vanguard, Fidelity, and others establish Web-based 401(k) plans with online tools—such as an "asset allocation planner"—even for small firms. Employers must also monitor 401(k) housekeeping issues such as late deposits and incorrect employer matching contributions.[109]

Firms such as Vanguard, Fidelity, and others can establish online, fully Web-based 401(k) plans even for small firms with 10 to 50 employees.

DNY59/Getty Images

savings and thrift plan
Plan in which employees contribute a portion of their earnings to a fund; the employer usually matches this contribution in whole or in part.

deferred profit-sharing plan
A plan in which a certain amount of profits is credited to each employee's account, payable at retirement, termination, or death.

employee stock ownership plan (ESOP)
A qualified, tax-deductible stock bonus plan in which employers contribute stock to a trust for eventual use by employees.

cash balance plans
Plans under which the employer contributes a percentage of employees' current pay to employees' pension plans every year, and employees earn interest on this amount.

Under the Pension Protection Act of 2006, employers who sponsor plans that facilitate both *automatic enrollment* and allocation to *default investments* (such as age-appropriate "lifestyle funds") reduce their compliance burdens.[110] Google's 401(k) plan automatically enrolls employees to contribute 10% of their eligible compensation. (The employee can decline).[111] After the president signed the 2017 tax law, many large and midsize companies, including Honeywell and AFLAC, increased their 401(k) contributions (to get the higher tax deduction that year).[112]

OTHER PLANS The 401(k) plan is one example of a **savings and thrift plan.**[113] In any such plan, employees contribute a portion of their earnings to a fund, and the employer usually matches this contribution completely or in part.

As discussed in Chapter 12 (Incentives), employers use a **deferred profit-sharing plan** to contribute a portion of their profits in cash to a pension fund, regardless of the level of employee contribution. An **employee stock ownership plan (ESOP)** is a qualified, tax-deductible defined contribution plan in which employers contribute stock to a trust for eventual use by employees who retire.

CASH BALANCE PENSION PLANS With *defined benefits* plans, to get your maximum pension, you generally must stay with your employer until you retire—the formula takes the number of years you work into consideration. With *defined contribution* plans, your pension is more portable—you can leave with it at any time. **Cash balance plans** are a hybrid; they have defined benefit plans' more predictable benefits, but the portability of defined contribution plans. The employer contributes a percentage of employees' current pay (usually 5%) to the employees' pension plans every year, and employees earn interest on this amount.[114]

KNOW YOUR EMPLOYMENT LAW

KNOWLEDGE BASE

Pension Planning and the Law

Various federal laws regulate pension planning and administration. As a rule, pension planning requires expert help.[115]

Employee Retirement Income Security Act of 1974 (ERISA)
Signed into law by President Ford to require that pension rights be vested and protected by a government agency, the PBGC.

The **Employee Retirement Income Security Act of 1974 (ERISA)** requires that employers have written pension plan documents and adhere to certain guidelines, such as regarding eligibility.[116] ERISA protects the employer's pension or health plans' assets by requiring that those who control the plans act responsibly. The *fiduciary's* responsibility is to run the plan solely in the interest of participants and beneficiaries.

Employers (and employees) also want their pension contributions to be "qualified," or tax deductible, so must adhere to the *income tax codes*. Under *labor relations laws*, the employer must let its unions participate in pension plan administration. The *Job Creation and Worker Assistance Act* provides guidelines regarding what rates of return employers should use in computing their pension plan values. ■

Pension Benefits Guarantee Corporation (PBGC)
Established under ERISA to ensure that pensions meet vesting obligations; also insures pensions should a plan terminate without sufficient funds to meet its vested obligations.

ERISA established the **Pension Benefits Guarantee Corporation (PBGC)** to oversee and insure a pension if a plan terminates without sufficient funds. Thousands of benefits plans, both private and public, are worryingly underfunded.[117] However, the PBGC guarantees only defined benefit plans, not defined contribution plans. And it will only pay a pension of up to about $5,420 per month for someone 65 years of age with a plan terminating as of 2018.[118] So, high-income workers still face reduced pensions if their employers go bankrupt.

MEMBERSHIP REQUIREMENTS When does the employee become eligible for a pension? Under the Tax Reform Act of 1986, an employer can require that an employee complete a period of no more than 2 years' service to the company before becoming eligible to participate in the plan. However, if it requires more than 1 year of service before eligibility, the plan must grant employees full and immediate vesting rights at the end of that period.

VESTING *Vested funds* are the money employer and employee have placed in the latter's pension fund that cannot be forfeited for any reason. The employees' contributions are always theirs. However, until ERISA, the *employers'* contribution in many pension plans didn't vest until the employee retired. Someone could have worked for a company for 30 years and been left with no pension if the company went bust a year before the person retired.

Employers can choose one of two minimum vesting schedules (employers can allow funds to vest faster if they wish). With *cliff vesting*, the period for acquiring a nonforfeitable right to employer matching contributions (if any) is 3 years. So, the employee must have nonforfeitable rights to these funds by the end of 3 years. With the second *(graded vesting)* option, pension plan participants must receive nonforfeitable rights to the matching contributions as follows: 20% after 2 years, and then 20% for each succeeding year, with a 100% nonforfeitable right by the end of 6 years.

Pensions and Early Retirement

early retirement window
A type of offering by which employees are encouraged to retire early, the incentive being liberal pension benefits plus perhaps a cash payment.

To trim their workforces or for other reasons, some employers encourage employees to retire early. Many such programs take the form of **early retirement window** arrangements for specific employees (often age 50+). The "window" means that for a limited time, the employees can retire early, generally with a combination of improved or liberalized pension benefits plus a cash payment.

Early retirement programs can backfire, however. In the early 2000s Verizon offered enhanced pensions to encourage 12,000 employees to retire. When over 21,000 took the plan, the company had to replace 16,000 managers.[119] Furthermore, unless structured properly, older employees can challenge early retirement programs for forcing them to retire involuntarily. Although it is generally legal to use incentives to encourage individuals to choose early retirement, the employee's decision must be voluntary. Under the Older Workers' Benefit Protection Act (OWBPA), the employee's waiver must be knowing and voluntary, and the employee must have ample time to consider the agreement and seek legal advice.

IMPROVING PERFORMANCE: *THROUGH HRIS*

Online Benefits Management Systems

It can be enormously time-consuming answering benefits questions such as, "If I retire in 5 years, what will be my monthly retirement income?" Most employers therefore opt for online self-service applications.

For example, when the organization that assists Pennsylvania school districts with their insurance needs decided to help the school boards automate their benefits administration, they chose a company called Benelogic.[120] The solution, called the "Employee Benefit Electronic Service Tool," lets users manage all aspects of benefits administration, including enrollment, plan descriptions, eligibility, and premium reconciliation, via their browsers.[121]

Benelogic hosts and maintains the Web application on its servers, and creates customized, Web-based applications for each school district. The system facilitates online employee benefit enrollment, and provides centralized call center support for benefit-related questions. It even handles benefits-related payroll and similar functions by collaborating with companies like ADP (for payroll). Each school board employee accesses the Benelogic site via a link on his or her own board's Web site. ■

TRENDS SHAPING HR: *DIGITAL AND SOCIAL MEDIA*

Communicating with employees about their benefits once required time-consuming HR assistance, but with digital and social media that's no longer the case.[122] Some use their Facebook and LinkedIn pages to publicize their benefits to a wider audience. Siemens created an internal social media Web site for its 13,000 UK employees. Siemens UK uses it to keep its employees up-to-date about its latest employee benefits offerings, to run real-time employee feedback polls about Siemens benefits, and to remind employees about the availability of various benefits. (For example, that each employee has points to use as part of the Siemens employee recognition program.)

To facilitate employee benefits self-management, other employers provide workers with mobile apps.[123] For example, clients of Discovery Benefits Inc., a benefits administrator, reportedly logged in through its app about 25,000 times in one year, saving Discovery the time it would have spent dealing with call-ins.[124]

Social media sites can also get workers in trouble. In one case, an employee took a sick day, saying that chronic pain prevented her from coming to work. Unfortunately, she posted pictures of herself drinking at a festival the day she was supposed to be home sick. One of her Facebook "friends" got the photo and showed it to a company supervisor. The company fired her for absence, and an appeals court upheld the employer's decision.[125] ■

Personal Services and Family-Friendly Benefits

LEARNING OBJECTIVE 13-4
Outline the main employees' services benefits.

Although time off, insurance, and retirement account for the lion's share of benefits costs, most employers also provide various services benefits. These include personal services (such as legal and personal counseling), "family-friendly" services (such as child-care facilities), educational subsidies, and executive perquisites (such as company cars for executives).

Personal Services

Personal services benefits include credit unions, legal services, counseling, and social and recreational opportunities. All are voluntary benefits, rather than required or mandatory under the law.

employee assistance program (EAP)
A formal employer program for providing employees with counseling and/or treatment programs for problems such as alcoholism, gambling, or stress.

Perhaps most notably, **employee assistance programs (EAPs)** provide counseling and advisory services, such as personal legal services, adoption assistance, or mental health counseling, for personal problems that may adversely affect the employee's work life. As the EAP site for one such plan at Sutter Health says, "Life's journey isn't always a smooth one. Sutter Health recognizes this and wants to help you overcome obstacles through the Employee Assistance Program."[126] Its EAP offers consulting on: child-care and parenting issues, elder care and disabled adult issues, pet care needs, adoptions, school, high school and college selection, and financial planning.[127]

Few but the largest employers establish their own EAPs. Most contract with vendors such as Ceridian Life Works, Comps Sync, and Integrated Behavioral Health.[128]

In either case, everyone involved, including supervisors and EAP staff, must respect *confidentiality*. Also keep files locked, limit access, and minimize identifying information. *Be aware of legal issues*. For example, in most states counselors must disclose suspicions of child abuse to state agencies. *Define* the program's purpose, employee eligibility, the roles and responsibilities of EAP and employer personnel, and procedures for using the plan. Ensure your EAP vendors fulfill *professional and state licensing requirements.*

Family-Friendly Benefits

family-friendly (or work–life) benefits
Benefits such as child care that make it easier for employees to balance their work and family responsibilities.

Family-related distractions—a sick child or parent, for instance—can make it difficult for employees to work effectively. Therefore, creating a family-friendly workplace through **family-friendly (or "work–life") benefits** is important. Such benefits include, for instance, child care, elder care, flexible work schedules, paid family leave, and concierge services (for help with tasks like grocery shopping).[129]

SUBSIDIZED CHILD CARE A recent study by the Brookings Institution listed some consequences of inadequate child care, including deleterious effects on children, lost productivity for employers due to parents missing work, and lost wages for parents.[130] Employers who want to reduce the distractions associated with finding reliable child care can help. Some simply investigate the day care facilities in their communities and recommend certain ones to employees. Others set up company-sponsored and subsidized day care facilities. For example, Goldman Sachs established its Children's Centre

bearmoney/Shutterstock

Software giant SAS Institute, Inc., is one company that offers generous employee benefits. The North Carolina firm keeps turnover at 4% in an industry where 20% is typical, partly by offering family-friendly and other benefits like paid maternity leave, day care on site, lunchtime piano concerts, massages, and yoga classes like this one.

at its London facility to offer backup child-care services for Goldman staff; the Centre takes children between three months and 12 years old.[131]

For many Millennials, benefits like child care reportedly often trump higher pay. Netflix recently told employees they can take a year off for child care.[132] Polices like those of Goldman and Netflix not only benefit employees. Employers may gain in improved recruiting results, lower absenteeism, improved morale, and lower turnover. As usual, start by surveying employees to assess their needs and perhaps what they'd be willing to pay.

SICK CHILD BENEFITS Sick child benefits are important. Sending a sick child with flulike symptoms to school because the parents must work risks worsening the child's condition and exposing classmates and teacher to illness. Yet only about half of U.S. workers are eligible for paid sick days that they can use for family members, so they risk pay loss and job loss by staying home.[133] By one estimate, sick children, sick nannies, and snow days cause about 2.8 million days of absences per year for U.S. employers.[134] The FMLA provides only unpaid leave, and not all employees are even eligible for that. Several states and cities including California, New Jersey, and New York City do provide for family-related paid sick leave.[135]

Employers can do several things. To use paid sick days, some employees claim they themselves are ill, but the better alternative is a policy allowing use for sick children too. Paid time off banks facilitate this. Flexible schedules and telecommuting policies can help. Some employers offer last-minute backup care, either with on-site centers (like Goldman Sachs'), or by making available last-minute in-home nannies.[136]

ELDER CARE By one estimate, 80% of elderly care is done by family members.[137] As with child care, female employees tend to bear the brunt of providing care for elderly parents. Helpful benefits for them (as well as male workers) include 10 to 15 days of backup elder care,[138] scheduling flexibility, and sabbaticals (for those needing extended time off).[139] About 43% of employers in one survey provide information on available elder care services.[140] When Pfizer discovered from a survey how many employees needed elder care services, it improved flexible schedule options, trained managers in how to handle such requests, and offered geriatric assessments.[141] Companies including Facebook and Vanguard instituted paid time off benefits to care for sick relatives.[142]

Finally, don't ignore employees who do *not* have family members to care for. For example, treat requests for schedule flexibility or time off seriously, regardless of the employee's family or marital status.[143]

EDUCATIONAL SUBSIDIES Employers use educational subsidies (usually tuition assistance) to help employees pursue educational course work, usually at the undergraduate or graduate college level, but also for basic learning, such as high school equivalency degrees.[144] By one estimate, almost 90% of U.S. employers provide such subsidies. About 5.6% of undergraduate students received such employer support a few years ago, and about 14.5% of graduate students did. (Almost 22% of MBA students receive such support). However, the benefit seems to be somewhat less popular than it used to be.

It may at first seem counterintuitive to subsidize an employee to get a degree that might then prompt him or her to move to a better job somewhere else, and educational benefits can have such unintended effects. But in general, educational subsidies seem to more than pay for themselves, in terms of improved employee recruiting and retention, and by improving productivity by raising employees' skills.

Introducing such a program requires policy decisions. For example, some employers only reimburse the employee after the course is completed, or if a particular grade is obtained. Some pay part of the tuition up front and then the remainder after completion. Some require repayment if the employee leaves the firm within a specific time period.

Other Personal Services Benefits

Employers provide other personal services benefits.[145] Google, perennially one of the "100 best companies to work for," is famous for its personal services benefits. Google arranges with local vendors to provide on-Google-site programs such as ATMs, mobile libraries, bike repair, car wash and oil change, dry cleaning, haircuts and salons, and organic grocery delivery.[146] Free though they are to Google, why does Google even bother? Largely because their on-site availability boosts employees' efficiency by reducing the need for them to seek services off-site. (It also offers the Google Child Care Center, and free shuttle service from San Francisco, for instance.)[147] CVS Caremark, seeking to retain older employees, offers various elder-friendly benefits. Its "snowbird" program lets pharmacists winter in Florida and work in the Northeast when it's warmer, for instance.[148] Nestlé Purina Pet Care's St. Louis headquarters lets employees bring their dogs to work.[149] PriceWaterhouseCoopers helps employees pay off student loans.[150] Most *Fortune* 500 companies offer donation-matching programs.[151]

Diversity Counts: Domestic Partner Benefits

When employers provide *domestic partner benefits* the employees' same-sex or opposite-sex domestic partners are eligible to receive the same benefits (health care, life insurance, and so forth) as do the husband, wife, or legal dependent of one of the firm's employees. In 2013, the U.S. Supreme Court struck down part of the Defense of Marriage Act. Under its ruling, gay couples married in states where it is legal must receive the same federal health, tax, Social Security, and other benefits heterosexual couples receive.[152] Then, in 2015, the U.S. Supreme Court held that same-sex couples can marry nationwide.[153]

After the 2015 decision, the percentage of employers providing same-sex domestic partner benefits dropped, from 59% to 48%.[154] Some employers such as IBM and Verizon said they would phase out domestic partner benefits, but gave employees who were receiving such benefits time to consider getting married. With same sex marriage legal in all 50 states, the trend, says one expert, is to "not differentiate between types of spouses" in offering benefits.[155] ■

The Strategic Context feature illustrates how one employer uses benefits to support its strategic goals.

IMPROVING PERFORMANCE: *THE STRATEGIC CONTEXT*

Gary Erickson started Clif Bar as a small bakery and grew it into a company that's been growing 20% per year. Central to his "healthy foods" strategy is the idea that his hundreds of employees should live the values of sustainability, healthiness, and eco-friendliness.[156] Therefore, he put together a benefits package that encouraged just such values. For example, the company encourages eco-friendliness by reimbursing employees up to $6,500 if they buy hybrid or electric vehicles. Those who bike or walk to work receive $1,500 per year. Clif Bar's subsidized cafeteria serves meals cooked with local organic ingredients. Employees become eligible for 6-week paid sabbaticals after 7 years working for the company. He put in place an employee stock option plan (ESOP). With employee turnover only 3% per year, Clif Bar received over 7,500 applications for 114 open jobs one year, so his benefits plan also seems to be helping keep workforce costs under control.

MyLab Management Talk About It 3

If your professor has assigned this, go to the Assignments section of **www.pearson.com/mylab/management** to complete this discussion question. How do you think offering benefits like these affects Clif Bar's recruiting and selection process and helps the company to keep costs down?

Executive Perquisites

When you reach the pinnacle of the organizational pyramid—or close to the top—you will find, waiting for you, the "executive perk." Perquisites (perks for short) are special benefits for top executives. They range from company planes to private bathrooms.

Most fall between these extremes. Perks include *management loans* (typically to exercise executives' stock options); *financial counseling*; and *relocation benefits*, often including subsidized mortgages, purchase of the executive's current house, and payment for the move. Publicly traded companies must itemize all executives' perks (if they total more than $100,000). Many popular perks (such as entertainment expenses) lost their tax breaks under the 2017 tax law, and many employers are reducing or phasing them out.[157]

Flexible Benefits Programs

LEARNING OBJECTIVE 13-5
Explain the main flexible benefit programs.

In a report titled "Employee Benefits: What Each Generation Wants," Glassdoor says employees increasingly seek flexibility.[158] They say baby boomers value salary level, health insurance, and retirement plans. Gen Xers (born roughly from the 1960s to the early 1980s) value salary level, a 401K plan with matching benefits, job security, advancement, and work–life balance. Millennials (born roughly from the early 1980s to early 2000s) value benefits choices, paid time off, ability to work remotely, control over their schedules, and flexibility. Offering flexibility thus makes sense. However, first survey employees' preferences, perhaps with a form as in Figure 13-4.[159]

The Cafeteria Approach

cafeteria benefits plan
Individualized tax-qualified plans allowed by employers to accommodate employee preferences for benefits.

One way to provide choice is with an aptly named *cafeteria benefits plan*. To paraphrase the U.S. Internal Revenue Service, a **cafeteria plan** provides participants an opportunity to receive a choice of certain benefits on a pretax basis. Qualified benefits include, for instance, accident and health benefits, adoption assistance, dependent care assistance, and group-term life insurance coverage.[160]

Cafeteria plans come in several varieties.[161] For example, *flexible spending accounts* are a form of cafeteria plan that reimburses employees for expenses they incur for buying certain qualified benefits;[162] the employees pay for the benefits with pretax dollars. With a *core plus option plan*, the employer specifies a core set of benefits (such as medical insurance), which are required; beyond those the employee can choose (up to a limit) which other benefits he or she wants.

FIGURE 13-4 One Page from Online Survey of Employees' Benefits Preferences

Source: Reprinted with permission from GrapeVine solutions.

Your Logo Here. 125 px

300 px

Human Resources - Employee Benefits Survey

Please take a moment to tell us your thoughts on the Company benefits plan. Your input is valued and will help us make this better.

Health care

1 **Please rate the following.**
1-Very Satisfied, 5-Very Dissatisfied

	1	2	3	4	5
Medical plan	1	2	3	4	5
Dental plan	1	2	3	4	5
Vision plan	1	2	3	4	5

Retirement and Savings Plan

The accompanying HR Tools feature explains how many smaller employers manage the costs of their various benefits.

IMPROVING PERFORMANCE: *HR TOOLS FOR LINE MANAGERS AND SMALL BUSINESSES*

Benefits and Employee Leasing

Many businesses—particularly smaller ones—don't have the resources or employee base to support the cost of many of the benefits we've discussed in this chapter. That's one big reason they turn to "employee leasing."

In brief, employee leasing firms (also called *professional employer organizations* or *staff leasing firms*) assume all or most of the employer's human resources chores. In doing so, they also become the employer of record for the employer's employees, by transferring them all to the employee leasing firm's payroll. The leasing firm thus becomes the employees' legal employer, and usually handles employee-related activities such as recruiting, hiring (with client firms' supervisors' approvals), and paying taxes (Social Security payments, unemployment insurance, and so on).

But insurance and benefits are usually the big attraction. Even group rates for life or health insurance can be quite high when only 20 or 30 employees are involved. That's where leasing comes in. Remember that the leasing firm is now the legal employer. The employees are thus part of a larger insurable group, along with other employers' former employees. The small business owner may get insurance it couldn't otherwise afford.

As in dealing with all vendors, the employer should have a detailed negotiated agreement with the employee leasing firm. Define what the services will be; include priorities, responsibilities, and warranties.[163] Understand that if the leasing firm merges into another firm, the new parent may require you to change your systems once the contract period expires.[164] ■

> MyLab Management Talk About It 4
>
> If your professor has assigned this, go to the Assignments section of **www.pearson.com/mylab/management** to complete this discussion. Explain how you believe you'd react to having your employer switch you to a leasing firm, and why.

Flexible Work Schedules

Flexible work schedules are popular.[165] In one survey about 70% of surveyed employees called flexible work hours "very important."[166]

flextime
A work schedule in which employees' workdays are built around a core of midday hours, and employees determine, within limits, what other hours they will work.

Flextime is a plan whereby employees' workdays are built around a core of midday hours, such as 11:00 A.M. to 2:00 P.M. Thus, workers may opt to work from 8:00 A.M. to 4:00 P.M. or from 11:00 A.M. to 7:00 P.M. In one survey of employers about 57% offered flextime.[167]

Some writers suggest that inflexible schedules help explain both the gender pay gap and the fact that women hold few top management jobs. A new job search site (www.saywerk.com) negotiates ahead of time with employers to provide flexible schedules for any jobs listed on its site.[168]

Telecommuting—using technology to work away from the office—is popular. Almost two-thirds (62%) of employers offer at least some telecommuting.[169] Some jobs have much higher rates than others. Historically, for example, almost 45% of medical transcription is reportedly work from home.[170] Just over 13 million Americans work from home at least one day per week, with Fridays and Mondays the favorite days to stay home.[171]

Employers that offer telecommuting must calculate the program's benefits and costs. Thus, Delta Airlines spends an initial $2,500 for each home-based reservation agent for computer and software licenses, but pays each such agent $1.50 per hour less than call-center counterparts. Less obvious expenses include having IT answer telecommuters' technical questions.[172] Telecommuting's effects on the environment, of course, are positive, given the reduced commuting.

Studies of telecommuting's effects on productivity are mixed. A program at Capital One Bank apparently led to about a 41% increase in workplace satisfaction, and a 53% increase in those who say their workplace enhances group productivity.[173] Another study concluded that telecommuting had positive effects for creative jobs but negative effects for dull jobs.[174] Detractors contend that telecommuting reduces camaraderie and opportunities for collaboration and synergies at work.[175] Yahoo! famously said a few years ago that it needed its employees "working side by side" and brought them back to the office.[176]

COMPRESSED WORKWEEKS Many employees, like airline pilots, don't work conventional 5-day, 40-hour workweeks.[177]

compressed workweek
Schedule in which employee works fewer but longer days each week.

Workers like these typically have **compressed workweek** schedules—they work fewer days each week, but each day they work longer hours. Some firms have four 10-hour day workweeks. Some workers—in hospitals, for instance—work three 12-hour shifts, and then take off for 4 days.[178] About 29% of employers in one survey reported using compressed workweeks.[179] Some experts argue that 12-hour shifts increase fatigue and accidents. To reduce potential side effects, some employers install treadmills, exercise bikes, and special lights that mimic daylight.

job sharing
Allows two or more people to share a single full-time job.

work sharing
Refers to a temporary reduction in work hours by a group of employees during economic downturns as a way to prevent layoffs.

OTHER FLEXIBLE WORK ARRANGEMENTS **Job sharing** allows two or more people to share a single full-time job. For example, two people may share a 40-hour-per-week job, with one working mornings and the other working afternoons. For example, two retired friends arranged to share a job (working alternate days) at a library.[180] About 11% of the firms questioned recently indicated that they allow job sharing, down from 22% several years ago.[181] **Work sharing** refers to a temporary reduction in work hours by a group of employees during economic downturns as a way to prevent layoffs. Thus, 400 employees may all agree to work (and be paid for) only 35 hours per week, to avoid a layoff of 30 workers.[182]

LEARNING OBJECTIVE 13-6
Explain how to use benefits to improve engagement, productivity, and performance.

Employee Engagement Guide for Managers

Costco's Compensation Plan

Costco's HR strategy is to deflect Walmart's famously low costs and wages by paying employees more, and thereby producing improved employee engagement, productivity, and customer service.[183]

For example, Costco pays its employees on average about $21 per hour (not including overtime,) almost triple the federal minimum wage.[184] That compares with Walmart's average wage for full-time employees in the United States of $12.67 an hour.[185]

Costco's employee benefits are also highly competitive, particularly compared with the typically sparse offerings in the retail industry.[186] For example, Costco pays about 90% of the health insurance costs of its over 90,000 domestic employees.[187] Its other benefits include (as examples) dental care, a pharmacy/prescriptions program, a vision program, a 401(k) plan, a dependent care assistance plan, an external network of professional counselors, voluntary short-term disability, long-term disability, and life insurance.[188] Costco also extends these benefits to employees' spouses, children, and domestic partners.

Costco doesn't directly measure employee engagement; it says it tracks engagement by "by-products," such as turnover and productivity.[189] By those criteria, Costco's engagement efforts seem to be working. Its sales per employee are about $500,000 a year versus $340,000 at Walmart's Sam's Club.[190] Costco's turnover is far below the retail industry average, and employee retention is higher.[191] Costco, by the way, is not alone. Other large chains with traditionally excellent customer service, like Nordstrom and the Container Store, also do well financially, in part by treating employees well and keeping engagement up.[192]

Chapter Review

Chapter Section Summaries

13-1. Employers provide numerous **pay for time not worked benefits.** These include unemployment insurance, vacation and other leave days, and sick pay. Minimizing sick leave pay is important, and here cost reduction tactics include paid leave plans that lump sick leave, vacation, and holidays into one leave pool. The Family and Medical Leave Act requires larger employers to provide up to 12 weeks of unpaid leave for family-related issues.

13-2. Most employers also provide required or voluntary **insurance benefits.** Workers' compensation laws aim to provide sure, prompt medical benefits to work-related accident victims or their dependents, regardless of fault. Most employer health plans provide at least basic hospitalization and surgical and medical insurance for eligible employees. When an employee is terminated or terminates his or her employment, it is essential that the employer make the person aware of his or her COBRA rights. Employers generally work hard to keep the rising cost of health-care insurance under control.

13-3. **Retirement benefits** are important to employees today. Social Security is a federal program that provides retirement income at the age of 62 and thereafter, as well as other benefits. Many employers make available pension plans; these provide an income when employees reach retirement age or when they can no longer work due to disability. Defined benefit plans contain a formula for determining retirement benefits, while defined contribution plans are plans in which the contribution to employees' retirement savings plans is specified. The most well-known of the latter are 401(k) plans. The Employee Retirement Income Security Act of 1974 requires that employers have written pension plan documents, and established the Pension Benefits Guarantee Corporation to oversee employers' pension plans. Key pension policy issues include membership requirements and testing.

13-4. Most employers also provide various **personal services and family-friendly benefits.** These include credit unions, employee assistance programs, and subsidized child care and elder care.

13-5. Employees prefer choice in their benefits plans, so **flexible benefits programs** are important. Flexible benefits or cafeteria benefits plans are individual plans that accommodate employee preferences for benefits. Some employers turn to employee leasing companies to capitalize on the advantage of the leasing firm's large employee base to get better employee benefits for their employees. Employers also are implementing various types of flexible work schedules, including flextime, compressed workweeks, and other flexible work arrangements such as job sharing.

13-6. Costco's HR strategy is to deflect Walmart's low wages by paying employees more, thereby producing more **employee engagement,** higher productivity, and better customer service. As one example, Costco pays about 90% of the health insurance costs of its over 90,000 domestic employees.

Discussion Questions

13-1. What is unemployment insurance? Is an organization required to pay unemployment benefits to all dismissed employees? Explain how you would go about minimizing your organization's unemployment insurance tax.

13-2. Explain how ERISA protects employees' pension rights.

13-3. Describe the main retirement benefits.

13-4. What are the main provisions of the FMLA?

Individual and Group Activities

13-5. Working individually or in groups, research the unemployment insurance rate and laws of your state. Write a summary detailing your state's unemployment laws. Assuming Company X has a 30% rate of annual personnel terminations, calculate Company X's approximate unemployment tax rate in your state.

13-6. Assume you run a small business. Working individually or in groups, visit the Web site www.dol.gov/elaws. See the Small Business

Retirement Savings Advisor. Write a two-page summary explaining: (1) the various retirement savings programs available to small business employers, and (2) which retirement savings program you would choose for your small business, and why.

13-7. You are the HR consultant to a small business with about 40 employees. Now the firm offers only 5 days of vacation, 5 paid holidays, and legally mandated benefits such as unemployment insurance payments. Develop a list of other benefits you believe it should offer, along with your reasons for suggesting them.

13-8. Appendices A and B at the end of this book (pages 614–634) list the knowledge someone studying for the HRCI (Appendix A) or SHRM (Appendix B) certification exam needs to have in each area of human resource management (such as in Strategic Management and Workforce Planning). In groups of several students, do four things: (1) review Appendix A and/or B; (2) identify the material in this chapter that relates to the Appendix A and/or B required knowledge lists; (3) write four multiple-choice exam questions on this material that you believe would be suitable for inclusion in the HRCI exam and/or the SHRM exam; and (4) if time permits, have someone from your team post your team's questions in front of the class, so that students in all teams can answer the exam questions created by the other teams.

KNOWLEDGE BASE

Experiential Exercise

Revising the Benefits Package

Written and copyrighted by Gary Dessler, PhD.

Purpose: The purpose of this exercise is to provide practice in developing a benefits package for a small business.

Required Understanding: Be very familiar with the material presented in this chapter. In addition, review Chapter 11 to reacquaint yourself with sources of compensation survey information, and come to class prepared to share with your group the benefits package for the small business in which you work or in which someone with whom you're familiar works.

How to Set Up the Exercise/Instructions: Divide the class into groups of four or five students. Your assignment is as follows: Maria Cortes runs a small personnel recruiting office in Miami and has decided to start offering an expanded benefits package to her 25 employees. At the current time, the only benefits are 7 paid holidays per year and 5 sick days per year. In her company, there are 2 other managers, as well as 17 full-time recruiters and 5 secretarial staff members. Your assignment is as follows:

- In the time allotted, your group should create a benefits package in keeping with the size and requirements of this firm.

Application Case

Striking for Benefits[193]

Written and copyrighted by Gary Dessler, PhD.

When the Southern California grocery workers went on strike against the state's major supermarket chains, the main issue was employee benefits, and specifically how much of their health-care costs the employees should pay themselves. Based on their existing contract, the workers had unusually good health benefits. For example, they paid nothing toward their health insurance premiums, and paid only $10 co-payments for doctor visits. However, supporting these excellent health benefits cost the big Southern California grocery chains over $4 per hour per worker.

The big grocery chains were not proposing cutting health-care insurance benefits for their existing employees. Instead, they proposed putting any new employees hired after the new contract went into effect into a separate insurance pool, and contributing $1.35 per hour for their health insurance coverage. That meant new employees' health insurance would cost each new employee perhaps $10 per week. And, if that $10 per week wasn't enough to cover the cost of health care, then the employees would have to pay more, or do without some of their benefits.

It was a difficult situation for all involved. For the grocery chain employers, skyrocketing health-care costs were undermining their competitiveness; the current employees feared any step down the slippery slope that might eventually mean cutting their own health benefits. The unions didn't welcome a situation in which they'd end up representing two classes of employees, one (the existing employees) who had excellent health insurance benefits, and another (newly hired employees) whose benefits were relatively meager, and who might therefore be unhappy from the moment they took their jobs and joined the union.

Questions

13-9. Assume you are mediating this dispute. Discuss five creative solutions you would suggest for how the grocers could reduce the health insurance benefits and the cost of their total benefits package without making any employees pay more.

13-10. From the grocery chains' point of view, what is the downside of having two classes of employees, one of which has superior health insurance benefits? How would you suggest they handle the problem?

13-11. Similarly, from the point of view of the union, what are the downsides of having to represent two classes of employees, and how would you suggest handling the situation?

Continuing Case

Carter Cleaning Company

Written and copyrighted by Gary Dessler, PhD.

The New Benefit Plan

Carter Cleaning Centers has traditionally provided only legislatively required benefits for its employees. These include unemployment compensation, Social Security, and workers' compensation (which is provided through the same insurance carrier that insures the stores for such hazards as theft and fire). The principals of the firm—Jack, Jennifer, and their families—have individual, family-supplied health and life insurance.

Jennifer can see several potential problems with the company's policies regarding benefits and services. One is turnover. She wants to study whether similar companies' experiences with providing health and life insurance benefits enable these firms to reduce employee turnover and perhaps pay lower wages. Jennifer is also concerned that her company has no formal vacation or paid days off or sick leave policies. Informally, at least, it is understood that employees get 1 week's vacation after 1 year's work, but in the past the policy regarding paid vacations for days such as New Year's Day and Thanksgiving Day has been very inconsistent. Sometimes employees who had been on the job only 2 or 3 weeks were paid fully for one of these holidays, while at other times employees who had been with the firm for 6 months or more had been paid for only half a day.

She also wonders whether it would be advisable to establish some type of day care center for the employees' children. Many of them have no place to go during the day (they are preschoolers) or have no place to go after school; she wonders whether a day care benefit would be in the best interests of the company.

Questions

13-12. Draw up a policy statement regarding vacations, sick leave, and paid days off for Carter Cleaning Centers.

13-13. What would you tell Jennifer are the advantages and disadvantages to Carter Cleaning Centers of providing its employees with health, hospitalization, and life insurance programs?

13-14. Would you advise establishing some type of day care center for the Carter Cleaning employees? Why or why not?

Translating Strategy into HR Policies and Practices Case*,§

** The accompanying strategy map for this chapter is in MyLab Management; the overall map on the inside back cover of this text outlines the relationships involved.*

Improving Performance at the Hotel Paris

The New Benefits Plan

The Hotel Paris's competitive strategy is "To use superior guest service to differentiate the Hotel Paris properties, and to thereby increase the length of stay and return rate of guests, and thus boost revenues and profitability." HR manager Lisa Cruz must now formulate functional policies and activities that support this competitive strategy by eliciting the required employee behaviors and competencies.

While the Hotel Paris's benefits (in terms of things like holidays and health care) were comparable to other hotels', Lisa knew they weren't good enough to support the high-quality service behaviors her company sought. Indeed, the fact that they were roughly comparable to those of similar firms didn't seem to impress the Hotel Paris's employees. Sixty percent of them consistently said they were dissatisfied with their benefits. Lisa's concern (with which the CFO concurred) was that dissatisfaction with benefits contributed to low morale and engagement, and thus to inhibiting the Hotel Paris from achieving its strategic aims. Lisa therefore turned to the task of assessing and redesigning the company's benefits plans.

As they reviewed the benefits numbers, Lisa and the CFO became concerned. They computed several benefits-related metrics for their firm, including benefits costs as a percentage of payroll, sick days per full-time-equivalent employee per year, benefits cost/competitor's benefits cost ratio, and workers' compensation experience ratings. The results, said the CFO, offered a "good news–bad news" situation. On the good side, as noted, the ratios were similar to most competing hotels'. The bad news was that the measures were well below those for high-performing service businesses. The CFO authorized Lisa to design and propose a new benefits plan.

Lisa knew there were several things she wanted to accomplish. She wanted a plan that contributed to improved employee morale and engagement. And, she wanted the plan to include elements that made it easier for her employees to do their jobs—so that, as she put it, "they could come to work and give their full attention to giving our guests great service, without worrying about child care and other family distractions."

The new plan's centerpiece was a proposal for much better family-friendly benefits. Because so many of each hotel's employees were single parents, and because each hotel had to run 24 hours a day, Lisa's team proposed, and the board approved, setting aside a room in each hotel for an on-site child-care facility and for hiring a trained professional attendant. They considered instituting a flexible work schedule program, but for most of the jobs, this was impractical, because each front-line employee simply had to be there at his or her appointed hour. However, they did institute a new job-sharing program. Now two people could share one housekeeping or front-desk clerk job, as long as the job was covered.

One of the metrics Lisa and her team specifically wanted to address was the relatively high absence rate at the Hotel Paris. Because so many of these jobs are front-line jobs—valets, limousine drivers, and front-desk clerks, for instance—absence had a particularly serious effect on metrics like overtime pay and temporary help costs. Here, at the urging of her compensation consultant, Lisa decided to opt for a system similar to Marriott's BENETRADE. With this benefit program, employees can trade the value of some sick days for other benefits. As Lisa put it, "I'd rather see our employees using their sick day pay for things like additional health-care benefits, if it means they'll think twice before taking a sick day to run a personal errand."

§ Written and copyrighted by Gary Dessler, PhD.

After just less than a year, Lisa and the CFO believe the new program is successful. Their studies suggest that the improved benefits are directly contributing to improved employee morale and commitment, sick days have diminished by 40%, and employee turnover is down 60%. And when they advertise for open positions, over 60% of the applicants cite "family-friendly benefits" as a top reason for applying to work at the Hotel Paris.

Questions

13-15. What is your opinion of the new Hotel Paris benefits plan?

13-16. Because employers typically make benefits available to all employees, they may not have the motivational effects of incentive plans. Given this, list five employee behaviors you believe Hotel Paris could try to improve through an enhanced benefits plan, and explain why you chose them.

13-17. Given your answer to question 13-16 and what you read in this chapter of Dessler *Human Resource Management*, explain specifically what other benefits you would recommend the Hotel Paris implement to achieve these behavioral improvements.

Writing Assignments

13-18. You are applying for a job as a manager and are at the point of negotiating salary and benefits. What questions would you ask your prospective employer concerning benefits? Describe the benefits package you would try to negotiate for yourself.

13-19. Your clients want to know how they can use their employee benefits package to improve employee engagement. What would you tell them?

Key Terms

benefits, 421
supplemental pay benefits, 422
unemployment insurance (or compensation), 422
sick leave, 424
severance pay, 427
supplemental unemployment benefits, 427
workers' compensation, 428
health maintenance organization (HMO), 429
group life insurance, 434
Social Security, 434
pension plans, 435
defined benefit pension plan, 435
defined contribution pension plan, 435
portability, 435
401(k) plan, 435
savings and thrift plan, 436
deferred profit-sharing plan, 436
employee stock ownership plan (ESOP), 436
cash balance plans, 436
Employee Retirement Income Security Act 1974 (ERISA), 437
Pension Benefits Guarantee Corporation (PBGC), 437
early retirement window, 437
employee assistance program (EAP), 439
family-friendly (or work–life) benefits, 439
cafeteria benefits plan, 442
flextime, 443
compressed workweek, 444
job sharing, 444
work sharing, 444

Endnotes

1. J. P. Mangalindan, "A Healthier, More Rewarding Workplace," *Fortune*, October 6, 2014, pp. 49–50; www.clifbar.com/article/family-and-employee-ownership-shares-prosperity-at-clif-bar, accessed March 30, 2018.
2. "Introduction to the Human Resources Discipline of Employee Benefits," July 27, 2015, https://www.shrm.org/resourcesandtools/tools-and-samples/toolkits/pages/employeebenefits.aspx, accessed March 29, 2018.
3. Kerry Jones, "The Most Desirable Employee Benefits," *Harvard Business Review*, February 15, 2017, https://hbr.org/2017/02/the-most-desirable-employee-benefits, accessed March 29, 2018.
4. Frank Giancola, "Are Employee Benefit Programs Being Given Enough Credit for Their Effect on Employee Attitudes?" *Compensation & Benefits Review* 44, no. 5 (2012), pp. 291–297.
5. Joseph Martocchio, *Strategic Compensation* (Upper Saddle River, NJ: Prentice Hall, 2001), p. 262; for an example of an actual benefits policies and procedures manual, see http://www.stancounty.com/riskmgmt/docs/eb-forms/manual.pdf, accessed March 29, 2018.
6. "HR Plays a Major Role in Curbing Company Unemployment Insurance Costs, Analysts Say," *Bloomberg BNA Bulletin to Management*, August 3, 2010, pp. 241–242; www.dllr.state.md.us/employment/uitrustfundpoints.shtml, accessed April 22, 2017.
7. www.bls.gov/opub/perspectives/issue2.pdf, accessed September 8, 2014.
8. Ibid.
9. www.bls.gov/opub/perspectives/issue2.pdf, accessed June 1, 2011.
10. Aron Ain, "The CEO of Kronos on Launching an Unlimited Vacation Policy," *Harvard Business Review*, November–December 2017, pp. 37–42.
11. Ibid., p. 41.
12. Madison Alder and Kristin Knebel, "Blackrock's Unlimited Time Off a Rarity for Finance Industry," *Bloomberg BNA Bulletin to Management*, January 30, 2018.
13. http://www-01.ibm.com/employment/us/benefits/top01.shtml, accessed March 29, 2018.
14. Robert Grossman, "Gone but Not Forgotten," *HR Magazine*, September 2011, p. 44; then put in place solutions such as rigorous absenteeism claims reviews.
15. Carmen Castro-Pagan, "United, JetBlue, Others Seek to Stop Washington Sick Leave Law," *Bloomberg BNA Bulletin to Management*, February 13, 2018; Kristin Knebel, "Austin Is First Texas City with Paid Sick Leave Mandate," *Bloomberg BNA Bulletin to Management*, February 20, 2018.
16. "National Compensation Survey: Employee Benefits in Private Industry in the United States, March 2006," U.S. Bureau of Labor Statistics,

August 2006, p. 116. Job absence rates haven't changed appreciably for years; they averaged about 0.8% of scheduled worker days in one recent year. "Employee Absenteeism through All of 2016 Remains Low by Historical Standards," *Bloomberg BNA Bulletin to Management*, February 28, 2017.

17. "Managing Employee Attendance," February 17, 2016, https://www.shrm.org/resourcesandtools/tools-and-samples/toolkits/pages/managingemployeeattendance.aspx, accessed March 29, 2018.
18. "2016 Paid Leave in the Workplace," October 6, 2016, https://www.shrm.org/hr-today/trends-and-forecasting/research-and-surveys/pages/2016-paid-leave-in-the-workplace.aspx, accessed March 29, 2018.
19. Society for Human Resource Management 2009 Employee Benefits Survey, quoted in Martha Frase, "Taking Time Off to the Bank," *HR Magazine*, March 2010, p. 42. See also Marissa Warford, "Does Paid Time Off Pay Off?" *Workforce*, August 2014, pp. 26–29, 48.
20. "Making Up for Lost Time: How Employers Can Curb Excessive Unscheduled Absences," *BNA Human Resources Report*, October 20, 2003, p. 1097. See also W. H. J. Hassink et al., "Do Financial Bonuses Reduce Employee Absenteeism? Evidence from a Lottery," *Industrial and Labor Relations Review* 62, no. 3 (April 2009), pp. 327–342.
21. Based on "Creating Holistic Time Off Programs Can Significantly Reduce Expenses," *Compensation & Benefits Review*, July/August 2007, pp. 18–19; Rita Zeidner, "Strategies for Saving in a Down Economy," *HR Magazine*, February 2009, p. 28. Judith Whitaker, "How HR Made a Difference," *People Management* 27 (October 28, 2010).
22. See, for example, Rita Zeidner, "Strategies for Saving in a Down Economy," p. 28.
23. Judith Whitaker, "How HR Made a Difference."
24. Ibid.
25. http://en.wikipedia.org/wiki/Driver_and_Vehicle_Licensing_Agency, accessed April 13, 2013.
26. See www.dol.gov/whd/regs/compliance/posters/fmlaen.pdf, accessed March 29, 2018.
27. For recent regulations for administering the Family and Medical Leave Act, see https://www.dol.gov/whd/fmla/, accessed April 23, 2017.
28. Jill Fisher, "Reconciling the Family Medical Leave Act with Overlapping or Conflicting State Leave Laws," *Compensation & Benefits Review*, September/October 2007, pp. 39–44. President Obama issued an executive order requiring federal contractors to provide their employees with mandatory sick leave; initially, at least, it appeared that the Trump administration would let that rule stand. Ben Penn, "Obama Sick Leave Order Survives under Trump, for Now," *Bloomberg BNA Bulletin to Management*, April 18, 2017; https://www.workplacefairness.org/sick-leave#1, accessed March 29, 2018.
29. https://www.dol.gov/whd/fmla/employerguide.pdf, accessed March 29, 2018.
30. Martin Berman-Gorvine, "FMLA Leave, Legitimate or Not, Can Create Headaches for Employers," *Bloomberg BNA Bulletin to Management*, July 4, 2017.
31. Sue Shellenbarger, "The Mommy Drain: Employers Beef Up Perks to Lure New Mothers Back to Work," *The Wall Street Journal*, September 28, 2006, p. D1.
32. John Herzfeld, "New York Ramping Up for 2018 Paid Family Leave Start," *Bloomberg BNA Bulletin to Management*, February 28, 2017.
33. See, for example, Genevieve Douglas, "Low-Income Workers Need, Want Federal Paid Parental Leave," *Bloomberg BNA Bulletin to Management*, April 4, 2017.
34. Historically, employers offer severance pay partly to avoid litigation. However the U.S. Securities and Exchange Commission (SEC), and the Equal Employment Opportunity Commission are pressuring employers to stop requiring employees to waive their rights to sue in return for severance, Some employers are therefore reviewing their severance policies. Rita Zeidner, "Severance under Scrutiny," *HR Magazine*, June/July 2017, pp. 90–98.
35. http://www.natlawreview.com/article/does-your-severance-trigger-erisa-why-you-should-care-and-what-you-should-do, accessed April 23, 2017.
36. *Severance and separation policies*, Lee Hecht Harrison, www.lhh.com/~/media/adeccogroup/brands/lhh-brand/.../severance-study.pdf Accessed April 23, 2017.
37. Terry Baglieri, "Severance Pay," www.shrm.org, accessed December 23, 2006. See also www.shrm.org/hrdisciplines/compensation/articles/pages/cms_022345.aspx, accessed July 15, 2015.
38. Carol Matlack, "Severance a la Francaise," *Bloomberg Businessweek*, October 2, 2017, pp. 34–35.
39. However, if the employee was intoxicated or under the influence of drugs, or intentionally caused the injury, he or she may lose their rights to payments. See, for example, http://www.wcb.ny.gov/content/main/onthejob/WCLawIntro.jsp, accessed March 29, 2018.
40. https://www.thehartford.com/resources/construction/claims, accessed March 29, 2018.
41. Ibid.
42. "Workers' Comp Claims Rise with Layoffs, but Employers Can Identify, Prevent Fraud," *BNA Bulletin to Management*, October 4, 2001, p. 313.
43. "Using Case Management in Workers' Compensation," *BNA Bulletin to Management*, June 6, 1996, p. 181; Sharron Edgar. "Effective Workers' Compensation Nurse Case Management," *Professional Case Management*, 12, no. 2 (March–April 2007), pp. 123–124.
44. "Workers Comp Research Provides Insight into Curbing Health Care Costs," *EHS Today*, February 2010, p. 18.
45. In one recent survey, 53% of workers said they would trade some pay for better retirement benefits: "Employees Willing to Trade Pay for More Benefits, Survey Finds," *Bloomberg BNA Bulletin to Management*, March 6, 2012, p. 78.
46. Sara Hansard, "Employers Taking Action to Control Healthcare Costs," *Bloomberg BNA Bulletin to Management*, September 5, 2017.
47. Emily Jane Fox, "Health Insurance Premiums Climb 4% in 2012," http://money.cnn.com/2012/09/11/pf/insurance/health-insurance-premiums/index.html, accessed April 12, 2013. See also "Costs This Year Increased at Highest Rate Since 2004, Survey Reveals," *HR Focus* 88, no. 1 (January 10, 2011); "Health Costs," http://kff.org/health-costs/, accessed April 20, 2015.
48. Frederick Hills, Thomas Bergmann, and Vida Scarpello, *Compensation Decision Making* (Fort Worth, TX: The Dryden Press, 1994), p. 137.
49. "Costs This Year Increased at Highest Rate Since 2004, Survey Reveals," *HR Focus* 88, no. 1 (January 10, 2011); "Health Costs," http://kff.org/health-costs/, accessed April 20, 2015.
50. Society for Human Resource Management, "Mental Health Trends," *Workplace Visions*, no. 2, http://moss07.shrm.org/Research/FutureWorkplaceTrends/Pages/0303.aspx, accessed July 28, 2009.
51. Genevieve Douglas, "Millennial's Report Higher Rates of Depression, Need Support," *Bloomberg BNA Bulletin to Management*, February 21, 2017.
52. "Mental-Health Parity Measure Enacted as Part of Financial Rescue Signed by Bush," *Bloomberg BNA Bulletin to Management*, October 7, 2008, p. 321. Because the act requires employers who offer mental health coverage to make that coverage similar to their medical and surgical health coverage benefits, some employers drop health-care coverage. Alice Andors, "This Parity Pay Off?" *HR Magazine*, September 2012, pp. 45–46.
53. "IRS Unveils Proposed Rules of 'Shared Responsibility,'" *Bloomberg BNA Bulletin to Management*, January 18, 2013, p. 12. See also Wendy Voss and Jesse Noa, "The ACA's Employer Mandate: What Are the Implications?" *Bloomberg BNA Bulletin to Management*, June 17, 2014, pp. S1–S12.
54. "Deadlines Vary for Implementing Provisions of Health Care Law," *Bloomberg BNA Bulletin to Management*, May 4, 2010, p. 143; "Ruling Means Employers Now Face Various PPACA Deadlines," *Bloomberg BNA Bulletin to Management*, August 10, 2012, p. 222.
55. "Regulation Will Allow Young Adults Up to Age 26 to Retain Dependent Coverage," *Bloomberg BNA Bulletin to Management*, May 18, 2010, p. 153.
56. Sara Hansard, "Employers Taking Action to Control Healthcare Costs," *Bloomberg BNA Bulletin to Management*, September 5, 2017.
57. "Lavish Cadillac Health Plans Dying Out as ACA Tax Looms Three Years Hence," *Bloomberg BNA Bulletin to Management*, January 13, 2015, p. 9.
58. Anna Mathews and Julie Jargon, "Firms Try to Escape Health Penalties," *The Wall Street Journal*, October 22, 2014, pp. A1, A2.
59. Ibid.
60. "The Insured and the Unsure," *The Economist* 6 (January 20, 2013), p. 59.
61. Mark Lutes and Adam Solander, "Cadillac Tax Could Jeopardize Viability of Employer-Based Plans," *Bloomberg BNA Bulletin to Management*, November 27, 2012, p. 382.
62. Joanne Sammer, "How to Choose Health Insurance Exchanges," *HR Magazine*, October 2012, pp. 47–52.
63. Sara Hansard, "Obama Care Premiums Estimated to Rise 10 to 20% in 2018," *Bloomberg BNA Bulletin to Management*, April 20, 2017.
64. Margot Sanger Katz, "A New Republican Proposal That Evokes the Old Days," *The New York Times*, April 21, 2017, p. A16; Stephanie Armour and Christina Peterson, "GOP Shifts Help Strategy," *The Wall Street Journal*, April 5, 2017, p. A6.
65. Zachary Tracer and Anna Edney, "Obama Care Insurers

Struggle for Stability Amid Trump Threats," *Bloomberg BNA Bulletin to Management*, April 18, 2017; see also Kristin Knebel, "IRS Expands Deadlines for Providing Health Coverage Notice," *Bloomberg BNA Bulletin to Management*, January 2, 2018.
66. Sean Forbes, "Employers Make Tweaks While Watching Health Overhaul," *Bloomberg BNA Bulletin to Management*, July 18, 2017.
67. https://www.dol.gov/general/topic/health-plans/cobra, accessed March 29, 2018.
68. https://www.dol.gov/general/topic/health-plans/erisa, accessed March 29, 2018.
69. Larri Short and Eileen Kahanar, "Unlocking the Secrets of the New Privacy Rules," *Occupational Hazards*, September 2002, pp. 51–54. See also http://www.hipaasurvivalguide.com/hipaa-privacy-rule.php, accessed April 23, 2017.
70. Kevin Maroney, "Prognosis Negative? GINA's Interim Incentives Ruling a Concern for Wellness Programs," *Compensation & Benefits Review* 42, no. 2 (2010), pp. 94–101.
71. Joanne Deschenaux, "Managing Leaves of Absence in California Is Complicated," *HR Magazine*, June 2011, p. 23.
72. http://insight.aon.com/?elqPURLPage=6567, accessed April 11, 2013.
73. James Curcio, "Creating Standardized Metrics and Benchmarking for Health, Absence and Productivity Management Programs: The EMPAQ Initiative," *Compensation & Benefits Review* 42, no. 2 (2010), pp. 109–126.
74. Vanessa Fuhrmanns, "Oops! As Health Plans Become More Complicated, They're Also Subject to a Lot More Costly Mistakes," *The Wall Street Journal*, January 24, 2005, p. R4; "Healthcare Claims Audit," http://www.costrecoverysolutions.com/auditing_services/healthcare_audit.html, accessed March 29, 2018.
75. Jerry Geisel, "Employers Accelerate Health Care Cost-Shifting," *Business Insurance* 45, no. 21 (May 23, 2011), pp. 3, 21; http://kff.org/report-section/ehbs-2014-summary-of-findings/, accessed July 15, 2015.
76. In contrast, with health reimbursement arrangements (HRA) only the employer makes contributions. See "Types of Tax Favored Health Accounts," *HR Magazine*, August 2008, p. 76.
77. David Tobenkin, "Spousal Exclusions on the Rise," *HR Magazine*, November 2011, pp. 55–56.
78. "To Cut Costs, Employers Considering Defined Contribution Health Insurance Plans," *Bloomberg BNA Bulletin to Management*, November 20, 2011, p. 377.
79. Tamara Lytle, "Strategic Moves," *HR Magazine*, March 2016, pp. 39–42.
80. Sandra Yin, "A New Breed," *American Way*, May 1, 2013, pp. 40–41.
81. Madison Alder, "Skimpy Coverage Concern Takes Center Stage in Health Rules Debate," *Bloomberg BNA Bulletin to Management*, March 13, 2018.
82. Martin Berman-Gorvine, "At Work Health Centers a Popular Prescription," *Bloomberg BNA Bulletin to Management*, September 19, 2017.
83. Rebecca Vesely, "A New Remedy Emerges for Spiraling Health Costs," *Workforce Management*, June 2012, p. 14.
84. Alan Cohen, "Decision-Support in the Benefits Consumer Age," *Compensation & Benefits Review*, March/April 2006, pp. 46–51.
85. http://insight.aon.com/?elqPURLPage?6567, accessed April 11, 2013.
86. "Employer Partners to Launch a Three-Year Wellness Initiative," *BNA Bulletin to Management*, August 7, 2007, p. 255; Leonard L. Berry, Ann M. Mirabito, and William B. Baun, "What's the Hard Return on Employee Wellness Programs?" *Harvard Business Review*, December 2010, https://hbr.org/2010/12/whats-the-hard-return-on-employee-wellness-programs, accessed March 29, 2018. Some employers, such as Cisco Systems, take a broad view of "wellness." For instance, at Cisco, wellness also includes personal financial counselling, time off for volunteer work, and hiking and biking paths. Usan Milligan, "Wellness Blows Up," *HR Magazine*, September 2017, pp. 61–67.
87. "Employer Partners to Launch a Three-Year Wellness Initiative," *BNA Bulletin to Management*, August 7, 2007, p. 255. See also Drew Robb, "Benefits Choices: Educating the Consumer," *HR Magazine*, March 2011, pp. 29–30.
88. "On-Site Clinics Aimed at Cutting Costs, Promoting Wellness," *Bloomberg BNA Bulletin to Management*, March 25, 2008, p. 103. See also Susan Wells, "Navigating the Expanding Wellness Industry," *HR Magazine*, March 2011, pp. 45–50.
89. Susan Wells, "Getting Paid for Staying Well," *HR Magazine*, February 2010, p. 59. See also Martin Berman-Gorvine, "For Wellness Programs, Winning Hearts May Beat Stuffing Wallets," *Bloomberg BNA Bulletin to Management*, November 14, 2017.
90. Rebecca Greenfield, "Do Standing Desks Really Help You Lose Weight?" *Bloomberg BNA Bulletin to Management*, February 6, 2018.
91. Rebecca Greenfield, "Workplace Wellness Programs Really Don't Work," *Bloomberg BNA Bulletin to Management*, January 30, 2018.
92. Hector De La Torre and Ron Goetzel, "How to Design a Corporate Wellness Plan That Actually Works," *Harvard Business Review*, March 31, 2016, https://hbr.org/2016/03/how-to-design-a-corporate-wellness-plan-that-actually-works, accessed March 29, 2018.
93. Susan Galactica, "There's a Doctor on the Phone? Employers Dial-Up Telemedicine," *Workforce Management*, September 2012, p. 8. See also "Speakers Tout Advantages, $6 Billion Potential of Telemedicine," *Bloomberg BNA Bulletin to Management*, December 16, 2014, p. 399.
94. http://www.aaltci.org/long-term-care-insurance/learning-center/tax-for-business.php, accessed March 29, 2018.
95. http://www.bls.gov/news.release/empsit.t08.htm, accessed September 17, 2015.
96. See, for example, Nancy Woodward, "Part-Time Benefits: A Moving Target," *HR Magazine*, November 2012, pp. 61–64.
97. Gig businesses often resist giving benefits like retirement plans to their gig workers, lest doing so make the gig workers seem more like regular employees to courts. However advocates are pressing U.S. Senate members to make it easier to offer retirement and other benefits to gig workers. Tyrone Richardson, "Retirement Plan Advocates Urge Senate to Help Gig Workers," *Bloomberg BNA Bulletin to Management*, February 13, 2018.
98. Josh Eidelson, "Unionize Me," *Bloomberg Businessweek*, January 12, 2017, pp. 26–27.
99. See also Jeff Wald, "The Benefits or Lack Thereof of the Gig," *Workforce*, August 2016, pp. 22–25.
100. Mark Feffer, "What Benefits Can Companies Offer Gig Workers?" March 21, 2017, www.shrm.org/resourcesandtools/hr-topics/benefits/pages/What-benefits-can-companies-offer-gig-workers, accessed April 23, 2017.
101. https://www.ssa.gov/OACT/COLA/cbb.html, accessed March 29, 2018.
102. https://www.ssa.gov/planners/retire/1960.html, accessed March 29, 2018.
103. "What Are the Different Types of Pension Plans?" http://www.gasb.org/jsp/GASB/Page/GASBSectionPage%26cid=1176163527901, accessed March 29, 2018.
104. Patty Kujawa, "The Young and Not So Restless," *Workforce Management*, May 2012, p. 6. See also Joanne Sammer, "Are Defined Benefit Plans Dead?" *HR Magazine*, July 2012, pp. 29–32.
105. Patty Kujawa, "Young Workers Craving Defined Benefit Plans," *Workforce Management*, March 2011, p. 16.
106. "Target CEO's $47 Million Package Shows Gap with Workers," *Bloomberg BNA Bulletin to Management*, January 13, 2015, p. 12.
107. Nancy Pridgen, "The Duty to Monitor Appointed Fiduciaries under ERISA," *Compensation & Benefits Review*, September/October 2007, pp. 46–51; "Individual 401(k) Plan Participant Can Sue Plan Fiduciary for Losses, Justices Rule," *Bloomberg BNA Bulletin to Management*, February 20, 2008, p. 65. A federal judge recently ruled that a Florida construction company's co-owners are liable under ERISA after they allegedly improperly withdrew about $112,000 from the firm's profit-sharing plan. Jaclyn Wille, "Owners of Florida Company Liable for $112k Benefit Plan Theft," *Bloomberg BNA Bulletin to Management*, April 18, 2017.
108. "Benefit Trends: Automatic Enrollment Takes Off," *Compensation & Benefits Review*, September/October 2008, p. 14.
109. For a discussion, see Jewel Esposito, "Avoiding 401(k) ERISA Disasters," *Compensation & Benefits Review* 42, no. 1 (January/February 2010), pp. 39–45. After the U.S. Supreme Court made it easier for employees to sue their employer if any stock in the firm's 401(k) plan lost money, several companies, including Target and Comcast, cut the amount of company stock in their retirement funds. Jacklyn Wille, "Target, Microsoft Lead Move Away from 401(k) Stock Investments," *Bloomberg BNA Bulletin to Management*, March 20, 2018.
110. Jack VanDerhei, "The Pension Protection Act and 401(k)s," *The Wall Street Journal*, April 20, 2008, p. 12.
111. "Google Sets Employees Up for a Successful Retirement," www.brightscope.com, accessed March 23, 2018.
112. David Brandolph, "Companies See Tax Law as Quick Trigger for Worker Benefits," *Bloomberg BNA Bulletin to Management*, January 30, 2018.
113. Wyatt, "401(k) Conversion," p. 20.
114. "What Is a Cash-Balance Plan?" http://money.cnn.com/retirement/guide/pensions_cashbalanceplans.moneymag/index.htm, accessed

March 29, 2018; "Cash Balance Plans," https://www.irs.gov/pub/irs-tege/epchd1104.pdf, accessed March 29, 2018.

115. Rita Pyrillis, "Picking a PBM for '13," *Workforce Management*, June 2012, p. 8.

116. This is based on Eric Parmenter, "Employee Benefit Compliance Checklist," *Compensation & Benefits Review*, May/June 2002, pp. 29–38. Also see "Retirement Plans and ERISA FAQs," https://www.dol.gov/agencies/ebsa/about-ebsa/our-activities/resource-center/faqs/retirement-plans-and-erisa-consumer, accessed April 23, 2017.

117. John Kilgour, "Public Pension Underfunding in California: A Perfect Storm Likely to Sweep the Nation," *Compensation & Benefits Review* 44, no. 6 (2013), pp. 345–351. With more pension plans going bust, at least one study concludes that "while the numerous PBGC insurance premium increases will allow some short-term respite, the long-run prospects of the PBGC are bleak." John Kilgour, "The Plight of the Pension Benefit Guarantee Corporation," *Compensation & Benefits Review* 47, no. 1 (2015), pp. 39–49. The Pension Benefit Guarantee Corporation also helps employers locate workers who still have money in closed plans. Kristin Knebel, "Pension Insurer Expands Program to Reunite Workers with Benefits," *Bloomberg BNA Bulletin to Management*, January 2, 2018.

118. https://www.pbgc.gov/wr/benefits/guaranteed-benefits/maximum-guarantee, accessed March 29, 2018.

119. Patrick Kiger, "Early-Retirement Plans Backfire, Driving Up Costs Instead of Cutting Them," *Workforce Management*, January 2004, pp. 66–68.

120. Johanna Rodgers, "Web Based Apps Simplify Employee Benefits," *Insurance and Technology* 28, no. 11 (November 2003), p. 21. See also www.benelogic.com, accessed March 29, 2018.

121. Ibid.

122. The following is based on www.tlnt.com/2012/04/26/the-5-best-social-media-tools-for-employee-benefits-communication/, www.abenity.com/celebrate/how-to-use-social-media-to-communicate-employee-perks-benefits/, www.benefitspro.com/2013/04/19/social-media-a-tool-to-boost-employee-engagement-p, and www.employeebenefits.co.uk/benefits/communication/siemens-launches-social-media-website/105812.article, all accessed April 20, 2015.

123. See, for example, http://appfinder.lisisoft.com/tag/employee-benefits.html, accessed March 29, 2018.

124. Michelle Rafter, "Mobile Apps for Benefits Go from Luxury to Necessity," *Workforce Management*, June 2012, p. 3.

125. "Employee Whose Facebook Photos Suggested Fraud Lacks FMLA Claims, Sixth Circuit Rules," *Bloomberg BNA Bulletin to Management*, November 20, 2012, p. 371.

126. https://www.sutterhealth.org/for-employees/employee-assistance-program, accessed March 29, 2018.

127. Ibid,

128. Rita Pyrillis, "Devoid of Data," *Workforce*, June 2014, pp. 48–50.

129. Paula Fernandes, "Support Your Employees by Creating a Family-Friendly Workplace," *Business News Daily*, December 7, 2016, https://www.businessnewsdaily.com/9614-family-friendly-workplace.html, accessed March 29, 2018.

130. Grover J. Whitehurst, "Why the Federal Government Should Subsidize Childcare and How to Pay for It," March 9, 2017, https://www.brookings.edu/research/why-the-federal-government-should-subsidize-childcare-and-how-to-pay-for-it/, accessed March 29, 2018.

131. Katie Prescott, "A Glimpse Inside the Goldman Sachs Nursery," July 20, 2017, http://www.bbc.com/news/business-40658619, accessed March 29, 2018.

132. Jeff Green and Rick Clough, "GE Considers Scrapping the Annual Raise," https://www.bloomberg.com/news/articles/2016-06-06/ge-studies-scrapping-annual-raise-in-nod-to-shifting-priorities, accessed August 11, 2018.

133. Mark Schuster and Paul Chung, "Time Off to Care for a Sick Child—Why Family Leave Policies Matter," *New England Journal of Medicine* 371 (2014), 493–495; http://www.nejm.org/doi/full/10.1056/NEJMp1404860, accessed March 29, 2018.

134. https://solutionsatwork.brighthorizons.com/employer-back-up-child-care/roi-employer-backup-care, accessed March 29, 2018.

135. Schuster and Chung, "Time Off to Care for a Sick Child," op cit.

136. https://solutionsatwork.brighthorizons.com/employer-back-up-child-care/backup-in-home-child-care, accessed March 29, 2018.

137. Brigid Schulte, "Aging Population Prompts More Employers to Offer Elder-Care Benefits to Workers," *The Washington Post*, November 16, 2014, https://www.washingtonpost.com/local/aging-population-prompts-more-employers-to-offer-elder-care-benefits-to-workers/2014/11/16/25f9c8e6-6847-11e4-a31c-77759fc1eacc_story.html?utm_term=.6b0b2bb17cf9, accessed March 29, 2018.

138. Last minute help such as a list of available caregivers who can come in if there's an unexpected need one day. See, for example, http://www.parentsinapinch.com/companies/corporate-backupcare/, accessed March 30. 2018.

139. Martin Berman-Gorvine, "Women Workers Caring for Parents Need Employer Help," *Bloomberg BNA Bulletin to Management*, July 4, 2017.

140. Brigid Schulte, "Aging Population Prompts More Employers to Offer Elder-Care Benefits to Workers," op cit.

141. Ibid.

142. Rebecca Greenfield, "Employers Are Finally Starting to Deal with Death and Dying," *Bloomberg BNA Bulletin to Management*, February 14, 2017.

143. Clif Boutelle, "Singled Out," *Workforce*, May/June 2017, pp. 48–52.

144. This is based on "Employer Tuition Assistance," https://www.edvisors.com/education-tax-benefits/tuition-and-fees/employer-tuition-assistance/, accessed August 11, 2018; Richard Buddin and Kanika Kapur, "The Effect of Employer-Sponsored Education on Job Mobility: Evidence from the U.S. Navy," *Industrial Relations* 44, no. 2 (April 2005), pp. 341–363; "Designing and Managing Educational Assistance Programs," Society for Human Resource Management, November 14, 2015, www.Sherm.org/ ; "Why Companies Pay for College," the National Bureau of Economic Research, www.nber.org, all accessed March 30, 2018.

145. "Rising Gas Prices Prompting Employers to Consider Varied Computer Benefit Options," *Bloomberg BNA Bulletin to Management*, June 20, 2008, p. 201.

146. Laszlo Bock, *Work Rules!* (New York: 12, 2015), p. 274.

147. See "The 100 Best Companies to Work For," *Fortune*, February 6, 2012, p. 117.

148. Tamera Lionel, "Benefits for Older Workers," *HR Magazine*, March 2012, pp. 53–58.

149. "Perks at Work," *Workforce*, September 2014, pp. 40–43.

150. Susan Milligan, "The Royal Treatment," *HR Magazine*, September 2016, pp. 30–35.

151. Genevieve Douglas, "Boeing, GE Donation-Matching Programs Energized Talent Recruiting," *Bloomberg BNA Bulletin to Management*, February 27, 2018.

152. http://articles.washingtonpost.com/2013-06-26/politics/40195683_1_gay-couples-edith-windsor-doma, accessed August 1, 2013.

153. www.cnn.com/2015/06/26/politics/supreme-court-same-sex-marriage-ruling/index.html; www.nytimes.com/2015/06/27/us/supreme-court-same-sex-marriage.html?_r=0, both accessed July 15, 2015.

154. Stephen Miller, "Employers Are Dropping Domestic Partner Health Care Benefits," SHRM, August 18, 2017, https://www.shrm.org/resourcesandtools/hr-topics/benefits/pages/employers-dropping-domestic-partner-benefits.aspx, accessed March 30, 2018.

155. Ibid.

156. Mangalindan, "A Healthier, More Rewarding Workplace;" http://www.clifbar.com/article/family-and-employee-ownership-shares-prosperity-at-clif-bar, accessed March 30, 2018.

157. Lydia O'Neal, "Will Employee Perks Survive the Tax Law?" *Bloomberg BNA Bulletin to Management*, March 6, 2018.

158. "Employee Benefits: What Each Generation Wants," October 25, 2016. https://www.glassdoor.com/employers/blog/employee-benefits-what-each-generation-wants/, accessed March 30, 2018.

159. Martin Berman-Gorvine, "Bright Ideas on Benefits: Ask Employees What They Want," *Bloomberg BNA Bulletin to Management*, September 19, 2017.

160. https://www.irs.gov/government-entities/federal-state-local-governments/faqs-for-government-entities-regarding-cafeteria-plans, accessed March 30, 2018.

161. Martocchio, *Strategic Compensation*, pp. 217–219.

162. https://www.irs.gov/government-entities/federal-state-local-governments/faqs-for-government-entities-regarding-cafeteria-plans, accessed March 30, 2018.

163. Bill Roberts, "Good Vendor Relations," *HR Magazine*, September 2011, p. 110.

164. Ibid.

165. Elka Maria Torpey, "Flexible Work: Adjusting the When and Where of Your Job," *Occupational Outlook Quarterly*, Summer 2007, pp. 14–27.

166. Genevieve Douglas, "Flexibility Outpacing Time Off, Paid in Valued Benefits," *Bloomberg BNA Bulletin to Management*, February 14, 2017.

167. "2017 Employee Benefits," Society for Human Resource Management, p. 12.

168. Claire Miller, "How to Close the Gender Gap: True Job Flexibility," *The New York Times*, February 7, 2017, p. 83.

169. "2017 Employee Benefits," Society for Human Resource Management, p. 12.

170. "Telework among Full-Time Employees Almost Doubled in

the Last Decade, Study Says," *Bloomberg BNA Bulletin to Management*, June 12, 2012, p. 187.

171. "13.4 Million Work from Home in 2010, Census Bureau Reports," *Bloomberg BNA Bulletin to Management*, October 16, 2012, p. 330; "How Do We Know? Working at Home is on the Rise," U.S. Census Bureau, June 3, 2013, https://www.census.gov/library/visualizations/2013/comm/home_based_workers.html, accessed March 30, 2018.
172. Dori Meinert, "Make Telecommuting Pay Off," *HR Magazine*, June 2011, pp. 33–37.
173. Ann Pomeroy, "The Future Is Now," *HR Magazine*, September 2007, pp. 46–52. See also "Telework among Full-Time Employees Almost Doubled in the Last Decade," p. 187.
174. E. Glenn Dutcher, "The Effects of Telecommuting on Productivity: An Experimental Examination: The Role of Dull and Creative Tasks," *Journal of Economic Behavior & Organization* 84, no. 1 (September 2012), pp. 355–363.
175. For example, Michael Ortner, "Why Telecommuting Can Be Dangerous for Your Company Culture," *Fast Company*, January 13, 2015, https://www.fastcompany.com/3040750/why-telecommuting-can-be-dangerous-for-your-company-culture, accessed March 30, 2018.
176. Martha White, "One Part Gone: Yahoo Says No to Telecommuting," www.CNBC.com/ID/100492123, accessed February 25, 2013.
177. For many employees the ultimate flextime schedule is not having to come to work at all. The government in Gothenburg, Sweden, recently studied the effects of giving workers a 5-day 6-hour (instead of 8-hour) workday schedule. Most employees were very happy and more productive with their shorter workdays. The problem was, it was too expensive. For the 2-year study, the employer (a municipal retirement home) had to hire 17 new employees to cover the hours that the other employees were not working; this cost over $700,000 extra per year, too much to continue. Liz Aldernan., "In Sweden, Happiness from Shorter Workday Can't Overcome the Cost," *The New York Times*, January 7, 2017, p. B2.
178. See, for example, "Compressed Workweeks Gain Popularity, but Concerns Remain about Effectiveness," *Bloomberg BNA Bulletin to Management*, September 16, 2008, p. 297. In a related change, more employers, including Disney, David's Tea, and Aeropostale, have stopped requiring employees to stay "on call" and stopped scheduling them for work at the last minute, Michael Bologna, "Disney, Five Other Retailers Relent on Employee Scheduling," *Bloomberg BNA Bulletin to Management*, January 3, 2017.
179. 2017 Employee Benefits, SHRM, op cit.
180. See, for example, Kerry Hannon, "Part-Time Jobs for Retirees: If You're Retired but Miss Working, These 5 Jobs Offer Decent Pay, Flexible Hours," https://www.aarp.org/work/working-after-retirement/info-10-2010/5-great-part-time-jobs-for-retirees.html#quest1, accessed March 29, 2018.
181. SHRM, "2003 Benefits Survey," p. 2; 2017 Employee Benefits, SHRM, op cit.
182. See, for example, http://www.ncsl.org/research/labor-and-employment/work-share-programs.aspx, accessed March 30, 2018.
183. http://articles.moneycentral.msn.com/Investing/Extra/CostcoTheAntiWalMart.aspx?page?1, accessed September 15, 2011; and, Hamilton Nolan, "The Anti-Wal-Mart," http://gawker.com/costco-the-anti-wal-mart-511739135, accessed August 7, 2013.
184. Tavia Grant, "How One Company Levels the Pay Slope of Executives and Workers," *Globe and Mail*, November 16, 2013, www.theGlobeandMail.com/news/national, accessed April 1, 2014.
185. Brad Stone, "Costco CEO Craig Jelinek Leads the Cheapest, Happiest Company in the World," *Bloomberg Businessweek*, June 6, 2013, www.BusinessWeek.com/articles/2013-06-06/Costco-CEO-Craig-Jelinek-leads-the-cheapest-happiest-company-in-the-world, accessed March 31, 2014.
186. www.Costco.com/benefits.HTML, accessed April 1, 2014.
187. Ibid.
188. Ibid.
189. Garry Kranz, "Special Report on Employee Engagement Losing Lifeblood," *Workforce*, July 21, 2011, www.workforce.com/articles/special-report-on-employee-engagement-losing-lifeblood, accessed April 10, 2014.
190. http://articles.moneycentral.msn.com/Investing/Extra/CostcoTheAntiWalMart.aspx?page?1, accessed September 15, 2011; and Hamilton Nolan, "The Anti-Wal-Mart," http://gawker.com/costco-the-anti-wal-mart-511739135, accessed August 7, 2013.
191. Ibid. See also Stone, "Costco CEO Craig Jelinek Leads the Cheapest, Happiest Company in the World."
192. Ibid. Engaged workers also had more positive interactions with their families, for instance, in terms of sharing their work progress with their spouses. Remus Ilies et al., "Why Do Employees Have Better Family Lives When They Are Highly Engaged at Work?" *Journal of Applied Psychology* 102, no. 6 (2017), pp. 956–970.
193. Based on "Settlement Nears for Southern California Grocery Strike," *Knight-Ridder/Tribune Business News*, February 26, 2004, item 04057052.

PART FIVE Enrichment Topics in Human Resource Management

PRESSLAB/Shutterstock

14 Building Positive Employee Relations

LEARNING OBJECTIVES

When you finish studying this chapter, you should be able to:

14-1 **Define** *employee relations*.

14-2 **Discuss** at least four methods for managing employee relations.

14-3 **Explain** what is meant by ethical behavior.

14-4 **Explain** what is meant by fair disciplinary practices.

14-5 **Answer** the question, "How do companies become 'Best Companies to Work For'?"

After a worker uprising over pay and work rules at Apple Inc.'s Foxconn iPhone assembly plant in Shenzhen, China, Apple asked the plant's owner to have the Fair Labor Association (FLA) survey the plant's workers. The FLA found "tons of issues."[1] We'll see what they found and what Foxconn's management did to improve the situation.

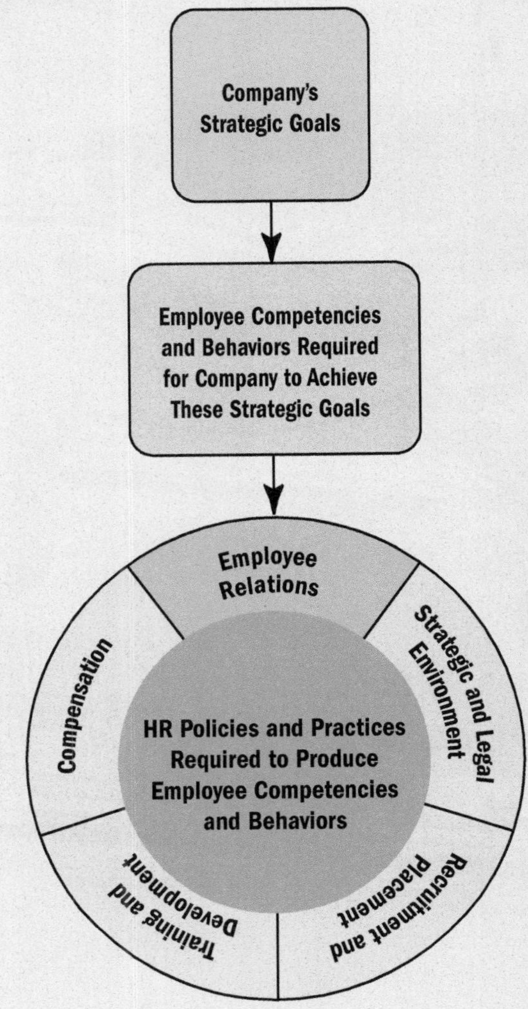

WHERE ARE WE NOW . . .

Although people tend to view recruitment, selection, appraisal, training, and compensation as the heart of human resource management, most employees expect something more. For example, they expect to be treated fairly, and to have a safe work environment. Now, in Part Five, we therefore turn to ethics, employee fairness, safety, and union relations. The main purpose of this chapter is to explain the building blocks of positive employee relations. Our topics include **What Is Employee Relations, Managing Employee Relations, Using Human Resource Management Tools to Promote Ethics and Fair Treatment, Managing Employee Discipline,** and **Employee Engagement Guide for Managers**.

What Is Employee Relations?

LEARNING OBJECTIVE 14-1
Define *employee relations.*

employee relations
The activity that involves establishing and maintaining the positive employee–employer relationships that contribute to satisfactory productivity, motivation, morale, and discipline, and to maintaining a positive, productive, and cohesive work environment.

Anyone who has worked knows that some companies are better to work for than are others. Some companies we've touched on in this book—Wegmans, SAS, and Google, for instance—show up repeatedly on "Best Companies to Work For" lists, while others always seem to have labor problems and negative press. This commonsense observation reflects the fact that some companies do have better employee relations than do others.

Employee relations is the managerial activity that involves establishing and maintaining the positive employee–employer relationships that contribute to satisfactory productivity, motivation, morale, and discipline, and to maintaining a positive, productive, and cohesive work environment.[2] Whether you're recruiting employees, managing union organizing campaigns, asking employees to work overtime, or doing some other task, it obviously makes sense to have employees "on your side." Many employers therefore endeavor to build positive employee relations, on the sensible assumption that doing so beats building negative ones. Managing employee relations is usually assigned to HR, and is a topic that both the SHRM and HRCI exams address.

Employers can do many things to build positive employee relations. Some examples include good training, fair appraisals, and competitive pay and benefits (all of which we discussed in previous chapters). However, most employers also institute special "employee relations programs" to maintain positive employee relations. These include employee fair treatment programs, improving employee relations through improved communications, developing employee recognition/relations programs, and having fair and predictable disciplinary procedures.

Employee Relations Programs for Building and Maintaining Positive Employee Relations

LEARNING OBJECTIVE 14-2
Discuss at least four methods for managing employee relations.

We'll begin with how to ensure fair treatment.

Ensuring Fair Treatment

fair treatment
Reflects concrete actions, such as "employees are treated with respect," and "employees are treated fairly."

Anyone who has suffered unfair treatment at work knows it is demoralizing. It reduces morale, poisons trust, and negatively impacts employee relations and performance.[3] Employees of abusive supervisors are more likely to quit, and to report lower job and life satisfaction and higher stress.[4] The effects on employees of such abusiveness are particularly pronounced where the abusive supervisors seem to have support from higher-ups.[5] Even when someone just witnesses abusive supervision—for instance, seeing a coworker abused—it triggers adverse reactions including unethical behavior.[6] At work, **fair treatment** reflects concrete actions such as "employees are treated with respect," and "employees are treated fairly" (see Figure 14-1).[7]

There are many reasons why managers should be fair. The golden rule is one obvious reason. What may not be so obvious is that unfairness can backfire on the company. For example, victims of unfairness exhibit more workplace deviance, such as theft and sabotage.[8] Victims of unfairness also suffer a range of ill effects including poor health, strain, and psychological conditions.[9] Unfairness leads to increased tensions between the employee and his or her family or partner.[10] Abusive supervisors undermine their subordinates' effectiveness and may prompt them to act destructively.[11] Witnessing disrespectful behavior in the morning contaminated employees' perceptions all day, making even innocent interactions seem rude.[12]

In terms of employee relations, employees' perceptions of fairness relate *positively* to employee commitment; job involvement; satisfaction with the company, job, and leader; and organizational citizenship behaviors; and *negatively* to employees' turnover intention.[13]

The employer and its managers are responsible for ensuring that employees are treated fairly and with respect. Techniques for minimizing unfairness discussed in previous chapters include hire competent employees and supervisors, ensure equitable pay, have fair performance appraisal systems, and have policies requiring fair treatment. Communications systems (such as periodic attitude surveys), and disciplinary appeals programs (both discussed later in this chapter) also reduce unfairness.

FIGURE 14-1 Perceptions of Fair Interpersonal Treatment Scale

Source: "The Perceptions of Their Interpersonal Treatment Scale: Development and Validation of a Measure of Interpersonal Treatment in the Workplace" by Michelle A. Donovan, from *Journal of Applied Psychology* 83, no. 5 (1998).

What is your organization like most of the time? Circle yes if the item describes your organization, No if it does not describe your organization, and ? if you cannot decide.

IN THIS ORGANIZATION:			
1. Employees are praised for good work	Yes	?	No
2. Supervisors yell at employees (R)	Yes	?	No
3. Supervisors play favorites (R)	Yes	?	No
4. Employees are trusted	Yes	?	No
5. Employees' complaints are dealt with effectively	Yes	?	No
6. Employees are treated like children (R)	Yes	?	No
7. Employees are treated with respect	Yes	?	No
8. Employees' question and problems are responded to quickly	Yes	?	No
9. Employees are lied to (R)	Yes	?	No
10. Employees' suggestions are ignored (R)	Yes	?	No
11. Supervisors swear at employees (R)	Yes	?	No
12. Employees' hard work is appreciated	Yes	?	No
13. Supervisors threaten to fire or lay off employees (R)	Yes	?	No
14. Employees are treated fairly	Yes	?	No
15. Coworkers help each other out	Yes	?	No
16. Coworkers argue with each other (R)	Yes	?	No
17. Coworkers put each other down (R)	Yes	?	No
18. Coworkers treat each other with respect	Yes	?	No

Note: R = the item is reverse scored

procedural justice
Refers to just procedures in the allocation of rewards or discipline, in terms of the actual procedures being evenhanded and fair.

distributive justice
Refers to a system of distributing rewards and discipline in which the actual results or outcomes are evenhanded and fair.

RESEARCH INSIGHT A study illustrates the effects of unfairness. College instructors first completed surveys concerning the extent to which they saw their colleges as treating them with *procedural* and *distributive* justice. (**Procedural justice** refers to justice in the allocation of rewards or discipline, in terms of the *procedures* being evenhanded and fair; **distributive justice** refers to a system for distributing rewards and discipline in which *the actual results* or outcomes are evenhanded and fair.) Procedural justice items included, for example, "In general, the department/college's procedures allow for requests for clarification or for additional information about a decision." Distributive justice items included, "I am fairly rewarded considering the responsibilities I have."

Then the instructors completed organizational commitment questionnaires, with items such as "I am proud to tell others that I am part of this department/college." Their students then completed surveys, with items such as "The instructor was sympathetic to my needs," and "The instructor treated me fairly."

The results were impressive. Instructors who perceived high distributive and procedural justice were more committed. Furthermore, these instructors' students reported higher levels of instructor effort, prosocial behaviors, and fairness, and had more positive reactions to their instructors.[14] So in this case, treating some professors badly backfired on the university. Treating others fairly produced improved employee commitment and results.

The accompanying Strategic Context feature shows how one employer in China improved the fairness with which it treated employees.

IMPROVING PERFORMANCE: *THE STRATEGIC CONTEXT*

A New HR Strategy at the Foxconn Plant in Shenzhen, China

The phrase *social responsibility* tends to trigger images of charitable contributions, but it actually refers to much more. For example, it refers to the honesty of the company's ads; to the quality of the parts it builds into its products; and to the honesty, ethics, fairness, and "rightness" of

social responsibility
Refers to the extent to which companies should and do channel resources toward improving one or more segments of society other than the firm's owners or stockholders.

its dealings with customers, suppliers, and, of course, employees. The basic question is always whether the company is serving all its constituencies (or "stakeholders") fairly and honestly. Corporate **social responsibility** thus refers to the extent to which companies should and do channel resources toward improving one or more segments of society other than the firm's owners or stockholders.[15]

A worker uprising at Apple's Foxconn iPhone assembly plant in Shenzhen, China, shows that workers around the globe want their employers to treat them in a fair and socially responsible manner.

Producing quality products as efficiently as possible was long the strategy at this plant. However, after the uprising over pay and work rules at the Foxconn plant, Apple asked the plant's owner to have the Fair Labor Association (FLA) survey the workers. It found "tons of issues."[16] For example, employees faced "overly strict" product-quality demands: "Every job is tagged to time, there are targets on how many things must be completed within an hour," said Xie Xiaogang, 22, who worked at Foxconn's Shenzhen plant. "In this environment, many people cannot take it."[17] Heavy overtime work and having to work through a holiday week were other examples.

To foster the improved behaviors that the plant's performance required, Hon Hai, the Foxconn plant's owner, tweaked its efficiency-first strategy and changed its plant human resource strategy and practices. It made 284 changes altogether, including raising salaries and cutting mandatory overtime.[18] The changes show that fair treatment is a global obligation.

MyLab Management Talk About It 1

If your professor has assigned this, go to the Assignments section of **www.pearson.com/mylab/management** to complete this discussion question. How would you explain the fact that workers in such diverse cultures as America and China seem to crave fair treatment?

Bullying and Victimization

Some workplace unfairness, such as bullying, is blatant. Bullying and victimization—singling out someone to harass and mistreat—is a serious problem. For example, a survey of 1,000 U.S. employees concluded that about 45% said they'd worked for abusive bosses.[19] Victims will often suffer in silence in fear of retribution.[20] The U.S. government (www.stopbullying.gov) says most would agree that bullying involves three things:

- ***Imbalance of power.*** People who bully use their power to control or harm, and the people being bullied may have a hard time defending themselves.
- ***Intent to cause harm.*** Actions done by accident are not bullying; the person bullying has a goal to cause harm.
- ***Repetition.*** Incidents of bullying happen to the same person over and over by the same person or group, and that bullying can take many forms, such as:
  - ***Verbal:*** name-calling, teasing
  - ***Social:*** spreading rumors, leaving people out on purpose, breaking up friendships
  - ***Physical:*** hitting, punching, shoving
  - ***Cyberbullying:*** using the Internet, mobile phones, or other digital technologies to harm others

Undoubtedly, the perpetrator is to blame for bullying. However, how some people behave does make them more likely victims.[21] These include submissive victims (who seem more anxious, cautious, and sensitive), provocative victims (who show more aggression), and victims low in self-determination (who leave it to others to make decisions for them). Similarly, high performers can earn colleagues' envy and thus suffer victimization.[22] Using team-building training, social gatherings, and interteam competition to build team cohesion can reduce envy and victimization.[23] Other suggestions include identify bullying through morale surveys, train employees to recognize bullying, and have a code of conduct.[24]

Beyond this, maintaining positive employee relations entails having communications programs that let employees both express their opinions, and let management know if there's a problem. We turn to these programs next.

Improving Employee Relations through Communications Programs

Many employers use communications programs, on the reasonable assumption that employees feel better about their employers when they're "kept in the loop." For example, one university's Web site emphasizes its intention to keep employees in the loop regarding matters like policies and benefits.[25] This employer uses an *open-door policy* to encourage communication between employees and managers, an *employee handbook* covering basic employment information, as well as abundant *e-mail* and *hard copy notes and memos*.[26]

Two-way communication also helps management know what's bothering employees. To paraphrase one writer, soliciting complaints is vital for employers who want to short-circuit inequitable treatment and maintain positive employee relations.[27] Tactics include hosting employee *focus groups*, making available *ombudsman* and *suggestion boxes*, and implementing telephone, messaging, and Web-based *hotlines*. (Some employers use hotline providers to manage their hotlines. A vendor sets up the hotlines for the employer; it also receives the employees' comments, and provides ongoing feedback to the employer about employees' concerns, as well as periodic summaries of comments and trends.) *Exit interviews*, discussed in an earlier chapter, should enable the manager to sample the quality of employee relations and identify potential problem areas.[28] Managers also use *open-door policies* and "management by walking around" to informally ask employees "how things are going."

USING ORGANIZATIONAL CLIMATE SURVEYS Similarly, employers use attitude, morale, or *climate surveys* to support employee relations efforts. They use the surveys to "take the pulse" of their employees' attitudes toward a variety of organizational issues including leadership, safety, role clarity, fairness, and pay, and to thereby get a sense of whether their employee relations need improvement. The dividing lines between attitude surveys, satisfaction or morale surveys, and climate surveys are somewhat arbitrary; we can define **organizational climate** as the perceptions employees have of and the meaning that attach to a company's psychological environment, in terms of dimensions such as concern for employee well-being, supervisory behavior, political behaviors, and rewards.[29]

organizational climate
The perceptions a company's employees share about the firm's psychological environment, for instance, in terms of things like concern for employees' well-being, supervisory behavior, flexibility, appreciation, ethics, empowerment, political behaviors, and rewards.

Many employers use online surveys from firms like Know Your Company (http://knowyourcompany.com), focusing on questions such as "Are you proud to work here?"[30] Google conducts an annual "Googlegeist" survey of its employees. This survey measures things such as employees' willingness to leave.[31] Other surveys are available off the shelf. For instance, one SHRM sample survey has employees use a scale from 1 ("to a very little extent") to 5 ("to a very great extent") to answer survey questions. Questions include, "Overall, how satisfied are you with your supervisor?," "Overall, how satisfied are you with your job?," and "Does doing your job well lead to things like recognition and respect from those you work with?"[32]

Develop Employee Recognition/Relations Programs

In addition to communications programs, company-wide employee recognition and award programs improve employee relations. As one example, a trade journal notes how the Murray Supply Co. held a special dinner for all its employees, at which it gave out special awards for things like safe driving, tenure with the company, and branch employee of the year.[33] Employers often distribute such awards with much fanfare at special events such as awards dinners. One SHRM survey found that 76% of organizations surveyed had such employee recognition programs, and another 5% planned to implement one soon.[34]

Recognition and service award programs requires planning.[35] For example, starting a *service award program* requires reviewing employee tenure and setting meaningful award periods (1 year, 5 years, etc.). It also requires setting a budget, selecting awards, having a procedure for monitoring what awards to actually award, having a process for giving awards (such as special dinners or staff meetings), and measuring program success. Similarly, starting a *recognition program* requires developing criteria (such as customer service, and cost savings), creating forms and procedures for submitting and reviewing nominations, selecting awards, and having a process for awarding the awards.

There are online tools for automating the employee recognition process. Employees use these to recognize each other's contributions, for instance through peer recognition, spot awards, e-Cards, and incentives.[36] For example Globoforce.com organized a "Lift" recognition program for JetBlue. Employees nominate colleagues for their everyday contributions, and for outstanding work.[37]

Use Employee Involvement Programs

Employee relations also tend to improve when employees are *involved* with the company in positive ways.

Employers encourage involvement in various ways. Some organize focus groups. A *focus group* is a small sample of employees who are presented with a specific issue and who interactively express their opinions and attitudes on that issue with the group's assigned facilitator. Many employers use *social media* such as the photo-sharing Web site Pinterest to encourage involvement.[38] One survey found that about half of employers use social media to communicate with employees and to develop a sense of community.[39] For example, Red Door Interactive used a Pinterest-based project it called "San Diego Office Inspiration." This encouraged employees to contribute interior design and decor ideas for its new offices.[40]

suggestion teams
Temporary teams whose members work on specific analytical assignments, such as how to cut costs or raise productivity.

problem-solving teams
Teams that identify and research work processes and develop solutions to work-related problems.

quality circle
A special type of formal problem-solving team, usually composed of 6 to 12 specially trained employees who meet once a week to solve problems affecting their work area.

self-managing/self-directed work team
A small (usually 8 to 10 members) group of carefully selected, trained, and empowered employees who basically run themselves with little or no outside supervision, usually for the purpose of accomplishing a specific task or mission.

USING EMPLOYEE INVOLVEMENT TEAMS Employers have long used special teams to encourage employee involvement and boost productivity. **Suggestion teams** are temporary teams whose members work on specific analytical assignments, such as how to cut costs or raise productivity. One airline split employees (such as baggage handlers and ground crew) into teams, linking team members via its Web site for brainstorming and voting on ideas.[41] Semi-permanent **problem-solving teams** research work processes, and develop solutions to work problems.[42] A **quality circle** is a permanent problem-solving team, more popular in the past than now. They are usually composed of 6 to 12 specially trained employees who meet weekly to solve problems affecting their work area.[43] The team gets training in problem-analysis techniques (including basic statistics).

A **self-managing/self-directed work team** is a small (usually 8 to 10 members) group of carefully selected, trained, and empowered employees who supervise themselves with little or no outside supervision, usually for the purpose of accomplishing a specific mission.[44] For example, at the GE aircraft engine plant in Durham, North Carolina, employees work in teams, all of which report to the factory manager.[45] Teams like these usually function with minimal supervisory oversight, collectively voting on who could join the team, training each other, and handling quality control, for instance. Several years ago, GE expanded its footprint in North Carolina, opening new aircraft facilities. GE partnered with a local community college to do the preliminary training for its new employees.[46]

USING SUGGESTION SYSTEMS Employee suggestion plans can produce significant savings (and, through involvement and rewards, improve employee relations). For example, one study several years ago of 47 companies concluded that the firms had saved more than $624 million in one year from their suggestion programs; more than 250,000 suggestions were submitted, of which employers adopted over 93,000 ideas.[47] The accompanying HR as a Profit Center feature provides an example.

IMPROVING PERFORMANCE: *HR AS A PROFIT CENTER*

The Cost-Effective Suggestion System[48]

A Lockheed Martin unit in Oswego, New York, developed its "Cost-Effectiveness Plus" suggestion program to encourage and recognize employees for streamlining processes. With the Cost-Effectiveness Plus program, employees electronically submit their ideas. These are then evaluated and approved by the local manager and the program's coordinator (and by higher management when necessary). This program reportedly saves this facility about $77,000 per implemented idea, or more than $100 million each year.

Today's suggestion systems are more sophisticated than the "suggestion boxes" of years ago.[49] The main improvements are in how the employer formalizes and communicates the suggestion process. The essential elements of an effective employee suggestion system include the following:[50]

✓ Senior staff support
✓ A simple, easy process for submitting suggestions
✓ A strong process for evaluating and implementing suggestions
✓ An effective program for publicizing and communicating the program
✓ A program focus on key organizational goals ■

MyLab Management Talk About It 2

If your professor has assigned this, go to the Assignments section of **www.pearson.com/mylab/management** to complete this discussion. Based on this, write a one-page outline describing an employee suggestion system for a small department store.

HR AND THE GIG ECONOMY: *EMPLOYEE RELATIONS AND GIG WORKERS*[51]

Employers can take steps to improve employee relations with gig workers.

First understand that gig workers each come to their jobs with their own needs. For example, one researcher interviewed Uber and Lyft drivers. He found that how drivers reacted to things like pay cuts depended on why they were driving. Some were driving mostly for social interaction and to relax from their full-time jobs. (One psychotherapist wasn't too upset by Uber's pay cuts. He was just happy to unwind from 40 hours per week of counseling people). On the other hand, drivers who *were* financially dependent on driving were understandably quite upset by the cuts.

In any case, here are suggestions for improving gig-worker employee relations:

- Don't treat gig workers like they're disposable. Even if it's a short gig, communicate with the worker, and get to know him or her. Recognize their contributions.
- Make signing on as frictionless as possible. Many gig workers are looking for part-time flexible gigs, and want work, not paperwork.
- Research shows that most employers put little time into onboarding gig workers, which is a mistake: even an abbreviated onboarding process is better than none. Give them a brief background on your company and/or project, and make them feel part (albeit an independent-contractor part) of your business.
- It is important legally to make it clear that they are independent contractors. However, to the extent possible, share company news with and seek feedback from your gig workers. Include them in intracompany communications and to the extent possible in company social and educational events.

LEARNING OBJECTIVE 14-3

Explain what is meant by ethical behavior.

The Ethical Organization

People face ethical choices every day. Is it wrong to use a company credit card for personal purchases? Is a $50 gift to a client unacceptable? Compare your answers by doing the quiz in Figure 14-2.

Most of those reading this book rightfully view themselves as ethical people, so why include ethics in a human resource management book? For three reasons: First, ethics is not theoretical. Instead, it greases the wheels that make businesses work. Managers who promise raises but don't deliver, salespeople who say "The order's coming" when it's not, production managers who take kickbacks from suppliers—they all corrode the trust that day-to-day business transactions rely on.

Second, it is hard to even imagine an *un*ethical company with good employee relations.

The spread of technology into the workshop has raised a variety of new ethical questions and many old ones still linger. Compare your answers with those of other Americans surveyed, on page 479.

Office Technology

1. Is it wrong to use company e-mail for personal reasons?
   ❑ Yes ❑ No
2. Is it wrong to use office equipment to help your children or spouse do schoolwork?
   ❑ Yes ❑ No
3. Is it wrong to play computer games on office equipment during the workday?
   ❑ Yes ❑ No
4. Is it wrong to use office equipment to do Internet shopping?
   ❑ Yes ❑ No
5. Is it unethical to blame an error you made on a technological glitch?
   ❑ Yes ❑ No
6. Is it unethical to visit pornographic Web sites using office equipment?
   ❑ Yes ❑ No

Gifts and Entertainment

7. What's the value at which a gift from a supplier or client becomes troubling?
   ❑ $25 ❑ $50 ❑ $100
8. Is a $50 gift to a boss unacceptable?
   ❑ Yes ❑ No
9. Is a $50 gift *from* the boss unacceptable?
   ❑ Yes ❑ No
10. Of gifts from suppliers: Is it OK to take a $200 pair of football tickets?
    ❑ Yes ❑ No
11. Is it OK to take a $120 pair of theater tickets?
    ❑ Yes ❑ No
12. Is it OK to take a $100 holiday food basket?
    ❑ Yes ❑ No
13. Is it OK to take a $25 gift certificate?
    ❑ Yes ❑ No
14. Can you accept a $75 prize won at a raffle at a supplier's conference?
    ❑ Yes ❑ No

Truth and Lies

15. Due to on-the-job pressure, have you ever abused or lied about sick days?
    ❑ Yes ❑ No
16. Due to on-the-job pressure, have you ever taken credit for someone else's work or idea?
    ❑ Yes ❑ No

FIGURE 14-2 ***The Wall Street Journal* Workplace Ethics Quiz**

Source: Ethics and Compliance Officer Association, Waltham, MA, and the Ethical Leadership Group, Global Compliance's Expert Advisors, Wilmette, IL. (printed in *The Wall Street Journal*, October 21, 1999, pp. B1–B4).

Third, many ethical predicaments involve human resource management. For example, one HR manager described how employees at one plant were told to "vent poisonous gas into the air," something that could have killed them.[52] A survey found that 6 of the 10 most serious ethical work issues—workplace safety, employee records security, employee theft, affirmative action, comparable work, and employee privacy rights—were HR-related.[53]

ethics
The study of standards of conduct and moral judgment; also the standards of right conduct.

Ethics are "the principles of conduct governing an individual or a group"—the principles people use to decide what their conduct should be.[54] Of course, not all conduct involves ethics.[55] For example, buying an iPad usually isn't an ethical decision. Instead, ethical decisions are those rooted in *morality*. Morality refers to society's accepted standards of behavior. To be more precise, morality (and therefore ethical decisions) always involves the most fundamental questions of what is right and wrong, such as stealing, murder, and how to treat other people.

Ethics and Employee Rights

Societies don't rely just on employers' ethics or sense of fairness or morality to ensure that they do what's right. Societies also institute laws, and procedures for enforcing these laws. These laws lay out what employers can and cannot do, for instance, in terms of discriminating based on race. In so doing, these laws also carve out explicit rights for employees. For example, Title VII of the Civil Rights Act gives employees the right to bring legal charges against an employer who they believe discriminated against them due to race. And, the Fair Labor Standards Act gave employees the right to a minimum wage and overtime pay. The bottom line is that although ethics, fairness, and morality help govern how employers treat their employees, the enforceable rights embedded in employment law also govern what employers and employees can do.

What Shapes Ethical Behavior at Work?

Why do people do bad things? It's complicated. However, one review of over 30 years of ethics research concluded that three factors combine to determine the ethical choices we make.[56] The authors titled their paper "Bad Apples, Bad Cases, and Bad Barrels." This title highlighted their conclusion that when

"Bad apples" (people who are inclined to make unethical choices), must deal with

"Bad cases" (ethical situations that are ripe for unethical choices), while working in

"Bad barrels" (company environments that foster or condone unethical choices), . . . then people tend to act unethically.

Here's a closer look at what they found.

THE PERSON (WHAT MAKES BAD APPLES?) First, because people bring to their jobs their own ideas of what is morally right and wrong, each person must shoulder much of the credit (or blame) for his or her ethical choices.

For example, researchers surveyed CEOs to study their intentions to engage in two questionable practices: soliciting a competitor's technological secrets, and making illegal payments to foreign officials. The researchers concluded that the CEOs' personal predispositions more strongly affected their decisions than did outside pressures or characteristics of their firms.[57] The most principled people, with the highest level of "cognitive moral development," think through the implications of their decisions and apply ethical principles. They have "moral attentiveness," and are aware of the ethical dilemma at hand.[58] How would you rate your own ethics? Figure 14-2 (page 461) presented a short self-assessment survey (you'll find typical survey takers' answers on page 479).

WHICH ETHICAL SITUATIONS MAKE FOR ETHICALLY DANGEROUS SITUATIONS (BAD CASES)? It's not just the person but the situation that's important. For example, the researchers found that "smaller" ethical dilemmas prompt more bad choices. What determines "small"? Basically, how much harm can befall victims of the choice, or the number of people potentially affected. People seemed more likely to "do the wrong thing" in "less serious" situations, in other words. That obviously doesn't mean that some people don't do bad things when huge consequences are involved; it just means that people cut more ethical corners on small things. The problem is that one thing leads to another; people start by doing small bad things and then "graduate" to larger ones.[59]

WHAT ARE THE "BAD BARRELS"?—THE OUTSIDE FACTORS THAT MOLD ETHICAL CHOICES Finally, the study found that some companies produce more poisonous social environments ("outside factors" or "barrels") than do others; these bad environments in turn encourage unethical choices.[60] For example, companies that promoted an "everyone for him- or herself" culture were more likely to suffer unethical choices. Those that encouraged employees to consider the well-being of everyone had more ethical choices. Most important, companies whose managers put in place "a strong ethical culture that clearly communicates the range of acceptable and unacceptable behavior" suffered fewer unethical decisions.[61]

How Any Manager Can Create an Ethical Environment

We can translate findings like these into the following specific steps managers can take to create more ethical environments.

REDUCE JOB-RELATED PRESSURES If people did unethical things at work solely for personal gain or because they were "bad people," it perhaps would be understandable (though inexcusable). The scary thing is that it's often not personal interests but the pressures of the job. As one former executive said at his trial, "I took these actions, knowing they were wrong, in a misguided attempt to preserve the company to allow it to withstand what I believed were temporary financial difficulties."[62]

One study illustrates this. It asked employees to list their reasons for taking unethical actions at work.[63] For most of these employees, "meeting schedule pressures," "meeting overly aggressive financial or business objectives," and "helping the company survive" were the three top causes. "Advancing my own career or financial interests" ranked about last.[64] So first, reducing such "outside" pressures helps head off ethical lapses.

MAKE IT CLEAR WHAT'S OKAY AND NOT OKAY[65] If your company has an ethics code, make it clear you take it seriously; if there is no code, show by your own actions and words what's acceptable and not acceptable.

MODEL THE DESIRED BEHAVIOR ("WALK THE TALK") It's hard to resist even subtle pressure from a boss. In one report, "the level of misconduct at work dropped dramatically when employees said their supervisors exhibited ethical behavior."[66] Examples of how supervisors lead subordinates astray include the following:

- Tell them to do "whatever is necessary" to achieve results.
- Look the other way when wrongdoing occurs.
- Take credit for others' work or shift blame.[67]

Put another way, managers must walk the talk—not just pay lip service to ethics but behave ethically. Some managers urge employees to apply a quick "ethics test" to evaluate whether what they're about to do fits the company's code of conduct. For example, Raytheon Co. asked employees to ask:

- Is the action legal?
- Is it right?
- Who will be affected?
- Does it fit Raytheon's values?
- How will it "feel" afterward?
- How will it look in the newspaper?
- Will it reflect poorly on the company?[68]

REINFORCE THE DESIRED BEHAVIOR, NOT THE UNDESIRABLE BEHAVIOR[69] People tend to do what they get positive reinforcement for, and gradually stop doing what's not reinforced. Do not inadvertently reinforce unethical behavior (nor punish ethical behavior).

TAKE IT SERIOUSLY When students complained of inappropriate behavior by an osteopathic medical school administrator, university administrators (including an attorney) put a letter in his file and got his agreement to change. It transpired that they should have taken stronger action. The moral is, investigate ethics-related accusations vigorously and make sure you correct the problem.

How Human Resource Managers Can Create More Ethical Environments

There are also steps human resource managers can take.

INSTITUTE ETHICS POLICIES AND CODES Employers use ethics policies and codes to signal that their companies are serious about ethics. For example, IBM's code of ethics says, in part:

> Neither you nor any member of your family may, directly or through others, solicit or accept from anyone money, a gift, or any amenity that could influence or could reasonably give the appearance of influencing IBM's business

relationship with that person or organization. If you or your family members receive a gift (including money), even if the gift was unsolicited, you must notify your manager and take appropriate measures, which may include returning or disposing of what you received.[70]

ENFORCE THE RULES Codifying rules without enforcing them is useless. To paraphrase one study, managers' statements can reduce unethical behavior on the part of employees, but knowing that behavior is actually monitored and enforced has the biggest impact.[71] *Ethics audits* address topics like conflicts of interest, giving and receiving gifts, and employee discrimination.[72] One study found that fraud controls such as hotlines, surprise audits, fraud training for employees, and mandatory vacations can each reduce internal theft by around 50%.[73] Lockheed Martin Corp. has a chief ethics officer.[74]

ENCOURAGE WHISTLEBLOWERS Some companies encourage employees to use hotlines and other means to "blow the whistle" on the company when they discover fraud. Several U.S. laws, including Dodd–Frank, the False Claims Act, the U.S. Financial Institutions Reform, Recovery, and Enforcement Act, and U.S. federal sentencing guidelines address whistleblowing.[75] Under the U.S. Securities and Exchange Commission's whistleblower program, awards are not limited to company employees. Consultants, independent contractors, vendors, and sometimes audit and compliance personnel are also eligible.[76]

MyLab Management Apply It!

What steps did an actual company take to tighten its ethics processes after confronting accusations of corporate misdeeds? If your professor has chosen to assign this activity, go to **www.pearson.com/mylab/management** to complete the video exercise.

organizational culture
The characteristic values, traditions, and behaviors a company's employees share.

FOSTER AN ETHICAL CULTURE[77] Several years ago Uber faced multiple harassment claims, in part due to the company's uninhibited culture.[78] **Organizational culture** is the "characteristic values, traditions, and behaviors a company's employees share." A *value* is a basic belief about what is right or wrong, or about what you should or shouldn't do. ("Honesty is the best policy" would be a value.) Managing people and shaping their behavior depends on shaping the values they use as behavioral guides. For example, if management really believes "honesty is the best policy," the actions it takes should reflect this value. Managers therefore should think through how to send the right signals to their employees—in other words, create the right culture. Doing so includes:

- ***Choose as leaders*** people who reflect the culture you're trying to achieve.[79]
- ***Clarify expectations.*** Make it clear what values you want subordinates to adhere to. For example, IBM's ethics statement shows the company takes ethics seriously.
- ***Use signs and symbols.*** *Symbolism*—what the manager actually does—ultimately does the most to create and sustain the company's culture. As we said earlier, managers should "walk the talk." They can't say "don't falsify the financials" and then do so themselves.
- ***Provide physical support.*** The physical signs of the employer's values—its incentive plan, appraisal system, and disciplinary procedures, for instance—send strong signals regarding what employees should and should not do. For example, do promotions reward ethical behavior or penalize it?[80]
- ***Interact frequently*** with employees to explain the values that are important.[81]

The accompanying HR Tools feature illustrates ethics management in small businesses.

IMPROVING PERFORMANCE: *HR TOOLS FOR LINE MANAGERS AND SMALL BUSINESSES*

Small Business Ethics

When people think of unethical corporate behavior, big companies come to mind, because they're usually in the headlines. Yet studies show that small enterprises are prone to the same unethical behavior as big firms.

For example, one study of 20 small to midsize firms found that bribery, corrupt dealings, and a general tone of dishonesty were all "business as usual" at many of these firms.[82] Some were clever about it. When doing business abroad, one U.S. business kept its hands "clean" by partnering with a local firm. The latter did the dirty work, for example, the local bribes, while the U.S. firm's managers looked the other way.

Smaller firms should be alert to unethical behavior. They don't have the resources for ethics officers, ethics hotlines, or the ethics training that big firms have. Furthermore, having an unethical accountant in a billion-dollar firm embezzle $10 million is a nuisance. Having the bookkeeper of a $10 million firm abscond with $1 million could be the end.

Small business owners can take several steps. First, *size up your company's current ethics-related activities.*[83] Even a self-audit based on guidelines like those in this chapter (having an ethics code, ethics training, controls to monitor ethical behavior, and so on) are worthwhile. Second, *create a code of conduct (Googling "code of conduct" reveals thousands of examples)*, and show you take it seriously. Third, *train your people*. Training needn't be complicated. For example, one expert suggests having your managers develop scenarios, relevant to your business, illustrating which behaviors are ethical and which are not; then meet to discuss these. Fourth, make it easier to *solicit feedback* from your employees, to report unethical behavior. ("Open door" polices and suggestion boxes are examples.) Finally, *walk the talk*. In a small business, the owner is so visible that employees will take their ethical signals from him or her. ■

> **MyLab Management Talk About It 3**
>
> If your professor has assigned this, go to the Assignments section of **www.pearson.com/mylab/management** to complete this discussion. Create a 50-word ethics code for a small business. Then, explain how the owner might use an ethics code to help avoid mistreatment of employees.

HIRE RIGHT The most straightforward way an HR manager can build an ethical organization is to attract and hire ethical people. Start with recruitment ads that highlight your firm's commitment to ethics. Then screen carefully. An integrity test "is a specific type of personality test designed to assess an applicant's tendency to be honest, trustworthy, and dependable."[84] Use interview questions (such as "Have you ever observed someone doing something dishonest at work? What did you do?").[85] Check backgrounds thoroughly.

Also treat job applicants fairly. "If prospective employees perceive that the hiring process does not treat people fairly, they may assume that ethical behavior is not important in the company."[86] What exactly to do? Here:

- Applicants tend to view the *formal procedure* (such as the interview) as fair to the extent that it tests job-related criteria and provides an opportunity to demonstrate competence.
- Applicants expect respect. *Fair interpersonal treatment* reflects things like the propriety of the questions, the politeness of interviewer, and the degree of two-way communication.
- Applicants see a selection system as fair to the extent that the employer provides *useful feedback* about the candidate's own performance.[87]

USE ETHICS TRAINING Ethics training is basically mandatory. Since 1991, federal sentencing guidelines have prescribed reduced penalties for employers accused of misconduct who implement codes of conduct and ethics training.[88] The Sarbanes–Oxley Act of 2002 makes ethics training even more important.

Ethics training involves showing employees how to recognize ethical dilemmas, how to apply codes of conduct to resolve problems, and how to use personnel activities like discipline in ethical ways.[89] The training should illustrate the moral underpinnings of the ethical choice, and the company's commitment to integrity and ethics. Include participation by top managers to emphasize that commitment.[90]

Lockheed Martin's annual *Giving Voice to Values* ethics training program is an example.[91] Lockheed Martin's CEO, Marillyn Hewson, first trains her immediate staff. They in turn train their subordinates. The program first reviews Lockheed Martin's business conduct code. It then prepares employees to recognize and react to ethics-laden situations. To do this, trainees review videos of actual ethics cases from the company's Ethics Office. Then they discuss the cases and how to react to them.

USE REWARDS AND DISCIPLINE Employees expect employers to punish unethical conduct and to reward ethical conduct, (including executives', not just underlings').[92] A code of conduct generally describes what employees should and should not do ethically.[93] Employers often put their code of conduct policies in the employee manual.[94] For example, one university lists "penalties ranging from a formal written warning notice up to, and including, discharge" for violations such as "immoral or indecent conduct."[95]

INSTITUTE EMPLOYEE PRIVACY POLICIES With Facebook and others routinely marketing users' personal information, privacy seems to be going out of style; as one cybersecurity expert said, "surveillance is the business model of the internet."[96]

But while some online users willingly share personal information as the price of freely staying in touch, privacy still matters at work.[97] Here employee privacy violations include *intrusion* (such as locker room and e-mail surveillance), *publication* of private matters, and *disclosure* of medical records.[98] In practice, background checks, monitoring off-duty conduct and lifestyle, drug testing, workplace searches, and workplace monitoring trigger most privacy violations.[99] Such activities have legitimate business purposes; however, they can be abused—as when erroneous background information leads to unjust treatment.[100] Many employers therefore include privacy policies in their ethics programs. For example, Ceridian's Privacy Policy Web site starts with "Ceridian is committed to protecting the privacy of our employees, our customers, and their employees."[101]

KNOW YOUR EMPLOYMENT LAW

Electronic Monitoring

Electronic Communications Privacy Act (ECPA)
The ECPA is a federal law intended to help restrict interception and monitoring of oral and wire communications.

There are two main restrictions on workplace monitoring. One is the **Electronic Communications Privacy Act (ECPA).** The other are *common-law protections* (protections that evolved from court decisions, for instance, decisions against defaming employees by publicizing highly personal matters about them). The ECPA is a federal law intended to help restrict interception and monitoring of oral and wire communications. (Several states have similar laws.) It contains two exceptions. The "business purpose exception" permits employers to monitor communications if they can show a legitimate business reason for doing so. The second, "consent exception," lets employers monitor communications if they have their employees' consent to do so.[102]

In one survey several years ago, 41% of employers with more than 20,000 employees had someone reading employee e-mails.[103] Ninety-six percent block access to adult Web sites, 61% to game sites.[104] (A court found one employer liable when one employee used his company computer at work to distribute child pornography.)[105] Some check employees' personal blogs or Facebook sites to see if they're publicizing work-related matters.[106]

More employers are using iris scanning to verify employee identity.

Monty Rakusen/Cultura/Getty Images

Electronic eavesdropping is legal—up to a point. For example, federal law and most state laws allow employers to monitor employees' phone calls in the ordinary course of business. However, they must stop listening when it becomes clear the conversation is personal. You can also intercept e-mail to protect the property rights of the e-mail provider. Many employees assume that their messages using the company's e-mail system are open to review, but that e-mails they send via the employer's system but using personal e-mail like Gmail aren't. However, that's not necessarily true.

To be safe, employers issue e-mail and online service usage policies. These warn employees that their systems should be used for business only. Employers also have employees sign e-mail and telephone monitoring acknowledgment statements like that in Figure 14-3.

Monitoring raises privacy issues, but can also boost profits. For example, employers routinely use software to monitor what their employees are doing online. When one employer noticed high employee overtime claims, it installed new software, and discovered many employees spent hours daily shopping online instead of working. Computer monitoring usually involves loading software directly onto the device. It then keeps logs of keystrokes, screenshots, and URLs visited by individuals.[107]

FIGURE 14-3 Sample E-Mail Monitoring Acknowledgment Statement

I understand that XYZ Company periodically monitors any e-mail communications created, sent, or retrieved using this company's e-mail system. Therefore, I understand that my e-mail communications may be read by individuals other than the intended recipient. I also understand that XYZ Company periodically monitors telephone communications, for example to improve customer service quality.

____
Signature Date

____
Print Name Department

An attorney should review the company's e-mail policy. At a minimum, make it clear that employees should have no expectation of privacy in their e-mail and Internet usage.[108] Also emphasize that all messages sent and received on the employer's e-mail system are company property and not confidential.[109] Employee monitoring best practices include: don't target a legally protected class or monitor in nonwork areas, do be consistent in how you monitor employees, and get legal advice before installing a monitoring system.[110]

Videotaped workplace monitoring requires more caution. Continuous video surveillance of employees in an office setting may not be a problem. But a Boston employer had to pay over $200,000 to five workers it secretly videotaped in an employee locker room, after they sued.[111]

More companies are monitoring in part due to the proliferation of online and smart devices and social media. For example, a thumb drive can carry off huge amounts of corporate data. And, increasingly, disgruntled employees are using their companies' cloud services to hack into and undermine their computer systems.[112]

Monitoring goes beyond work stations and phones. One hospital uses biometric scanners to ensure that employees who clock in really are who they say they are. The Federal Aviation Administration uses iris scanning to control employees' access to their network information systems. One restaurant monitors most everything waiters do, for instance, tracking every ticket, dish, and drink that they process.[113] (This makes it easier to track employee theft, but also helps identify conscientious waiters). The British grocer Tesco has some distribution center employees wear armbands that track how quickly employees are unloading and scanning goods.[114] ■

> **MyLab Management Talk About It 4**
>
> If your professor has assigned this, go to the Assignments section of **www.pearson.com/mylab/management** to complete these discussion questions. How would you feel if your employer told you to wear an armband monitor? Why? How would you react?

Managing Employee Discipline

LEARNING OBJECTIVE 14-4

Explain what is meant by fair disciplinary practices.

The purpose of *discipline* is to encourage employees to behave sensibly at work (where *sensible* means adhering to rules and regulations). Discipline is required when an employee violates a rule.[115]

Proper disciplinary procedures are important for several reasons. For one thing, positive employee relations requires trust, and few personnel actions will undermine trust as will arbitrary discipline. Legal concerns are important too. One study surveyed 45 published arbitration awards in which tardiness had triggered discipline and/or discharge. When arbitrators overturned employers' decisions, it was usually due to inadequate disciplinary procedures—for example, the employer failed to clarify what "tardy" meant. Unfair disciplinary procedures can backfire in other ways. For example, it can trigger retaliatory employee misbehavior.

The Three Pillars of Fair Discipline

Disciplining employees is often unavoidable, but any such discipline should be rooted in the need to be fair. The manager builds a fair discipline process on three pillars: rules and regulations, a system of progressive penalties, and an appeals process.[116]

RULES AND REGULATIONS An acceptable disciplinary process begins with a set of clear disciplinary rules and regulations. The rules should cover problems such as theft, destruction of company property, drinking on the job, and insubordination. Examples of rules include:

Poor performance is not acceptable. Each employee is expected to perform his or her work properly and efficiently and to meet established standards of quality.

Alcohol and drugs do not mix with work. The use of either during working hours and reporting for work under the influence of either are both strictly prohibited.

The purpose of the rules is to inform employees ahead of time what is and is not acceptable behavior. Tell employees, preferably in writing, what is not permitted. The employee handbook should contain the rules and regulations.

PROGRESSIVE PENALTIES A system of progressive penalties is the second pillar of effective discipline. The severity of the penalty usually depends on the offense and the number of times it has occurred. For example, most companies issue warnings for the first unexcused lateness. However, for a fourth offense, discharge is the usual disciplinary action.

APPEALS PROCESS Third, the aim of an appeals process is to ensure that supervisors mete out discipline fairly. FedEx's *guaranteed fair treatment* multistep program illustrates this. We'll look at it in a moment.

An appeals process is essential but is no panacea. Often employers can mitigate the effects of unfair discipline by catching it during an appeal. However, some supervisory behavior may be impossible to overcome. For example, behaviors that attack the employee's personal and/or social identity are difficult to remedy.[117] Remember that punishment is particularly objectionable when it seems motivated by revenge.[118]

Diversity Counts: Comparing Males and Females in a Discipline Situation

A well-known study about 20 years ago concluded that when a woman doesn't act the way other men and women expect she should act, they tend to treat her more harshly than they might if a man acted unexpectedly.[119]

The study involved 360 graduate and undergraduate business school students. They reviewed a labor arbitration case. The case involved two employees, one male and one female, with similar work records and tenure with their employers. Both were discharged for violation of company rules related to alcohol and drugs. The case portrays one worker's behavior as a more serious breach of company rules: The more culpable worker (a male in half the study and a female in the other half) had brought the intoxicant to work. The students had to express their agreement with two alternative approaches (tough or not-so-tough) to settling the dispute that arose after the discharge.

The researchers found bias against the female "employee" by both the male and female students. Both the male and female students recommended harsher treatment for the "culpable" female employee in the case than they did for the "culpable" man. As the researchers conclude, "women, as decision makers, appear to be as willing as men to impose harsher discipline on women than upon men." ■

How to Discipline an Employee

Even if you're a manager in a *Fortune* 500 company, you may find yourself without company guidelines when you have to discipline an employee. An error could trigger a costly appeal, or even litigation. To help head off errors, fair discipline guidelines would include:[120]

- Make sure the evidence supports the charge of employee wrongdoing.
- Adequately warn the employee of the disciplinary consequences of his or her alleged misconduct. Have the employee sign a form as in Figure 14-4.
- The rule that allegedly was violated should be "reasonably related" to the facility's efficient and safe operation.
- Objectively investigate the matter before disciplining.
- The investigation should produce substantial evidence of misconduct.
- Apply applicable rules, orders, or penalties *without discrimination*.
- The U.S. Constitution contains the *due process* clause, specifically that no one shall be "deprived of life, liberty or property without due process of law."[121] Most basically, due process means that anyone accused or suspected deserves to have his or her case reviewed through a fair process. For example, did the person have a chance to defend himself or herself? Was there an appeals process?

FIGURE 14-4 **Report of Employee Discipline**

Apex Telecommunications Corporation
Report of Disciplinary Action and Warning

Employee's Name____________________
Employee's Department____________________
Date of Misconduct_______________ Today's Date_______________

Description of incident and misconduct (including witnesses, if any)_______________

Witnesses to incident_______________

If the misconduct violated an Apex Co. policy or rule, state the policy or rule_______________

Employee's explanation for misconduct, if any_______________

Disciplinary action taken, if any_______________

The employee was warned today that if misconduct such as this reoccurs at any time during the next_____ weeks, he or she may be subject to the following disciplinary action_______________

_______________ _______________
Supervisor's signature Employee's signature

_______________ _______________
Print name Print name

- Maintain the employee's right to counsel. For example, all union employees generally have the right to bring a representative to a disciplinary interview.
- Don't rob your subordinate of his or her dignity, for instance by disciplining in public.
- Listen to what the person has to say.
- Remember that the burden of proof is on you. In U.S. society, a person is considered innocent until proven guilty.
- Get the facts. Don't base your decision on hearsay evidence or on your general impression.
- Don't act while angry.

Discipline without Punishment

Traditional discipline processes have two main drawbacks. First, no one likes being punished. Second, punishment tends to gain short-term compliance, but not long-term cooperation.

Discipline without punishment (or alternative or nonpunitive discipline) aims to avoid these drawbacks by reducing the punitive nature of the discipline. Steps include:[122]

1. ***Issue an oral reminder for a first infraction.*** Have a private discussion with the employee.
2. ***Should another incident arise within 6 weeks, issue a formal written reminder, and place a copy in the employee's personnel file.*** Also, hold a second private discussion with the employee.

3. ***Give a paid, one-day "decision-making leave."*** If another incident occurs in the next 6 weeks or so, tell the employee to take a 1-day leave with pay, and to consider whether he or she wants to abide by the rules. When the employee returns to work, he or she meets with you and gives you a decision.
4. ***If no further incidents occur in the next year or so, purge the 1-day paid suspension from the person's file.*** If the behavior is repeated, the next step is dismissal.

The process would not apply to exceptional circumstances. Criminal behavior or in-plant fighting might be grounds for immediate dismissal, for instance.

Employee Engagement Guide for Managers

How Companies Become "Best Companies to Work For"

LEARNING OBJECTIVE 14-5
Answer the question, "How do companies become 'Best Companies to Work For'?"

We began this chapter by noting that some companies are better to work for than are others, and we therefore focused on programs managers use to cultivate the positive employee relations that contribute to being a best place to work. This final section zeroes in on three companies that are known in part for actually being best places to work.

The "Best Companies to Work For"

Each year, several organizations publish "Best Companies to Work For" lists, the most notable of which is probably "*Fortune* Magazine's 100 Best Companies to Work For®."[123] Based on an extensive multinational survey of employees by the Great Place to Work® Institute (www.greatplacetowork.com), the survey seeks to identify the best companies to work for, based on how the employees working in them actually feel about working there. The Great Place to Work Institute defines a great workplace as one where employees trust the people they work for, have pride in the work they do, and enjoy the people they work with.[124] They say that these companies "have the highest levels of trust, strongest evidence of employee engagement and demonstrate the best applied management practices and programs" as defined by the institute's proprietary models.[125] We'll look at three recent "*Fortune* Magazine's 100 Best Companies to Work For"—SAS, Google, and FedEx.[126]

SAS: Great Benefits, Trust, and Work–Life Balance

SAS, headquartered in Cary, North Carolina, is a leader in providing business analytics software and services to companies that include 90 of the top 100 companies on the *Fortune* global 500 list.[127] Founded in the 1970s, the company is privately owned and has long been known for the quality of its benefits and for the support it provides for its employees' work–life balance. It has annual revenues of over $2.3 billion, and a worldwide workforce of over 13,000 people, about half at the company's North Carolina campus.

When people think about employee relations at SAS, the first thing that comes to mind is probably its employee benefits, which are extraordinary. To paraphrase its CEO, the firm's employees are happier and healthier because SAS's extensive benefits remove unnecessary distractions and stress.[128] They include (for example) 3 to 4 weeks per year company-paid vacations, paid sick days, flexible work schedules, 11 paid holidays, competitive pay, company-paid life insurance and accidental death insurance, retirement plans, an on-site fitness center, employee assistance programs, domestic partner benefits, and subsidized on-site child-care centers in Cary.[129]

In a larger sense, such benefits symbolize SAS's approach to employee relations. While many employers talk about "putting their employees first," SAS puts its money where its mouth is. For example, late in 2008, as the recession was gaining speed, most employers were laying off employees. SAS's founder and CEO, Dr. Jim Goodnight, held a special global webcast to announce to employees that none of SAS's 13,000 worldwide employees would lose their jobs.[130] They have reportedly never laid off an employee.[131] SAS goes to great lengths to foster trust in other ways, for instance by giving employees abundant freedom in the hours they work. They also have the Great Place to Work Institute survey employees on important characteristics of trust including open communication, respect, and career paths.[132]

What does all this do for SAS? As one long-term employee put it, "I just can't imagine leaving SAS, and I felt that way for a very long time . . . if somebody offered to double my salary, I wouldn't even think about it."[133] Employee turnover, about 20% in software companies, is about 3% at SAS, which highlights another important facet of the SAS benefits programs.[134] One expert estimates that the lower turnover alone saves SAS $60 million to $80 million a year. As another example, letting employees visit on-campus health professionals (as SAS does) cuts hours out of the average employee's time away from work.[135] And, of course, the effect on engagement, morale, and productivity may be priceless.

Google: Happiness and People Analytics

When Google founders Larry Page and Sergey Brin began building Google, they wanted to make it a great place to work, so they turned to SAS. They met with SAS executives and sent a team there to better understand what made SAS consistently a "Best Company to Work For."[136]

It's therefore not surprising that Google is one of the few employers whose employee benefits equal or exceed those at SAS. In addition to things like health-care benefits and flexible work hours (and the possibility of making millions on stock options), its benefits include on-site dry cleaners, bowling alleys, cafés, transportation to and from campus, and nap pods.[137] As Google puts it, "It's all about removing barriers so Googlers can focus on the things they love, both inside and outside of work. We're constantly searching for unique ways to improve the health and happiness of our Googlers."[138]

Aside from its benefits, what sets Google apart is the scientific way it decides how to "improve the health and happiness" of Google employees. At Google, maintaining positive employee relations is highly analytical (one writer calls Google "The Happiness Machine").[139] Google calls its human resource department, "People Operations" (employees call it "POPS"). It hired social scientists to create what they call the People & Innovation Lab, with a Google "people analytics team" charged with finding out how to make Googlers happy.[140] Google "monitors its employees' well-being to a degree that can seem absurd to those who work outside [Google's headquarters in] Mountain View [California]."[141] The social scientists run experiments, for instance, to determine if successful middle managers have certain skills, and what's the best way to remind people to contribute to their 401(k)s.[142] In one example, when the analytics team found that women staffers' turnover was too high, they concluded that new mothers were leaving at twice Google's average departure rate.[143] This led to a redesigned maternity leave plan including 5 months off at full pay and full benefits. The new plan cut female Googler turnover in half.[144] To support its analytical approach, Google "solicits employee feedback on everything from how they prefer to be compensated, to the design of new bicycles used throughout the expansive headquarters campus."[145] So, it's little wonder why Googlers are happy.

FedEx: Guaranteed Fair Treatment

FedEx has been one of the "*Fortune* Magazine's 100 Best Companies to Work For" for 12 of the past 15 years. Several things—excellent benefits, competitive salaries, and (as we discussed in Chapter 5) a focus on promoting from within help to explain this; however, it may be FedEx's emphasis on building trust through communications that most sets it apart.

SURVEY FEEDBACK ACTION (SFA) The FedEx survey feedback action (SFA) program is one example. SFA includes an anonymous survey that allows employees to express feelings about the company and their managers, and to some extent about service, pay, and benefits. Each manager then has an opportunity to use the results to help design a blueprint for improving workgroup engagement and commitment.[146]

SFA has three phases. First, the survey itself is a standard, anonymous questionnaire given each year to every employee. The questions are designed to gather information about what helps and hinders employees in their work environment. Sample items include: "I can tell my manager what I think" and "My manager tells me what was expected." A workgroup's survey results are compiled and sent anonymously to the manager.

The second phase is a feedback session between the manager and his or her workgroup. The goal here is to identify specific concerns or problems, examine causes for these problems, and devise action plans to correct the problems.

The feedback meeting should lead to a third, "action plan" phase. This produces a list of actions that the manager will take to address employees' concerns and boost results. It includes: What is the concern? What's your analysis? What's the cause? and What should be done?

THE FEDEX GUARANTEED FAIR TREATMENT PROCESS FedEx's Guaranteed Fair Treatment Process (GFTP) goes beyond most grievance procedures in several ways, perhaps most notably in that an appeal can go all the way to FedEx's top executives. The effect is twofold: Complaints don't get a chance to fester, and managers think twice before acting unfairly.[147] GFTP is available to all permanent FedEx employees. It covers concerns regarding matters such as disputed performance reviews, disciplinary actions, and terminations.[148]

Employees use Guaranteed Fair Treatment Process packets, available from the HR department, to file GFTP complaints. These include a fact sheet listing the complainant's name and work history; a GFTP tracking sheet to track the complaint at each step; management's rationale (for instance, in terms of applicable policies and procedures); a write-up from the HR department; space for key documents (termination letters, and so on); and space for backup information including witness statements. The employee must try to resolve the problem with his or her supervisor before filing a GFTP appeal.

GFTP contains three steps.[149] In step one, *management review*, the complainant submits a written complaint to a manager, senior manager, or managing director, within seven calendar days of the occurrence of the eligible issue. Then the manager, senior manager, and managing director of the employee's group review all relevant information; hold a telephone conference and/or meeting with the complainant; make a decision to either uphold, modify, or overturn management action; and communicate their decision in writing to the complainant.

If turned down in step one, then in step two, *officer complaint*, the complainant submits a written complaint to an officer (VP or senior vice president) of the division within 7 calendar days of the step one decision.

Finally (if necessary), in step three, *executive appeals review*, the complainant submits a written complaint within 7 calendar days of the step two decision to the employee relations department. This department investigates and prepares a GFTP case file for the appeals board executive review. The appeals board—the CEO, the COO, the chief personnel officer, and senior vice presidents—then reviews all relevant information and makes a decision to either uphold, overturn, or initiate a board of review or to take other appropriate action; the appeals board's decision is final.

A "Best Company" Human Resource Philosophy?

SAS, Google, and FedEx are different from each other, and from other companies, so there's no guarantee that what works for them will work for other firms. For example, SAS is privately owned. Its owners can therefore more easily absorb the short-term fluctuations in profits that great benefits and no layoffs engender than can most publicly traded companies. Google has grown fast through a series of smart strategic moves, and, when the economy turns down, its managers generally still have to focus more on retaining great employees than on laying them off. FedEx, still a "Best Company to Work For," has run into some labor relations problems recently, for instance, from drivers who don't want to be independent contractors.

However, there are several things that any manager intent on building positive employee relations can learn from studying any of these three companies. For example, their managers work hard to cultivate trust and to ensure—for instance, by monitoring employees' attitudes and by instituting open-door and guaranteed fair treatment–type grievance processes—that employees are treated fairly. And, in numerous ways (such as in their recognition programs, involvement programs, ethical standards, benefits, and climate surveys and other two-way communications programs), they all exhibit a deep and evident respect for their employees and to "putting employees first."

But perhaps the single most important thing a manager can glean from these three companies is the human resource philosophy on which they built their human resource management practices. In Chapter 1, we said that people's actions are always based in part on the basic assumptions they make, and that this is especially true in regard to human resource management. The basic assumptions you make about people—Can they be trusted? Do they dislike work? Why do they act as they do? How should they be treated?—together comprise your philosophy of human resource management. And every personnel decision you make—the people you hire, the training you provide, your leadership style, and the like—reflects (for better or worse) this basic philosophy.

One of the things molding your own philosophy is that of your organization's top management. While it may or may not be stated, it is usually communicated by their actions and permeates every level and department. Google's founders want their employees to be happy, and they've worked since Google's founding to make sure that they are. FedEx founder and CEO Frederick Smith is famous for (among many other things) his P-S-P mantra, namely that when you treat your People well they will provide great Service, and Profits will follow.[150] Similarly, the founder and CEO of SAS has said, "We've worked hard to create a corporate culture that is based on trust between our employees and the company . . . a culture that rewards innovation, encourages employees to try new things and yet doesn't penalize them for taking chances, and a culture that cares about employees' personal and professional growth."[151] Such HR philosophies may well be the "magic sauce" that explains why great companies to work for are great.

Chapter Review

Chapter Section Summaries

14-1. **Employee relations** is the activity that involves establishing and maintaining the positive employee–employer relationships that contribute to satisfactory productivity, motivation, morale, and discipline, and to maintaining a positive, productive, and cohesive work environment.

14-2. Managers and HR management use **programs to develop positive employee relations.** Unfair treatment reduces morale, increases stress, and has negative effects on employees and should be weeded out. Managers also use communications programs, recognition programs, and employee involvement programs to build positive employee relations.

14-3. **Ethics** refers to the principles of conduct governing an individual or a group, and specifically to the standards you use to decide what your conduct should be. Numerous factors shape ethical behavior at work. These include individual factors, organizational factors, the boss's influence, ethics policies and codes, and the organization's culture. HR management can influence ethical behavior. Having a fair and open selection process, establishing special ethics training programs, and rewarding (or disciplining) ethical (or unethical) work-related behavior are some examples.

14-4. A fair and just **discipline** process is based on rules and regulations, a system of progressive penalties, and an appeals process. A number of discipline guidelines are important, including discipline should be in line with the way management usually responds to similar incidents, management must adequately investigate the matter, and do not rob a subordinate of his or her dignity.

14-5. There are several things that any manager intent on building positive employee relations and **employee engagement** can draw from studying "Best Companies to Work For" such as SAS, Google, and FedEx. Their managers cultivate trust and ensure that employees are treated fairly. They all exhibit a deep and evident respect for their employees and to "putting employees first." Their human resource philosophy emphasizes trust, respect, and caring about their employees' personal and professional growth.

Discussion Questions

14-1. Explain how you would ensure fairness in disciplining, discussing particularly the prerequisites to disciplining, disciplining guidelines, and the discipline without punishment approach.

14-2. Why is it important in our litigious society to manage electronic monitoring properly?

14-3. Provide two examples of behaviors that would probably be unethical but legal, and three that would probably be illegal but ethical.

14-4. List 10 things your college or university does to encourage ethical behavior by students and/or faculty.

14-5. You need to select a nanny for your or a relative's child, and want someone ethical. What would you do to help ensure you ended up hiring someone ethical?

14-6. You believe your coworker is being bullied. How would you verify this, and what would you do about it if it is true?

14-7. Define *employee relations*, and discuss at least four methods for managing it.

Individual and Group Activities

14-8. Working individually or in groups, interview managers or administrators at your employer or college in order to determine the extent to which the employer or college endeavors to build two-way communication, and the specific types of programs used. Do the managers think they are effective? What do the employees (or faculty members) think of the programs in use at the employer or college?

14-9. Working individually or in groups, obtain copies of the student handbook for your college and determine to what extent there is a formal process through which students can air grievances. Based on your contacts with other students, has it been an effective grievance process? Why or why not?

14-10. Working individually or in groups, determine the nature of the academic discipline process in your college. Do you think it is effective? Based on what you read in this chapter, would you recommend any modifications?

14-11. Appendices A and B at the end of this book (pages 614–634) list the knowledge someone studying for the HRCI (Appendix A) or SHRM (Appendix B) certification exam needs to have in each area of human resource management (such as in Strategic Management and Workforce Planning). In groups of several students, do four things: (1) review Appendix A and/or B; (2) identify the material in this chapter that relates to the Appendix A and/or B required knowledge lists; (3) write four multiple-choice exam questions on this material that you believe would be suitable for inclusion in the HRCI exam and/or the SHRM exam; and (4) if time permits, have someone from your team post your team's questions in front of the class, so that students in all teams can answer the exam questions created by the other teams.

KNOWLEDGE BASE

14-12. In a research study at Ohio State University, a professor found that even honest people, left to their own devices, would steal from their employers.[152] In this study, the researchers gave financial services workers the opportunity to steal a small amount of money after participating in an after-work project for which the pay was inadequate. Would the employees steal to make up for the underpayment? In most cases, yes. Employees who scored low on an honesty test stole whether or not their office had an ethics program that said stealing from the company was illegal. Employees who scored high on the honesty test also stole, but only if their office did not have such an employee ethics program—the "honest" people didn't steal if there was an ethics policy.

Individually or in groups, answer these questions: Do you think findings like these are generalizable? In other words, would they apply across the board to employees in other types of companies and situations? If your answer is yes, what do you think this implies about the need for and wisdom of having an ethics program?

Experiential Exercise

Discipline or Not?

Written and copyrighted by Gary Dessler, PhD.

Purpose: The purpose of this exercise is to provide you with some experience in analyzing and handling an actual disciplinary action.

Required Understanding: Students should be thoroughly familiar with the facts of the following incident, titled "Botched Batch." **Do not read the "award" or "discussion" sections until after the groups have completed their deliberations.**

How to Set Up the Exercise/Instructions: Divide the class into groups of four or five students. Each group should take the arbitrator's point of view and assume that they are to analyze the case and make the arbitrator's decision. Review the case again at this point, but please do not read the award and discussion sections.

Each group should answer the following questions:

14-13. Based on what you read in this chapter, including all relevant guidelines, what would your decision be if you were the arbitrator? Why?

14-14. Do you think that after their experience in this arbitration the parties involved will be more or less inclined to settle grievances by themselves without resorting to arbitration?

Botched Batch:

Facts: A computer department employee made an entry error that botched an entire run of computer reports. Efforts to rectify the situation produced a second set of improperly run reports. Because of the series of errors, the employer incurred extra costs of $2,400, plus a weekend of overtime work by other computer department staffers. Management suspended the employee for 3 days for negligence, and revoked a promotion for which the employee had previously been approved.

Protesting the discipline, the employee stressed that she had attempted to correct her error in the early stages of the run by notifying the manager of computer operations of her mistake. Maintaining that the resulting string of errors could have been avoided if the manager had followed up on her report and stopped the initial run, the employee argued that she had been treated unfairly because the manager had not been disciplined even though he compounded the problem, whereas she was severely punished. Moreover, citing her "impeccable" work record and management's acknowledgment that she had always been a "model employee," the employee insisted that the denial of her previously approved promotion was "unconscionable."

(Please do **not** *read beyond this point until after you have answered the two questions.)*

Award: The arbitrator upholds the 3-day suspension, but decides that the promotion should be restored.

Discussion: "There is no question," the arbitrator notes, that the employee's negligent act "set in motion the train of events that resulted in running two complete sets of reports reflecting improper information." Stressing that the employer incurred substantial cost because of the error, the arbitrator cites "unchallenged" testimony that management had commonly issued 3-day suspensions for similar infractions in the past. Thus, the arbitrator decides, the employer acted with just cause in meting out an "evenhanded" punishment for the negligence.

Turning to the denial of the already approved promotion, the arbitrator says that this action should be viewed "in the same light as a demotion for disciplinary reasons." In such cases, the arbitrator notes, management's decision normally is based on a pattern of unsatisfactory behavior, an employee's inability to perform, or similar grounds. Observing that management had never before reversed a promotion as part of a disciplinary action, the arbitrator says that by tacking on the denial of the promotion in this case, the employer substantially varied its disciplinary policy from its past practice. Because this action on management's part was not "evenhanded," the arbitrator rules, the promotion should be restored.[153]

Application Case

Enron, Ethics, and Organizational Culture

Written and copyrighted by Gary Dessler, PhD.

For many people, a company called Enron Corp. still ranks as one of history's classic examples of ethics run amok. During the 1990s and early 2000s, Enron was in the business of wholesaling natural gas and electricity. Enron made its money as the intermediary (wholesaler) between suppliers and customers. Without getting into all the details, the nature of Enron's business—and the fact that Enron didn't actually own the assets—meant that its profit statements and balance sheets listing the firm's assets and liabilities were unusually difficult to understand.

It turned out that the lack of accounting transparency enabled the company's managers to make Enron's financial performance look much better than it actually was. Outside experts began questioning Enron's financial statements in 2001. In fairly short order, Enron collapsed, and courts convicted several of its top executives of things like manipulating Enron's reported assets and profitability. Many investors (including former Enron employees) lost all or most of their investments in Enron. In Enron's case, this breakdown is perhaps more perplexing than usual. As one writer said,

> Enron had all the elements usually found in comprehensive ethics and compliance programs: a code of ethics, a

reporting system, as well as a training video on vision and values led by [the company's top executives].[154]

Experts subsequently put forth many explanations for how a company that was apparently so ethical outwardly could actually have been making so many bad ethical decisions without other managers (and the board of directors) noticing. The explanations ranged from a "deliberate concealment of information by officers," to more psychological explanations (such as employees not wanting to contradict their bosses) and the "surprising role of irrationality in decision-making."[155]

But perhaps the most persuasive explanation of how an apparently ethical company could go so wrong concerns organizational culture. The reasoning here is that it's not the rules but what employees feel they should do that determines ethical behavior. For example (speaking in general, not specifically about Enron), the executive director of the Ethics Officer Association put it this way:

> We're a legalistic society, and we've created a lot of laws. We assume that if you just knew what those laws meant that you would behave properly. Well, guess what? You can't write enough laws to tell us what to do at all times every day of the week in every part of the world. We've got to develop the critical thinking and critical reasoning skills of our people because most of the ethical issues that we deal with are in the ethical gray areas.

Questions

14-15. Based on what you read in this chapter, summarize in one page or less how you would explain Enron's ethical meltdown.

14-16. It is said that when one securities analyst tried to confront Enron's CEO about the firm's unusual accounting statements, the CEO publicly used vulgar language to describe the analyst, and that Enron employees subsequently thought doing so was humorous. If true, what does that say about Enron's ethical culture?

14-17. This case and chapter had something to say about how organizational culture influences ethical behavior. What role do you think culture played at Enron? Give five specific examples of things Enron's CEO could have done to create a healthy ethical culture.

Continuing Case

Carter Cleaning Company

Written and copyrighted by Gary Dessler, PhD.

Guaranteeing Fair Treatment

Being in the laundry and cleaning business, the Carters feel strongly about not allowing employees to smoke, eat, or drink in their stores. Jennifer was therefore surprised to walk into a store and find two employees eating lunch at the front counter. There was a large pizza in its box, and the two of them were sipping colas and eating slices of pizza and submarine sandwiches off paper plates. Not only did it look messy, but there were grease and soda spills on the counter, and the store smelled from onions and pepperoni, even with the exhaust fan pulling air out through the roof. In addition to being a turnoff to customers, the mess on the counter meant that a customer's order might actually become soiled in the store.

Although this was a serious matter, Jennifer didn't feel that what the counter people were doing was grounds for dismissal (partly because the store manager had apparently condoned their actions). It seemed to her that the matter called for more than just a warning but less than dismissal.

Questions

14-18. What would you do if you were Jennifer, and why?

14-19. Should a disciplinary system be established at Carter Cleaning?

14-20. If so, what should it cover? How would you suggest it deal with a situation such as the one with the errant counter people?

14-21. How would you deal with the store manager?

Translating Strategy into HR Policies and Practices Case*,§

**The accompanying strategy map for this chapter is in MyLab Management; the overall map in the inside back cover of this text outlines the relationships involved.*

Improving Performance at the Hotel Paris

The Hotel Paris's New Ethics, Justice, and Fair Treatment Process

The Hotel Paris's competitive strategy is "To use superior guest service to differentiate the Hotel Paris properties, and to thereby increase the length of stay and return rate of guests, and thus boost revenues and profitability." HR manager Lisa Cruz must now formulate functional policies and activities that support this competitive strategy, by eliciting the required employee behaviors and competencies.

As the head of HR for the Hotel Paris, Lisa Cruz was especially concerned about her company maintaining the highest ethical standards. Her concerns were twofold. First, there are, in any single hotel each day, at least a dozen people (including housekeepers, front-desk clerks, security guards, and so on) with easy access to guests' rooms, and to their personal belongings. Guests—many younger, and many unwary—are continually walking the halls unprotected. So, in a service company like this, there is simply no margin for ethical errors.

But she was concerned about ethics for a second reason. She knew that employees do not like being treated unfairly, and that unfairness in any form could manifest itself in low morale and in diminished performance. She wondered if her employees' low morale and engagement—as measured by her firm's attitude surveys—stemmed, in part, from what they perceived as unjust treatment. Lisa therefore turned to the task of assessing and redesigning the Hotel Paris's ethics, justice, and fair treatment practices.

When she sat with the CFO to discuss her proposal for the Hotel Paris's fairness, justice, and ethics system, Lisa came armed with some research. In 2003, the *Journal of Applied Psychology* published a study that showed how improving the level of interpersonal and procedural justice in a service company can lead to improved employee attitudes and performance and thus to improved hotel performance.[156] And the study was done in a hotel chain.

In this study, the researchers collected employee survey data from a hotel chain's 111 different hotels in the United States and Canada. The employee services department of this hotel chain obtained completed

§ Written and copyrighted by Gary Dessler, PhD.

surveys from 8,832 of the hotel's employees. The researchers also obtained data on employee turnover as well as on the employees' commitment, employees' intentions to remain with the organization, and guest satisfaction.

Clearly, having fair and just procedures in place affected these hotels' employee morale and behavior, and thus company performance—they could even measure the links. For example, procedural justice and interpersonal justice were related to increased levels of employees' satisfaction with supervision.

For Lisa and the CFO, these results supported, in a measurably defensible way, the idea that spending the money required to improve procedural and interpersonal justice would likely improve employee attitudes and behaviors (employee commitment, discretionary service behavior, and employee turnover), and, thereby, improve guest satisfaction and company performance.

Lisa and her HR team took steps to institute new ethics, justice, and fair treatment practices at the Hotel Paris. Working with the company's general counsel, they produced and presented to the CEO a new Hotel Paris code of ethics, as well as a more complete set of ethical guidelines. These now appear on the Hotel Paris's careers Web site link, and are part of each new employee's orientation packet. They contracted with a vendor to provide a customized, Web-based ethics training program, and made it clear that the first employees to participate in it were the company's top executives.

Lisa and her team then proceeded methodically through the company's entire HR process, starting with recruitment and selection. The selection process now includes an honesty test. New guidelines ensure an open and fair performance appraisal process. The team completely revamped the hotel's disciplinary process. They instituted a new appeals process that included appeals to each hotel's manager, and then to Lisa Cruz, and finally to a top management executive appeals committee. They instituted a new discipline without punishment system.

After 6 months of operating under the new system, several changes are evident. Surveys Lisa took before the new program, and now, indicate a significant upward movement in the employees' perceptions of "consistent and equitable treatment of all employees." Grievances are down by 80%, 95% of employees are able to quote the ethics code, employee morale and commitment are up, and, in general, employee service–type behaviors (such as greeting guests in a friendly manner) have increased, too. Lisa and the CFO are pleased with the new system, and are optimistic it will also help to improve customer service satisfaction.

Questions

14-22. Based on what you learned in this chapter of Dessler *Human Resource Management*, what do you think of the adequacy and effectiveness of the steps Lisa has taken so far?

14-23. List three more specific steps Hotel Paris should take with respect to each individual human research function (selection, training, and so on) to improve the level of ethics in the company.

14-24. Based on what you learned in this chapter, write a short (less than one page) explanation Lisa can use to sell to top management the need to further improve the hotel chain's fairness and justice processes.

Writing Assignments

14-25. What techniques would you use as alternatives to traditional discipline? Why do you think alternatives like these are important, given industry's need today for highly engaged and committed employees?

14-26. Using several "Best Companies to Work For" as examples, explain what you would do to improve employee relations in an organization.

MyLab Management Try It!

How would you apply the concepts and skills you learned in this chapter? If your professor has assigned this activity, go to the Assignments section of **www.pearson.com/mylab/management** to complete the simulation.

PERSONAL INVENTORY ASSESSMENTS

Go to **www.pearson.com/mylab/management** to complete the Personal Inventory Assessment related to this chapter.

Key Terms

employee relations, 455
fair treatment, 455
procedural justice, 456
distributive justice, 456
social responsibility, 457
organizational climate, 458
suggestion teams, 459
problem-solving teams, 459
quality circle, 459
self-managing/self-directed work team, 459
ethics, 461
organizational culture, 464
Electronic Communications Privacy Act (ECPA), 466

Ethics Quiz Answers

Quiz is on page 461.

1. 34% said personal e-mail on company computers is wrong.
2. 37% said using office equipment for schoolwork is wrong.
3. 49% said playing computer games at work is wrong.
4. 54% said Internet shopping at work is wrong.
5. 61% said it's unethical to blame your error on technology.
6. 87% said it's unethical to visit pornographic sites at work.
7. 33% said $25 is the amount at which a gift from a supplier or client becomes troubling, while 33% said $50, and 33% said $100.
8. 35% said a $50 gift to the boss is unacceptable.
9. 12% said a $50 gift from the boss is unacceptable.
10. 70% said it's unacceptable to take the $200 football tickets.
11. 70% said it's unacceptable to take the $120 theater tickets.
12. 35% said it's unacceptable to take the $100 food basket.
13. 45% said it's unacceptable to take the $25 gift certificate.
14. 40% said it's unacceptable to take the $75 raffle prize.
15. 11% reported they lie about sick days.
16. 4% reported they take credit for the work or ideas of others.

Endnotes

1. "When the Jobs Inspector Calls," *The Economist*, March 31, 2012, p. 73. For an in-depth description of this situation, see www.theguardian.com/technology/2017/jun/18/foxconn-life-death-forbidden-city-longhua-suicide-apple-iphone-brian-merchant-one-device-extract, accessed May 12, 2018.
2. "Workforce Compensation and Performance Service, Office of Performance and Compensation Systems Design, Classification Programs Division," July 1999, HRCD-7; "Employee Relations," *HR Magazine* 55, no. 7 (July 2010), p. SS-4.
3. See, for example, Chris Long et al., "Fairness Monitoring: Linking Managerial Controls and Fairness Judgments in Organizations," *Academy of Management Journal* 54, no. 3 (2012), pp. 1045–1068. Furthermore, it's not just how management treats its own employees; employees also take their signals from how it treats external parties such as customers and the general public. Benjamin Dunford, Christine Jackson, Alan Boss, Louis Tay, and R. Wayne Boss, "Be Fair, Your Employees Are Watching: A Relational Response Model of External Third-Party Justice," *Personnel Psychology*, 68 (2015), pp. 319–352.
4. Bennett Tepper, "Consequences of Abusive Supervision," *Academy of Management Journal* 43, no. 2 (2000), pp. 178–190. See also Samuel Aryee et al., "Antecedents and Outcomes of Abusive Supervision: A Test of a Trickle-Down Model," *Journal of Applied Psychology* 92, no. 1 (2007), pp. 191–201; and Lingyan Hu and Yan Liu, "Abuse for Status: A Social Dominance Perspective of Abusive Supervision," *Human Resource Management Review* 27 (2017), pp. 328–337.
5. Mindy Shoss et al., "Blaming the Organization for Abusive Supervision: The Roles of Perceived Organizational Support and Supervisor's Organizational Embodiment," *Journal of Applied Psychology* 98, no. 1 (2013), pp. 158–168.
6. Sean Hannah et al., "Joint Influences of Individual and Work Unit of Abusive Supervision on Ethical Intentions and Behaviors: A Moderated Mediation Model," *Journal of Applied Psychology* 98, no. 4 (2013), pp. 579–592.
7. Michelle Donovan et al., "The Perceptions of Fair Interpersonal Treatment Scale: Development and Validation of a Measure of Interpersonal Treatment in the Workplace," *Journal of Applied Psychology* 83, no. 5 (1998), pp. 683–692. For another example of such a scale, see James F. Devlin et al., "Perceptions of Fair Treatment in Financial Services: Development, Validation and Application of a Fairness Measurement Scale," *European Journal of Marketing*, July 2014.
8. Bennett Tepper et al., "Abusive Supervision and Subordinates' Organization Deviance," *Journal of Applied Psychology* 93, no. 4 (2008), pp. 721–732.
9. Jordan Robbins et al., "Perceived Unfairness and Employee Health: A Meta-Analytic Integration," *Journal of Applied Psychology* 97, no. 2 (2012), pp. 235–272.
10. Dawn Carlson et al., "The Fallout from Abusive Supervision: An Examination of Subordinates and Their Partners," *Personnel Psychology* 60, no. 4 (2011), pp. 937–961.
11. Marie Mitchell and Maureen Ambrose, "Employees' Behavioral Reactions to Supervisor Aggression: An Examination of Individual and Situational Factors," *Journal of Applied Psychology* 97, no. 6 (2012), pp. 1148–1170.
12. Andrew Woolum et al. "Rude Colored Glasses: The Contaminating Effects of Witnessed Morning Rudeness on Perceptions and Behaviors throughout the Workday," *Journal of Applied Psychology* 102, no. 12 (2017), pp. 1658–1672.
13. Gary Weaver and Linda Treviño, "The Role of Human Resources in Ethics/Compliance Management: A Fairness Perspective," *Human Resource Management Review* 11 (2001), p. 117; Shahidul Hassan, "Does Fair Treatment in the Workplace Matter? An Assessment of Organizational Fairness and Employee Outcomes in Government," *The American Review of Public Administration* 43, no. 5 (September 1, 2013), pp. 539–557.
14. Suzanne Masterson, "A Trickle-Down Model of Organizational Justice: Relating Employees' and Customers' Perceptions of and Reactions to Fairness," *Journal of Applied Psychology* 86, no. 4 (2001), pp. 594–601. See also Jane O'Reilly, Karl Aquino, and Daniel Skarlicki, "The Lives of Others: Third Parties Responses to Others' Injustice," *Journal of Applied Psychology* 101, no. 2 (2016), pp. 171–189.
15. Based on Daniel Denison, *Corporate Culture and Organizational Effectiveness* (New York: Wiley, 1990), p. 155. See also Christian Voegetlin and Michele Greenwood, "Corporate Social Responsibility and Human Resource Management: A Systematic Review and Conceptual Analysis," *Human Resource Management Review* 26 (2016), pp. 181–197.
16. "When the Jobs Inspector Calls," p. 73. See also, www.theguardian.com/technology/2017/jun/18/foxconn-life-death-forbidden-city-longhua-suicide-apple-iphone-brian-merchant-one-device-extract, accessed May 12, 2018.
17. Alexandra Ho and Tim Culpan, with assistance from Jun Yang in Seoul, Andrea Wong in Taipei, Tian Ying in Beijing, and Jasmine Wang in Hong Kong, "Foxconn Labor Disputes Disrupt IPhone Output for 2nd Time," *Bloomberg News*, October 8, 2012, www.bloomberg.com/news/2012-10-07/foxconn-labor-disputes-disrupt-iphone-output-for-2nd-time.html, accessed April 14, 2013. See also, "Foxconn Confirms Dispute between Workers at China Factory," https://www.cnet.com/news/foxconn-confirms-dispute-between-workers-at-china-factory/, accessed March 30, 2017.
18. Ibid.
19. Teresa Daniel, "Tough Boss or Workplace Bully?" *HR Magazine*, June 2009, pp. 83–86.
20. Christian Kiewitz et al., "Suffering in Silence: Investigating the Role of Fear in the Relationship between Abusive Supervision and Defensive Silence," *Journal of Applied Psychology* 101, no. 5 (2016), pp. 731–742; see also Christopher Rosen et al., "Who Strikes Back? A Daily Investigation of When and Why Incivility Begets Incivility," *Journal of Applied Psychology* 101, no. 11 (2016), pp. 1620–1634.
21. Eugene Kim and Theresa Glomb, "Get Smarty-Pants: Cognitive Ability, Personality, and Victimization," *Journal of Applied Psychology* 95, no. 3 (2010), pp. 889–901. See also Jaclyn Jensen et al., "Is It Better to Be Average? High and Low Performance as Predictors of Employee Victimization," *Journal of Applied Psychology* 90, no. 2 (2014), pp. 296–309.
22. Eugene Kim and Teresa Glomb, "Victimization of High Performers: The Roles of Envy and Work Group Identification," *Journal of Applied Psychology* 9, no. 4 (2014), pp. 619–634.

23. Kiewitz, "Suffering in Silence," op. cit. In another study, high-performing employees were more likely to become victims of covert victimization, while low performers were more often victims of overt victimization. Jaclyn Jensen, Jana Raver, and Pankaj Patel, "Is It Better to Be Average? High and Low Performance as Predictors of Employee Victimization," *Journal of Applied Psychology* 99, no. 2 (2014), pp. 296–309.
24. Martin Berman-Gorvine, "It Takes More Than Words to Stop Workplace Bullying," *Bloomberg BNA Bulletin to Management*, June 20, 2017.
25. http://view.fdu.edu/default.aspx?id?3529, accessed September 6, 2012.
26. Ibid.
27. Carolyn Hirschman, "Giving Voice to Employee Concerns: Encouraging Employees to Speak Out Requires Respectful Treatment and Appropriate Action," *HR Magazine* 53, no. 8 (August 2008), pp. 50–54.
28. Everett Spain and Boris Groysberg, "Making Exit Interviews Count," *Harvard Business Review*, April 2016, https://hbr.org/2016/04/making-exit-interviews-count, accessed April 3, 2018.
29. See, for example, Benjamin Schneider et al, "Organizational Climate and Culture," *Annual Review of Psychology* 64 (2013), pp. 361–388.
30. Rachel Silverman, "Are You Happy in Your Job? Bosses Push Weekly Surveys," *The Wall Street Journal*, December 3, 2014, pp. B1, B4.
31. Laszlo Bock, *Work Rules!* (New York: 12, 2015), pp. 140–142.
32. "Survey: Employee Survey Number One," www.shrm.org/templatestools/samples/HRforms, accessed April 11, 2012.
33. Pat Lenius, "Murray Supply Host Recognition Dinner," *Supply House Times*, May 2011, p. 70.
34. SHRM Survey Findings: Employee Recognition Programs, Winter 2012. In collaboration with and commissioned by Globoforce (www.globoforce.com).
35. This is based on "Recognition: Awards Checklist," August 22, 2014, https://www.shrm.org/resourcesandtools/tools-and-samples/hr-forms/pages/recognition_awardschecklist.aspx, accessed April 3, 2018.
36. https://online-rewards.com/program/employee-recognition/; www.globoforce.com/how-it-works/; and www.thanksbox.co/solutions/reward-and-recognition/, all accessed April 2, 2018.
37. Martin Berman-Gorvine, "Honoring Workers Can Boost Employer's Bottom Line," *Bloomberg BNA Bulletin to Management*, July 18, 2017.
38. http://mashable.com/follow/topics/pinterest, accessed April 15, 2012.
39. "Over Half of Employers Use Social Media for Internal Communications, Survey Reveals," *Bloomberg BNA Bulletin to Management*, June 4, 2013, p. 179.
40. http://mashable.com/2012/04/06/pinterest-employee-engagement/, accessed April 15, 2012.
41. Tamara Lytle, "Giving Employees a Say: Getting—and Acting on—Ideas Offered by Employees Can Save Employers Money and Build a Sense of Ownership among Workers," *HR Magazine* 56, no. 10 (October 2011), pp. 69–74.
42. James H. Shonk, *Team-Based Organizations* (Chicago: Irwin, 1997), pp. 27–33.
43. Everett Adams Jr., "Quality Circle Performance," *Journal of Management* 17, no. 1 (1991), pp. 25–39; "Quality Circle", https://www.economist.com/node/14301388, accessed April 3, 2018.
44. See, for example, Jack Orsburn et al., *Self-Directed Teams* (Homewood, IL: Business One Irwin, 1990), p. 8; http://sloanreview.mit.edu/article/how-to-lead-a-selfmanaging-team/, accessed July 14, 2014.
45. Charles Fishman, "Engines of Democracy," *Fast Company*, October 1999, pp. 173–202.
46. "GE Aviation Plans to Open New Plant in NC," June 17, 2013, https://www.yahoo.com/news/ge-aviation-plans-open-plant-162304601.html, accessed April 3, 2018.
47. Susan Wells, "From Ideas to Results: To Get the Most from Your Company's Suggestion System, Move Ideas up the Ladder through a Formal Process," *HR Magazine* 50, no. 2 (February 2005), pp. 54–59; Rebecca Hastings, "Survey: Employees Have Plenty of Suggestions," www.shrm.org/HRdisciplines/employeerelations/articles, February 29, 2012, accessed April 15, 2012.
48. Based on Wells, "From Ideas to Results."
49. Ibid.
50. This is quoted from ibid. For another example, see H. Goa, "Application of the Suggestion System in the Improvement of the Production Process and Product Quality Control," *Materials Science and Engineering*, 2016; http://iopscience.iop.org/article/10.1088/1757-899X/145/6/062005/pdf, accessed April 3, 2018.
51. Alex Rosenblat, "What Motivates Gig Economy Workers," https://hbr.org/2016/11/what-motivates-gig-economy-workers, accessed March 30, 2017; Mark Feffer, "What Benefits Can Companies Offer Gig Workers?" March 21, 2017, https://www.shrm.org/resourcesandtools/hr-topics/benefits/pages/what-benefits-can-companies-offer-gig-workers.aspx, accessed March 30, 2017; Mukesh Gupta, "Strategies for Employee Engagement in a Gig Economy," http://www.digitalistmag.com/future-of-work/2017/02/03/strategies-for-employee-engagement-in-gig-economy-04887378, accessed March 30, 2017; Jenny Perkins, "Employee Engagement in the Gig Economy," http://www.cirrus-connect.com/blog/employee-engagement-in-the-gig-economy-10875, accessed March 30, 2017.
52. Mark Feffer, "Ethical vs. Legal Responsibilities for HR Professionals," Society for Human Resource Management, March 30, 2017, https://www.shrm.org/resourcesandtools/hr-topics/behavioral-competencies/ethical-practice/pages/ethical-and-legal-responsibilities-for-hr-professionals.aspx, accessed April 3, 2018.
53. Kevin Wooten, "Ethical Dilemmas in Human Resource Management: An Application of a Multidimensional Framework, A Unifying Taxonomy, and Applicable Codes," *Human Resource Management Review* 11 (2001), p. 161. See also Sean Valentine et al., "Employee Job Response as a Function of Ethical Context and Perceived Organization Support," *Journal of Business Research* 59, no. 5 (2006), pp. 582–588.
54. Manuel Velasquez, *Business Ethics: Concepts and Cases* (Upper Saddle River, NJ: Prentice Hall, 1992), p. 9. See also O. C. Ferrell, John Fraedrich, and Linda Ferrell, *Business Ethics* (Boston: Houghton Mifflin, 2008).
55. For further discussion of ethics and morality, see Tom Beauchamp and Norman Bowie, *Ethical Theory and Business* (Upper Saddle River, NJ: Prentice Hall, 2001), pp. 1–19.
56. Jennifer Kish-Gephart, David Harrison, and Linda Trevino, "Bad Apples, Bad Cases, and Bad Barrels: Meta-Analytic Evidence about Sources of Unethical Decisions at Work," *Journal of Applied Psychology* 95, no. 1 (2010), pp. 1–31.
57. Sara Morris et al., "A Test of Environmental, Situational, and Personal Influences on the Ethical Intentions of CEOs," *Business and Society*, August 1995, pp. 119–147. See also Dennis Moberg, "Ethics Blind Spots in Organizations: How Systematic Errors in Person's Perception Undermine Moral Agency," *Organization Studies* 27, no. 3 (2006), pp. 413–428; and Scott Reynolds et al., "Automatic Ethics: The Effects of Implicit Assumptions and Contextual Cues on Moral Behavior," *Journal of Applied Psychology* 95, no. 5 (2010), pp. 752–760.
58. David De Cremer, "6 Traits That Predict Ethical Behavior at Work," *Harvard Business Review*, December 22, 2016, https://hbr.org/2016/12/6-traits-that-predict-ethical-behavior-at-work, accessed April 3, 2018.
59. David Welsh, Deidre Snyder, Michael Christian, and Lisa Ordonez, "The Slippery Slope: How Small Ethical Transgressions Pave the Way for Larger Future Transgressions," *Journal of Applied Psychology* 100, no. 1 (2015), pp. 114–127.
60. Ibid., p. 21.
61. Ibid.
62. "Former CEO Joins WorldCom's Indicted," *Miami Herald*, March 3, 2004, p. 4C.
63. Ferrell and Fraedrich, *Business Ethics*, p. 28; adapted from Rebecca Goodell, *Ethics in American Business: Policies, Programs, and Perceptions* (Washington, DC: Ethics Resource Center, 1994), p. 54. For other insights into unethical behavior's causes, see, for example, F. Gino et al., "Nameless + Harmless = Blameless: When Seemingly Irrelevant Factors Influence Judgment of (Un)ethical Behavior," *Organizational Behavior and Human Decision Processes* 111, no. 2 (March 2010), pp. 93–101; and J. Camps et al., "Learning Atmosphere and Ethical Behavior, Does It Make Sense?" *Journal of Business Ethics* 94, no. 1 (June 2010), pp. 129–147.
64. One study suggests that people may not be so selfless. Elizabeth Umphress, John Bingham, and Marie Mitchell, "Unethical Behavior in the Name of the Company: The Moderating Effect of Organizational Identification and Positive Reciprocity Beliefs on Unethical Pro-organizational Behavior," *Journal of Applied Psychology* 95, no. 4 (2010), pp. 769–770.
65. Thomas G. Plante, "Six Ways to Create a Culture of Ethics in Any Organization," *Psychology Today*, July 1, 2015, https://www.psychologytoday.com/us/blog/do-the-right-thing/201507/six-ways-create-culture-ethics-in-any-organization, accessed April 3, 2018.
66. "Ethics Policies Are Big with Employers, but Workers See Small Impact on the Workplace," *BNA Bulletin to Management*, June 29, 2000, p. 201.
67. Guy Brumback, "Managing above the Bottom Line of

Ethics," *Supervisory Management*, December 1993, p. 12. See also E. E. Umphress et al., "The Influence of Distributive Justice on Lying for and Stealing from a Supervisor," *Journal of Business Ethics* 86, no. 4 (June 2009), pp. 507–518; and S. Chen, "The Role of Ethical Leadership versus Institutional Constraints: A Simulation Study of Financial Misreporting by CEOs," *Journal of Business Ethics* 93, part supplement 1 (June 2010), pp. 33–52.

68. Dayton Fandray, "The Ethical Company," *Workforce* 79, no. 12 (December 2000), pp. 74–77. To review Ratheon's ethics code, see https://www.raytheon.com/ourcompany/rtnwcm/groups/gallery/documents/digitalasset/rtn_160603.pdf, accessed April 3, 2018.
69. Plante, "Six Ways to Create a Culture of Ethics in Any Organization."
70. IBM Business Conduct Guidelines, www.ibm.com/investor/pdf/BCG2012.pdf, accessed August 2, 2013.
71. Richard Beatty et al., "HR's Role in Corporate Governance: Present and Prospective," *Human Resource Management* 42, no. 3 (Fall 2003), p. 268.
72. Eric Krell, "How to Conduct an Ethics Audit," *HR Magazine*, April 2010, pp. 48–51.
73. Betsy Shepherd, "Occupational Fraud," *Workforce Management*, April 2012, p. 18.
74. "Ethics Supplier Mentoring Program," https://www.lockheedmartin.com/us/suppliers/ethics.html, accessed April 3, 2018.
75. Richard Girgenti, "As Whistleblowing Surges, Internal Reporting Must Keep Up," *Bloomberg BNA Bulletin to Management*, May 19, 2015, p. 158.
76. Dodd–Frank requires that whistleblowers report concerns of securities law violations to the Securities and Exchange Commission. Sarbanes–Oxley permits claims to the U.S. Labor Department. Greg Stohr, "Corporate Whistleblower Protections Cut by US High Court," *Bloomberg BNA Bulletin to Management*, February 27, 2018.
77. David Mayer et al., "Who Displays Ethical Leadership, and Why Does It Matter? An Examination of Antecedents and Consequences of Ethical Leadership," *Academy of Management Journal* 55, no. 1 (2012), p. 167.
78. Martin Berman-Gorvine, "Culture Is Critical to Prevent Employers Behaving Badly," *Bloomberg BNA Bulletin to Management*, July 4, 2017.
79. Boris Groysberg et al., "The Leader's Guide to Corporate Culture," *Harvard Business Review*, January–February 2018, pp. 51–53.
80. Sometimes the most straightforward way of changing a company's culture is to move fast to change its top management. See Jeremy Smerd, "A Stalled Culture Change?" *Workforce Management*, December 14, 2009, pp. 1, 3.
81. Groysberg et al., "The Leader's Guide to Corporate Culture."
82. "Ethics: It Isn't Just the Big Guys," *The American Intelligence Wire*, July 28, 2003, p. 10.
83. Based on "Ethics: It Isn't Just the Big Guys."
84. "Assessment & Selection," https://www.opm.gov/policy-data-oversight/assessment-and-selection/other-assessment-methods/integrityhonesty-tests/, accessed April 3, 2018.
85. "Ethical Issues in the Management of Human Resources," *Human Resource Management Review* 11 (2001), p. 6; Joel Lefkowitz, "The Constancy of Ethics amidst the Changing World of Work," *Human Resource Management Review* 16 (2006), pp. 245–268; William Byham, "Can You Interview for Integrity?" *Across the Board* 41, no. 2 (March/April 2004), pp. 34–38; Evan Offstein and Ronald Dufresne, "Building Strong Ethics and Promoting Positive Character Development: The Influence of HRM at the United States Military Academy at West Point," *Human Resource Management* 46, no. 1 (Spring 2007), pp. 95–114.
86. Gary Weaver and Linda Treviño, "The Role of Human Resources in Ethics/Compliance Management: A Fairness Perspective," *Human Resource Management Review* 11 (2001), p. 123. See also Linda Andrews, "The Nexus of Ethics," *HR Magazine*, August 2005, pp. 53–58.
87. Russell Cropanzano and Thomas Wright, "Procedural Justice and Organizational Staffing: A Tale of Two Paradigms," *Human Resource Management Review* 13, no. 1 (2003), pp. 7–40.
88. Kathryn Tyler, "Do the Right Thing: Ethics Training Programs Help Employees Deal with Ethical Dilemmas," *HR Magazine*, February 2005, pp. 99–102; Diana E. Murphy, "The Federal Sentencing Guidelines for Organizations: A Decade of Promoting Compliance and Ethics," https://www.ussc.gov/sites/default/files/pdf/training/organizational-guidelines/selected-articles/Murphy1.pdf, accessed April 3, 2018.
89. "Ethical Issues in the Management of Human Resources," p. 6.
90. Weaver and Treviño, "The Role of Human Resources in Ethics/Compliance Management," p. 123.
91. https://www.lockheedmartin.com/us/who-we-are/ethics/training.html, accessed April 3, 2018.
92. Robert Grossman, "Executive Discipline," *HR Magazine*, August 2005, pp. 46–51. See also Jean Thilmany, "Supporting Ethical Employees," *HR Magazine* 52, no. 9 (September 2007), pp. 105–106, 108, 110, 112.
93. See, for example, https://www.raytheon.com/rtnwcm/groups/public/documents/content/rtn_ethics-code.pdf accessed April 4, 2018; https://www.lockheedmartin.com/content/dam/lockheed/data/corporate/documents/ethics/code-of-conduct.pdf, accessed April 4, 2018.
94. Lisa Bigelow, "What Happens to an Employee If He Violated the Code of Conduct?" http://smallbusiness.chron.com/happens-employee-violated-code-conduct-16118.html, accessed April 4, 2018.
95. https://wmich.edu/hr/handbook-conduct, accessed April 4, 2018.
96. Liz Mineo, "On Internet Privacy, Be Very Afraid," *The Harvard Gazette*, August 24, 2017.
97. Lee Rainie, "The State of Privacy in Post-Snowden America," Pew Research Center, September 21, 2016, http://www.pewresearch.org/fact-tank/2016/09/21/the-state-of-privacy-in-america/, accessed April 4, 2018.
98. Morris Attaway, "Privacy in the Workplace on the Web," *Internal Auditor* 58, no. 1 (February 2010), p. 30. See also, Kenny Brown, "What Are Employee Privacy Rights?" http://smallbusiness.chron.com/employee-privacy-rights-1239.html, accessed March 30, 2017.
99. Declam Leonard and Angela France, "Workplace Monitoring: Balancing Business Interests with Employee Privacy Rights," *Society for Human Resource Management Legal Report*, May–June 2003, pp. 3–6. See also, "Workplace Privacy," The American Civil Liberties Union, https://www.aclu.org/issues/privacy-technology/workplace-privacy, accessed April 4, 2018.
100. "Workplace Privacy," The American Civil Liberties Union, https://www.aclu.org/issues/privacy-technology/workplace-privacy, accessed April 4, 2018.
101. https://www.ceridian.com/company/corporate/corporate-privacy-policy, accessed April 4, 2018.
102. *Vega-Rodriguez v. Puerto Rico Telephone Company*, CA1, #962061, 4/8/97, discussed in "Video Surveillance Withstands Privacy Challenge," *BNA Bulletin to Management*, April 17, 1997, p. 121. Also see, J. Greenwald, "Monitoring Communications? Know Legal Pitfalls," *Business Insurance* 45, no. 6 (February 7, 2011), pp. 1, 17; and Workplace Monitoring Laws, SHRM, https://www.shrm.org/ResourcesAndTools/hr-topics/employee-relations/Documents/State%20surveillance%20and%20monitoring%20laws.pdf, accessed April 4, 2018.
103. Fredric Leffler and Lauren Palais, "Filter Out Perilous Company E-Mails," *Society for Human Resource Management Legal Report*, August 2008, p. 3. A survey of 220 large U.S. firms suggests that about 38% of them have people reading or otherwise analyzing employees' outgoing e-mail. See Dionne Searcey, "Some Courts Raise Bar on Reading Employee Email," *The Wall Street Journal*, November 19, 2009, p. A17.
104. Bill Roberts, "Stay Ahead of the Technology Use Curve," *HR Magazine*, October 2008, pp. 57–61.
105. "After Employer Found Liable for Worker's Child Porn, Policies May Need to Be Revisited," *BNA Bulletin to Management*, March 21, 2006, p. 89.
106. One attorney notes that problems can arise with the Federal Stored Communications Act if the employer uses illicit or coercive means to access the employee's private social media accounts. *Bloomberg BNA Bulletin to Management*, July 21, 2009, p. 225.
107. Brittany Petersen, "Employee Monitoring: It's Not Paranoia; You Really Are Being Watched!" *PC Magazine*, May 26, 2008, https://www.pcmag.com/article2/0,2817,2308363,00.asp, accessed April 4, 2018; For one such software package, see https://www.veriato.com/?utm_source=ss2018&utm_medium=redirect&utm_campaign=ssredirect, accessed April 4, 2018.
108. Searcey, "Some Courts Raise Bar on Reading Employee E-mail."
109. "When Can an Employer Access Private E-Mail on Its System?" *Bloomberg BNA Bulletin to Management*, July 14, 2009, p. 224; one employment lawyer says that courts look to whether the employer's process is reasonable when determining if the employer's monitoring practices are acceptable. Electronic monitoring is generally reasonable "where there is a legitimate business purpose, where policies exist to set the privacy expectations of employees, and where employees are informed of the rules and understand the

methods used to monitor the workplace." Nicole Kamm, "Bodyguard for Electronic Information," *HR Magazine*, January 2010, pp. 57–58.
110. Lee Michael Katz, "Big Employer Is Watching," *HR Magazine*, June 2015, pp. 67–74.
111. Bill Roberts, "Are You Ready for Biometrics?" *HR Magazine*, March 2003, pp. 95–96.
112. "Disgruntled Workers' Hacking of Employers Is on the Rise, FBI–DHS Public Alert Says," *Bloomberg BNA Bulletin to Management*, October 7, 2014, p. 315.
113. Steve Lohr, "Unblinking Eyes Track Employees," *The New York Times*, June 22, 2014, pp. 1, 15.
114. Claire Suddath, "Tesco Monitors Employees with Motorola on Bands," www.BusinessWeek.com/articles/2013-02-13/Tescomonitors_employees-withMotorola-arm-bands, accessed February 14, 2013.
115. Lester Bittel, *What Every Supervisor Should Know* (New York: McGraw-Hill, 1974), p. 308; and Thomas Salvo, "Practical Tips for Successful Progressive Discipline," SHRM White Paper, July 2004, www.shrm.org/hrresources/whitepapers_published/CMS_009030.asp, accessed January 5, 2008.
116. For fair discipline guidelines, see Bittel, *What Every Supervisor Should Know*, p. 308; Paul Falcone, "Fundamentals of Progressive Discipline," *HR Magazine*, February 1997, pp. 90–92; and "How to Discipline and Fire Employees," www.entrepreneur.com/article/79928, accessed May 3, 2012.
117. David Mayer et al., "When Do Fair Procedures Not Matter? A Test of the Identity Violation Effect," *Journal of Applied Psychology*, 94, no. 1 (2009), pp. 142–161.
118. Long Wang and J. Keith Murnighan, "The Dynamics of Punishment and Trust," *Journal of Applied Psychology* 102, no. 10 (2017), pp. 1385–1402.
119. Grossman, "Executive Discipline," pp. 46–51; "The Evil Women Theses," based on Sandra Hartman et al., "Males and Females in a Discipline Situation Exploratory Research on Competing Hypotheses," *Journal of Managerial Issues* 6, no. 1 (Spring 1994), pp. 57, 64–68; "A Woman's Place," *Economist* (August 19, 2000), p. 56.
120. For fair discipline guidelines, see Bittel, *What Every Supervisor Should Know*, p. 308; Falcone, "Fundamentals of Progressive Discipline," pp. 90–92; and "How to Discipline and Fire Employees."
121. https://www.law.cornell.edu/wex/due_process, accessed April 4, 2018.
122. Dick Grote, "Discipline without Punishment," *Across the Board* 38, no. 5 (September 2001), pp. 52–57.
123. http://www.greatplacetowork.com.sg/our-approach/what-is-a-great-workplace, accessed April 12, 2018. For 2017, *Fortune* Magazine's "Best Companies to Work For" included (from 1 to 10) Google, Wegmans Food Markets, Boston Consulting Group, Baird, Edward Jones, Genentech, Ultimate Software, Salesforce, Acuity, and Quicken Loans. *Fortune*, March 15, 2017, pp. 84–87.
124. http://www.greatplacetowork.com/best-companies#sthash.ECoNqRRH.dpbs, accessed July 17, 2015.
125. Ibid. Another thing that makes these companies "great places to work" is an emphasis on building a sense of community; see Ed Frauenheim, "Community Outreach," *Workforce*, January 2016, pp. 32–35, 49. See also, Martin Berman-Gorvine, "Employee Engagement Starts at The Top," *Bloomberg BNA Bulletin to Management*, January 3, 2017.
126. In *Fortune* Magazine's 2017 listing, SAS was number 15, Google 1, and FedEx 99. *Fortune*, March 15, 2017, pp. 84–136. In their 2018 list, Google (Alphabet) was, oddly, off the list. Michael Bush and Cheryl Lewis-Kulin, "100 Best Companies to Work For 2018," *Fortune*, March 1, 2018, pp. 53–78. However, Alphabet was listed as the number one employer that people want to work for according to LinkedIn (Amazon by that measure was first). https://www.linkedin.com/pulse/linkedin-top-companies-2018-where-us-wants-work-now-daniel-roth, accessed April 1, 2018.
127. http://www.sas.com/en_us/company-information/great-workplace.html, accessed July 17, 2015.
128. https://www.sas.com/en_us/careers.html, accessed March 30, 2017.
129. www.sas.com/content/dam/SAS/en_us/doc/other1/benefits-brochure.pdf; also see www.sas.com/en_us/news/pressreleases/2014/january/greatworkplace-US-Fortune-2014.html, accessed September 8, 2014.
130. Mark Crowley, "How SAS Became the World's Best Place to Work," www.fastcompany.com/300-4953/how-SAS-became-worlds-best-place-to-work, accessed April 8, 2014.
131. Rebecca Leung, "Working the Good Life," www.CBSnews.com/news/working-the-good-life/, accessed July 17, 2015.
132. Ibid.
133. Ibid.
134. Ibid.
135. Ibid.
136. Mark Crowley, "Not a Happy Accident: How Google Deliberately Designed Workplace Satisfaction," www.fastcompany.com/300-7268/where-are-they-now, accessed April 8, 2014.
137. http://US.Greatrated.com/Googlean, accessed April 6, 2014.
138. From "Benefits," Google Careers, https://www.google.co.in/about/careers/lifeatgoogle/benefits/, accessed April 7, 2014. Used by permission from Google Press.
139. Farhad Manjoo, "The Happiness Machine," January 21, 2013, www.slate.com, accessed April 6, 2014.
140. Ibid.; and Greta Roberts, "Why Google's Employee Engagement Programs Are Bad for Your Business," www.talentanalytics.com/blog, accessed April 5, 2014.
141. Manjoo, "The Happiness Machine."
142. Ibid.
143. Ibid.
144. Ibid.
145. Crowley, "Not a Happy Accident: How Google Deliberately Designs Workplace Satisfaction."
146. This is based on Gary Dessler, *Winning Commitment* (New York: McGraw-Hill, 1993), pp. 37–51; "The Federal Express Employee Handbook," August 7, 1989, p. 89; and "FedEx Attributes Success to People-First Philosophy," www.fedex.com/ma/about/overview/philosophy.html, accessed July 18, 2015.
147. Ibid.
148. Ibid.
149. Ibid.
150. http://www.fedex.com/cz_english/about/overview/philosophy.html, accessed July 14, 2014.
151. "Working at SAS: An Ideal Environment for New Ideas," SAS Web site, April 20, 2012. Copyright © SAS Institute Inc., Cary, NC, USA. All Rights Reserved. Used with permission.
152. Based on "Theft Is Unethical," *HR Solutions* 34 (October 2002), p. 66.
153. Bureau of National Affairs, *BNA Bulletin to Management*, September 13, 1985, p. 3.
154. David Gebler, "Is Your Culture a Risk Factor?" *Business and Society Review* 111, no. 3 (Fall 2006), pp. 337–362.
155. John Cohan, "'I Didn't Know' and 'I Was Only Doing My Job': Has Corporate Governance Careened Out of Control? A Case Study of Enron's Information Myopia," *Journal of Business Ethics* 40, no. 3 (October 2002), pp. 275–299.
156. Tony Simons and Quinetta Roberson, "Why Managers Should Care about Fairness: The Effects of Aggregate Justice Perceptions on Organizational Outcomes," *Journal of Applied Psychology* 88, no. 3 (2003), p. 432.

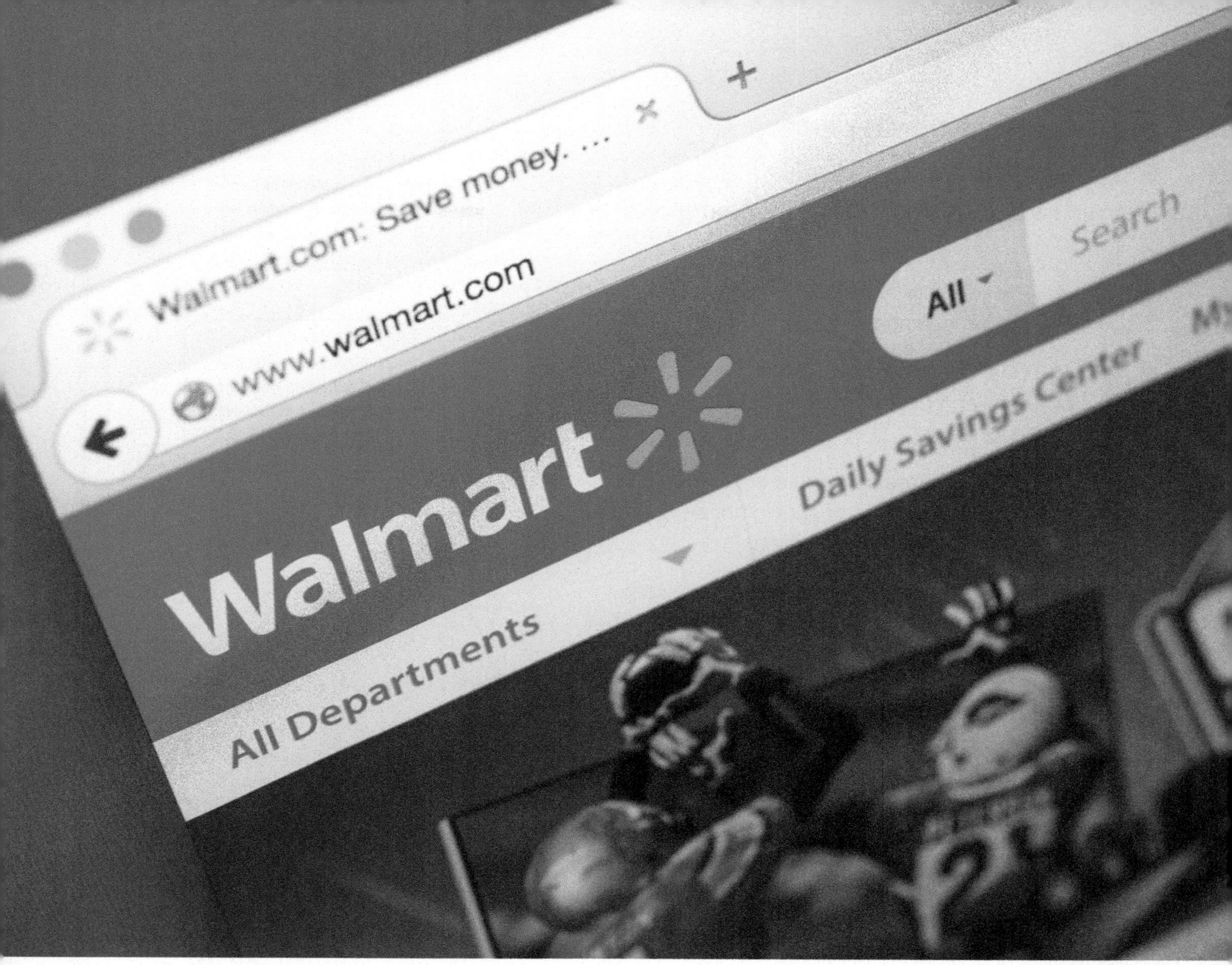

Chrisdorney/Shutterstock

15 Labor Relations and Collective Bargaining

LEARNING OBJECTIVES

When you finish studying this chapter, you should be able to:

15-1 **Present** a brief history of the American labor movement.

15-2 **Give five** examples of unfair union practices and of unfair employer practices in labor law.

15-3 **Present three examples** of what a supervisor should or should not do during the union drive and election.

15-4 **Illustrate with five examples** bargaining that is not in good faith.

15-5 **Develop** a grievance procedure.

15-6 **Give an example** of cooperative labor relations.

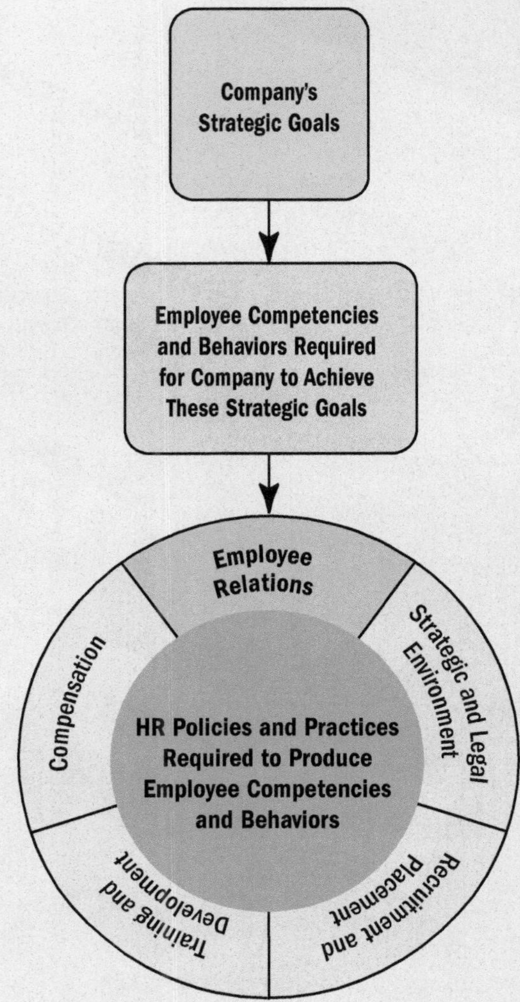

In early 2018, Walmart raised its starting hourly wages to $11 and gave $1,000 bonuses to employees.[1] Walmart's low-cost leader strategy has long meant low wages and personnel costs and difficult labor relations.[2] Walmart's recent pay and bonus moves suggest that its labor relations strategies may be evolving. We'll see if this is happening, and if so, why.

WHERE ARE WE NOW . . .

Chapter 14 focused on employee relations, ethics, and justice—important issues in determining employees' tendencies to join unions. The main purpose of this chapter is to help you deal effectively with unions and grievances. After briefly discussing the **History of the American Labor Movement**, we describe the **Basic Labor Law**, including unfair labor practices. We explain labor negotiations, including the union actions you can expect during **The Union Campaign and Election**. And we explain what you can expect during the actual **Collective Bargaining** sessions, **How to Handle Grievances**, and finally, **Cooperative Labor Relations**.

LEARNING OBJECTIVE 15-1

Present a brief history of the American labor movement.

The Labor Movement

Unions remain influential. Almost 15 million U.S. workers belong to unions—about 11.1% of the total number of men and women working in America.[3] About 36% of public-sector workers belong to unions. In some private-sector industries like utilities (22.3% unionization), and transportation and warehousing (19.6%), it can still be hard to get jobs without joining unions. Unionization also varies widely by state, from a high of 23.8% in New York down to 2.6% in South Carolina.[4]

Furthermore, don't assume that unions affect employers only negatively. For example, perhaps by professionalizing the staff and/or systematizing practices, heart attack mortality among patients in hospitals with unionized nurses was 5% to 9% lower than in nonunion hospitals.[5] Often, employers' labor relations policies evolve, as the accompanying Strategic Context feature illustrates.

IMPROVING PERFORMANCE: *THE STRATEGIC CONTEXT*

Walmart's New HR Strategy

Walmart aims to be retailing's low-cost leader. It minimizes purchasing, site location, distribution, and personnel costs to offer the lowest prices.[6] It consistently blocked entry to unions.

Recently, Walmart revised its strategies, for several reasons. Amazon was pressuring it on prices. The U.S. labor market tightened, which made hiring more challenging. Negative stories about "below living wage" wages and last-minute employee scheduling undermined Walmart's appeal for many consumers. Costco has long parried Walmart's low labor costs by eliciting higher productivity from higher-paid and engaged employees and by maintaining good union relations. Walmart's year-on-year same-store sales drifted down. Its top management had to do something.

Walmart changed its strategy in two ways. First, it bought jet.com for $3.3 billion, in a bid to expand its online efforts. Second, it instituted new HR policies. It raised starting employees' hourly wages to $11 per hour, and awarded up to $1,000 bonuses to most employees. It instituted a new "Pathways" training program to help employees plan Walmart careers and to help them better understand their jobs. Employees also started getting more choice in scheduling their hours.

Early results are promising. Same-store sales are rising, associates' feedback is good, and employment applications are up 5–10%. Whether Walmart's stance toward unions evolves should become apparent over time.

MyLab Management Talk About It 1

If your professor has assigned this, go to the Assignments section of **www.pearson.com/mylab/management** to complete this discussion question. Even before it instituted its new HR policies, Walmart effectively blocked union organizing efforts at its store. If pay was so low and scheduling so troublesome, how do you think they were able to keep unions out?

Support for unions has always ebbed and flowed in America, and today pressures are building against unions. For example, many public employees are unionized, and budget problems prompted several states to reduce public employees' numbers, pensions, and pay.

We'll look at unions and dealing with them in this chapter.

Why Do Workers Organize?

Experts have spent much time and money trying to figure out why workers unionize, and they've proposed many theories. Yet there is no simple answer.

Pay is still important. For example, recent median weekly wages for union workers was $980, versus $776 for nonunion workers.[7] Union workers also generally receive more holidays, sick leave, unpaid leave, health plan benefits, and other benefits—about $14.50 per hour in benefits compared with about $7.50 per hour for nonunion workers.[8]

But it's not just the money. Instead the urge to unionize often comes down to the belief on the part of workers that it's only through unity that they can get their fair share of the "pie" and also protect themselves from the arbitrary whims of management.

VintageCorner/Alamy Stock Photo

Workers at an early Ford factory. In addition to heavy physical labor, workers faced health hazards—poor lighting, dust, and dangerous machinery.

The bottom line is that low morale, fear of job loss, and poor communication (in other words, poor employee relations) also foster unionization. When Kaiser Permanente cut back on vacation and sick leave for its pharmacists, the Guild for Professional Pharmacists won back the lost vacation days. Said one, "Kaiser is a pretty benevolent employer, but there's always the pressure to squeeze a little."[9] One labor relations lawyer says, "The one major thing unions offer is making you a 'for cause' instead of an 'at will' employee, which guarantees a hearing and arbitration if you're fired."[10] So, in practice, low morale, fear of job loss, and arbitrary management actions help foster unionization.[11]

In some respects, things haven't changed much in decades. Here is how one writer describes the motivation behind the early (1900s) unionization of automobile workers:

> In the years to come, economic issues would make the headlines when union and management met in negotiations. But in the early years, . . . the principal grievances of the autoworkers were the speed-up of production and the lack of any kind of job security. As production tapered off, the order in which workers were laid off was determined largely by the whim of foremen and other supervisors. . . . Generally, what the workers revolted against was the lack of human dignity and individuality, and a working relationship that was massively impersonal, cold, and nonhuman. They wanted to be treated like human beings—not like faceless clock card numbers.[12]

HR AND THE GIG ECONOMY: *WILL UBER DRIVERS ORGANIZE?*

For many gig workers, being at the employer's mercy is the biggest downside of gig work. For example, low user ratings can lead to Uber summarily deactivating drivers. Would unionizing help?

Many Uber drivers think so. In New York City pressure from drivers prompted Uber to create a union-like entity known as the Independent Drivers Guild (IDG).[13] The IDG isn't really a union under the law. For instance, Uber funds the Guild, Uber drivers are independent contractors and didn't vote to have the Guild represent them, and the Guild itself agreed not to instigate strikes or to push for forming a union prior to 2021. However, the IDG has established a mechanism through which Uber drivers can appeal deactivations (staffed by other drivers and overseen by the American Arbitration Association) and also provides other types of driver assistance.[14]

MyLab Management Talk About It 2

If your professor has chosen to assign this, go to the Assignments section of **www.pearson.com/mylab/management** to complete these discussion questions. Based on your experience, do you think drivers like those for Uber, Via, and Lyft need union representation? Why?

Employee Engagement and Unionization

Why else do workers unionize? *Modern Survey* conducted a study that measured things such as employees' interest in being represented by a union, confidence in senior management, and employee engagement. It concluded that 50% of "actively disengaged" employees would vote "yes" to unionize, while only 20% of such employees would vote "no union." It concludes that "paying attention to employee engagement levels within your organization helps to foster positive relationships between employees and management and decreases the likelihood of a workforce seeking union representation."[15]

Gallup surveys complement these conclusions. For example, among the over 500 organizations in which Gallup measures employee engagement, 45% of *non*union employees were engaged, while fewer—38%—of unionized employees were engaged.[16]

Findings like these don't prove that engaged employees are less likely to support a unionization effort in their companies, or that unionized employees are less engaged. The findings are correlational, so they only "prove" that when employee engagement goes up, unionization goes down. It could be that the same management policies (such as guaranteed fair treatment systems) affect both employee engagement and nonunionization. But on the whole such findings do suggest that the same sorts of policies (such as good benefits, building trust, and guaranteeing fair treatment) that improve employee engagement may also reduce the likelihood of being unionized.

What Do Unions Want?

We can generalize by saying that unions have two sets of aims, for *union security* and for *improved wages, hours, working conditions, and benefits* for their members.

UNION SECURITY First and probably foremost, unions seek security for themselves. They fight hard for the right to represent a firm's workers, and to be the exclusive bargaining agent for all employees in the unit. (As such, they negotiate contracts for all employees, including those not members of the union.) Five types of union security are possible:

closed shop
A form of union security in which the company can hire only union members. This was outlawed in 1947 but still exists in some industries (such as printing).

union shop
A form of union security in which the company can hire nonunion people, but they must join the union after a prescribed period of time and pay dues. (If they do not, they can be fired.)

agency shop
A form of union security in which employees who do not belong to the union must still pay union dues on the assumption that union efforts benefit all workers.

preferential shop
Union members get preference in hiring, but the employer can still hire nonunion members.

right to work
A term used to describe state statutory or constitutional provisions banning the requirement of union membership as a condition of employment.

1. **Closed shop.**[17] The company can hire only current union members. Congress outlawed closed shops in interstate commerce, but they still exist in some states for particular industries (such as printing). They account for fewer than 5% of union contracts.
2. **Union shop.** The company can hire nonunion people, but they must join the union after a prescribed period and pay dues. (If not, they can be fired.) These account for about 73% of union contracts.
3. **Agency shop.** Employees who do not belong to the union still must pay the union an amount equal to union dues (on the assumption that the union's efforts benefit *all* the workers).
4. **Preferential shop.** Union members get preference in hiring, but the employer can still hire nonunion members.
5. **Maintenance of membership arrangement.** Employees do not have to belong to the union. However, union members employed by the firm must maintain membership in the union for the contract period. These account for about 4% of union agreements.

Not all states give unions the right to require union membership as a condition of employment. **Right to work** is a term used to describe "state statutory or constitutional provisions banning the requirement of union membership as a condition of employment."[18] *Right-to-work laws* don't outlaw unions. They do outlaw (within those states) any form of union security. Recently, there were 28 right-to-work states.[19] Right to work adversely affects union membership levels.[20] After Oklahoma passed right-to-work legislation, its union membership dropped dramatically in the next three years.[21]

IMPROVED WAGES, HOURS, AND BENEFITS Once the union ensures its security at the employer, it fights to improve its members' wages, hours, working conditions, and benefits. The typical labor agreement also gives the union a role in other human resource activities, including recruiting, selecting, compensating, promoting, training, and discharging employees.

The AFL–CIO and the SEIU

The American Federation of Labor and Congress of Industrial Organizations (AFL–CIO) is a voluntary federation of about 57 national and international labor unions in the United States. For many people in the United States, the AFL–CIO is still synonymous with the word *union*.

There are three layers in the AFL–CIO and most other U.S. unions. The worker joins the local union, to which he or she pays dues. The local is in turn a single chapter in the national union. For example, if you were a teacher in Detroit, you would belong to the local union there, which is one of hundreds of local chapters of the American Federation of Teachers, their national union (most unions actually call themselves international unions). The third layer is the national federation, in this case, the AFL–CIO.

The Service Employees International Union (SEIU) is an organization of more than 2.2 million members. It includes the largest health-care union, with more than 1.1 million members, including nurses, LPNs, and doctors, and the second-largest public employees union, with more than 1 million local and state government workers.[22]

Union federation membership is in flux. Some years ago, the SEIU, the International Brotherhood of Teamsters, and UNITE HERE left the AFL–CIO and established their own federation, called the Change to Win Coalition. Together, the departing unions represented over a quarter of the AFL–CIO's membership and budget. Change to Win plans to be more aggressive about organizing workers than they say the AFL–CIO was.[23] More recently UNITE HERE left Change to Win and rejoined the AFL–CIO.

Unions and the Law

LEARNING OBJECTIVE 15-2
Give five examples of unfair union practices and of unfair employer practices in labor law.

The history of the American labor movement is one of expansion and contraction in response to public policy changes. Until about 1930, there were no special labor laws. Employers were not required to engage in collective bargaining with employees and were virtually unrestrained in their behavior toward unions; the use of spies and firing of union agitators were widespread. "Yellow dog" contracts, whereby management could require nonunion membership as a condition for employment, were widely enforced. Most union weapons—even strikes—were illegal.

This situation lasted until the Great Depression (around 1930).[24] Since then, in response to changing public attitudes and economic conditions, labor law has gone through three clear periods: from "strong encouragement" of unions, to "modified encouragement coupled with regulation," and finally to "detailed regulation of internal union affairs."[25]

Norris–LaGuardia Act of 1932
This law marked the beginning of the era of strong encouragement of unions and guaranteed to each employee the right to bargain collectively "free from interference, restraint, or coercion."

National Labor Relations (or Wagner) Act
This law banned certain types of unfair practices and provided for secret-ballot elections and majority rule for determining whether a firm's employees want to unionize.

Period of Strong Encouragement: The Norris–LaGuardia (1932) and National Labor Relations (or Wagner) Acts (1935)

The **Norris–LaGuardia Act of 1932** set the stage for a new era in which union activity was encouraged. It guaranteed to each employee the right to bargain collectively "free from interference, restraint, or coercion." It declared yellow dog contracts unenforceable. And it limited the courts' abilities to issue injunctions (stop orders) for activities such as peaceful picketing and payment of strike benefits.

Yet this act did little to restrain employers from fighting labor organizations. So, in 1935, Congress passed the **National Labor Relations (or Wagner) Act** to add teeth to Norris–LaGuardia. It did this by (1) banning certain unfair labor practices, (2) providing for secret-ballot elections and majority rule for determining whether a firm's employees would unionize, and (3) creating the **National Labor Relations Board (NLRB)** to enforce these two provisions.[26]

National Labor Relations Board (NLRB)
The agency created by the Wagner Act to investigate unfair labor practice charges and to provide for secret-ballot elections and majority rule in determining whether a firm's employees want a union.

UNFAIR EMPLOYER LABOR PRACTICES The Wagner Act deemed "statutory wrongs" (but not crimes) five unfair labor practices used by employers:

1. It is unfair for employers to "interfere with, restrain, or coerce employees" in exercising their legally sanctioned right of self-organization.
2. It is unfair for company representatives to dominate or interfere with either the formation or the administration of labor unions. Among other specific management actions found to be unfair under these first two practices are bribing employees, using company spy systems, moving a business to avoid unionization, and blacklisting union sympathizers.

3. Employers are prohibited from discriminating in any way against employees for their legal union activities.
4. Employers are forbidden to discharge or discriminate against employees simply because the latter file unfair practice charges against the company.
5. Finally, it is an unfair labor practice for employers to refuse to bargain collectively with their employees' duly chosen representatives.

Unions file an unfair labor practice charge (see Figure 15-1) with the National Labor Relations Board. (For example, the American Guild of Musical Artists said it would file an unfair labor charge against the New York City Opera if it cut staff

FIGURE 15-1 NLRB Form 501: Filing an Unfair Labor Practice

Source: From Unfair Labor Practice (ULP) Case Forms, National Labor Relations Board, www.nlrb.gov.

FORM NLRB 501
(2 81)

FORM EXEMPT UNDER
44 U.S.C. 3512

UNITED STATES OF AMERICA
NATIONAL LABOR RELATIONS BOARD
CHARGE AGAINST EMPLOYER

INSTRUCTIONS: File an original and 4 copies of this charge with NLRB Regional Director for the region in which the alleged unfair labor practice occurred or is occurring.	DO NOT WRITE IN THIS SPACE	
	CASE NO.	DATE FILE

1. EMPLOYER AGAINST WHOM CHARGE IS BROUGHT

a. NAME OF EMPLOYER	b. NUMBER OF WORKERS EMPLOYED	
c. ADDRESS OF ESTABLISHMENT (*street and number, city, state, and ZIP code*)	d. EMPLOYER REPRESENTATIVE TO CONTACT	e. PHONE NO.
f. TYPE OF ESTABLISHMENT (*factory, mine, wholesaler, etc.*)	g. IDENTIFY PRINCIPAL PRODUCT OR SERVICE	

h. THE ABOVE-NAMED EMPLOYER HAS ENGAGED IN AND IS ENGAGING IN UNFAIR LABOR PRACTICES WITHIN THE MEANING OF SECTION 8(a), SUBSECTIONS (1) AND ____________ (*list subsections*) OF THE NATIONAL LABOR RELATIONS ACT, AND THESE UNFAIR LABOR PRACTICES ARE UNFAIR LABOR PRACTICES AFFECTING COMMERCE WITHIN THE MEANING OF THE ACT.

2. BASIS OF THE CHARGE (*be specific as to facts, names, addresses, plants involved, dates, places, etc.*)

BY THE ABOVE AND OTHER ACTS, THE ABOVE-NAMED EMPLOYER HAS INTERFERED WITH, RESTRAINED, AND COERCED EMPLOYEES IN THE EXERCISE OF THE RIGHTS GUARANTEED IN SECTION 7 OF THE ACT.

3. FULL NAME OF PARTY FILING CHARGE (*if labor organization, give full name, including local name and number*)

4a. ADDRESS (*street and number, city, state, and ZIP code*)	4b. TELEPHONE NO.

5. FULL NAME OF NATIONAL OR INTERNATIONAL LABOR ORGANIZATION OF WHICH IT IS AN AFFILIATE OR CONSTITUENT UNIT (*to be filled in when charge is filed by a labor organization*)

6. DECLARATION

I declare that I have read the above charge and that the statements therein are true to the best of my knowledge and belief.

By ____________________
(signature of representative or person filing charge) (title, if any)

Address ____________________
(telephone number) (date)

WILLFULLY FALSE STATEMENTS ON THIS CHARGE CAN BE PUNISHED BY FINE AND IMPRISONMENT
(U.S. CODE, TITLE 18, SECTION 1001)

and moved.) The Board then decides whether to take action. Possible actions include dismissal of the complaint, request for an injunction against the employer, or an order that the employer cease and desist.

FROM 1935 TO 1947 Union membership increased quickly after passage of the Wagner Act. Other factors such as an improving economy and aggressive union leadership contributed to this rise. But by the mid-1940s, largely due to massive postwar strikes, public policy began to shift against what many viewed as union excesses. The stage was set for passage of the Taft–Hartley Act.

Period of Modified Encouragement Coupled with Regulation: The Taft–Hartley Act (1947)

Taft–Hartley Act of 1947
Also known as the *Labor Management Relations Act*, this law prohibited unfair union labor practices and enumerated the rights of employees as union members. It also enumerated the rights of employers.

The **Taft–Hartley (*or Labor Management Relations*) Act of 1947** reflected the public's less enthusiastic attitude toward unions. It amended the National Labor Relations (Wagner) Act by limiting unions in four ways: (1) prohibiting unfair union labor practices, (2) enumerating the rights of employees as union members, (3) enumerating the rights of employers, and (4) allowing the president of the United States to bar temporarily national emergency strikes.

Unfair Union Labor Practices

The Taft–Hartley Act enumerated several labor practices that unions were prohibited from engaging in:

1. First, it banned *unions* from *restraining or coercing employees* from exercising their guaranteed bargaining rights. (Some union actions that courts have held illegal include telling an anti-union employee that he or she will lose his or her job once the union gains recognition, and issuing patently false statements during union organizing campaigns.)
2. It is also an unfair labor practice for a union to *cause an employer to discriminate* in any way against an employee so as to encourage or discourage his or her union membership. For example, the union cannot try to force an employer to fire a worker because he or she doesn't attend union meetings or refuses to join a union. There is one exception: Suppose a closed or union shop prevails (and union membership is therefore a prerequisite to employment). Then the union may demand the discharge of someone who fails to pay his or her initiation fees and dues.
3. It is an unfair labor practice for a union to *refuse to bargain in good faith* with the employer about wages, hours, and other employment conditions.
4. It is an unfair labor practice for a union to engage in *featherbedding* (requiring an employer to pay an employee for services not performed).

RIGHTS OF EMPLOYEES The Taft–Hartley Act protected the rights of employees against their unions in other ways. For example, many people felt that compulsory unionism violated the right of freedom of association. Legitimized by Taft–Hartley, new right-to-work laws sprung up in 19 (now 28) states (mainly in the South and Southwest). In New York, for example, in many printing firms you can't work as a press operator unless you belong to a printers' union. In Florida, a right-to-work state, printing shops typically employ both union and nonunion operators. Even today, union membership varies widely by state, from a high of 23.8% in New York to a low of 2.6% in South Carolina.[27] The Taft–Hartley act also required the employee's authorization before the union could subtract dues from his or her paycheck.

In general, the Labor Relations (Taft–Hartley) Act does not restrain unions from unfair labor practices to the extent that the law does employers. It says unions may not restrain or coerce employees. However, "violent or otherwise threatening behavior or clearly coercive or intimidating union activities are necessary before the NLRB will find an unfair labor practice."[28] Examples include physical assaults or threats, economic reprisals, and mass picketing that restrains lawful entry or leaving.

RIGHTS OF EMPLOYERS The Taft–Hartley Act also explicitly gave *employers* certain rights. First, it gave them full freedom to express their views concerning union organization. For example, as a manager you can tell your employees that in your opinion unions are worthless, dangerous to the economy, and immoral. You can even (generally) hint that unionization and high-wage demands might result in the permanent closing of the plant (but not its relocation). Employers can set forth the union's record concerning violence and corruption, if appropriate. In fact, the only major restraint is that employers must avoid threats, promises, coercion, and direct interference with workers who are trying to reach a decision. There can be no threat of reprisal or force or promise of benefit.[29]

Furthermore, the employer (1) cannot meet with employees on company time within 24 hours of an election or (2) suggest to employees that they vote against the union while they are at home or in the employer's office (although he or she can do so while in their work area or where they normally gather).

national emergency strikes
Strikes that might "imperil the national health and safety."

NATIONAL EMERGENCY STRIKES The Taft–Hartley Act also allows the U.S. president to intervene in **national emergency strikes.** These are strikes (for example, by railroad workers) that might "imperil the national health and safety." The president may appoint a board of inquiry and, based on its report, apply for an injunction restraining the strike for 60 days. If the parties don't reach a settlement during that time, the president can have the injunction extended for another 20 days. During this last period, employees take a secret ballot to ascertain their willingness to accept the employer's last offer.

Landrum–Griffin Act of 1959
Also known as the *Labor Management Reporting and Disclosure Act*, this law aimed at protecting union members from possible wrongdoing on the part of their unions.

PERIOD OF DETAILED REGULATION OF INTERNAL UNION AFFAIRS: THE LANDRUM–GRIFFIN ACT (1959) In the 1950s, Senate investigations revealed unsavory practices on the part of some unions, and the result was the **Landrum–Griffin Act (officially, the *Labor Management Reporting and Disclosure Act*) of 1959.** An overriding aim of this act was to protect union members from possible union wrongdoing. Like Taft–Hartley, it also amended the National Labor Relations (Wagner) Act.

First, the act contains a *bill of rights* for union members. It provides for certain rights in the nomination of candidates for union office. It also affirms a member's right to sue his or her union and ensures that the union cannot fine or suspend a member without due process.

This act also laid out rules regarding union elections. For example, national and international unions must elect officers at least once every 5 years, using a secret-ballot mechanism. And the act regulates the kind of person who can serve as a union officer. For example, it bars for a time persons convicted of felonies from holding union officer positions.

Senate investigators also discovered flagrant examples of employer wrongdoing. Employers and their "labor relations consultants" had bribed union agents and officers, for example. Landrum–Griffin therefore expanded the list of unlawful employer actions. For example, companies can no longer pay their own employees to entice them not to join the union.

KNOWLEDGE BASE

The Union Drive and Election

LEARNING OBJECTIVE 15-3
Present three examples of what a supervisor should or should not do during the union drive and election.

It is through the union drive and election that a union tries to be recognized to represent employees. To protect themselves and their employers, supervisors need to understand this process. It has five basic steps.[30]

Step 1. Initial Contact

During the initial contact stage, the union determines the employees' interest in organizing, and establishes an organizing committee.

The initiative for the first contact between the employees and the union may come from the employees, from a union already representing other employees of the firm, or from another union. In any case, there is an initial contact.

Once an employer becomes a target, a union official usually assigns a representative to assess employee interest. The representative visits the firm to determine if enough employees are interested in a campaign, identifies employees who would make good leaders in the organizing campaign, and creates an organizing committee. The aim is to educate the committee about the benefits of forming a union and the law and procedures for forming a local union.

The union must follow certain rules when it starts contacting employees. The law allows organizers to solicit employees for membership as long as the effort doesn't endanger the performance or safety of the employees. Therefore, much contact takes place off the job, perhaps at home or at places near work. Organizers can also safely contact employees on company grounds during off hours (such as lunch or break time). Yet, in practice, there will be much informal organizing going on at the workplace as employees debate organizing. Sometimes the first inkling management has is the distribution of handbills soliciting union membership.

Much soliciting will be via e-mail, but prohibiting employees from sending pro-union e-mail messages using company e-mail isn't easy. You can't discriminate against union activities. Therefore, prohibiting only union e-mail may violate NLRB rules. And barring workers from using e-mail for all non-work-related topics may be futile if the company actually does little to stop it.

LABOR RELATIONS CONSULTANTS Both management and unions typically use "labor relations consultants." These may be law firms, researchers, psychologists, labor relations specialists, or public relations firms. Some are former union organizers.[31]

For the employer, the consultant's services may range from ensuring that the firm properly fills out routine labor relations forms to managing the union campaign. Unions may use public relations firms to improve their image, or specialists to manage corporate campaigns. (These pressure shareholders and creditors to get management to agree to the union's demands.)

Some say consultants encourage questionable tactics. One tactic is to delay the union vote with lengthy hearings at the NLRB. The longer the delay in the vote, they argue, the more time the employer has to drill anti-union propaganda into the employees.

union salting
A union organizing tactic by which workers who are in fact employed full-time by a union as undercover organizers are hired by unwitting employers.

UNION SALTING Unions are not without creative ways to win elections. The National Labor Relations Board defines **union salting** as "placing of union members on non-union job sites for the purpose of organizing." Critics claim that "salts" interfere with business operations and harass employees.[32] The U.S. Supreme Court ruled that union salts are "employees" under the National Labor Relations Act; the NLRB will require that employers pay salts if they fire them for trying to organize.[33] The solution is to know whom you're hiring. However, not hiring someone solely because he or she might be pro-union or a union salt would be discriminatory.[34]

Unions also use *public pressure*. For example, in the past few years, unions have organized about 5,000 Silicon Valley contract workers (such as Facebook shuttle drivers), most of whom are employed by contractors.[35]

When the Unite union set out to organize Facebook shuttle workers, they didn't just pressure the employment contractor (Loop Transportation Inc.). Instead, Unite's campaign publicized how Facebook shuttle drivers had to sleep in their cars to make ends meet; news organizations worldwide ran the story. Soon, with Facebook's acquiescence, Loop Transportation signed a contract with the union and boosted drivers' pay.

Step 2. Obtaining Authorization Cards

authorization cards
In order to petition for a union election, the union must show that at least 30% of employees may be interested in being unionized. Employees indicate this interest by signing authorization cards.

For the union to petition the NLRB for the right to hold an election, it must show that a sizable number of employees may be interested in organizing. Therefore, the next step for union organizers is to try to get the employees to sign **authorization cards** (see Figure 15-2). Among other things, these usually authorize the union to seek a representation election, and state that the employee has applied to join the union. Thirty percent of the eligible employees in an appropriate bargaining unit must sign before the union can petition the NLRB for an election (although that figure may rise to over

FIGURE 15-2 Sample Authorization Card

Source: Gary Dessler, *Fundamentals of Human Resource Management*, Pearson Education, 2019.

SAMPLE UNION of AMERICA
Authorization for Representation

I hereby authorize Local 409 of the SAMPLE union to be my exclusive representative for the purposes of collective bargaining with my employer. I understand that my signature on this card may be used to obtain certification of Local 409 as our exclusive bargaining representative without an election.

This card will verify that I have applied for union membership and that effective ________________ I hereby authorize you to deduct each pay period from my earnings an amount equal to the regular current rate of monthly union dues and initiation fee.

Employer: ______________________ **Worksite:** ______________________

Date: ____________ **Name:** ______________________________________

Street Address: ______________________ **City:**________ **Zip Code:** __________

Home Phone: ___________ **Cell Phone:** _________ **Home E-Mail:** ____________

Department: _______________________

Job Title/Classification: _________________________

Signature: ___________________________________

You must print and mail in this authorization card for it to be recognized. Only original cards are valid and should be submitted. Mail to:

SAMPLE UNION of America, Local 409

301 Sample Way

Miami, FL 33101

50% if the employer has agreed to recognize the union if a majority of employees sign the authorization cards).

This is a dangerous time for supervisors. During this stage, both union and management use propaganda. The union claims it can improve working conditions, raise wages, increase benefits, and generally get the workers better deals. Management can attack the union on ethical and moral grounds and cite the cost of union membership. Management can also explain its accomplishments, express facts and opinions, and explain the law applicable to organizing campaigns. However, neither side can threaten, bribe, or coerce employees. And an employer (or supervisor) may not make promises of benefits to employees or make unilateral changes in terms and conditions of employment that were not planned to be implemented prior to the onset of union organizing activity.

STEPS TO TAKE Management can take several steps with respect to the authorization cards. For example, the NLRB ruled an employer might lawfully inform employees of their right to revoke their authorization cards, even when employees have not asked for such information. The employer can also distribute pamphlets that explain just how employees can revoke their cards. However, the law prohibits any material assistance to employees such as postage or stationery.

Similarly, it is an unfair labor practice to tell employees they can't sign a card. What you *can* do is prepare supervisors so they can explain what the card actually authorizes the union to do—including subjecting the employee to union rules. The union, for instance, may force the employee to picket and fine any member who does not comply. Such explanations can be an effective weapon.

One thing managers should *not* do is look through signed authorization cards if confronted with them by union representatives. The NLRB could construe that as an unfair labor practice, as spying on those who signed. Doing so could also later form the basis of a charge alleging discrimination due to union activity, if the firm subsequently disciplines someone who signed a card.

During this stage, unions can picket the company, subject to three constraints: (1) The union must file a petition for an election within 30 days after the start of picketing; (2) the firm cannot already be lawfully recognizing another union; and (3) there cannot have been a valid NLRB election during the past 12 months.

MyLab Management Apply It!

If your professor has assigned this activity, go to the Assignments section of **www.pearson.com/mylab/management** to complete the video exercise.

Step 3. Hold a Hearing

Once the union collects the authorization cards, one of three things can occur. If the employer chooses *not to contest union recognition* at all, then the parties need no hearing, and a special "consent election" is held. If the employer chooses not to contest the union's *right to an election*, and/or the scope of the bargaining unit, and/or which employees are eligible to vote in the election, no hearing is needed and the parties can stipulate an election. If an employer *does* wish to contest the union's right, it can insist on a hearing to determine those issues. An employer's decision about whether to insist on a hearing is a strategic one. Management bases it on the facts of each case, and on whether it feels it needs more time to try to persuade employees not to elect a union.

Most companies do contest the union's right to represent their employees, claiming that a significant number don't really want the union. It is at this point that the NLRB gets involved. The union usually contacts the NLRB, which requests a hearing. It then sends a hearing officer to investigate. The examiner sends both management and union a notice of representation hearing (NLRB Form 852) that states the time and place of the hearing.

The hearing addresses several issues. First, does the record indicate there is enough evidence to hold an election? (For example, did 30% or more of the employees in an appropriate bargaining unit sign the authorization cards?) Second, the examiner decides what the bargaining unit will be. The **bargaining unit** is the group of employees that the union will be authorized to represent and bargain for collectively. If the entire organization is the bargaining unit, the union will represent all nonsupervisory, nonmanagerial, and nonconfidential employees, even though the union may be oriented mostly toward blue-collar workers. (Professional and nonprofessional employees can be included in the same bargaining unit only if the professionals agree.) If your firm disagrees with the examiner's bargaining unit decision, it can challenge the decision. This will require a separate NLRB ruling.

bargaining unit
The group of employees the union will be authorized to represent.

The NLRB hearing addresses other issues. These include, "Does the employer qualify for coverage by the NLRB?" and "Is the union a labor organization within the meaning of the National Labor Relations Act?"

If the results of the hearing are favorable for the union, the NLRB will order holding an election. It will issue a Notice of Election (NLRB Form 707) to that effect for the employer to post.

Step 4. The Campaign

During the campaign that precedes the election, union and employer appeal to employees for their votes. The union will emphasize that it will prevent unfairness, set up grievance and seniority systems, and improve wages. Union strength, they'll say, will give employees a greater voice in disciplinary matters and in determining wages and working conditions. Management will stress that improvements like those don't require unions and that wages are equal to or better than with a union. Management will also emphasize the cost of union dues; the fact that the union is an "outsider"; and that if the union wins, a strike may follow. It can even attack the union on ethical and moral grounds, while insisting that employees will not be as well off and may lose freedom. But neither side can threaten, bribe, or coerce employees.

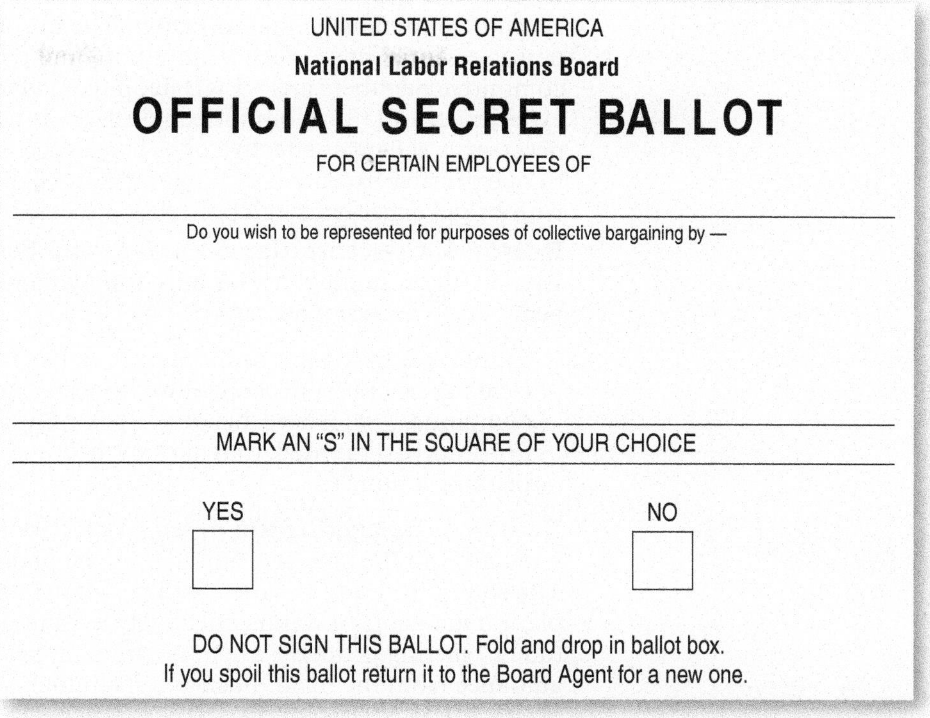

FIGURE 15-3 Sample NLRB Ballot

UNITED STATES OF AMERICA

National Labor Relations Board

OFFICIAL SECRET BALLOT

FOR CERTAIN EMPLOYEES OF

Do you wish to be represented for purposes of collective bargaining by —

MARK AN "S" IN THE SQUARE OF YOUR CHOICE

YES ☐ NO ☐

DO NOT SIGN THIS BALLOT. Fold and drop in ballot box.
If you spoil this ballot return it to the Board Agent for a new one.

Step 5. The Election

The election occurs within 30 to 60 days after the NLRB issues its Decision and Direction of Election. The election is by secret ballot; the NLRB provides the ballots (see Figure 15-3), voting booth, and ballot box; counts the votes; and certifies the results.

The union becomes the employees' representative if it wins the election, and winning means getting a majority of the votes *cast*, not a majority of the total workers in the bargaining unit. (Also keep in mind that if an employer commits an unfair labor practice, the NLRB may reverse a "no union" election. Supervisors must therefore be careful not to commit unfair practices.)

Several things influence whether the union wins the certification election. Unions have a higher probability of success in geographic areas with a higher percentage of union workers. High unemployment seems to lead to poorer results for the union, perhaps because employees fear that unionization efforts might result in reduced job security or employer retaliation. Unions usually carefully pick the size of their bargaining unit (all clerical employees in the company, only those at one facility, and so on) because the larger the bargaining unit, the smaller the probability of union victory. The more workers vote, the less likely a union victory, probably because more workers who are not strong supporters vote.

How to Lose an NLRB Election

In recent years, unions have won about 69% of elections held each year (and as we'll see, somewhat fewer decertifications).[36] According to expert Matthew Goodfellow, there is no sure way employers can win elections, but several sure ways to lose one.[37]

Reason 1. Asleep at the switch. In one study, in 68% of the companies that lost to the union, executives were caught unaware. In these companies, turnover and absenteeism had increased, productivity was erratic, and safety was poor. Grievance procedures were rare. But ironically when the first reports of authorization cards began trickling in, management usually responded with letters describing the company as "one big family."[38]

Reason 2. Appointing a committee. Of the losing companies, 36% formed a committee to manage the campaign. The problems here are that: (1) promptness is essential in an election situation, and committees move slowly; (2) most committee members are NLRB neophytes, whose views reflect hope rather than experience; and (3) a committee's decision is usually a compromise decision, not necessarily the most effective one. This expert suggests giving full responsibility to one decisive executive. A human resource director and a consultant or advisor with broad experience in labor relations should assist this person.

Reason 3. Concentrating on money and benefits. In 54% of the elections studied, the company lost because top management concentrated on money and benefits. As Goodfellow says:

> Employees may want more money, but quite often, if they feel the company treats them fairly, decently, and honestly, they are satisfied with reasonable, competitive rates and benefits. It is only when they feel ignored, uncared for, and disregarded that money becomes a major issue to express their dissatisfaction.[39]

Reason 4. Delegating too much to divisions. For companies with plants scattered around the country, unionizing one plant tends to lead to unionizing others. The solution is, don't abdicate all personnel and industrial relations decisions to plant managers.[40] Dealing effectively with unions—monitoring employees' attitudes, reacting properly when the union appears, and so on—requires centralized guidance from the main office and its human resources staff.

Evidence-Based HR: What to Expect the Union to Do to Win the Election

The other side of the coin is this: What can unions do to boost their chances they'll win the election? A researcher analyzed data from 261 NLRB elections. She found that the best way for unions to win is a "rank-and-file strategy." This includes:[41]

1. "Reliance on a slow, underground, person-to-person campaign using house calls, small group meetings, and pre-union associations to develop leadership and union commitment, and prepare workers for employer anti-union strategies before the employer becomes aware of the campaign."
2. The union will focus on building active rank-and-file participation, including an organizing committee reflecting the different interest groups in the bargaining unit.
3. The union will press for a first contract early in the organizing process.
4. The union will use "inside and outside pressure tactics to build worker commitment and compel the employer to run a fair campaign."
5. There will be an emphasis during the organizing campaign on issues such as respect, dignity, and fairness, not just traditional bread-and-butter issues like wages.

The Supervisor's Role

After Target won a unionization election at a New York store, a federal judge overturned it and required a new election. The judge found that Target managers had violated labor law by telling employees they couldn't wear union buttons or distribute flyers, and by threatening to discipline workers who discussed union matters.[42]

Supervisors are an employer's first line of defense in the unionizing effort. They are often in the best position to sense employee attitude problems, and to discover the first signs of union activity. However, supervisors can also inadvertently undermine their employer's union efforts. Supervisory unfair labor practices could then (1) cause the NLRB to hold a new election after your company has won a previous election, or (2) cause your company to forfeit the second election and go directly to contract negotiation.

For example, one plant superintendent reacted to a union's initial organizing attempt by prohibiting distribution of union literature in the plant's lunchroom. Since solicitation of off-duty workers in nonwork areas is generally legal, the company subsequently allowed the union to post literature on the company's bulletin board and to distribute literature in nonworking areas inside the plant. However, the NLRB still ruled that the initial act of prohibiting distribution of the literature was an unfair labor practice, one not "made right" by the company's subsequent efforts. The NLRB used the superintendent's action as one reason for invalidating an election that the company had won.[43] (Today certain "supervisors" may no longer be excluded from the bargaining unit. The employer could trigger an unfair labor practice charge if it tries to use those people to assist in its campaign.)[44]

SOME TIPS Supervisors can use the acronym TIPS to remember what *not* to do during the campaigns.[45] *Do not* Threaten, Interrogate, make Promises to, or Spy on employees (for instance, do not threaten that you will close or move the business, cut wages, reduce overtime, or lay off employees). FORE outlines what you may do. *You may* give employees Facts (like what signing the authorization card means), express your Opinion about unions, explain factually correct Rules (such as that the law permits permanently replacing striking employees), and share your Experiences about unions. The Know Your Employment Law discussion expands on this.

KNOW YOUR EMPLOYMENT LAW

Rules Regarding Literature and Solicitation

To avoid legal problems, employers need rules governing distribution of literature and solicitation of workers, and should show supervisors how to apply them.[46] For example:

1. Employers can always bar nonemployees from soliciting employees when the employee is on duty and not on a break.
2. Employers can usually stop employees from soliciting other employees for any purpose if one or both employees are on paid-duty time and not on a break.
3. Most employers (generally not including retail stores, shopping centers, and certain other employers) can bar nonemployees from the building's interiors and work areas as a right of private property owners.[47]
4. Employers can deny on- or off-duty employees access to interior or exterior areas only if they can show the rule is required for reasons of production, safety, or discipline.

Again, such restrictions are valid only if the employer doesn't discriminate against the union. Thus, if the employer lets employees collect money for baby gifts, to sell products, or to engage in other solicitation during their working time, it may not be able lawfully to prohibit them from union soliciting during work time. Here is one example of a specific rule aimed at limiting union organizing or activity:

> Solicitation of employees on company property during working time interferes with the efficient operation of our business. Nonemployees are not permitted to solicit employees on company property for any purpose. Except in break areas where both employees are on break or off the clock, no employee may solicit another employee during working time for any purpose.[48] ■

Decertification Elections: Ousting the Union

decertification
Legal process for employees to terminate a union's right to represent them.

Winning an election and signing an agreement don't necessarily mean that the union is in the company to stay. The same law that grants employees the right to unionize also gives them a way to terminate legally (decertify) their union's right to represent them. There were 180 such **decertification** elections in one recent year, of which unions won about 39%.[49] (That's actually a more favorable win rate for employers than that for the original, representation elections).

Decertification campaigns are similar to certification campaigns.[50] The union organizes membership meetings and house-to-house visits, mails literature into the homes, and uses phone calls, e-mails, NLRB appeals, and (sometimes) threats and harassment to win the election. Employers can't legally start the decertification process, but once started management uses meetings—including one-on-one meetings, small-group meetings, and meetings with entire units—as well as legal or expert assistance, letters, improved working conditions, and subtle or not-so-subtle threats to try to influence the votes.[51]

Globalization complicates the employer's union relations challenges, as the accompanying HR Practices Around the Globe feature shows.

IMPROVING PERFORMANCE: *HR PRACTICES AROUND THE GLOBE*[52]

France Comes to the Workers' Aid

Employers planning to expand abroad should ponder the experience of drug maker Sanofi SA in France. Because of the relatively high cost of running its research facility in southwestern France, Sanofi told its researchers there it was closing their facility.[53] Employees began staging weekly protests, supported by the French government, which opposes profitable companies slashing jobs. After 9 months, the company was still waiting for a government report on the situation so it could finish negotiating with its unions and try to get some of them other jobs elsewhere. As one Sanofi manager said, "In France, the politics, the labor laws are extremely different than in any other regions. . . . It means that for sites like Toulouse . . . anything you want to do differently gets to be a confrontational issue."[54]

MyLab Management Talk About It 3

If your professor has assigned this, go to the Assignments section of **www.pearson.com/mylab/management** to complete this discussion question. With government policies like this, how do you think French companies remain competitive with those, say, in the United States?

The Collective Bargaining Process

LEARNING OBJECTIVE 15-4

Illustrate with five examples bargaining that is not in good faith.

What Is Collective Bargaining?

When and if the union becomes your employees' representative, a day is set for management and labor to meet and negotiate a labor agreement. This agreement will contain specific provisions covering wages, hours, and working conditions.

collective bargaining
The process through which representatives of management and the union meet to negotiate a labor agreement.

What exactly is **collective bargaining?** According to the National Labor Relations Act:

> For the purpose of [this act,] to bargain collectively is the performance of the mutual obligation of the employer and the representative of the employees to meet at reasonable times and confer in good faith with respect to wages, hours, and terms and conditions of employment, or the negotiation of an agreement, or any question arising thereunder, and the execution of a written contract incorporating any agreement reached if requested by either party, but such obligation does not compel either party to agree to a proposal or require the making of a concession.

In plain language, this means that both management and labor are required by law to negotiate wages, hours, and terms and conditions of employment "in good faith."

What Is Good Faith?

good faith bargaining
Both parties are making every reasonable effort to arrive at agreement; proposals are being matched with counterproposals.

Good faith bargaining is the cornerstone of effective labor–management relations. It means that both parties communicate and negotiate, match proposals with counterproposals, and make a reasonable effort to arrive at an agreement. It does not mean that one party compels another to agree. Nor does it require that either party make any specific concessions (although some may be necessary).[55]

How can you tell if bargaining is *not* in good faith? Here are some examples.[56]

Surface bargaining. Going through the motions of bargaining without any real intention of completing an agreement.

Inadequate concessions. Unwillingness to compromise.

Inadequate proposals and demands. The NLRB considers the advancement of proposals to be a positive factor in determining overall good faith.

Dilatory tactics. The law requires that the parties meet and "confer at reasonable times and intervals." Obviously, refusal to meet with the union does not satisfy the positive duty imposed on the employer.

Imposing conditions. Attempts to impose conditions that are so onerous or unreasonable as to indicate bad faith.

Making unilateral changes in conditions. This is a strong indication that the employer is not bargaining with the required intent of reaching an agreement.

Bypassing the representative. The duty of management to bargain in good faith involves, at a minimum, recognition that the union representative is the one with whom the employer must deal in conducting negotiations.

Withholding information. An employer must supply the union with information, upon request, to enable it to discuss the collective bargaining issues intelligently.

Of course, requiring good faith bargaining doesn't mean that negotiations can't grind to a halt. For example, a few years ago the National Football League accused the Players Association of not bargaining in good faith, using delays to "run out the clock" so that the players could bring suit against the NFL.[57]

The Negotiating Team

Both union and management send negotiating teams to the bargaining table, and both go into the bargaining sessions having "done their homework."

First, they acquire data on which to build their bargaining positions.[58] From compensation surveys they compile data on pay and benefits, including comparisons with local pay rates and to rates for similar jobs in the industry. Data on the distribution of the workforce (in terms of age, sex, and seniority, for instance) are important, because it determines benefits. Internal economic data regarding benefits, earnings, and the cost of overtime are important too. Union representatives will have sounded out union members on their desires and conferred with representatives of related unions.

Management will also "cost" the current labor contract and determine the increased cost—total, per employee, and per hour—of the union's demands. It will use information from grievances and feedback from supervisors to determine what the union's demands might be, and prepare counteroffers and arguments.[59] Other popular tactics include attitude surveys to test employee reactions to various sections of the contract that management may feel require change, and informal conferences with local union leaders to discuss the operational effectiveness of the contract and to send up trial balloons on management ideas for change.

Costing the Contract

Collective bargaining experts emphasize the need to cost the union's demands carefully. One says,

> The mistake I see most often is [HR professionals who] enter the negotiations without understanding the financial impact of things they put on the table. For example, the union wants three extra vacation days. That doesn't sound like a lot, except that in some states, if an employee leaves, you have to pay them for unused vacation time. [So] now your employer has to carry that liability on their books at all times.[60]

Bargaining Items

Labor law sets out categories of specific items that are subject to bargaining: These are mandatory, voluntary, and illegal items.

TABLE 15-1 Illustrative Bargaining Items

Mandatory	Permissible	Illegal
Rates of pay	Indemnity bonds	Closed shop
Hours of employment	Management rights as to union affairs	Separation of employees based on race
Overtime pay	Pension benefits of retired employees	Discriminatory treatment
Holidays	Scope of the bargaining unit	
Vacations	Including supervisors in the contract	
Severance pay	Additional parties to the contract such as the international union	
Pensions	Use of union label	
Insurance benefits	Settlement of unfair labor charges	
Profit-sharing plans	Prices in cafeteria	
Christmas bonuses	Continuance of past contract	
Employee security	Membership of bargaining team	
Job performance	Employment of strikebreaker	
Union security		
Drug testing of employees		

Source: Michael R. Carrell and Christina Heavrin, *Labor Relations and Collective Bargaining: Cases, Practices, and Law*, 6th edition, © 2001. Reprinted by permission of Pearson Education, Inc. Upper Saddle River, NJ.

voluntary (or permissible) bargaining items
Items in collective bargaining over which bargaining is neither illegal nor mandatory—neither party can be compelled against its wishes to negotiate over those items.

Voluntary (or permissible) bargaining items are neither mandatory nor illegal; they become a part of negotiations only through the joint agreement of both management and union. Neither party can compel the other to negotiate over voluntary items. You cannot hold up signing a contract because the other party refuses to bargain on a voluntary item, such as benefits for retirees.

Illegal bargaining items are forbidden by law. A clause agreeing to hire union members exclusively would be illegal in a right-to-work state, for example.

Table 15-1 presents some of the 70 or so **mandatory bargaining items** over which bargaining is mandatory under the law. They include wages, hours, rest periods, layoffs, transfers, benefits, and severance pay. Others, such as drug testing, are added as the law evolves.

illegal bargaining items
Items in collective bargaining that are forbidden by law; for example, a clause agreeing to hire "union members exclusively" would be illegal in a right-to-work state.

mandatory bargaining items
Items in collective bargaining that a party must bargain over if they are introduced by the other party—for example, pay.

Building Negotiating Skills

Hammering out a satisfactory labor agreement requires negotiating skills. Experienced negotiators use *leverage, desire, time, competition, information, credibility*, and *judgment* to improve their bargaining positions.[61] Things you can *leverage* include *necessity, desire, competition*, and *time*.[62] For example, the union knows that an employer who must fill a big order fast (*necessity*) is at a disadvantage.

Similarly, the employer who makes its *desires* too obvious undercuts its position. *Competition* is important too. There is no more convincing ploy than subtly hinting you've got an alternative (like shifting services abroad). *Time* (particularly deadlines) can also tilt things for or against you.

"Knowledge is power" when negotiating, so having *information* is advantageous, as is *credibility*. Finally, good negotiators need *judgment*: the ability to "strike the right balance between gaining advantages and reaching compromises, in the substance as well as in the style of [their] negotiating technique."[63]

Bargaining Guidelines

Expert Reed Richardson has the following advice for bargainers:

1. Be sure to set clear objectives for every bargaining item, and be sure you understand the reason for each.
2. Do not hurry.
3. When in doubt, caucus with your associates.

4. Be well prepared with firm data supporting your position.
5. Strive to keep some flexibility in your position.
6. Don't concern yourself just with what the other party says and does; find out why.
7. Respect the importance of face saving for the other party.
8. Be alert to the real intentions of the other party—not only for goals, but also for priorities.
9. Be a good listener.
10. Build a reputation for being fair but firm.
11. Learn to control your emotions and use them as a tool.
12. As you make each bargaining move, be sure you know its relationship to all other moves.
13. Measure each move against your objectives.
14. Remember that collective bargaining is a compromise process. There is no such thing as having all the pie.
15. Try to understand the people and their personalities.[64]
16. Remember that excessive bargainer transparency and openness can backfire.[65]

Impasses, Mediation, and Strikes

In collective bargaining, an **impasse** (or stalemate) occurs when the parties are not able to move further toward settlement. This usually occurs because one party is demanding more than the other will offer. For example, after reaching agreement with its unions on many issues after several months of bargaining, the Polk County (Florida) School District declared an impasse. It said that although it had negotiated in good faith with its two unions, it could not reach agreement on several issues, including wages and teacher evaluations.[66] Sometimes a third party, such as a mediator, can resolve an impasse. If the impasse is not resolved, the union may call a work stoppage, or *strike*.[67]

impasse
Collective bargaining situation that occurs when the parties are not able to move further toward settlement, usually because one party is demanding more than the other will offer.

mediation
Intervention in which a neutral third party tries to assist the principals in reaching agreement.

fact finder
A neutral party who studies the issues in a dispute and makes a public recommendation for a reasonable settlement.

arbitration
The most definitive type of third-party intervention, in which the arbitrator usually has the power to determine and dictate the settlement terms.

interest arbitration
Arbitration enacted when labor agreements do not yet exist or when one or both parties are seeking to change the agreement.

rights arbitration
Arbitration that interprets existing contract terms, for instance, when an employee questions the employer's right to take some disciplinary action.

THIRD-PARTY INVOLVEMENT Negotiators use three types of third-party interventions to overcome an impasse. With **mediation,** a neutral third party tries to assist the principals in reaching agreement. The mediator meets with each party to determine where each stands, and then uses this information to find common ground for bargaining. When Hostess Brands couldn't reach agreement with its unions, its bankruptcy judge had them join him for a mediation session, where he tried (unsuccessfully) to broker a new contract.[68]

In certain situations, as in a national emergency dispute, a **fact finder** is a neutral party who studies the issues in a dispute and makes a public recommendation for a reasonable settlement.[69] Presidential emergency fact-finding boards resolved impasses in certain critical transportation disputes.

Arbitration is the most definitive third-party intervention, because the arbitrator may have the power to determine and dictate the settlement terms. With *binding arbitration*, both parties are committed to accepting the arbitrator's award. With *nonbinding arbitration*, they are not. Arbitration may also be voluntary or compulsory (imposed by a government agency). In the United States, voluntary binding arbitration is the most prevalent.

There are two main topics of arbitration. **Interest arbitration** centers on working out a labor agreement; the parties use it when such agreements do not yet exist or when one or both parties are seeking to change the agreement. **Rights arbitration** really means "contract interpretation arbitration." It usually involves interpreting existing contract terms, for instance, when an employee questions the employer's right to have taken some disciplinary action.[70] Mediators will often use *alternative dispute resolution* tactics (such as asking if the parties want to take a break, or are willing to set the issue at hand aside temporarily) to head off or deal with an impasse.[71]

SOURCES OF THIRD-PARTY ASSISTANCE Various public and professional agencies make arbitrators and mediators available. For example, the American Arbitration Association (AAA) represents and provides the services of thousands of arbitrators and mediators to employers and unions. The U.S. government's Federal Mediation and Conciliation Service provides both arbitrators and mediators (see Figure 15-4).[72] In addition, most states provide arbitrator and mediation services.

FIGURE 15-4 Form to Request Mediation Services

Source: Federal Mediation and Conciliation Service.

FMCS Form F-53
Revised 5-92

Form Approved
OMB No. 3076-0005

FEDERAL SECTOR LABOR RELATIONS
NOTICE TO FEDERAL MEDIATION AND CONCILIATION SERVICE

Mail To:
Notice Processing Unit
FEDERAL MEDIATION AND CONCILIATION SERVICE
2100 K Street, N.W.
Washington, D.C. 20427

THIS NOTICE IS IN REGARD TO: (MARK "X")

(1) ☐ AN INITIAL CONTRACT (INCLUDED FLRA CERTIFICATION NUMBER) # ______
☐ A CONTRACT REOPENER REOPENER DATE ______
☐ THE EXPIRATION OF AN EXISTING AGREEMENT EXPIRATION DATE: ______

(2) ☐ ***OTHER REQUESTS FOR THE ASSISTANCE OF FMCS IN BARGAINING*** ***(MARK "X")***
SPECIFY TYPE OF ISSUE(S)

(3) ☐ ***REQUEST FOR GRIEVANCE MEDIATION (SEE ITEM #10)*** ***(MARK "X")***
ISSUE(S)

(4) NAME OF FEDERAL AGENCY | NAME OF SUBDIVISION OR COMPONENT, IF ANY
STREET ADDRESS OF AGENCY | CITY | STATE | ZIP
AGENCY OFFICIAL TO BE CONTACTED | AREA CODE & PHONE NUMBER

(5) NAME OF NATIONAL UNION OR PARENT BODY | NAME AND/OR LOCAL NUMBER
STREET ADDRESS | CITY | STATE | ZIP
UNION OFFICIAL TO BE CONTACTED | AREA CODE & PHONE NUMBER

LOCATION OF NEGOTIATIONS OR WHERE MEDIATION WILL BE HELD
(6) STREET ADDRESS | CITY | STATE | ZIP

(7) APPROX. # OF EMPLOYEES IN BARGAINING UNIT(S) >> | IN ESTABLISHMENT>>

(8) THIS NOTICE OR REQUEST IS FILED ON BEHALF OF ***(MARK "X")*** ☐UNION ☐AGENCY

(9) NAME AND TITLE OF OFFICIAL(S) SUBMITTING THIS NOTICE OR REQUEST | AREA CODE AND PHONE NUMBER
STREET ADDRESS | CITY | STATE | ZIP

FOR GRIEVANCE MEDIATION, THE SIGNATURES OF BOTH PARTIES ARE REQUIRED:*

(10) SIGNATURE (AGENCY) | DATE | SIGNATURE (UNION) | DATE

*Receipt of this form does not commit FMCS to offer its services. Receipt of this form will not be acknowledged in writing by FMCS. While use of this form is voluntary, its use will facilitate FMCS service to respondents. Public reporting burden for this collection of information is estimated to average 10 minutes per response, including time for reviewing the collection of information. Send comments regarding this burden estimate or any other aspect of this collection of information, including suggestions for reducing this burden, to FMCS Division of Administrative Services, Washington, D.C. 20427, and to the Office of Management and Budget, Paperwork Reduction Project. Washington, D.C. 20603

For Instructions, See Back

strike
A withdrawal of labor.

economic strike
A strike that results from a failure to agree on the terms of a contract that involves wages, benefits, and other conditions of employment.

unfair labor practice strike
A strike aimed at protesting illegal conduct by the employer.

wildcat strike
An unauthorized strike occurring during the term of a contract.

sympathy strike
A strike that takes place when one union strikes in support of the strike of another.

STRIKES A **strike** is a withdrawal of labor. There are four main types of strikes. An **economic strike** results from a failure to agree on the terms of a contract. Unions call **unfair labor practice strikes** to protest illegal conduct by the employer. A **wildcat strike** is an unauthorized strike occurring during the term of a contract. A **sympathy strike** occurs when one union strikes in support of the strike of another union.[73] For example, in sympathy with South Korean Hyundai workers, the United Auto Workers organized a rally outside of Hyundai's technical center in Superior Township, Michigan, and took steps to hold other rallies.[74]

Resisting unions isn't unique to American employers, of course. For example, in December 2017, the European airline Ryanair suffered its first-ever pilot strike, just after union talks broke down.[75]

Stacy Walsh Rosenstock/Alamy Stock Photo

Picketing is one of the first activities to occur during a strike. The purpose is to inform the public about the labor dispute.

The likelihood of and severity of a strike depend partly on the parties' willingness to "take a strike."[76] The number of major work stoppages (strikes involving 1,000 workers or more) peaked at about 400 per year between 1965 and 1975, and today average around 20.

Picketing, or having employees carry signs announcing their concerns near the employer's place of business, is one of the first activities to appear during a strike. Its purpose is to inform the public about the existence of the labor dispute and often to encourage them to refrain from doing business with the struck employer.

picketing
Having employees carry signs announcing their concerns near the employer's place of business.

Employers have several options when employees strike. One is to temporarily shut down the affected area and halt operations. A second is to contract out work to blunt the effects of the strike. A third is to continue operations, perhaps using supervisors and other nonstriking workers. A fourth alternative is hiring replacements for the strikers.

Diminished union influence plus competitive pressures now prompt more employers to replace (or consider replacing) strikers with permanent replacement workers. When the United Steel Workers struck refineries, BP quickly began training replacement workers.[77] And in a labor dispute a few years ago, the NFL implied even they might use replacement players.[78]

Employers generally can replace strikers. In one case known as *Mackay*, the U.S. Supreme Court ruled that although the National Labor Relations Act does prohibit employers from interfering with employees' right to strike, employers still have the right to continue their operations and to replace strikers. Subsequent decisions by the National Labor Relations Board put some limitations on *Mackay*. For example, employers cannot permanently replace strikers who are protesting unfair labor practices; they must rehire strikers who unconditionally apply for reinstatement.

IMPROVING PERFORMANCE: *HR TOOLS FOR LINE MANAGERS AND SMALL BUSINESSES: STRIKE GUIDELINES*

As negotiations between the Hibbing Taconite Steel Plant in Minnesota and the United Steelworkers of America headed toward a deadline, the firm brought in security workers and trailers to house them.

Two experts say that, with a strike imminent, following these guidelines is advisable:

- Pay all striking employees what you owe them on the first day of the strike.
- Secure the facility. Management should control access to the property. Some employers make preparations with special strike security companies to provide security during the strike.[79]
- Notify all customers, and prepare a standard official response to all queries.
- Contact all suppliers and others who will have to cross the picket line. Establish alternative methods of obtaining supplies.
- Arrange for overnight stays in the facility and for delivered meals, if necessary.
- Notify the local unemployment office of your need for replacement workers.
- Photograph the facility before, during, and after picketing. If necessary, install video equipment to monitor picket lines.
- Record all facts concerning strikers' demeanor and activities and such incidents as violence, threats, mass pickets, property damage, or problems.
- Gather the following evidence: number of pickets and their names; time, date, and location of picketing; wording on every sign carried by pickets; and descriptions of picketers' cars and license numbers.[80] ■

corporate campaign
An organized effort by the union that exerts pressure on the corporation by pressuring the company's other unions, shareholders, directors, customers, creditors, and government agencies, often directly.

OTHER "WEAPONS" Management and labor each have other weapons to break an impasse. The union, for example, may resort to a corporate campaign. A **corporate campaign** is an organized effort by the union to exert pressure on the employer by pressuring the company's other unions, shareholders, corporate directors, customers, creditors, and government agencies.[81] Thus, the union might surprise members of the board of directors by picketing their homes and organizing a **boycott** of the company's banks.[82]

boycott
The combined refusal by employees and other interested parties to buy or use the employer's products.

TRENDS SHAPING HR: *DIGITAL AND SOCIAL MEDIA*

Unions Go Digital

When it comes to organizing just about any sort of campaign, communication is king, a fact that hasn't been lost on unions. For example, in one survey, 49% of unions said they used Facebook to communicate with members and employees, 23% used Twitter, and 13% used YouTube.[83] About 92% of unions have a Web site, while 78.1% use e-mail newsletters.[84] The group trying to organize Starbucks workers (the *Starbucks Workers' Union*) started their own Web site (starbucksunion.org).[85] In another recent campaign, the employer restricted the use of its electronic systems (including e-mail) to "business purposes only." The union filed objections. The NLRB held that nonmanagement employees who normally have access to an employer's e-mail system as part of their jobs may use the system to communicate about union matters when not working, such as during lunch or break times.[86] ■

inside games
Union efforts to convince employees to impede or to disrupt production—for example, by slowing the work pace.

lockout
A refusal by the employer to provide opportunities to work.

Inside games are union efforts to convince employees to impede or to disrupt production—for example, by slowing the work pace or refusing to work overtime.[87] Inside games are basically strikes—albeit "strikes" in which the company continues to pay the employees. In one inside game at a Caterpillar plant, UAW grievances rose from 22 to 336. This tied up workers and management on company time.[88]

For their part, employers can try to break an impasse with lockouts. A **lockout** is a refusal by the employer to provide opportunities to work. It (sometimes literally) locks out employees and prohibits them from doing their jobs (and being paid). Faced with a new contract that might slash their wages by 50%, Canadian Auto Workers Union employees from one Caterpillar plant found themselves locked out after negotiations failed to produce a settlement.[89]

The NLRB views lockouts as an unfair labor practice only when the employer acts for a prohibited purpose. Trying to bring about a settlement on terms favorable to the employer is not a prohibited purpose. Lockouts are not widely used; employers are usually reluctant to cease operations when employees are willing to continue working.

Employers exert other pressure. When Boeing's union resisted accepting new labor concessions at its Washington assembly facility, Boeing began actively considering moving the planned assembly of its new Boeing 777X long-range jet to South Carolina. Boeing's Washington state workers approved a new agreement.[90]

injunction
A court order compelling a party or parties either to resume or to desist from a certain action.

Both employers and unions can seek a court injunction if they believe the other side is causing irreparable harm to the other party. An **injunction** is a court order compelling a party or parties either to resume or to desist from a certain action.[91]

The Contract Agreement

The actual contract agreement may be a 20- or 30-page document, or longer. It may contain just general declarations of policy, or detailed rules and procedures. The tendency today is toward the longer contract.

The main sections of a typical contract cover subjects such as these: (1) management rights; (2) union security and automatic payroll dues deduction; (3) grievance procedures; (4) arbitration of grievances; (5) disciplinary procedures; (6) compensation rates; (7) hours of work and overtime; (8) benefits: vacations, holidays, insurance, pensions; (9) health and safety provisions; (10) employee security seniority provisions; and (11) contract expiration date.

Dealing with Disputes and Grievances

LEARNING OBJECTIVE 15-5
Develop a grievance procedure.

Signing the labor agreement is not the last step in collective bargaining. No labor contract can cover all contingencies and answer all questions. For example, suppose the contract says you can only discharge an employee for "just cause." You subsequently discharge someone for speaking back to you. Was speaking back to you "just cause?"

The *grievance process* is the process or steps that the employer and union agreed to follow to ascertain whether some action violated the collective bargaining agreement. It is the vehicle for administering the contract day to day. However, this usually involves interpretation only, not negotiating new terms or altering existing ones. The aim is to clarify what those contract points really mean, in the context of addressing grievances regarding things like time off, disciplinary action, and pay. When the Cleveland Browns' head coach fined one of his players $1,701 for not paying the hotel's bill for a $3 bottle of water, players quickly filed grievances with the NFL.[92]

Sources of Grievances

In practice, it's probably easier to list those items that *don't* precipitate grievances than the ones that do. Employees may use just about anything involving wages, hours, or conditions of employment as the basis of a grievance.

Discipline cases and seniority problems including promotions, transfers, and layoffs would top this list. Others would include grievances growing out of job evaluations and work assignments, overtime, vacations, incentive plans, and holidays.[93] Here are three examples of grievances:

- ***Absenteeism.*** An employer fired an employee for excessive absences. The employee filed a grievance stating that there had been no previous warnings related to excessive absences.
- ***Insubordination.*** An employee on two occasions refused to obey a supervisor's order to meet with him, unless a union representative was present at the meeting. As a result, the employee was discharged and subsequently filed a grievance protesting the discharge.
- ***Plant rules.*** The plant had a posted rule barring employees from eating or drinking during unscheduled breaks. The employees filed a grievance claiming the rule was arbitrary.[94]

Grievances are often symptoms of underlying problems. Sometimes bad relationships between supervisors and subordinates are to blame: This is often the cause of grievances over "fair treatment," for instance. Organizational factors like ambiguous instructions also cause frustration and grievances. Union activism is another cause; the union may solicit grievances from workers to underscore ineffective supervision. Some people are by their nature dissatisfied and prone to complaints. Discipline and dismissal are two major sources of grievances.

The Grievance Procedure

grievance procedure
Formal process for addressing any factor involving wages, hours, or conditions of employment that is used as a complaint against the employer.

Most collective bargaining contracts contain a **grievance procedure.** It lists the steps in the procedure, time limits associated with each step, and specific rules such as "all charges of contract violation must be reduced to writing." Nonunionized employers need such procedures, too.

Grievance procedures differ from firm to firm. Some are simple, two-step procedures. Here, the grievant, union representative, and company representative meet to discuss the grievance. If they don't find a satisfactory solution, the grievance goes

FIGURE 15-5 **Sample Online Grievance Form**

EMPLOYEE GRIEVANCE FORM

Aggrieved employee ______________________________ Date______________

Department______________________ Employee's job title ________________

Employee's work email address and/or other contact information ____________________

____

Statement of grievance: Briefly state what happened to lead you to grieve, including for instance situation leading to the complaint, who was involved (names and titles), when the occurrence/situation took place (date and time), and where it took place

____

____

____

____

____

____

____

____

Why do you consider this a grievance? (please check one) __Contract violation __Unfair treatment

If you checked contract violation, please list contract articles and sections you believe apply

____

What remedy are you seeking?

____

____

____

Aggrieved employee's signature____________________________ Date__________

HR officer signature ______________________________ Date

before a third-party arbitrator, who hears the case, writes it up, and makes a decision. Figure 15-5 shows a grievance form.

At the other extreme, the grievance procedure may contain six or more steps. The first step might be for the grievant and shop steward to meet informally with the supervisor of the grievant to try to find a solution. The next steps involve the grievant and union representatives meeting with higher-level managers. Finally, if top management and the union can't reach agreement, the grievance may go to arbitration.

Guidelines for Handling Grievances

The best way for a supervisor to handle a grievance is to develop a work environment in which grievances don't arise in the first place. Hone your ability to avoid, recognize, diagnose, and correct the causes of potential employee dissatisfaction (such as unfair appraisals or poor communications) before they become grievances.

Given that many factors including union pressures prompt grievances, it would be naïve to think that grievances arise only due to supervisor unfairness. However, there's little doubt that the quality of the interpersonal relations among you and your subordinates will influence your team's grievance rate. The supervisor is on the firing line and must steer a course between treating employees fairly and maintaining management's rights and prerogatives. The HR Tools feature presents some guidelines.

IMPROVING PERFORMANCE: *HR TOOLS FOR LINE MANAGERS AND SMALL BUSINESSES: HOW TO HANDLE A GRIEVANCE SITUATION*

Grievances cost money, in terms of lost work time, productivity, and (possibly) arbitrators' fees. One expert has developed a list of supervisor do's and don'ts as useful guides in handling grievances.[95] Some critical ones include:

Do:

1. Investigate and handle each case as though it may eventually result in arbitration.
2. Talk with the employee about his or her grievance; give the person a full hearing.
3. Require the union to identify specific contractual provisions allegedly violated.
4. Comply with the contractual time limits for handling the grievance.
5. Visit the work area of the grievance.
6. Determine whether there were any witnesses.
7. Examine the grievant's personnel record.
8. Fully examine prior grievance records.
9. Treat the union representative as your equal.
10. Hold your grievance discussions privately.
11. Fully inform your own supervisor of grievance matters.

Don't:

1. Discuss the case with the union steward alone—the grievant should be there.
2. Make arrangements with individual employees that are inconsistent with the labor agreement.
3. Hold back the remedy if the company is wrong.
4. Admit to the binding effect of a past practice.
5. Relinquish to the union your rights as a manager.
6. Settle grievances based on what is "fair." Instead, stick to the labor agreement.
7. Bargain over items not covered by the contract.
8. Treat as subject to arbitration claims demanding the discipline or discharge of managers.
9. Give long written grievance answers.
10. Trade a grievance settlement for a grievance withdrawal.
11. Deny grievances because "your hands have been tied by management."
12. Agree to informal amendments in the contract. ■

MyLab Management Talk About It 4

If your professor has assigned this, go to the Assignments section of **www.pearson.com/mylab/management** to complete this discussion. Write a 30-word guide that summarizes the essence of these do's and don'ts.

LEARNING OBJECTIVE 15-6

Give an example of cooperative labor relations.

The Union Movement Today and Tomorrow

Union membership has decreased from about 20% of the U.S. workforce in 1983 (when 17.8 million workers belonged to unions) to about 11.1 % (just over 14 million workers) recently.[96]

Several factors contributed to the decline. Unions traditionally appealed mostly to blue-collar workers, and the proportion of blue-collar jobs has been decreasing. Globalization increased competition and pressured employers to cut costs and boost productivity, often by shifting production offshore. Other factors pressuring employers and unions included the deregulation of trucking, airlines, and communications, and laws (such as occupational safety) that somewhat reduced the need for unions. Automation displaced still more blue-collar (and other) workers. The poor economy after the 2007–2008 recession triggered public- and private-sector budget cuts and the

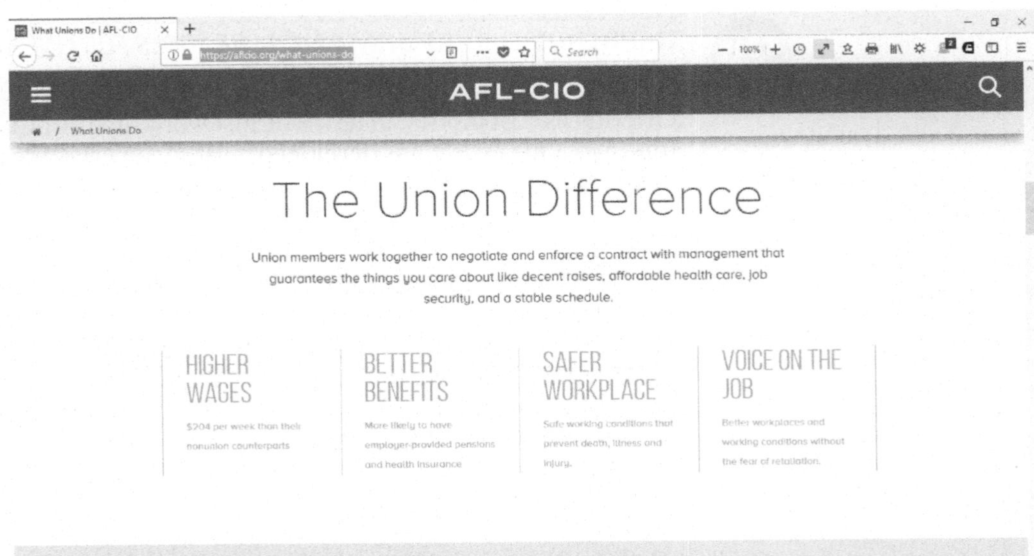

The AFL–CIO says unions want higher wages, better benefits, safer workplaces, and to give workers a voice on the job.

Source: https://aflcio.org/what-unions-do, accessed January 9, 2018.

loss of about one million public-sector union jobs. And, bankruptcies often end with courts imposing less-favorable contract terms on union employees.[97] For example, a bankruptcy court judge let Patriot Coal Corp. drastically reduce pay and benefits for thousands of miners, retirees, and dependents.[98]

The net effect has been the permanent layoff of hundreds of thousands of union members, the permanent closing of company plants, the relocation of companies to nonunion settings (either in the United States or abroad), and mergers and acquisitions that eliminated union jobs and affected collective bargaining agreements. That's why union membership as a percentage of people working has dropped by about two-thirds over 50 years, to about 11%.[99]

What Are Unions Doing About It?

Of course, unions aren't sitting idly by. For example, the Change to Win Coalition (representing about 5.5 million workers) will strive, through "innovative campaigns in the private-sector economy . . . to ensure that every working person has a living wage, benefits to support their family and dignity in retirement."[100] The AFL–CIO also continues to press its case, for instance opposing new tax laws that it said would "kill jobs," and opposing a bill that would "slash support for health programs that benefit working families."[101]

Unions are also increasingly successful organizing new-economy firms. For example, writers at Slate and Salon joined the Writers Guild of America East.[102] Why are these workers unionizing? The companies may be "new," but the reasons are pretty traditional. For example, at Vice Media, fair wages reportedly played a big role. And when the publisher Ziff Davis bought Mashable, it laid off 50 employees; those staying may have read this as a sign that they had to protect themselves.[103]

Unions are also becoming more proactive in coordinating their efforts. For example, to support its efforts to unionize Nissan autoworkers in the United States, the UAW enlisted union members in Brazil to picket Nissan dealerships there.[104] The same is happening in reverse. When Daimler said it was going to phase out producing its "C" cars in Germany and begin producing them in the United States, its German union, IG Metall, began cooperating with the UAW to unionize Daimler's American plants.[105]

RECENT TRENDS IN LABOR LAWS As mentioned earlier, support for unions has always ebbed and flowed in America, and the past few years have been no different. For example, in late 2014 the NLRB published its Final Rule on so-called quickie union elections. By allowing unions to call elections in as little as 13 days after filing a representation petition, labor experts expected this rule to make it more difficult for employers to present their arguments against the union.[106] And after being exempted for many years from having to disclose their participation with each other in a union campaign, employers and their union campaign consultants and attorneys now must report their relationship.[107]

Then in 2017 President Trump appointed a Republican labor law attorney for a vacancy on the NLRB; experts assume the board will now move to reverse some of its Obama-era decisions.[108] And in 2018, Republicans in the House of Representatives were pushing for country-wide "right-to-work" legislation.[109]

Cooperative Labor–Management Relations

News reports tend to highlight adversarial labor–management relations, but the history of labor–management relations is also sprinkled with cooperation.

For example, more than 50 years ago, General Motors and Toyota created a joint venture they called New United Motor Manufacturing Inc. (NUMMI). NUMMI reopened a former GM plant (in what today produces Tesla automobiles) in Fremont, California, The GM plant had suffered from such poisonous labor relations that GM had to close it. The new partners hoped to merge GM's marketing expertise with Toyota's famous team-based management system.[110] NUMMI and the UAW agreed that management and labor would work together as a team, give workers a voice in decision making, and build the highest-quality cars at the lowest cost. The plant was soon very successful (although the parties ultimately ended their joint venture).

Since then, many labor–management agreements have included cooperative agreements and clauses, such as a statement of commitment to cooperate, and/or setting up committees to review mutual concerns that arise, and/or guarantees of employment security. But with or without such contractual commitments, there's little doubt, as one study argues, that unions "that have a cooperative relationship with management can play an important role in overcoming barriers to the effective adoption of practices that have been linked to organizational competitiveness."[111] However employers who want to capitalize on that potential must change how they think, by emphasizing a cooperative partnership.[112]

Chapter Review

Chapter Section Summaries

15-1. The **labor movement** is important. About 15 million U.S. workers belong to unions—about 11% of the total. Workers unionize not just to get more pay or better working conditions; employer unfairness and the union's power are also important. Unions aim for union security, and then for improved wages, hours, and working conditions and benefits for their members. Union security options include the closed shop, union shop, agency shop, preferential shop, and maintenance of membership arrangement.

15-2. To understand how to deal with unions, one should understand labor law and **unfair labor practices.** The laws encouraging the union movement included the Norris–LaGuardia and National Labor Relations (Wagner) Acts of the 1930s. These outlawed certain unfair employer labor practices and made it easier for unions to organize. The Taft–Hartley or Labor Management Relations Act of 1947 addressed keeping unions from restraining or coercing employees, and listed certain unfair union labor practices. In the 1950s, the Landrum–Griffin Act (the Labor Management Reporting and Disclosure Act) further protected union members from possible wrongdoing on the part of their unions.

15-3. When unions begin organizing, any manager may get involved, so one must understand the mechanics of **the union drive and election.** The main steps include initial contact, obtaining authorization cards, holding a hearing, the campaign itself, and the election. Supervisors can follow the acronym TIPS—do not Threaten, Interrogate, make Promises, or Spy. And follow

FORE—provide Facts, express your Opinions, explain factually correct Rules, and share your Experiences.

15-4 The employer and union hammer out an agreement via the **collective bargaining process.** The heart of collective bargaining is good faith bargaining, which means both parties must make reasonable efforts to arrive at agreement, and proposals are matched with counterproposals. There are mandatory bargaining items such as pay, illegal bargaining items, and voluntary bargaining items such as benefits for retirees. If things don't go smoothly during bargaining, the parties may utilize third-party intermediaries, including mediators, fact finders, and arbitrators. Strikes represent a withdrawal of labor.

15-5. A manager may become involved with **disputes and grievances.** Collective bargaining agreements contain a specific grievance procedure listing the steps in the procedure. The best way to handle a grievance is to create an environment in which grievances don't occur. If one does occur, investigate, handle each case as though it may lead to arbitration, talk with the employee about the grievance, and comply with the contractual grievance-handling time limits.

15-6. Union federations, such as Change to Win, continue to be aggressive about organizing workers, and unions are going global, so **cooperative labor relations** is both possible and a sensible aim.

Discussion Questions

CHAPTER 15

15-1. Why do employees join unions? What are the advantages and disadvantages of being a union member?

15-2. Discuss four sure ways to lose an NLRB election.

15-3. Briefly illustrate how labor law has gone through a cycle of repression and encouragement.

15-4. Explain in detail each step in a union drive and election.

15-5. Define impasse, mediation, and strike, and explain the techniques that are used to overcome an impasse.

Individual and Group Activities

15-6. You are the manager of a small manufacturing plant. The union contract covering most of your employees is about to expire. Working individually or in groups, discuss how to prepare for union contract negotiations.

15-7. Working individually or in groups, use Internet resources to find situations where company management and the union reached an impasse at some point during their negotiation process, but eventually resolved the impasse. Describe the issues on both sides that led to the impasse. How did they move past the impasse? What were the final outcomes?

15-8. Appendices A and B at the end of this book (pages 614–634) list the knowledge someone studying for the HRCI (Appendix A) or SHRM (Appendix B) certification exam needs to have in each area of human resource management (such as in Strategic Management and Workforce Planning). In groups of several students, do four things: (1) review Appendix A and/or B; (2) identify the material in this chapter that relates to the Appendix A and/or B required knowledge lists; (3) write four multiple-choice exam questions on this material that you believe would be suitable for inclusion in the HRCI exam and/or the SHRM exam; and (4) if time permits, have someone from your team post your team's questions in front of the class, so that students in all teams can answer the exam questions created by the other teams.

KNOWLEDGE BASE

15-9. Several years ago, 8,000 Amtrak workers agreed not to disrupt service by walking out, at least not until a court hearing was held. Amtrak had asked the courts for a temporary restraining order, and the Transport Workers Union of America was actually pleased to postpone its walkout. The workers were apparently not upset at Amtrak, but at Congress for failing to provide enough funding for Amtrak. What, if anything, can an employer do when employees threaten to go on strike, not because of what the employer did, but what a third party—in this case, Congress—has done or not done? What laws would prevent the union from going on strike in this case?

Experiential Exercise

The Organizing Campaign at Sam's Cupcake Shop

Written and copyrighted by Gary Dessler, PhD.

Purpose: The purpose of this exercise is to give you practice in dealing with some of the elements of a union-organizing campaign.[113]

Required Understanding: You should be familiar with the material covered in this chapter, as well as the following incident, "The Organizing Campaign at Sam's Cupcake Shop."

Incident: Sam's Cupcake Shop sells baked goods (croissants, cupcakes, rolls, cakes, etc.) and serves light meals such as breakfast and salads through its chain of ten small retail stores in the borough of Manhattan, in New York City. Each store is staffed with about 9 employees (plus one manager), some of whom do the cooking and some of whom staff the counter and sell the food items. As with Sam's other stores, the Sam's Cupcake Shop on First Avenue is staffed mostly with recent (legal) immigrants to America, all of whom are paid at or just above the minimum wage. Everything at the First Avenue store seemed to be going smoothly, but that apparent tranquility ended abruptly on July 27, 2018. That was the day that Anesha, the First Avenue store's manager, called Taylor Brooke, Sam's Cupcake's human resource manager, to tell her that they had "an employee problem."

The problem, Anesha said, was that she'd heard from a few employees that the Service Employees International Union was trying to organize Sam's Cupcake Shop employees. Taylor's first reaction was one of caution, particularly because food service employees are historically difficult to organize—"they don't stay in their jobs long enough to unionize them," to paraphrase one union leader.[114] Unfortunately, Anesha said she had already taken what she called "sensible steps" to blunt the unionization effort. She had, first, explained to her employees that if costs went up because they unionized, then "we'd probably have to close this shop." She said she also promised better work schedules if they "ignored" the union, and told them they were prohibited from discussing union matters during work time. "And don't worry" she said to Taylor, "I've got a list of the employees who are pushing for the union."

The more Anesha talked, the more concerned Taylor became, not just with the union but with the possible consequences of Anesha's efforts. She wondered particularly if Anesha's actions could cause problems down the road for Sam's Cupcakes with the NLRB.

She didn't have long to wait for an answer. The following week pickets from the union and its supporters appeared in front of the First Avenue store carrying signs decrying the company's "unfair labor practices." At that point Sam came into Taylor's office and said, "If they think they can railroad me into giving them big raises they are wrong; I am closing that store down." Taylor was in a quandary as to how to reply to Sam, and in general, what she should do.

How to Set Up the Exercise/Instructions: Divide the class into groups of several students. Assume that you are labor relations consultants retained by Taylor to identify the problems and issues involved and to advise Taylor and Sam of the company's rights and obligations, as well as the implications of what's transpired so far, and finally what to do next. Each group will spend the time allotted discussing the issues. Then, outline those issues, as well as an action plan for Taylor and Sam. What should they do next? Can Sam really close the store down?

If time permits, a spokesperson from each group should list on the board the issues involved and the group's recommendations.

Application Case

Organizing New Media Employees at Vice Media

Written and copyrighted by Gary Dessler, PhD.

In 2016 Vice Media and the Writers Guild of America (WGA) agreed on a contract covering about 70 people in Vice Media digital businesses.[115] In 2017 another 430 Vice Media employees voted to unionize. Many of them work on video content for Vice.com and Vice-branded HBO programs. Some joined the WGA East, and some the Motion Pictures Editors Guild. With "new media" growing fast, what's happening at Vice Media illustrates the union challenges new media firms face today.

Vice Media began as an edgy magazine in the 1990s. Today, in addition to its print arm, it has morphed into an online news source with channels including Noisey, Garage, and Motherboard, a Viceland cable channel (among others), and mobile platforms. Walt Disney Company made a $400 million investment in Vice, and Vice Media recently got a $450 million investment from a private equity firm. Some of this new money will go to developing scripted programming for Vice's Viceland cable channel and mobile platforms. In any case, it's obvious that, as at other new-media firms like Buzzfeed and Vox, content creators—writers, editors, and so on—are the lifeblood of the company. That makes labor relations a central issue for companies like these.

For unions, the new-media workforce represents one of the best opportunities in years for union membership to start growing again.

Unions like the WGA are therefore pursuing these employees. In doing so, they're emphasizing the things millennial workers seem to care about the most, not just wage increases, but editorial independence and diversity.

To help unionize firms like these, unions are holding networking events, and headlining them with employees from new-media firms that they've organized. For example, one union let unionized writers from *The Daily Show* explain the advantages of union membership.

Some new-media companies (including Vice Media) were fairly welcoming of the unions, while others were more combative. For example, Buzzfeed's CEO reportedly took a strong stance against the "adversarial" nature of unionization.

Therefore, things don't always go well for new-media employees who do organize. For example, the owner of Gothamist and DNAinfo closed both sites after employees voted to unionize. The owner had warned that it was already running both sites at a loss.

Unions and new-media employers therefore have to understand what new-media employees—many or most of whom are millennials—want from employers. And it turns out that what they want isn't that different from what workers have always wanted. In addition to editorial independence, they want good pay and benefits, fair treatment, and the ability to be heard.

Employers who hoped that the glamour of writing for a fast-growing new-media firm might be enough to keep workers from unionizing were wrong. For one thing (to paraphrase one Vice Media channel editor), after Mashable laid off 50 employees and Buzzfeed fired 100, anxiety began prompting employees to unionize. Many (or most) of these employees went to good schools and got good jobs, only to find that journalists' average pay is low and turnover is high: Many were on their second or third jobs just a few years after college. It's probably not surprising that one study found that 46% of people 30 and over view unions favorably, while 55% of those 18 to 29 have favorable views.

Furthermore, both the new-media firms and their employees have evolved. For example, many firms, including Vice Media, began as what one writer called the "lawless cowboys" of new media. But as they and their employees aged, the writers and employees wanted more stability.

Questions

15-10. The WGA did not have to call a strike at Vice. Why do you think that is? If they struck, what employer tactics would you have suggested to fight back once the strike began?

15-11. What do you think accounts for the fact that Vice Media agreed fairly quickly to recognize the union, whereas other new-media firms simply closed down? What does this mean for unions like the WGA?

15-12. The organizing campaigns at new-media firms like Vice and Buzzfeed are essentially conflicts between professional and creative people (the WGA) and owners and TV and movie producers. Do you think such conflicts are different in any way than are the conflicts between, say, the United Autoworkers or Teamsters unions against auto and trucking companies? Why?

15-13. If you owned a start-up new-media company, how would you react to a union coming in to demand recognition, and why?

CHAPTER 15

Continuing Case

Carter Cleaning Company

Written and copyrighted by Gary Dessler, PhD.

The Grievance

On visiting one of Carter Cleaning Company's stores, Jennifer was surprised to be taken aside by a long-term Carter employee, who met her as she was parking her car. "Murray (the store manager) told me I was suspended for 2 days without pay because I came in late last Thursday," said George. "I'm really upset, but around here the store manager's word seems to be law, and it sometimes seems like the only way anyone can file a grievance is by meeting you or your father like this in the parking lot." Jennifer was very disturbed by this revelation and promised the employee she would look into it and discuss the situation with her father. In the car heading back to headquarters, she began mulling over what Carter Cleaning Company's alternatives might be.

Questions

15-14. Do you think it is important for Carter Cleaning Company to have a formal grievance process? Why or why not?

15-15. Based on what you know about the Carter Cleaning Company, outline the steps in what you think would be the ideal grievance process for this company.

15-16. In addition to the grievance process, can you think of anything else that Carter Cleaning Company might do to make sure grievances and gripes like this one are expressed and are heard by top management?

Translating Strategy into HR Policies and Practices Case*,§

** The accompanying strategy map for this chapter is in MyLab Management; the overall map on the inside back cover of this text outlines the relationships involved.*

Improving Performance at the Hotel Paris

The Hotel Paris's New Labor Relations Practices

The Hotel Paris's competitive strategy is "To use superior guest service to differentiate the Hotel Paris properties, and to thereby increase the length of stay and return rate of guests, and thus boost revenues and profitability." HR manager Lisa Cruz must now formulate functional policies and activities that support this competitive strategy and boost performance by eliciting the required employee behaviors and competencies.

Lisa Cruz's parents were union members, and she had no strong philosophical objections to unions, per se. However, as the head of HR for the Hotel Paris, she did feel very strongly that her employer should do everything legally possible to remain union-free. She knew that this is what the hotel chain's owners and top executives wanted, and that achieving their strategic goals would be best accomplished by

§ Written and copyrighted by Gary Dessler, PhD.

staying union-free. Furthermore, the evidence seemed to support their position. At least one study that she'd seen concluded that firms with 30% or more of their eligible workers in unions were in the bottom 10% in terms of performance, while those with 8% to 9% of eligible workers in unions scored in the top 10%.[116] The problem was that the Hotel Paris really had no specific policies and procedures in place to help its managers and supervisors deal with union activities. With all the laws regarding what employers and their managers could and could not do to respond to a union's efforts, Lisa knew her company was "a problem waiting to happen." She turned her attention to deciding what steps she and her team should take with regard to labor relations and collective bargaining.

Lisa and the CFO knew that unionization was a growing reality for the Hotel Paris. Some of the hotel chain's U.S. employees were already unionized, and unions in this industry were quite active. For example, as they were surfing the Internet to better gauge the situation, Lisa and the CFO came across the Web site from the Hotel Employees Restaurant Union, Local 26. It describes their success in negotiating a contract at several local hotels including ones managed by the Westin and Hilton chains. The CFO and Lisa agreed that it was important that she and her team develop and institute a new set of policies and practices that would enable the Hotel Paris to deal more effectively with unions.

Together with a labor–management attorney, the team developed a 20-page "What You Need to Know When the Union Calls" manual for Hotel Paris managers and supervisors. This contained three sets of information. First, it provided a succinct outline of *labor relations law*, particularly as it relates to the company's managers. Second, it laid out a *detailed set of guidelines* regarding what supervisors could and could not do with respect to union-organizing activities. Third, it identified all line supervisors as the company's "*front-line eyes and ears*" with respect to union organizing activity. Here, the manual provided examples of activities that might suggest that a union was trying to organize the hotel's employees, and whom the supervisor should notify.

Lisa and her team also decided to ensure that the company was responsive to its employees' concerns. Lisa and her team believed that many of the steps they'd taken earlier should help. For example, improving salaries and wages, providing financial incentives, and instituting the new ethics, justice, and fairness programs already seemed to be having a measurable effect on employee morale.

Questions

15-17. List and briefly describe what you believe are the three most important steps Hotel Paris management can take now to reduce the likelihood unions will organize more of its employees.

15-18. Write a detailed two-page outline for a "What You Need to Know When the Union Calls" manual. Lisa will distribute this manual to her company's supervisors and managers, telling them what they need to know about looking out for possible unionizing activity, and how to handle actual organizing process-related supervisory tasks.

CHAPTER 15

Writing Assignments

15-19. Describe important tactics you would expect the union to use during the union drive and election.

15-20. Why, would you say, workers join unions, and what would you as a manager do to make it less likely your employees would want to join a union at your workplace?

PERSONAL INVENTORY ASSESSMENTS

Go to **www.pearson.com/mylab/management** to complete the Personal Inventory Assessment related to this chapter.

Key Terms

closed shop, 487
union shop, 487
agency shop, 487
preferential shop, 487
right to work, 487
Norris–LaGuardia Act of 1932, 488
National Labor Relations (or Wagner) Act, 488
National Labor Relations Board (NLRB), 488
Taft–Hartley Act of 1947, 490
national emergency strikes, 491
Landrum–Griffin Act of 1959, 491
union salting, 492
authorization cards, 492
bargaining unit, 494
decertification, 497
collective bargaining, 498
good faith bargaining, 498
voluntary (or permissible) bargaining items, 500
illegal bargaining items, 500
mandatory bargaining items, 500
impasse, 501
mediation, 501
fact finder, 501
arbitration, 501
interest arbitration, 501
rights arbitration, 501
strike, 502
economic strike, 502
unfair labor practice strike, 502
wildcat strike, 502
sympathy strike, 502
picketing, 503
corporate campaign, 504
boycott, 504
inside games, 504
lockout, 504
injunction, 504
grievance procedure, 505

Endnotes

1. https://www.cnbc.com/2018/01/11/walmart-to-boost-starting-wage-give-employees-bonus-after-tax-bill.html, accessed January 11, 2018.
2. For example, see http://articles.moneycentral.msn.com/Investing/Extra/CostcoTheAntiWalMart.aspx?page=1, accessed June 29, 2011; and Hamilton Nolan, "The Anti-Wal-Mart," http://gawker.com/costco-the-anti-wal-mart-511739135, accessed August 7, 2013.
3. Steven Greenhouse, "Share of the Workforce in a Union Falls to a 97 Year Low, 11.3%," *The New York Times*, January 24, 2013, B1; https://www.bls.gov/news.release/union2.nr0.htm, accessed January 9, 2017.
4. https://www.bls.gov/news.release/union2.t05.htm, accessed June 11, 2018. And increasingly unions are organizing workers at tech and new media firms like Facebook and salon.com. Lukas Alpert, "Labor Unions Move into New Media as Investors Circle," *The Wall Street Journal*, August 30, 2015, p. B6.
5. Michael Ash and Jean Seago, "The Effect of Registered Nurses' Unions on Heart Attack Mortality," *Industrial and Labor Relations Review* 57, no. 3 (April 2004), pp. 422–442.
6. Source: Hamilton Nolan, "The Anti-Wal-Mart," http://gawker.com/costco-the-anti-wal-mart-511739135, accessed August 7, 2013; http://articles.moneycentral.msn.com/Investing/Extra/CostcoTheAntiWalMart.aspx?page 1; Dale Busa, "A Look at Walmart's HR Strategy from the Inside Out: Would It Work for Your Company?" chiefexecutive.net, May 8, 2016; Lauren Thomas and Courtney Reagan, "Walmart to Raise Its Starting Wage to $11, Give Some Employees Bonuses Following Tax Bill Passage," www.CNBC.com/2018/01/11; Leslie Picker and Rachel Abrams, "Walmart Rewrites Its e-Commerce Strategy with $3.3 Billion Deal for jet.com," www.NYTimes.com/2016/08/09; all accessed January 11, 2018; https://blog.walmart.com/business/20160919/five-big-reasons-walmart-bought-jetcom, accessed June 11, 2018.
7. https://stats.bls.gov/cps/cpsaat43.pdf, accessed \January 9, 2017.
8. "Union Benefit Costs Prevailing," *Bloomberg BNA Bulletin to Management*, May 14, 2013, p. 156.
9. Kris Maher, "The New Union Worker," *The Wall Street Journal*, September 27, 2005, pp. B1, B11.
10. Robert Grossman, "Unions Follow Suit," *HR Magazine*, May 2005, p. 49.
11. Not surprisingly, the big questions facing employees are whether the union can be helpful in getting the workers what they want, and the likelihood that collective action will succeed. M. Teresa Cardador et al., "To Be or Not to Be Unionized? A Social Dilemma Perspective on Worker Decisions to Support Union Organizing," *Human Resource Management Review*, 27, no. 3 (September 2017), p. 559.
12. Warner Pflug, *The UAW in Pictures* (Detroit: Wayne State University Press, 1971), pp. 11–12.
13. Josh Eidelson, "What Do We Want? Uber Union," *Bloomberg Businessweek*, October 31, 2016, pp. 33–34. Unions are still far from unanimous about how to handle gig worker unions, but are working with legislatures to find solutions. See, for example, Chris Opfer, "Gig Worker Organizers Still Looking for a Roadmap," *Bloomberg Labor & Employment on Bloomberg Law*, May 26, 2017.
14. Eidelson, "What Do We Want? Uber Union." Other cities are moving to let drivers from companies like Uber and Lyft organize. For example, the Seattle City Council approved a bill that, if passed, would let drivers form unions, and in California the group California App-Based Drivers Association has pushed for legislation allowing drivers to organize. Nick Wingfield and Mike Isaac, "Seattle Will Allow Uber and Lyft Drivers to Form Unions," *The New York Times*, www.NYTimes.com/2015/12/15/technology/ December 14, 2015, accessed January 8, 2017; Dennis Romero, "Uber Drivers Team Up with Teamsters Union," *LA Weekly*, August 28, 2014, http://www.laweekly.com/news/uber-drivers-team-up-with-teamsters-union-5040562, accessed June 14, 2018.
15. "Employee Engagement: A New Union Avoidance Strategy," June 28, 2011, www.modernsurvey.com, accessed April 12, 2014.
16. This is based on Jessica Tyler, "Employee Engagement and Labor Relations," *Gallup Business Journal*. http://businessJournal.Gallup.com, accessed April 9, 2014.
17. Arthur Sloane and Fred Witney, *Labor Relations* (Upper Saddle River, NJ: Prentice Hall, 2007), pp. 335–336.
18. Benjamin Taylor and Fred Witney, *Labor Relations Law* (Upper Saddle River, NJ: Prentice Hall, 1992), pp. 170–171; www.dol.gov/whd/state/righttowork.htm, accessed June 5, 2010.
19. http://www.ncsl.org/research/labor-and-employment/right-to-work-laws-and-bills.aspx, accessed June 11, 2018.
20. "Research Inconclusive About Effective Right to Work on Economy," *Bloomberg BNA Bulletin to Management*, January 8, 2013, p. 14.
21. "Unions Hit Hard by Job Losses, Right to Work," *Daily Oklahoman* (via *Knight Ridder/Tribune Business News*), February 1, 2005. See also www.dol.gov/whd/state/righttowork.htm, accessed September 11, 2014.
22. www.seiu.org/our-union/, accessed June 1, 2011.
23. Steven Greenhouse, "4th Union Quits AFL–CIO in a Dispute Over Organizing," *The New York Times*, September 15, 2005, p. A14.
24. Some trace early U.S. labor relations legislation back to a fire at the Triangle Shirtwaist factory in 1911. Following that tragedy, New York City and New York State soon adopted 36 new laws, and many view these laws as the basis for and precursor to the U.S. labor legislation efforts that began in earnest in the 1930s. "The Birth of the New Deal," *The Economist*, March 19, 2011, p. 39.
25. The following material is based on Sloane and Witney, *Labor Relations*, pp. 46–124.
26. Michael Carrell and Christina Heavrin, *Labor Relations and Collective Bargaining* (Upper Saddle River, NJ: Prentice Hall, 2004), p. 7. The word *union* doesn't appear in the National Labor Relations Act, which just refers to "labor organizations." Many unions, such as the Fraternal Order of Police, don't have "union" in their names. Similarly, workers can "organize" without forming a union. In one case employees of a car wash formed a workers' committee and sent a letter to their employer requesting better treatment. The employer reacted by terminating their employment. Federal labor law prohibits employers from retaliating against workers who band together to try to improve their working conditions. Under pressure from the NLRB the employer reinstated the employees, paid their back wages, and improved the workers' treatment and working conditions. Steven Greenhouse, "Workers Organize, but Don't Unionize, to Get Protection Under Labor Law," *The New York Times*, September 7, 2015, pp. B1, B4.
27. https://www.bls.gov/news.release/union2.t05.htm, accessed June 11, 2018.
28. Carrell and Heavrin, *Labor Relations and Collective Bargaining*, p. 180.
29. Sloane and Witney, *Labor Relations*, p. 121.
30. For organizing examples from the unions' point of view, see www.twu.org/international/steps, accessed June 29, 2011; www.opeiu.org/NeedAUnion/StepstoCreatingaUnionWorkplace/tabid/71/Default.aspx, accessed June 29, 2011; and particularly http://ufcwone.org/steps-form-union, accessed August 7, 2013.
31. Kris Maher, "Unions' New Foe: Consultants," *The Wall Street Journal*, August 15, 2005, p. B1.
32. "Some Say Salting Leaves Bitter Taste for Employers," *BNA Bulletin to Management*, March 4, 2004, p. 79; www.nlrb.gov/global/search/index.aspx?mode=s&qt=salting&col=nlrb&gb=y, accessed January 14, 2008. For a management lawyer's perspective, see www.fklaborlaw.com/union_salt-objectives.html, accessed May 25, 2007.
33. "Spurned Union Salts Entitled to Back Pay, D.C. Court Says, Affirming Labor Board," *BNA Bulletin to Management*, June 21, 2001, p. 193.
34. D. Diane Hatch and James Hall, "Salting Cases Clarified by NLRB," *Workforce*, August 2000, p. 92. See also www.fklaborlaw.com/union_salt-objectives.html, accessed May 25, 2007.
35. Josh Eidelson, "Workers of Silicon Valley Unite!" *Bloomberg Businessweek*, September 18, 2017, pp. 22–24.
36. http://www.laborandcollective-bargaining.com/2014/11/articles/unions-and-organizing/unions-winning-more-elections-but-facing-diminishing-returns/, accessed September 20, 2015.
37. This section is based on Matthew Goodfellow, "How to Lose an NLRB Election," *Personnel Administrator* 23 (September 1976), pp. 40–44. See also Matthew Goodfellow, "Avoid Unionizing: Chemical Company Union Election Results for 1993," *Chemical Marketing Reporter* 246 (July 18, 1994), p. SR14; Gillian Flynn, "When the Unions Come Calling," *Workforce*, November 2000, pp. 82–87.

38. Ibid.
39. Ibid.
40. Harry Katz, "The Decentralization of Collective Bargaining: A Literature Review and Comparative Analysis," *Industrial and Labor Relations Review* 47, no. 1 (October 1993), p. 11; F. Traxler, "Bargaining (De)centralization, Macroeconomic Performance and Control over the Employment Relationship," *British Journal of Industrial Relations* 41, no. 1 (March 2003), pp. 1–27.
41. The following are adapted and/or quoted from Kate Bronfenbrenner, "The Role of Union Strategies in NLRB Certification Elections," *Industrial and Labor Relations Review* 50 (January 1997), pp. 195–212; see also J. Fiorito et. al., "Understanding Organising Activity Among US National Unions," *Industrial Relations Journal* 41, no. 1 (January 2010), pp. 74–92.
42. Stephen Greenhouse, "Union Gets New Election at a Target," *The New York Times*, May 22, 2012, B3.
43. Frederick Sullivan, "Limiting Union Organizing Activity Through Supervisors," *Personnel* 55 (July/August 1978), pp. 55–65. See also Edward Young and William Levy, "Responding to a Union-Organizing Campaign: Do You and Your Supervisors Know the Legal Boundaries in a Union Campaign?" *Franchising World* 39, no. 3 (March 2007), pp. 45–49.
44. www.hreonline.com/HRE/view/story.jhtml?id=534358235, accessed April 25, 2015.
45. Carrell and Heavrin, *Labor Relations and Collective Bargaining*, pp. 167–168.
46. Jonathan Segal, "Unshackle Your Supervisors to Stay Union Free," *HR Magazine*, June 1998, pp. 62–65. See also www.nlrb.gov/rights-we-protect/employerunion-rights-and-obligations, accessed September 11, 2014.
47. Whether employers must give union representatives permission to organize on employer-owned property at shopping malls is a matter of legal debate. See, for example, "Union Access to Employer's Customers Restricted," *BNA Bulletin to Management*, February 15, 1996, p. 49; "Workplace Access for Unions Hinges on Legal Issues," *BNA Bulletin to Management*, April 11, 1996, p. 113.
48. "Union Access to Employer's Customers Restricted," pp. 4–65. The appropriateness of these sample rules may be affected by factors unique to an employer's operation, and they should therefore be reviewed by the employer's attorney before implementation.
49. https://www.bna.com/nlrb-conducted-elections-n57982068022/, accessed January 10, 2017.
50. Carrell and Heavrin, *Labor Relations and Collective Bargaining*, pp. 120–121.
51. See, for example, David Meyer and Trevor Bain, "Union Decertification Election Outcomes: Bargaining Unit Characteristics and Union Resources," *Journal of Labor Research* 15, no. 2 (Spring 1994), pp. 117–136; Sloane and Witney, Labor Relations, p. 96.
52. Based on Nick Wingfield and Melissa Eddy, "In Germany, Union Culture Clashes with Amazon's Labor Practices," *The New York Times*, August 5, 2013, pp. B1, B4.
53. Mimosa Spencer and Jeanne Whalen, "Change France? Sanofi Finds It Can't," *The Wall Street Journal*, April 11, 2013, pp. B1, D5.
54. Ibid., B1. Similarly, workers in Germany are resisting what they call Amazon's American-style business practices. Nick Wingfield and Melissa Eddy, "In Germany, Union Culture Clashes with Amazons' Labor Practices," *The New York Times*, August 5, 2013, pp. B1, B4.
55. www.nlrb.gov/nlrb/shared_files/brochures/basicguide.pdf, accessed January 14, 2008.
56. Carrell and Heavrin, *Labor Relations and Collective Bargaining*, pp. 176–177.
57. www.bloomberg.com/news/2011-02-14/nfl-files-unfair-labor-practice-charge-against-union.html, accessed June 1, 2011.
58. John Fossum, *Labor Relations* (Dallas: BPI, 1982), pp. 246–250; Sloane and Witney, *Labor Relations*, pp. 197–205.
59. *Boulwareism* is the name given to a strategy, now held in disfavor, by which the company, based on an exhaustive study of what it believed its employees wanted, made but one offer at the bargaining table and then refused to bargain any further unless convinced by the union on the basis of new facts that its original position was wrong. Fossum, *Labor Relations*, p. 267.
60. Kathryn Tyler, "Good-Faith Bargaining," *HR Magazine*, January 2005, p. 52.
61. These are based on James C. Freund, *Smart Negotiating* (New York: Simon & Schuster, 1992), pp. 42–46.
62. Freund, *Smart Negotiating*, pp. 42–46.
63. Ibid., 33. One interesting observation: Communicating threats is more effective than communicating anger. See Marwan Sineceure et al., "Hot or Cold: Is Communicating Anger or Threats More Effective in Negotiation?" *Journal of Applied Psychology* 96, no. 5 (2011), pp. 1019–1032.
64. Reed Richardson, *Collective Bargaining by Objectives* (Upper Saddle River, NJ: Prentice Hall, 1977), p. 150. Both sides will try to manipulate the media to jockey for better positions; for example, see J. McCafferty, "Labor-Management Dispute Resolution and the Media," *Dispute Resolution Journal* 56, no. 3 (August/October 2001), pp. 40–47.
65. Many negotiators pride themselves on being open, honest, and straightforward in their negotiations, but at least one study suggests that this can lead to excessive concessions. D. Scott DeRue et al., "When Is Straightforwardness a Liability in Negotiations? The Role of Integrative Potential and Structural Power," *Journal of Applied Psychology* 94, no. 4 (2009), pp. 1032–1047.
66. Tori Walker, "Polk School District Reaches Impasse with Unions," January 6, 2017, http://www.theledger.com/news/20170106/polk-school-district-reaches-impasse-with-unions, accessed January 10, 2017.
67. With or without reaching a solution, impasses and union–management conflict can leave union members demoralized. See, for example, Jessica Marquez, "Taking Flight," *Workforce*, June 9, 2008, pp. 1, 18.
68. Jacqueline Palank et al., "Last Chance to Save the Twinkie," *The Wall Street Journal*, November 20, 2012, p. B1.
69. Fossum, *Labor Relations*, p. 312.
70. Carrell and Heavrin, *Labor Relations and Collective Bargaining*, p. 501.
71. Alternative Dispute Resolution (ADR), http://www.va.gov/ADR/Impasse.asp, accessed January 10, 2017.
72. http://fmcs.gov/assets/files/annual%20reports/FY2006_Annual_Report.pdf, accessed January 14, 2008.
73. Fossum, *Labor Relations*, p. 317.
74. www.autoblog.com/2010/12/06/report-uaw-to-hold-sympathy-strike-for-hyundai-workers-in-korea/, accessed June 1, 2011.
75. Amie Tsang, "Ryanair Hit by Its First Pilot Strike, Days After Collapse of Union Talks," *The New York Times*, December 23, 2017, p. B3.
76. This is based on Sloane and Whitney, *Labor Relations*, p. 213.
77. http://fuelfix.com/blog/2015/02/18/strike-update-bp-training-additional-replacement-workers/#30249101=0, accessed July 24, 2015.
78. http://profootballtalk.nbcsports.com/2011/03/21/league-doesnt-rule-out-replacement-players-during-lockout/, accessed June 29, 2011.
79. See, for example, www.afimac-us.com/what-we-do/labor-disputes-and-plant-closures/strike-security/, accessed April 11, 2014.
80. Stephen Cabot and Gerald Cuerton, "Labor Disputes and Strikes: Be Prepared," *Personnel Journal* 60 (February 1981), pp. 121–126. See also Brenda Sunoo, "Managing Strikes, Minimizing Loss," *Personnel Journal* 74, no. 1 (January 1995), p. 50ff.
81. Some labor lawyers report an increase in the use by unions of corporate campaigns. Janet Walthall, "Unions Increasingly Using Corporate Campaigns," *Bloomberg BNA Bulletin to Management*, February 16, 2010, p. 55.
82. For a discussion, see Herbert Northrup, "Union Corporate Campaigns and Inside Games as a Strike Form," *Employee Relations Law Journal* 19, no. 4 (Spring 1994), pp. 507–549.
83. www.blogging4jobs.com/wp-content/uploads/2012/02/unions-social-media.png, accessed April 25, 2015.
84. www.bna.com/social-media-new-b17179923064/, accessed April 25, 2015.
85. www.starbucksunion.org, accessed August 7, 2013.
86. www.hreonline.com/HRE/view/story.jhtml?id=534358235, accessed April 25, 2015.
87. Northrup, "Union Corporate Campaigns and Inside Games," p. 513.
88. Ibid., p. 518.
89. James Hagerty and Caroline Van Hasselt, "Lockout Tests Union's Clout," *The Wall Street Journal*, January 30, 2012, p. B-1.
90. Jon Ostrower, "Boeing Considers Nonunion Plant for 777X," *The Wall Street Journal*, October 20, 2013, p. B3; Jon Ostrower, "Boeing Prods Unions on Pact," *The Wall Street Journal*, November 9–10, 2013, p. B3.
91. Clifford Koen Jr., Sondra Hartman, and Dinah Payne, "The NLRB Wields a Rejuvenated Weapon," *Personnel Journal*, December 1996, pp. 85–87; D. Silverman, "The NLRA at 70: A New Approach to Processing 10(j)s [NLRA at Seventy conference in New York City, 2005]," *Labor Law Journal* 56, no. 3 (Fall 2005), pp. 203–206.
92. http://sports.espn.go.com/nfl/news/story?id=4508545, accessed November 17, 2009.

93. Carrell and Heavrin, *Labor Relations and Collective Bargaining*, pp. 417–418.
94. Richardson, *Collective Bargaining by Objectives*.
95. Based on M. Gene Newport, *Supervisory Management* (St. Paul, MN: West Group, 1976), p. 273; see also Walter Baer, *Grievance Handling: 101 Guides for Supervisors* (New York: American Management Association, 1970); and Mark Lurie, "The Eight Essential Steps in Grievance Processing," *Dispute Resolution Journal* 54, no. 4 (November 1999), pp. 61–65.
96. https://www.bls.gov/news.release/union2.nr0.htm, accessed January 9, 2017.
97. Susan Carey and Jack Nicas, "AMR Will Ask the Judge to Toss Labor Pacts," *The Wall Street Journal*, March 23, 2012, p. B3.
98. Kris Maher and Jacqueline Palank, "Patriot Coal Allowed to Win Union PACs," *The Wall Street Journal*, May 30, 2013, p. B1.
99. www.bls.gov/news.release/union2.nr0.htm, accessed April 2, 2009.
100. http://www.changetowin.org/about-us/ accessed January 9, 2018.
101. https://aflcio.org/, accessed January 9, 2018.
102. Matthew Sedacca, "Labor Unions Gain Foothold at News Sites," *The New York Times*, December 27, 2017, pp. B1, B2.
103. Ibid.
104. Steven Greenhouse, "At a Nissan Plant in Mississippi, a Battle to Shape the UAW's Future," *The New York Times*, October 7, 2013, pp. B1, B3.
105. Neal Boudette, "A New Alliance: UAW in Germany," *The Wall Street Journal*, November 8, 2013, pp. B1, B2.
106. www.littler.com/publication-press/publication/nlrb-issues-its-long-anticipated-quickie-election-rule-making-union-or, accessed April 25, 2015.
107. Ibid.
108. Eric Morath, "Trump to Nominate Attorney William Emanuel to National Labor Relations Board," *The Wall Street Journal*, June 28, 2017, www.wsj.com/articles/trump-to-nominate-attorney-william-emanuel-to-national-labor-relations-board-1498650169, accessed June 28, 2017.
109. David Jamieson, "Republicans Want to Pass a National Right To Work Law," https://www.huffingtonpost.com/entry/republicans-pursue-national-right-to-work-law-while-they-hold-the-reins-in-washington_us_5891fb30e4b0522c7d3e354d, accessed June 11, 2018.
110. Carrell and Heavrin, *Labor Relations and Collective Bargaining*, pp. 62–63.
111. Carol Gill, "Union Impact on the Effective Adoption of High Performance Work Practices," *Human Resource Management Review* 19 (2009), pp. 39–50.
112. See also Thomas Kochan, "A Jobs Compact for America's Future," *Harvard Business Review*, March 2012, pp. 64–70.
113. © Gary Dessler, PhD. For information on what employers should not do, see https://www.nlrb.gov/rights-we-protect/whats-law/employers/interfering-employee-rights-section-7-8a1, accessed January 16, 2018.
114. Ibid.
115. Copyright Gary Dessler, PhD. Sources for this case include Matthew Sedacca, "Labor Unions Gain Foothold at News Sites," *The New York Times*, December 27, 2017, pp. B1, B2; Lucas Alpert and Shalini Ramachandran, "Vice Media Secures $450 Million Investment from Private Equity Firm TPG," www.WSJ.com/articles, accessed January 11, 2018; Matthew Ingram, "Vice Media Joins The Waiver Unionization Rolling over New-Media Companies," Fortune.com, accessed January 11, 2018; Gary Weiss, "An Unlikely Big Player in Digital Media: Unions," *Columbia Journalism Review*, www.CJR.org/, accessed January 11, 2018; Noah Kulwin, "vice media is the Second Big Digital Publisher to Unionize," https://www.recode.net/2016/4/15/11586166/vice-media-union-contract, accessed June 11, 2018; Dave McNary, "Vice Media Video Employees Unionize with Writers Guild East and Editors Guild," http://variety.com, accessed January 11, 2018; Maxwell Tani, "Fox Media Voluntarily Recognizes Employee Editorial Union," www.businessinsider.com, accessed January 11, 2018.
116. Brian Becker et al., *The HR Scorecard* (Boston: Harvard Business School Press, 2001), p. 16.

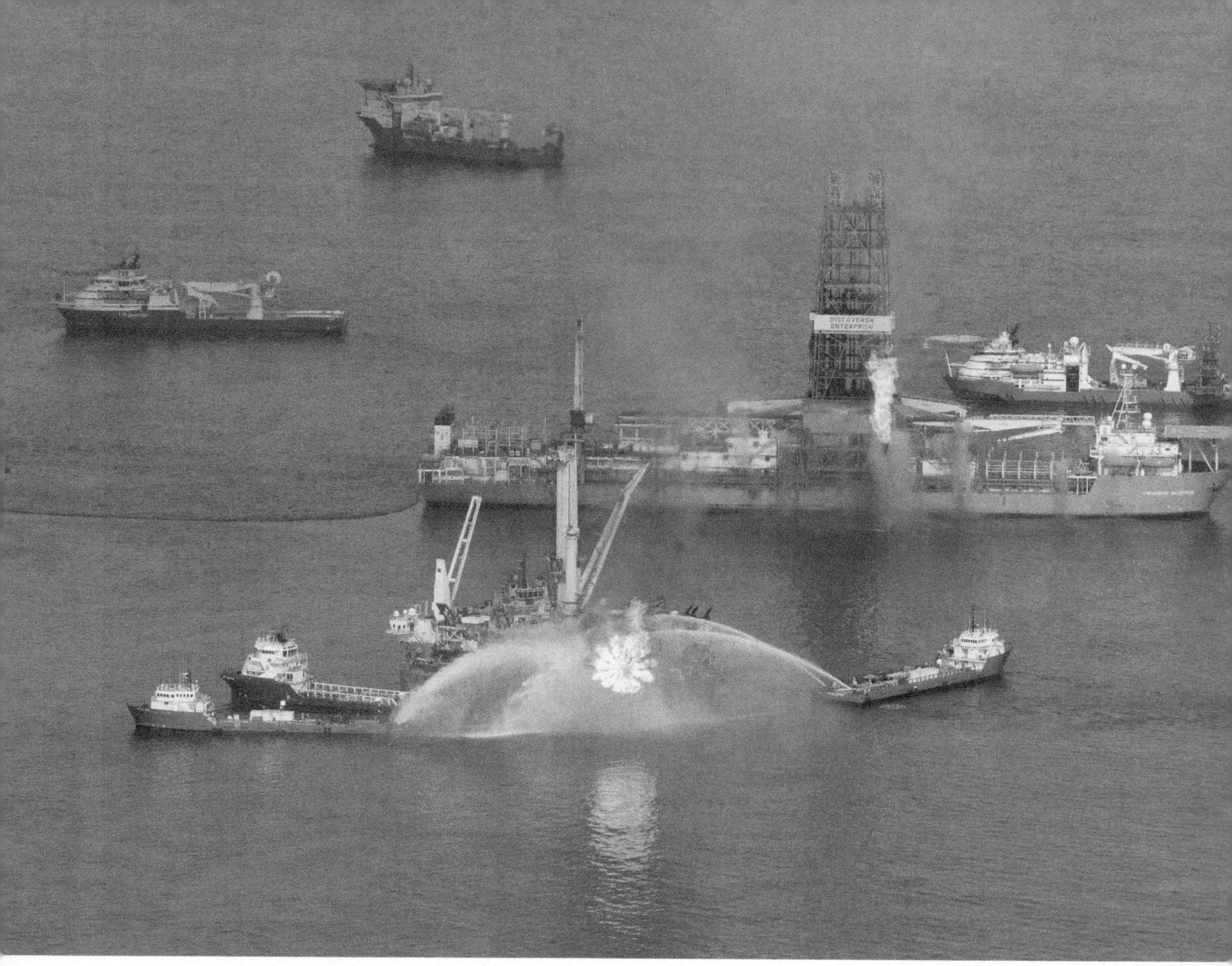

Breck P. Kent/Shutterstock

16 Safety, Health, and Risk Management

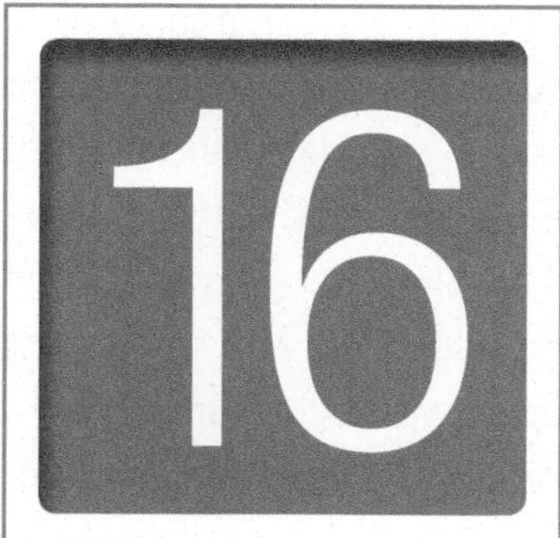

LEARNING OBJECTIVES

When you finish studying this chapter, you should be able to:

16-1 **Explain** the supervisor's role in safety.

16-2 **Explain** the basic facts about safety law and OSHA.

16-3 **Answer** the question, "What causes accidents?"

16-4 **List and explain** five ways to prevent accidents at work.

16-5 **Describe** how one company uses employee engagement to improve workplace safety.

16-6 **List** five workplace health hazards and how to deal with them.

16-7 **Discuss** the prerequisites for a security plan and how to set up a basic security program.

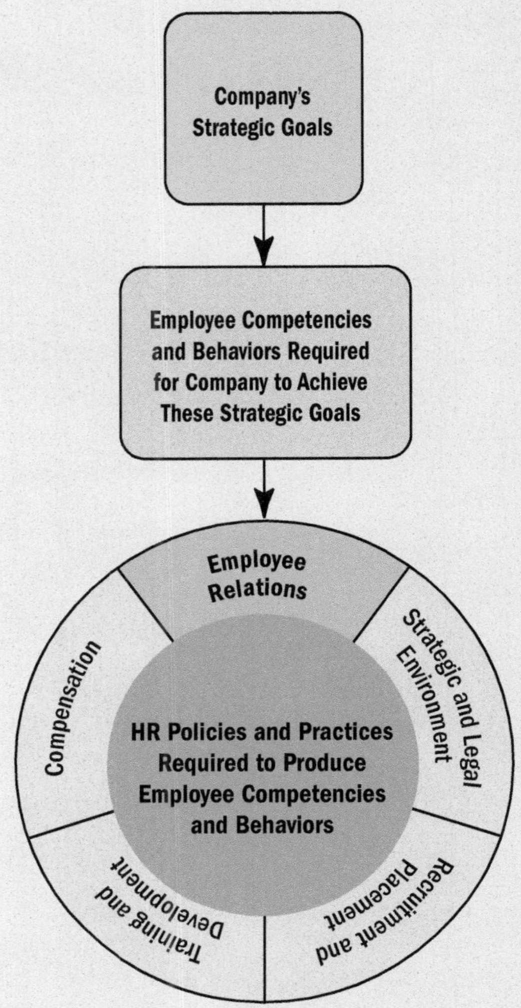

When it comes to safety strategy, the, explosion and fire on British Petroleum's (BP's) Deepwater Horizon rig in the Gulf of Mexico back in 2010 still epitomizes what can go wrong. The blast took the lives of 11 workers.[2] Reports from the scene said a malfunctioning blowout preventer failed to activate, causing the disaster. Past critics of BP's safety practices weren't so sure.

WHERE ARE WE NOW . . .

Over 80% of the workers in one survey ranked workplace safety more important than minimum wages, sick days, and maternity leave.[1] The main purpose of this chapter is to provide you with knowledge managers need to reduce workplace safety and health problems. The main topics we discuss are **Safety and the Manager, Manager's Briefing on Occupational Safety Law, What Causes Accidents, How to Prevent Accidents, Employee Engagement–Based Safety Programs, Workplace Health Hazards—Problems and Remedies**, and **Occupational Security and Risk Management**.

LEARNING OBJECTIVE 16-1
Explain the supervisor's role in safety.

Introduction: Safety and the Manager

Why Safety Is Important

Several years ago while filming *Star Wars/The Force Awakens*, a hydraulic door on the Millennium Falcon spaceship slammed Harrison Ford. He couldn't work for several weeks, but thankfully wasn't injured seriously.[3]

Safety and accident prevention concern managers for several reasons, one of which is the staggering number of workplace accidents. For example, in one recent year, at least 5,190 people died at work, up from about 4,800 the year before.[4] Workplace accidents caused about 2.9 million occupational injuries and illnesses.[5]

Such figures probably underestimate injuries and illnesses by two or three times.[6] And they ignore the suffering the accidents cause the employee and his or her loved ones.[7] Safety also affects costs and profits, as the accompanying Profit Center feature illustrates.

IMPROVING PERFORMANCE: *HR AS A PROFIT CENTER*

Improving Safety Boosts Profits

Many people assume that when employers economize on safety programs the money they save improves profits, but that's not the case. For one thing, poor safety practices raise wage rates, because wage rates are higher on jobs with riskier working conditions, other things equal.[8] And poor safety and the injuries and illnesses it begets actually drive up costs, including medical expenses, workers' compensation, and lost productivity.[9]

Consider the evidence. One study found a 9.4% drop in injury claims and a 26% average savings on workers' compensation costs over 4 years in companies inspected by California's occupational safety and health agency.[10] A survey of chief financial officers concluded that for every one dollar invested in injury prevention, the employer earns two dollars; 40% said "productivity" was the top benefit of effective workplace safety.[11] One forest products company saved over $1 million over 5 years by investing only about $50,000 in safety improvements and employee training. In the United States, work-related hearing loss costs employers about $242 million a year in workers' compensation claims alone, costs that are probably avoidable through earmuffs, earplugs, and training.[12] So one of the easiest ways to cut costs and boost profits is to spend money improving safety. ■

MyLab Management Talk About It 1

If your professor has assigned this, go to the Assignments section of **www.pearson.com/mylab/management** to complete this discussion question. Assuming this is true, why do so many employers apparently cut corners on safety?

Injuries aren't just a problem in dangerous industries like construction. For example, computers contribute to airtight "sick building" symptoms like headaches. And office work is susceptible to problems like repetitive trauma injuries.

Top Management's Role in Safety

Several years ago an energy company's CEO was convicted over the deaths of 29 workers in a coal mine.[13] His conviction highlights the fact that the people at the top—the CEO, president, and board members—must set the tone for occupational safety.[14]

We will see that reducing accidents often boils down to reducing accident-causing conditions and accident-causing acts. However, telling employees to "work safely" is futile unless everyone knows management takes safety seriously.[15] Historically, for instance, Milliken & Company's accident rate has been lower than that of the chemical industry as a whole. Its safety record largely reflects Milliken's organizational commitment to safety, as reflected in this quote from a Milliken company blog:

> We've all heard the saying, "lead by example," and when it comes to creating a successful safety culture, this saying still rings true. In fact, the tone for safety is usually set from the top. Moving safety from "just another program" to an uncompromised value within the organization that everyone respects and follows will ensure its success.[16]

The Strategic Context feature further illustrates this.

IMPROVING PERFORMANCE: *THE STRATEGIC CONTEXT*

Deepwater Horizon

To critics of BP's safety practices, the Deepwater Horizon disaster in the Gulf wasn't just due to a malfunctioning blowout preventer.[17] To them, rightly or wrongly, the accident reflected the fact that BP's corporate strategy had long emphasized cost-cutting and profitability at the expense of safety. For example, 5 years earlier, a report by the Chemical Safety Board blamed a huge blast at BP's Texas City, Texas, oil refinery on cost-cutting, and on a safety strategy that aimed to reduce accidents but left in place "unsafe and antiquated equipment." To that board and to some others who studied BP's safety practices, Deepwater was another example of how encouraging safe employee behavior must start at the top, and how top management's strategy can trump even earnest efforts to improve employee safety behaviors.[18] A subsequent movie, *Deepwater Horizon*, depicts a BP executive, visiting the rig and annoyed by drilling delays, pressing the crew to ignore test results that in fact accurately showed the rig about to blow.

MyLab Management Talk About It 2

If your professor has assigned this, go to the Assignments section of **www.pearson.com/mylab/management** to complete these discussion questions. How would you make the case to BP's management that boosting safety can actually support an "improve profits" strategy? What evidence could you offer?

In sum, employers should institutionalize their commitment with a safety policy, publicize it, and give safety matters high priority. Louisiana-Pacific Corp. starts all meetings with a brief safety message.[19] Georgia-Pacific reduced its workers' compensation costs by requiring that managers halve accidents or forfeit 30% of their bonuses. ABB Inc. requires its top executives to make safety observation tours of the company's facilities, sites, and projects at least quarterly.[20]

The Supervisor's Role in Accident Prevention

After inspecting a work site in which workers were installing sewer pipes in a 4-foot trench, the Occupational Safety & Health Administration (OSHA) inspector cited the employer for violating the OSHA rule requiring employers to have a "stairway, ladder, ramp or other safe means of egress."[21] In the event the trench caved in, workers needed a quick way out.[22]

As in most such cases, the employer had the primary responsibility for safety, but the local supervisor was responsible for day-to-day inspections. Here, the supervisor did not properly do his daily inspection. The trench did cave in, injuring workers (and, secondarily, costing his company many thousands of dollars).

Whether you're an IT department manager in a *Fortune* 500 company or managing an excavation or dry-cleaning store, daily safety inspections should be part of your routine. As one safety recommendation put it, "a daily walk-through of your workplace—whether you are working in outdoor construction, indoor manufacturing, or any place that poses safety challenges—is an essential part of your work."[23]

What to look for depends on the workplace. For example, construction sites and dry-cleaning stores have hazards all their own. But in general, you can use a checklist of unsafe conditions such as the one in Figure 16-6 (pages 529–531) to spot problems. We present another, more extensive checklist in Figure 16-8 (pages 551–554) at the end of this chapter. (Note: Please stop what you are reading and look around where you are now: Can you list four potential safety hazards?)

Manager's Briefing on Occupational Safety Law

LEARNING OBJECTIVE 16-2

Explain the basic facts about safety law and OSHA.

Congress passed the **Occupational Safety and Health Act of 1970**[24] "to assure so far as possible every working man and woman in the nation safe and healthful working conditions and to preserve our human resources."[25] The only employers it

Occupational Safety and Health Act of 1970
The law passed by Congress in 1970 "to assure so far as possible every working man and woman in the nation safe and healthful working conditions and to preserve our human resources."

Occupational Safety and Health Administration (OSHA)
The agency created within the Department of Labor to set safety and health standards for almost all workers in the United States.

doesn't cover are self-employed persons, farms in which only immediate members of the employer's family work, and some workplaces already protected by other federal agencies or under other statutes. The act covers federal agencies, but usually not state and local governments.

The act created the **Occupational Safety and Health Administration (OSHA)** within the Department of Labor. OSHA's basic purpose is to administer the act and to set and enforce the safety and health standards that apply to almost all workers in the United States. OSHA has about 2,200 inspectors working from branches around the country.[26] Its exact enforcement direction was recently in flux. However, OSHA and many employers continue to emphasize OSHA's cooperative programs, such as its Voluntary Protection Program (VPP). VPP exempts from routine inspections those employers who have OSHA-approved policies and programs *and* below-average injury and illness rates.[27]

OSHA Standards and Record Keeping

OSHA operates under the "general" standard clause that each employer:

> . . . shall furnish to each of his [or her] employees employment and a place of employment which are free from recognized hazards that are causing or are likely to cause death or serious physical harm to his [or her] employees.

To carry out this basic mission, OSHA promulgates detailed legally enforceable standards. (Employers also follow standards from the International Safety Equipment Association and from the American National Standards Institute.)[28] Figure 16-1 shows part of the OSHA standard governing scaffold handrails.[29]

The regulations don't just list standards to which employers should adhere, but "how." For example, OSHA's respiratory protection standard also covers employee training.

Under OSHA, employers with 11 or more employees must maintain records of and report certain occupational injuries and occupational illnesses. An **occupational illness** is any abnormal condition or disorder caused by exposure to environmental factors associated with employment. This includes acute and chronic illnesses caused by inhalation, absorption, ingestion, or direct contact with toxic substances or harmful agents.

occupational illness
Any abnormal condition or disorder caused by exposure to environmental factors associated with employment.

WHAT THE EMPLOYER MUST REPORT Employers must report *all* occupational illnesses. As in Figure 16-2,[30] they must also report most occupational injuries, specifically those that result in medical treatment (other than first aid), loss of consciousness, restriction of work (one or more lost workdays), restriction of motion, or transfer to another job.[31] If an on-the-job accident results in the death of an employee, all employers, regardless of size, must report the accident to the nearest OSHA office. If even one employee is hospitalized for inpatient treatment because of a work-related incident, the employer must notify OSHA within 24 hours.[32]

Similarly, OSHA's record-keeping requirements are broad.[33] Examples of recordable conditions include any work-related fatality, any work-related injury or illness that results in loss of consciousness, days away from work, restricted work, or transfer to another job, and any work-related injury or illness requiring medical treatment beyond first aid.

Figure 16-3 shows the OSHA form for reporting occupational injuries or illness.

FIGURE 16-1 OSHA Standards Example
Source: From Occupational Safety and Hazard Administration (OSHA). Retrieved from https://www.osha.gov/pls/oshaweb/owadisp.show_document?p_table=STANDARDS&p_id=9720.

Guardrails not less than 2″ × 4″ or the equivalent and not less than 36″ or more than 42″ high, with a midrail, when required, of a 1″ × 4″ lumber or equivalent, and toeboards, shall be installed at all open sides on all scaffolds more than 10 feet above the ground or floor. Toeboards shall be a minimum of 4″ in height. Wire mesh shall be installed in accordance with paragraph [a] (17) of this section.

FIGURE 16-2 What Accidents Must Be Reported Under the Occupational Safety and Health Act (OSHA)?

Source: https://www.osha.gov/recordkeeping2014/blog-OSHA-flow.pdf.

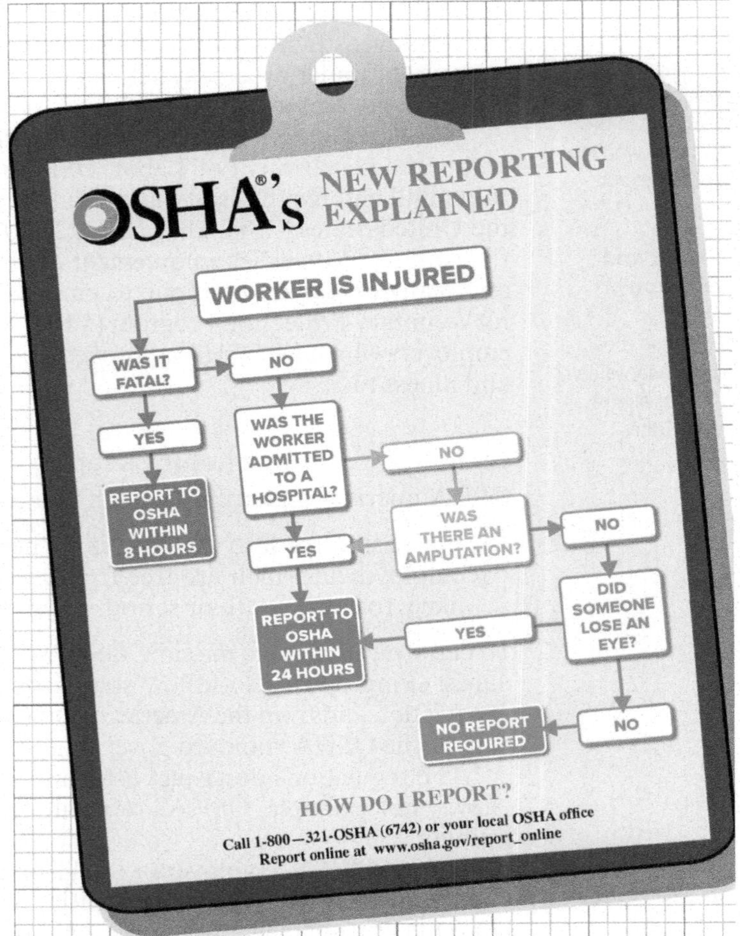

Inspections and Citations

OSHA enforces its standards through inspections and (if necessary) citations. The inspection is usually unannounced. OSHA may not conduct warrantless inspections without an employer's consent. It may inspect with an authorized search warrant.[34] With a limited number of inspectors, OSHA has focused on "fair and effective enforcement," combined with outreach, education and compliance assistance, and OSHA–employer cooperative programs (such as its Voluntary Protection Programs).[35]

INSPECTION PRIORITIES In inspections, OSHA takes a "worst-first" approach. Priorities include, from highest to lowest, imminent dangers, severe injuries and illnesses, worker complaints, referrals of hazards from other agencies, targeted high-hazard industries inspections, and follow-up inspections.[36] In one recent year, OSHA conducted about 32,400 inspections, and there were about 43,500 state inspections.[37] OSHA publicly posts employers' safety and health data in an effort to encourage safer practices.[38]

OSHA conducts an inspection within 24 hours when a complaint indicates an immediate danger, and within 3 working days when a serious hazard exists. For a "nonserious" complaint filed in writing by a worker or a union, OSHA will respond within 20 working days. OSHA handles other nonserious complaints by writing to the employer and requesting corrective action. OSHA told almost 15,000 U.S. employers that because of their higher-than-average injury and illness rates, they may be subject to inspections.[39]

THE INSPECTION The inspection begins when the OSHA officer arrives at the workplace.[40] He or she displays credentials and asks to meet an employer representative. (The credentials must include photograph and serial number.) The officer explains

OSHA's FORM 301

Injury and Illness Incident Report

Attention: This form contains information relating to employee health and must be used in a manner that protects the confidentiality of employees to the extent possible while the information is being used for occupational safety and health purposes.

U.S. Department of Labor
Occupational Safety and Health Administration

Form approved OMB no. 1218-0176

This *Injury and Illness Incident Report* is one of the first forms you must fill out when a recordable work-related injury or illness has occurred. Together with the *Log of Work-Related Injuries and Illnesses* and the accompanying *Summary*, these forms help the employer and OSHA develop a picture of the extent and severity of work-related incidents.

Within 7 calendar days after you receive information that a recordable work-related injury or illness has occurred, you must fill out this form or an equivalent. Some state workers' compensation, insurance, or other reports may be acceptable substitutes. To be considered an equivalent form, any substitute must contain all the information asked for on this form.

According to Public Law 91-596 and 29 CFR 1904, OSHA's recordkeeping rule, you must keep this form on file for 5 years following the year to which it pertains.

If you need additional copies of this form, you may photocopy and use as many as you need.

Completed by ____________

Title ____________

Phone (____) ____-______ **Date** ___/___/___

Information about the employee

1) Full name ____________

2) Street ____________

City ____________ State ______ ZIP ______

3) Date of birth ___/___/___

4) Date hired ___/___/___

5) ☐ Male
☐ Female

Information about the physician or other health care professional

6) Name of physician or other health care professional ____________

7) If treatment was given away from the worksite, where was it given?

Facility ____________

Street ____________

City ____________ State ______ ZIP ______

8) Was employee treated in an emergency room?
☐ Yes
☐ No

9) Was employee hospitalized overnight as an in-patient?
☐ Yes
☐ No

Information about the case

10) Case number from the *Log* ____________ *(Transfer the case number from the Log after you record the case.)*

11) Date of injury or illness ___/___/___

12) Time employee began work ________ AM/PM

13) Time of event ________ AM/PM
☐ Check if time cannot be determined

14) ***What was the employee doing just before the incident occurred?*** Describe the activity, as well as the tools, equipment, or material the employee was using. Be specific. *Examples:* "climbing a ladder while carrying roofing materials"; "spraying chlorine from hand sprayer"; "daily computer key-entry."

15) ***What happened?*** Tell us how the injury occurred. *Examples:* "When ladder slipped on wet floor, worker fell 20 feet"; "Worker was sprayed with chlorine when gasket broke during replacement"; "Worker developed soreness in wrist over time."

16) ***What was the injury or illness?*** Tell us the part of the body that was affected and how it was affected; be more specific than "hurt," "pain," or sore." *Examples:* "strained back"; "chemical burn, hand"; "carpal tunnel syndrome."

17) ***What object or substance directly harmed the employee?*** *Examples:* "concrete floor"; "chlorine"; "radial arm saw," *If this question does not apply to the incident, leave it blank.*

18) ***If the employee died, when did death occur?*** Date of death ___/___/___

Public reporting burden for this collection of information is estimated to average 22 minutes per response, including time for reviewing instructions, searching existing data sources, gathering and maintaining the data needed, and completing and reviewing the collection of information. Persons are not required to respond to the collection of information unless it displays a current valid OMB control number. If you have any comments about this estimate or any other aspects of this data collection, including suggestions for reducing this burden, contact: US Department of Labor, OSHA Office of Statistical Analysis, Room N-3644, 200 Constitution Avenue, NW, Washington, DC 20210. Do not send the completed forms to this office.

FIGURE 16-3 **Form Used to Record Occupational Injuries and Illnesses**

Source: U.S. Department of Labor.

the visit's purpose, the scope of the inspection, and the standards that apply. An authorized employee representative accompanies the officer during the inspection. The inspector can also stop and question workers (in private, if necessary). The act protects each employee from retaliation for exercising his or her whistleblower rights.[41]

OSHA inspectors look for all types of violations, but some areas grab more attention. The five most frequent OSHA inspection violations were for fall protection, hazard communication, scaffolding, respiratory protection, and lockout/tagout.[42]

Finally, the inspector holds a closing conference with the employer's representative. Here the inspector discusses apparent violations for which OSHA may issue or recommend a **citation** and penalty. At this point, the employer can produce records to show compliance efforts. Figure 16-4 lists a manager's inspection guidelines.

citation
Summons informing employers and employees of the regulations and standards that have been violated in the workplace.

OSHA provides a free On-Site Consultation Program, offering confidential occupational safety and health services to small- and medium-sized businesses. It uses safety experts from state agencies and is completely separate from the OSHA inspection effort; no citations are issued or penalties proposed.[43]

PENALTIES OSHA can impose penalties. These generally range from $5,000 up to $150,000 for willful or repeat serious violations but can be far higher—$13 million after a tragedy at BP's Texas City plant, for instance.[44] (The parties settle many OSHA cases before litigation, in "precitation settlements.")[45] OSHA issues the citation and agreed-on penalties simultaneously, after the employer initiates negotiation settlements.[46] Nonserious violations may carry no penalties.

In general, OSHA calculates penalties based on the gravity of the violation, usually taking into consideration things like the size of the business, the firm's compliance history, and the employer's good faith (although not for willful violations).[47] OSHA must have a final order from the independent Occupational Safety and Health Review Commission to enforce a penalty.[48] An employer who files a notice of contest can drag out an appeal for years.[49] OSHA publicizes its inspection results online. Its Web

FIGURE 16-4 Manager's OSHA Inspection Guidelines

Source: Patricia Polle, "When OSHA Knocks," *Occupational Hazards,* February 2008, pp. 59–61; Robert Grossman, "Handling Inspections: Tips From Insiders," *HR Magazine,* October 1999, pp. 41–50; and "OSHA Inspections," https://www.osha.gov/OshDoc/data_General_Facts/factsheet-inspections.pdf, accessed August 18, 2018

Initial Contact

- Refer the inspector to your OSHA coordinator.
- Check the inspector's credentials.
- Ask why he or she is inspecting. Is it a complaint? Programmed visit? Fatality or accident follow-up? Imminent danger investigation?
- If the inspection is the result of a complaint, the inspector won't identify the complainant, but you are entitled to know whether the person is a current employee.
- Notify your OSHA counsel, who should review all requests from the inspector for documents and information. Your counsel also should review the documents and information you provide to the inspector.

Opening Conference

- Establish the focus and scope of the planned inspection: Does the inspector want to inspect the premises or simply study your records?
- Discuss the procedures for protecting trade-secret areas, conducting employee interviews, and producing documents.
- Show the inspector that you have safety programs in place. He or she may not go to the work floor if paperwork is complete and up-to-date.

Walk-Around Inspection

- Accompany the inspector and take detailed notes.
- If the inspector takes a photo or video, you should too.
- Ask the inspector for duplicates of all physical samples and copies of all test results.
- Be helpful and cooperative, but don't volunteer information.
- To the extent possible, immediately correct any violation the inspector identifies.

site (www.osha.gov) provides easy access to most companies' (or competitors') OSHA enforcement history.[50]

Responsibilities and Rights of Employers and Employees

Both employers and employees have responsibilities and rights under the Occupational Safety and Health Act. *Employers* are responsible for providing "a workplace free from recognized hazards," for being familiar with mandatory OSHA standards, and for examining workplace conditions to make sure they conform to OSHA standards.[51] Employers have the right to seek advice and off-site consultation from OSHA, request and receive proper identification of the OSHA compliance officer before inspection, and to be advised by the compliance officer of the reason for an inspection.

Employees also have rights and responsibilities, but OSHA can't cite them for violations of their responsibilities. Employees are responsible, for example, for complying with all applicable OSHA standards, for following all employer safety and health rules and regulations, and for reporting hazardous conditions to the supervisor. They have the right to demand safety and health on the job without fear of punishment. Retaliating against employees for reporting injuries or safety problems is illegal (see the OSHA safety poster in Figure 16-5).[52]

DEALING WITH EMPLOYEE RESISTANCE Although employees are responsible to comply with OSHA standards, they often resist; the employer usually remains liable for any penalties. The refusal of some workers to wear hard hats typifies this problem.

Employers have attempted to defend themselves by citing worker intransigence. In most cases, courts still hold employers liable for workplace safety violations. The independent three-member Occupational Safety and Health Review Commission says employers must make "a diligent effort to discourage, by discipline if necessary, violations of safety rules by employees."[53] Cited for a workplace injury, the employer may claim employee misconduct. The key here is to provide documented evidence that the employee was properly trained to do the job the right way but did not.[54] But the only sure way to eliminate liability is to make sure that no accidents occur.

Polina Petrenko/Shutterstock

Employees have rights and responsibilities under OSHA standards, such as to wear their hard hats, but OSHA can't cite them if they violate their responsibilities.

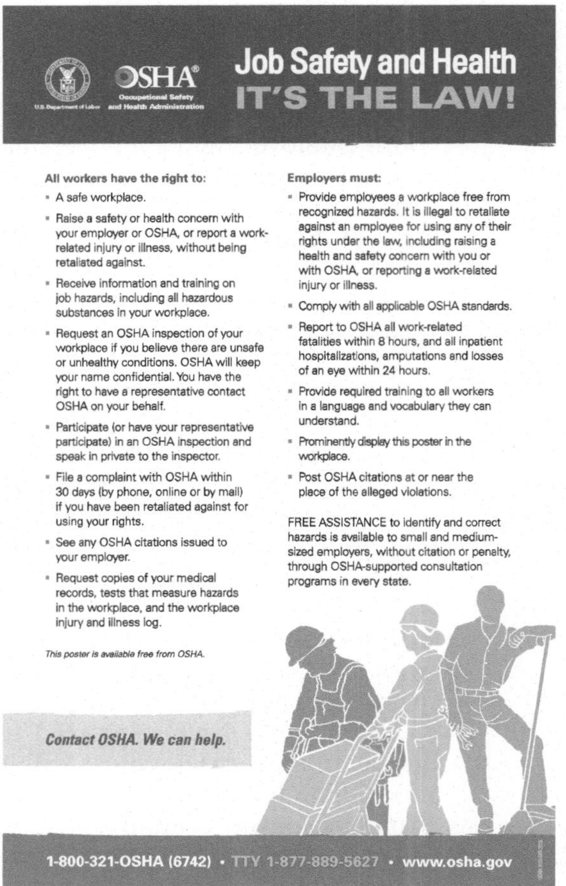

FIGURE 16-5 OSHA Safety Poster

Source: From Job Safety and Health: It's the Law! U.S. Department of Labor. www.osha.gov/Publications/osha3165.pdf, accessed September 9, 2018.

TRENDS SHAPING HR: *DIGITAL AND SOCIAL MEDIA*

Sitedocs Digital Workplace Safety

Safety compliance usually has been managed centrally, by human resource managers or by a specialized safety unit. However, new digital mobile device–based safety systems now give managers and even employees more influence over safety. For example, the SiteDocs digital safety management system lets the employer digitize, move, store, work with, and access safety documents via mobile devices (iPad) and the Web.[55] Employees can login via the mobile device and view and complete their safety documentation (such as OSHA reports). These become available immediately to management. This enables management to monitor in real time whether employees are completing their documentation and to identify almost at once workplace hazards and incidents. ■

What Causes Accidents?

LEARNING OBJECTIVE 16-3

Answer the question, "What causes accidents?"

There are three basic causes of workplace accidents: chance occurrences, unsafe conditions, and employees' unsafe acts. Chance occurrences (such as walking past a tree just when a branch falls) are more or less beyond management's control. We will therefore focus on unsafe conditions and unsafe acts.

What Causes Unsafe Conditions?

unsafe conditions
The mechanical and physical conditions that cause accidents.

Unsafe conditions are a main cause of accidents. They include[56]

- Improperly guarded equipment
- Defective equipment
- Hazardous procedures around machines or equipment

- Unsafe storage—congestion, overloading
- Improper illumination—glare, insufficient light
- Spills on floors
- Tripping hazards, such as blocked aisles
- Working from heights, including ladders and scaffolds
- Electrical hazards like frayed cords

The solution here is to identify and eliminate the unsafe conditions. The main purpose of OSHA standards is to address such mechanical and physical accident-causing conditions. The employer's safety department (if any) and its human resource managers and top managers should have responsibility for identifying unsafe conditions.

While accidents can happen anywhere, there's little mystery about where the worst ones occur:[57] around metal and woodworking machines and saws, transmission machinery (like gears), cutting machines, and conveyors. For example, when a conveyor with liquid chocolate suddenly started, it pulled in and mangled the arm of a worker who was cleaning it.[58]

About one-third of industrial accidents occur around forklift trucks, wheelbarrows, and other handling and lifting areas. Construction accounts for a disproportionate share of accidents, with falls the major problem.[59]

SAFETY SCHEDULES AND CLIMATE Work schedules and fatigue also affect accident rates. Accident rates usually don't increase too noticeably during the first 5 or 6 hours of the workday. But after that, the accident rate increases faster. This is due partly to fatigue and partly to the fact that accidents occur more often during night shifts. With reduced headcount and more people with second jobs, employee fatigue is a growing problem.[60] Many employers therefore take steps to reduce employee fatigue, such as banning mandatory overtime.

The workplace "climate" or psychology is very important. In one classic study in the 1990s, a researcher reviewed the fatal accidents offshore oil workers suffered in the British North Sea.[61] A strong pressure to complete the work as quickly as possible, employees who are under stress, and a poor safety climate—for instance, supervisors who never mentioned safety—were some of the psychological conditions leading to accidents. Similarly, accidents occur more frequently in plants with high seasonal layoff rates, hostility among employees, many garnished wages, and blighted living conditions.

What Causes Unsafe Acts?

Unsafe employee acts (such as running) will undo your efforts to banish unsafe conditions, but there are no easy answers to what causes people to act unsafely.

There is no one explanation for why people behave unsafely. Sometimes the working conditions prompt unsafe acts, as with stressed-out oil rig workers. Sometimes employees don't get the required training, nor learn safe procedures.[62]

One might assume that some people are just accident prone, but the research isn't clear.[63] On closer inspection some "accident repeaters" were just unlucky, or may have been more meticulous about reporting their accidents.[64] However, there is evidence that people who are impulsive, sensation seeking, extremely extroverted, less agreeable, and less conscientious (in terms of being less fastidious and dependable) do have more accidents.[65] (*Psychology Today* offers an accident-proneness test for about $7.00.)[66]

Furthermore, someone accident prone on one job may not be so on another. For example, personality traits that correlate with filing vehicular insurance claims include *entitlement* ("think there's no reason they should not speed"), *impatience* ("were 'always in a hurry'"), *aggressiveness* ("the first to move when the light turns green"), and *distractibility* ("frequently distracted by cell phones, eating, and so on").[67]

HR in Action at the Hotel Paris Lisa and the CFO reviewed their company's safety records, and what they found disturbed them deeply. In terms of every safety-related metric they could find, including accident costs per year, lost time due to accidents, workers' compensation per employee, and number of safety training programs per year, the Hotel Paris compared unfavorably with most other hotel chains and service firms. To see how they handled this, see the case on page 555 of this chapter.

How to Prevent Accidents

LEARNING OBJECTIVE 16-4
List and explain five ways to prevent accidents at work.

In practice, accident prevention boils down to reducing unsafe conditions and reducing unsafe acts. Larger firms generally have a chief safety officer (or "environmental health and safety officer"). But in smaller firms, managers, including those from human resources, plant managers, and first-line managers, share these responsibilities.

Small business safety can be particularly problematical: for example, owners might naively overlook crucial safety activities, such as chemical hazards training. There are no easy solutions. However, the firm's HR manager should make sure top management (1) understands the potential problem, and (2) actively seeks solutions, such as having OSHA conduct a safety audit and make recommendations.[68]

Reducing Unsafe Conditions

Reducing unsafe conditions (like those OSHA addresses) is the employer's first line of defense. Safety engineers should design jobs to remove or reduce physical hazards. Supervisors play an important role. Checklists as in Figure 16-6 and Figure 16-8 (pages 529–531 and 551–554, respectively) can help identify and remove potential hazards.

Sometimes the solution for an unsafe condition is obvious, and sometimes it's not. For example, obvious remedies for slippery floors include keeping them dry, floor mats, and better lighting. Perhaps less obviously, personal safety gear like slip-resistant footwear can also reduce falls. Cut-resistant gloves reduce the hazards of working with sharp objects.[69] (Hand injuries account for about 1 million emergency department visits annually by U.S. workers.)[70] Employees can use stop button devices to cut power to machines.[71] *Lockout/tagout* is a formal procedure to disable equipment such as power saws, to avoid unexpected activation. It involves disarming the device and affixing a "disabled" tag to the equipment.[72] For wearable digital devices such as motion monitors, the employer should determine the device's usability and ascertain that it won't cause unanticipated safety problems.[73]

Reducing unsafe conditions is important in offices too.[74] For example, get written confirmation that the space meets all building codes; make sure the builder, contractors, and/or landlord follow OSHA standards (for instance, unblocked exits); make sure the lease lets you compel the landlord to fix safety problems; and make sure air ducts are cleaned.

TRENDS SHAPING HR: *ROBOTS*

With more employees working alongside robots, safety standards are evolving. For example, industrial robots have speed and separation monitoring and safety stops so humans can "hand" them parts without the robot arm hitting them.[75] Many of the new so-called cobots have digital screen faces with human characteristics. For example, one cobot "glances" in the direction when it's about to pick something up, to forewarn its human "colleagues."[76] ■

job hazard analysis
A systematic approach to identifying and eliminating workplace hazards before they occur.

JOB HAZARD ANALYSIS A Yale University science student, working late in a lab, was critically injured when her hair was caught in a spinning lathe. **Job hazard analysis** involves a systematic approach to identifying and eliminating such hazards before they cause accidents.[77]

Consider a safety analyst looking at the Yale science lab, with the aim of identifying potential hazards. Performing a job hazard analysis here might involve looking at the situation and asking four questions:

- ***What can go wrong?*** A student's hair or clothing could become caught in the lathe, a rotating object that "catches" it and pulls it into the machine.
- ***What are the consequences?*** The student could receive a severe injury as his or her body part or hair is caught and drawn into the spinning lathe.

FIGURE 16-6 Supervisor's Safety Checklist

Source: Office of the Chief Information Officer, United States Department of Commerce, http://ocio.os.doc.gov/s/groups/public/@doc/@os/@ocio/@oitpp/documents/content/dev01_002574.pdf, assessed October 15, 2013.

FORM **CD-574**
(9/02)

U.S. Department of Commerce
Office Safety Inspection Checklist for
Supervisors and Program Managers

Name:	**Division:**
Location:	**Date:**
Signature:	

This checklist is intended as a guide to assist supervisors and program managers in conducting safety and health inspections of their work areas. It includes questions relating to general office safety, ergonomics, fire prevention, and electrical safety. Questions which receive a "**NO**" answer require corrective action. If you have questions or need assistance with resolving any problems, please contact your safety office. More information on office safety is available through the Department of Commerce Safety Office website at http://ohrm.doc.gov/safetyprogram/safety.htm.

Work Environment

Yes	No	N/A	
○	○	⊙	Are all work areas clean, sanitary, and orderly?
○	○	⊙	Is there adequate lighting?
○	○	⊙	Do noise levels appear high?
○	○	⊙	Is ventilation adequate?

Walking / Working Surfaces

Yes	No	N/A	
○	○	⊙	Are aisles and passages free of stored material that may present trip hazards?
○	○	⊙	Are tile floors in places like kitchens and bathrooms free of water and slippery substances?
○	○	⊙	Are carpet and throw rugs free of tears or trip hazards?
○	○	⊙	Are hand rails provided on all fixed stairways?
○	○	⊙	Are treads provided with anti-slip surfaces?
○	○	⊙	Are step ladders provided for reaching overhead storage areas and are materials stored safely?
○	○	⊙	Are file drawers kept closed when not in use?
○	○	⊙	Are passenger and freight elevators inspected annually and are the inspection certificates available for review on-site?
○	○	⊙	Are pits and floor openings covered or otherwise guarded?
○	○	⊙	Are standard guardrails provided wherever aisle or walkway surfaces are elevated more than 48 inches above any adjacent floor or the ground?
○	○	⊙	Is any furniture unsafe or defective?
○	○	⊙	Are objects covering heating and air conditioning vents?

Ergonomics

Yes	No	N/A	
○	○	⊙	Are employees advised of proper lifting techniques?
○	○	⊙	Are workstations configured to prevent common ergonomic problems? (Chair height allows employees' feet to rest flat on the ground with thighs parallel to the floor, top of computer screen is at or slightly below eye level, keyboard is at elbow height. Additional information on proper configuration of workstations is available through the Commerce Safety website at http://ohrm.doc.gov/safetyprogram/safety.htm)
○	○	⊙	Are mechanical aids and equipment, such as; lifting devices, carts, dollies provided where needed?
○	○	⊙	Are employees surveyed annually on their ergonomic concerns?

(*Continued*)

FIGURE 16-6 ***Continued***

FORM **CD-574**
(9/02)

Emergency Information (Postings)

Yes	No	N/A	
○	○	⊙	Are established emergency phone numbers posted where they can be readily found in case of an emergency?
○	○	⊙	Are employees trained on emergency procedures?
○	○	⊙	Are fire evacuation procedures/diagrams posted?
○	○	⊙	Is emergency information posted in every area where you store hazardous waste?
○	○	⊙	Is established facility emergency information posted near a telephone?
○	○	⊙	Are the OSHA poster, and other required posters displayed conspicuously?
○	○	⊙	Are adequate first aid supplies available and properly maintained?
○	○	⊙	Are an adequate number of first aid trained personnel available to respond to injuries and illnesses until medical assistance arrives?
○	○	⊙	Is a copy of the facility fire prevention and emergency action plan available on site?
○	○	⊙	Are safety hazard warning signs/caution signs provided to warn employees of pertinent hazards?

Fire Prevention

Yes	No	N/A	
○	○	⊙	Are flammable liquids, such as gasoline, kept in approved safety cans and stored in flammable cabinets?
○	○	⊙	Are portable fire extinguishers distributed properly (less than 75 feet travel distance for combustibles and 50 feet for flammables)?
○	○	⊙	Are employees trained on the use of portable fire extinguishers?
○	○	⊙	Are portable fire extinguishers visually inspected monthly and serviced annually?
○	○	⊙	Is the area around portable fire extinguishers free of obstructions and properly labeled ?
○	○	⊙	Is heat-producing equipment used in a well ventilated area?
○	○	⊙	Are fire alarm pull stations clearly marked and unobstructed?
○	○	⊙	Is proper clearance maintained below sprinkler heads (i.e., 18" clear)?

Emergency Exits

Yes	No	N/A	
○	○	⊙	Are doors, passageways or stairways that are neither exits nor access to exits and which could be mistaken for exits, appropriately marked "NOT AN EXIT," "TO BASEMENT," "STOREROOM," etc.?
○	○	⊙	Are a sufficient number of exits provided?
○	○	⊙	Are exits kept free of obstructions or locking devices which could impede immediate escape?
○	○	⊙	Are exits properly marked and illuminated?
○	○	⊙	Are the directions to exits, when not immediately apparent, marked with visible signs?
○	○	⊙	Can emergency exit doors be opened from the direction of exit travel without the use of a key or any special knowledge or effort when the building is occupied?
○	○	⊙	Are exits arranged such that it is not possible to travel toward a fire hazard when exiting the facility?

FIGURE 16-6 ***Continued***

FORM **CD-574**
(9/02)

Electrical Systems
(Please have your facility maintenance person or electrician accompany you during this part of the inspection)

Yes	No	N/A	
○	○	⦿	Are all cord and cable connections intact and secure?
○	○	⦿	Are electrical outlets free of overloads?
○	○	⦿	Is fixed wiring used instead of flexible/extension cords?
○	○	⦿	Is the area around electrical panels and breakers free of obstructions?
○	○	⦿	Are high-voltage electrical service rooms kept locked?
○	○	⦿	Are electrical cords routed such that they are free of sharp objects and clearly visible?
○	○	⦿	Are all electrical cords grounded?
○	○	⦿	Are electrical cords in good condition (free of splices, frays, etc.)?
○	○	⦿	Are electrical appliances approved (Underwriters Laboratory, Inc. (UL), etc)?
○	○	⦿	Are electric fans provided with guards of not over one-half inch, preventing finger exposures?
○	○	⦿	Are space heaters UL listed and equipped with shutoffs that activate if the heater tips over?
○	○	⦿	Are space heaters located away from combustibles and properly ventilated?
○	○	⦿	In your electrical rooms are all electrical raceways and enclosures securely fastened in place?
○	○	⦿	Are clamps or other securing means provided on flexible cords or cables at plugs, receptacles, tools, equipment, etc., and is the cord jacket securely held in place?
○	○	⦿	Is sufficient access and working space provided and maintained about all electrical equipment to permit ready and safe operations and maintenance? (This space is 3 feet for less than 600 volts, 4 feet for more than 600 volts)

FORM **CD-574**
(9/02)

Material Storage

Yes	No	N/A	
○	○	⦿	Are storage racks and shelves capable of supporting the intended load and materials stored safely?
○	○	⦿	Are storage racks secured from falling?
○	○	⦿	Are office equipment stored in a stable manner, not capable of falling?

- ***How could it happen?*** The accident could happen as a result of the student leaning too close to the lathe while working at the bench, or walking too close to the lathe, or bending to reach for an article that fell close to the lathe.
- ***What are other contributing factors?*** Speed is one contributing factor. The problem would occur so quickly that the student would be unable to take evasive action once the lathe ensnarled the hair.

The job hazard analysis should provide the basis for creating countermeasures. For example, given the speed with which such a lathe accident would occur, it's unlikely that training by itself would suffice. Instead, the lathe area should be ensconced in its own protective casing, and changes made to ensure that the lathe can't spin unless the student takes action via a foot pedal.

Surprisingly, while workplace injuries are declining, *serious* injuries and fatalities are not. For example, the injury and illness rate dropped by about 40% from 2003 to 2015, but the fatality rate dropped only 15%.[78]

Employers therefore should particularly focus on serious injuries and fatalities. This starts with identifying high hazard events. For example, accidentally cutting one's finger with a knife is not as potentially catastrophic as cutting it by catching it in an automated slicing machine. So first identify such potential high hazard events. Then conduct job hazard analyses, and implement preventive steps.[79]

OPERATIONAL SAFETY REVIEWS After Japan's Fukushima nuclear power plant exploded back in 2011, many wondered if the International Atomic Energy Agency (IAEA) had conducted the necessary operational safety reviews. **Operational safety reviews** (or safety operations reviews) are conducted by agencies to ascertain whether units under their jurisdiction are complying with all the applicable safety laws, regulations, orders, and rules. For example, under IAEA's Operational Safety Review Program, "international teams of experts conduct in-depth reviews of operational safety performance at a nuclear power plant."[80]

operational safety reviews Reviews conducted by agencies to ascertain whether units under their jurisdiction are complying with all the applicable safety laws, regulations, orders, and rules.

PERSONAL PROTECTIVE EQUIPMENT While it can reduce the perils of some unsafe conditions, getting employees to wear personal protective equipment (PPE) like hard hats is famously difficult.[81] Wearability is important. OSHA says it "should fit comfortably, encouraging worker use."[82] In addition to providing protection, PPE should fit properly; be easy to care for; be flexible and lightweight; and be maintained in a clean and reliable fashion, for instance. Companies such as Kimberly-Clark are using new fibers and fabrics to design easier-wearing high-tech solutions.[83] And it's not just wearability. For example, some workers resist hearing protection because they're afraid it may interfere with hearing their colleagues.[84] It's therefore important to solicit workers' opinions.

Of course, the manager should require wearing the protective equipment before the accident, not just after it. For example, a combustible dust explosion at a sugar refinery killed 14 employees and burned many others. The employer subsequently required that all employees wear fire-resistant clothing, unfortunately too late for the victims.[85]

Similarly, cold weather means employers should protect their outdoor workers.[86] This should include, among other things, monitoring temperature and wind chill conditions, making sure workers are supplied with cold-weather apparel, monitoring workers for signs of frostbite, and providing adequate indoor breaks.[87]

But again, reducing unsafe conditions is the first line of defense. OSHA says, "[e]mployers must institute all feasible engineering and work practice controls to eliminate and reduce hazards before using PPE to protect against hazards."[88]

TRENDS SHAPING HR: *LOCATION BEACONS*

Beacons—tiny devices that continuously transmit radio signals identifying themselves—are becoming valuable occupational safety tools. Employers use beacons to keep track of employees, particularly if they're in distress. Others use them to warn employees, such as when they're too close to a danger zone.[89] ■

Diversity Counts: Protecting Vulnerable Workers

In designing safe environments, employers need to pay special attention to vulnerable workers, such as young, immigrant, aging, and women workers.[90] For example, although 14- and 15-year-olds can generally only legally work at jobs like cashier and office work, 16- and 17-year-olds may take jobs like cooking and construction. In one recent year, about 550 16- and 17-year-olds were injured at work.[91] Similarly, as one safety engineering company CEO said, "For decades, women essentially were ignored when it came to designing eye and face protection." Today, more products are available in smaller sizes.[92]

With more workers postponing retirement, older workers often fill manufacturing jobs.[93] They can do these jobs effectively. However, there are numerous physical changes associated with aging, including loss of strength, loss of muscular flexibility, and reduced reaction time.[94] The fatality rate for older workers is about three times that of younger workers.[95] Employers should make special provisions. For example, boost lighting levels and reduce heavy lifting.[96]

One also needs plans for dealing with health issues.[97] Thus, in the case of a cardiac arrest emergency, early CPR and external defibrillators are essential. These should be available and one or more employees trained to use them.[98] ■

Reducing Unsafe Acts

While reducing unsafe conditions is the first line of defense, human misbehavior will short-circuit even the best safety efforts.[99]

Sometimes the misbehavior is intentional, but often it's not. For example, distractions contribute to about half of all car accidents. The National Safety Council estimates that cell phone use was involved in 24% of all motor vehicle crashes.[100] (Drivers of commercial interstate motor vehicles are banned from using handheld mobile telephones while driving.)[101] At work, not noticing moving or stationary objects or that a floor is wet often causes accidents.[102] And, ironically, "making a job safer with machine guards or PPE lowers people's risk perceptions and thus can lead to [more] at-risk behavior."[103]

Unfortunately, telling employees to "pay attention" isn't enough. First try to eliminate potential risks, such as unguarded equipment. Next, reduce potential distractions such as noise, heat, and stress. Then, carefully screen and train employees, as we explain next.

Reducing Unsafe Acts through Screening

In reducing unsafe acts through screening, the employer's aim is to identify the traits that predict accidents on the job and then test candidates for these traits. For example, the Employee Reliability Index (ERI) measures dimensions such as emotional maturity, conscientiousness, and safe job performance.[104] Employers also use *work sample* tests and tests of *physical abilities* to determine if the person can do the job. Some employers conduct *physical demands assessments* (PDAs). These itemize a job's physical demands, such as "lifting 40 pounds an hour," and "working in 90 degree heat." The employer then uses this to develop more precise screening and training for the job.[105]

Behavioral interview questions can also be revealing. For example, ask, "What would you do if your supervisor told you to do something you knew was unsafe?

Reducing Unsafe Acts through Training

Studies by the Hartford Insurance Company found that injury rates for workers in their first month on the job were four to six times higher than for other workers.[106]

Safety training reduces unsafe acts, especially for new employees.[107] Here the employer should instruct employees in safe practices and procedures, warn them of potential hazards, and work to develop a safety-conscious employee attitude. OSHA's standards don't just require training. Employees must demonstrate that they actually learned what to do. (For example, OSHA's respiratory standard requires that each employee demonstrate how to inspect, put on, and remove respirator seals.[108] OSHA has two booklets, *Training Requirements under OSHA* and *Teaching Safety and Health in the Workplace*.) Because temporary workers account for a disproportionate share of workplace accidents, the employer should take particular care to train them.[109]

The main aim of safety training is not to meet OSHA training standards, but to impart knowledge and skills to reduce accidents. One study found that the most effective safety training elicited employee engagement.[110] The "least engaging" programs included lectures, films, reading materials, and video-based training. "Moderately engaging" programs included computer interface instruction with feedback. "Engaging" ones included behavioral modeling, simulation, and hands-on training.

Employers also use training vendors' online safety programs.[111] Online safety course and video vendors include, for example, https://safetyskills.com/, PureSafety (www.ulworkplace.com), and https://vividlearningsystems.com/courses. When the University of California system wanted safety training for its 50,000 employees on 10 different campuses, it developed an online program with Vivid Learning Systems. The 2-hour custom online lab safety course covers OSHA regulations, with exercises for participants.[112] OSHA, the National Institute for Occupational Safety and Health (NIOSH), and other private vendors also offer online safety training solutions.[113]

Ekkaluck Sangkla/Alamy Stock Photo

Emergency stop devices, such as buttons, override other machine controls to remove power from hazardous machine motion.

Reducing Unsafe Acts through Posters, Incentives, and Positive Reinforcement

Employers also use various tools to motivate worker safety.[114] Safety posters are one, but are no substitute for comprehensive safety programs. Employers should combine posters with other techniques (like screening and training) to reduce unsafe conditions and acts, and change the posters often. Posters should be easily visible, legible, and well-lit.[115]

Incentive programs are also useful. In one survey several years ago, about 75% of U.S. manufacturers surveyed said they had safety incentive programs.[116] Most such programs pay incentives for safety-related worker behaviors such as participating in a safety meeting, reporting a near miss, or reporting unsafe conditions.[117] Vendors also offer turnkey safety incentive programs. For example, safety incentive programs from $afety Pay$ (www.safetypays.com/) include programs for incentivizing employees' safety awareness.

OSHA has argued that such programs don't reduce injuries or illnesses, but only injury and illness *reporting*. OSHA rules prohibit employers from using incentive programs that in any way penalize workers for reporting accidents or injuries.[118] OSHA might question any safety incentive payment that is so high that the award might dissuade reasonable workers from reporting safety problems.[119]

One option (see accompanying Profit Center discussion) is to emphasize behavioral incentives like recognition.[120] In any case, the incentive program should be part of a comprehensive safety program.[121]

IMPROVING PERFORMANCE: *HR AS A PROFIT CENTER*

Using Positive Reinforcement

Many employers successfully use *positive reinforcement programs* to improve safety. Such programs provide workers with continuing positive feedback, usually in the form of graphical performance reports and supervisory support, to shape the workers' safety-related behavior.

Researchers introduced one program in a wholesale bakery.[122] The new safety program included training and positive reinforcement. The researchers set and communicated a reasonable safety goal (in terms of observed incidents performed safely).

Next, employees participated in a 30-minute training session by viewing pairs of slides depicting scenes that the researchers staged in the plant. One slide, for example, showed the supervisor climbing over a conveyor; the parallel slide showed the supervisor walking around the conveyor. After viewing an unsafe act, employees had to describe, "What's unsafe here?" Then the researchers demonstrated the same incident again but performed in a safe manner, and explicitly stated the safe-conduct rule ("go around, not over or under, conveyors").

At the conclusion of the training phase, supervisors showed employees a graph with their pretraining safety record (in terms of observed incidents performed safely) plotted. Supervisors then encouraged workers to consider increasing their performance to the new safety goal for their own protection, to decrease costs, and to help the plant get out of its last-place safety ranking. Then the researchers posted the graph and a list of safety rules.

Whenever observers walked through the plant collecting safety data, they posted on the graph the percentage of incidents they had seen performed safely by the group as a whole, thus providing the workers with positive feedback. Workers could compare their current safety performance with both their previous performance and their assigned goal. In addition, supervisors praised workers when they performed selected incidents safely. Safety in the plant subsequently improved markedly. ■

> **MyLab Management Talk About It 3**
>
> If your professor has assigned this, go to the Assignments section of **www.pearson.com/mylab/management** to complete this discussion. List six more unsafe incidents you believe might occur in a bakery, and a "safe manner" for doing each.

Reducing Unsafe Acts by Fostering a Culture of Safety

Employers and supervisors should create a culture of safety by showing they take safety seriously. One study measured safety culture in terms of questions like "my supervisor says a good word whenever he sees the job done according to the safety rules" and "my supervisor approaches workers during work to discuss safety issues."[123]

According to one safety expert, a workplace with a safety-oriented culture exhibits:

1. *Teamwork*, in the form of management and employees both involved in safety;
2. Highly visible and interactive *communication and collaboration* on safety matters;

caia image/Alamy Stock Photo

Particularly in situations like this where employees are relatively unsupervised, employers should create a safety-conscious culture by showing that they take safety seriously.

3. A *shared vision* of safety excellence (specifically, an overriding attitude that all accidents and injuries are preventable);
4. *Assignment* of critical safety functions to specific individuals or teams;
5. A *continuous effort* toward identifying and correcting workplace safety problems and hazards;[124] and,
6. *Encouragement* of incident reporting.[125]

Reducing Unsafe Acts by Creating a Supportive Environment

Supportive supervisors' teams seem to have better safety records. "Organizations can develop a supportive environment by training supervisors to be better leaders, emphasizing the importance of teamwork and social support, and establishing the value of safety."[126]

Reducing Unsafe Acts by Establishing a Safety Policy

The company's written safety policy should emphasize that accident prevention is of the utmost importance, and that the firm will do everything practical to eliminate or reduce accidents and injuries.

Reducing Unsafe Acts by Setting Specific Loss Control Goals

Set specific safety goals to achieve. For example, set safety goals in terms of frequency of lost-time injuries per number of full-time employees.

Reducing Unsafe Acts through Behavior-Based Safety and Safety Awareness Programs

behavior-based safety
Identifying the worker behaviors that contribute to accidents and then training workers to avoid these behaviors.

Behavior-based safety means identifying the worker behaviors that contribute to accidents and then training workers to avoid these behaviors. Tenneco Corporation implemented one such program. The firm selected internal consultants from among its quality managers, training managers, engineers, and production workers. After training, the internal consultants identified five critical behaviors for Tenneco's first safety program, such as *Eyes on task: Does the employee watch his or her hands while performing a task?* The consultants made observations and collected data on the behaviors. Then they instituted training programs to get employees to perform these five behaviors properly.[127]

safety awareness program
Program that enables trained supervisors to orient new workers arriving at a job site regarding common safety hazards and simple prevention methods.

Employers also use *safety awareness* programs. In a **safety awareness program** new workers receive critical information regarding the job's common safety hazards and simple prevention methods, often when first arriving at a job site. For example, the Roadway Safety Awareness Program from the American Road & Transportation Builders Association addresses trucker safety issues such as stopping distances required at various speeds.

Reducing Unsafe Acts through Employee Participation

Employee participation plays a central role in safety programs. As OSHA says, "To be effective, any safety and health program needs the meaningful participation of workers and their representatives. . . . Worker participation means that workers are involved in establishing, operating, evaluating, and improving the safety and health program."[128] Ideally, the employer should encourage all workers to participate, to feel comfortable reporting safety or health concerns, and to have access to the information they need to participate in the program.[129] The employee engagement section in this chapter illustrates this.

TRENDS SHAPING HR: *DIGITAL AND SOCIAL MEDIA*

Conducting Safety and Health Audits and Inspections

Safety managers know that good intentions aren't enough: the employer must audit safety compliance. First, line managers should periodically inspect their areas using safety audit/checklists (as in Figure 16-6, pages 529–531), including investigating all accidents and "near misses."

A company/facility-wide safety audit is also in order. OSHA provides a safety self-audit tool.[130] It contains items to check off, such as "Management implements and communicates a written policy supporting the safety and health program," and "Management defines specific goals and expectations for the program."[131]

Employers expedite and enable safety audits with mobile digital tools. For example, managers and employees use iAuditor—Safety Audit and Checklist App,[132] available via iTunes, to facilitate safety audits. iAuditor contains safety checklists and tools that let employers take action depending on the checklist response.[133] AssessNET is cloud-based safety software that lets employers remotely manage risk assessments, accident records, and safety audits.[134] Employees use AssessNET from their desktops and mobile devices. It provides them with quick access to safety records, lets them quickly report hazards, and alerts management of safety incidents.[135] With safety audits, safety-related metrics would include, for instance, injury and illness rates, workers' compensation cost per employee, at-risk behavior reduction, and safety training exercises.[136] Ideally, *trend the audit data* (for instance, to see if accident rates are rising or falling or steady), and *track the corrective actions* through to completion.[137] ■

Table 16-1 summarizes suggestions for reducing unsafe conditions and acts.

LEARNING OBJECTIVE 16-5

Describe how one company uses employee engagement to improve workplace safety.

Employee Engagement Guide for Managers

Milliken & Company—World-Class Safety through Employee Engagement

Milliken & Company designs, manufactures, and markets chemicals, floor coverings, protective fabrics, and textiles. It has about 7,000 employees in more than 39 facilities around the world. The privately owned Milliken has received widespread recognition for the quality of its innovative products, for its high employee engagement, and for its world-class employee engagement-based safety program. It's also the only company to consistently rank as a "most ethical company" for 15 years running.[138] A survey of Milliken's employees found an 80% positive engagement level, based on questions concerning employees' commitment, pride in company, and empowerment efforts.[139] Its extraordinarily low workplace illness and injury rates make it one of the safest companies in which to work.[140]

Involvement-Based Employee Engagement

The centerpiece of Milliken's safety process is its *involvement-based employee engagement* program. For example, employees staff the safety steering and safety subcommittee

TABLE 16-1 Reducing Unsafe Conditions and Acts: A Summary

Reduce Unsafe Conditions
Identify and eliminate unsafe conditions.
Use administrative means, such as job rotation.
Use personal protective equipment.
Reduce Unsafe Acts
Emphasize top management commitment.
Emphasize safety.
Establish a safety policy.
Reduce unsafe acts through selection.
Provide safety training.
Use posters and other propaganda.
Use positive reinforcement.
Set specific safety goals to achieve.
Use behavior-based safety programs.
Encourage worker participation.
Conduct safety and health audits and inspections regularly.

system, submit "opportunity for improvement" suggestions weekly, review each of these suggestions, and provide feedback on every suggestion.[141] The safety process depends on *cascading goals* deriving from federal, state, and Milliken-based safety guidelines. These goals are translated through weekly meetings into specific metrics (for instance, "accidents per employee hour worked") to be achieved by each plant's subcommittees. Each subcommittee then performs weekly *audits*, to ensure compliance and that the plant's safety activities are continuously improved. Plant employees get checklists to familiarize themselves with the safety measures associated with their machines.[142]

Each Milliken employee's safety program involvement is quantified, for instance in terms of serving on safety subcommittees, or conducting safety audits.[143] Also, to help foster engagement, the program *empowers* employees, for instance, by training each to be knowledgeable about OSHA safety regulations. Milliken also trains employees to give and receive peer-to-peer safety comments. Each is authorized to act by providing "constructive feedback" or "appreciative feedback" when observing another employee doing something safely (or not). Milliken's safety tracking tool helps employees make sure that safety suggestions, safety audit findings, or other safety agenda items are each tracked and finalized; each item gets a number, date, and the name of the responsible Milliken employee.[144] Milliken's programs are consistent with OSHA's Voluntary Protection Program, and many of its U.S. facilities are VPP certified.[145]

Members of each plant's employee safety steering committee investigate all safety incidents to identify the causes.[146] Milliken recognizes employees' safety efforts in formal celebratory events throughout the year, such as having "cheerleaders" provide safety cheers as engineers enter the plant.[147]

LEARNING OBJECTIVE 16-6

List five workplace health hazards and how to deal with them.

Workplace Health Hazards: Problems and Remedies

Many workplace hazards aren't as obvious as slippery floors. Many are unseen hazards that the company may use or produce as part of its production processes. Typical here are chemicals, temperature extremes, biohazards (such as mold and anthrax), and ergonomic hazards (such as misaligned computer screens). OSHA and other safety standards cover many of them.[148]

Chemicals and Industrial Hygiene

For example, OSHA standards list exposure limits for about 600 chemicals, such as asbestos and lead. Such hazardous substances require air sampling and other precautionary measures.

Managing such hazards comes under the purview of *industrial hygiene*, and involves recognition, evaluation, and control. First, the facility's safety officers (often working with supervisors and employees) must *recognize* possible exposure hazards. This typically means conducting plant/facility walk-around surveys, employee interviews, records reviews, and reviews of government (OSHA) and nongovernmental standards.

Once the manager identifies a possible hazard, *evaluation* involves determining how severe it is. This requires measuring the exposure, comparing the measure to some benchmark (such as 0.10 fibers per cubic centimeter for asbestos), and determining if the risk is within standard.[149]

Hazard *control* involves eliminating or reducing the hazard. Here personal protective gear should be the *last* option. The employer must first install engineering controls (such as enclosures or ventilation) and administrative controls (including training and improved housekeeping).

KNOW YOUR EMPLOYMENT LAW

Hazard Communication

In, say, a dry cleaning store, it might not be apparent by looking at it that the clear cleaning chemical hydrofluoric acid will eat through glass and blind an unsuspecting worker. Under OSHA's *hazard communication standard*, "in order to ensure chemical safety in the workplace, information about the identities and hazards of the chemicals must be available and understandable to workers." As a result, chemical manufacturers and importers must label and provide hazard safety data sheets to their customers. All employers must have labels and safety data sheets available for their exposed workers, and train workers to handle the chemicals appropriately.[150]

HR AND THE GIG ECONOMY: *TEMP EMPLOYEE SAFETY*[151]

Temp workers in the United States account for as much as five times the workplace fatalities than one might expect.

Why? First, new employees tend to have higher accident rates, and temp or gig workers are often new. Furthermore, temp or gig workers lack some familiar legal employment protections (for example, they generally don't get unemployment insurance or workers' compensation).[152] This may in turn prompt some employers to ignore temps' safety training (on the mistaken assumption that they need not provide it). Temps may also lack the workmates who might otherwise provide safety guidance. Some experts also believe that temp workers often get the "dirtiest most hazardous" jobs.

However, temp/gig workers *are* covered by occupational health and safety laws, and companies have the same safety obligations to them as to their own employees. For example, the host employer has the primary responsibility for providing temp workers with site-specific hazard communications information and training, and safety training must be identical to what it gives its own employees. As other examples, the host employer must ensure appropriate labeling of chemical containers, and provide appropriate personal protective equipment (PPE). Many host employers hire temps through staffing agencies. According to OSHA, these agencies should, for example, provide generic hazard communications and visit the facility to review the adequacy of its hazard safety processes.

We'll look at several important workplace hazards next.

Asbestos Exposure at Work and Air Quality

Asbestos is a major source of occupational respiratory disease. Efforts are still underway to rid old buildings of the substance.

OSHA standards require several actions with respect to asbestos. Employers must monitor the air whenever they expect the level of asbestos to rise to one-half the allowable limit (0.10 fibers per cubic centimeter). Engineering controls—walls, special filters, and so forth—are required to maintain a compliant asbestos level. Only then can employers use respirators if additional efforts are required to achieve compliance.

Krzysztof Slusarczyk/Shutterstock

Exposure to asbestos is a major potential source of occupational respiratory disease. Workers need to wear protective clothing and a respirator to remove asbestos from buildings.

Alcoholism and Substance Abuse

About two-thirds of all drug users and people with alcohol disorders are employed.[153] One estimate around 10 years ago was that about 15% of the U.S. workforce "has either been hung over at work, been drinking shortly before showing up for work, or been drinking or impaired while on the job at least once during the previous year."[154] Breathalyzer tests detected alcohol in 16% of emergency room patients injured at work.[155] Employee alcoholism may cost U.S. employees about $226 billion per year, for instance in absenteeism and accidents.[156] Deaths from opioids about tripled in one recent 5-year period.[157]

SUBSTANCE ABUSE TESTING Dealing with substance abuse often involves *substance abuse testing*.[158] It's unusual to find employers who don't at least test job candidates for substance abuse before formally hiring them. And many states have mandatory random drug testing for high-hazard workers. For example, New Jersey requires random drug testing of electrical workers.[159]

Yet there is debate about whether drug tests reduce workplace accidents. One study, in three hotels, concluded that preemployment drug tests seemed to have little effect on workplace accidents. However, a combination of preemployment and random ongoing testing was associated with a significant reduction in workplace accidents.[160]

With a tighter U.S. job market and more states legalizing marijuana, many employers are ratcheting down their drug testing programs, at least with respect to marijuana.[161] For example, AutoNation recently said it would no longer refuse job offers because someone tested positive for marijuana.

However, employers with critical safety issues (like those with heavy equipment or in transportation) continue to test. Others do as well: Burger King and Ford Motor Company still treat marijuana as illegal. AutoNation continues to bar those who test positive for other illegal drugs. And at factories (particularly with heavy machinery), a zero-tolerance policy remains the rule. One food processing plant randomly tests one employee every month, "and we're going to move it to two,"[162]

Some applicants or employees may try to evade testing by purchasing "clean" specimens. Several states—including New Jersey, North Carolina, Virginia, Oregon, South Carolina, Pennsylvania, Louisiana, Texas, and Nebraska—have laws making drug-test fraud a crime.[163] The oral fluid drug test eliminates the "clean specimen" problem.[164] However, given the problem, ongoing random testing is still advisable.

DEALING WITH SUBSTANCE ABUSE Ideally, a drug-free workplace program includes five components:[165]

1. A drug-free workplace policy
2. Supervisor training
3. Employee education
4. Employee assistance
5. Drug testing

The policy should state, at a minimum, "The use, possession, transfer, or sale of illegal drugs by employees is prohibited." It should also explain the policy's rationale, and the disciplinary consequences. Supervisors should be trained to monitor employees' performance, and to stay alert to drug-related performance problems. As in Table 16-2, alcohol-related symptoms range from tardiness in the earliest stages of alcohol abuse to prolonged, unpredictable absences in its later stages.[166]

Several tools are available to screen for alcohol or drug abuse. The most widely used self-reporting screening instruments for alcoholism are the 4-item CAGE and the 25-item Michigan Alcoholism Screening Test (MAST). The former asks questions like these: Have you ever (1) attempted to Cut back on alcohol, (2) been Annoyed by comments about your drinking, (3) felt Guilty about drinking, (4) had an Eye-opener first thing in the morning to steady your nerves?[167]

In general, disciplining, discharge, in-house counseling, and referral to an outside agency are the traditional prescriptions when *current* employees test positive; repeated test failures often incur harsher penalties. However federal and state laws govern what employers can and can't do.[168] For example federal transportation law basically requires

TABLE 16-2 Observable Behavior Patterns Indicating Possible Alcohol-Related Problems

Alcoholism Stage	Some Possible Signs of Alcoholism Problems	Some Possible Alcoholism Performance Issues
Early	Arrives at work late Untrue statements Leaves work early	Reduced job efficiency Missed deadlines Careless, sloppy work
Middle	Frequent absences, especially Mondays Colleagues mentioning erratic behavior Mood swings Anxiety Late returning from lunch Frequent multiday absences	Accidents Warnings from boss Noticeably reduced performance Many excuses for incomplete assignments or missed deadlines
Advanced	Personal neglect Unsteady gait Violent outbursts Blackouts and frequent forgetfulness Possible drinking on job	Frequent falls, accidents Strong disciplinary actions Basically incompetent performance

Source: Based on Gopal Patel and John Adkins Jr., "The Employer's Role in Alcoholism Assistance," *Personnel Journal* 62, no. 7 (July 1983), p. 570; Mary-Anne Enoch and David Goldman, "Problem Drinking and Alcoholism: Diagnosis and Treatment," *American Family Physician*, February 1, 2002, www.aafp.org/afp/20020201/441.html, accessed July 20, 2008; and Ken Pidd et al., "Alcohol and Work: Patterns of Use, Workplace Culture, and Safety," www.nisu.flinders.edu.au/pubs/-reports/2006/injcat82.pdf, accessed July 20, 2008; www.ncadd.org/about-addiction/addiction-update/drugs-and-alcohol-in-the-workplace, accessed April 12, 2017; www.opm.gov/policy-data-oversight/worklife/reference-materials/alcoholism-in-the-workplace-a-handbook-for-supervisors/, accessed April 9, 2018.

that a truck driver who fails (or refuses to take) a drug test be immediately removed from driving until successful completion of qualified counseling.[169] And in Vermont and Minnesota, someone who fails a first drug test can't be fired if he or she completes a rehabilitation program.[170]

According to the EEOC, the Americans with Disabilities Act "specifically provides that employers may require an employee who is an alcoholic or who engages in the illegal use of drugs to meet the same standards of performance and behavior as other employees."[171] So, for example, the employer generally need not tolerate substance abuse-related behavior such as absenteeism.[172] However there may be exceptions, such as whether the test results involved prescription drugs or medical marijuana. And suits for invasion of privacy and defamation are always possible. Therefore, it's prudent to publicize the substance abuse policy and procedures, for instance in the employee manual.[173]

Stress, Burnout, and Depression

Many things about one's job can be stressful. These include belligerent bosses or colleagues, poor job security, low pay, unpredictable schedules, workplace noise, excessive workloads, inadequate control over job-related decisions, unclear performance expectations, and arrogant customers.[174]

Furthermore, personality affects stress. For example, Type A personalities—workaholics who feel driven to meet deadlines—normally place themselves under greater stress. Add to job stress the stress caused by nonjob problems like divorce, and many workers are problems waiting to happen.

Human consequences of job stress include anxiety, depression, anger, cardiovascular disease, headaches, accidents, and even early onset Alzheimer's disease.[175] One study found that nurses working under excessive pressure had double the risk for heart attacks.[176] For the employer, consequences include diminished performance and increased absenteeism and turnover. One report estimates that work stress costs an extra $125 to $190 billion dollars per year in health-care spending.[177]

REDUCING JOB STRESS There are several ways to alleviate dysfunctional stress. These range from commonsense remedies (getting more sleep) to biofeedback and meditation. Finding a more suitable job, getting counseling, and planning each day's activities are other sensible responses.[178] In his book *Stress and the Manager*, Dr. Karl Albrecht suggests the following ways for a person to reduce job stress:[179]

- Build rewarding, pleasant, cooperative relationships with colleagues and employees.
- Don't bite off more than you can chew.
- Talk to your supervisor, for instance to clear the air if the relationship has become tense.
- Negotiate with your boss for realistic deadlines on important projects.
- Learn as much as you can about upcoming events, and get as much lead time as possible to prepare for them.
- Find time every day for detachment and relaxation.
- Take a walk around the office to keep your body refreshed and alert.
- Find ways to reduce unnecessary noise.
- Reduce the amount of trivia in your job; delegate routine work when possible.
- Limit interruptions.
- Don't put off dealing with distasteful problems.
- Make a constructive "worry list" that includes solutions for each problem.
- Get more and better quality sleep.[180]
- Establish boundaries, such as by not checking email from home after 10 P.M.
- Get some support, by speaking with a trusted friend or counselor.

Meditation is an option. Choose a quiet place with soft light and sit comfortably. Then focus your thoughts (for example, count breaths or visualize a calming location such as a beach). When your mind wanders, bring it back to focusing your thoughts on your breathing or the beach.[181]

WHAT THE EMPLOYER CAN DO Employers and supervisors play roles in reducing stress. Supportive supervisors and fair treatment are important; rein in bullying-prone supervisors. Other steps include reducing personal conflicts on the job and encouraging open communication between management and employees. One hospital in California introduced an on-site concierge service to help its employees reduce work-related stress. It handles tasks like making vacation plans for employees.[182] Some employers use "resilience training" to help employees deal with stress. As one example, "participants consider previous stressful situations in their lives that they have overcome and identify factors that made the situations manageable."[183]

One British firm has a three-tiered employee stress-reduction program.[184] First is *primary prevention.* This focuses on ensuring that things like job designs and workflows are correct. Second is *intervention.* This includes individual employee assessment, attitude surveys to find sources of stress, and supervisory intervention. Third is *rehabilitation*, which includes employee assistance programs and counseling.

burnout
The total depletion of physical and mental resources caused by excessive striving to reach an unrealistic work-related goal.

BURNOUT Experts define **burnout** as the total depletion of physical and mental resources caused by excessive striving to reach an unrealistic work-related goal. Burnout manifests itself in symptoms like irritability, discouragement, exhaustion, cynicism, entrapment, and resentment.[185]

Employers can head off burnout, for instance, by monitoring employees in potentially high-stress jobs.[186] What can a burnout candidate do? First, watch for warning signs such as tiredness, lack of focus, and depressed mood.[187] In his book *How to Beat the High Cost of Success*, Dr. Herbert Freudenberger suggests:

- ***Break your patterns.*** The more well-rounded your life is, the better protected you are against burnout.
- ***Get away from it all periodically.*** Schedule occasional periods of introspection where you can get away from your usual routine.[188] Another way to reduce burnout is to (try to) put your job aside once you go home.[189] Similarly, take your vacation time: only about 47% of workers used all their paid vacation days recently.[190]

- ***Reassess your goals in terms of their intrinsic worth.*** Are the goals you've set for yourself attainable? Are they really worth the sacrifices?
- ***Think about your work.*** Could you do as good a job without being so intense?
- ***Stay active.*** One study concluded that "the increase in job burnout and depression was strongest among employees who did not engage in physical activity and weakest to the point of non-significance among those engaging in high physical activity."[191]

EMPLOYEE DEPRESSION *Employee depression* is a serious work problem. Experts estimate that depression results in about 200 million lost workdays each year, costing employers $17 to $44 billion annually.[192] Depressed people also tend to have worse safety records.[193]

One survey found that while about two-thirds of large firms offered employee assistance programs covering depression, only about 14% of employees with depression said they ever used one.[194] Employers therefore need to train supervisors to identify depression's warning signs and to counsel those who may need such services to use them.[195] Depression is a disease. It does no more good to tell a depressed person to "snap out of it" than it would to tell someone with a heart condition to stop acting tired. Typical depression warning signs (if they last for more than 2 weeks) include persistent sad, anxious, or "empty" moods; sleeping too little; reduced appetite; loss of interest in activities once enjoyed; restlessness or irritability; and difficulty concentrating.[196]

Solving Computer-Related Ergonomic Problems

OSHA provides an e-Tool for designing computer workstations.[197] Its prescriptions include, place the monitor directly in front of you, ensure it's at arm's length, and look away from the monitor every 20 minutes while focusing on something at least 20 feet away.[198]

NIOSH (the National Institute for Occupational Safety and Health) provides general recommendations. Most relate to *ergonomics* or design of the worker–equipment interface. These include the following:

- Employees should take a 3- to 5-minute break from working at the computer every 20–40 minutes, using the time for other tasks.
- Design maximum flexibility into the workstation so it can be adapted to the person. For example, use adjustable chairs with midback supports. Don't stay in one position too long.
- Reduce glare with devices such as shades over windows and indirect lighting.
- Give workers a preplacement vision exam to ensure properly corrected vision for reduced visual strain.[199]
- Allow the user to position his or her wrists at the same level as the elbow.
- Put the screen at or just below eye level, at a distance of 18 to 30 inches from the eyes.
- Let the wrists rest lightly on a pad for support.
- Put the feet flat on the floor or on a footrest.[200]

Repetitive Motion Disorders

Repetitive motion disorders include carpal tunnel syndrome and tendonitis. They result from too many uninterrupted repetitions of an activity or motion, or from unnatural motions such as twisting the arm or wrist. It affects people who perform repetitive tasks such as assembly line or computer work. Employers can reduce the problem, for instance, with programs to help workers adjust their pace of work.[201]

Sitting

Studies suggest that people who sit a lot are in poorer health, and need to get up and walk around about 30 or 40 times a day; that's why apps (such as iPhone's health app) prompt users to walk around hourly.[202] Standing desks and slow treadmills (up to 3–4 miles/hour) are other options.[203]

Infectious Diseases

Employers can take steps to prevent the entry or spread of infectious diseases.[204] These steps include

1. Monitor the Centers for Disease Control and Prevention (www.cdc.gov) travel alerts.
2. Encourage employees to receive immunizations.
3. Provide daily medical screenings for employees returning from infected areas.
4. Deny access for 10 days to employees or visitors who have had contact with suspected infected individuals.
5. Tell employees to stay home if they have a fever or respiratory system symptoms.
6. Clean work areas and surfaces regularly.
7. Practice hand hygiene, and make sanitizers easily available.
8. Stagger breaks. Offer several lunch periods to reduce overcrowding.[205]

Workplace Smoking

Smoking is a serious health and cost problem. For employers, costs derive from higher health and fire insurance, increased absenteeism, and reduced productivity (as when smokers take a 10-minute break behind the store).

The manager can probably deny a job to a smoker as long as smoking isn't used as a surrogate for other discrimination.[206] Federal laws don't expressly prohibit discrimination against smokers. However, if a majority of a company's smokers also happen to be minorities, antismoking activities could be viewed as discriminatory. Seventeen states and the District of Columbia ban discriminating against smokers.[207] Most employers these days ban indoor smoking, often designating small outdoor areas where smoking is permitted. Many states and municipalities now ban indoor smoking in public areas.[208] With vaping laws in flux, employers should check the status of their local and state laws.[209] NIOSH suggests prohibiting both tobacco smoke and e-cigarettes from the workplace.[210] While marijuana use is still illegal by federal law, it is legal in about 26 states, some of which have safety standards to protect cannabis industry workers.[211]

MyLab Management Apply It!

If your professor has assigned this activity, go to the Assignments section of **www.pearson.com/mylab/management** to complete the video exercise.

Occupational Security and Risk Management

LEARNING OBJECTIVE 16-7

Discuss the prerequisites for a security plan and how to set up a basic security program.

Workplace *safety* relates to risks of injury or illness to employees. Workplace *security* relates to protecting employees from internal and external security risks such as criminal acts by visitors and terrorism.[212] The employer's workplace security plans should address things like establishing a formal security team, protecting the firm's intellectual property (for instance, through noncompete agreements), protecting against cyber threats (personnel information can be a "gold mine" for hackers),[213] developing crisis management plans, establishing theft and fraud prevention procedures, preventing workplace violence, and installing facility security systems.[214] Many firms of course also have special handling procedures for mail packages and hold regular emergency evacuation drills.

Enterprise Risk Management

Enterprise risk management is "the process of assessing exposures to loss within an operation and determining how best to eliminate, manage or otherwise reduce the risk of an adverse event from having a negative impact on the business."[215]

Companies face a wide variety of risks, only some of which are OSHA-type direct risks to employees' health and safety. Other risks include, for instance, natural disaster risks, financial risks, and risks to the firm's computer systems. *Human capital risks* rank high. These include safety risks like those we discussed earlier in this chapter but also, for instance, "risks" from unionization and from inadequate staffing plans.[216]

How the employer manages a risk depends on the type of risk. For example, *internal preventable* risks arise from actions within the company and include things like employees' illegal conduct or workplace accidents.[217] Employers manage these risks with methods such as codes of conduct, disciplinary procedures, and safety rules. *Strategy risks* are risks that managers accept as part of executing their strategies, such as the risk a banker takes that a borrower defaults. Employers manage some strategy risks with independent experts (like those who assess insurance risks) and with in-house experts, like the risk managers who help to oversee banks' loan portfolios. *External risks* come from outside the company and include things like political and natural disasters and terrorism. Managing external risks might involve methods like scenario planning, in which the company endeavors to identify, analyze, and plan for multiple possible eventualities.

Preventing and Dealing with Violence at Work

Violence against employees is an internal preventable risk, and a huge problem.[218] According to OSHA, homicide is the fourth-leading cause of fatal occupational injuries in the United States.[219] Customers are often the perpetrators.[220] Many other assaults involve coworkers or a current or a former partner or spouse.[221]

Workplace violence incidents by coworkers are predictable and avoidable. *Risk Management Magazine* estimates that about 86% of past workplace violence incidents were anticipated by coworkers, who had brought them to management's attention prior to the incidents actually occurring. Yet management usually did little or nothing.[222] Human resource managers can take several steps to reduce workplace violence risks.

HEIGHTEN SECURITY MEASURES Heightened security measures are the first line of defense, whether the violence is from coworkers, customers, or outsiders. According to OSHA, measures should include those in Figure 16-7.

IMPROVE EMPLOYEE SCREENING With about 30% of workplace attacks committed by coworkers, screening out potentially violent applicants is the employer's next line of defense.

Both personal and situational factors correlate with workplace aggression. Men and individuals scoring higher on "trait anger" (the predisposition to respond to situations with hostility) are more likely to exhibit aggression. In terms of the situation, interpersonal injustice and poor leadership can trigger aggression against supervisors.[223]

Employers can screen out potentially violent workers before they're hired. Obtain an employment application, and check the applicant's employment history, education, and references.[224] Sample interview questions include "What frustrates you?" and "Who was your worst supervisor and why?"[225] Certain background circumstances, such as the following, may call for more in-depth background checking:[226]

- An unexplained gap in employment
- Incomplete or false information on the résumé or application
- A negative, unfavorable, or false reference
- Prior insubordinate or violent behavior on the job[227]
- A criminal history involving harassing or violent behavior
- A prior termination for cause with a suspicious (or no) explanation
- History of drug or alcohol abuse

FIGURE 16-7 How to Heighten Security in Your Workplace

Source: See "Creating a Safer Workplace: Simple Steps Bring Results," *Safety Now September 2002*, pp. 1–2. See also www.osha.gov/OshDoc/data_General_Facts/factsheet-workplaceviolence.pdf, accessed September 22, 2015.

- Improve external lighting.
- Use drop safes to minimize cash on hand.
- Post signs noting that only a limited amount of cash is on hand.
- Install silent alarms and surveillance cameras.
- Increase the number of staff on duty.
- Provide staff training in conflict resolution and nonviolent response.
- Close establishments during high-risk hours late at night and early in the morning.
- Issue a weapons policy; for instance, "firearms or other dangerous or deadly weapons cannot be brought onto the facility either openly or concealed."

- Strong indications of instability as indicated, for example, by frequent job changes or geographic moves
- Lost licenses or accreditations[228]
- Past conflicts (especially if violence was involved) with coworkers
- Past convictions for violent crimes

ESTABLISH A ZERO-TOLERANCE POLICY TOWARD WORKPLACE VIOLENCE This should cover all workers and *anyone* who may come in contact with company personnel.[229]

USE WORKPLACE VIOLENCE TRAINING You can also train supervisors to notice the clues that typify potentially violent current employees. Common clues include[230]

- An act of violence on or off the job
- Erratic behavior evidencing a loss of perception or awareness of actions
- Overly confrontational or antisocial behavior
- Sexually aggressive behavior
- Isolationist or loner tendencies
- Insubordinate behavior with a threat of violence
- Tendency to overreact to criticism
- Exaggerated interest in war, guns, violence, mass murders, catastrophes, and so on
- Commission of a serious breach of security
- Possession of weapons, guns, knives, or like items in the workplace
- Violation of privacy rights of others, such as searching desks or stalking
- Chronic complaining and the raising of frequent, unreasonable grievances
- A retributory or get-even attitude

GUIDELINES FOR FIRING A HIGH-RISK EMPLOYEE When firing a high-risk employee:

- Plan all aspects of the meeting, including its time, location, the people to be present, and agenda.
- Involve security enforcement personnel.
- Conduct the meeting in a room with a door leading to the outside of the building.
- Advise the employee that he or she is no longer permitted onto the employer's property.
- Keep the termination brief and to the point.
- Make sure he or she returns all company-owned property at the meeting.
- Don't let the person return to his or her workstation.
- Conduct the meeting early in the week and early in the morning so he or she has time to meet with employment counselors or support groups.
- Offer as generous a severance package as possible.
- Protect the employee's dignity by not advertising the event.[231]
- Managers associated with the dismissal should for a time exercise personal caution.[232]
- Employers should consider hiring a security expert to monitor, for a time, the former employee's social media for threats.[233]

VIOLENCE TOWARD WOMEN AT WORK Homicides accounted for 10% of those who died at work in one recent year.[234] Men have more fatal occupational injuries than do women, but the proportion of female victims of assault is much higher. The Gender-Motivated Violence Act (part of the Violence Against Women Act) imposes liabilities on employers whose women employees become violence victims.[235] Of all females murdered at work, more than three-fourths are victims of random criminal violence by assailants unknown to the victims. Family members, coworkers, or acquaintances commit the rest. Tangible security improvements including better lighting, cash-drop boxes, and similar steps can help. Women (and men) should have access to domestic crisis hotlines,[236] and to employee assistance programs.

Securing the Facility

As noted, workplace security relates to protecting employees from internal and external security risks (such as robberies and terrorism). This often starts with facilities security.

In simplest terms, instituting a basic facility security program requires four steps: analyzing the current *level* of risk, and then installing *mechanical, natural*, and *organizational* security systems.[237]

At one university, threat assessment team members meet periodically to review potential threats to university students and employees.[238] Such teams ideally start with an analysis of the facility's *current level of risk.* Here, start with the obvious. For example, what is the neighborhood like? Is the facility adjacent to railyards, or roads?[239] Does your facility (such as your office building) house other businesses or individuals that might bring unsafe activities? As part of this initial threat assessment, also review these six matters:

1. ***Reception area access***, including need for a "panic button";
2. ***Interior security***, including secure restrooms, and better identification of exits;
3. ***Authorities' involvement***, in particular emergency procedures developed with local law enforcement;
4. ***Mail handling***, including screening and opening mail;
5. ***Evacuation***, including evacuation procedures and training; and
6. ***Backup systems***, such as storing data off site.

Having assessed the potential current level of risk, the employer then turns to assessing and improving natural, mechanical, and organizational security.[240]

Natural security means capitalizing on the facility's natural or architectural features to minimize security problems. For example, do too many entrances hamper controlling facility access?

Mechanical security is the utilization of security systems such as locks, intrusion alarms, access control systems, and surveillance systems.[241] Here make sure to train local employees to use the security devices and that the devices (cameras, and so on) are maintained.[242]

Finally, *organizational security* means using good management to improve security. For example, it means properly training and motivating security staff and lobby attendants. Ensure that the security staff has written orders that define their duties,

Many employers install video security cameras to monitor areas in and around their premises.

Andrey Popov/Shutterstock

especially in situations such as fire, elevator entrapment, hazardous materials spills, medical emergencies, hostile intrusions, suspicious packages, civil disturbances, and workplace violence.[243]

Remember, however, that facility security *systems* are not enough. In particular, having security personnel who should be watching your monitors staring at their smart phone screens, or guards who should be challenging visitors nonchalantly letting all through, will defeat your systems. At the end of the day, security is as much (or more) an employee selection, training, evaluation, and motivation problem as a mechanical one.

Terrorism

The employer can take several steps to protect its employees and physical assets from the risk of terrorist attack. These steps, now familiar at many workplaces, include the following:

- Screen the identities of everyone entering the premises.[244]
- Check mail carefully.
- Identify ahead of time a lean interim "crisis organization" that can run the company after a terrorist threat.
- Identify in advance under what conditions you will close the company down, as well as the shutdown process.
- Institute a process to put a crisis management team together.
- Prepare evacuation plans, and make sure exits are well marked and unblocked.
- Designate an employee who will communicate with families and off-site employees.
- Identify an upwind, off-site location near your facility as a staging area for all evacuated personnel.
- Designate in advance several employees who will do headcounts at the staging area.
- Establish an emergency communications procedure, for instance based on text messaging or Twitter.

Cybersecurity

Securing the employer's physical facility may do little to prevent cyberattacks of the sort that hit Facebook a while ago; similarly, hackers got personal information of about 22 million U.S. federal employees from Office of Personnel Management (OPM) servers.[245]

Data protection and cybersecurity are specialized areas requiring special expertise. However, some basic guidelines would include: First, *data security is everyone's responsibility*.[246] IT installs firewalls and password systems. However, every employee plays a security role, from the CEO setting policy to first-line employees guarding their passwords. Second, "*old data is bad data.*" In other words, destroy unneeded old personal data (say from five years ago) unless it's absolutely required. Third, *encrypt*. That includes data in laptops employees carry with them. Fourth, *monitor*. The IT staff should periodically assess cyber risks. Two of many cybersecurity consultants include Kroll,[247] and KPMG.[248]

Business Continuity and Emergency Plans

One source estimates that 40% of companies never reopen after suffering business disruptions from a major catastrophe, so putting a disaster plan in place is imperative.[249] Emergency preparedness resources include www.ready.gov and the National Institute for Occupational Safety and Health (www.cdc.gov/niosh/). OSHA requires written emergency action plans.[250]

To help the employer prepare for potential disasters, the human resource department should develop a plan and identify key responsibilities, make sure all employees are aware of the plan, and train employees regularly.[251] Such plans should cover *early detection of a problem, methods for communicating the emergency externally*, and *communications plans for initiating an evacuation.* The initial alarm should come first. The employer should follow that with an announcement providing specific information about the emergency and letting employees know what action they should take.[252]

The employer also needs plans for *business continuity* in the event of a disaster. The employer can designate a secure area of the company Web site for emergency employee communications, listing such things as expected hours of operation, facilities opening schedules, and alternative work locations.[253] The disaster plans should include establishing a command center and identifying employees considered essential in the event of a disaster, including responsibilities for each. Business continuity information is available at www.preparemybusiness.org.

TRENDS SHAPING HR: *DIGITAL AND SOCIAL MEDIA*

Twitter Notifications

Social media such as Twitter are obvious choices for quickly communicating emergency information to large numbers of dispersed individuals. When a tornado hit Bridgeport, Connecticut, a few years ago, the city's administrators used Twitter to tell citizens about things like power outages and blocked roads. The Canadian Red Cross uses social media to publicize preparedness information and respond to questions from affected communities. And emergency managers, utility companies, and the public used social media to share updates on things like shelter locations when Hurricane Sandy struck the Northeast.[254] ■

Chapter Review

Chapter Section Summaries

16-1. The subject **safety and the manager** concerns managers for several reasons, one of which is the number of workplace accidents. Reducing accidents often boils down to reducing accident-causing conditions and accident-causing acts. However, safety always starts at the top.

16-2. Because of this, all managers need to be familiar with **occupational safety law.** The Occupational Safety and Health Act was passed by Congress in 1972 to assure so far as possible every working man and woman in the nation has safe and healthful working conditions, and to preserve human resources. The act created the Occupational Safety and Health Administration (OSHA).

16-3. There are three basic **causes of workplace accidents:** chance occurrences, unsafe conditions, and employees' unsafe acts. Unsafe conditions include things like improperly guarded equipment and hazardous procedures. Unsafe acts sometimes reflect personality traits such as impatience and distractibility.

16-4. In practice, **how to prevent accidents** boils down to reducing unsafe conditions and reducing unsafe acts. Reducing unsafe conditions is always the first line of defense and includes using checklists and following OSHA standards. There are then several basic approaches to reducing unsafe acts, for instance, through proper selection and placement, training, motivation and positive reinforcement, behavior-based safety, employee participation, and conducting safety and health audits.

16-5. The centerpiece of Milliken's safety process is its *involvement-based* employee engagement **program.** Milliken's employees staff the steering and safety subcommittee system, submit "opportunity for improvement" suggestions weekly, review each of these suggestions, and provide feedback on every suggestion.

16-6. Most **workplace health hazards** aren't obvious, like unguarded equipment. Typical exposure hazards include, for instance, chemicals, biohazards, and improperly designed equipment. Managing exposure hazards like these comes under the area of industrial hygiene, and involves recognition, evaluation, and control. Stress, burnout, and depression are more serious at work than many people realize, and both the employee and employer can take steps to deal with them. Employers especially need to train supervisors to identify depression's warning signs and to counsel those who may need special services.

16-7. Most employers today have **occupational security and risk management programs.** Heightened security measures are an employer's first line of defense against attacks on workers, and include, for instance, improving external lighting. Screening can reduce the risk of hiring potentially violent employees. Instituting a basic facility security program involves analyzing the current level of risk, and then installing mechanical, natural, and organizational security systems.

Discussion Questions

16-1. Explain how to reduce the occurrence of unsafe acts on the part of your employees.
16-2. Explain the supervisor's role in safety.
16-3. Explain what causes unsafe acts.
16-4. Describe at least five techniques for reducing accidents.
16-5. Explain how you would reduce stress at work.

Individual and Group Activities

16-6. Working individually or in groups, answer the question, "Is there such a thing as an accident-prone person?"

16-7. Working individually or in groups, compile a list of the factors at work or in school that create stress for you. What methods do you use for dealing with the stress?

16-8. Appendices A and B at the end of this book (pages 614–634) list the knowledge someone studying for the HRCI (Appendix A) or SHRM (Appendix B) certification exam needs to have in each area of human resource management (such as in Strategic Management and Workforce Planning). In groups of several students, do four things: (1) review Appendix A and/or B; (2) identify the material in this chapter that relates to the Appendix A and/or B required knowledge lists; (3) write four multiple-choice exam questions on this material that you believe would be suitable for inclusion in the HRCI exam and/or the SHRM exam; and (4) if time permits, have someone from your team post your team's questions in front of the class, so that students in all teams can answer the exam questions created by the other teams.

KNOWLEDGE BASE

16-9. A safety journal presented some information about what happens when OSHA refers criminal complaints about willful violations of OSHA standards to the U.S. Department of Justice (DOJ). In one 20-year period, of the 119 cases OSHA referred to the DOJ, only 9 resulted in prison time for at least one of the defendants. "The Department of Justice is a disgrace," charged the founder of an organization for family members of workers killed on the job. One possible explanation for this low conviction rate is that the crime in cases like these is generally a misdemeanor, not a felony, and the DOJ generally tries to focus its attention on felony cases. Given this information, what implications do you think this has for how employers and their managers should manage their safety programs, and why do you take that position?

16-10. A 315-foot-tall, 2-million-pound crane collapsed on a construction site in East Toledo, Ohio, killing four ironworkers. Do you think catastrophic failures like this are avoidable? If so, what steps would you suggest the general contractor take to avoid a disaster like this?

CHAPTER 16

Experiential Exercise

How Safe Is My University?

Written and copyrighted by Gary Dessler, PhD.

Purpose: The purpose of this exercise is to give you practice in identifying unsafe conditions.

Required Understanding: You should be familiar with material covered in this chapter, particularly that on unsafe conditions and that in Figures 16-6 and 16-8.

How to Set Up the Exercise/Instructions: Divide the class into groups of four. Assume that each group is a safety committee retained by your college's or university's safety engineer to identify and report on any possible unsafe conditions in and around the school building. Each group will spend about 45 minutes in and around the building you are now in for the purpose of identifying and listing possible unsafe conditions. (Make use of the checklists in Figures 16-6 and 16-8.)

Return to the class in about 45 minutes. A spokesperson for each group should list on the board the unsafe conditions you have identified. How many were there? Do you think these also violate OSHA standards? How would you go about checking?

GENERAL

	OK	ACTION NEEDED
1. Is the required OSHA workplace poster displayed in your place of business as required where all employees are likely to see it?	☐	☐
2. Are you aware of the requirement to report all workplace fatalities and any serious accidents (where five or more are hospitalized) to a federal or state OSHA office within 48 hours?	☐	☐
3. Are workplace injury and illness records being kept as required by OSHA?	☐	☐
4. Are you aware that the OSHA annual summary of workplace injuries and illnesses must be posted by February 1 and must remain posted until March 1?	☐	☐
5. Are you aware that employers with 10 or fewer employees are exempt from the OSHA record-keeping requirements, unless they are part of an official BLS or state survey and have received specific instructions to keep records?	☐	☐
6. Have you demonstrated an active interest in safety and health matters by defining a policy for your business and communicating it to all employees?	☐	☐
7. Do you have a safety committee or group that allows participation of employees in safety and health activities?	☐	☐
8. Does the safety committee or group meet regularly and report, in writing, its activities?	☐	☐
9. Do you provide safety and health training for all employees requiring such training, and is it documented?	☐	☐
10. Is one person clearly in charge of safety and health activities?	☐	☐
11. Do all employees know what to do in emergencies?	☐	☐
12. Are emergency telephone numbers posted?	☐	☐
13. Do you have a procedure for handling employee complaints regarding safety and health?	☐	☐

WORKPLACE

ELECTRICAL WIRING, FIXTURES, AND CONTROLS	OK	ACTION NEEDED
1. Are your workplace electricians familiar with the requirements of the National Electrical Code (NEC)?	☐	☐
2. Do you specify compliance with the NEC for all contract electrical work?	☐	☐
3. If you have electrical installations in hazardous dust or vapor areas, do they meet the NEC for hazardous locations?	☐	☐
4. Are all electrical cords strung so they do not hang on pipes, nails, hooks, etc.?	☐	☐
5. Is all conduit, BX cable, etc., properly attached to all supports and tightly connected to junction and outlet boxes?	☐	☐
6. Is there no evidence of fraying on any electrical cords?	☐	☐
7. Are rubber cords kept free of grease, oil, and chemicals?	☐	☐
8. Are metallic cable and conduit systems properly grounded?	☐	☐
9. Are portable electric tools and appliances grounded or double insulated?	☐	☐
10. Are all ground connections clean and tight?	☐	☐
11. Are fuses and circuit breakers the right type and size for the load on each circuit?	☐	☐
12. Are all fuses free of "jumping" with pennies or metal strips?	☐	☐
13. Do switches show evidence of overheating?	☐	☐
14. Are switches mounted in clean, tightly closed metal boxes?	☐	☐
15. Are all electrical switches marked to show their purpose?	☐	☐
16. Are motors clean and kept free of excessive grease and oil?	☐	☐
17. Are motors properly maintained and provided with adequate overcurrent protection?	☐	☐
18. Are bearings in good condition?	☐	☐
19. Are portable lights equipped with proper guards?	☐	☐
20. Are all lamps kept free of combustible material?	☐	☐
21. Is your electrical system checked periodically by someone competent in the NEC?	☐	☐

Develop your own checklist.

These are only sample questions.

FIGURE 16-8 **Self-Inspection Safety and Health Checklist**

Source: From OSHA Self-Inspection Checklist for General Industry, from http://www.safetyhouse.ir/safetyhouse/file/OSHA%20Self-Inspection%20Checklist%20for%20General%20Industry.pdf, accessed April 10, 2018.
Note: For a more extensive checklist, see "Self-Inspection Checklists," www.osha.gov/Publications/smallbusiness/small-business.html#check, accessed April 10, 2018.

Develop your own checklist.

These are only sample questions.

EXITS AND ACCESS

OK | ACTION NEEDED

1. Are all exits visible and unobstructed? ☐ ☐
2. Are all exits marked with a readily visible sign that is properly illuminated? ☐ ☐
3. Are there sufficient exits to ensure prompt escape in case of emergency? ☐ ☐
4. Are areas with restricted occupancy posted and is access/egress controlled by persons specifically authorized to be in those areas? ☐ ☐
5. Do you take special precautions to protect employees during construction and repair operations? ☐ ☐

FIRE PROTECTION

OK | ACTION NEEDED

1. Are portable fire extinguishers provided in adequate number and type? ☐ ☐
2. Are fire extinguishers inspected monthly for general condition and operability and noted on the inspection tag? ☐ ☐
3. Are fire extinguishers recharged regularly and properly noted on the inspection tag? ☐ ☐
4. Are fire extinguishers mounted in readily accessible locations? ☐ ☐
5. If you have interior standpipes and valves, are these inspected regularly? ☐ ☐
6. If you have a fire alarm system, is it tested at least annually? ☐ ☐
7. Are employees periodically instructed in the use of extinguishers and fire protection procedures? ☐ ☐
8. If you have outside private fire hydrants, were they flushed within the last year and placed on a regular maintenance schedule? ☐ ☐
9. Are fire doors and shutters in good operating condition? ☐ ☐
   Are they unobstructed and protected against obstruction? ☐ ☐
10. Are fusible links in place? ☐ ☐
11. Is your local fire department well acquainted with your plant, location, and specific hazards? ☐ ☐
12. Automatic sprinklers:
    Are water control valves, air, and water pressures checked weekly? ☐ ☐
    Are control valves locked open? ☐ ☐
    Is maintenance of the system assigned to responsible persons or a sprinkler contractor? ☐ ☐
    Are sprinkler heads protected by metal guards where exposed to mechanical damage? ☐ ☐
    Is proper minimum clearance maintained around sprinkler heads? ☐ ☐

HOUSEKEEPING AND GENERAL WORK ENVIRONMENT

OK | ACTION NEEDED

1. Is smoking permitted in designated "safe areas" only? ☐ ☐
2. Are NO SMOKING signs prominently posted in areas containing combustibles and flammables? ☐ ☐
3. Are covered metal waste cans used for oily and paint-soaked waste? ☐ ☐
   Are they emptied at least daily? ☐ ☐
4. Are paint spray booths, dip tanks, etc., and their exhaust ducts cleaned regularly? ☐ ☐
5. Are stand mats, platforms, or similar protection provided to protect employees from wet floors in wet processes? ☐ ☐
6. Are waste receptacles provided and are they emptied regularly? ☐ ☐
7. Do your toilet facilities meet the requirements of applicable sanitary codes? ☐ ☐
8. Are washing facilities provided? ☐ ☐
9. Are all areas of your business adequately illuminated? ☐ ☐
10. Are floor load capacities posted in second floors, lofts, storage areas, etc.? ☐ ☐
11. Are floor openings provided with toe boards and railings or a floor hole cover? ☐ ☐
12. Are stairways in good condition with standard railings provided for every flight having four or more risers? ☐ ☐
13. Are portable wood ladders and metal ladders adequate for their purpose, in good condition, and provided with secure footing? ☐ ☐
14. If you have fixed ladders, are they adequate, and are they in good condition and equipped with side rails or cages or special safety climbing devices, if required? ☐ ☐
15. For loading docks:
    Are dockplates kept in serviceable condition and secured to prevent slipping? ☐ ☐
    Do you have means to prevent car or truck movement when dockplates are in place? ☐ ☐

FIGURE 16-8 *Continued*

MACHINES AND EQUIPMENT

	OK	ACTION NEEDED
1. Are all machines or operations that expose operators or other employees to rotating parts, pinch points, flying chips, particles, or sparks adequately guarded?	☐	☐
2. Are mechanical power transmission belts and pinch points guarded?	☐	☐
3. Is exposed power shafting less than 7 feet from the floor guarded?	☐	☐
4. Are hand tools and other equipment regularly inspected for safe condition?	☐	☐
5. Is compressed air used for cleaning reduced to less than 30 psi?	☐	☐
6. Are power saws and similar equipment provided with safety guards?	☐	☐
7. Are grinding wheel tool rests set to within 1/8 inch or less of the wheel?	☐	☐
8. Is there any system for inspecting small hand tools for burred ends, cracked handles, etc.?	☐	☐
9. Are compressed gas cylinders examined regularly for obvious signs of defects, deep rusting, or leakage?	☐	☐
10. Is care used in handling and storing cylinders and valves to prevent damage?	☐	☐
11. Are all air receivers periodically examined, including the safety valves?	☐	☐
12. Are safety valves tested regularly and frequently?	☐	☐
13. Is there sufficient clearance from stoves, furnaces, etc., for stock, woodwork, or other combustible materials?	☐	☐
14. Is there clearance of at least 4 feet in front of heating equipment involving open flames, such as gas radiant heaters, and fronts of firing doors of stoves, furnaces, etc.?	☐	☐
15. Are all oil and gas fired devices equipped with flame failure controls that will prevent flow of fuel if pilots or main burners are not working?	☐	☐
16. Is there at least a 2-inch clearance between chimney brickwork and all woodwork or other combustible materials?	☐	☐
17. For welding or flame cutting operations:		
Are only authorized, trained personnel permitted to use such equipment?	☐	☐
Have operators been given a copy of operating instructions and asked to follow them?	☐	☐
Are welding gas cylinders stored so they are not subjected to damage?	☐	☐
Are valve protection caps in place on all cylinders not connected for use?	☐	☐
Are all combustible materials near the operator covered with protective shields or otherwise protected?	☐	☐
Is a fire extinguisher provided at the welding site?	☐	☐
Do operators have the proper protective clothing and equipment?	☐	☐

Develop your own checklist.

These are only sample questions.

MATERIALS

	OK	ACTION NEEDED
1. Are approved safety cans or other acceptable containers used for handling and dispensing flammable liquids?	☐	☐
2. Are all flammable liquids that are kept inside buildings stored in proper storage containers or cabinets?	☐	☐
3. Do you meet OSHA standards for all spray painting or dip tank operations using combustible liquids?	☐	☐
4. Are oxidizing chemicals stored in areas separate from all organic material except shipping bags?	☐	☐
5. Do you have an enforced NO SMOKING rule in areas for storage and use of hazardous materials?	☐	☐
6. Are NO SMOKING signs posted where needed?	☐	☐
7. Is ventilation equipment provided for removal of air contaminants from operations such as production grinding, buffing, spray painting and/or vapor degreasing, and is it operating properly?	☐	☐
8. Are protective measures in effect for operations involved with x-rays or other radiation?	☐	☐
9. For lift truck operations:		
Are only trained personnel allowed to operate forklift trucks?	☐	☐
Is overhead protection provided on high lift rider trucks?	☐	☐
10. For toxic materials:		
Are all materials used in your plant checked for toxic qualities?	☐	☐
Have appropriate control procedures such as ventilation systems, enclosed operations, safe handling practices, proper personal protective equipment (such as respirators, glasses or goggles, gloves, etc.) been instituted for toxic materials?	☐	☐

FIGURE 16-8 *Continued*

Develop your own checklist.

These are only sample questions.

EMPLOYEE PROTECTION	OK	ACTION NEEDED
1. Is there a hospital, clinic, or infirmary for medical care near your business?	☐	☐
2. If medical and first-aid facilities are not nearby, do you have one or more employees trained in first aid?	☐	☐
3. Are your first-aid supplies adequate for the type of potential injuries in your workplace?	☐	☐
4. Are there quick water flush facilities available where employees are exposed to corrosive materials?	☐	☐
5. Are hard hats provided and worn where any danger of falling objects exists?	☐	☐
6. Are protective goggles or glasses provided and worn where there is any danger of flying particles or splashing of corrosive materials?	☐	☐
7. Are protective gloves, aprons, shields, or other means provided for protection from sharp, hot, or corrosive materials?	☐	☐
8. Are approved respirators provided for regular or emergency use where needed?	☐	☐
9. Is all protective equipment maintained in a sanitary condition and readily available for use?	☐	☐
10. Where special equipment is needed for electrical workers, is it available?	☐	☐
11. When lunches are eaten on the premises, are they eaten in areas where there is no exposure to toxic materials, and not in toilet facility areas?	☐	☐
12. Is protection against the effect of occupational noise exposure provided when the sound levels exceed those shown in the OSHA noise standard?	☐	☐

FIGURE 16-8 ***Continued***

Application Case

The Dangerous Third Shift

Written and copyrighted by Gary Dessler, PhD.

More than 100 years ago, Upton Sinclair wrote his famous book, *The Jungle*, about the outrageous conditions in Chicago-area slaughterhouses. Although slaughterhouse conditions have undoubtedly improved, working in meatpacking plants can still be strikingly dangerous.[255]

In one such plant, in Kansas, the first two (daytime) work shifts oversee the actual processing of approximately 6,000 cows per day. After that, the third, 11 P.M shift starts as the sanitation crews arrive. These workers have to wade through slippery conditions, including grease and parts left over from the day shifts' work. The sanitation crew's job is to clean the plant and its machines and conveyors with boiling water and disinfectants.

Several years ago, a female sanitation crew worker was finishing cleaning the belt on one of the conveyors. She had shut down the conveyor when she cleaned it. However, after turning it back on, she noticed she had missed some animal fat dirt below the conveyor. With the belt still moving she reached under it to get the dirt. She lost her balance and tried to catch herself, but her hand and then her arm were drawn into the machine and completely mangled.

Questions

16-11. No doubt many problems contributed to this severe accident. However, if you had to choose just one thing that you would tell the meatpacking company to change, what would it be?

16-12. Would it be advisable for them to set up a procedure for screening out accident-prone individuals? Why or why not? If so, how should they screen them?

16-13. Write a short position paper on the subject, "What should we do in this plant to get all our employees to behave more safely at work?"

16-14. Based on what you learned from this chapter, write a short position paper on the subject, "What should we do to reduce the chances of accidents like this in our meatpacking plant? Please make sure to list at least 5–10 specific things you would suggest.

Continuing Case

Carter Cleaning Company

Written and copyrighted by Gary Dessler, PhD.

The New Safety Program

Employees' safety and health are very important matters in the laundry and cleaning business. Each facility is a small production plant in which machines, powered by high-pressure steam and compressed air, work at high temperatures washing, cleaning, and pressing garments, often under very hot, slippery conditions. Chemical vapors are produced continually, and caustic chemicals are used in the cleaning process. High-temperature stills are almost continually "cooking down" cleaning solvents in order to remove impurities so that the solvents can be reused. If a mistake is made in this process—like injecting too much steam into the still—a boilover occurs, in which boiling chemical solvent erupts out of the still and over the floor, and on anyone who happens to be standing in its way.

As a result of these hazards and the fact that chemically hazardous waste is continually produced in these stores, several government agencies (including OSHA and the Environmental Protection Agency) have instituted strict guidelines regarding the management of these plants. For example, posters have to be placed in each store notifying employees of their right to be told what hazardous chemicals they are dealing with and what the proper method for handling each chemical is. Special waste-management firms must be used to pick up and properly dispose of the hazardous waste.

A chronic problem the Carters (and most other laundry owners) have is the unwillingness on the part of the cleaning/spotting workers to wear safety goggles. Not all the chemicals they use require safety goggles, but some—like the hydrofluoric acid used to remove rust stains from garments—are very dangerous. The latter is kept in special plastic containers, since it dissolves glass. The problem is that wearing safety goggles can be troublesome. They are somewhat uncomfortable, and they become smudged easily and thus cut down on visibility. As a result, Jack has always found it almost impossible to get these employees to wear their goggles.

Questions

16-15. How should the firm go about identifying hazardous conditions that should be rectified? Use checklists such as those in Figures 16-6 and 16-8 to list at least 10 possible dry cleaning store hazardous conditions.

16-16. Would it be advisable for the firm to set up a procedure for screening out accident-prone individuals? How should they do so?

16-17. How would you suggest the Carters get all employees to behave more safely at work? Also, how would you advise them to get those who should be wearing goggles to do so?

Translating Strategy into HR Policies and Practices Case*,§

** The accompanying strategy map for this chapter is in MyLab Management; the overall map on the inside back cover of this text outlines the relationships involved.*

Improving Performance at the Hotel Paris

The New Safety and Health Program

The Hotel Paris's competitive strategy is "To use superior guest service to differentiate the Hotel Paris properties, and to thereby increase the length of stay and return rate of guests, and thus boost revenues and profitability." HR manager Lisa Cruz must now formulate functional policies and activities that support this competitive strategy and boost performance, by eliciting the required employee behaviors and competencies.

While "hazardous conditions" might not be the first thing that comes to mind when you think of hotels, Lisa Cruz knew that hazards and safety were in fact serious issues for the Hotel Paris. Indeed, everywhere you look—from the valets leaving car doors open on the driveways to slippery areas around the pools, to thousands of pounds of ammonia, chlorine, and other caustic chemicals that the hotels use each year for cleaning and laundry, hotels provide a fertile environment for accidents. Obviously, hazardous conditions are bad for the Hotel Paris. They are inhumane for the workers. High accident rates probably reduce employee morale and thus service. And accidents raise the company's costs and reduce its profitability, for instance, in terms of workers' compensation claims and absences. Lisa knew that she had to clean up her firm's occupational safety and health systems, for its employees' well-being, and to achieve the company's strategic goals.

Lisa and the CFO reviewed their company's safety records, and what they found disturbed them. In terms of every safety-related metric they could find, including accident costs per year, lost time due to accidents, workers' compensation per employee, and number of safety training programs per year, the Hotel Paris compared unfavorably with most other hotel chains and service firms. "Just in terms of extra workers' compensation costs, the Hotel Paris must be spending $500,000 a year more than we should be," said the CFO. And that didn't include lost time due to accidents, or the negative effect accidents had on employee morale, or the cost of litigation (as when, for instance, one guest accidentally burned himself with chlorine that a pool attendant had left unprotected). The CFO authorized Lisa to develop a new safety and health program.

Lisa and her team began by hiring a safety and health consultant, someone who had been an inspector and then manager with OSHA. Based on the analysis, the team then took numerous steps, including the following. First, specially trained teams consisting of someone from Lisa's HR group, the local hotel's assistant manager, and three local hotel employees went through each local hotel "with a fine-tooth comb," as Lisa put it. They used an extensive checklist to identify and eliminate unsafe conditions.

Lisa's team took other steps. They convinced the Hotel Paris's board of directors and chairman and CEO to issue a joint statement emphasizing the importance of safety, and the CEO, during a one-month period, visited each hotel to meet with all employees and emphasize safety. The Hotel Paris also contracted with a safety training company. This firm created special online safety programs for the company's managers, and developed five-day training seminars for the hotels' staffs.

The new programs seem to be effective. Lisa and the CFO were pleased to find, after about a year, that accident costs per year, lost time due to accidents, and workers' compensation expenses were all down at least 40%. And anecdotal evidence from supervisors suggested that employees feel better about the company's commitment to them and were providing better service as a result.

Questions

16-18. Based on what you read in this chapter of Dessler *Human Resource Management*, what's the first step you would have advised the Hotel Paris to take as part of its new safety and health program, and why?

16-19. List 10 specific high-risk areas in a typical hotel you believe Lisa and her team should look at now, including examples of the safety or health hazards that they should look for there.

16-20. Give three specific examples of how the Hotel Paris can use HR practices to improve its safety efforts.

16-21. Write a one-page summary addressing the topic, "How improving safety and health at the Hotel Paris will contribute to us achieving our strategic goals."

§ Written and copyrighted by Gary Dessler, PhD.

Writing Assignments

16-22. Based on everything you read in this chapter, what is Milliken doing "right" that you believe helps to explain why they have such a good safety record?

16-23. Describe the steps employers can take to reduce workplace violence.

PERSONAL INVENTORY ASSESSMENTS

Go to **www.pearson.com/mylab/management** to complete the Personal Inventory Assessment related to this chapter.

Key Terms

Occupational Safety and Health Act of 1970, 521
Occupational Safety and Health Administration (OSHA), 521
occupational illness, 521
citation, 524
unsafe conditions, 526
job hazard analysis, 528
operational safety reviews, 532
behavior-based safety, 536
safety awareness program, 536
burnout, 542

Endnotes

1. "Workers Rate Safety Most Important Workplace Issue," *EHS Today*, October 2010, p. 17.
2. "BP Oil Spill Timeline," July 22, 2010, www.guardian.co.uk/environment/2010/jun/29/bp-oil-spill-timeline-deepwater-horizon, accessed June 29, 2011.
3. "Film Company Fined over Harrison Ford Injury on Star Wars Set," p. 6 .com/2016/10/12/film–company–fine–over–Harrison–ford–injury–on–star–wars.
4. Bruce Rolfsen, "Workplace Death Rates in 2016 Jump to Highest Level since 2010," *Bloomberg BNA Bulletin to Management*, January 2, 2018.
5. Figures for 2015; https://www.bls.gov/news.release/osh.nr0.htm, accessed April 20, 2017.
6. "BLS Likely Underestimating Injury and Illness Estimates," May 2006, p. 16; Tahira Probst et al., "Organizational Injury Rate Underreporting: The Moderating Effect of Organizational Safety Climate," *Journal of Applied Psychology* 93, no. 5 (2008), pp. 1147–1154.
7. For example, workers' compensation typically covers only about 21% of the total cost of a worker's injuries. Various federal, state, and local government programs pay about 16%, private health insurance 13%, and the worker and his or her family pay about 50% of the total costs out of pocket. "Adding Inequality to Injury: The Cost of Failing to Protect Workers on the Job," Occupational Safety & Health Administration, https://www.dol.gov/osha/report/20150304-inequality.pdf, accessed May 14, 2018.
8. Russell Sobel, "Occupational Safety and Profit Maximization: Friends or Foes?" *The Journal of Socioeconomics* 30, no. 9 (2010), pp. 429–433.
9. www.osha.gov/dcsp/products/topics/businesscase/, accessed April 16, 2013.
10. David Levine et al., "Randomized Government Safety Inspections Reduce Worker Injuries with No Detectable Job Loss," *Science* 336 (May 18, 2012), pp. 907–911.
11. Chief Financial Officer Survey, Liberty Mutual Insurance Co., 2005.
12. Mike Rich, "Preventing Hearing Loss," www.adhesivesmag.com, January 2012, pp. 40–41.
13. Kristen Ferguson, "The Role of Senior Executives and Board Directors in Safety Leadership," *EHS Today*, January 2016, pp. 17–20.
14. See, for example, Len Jannaman, "Are Your Top Leaders Engaged in Driving Safety Performance?" *EHS Today*, January 2017, pp. 14–17.
15. One study concluded that "employee perceptions of the extent to which managers and supervisors are committed to workplace safety likely influence employee safety behavior and, subsequently, injuries." Jeremy Beus et al., "Safety Climate and Juries: An Examination of Theoretical and Empirical Relationships," *Journal of Applied Psychology* 95, no. 4 (2010), pp. 713–727. See also Sean Tucker et al., "Safety in the C Suite: How Chief Executive Officers Influence Organizational Safety Climate and Employee Injuries," *Journal of Applied Psychology* 101, no. 9 (2016), pp. 1228–1239.
16. https://www.westex.com/blog/is-safety-an-initiative-or-a-value-at-your-organization/, accessed April 9, 2018.
17. Based on Chip Cummins, U.S. Cites Cost Cuts' Role in BP Refinery Blast, Safety Board Lays Blame with Top-Level Decisions, Raising Firm's Legal Risks, www.wsj.com/articles/SB116222460245007872.
18. See the BP case in the Appendix for further discussion.
19. Sandy Smith, "Louisiana-Pacific Corp. Builds Safety into Everything It Does," *Occupational Hazards*, November 2007, pp. 41–42.
20. Sandy Smith, "ABB Inc. Relies on Leadership and Accountability for Safety Performance," *EHS Today*, November 2012, p. 38.
21. "Did This Supervisor Do Enough to Protect Trench Workers?" *Safety Compliance Letter*, October 2003, p. 9; https://www.osha.gov/pls/oshaweb/owadisp.show_document?p_table=STANDARDS&p_id=10775, accessed April 9, 2018.
22. Possibly because they provide more apprenticeship training and make it easier to report dangers, unionized facilities tend to have fewer accidents than nonunionized ones. For example, Dominique Bravo, "Death on the Construction Site," *The New York Times*, January 17, 2017, p. 821.
23. Ibid.
24. Based on "All About OSHA," rev. ed. (Washington, DC: U.S. Department of Labor, 1980), www.osha.gov/law-regs.html, accessed September 11, 2014.
25. Ibid.
26. https://www.osha.gov/dep/index.html, accessed April 12, 2017.
27. Bruce Rolfson, "Employer Still Await Guidance on Worker Safety Incentive Programs," *Bloomberg BNA Bulletin to Management*, February 13, 2018.
28. Stefanie Valentic, "Protecting Those Peepers: A Guide to Eye Wash and Emergency Shower Stations," *EHS Today*, March 2017, p. 21.
29. Such specificity is not excessive, because even choosing a ladder requires expertise. One must consider its weight rating, material (such as fiberglass for nonconductivity), and length or height (to allow workers to work without

CHAPTER 16

climbing on the top rung), David Francis, "The Future of Fall Prevention," *EHS Today*, March 2017, pp. 13–16.

30. "OSHA Hazard Communication Standard Enforcement," *BNA Bulletin to Management*, February 23, 1989, p. 13; https://www.osha.gov/report.html, accessed April 9, 2018. Flowchart based on https://www.osha.gov/recordkeeping2014/blog-OSHA-flow.pdf, accessed April 9, 2018.
31. "What Every Employer Needs to Know about OSHA Record Keeping," U.S. Department of Labor, Bureau of Labor Statistics, Washington, DC, report 412–413, p. 3, www.osha.gov/recordkeeping/index.html, accessed September 11, 2014.
32. "New OSHA Recordkeeping Rule in Effect with the New Year," *Bloomberg BNA Bulletin to Management*, January 6, 2015, p. 2.
33. https://www.osha.gov/recordkeeping/index.html, accessed April 9, 2018.
34. Steve Hollingsworth, "How to Survive an OSHA Inspection," *Occupational Hazards*, March 2004, pp. 31–33; https://www.osha.gov/OshDoc/data_General_Facts/factsheet-inspections.pdf, accessed April 9, 2018.
35. www.osha.gov/as/opa/oshafacts.html, accessed January 19, 2008; Edwin Foulke Jr., "OSHA's Evolving Role in Promoting Occupational Safety and Health," *EHS Today*, November 2008, pp. 44–49; www.osha.gov/dcsp/compliance_assistance/index_programs.html, accessed August 8, 2013.
36. https://www.osha.gov/dep/index.html, accessed April 12, 2017.
37. https://www.osha.gov/oshstats/commonstats.html, accessed April 8, 2018.
38. Chris Mancillas, "OSHA" New Injury Data Disclosure Rule—Good Intentions but Questions on Execution," *EHS Today*, September 2016, pp. 28–29. As of 2017, many employers are required to electronically submit workplace injury and illness data, which OSHA may then post publicly. "New Rule Allows OSHA to Cite Employers' Incentive Programs, Post Injury Data Online," *Bloomberg BNA Bulletin to Management*, May 17, 2016, p. 153.
39. See "Site-Specific Targeting Program Letters Mailed to High Injury/Illness Rate Employers," *Bloomberg BNA Bulletin to Management*, April 10, 2012, p. 113.
40. This section is based on "All About OSHA," pp. 23–25; and https://www.osha.gov/OshDoc/data_General_Facts/factsheet-inspections.pdf, accessed April 9, 2018.
41. "Your Rights as a Whistleblower," https://www.osha.gov/OshDoc/data_General_Facts/whistleblower_rights.pdf, accessed April 9, 2018.
42. Bruce Rolfson, "Worker Safety Violations Fall across the Board and Top 10 List," *Bloomberg BNA Bulletin to Management*, October 10, 2017.
43. https://www.osha.gov/dcsp/smallbusiness/consult.html, accessed April 9, 2018.
44. It was not until July 12, 2012, that British Petroleum and the U.S. government agreed on $13 million in OSHA fines and resolving outstanding citations against the company for the Texas City explosion. "BP to Pay $13 Million in OSHA Penalties," *EHS Today*, August 2012, p. 12.
45. www.osha.gov/Publications/osha2098.pdf+OSHA+inspection+priorities&hl=en&ct=clnk&cd=1&gl=us, accessed January 19, 2008.
46. www.osha.gov/Publications/osha2098.pdf, accessed April 27, 2008; www.osha.gov/ooc/citations/Cits330085.pdf, accessed September 11, 2014.
47. https://www.osha.gov/OshDoc/data_General_Facts/factsheet-inspections.pdf, accessed April 9, 2018.
48. Ibid.
49. For a discussion of how to deal with citations and proposed penalties, see, for example, Michael Taylor, "OSHA Citations and Proposed Penalties: How to Beat the Rap," *EHS Today*, December 2008, pp. 34–36.
50. Employers with high injury rates may also be subject to additional monitoring. For example, OSHA sent about 15,000 letters to employers telling them that their injury and illness rates were much higher than the national average. "OSHA Sends 15,000 Letters to Employers with High Injury Rates and Offers Assistance," *Bloomberg BNA Bulletin to Management*, March 16, 2010, p. 83.
51. Knowing OSHA's rules is not enough. The employer should develop and communicate its own written safety and health rules to employees, monitor violations, and discipline employees who violate the rules. Michael Taylor, "OSHA Compliance Mistakes," *EHS Today*, July 2012, pp. 29–31.
52. "New OSHA Enforcement Memo Target Safety Incentive Programs, Retaliation," *Bloomberg BNA Bulletin to Management*, March 27, 2012, p. 99.
53. Arthur Sapper, "The Oft-Missed Step: Documentation of Safety Discipline," *Occupational Hazards*, January 2006, p. 59. See also Arthur Sapper, "Three Decisions Show the Importance of Documenting Safety Discipline," *EHS Today*, October 2016, pp. 23–26.
54. Courtney Malveaux and J. A. Rodriguez Jr., "Can You Claim Employee Misconduct? Take the Legal Test," *EHS Today*, November 2014, pp. 37–41.
55. The following is based on www.sitedocs.com, accessed May 5, 2015.
56. https://www.osha.gov/dte/grant_materials/fy10/sh-20839-10/circle_chart.pdf, accessed April 9, 2018.
57. "Year One of OSHA's Severe Injury Reporting Program," March 17, 2016, https://www.osha.gov/injuryreport/2015.pdf, accessed April 9, 2018.
58. Ibid.
59. "Four Ways a Construction Job Can Kill You," *EHS Today*, February 2015, pp. 23–24.
60. "The Dawning of a New Era," *Workforce Management*, December 2010, p. 3.
61. For a discussion, see David Hofmann and Adam Stetzer, "A Cross-Level Investigation of Factors Influencing Unsafe Behaviors and Accidents," *Personnel Psychology* 49 (1996), pp. 307–308. See also David Hofman and Barbara Mark, "An Investigation of the Relationship Between Safety Climate and Medication Errors as Well as Other Nurse and Patient Outcomes," *Personnel Psychology* 50, no. 9 (2006), pp. 847–869.
62. See, for example, E. Scott Keller, "Should Safe Behavior Become a Habit?" *EHS Today*, July 2013, pp. 31–32; and Esteban Tristan, "Is Your Brain Hardwired for Safety?" *EHS Today*, April 2017, pp. 12–15.
63. Duane Schultz and Sydney Schultz, *Psychology and Work Today* (Upper Saddle River, NJ: Prentice Hall, 2002), p. 332.
64. Robert Pater and Robert Russell, "Drop That 'Accident Prone' Tag: Look for Causes Beyond Personal Issues," *Industrial Safety and Hygiene News* 38, no. 1 (January 2004), p. 50, http://findarticles.com/p/articles/mi_hb5992/is_200401/ai_n24195869/, accessed August 11, 2009.
65. Discussed in Douglas Haaland, "Who's the Safest Bet for the Job? Find Out Why the Fun Guy in the Next Cubicle May Be the Next Accident Waiting to Happen," *Security Management* 49, no. 2 (February 2005), pp. 51–57; Jeremy Beus et al., "A Meta-Analysis of Personality and Workplace Safety: Addressing Unanswered Questions," *Journal of Applied Psychology* 100, no. 2, 2015, p. 41.
66. https://www.psychologytoday.com/us/tests/personality/accident-proneness-test, accessed April 9, 2018.
67. "Thai Research Points to Role of Personality in Road Accidents," www.driveandstayalive.com/info%20section/news/individual%20news%20articles/x_050204_personality-in-crash-causation_thailand.htm, February 2, 2005, accessed August 11, 2009; Donald Bashline et al., "Bad Behavior: Personality Tests Can Help Underwriters Identify High-Risk Drivers," *Best's Review* 105, no. 12 (April 2005), pp. 63–64. Research suggests that up to 80% of traffic accidents involve drivers who were not looking at the road. Sandy Smith, "Deadly Distractions: Advice to Stay Safe in Highway Work Zones," *EHS Today*, May 2016, p. 17.
68. Rick Taft, "Safety as a Collateral Duty Managing Your Part-Time Job," *DHS Today*, July 2017, pp. 17–19.
69. See, for example, Laura Walter, "What's in a Glove?" *Occupational Hazards*, May 2008, pp. 35–36.
70. Donald Groce, "Keep the Gloves On!" *Occupational Hazards*, June 2008, pp. 45–47.
71. Mike Carlson, "Machine Safety Solutions for Protecting Employees and Safeguarding against Machine Hazards," *EHS Today*, July 2009, p. 24.
72. Benjamin Mangan, "Lockout/Tagout Prevents Workplace Injuries and Saves Lives," *Occupational Hazards*, March 2007, pp. 59–60. See also Todd Grover, "Effective Group Lockout Techniques," *EHS Today*, October 2016, pp. 16–17.
73. Tracy Moon Junior, "Wearable Technology in the Workplace," *EHS Today*, December 2014, pp. 28–29.
74. Howard Mavity, "What Should Be Your Safety Concerns When Buying or Leasing Office Space?" *EHS Today*, July 2014, pp. 20–22.
75. Ginger Christ, "Collaborative Robots: Safety within Arm's Reach," *EHS Today*, January 2016, pp. 14–17. Some experts call these worker-friendly collaborative robots "cobots." Thomas Black, "Armed with Don't Hurt Humans Sensors, Robots Hit Small Factories," *Bloomberg BNA Bulletin to Management*, May 16, 2017.
76. "Your Plastic Pal Who's Fun to Be With," *The Economist*, August 19, 2017, pp. 67–68.
77. Identify Problems, Occupational Safety and Health Administration. US Department of Labor. Accessed from https://www.osha.gov/SLTC/ergonomics/identifyprobs.html.
78. Bruce Rolfson, "Employers Change Safety Efforts to Focus on High Hazard Incidents,"

Bloomberg BNA Bulletin to Management, November 14, 2017.

79. Ibid.
80. www-ns.iaea.org/reviews/op-safety-reviews.asp, accessed April 21, 2011.
81. For example, when asked what accounted for injuries such as cuts and lacerations, contusions, and chemical exposure at their facilities, most employees concluded either that workers were not wearing the proper protective equipment or had been given the wrong protection for the task. Brian Perry, "Don't Invite an OSHA Citation with Lower Quality PPE," *EHS Today*, January 2011, p. 23.
82. https://www.osha.gov/SLTC/personalprotectiveequipment/, accessed April 9, 2018.
83. Sandy Smith, "Protective Clothing and the Quest for Improved Performance," *Occupational Hazards*, February 2008, pp. 63–66. Note that the vast array of available personal protective equipment makes choosing the appropriate equipment what one expert calls "complex and sometimes confusing." See Scott Larsen, "Integrated Use of Personal Protective Equipment," *EHS Today*, June 2012, p. 31.
84. Brad Witt, "connecting the worker to hearing protection," *EHS Today*, May 2017, pp. 26–29.
85. Laura Walter, "FR Clothing: Leaving Hazards in the Dust," *EHS Today*, January 2010, pp. 20–22.
86. Roger Paquette, "Staying Safe and Warm in Cold Weather Environments," *EHS Today*, January 2015, pp. 19–22.
87. Everything must be considered. For example, if the employees work outdoors during the winter they should dress for the cold. This might include knit hats under their hardhats, ultraviolet eye protection, a brightly covered outer layer to protect against cold and wet, and gloves that both insulate from the cold and protect against hazards such as cuts. "8 Winter Essentials for Outdoor Workers," *EHS Today*, December 2016, p. 11.
88. "Assessing the Need for Personal Protective Equipment (PPE)," OSHA, https://www.osha.gov/dte/library/ppe_assessment/ppe_assessment.pdf, accessed April 9, 2018.
89. Raghu Arunachalam and Scott Jubeck, "Beacons in the Internet of Industrial Things: A New Tool to Enhance Worker Safety," *EHS Today*, August 2016, pp. 27–30.
90. Sandy Smith, "Protecting Vulnerable Workers," *Occupational Hazards*, April 2004, pp. 25–28.
91. "Teen Workplace Injuries and the Importance of Training," *EHS Today*, July 2015, p. 19.
92. J. P. Sankpill, "A Clear Vision for Eye and Face Protection," *EHS Today*, November 2010, p. 29.
93. See, for instance, Laura Walter, "Training the Older Worker," *EHS Today*, February 2011, p. 39.
94. Robert Pater, "Boosting Safety with an Aging Workforce," *Occupational Hazards*, March 2006, p. 24.
95. Elizabeth Rogers and William Wiatrowski, "Injuries, Illnesses, and Fatalities among Older Workers," *Monthly Labor Review* 128, no. 10 (October 2005), pp. 24–30. Actually, studies suggest that workers under 25, especially with less experience on the job, are much more likely to have more injuries and more serious injuries than older workers. Steve Ludwig, "How an Aging Workforce Will Affect Your Productivity and Safety (and What You Can Do about It)," *EHS Today*, April 2015, pp. 21–24.
96. Michael Silverstein, M.D., "Designing the Age Friendly Workplace," *Occupational Hazards*, December 2007, pp. 29–31.
97. "Swine Flu Tests Employer Emergency Plan; Experts Urge Communicating Best Practices," *Bloomberg BNA Bulletin to Management*, May 5, 2009, pp. 137–144.
98. Sandy Devine, "Are You Ready for a Sudden Cardiac Arrest Emergency?" *EHS Today*, April 2009, pp. 26–29.
99. Bill Sims Jr., "Employee Engagement and Commitment: The Super Bowl of Safety," *EHS Today*, July 2014, pp. 28–29.
100. "Cell Phone Use Contributes to 24% of Crashes," *EHS Today*, May 2012, p. 22.
101. "DOT Final Rule Bans Cell Phone Use by Commercial Bus Drivers, Truckers," *Bloomberg BNA Bulletin to Management*, December 6, 2011, p. 387.
102. Robert Pater and Ron Bowles, "Directing Attention to Boost Safety Performance," *Occupational Hazards*, March 2007, pp. 46–48.
103. E. Scott Geller, "The Thinking and Seeing Components of People-Based Safety," *Occupational Hazards*, December 2006, pp. 38–40. See also David Lynn, "Principle to Practice Safety Transformation," *EHS Today*, June 2015, pp. 37–39.
104. See www.ramsaycorp.com/catalog/view/?productid=208; https://www.psychometrics.com/assessments/employee-reliability-inventory/, accessed April 8, 2018.
105. Christina Bergman and Rachel Michael, "The PDA: One Tool with Multiple Applications," *EHS Today*, August 2017, pp. 26–28.
106. "Reduce Your Risk of Workers Comp Claims with Employee Selection, Placement and on Boarding Best Practices," 2014, The Hartford financial services group, Inc. Caterina Saralva et al., "Overdosing on the Job: Opioid Crisis Spills into the Workplace," *Bloomberg BNA Bulletin to Management*, September 26, 2017.
107. Safety training draws on a range of training methods, from face-to-face training to online/on-demand training, video training (online videos available on demand), computer-based training, and safety training apps. Jerry DaValle, "Get Lifesaving Training, Whenever, Wherever," *EHS Today*, February 2017, pp. 11, 12.
108. John Rekus, "Is Your Safety Training Program Effective?" *Occupational Hazards*, August 1999, pp. 37–39; see also www.osha.gov/-Publications/osha2254.pdf, accessed October 25, 2011.
109. Kathryn Tyler, "Better Safe Than Sorry," *HR Magazine*, December 2014, pp. 44–45.
110. Michael Burke et al., "The Dread Factor: How Hazards and Safety Training Influence Learning and Performance," *Journal of Applied Psychology* 96, no. 1 (2011), pp. 46–70.
111. See, for example, Ron Bruce, "Online from Kazakhstan to California," *Occupational Hazards*, June 2008, pp. 61–65.
112. Dave Zielinski, "Putting Safety Training Online," *HR Magazine*, January 2013, p. 51.
113. Laura Walter, "Surfing for Safety," *Occupational Hazards*, July 2008, pp. 23–29.
114. In a survey of about 2,600 employees, roughly one-fourth said they would not intervene if they saw a coworker acting unsafely, for fear the coworker would be defensive or angry. Phillip Ragain et al., "The Causes and Consequences of Employees' Silence," *EHS Today*, July 2011, pp. 36–38.
115. Jack Rubinger, "Signs, Labels and Lighting for a Safe and Productive Workplace," *EHS Today*, October 2012, p. 67.
116. "Designing a Safety Incentive Program," *Safety and Health Magazine*, August 1, 2012, http://www.safetyandhealthmagazine.com/articles/designing-a-safety-incentive-program-2, accessed April 9, 2018.
117. Ibid.
118. Jon Hyman, "OSHA Buffers against Retaliation," *Workforce*, January/February 2017, p. 24.
119. "Are Traditional Incentive Programs Illegal?" *EHS Today*, April 2012, p. 12. See also Howard Mavity, "OSHA: Don't Get Caught in the Trap of Rewarding Employees for Reducing Recordables!" *EHS Today*, September 2012, pp. 39–41; and James Stanley, "OSHA's Warning on Safety Incentive Programs Are Wide of the Mark," *EHS Today*, October 2012, p. 63.
120. James Nash, "Construction Safety: Best Practices in Training Hispanic Workers," *Occupational Hazards*, February 2004, pp. 35–38.
121. Ibid., p. 37.
122. Based on Judi Komaki, Kenneth Barwick, and Lawrence Scott, "A Behavioral Approach to Occupational Safety: Pinpointing and Reinforcing Safe Performance in a Food Manufacturing Plant," *Journal of Applied Psychology* 63 (August 1978), pp. 434–445. See also Anat Arkin, "Incentives to Work Safely," *Personnel Management* 26, no. 9 (September 1994), pp. 48–52; Sandy Smith, "Why Cash Isn't King," *Occupational Hazards*, March 2004, pp. 37–38.
123. Dov Zohar, "A Group Level Model of Safety Climate: Testing the Effect of a Group Climate on Students in Manufacturing Jobs," *Journal of Applied Psychology* 85, no. 4 (2000), pp. 587–596. See also Steven Yule, Rhona Flin, and Andy Murdy, "The Role of Management and Safety Climate in Preventing Risk-Taking at Work," *International Journal of Risk Assessment and Management* 7, no. 2 (December 20, 2006), p. 137; and Judy Agnew, "Building the Foundation for a Sustainable Safety Culture," *EHS Today*, February 2013, pp. 41–43.
124. Quoted from Sandy Smith, "Breakthrough Safety Management," *Occupational Hazards*, June 2004, p. 43. For a discussion of developing a safety climate survey, see also Sara Singer et al., "Workforce Perceptions of Hospital Safety Culture: Development and Validation of the Patient Safety Climate in Healthcare Organizations Survey," *Health Services Research* 42, no. 5 (October 2007), pp. 19–23.
125. "Encourage Incident Reporting to Improve Safety Culture," *EHS Today*, December 2012, p. 16.
126. Jennifer Nahrgang et al., "Safety at Work: A Meta-Analytic Investigation of the Link between Job Demands, Job Resources, Burnout, Engagement, and Safety Outcomes," *Journal of Applied Psychology* 96, no. 1 (2011), p. 86.
127. Stan Hodson and Tim Gordon, "Tenneco's Drive to Become Injury Free," *Occupational*

Hazards, May 2000, pp. 85–87. For another example, see Terry Mathis, "Lean Behavior-Based Safety," *Occupational Hazards*, May 2005, pp. 33–34.
128. "Worker Participation," https://www.osha.gov/shpguidelines/worker-participation.html, accessed April 9, 2018.
129. Ibid.
130. https://www.osha.gov/shpguidelines/docs/SHP_Audit_Tool.pdf, accessed April 9, 2018.
131. Ibid.
132. https://itunes.apple.com/us/app/iauditor-safety-audit-checklist/id499999532?mt=8, accessed May 6, 2015; https://safetyculture.com/iauditor/, accessed April 9, 2018.
133. http://download.cnet.com/iAuditor-Safety-Audit-and-Checklist/3000-2064_4-75728239.html, accessed May 6, 2015.
134. www.digitalmarketplace.service.gov.uk/service/5-g1-0377-007, accessed May 6, 2015.
135. www.assessnet.co.uk, accessed May 6, 2015.
136. John Garber, "Introduction to the Human Resource Discipline of Safety and Security," www.shrm.org/templates_tools/toolkits, accessed May 27, 2012.
137. Mike Powell, "Sustaining Your Safety Sweep Audit Process," *EHS Today*, December 2012, pp. 35–36.
138. "World-Class Safety: DuPont and Milliken Share Their Proven Successes," BLR, August 23, 2013, http://safety.blr.com/, accessed April 15, 2014.
139. Carey Tebbetts and Robert Allen, "Milliken's Keys to Employee Engagement, Increased Workplace Safety and Productivity," *EHS Today*, January 9, 2013: http://ehstoday.com/safety/millikens-keys-employee-engagement-increased-workplace-safety-and-productivity, accessed July 24, 2015.
140. Ibid.
141. Ibid.
142. Milliken Company: "America's Safest Companies," *EHS Today*, November 2017, p. 13.
143. Ibid.
144. Ibid.
145. https://autovation.milliken.com/hillcrest-plant-is-an-osha-vpp-star-site-again/, accessed May 14, 2018.
146. Mike Powell, "Harness the Full Power of Your Incident Investigation Process," *EHS Today*, September 2013, p. 71.
147. www.performancesolutionsbymilliken.com, accessed April 15, 2014. As part of its safety program, Milliken has partnered with the Occupational Safety and Health Administration and follows the latter's voluntary protection program's (VPP's) guidelines to help it reach its safety goals. "Milliken and Company VPP Star Site Elm Facility Receiving VPP Recognition," www.osha.gov, accessed April 14, 2014. For another example of how employee engagement impacts occupational safety, see "How Employee Engagement Can Improve the Hospital's Health," *Gallup Business Journal*, http://businessjournal.gallup.com, accessed April 14, 2014.
148. This is based on Paul Puncochar, "The Science and Art to Identifying Workplace Hazards," *Occupational Hazards*, September 2003, pp. 50–54; "Chemical Hazards and Toxic Substances," https://www.osha.gov/SLTC/hazardoustoxicsubstances/, accessed April 9, 2018.
149. Ibid., p. 52; "Chemical Hazards and Toxic Substances," https://www.osha.gov/SLTC/hazardoustoxicsubstances/, accessed April 9, 2018.
150. "Hazard Communication," www.osha.gov/dsg/hazcom/index.HTML, accessed May 26, 2012.
151. Based on, Beverley Sunderland, "Ensuring Legal Safety for Gig Economy Workers," *People Management*, February 2017, http://www2.cipd.co.uk/pm/peoplemanagement/b/weblog/archive/2017/02/06/ensuring-legal-safety-for-gig-economy-workers.aspx; Elizabeth Grossman, "Hazards of the Gig Economy—Temp Workers at Greater Risk for Workplace Injury but Poorly Protected, Say Labor Advocates," *Pump Handle*, November 4, 2016, http://scienceblogs.com/thepumphandle/2016/11/04/hazards-of-the-gig-economy-temp-workers-at-greater-risk-for-workplace-injury-but-poorly-protected-say-labor-advocates/; Roger Marks, "Who's Responsible for Training Temp Workers on GHS?" May 6, 2016, https://www.lion.com/lion-news/may-2016/who-s-responsible-for-training-temp-workers-on-ghs; *Hazard Communication*, https://www.osha.gov/Publications/OSHA3860.pdf; "Temporary Worker Safety," https://www.jjkeller.com/learn/temporary-workers; all accessed April 8, 2017.
152. If hired by a staffing agency, it, not the host hiring company, would probably pay for workers' compensation insurance.
153. Based on the report "Workplace Screening and Brief Intervention: What Employers Can and Should Do about Excessive Alcohol Use," www.ensuringsolutions.org/resources/resources_show.htm?doc_id=673239, accessed August 11, 2009; "Workplace Drug Abuse," https://drugabuse.com/library/workplace-drug-abuse/, accessed April 9, 2018.
154. "15% of Workers Drinking, Drunk, or Hungover While at Work, according to New University Study," *BNA Bulletin to Management*, January 24, 2006, p. 27.
155. https://www.ncadd.org/about-addiction/addiction-update/drugs-and-alcohol-in-the-workplace, accessed April 12, 2017.
156. Samuel Bacharach et al., "Alcohol Consumption and Workplace Absenteeism: The Moderating Effect of Social Support," *Journal of Applied Psychology*, 95, no. 2 (2010), pp. 334–348.
157. Saralva et al., "Overdosing on the Job."
158. See, for example, L. Claussen, "Can You Spot the Meth Addict?" *Safety & Health* 179, no. 4, April 2009, pp. 48–52.
159. "New Jersey Union Takes on Mandatory Random Drug Tests," *Record* (Hackensack, NJ), January 2, 2008.
160. Frank Lockwood et al., "Drug Testing Programs and Their Impact on Workplace Accidents: A Time Series Analysis," *Journal of Individual Employment Rights*, 8, no. 4 (2000), pp. 295–306; Sally Roberts, "Random Drug Testing Can Help Reduce Accidents for Construction Companies; Drug Abuse Blamed for Heightened Risk in the Workplace," *Business Insurance*, 40, October 23, 2006, p. 6.
161. Rebecca Greenfield and Jennifer Kaplan, "The Coming Decline of the Employment Drug Test," *Bloomberg BNA Bulletin to Management*, March 6, 2018; Jennifer Kaplan and Jamie Butters, "AutoNation Looks Other Way When Applicants Test Positive for Pot," *Bloomberg BNA Bulletin to Management*, February 6, 2018.
162. Saralva et al., "Overdosing on the Job."
163. Diane Cadrain, "Are Your Employees' Drug Tests Accurate?" *HR Magazine*, January 2003, pp. 41–45.
164. Sally Roberts, "Random Drug Testing Can Help Reduce Accidents for Construction Companies; Drug Abuse Blamed for Heightened Risk in the Workplace," *Business Insurance* 40 (October 23, 2006), p. 6.
165. See for example, http://workplacedrugpolicy.com/program-components.htm; http://www.workingpartners.com/understanding-dfwp/elements-of-dfwp.asp; and http://www.dol.gov/elaws/asp/drugfree/drugs/screen15.asp, accessed July 27, 2015.
166. Gopal Pati and John Adkins Jr., "The Employer's Role in Alcoholism Assistance," *Personnel Journal* 62, no. 7 (July 1983), p. 570. See also Commerce Clearing House, "How Should Employers Respond to Indications an Employee May Have an Alcohol or Drug Problem?" *Ideas and Trends*, April 6, 1989, pp. 53–57; https://www.opm.gov/policy-data-oversight/worklife/reference-materials/alcoholism-in-the-workplace-a-handbook-for-supervisors/, accessed April 9, 2018.
167. www.dol.gov/asp/programs/drugs/workingpartners/sab/screen.asp, accessed April 27, 2008; www.dol.gov/whd/FOH/ch64/64a01.htm, accessed September 11, 2014; Michigan Alcoholism Screening Test (MAST), https://pubs.niaaa.nih.gov/publications/AssessingAlcohol/InstrumentPDFs/42_MAST.pdf, accessed April 9, 2018.
168. Lisa Nagele-Piazza, "An Employee Failed a Drug Test. Now What? Workplace Drug-Testing Rules Vary from State to State," SHRM, August 21, 2017, https://www.shrm.org/resourcesandtools/legal-and-compliance/state-and-local-updates/pages/an-employee-failed-a-drug-test-.aspx, accessed April 10, 2018.
169. "What If My Driver Fails or Refuses a Test?" https://www.fmcsa.dot.gov/regulations/drug-alcohol-testing/what-if-my-driver-fails-or-refuses-test, accessed April 10, 2018.
170. Nagele-Piazza, "An Employee Failed a Drug Test. Now What?"
171. "The Americans with Disabilities Act: Applying Performance and Conduct Standards to Employees with Disabilities," https://www.eeoc.gov/facts/performance-conduct.html#alcohol, accessed April 10, 2018.
172. Ibid.
173. Beth Andrus, "Accommodating the Alcoholic Executive," *Society for Human Resource Management Legal Report*, January 2008, pp. 1, 4.
174. Eric Sundstrom et al., "Office Noise, Satisfaction, and Performance," *Environment and Behavior* no. 2 (March 1994), pp. 195–222; "Stress: How to Cope with Life's Challenges," *American Family Physician* 74, no. 8 (October 15, 2006); Sarah Ponczek, "Unpredictable Hours Found to Hurt Workers' Well-Being and Income Stability," *Bloomberg BNA Bulletin to Management*, August 27, 2016, p. 307; "Coping with Stress at Work," American Psychological Association, http://www.apa.org/helpcenter/work-stress.aspx, accessed April 10, 2018.

175. "Failing to Tackle Stress Could Cost You Dearly," *Personnel Today*, September 12, 2006; www.sciencedaily.com/-releases/2007/06/070604170722.htm, accessed November 3, 2009.
176. Tara Parker-Pope, "Time to Review Workplace Reviews?" *The New York Times*, May 18, 2010, p. D5. A recent study illustrates the potential fatal effects of one's work environment. The researchers measured *job demands* with questions such as "To what extent do you agree that your job requires working very hard?" They measured *job control* with questions such as "To what extent do you agree that you have a lot of say about what happens on your job?" They studied more than 2,300 individuals over seven years. For individuals who said they felt they had little control over how they did their jobs, high job demands were associated with a 15.4% increase in the odds of death compared to low job demands. As the researchers conclude, " . . . employers of individuals in highly demanding jobs in which employees also have little control should be aware of the increased risk of mortality facing their employees." Eric Gonzalez-Mule and Bethany Cockburn, "Worked to Death: The Relationships of Job Demands and Job Control with Mortality," *Personnel Psychology*, 70, 2017, pp. 73–112.
177. "Workplace Stress Responsible for Up to $190B in Annual U.S. Healthcare Costs," *Forbes*, January 26, 2015, https://www.forbes.com/sites/hbsworkingknowledge/2015/01/26/workplace-stress-responsible-for-up-to-190-billion-in-annual-u-s-heathcare-costs/#310d1ef2235a, accessed April 10, 2018.
178. See, for example, Elizabeth Bernstein, "When a Coworker Is Stressed Out," *The Wall Street Journal*, August 26, 2008, pp. B1, B2.
179. Karl Albrecht, *Stress and the Manager* (Englewood Cliffs, NJ: Spectrum, 1979); and, "Coping with Stress at Work," American Psychological Association, http://www.apa.org/helpcenter/work-stress.aspx, accessed April 10, 2018.
180. Sabine Sonnentag et al., "'Did You Have a Nice Evening?' A Day-Level Study on Recovery Experiences, Sleep, and Affect," *Journal of Applied Psychology* 93, no. 3 (2008), pp. 674–684.
181. "Meditation Gives Your Mind Permanent Working Holiday; Relaxation Can Improve Your Business Decisions and Your Overall Health," discussed in *Investors Business Daily*, March 24, 2004, p. 89. See also "Meditation Helps Employees Focus, Relieve Stress," *BNA Bulletin to Management*, February 20, 2007, p. 63.
182. Kathryn Tyler, "Stress Management," *HR Magazine*, September 2006, pp. 79–82.
183. William Atkinson, "Turning Stress into Strength," *HR Magazine*, January 2011, p. 51.
184. "Going Head to Head with Stress," *Personnel Today*, April 26, 2005, p. 1.
185. See, for example, Christina Maslach and Michael Leiter, "Early Predictors of Job Burnout and Engagement," *Journal of Applied Psychology* 93, no. 3 (2008), pp. 498–512; Monique Valcour, "Managing Yourself: Beating Burnout Strategies to Recognize, Recover From, and Prevent It," *Harvard Business Review*, November 2016, pp. 98–100.
186. Christina Maslach and Michael Leiter, "Early Predictors of Job Burnout and Engagement," *Journal of Applied Psychology* 93, no. 3 (2008), pp. 498–512.
187. Valcour, "Managing Yourself."
188. Experts argue that there are pros and cons to the open office spaces that many employees work in. Pros include encouraging collaboration and reducing unproductiveness. Cons include reduced privacy, the pressure to always be performing, and possibly job dissatisfaction. Genevieve Douglas, "Office Space Design May Affect Worker Productivity," *Bloomberg BNA Bulletin to Management*, March 14, 2017.
189. Sabine Sonnentag et al., "Staying Well and Engaged When Demands Are High: The Role of Psychological Detachment," *Journal of Applied Psychology* 95, no. 5 (2010), pp. 965–976.
190. Genevieve Douglas, "US Workers Choosing Burnout over Vacation?" *Bloomberg BNA Bulletin to Management*, March 28, 2017.
191. Sharon Toker and Michael Biron, "Job Burnout and Depression: Unraveling Their Temporal Relationship and Considering the Role of Physical Activity," *Journal of Applied Psychology* 97, no. 3 (2012), p. 699.
192. "Depression Evaluation Measures," Centers for Disease Control, https://www.cdc.gov/workplacehealthpromotion/health-strategies/depression/evaluation-measures/index.html, accessed April 10, 2018.
193. Todd Nighswonger, "Depression: The Unseen Safety Risk," *Occupational Hazards*, April 2002, pp. 38–42; http://www.huffingtonpost.com/2013/07/25/depression-missed-work-days-absent_n_3652888.html, accessed July 27, 2015.
194. "Employers Must Move from Awareness to Action in Dealing with Worker Depression," *BNA Bulletin to Management*, April 29, 2004, p. 137. A similar point is made in Steve Albrecht, "Why Don't Employees Use EAP Services?" *Psychology Today*, February 7, 2014, https://www.psychologytoday.com/us/blog/the-act-violence/201402/why-dont-employees-use-eap-services, accessed April 10, 2018.
195. See, for example, Felix Chima, "Depression and the Workplace: Occupational Social Work Development and Intervention," *Employee Assistance Quarterly* 19, no. 4 (2004), pp. 1–20.
196. Ibid.
197. https://www.osha.gov/SLTC/etools/computerworkstations/index.html, accessed April 9, 2017.
198. Mark Christian et al., "Single and Dual Monitor Computer Set Up: Ergonomic Tips," *EHS Today*, April 2016, pp. 20–22.
199. Anne Chambers, "Computer Vision Syndrome: Relief Is in Sight," *Occupational Hazards*, October 1999, pp. 179–184; www.osha.gov/etools/computerworkstations/index.html, accessed May 28, 2005.
200. Sandra Lotz Fisher, "Are Your Employees Working Ergosmart?" *Personnel Journal*, December 1996, pp. 91–92. See also www.cdc.gov/od/ohs/Ergonomics/compergo.htm, accessed May 26, 2007.
201. www.ninds.nih.gov/disorders/repetitive_-motion/repetitive_motion.htm, accessed February 28, 2010.
202. Mike Stearns, "Silence of the Limbs: The Toll of Inactivity on Our Sedentary Workforce," *EHS Today*, August 2016, pp. 11–14. Walking around briefly a few times each hour can have significant health benefits. One expert estimates that an employer will derive between $3 and $7 in savings (for instance, in insurance costs) for each dollar it invests in getting workers to be more active on the job. Tamara Lytle, "Stand Up and Get Moving," *HR Magazine*, March 2017, p. 46.
203. Jon Fitch, "EHS Today Takes Workplace Wellness to a Whole New Level," *EHS Today*, January 2017, pp. 21–22.
204. Sandy Smith, "SARS: What Employers Need to Know," *Occupational Hazards*, July 2003, pp. 33–35; "Infectious Diseases," OSHA, https://www.osha.gov/SLTC/healthcarefacilities/infectious_diseases.html, accessed April 10, 2018; "Chapter 10: Controlling the Spread of Infectious Diseases," www.who.int/healthsystems/topics/health-law/chapter10.pdf, accessed April 10, 2018.
205. "CDC Recommends Respirators in Revised H1N1 Flu Guidance for Healthcare Workers," *Bloomberg BNA Bulletin to Management*, October 20, 2009, pp. 329–336; Pamela Ferrante, "H1N1: Spreading the Message," *EHS Today*, January 2010, pp. 25–27.
206. However, note that some experts believe that in some circumstances the EEOC might see a smoking addiction as similar to use of illegal drugs, and thus possibly covered by the ADA. "Policies to Not Hire Smokers Raise Privacy, Bias Issues," *Bloomberg BNA Bulletin to Management*, December 14, 2010, p. 399.
207. Joan Deschenauxh, "Is a 'Smoker-Free' Workplace Right for You?" *HR Magazine*, July 2011, pp. 43–45.
208. See http://en.wikipedia.org/wiki/List_of_smoking_bans#United_States for a list.
209. Sarah Sipek, "Vaping Decision Up in the Air, but Some Fuming about Potential e-Cigarette Regulation," *Workforce*, November 2014, p. 15.
210. "No Tobacco or E-Cigarettes in the Workplace, NIOSH Says in Updated Recommendations," *Bloomberg BNA Bulletin to Management*, April 14, 2015, p. 113.
211. Bruce Rolfsen, "Hazy Marijuana Laws Stir Confusion over Worker Protection," *Bloomberg BNA Bulletin to Management*, April 18, 2017.
212. Garber, "Introduction to the Human Resource Discipline of Safety and Security."
213. Genevieve Douglas, "HR Must Evolve to Fight Complex Cyber Threats," *Bloomberg BNA Bulletin to Management*, January 10, 2017.
214. Ibid. See also, "New Challenges for Health and Safety in the Workplace," *Workplace Visions* (Society for Human Resource Management), no. 3 (2003), pp. 2–4, and J. L. Nash, "Protecting Chemical Plants from Terrorists: Opposing Views," *Occupational Hazards*, February 2004, pp. 18–20.
215. Garber, "Introduction to the Human Resource Discipline of Safety and Security."
216. "Study: Don't Silo Human Capital Risk," www.shrm.org/hrdisciplines/ethics/articles, accessed May 27, 2012.
217. Robert Kaplan and Anette Mikes, "Managing Risks: A New Framework," *Harvard Business Review*, June 2012, pp. 48–60.
218. "Workplace Violence Takes a Deadly Toll," *EHS Today*, December 2009, p. 17; "Workplace Violence," www.osha.gov/SLTC/workplaceviolence, accessed September 11, 2014.

219. "Workplace Violence," OSHA, https://www.osha.gov/SLTC/workplaceviolence/, accessed April 10, 2018.
220. Jerry Hoobler and Jennifer Swanberg, "The Enemy Is Not Us," *International Personnel Management Association for HR* 35, no. 3 (Fall 2006), pp. 229–246.
221. www.cdc.gov/ncipc/dvp/ipv_factsheet.pdf, accessed August 8, 2013.
222. Paul Viollis and Doug Kane, "At-Risk Terminations: Protecting Employees, Preventing Disaster," *Risk Management Magazine* 52, no. 5 (May 2005), pp. 28–33.
223. M. Sandy Hershcovis et al., "Predicting Workplace Aggression: A Meta-Analysis," *Journal of Applied Psychology* 92, no. 1 (2007), pp. 228–238.
224. Alfred Feliu, "Workplace Violence and the Duty of Care: The Scope of an Employer's Obligation to Protect Against the Violent Employee," *Employee Relations Law Journal* 20, no. 3 (Winter 1994/95), p. 395; see also, "Workplace Violence," The Federal Bureau of Investigation, Critical Incident Response Group National Center for the Analysis of Violent Crime, FBI Academy, Quantico, Virginia.
225. Dawn Anfuso, "Deflecting Workplace Violence," *Personnel Journal*, October 1994, pp. 66–77.
226. Feliu, "Workplace Violence and the Duty of Care," p. 395; see also, "Workplace Violence," The Federal Bureau of Investigation, Critical Incident Response Group National Center for the Analysis of Violent Crime, FBI Academy, Quantico, Virginia.
227. See, for example, James Thelan, "Is That a Threat?" *HR Magazine*, December 2009, pp. 61–63.
228. Feliu, "Workplace Violence and the Duty of Care."
229. "Workplace Violence," OSHA, https://www.osha.gov/SLTC/workplaceviolence/, accessed April 10, 2018.
230. Feliu, "Workplace Violence and the Duty of Care."
231. Viollis and Kane, "At-Risk Terminations," pp. 28–33.
232. Martin Berman-Gorvine, "When Ex-Employees Turn Violent, HR Is on the Front Line," *Bloomberg BNA Bulletin to Management*, July 11, 2017.
233. Ibid.
234. Bruce Rolfson, "Workplace Death Rates in 2016 Jump the Highest Level since 2010," *Bloomberg BNA Bulletin to Management*, January 2, 2018.
235. Kenneth Diamond, "The Gender-Motivated Violence Act: What Employers Should Know," *Employee Relations Law Journal* 25, no. 4 (Spring 2000), pp. 29–41; "Bush Signs 'Violence Against Women Act'; Funding Badly Needed Initiatives to Prevent Domestic & Sexual Violence, Help Victims," *The America's Intelligence Wire*, January 5, 2006.
236. For example, see www.womenshealth.gov/violence-against-women/get-help-for-violence/violence-help-hotlines.html, accessed April 9, 2018.
237. Unless otherwise noted, the following including the six matters to address is based on Richard Maurer, "Keeping Your Security Program Active," *Occupational Hazards*, March 2003, pp. 49–52.
238. http://view.fdu.edu/default.aspx?id=3705, accessed February 28, 2010.
239. S. Steven Oplinger, "Physical Security Planning," *Facility Executive*, April 7, 2016, https://facilityexecutive.com/2016/04/physical-security-planning/, accessed April 10, 2018.
240. Maurer, "Keeping Your Security Program Active," p. 50.
241. Ibid.
242. Oplinger, "Physical Security Planning."
243. Maurer, "Keeping Your Security Program Active," p. 52.
244. See also Shari Lau, "Terrorist Screening, Bonus Pay, Labor Department Audits," *HR Magazine*, October 2012, p. 28.
245. George Russel, "Cybersecurity Fiasco: Interior Department Computers Trying to Talk to Russia, Inspectors Say," Fox News, http://www.foxnews.com/politics/2018/04/05/cybersecurity-fiasco-interior-department-computers-trying-to-talk-to-russia-inspectors-say.html, accessed April 10, 2018.
246. This is based on, "5 Key Steps for Data Breach Risk Prevention," http://www.cpamutual.com/resources/industry-news/articles/5-key-steps-data-breach-risk-prevention, accessed April 10, 2018.
247. https://www.kroll.com/en-us/how-we-help/respond-investigate-data-breaches, accessed April 10, 2018.
248. https://advisory.kpmg.us/kpmg-cyber.html?utm_source=kpmgcybrlndngpgg_0131&utm_medium=search&mid=m-00002752&utm_campaign=c-00047102&cid=c-00047102&gclid=EAIaIQobChMI84PZhpKw2gIVh4p-Ch3sqAA7EAAYAiAAEgLJPfD_BwE, accessed April 10, 2018.
249. Craig Schroll, "Evacuation Planning: A Matter of Life and Death," *Occupational Hazards*, June 2002, pp. 49–51. See also "Thorough Preparation for Natural Disasters Is Most Effective Way to Reduce Risks, Costs," *Bloomberg BNA Bulletin to Management*, November 20, 2012, p. 369.
250. Kelsey Rzepecki, "Four Steps to Keep Your Workers & Facilities Safe This Winter," *EHS Today*, December 2017, pp. 9–10.
251. "HR Plays Key Role in Preparing Organizations for Disasters," *Bloomberg BNA Bulletin to Management*, June 25, 2013, p. 206.
252. Maurer, "Keeping Your Security Program Active," p. 52; Li Yuan et al., "Texting When There's Trouble," *The Wall Street Journal*, April 18, 2007, p. B1.
253. "Business Continuity: What Is the Best Way to Plan for Disasters That May Affect Our Business, Like the Gulf Oil Spill?" www.shrm.org/templates_tools, accessed May 27, 2012.
254. *PR Newswire*, April 2, 2013 pNA; "Get Tips on Using Social Media for Disaster Recovery," *The Public Manager* 42, no. 1 (Spring 2013), p. 35(3); Joseph Porcelli, "How FEMA Drove 23,000 People to Join Its Online Community," *The America's Intelligence Wire*, October 28, 2012; "Officials Take to Social Media to Share Emergency Information: Canadians Tapped into Social Networks, Expect Emergency Responders to Use Social Media: New Red Cross Survey," *CNW Group*, October 9, 2012.
255. This case is based on, Peter Waldman and Kartikay Mehrotra, "Life and Death on the Third Shift," *Bloomberg Businessweek*, January 8, 2018, pp. 36–41.

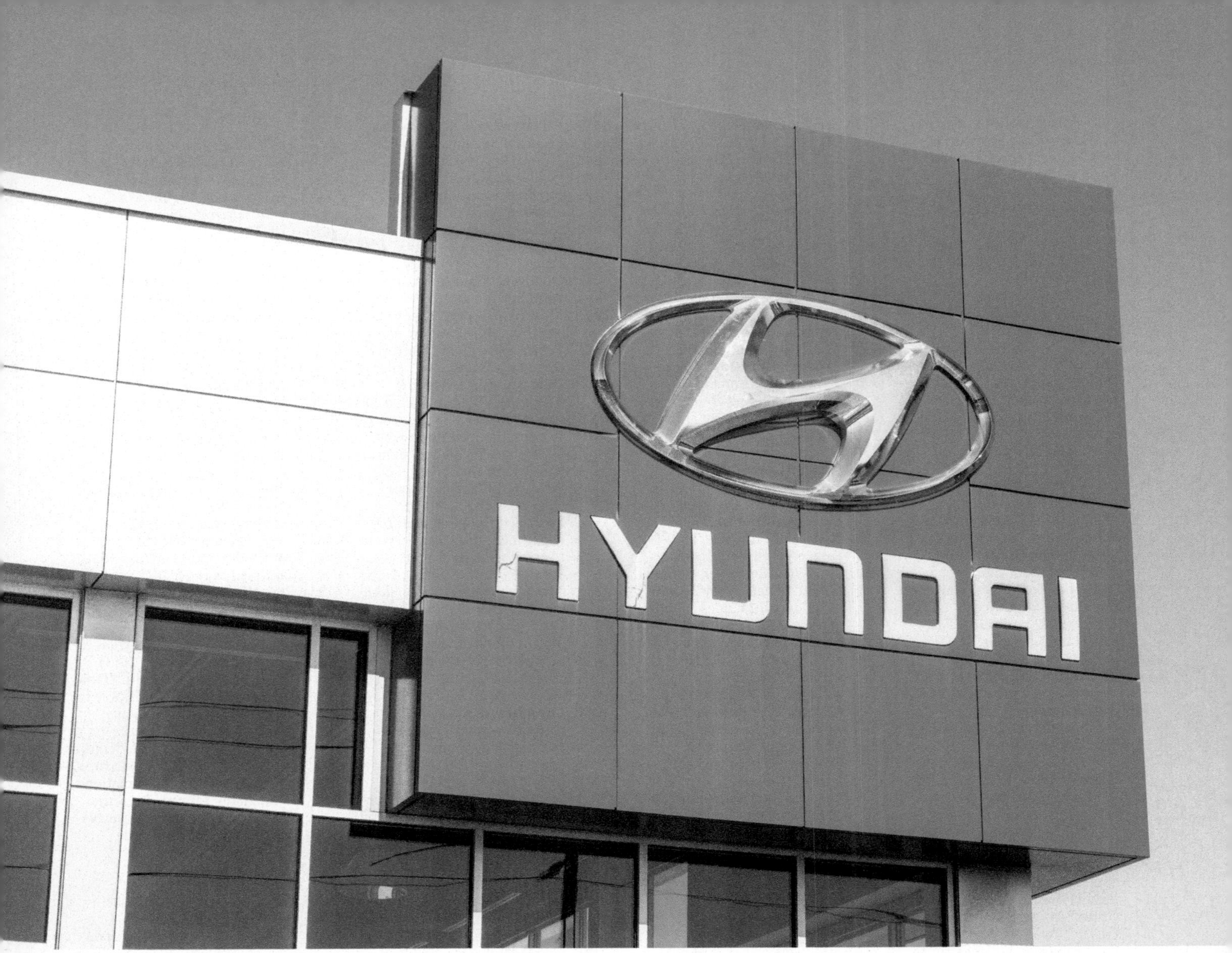

Jonathan Weiss/Shutterstock

17 Managing Global Human Resources

LEARNING OBJECTIVES

When you finish studying this chapter, you should be able to:

17-1 **List** the HR challenges of international business.

17-2 **Illustrate** with examples how intercountry differences affect HRM.

17-3 **List and briefly describe** the main methods for staffing global organizations.

17-4 **Discuss** some important issues to keep in mind in training, appraising, and compensating international employees.

17-5 **Discuss** similarities and differences in employee engagement around the globe.

17-6 **Explain** with examples how to implement a global human resource management program.

Hyundai Capital's strategy includes becoming what it calls a "Global One Company." For example, it is unifying its organizational structure, products and services, and management practices worldwide.[1] Its HR group needed a new human resource strategy to similarly ensure that its human resource practices in countries around the world were standardized. We'll see what they did.

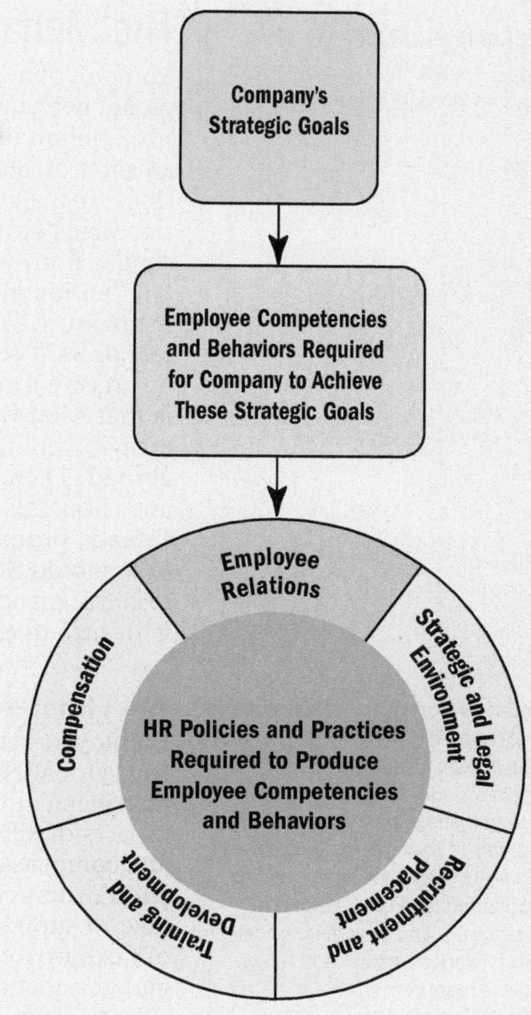

WHERE ARE WE NOW . . .

More managers today are managing people internationally. The purpose of this chapter is to improve your effectiveness at applying your human resource knowledge and skills when global challenges are involved. The topics we'll discuss include **The Manager's Global Challenge, Adapting Human Resource Activities to Intercountry Differences, Staffing the Global Organization, Training and Maintaining Employees Abroad, Employee Engagement Globally**, and **Managing HR Locally: How to Implement a Global HR System.**

LEARNING OBJECTIVE 17-1

List the HR challenges of international business.

The Manager's Global Challenge

You don't have to dig very far to see how important international business is to companies here and abroad. For example, the total of U.S. imports plus exports rose from $562 billion in 1980, to about $5.2 *trillion* recently.[2] That growth has been great for all sorts of businesses, but also confronts managers with special challenges. For one thing, managers have to formulate and execute their marketing, product, and production plans on a global basis. Ford Motor, for instance, has a strategy aimed at offering similar Ford vehicles globally.

"Going global" also requires addressing international human resource management issues. For example, "Should we staff our local offices in Japan with local or U.S. managers?" And, "How should we appraise and pay our China employees?"

As we'll see in a moment, the challenging thing about managing HR globally is that what works in one country may not work in another. The employer faces an array of political, social, legal, and cultural differences among countries and people abroad. Therefore, for instance, telling employees in Russia that they're "empowered" and should use their initiative may prompt stony silence, while the same suggestion in Canada prompts initiatives and ideas. Distance adds to the challenge. For example, how should Starbucks' chief HR officer, based in Seattle, monitor Starbucks' human resource managers in China? Yet, challenging or not, the employer needs a way to deal with such questions.

What Is International Human Resource Management?

international human resource management (IHRM)
The human resource management concepts and techniques employers use to manage the human resource aspects of their international operations, including acquiring, training, appraising, and compensating employees, and attending to their labor relations, health and safety, and fairness concerns.

Employers rely on **international human resource management (IHRM)** to deal with global HR challenges like these.[3] We can define IHRM as the human resource management concepts and techniques employers use to manage the human resource aspects of their international operations, including acquiring, training, appraising, and compensating employees, and attending to their labor relations, health and safety, and fairness concerns. IHR managers address questions such as "What steps can we take to support the company's global strategy?" "What's the best way for us to pay our expatriate employees?" and "How can we best staff our assignments abroad with global leaders?"[4]

Adapting Human Resource Activities to Intercountry Differences

LEARNING OBJECTIVE 17-2

Illustrate with examples how intercountry differences affect HRM.

As we said, the challenges of international human resource management don't just stem from the distances involved (though this is important). The bigger issue is dealing with the cultural, political, legal, and economic differences among countries and their people. The result is that what works in one country might fail in another.

Companies operating only within the United States generally have the luxury of dealing with a relatively limited set of economic, cultural, and legal variables. Economically the United States is a capitalist, competitive society. And while the U.S. workforce reflects a multitude of cultural and ethnic backgrounds, shared values (such as an appreciation for democracy) help to blur cultural differences. Different states and municipalities certainly have their own employment laws. However, a basic federal framework helps produce a predictable set of legal guidelines regarding matters such as employment discrimination and labor relations.

A company operating multiple units abroad doesn't face such homogeneity. For example, minimum legally mandated holidays range from none in the United Kingdom to 5 weeks in Luxembourg. Italy has no formal requirements for employee representatives on boards of directors, but they're usually required in Denmark. The point is that managers have to adapt their human resource policies and practices to the countries in which they're operating. Figure 17-1 sums up critical intercountry differences.

FIGURE 17-1 Critical Intercountry Differences That Influence International HR Practices

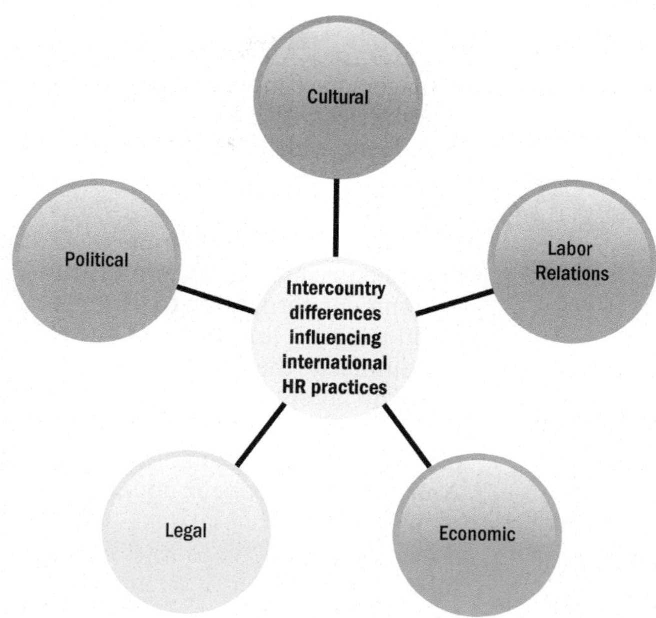

Cultural Factors

For example, countries differ widely in their *cultures*—in other words, in the basic values, assumptions, and understandings their citizens share.[5] Peoples' values and assumptions tend to drive what they do, and so cultural differences manifest themselves in how people in different countries think and act. For example, one Michelin executive said that when he gives performance feedback in France, employees don't think it's necessary to mention what's right because they know what they've done right. He focuses instead on what's wrong.[6] That approach would surprise most U.S. employees, so there's a tendency for U.S. managers to sugarcoat what's wrong. In China, heads of companies are inclined to see employees as members of their family, but in turn demand much of them.[7]

As another example, one expert says that workers around the world tend to have differing attitudes toward authority and decision making.[8] With respect to *authority*, countries range from egalitarian to hierarchical. For example, in the more egalitarian United States and Canada, managers emphasize worker empowerment and soliciting input, while in hierarchical countries like Saudi Arabia and Russia authority clearly resides in top managers. Similarly, differences in how they *make decisions* characterize cultures around the world. Thus, in the United States and Mexico, top-down decision making tends to be the rule, while in Sweden and Japan the emphasis is on consensus decisions.

Such differences can cause consternation for multinational employers. For example, employees in hierarchical countries such as Indonesia might react negatively to a manager from the U.S. soliciting their opinions. Similarly, employees in egalitarian countries like Sweden, (where even schoolchildren call their teachers by their first name) might react negatively to a boss from abroad who emphasizes his or her "bossiness."

THE HOFSTEDE STUDY Studies by Professor Geert Hofstede further illustrate international cultural differences. Hofstede says societies differ in five values, which he calls *power distance, individualism, masculinity, uncertainty avoidance,* and *long-term orientation.* For example, power distance represents the degree to which less-powerful people accept the unequal distribution of power in society.[9] He concluded that acceptance of such inequality was higher in some countries (such as Mexico) than in others (such as Sweden).[10] In turn, such differences manifest themselves in different behaviors. To see how your country's culture compares with others, go to https://geerthofstede.com/culture-geert-hofstede-gert-jan-hofstede/6d-model-of-national-culture/.

Such cultural differences influence human resource policies and practices. For example, Americans' emphasis on individuality may help explain why European managers have more constraints, such as in dismissing workers.[11] As another example, in countries with a history of autocratic rule, employees often had to divulge information. Here, whistle-blower rules are less popular.[12]

Legal Factors

Employers expanding abroad must also be familiar with the labor laws in the countries they're entering. For example, in India, companies with more than 100 workers need government permission to fire anyone.[13] In Brazil, firing someone without "just cause" could trigger a fine of 4% of the total amount the worker ever earned.[14]

Similarly, the U.S. practice of employment at will doesn't exist in Europe, where firing or laying off workers is usually expensive. One firm there hired someone as an independent contractor, only to find later that they owed the person hundreds of thousands of dollars in back taxes and penalties for misclassifying the person.[15] And in many European countries, **works councils**—formal, employee-elected groups of worker representatives—meet monthly with managers on topics ranging from no-smoking policies to layoffs.[16] *Codetermination* is the rule in Germany and several other countries. **Codetermination** means workers have the right to have their own elected representatives on the employer's supervisory board.[17]

works councils
Formal, employee-elected groups of worker representatives.

codetermination
Employees have the legal right to a voice in setting company policies.

Economic Systems

Similarly, differences in *economic systems* translate into differences in intercountry HR practices. In *market* economies (such as the United States), governments play a relatively restrained role in deciding what will be produced and sold at what prices. In *planned* economies (such as North Korea), the government decides and plans what to produce and sell at what price. In *mixed* economies (such as China), many companies are still state owned, while others make decisions based on market demand.

Differences in economic systems tend to translate into differences in human resource management policies. For instance, dismissing employees in China or Europe is more difficult than in the United States. Labor costs also vary widely. For example, hourly compensation costs (in U.S. dollars) for production workers range from

Employers need to adapt their HR practices to the cultures of the countries where they do business.

Shafiqul Alam/Alamy Stock Photo

$2.10 in the Philippines to $9.46 in Taiwan, $35.67 in the United States, $45.79 in Germany, to $63.86 in Norway.[18]

KNOWLEDGE BASE

HR Abroad Example: The European Union

To appreciate the employment effects of cultural, economic, and legal differences like these, consider Europe and China. The separate countries of the former European Community (EC) unified into a common market for goods, services, capital, and even labor called the *European Union (EU)*. Tariffs for goods moving across borders from one EU country to another generally disappeared, and employees generally move freely between jobs in EU countries. The introduction of a single currency (the euro) by a subset of EU countries further blurred differences. Despite (or perhaps partly because of) Greece's fiscal problems, EU countries today are discussing moving toward increased economic integration.

Companies doing business in Europe must adjust their human resource policies and practices to EU directives (laws), as well as to country-specific employment laws. The directives are binding on all member countries, but each country can implement them as they wish. Some laws are applied fairly similarly across Europe. For example, Germany has high barriers to dismissal, in Italy poor performance is not a reason for dismissal, and in Norway a dismissal must be justified based on the evidence.[19] (Whirlpool Corporation spent more than 3 years trying to eliminate 500 jobs in Italy, while [for better or worse] it took them less than a year to dismiss 1,000 people in Arkansas.)[20] Other details, such as whether job offers must be in writing, and whether there is a mandatory minimum wage (yes in Germany, no in Austria) vary among European countries.[21]

HR Abroad Example: China

For years, employers relied on China's huge workforce to provide products and services at low cost. Part of the reason for the low labor cost was the dearth of labor laws on things like severance pay, minimum wages, and benefits.

But things are changing. For one thing, China's workforce, while still huge, is growing less quickly. For another, China enacted a labor law. This adds many new employment protections for employees, and makes it more expensive for employers in China to implement personnel actions such as layoffs. Multinational companies doing business in China argue that the law will raise labor costs and make it difficult to lay off employees, by instituting new severance package rules.[22] Local firms, including the remaining state-owned enterprises, tend to use fewer modern human resource management tools than do private Chinese multinationals like Lenovo, but they must all deal with the fallout of the labor law. There are therefore wide variations in how companies in China deal with HR issues such as the following.[23]

RECRUITING Compared to some Western countries, it is still relatively difficult to recruit, hire, and retain good employees. China's employment contract law requires, among many other things, that employers report the names, sexes, identification numbers, and contract terms for all employees they hire within 30 days of hiring to local labor bureaus.[24]

In China, recruiting effectiveness depends on nonrecruitment human resource management issues. Employees gravitate toward employers that provide the best career advancement training and opportunities.[25] Firms like Siemens China, with impressive training and development programs, have the least difficulty attracting good candidates. Poaching employees is a serious matter in China. The employer must verify that the applicant is free to sign a new employment agreement.

SELECTION The dominant employee selection method involves analyzing the applicant's résumé and then interviewing him or her. The ideal way to do this is to institute a structured interview process, as many of the foreign firms in China have done.

COMPENSATION Although many managers endorse performance-based pay in China, other employers, to preserve group harmony, make incentive pay a small part of the pay package. And, as in other parts of Asia, team incentives are advisable.[26]

LABOR UNIONS Chinese facilities of IBM, PepsiCo, Walmart, and others have seen extensive strikes by Chinese workers.[27] Several things may be contributing to the strikes. China's new labor law expands workers' rights. An aging population in China means a diminishing supply of factory workers. And China's government may see the strikes as a way of raising workers' incomes and thus boosting consumer spending. China's All-China Federation of Trade Unions is closely tied to the government.

Staffing the Global Organization

LEARNING OBJECTIVE 17-3
List and briefly describe the main methods for staffing global organizations.

International employers' focus today is increasingly on managing human resource activities locally. In other words, their main concern is on selecting, training, appraising, and managing the in-country employees where they do business. However, deciding whether to fill local positions with local versus expatriate ("imported") employees remains a major concern.

HR in Action at the Hotel Paris On reviewing the data, it was apparent to Lisa and the CFO that the company's global human resource practices were probably inhibiting the Hotel Paris from being the world-class guest services company that it sought to be. To see how they handled this, see the case on page 585 of this chapter.

International Staffing: Home or Local?

In general, we can staff an international company with *expatriates, parent (or home-country) nationals, locals (host-country nationals),* or *third-country nationals*.[28] **Expatriates (expats)** are noncitizens of the countries in which they are working. In terms of where they come from, expatriates may also be **parent** or **home-country nationals,** citizens of the country in which the company is headquartered. Expatriates may also be **third-country nationals** —citizens of a country other than the parent or the host country—for example, a French executive working in the Beijing office of IBM. (And not all expatriates are sent there by employers; many recent graduates, academics, and business professionals decide to move, live, and work abroad.)[29] **Locals** (also known as *host-country nationals*) work for the company abroad and are citizens of the countries where they are working.

expatriates (expats)
Noncitizens of the countries in which employees are working.

parent or home-country nationals
Citizens of the country in which the multinational company has its headquarters.

third-country nationals
Citizens of a country other than the parent or the host country.

locals
Citizens of the countries in which employees are working; also called *host-country nationals*.

Internationalization Stage, Values, and Staffing Policy

Whether to use expatriates, locals, or some other type generally depends on quantifiable considerations (such as cost). However, it's not just hard facts that influence such decisions. Top management's personal inclinations and the company's stage in internationalization affect these decisions too. As a result, some companies are just more expat-oriented or local-oriented. Experts here distinguish among *ethnocentric, polycentric*, or *global* companies.

In an **ethnocentrically** oriented company, the company tends to staff its positions abroad with employees from its headquarters—with parent-country nationals, in other words.[30] The **polycentric** company staffs positions abroad with local or host-country employees. And the **global** company aims to attract the best candidates globally, including freely using third-country nationals to staff its positions around the world with the best people available.

ethnocentric
Here the company staffs its positions abroad with employees from its headquarters—with parent-country nationals, in other words.

polycentric
Here the company staffs positions abroad with local or host-country employees.

global
The global company aims to attract the best candidates globally, including freely using third-country nationals to staff its positions around the world with the best people available.

The company's stage in internationalization and its managers' inclinations both affect whether the company is inclined toward being ethnocentric, polycentric, or global in its staffing.[31] Companies new to the international arena may well run their international operations from "international" units within their corporate headquarters.[32] Here, the practical need to quickly transfer know-how abroad and to maintain a unified corporate culture and tighter control argue for an ethnocentric approach:[33] The company transfers abroad people (as expatriates) it knows well.

That "international" structure may evolve into a "multinational" structure, where subsidiaries abroad (often with their own HR units) largely control themselves. This tends to favor a polycentric staffing approach, wherein local, host-country employees, who know the local conditions best, staff the company's local positions.

Today, for many companies, the trend is toward being "global" companies. Global companies seek to be fully integrated. For example, a car to be sold throughout the world might be designed in France and manufactured in China and the United States with parts from Japan. Global companies not surprisingly tend to use a global philosophy in staffing its positions around the world, by filling positions with the best people—whether host-country nationals, locals, or third-country nationals.

EXPATS VERSUS LOCALS There are other considerations in using expats over locals. The employer may be unable to find local candidates with the required qualifications. Companies like GE traditionally viewed a successful stint abroad as a required step in developing top managers. Furthermore, home-country managers are already steeped in the firm's policies and culture, and thus more likely to apply headquarters' ways of doing things. Expatriates may also find it easier to coordinate with their former colleagues at the company's parent-country headquarters than would host-country locals.[34]

However, posting expatriates abroad is expensive, security problems give potential expatriates pause, returning expatriates often leave for other employers within a year or two, and educational facilities are turning out top-quality candidates abroad. As a result, new expatriate postings tend to be down. A survey several years ago found that about 47% of U.S. multinationals were maintaining the size of their expat workforces, 18% were increasing it, and 35% were decreasing it.[35] However, about half the global companies in another survey said they were doubling the number of expats they send to fast-growing countries such as China.[36]

From a practical point of view, most employees will be locals, for good reason. First, the cost of using expatriates is usually far greater than that of local workers.[37] Furthermore, in one survey, employers reported a 21% attrition rate for expatriate employees, compared with 10% for their general employee populations.[38] Local people will also probably better deal with local political issues than will expatriates.[39]

TRENDS SHAPING HR: *DIGITAL AND SOCIAL MEDIA*

Job Boards Abroad

Although a few U.S.-based job boards (like Indeed, and Monster) are global, most countries have their own major job boards. For instance, there is www.51job.com in China, www.careerone.com.au in Australia and New Zealand, and www.laborum.cl in Latin America.[40] ■

OTHER SOLUTIONS The choice is not just between expatriate versus local employees. For example, there are "commuter" solutions, involving frequent international travel but no formal relocation.[41]

One survey found that about 78% of surveyed employers had some form of "localization" policy. This is a policy of transferring a home-country national employee to a foreign subsidiary as a "permanent transferee."[42] For example, U.S. IBM employees originally from India eventually filled many of the 5,000 jobs that IBM shifted from the United States to India. These employees elected to move back to India, albeit at local India pay rates. The human resource team needs to control expat expenses, as the accompanying Profit Center feature explains.

IMPROVING PERFORMANCE: *HR AS A PROFIT CENTER*

Reducing Expatriate Costs

Given the expense of sending employees abroad for overseas assignments, the employer's human resource team plays a big role in controlling and reducing expatriate costs. A survey shows some of the steps HR managers are taking to reduce these expenses.[43] First, companies are upping the numbers of short-term assignments they make. This lets them use short-term expats to replace some long-term expats (and their families) who the company must maintain abroad for extended periods. Fifty percent of the companies surveyed are also replacing some expatriate postings with local hires. With an eye on cutting costs, many employers were also reviewing their firms' policies regarding such things as housing, education, and home leave, along with expatriate allowances and premiums (cost-of-living allowance and mobility/quality-of-living premiums).[44] The bottom line is that there's a lot human resource managers can do to cut costs and boost profits by better managing expat assignments. ■

> **MyLab Management Talk About It 1**
>
> If your professor has assigned this, go to the Assignments section of **www.pearson.com/mylab/management** to complete this discussion question. What else would you do to cut expat expenses?

OFFSHORING As we explained in Chapter 5, *offshoring*—moving business processes such as manufacturing or call-center operations abroad, and thus having local employees abroad do jobs that the firm's domestic employees previously did in-house—is another staffing option.

IBM Business Consulting Services surveyed employers to see what roles HR was playing in offshoring and overseas site selection decisions.[45] Here, human resource managers help top management:[46]

- To understand the *local labor markets*, for example, in terms of their size, education levels, and unions.
- To understand how the firm's current *employment-related reputation* in the locale may affect outsourcing to here.
- To decide how much the firm should *integrate the local workforce* into the parent firm's corporate organization. For example, engineers might best become employees. Others (such as call centers) might best remain employees of vendor firms.
- To deal with skill shortages.[47] This often requires using signing bonuses, higher wages, and improved promotion opportunities.
- To identify how to reduce attrition. This might include more training and development, better compensation, and improved career opportunities.

TRENDS SHAPING HR: *DIGITAL AND SOCIAL MEDIA*

Using Global Virtual Teams

virtual teams
Groups of geographically dispersed and generally same-level coworkers who meet and interact using information technologies to accomplish an organizational task.

Advances in telecommunications make it far easier today to carry out international projects and operations using global virtual teams. Global **virtual teams** are groups of geographically dispersed and generally same-level coworkers who meet and interact using information technologies to accomplish an organizational task.[48] For example, two multinational pharmaceutical companies used a multinational team with members from four continents to address detailed postmerger operational integration problems.

In a Skype and FaceTime world, virtual teams are both practical and popular. Collaborative software systems such as Microsoft NetMeeting conference system,[49] Cisco WebEx,[50] and GoToMeeting[51] enable virtual teams to hold live project reviews and discussions, share documents and exhibits, and store the sessions on the project's Web site. Cloud-based tools such as Huddle[52] allow team members to attend from wherever they are using mobile devices, Microsoft Project lets project team members manage tasks and flag issues and risks,[53] and Dropbox[54] facilitates cloud-based document storage. If necessary, large-screen tools such as Cisco Immersive TelePresence[55] make it seem as if team members are together in the same room, although they may be thousands of miles apart.

The main challenges virtual teams face are often people related. Challenges include building trust, cohesion, and team identity, and overcoming the isolation among team members. Similarly, if most team members reside in one country, the others may assume that the real power also lays in that country. Here the solution is to stress that the team has a unified goal and a common purpose.[56] The point is that human resource management plays an important role in such teams' success. Selecting virtual team members for their interpersonal skills, and then training them to deal with potential problems such as conflict avoidance and how to build trust is important. ■

Selecting International Managers

In most respects, screening managers for jobs abroad is similar to screening them for domestic jobs. Candidates need the technical knowledge and skills to do the job, and the required intelligence and people skills. Testing is widely used.

However, foreign assignments are different. The expatriate and his or her family will have to cope with and adapt to colleagues whose culture may be very different from their own. And, there's the stress of being in a foreign land. Ironically, one study a while ago concluded, "Traditionally, most selection of expatriates appears to be done solely on the basis of successful records of job performance in the home country."[57] The candidate's ability to adapt to a new culture is often secondary. That's exactly opposite from what it should be.

REALISTIC PREVIEWS Ideally, international assignee selection should therefore include *realistic previews*, and *adaptability screening procedures*.[58] Even in the most familiar countries there will be language barriers, and challenges for the family including homesickness and the need to adapt to new friends. It's important here to both reduce unrealistic expectations and familiarize the expat with potential challenges and benefits.[59] Realistic previews about what to expect, covering both problems and benefits, are therefore important. Many employers have prospective expat families meet with recently returned expats and their spouses to get that sort of information. Beyond that, social media such as www.linkedin.com (see their global expat network) and www.expatfinder.com are excellent sources of information, suggestions, support, and employment leads and connections for expats or for those considering a job abroad. A typical link you'll find at those sites is https://www.linkedin.com/company/aramco-expats.[60]

adaptability screening
A process that aims to assess the assignees' (and spouses') probable success in handling a foreign transfer.

ADAPTABILITY SCREENING Similarly, with adaptability important, **adaptability screening** should be part of the screening process. Employers often use psychologists for this. Adaptability screening aims to assess the assignee's (and spouse's) probable success in handling the foreign transfer, and to alert them to issues (such as the impact on children) the move may involve. Here, companies often look for overseas candidates whose work and nonwork experience, education, and language skills already demonstrate living and working with different cultures. Even several summers traveling overseas or in foreign study programs can provide some basis to believe the candidate can adjust abroad.

TESTING Selection testing is useful for expat selection. In terms of personality, sociable, outgoing, conscientious people seem more likely to fit into new cultural settings.[61] Similarly, expatriates who are more satisfied with their jobs abroad are more likely to adapt to the foreign assignment.[62] Employers have used the Overseas Assignment Inventory (OAI) for many years to help assess, select, and develop expatriates for assignments abroad. The OAI is an online assessment that measures attributes crucial for successful adaptation to another culture.[63] As another example, expat success also requires an "international mind-set." Employers sometimes measure this with the "Global Mindset Inventory." Sample questions include "Knows how to work well with people from different parts of the world?" And "Enjoys exploring different parts of the world?"[64]

Diversity Counts: Sending Women Managers Abroad

While women represent about half of the middle managers in U.S. companies, they represent only about 20% of managers sent abroad.[65] That's up from about 3% in the 1980s and 15% in 2005, but still low.[66] What accounts for this?

For one thing, misperceptions abound.[67] Line managers make these assignments, and many still probably assume that many women don't want to work abroad, or can't get their spouses to join them. However, a survey of female expatriates found enthusiasm. Why did they take their assignments? "Career development" was number one. Other reasons included "cultural understanding," "gaining experience," "doing something different," "personal goals," and "development learning."[68]

Fear of cultural prejudices against women is another issue. In some cultures, women do have to follow different rules, for instance, in terms of attire. But as one expat said, "Even in the more harsh cultures, once they recognize that the women can do the job . . . it becomes less of a problem."[69] Safety is another concern. Employers tend to assume that women abroad are more likely to become crime victims. However, most surveyed women expats said that safety was no more an issue with women than it was with men.[70]

Employers can take several steps to identify more women to assign abroad. For example, *formalize a process* for identifying employees who are willing to take assignments abroad. (At Gillette, for instance, supervisors use the performance review to identify the subordinate's career interests, including for assignments abroad.) *Train managers* to understand how their employees really feel about going abroad. And let successful female expats *help recruit* prospective female expats. And provide the expat's spouse with *employment assistance*.[71] ■

LEGAL ISSUES There are various legal considerations when hiring for assignments abroad. For example, as we explained in Chapter 2 (Equal Opportunity), American equal employment opportunity laws, including Title VII, the ADEA, and the ADA, do affect qualified employees of U.S. employers doing business abroad, and foreign firms doing business in the United States or its territories. If equal employment opportunity laws conflict with the laws of the country in which the U.S. employer is operating, the laws of the local country generally take precedence.[72]

Avoiding Early Expatriate Returns

As a rule, "expatriates typically experience a gradual increase in work adjustment over time."[73] However, many expat assignments do fail, usually ending in an early unplanned return. Determining why the foreign assignment of a technically qualified expat failed is a cottage industry, but two factors loom large—the expat's personality, and family pressures.

As noted, a big part of the problem is how they're chosen in the first place. The tendency is to choose expats for their technical expertise and successful work achievements, but going abroad actually requires an expanded skill set (including adaptability). For example, as noted, sociable, outgoing, conscientious people seem more likely to fit into new cultural settings.[74] Studies also suggest that it's not how different culturally the host country is from the person's home country that causes problems; it's the person's cross-cultural awareness and ability to adapt.[75] Some people are so culturally at ease that they do fine transferred anywhere; others will fail anywhere.[76] Careful selection is therefore in order.

Violations of what the expatriate sees as his or her psychological contract with the employer (the unwritten rules, agreements, and expectations governing the person's position abroad) may add to expatriate failure.[77] Similarly, expatriates who are more satisfied with their jobs abroad are more likely to adapt to the foreign assignment.[78] Therefore, realistic previews and then monitoring and communicating with the expat are important.

FAMILY PRESSURES However, it is usually not technical or personality factors but family and personal ones that undermine international assignees. One solution here is to provide *realistic previews* of what to expect abroad, careful *screening* (of both the prospective expat and his or her spouse), and improved *orientation* (discussions with recent returnees about the challenges of the foreign posting, for instance). Other suggestions include: *shorten the* *length* of the assignment;[79] and form *"global buddy"* programs, wherein local managers and their spouses assist new expatriates and their families with advice on things such as office politics, norms of behavior, and emergency medical care.[80] Most expatriates and their families make use of medical care while abroad; their main concern isn't the cost, but rather the quality of health care.[81] Providing site-specific orientation and language training are also valuable. The HR Tools feature sums up some suggestions.

IMPROVING PERFORMANCE: *HR TOOLS FOR LINE MANAGERS AND SMALL BUSINESSES*

Some Practical Solutions to the Expatriate Challenge

Expat failure is expensive; managers can take several practical steps to improve the expat's success abroad.

- ✓ *Carefully select* expatriates, using expat-relevant criteria such as sociability and adaptability, rather than just technical skills.
- ✓ *Provide realistic previews* of what to expect abroad, *careful screening* (of both the prospective expat and his or her spouse), *improved orientation,* and *improved benefits* packages.
- ✓ *Shorten the length* of the assignment.
- ✓ *Form "global buddy"* programs. Here local managers assist new expatriates with advice on things such as office politics, norms of behavior, and where to receive emergency medical assistance.[82]
- ✓ *Use executive coaches* to mentor and work with expatriate managers.[83] ■

> MyLab Management Talk About It 2
>
> If your professor has assigned this, go to the Assignments section of **www.pearson.com/mylab/management** to complete this discussion topic. Choose one country abroad, and write 200 words on this topic: "Here is what we should cover in our realistic preview to someone we are sending to this country."

Training and Maintaining Employees Abroad

LEARNING OBJECTIVE 17-4

Discuss some important issues to keep in mind in training, appraising, and compensating international employees.

Orienting and Training Employees on International Assignment

When it comes to the orientation and training required for expatriate success abroad, the practices of many U.S. employers reflect more talk than substance. Executives agree that international assignees do best when they receive the special training (in things like language and culture) that they require. Few provide it.

Many vendors offer packaged predeparture training. In general, the programs use on- and offline lectures, simulations, videos, and readings to prepare trainees. Their offerings illustrate the aim and content of such programs. One program aims to provide the trainee with (1) the basics of the new country's history, politics, business norms, education system, and demographics; (2) an understanding of how cultural values affect perceptions, values, and communications; and (3) examples of why moving to a new country can be difficult, and how to manage these challenges.[84] Others aim to build cross-cultural understanding, cross-cultural relationships and trust, and one's ability to communicate across cultures.[85] Global LT's "Living and Working Successfully" courses (https://global-lt.com/) "allow expatriate individuals and their families to gain a comprehensive understanding of the culture and business practices of their destination country. This course will help assignees more readily adjust to the work style and culture of an international assignment destination."[86]

Some employers use returning managers to cultivate the global mind-sets of those departing. For example, Bosch holds regular seminars, where newly arrived returnees pass on their experience to managers and their families going abroad.

ONGOING TRAINING Beyond such predeparture training, many firms provide continuing, in-country cross-cultural, and other training, particularly during the early stages of an overseas assignment.

For example, managers abroad (both expats and locals) continue to need traditional skills-oriented development. At many firms, including IBM, this includes rotating assignments, which help overseas managers grow professionally. IBM and other firms also have management development centers around the world where executives can hone their skills. And classroom programs (such as those at the London Business School or at INSEAD in France) provide overseas executives the educational opportunities (to acquire MBAs, for instance) that stateside colleagues have. PepsiCo encourages expatriates to engage in local social activities, such as table tennis tournaments in China, to help them become acclimated faster to local cultures.[87] Starbucks brings new management trainees from abroad to its Seattle, Washington, headquarters. This gives them "a taste of the West Coast lifestyle and the company's informal culture," as well as the technical knowledge required to manage their local stores.[88]

International development activities can have other, less-tangible benefits. For example, rotating their assignments helps managers form bonds with colleagues around the world. These can help the managers form the informal networks they need to make cross-border decisions more expeditiously.

Ethics and Codes of Conduct

Employers also need to make sure their employees abroad are adhering to their firm's ethics codes. However, exporting a firm's ethics rules requires more than giving employees abroad versions of a U.S. employee handbook. For example, few countries abroad adhere to "employment at will." Therefore, even handbooks that say, "We can fire employees at will" won't enable one to dismiss employees.[89] Instead of exporting the employee handbook, some distribute and publicize a global code of conduct.

Often, the employer's main concern is establishing global standards for adhering to U.S. laws that have cross-border impacts. For example, IBM paid $10 million to settle accusations that it had bribed Chinese and South Korean officials to get $54 million in government contracts.[90] Global employers need global codes of conduct on things like discrimination, harassment, bribery, and Sarbanes–Oxley.

Performance Appraisal of International Managers

Given the high costs of expatriate failure, appraising the expat is important.[91] However, several things complicate appraising an expatriate's performance. Cultural differences are one. For example, a candid exchange is often the norm in France, but sometimes less so in Japan, where "face" is a concern. Furthermore, the "cultural distance" in terms of basic values and ways of doing things is much wider between some countries (such as between Japan and South Africa) than others (such as between the United States and England). With more people involved, such cultural differences can particularly distort the multisource or "360-degree" feedback one gets from peers and subordinates. Therefore, particularly for expatriate employees, "peer and subordinate ratings should be used for feedback related to development, and only supervisor ratings should be used to make HR administrative decisions such as performance appraisal and merit pay."[92]

Furthermore, who does the appraisal? Local managers must have some input, but, again, cultural differences may distort the appraisals. On the other hand, home-office managers may be so out of touch that they can't provide useful input. The sensible alternative is probably to let both have some input, but most companies probably emphasize the local manager's opinion. Some suggestions for improving the expatriate appraisal process include the following:

1. Adapt the performance criteria to the local job and situation.
2. Weigh the evaluation more toward the on-site manager's appraisal than toward the home-site manager's.
3. If the home-office manager does the appraisal, have him or her use a former expatriate from the same location abroad for advice.

Many global employers bring their international managers together periodically for training seminars.

Cathy Yeulet/123RF

Compensating Managers Abroad

As discussed in Chapter 11 (Compensation), the usual way to formulate expatriate pay is to equalize purchasing power across countries, a technique known as the *balance sheet* approach; about 78% of respondents in one survey used it.[93] The basic idea is that each expatriate should enjoy the same standard of living he or she would have at home. Some use a *localization* compensation policy—they pay the incoming expat a salary comparable to what a local person would earn, but supplement that with payments to let the expat maintain his or her home-country standard of living.[94] In any case, the bottom line is that the pay plan must be competitive enough to get the person to move.

In practice, this usually boils down to building the expatriate's total compensation around five or six separate components. Table 17-1 illustrates the balance sheet approach. In this case, the manager's annual earnings are $160,000, and she faces a U.S. income tax rate of 28%. (Multiple-nation taxation can be a problem. Respondents often list "tax compliance" as the top challenge in sending employees abroad.)[95] Other costs are based on the index of living costs abroad published in the "U.S. Department of State Indexes of Living Costs Abroad, Quarters Allowances, and Hardship Differentials," available via the www.state.gov Web site.[96]

To help the expatriate manage his or her home and foreign financial obligations, most employers use a *split pay* approach; they pay, say, half a person's actual pay in home-country currency and half in the local currency.[97] For compensating *host country*

TABLE 17-1 The Balance Sheet Approach (Assumes U.S. Base Salary of $160,000)

Annual Expense	Home Assignment Chicago, U.S.	Shanghai, China (US $ Equivalent)	Allowance
Housing and utilities	$35,000	$ 44,800	$ 9,800
Goods and services	6,000	7,680	1,680
Taxes	44,800	57,344	12,544
Discretionary income	10,000	12,800	2,800
Total	$95,800	$122,624	$26,824

nationals, employers tend to use a similar process to what they use at home, namely methods like job grading to create equitable pay plans adjusted for local market conditions.[98]

Determining pay rates abroad isn't easy. Although there is a wealth of compensation survey data available in the United States, such data are not as easy to come by overseas. Some multinationals therefore conduct their own local annual compensation surveys. For example, Kraft has conducted one of total compensation in Europe. However, most employers abroad do probably purchase one or more of various international salary surveys such as the Call Centre Remuneration Report/Australia, from Aon Hewitt, or the International Salary Survey Database/United Arab Emirates, from Executive Resources Limited.[99]

EXPATRIATE PAY EXAMPLE As one expat pay example, those working for the company CEMEX (a multinational building supplies company)

> . . . get foreign service premium equal to a 10% increase in salary. Some get a hardship premium, depending on the country; it ranges from zero in a relatively comfortable posting to, for example, 30% in Bangladesh. We pay for their housing. We pay for their children's schooling up to college. There's home leave—a ticket back to their home country for the entire family once a year. There are language lessons for the spouse. And we gross up the pay of all expats, to take out the potential effects of local tax law. Say you have an executive earning $150,000. This person would cost close to $300,000 as an ex-pat.[100]

foreign service premiums
Financial payments over and above regular base pay, typically ranging between 10% and 30% of base pay.

hardship allowances
Payments that compensate expatriates for exceptionally hard living and working conditions at certain locations.

mobility premiums
Typically, lump-sum payments to reward employees for moving from one assignment to another.

INCENTIVES Employers use various incentives to encourage the employee to take the job abroad.[101] For example, **foreign service premiums** are financial payments over and above regular base pay. These typically range from 10% to 30% of base pay, and appear as weekly or monthly salary supplements. **Hardship allowances** compensate expatriates for hard living and working conditions at certain foreign locations. (U.S. diplomats posted to Iraq receive about a 70% boost in base salary, among other incentives.)[102] **Mobility premiums** are typically lump-sum payments to reward employees for moving from one assignment to another. In at least one way, executive compensation systems around the world are becoming more similar.[103] Specifically, U.S. firms that offer overseas managers long-term incentives often use overall corporate performance criteria (like worldwide profits) when awarding incentive pay.

STEPS IN ESTABLISHING A GLOBAL PAY SYSTEM Balancing global consistency in compensation with local considerations starts with establishing a rewards program that makes sense in terms of the employer's strategic aims.[104] Then the employer turns to more micro issues, such as, is how we're paying our employees abroad competitive?[105] Steps to follow in creating a global pay system include these:[106]

Step 1. **Set strategy.** First, formulate longer-term strategic goals, for instance, in terms of improving productivity or boosting market share.

Step 2. **Identify crucial executive behaviors.** Next, list the actions you expect your executives to exhibit in order to achieve these strategic goals.

Step 3. **Global philosophy framework.** Next, step back and ask how you want *each pay component* (salary, bonus, incentives, and so forth) to contribute to prompting those executive actions.

Step 4. **Identify gaps.** Next, ask, "To what extent do our pay plans around the world now support these actions, and what changes if any are required?"

Step 5. **Systematize pay systems.** Next, create more consistent performance assessment practices, and establish consistent job requirements and performance expectations for similar jobs worldwide.

Step 6. **Adapt pay policies.** Finally, review your global pay policies (for setting salary levels, incentives, and so forth). Conduct surveys and analyses to assess local pay practices. Then fine-tune your global pay policies so they make sense for each location.

Union Relations Abroad

A manager flying either East or West from the United States would most likely land in a country with a much stronger union movement than in the United States. For example, Walmart successfully neutralized unionization attempts in the United States, but had to accept unions in China. And collective bargaining in Western Europe tends to be industry-wide, whereas in the United States it generally occurs at the company or plant level. Furthermore, union recognition in Europe is less restrictive than in the United States. For example, even if one union represents 80% of an employer's workers, another union in Europe can try to organize the other 20%. The bottom line, as noted earlier, is that managers should steel themselves to more vigorous collective bargaining negotiations abroad then they may be used to in the United States.

Safety Abroad

Employers need to address at least two matters in developing their international safety policies and practices.

First is the question of local worker safety. Recently, for instance, at a plant that manufactures iPhone casings not far from Shanghai China, workers reportedly were using noxious chemicals, sometimes without proper personal protective equipment.[107] The United States has often taken the lead in occupational safety. However, other countries have such laws, with which all employers must comply. And in any case, it's hard to make a case for being less safety conscious or fair with workers abroad than you are with those at home.

The second matter is protecting their own international assignees and international travelers. (Legally, employers have a duty of care for protecting international assignees and their dependents and international business travelers.)[108] For example, the threat of terrorism is prompting more employers to use special mobile safety tools to track and communicate with workers in real time.[109] Security firm International SOS provides its clients with online and smart phone tools. These let the client quickly notify employees traveling abroad of potential problems and what to do about them. Many employers use intelligence services for monitoring potential terrorist threats abroad. The head of one intelligence firm estimated such services cost around $10,000 per year.[110] Some employers retain crisis management teams' services. They then call on these teams, for instance, when criminals kidnap one of their managers.

Hiring crisis teams and paying ransoms can be prohibitively expensive for all but the largest firms, so many employers buy kidnapping and ransom (K&R) insurance. Various events may trigger payments under such policies, including kidnapping/hostage situations, extortion, and detention.

The HR Practices Around the Globe feature provides some practical suggestions.

IMPROVING PERFORMANCE: *HR PRACTICES AROUND THE GLOBE*

Business Travel

Keeping business travelers safe is a specialty all its own, but suggestions here include[111]

- ✓ Provide expatriates with training about the place they're going to, so they're more oriented.
- ✓ Tell them not to draw attention to the fact they're Americans—by wearing T-shirts with American names, for instance.
- ✓ Have travelers arrive at airports as close to departure time as possible and wait in areas away from the main flow of traffic.
- ✓ Equip the expatriate's car and home with security systems.
- ✓ Tell employees to vary their departure and arrival times and take different routes.
- ✓ Keep employees current on crime and other problems by regularly checking, for example, the State Department's travel advisories and warnings at http://travel.state.gov.[112] Click on "Travel Alerts" and "Country Information."
- ✓ Advise employees to act confident at all times. Body language can attract perpetrators, and those who look like victims often become victimized.[113]

Increased terrorism worldwide is causing more employers to use special travel safety tools to track and communicate with workers in real time.[114] For example, as noted, International SOS provides its clients with online and smart phone tools.

MyLab Management Talk About It 3

If your professor has assigned this, go to the Assignments section of **www.pearson.com/mylab/management** to complete these discussion questions. Have you traveled abroad and violated any of these suggestions? Which? Would you do things differently now, knowing what you know?

Repatriation: Problems and Solutions

Too many employers waste the investment they've made in the employees they've sent abroad. For one thing, as we summarized in Table 17.1, a three-year assignment abroad for an employee with a salary of about $160,000 may cost the employer $800,000 or more, once extra living costs and taxes, (plus transportation and the person's regular benefits) are added up. Furthermore, losing the returnee also means losing the knowledge and experience he or she gained while abroad.[115] One survey several years ago found some employers lost 30% or more of their returning expats (although the attrition rates for most employers were much lower).[116]

Given the investment, it obviously makes sense to keep such employees with the firm. Formal repatriation programs are useful. For instance, one survey found that of the employers with excessive expat returnee attrition rates, about two-thirds had no formal repatriation plans in place.[117] About a quarter of employers don't even know if their recently returned expatriates quit within 12 months of returning.[118]

STEPS IN REPATRIATION Successful repatriation programs have several characteristics. The best begin before the person is even sent abroad, by making sure he or she sees that the position is an integral part of a sensible career plan.[119] Discussions about the return should begin 6–12 or more months before the actual repatriation, and include discussions of the person's next career moves.[120] It is essential that the expatriate and his or her family not feel that the company has forgotten them.

As an example, one firm has a three-part repatriation program.[121]

TunedIn by Westend61/Shutterstock

It is prudent to make sure that the employee always feels that he or she is still "in the loop" with what's happening back at the home office.

First, the firm matches the expat and his or her family with a psychologist trained in repatriation issues. The psychologist meets with the family before they go abroad. The psychologist discusses the challenges they will face abroad, assesses with them how well they think they will adapt to their new culture, and stays in touch with them throughout their assignment.

Second, the program ensures that the employee always feels that he or she is still "in the home-office loop." For example, the expat gets a mentor, and travels back to the home office periodically for meetings.

Third, once it's time for the expat employee and his or her family to return home, there's a formal repatriation service. About six months before the overseas assignment ends, the psychologist and an HR representative meet with the expat and the family to start preparing them for return. For example, they help plan the employee's next career move, help the person update his or her résumé, and begin putting the person in contact with supervisors back home.[122]

At the end of the day, probably the simplest thing employers can do to retain the returnee is value the expat's experience. As one returnee put it: "My company was, in my view, somewhat indifferent to my experience in China as evidenced by a lack of monetary reward, positive increase, or leverage to my career in any way." Such feelings prompt former expats to look elsewhere.[123] Having a system that facilitates keeping track of employees as they move from position to position in a global organization is essential. One reason for returnees' high attrition rates is that employers simply lose track of their returnees' new skills and competencies.[124]

LEARNING OBJECTIVE 17-5
Discuss similarities and differences in employee engagement around the globe.

Employee Engagement Guide for Managers

Engagement around the Globe

A survey of employee engagement around the globe provides some useful observations.[125]

On average, the percent of engaged employees (including highly engaged and moderately engaged) was 70% in Latin America, 65% in North America, 61% in Asia/Pacific and Africa/Middle East, and 57% in Europe. The percentage of actively disengaged employees was highest in Europe (19%), lowest in Latin America (12%), and 15%–16% in North America, Asia/Pacific, and Africa/Middle East. The trend was for employee engagement (highly and moderately engaged) in all regions of the world to be converging around the current global average of about 61% of employees engaged. So, workers everywhere are becoming about equally engaged.

What are the top drivers of employee engagement around the globe? Career opportunities was the number-one key driver of employee engagement in all regions of the world, underscoring the universal importance of providing such opportunities. But beyond that point of agreement, the other key drivers varied by geographic area. For example, setting goals/managing performance was the number two key driver of employee engagement in North America but was much less important in Europe; the reputation of the organization was number two in Europe, pay was number two in Asia/Pacific, and recognition was number two in Latin America. So, the management actions that drive engagement vary somewhat by region.

One thing that did not seem to vary much was the global importance of employee engagement. The best-performing companies' employees were in the top quartile in employee engagement.

LEARNING OBJECTIVE 17-6
Explain with examples how to implement a global human resource management program.

Managing HR Locally: How to Put into Practice a Global HR System

A noted earlier, companies tend to evolve from running their international operations from home-based "international" units, to a "multinational" structure where subsidiaries abroad largely control themselves, to fully unified "global" companies with a unified management structure worldwide. Here, for instance, a car to be sold worldwide might be designed in France and manufactured in China and the U.S. with parts from Japan.[126]

Being "global" affects how the company organizes and manages its human resource management function. The global firm's emphasis will likely be on standardizing HR practices worldwide. In practice, technology—and particularly cloud computing—means most employers are moving to such unified global HR functions.[127] For example, BP recently adopted the cloud-based "Workday HCM" (Human Capital Management) in order to support BP's global HR modernization strategy.[128] Among other things, adopting Workday HCM enabled BP to standardize its human capital management processes around the world, and gave employees worldwide access to information such as regarding their benefit status. It also provides top management with better insights into worldwide staffing levels and employee performance. And, it enabled BP's human resource management staff to transition from doing administrative HR tasks to supporting BP's strategic initiatives. The Strategic Context feature provides another example.[129]

IMPROVING PERFORMANCE: *THE STRATEGIC CONTEXT*

Hyundai Capital

Hyundai Capital strategically is moving to what it calls a "Global One Company." For example, it is unifying its organizational structure, products and services, and management practices worldwide.[130] To standardize its HR practices globally, it therefore recently moved its human resource management system from one that relied on separate HR systems in areas around the world, to a unified system based on Oracle HCM (Human Capital Management) Fusion Cloud. The new system, for example, enables employees around the globe to update their HR data and access improved training, onboarding, and other talent management tools. Oracle's system also helps employers adapt to legal and labor relations differences around the world. For example, it handles multiple unique union and worker agreements in different countries, and helps management make local hiring and dismissal decisions consistent with local laws.

MyLab Management Talk About It 4

If your professor has assigned this, go to the Assignments section of **www.pearson.com/mylab/management** to complete these discussion questions. What problems would you expect Hyundai Capital to face in achieving standardization? How would you suggest they handle them?

Yet, even with cloud-computing, one could reasonably ask, "With the large cross-cultural differences involved, what is the best way to institute a standardized human resource management system in our facilities around the world? A study conducted a number of years ago sheds some light on this. In brief, the study's results show that employers may have to defer to local managers for fine-tuning human resource management policies.

In this study, the researchers interviewed human resource personnel from six global companies—Agilent, Dow, IBM, Motorola, Procter & Gamble, and Shell Oil Co.—as well as international human resources consultants.[131] The study's overall conclusion was that employers who successfully implement global HR systems do so by applying several best practices. The basic idea is to *develop* systems that are *acceptable* to employees in units around the world, and ones that the employers can *implement* more effectively. Figure 17-2 summarizes this.

Developing a More Effective Global HR System

First, these employers engage in two best practices in *developing* their worldwide human resource policies and practices.

Form global HR networks. To head off resistance, human resource managers around the world should feel part of the firm's global human resource management team. Treat the local human resource managers as equal partners. For instance, form global teams to develop the new human resources system. Create

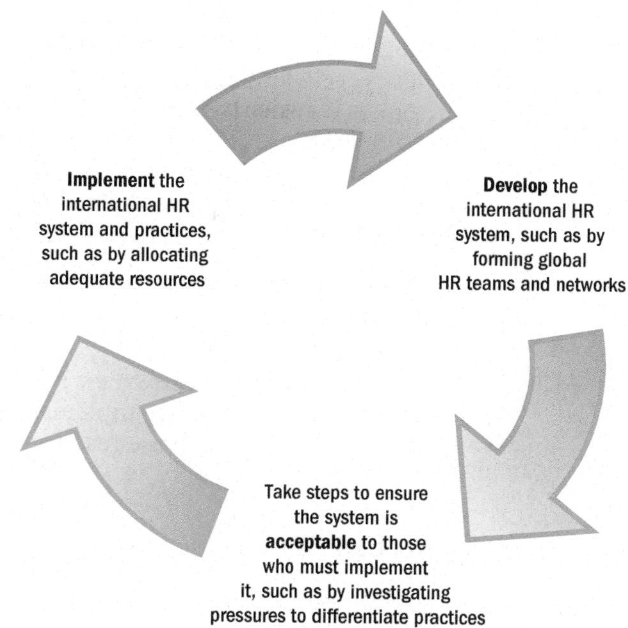

FIGURE 17-2 Best Practices for Creating Global HR Systems

"an infrastructure of partners around the world that you use for support, for buy-in, for organization of local activities, and to help you better understand their own systems and their own challenges."[132]

Remember that it's more important to standardize ends and competencies than specific methods. For example, IBM uses a basically standardized recruitment and selection process worldwide. However, "details such as who conducts the interview (hiring manager vs. recruiter), or whether the prescreen is by phone or in person, differ by country."[133]

Making the Global HR System More Acceptable

Next, employers engage in three best practices so that the global human resource systems they develop will be *acceptable* to local managers around the world. These practices are

Remember that truly global organizations find it easier to install global systems. For example, their managers work on global teams, and the firms identify, recruit, and place employees globally. As one Shell manager said, "If you're truly global, then you are hiring here [the United States] people who are going to immediately go and work in the Hague, and vice versa."[134] Doing so makes it easier for managers everywhere to accept the wisdom of having a standardized human resource management system.

Investigate pressures to differentiate and determine their legitimacy. Local managers will insist, "You can't do that here, because we are different culturally." These "differences" aren't usually persuasive. For example, when Dow wanted to implement an online recruitment and selection tool abroad, the hiring managers there said that their managers would not use it. After investigating the supposed cultural roadblocks, Dow successfully implemented the new system.[135]

However, first carefully assess whether the local culture or other differences might in fact undermine the new system. Be knowledgeable about local legal issues, and be willing to differentiate where necessary.

Try to work within the context of a strong corporate culture. Companies that do so find it easier to obtain agreement among far-flung employees. For example, because of how P&G recruits, selects, trains, and rewards them, its managers have a strong sense of shared values. For instance, new recruits quickly learn to think in terms of "we" instead of "I." They learn to value thoroughness, consistency, self-discipline, and a methodical approach. Having such global unanimity makes it easier to implement standardized human resource practices.

Implementing the Global HR System

Finally, two best practices helped ensure success in actually *implementing* the globally consistent human resource policies and practices.

"You can't communicate enough." "There's a need for constant contact with the decision makers in each country, as well as the people who will be implementing and using the system."[136]

Dedicate adequate resources. For example, don't require the local human resource management offices to implement new job analysis procedures unless the head office provides adequate resources for these additional activities.

MyLab Management Apply It!

How does a company actually go about managing its international human resource management function? If your professor has assigned this activity, go to the Assignments section of **www.pearson.com/mylab/management** to complete the video exercise.

Chapter Review

Chapter Section Summaries

17-1. Dealing with **global human resource challenges as a manager** isn't easy. The employer faces an array of political, social, legal, and cultural differences among countries abroad. What works in one country may not work in another.

17-2. **The need for adapting human resource activities to intercountry differences** influences employers' HR processes. For example, citizens of different countries adhere to different values, and countries have differing economic systems as well as different legal, political, and labor relations systems.

17-3. **Staffing the global organization** is a major challenge. Companies may use expatriates, home-country nationals, locals, or third-country nationals. Ethnocentric companies tend to emphasize home-country attitudes, polycentric companies focus more on host-country employees, and global employers try to pick the best candidates from wherever they might be. Selecting employees to successfully work abroad depends on several things, most important on adaptability screening and on making sure that each employee's spouse and family get the realistic previews and support necessary to make the transition.

17-4. After selecting the employees to send abroad, attention turns to **training and maintaining your expatriate employees.**

In terms of predeparture preparation, training efforts ideally first cover the impact of cultural differences; then, the focus moves to getting participants to understand how attitudes influence behavior, providing factual knowledge about the target country, and developing skills in areas like language and adjustment.

In compensating expatriates, most employers use the balance sheet approach; this focuses on four groups of expenses: income taxes, housing, goods and services, and discretionary expenses, and aims to ensure that the employee's standard of living abroad is about what it would have been at home.

With terrorism a threat, most employers today take protective measures, including buying kidnapping and ransom insurance.

Well-thought-out repatriation programs emphasize keeping employees in the loop as far as what's happening in their home offices, bringing them back to the office periodically, and providing formal repatriation services for the expatriate and his or her family to start preparing them for the return.

17-5. The worldwide trend is for employee engagement to converge around the current global average of about 61% of **employees engaged**. Career opportunities was the number-one key driver of employee engagement in all regions of the world, underscoring its universal importance.

17-6. With employers increasingly relying on local rather than expatriate employees, it's important for managers to understand **how to implement a global HR system.** The basic approach involves: (1) Develop a more effective global HR system; (2) Make the global HR system more acceptable; and (3) Implement the global system.

Discussion Questions

17-1. You are the president of a small business. What are some of the ways you expect "going international" will affect HR activities in your business?

17-2. What are some of the specific, uniquely international activities an international HR manager typically engages in?

17-3. What intercountry differences affect HRM? Give several examples of how each may affect HRM.

17-4. You are the HR manager of a firm that is about to send its first employees overseas to staff a new subsidiary. Your boss, the president, asks you why such assignments often fail, and what you plan to do to avoid such failures. How do you respond?

17-5. As an HR manager, what program would you establish to reduce repatriation problems of returning expatriates and their families?

Individual and Group Activities

17-6. Working individually or in groups, outline an expatriation and repatriation plan for your professor, whom your school is sending to Bulgaria to teach HR for the next 3 years.

17-7. Give three specific examples of multinational corporations in your area. Check on the Internet or with each firm to determine in what countries these firms have operations. Explain the nature of some of their operations, and summarize whatever you can find out about their international employee selection and training HR policies.

17-8. Choose three traits useful for selecting international assignees, and create a straightforward test to screen candidates for these traits.

17-9. Use a library or Internet source to determine the relative cost of living in five countries as of this year, and explain the implications of such differences for drafting a pay plan for managers being sent to each country.

17-10. Appendices A and B at the end of this book (pages 614–634) list the knowledge someone studying for the HRCI (Appendix A) or SHRM (Appendix B) certification exam needs to have in each area of human resource management (such as in Strategic Management and Workforce Planning).

KNOWLEDGE BASE

In groups of several students, do four things: (1) review Appendix A and/or B; (2) identify the material in this chapter that relates to the Appendix A and/or B required knowledge lists; (3) write four multiple-choice exam questions on this material that you believe would be suitable for inclusion in the HRCI exam and/or the SHRM exam; and (4) if time permits, have someone from your team post your team's questions in front of the class, so that students in all teams can answer the exam questions created by the other teams.

17-11. An issue of *HR Magazine* contained an article titled "Aftershocks of War," which said that soldiers returning to their jobs from Iraq would likely require HR's assistance in coping with "delayed emotional trauma." The term *delayed emotional trauma* refers to the personality changes such as anger, anxiety, or irritability that exposure to the traumatic events of war sometimes triggers in returning veterans. Assume you are the HR manager for the employer of John Smith, who is returning to work next week after 1 year in Iraq. Based on what you read in this chapter, what steps would you take to help smooth John's reintegration into your workforce?

Experiential Exercise

A Taxing Problem for Expatriate Employees

Written and copyrighted by Gary Dessler, PhD.

Purpose: The purpose of this exercise is to give you practice identifying and analyzing some of the factors that influence expatriates' pay.

Required Understanding: You should be thoroughly familiar with this chapter and with the Web site www.irs.gov.

How to Set Up the Exercise/Instructions: Divide the class into teams of four or five students. Each team member should read the following: One of the trickiest aspects of calculating expatriates' pay relates to the question of the expatriate's U.S. federal income tax liabilities. Go to the Internal Revenue Service's Web site, https://www.irs.gov/individuals/international-taxpayers/taxpayers-living-abroad. Your team is the expatriate-employee compensation task force for your company, and your firm is about to send several managers and engineers to, say, Japan, England, and Hong Kong. What information did you find on the site that will help your team formulate expat tax and compensation policies? Based on that, what are three important things your firm should keep in mind in formulating a compensation policy for employees you're about to send abroad?

Application Case

"Boss, I Think We Have a Problem"

Written and copyrighted by Gary Dessler, PhD.

Central Steel Door Corporation has been in business for about 20 years, successfully selling a line of steel industrial-grade doors. The company had gradually increased its presence from the New York City area, first into New England and then down the Atlantic Coast, then through the Midwest and West, and finally into Canada. The company's basic expansion strategy was always the same: Choose an area, open a distribution center, hire a regional sales manager, and then let that regional sales manager help staff the distribution center and hire local sales reps.

Unfortunately, the company's traditional success in finding sales help did not extend to its overseas operations, when Mel Fisher, president of Central Steel Door, decided to expand his company into Europe. He tried for 3 weeks to find a sales manager by advertising in the *International New York Times*, which is read by businesspeople in Europe and by American expatriates living and working in Europe. Although the ads placed in the *Times* also ran for about a month on the *Times*'s Web site, Mr. Fisher so far has received only five applications. One came from a possibly viable candidate, whereas four came from candidates whom Mr. Fisher refers to as "lost souls"—people who seem to have spent most of their time traveling aimlessly from country to country, sipping espresso in sidewalk cafés. When asked what he had done for the last 3 years, one told Mr. Fisher he'd been on a "walkabout."

Other aspects of his international HR activities have been equally problematic. Fisher alienated two of his U.S. sales managers by sending them to Europe to temporarily run the European operations, but neglecting to work out a compensation package that would cover their relatively high living expenses in Germany and Belgium. One ended up staying the better part of the year, and Mr. Fisher was rudely surprised to be informed by the Belgian government that his sales manager owed thousands of dollars in local taxes. The two managers had hired about 10 local people to staff each of the two distribution centers. However, the level of sales was disappointing, so Fisher decided to fire about half the distribution center employees. That's when he got an emergency phone call from his temporary sales manager in Germany: "I've just been told that all these employees should have had written employment agreements and that in any case we can't fire anyone without at least 1 year's notice, and the local authorities here are really up in arms. Boss, I think we have a problem."

Questions

17-12. Based on this chapter and the case incident, compile a list of 10 international HR mistakes Mr. Fisher has made so far.

17-13. How would you have gone about hiring a European sales manager? Why?

17-14. What would you do now if you were Mr. Fisher?

Continuing Case

Carter Cleaning Company

Written and copyrighted by Gary Dessler, PhD.

Going Abroad

Jack Carter decided to take his first long vacation in years and go to Mexico for a month a few years ago. What he found surprised him: He spent time in Mexico City and was surprised at the dearth of cleaning stores, particularly considering the amount of air pollution. Traveling north, he passed through Juarez, Mexico, and was similarly surprised at the relatively few cleaning stores he found there. As he drove back into Texas, and back toward home, he began to think about whether it would be advisable to consider expanding his chain of stores into Mexico.

Aside from the possible economic benefits, he liked what he saw in Mexico. Starting a new business again also appealed to him. "I guess entrepreneurship is in my blood," is the way he put it.

As he drove home to have dinner with Jennifer, he began to formulate the questions he would have to ask before deciding whether to expand abroad.

Questions

17-15. Assuming they began by opening just one or two stores in Mexico, what do you see as the main HR-related challenges Jack and Jennifer would have to address?

17-16. How would you go about choosing a manager for a new Mexican store if you were Jack or Jennifer? For instance, would you hire someone locally or send someone from one of your existing stores? Why?

17-17. The cost of living in Mexico is substantially below that of where Carter is now located: How would you go about developing a pay plan for your new manager if you decided to send an expatriate to Mexico?

17-18. Present a detailed explanation of the factors you would look for in your candidate for expatriate manager to run the stores in Mexico.

Translating Strategy into HR Policies and Practices Case*,§

** The accompanying strategy map for this chapter is in MyLab Management; the overall map on the inside back cover of this text outlines the relationships involved.*

Improving Performance at the Hotel Paris

Managing Global Human Resources

The Hotel Paris's competitive strategy is, "To use superior guest service to differentiate the Hotel Paris properties, and to thereby increase the length of stay and return rate of guests, and thus boost revenues and profitability." HR manager Lisa Cruz must now formulate functional policies and activities that support this competitive strategy and boost performance by eliciting the required employee behaviors and competencies.

With hotels in 11 cities in Europe and the United States, Lisa knew that the company had to do a better job of managing its global human resources. For example, there were no formal means of identifying or training management employees for duties abroad (for those going either to the United States or to Europe). As another example, after spending upward of $200,000 on sending a U.S. manager and her family abroad, they had to return her abruptly when the family complained of missing their friends back home. Lisa knew this was no way to run a multinational business. She turned her attention to developing the HR practices her company required to do business more effectively internationally.

On reviewing the data, it was apparent to Lisa and the CFO that the company's global human resource practices were probably inhibiting the Hotel Paris from being the world-class guest services company that it sought to be. For example, high-performing service and hotel firms had formal departure training programs for at least 90% of the employees they sent abroad; the Hotel Paris had no such programs. Similarly, with each city's hotel operating its own local hotel HR information system, there was no easy way for Lisa, the CFO, or the company's CEO to obtain reports on metrics like turnover, absences, or workers' compensation costs across all the different hotels. As the CFO summed it up, "If we can't measure how each hotel is doing in terms of human resource metrics like these, there's really no way to manage these activities, so there's no telling how much lost profits and wasted efforts are dragging down each hotel's performance." Lisa received approval to institute new global human resources programs and practices.

In instituting these new programs and practices, Lisa had several goals in mind. She wanted an integrated human resource information system (HRIS) that allowed her and the company's top managers to monitor and assess, on an ongoing basis, the company's global performance on strategically required employee competencies and behaviors such as attendance, morale, commitment, and service-oriented behavior. To address this need, she received approval to contract with a company that integrated, via the Internet, the separate hotels' HR systems, including human resource and benefits administration, applicant tracking and résumé scanning, and employee morale surveys and performance appraisals.

She also contracted with an international HR training company to offer expatriate training for Hotel Paris employees and their families before they left for their foreign assignments, and to provide short-term support after they arrived. That training company also helped create a series of weeklong "Managers' Seminars." Held once every 6 months at a different hotel in a different city, these gave selected managers from throughout the Hotel Paris system an opportunity to meet and to learn more about the numerous new HR programs and practices that Lisa and her team had been instituting for the purpose of supporting the company's strategic aims. With the help of their compensation specialist, Lisa and her team also instituted a new incentive program for each of the company's local managers, to focus their attention more fully on the company's service-oriented strategic aims. By the end of the year, the Hotel Paris's performance on metrics such as percent of expatriates receiving predeparture screening, training, and counseling were at or above those of high-performing similar companies. She and the CFO believed, rightly, that they had begun to get their global HR system under control.

Questions

17-19. Provide a one-page summary of what individual hotel managers should know in order to make it more likely incoming employees from abroad will adapt to their new surroundings.

17-20. In previous chapters of Dessler *Human Resource Management* you recommended various human resource practices the Hotel Paris should use. Choose one of these, and explain why you believe they could take this program abroad, and how you suggest they do so.

17-21. Choose one Hotel Paris human resource practice that you believe is essential to the company specifically for achieving its high-quality-service goal, and explain how you would implement that practice in the firm's various hotels worldwide.

§ Written and copyrighted by Gary Dessler, PhD.

Writing Assignments

17-22. What special training do overseas candidates need? In what ways is such training similar to and different from traditional diversity training?

17-23. Your boss wants you to transfer from headquarters in Columbus, Ohio, to the firm's Moscow, Russia, office. You're pretty sure you're suited to work abroad, but to be sure you decide to write a short essay based on what you learned in this chapter titled "Why I think I would be successful in an overseas assignment." What would you say in your essay?

MyLab Management Try It!

How would you apply the concepts and skills you learned in this chapter? If your professor has assigned this activity, go to the Assignments section of **www.pearson.com/mylab/management** to complete the simulation.

PERSONAL INVENTORY ASSESSMENTS

Go to **www.pearson.com/mylab/management** to complete the Personal Inventory Assessment related to this chapter.

Key Terms

international human resource management (IHRM), 564
works councils, 566
codetermination, 566
expatriates (expats), 568
parent or home-country nationals, 568
third-country nationals, 568
locals, 568
etãocentric, 568
polycentric, 568
global, 568
virtual teams, 570
adaptability screening, 571
foreign service premiums, 576
hardship allowances, 576
mobility premiums, 576

Endnotes

1. "Hyundai Capital Selects Oracle HCM Cloud Solutions for Global HR Transformation," http://markets.businessinsider.com/news/stocks/hyundai-capital-selects-oracle-hcm-cloud-solutions-for-global-hr-transformation-1011612997, accessed July 16, 2018; "Oracle Global Human Resources Cloud," https://cloud.oracle.com/en_US/global-human-resources-cloud/features, accessed April 12, 2018.
2. www.census.gov/foreign-trade/statistics/historical/gands.pdf, accessed March 9, 2018.
3. For example, see Chris Brewster, Wolfgang Mayrhofer, and Adam Smale, "Crossing the Streams: HRM in Multinational Enterprises and Comparative HRM," *Human Resource Management Review* 26 (2016), pp. 285–297.
4. See, for example, Helen Deresky, *International Management* (Boston: Pearson, 2017), p. 286.
5. Deresky, p. 77.
6. "Voices from the Front Lines," *Harvard Business Review*, September 2014, pp. 77–83.
7. Thomas Hout and David Michael, "A Chinese Approach to Management," *Harvard Business Review*, September 2014, pp. 103–107.
8. Erin Meyer, "Being the Boss in Brussels, Boston, and Beijing," *Harvard Business Review*, July–August 2017, pp. 70–78.
9. www.geert-hofstede.com/, accessed April 12, 2018.
10. See Vas Taras, Bradley Kirkman, and Piers Steel, "Examining the Impact of Culture's Consequences: A Three-Decade, Multilevel, Multi-Analytic Review of Hofstadter's Cultural Value Dimensions," *Journal of Applied Psychology* 95, no. 3 (2010), pp. 405–439.
11. Chris Brewster, "European Perspectives on Human Resource Management," *Human Resource Management Review* 14 (2004), pp. 365–382.
12. "SOX Compliance, Corporate Codes of Conduct Can Create Challenges for U.S. Multinationals," *BNA Bulletin to Management*, March 28, 2006, p. 97.
13. "In India, 101 Employees Pose Big Problems," *Bloomberg Businessweek*, January 17–23, 2011, p. 13.
14. "Employer Beware," *The Economist*, March 12, 2011, p. 43.
15. Stephenie Overman, "Tapping Talent around the Globe," *HR Magazine*, February 2016, pp. 47–51.
16. See, for example, "Works Councils in the European Union (EU)," http://www.acc.com/legalresources/quickcounsel/wciteu.cfm, accessed August 20, 2018.
17. Deresky, op cit, p. 140.
18. 2012 figures, International Comparisons of Hourly Compensation Costs, 2012, https://www.bls.gov/fls/ichcc.pdf, accessed April 12, 2018.
19. "An International Guide to Employment Law across 28 Countries—Europe Highlights," Clyde & Co., https://www.lexology.com/library/detail.aspx?g=6e59f071-8bdf-4ee8-8003-523daf192c4a, accessed April 12, 2018.
20. Deborah Ball and James Haggerty, "How to Cut a Job in Italy? Wait, and Wait Some

More," *The Wall Street Journal*, May 21, 2013, pp. B1, B2.

21. Phillips Taft and Cliff Powell, "The European Pensions and Benefits Environment: A Complex Ecology," *Compensation & Benefits Review*, January/February 2005, pp. 37–50; and "An International Guide to Employment Law across 28 Countries."
22. Lisbeth Claus, "What You Need to Know about the New Labor Contract Law of China," *SHRM Global Law Special Report*, October–November 2008.
23. See, for example, Syed Akhtar et al., "Strategic HRM Practices and Their Impact on Company Performance in Chinese Enterprises," *Human Resource Management* 47, no. 1 (Spring 2008), pp. 15–32.
24. Andreas Lauffs, "Chinese Law Spurs Reforms," *HR Magazine*, June 2008, pp. 92–98.
25. See, for example, Kathryn King-Metters and Richard Metters, "Misunderstanding the Chinese Worker," *The Wall Street Journal*, July 7, 2008, p. R11.
26. Gary Dessler, "Expanding into China? What Foreign Employers Entering China Should Know about Human Resource Management Today," *SAM Advanced Management Journal*, August 2006. See also Joseph Gamble, "Introducing Western-Style HRM Practices to China: Shop Floor Perceptions in a British Multinational," *Journal of World Business* 41, no. 4 (December 2006), pp. 328–340; and Adrienne Fox, "China: Land of Opportunity and Challenge," *HR Magazine*, September 2007, pp. 38–44.
27. "Striking Chinese Workers Are Headache for Nike, IBM, Secret Weapon for Beijing," *Bloomberg News*, May 6, 2014.
28. Anne Marie Francesco and Barry Gold, *International Organizational Behavior* (Upper Saddle River, NJ: Prentice Hall, 2005), p. 145.
29. Vlad Vainan et al., "Recognizing the Important Role of Self-Initiated Expatriates and Effective Global Talent Management," *Human Resource Management Review* 25 (2015), pp. 280–286.
30. Deresky, pp. 288–299.
31. Ibid.
32. Yaarit Silverstone, Claira Yang, Colin Sloman, and Susan Cantrell, "Trends Reshaping the Future of HR: Reconfiguring the Global Talent Landscape," *Top Trends That Will Reshape the Future of HR: The Future of HR*, Accenture, www.Accenture.com/us-en/Pages/insight-future-HR.aspx, accessed March 6, 2015.
33. Deresky, p. 188.
34. Ibid. p. 189
35. See "Workforce Trends: Companies Continue to Deploy Ex-Pats," *Compensation & Benefits Review* 42, no. 1 (January/February 2010), p. 6.
36. "Expatriate Assignments in Growth Markets to Soar," *HR Magazine*, January 2013, p. 20.
37. Deresky, p. 189.
38. "Survey Says Expatriates Twice as Likely to Leave Employer as Home-Based Workers," *BNA Bulletin to Management*, May 9, 2006, p. 147.
39. Deresky, p. 289.
40. Overman, "Tapping Talent around the Globe."
41. Helene Mayerhofer et al., "Flexpatriate Assignments: A Neglected Issue in Global Staffing," *International Journal of Human Resource Management* 15, no. 8 (December 2004), pp. 1371–1389; and Martha Frase, "International Commuters," *HR Magazine*, March 2007, pp. 91–96.
42. Timothy Dwyer, "Localization's Hidden Costs," *HR Magazine*, June 2004, pp. 135–144.
43. "Mercer's International Assignments Survey 2010," www.imercer.com/products/2010/intl-assignments-survey.aspx, accessed June 2, 2011; "Companies Juggle Cost Cutting with Maintaining Competitive Benefits for International Assignments," www.amanet.org/training/articles/Companies-Juggle-cost-cutting-with-Maintaining-Competitive-Benefits-for-International-Assignments.aspx, accessed June 2, 2011.
44. "Mercer's International Assignments Survey 2010"; "Companies Juggle Cost Cutting with Maintaining Competitive Benefits for International Assignments."
45. The following is based on "Back-Office and Customer Care Centers in Emerging Economies: A Human Capital Perspective," IBM Business Consulting Services, http://www-07.ibm.com/innovation/includes/pdf/ge510-3967-back-office-asiapac.pdf, accessed August 19, 2018.
46. Ibid., pp. 3, 4.
47. Ibid., pp. 5, 6.
48. See, for example, Deresky, p. 325.
49. www.microsoft.com/en-us/download/details.aspx?id=23745, accessed May 6, 2015.
50. https://signup.webex.com/webexmeetings/US/sem_-acquisition.html?CPM=KNC-sem&TrackID=1031986&country=US&psearch ID=webex%20collaboration%20meeting%20room, accessed May 6, 2015.
51. www1.gotomeeting.com/m/g2msem3.tmpl?Portal=www.gotomeeting.com&c_name=msns&c_mark=NAPPC&c_kwd=go_to_meeting_software_download-Broad&c_prod=GTM&c_cmp=sf-70150000000add7&c_date=CATnumber&c_cell=CMjwmL3KrcUCFUIZ7AodlRIAgQ&gclid=CMjwmL3KrcUCFUIZ7AodlRIAgQ&gclsrc=ds, accessed May 6, 2015.
52. www.huddle.com, accessed May 6, 2015.
53. https://products.office.com/en-us/project?legRedir=true&CorrelationId=20cd3b87-4cc5-4e30-ad86-c713d2a47abd, accessed May 6, 2015.
54. www.dropbox.com, accessed May 6, 2015.
55. www.cisco.com/c/en/us/products/collaboration-endpoints/immersive-telePresence/index.html, accessed May 6, 2015.
56. Tsedal Neeley, "Global Teams That Work," *Harvard Business Review*, October 2015, pp. 75–85.
57. Mary G. Tye and Peter Y. Chen, "Selection of Expatriates: Decision-Making Models Used by HR Professionals," *Human Resource Planning* 28, no. 4 (December 2005), pp. 15–20.
58. Paula Caligiuri et al., "Selection for International Assignments," *Human Resource Management Review* 19 (2009), pp. 251–262.
59. See, for example, Michael Harvey et al., "Aligning Expatriate Managers' Expectations with Complex Global Assignments," *Journal of Applied Social Psychology* 42, no. 2 (December 2012), pp. 3026–3050.
60. For others, see www.linkedin.com/groups/Global-Expat-Professional-Network-4763493 and www.linkedin.com/groups/Forum-Expatriate-Management-1056387, both accessed July 29, 2015.
61. Quoted in Meredith Downes, Iris I. Varner, and Luke Musinski, "Personality Traits as Predictors of Expatriate Effectiveness: A Synthesis and Reconceptualization," *Review of Business* 27, no. 3 (Spring/Summer 2007), p. 16.
62. Hung-Wen Lee and Ching-Hsing, "Determinants of the Adjustment of Expatriate Managers to Foreign Countries: An Empirical Study," *International Journal of Management* 23, no. 2 (2006), pp. 302–311.
63. www.brookfieldgrs.com/intercultural, accessed September 7, 2013.
64. Mansour Javidan, Amanda Bullough, and Rebekah Dibble, "Mind the Gap: Gender Differences in Global Leadership Self-Efficacies," *Academy of Management Perspectives* 30, no. 1 (2016), pp. 59–73.
65. "More Women, Young Workers on the Move," *Workforce Management*, August 20, 2007, p. 9; Andy Smailes, "Women Abroad—How to Get the Most from an International Assignment," *Living Abroad*, January 18, 2013, www.livingabroad.com/women-abroad-how-to-get-the-most-from-an-international-assignment/, accessed July 28, 2015; "BGRS 2015 Global Mobility Trends Survey," https://www.bgrs.com/insights-articles/female-expatriates-continue-to-be-underrepresented/, accessed April 13, 2018.
66. "More Women . . . ," op. cit.; Tina Vasquez, "Women Abroad: How to Get the Most from an International Assignment," May 31, 2012, www.theglasshammer.com/news/2012/05/31/women-abroad-%E2%80%93-how-to-get-the-most-from-an-international-assignment/, accessed July 17, 2014; "BGRS 2015 Global Mobility Trends Survey," http://www.bgrs.com/insights-articles/female-expatriates-continue-to-be-underrepresented/, accessed April 13, 2018.
67. For a good discussion of this, see Yochanan Altman and Susan Shortland, "Women and International Assignments: Taking Stock—A 25 Year Review," *Human Resource Management* 47, no. 2 (Summer 2008), pp. 199–216.
68. Susan Shortland, "The Purpose of Expatriation: Why Women Undertake International Assignments," *Human Resource Management*, 55, no. 4, July–August 2016, pp. 655–678.
69. Kathryn Tyler, "Don't Fence Her In," *HR Magazine*, 46, no. 3, March 2001, pp. 69–77.
70. Ibid.
71. See Nancy Napier and Sully Taylor, "Experiences of Women Professionals Abroad," *International Journal of Human Resource Management* 13, no. 5 (August 2002), pp. 837–851; Iris Fischlmayr, "Female Self-Perception as a Barrier to International Careers?" *International Journal of Human Resource Management* 13, no. 5 (August 2002), pp. 773–783; Wolfgang Mayrhofer and Hugh Scullion, "Female Expatriates in International Business: Evidence from the German Clothing Industry," *International Journal of Human Resource Management* 13, no. 5 (August 2002),

pp. 815–836; and Altman and Shortland, "Women and International Assignments."

72. See Donald Dowling Jr., "Choice of Law Contract Clauses May Not Fly Abroad," *Society for Human Resource Management Legal Report*, October-November 2008, pp. 1–2.
73. Jing Zhu et al., "Ups and Downs of the Expatriate Experience? Understanding Work Adjustment Trajectories and Career Outcomes," *Journal of Applied Psychology* 101, no. 4 (2016), pp. 549–568.
74. Quoted in Meredith Downes, Iris I. Varner, and Luke Musinski, "Personality Traits as Predictors of Expatriate Effectiveness: A Synthesis and Reconceptualization," *Review of Business* 27, no. 3 (Spring/Summer 2007), p. 16.
75. Deresky, p. 295.
76. Sunkyu Jun and James Gentry, "An Exploratory Investigation of the Relative Importance of Cultural Similarity and Personal Fit in the Selection and Performance of Expatriates," *Journal of World Business* 40, no. 1 (February 2005), pp. 1–8. See also Jan Selmer, "Cultural Novelty and Adjustment: Western Business Expatriates in China," *International Journal of Human Resource Management* 17, no. 7 (2006), pp. 1211–1222.
77. Hasuli Kumarika Perera et al., "A Psychological Contract Perspective of Expatriate Failure," *Human Resource Management* 56, no. 3 (May–June 2017), pp. 479–499.
78. Hung-Wen Lee and Ching-Hsing, "Determinants of the Adjustment of Expatriate Managers to Foreign Countries: An Empirical Study," *International Journal of Management* 23, no. 2 (2006), pp. 302–311.
79. M. Harvey et al., "Global Virtual Teams: A Human Resource Capital Architecture," *International Journal of Human Resource Management* 16, no. 9 (September 2005), pp. 1583–1599.
80. Eric Krell, "Budding Relationships," *HR Magazine* 50, no. 6 (June 2005), pp. 114–118. See also Jill Elswick, "Worldly Wisdom: Companies Refine Their Approach to Overseas Assignments, Emphasizing Cost-Cutting and Work-Life Support for Expatriates," *Employee Benefit News*, June 15, 2004, Item 0416600B.
81. Rita Pyrillis, "Quality Quandary," *Workforce,* February 2016, p. 17.
82. Eric Krell, "Budding Relationships," *HR Magazine* 50, no. 6 (June 2005), pp. 114–118. See also Jill Elswick, "Worldly Wisdom: Companies Refine Their Approach to Overseas Assignments, Emphasizing Cost-Cutting and Work-Life Support for Expatriates," *Employee Benefit News*, June 15, 2004, Item 0416600B.
83. Geoffrey Abbott et al., "Coaching Expatriate Managers for Success: Adding Value Beyond Training and Mentoring," *Asia-Pacific Journal of Human Resources* 44, no. 3 (December 2006), pp. 295–317.
84. Adapted from www.interchangeinstitute.org/html/cross_cultural.htm, accessed July 1, 2011.
85. https://www.communicaid.com/cross-cultural-training/managing-expatriate-staff/, accessed August 19, 2018.
86. https://global-lt.com/?s=living, accessed August 20, 2018.
87. Lynette Clemetson, "The Pepsi Challenge: Helping Ex-Pats Feel at Home," *Workforce Management*, December 2010, p. 36.
88. Ibid., p. 359. Some suggest adapting the training program to the cultures and values of the trainees. For example, ask whether the trainees come from a more individualistic or collectivist society because this may affect the degree to which you want training to be participatory versus nonparticipatory. Baiyin Yang, Yingchun Wang, and Anne Wang Drewry, "Does It Matter Where to Conduct Training? Accounting for Cultural Factors," *Human Resource Management Review* 19, no. 4 (2009), pp. 324–333. See also Laura Rodriguez-Costacamps, "Training Goes Global," *TD*, April 2016, pp. 38–42.
89. Donald Dowling Jr., "Export Codes of Conduct, Not Employee Handbooks," *Society for Human Resource Management Legal Report*, January/February 2007, pp. 1–4.
90. www.nytimes.com/2011/03/19/business/global/19blue.html, accessed June 30, 2011.
91. See, for example, "Managing International Assignments," SHRM, May 1, 2017, https://www.shrm.org/resourcesandtools/tools-and-samples/toolkits/pages/cms_010358.aspx, accessed April 13, 2018.
92. Ellen Ernst Kossek, et al., "Rating Expatriate Leader Effectiveness in Multisource Feedback Systems: Cultural Distance and Hierarchical Effects," *Human Resource Management* 56, no. 1 (January–February 2017), p. 165.
93. Joseph Martocchio, *Strategic Compensation* (Upper Saddle River, NJ: Pearson, 2006), pp. 402–403; Deresky, op cit, p. 305.
94. Deresky, op cit, p. 305.
95. "Expatriate Assignments in Growth Markets to Soar," *HR Magazine*, January 2013, p. 20.
96. https://aoprals.state.gov/content.asp?content_id=186&menu_id=81, accessed April 13, 2018.
97. Thomas Shelton, "Global Compensation Strategies: Managing and Administering Split Pay for an Expatriate Workforce," *Compensation & Benefits Review*, January/February 2008, pp. 56–59.
98. Ibid.; Helen Deresky, *International Management* (Boston: Pearson, 2017), p. 309.
99. www.erieri.com/SurveySources/International, accessed July 28, 2015.
100. Luis Hernandez, "On Why Ex-Pat Assignments Succeed—or Fail," *Harvard Business Review*, March 2011, p. 73.
101. For example, see Joseph Martocchio, *Strategic Compensation* (Boston: Pearson, 2017), pp. 313–314.
102. Mark Schoeff Jr., "Danger and Duty," *Workforce*, November 19, 2007, pp. 1, 3.
103. See, for example, "More Multinational Organizations Are Taking a Global Approach to Compensation," *Compensation & Benefits Review*, May/June 2008, p. 5.
104. Robin White, "A Strategic Approach to Building a Consistent Global Rewards Program," *Compensation & Benefits Review*, July/August 2005, p. 25.
105. "Recommendations for Managing Global Compensation Clause in a Changing Economy," Hewitt Associates, www.hewittassociates.com/_MetaBasicCMAssetCache_/Assets/Articles/2009/hewitt_pov_globalcomp_0109.pdf, accessed March 22, 2009.
106. White, "A Strategic Approach," pp. 23–40.
107. "Apple Supplier Workers Describe Noxious Hazards at China Factory," *Bloomberg News*, January 16, 2018, https://www.bloomberg.com/news/articles/2018-01-16/workers-at-apple-supplier-catcher-describe-harsh-conditions, accessed April 13, 2018.
108. Lisbeth Claus, "International Assignees at Risk," *HR Magazine*, February 2010, p. 73.
109. Jane Levere, "Putting Safety First," *The New York Times*, January 27, 2015, p. B4.
110. Fay Hansen, "Skirting Danger," *Workforce Magazine*, January 19, 2009, pp. 1, 3.
111. Based on Samuel Greengard, "Mission Possible: Protecting Employees Abroad," *Workforce*, August 1997, pp. 30–32. See also Z. Phillips, "Global Firms Consider Additional Cover for Overseas Execs," *Business Insurance* 43, no. 23 (June 15–22, 2009), pp. 4, 22.
112. http://travel.state.gov/content/passports/english/alertswarnings.html, accessed September 11, 2014.
113. Greengard, "Mission Possible," p. 32.
114. Jane Levere, "Putting Safety First," *The New York Times*, January 27, 2015, p. B4.
115. Deresky, p. 322.
116. Amy Gulati, "Protect Your Expat Investment with Effective Repatriation," SHRM, October 23, 2014, https://www.shrm.org/ResourcesAndTools/hr-topics/global-hr/Pages/Protect-Expat-Effective-Repatriation.aspx accessed April 13, 2018.
117. Ibid.
118. Deresky, *International Management*, p. 320.
119. Deresky, p. 324.
120. Amy Gulati, "Protect Your Expat Investment with Effective Repatriation," SHRM, October 23, 2014, https://www.shrm.org/ResourcesAndTools/hr-topics/global-hr/Pages/Protect-Expat-Effective-Repatriation.aspx, accessed April 13, 2018.
121. Leslie Klaff, "The Right Way to Bring Expats Home," *Workforce*, July 2002, p. 43.
122. Ibid.
123. Maria Kraimer et al., "The Influence of Expatriate and Repatriate Experiences on Career Advancement and Repatriate Retention," *Human Resource Management* 48, no. 1 (January–February 2009), pp. 27–47.
124. "Survey: Practitioners Say Methods at Global Employers Need Overhaul," *Bloomberg BNA Bulletin to Management*, December 17, 2013, p. 406.
125. "2014 Global Trends in Employee Engagement," Aon Hewitt, www.aon.com/attachments/human-capital-consulting/2014-trends-in-global-employee-engagement-report.pdf, accessed May 5, 2015.
126. Yaarit Silverstone, Claira Yang, Colin Sloman, and Susan Cantrell, "Trends Reshaping the Future of HR: Reconfiguring the Global Talent Landscape," *Top Trends That Will Reshape the Future of HR*, Accenture, www.Accenture.com/us-en/Pages/insight-future-HR.aspx, accessed March 6, 2015.
127. Hyundai Capital Selects Oracle HCM Cloud Solutions for Global HR Transformation," http://markets.businessinsider.com/news/stocks/hyundai-capital-selects-oracle-hcm-

cloud-solutions-for-global-hr-transformation-1011612997, accessed July 16, 2018; "Oracle Global Human Resources Cloud," https://cloud.oracle.com/en_US/global-human-resources-cloud/features, accessed April 12, 2018.
128. See, for example, https://hrdailywire.com/stories/511086653-bp-selects-workday-hcm-as-part-of-hr-modernization-efforts, accessed April 22, 2018.
129. "Hyundai Capital Utilizes Oracle HCM Cloud Solutions for Global HR Transformation"; "Nissan Expands Its Global HR System"; "BP Taps Workday to Support Global HR Modernisation"; "Oracle Global Human Resources Cloud."
130. Ibid.
131. Ann Marie Ryan et al., "Designing and Implementing Global Staffing Systems: Part 2—Best Practices," *Human Resource Management* 42, no. 1 (Spring 2003), pp. 85–94.
132. Ibid., p. 89.
133. Ibid., p. 90.
134. Ibid., p. 86. See also M. Schoeff, "Adopting an HR Worldview," *Workforce Management* 87, no. 19 (November 17, 2008), p. 8.
135. Ryan et al., "Designing and Implementing Global Staffing Systems," p. 87.
136. Ibid., p. 92.

Aleksei Gorodenkov/Alamy Stock Photo

Managing Human Resources in Small and Entrepreneurial Firms

LEARNING OBJECTIVES

When you finish studying this chapter, you should be able to:

18-1 **Explain** why HRM is important to small businesses and how small business HRM is different from that in large businesses.

18-2 **Give** four examples of how entrepreneurs can use Internet and government tools to support the HR effort.

18-3 **List** five ways entrepreneurs can use their small size to improve their HR processes.

18-4 **Discuss** how you would choose and deal with a professional employer organization.

18-5 **Describe** how you would create a start-up human resource system for a new small business.

San Francisco-based apparel company Everlane's strategy involves building its brand around ethical manufacturing and transparency in all they do.[1] For example their Web site shows photos of the factories abroad that make their clothes, they give voice to the factories' workers, and they list for every item its costs, so you can better judge the worth of what you're buying. A strategy like that requires a set of recruitment, selection, and compensation practices that fit. We'll see what they did.

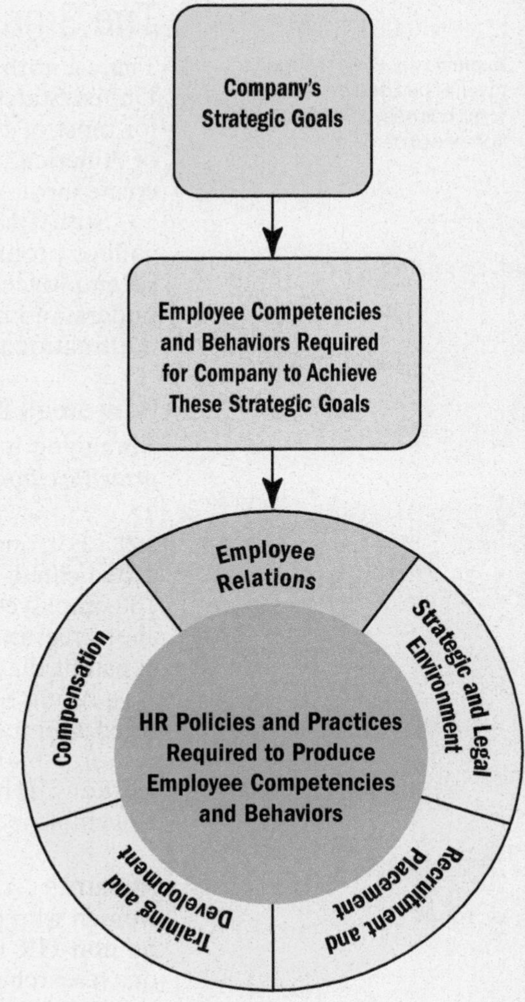

WHERE ARE WE NOW . . .

Small businesses have special human resource management needs. The main purpose of this chapter is to help you apply what you know about human resource management to running a small business. The main topics we'll address include **The Small Business Challenge; Using Internet, Government, and Other Tools to Support the HR Effort; Leveraging Small Size with Familiarity, Flexibility, Fairness, and Informality; Using Professional Employer Organizations;** and **Managing HR Systems, Procedures, and Paperwork.**

LEARNING OBJECTIVE 18-1

Explain why HRM is important to small businesses and how small business HRM is different from that in large businesses.

The Small Business Challenge

There's nothing small about *small business*. About half the people working in the United States today work for small firms.[2] Small businesses as a group also account for most of the 650,000 or so new businesses created every year,[3] as well as for most of America's business growth (small firms grow faster than big ones). And small firms create most of the new jobs in the United States.[4]

Statistically speaking, therefore, many (or most) people graduating from college probably do or will work for small businesses—firms with less than 200 or so employees. Anyone interested in human resource management thus needs to understand how managing human resources in small firms differs from that in huge multinationals.

How Small Business Human Resource Management Is Different

Managing human resources in small firms is different for four main reasons: *size, priorities, informality,* and the nature of the *entrepreneur*.

SIZE For one thing, it's unusual to find a business under 90 or so employees with a dedicated HR professional.[5] *As a rule*, it's not until a company reaches about 100 employees that it can afford an HR specialist. Yet even five- or six-person retail shops recruit, select, train, and pay employees. So, it's usually the owner or his or her assistant that does the HR tasks; the bookkeeper might handle payroll, for instance. As a result, SHRM found several years ago that even firms with under 100 employees often spend the equivalent of two or so people's time each year addressing human resource management issues.[6] Those hours usually come out of the owner's long workday. (However, about 10% of SHRM members work in firms with less than 100 employees, so there are exceptions.)[7]

PRIORITIES At the same time, business realities drive many entrepreneurs (the men and women who provide the vision and "spark" that starts a new business) to focus more on non-HR issues. After studying small e-commerce firms in the United Kingdom, one researcher concluded that, as important as human resource management is, it just wasn't a high priority for these firms:

> Given their shortage of resources in terms of time, money, people and expertise, a typical SME *[small- and medium-size enterprise]* manager's organizational imperatives are perceived elsewhere, in finance, production and marketing, with HR of diminished relative importance.[8]

INFORMALITY One effect of this is that human resource management tends to be more informal in smaller firms. Thus, one study analyzed training practices in about 900 family and nonfamily small companies.[9] Training tended to be informal, with an emphasis on methods like coworker and supervisory on-the-job training.

Such informality isn't just due to a lack of resources, it's a "matter of survival." Entrepreneurs must react fast to changing competitive conditions. So, there's logic in keeping things like compensation policies flexible. The need for small businesses to adapt quickly often means handling matters like raises, appraisals, and time off "on an informal, reactive basis with a short time horizon."[10]

THE ENTREPRENEUR *Entrepreneurs* are people who create businesses under risky conditions, and starting new businesses is always risky. Entrepreneurs therefore tend to be dedicated and visionary, and somewhat controlling. Researchers believe that small firms' informality partly stems from entrepreneurs' tendency to control things. For example, "Owners tend to want to impose their stamp and personal management style on internal matters, including the primary goal and orientation of the firm, its working conditions and policies, and the style of internal and external communication and how this is communicated to the staff."[11]

IMPLICATIONS This combination of small size, priorities, informality, and entrepreneurial tendencies can easily translate into several problems for a small firm's human resource management practices.[12]

- First, inadequate human resource practices may put small business owners at *legal risk*. For example, Outback Steakhouse long had no human resource department. That changed after an EEOC suit led Outback to pay a $19 million sex discrimination settlement. They hired an executive-level HR professional. Similar legal risks abound for violating Family Medical Leave Act regulations, and not paying for overtime hours worked, to name a few.
- Second, not having a dedicated HR person can *slow company decisions* and *overwhelm* its managers. After LRN Corp. eliminated its human resource department, tasks like hiring became convoluted as line managers tried to figure out what skills jobs required, and how to find and select the best people. Soon managers were pushing all these decisions up the ladder to the top manager.
- Third, without human resource information systems, paperwork is *time consuming*, and duplication may create *data entry errors*. Employee data (name, address, marital status, and so on) often appears on multiple human resource forms (medical enrollment forms, W-4 forms, and so on). Any personal data change then requires manually changing all forms. This is inefficient, and causes errors.
- Fourth, if the small business can't efficiently hire, train, appraise, and compensate employees, how will it compete with companies that can? It could be at a *competitive disadvantage*.

Diversity Counts: Necessity and the Entrepreneur

More men than women start new businesses, but according to one study, about 100 million women in 59 countries still started new businesses in one year.[13] Interestingly, most of the women who did start businesses were not in the developed world. The most likely countries for women to start businesses were in Latin America and sub-Saharan Africa. This may be because in developed economies, women have more career options. In developing economies such as Ghana, necessity infuses a confidence that drives more women to make it on their own. ■

Why HRM Is Important to Small Businesses

A small software start-up experienced turmoil when social media postings from one employee accused another of harassment. The moral, says one expert, is that start-ups can't assume that all they need is an employee handbook; they also need a functioning HR system.[14]

In fact, small firms with effective HR practices do better than those without them. For example, a study in the UK found a direct positive relationship between small companies' use of formal human resource practices and the companies' financial performance and labor productivity.[15] An earlier study focused on 168 family-owned high-growth small and medium-size enterprises (SMEs). The successful SMEs placed more emphasis on training and development, performance appraisal, recruitment packages, maintaining morale, and setting competitive compensation levels than did less successful ones.[16]

For many small firms, effective human resource management is also required for getting and keeping big customers. For example, to comply with international ISO-9000 quality standards, many large customers check that their small vendors follow the necessary HR standards.[17]

We devote this chapter to methods small business managers can use to improve their human resource management practices, starting with Internet and government tools.

LEARNING OBJECTIVE 18-2

Give four examples of how entrepreneurs can use Internet and government tools to support the HR effort.

Using Internet, Government, and Other Tools to Support the HR Effort

No small business need cede the "HR advantage" to big competitors. Knowledgeable small business managers can level the terrain by using Internet-based HR resources, including free online resources from the U.S. government. For example, the Small

Business Administration (SBA) provides (under Manage Your Business) a *Hire and Manage Employees* page, with a list of HR items to address.[18] Other useful sites include the following.

Government Tools for Complying with Employment Laws

Complying with federal (and state and local) employment law is a thorny issue for entrepreneurs. For example, the entrepreneur needs to know, "Must I pay this person overtime?" and, "Must I report this injury?"

Start by knowing which federal employment laws apply. For example, Title VII of the 1964 Civil Rights Act applies to employers with 15 or more employees, while the Age Discrimination in Employment Act of 1967 applies to those with 20 or more.[19] Small business owners will find the legal answers they need to answer questions like these online at federal agencies' Web sites.

DOL ONLINE ELAWS ADVISORS The U.S. Department of Labor provides "elaws Advisors" (such as its Health Benefits Advisor) for laws covering matters like pay and benefits, and health and safety. Using elaws Advisors is a bit like having an expert for advice, for example "is this employee exempt from overtime pay requirements?"[20] Thus, as in Figure 18-1 click "Begin FirstStep-Employment Law Overview Advisor Now." The wizard takes you through questions like "What best describes the nature of your business?"

Proceeding through the wizard, the owner arrives at "results." This says, "Based on the information you provided . . . the following employment laws administered by the Department of Labor (DOL) may apply to your business or organization."[21] Typically, these laws might include the Consumer Credit Protection Act, Employee

FIGURE 18-1 *FirstStep* Employment Law Advisor

Source: U.S. Department of Labor, https://webapps.dol.gov/elaws/firststep/, accessed August 24, 2018.

elaws® - *FirstStep* Employment Law Advisor

The *FirstStep* Employment Law Advisor helps employers determine which major Federal employment laws administered by the U.S. Department of Labor (DOL) apply to their business or organization, what recordkeeping and reporting requirements they must comply with, and which posters they need to post. The Advisor can help all employers, including non-profit organizations, private sector businesses and government agencies.

If employers already know which Federal employment laws apply to them, the Advisor can quickly provide basic information about how to comply with these laws, including the requirements for recordkeeping, reporting, and posters and other notices. This information can also be printed off as a reference guide.

This Advisor provides three basic starting points depending on your interests and needs:

- FirstStep - Employment Law Overview Advisor provides a short primer on each law's basic provisions as well as any related recordkeeping, reporting and notice requirements.
- FirstStep - Recordkeeping, Reporting, and Notices Advisor provides detailed explanations of each law's recordkeeping, reporting and notice requirements.
- FirstStep - Poster Advisor provides access to short descriptions of DOL poster requirements and links to printable posters.

Please note that the *FirstStep* Employment Law Advisor is intended as a guide on major DOL laws - it does not cover all laws administered by DOL. In addition, the system will not identify laws administered by other Federal agencies that might be applicable to your business or organization.

You may want to contact your State Labor Office to obtain information about your state's requirements, or other Federal agencies that enforce employment laws such as the Equal Employment Opportunity Commission (EEOC), the National Labor Relations Board (NLRB), and the National Mediation Board (NMB).

The *FirstStep* Employment Law Advisor is one of a series of **elaws** (Employment Laws Assistance for Workers and Small Businesses) Advisors developed by the U.S. Department of Labor (DOL) to help employers and employees understand their rights and responsibilities under Federal employment laws. To view the entire list of **elaws** Advisors please visit the elaws website.

Begin FirstStep - Employment Law Overview Advisor Now

Polygraph Protection Act, Fair Labor Standards Act, Immigration and Nationality Act, Occupational Safety and Health Act, Uniformed Services Employment and Reemployment Rights Act, and Whistleblower Act.

A linked DOL site (www.dol.gov/whd/flsa/index.htm) provides information on the Fair Labor Standards Act (FLSA).[22] It also contains several specific FLSA "elaws Advisors." Each provides practical guidance on questions such as when to pay overtime. Figure 18-2 presents, from this Web site, a list of elaws Advisors.[23]

EEOC ONLINE TOOLS The U.S. Equal Employment Opportunity Commission administers Title VII of the Civil Rights Act of 1964 (Title VII), the Age Discrimination in Employment Act of 1967 (ADEA), Title I of the Americans with Disabilities Act of 1990 (ADA), and the Equal Pay Act of 1963 (EPA). As the EEOC says, "While the information in this section of our website applies to all employers, it has been specifically designed for small businesses which may not have a human resources department or a specialized EEO staff" (www.eeoc.gov/employers). The site provides small business owners with practical advice. For example, "What should I do when someone files a charge against my company?" Its Web site (www.eeoc.gov/employers) contains important information regarding matters such as:

- How do I determine if my business is covered by EEOC laws?
- Who may file a charge of discrimination with the EEOC?
- Can a small business resolve a charge without undergoing an investigation or facing a lawsuit?

OSHA ONLINE TOOLS FOR SMALL BUSINESSES The DOL's Occupational Safety and Health Administration site (www.osha.gov) provides specific guidance and checklists for small business managers (see Figure 18-3). OSHA's site provides, among other things, easy

FIGURE 18-2 Sample DOL elaws Advisors

Source: U.S. Department of Labor, http://webapps.dol.gov/elaws/, accessed September 21, 2017.

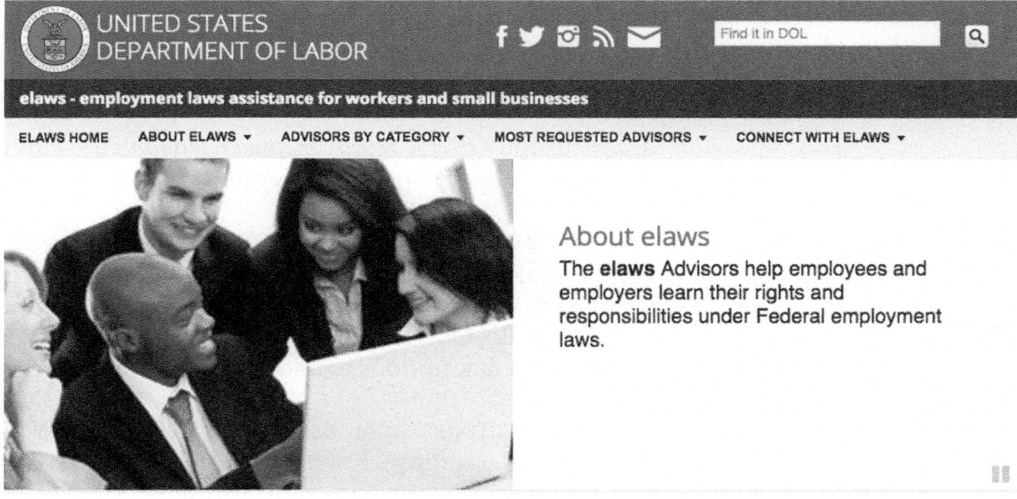

ELAWS ADVISORS BY CATEGORY

- Pay and Benefits
- Safety and Health
- Posters and Recordkeeping
- Youth Employment
- Veterans' Issues
- Federal Contractor
- Mining Industry
- All Advisors

MOST REQUESTED ELAWS ADVISORS

- Fair Labor Standards Act (FLSA) Advisor
- Family and Medical Leave Act (FMLA) Advisor
- *FirstStep* Poster Advisor
- Veterans' Preference Advisor
- Uniformed Services Employment and Reemployment Rights Act (USERRA) Advisor

ALL ELAWS ADVISORS

- Disability Nondiscrimination Law Advisor
- Drug-Free Workplace Advisor
- ERISA Fiduciary Advisor
- Family and Medical Leave Act (FMLA) Advisor
- Medical and Disability Related Leave Advisor
- MSHA Online Forms Advisor
- MSHA Training Plan Advisor
- MSHA Fire Suppression and Fire Protection Advisor

FIGURE 18-3 OSHA Small Business Web Site

Source: U.S. Department of Labor, https://www.osha.gov/dcsp/smallbusiness/index.html.

access to the *OSHA Small Business Handbook*. This contains practical information, including industry-specific safety and accident checklists.

Online Employment Planning and Recruiting Tools

Online tools can make small business owners as effective as their large competitors at writing job descriptions and recruiting applicants. For example, as we saw in Chapter 4 (Job Analysis), O*NET (http://online.onetcenter.org) enables business owners to create accurate job descriptions and job specifications quickly.

ONLINE RECRUITING Small business owners can also use the online recruiting tools in Chapter 5 (Recruiting). For example, it's easy to scour LinkedIn.com, and to post jobs on Careerbuilder.com, and on professional associations' job boards. Similarly, the best applicant tracking software does more than track job candidates.[24] They also automatically post open jobs to job Web sites. Some, like Bullhorn (www.bullhorn.com/) post jobs to social media sites including LinkedIn, Twitter, and Facebook.

TRENDS SHAPING HR: *DIGITAL AND SOCIAL MEDIA*[25]

Many small businesses use social media to recruit applicants. For example, LinkedIn lets employers post job openings and facilitates business networking. One recruiter reportedly looks for LinkedIn members who have compelling summaries, excellent recommendations, and memberships in industry groups. On Twitter, recruiters see if a potential candidate has an appropriate username and photos. But also check Twitter for things like the person's status updates and retweets, to see (for instance) if he or she shares useful information. Small business recruiters should also focus on the social media that makes sense for them. For example, if you're looking for a Facebook marketing expert, look on Facebook. Or look for a photographer on Instagram. And on Facebook and LinkedIn, focus recruiting efforts on industry groups that make sense for your company. Check to see how your competitors use social media, and which communities they use.

Social media recruiting entails risks. For example, conversing with someone whose Facebook profile reveals their ethnic background could expose the employer to a discrimination suit if that applicant isn't hired. And many agree that at the end of the day, social media recruiting can't substitute for in-person interactions. ■

Small Business Employee Selection Tools

Some tests are so easy to use they're particularly helpful for small firms. One is the *Wonderlic Personnel Test* (www.wonderlic.com/), which measures general mental ability. With questions somewhat similar to the SAT, it takes less than 15 minutes to administer. The tester reads the instructions, and keeps time as the candidate works through the 50 problems. The tester scores the test by totaling the number of correct answers. Comparing the person's score with the minimum scores recommended for various occupations shows whether he or she achieved the minimum score for the job in question.

The *Predictive Index* is another example. It measures work-related personality traits, drives, and behaviors—in particular, dominance, extroversion, patience, and blame avoidance. A template makes scoring simple. The Predictive Index program includes 15 standard benchmark personality patterns. For example, there is the "social interest" pattern, for a person who is generally unselfish, congenial, persuasive, patient, and unassuming. This person would be a good personnel interviewer, for instance.

Many vendors, including Wonderlic and Predictive Index, offer online applicant testing and screening services. Wonderlic's service (which costs about $9,000 per year for a small firm) first provides job analyses for the employer's jobs. Wonderlic then provides a Web site the small business applicants can log into to take one or several selection tests. It will also help set up a testing procedure.

Some other small business recruiting and selection suggestions would include

- ***Don't forgot the obvious.*** Sometimes the easiest way to get good candidates is a "Help Wanted" sign on the door.

aodaodaodaod/Shutterstock

Use online tests, for instance, to test an applicant's typing speed proficiency at Quickbooks, or even ability to sell over the phone.

- ***Keep it local, and in the industry.*** Use online job boards that target a particular industry or city to minimize irrelevant applicants.[26] For example, Jobing.com maintains city-specific job sites in over 19 states.[27] Smartrecruiters.com[28] lists dozens of job boards for specific industries or types of jobs, such as Dice.com for technical professionals (go to www.smartrecruiters.com, then Marketplace, then Job Boards).
- ***Test online.*** Use online tests, for instance, to test an applicant's proficiency at QuickBooks, or even at selling over the phone. Vendors include (as a small sample) IBM's Kenexa, eskill.com/, selectivehiring.com, and berkeassessment.com.[29]
- ***Poll your contacts.*** Tap friends and employees for recommendations, and use social networking sites such as LinkedIn. One employer says, "I get people vouching for each applicant, so I don't have to spend hours sorting through résumés."[30]
- ***Send a recording.*** InterviewStream is one of several vendors that records online video interviews for about $30 to $60.[31] It sends the candidate an e-mail invitation with a link. When he or she clicks the link, a video interviewer asks the company's prerecorded questions. Hiring managers can review the videos at their leisure.[32]

The following feature shows how one company recruits employees.

IMPROVING PERFORMANCE: *THE STRATEGIC CONTEXT*

Everlane

Everlane's strategy builds its brand around ethical manufacturing and transparency. For example, ethical manufacturing meant they spent months finding a factory to make their new jeans in Vietnam, choosing it because it recycles 98% of the water used in denim manufacturing. Everlane's Web site lists the material and labor costs of each item they sell.[33]

A strategy like that requires recruitment, selection, and compensation practices that fit, so when Everlane decided to emphasize transparency in its hiring no one was surprised. For example, they recently started recruiting job candidates by having them submit 60- to 90-second Snapchat stories, to show why they're a good candidate for Everlane. The idea is to create the story, tweet Everlane your snap code, and save the story before 24 hours run out, and mail it to Everlane.

A big reason they use social media to recruit is that it's likely to attract people who are already following Everlane. It seems to be working. For example, candidates are sending those Snapchat stories, taking them step-by-step through their presentations. That way, Everlane is getting applications from already engaged prospective employees for whom the company's goals resonate. Similarly, Everlane's career Web site page addresses itself to "rule breakers, questioners, and straight A students who skipped out of class." The site's also forthright in laying out Everlane's basic values, such as "everyone can, and should, make a difference," and "the ethical choice is the right one." The result of such recruiting is that Everlane is building a team that's deeply engaged in the company's values and goals.

MyLab Management Talk About It 1

If your professor has assigned this, go to the Assignments section of **www.pearson.com/mylab/management** to complete this discussion question. What other tools and techniques discussed in this chapter would you recommend Everlane use, and why?

Small Business Training Tools

Small companies can't compete with the training resources of giants like Google. However, as explained in Chapter 7 (Training), online training can provide employee training that used to be beyond most small employers' reach. Online sources (see Chapter 7) range from private vendors (such as www.PureSafety.com and www.skillsoft.com) to the small business administration (www.sba.gov/sitemap) and the National Association of Manufacturers (NAM). The buyer's guide from the Association for Talent Development (www.td.org/) lists many vendors (check under Resources).[34] Online learning platforms like Docebo's (www.docebo.com/) make it easy for a company's employees to access off-the-shelf and customized online learning courses and programs.[35]

Employment Appraisal and Compensation Online Tools

Small employers have easy access to computerized and online appraisal and compensation services. For example, Oracle Corporation's ePerformance[36] lets managers formalize the employee's goals and then assess progress toward meeting those goals. The eAppraisal system from Halogen Software[37] is another example. SAP Success Factors (www.successfactors.com/en_us.html) provides particularly effective performance management assistance. It facilitates assigning and monitoring goals, helps management provide feedback to employees, and makes it easy to review goal attainment as part of performance appraisal.[38]

Similarly, lack of easy access to high-priced salary surveys once made it difficult for small businesses to adjust their pay scales. Today, sites like www.salary.com and www.Glassdoor.com make it easy to determine local and national pay rates. Benefits administration packages, as from Zenefits (www.zenefits.com/), make it easy for employees to register for benefits, and to access their insurance and benefits information.[39]

Employment Safety and Health Tools

Average injury rates for small businesses are somewhat lower than in big companies.[40] However, most people work for small businesses, so that's still a huge number of total accidents. Small business managers should have a command of the tools and techniques in Chapter 16 (Safety). As also explained there, OHSA provides free services for small employers.[41] These include free on-site safety services for small businesses, and the OSHA Sharp program, a process through which OSHA certifies that small employers have achieved commendable levels of safety awareness.[42]

LEARNING OBJECTIVE 18-3
List five ways entrepreneurs can use their small size to improve their HR processes.

Leveraging Small Size with Familiarity, Flexibility, Fairness, and Informality

Because small businesses need to capitalize on their strengths, it makes sense for them to capitalize on their smallness when dealing with employees. For example, smallness can mean more personal *familiarity* with each employee's strengths, needs, and family situation. And it can mean being *flexible* and *informal* in its human resource management policies and practices.[43]

Simple, Informal Employee Selection Procedures

In addition to online recruitment and selection tools,[44] small business managers shouldn't forget simple, low-tech selection aids. For example, the Work Sampling Test we explained in Chapter 6 involves having the candidate show how he or she would actually do one of the job's tasks—such as a marketing candidate spending 30 minutes outlining an ad for a product. The accompanying HR Tools feature presents a more informal selection interview procedure the small business manager may find useful.

IMPROVING PERFORMANCE: *HR TOOLS FOR LINE MANAGERS AND SMALL BUSINESSES*

A Streamlined Interviewing Process[45]

The small business owner, pressed for time, may use the following practical, streamlined employment interview process.[46] One way to do so is to focus on four basic required factors: knowledge and experience, motivation, intellectual capacity, and personality. To proceed this way, interviewing expert John Drake suggests asking the following questions:

✓ **Knowledge and experience.** What must the candidate know to perform the job? What experience is necessary to perform the job? For example, ask a combination of situational questions plus open-ended questions to probe the candidate's suitability for the job, such as, "How would you organize such a sales effort?" or "How would you design that kind of Web site?"

- ✓ **Motivation.** What should the person like doing to enjoy this job? Is there anything the person should not dislike? Are there any essential goals or aspirations the person should have? For example, probe such areas as the person's likes and dislikes (for each thing done, what he or she liked or disliked about it).
- ✓ **Intellectual capacity.** Are there any specific intellectual aptitudes required (mathematical, mechanical, and so on)? How complex are the problems the person must solve? What must a person be able to demonstrate intellectually? For example, ask questions that judge such things as complexity of tasks the person has performed, and grades in school.
- ✓ **Personality.** What are the critical personality qualities needed for success on the job (ability to withstand boredom, decisiveness, stability, and so on)? How must the job incumbent handle stress, pressure, and criticism? What kind of interpersonal behavior is required in the job? For example, probe by looking for self-defeating behaviors (aggressiveness, compulsive fidgeting, and so on) and by exploring the person's past interpersonal relationships, such as leading the work team on the last job. Is the candidate personable? Shy? Outgoing?

How to Organize the Interview

- ✓ Have a plan. Devise and use a plan to guide the interview. Drake says that significant areas to touch on include the candidate's:
  - ✓ College experiences
  - ✓ Work experience—summer, part-time
  - ✓ Work experience—full-time (one by one)
  - ✓ Goals and ambitions
  - ✓ Reactions to the job you are interviewing for
  - ✓ Self-assessments (by the candidate of his or her strengths and weaknesses)
  - ✓ Military experiences
  - ✓ Present outside activities[47]
- ✓ Follow your plan. Start with an open-ended question for each topic, such as "Could you tell me about what you did in college?" Then probe for information about the person's knowledge and experience, motivation, intelligence, and personality.

Match the Candidate to the Job

You should now be able to draw conclusions about the person's knowledge and experience, motivation, intellectual capacity, and personality, and to summarize the candidate's strengths and limits. This should provide a rational basis for matching the candidate to the job—one based on the traits and aptitudes the job actually requires. ■

> MyLab Management Talk About It 2
>
> If your professor has assigned this, go to the Assignments section of **www.pearson.com/mylab/management** to complete these discussion questions. List two situational questions (what would you do . . . ?) and two behavioral questions (what did you do . . . ?) that you might ask to unearth insights into the candidate's motivation.

Flexibility in Training

Two things characterize training in small businesses. First, small businesses focus on what the training will do *for their bottom lines*, rather than how employees may benefit.[48] (Similarly, they focus management development on teaching specific firm-related skills, such as how to sell the firm's products).[49]

Second, a study several years ago in Europe found that small firms were also *relatively informal* in how they trained employees.[50] This probably isn't surprising, since (as explained in Chapter 8), training experts estimate that on average about 70% of all training is in fact "informal."

ENCOURAGING INFORMAL TRAINING Given the importance of informal learning, small business managers should take steps to encourage and facilitate it.

Several things contribute to building an environment in which informal learning thrives. Informal learning occurs when employees *have something they need to learn*, are *motivated to learn it*, and are given *the opportunity to learn*.[51] Informal learning tends to take place as *a by-product of employees' other activities*, and so usually occurs during day-to-day conversations, networking, and through teamwork and mentoring.[52] (To paraphrase one expert, workers learn more over coffee than they do taking courses.)[53] The best informal learning also tends to be *goal directed*, as when a manager who needs to recruit an engineer asks LinkedIn group colleagues how to do so; informal learning is thus often *triggered by something at work* that motivates the employee to initiate an informal learning interaction.[54] And, informal learning occurs best where employees know that top *management encourages and supports* such learning.[55]

Given all this, the small business owner can do several things to encourage and facilitate informal learning. These include

- Make it clear that you encourage employees to learn on the job, particularly when they're faced with a work problem.[56]
- Make high-quality content available. For example, while much on the Internet is free, sometimes the job-relevant content for your company requires a subscription; if so, provide such subscriptions.[57]
- Encourage supervisors to provide informal learning through coaching.[58]
- Offer to cover tuition for special classes.[59]
- Identify online training opportunities.[60]
- Encourage and facilitate (for instance, through a dedicated page on the company intranet) the sharing of best practices.[61]
- Send employees to special seminars and meetings for learning and networking.[62]
- Provide plenty of opportunities for informal learning at work, such as chalkboards at worksites and lunch areas.

Flexibility in Benefits and Rewards

The Family and Work Institute surveyed the benefits practices of about 1,000 small and large companies.[63] Not surprisingly, they found that large firms offer more *extensive* benefits packages than do smaller ones. For example, larger employers offered more wellness programs, and asked their employees to pay a smaller share of health premiums than did small firms, on average.

However, small firms offered more flexibility. For example, employees at small employers (50–99 employees) were more likely than large employers (1,000 or more employees) to (1) take time off during the workday to attend to important family or personal needs without loss of pay; (2) have control over when to take breaks; and (3) periodically change starting and quitting times within some range of hours.[64]

Some small businesses also "discovered how to turn tiny into tight-knit, earning employees' trust by keeping them in the loop on company news and financials, and their loyalty by providing frequent feedback on performance." [65] For example, ID Media, with 90 employees, gives all new employees a welcome breakfast on their first day.[66]

Wards Furniture in Long Beach, California, further illustrates this. Many of its 17 employees have been with the firm for 10 to 20 years. Brad Ward, an owner, attributes this partly to his firm's willingness to adapt to its workers' needs. For example, workers can share job responsibilities and work part-time from home. As a result, Wards Furniture is a good example of using small size to create valuable work–life benefits such as extra time off, compressed workweeks, schedule flexibility, and recognition for employees.

Here are other examples of what Wards and other small employers can offer:[67]

- ***Extra time off.*** For example, Friday afternoons off in the summer.
- ***Compressed workweeks.*** For example, compressed summer workweeks.
- ***Bonuses at critical times.*** Small business owners are more likely to know what's happening in their employees' lives. Use this knowledge to provide special bonuses, for instance, if an employee has a new baby.

At Wards Furniture, workers can share job responsibilities and work part-time from home.

Thomas Barwick/DigitalVision/Getty Images

- ***Flexibility.*** For example, "If an employee is having a personal problem, help create a work schedule that allows the person to solve problems without feeling like they're going to be in trouble."[68]
- ***Sensitivity to employees' strengths and weaknesses.*** The small business owner should stay attuned to his or her employees' strengths, weaknesses, and aspirations. For example, give them an opportunity to train for and move into the jobs they desire.
- ***Help them better themselves.*** For example, pay employees to take a class to help them develop their job skills.
- ***Feed them.*** Provide free meals occasionally, perhaps by taking your employees to lunch.
- ***Make them feel like owners.*** For example, give employees input into major decisions, let them work directly with clients, get them client feedback, share company performance data with them, and let them share in the company's financial success.
- ***Make sure they have what they need to do their jobs.*** Having motivated employees is only half the challenge. Also ensure they have the necessary training, procedures, computers, and so on.
- ***Constantly recognize a job well done.*** Capitalize on your day-to-day interactions with employees to "never miss an opportunity to give your employees the recognition they deserve."[69]

SIMPLE RETIREMENT BENEFITS About the same percentage of small firms (93%) as large ones (98%) offer defined contribution 401(k) plans, but more large firms (35%) offer *defined benefits* plans than do small firms (15%).[70]

An easy way for small businesses to provide retirement benefits is through a SIMPLE IRA plan.[71] With the SIMPLE (for Savings Incentive Match Plan for Employees) IRA, employers must (and employees may) make contributions to traditional employee IRAs. These plans are for employers or small businesses with 100 or fewer employees and no other retirement plan.

SIMPLE IRAs are inexpensive and easy. The owner contacts an eligible financial institution and fills out several IRS forms.[72] Most banks, mutual funds, and insurance companies that issue annuity contracts are generally eligible.[73] The plan has very low administrative costs. Employer contributions are tax deductible.[74] A typical employer contribution might match employee contributions dollar for dollar up to 3% of pay. The financial institution usually handles the IRS paperwork and reporting.

Fairness and the Family Business

Most small businesses are "family businesses," since the owner (and often some employees) are family members.

Being a nonfamily employee here isn't easy. The tendency is to treat family and nonfamily employees differently. If so, as one writer puts it, "It's a sure bet that their lower morale and simmering resentments are having a negative effect on your operations and sapping your profits."[75] Differential treatment of nonfamily versus family employees is so widespread that it is an area of small business research. Two experts suggest family business owners follow a four-step program to ensure fairness.[76]

- First, the family *commits* to the idea that all employees, family and nonfamily, should be treated fairly and consistently.[77] Work hard to avoid "any appearance that family members are benefiting unfairly from the sacrifice of others."[78] Avoid "any behavior that would lead people to the conclusion that they are demanding special treatment in terms of assignments or responsibilities."[79]
- Second, the family *communicates* their commitment that all employees are entitled to fair practices.[80]
- Third, before they sign on, all employees must know that they can "freely and safely" *discuss and report* perceived unfair decisions.[81] Particularly inform management applicants as to whether they will have potential for promotion. Make the expectations clear, regarding matters such as the authority the person will have and can attain.[82]
- Fourth, have a *committee* that meets monthly to correct any alleged unfair decision voiced by family or nonfamily employees.[83]

LEARNING OBJECTIVE 18-4

Discuss how you would choose and deal with a professional employer organization.

Using Professional Employer Organizations

As we explained in Chapter 13 (Benefits), many small business owners—pressed for time and concerned about the legal pitfalls of personnel blunders—opt to outsource all or most of their human resource functions to vendors. These vendors go by the names *professional employer organizations* (PEOs), *human resource outsourcers* (HROs), or sometimes *employee* or *staff leasing firms*.

How Do PEOs Work?

PEOs range from specialized payroll companies to ones that handle all an employer's human resource management needs.

In determining which personnel tasks to outsource, the small business manager has many choices. At a minimum, these firms take over the employer's payroll tasks. Usually, however, PEOs shoulder most of the employer's human resources chores. By transferring the client firm's employees to the PEO's payroll, PEOs become co-employers of record for the employer's employees. The PEO can then fold the client's employees into the PEO's insurance and benefits program, usually at a lower cost.[84] The PEO usually handles employee-related activities such as recruiting, hiring (with client firms' supervisors' approvals), and payroll and taxes. PEO companies like Paychex (www.paychex.com/) provide payroll, tax, and benefits processing but also handle recruiting and training. Oasis Outsourcing (www.oasisadvantage.com/) can handle the full human resource process for very small companies, ranging from recruitment through selection, training, appraisal, and compensation. ADP total source (https://totalsource.adp.com/ts/logout.do) handles payroll processing for thousands of employers, but can also manage the entire HR process, even including initial candidate interviews.[85]

Most PEOs focus on smaller employees, often those with under 100 employees (although some handle clients of 5,000 employees or more).[86] They typically charge fees of 2% to 4% of a company's payroll; alternatively, some charge monthly per-employee fees of $40-$125, depending on the services they provide.[87]

Why Use a PEO?

Some small business owners turn to PEOs to avoid the sorts of personnel-related problems we itemized earlier in this chapter. These were: (1) inadequate human resource practices may put small business owners at *legal risk*; (2) not having a dedicated HR person can slow down company decision making and overwhelm its managers; (3) without human resource information systems, paperwork duplication is time consuming and creates *data entry errors*; and (4) if the small business can't efficiently hire, train, appraise, and compensate employees, it may find itself at a *competitive disadvantage*.

INSURANCE AND BENEFITS However *insurance and benefits* are often the big PEO attraction. Getting health and other insurance is often a problem for smaller firms. That's where employee leasing comes in. The PEO absorbs the client firm's employees as its own. That often enables the PEO to offer larger benefits packages more cheaply than a small business could get on its own.

CAVEATS There are several potential downsides to PEOs. Many employers view their human resource management practices (like training new engineers) as strategic, and aren't inclined to turn them over to outsiders (let alone accept having outsiders be their employees' legal employer). Furthermore, the fact that your (former) employees get their health insurance through the PEO has cons as well as pros.[88] For example, if the PEO goes out of business, its small business clients may scramble to replace their insurance. And if the PEO decides to switch insurance plans, your own employees may not be pleased with the new health providers. There can also be some tax disadvantages, although 2014's Small Business Efficiency Act reduces these. Figure 18-4 summarizes guidelines for finding and working with PEOs.

FIGURE 18-4 Guidelines for Finding and Working with PEOs

Source: Based on Robert Beck and J. Starkman, "How to Find a PEO That Will Get the Job Done," *National Underwriter* 110, no. 39 (October 16, 2006), pp. 39, 45; Lyle DeWitt, "Advantages of Human Resource Outsourcing," *The CPA Journal* 75, no. 6 (June 2005), p. 13; www.peo.com/dmn, accessed April 28, 2008; Layne Davlin, "Human Resource Solutions for the Franchisee," *Franchising World* 39, no. 10 (October 2007), p. 27; and see, for example, www.adp.com/solutions/employer-services/totalsource/what-is-a-peo.aspx, accessed September 24, 2015.

Employers should choose and manage the PEO relationship carefully. Guidelines for doing so include:

- *Conduct a needs analysis.* Know ahead of time exactly what human resource concerns your company wants to address.
- *Review the services* of all PEO firms you're considering. Determine which can meet all your requirements.
- *Determine if the PEO is accredited.* There is no rating system. However, the Employer Services Assurance Corporation of Little Rock, Arkansas (https://www.esac.org/), imposes higher financial, auditing, and operating standards on its members. Also check the National Association of Professional Employer Organizations (www.NAPEO.org), and www.PEO.com.
- Check the provider's bank, credit, insurance, and professional references.
- Understand how the *employee benefits will be funded*. Is it fully insured or partially self-funded? Who is the carrier? Confirm that employers will receive first-day coverage.
- See if under the contract the PEO assumes the *compliance liabilities in the applicable states*.
- *Review the service agreement carefully.* Are the respective parties' responsibilities and liabilities clear?
- Investigate how long the *PEO has been in business*.
- *Check out the prospective PEO's staff. Do they seem to have the expertise to deliver on its* promises?
- Ask, *how will the firm deliver its services?* In person? By phone? Via the Web?
- Ask about upfront fees and how these are determined.
- *Periodically get proof that payroll taxes and insurance premiums are being paid properly* and that any legal issues are handled correctly.

MyLab Management Apply It!

How does a small company actually carry out its human resource management tasks? If your professor has assigned this activity, go to the Assignments section of **www.pearson.com/mylab/management** to complete the video exercise.

What Is the Alternative?

If it does not want to use a PEO, what should the small business do? Most owners simply handle it all themselves. Some retain HR-savvy consultants who provide, on an hourly basis, the knowledgeable assistance in job analysis, recruiting, selection, and other matters that the small business owner needs. The advent of new HR software that provides services including applicant tracking, automatic recruitment ad placement, online selection testing, and performance management, plus employee data management is another smart option.[89] The following section looks closer at such software systems.

LEARNING OBJECTIVE 18-5

Describe how you would create a start-up human resource system for a new small business.

Managing HR Systems, Procedures, and Paperwork

Introduction

Consider the paperwork required to run a five-person retail shop. Just to start with, recruiting and hiring an employee might require a help wanted advertising listing, an employment application, an interviewing checklist, various verifications—of education and immigration status, for instance—and a telephone reference checklist. You then might need an employment agreement, confidentiality and noncompetition agreements, and an employer indemnity agreement. To process the new employee you might need a background verification, a new employee checklist, and forms for withholding tax and to obtain new employee data. And to keep track of the employee once on board, you'd need—just to start—a personnel data sheet, daily and weekly time records, an hourly employee's weekly time sheet, and an expense report. Then come all the performance appraisal forms, a disciplinary notice, an employee orientation record, separation notice, and employment reference response.

In fact, this list barely scratches the surface of the policies, procedures, and paperwork you'll need to run the human resource management part of your business. Perhaps with just one or two employees you could track everything in your head, or just write a separate memo for each HR action, placing it in a folder for each worker. But with more employees, you'll need a human resource system comprised of standardized forms. Then as the company grows, you'll computerize various parts of the HR system—payroll, or appraising, for instance.

Basic Components of Manual HR Systems

Very small employers (say, with 10 employees or less) may start with a manual human resource management system. In practice, this generally means obtaining and organizing a set of standardized personnel forms covering each aspect of the HR process—recruitment, selection, training, appraisal, compensation, safety—as well as some means for organizing all this information for each of your employees.

The number of forms you would conceivably need even for a small firm is quite large, as the illustrative list in Table 18-1 shows.[90] One simple way to obtain a manual system's basic forms is from Web sites (such as www.hr.com/en/free_forms/) or books or CDs that provide compilations of HR forms.[91] The forms can then be adapted from these sources for your particular situation. Office supply stores also sell packages of personnel forms. For example, Office Depot sells packages of personnel forms such as: Application, Employment Interview, Reference Check, Employee Record, Performance Evaluation, Warning Notice, Exit Interview, and Vacation Request, plus a Lawsuit-Prevention Guide.[92] Also available is a package of Employee Record Folders. Use the folders to maintain a file on each individual employee; on the outside of the pocket is printed a form for recording name, start date, company benefits, and so on.

TABLE 18-1 Some Important Employment Forms

New Employee Forms	Current Employee Forms	Employee Separation Forms
Application	Employee Status Change Request	Retirement Checklist
New Employee Checklist	Employee Record	Termination Checklist
Employment Interview	Performance Evaluation	COBRA Acknowledgment
Reference Check	Warning Notice	Unemployment Claim
Telephone Reference Report	Vacation Request	Employee Exit Interview
Employee Manual Acknowledgment	Probation Notice	
Employment Agreement	Job Description	
Employment Application Disclaimer	Probationary Evaluation	
Employee Secrecy Agreement	Direct Deposit Acknowledgment	
	Absence Report	
	Disciplinary Notice	
	Grievance Form	
	Expense Report	
	401(k) Choices Acknowledgment	
	Injury Report	

OTHER SOURCES Numerous direct-mail catalog companies also sell HR materials. For example, HRdirect (www.hrdirect.com) offers packages of personnel forms.[93] These include, for instance, Short- and Long-Form Employee Applications, Applicant Interviews, Employee Performance Reviews, Job Descriptions, Exit Interviews, and Absentee Calendars and Reports. There are also various legal-compliance forms, including standardized Harassment Policy and FMLA Notice forms, as well as posters (for instance, covering legally required postings for matters such as the Americans with Disabilities Act and Occupational Safety and Health Act) available.

Automating Individual HR Tasks

As the small business grows, it becomes impractical to rely on manual HR systems. It is at this point that most small to medium-sized firms begin computerizing individual human resource management tasks.

HR in Action at the Hotel Paris Lisa had managed to install several separate information systems, such as for performance appraisals. However, as she discussed one day over lunch with the CFO, these systems were not integrated. To see how she handled this, see the case on page 611 of this chapter.

PACKAGED SYSTEMS[94] Web sites such as www.capterra.com/ itemize HR software available from vendors such as Zenefits, Halogen TalentSpace, Fairsail HRIS, and Cezanne HR.[95] These vendors provide software solutions for virtually all personnel tasks, ranging from benefits management to compensation, compliance, employee relations, outsourcing, payroll, and time and attendance systems.

HRdirect sells software packages for monitoring attendance, employee record keeping, writing employee policy handbooks, and conducting computerized employee appraisals. The sites www.hrdirect.com, www.effortlesshr.com, and others offer software and online solutions for writing employee policy manuals, maintaining employee records (including name, address, marital status, number of dependents, emergency contact and phone numbers, hire date, and job history), writing performance reviews, creating job descriptions, tracking attendance and hours worked for each employee, employee scheduling, writing organizational charts, managing payroll, conducting employee surveys, scheduling and tracking employee training activities, and managing OSHA compliance, often cloud-based.[96]

Human Resource Information Systems (HRIS)

As the company grows, a more comprehensive and integrated system becomes advisable. We can define a Human Resource Information System (HRIS) as human resource software that unifies HR management processes such as applicant tracking, hiring, training, performance management, benefits administration, and payroll into one automated system.[97] *PC Magazine* recently listed several top HR software packages; they include Gusto (https://gusto.com/) BambooHR (www.bamboohr.com/), Namely (www.namely.com/), Sage Business Cloud People (www.sagepeople.com/), Kronos Workforce (www.kronos.com/), and SAP Success Factors (www.successfactors.com/).[98]

As an example, Bamboo HR handles personnel tasks including *applicant tracking* (including automatically sending *recruitment* ads to job boards), employee *time off tracking, HR reporting* (in terms of detailed reports on employment levels, and so on), online employee *self on boarding*, and *performance management* in terms of tracking goals and helping managers appraise subordinates based on those goals.[99] As with Bamboo HR, there are several benefits to be gained by installing an HRIS. The first is improved transaction processing.

Improved Transaction Processing

The day-to-day minutiae of maintaining and updating employee records take an enormous amount of time. Small businesses therefore first adopt HR software packages to manage their personal records. And, by interacting with the company's employee database, these packages also produce employment data-related trend graphs and reports on personnel metrics such as turnover and compensation costs. *PC Magazine* recently rated BambooHR as an "Editor's choice" for these tasks.[100]

Online Self-Processing

HR information systems also facilitate employee self-processing. For example, with systems like that from Zenefits (www.zenefits.com), "[n]ew hires can self-enroll in medical, dental and vision benefits during onboarding, and employees can easily sign up during open enrollment."[101] Zenefits' system also facilitates employees signing up for Flexible Spending Accounts: It "makes enrolling a snap, issues all plan participants a debit card, and allows employees to track and manage their funds through our online dashboard."[102]

Improved Reporting Capability

By integrating numerous individual HR tasks (training records, appraisals, employee personal data, and so on), the HRIS improves HR's reporting capabilities. For example, reports might be available (company-wide and by department) for health-care cost per employee, pay and benefits as a percent of operating expense, cost per hire, report on training, volunteer turnover rates, turnover costs, time to fill jobs, and return on human capital invested (in terms of training and education fees, for instance).

HR System Integration

Because the HRIS's software components (record keeping, payroll, appraisal, and so forth) are integrated, they enable the employer to reengineer its HR function. For example, Oracle's PeopleSoft's HRIS[103] electronically routes salary increases, transfers, and other e-forms through the organization to the proper managers for approval. As one person signs off, it's routed to the next. If someone forgets to process a document, a smart agent issues reminders. The HRIS thus automates what might otherwise be a time-consuming manual process.

HRIS Vendors

Many firms today offer HRIS packages. Capterra.com, mentioned earlier, lists many vendors. The Web site for the International Association for Human Resource Information Management (www.ihrim.org) lists vendors such as Automatic Data Processing, Inc., Business Information Technology, Inc., Human Resource Microsystems, Lawson Software, Oracle Corporation, SAP America, Inc., and many other HRIS vendors. *PC Magazine* provides annual HR Software "Editor's Choice" lists.[104]

There are several practical considerations in choosing a software vendor.[105] For example, does the software provide *software-as-a-service* (SAaS) capability, or must it be kept and managed on the company's in-house servers? Does the package provide an intuitive user interface? Can you integrate it with your existing HR systems? And (particularly if it's stored in the cloud), security—mainly protecting personal data—is essential.

TRENDS SHAPING HR: *DIGITAL AND SOCIAL MEDIA*

HR on the Cloud

Most suppliers of human resource management systems, such as ADP, Kronos, Oracle, and SAP, offer cloud-based systems. Particularly for small business owners, the advantages of cloud systems are that the vendors can easily update them with the latest features—saving the small business owner much time and expense—and that the owner and employees can access the information anywhere they are.[106]

BambooHR illustrates an HR system especially designed for small and medium-sized businesses (www.bamboohr.com). This system enables authorized managers and employees to securely and remotely access company information on matters like time off and personal information, and to produce reports and/or follow trends on the system's customizable dashboards. It was also designed to be integrated with compatible applications, so it can be integrated with the small business's existing payroll systems, applicant tracking systems, benefits enrollment systems, and performance review systems.[107]

As another example, many employers outsource benefits administration to cloud-based services offered by firms like Zenefits. A new employee uses his or her laptop or smartphone to access the Zenefits Web site. He or she can then input personal information and sign documents via a touchscreen, and register for specific benefits.[108] ■

Chapter Review

Chapter Section Summaries

18-1. Many people reading this book will work for or own their own small businesses, so it's important to understand the **small business challenge.** Without effective human resource management, small business owners run the risk that they'll be at a competitive disadvantage or that without the necessary HR expertise they may commit mistakes that lead to litigation.

18-2. Being small, small businesses can particularly capitalize on freely available **Internet and government tools to support their HR efforts.** For example, you can use Department of Labor elaws Advisors to answer overtime questions, the EEOC's Web sites for answers on questions like "How can we resolve the charge?" and the Department of Labor's OSHA Web site to review, for instance, your small business handbook. To better compete, small business owners can also use online recruiting tools like those we discussed in Chapter 5 and training programs available online from companies such as PureSafety.

18-3. Small businesses need to capitalize on their strengths, and in this case, it means capitalizing on **familiarity, flexibility, and informality.** For example, be flexible about extra time off, compressed workweeks, and job enrichment. They can also use relatively informal but still effective employee selection procedures such as a work-sampling test. Informal training methods include online training opportunities, encouraging the sharing of best practices among associates, and sending employees to seminars. Because small businesses are often family businesses, it's important to treat nonfamily members fairly.

18-4. After reviewing all the challenges of managing human resources, many small business owners turn to **using professional employer organizations.** Also called *human resource outsourcers or employee* or *staff leasing firms*, these firms generally transfer the client firm's employees to the PEO's own payroll and thus become the employer of record for the employer's employees.

18-5. Small business managers need to understand how their **HR systems, procedures, and paperwork** will evolve. At first, there may be a simple manual human resource management system, for instance, with employee records compiled on forms from office supply companies and maintained in manual files. The employer then may purchase one or more packaged systems for automating individual HR tasks, for instance, such as applicant tracking and performance appraisal. As companies grow, they will look to integrate the separate systems with a human resource information system.

Discussion Questions

18-1. How and why is HR in small businesses different than that in large firms?

18-2. Explain why HRM is important to small businesses.

18-3. Explain and give at least five examples of ways entrepreneurs can use small size—familiarity, flexibility, and informality—to improve their HR processes.

18-4. Describe with examples how you would create a start-up, paper-based human resource system for a new small business.

Individual and Group Activities

18-5. Form teams of five or six persons, each with at least one person who owns or has worked for a small business. Based on their experiences, make a list of the "inadequate-HR risks" the business endured, in terms of competitive disadvantage, lack of specialized HR expertise, workplace litigation, compensation laws compliance, and paperwork/data-entry errors.

18-6. You own a small business, and you are confused about which of your employees is eligible for overtime pay. The employees in question include your secretary, two accounting clerks, one engineer, and two inside salespeople. Individually or in groups of four or five students, use the DOL's Overtime Security Advisor and DOL's Calculator to determine who gets overtime pay.

18-7. You have about 32 employees working in your factory. Working individually or in teams of four or five students, find and create a list of five online sources you could use to provide training to them, at no cost to you or to them.

18-8. Appendices A and B at the end of this book (pages 614–634) list the knowledge someone studying for the HRCI (Appendix A) or SHRM (Appendix B) certification exam needs to have in each area of human resource management (such as in Strategic Management and Workforce Planning). In groups of several students, do four things: (1) review Appendix A and/or B; (2) identify the material in this chapter that relates to the Appendix A and/or B required knowledge lists; (3) write four multiple-choice exam questions on this material that you believe would be suitable for inclusion in the HRCI exam and/or the SHRM exam; and (4) if time permits, have someone from your team post your team's questions in front of the class, so that students in all teams can answer the exam questions created by the other teams.

KNOWLEDGE BASE

Experiential Exercise

Building an HRIS

Written and copyrighted by Gary Dessler, PhD.

Purpose: The purpose of this exercise is to give you practice in creating a human resource management system (HRIS).

Required Understanding: You should be fully acquainted with the material in this chapter.

How to Set Up the Exercise/Instructions: Divide the class into teams of several students. Each team will need access to the Internet.

Assume that the owners of a small business come to you with the following problem. They have a company with less than 40 employees. They have been taking care of all HR paperwork informally, mostly on slips of paper and with memos. They want you to supply them with a human resource management information system—how computerized it is will be up to you, but they can only afford a budget of $5,000 upfront (not counting your consulting), and then about $500 per year for maintenance. You know from your HR training that there are various sources of paper-based and online systems. Write a two-page proposal telling them exactly what your team would suggest, based on its accumulated existing knowledge, and from online research.

Application Case

Netflix Breaks the Rules[109]

Written and copyrighted by Gary Dessler, PhD.

Why did Netflix survive as a start-up when the dot-com bubble burst in the late 1990s? Probably because, from the day he started Netflix, founder Reed Hastings believed in breaking the rules. His direct-to consumer mail and video streaming business model certainly helped Netflix to survive. But the firm's unorthodox human resource management practices helped the company to attract and keep the high producers who design the products that are the firm's lifeblood. Hastings knew that top Silicon Valley workers could choose where they worked, and high pay is pretty much standard throughout the Valley's industries. How to set oneself apart? Hastings and his start-up colleagues believed that a culture that balanced a flexible work environment with few constraints and high responsibility was the answer. They called the policy "Freedom and Responsibility."

Just how unorthodox are the Netflix HR practices? Consider this: As a Netflix professional you get unlimited vacations. One engineer takes 5-week vacations to Europe, because he likes (as he says) to take his time off in big chunks. (An HR officer must approve time off in excess of 30 days annually.) As a Netflix employee, your pay isn't tied to performance appraisals, or even to a compensation plan. Frequent market salary surveys and pay hikes keep everyone's pay aligned with Silicon Valley competitors'. Each employee decides whether to take his or her pay in cash or in Netflix stock. Options vest immediately. Netflix doesn't recruit much at college job fairs, instead hiring mostly highly experienced professionals. There's no training, professional development, or career planning at Netflix (except for legally required training, such as diversity training). You're in charge of your own career.

But with freedom like that comes responsibilities. The company expects its salaried employees to work hard—to "do the jobs of three or four people," as one report put it. And Netflix doesn't have the "frat party" free-wheeling atmosphere that many dot-coms do. It's an adult environment. Netflix does not coddle underperformers. Yearly 360-degree performance reviews provide "direct and honest feedback." Those that aren't cutting it are quickly let go, but (whenever possible) amicably. Rather than the sorts of litigiousness that often characterize dismissals in other firms (having to prove the person was incompetent, for instance), Netflix writes a check. The company believes that a handsome severance payment helps maintain the person's dignity, makes it easier for supervisors to make tough calls with underperformers, and, of course, minimizes blowback from those it dismisses. It's more like a "no-fault divorce," as one observer put it.

Questions

In many respects, the Netflix HR strategy seems like a dream come true for small businesses. You don't need a pay plan; instead, you just update each person's pay every few months based on market surveys. You offer no training and development. And you don't track vacation time, more or less. If someone's not doing well, you just pay him or her to leave, with no hassles. Netflix seems to have hit upon its own version of "Netflix High-Performance Work Practices." Given that, answer the following questions (please be specific).

18-9. What (if anything) is it about Netflix that makes its HR practices work for it?

18-10. Would you suggest using similar practices in other businesses, such as, say, a new restaurant? Why?

18-11. List the criteria you would use for deciding whether another company is right for Netflix-type HR practices.

18-12. What argument would you make in response to the following: "Netflix just lucked out; they'd have done even better with conventional HR practices."

Continuing Case

Carter Cleaning Company

Written and copyrighted by Gary Dessler, PhD.

Cleaning in Challenging Times

As the economic downturn worsened a few years ago, revenues at the Carter stores fell steeply. Many of their customers were simply out of work and didn't need (or couldn't afford) dry cleaning. The Carters actually found themselves giving away some free cleaning services. They started a new program wherein existing customers could get one suit or dress cleaned free each month if they needed it for a job interview.

In the midst of this downturn, the Carters knew they had to get their employment costs under control. The problem was that, realistically, there wasn't much room for cutting staffing in a store. Of course, if a store got very slow, they could double up by having a cleaner/spotter spend some time pressing, or having the manager displace the counter person. But if sales only fell 15% to 20% per store, there really wasn't much room for reducing employee head count because each store never employed many people in the first place.

The question, therefore, naturally arose as to whether the Carters could cut their employment expenses without dismissing too many people. Jennifer Carter has several questions for you.

Questions

18-13. Assume that we don't want to terminate any of our employees. What work-scheduling-related changes could we make that would reduce our payrolls by, say, 20% per week but still keep all our employees on board?

18-14. We are currently handling most of our personnel-related activities, such as sign-ons, benefits administration, and appraisals, manually. What specific suggestions would you have for us in terms of using software systems to automate our HR processes?

18-15. Suggest at least five free Internet-based sources we could turn to for helping us to lower our total employment costs.

Translating Strategy into HR Policies and Practices Case*,§

**The accompanying strategy map for this chapter is in MyLab Management; the overall map on the inside back cover of this text outlines the relationships involved.*

Improving Performance at the Hotel Paris

The New HRIS

The Hotel Paris's competitive strategy is "To use superior guest service to differentiate the Hotel Paris properties, and to thereby increase the length of stay and return rate of guests, and thus boost revenues and profitability." HR manager Lisa Cruz must now formulate functional policies and activities that support this competitive strategy and boost performance by eliciting the required employee behaviors and competencies.

Challenging economic times in the past few years brought the drawbacks of the Hotel Paris's relatively small size into sharp relief. Large chains like Marriott had vast online reservations capabilities with huge centralized systems that easily and economically handled reservations requests from throughout the world. By comparison, the Hotel Paris still handled reservations much as hotels did 15 years ago, either with separate Web sites for each of their hotel locations, e-mail, or an 800 number.

Their human resource management information systems were similarly primitive. Lisa had managed to install several separate information systems, such as for performance appraisals. However, as she discussed one day over lunch with the CFO, the HR systems were not integrated. Therefore, if an employee changed his or her name, for instance, through marriage, people in Lisa's office had to execute all those name changes manually on all the various employee rosters and benefits plans.

This lack of integration was bad enough in boom times, but was worse as the economy soured. The CFO pointed out to her that the amount of money they were spending on human resource management administration was about 30% higher than it was at larger chains such as Marriott. He understood that large size brings economies of scale. But he believed there had to be something they could do to reduce the cost of administering human resource management.

Lisa's solution was to get the CFO's approval to have several software consulting firms including IBM, Accenture, and Oracle provide proposals for how to integrate the hotel's HR information systems. After getting the CFO's and CEO's approval, they contracted with one vendor and installed the system.

Questions

18-16. Using any benchmark data that you can find, including information from this book, what are some benchmark metrics that Lisa could be using to assess the efficiency of her human resource management operations? To what extent does the Hotel Paris's quality service orientation enter into how Lisa's metrics should compare?

18-17. Throughout this book, we've discussed various specific examples of how human resource management departments have been reducing the cost of delivering their services. Keeping in mind the Hotel Paris's quality service orientation, please list and explain with examples how Lisa Cruz could use at least five of these.

18-18. Focusing only on human resource information systems for a moment, what sorts of systems would you suggest Lisa consider recommending for the Hotel Paris? Why?

18-19. Explain with detailed examples how Lisa can use free online and governmental sources to accomplish at least part of what you propose in your previous answers.

18-20. Give three examples of fee-based online tools you suggest Lisa use.

18-21. Based on what you read in this chapter of Dessler, *Human Resource Management*, do you suggest Lisa use a PEO? Why?

§ Written and copyrighted by Gary Dessler, PhD.

Writing Assignments

18-22. Explain and give at least four examples of how entrepreneurs can use Internet and government tools to support the HR effort.

18-23. This chapter explained that to compete with larger employers, the small business owner should capitalize on familiarity, flexibility, and informality. What does this mean, and how as a small business owner would you do that?

MyLab Management Try It!

How would you apply the concepts and skills you learned in this chapter? If your professor has assigned this activity, go to the Assignments section of **www.pearson.com/mylab/management** to complete the simulation.

PERSONAL INVENTORY ASSESSMENTS

Go to **www.pearson.com/mylab/management** to complete the Personal Inventory Assessment related to this chapter.

Endnotes

1. Elizabeth Segran, "For Building the Next-Gen Clothing Brand," *Fast Company*, March/April 2018, pp. 79–81; Jessica Schiffer, "The New Ways Fashion Companies Are Recruiting in 2016," http://www.whowhatwear.com/social-media-recruiting-in-fashion; www.glassdoor.com; www.Everlane.com/careers; Cady Lang, "This Company Actually Wants You to Snapchat Your Job Application," http://time.com, all URLs accessed April 17, 2018.
2. Historically, most U.S. employees have worked for small employers with fewer than 100 workers. However, around 2005 that changed. Today somewhat more employees work for larger employers (2,500 or more) than for small ones. Theo Francis, "Why You Probably Work for a Giant Company," *The Wall Street Journal*, April 7, 2017, p. A-10. As a rough rule, depending on the business, the SBA defines small business as less than 500 employees, or less than $7.5 million in sales: www.sba.gov/blogs/how-and-why-determine-if-your-business-small, accessed May 19, 2018. The SBA has an online tool for determining if a particular business qualifies as small: https://www.sba.gov/tools/size-standards-tool\?ms=nid4788, accessed May 19, 2018.
3. See, for example, https://www.bls.gov/bdm/entrepreneurship/entrepreneurship.htm, accessed April 17, 2017.
4. http://www.nber.org/digest/feb11/w16300.html, accessed May 4, 2017.
5. See, for example, Peter Hausdorf and Dale Duncan, "Firm Size and Internet Recruiting in Canada: A Preliminary Investigation," *Journal of Small-Business Management* 42, no. 3 (July 2004), pp. 325–334. SHRM found the average HR professional per 100 employees in businesses up to 250 employees was 3.54; however, that figure may be skewed by the higher HR/employee ratio in firms over 100 employees. https://www.shrm.org/ResourcesAndTools/business-solutions/Documents/Organizational%20Staff%20Size.pdf, accessed April 15, 2018.
6. *SHRM Human Capital Benchmarking Study 2009*, Society for Human Resource Management, p. 12, www.shrm.org/research/surveyfindings/articles/documents/09-0620_human_cap_benchmark_full_fnl.pdf, accessed July 17, 2014.
7. Mark Feffer, "Lessons from HR Departments of One: Small but Mighty, HR Departments of One Share How They Manage It All—and Prove Their Value in the Process," SHRM, November 1, 2015, https://www.shrm.org/hr-today/news/hr-magazine/pages/1115-hr-department-of-one.aspx, accessed April 15, 2018.
8. Graham Dietz et al., "HRM inside UK E-commerce Firms," *International Small Business Journal* 24, no. 5 (October 2006), pp. 443–470.
9. Bernice Kotey and Cathleen Folker, "Employee Training in SMEs: Effect of Size and Firm Type—Family and Nonfamily," *Journal of Small-Business Management* 45, no. 2 (April 2007), pp. 14–39.
10. Dietz et al., "HRM inside UK E-commerce Firms."
11. Ibid. See also Noam Wasserman, "Planning a Start-Up? Seize the Day . . . Then Expect to Work All Night," *Harvard Business Review* 87, no. 1 (January 2009), pp. 27.
12. Based on Kathy Williams, "Top HR Compliance Issues for Small Businesses," *Strategic Finance* (February 2005), pp. 21–23; and Lauren Weber and Rachel Feintzeig, "Companies Say No to Having an HR Department," *The Wall Street Journal*, April 9, 2014, https://www.wsj.com/articles/companies-say-no-to-having-an-hr-department-1396994461, accessed April 15, 2018.
13. "Entrepreneurs: The Gender Gap," https://diversitywoman.com/entrepreneurs-the-gender-gap, accessed April 20, 2013.
14. Evelyn Rusli, "Torment Claims Make GitHub Grow Up," *The Wall Street Journal*, July 18, 2014, pp. B1, B5.
15. Yanqing Lai, et al., "Human Resource Practices, Employee Attitudes and Small Firm Performance," *International Small Business Journal*, April 2016.
16. Dawn Carlson et al., "The Impact of Human Resource Practices and Compensation Design on Performance: An Analysis of Family-Owned SMEs," *Journal of Small Business Management* 44, no. 4 (October 2006), pp. 531–543. See also Jake Messersmith and James Guthrie, "High Performance Work Systems in Emergent Organizations: Implications for Firm Performance," *Human Resource Management* 49, no. 2 (March–April 2010), pp. 241–264.
17. Dietz et al., "HRM inside UK E-commerce Firms." See also, Diana Wicks, "Checklist of Audit Questions for ISO Internal Audits of Human Resources," http://smallbusiness.chron.com/checklist-audit-questions-iso-internal-audits-human-resources-12265.html, accessed July 30, 2015.
18. https://www.sba.gov/business-guide/manage-your-business/hire-manage-employees, accessed April 16, 2018.
19. www.eeoc.gov/employers/overview.html, accessed February 10, 2008.
20. http://webapps.dol.gov/elaws/firststep/, accessed May 4, 2017.
21. See, for example, http://webapps.dol.gov/elaws/firststep/results.htm?fs=AA0000000C0YYY0 0000NNNNNN00000000NY, accessed May 4, 2017.
22. https://www.dol.gov/whd/flsa/index.htm, accessed May 4, 2017.
23. http://webapps.dol.gov/elaws/, accessed May 4, 2017.
24. Michelle Rafter and Juan Martinez, "The Best HR Software of 2018," January 2018, https://www.pcmag.com/article2/0,2817,2492792,00.asp, accessed April 15, 2018.
25. "Six Common Mistakes Small Businesses Make When Incorporating Social Media into Their Recruiting Efforts," www.roberthalf.us/SocialMediaRecruitingMistakes; Rieva Lesonsky, "Find the Perfect Hire by Tapping into Social Media," *Employment Trends*, January 30, 2013, http://smallbiztrends.com/2013/01/3-ways-find-perfect-hire-social-media.html; and Emily Bennington, "Social Media Recruitment: Social Media Platforms and Your Next Hire," http://hiring.monster.com/hr/hr-best-practices/small-business/social-media-trends/social-media-recruitment.aspx, all accessed April 20, 2013.
26. Daren Dahl, "Recruiting: Tapping the Talent Pool . . . Without Drowning in Resumes," *Inc.* 31, no. 3 (April 2009), pp. 121–122.
27. Jobing.com, accessed May 4, 2017.
28. https://www.smartrecruiters.com/blog/best-50-niche-job-boards/, accessed April 15, 2018.
29. For example, https://www.berkeassessment.com/, accessed May 4, 2017.
30. Dahl, op. cit.
31. http://interviewstream.com/, accessed May 4, 2017.
32. Ibid.
33. Segran, "For Building the Next-Gen Clothing Brand"; Schiffer, "The New Ways Fashion Companies Are Recruiting in 2016"; Lang, "This Company Actually Wants You to Snapchat Your Job Application."
34. http://webcasts.td.org/sites, accessed May 4, 2017.
35. Rafter and Martinez, "The Best HR Software of 2018."
36. www.oracle.com/us/products/applications/peoplesoft-enterprise/hcm-resource-library/051027.pdf, accessed April 15, 2018.
37. www.halogensoftware.com/products/halogen-eappraisal, accessed August 17, 2013.
38. Rafter and Martinez, "The Best HR Software of 2018."
39. Ibid.
40. https://www.bls.gov/iif/oshsum.htm#16Quartile_Data, accessed April 15, 2018.
41. https://www.osha.gov/dcsp/smallbusiness/consult.html, accessed April 15, 2018.
42. https://www.osha.gov/dcsp/smallbusiness/sharp.html, accessed May 4, 2017.
43. Dietz et al., "HRM inside UK E-commerce Firms."
44. Adrienne Fox, "McMurray Scouts Top Talent to Produce Winning Results," *HR Magazine* 51, no. 7 (July 2006), pp. 57.
45. Based on John Drake, *Interviewing for Managers: A Complete Guide to Employment Interviewing* (New York, AMACOM, 1982).
46. This is based on John Drake, *Interviewing for Managers: A Complete Guide to Employment Interviewing* (New York: AMACOM, 1982).
47. Ibid.
48. See, for example, Yin Bai, Jiajian Yuan, and Jingzhou Pan, "Why SMEs in Emerging Economies Are Reluctant to Provide Employee Training: Evidence from China," *International Small Business Journal: Researching Entrepreneurship* 3,5nNo 6 (September 2017), p. 751+.
49. See, for example, Essi Saru, "Organizational Learning and HRD: How Appropriate Are They for Small Firms?" *Journal of European Industrial Training* 31, no. 1 (January 2007), pp. 36–52.
50. Colin Gray and Christopher Mabey, "Management Development: Key Differences between Small and Large Businesses in Europe," *International Small Business Journal* 23, no. 5 (October 2005), pp. 467–485.
51. Megan LeClus, "Informal Learning in the Workplace: A Review of the Literature," ECU Publications, 2011, http://ro.ecu.edu.au/cgi/viewcontent.cgi?article=1152&context=ecuworks2011, accessed April 15, 2018.
52. Ibid.
53. Francisco J. Garcia-Penalvo, Ricardo Colomo-Palacios, and Miltiadis D. Lytras, "Informal Learning in Work Environments: Training with the Social Web in the Workplace," *Behaviour and Information Technology* 1, no. 3 (March 2012), pp. 1–3.
54. Saul Carliner, "7 Informal Learning Lessons," *Training*,

https://trainingmag.com/trgmag-article/7-informal-learning-lessons, accessed April 15, 2018.
55. Ibid.
56. Ibid.
57. Ibid.
58. Ibid.
59. From Stephen Covey, "Small Business, Big Opportunity," *Training* 43, no. 11 (November 2006), p. 40 www.Trainingmag.com. Used by permission from Lakewood Media Group.
60. Ibid.
61. Ibid.
62. Ibid.
63. "National Study of Employers," 2016, https://www.shrm.org/hr-today/trends-and-forecasting/research-and-surveys/Documents/National%20Study%20of%20Employers.pdf, accessed April 15, 2018.
64. Ibid.
65. Kira Bindrum, "Little Firms Redefine Culture of Work," *Crain's New York Business* 25, no. 49 (December 7–13, 2009), p. 20.
66. Ibid., pp. 7–13.
67. These are from Ty Freyvogel, "Operation Employee Loyalty," *Training Media Review*, September–October 2007.
68. Ibid.
69. Ibid.
70. "National Study of Employers," 2016, https://www.shrm.org/hr-today/trends-and-forecasting/research-and-surveys/Documents/National%20Study%20of%20Employers.pdf, accessed April 15, 2018.
71. See, for example, https://www.irs.gov/retirement-plans/choosing-a-retirement-plan-simple-ira-plan, accessed April 18, 2018.
72. Forms are accessed at https://www.irs.gov/retirement-plans/establishing-a-simple-ira-plan, accessed April 15, 2018.
73. https://www.irs.gov/retirement-plans/establishing-a-simple-ira-plan,accessed April 15, 2018.
74. Ibid. www.irs.gov/Retirement-Plans/Plan-Sponsor/SIMPLE-IRA-Plan, accessed August 17, 2013.
75. Phillip Perry, "Welcome to the Family," *Restaurant Hospitality* 90, no. 5 (May 2006), pp. 73, 74, 76,78. Used by permission from Phillip Perry.
76. Georges Samara and Daniel Arenas, "Practicing Fairness in the Family Business Workplace," *Business Horizons* 60 (2017), pp. 647–655.
77. Ibid.
78. Perry, "Welcome to the Family." Used by permission from Phillip Perry.
79. Ibid.
80. Samara and Arenas, "Practicing Fairness in the Family Business Workplace."
81. Ibid.
82. Perry, "Welcome to the Family." Used by permission from Phillip Perry.
83. Samara and Arenas, "Practicing Fairness in the Family Business Workplace."
84. Layne Davlin, "Human Resource Solutions for the Franchisee," *Franchising World* 39, no. 10 (October 2007), pp. 27–28.
85. Rebecca Baldrige, "Best HR Outsourcing for Small Business in 2018," *Inc.*, October 3, 2017.
86. For example, see https://www.insperity.com/, accessed April 16, 2018.
87. http://thehro.com/; http://www.employeeleasingquotes.com/what-are-the-costs; https://fitsmallbusiness.com/professional-employer-organization-peo/; all accessed April 16, 2018.
88. See, for example, https://www.paycom.com/our-solution/, accessed April 16, 2018.
89. For example, see, www.paycom.com/our-solution/, accessed April 16, 2018.
90. For a more complete list, see, for example, Sondra Servais, *Personnel Director* (Deerfield Beach, FL: Made E-Z Products, 1994); www.hr.com/en/free_forms/, accessed September 10, 2012; and www.entrepreneur.com/formnet/hrcareers.html, accessed September 10, 2012.
91. www.hr.com/en/free_forms, accessed May 4, 2017.
92. www.officedepot.com/a/browse/business-forms-tax-forms-andrecordkeeping/N=5+516208/;jsession id=0000zlVADjXrV18WJcAFM0Ped0:13ddq0u44, accessed May 4, 2017.
93. www.hrdirect.com, accessed May 4, 2017.
94. www.ihrim.org, accessed April 28, 2008; www.pmihrm.com/hr_software_vendors.html, accessed July 18, 2014.
95. www.capterra.com/human-resource-software/, accessed July 30, 2015.
96. See, for example, www.effortlesshr.com/hr-software/online-employee-management-software and www.capterra.com/human-resource-software, both accessed July 18, 2014.
97. As an example, see https://www.zenefits.com/blog/whats-value-hris/, accessed April 16, 2018.
98. Rafter and Martinez, "The Best HR Software of 2018."
99. "Bamboo HR overview," www.bambooHR.com/.
100. Rafter and Martinez, " The Best HR Software of 2018."
101. https://www.zenefits.com/benefits/insurance/, accessed April 16, 2018.
102. https://www.zenefits.com/benefits/, accessed April 16, 2018.
103. http://www.oracle.com/us/products/applications/peoplesoft-enterprise/overview/index.html, accessed April 16, 2018.
104. Rafter and Martinez, "The Best HR Software of 2018."
105. Ibid.
106. www.comparehris.com/BambooHR and www.bamboohr.com/tour.php, both accessed May 4, 2015; Sarah Fister Gale, "Hey, You, Get onto My Cloud . . . ," *Workforce*, August 2014, pp. 44–45.
107. "HR Execs Trade Notes on Human Resource Information Systems," *BNA Bulletin to Management*, December 3, 1998, p. 2. See also Ali Velshi, "Human Resources Information," *The Americas Intelligence Wire*, February 11, 2004.
108. Eric Newcomer, "This Time, It's HR Getting Fired," *Bloomberg Businessweek*, May 25–May 31, 2015, pp. 31–33.
109. Copyright Gary Dessler, PhD, 2011; based on information in Michelle Conlin, "Netflix: Flex to the Max," September 24, 2007, www.businessweek.com/magazine/content/07_39/b4051059.htm, accessed July 3, 2011; Robert J. Grossman, "Tough Love at Netflix," April 1, 2010, www.shrm.org/Publications/hrmagazine/EditorialContent/2010/0410/Pages/0410grossman3.aspx, accessed July 3, 2011; and David F. Larcker, Allan McCall, and Brian Tayan, "Equity on Demand: The Netflix Approach to Compensation," January 15, 2010, http://hbr.org/product/equity-on-demand-the-netflix-approach-to-compensat/an/CG19-PDF-ENG, accessed July 3, 2011.

APPENDIX A

HRCI's PHR® and SPHR® Certification Body of Knowledge

ABOUT THE HR CERTIFICATION INSTITUTE PHR AND SPHR BODY OF KNOWLEDGE

The HRCI PHR (Professional in Human Resources) and SPHR (Senior Professional in Human Resources) exams are created using the Institute's PHR and SPHR Body of Knowledge, which outlines the responsibilities of, and knowledge needed by, today's HR professional. The PHR and SPHR Body of Knowledge is updated periodically to ensure it is consistent with current practices in the HR field. All questions appearing on the exams are linked to the Body of Knowledge's responsibility and knowledge statements. The HRCI organizes its PHR and SPHR Body of Knowledge into six functional areas (such as Functional Area 01: Business Management and Strategy), each listing various responsibilities and knowledge statements. For brevity, we list just the required knowledge items here, alongside the corresponding chapters in this book that address each particular knowledge area. To see the entire Body of Knowledge (including responsibilities), please go to certification-handbook at HRCI.org.

You'll find two numbers after each functional area heading. The first number is the percentage of the PHR exam that is about that topic. The second number is the percentage of the SPHR exam that is about that topic.

Functional Area 01: Business Management and Strategy (PHR: 11%, SPHR: 30%)

Developing, contributing to and supporting the organization's mission, vision, values, strategic goals and objectives; formulating policies; guiding and leading the change process; and evaluating organizational effectiveness as an organizational leader.

ADDRESSED IN THIS BOOK IN CHAPTER(S):	KNOWLEDGE OF	
1, 3	01	The organization's mission, vision, values, business goals, objectives, plans and processes
2, 11, 14, 15, 16, and Know Your Employment Law features in Chapters 2–16	02	Legislative and regulatory processes
1, 3, strategic Hotel Paris cases in Chapters 3–18 with in-chapter call-outs, "strategic" chapter openers, and Improving Performance: The Strategic Context features in most chapters	03	Strategic planning process, design, implementation and evaluation
1, 3	04	Management functions, including planning, organizing, directing and controlling
12, 14	05	Corporate governance procedures and compliance (for example: Sarbanes–Oxley Act)
1, 3, 5	06	**SPHR only* Due diligence processes (for example: M&A, divestitures)

Addressed in this book in chapter(s)	No.	Knowledge of
1, 3, 5	07	**SPHR only* Transition techniques for corporate restructuring, M&A offshoring and divestitures
	08	Elements of a cost-benefit analysis during the life cycle of the business (such as scenarios for growth, including expected, economic stressed and worst-case conditions) and the impact to net worth/earnings for short-, mid- and long-term horizons
3, 11,14	09	Business concepts (for example: competitive advantage, organizational branding, business case development, corporate responsibility)
3, 14, 16, 18	10	Business processes (for example: operations, sales and marketing, data management)

Functional Area 02: Workforce Planning and Employment (PHR: 24%, SPHR: 17%)

Developing, implementing and evaluating sourcing, recruitment, hiring, orientation, succession planning, retention and organizational exit programs necessary to ensure a workforce's ability to achieve the organization's goals and objectives.

ADDRESSED IN THIS BOOK IN CHAPTER(S):		KNOWLEDGE OF
2, 4, 5, 6, 7, and Know Your Employment Law features in Chapters 1–14	11	Applicable federal laws and regulations related to workforce planning and employment activities (for example: Title VII, ADA, EEOC Uniform Guidelines on Employee Selection Procedures, Immigration Reform and Control Act)
3, 4, 5, 6, and HR as a Profit Center features in Chapters 1–14	12	Methods to assess past and future staffing effectiveness (for example: costs per hire, selection ratios, adverse impact)
5	13	Recruitment sources (for example: employee referral, social networking/social media) for targeting passive, semi-active and active candidates
5	14	Recruitment strategies
1, 5	15	Staffing alternatives (for example: outsourcing, job sharing, phased retirement)
3, 4, 5	16	Planning techniques (for example: succession planning, forecasting)
2, 6, 7	17	Reliability and validity of selection tests/tools/ methods
6	18	Use and interpretation of selection tests (for example: psychological/personality, cognitive, motor/physical assessments, performance, assessment center)
6	19	Interviewing techniques (for example: behavioral, situational, panel)
5, 10, 11, 12, 13, 14	20	Impact of compensation and benefits on recruitment and retention
5, 17, and HR Practices Around the Globe features in Chapters 4–17	21	**SPHR only* International HR and implications of global workforce for workforce planning and employment
5, 10, 14	22	Voluntary and involuntary terminations, downsizing, restructuring and outplacement strategies and practices
4, 5, 6, 7, 8, 9, 10	23	Internal workforce assessment techniques (for example: skills testing, skills inventory, workforce demographic analysis)
3, 8, 10, 18	24	Employment policies, practices and procedures (for example: orientation, on-boarding and retention)
5	25	Employer marketing and branding techniques
15	26	Negotiation skills and techniques

Functional Area 03: Human Resource Development (PHR: 18%, SPHR: 19%)

Developing, implementing and evaluating activities and programs that address employee training and development, performance appraisal and talent and performance management to ensure that the knowledge, skills, abilities and performance of the workforce meet current and future organizational and individual needs.

ADDRESSED IN THIS BOOK IN CHAPTER(S):		KNOWLEDGE OF
8 and in Know Your Employment Law features in this chapter and Chapters 2–18	27	Applicable federal laws and regulations related to HR development activities (for example: Title VII, ADA, Title 17 [Copyright law])
5, 8, 9, 10	28	Career development and leadership development theories and applications (for example: succession planning, dual career ladders)
8	29	Organizational development (OD) theories and applications
8	30	Training program development techniques to create general and specialized training programs
8	31	Facilitation techniques, instructional methods and program delivery mechanisms
4, 8	32	Task/process analysis
9	33	Performance appraisal methods (for example: instruments, ranking and rating scales)
9, 11, 12	34	Performance management methods (for example: goal setting, relationship to compensation, job placements/promotions)
HR Practices Around the Globe features in most chapters and Chapter 17 (Global HR)	35	**SPHR only* Applicable global issues (for example: international law, culture, local management approaches/practices, societal norms)
8	36	Techniques to assess training program effectiveness, including use of applicable metrics (for example: participant surveys, pre- and post-testing)
8, 10	37	Mentoring and executive coaching

Functional Area 04: Compensation and Benefits (PHR: 19%, SPHR: 13%)

Developing/selecting, implementing/administering and evaluating compensation and benefits programs for all employee groups in order to support the organization's goals, objectives and values.

ADDRESSED IN THIS BOOK IN CHAPTER(S):		KNOWLEDGE OF
2, 11, 12, 13, 15, and Know Your Employment Law features	38	Applicable federal laws and regulations related to compensation, benefits, and tax (for example: FLSA, ERISA, FMLA, USERRA)
11, 12, 13	39	Compensation and benefits strategies
	40	Budgeting and accounting practices related to compensation and benefits
11	41	Job evaluation methods
11	42	Job pricing and pay structures
5, 11	43	External labor markets and/or economic factors
11, 12	44	Pay programs (for example: variable, merit)
11, 12, 13	45	**SPHR only* Executive compensation methods
11, 12, 13, 14	46	Noncash compensation methods (for example: equity programs, noncash rewards)
11	47	Benefits programs (for example: health and welfare, retirement, Employee Assistance Programs [EAPs])

11, 12, 13, 17, and HR Around the Globe features	48	**SPHR only* International compensation laws and practices (for example: expatriate compensation, entitlements, choice of law codes)
11, 12, 13	49	Fiduciary responsibilities related to compensation and benefits

Functional Area 05: Employee and Labor Relations (PHR: 20%, SPHR: 14%)

Developing, implementing/administering and evaluating the workplace in order to maintain relationships and working conditions that balance employer/employee needs and rights in support of the organization's goals and objectives.

ADDRESSED IN THIS BOOK IN CHAPTER(S):	KNOWLEDGE OF	
2, 10, 14, 15	50	Applicable federal laws affecting employment in union and nonunion environments, such as laws regarding antidiscrimination policies, sexual harassment, labor relations, and privacy (for example: WARN Act, Title VII, NLRA)
14 (Building Positive Employee Relations), 15	51	Techniques and tools for facilitating positive employee relations (for example: employee surveys, dispute/ conflict resolution, labor/management cooperative strategies)
3, 4, 14	52	Employee involvement strategies (for example: employee management committees, self-directed work teams, staff meetings)
10, 14	53	Individual employment rights issues and practices (for example: employment at will, negligent hiring, defamation)
9, 10, 14, 15	54	Workplace behavior issues/practices (for example: absenteeism and performance improvement)
15	55	Unfair labor practices
15	56	The collective bargaining process, strategies and concepts (for example: contract negotiation, costing and administration)
10, 14, including Know Your Employment Law features	57	Legal disciplinary procedures
11, 12, 13, 14	58	Positive employee relations strategies and non-monetary rewards
3, 14, 15	59	Techniques for conducting unbiased investigations
10, 14, 15, including Know Your Employment Law features	60	Legal termination procedures

Functional Area 06: Risk Management (PHR: 8%, SPHR: 7%)

Developing, implementing/administering and evaluating programs, procedures and policies in order to provide a safe, secure working environment and to protect the organization from potential liability.

ADDRESSED IN THIS BOOK IN CHAPTER(S):	KNOWLEDGE OF	
2, 14, 16, including Know Your Employment Law features	61	Applicable federal laws and regulations related to workplace health, safety, security and privacy (for example: OSHA, Drug-Free Workplace Act, ADA, HIPAA, Sarbanes–Oxley Act)
16	62	Occupational injury and illness prevention (safety) and compensation programs
16	63	Investigation procedures of workplace safety, health and security enforcement agencies
13, 16	64	Return to work procedures (for example: interactive dialog, job modification, accommodations)
16	65	Workplace safety risks (for example: trip hazards, blood-borne pathogens)

16	66	Workplace security risks (for example: theft, corporate espionage, sabotage)
14, 16	67	Potential violent behavior and workplace violence conditions
16	68	General health and safety practices (for example: evacuation, hazard communication, ergonomic evaluations)
16	69	Organizational incident and emergency response plans
14, 16	70	Internal investigation, monitoring and surveillance techniques
13, 14, 16	71	Employer/employee rights related to substance abuse
16, 18	72	Business continuity and disaster recovery plans (for example: data storage and backup, alternative work locations, procedures)
14, 16, 18	73	Data integrity techniques and technology (for example: data sharing, password usage, social engineering)
3, 4, 5, 18, and Trends Shaping HR: Digital and Social Media and Improving Performance Through HRIS features in Chapters 3–16	74	Technology and applications (for example: social media, monitoring software, biometrics)
	75	Financial management practices (for example: procurement policies, credit card policies and guidelines, expense policies)

CORE KNOWLEDGE

3, 8	76	Needs assessment and analysis
13, 18	77	Third-party or vendor selection, contract negotiation and management, including development of requests for proposals (RFPs)
9, 10, 14	78	Communication skills and strategies (for example: presentation, collaboration, sensitivity)
2, 4, 6, 9, 15, 16, 18, and Know Your Employment Law features in Chapters 2–16	79	Organizational documentation requirements to meet federal and state guidelines
8	80	Adult learning processes
8, 12, 13, 14	81	Motivation concepts and applications
8	82	Training techniques (for example: virtual, classroom, on-the-job)
	83	Leadership concepts and applications
	84	Project management concepts and applications
2 and Diversity features in most chapters	85	Diversity concepts and applications (for example: generational, cultural competency, learning styles)
14	86	Human relations concepts and applications (for example: emotional intelligence, organizational behavior)
1, 14	87	Ethical and professional standards
3–18 plus Trends Shaping HR: Digital and Social Media and Improving Performance Through HRIS features in most chapters	88	Technology to support HR activities (for example: HR Information Systems, employee self-service, E-learning, applicant tracking systems)
1, 3, and HR as a Profit Center features in most chapters	89	Qualitative and quantitative methods and tools for analysis, interpretation and decision-making purposes (for example: metrics and measurements, cost/benefit analysis, financial statement analysis)
8	90	Change management theory, methods and application
4	91	Job analysis and job description methods
4, 5, 18	92	Employee records management (for example: electronic/paper, retention, disposal)

3, 4, Improving Performance: The Strategic Context features in most chapters, a continuing strategic Hotel Paris case with in-chapter callouts in Chapters 3–16, and "strategic" chapter openers	93	Techniques for forecasting, planning and predicting the impact of HR activities and programs across functional areas
1, 4	94	Types of organizational structures (for example: matrix, hierarchy)
3	95	Environmental scanning concepts and applications (for example: Strengths, Weaknesses, Opportunities and Threats [SWOT], and Political, Economic, Social and Technological [PEST])
8, 14	96	Methods for assessing employee attitudes, opinions and satisfaction (for example: surveys, focus groups/panels)
	97	Budgeting, accounting and financial concepts
16	98	Risk-management techniques

APPENDIX B

About the Society for Human Resource Management (SHRM) Body of Competency & Knowledge® Model and Certification Exams

In 2011, SHRM began a program of research involving thousands of HR professionals to identify the critical competencies needed for success as an HR professional. This research led to the development of the SHRM Competency Model, which defines eight key behavioral competencies (*Ethical Practice*, *Leadership & Navigation*, *Business Acumen*, *Relationship Management*, *Communication*, *Consultation*, *Critical Evaluation*, and *Global & Cultural Effectiveness*) and one technical competency (*HR Expertise*). The SHRM Competency Model provides HR professionals with a comprehensive roadmap for developing the capabilities they need to advance their careers and improve their effectiveness in the workplace.

The SHRM Body of Competency & Knowledge® (SHRM BoCK®), which is based on the SHRM Competency Model outlines the content of SHRM's certification examinations, the SHRM Certified Professional (SHRM-CP®) exam for early-career and mid-level practitioners, and the SHRM Senior Certified Professional (SHRM-SCP®) exam for senior-level and executive practitioners.

In brief, the SHRM Body of Competency & Knowledge® model is based on a foundation of 15 "HR functional areas" such as HR Strategic Planning, and Talent Acquisition, which SHRM then groups into three main domains—People, Organization, and Workplace. The SHRM Body of Competency & Knowledge® model then layers, on top of these 15 functional knowledge areas, eight behavioral competencies, such as *Leadership & Navigation*, *Business Acumen*, and *Ethical Practice*.

The HR competencies and knowledge that are assessed on the SHRM-CP® and SHRM-SCP® exams are detailed in the SHRM BoCK®, which consists of the following two sections: Section 1: Behavioral Competencies, and Section 2: HR Expertise (HR Knowledge).

SECTION 1: BEHAVIORAL COMPETENCIES

Behavioral competencies describe the behaviors and attributes necessary for HR professionals to operate with a strategic mindset and perform effectively in the workplace. They facilitate the application of technical knowledge (i.e., *HR Expertise*), which may be defined as the principles, practices and functions of effective HR management (see Section 2). Successful HR professionals must understand the behavioral components of HR practice in addition to being in command of technical HR knowledge.

Originally published as The SHRM Body of Competency and Knowledge. © 2014, Society for Human Resource Management, Alexandria, VA. Used with permission. All rights reserved. https://www.shrm.org/certification/Documents/SHRM-BoCK-FINAL.pdf, accessed September 14, 2018.

Organizing Framework of Behavioral Competency Clusters

CLUSTER	COMPETENCY	DEFINITION
Leadership	Leadership & Navigation	The knowledge, skills, abilities, and other characteristics (KSAOs) needed to navigate the organization and accomplish HR goals, to create a compelling vision and mission for HR that aligns with the strategic direction and culture of the organization, to lead and promote organizational change, to manage the implementation and execution of HR initiatives, and to promote the role of HR as a key business partner.
	Ethical Practice	The KSAOs needed to maintain high levels of personal and professional integrity, and to act as an ethical agent who promotes core values, integrity and accountability throughout the organization.
Interpersonal	Relationship Management	The KSAOs needed to create and maintain a network of professional contacts within and outside of the organization, to build and maintain relationships, to work as an effective member of a team, and to manage conflict while supporting the organization.
	Communication	The KSAOs needed to effectively craft and deliver concise and informative communications, to listen to and address the concerns of others, and to transfer and translate information from one level or unit of the organization to another.
	Global & Cultural Effectiveness	The KSAOs needed to value and consider the perspectives and backgrounds of all parties, to interact with others in a global context, and to promote a diverse and inclusive workplace.
Business	Business Acumen	The KSAOs needed to understand the organization's operations, functions and external environment, and to apply business tools and analyses that inform HR initiatives and operations consistent with the overall strategic direction of the organization.
	Consultation	The KSAOs needed to work with organizational stakeholders in evaluating business challenges and identifying opportunities for the design, implementation and evaluation of change initiatives, and to build ongoing support for HR solutions that meet the changing needs of customers and the business.
	Critical Evaluation	The KSAOs needed to collect and analyze qualitative and quantitative data, and to interpret and promote findings that evaluate HR initiatives and inform business decisions and recommendations.

SECTION 2: HR EXPERTISE (HR KNOWLEDGE)

Technical HR knowledge (i.e., *HR Expertise*) is defined as the principles, practices and functions of effective HR management. Its application is facilitated by behavioral competencies (see Section 1). Successful HR professionals must be in command of both technical HR knowledge and the behavioral components of HR practice. This approach, which is supported by SHRM research (see Introduction), emphasizes the critical and integrated roles played by technical HR knowledge (**what** you know) **and** by behavioral competencies (how you **apply** what you know) in contributing to effective HR practice.

Functional Area #1: HR Strategic Planning

Definition: *HR Strategic Planning* involves the activities necessary for developing, implementing and managing the strategic direction required to achieve organizational success and to create value for stakeholders.

ADDRESSED IN THIS BOOK IN CHAPTER(S):	KEY CONCEPTS:
	• Approaches to project management (e.g., traditional, Lean Six Sigma, agile, critical chain) and processes (e.g., initiating, planning and design, launching/executing, monitoring and controlling, closing).
	• Concepts of systems thinking (e.g., related parts, input-process-output) and components of an organizational system (e.g., interdependence, necessity of feedback, differentiation of units).
1, 3, strategic Hotel Paris cases in Chapters 3–18 with in-chapter call-outs, "strategic" chapter openers, and Improving Performance: The Strategic Context features in most chapters	• Organizational mission, vision and values, and their relation to strategic management and planning.
	• Project planning, monitoring and reporting methods and tools (e.g., critical path analysis, Gantt charts, variance analysis, outcome monitoring).
	• Project leadership, governance and structures (e.g., team roles, team management, work breakdown structures).
1, 3, strategic Hotel Paris cases in Chapters 3–18 with in-chapter call-outs, "strategic" chapter openers, and Improving Performance: The Strategic Context features in most chapters	• Role of strategic management and planning in creating and sustaining competitive advantage.
1, 3, strategic Hotel Paris cases in Chapters 3–18 with in-chapter call-outs, "strategic" chapter openers, and Improving Performance: The Strategic Context features in most chapters	• Strategic planning analysis frameworks (e.g., PESTLE analysis, SWOT analysis, industry analysis, scenario planning, growth-share matrix).
1, 3, strategic Hotel Paris cases in Chapters 3–18 with in-chapter call-outs, "strategic" chapter openers, and Improving Performance: The Strategic Context features in most chapters	• Strategic planning process (e.g., formulation, goal-setting, implementation, evaluation).
	• Systems theory and input-process-output models.

PROFICIENCY INDICATORS	
For All HR Professionals	For Advanced HR Professionals
• Uses the perspective of systems thinking to understand how the organization operates. • Informs business decisions with knowledge of the strategy and goals of HR and the organization. • Develops and implements an individual action plan for executing HR's strategy and goals. • Uses benchmarks, industry metrics and workforce trends to understand the organization's market position and competitive advantage. • Informs HR leadership of new or overlooked opportunities to align HR's strategy with the organization's. • Provides HR leadership with timely and accurate information required for strategic decision making.	• Identifies the ways in which the HR function can support the organization's strategy and goals. • Engages other business leaders in strategic analysis and planning. • Evaluates HR's critical activities in terms of value added, impact and utility, using cost-benefit analysis, revenue, profit-and-loss estimates and other leading or lagging indicators. • Provides HR-focused expertise to other business leaders when formulating the organization's strategy and goals. • Develops and implements HR strategy, vision and goals that align with and support the organization's strategy and goals. • Ensures that HR strategy creates and sustains the organization's competitive advantage.

Functional Area #2: Talent Acquisition

Definition: *Talent Acquisition* encompasses the activities involved in building and maintaining a workforce that meets the needs of the organization.

ADDRESSED IN THIS BOOK IN CHAPTER(S):	KEY CONCEPTS:
8	• Approaches to employee onboarding.
5	• Approaches to sourcing (e.g., external talent pipelines).
4, 5, 11	• Employment categories (e.g., salaried/ hourly, contract, temporary, interns).
4	• Job analysis and identification of job requirements
6	• Job offer contingencies (e.g., background investigations, credit checks).
6,11	• Job offer negotiations (e.g., salary).
1, 8, 9, 10, 11, 14, 15, 16	• Methods for creating and maintaining a positive employer value proposition (EVP) and employment brand.
5	• Methods for external and internal employee recruitment (e.g., job ads, career fairs).
2, 6, 7	• Methods for selection assessment (e.g., ability, job knowledge, non-cognitive tests, assessment centers, interviews).
3, 4, 5, 6	• Talent acquisition metrics (e.g., cost per hire, time to fill).

PROFICIENCY INDICATORS

For All HR Professionals

- Understands the talent needs of the organization or business unit.
- Uses a wide variety of talent sources and recruiting methods to attract qualified applicants.
- Uses technology (e.g., social media, applicant tracking software [ATS]) to support effective and efficient approaches to sourcing and recruiting employees.
- Promotes and uses the EVP and employment brand for sourcing and recruiting applicants.
- Uses the most appropriate hiring methods to best evaluate a candidate's technical skills, organizational fit and alignment with the organization's competencies needs.
- Conducts appropriate pre-employment screening.
- Implements effective onboarding and orientation programs for new employees.
- Designs job descriptions to meet the organization's resource needs.

For Advanced HR Professionals

- Analyzes staffing levels and projections, to forecast workforce needs.
- Develops strategies for sourcing and acquiring a workforce that meets the organization's needs.
- Establishes an EVP and employment brand that supports recruitment of high-quality job applicants.
- Designs and oversees effective strategies for sourcing, recruiting and evaluating qualified job candidates.
- Designs and oversees employee onboarding and assimilation processes.
- Designs and oversees valid and systematic programs for assessing the effectiveness of talent acquisition activities that meet the organization's needs.

Functional Area #3: Employee Engagement & Retention

Definition: *Employee Engagement & Retention* refers to activities aimed at retaining high-performing talent, solidifying and improving the relationship between employees and the organization, creating a thriving and energized workforce, and developing effective strategies to address appropriate performance expectations from employees at all levels.

ADDRESSED IN THIS BOOK IN SPECIAL EMPLOYEE ENGAGEMENT GUIDE FOR MANAGERS FEATURES IN CHAPTERS 3–16, AND IN THE FOLLOWING CHAPTERS:	KEY CONCEPTS:
1, 10, 11, 12, 13, 14, 15, 16	• Approaches to developing and maintaining a positive organizational culture (e.g., learning strategies, communication strategies, building values).
9, 10, 11, 12, 14	• Approaches to recognition (e.g., performance or service awards).
14	• Creation, administration, analysis and interpretation of employee attitude surveys.

Special engagement features in Chapters 1–16, and Chapter 14	• Creation, planning and management of employee engagement activities.
10	• Employee lifecycle phases (e.g., recruitment, integration, development, departure).
10	• Employee retention concepts (e.g., causes of turnover) and best practices (e.g., realistic job previews [RJP]).
8, 10, 14	• Influence of culture on organizational outcomes (e.g., organizational performance, organizational learning, innovation).
Engagement features in Chapters 1–6, and Chapter 14	• Interventions for improving job attitudes.
11, 12, 14	• Job attitude theories and basic principles (e.g., engagement, satisfaction, commitment).
4, 14	• Job enrichment/enlargement principles and techniques.
9	• Key components of, and best practices associated with, performance management systems.
8, 10, 14	• Methods for assessing employee attitudes (e.g., focus groups, stay interviews, surveys).
9	• Principles of effective performance appraisal (e.g., goal setting, giving feedback).
3, 10	• Retention and turnover metrics (e.g., voluntary turnover rate).
10, 14	• Types of organizational cultures (e.g., authoritarian, mechanistic, participative, learning, high performance).
13, 14	• Workplace flexibility programs (e.g., telecommuting, alternative work schedules).

PROFICIENCY INDICATORS

For All HR Professionals

- Designs, administers, analyzes and interprets surveys of employee attitudes (e.g., engagement, job satisfaction) and culture.
- Administers and supports HR and organizational programs designed to improve employee attitudes and culture (e.g., social events, telecommuting policies, recognition, job enlargement/enrichment, workplace flexibility).
- Identifies program opportunities to create more engaging or motivating jobs (e.g., job enrichment/enlargement).
- Monitors changes in turnover and retention metrics, and ensures that leadership is aware of such changes.
- Coaches supervisors on creating positive working relationships with their employees.
- Trains stakeholders on use of organization's performance management systems (e.g., how to enter performance goals, make ratings).
- Helps stakeholders understand the elements of satisfactory employee performance and performance management.
- Implements and monitors processes that measure effectiveness of performance management systems.

For Advanced HR Professionals

- In collaboration with other leaders, defines an organizational strategy to create an engaged workforce.
- Implements best practices for employee retention in HR programs, practices and policies (e.g., RJP, career development programs, employee socialization).
- Communicates to other senior leaders the results of surveys of employee attitudes and culture.
- Designs and oversees an action plan to address the findings of employee attitude surveys.
- Designs and oversees HR and organizational programs designed to improve employee attitudes (e.g., social events, telecommuting policies, recognition, job enlargement/enrichment, workplace flexibility).
- Holistically monitors the organization's metrics on employee attitudes, turnover and retention, and other information about employee engagement and retention.
- Designs and oversees best practices-based employee performance management systems that meet the organization's talent management needs.
- Designs and oversees processes to measure the effectiveness of performance management systems.

Functional Area #4: Learning & Development

Definition: *Learning & Development* activities enhance the knowledge, skills, abilities and other characteristics (KSAOs) and competencies of the workforce in order to meet the organization's business needs.

ADDRESSED IN THIS BOOK IN CHAPTER(S):	KEY CONCEPTS:
8, 9, 10	• Approaches to coaching and mentoring (e.g., formal, informal mentorship programs).
10	• Career development.
8, 9	• Developmental assessments (e.g., 360s).
8, 14	• Knowledge-sharing techniques and facilitation.
8	• Learning and development approaches and techniques (e.g., e-learning, leader development).
8	• Learning and development program design and implementation (e.g., ADDIE model).
8	• Learning evaluation (e.g., Kirkpatrick 4-level model).
8	• Learning theories (e.g., adult learning theory).
8	• Needs analysis types (e.g., person, organizational, training, cost-benefit) and techniques (e.g., surveys, observations, interviews).
3 and HR as a Profit Center features in many chapters	• Organizational analysis (e.g., performance analysis).
10	• Techniques for career development (e.g., career pathing, career mapping).

PROFICIENCY INDICATORS

For All HR Professionals

- Uses best practices to evaluate data on gaps in competencies.
- Creates individual development plans (IDPs) in collaboration with supervisors and employees.
- Uses best practices to develop and deliver learning and development activities that close gaps in employees' competencies and skills.
- Uses all available resources (e.g., vendors) to develop and deliver effective learning and development programs.
- Creates internal social networks to facilitate knowledge-sharing among employees.
- Administers and supports programs to promote knowledge transfer.

For Advanced HR Professionals

- Designs and oversees efforts to collect data on critical gaps in competencies.
- Provides guidance to identify and develop critical competencies that meet the organization's talent needs.
- Monitors the effectiveness of programs for emerging leaders and leadership development.
- Creates long-term organizational strategies to develop talent.
- Creates strategies to ensure the retention of organizational knowledge.

Functional Area #5: Total Rewards

Definition: *Total Rewards* refers to the design and implementation of compensation systems and benefit packages, which employers use to attract and retain employees.

ADDRESSED IN THIS BOOK IN CHAPTER(S):	KEY CONCEPTS:
11	• Approaches to gathering compensation- and benefits-related market and competitive intelligence (e.g., remuneration surveys).
11, 18	• Basic accounting and financial knowledge for managing payroll (e.g., total compensation statements).
11	• Compensation philosophies.
11, 12, 13, 17	• Compensation plans for common and special workforce groups (e.g., domestic, global/expatriate, executive, sales).
11	• Job evaluation for determining compensation and benefits.

Chapter(s)	Key Concepts
11, 13	• Leave plans and approaches (e.g., vacation, holiday, sick, paid/unpaid leave).
13	• Other benefits (e.g., disability, unemployment insurance, employee assistance programs, family, flex, wellness programs).
11, 12, 13	• Other compensation (e.g., deferred compensation, direct/indirect compensation, stock options).
11, 12, 13	• Pay practices and issues (e.g., pay increases, base pay, pay levels, banding, variable pay).
11	• Remuneration and labor market data collection and interpretation.
11	• Remuneration data analysis (e.g., comparable worth, determining compensation, internal alignment, external competitiveness).
10, 13	• Retirement planning and benefits (e.g., pension plans).
11	• Total rewards metrics and benchmarks.

PROFICIENCY INDICATORS

For All HR Professionals	For Advanced HR Professionals
• Collects, compiles and interprets compensation and benefits data from various sources (e.g., remuneration surveys, labor market trends). • Implements appropriate pay, benefit, incentive, separation and severance systems and programs. • Complies with best practices for and laws and regulations governing compensation and benefits. • Differentiates between government-mandated, government-provided and voluntary benefit approaches. • Performs accurate job evaluations to determine appropriate compensation.	• Designs and oversees organizational compensation and benefits philosophies, strategies and plans that align with the organization's strategic direction and talent needs. • Designs and oversees executive compensation approaches that directly connect individual performance to organizational success. • Ensures the internal equity of compensation systems.

Functional Area #6: Structure of the HR Function

Definition: *Structure of the HR Function* encompasses the people, processes, theories and activities involved in the delivery of HR-related services that create and drive organizational effectiveness.

When necessary, HR professionals should be able to recognize opportunities to improve HR operations or structure in response to such factors as changes in the workforce, globalization and organizational restructuring.

ADDRESSED IN THIS BOOK IN CHAPTER(S):	KEY CONCEPTS:
1, 4	• Approaches to HR operational integration (i.e., how HR structures work together).
1	• Approaches to HR function/service models (e.g., centralized vs. decentralized).
1	• Approaches to HR structural models (e.g., Center of Excellence [COE], shared services).
1, 4, 5, 6	• Elements of the HR function (e.g., recruiting, talent management, compensation, benefits).
1, 3	• HR-function metrics (e.g., HR staff per fulltime employee, customer satisfaction, key performance indicators, balanced scorecard).
1	• HR staff roles, responsibilities and functions (e.g., generalists, specialists, HR business partners).
1, 13, 18	• Outsourcing of HR functions.

PROFICIENCY INDICATORS

For All HR Professionals

- Adapts work style to fit the organization's HR service model (e.g., centralized vs. decentralized), to ensure timely and consistent delivery of services to stakeholders.
- Seeks feedback from stakeholders to identify opportunities for HR function improvements.
- Acts as HR point-of-service contact for key stakeholders within a division or group.
- Provides consultation on HR issues to all levels of leadership and management.
- Coordinates with other HR functions to ensure timely and consistent delivery of services to stakeholders.
- Ensures that outsourced and/or automated HR functions are integrated with other HR activities.
- Analyzes and interprets key performance indicators to understand the effectiveness of the HR function.

For Advanced HR Professionals

- Designs and implements the appropriate HR service model for the organization (e.g., centralized vs. decentralized), to ensure efficient and effective delivery of services to stakeholders.
- Creates long-term goals that address feedback from stakeholders identifying opportunities for HR function improvements.
- Ensures that all elements of the HR function (e.g., recruiting, talent management, compensation and benefits, learning and development) are aligned and integrated, and provide timely and consistent delivery of services to stakeholders.
- Identifies opportunities to improve HR operations by outsourcing work or implementing technologies that automate HR functions (e.g., time, payroll).
- Designs and oversees programs to collect, analyze and interpret key performance indicators (e.g., balanced scorecard) to evaluate the effectiveness of HR activities in supporting organizational success.

Functional Area #7: Organizational Effectiveness & Development

Definition: *Organizational Effectiveness & Development* concerns the overall structure and functionality of the organization, and involves measurement of long- and short-term effectiveness and growth of people and processes, and implementation of necessary organizational change initiatives.

ADDRESSED IN THIS BOOK IN CHAPTER(S):	KEY CONCEPTS:
6, 7	• Application of behavioral assessments (e.g., personality assessments).
8	• Intergroup dynamics (e.g., intergroup conflict).
8	• Intragroup dynamics (e.g., group formation, identity, cohesion, structure, influence on behavior).
4	• Organizational design structures and approaches (e.g., customer, functional, geographic, matrix, program).
1, 3	• Organizational performance theories, structures, and approaches.

PROFICIENCY INDICATORS

For All HR Professionals

- Ensures that key documents and systems (e.g., job postings and descriptions, performance management systems) accurately reflect workforce activities.
- Supports change initiatives to increase the effectiveness of HR systems and processes.
- Identifies areas in the organization's structures, processes and procedures that need change.
- Provides recommendations for eliminating barriers to organizational effectiveness and development.
- Collects and analyzes data on the value of HR initiatives to the organization.

For Advanced HR Professionals

- Aligns HR's strategy and activities with the organization's mission, vision, values and strategy.
- Regularly monitors results against performance standards and goals in support of the organization's strategy.
- Establishes measurable goals and objectives to create a culture of accountability.
- Consults on, plans and designs organizational structures that align with the effective delivery of activities in support of the organization's strategy.
- Assesses organizational needs to identify critical competencies for operational effectiveness.
- Designs and oversees change initiatives to increase the effectiveness of HR systems and processes.
- Ensures that HR initiatives demonstrate measurable value to the organization.

Functional Area #8: Workforce Management

Definition: *Workforce Management* refers to HR practices and initiatives that allow the organization to meet its talent needs (e.g., workforce planning, succession planning) and close critical gaps in competencies.

ADDRESSED IN THIS BOOK IN CHAPTER(S):	KEY CONCEPTS:
4, 5	• Analysis of labor supply and demand.
3	• Approaches to restructuring (e.g., mergers and acquisitions, downsizing).
8	• Best practices and techniques for knowledge management, retention and transfer.
8	• Leadership development and planning (e.g., high-potential development programs).
5, 8, 10	• Succession planning programs and techniques.
5	• Techniques for organizational need-gap analysis (e.g., examination of HR records, interviews, focus groups).
5, 10	• Workforce planning approaches, techniques and analyses (e.g., attrition, gap and solution, implementation and evaluation, reduction in force, supply and demand, workforce profile).

PROFICIENCY INDICATORS

For All HR Professionals

- Identifies gaps in workforce competencies and misalignment of staffing levels.
- Implements approaches (e.g., buy or build) to ensure that appropriate workforce staffing levels and competencies exist to meet the organization's goals and objectives.
- Plans short-term strategies to develop workforce competencies that support the organization's goals and objectives.
- Administers and supports approaches (e.g., succession plans, high-potential development programs) to ensure that the organization's leadership needs are met.
- Supports strategies for restructuring the organization's workforce (e.g., mergers and acquisitions, downsizing).

For Advanced HR Professionals

- Evaluates how the organization's strategy and goals align with future and current staffing levels and workforce competencies.
- Develops strategies to maintain a robust workforce that has the talent to carry out the organization's current and future strategy and goals.
- Coordinates with business leaders to create strategies (e.g., succession planning, leadership development, training) that address the organization's leadership needs.
- Develops strategies for restructuring the organization's workforce (e.g., mergers and acquisitions, downsizing).

Functional Area #9: Employee & Labor Relations

Definition: *Employee & Labor Relations* refers to any dealings between the organization and its employees regarding the terms and conditions of employment.

ADDRESSED IN THIS BOOK IN CHAPTER(S):	KEY CONCEPTS:
1, 2, 14	• Approaches to retaliation prevention.
15	• Approaches to union-organization relations (e.g., collective bargaining, contract negotiation, contract administration process).
14, 15	• Causes of and methods for preventing and addressing strikes, boycotts and work stoppages.
10, 14, 15	• Disciplinary procedures and approaches.
11, 14, 15	• Employment rights, standards and concepts (e.g., labor rights, living wage and fair wage concepts, standard workday), according to the International Labor Organization (ILO).

10, 14, 15 • Techniques for disciplinary investigations.

15 • Techniques for grievance and complaint resolution.

14 • Types and development of compliance and ethics programs (e.g., design, implementation, performance measures).

2, 14, 15 • Types and structures of organized labor (e.g., unions, works councils, trade union federations, other employee collectives).

15 • Types of alternative dispute resolution (ADR) (e.g., mediation, arbitration) and their advantages and disadvantages.

15 • Unfair labor practices, according to the ILO.

• Unionization approaches, methods and management (e.g., acceptance, avoidance strategies).

PROFICIENCY INDICATORS

For All HR Professionals

- Supports interactions with union and other employee representatives.
- Supports the organization's interests in union–management activities.
- Assists and supports the organization in the collective bargaining process.
- Participates in or facilitates ADR processes (e.g., arbitration, mediation).
- Makes recommendations for addressing other types of employee representation (e.g., governmental, legal).
- Develops and implements workplace policies, handbooks and codes of conduct.
- Provides guidance to employees on the terms and implications of their employment agreement and the organization's policies and procedures (e.g., employee handbook).
- Consults managers on how to supervise difficult employees, handle disruptive behaviors and respond with the appropriate level of corrective action.
- Conducts investigations into employee misconduct and suggests disciplinary action when necessary.
- Manages employee grievance and discipline processes.
- Resolves workplace labor disputes internally.

For Advanced HR Professionals

- Manages interactions and negotiations with union and other employe representatives (e.g., governmental, legal).
- Serves as the primary representative of the organization's interests in union–management activities (e.g., negotiations, dispute resolution).
- Manages the collective bargaining process.
- Consults on and develops an effective organized labor strategy (e.g., avoidance, acceptance, adaptation) to achieve the organization's desired impact on itself and its workforce.
- Educates employees, managers and leaders at all levels about the organization's labor strategy (e.g., avoidance, acceptance, adaptation and its impact on the achievement of goals and objectives.
- Educates employees at all levels about changes in the organization's policies.
- Coaches and counsels managers on how to operate within the parameters of organizational policy, labor agreements and employment agreements.
- Oversees employee investigations and discipline.

Functional Area #10: Technology Management

Definition: *Technology Management* involves the use of existing, new and emerging technologies to support the HR function, and the development and implementation of policies and procedures governing the use of technologies in the workplace.

ADDRESSED IN THIS BOOK IN CHAPTER(S):

KEY CONCEPTS:

Trends Shaping HR: Digital and Social Media features in many chapters, 11 • Approaches to electronic self-service for basic HR and people management functions (e.g., scheduling, timekeeping, benefit enrollment).

Trends Shaping HR: Digital and Social Media features in many chapters, 18 • Data and information management (e.g., data integrity, confidentiality, security, disclosure).

Trends Shaping HR: Digital and Social Media features in many chapters, 18 • HRIS capabilities and use.

18 and Improving Performance Through HRIS features in many chapters • Policies and procedures for procurement.

18, Trends Shaping HR: Digital and Social Media features, and Improving Performance Through HRIS features in many chapters	• Policies and practices for technology and social media use (e.g., bring-your-own-device, websites, computers for personal activity).
5, 6, 18 and Improving Performance Through HRIS features in many chapters	• Software for recruiting and applicant tracking.

PROFICIENCY INDICATORS

For All HR Professionals	For Advanced HR Professionals
• Implements and uses technology solutions that support or facilitate delivery of effective HR services and storage of critical employee data. • Implements HRIS that integrate with and complement other enterprise information systems. • Develops and implements organizational standards and policies for maintaining confidentiality of employee data. • Uses technologies in a manner that protects workforce data. • Provides guidance to stakeholders on effective standards and policies for use of technologies in the workplace (e.g., social media, corporate and personal e-mail, internet messaging). • Coordinates and manages vendors implementing HR technology solutions. • Uses technologies that collect, access and analyze data and information, in order to understand business challenges and recommend evidence-based solutions.	• Evaluates and implements technology solutions that support the achievement of HR's strategic direction, vision and goals. • Evaluates and selects vendors to provide HR technology solutions. • Designs and implements technology systems that optimize and integrate HR functional areas. • Develops and implements technology-driven self-service approaches that enable managers and employees to perform basic people-related transactions (e.g., scheduling, timekeeping, compensation administration, benefit enrollment, information changes).

Functional Area #11: HR in the Global Context

Definition: *HR in the Global Context* focuses on the role of the HR professional in managing global workforces to achieve organizational objectives.

ADDRESSED IN THIS BOOK IN CHAPTER(S):	KEY CONCEPTS:
17, and HR Around the Globe features in many chapters	• Best practices for international assignments (e.g., approaches and trends, effective performance, health and safety, compensation adjustments, employee repatriation, socialization).
17, and HR Around the Globe features in many chapters	• Requirements for moving work (e.g., co-sourcing, near-shoring, offshoring, on-shoring).

PROFICIENCY INDICATORS

For All HR Professionals	For Advanced HR Professionals
• Addresses global issues that influence day-to-day HR activities and makes recommendations for business solutions. • Maintains up-to-date knowledge of global political, economic, social, technological, legal and environmental (PESTLE) factors and their influence on the organization's workforce. • Administers and supports HR activities associated with a global workforce. • Implements and conducts audits of global HR practices. • Maintains knowledge of global HR trends and best practices. • Balances with local needs the organization's desire for standardization of HR programs, practices and policies. • Builds relationships with global stakeholders. • Manages the day-to-day activities associated with international (i.e., expatriate) assignments.	• Recognizes and responds to global issues that influence the organization's human capital strategy. • Consults with business leaders on global PESTLE factors and their influence on the organization's workforce. • Develops a comprehensive organizational strategy that addresses global workforce issues. • Consults with business leaders to define global competencies and embed them throughout the organization. • Identifies opportunities to achieve efficiencies and cost savings by moving work (e.g., offshoring, on-shoring, near-shoring). • Designs and oversees programs for international (i.e., expatriate) assignments that support the organization's human capital strategy.

Functional Area #12: Diversity & Inclusion

Definition: *Diversity & Inclusion* encompasses activities that create opportunities for the organization to leverage the unique backgrounds and characteristics of all employees to contribute to its success.

ADDRESSED IN THIS BOOK IN CHAPTER(S):	KEY CONCEPTS:
2, 5, 6, 7, Know Your Employment Law, and Diversity features	• Approaches to developing an inclusive workplace (e.g., best practices for diversity training).
2 and Diversity features	• Approaches to managing a multi-generational/aging workforce.
2, 6, 7, 10	• Demographic barriers to success (e.g., glass ceiling).
2, 10, 17, and Diversity features	• Issues related to acceptance of diversity, including international differences (i.e., its acceptance in foreign nations or by employees from foreign nations).
2	• Workplace accommodations (e.g., disability, religious, transgender, veteran, active-duty military).

PROFICIENCY INDICATORS

For All HR Professionals	For Advanced HR Professionals
• Provides mentoring, training, guidance and coaching on cultural differences and practices to employees at all levels of the organization. • Consults with managers about distinctions between performance issues and cultural differences. • Develops and maintains knowledge of current trends and HR management best practices relating to D&I. • Contributes to development and maintenance of an organizational culture that values a diverse and inclusive workforce (e.g., conducts diversity training). • Identifies opportunities to enhance the fairness of organizational policies and procedures to all employees (e.g., removes demographic barriers to success). • Identifies and implements workplace accommodations. • Demonstrates support to internal and external stakeholders for the organization's D&I efforts.	• Incorporates D&I goals into all HR programs, practices and policies. • Advocates for incorporation of diversity goals into the organization's strategic plan. • Develops, implements and oversees, in conjunction with other business leaders, enterprise-wide programs, practices and policies that lead to a diverse workforce. • Designs and oversees HR programs, practices and policies supporting the development and maintenance of an organizational culture that values and promotes a diverse and inclusive workforce. • Designs and oversees HR programs, practices and policies that encourage employees to take advantage of opportunities for working with those who possess a diverse set of experiences and backgrounds. • Ensures that HR staff members have up-to-date knowledge of current trends and HR management best practices relating to D&I.

Functional Area #13: Risk Management

Definition: *Risk Management* is the identification, assessment and prioritization of risks, and the application of resources to minimize, monitor and control the probability and impact of those risks accordingly.

ADDRESSED IN THIS BOOK IN CHAPTER(S):	KEY CONCEPTS:
16	• Approaches to a drug-free workplace (e.g., testing, treatment of substance abuse).
16	• Approaches to qualitative and quantitative risk assessment (e.g., single loss expectancy, annualized loss expectancy).
16	• Business recovery and continuity-of-operations planning.
16	• Emergency and disaster (e.g., communicable disease, natural disaster, severe weather, terrorism) preparation and response planning.

Chapter(s)	Key Concepts
16	• Enterprise risk management processes and best practices (e.g., understand context, identify risks, analyze risks, prioritize risks) and risk treatments (e.g., avoidance, reduction, sharing, retention).
16, 18	• Legal and regulatory compliance auditing and investigation techniques.
16	• Quality assurance techniques and methods.
16	• Risk sources (e.g., project failures) and types (e.g., hazard, financial, operational, strategic).
16, 18, and Improving Performance Through HRIS features	• Security concerns (e.g., workplace violence, theft, fraud, corporate espionage, sabotage, kidnapping and ransom) and prevention.
16	• Workplace/occupational injury and illness prevention (e.g., identification of hazards), investigations and accommodations.

PROFICIENCY INDICATORS

For All HR Professionals	For Advanced HR Professionals
• Monitors political, economic, social, technological, legal and environmental (PESTLE) factors and their influence on the organization. • Administers and supports HR programs, practices and policies that identify and/or mitigate workplace risk. • Implements crisis management, contingency and business continuity plans for the HR function and the organization. • Communicates critical information about risks (e.g., safety and security) and risk mitigation to employees at all levels. • Conducts due diligence investigations to evaluate risks and ensure legal and regulatory compliance. • Conducts workplace safety and health-related investigations (e.g., investigates workplace injuries). • Audits risk management activities and plans. • Maintains and ensures accurate reporting of internationally accepted workplace health and safety standards. • Incorporates into business cases the anticipated level of risk.	• Develops, implements and oversees formal and routinized processes for monitoring the organization's internal and external environments, to identify potential risks. • Monitors and evaluates macro-level labor market, industry and global trends for their impact on the organization. • Examines potential threats to the organization and guides senior leadership accordingly. • Develops, implements and oversees a comprehensive enterprise risk management strategy. • Develops crisis management, contingency, and business continuity plans for the HR function and the organization. • Communicates critical information about risks (e.g., safety and security) and risk mitigation to senior-level employees and external stakeholders. • Ensures that risk management activities and plans are audited and that the results inform risk mitigation strategies. • Oversees workplace safety- and health-related investigations and reporting. • Establishes strategies to address workplace retaliation and violence. • Leads after-action debriefs following significant workplace incidents (e.g., those involving employee safety and security). • Evaluates the anticipated level of risk associated with strategic opportunities.

Functional Area #14: Corporate Social Responsibility

Definition: *Corporate Social Responsibility* represents the organization's commitment to operate in an ethical and sustainable manner by engaging in activities that promote and support philanthropy, transparency, sustainability and ethically sound governance practices.

ADDRESSED IN THIS BOOK IN CHAPTER(S):	KEY CONCEPTS:
14	• Approaches to community inclusion and engagement (e.g., representation on community boards, joint community projects, employee volunteerism).
14	• Creating shared value (e.g., definition, best practices).
14	• Developing CSR-related volunteer programs (e.g., recruiting and organizing participants).

1, 3, 14, • Organizational philosophies and policies (e.g., development, integration into the organization).

14 • Principles of corporate citizenship and governance.

14 • Steps for corporate philanthropy and charitable giving (e.g., selecting recipients, types, donation amounts).

PROFICIENCY INDICATORS	
For All HR Professionals	For Advanced HR Professionals
• Acts as a professional role model and representative of the organization when interacting with the community. • Engages in community-based volunteer and philanthropic activities. • Identifies and promotes opportunities for HR and the organization to engage in CSR activities. • Helps staff at all levels understand the societal impact of business decisions and the role of the organization's CSR activities in improving the community. • Maintains transparency of HR programs, practices and policies, where appropriate. • Coaches managers to achieve an appropriate level of transparency in organizational practices and decisions. • Identifies opportunities for incorporation of environmentally responsible business practices, and shares them with leadership.	• Serves as a leader in community-based volunteer and philanthropic organizations. • Develops CSR strategies that reflect the organization's mission and values. • Ensures that the organization's CSR programs enhance the employee value proposition and have a beneficial impact on HR programs (e.g., recruitment and retention) and/or contribute to the organization's competitive advantage. • Creates CSR program activities that engage the organization's workforce and the community at large. • Coordinates with other business leaders to integrate CSR objectives throughout the organization. • Coordinates with other business leaders to develop and implement appropriate levels of corporate self-governance and transparency. • Develops, with other business leaders, strategies that encourage and support environmentally responsible business decisions.

Functional Area #15: U.S. Employment Law & Regulations

Important note: *Only examinees residing within the United States will be tested on these topics; examinees residing outside the U.S. will not be tested on it. All laws and regulations referenced are subject to change.*

Definition: *U.S. Employment Law & Regulations* refers to the knowledge and application of all relevant laws and regulations in the United States relating to employment—provisions that set the parameters and limitations for each HR functional area and for organizations overall.

ADDRESSED BY KNOW YOUR EMPLOYMENT LAW FEATURES IN MOST CHAPTERS AS WELL AS IN THE FOLLOWING CHAPTERS:

KEY CONCEPTS:

Below are six broad categories of U.S. laws, regulations and Supreme Court cases relating to employment, with selected examples. (Please note that this is **not** an exhaustive list of categories or examples.) State, municipal and other local-level laws, regulations and cases are not included.

11 • ***Compensation*** *Examples:* Employee Retirement Income Security Act of 1974 (ERISA); Fair Labor Standards Act of 1938 (FLSA; Wage-Hour Bill; Wagner–Connery Wages and Hours Act) and amendments; Equal Pay Act of 1963 (amending FLSA); Lilly Ledbetter Fair Pay Act of 2009; *Ledbetter v. Goodyear Tire & Rubber Co.* (2007).

14, 15 • ***Employee relations*** *Examples:* Labor Management Relations Act of 1947 (LMRA; Taft–Hartley Act); National Labor Relations Act of 1935 (NLRA; Wagner Act; Wagner–Connery Labor Relations Act); *NLRB v. Weingarten* (1975); *Lechmere, Inc. v. NLRB* (1992).

16 • ***Job safety and health*** *Examples:* Drug-Free Workplace Act of 1988; Guidelines on Sexual Harassment; Occupational Safety and Health Act of 1970.

2 • ***Equal employment opportunity*** *Examples:* Age Discrimination in Employment Act of 1967 (ADEA) and amendments; Americans with Disabilities Act of 1990 (ADA) and amendments; Civil Rights Acts; Equal Employment Opportunity Act of 1972; Uniform Guidelines on Employee Selection Procedures (1978) (29 CFR Part 1607); *Griggs v. Duke Power Co.* (1971); *Phillips v. Martin Marietta Corp.* (1971).

13 • ***Leave and benefits*** *Examples:* Family and Medical Leave Act of 1993 (FMLA; expanded 2008, 2010); Patient Protection and Affordable Care Act (ACA; "Obamacare"); *National Federation of Independent Business v. Sebelius* (2012).

2, 6, 7 • ***Miscellaneous protection laws*** *Examples:* Employee Polygraph Protection Act of 1988; Genetic Information Nondiscrimination Act of 2008 (GINA).

PROFICIENCY INDICATORS	
For All HR Professionals	For Advanced HR Professionals
• Maintains a current working knowledge of relevant domestic and global employment laws. • Ensures that HR programs, practices and policies align and comply with laws and regulations. • Coaches employees at all levels in understanding and avoiding illegal and noncompliant HR-related behaviors (e.g., illegal terminations or discipline, unfair labor practices). • Brokers internal or external legal services for interpretation of employment laws.	• Maintains current, expert knowledge of relevant domestic and global employment laws. • Establishes and monitors criteria for organizational compliance with laws and regulations. • Educates and advises senior leadership on HR-related legal and regulatory compliance issues. • Oversees fulfillment of compliance requirements for HR programs, practices and policies. • Ensures that HR technologies facilitate compliance and reporting requirements (e.g., tracking employee accidents, safety reports).

APPENDIX C

Comprehensive Cases

BANDAG AUTOMOTIVE*

Jim Bandag took over his family's auto supply business in 2012, after helping his father, who founded the business, run it for about 10 years. Based in Illinois, Bandag employs about 300 people, and distributes auto supplies (replacement mufflers, bulbs, engine parts, and so on) through two divisions, one that supplies service stations and repair shops, and a second that sells retail auto supplies through five "Bandag Automotive" auto supply stores.

Jim's father, and now Jim, have always endeavored to keep Bandag's organization chart as simple as possible. The company has a full-time controller, managers for each of the five stores, a manager who oversees the distribution division, and Jim Bandag's executive assistant. Jim (along with his father, working part-time) handles marketing and sales.

Jim's executive assistant administers the firm's day-to-day human resource management tasks, but the company outsources most HR activities to others, including an employment agency that does its recruiting and screening, a benefits firm that administers its 401(k) plan, and a payroll service that handles its paychecks. Bandag's human resource management systems consist almost entirely of standardized HR forms purchased from an HR supplies company. These include forms such as application and performance appraisal forms, as well as an "honesty" test Bandag uses to screen the staff that works in the five stores. The company performs informal salary surveys to see what other companies in the area are paying for similar positions, and use these results for awarding annual merit increases (which in fact are more accurately cost-of-living adjustments).

Jim's father took a fairly paternal approach to the business. He often walked around speaking with his employees, finding out what their problems were, and even helping them out with an occasional loan—for instance, when he discovered that one of their children was sick, or for part of a new home down payment. Jim, on the other hand, tends to be more abrupt, and does not enjoy the same warm relationship with the employees as did his father. Jim is not unfair or dictatorial. He's just very focused on improving Bandag's financial performance, and so all his decisions, including his HR-related decisions, generally come down to cutting costs. For example, his knee-jerk reaction is usually to offer fewer days off rather than more, fewer benefits rather than more, and to be less flexible when an employee needs, for instance, a few extra days off because a child is sick.

It's therefore perhaps not surprising that over the past few years Bandag's sales and profits have increased markedly, but that the firm has found itself increasingly enmeshed in HR/equal employment–type issues. Indeed, Jim now finds himself spending a day or two a week addressing HR problems. For example, Henry Jaques, an employee at one of the stores, came to Jim's executive assistant and told her he was "irate" about his recent firing and was probably going to sue. Henry's store manager stated on his last performance appraisal that Henry did the technical aspects of his job well, but that he had "serious problems interacting with his coworkers." He was continually arguing with them, and complaining to the store manager about working conditions. The store manager had told Jim that he had to fire Henry because he was making "the whole place poisonous," and that (although he felt sorry because he'd heard rumors that Henry suffered from some mental illness) he felt he had to go. Jim approved the dismissal.

* Written and copyrighted by Gary Dessler, PhD.

Gavin was another problem. Gavin had worked for Bandag for 10 years, the last two as manager of one of the company's five stores. Right after Jim Bandag took over, Gavin told him he had to take a Family and Medical Leave Act medical leave to have hip surgery, and Jim approved the leave. When Gavin returned from leave, Jim told him that his position had been eliminated. Bandag had decided to close his store and open a new, larger store across from a shopping center about a mile away, and had appointed a new manager in Gavin's absence. However, the company did give Gavin a (nonmanagerial) position in the new store as a counter salesperson, at the same salary and with the same benefits as he had before. Even so, "This job is not similar to my old one," Gavin insisted. "It doesn't have nearly as much prestige." His contention is that the FMLA requires that the company bring him back in the same or equivalent position, and that this means a supervisory position, similar to what he had before he went on leave. Jim said no, and they seem to be heading toward litigation.

In another sign of the times at Bandag, the company's controller, Miriam, who had been with the company for about six years, went on pregnancy leave for 12 weeks in 2012 (also under the FMLA), and then received an additional three weeks' leave under Bandag's extended illness days program. Four weeks after she came back, she asked Jim Bandag if she could arrange to work fewer hours per week, and spend about a day per week working out of her home. He refused, and about two months later fired her. Jim Bandag said, "I'm sorry, it's not anything to do with your pregnancy-related requests, but we've got ample reasons to discharge you—your monthly budgets have been several days late, and we've got proof you may have forged documents." She replied, "I don't care what you say your reasons are; you're really firing me because of my pregnancy, and that's illegal."

Jim felt he was on safe ground as far as defending the company for these actions, although he didn't look forward to spending the time and money that he knew it would take to fight each. However, what he learned over lunch from a colleague undermined his confidence about another case that Jim had been sure would be a "slam dunk" for his company. Jim was explaining to his friend that one of Bandag's truck maintenance service people had applied for a job driving one of Bandag's distribution department trucks, and that Jim had turned him down because the worker was deaf. Jim (whose wife has occasionally said of him, "No one has ever accused Jim of being politically correct") was mentioning to his friend the apparent absurdity of a deaf person asking to be a truck delivery person. His friend, who happens to work for UPS, pointed out that the U.S. Court of Appeals for the Ninth Circuit had recently decided that UPS had violated the Americans with Disabilities Act by refusing to consider deaf workers for jobs driving the company's smaller vehicles.

Although Jim's father is semiretired, the sudden uptick in the frequency of such EEO-type issues troubled him, particularly after so many years of labor peace. However, he's not sure what to do about it. Having handed over the reins of the company to his son, he was loath to inject himself back into the company's operational decision making. On the other hand, he was afraid that in the short run these issues were going to drain a great deal of Jim's time and resources, and that in the long run they might be a sign of things to come, with problems like these eventually overwhelming Bandag Automotive. He comes to you, who he knows consults in human resource management, and asks you the following questions.

Questions

1. Given Bandag Automotive's size, and anything else you know about it, should we reorganize the human resource management function, and if so, why and how?
2. What, if anything, would you do to change and/or improve upon the current HR systems, forms, and practices that we now use?

3. Do you think that the employee whom Jim fired for creating what the manager called a poisonous relationship has a legitimate claim against us, and if so, why and what should we do about it?
4. Is it true that we really had to put Gavin back into an equivalent position, or was it adequate to just bring him back into a job at the same salary, bonuses, and benefits as he had before his leave?
5. Miriam, the controller, is basically claiming that the company is retaliating against her for being pregnant, and that the fact that we raised performance issues was just a smokescreen. Do you think the EEOC and/or courts would agree with her, and, in any case, what should we do now?
6. An employee who is deaf has asked us to be one of our delivery people and we turned him down. He's now threatening to sue. What should we do, and why?
7. In the previous 10 years, we've had only one equal employment complaint, and now in the last few years we've had four or five. What should I do about it? Why?

Based generally on actual facts, but Bandag is a fictitious company. Bandag source notes: "The Problem Employee: Discipline or Accommodation?" *Monday Business Briefing*, March 8, 2005; "Employee Says Change in Duties after Leave Violates FMLA," *BNA Bulletin to Management*, January 16, 2007, p. 24; "Manager Fired Days After Announcing Pregnancy," *BNA Bulletin to Management*, January 2, 2007, p. 8; "Ninth Circuit Rules UPS Violated ADA by Barring Deaf Workers from Driving Jobs," *BNA Bulletin to Management*, October 17, 2006, p. 329.

ANGELO'S PIZZA*

Angelo Camero was brought up in the Bronx, New York, and basically always wanted to be in the pizza store business. As a youngster, he would sometimes spend hours at the local pizza store, watching the owner knead the pizza dough, flatten it into a large circular crust, fling it up, and then spread on tomato sauce in larger and larger loops. After graduating from college as a marketing major, he made a beeline back to the Bronx, where he opened his first Angelo's Pizza store, emphasizing its clean, bright interior; its crisp green, red, and white sign; and his all-natural, fresh ingredients. Within five years, Angelo's store was a success, and he had opened three other stores and was considering franchising his concept.

Eager as he was to expand, his four years in business school had taught him the difference between being an entrepreneur and being a manager. As an entrepreneur/small business owner, he knew he had the distinct advantage of being able to personally run the whole operation himself. With just one store and a handful of employees, he could make every decision and watch the cash register, check in the new supplies, oversee the takeout, and personally supervise the service.

When he expanded to three stores, things started getting challenging. He hired managers for the two new stores (both of whom had worked for him at his first store for several years) and gave them only minimal "how to run a store"–type training, on the assumption that, having worked with him for several years, they already knew pretty much everything they needed to know about running a store. However, he was already experiencing human resource management problems, and he knew there was no way he could expand the number of stores he owned, or (certainly) contemplate franchising his idea, unless he had a system in place that he could clone in each new store to provide the managers (or the franchisees) with the necessary management knowledge and expertise to run their stores. Angelo had no training program in place for teaching his store managers how to run their stores. He simply (erroneously, as it turned out) assumed that by working with him they would learn how to do things on the job. Since Angelo had no system in place, the new managers were, in a way, starting off below zero when it came to how to manage a store.

* Written and copyrighted by Gary Dessler, PhD.

There were several issues that particularly concerned Angelo. Finding and hiring good employees was number one. He'd read the new National Small Business Poll from the National Federation of Independent Business Education Foundation. It found that 71% of small business owners believed that finding qualified employees was "hard." Furthermore, "the search for qualified employees will grow more difficult as demographic and education factors" continue to make it more difficult to find employees. Similarly, reading the *Kiplinger Letter* one day, he noticed that just about every type of business couldn't find enough good employees to hire. Small firms were particularly in jeopardy; the *Letter* said that giant firms can outsource many (particularly entry-level) jobs abroad, and larger companies can also afford to pay better benefits and to train their employees. Small firms rarely have the resources or the economies of scale to allow outsourcing or to install the big training programs that would enable them to take untrained new employees and turn them into skilled ones.

Although finding enough employees was his biggest problem, finding enough honest ones scared him even more. Angelo recalled from one of his business school courses that companies in the United States are losing a total of well over $400 billion a year in employee theft. As a rough approximation, that works out to about $9 per employee per day and about $12,000 lost annually for a typical company. Furthermore, it was small companies like Angelo's that were particularly in the crosshairs, because companies with fewer than 100 employees are particularly prone to employee theft. Why are small firms particularly vulnerable? Perhaps they lack experience dealing with the problem. More importantly: Small firms are more likely to have a single person doing several jobs, such as ordering supplies and paying the delivery person. This undercuts the checks and balances managers often strive for to control theft. Furthermore, the risk of stealing goes up dramatically when the business is largely based on cash. In a pizza store, many people come in and buy just one or two slices and a cola for lunch, and almost all pay with cash, not credit cards.

And, Angelo was not just worried about someone stealing cash. They can steal your whole business idea, something he learned from painful experience. He had been planning to open a store in what he thought would be a particularly good location, and was thinking of having one of his current employees manage the store. Instead, it turned out that this employee was, in a manner of speaking, stealing Angelo's brain: what Angelo knew about customers, suppliers, where to buy pizza dough, where to buy tomato sauce, how much everything should cost, how to furnish the store, where to buy ovens, store layout—everything. This employee soon quit and opened up his own pizza store, not far from where Angelo had planned to open his new store.

That he was having trouble hiring good employees, there was no doubt. The restaurant business is particularly brutal when it comes to turnover. Many restaurants turn over their employees at a rate of 200% to 300% per year—so every year, each position might have a series of two to three employees filling it. As Angelo said, "I was losing two to three employees a month," adding, "We're a high-volume store, and while we should have about six employees per store [to fill all the hours in a week], we were down to only three or four, so my managers and I were really under the gun."

The problem was bad at the hourly employee level: "We were churning a lot at the hourly level," said Angelo. "Applicants would come in, my managers or I would hire them and not spend much time training them, and the good ones would leave in frustration after a few weeks, while often it was the bad ones who'd stay behind." But in the last two years, Angelo's three company-owned stores also went through a total of three store managers—"They were just blowing through the door," as Angelo put it, in part because, without good employees, their workday was brutal. As a rule, when a small business owner or manager can't find enough employees (or an employee doesn't show up for work), about 80% of the time the owner or manager does the job himself or herself. So, these managers often ended up working seven days a week, 10 to 12 hours a day, and many just burned out in the end. One night, working three jobs himself with customers leaving in anger, Angelo decided he'd never just hire someone because he was desperate again, but would start doing his hiring more rationally.

Angelo knew he should have a more formal screening process. As he said, "If there's been a lesson learned, it's much better to spend time up front screening out candidates who don't fit than to hire them and have to put up with their ineffectiveness." He also knew that he could identify many of the traits that his employees needed. For example, he knew that not everyone has the temperament to be a waiter (he has a small pizza/Italian restaurant in the back of his main store). As Angelo said, "I've seen personalities that were off the charts in assertiveness or overly introverted, traits that obviously don't make a good fit for a waiter or waitress."

As a local business, Angelo recruits by placing help wanted ads in two local newspapers, and he's been "shocked" at some of the responses and experiences he's had in response to the ads. Many of the applicants left voicemail messages (Angelo or the other workers in the store were too busy to answer), and some applicants Angelo "just axed" on the assumption that people without good telephone manners wouldn't have very good manners in the store, either. He also quickly learned that he had to throw out a very wide net, even if hiring only one or two people. Many people, as noted, he eliminated from consideration because of the messages they left, and about half the people he scheduled to come in for interviews didn't show up. He'd taken courses in human resource management, so (as he said) "I should know better," but he hired people based almost exclusively on a single interview (he occasionally made a feeble attempt to check references). In total, his HR approach was obviously not working. It wasn't producing enough good recruits, and the people he did hire were often problematic.

What was he looking for? Service-oriented courteous people, for one. For example, he'd hired one employee who used profanity several times, including once in front of a customer. On that employee's third day, Angelo had to tell her, "I think Angelo's isn't the right place for you," and he fired her. As Angelo said, "I felt bad, but also knew that everything I have is on the line for this business, so I wasn't going to let anyone run this business down." Angelo wants reliable people (who'll show up on time), honest people, and people who are flexible about switching jobs and hours as required. He calls his management style "trust and track." "I coach them and give them goals, and then carefully track results."

Angelo's Pizza business has only the most rudimentary human resource management system. Angelo bought several application forms at a local Office Depot, and rarely uses other forms of any sort. He uses his personal accountant for reviewing the company's books, and Angelo himself computes each employee's paycheck at the end of the week and writes the checks. Training is entirely on-the-job. Angelo personally trained each of his employees. For those employees who go on to be store managers, he assumes that they are training their own employees the way that Angelo trained them (for better or worse, as it turns out). Angelo pays "a bit above" prevailing wage rates (judging by other help wanted ads), but probably not enough to make a significant difference in the quality of employees whom he attracts. If you asked Angelo what his reputation is as an employer, Angelo, being a candid and forthright person, would probably tell you that he is a supportive but hard-nosed employer who treats people fairly, but whose business reputation may suffer from disorganization stemming from inadequate organization and training. He approaches you to ask you several questions.

Questions

8. My strategy is to (hopefully) expand the number of stores and eventually franchise, while focusing on serving only high-quality fresh ingredients. What are three specific human resource management implications of my strategy (including specific policies and practices)?

9. Identify and briefly discuss five specific human resource management errors that I'm currently making.

10. Develop a structured interview form that we can use for hiring (1) store managers, (2) wait staff, and (3) counter people/pizza makers.
11. Based on what you know about Angelo's, and what you know from having visited pizza restaurants, write a one-page outline showing specifically how you think Angelo's should go about selecting employees.

Based generally on actual facts, but Angelo's Pizza is a fictitious company. Angelo's Pizza source notes: Dino Berta, "People Problems: Keep Hiring from Becoming a Crying Game," *Nation's Business News*, 36, no. 20, May 20, 2002, pp. 72–74; Ellen Lyon, "Hiring, Personnel Problems Can Challenge Entrepreneurs," *Patriot-News*, October 12, 2004; Rose Robin Pedone, "Businesses' $400 Billion Theft Problem," *Long Island Business News*, 27, July 6, 1998, pp. 1B–2B; "Survey Shows Small-Business Problems with Hiring, Internet," *Providence Business News*, 16, September 10, 2001, pp. 1B; "Finding Good Workers Is Posing a Big Problem as Hiring Picks Up," *Kiplinger Letter*, 81, February 13, 2004; Ian Mount, "A Pizzeria Owner Learns the Value of Watching the Books," *The New York Times*, October 25, 2012, p. B8.

ALPHABET (GOOGLE)*

Fortune magazine named Google the best of the 100 best companies to work for, and there is little doubt why. Among the benefits it offers are free shuttles equipped with Wi-Fi to pick up and drop off employees from San Francisco Bay Area locations, unlimited sick days, annual all-expense-paid ski trips, free gourmet meals, five on-site free doctors, $2,000 bonuses for referring a new hire, free flu shots, a giant lap pool, on-site oil changes, on-site car washes, volleyball courts, TGIF parties, free on-site washers and dryers (with free detergent), Ping-Pong and foosball tables, and free famous people lectures. For many people, it's the gourmet meals and snacks that make Google stand out. For example, one human resources director loves the Irish oatmeal with fresh berries at the company's Plymouth Rock Cafe, near Google's "people operations" group. "I sometimes dream about it," she says. Engineer Jan Fitzpatrick loves the raw bar at Google's Tapis restaurant, down the road on the Google campus. Then, of course, there are the stock options—each new employee gets about 1,200 options to buy Google shares (recently worth about $480 per share). In fact, dozens of early Google employees ("Googlers") are already multimillionaires thanks to Google stock. The recession several years ago did prompt Google and other firms to cut back on some of these benefits (cafeteria hours are shorter today, for instance), but Google still pretty much leads the benefits pack.

For their part, Googlers share certain traits. They tend to be super smart, team oriented (teamwork is the norm, especially for big projects), and driven. *Fortune* describes them as people who "almost universally" see themselves as the most interesting people on the planet, and who are happy-go-lucky on the outside, but type A—highly intense and goal directed—on the inside. They're also super-hardworking (which makes sense, since it's not unusual for engineers to be in the hallways at 3 A.M. debating some new mathematical solution to a Google search problem). They're so team oriented that when working on projects, it's not unusual for Google team members to give up their larger, more spacious offices and to crowd into a small conference room, where they can "get things done." Historically, Googlers generally graduate with great grades from the best universities, including Stanford, Harvard, and MIT. For many years, Google wouldn't even consider hiring someone with less than a 3.7 average—while also probing deeply into the why behind any B grades. Google also doesn't hire lone wolves, but wants people who work together and people who also have diverse interests (narrow interests or skills are a turnoff at Google). Google also wants people with growth potential. The company is expanding so fast that it needs to hire people who are capable of being promoted multiple times—it's only, the company says, by hiring such overqualified people that it can be sure that the employees will be able to keep up as Google and their own departments expand.

* Written and copyrighted by Gary Dessler, PhD.

The starting salaries are highly competitive. Experienced engineers start at about $130,000 a year (plus about 1,200 shares of stock options, as noted), and new MBAs can expect between $80,000 and $120,000 per year (with smaller option grants). Software engineering managers average about $217,000 per year. Most recently, Google had about 72,000 staff members, up from its beginnings with just three employees in a rented garage.

Of course, in a company that's grown from 3 employees to 72,000 and from zero value to hundreds of billions of dollars, it may be quibbling to talk about "problems," but there's no doubt that such rapid growth does confront Google's management, and particularly its "people operations" group, with some big challenges. Let's look at these.

For one, Google, as noted earlier, is a 24-hour operation, and with engineers and others frequently pulling all-nighters to complete their projects, the company needs to provide a package of services and financial benefits that supports that kind of lifestyle, and that helps its employees maintain an acceptable work–life balance.

As another challenge, Google's enormous financial success is a two-edged sword. Although Google usually wins the recruitment race when it comes to competing for new employees against competitors like Microsoft or Facebook, Google does need some way to stem a rising tide of retirements. Most Googlers are still in their 20s and 30s, but many have become so wealthy from their Google stock options that they can afford to retire. One 27-year-old engineer received a million-dollar founder's award for her work on the program for searching desktop computers, and wouldn't think of leaving "except to start her own company." Similarly, a former engineering vice president retired (with his Google stock profits) to pursue his love of astronomy. The engineer who dreamed up Gmail retired at the age of 30.

Another challenge is that the work involves not only long hours but can also be very tense. Google is a very numbers-oriented environment. For example, consider a typical weekly Google user interface design meeting. Seated around a conference table are about a dozen Googlers, tapping on laptops. During the 2-hour meeting, the head of search products needs to evaluate various design proposals, ranging from minor tweaks to a new product's entire layout. She's previously given each presentation an allotted amount of time, and a large digital clock on the wall ticks off the seconds. The presenters must quickly present their ideas, but also handle questions such as "what do users do if the tab is moved from the side of the page to the top?" Furthermore, it's all about the numbers—no one at Google would ever say, for instance, "the tab looks better in red"—you need to prove your point. Presenters must come armed with usability experiment results, showing, for instance, that a certain percentage preferred red or some other color. While the presenters are answering these questions as quickly as possible, the digital clock is ticking, and when it hits the allotted time, the presentation must end, and the next team steps up to present. It is a tough and tense environment, and Googlers must have done their homework.

Growth can also undermine the "outlaw band that's changing the world" culture that fostered the services that made Google famous. Even cofounder Sergi Brin agrees that Google risks becoming less "zany" as it grows. To paraphrase one of its top managers, the hard part of any business is keeping that original innovative, small business feel even as the company grows. Several years ago (in 2015) Google appointed Sundar Pichai its new CEO.

Creating the right culture is especially challenging now that Google is truly global. For example, Google works hard to provide the same employee benefits every place it does business around the world, but it can't exactly match its benefits in every country because of international laws and international taxation issues. Yet offering the same benefits everywhere is more important than it might initially appear. All those benefits make life easier for Google staff, and help them achieve a work–life balance. Achieving the right work–life balance is the centerpiece of Google's culture, but this also becomes more challenging as the company grows. On the one hand, Google expects all of its employees to work super hard; on the other hand, it realizes that it needs to help them maintain a healthy balance.

As one manager says, Google acknowledges "that we work hard but that work is not everything."

Recruitment is another challenge. While Google certainly doesn't lack applicants, attracting the right applicants is crucial if Google is to continue to grow successfully. Working at Google requires a special set of traits, and screening employees is easier if it recruits the right people to begin with. For instance, Google needs to attract people who are very smart, love to work, have fun, can handle the stress, and who also have outside interests and flexibility.

As the company grows internationally, it also faces the considerable challenge of recruiting and building staff overseas. For example, Google introduced a new vertical market–based structure across Europe to attract more business advertisers to its search engine. (By vertical market–based structure, Google means focusing on key vertical industry sectors such as travel, retail, automotive, and technology.) To build these industry groupings abroad from scratch, Google promoted its former head of its U.S. financial services group to be the vertical markets director for Europe; he moved there several years ago. Google then had to find heads for each of its vertical industry groups for all of its key European territories. Each of these vertical market heads then have to educate their market sectors (retailing, travel, and so on) so Google can attract new advertisers. Google already has offices around the world.

However, probably the biggest challenge Google faces is evolving its employee selection system, given that the company must hire thousands of people per year. When Google started in business, job candidates typically suffered through a dozen or more in-person interviews, and the standards were so high that even applicants with years of great work experience often got turned down if they had just average college grades. But more recently, even Google's cofounders acknowledged to security analysts that setting such an extraordinarily high bar for hiring was holding back Google's expansion. For Google's early years, one of the company's cofounders interviewed nearly every job candidate before he or she was hired, and even today one of them still reviews the qualifications of everyone before he or she gets a final offer.

The experience of one candidate illustrates what Google was up against. A 24-year-old is interviewed for a corporate communications job at Google. Google first made contact with the candidate in May, and then, after two phone interviews, invited him to headquarters. There he had separate interviews with about six people and was treated to lunch in a Google cafeteria. They also had him turn in several "homework" assignments, including a personal statement and a marketing plan. In August, Google invited the candidate back for a second round, which it said would involve another four or five interviews. In the meantime, he decided he'd rather work at a start-up, and accepted another job at a new Web-based instant messaging provider.

Google's head of "people operations" says that Google is trying to strike the right balance between letting Google and the candidate get to know each other while also moving quickly. To that end, Google administered a survey to all Google's current employees in an effort to identify the traits that correlate with success at Google. In the survey, employees responded to questions relating to about 300 variables, including their performance on standardized tests, how old they were when they first used a computer, and how many foreign languages they speak. The Google survey team then went back and compared the answers against the 30 or 40 job performance factors they keep for each employee. They thereby identified clusters of traits that Google might better focus on during the hiring process. Google also moved from the free-form interviews it used in the past to a more structured process.

Questions

12. What do you think of the idea of Google correlating personal traits from the employees' answers on the survey to their performance, and then using that as the basis for screening job candidates? In other words, is it or is it not a good idea? Please explain your answer.

13. The benefits that Google pays obviously represent an enormous expense. Based on what you know about Google and on what you read in this book, how would you defend all these benefits if you're making a presentation to the security analysts who were analyzing Google's performance?
14. If you wanted to hire the brightest people around, how would you go about recruiting and selecting them? How does your proposed approach compare with how Google actually does it (based on this case and anything else you recall reading about Google in this book)?
15. To support its growth and expansion strategy, Google wants (among other traits) people who are very bright and who work hard, often round-the-clock, and who are flexible and maintain a decent work–life balance. List five specific HR policies or practices that you think Google has implemented or should implement to support its strategy, and explain your answer.
16. What sorts of factors do you think Google will have to take into consideration as it tries transferring its culture and reward systems and way of doing business to its operations abroad?
17. Given the sorts of values and culture Google cherishes, briefly describe four specific activities you suggest it pursue during new-employee orientation.

Source: Notes for Google: "Google Brings Vertical Structure to Europe," *New Media Age*, August 4, 2005, p. 2; Debbie Lovewell, "Employer Profile—Google: Searching for Talent," *Employee Benefits*, October 10, 2005, p. 66; "Google Looking for Gourmet Chefs," *Internet Week*, August 4, 2005; Douglas Merrill, "Google's 'Googley' Culture Kept Alive by Tech," *eWeek*, April 11, 2006; Robert Hof, "Google Gives Employees Another Option," *BusinessWeek Online*, December 13, 2005; Kevin Delaney, "Google Adjusts Hiring Process as Needs Grow," *The Wall Street Journal*, October 23, 2006, pp. B1, B8; Adam Lishinsky, "Search and Enjoy," *Fortune*, January 22, 2007, pp. 70–82; www.nypost.com/seven/10302008/business/frugal_google_cuts_perks_136011.htm, accessed July 12, 2009; Adam Bryant, "The Quest to Build a Better Boss," *New York Times*, March 13, 2011, pp. 1, 7; Mark C. Crowley, "Not a Happy Accident: How Google Deliberately Designs Workplace Satisfaction," www.fastcompany.com/3007268/where-are-they-now/not-happy-accident-how-google-deliberately-designs-workplace-satisfaction, accessed September 16, 2014; Google salaries in the United States, https://www.indeed.com/cmp/Google/salaries, accessed May 8, 2018; https://www.recode.net/2017/7/24/16022210/alphabet-google-employment-employees-doubled-headcount, accessed May 8, 2018; http://fortune.com/best-companies/2017/google/, accessed May 8, 2018.

MUFFLER MAGIC*

Muffler Magic is a fast-growing chain of 25 automobile service centers in Nevada. Originally started 20 years ago as a muffler repair shop by Ronald Brown, the chain expanded rapidly to new locations, and as it did so Muffler Magic also expanded the services it provided, from muffler replacement to oil changes, brake jobs, and engine repair. Today, one can bring an automobile to a Muffler Magic shop for basically any type of service, from tires to mufflers to engine repair.

Auto service is a tough business. The shop owner is basically dependent upon the quality of the service people he or she hires and retains, and the most qualified mechanics find it easy to pick up and leave for a job paying a bit more at a competitor down the road. It's also a business in which productivity is very important. The single largest expense is usually the cost of labor. Auto service dealers generally don't just make up the prices that they charge customers for various repairs; instead, they charge based on standardized industry rates for jobs like changing spark plugs or repairing a leaky radiator. Therefore, if someone brings a car in for a new alternator and the standard number of hours for changing the alternator is an hour, but it takes the mechanic 2 hours, the service center's owner may end up making less profit on the transaction.

Quality is a persistent problem as well. For example, "rework" has recently been a problem at Muffler Magic. A customer recently brought her car to a Muffler Magic to have the car's brake pads replaced, which the service center did for her. Unfortunately, when she left she drove only about two blocks before she discovered that she had no brake power at all. It was simply fortuitous that she was going so

* Written and copyrighted by Gary Dessler, PhD.

slowly she was able to stop her car by slowly rolling up against a parking bumper. It subsequently turned out that the mechanic who replaced the brake pads had failed to properly tighten a fitting on the hydraulic brake tubes and the brake fluid had run out, leaving the car with no braking power. In a similar problem the month before that, a (different) mechanic replaced a fan belt, but forgot to refill the radiator with fluid; that customer's car overheated before he got four blocks away, and Muffler Magic had to replace the whole engine. Of course problems like these not only diminish the profitability of the company's profits, but, repeated many times over, have the potential for ruining Muffler Magic's word-of-mouth reputation.

Organizationally, Muffler Magic employs about 300 people, and Ron runs his company with eight managers, including himself as president, a controller, a purchasing director, a marketing director, and the human resource manager. He also has three regional managers to whom the eight or nine service center managers in each area of Nevada report. Over the past two years, as the company has opened new service centers, company-wide profits have diminished rather than increased. In part, these diminishing profits probably reflect the fact that Ron Brown has found it increasingly difficult to manage his growing operation. ("Your reach is exceeding your grasp" is how Ron's wife puts it.)

The company has only the most basic HR systems in place. It uses an application form that the human resource manager modified from one that he downloaded from the Web, and the standard employee status change request forms, sign-on forms, I-9 forms, and so on, that it purchased from a human resource management supply house. Training is entirely on-the-job. Muffler Magic expects the experienced technicians that it hires to come to the job fully trained; to that end, the service center managers generally ask candidates for these jobs basic behavioral questions that hopefully provide a window into these applicants' skills. However, most of the other technicians hired to do jobs like rotating tires, fixing brake pads, and replacing mufflers are untrained and inexperienced. They are to be trained by either the service center manager or by more experienced technicians, on-the-job.

Ron Brown faces several HR-type problems. One, as he says, is that he faces the "tyranny of the immediate" when it comes to hiring employees. Although it's fine to say that he should be carefully screening each employee and checking his or her references and work ethic, from a practical point of view, with 25 centers to run, the centers' managers usually just hire anyone who seems to be breathing, as long as he or she can answer some basic interview questions about auto repair, such as, "What do you think the problem is if a 2001 Camry is overheating, and what would you do about it?"

Employee safety is also a problem. An automobile service center may not be the most dangerous type of workplace, but it is potentially dangerous. Employees are dealing with sharp tools, greasy floors, greasy tools, extremely hot temperatures (for instance, on mufflers and engines), and fast-moving engine parts including fan blades. There are some basic things that a service manager can do to ensure more safety, such as insisting that all oil spills be cleaned up immediately. However, from a practical point of view, there are few ways to get around many of the problems—such as when the technician must check out an engine while it is running.

With Muffler Magic's profits going down instead of up, Brown's human resource manager has taken the position that the main problem is financial. As he says, "You get what you pay for" when it comes to employees, and if you compensate technicians better than your competitors do, then you get better technicians, ones who do their jobs better and stay longer with the company—and then profits will rise. So, the HR manager scheduled a meeting between himself, Ron Brown, and a professor of business who teaches compensation management at a local university. The HR manager has asked this professor to spend about a week looking at each of the service centers, analyzing the situation, and coming up with a compensation plan that will address Muffler Magic's quality and productivity problems. At this meeting, the professor makes three basic recommendations for changing the company's compensation policies.

Number one, she says that she has found that Muffler Magic suffers from what she calls "presenteeism"—in other words, employees drag themselves into work even when they're sick, because the company does not pay them if they are out; the company offers no sick days. In just a few days the professor couldn't properly quantify how much Muffler Magic is losing to presenteeism. However, from what she could see at each shop, there are typically one or two technicians working with various maladies like the cold or flu, and it seemed to her that each of these people was probably really only working about half of the time (although they were getting paid for the whole day). So, for 25 service centers per week, Muffler Magic could well be losing 125 or 130 personnel days per week of work. The professor suggests that Muffler Magic start allowing everyone to take three paid sick days per year, a reasonable suggestion. However, as Ron Brown points out, "Right now, we're only losing about half a day's pay for each employee who comes in and who works unproductively; with your suggestion, won't we lose the whole day?" The professor says she'll ponder that one.

Second, the professor recommends putting the technicians on a skill-for-pay plan. Basically, she suggests the following. Give each technician a letter grade (A through E) based upon that technician's particular skill level and abilities. An "A" technician is a team leader and needs to show that he or she has excellent diagnostic troubleshooting skills, and the ability to supervise and direct other technicians. At the other extreme, an "E" technician would typically be a new apprentice with little technical training. The other technicians fall in between those two levels, based on their individual skills and abilities.

In the professor's system, the "A" technician or team leader would assign and supervise all work done within his or her area but generally not do any mechanical repairs himself or herself. The team leader does the diagnostic troubleshooting, supervises and trains the other technicians, and test drives the car before it goes back to the customer. Under this plan, every technician receives a guaranteed hourly wage within a certain range, for instance:

A tech = \$25–\$30 an hour
B tech = \$20–\$25 an hour
C tech = \$15–\$20 an hour
D tech = \$10–\$15 an hour
E tech = \$8–\$10 an hour

Third, to directly address the productivity issue, the professor recommends that each service manager calculate each technician-team's productivity at the end of each day and at the end of each week. She suggests posting the running productivity total conspicuously for daily viewing. Then, the technicians as a group get weekly cash bonuses based upon their productivity. To calculate productivity, the professor recommends dividing the total labor hours billed by the total labor hours paid to technicians; in other words, total labor hours billed *divided by* total hours paid to technicians.

Having done some homework, the professor says that the national average for labor productivity is currently about 60%, and that only the best-run service centers achieve 85% or greater. By her rough calculations, Muffler Magic was attaining about industry average (about 60%—in other words, they were billing for only about 60 hours for each 100 hours that they actually had to pay technicians to do the jobs). (Of course, this was not entirely the technicians' fault. Technicians get time off for breaks and for lunch, and if a particular service center simply didn't have enough business on a particular day or during a particular week, then several technicians may well sit around idly waiting for the next car to come in.) The professor recommends setting a labor efficiency goal of 80% and posting each team's daily productivity results in the workplace to provide them with additional feedback. She recommends that if at the end of a week the team is able to boost its productivity ratio from the current 60% to 80%, then that team would get an additional

10% weekly pay bonus. After that, for every 5% boost of increased productivity above 80%, technicians would receive an additional 5% weekly bonus. So, if a technician's normal weekly pay is $400, that employee would receive an extra $40 at the end of the week when his team moves from 60% productivity to 80% productivity.

After the meeting, Ron Brown thanked the professor for her recommendations and told her he would think about it and get back to her. After the meeting, on the drive home, Ron was pondering what to do. He had to decide whether to institute the professor's sick leave policy, and whether to implement the professor's incentive and compensation plan. Before implementing anything, however, he wanted to make sure he understood the context in which he was making his decision. For example, did Muffler Magic really have an incentive pay problem, or were the problems more broad? Furthermore, how, if at all, would the professor's incentive plan impact the quality of the work that the teams were doing? And should the company really start paying employees for sick days? Ron Brown had a lot to think about.

Questions

18. Write a one-page summary outline listing three or four recommendations you would make with respect to each HR function (recruiting, selection, training, and so on) that you think Ron Brown should be addressing with his HR manager.

19. Develop a 10-question structured interview form Ron Brown's service center managers can use to interview experienced technicians.

20. If you were Ron Brown, would you implement the professor's recommendation addressing the presenteeism problem—in other words, start paying for sick days? Why or why not?

21. If you were advising Ron Brown, would you recommend that he implement the professor's skill-based pay and incentive pay plan as is? Why? Would you implement it with modifications? If you would modify it, please be specific about what you think those modifications should be, and why.

Based generally on actual facts, but Muffler Magic is a fictitious company. This case is based largely on information in Drew Paras, "The Pay Factor: Technicians' Salaries Can Be the Largest Expense in a Server Shop, as Well as the Biggest Headache. Here's How One Shop Owner Tackled the Problem," *Motor Age*, November 2003, pp. 76–79; see also Jennifer Pellet, "Health Care Crisis," *Chief Executive*, June 2004, pp. 56–61; "Firms Press to Quantify, Control Presenteeism," *Employee Benefits*, December 1, 2002.

BP TEXAS CITY*

When British Petroleum's (BP) Horizon oil rig exploded in the Gulf of Mexico in 2010, it triggered tragic reminders for experts in the safety community. In March 2005, an explosion and fire at BP's Texas City, Texas, refinery killed 15 people and injured 500 people in the worst U.S. industrial accident in more than 10 years. That disaster triggered three investigations: one internal investigation by BP, one by the U.S. Chemical Safety Board, and an independent investigation chaired by former U.S. Secretary of State James Baker and an 11-member panel that was organized at BP's request.

To put the results of these three investigations into context, it's useful to understand that under its current management, BP had pursued, for the past 10 or so years before the Texas City explosion, a strategy emphasizing cost-cutting and profitability. The basic conclusion of the investigations was that cost-cutting helped compromise safety at the Texas City refinery. It's useful to consider each investigation's findings.

The Chemical Safety Board's (CSB) investigation, according to Carol Merritt, the board's chair, showed that "BP's global management was aware of problems with maintenance, spending, and infrastructure well before March 2005." Apparently,

* Written and copyrighted by Gary Dessler, PhD.

faced with numerous earlier accidents, BP did make some safety improvements. However, it focused primarily on emphasizing personal employee safety behaviors and procedural compliance, and thereby reducing safety accident rates. The problem (according to the CSB) was that "catastrophic safety risks remained." For example, according to the CSB, "unsafe and antiquated equipment designs were left in place, and unacceptable deficiencies in preventive maintenance were tolerated." Basically, the CSB found that BP's budget cuts led to a progressive deterioration of safety at the Texas City refinery. Said Merritt, "In an aging facility like Texas City, it is not responsible to cut budgets related to safety and maintenance without thoroughly examining the impact on the risk of a catastrophic accident."

Looking at specifics, the CSB said that a 2004 internal audit of 35 BP business units, including Texas City (BP's largest refinery), found significant safety gaps they all had in common, including, for instance, a lack of leadership competence, and "systemic underlying issues" such as a widespread tolerance of noncompliance with basic safety rules and poor monitoring of safety management systems and processes. Ironically, the CSB found that BP's accident prevention effort at Texas City had achieved a 70% reduction in worker injuries in the year before the explosion. Unfortunately, this simply meant that individual employees were having fewer accidents. The larger, more fundamental problem was that the potentially explosive situation inherent in the depreciating machinery remained.

The CSB found that the Texas City explosion followed a pattern of years of major accidents at the facility. In fact, there had apparently been an average of one employee death every 16 months at the plant for the last 30 years. The CSB found that the equipment directly involved in the most recent explosion was an obsolete design already phased out in most refineries and chemical plants, and that key pieces of its instrumentation were not working. There had also been previous instances where flammable vapors were released from the same unit in the 10 years prior to the explosion. In 2003, an external audit had referred to the Texas City refinery's infrastructure and assets as "poor" and found what it referred to as a "checkbook mentality," one in which budgets were not sufficient to manage all the risks. In particular, the CSB found that BP had implemented a 25% cut on fixed costs between 1998 and 2000 and that this adversely impacted maintenance expenditures and net expenditures, and refinery infrastructure. Going on, the CSB found that in 2004, there were three major accidents at the refinery that killed three workers.

BP's own internal report concluded that the problems at Texas City were not of recent origin, and instead were years in the making. It said BP was taking steps to address them. Its investigation found "no evidence of anyone consciously or intentionally taking actions or making decisions that put others at risk." Said BP's report, "The underlying reasons for the behaviors and actions displayed during the incident are complex, and the team has spent much time trying to understand them—it is evident that they were many years in the making and will require concerted and committed actions to address." BP's report concluded that there were five underlying causes for the massive explosion:

- A working environment had eroded to one characterized by resistance to change, and a lack of trust.
- Safety, performance, and risk-reduction priorities had not been set and consistently reinforced by management.
- Changes in the "complex organization" led to a lack of clear accountabilities and poor communication.
- A poor level of hazard awareness and understanding of safety resulted in workers accepting levels of risk that were considerably higher than at comparable installations.
- Adequate early warning systems for problems were lacking, and there were no independent means of understanding the deteriorating standards at the plant.

The report from the BP-initiated but independent 11-person panel chaired by former U.S. Secretary of State James Baker contained specific conclusions and recommendations. The Baker panel looked at BP's corporate safety oversight, the corporate safety culture, and the process safety management systems at BP at the Texas City plant as well as at BP's other refineries.

Basically, the Baker panel concluded that BP had not provided effective safety process leadership and had not established safety as a core value at the five refineries it looked at (including Texas City).

Like the CSB, the Baker panel found that BP had emphasized personal safety in recent years and had in fact improved personal safety performance, but had not emphasized the overall safety process, thereby mistakenly interpreting "improving personal injury rates as an indication of acceptable process safety performance at its U.S. refineries." In fact, the Baker panel went on, by focusing on these some what misleading improving personal injury rates, BP created a false sense of confidence that it was properly addressing process safety risks. It also found that the safety culture at Texas City did not have the positive, trusting, open environment that a proper safety culture required. The Baker panel's other findings included the following.

- BP did not always ensure that adequate resources were effectively allocated to support or sustain a high level of process safety performance.
- BP's refinery personnel are "overloaded" by corporate initiatives.
- Operators and maintenance personnel work high rates of overtime.
- BP tended to have a short-term focus and its decentralized management system and entrepreneurial culture delegated substantial discretion to refinery plant managers "without clearly defining process safety expectations, responsibilities, or accountabilities."
- There was no common, unifying process safety culture among the five refineries.
- The company's corporate safety management system did not make sure there was timely compliance with internal process safety standards and programs.
- BP's executive management either did not receive refinery-specific information that showed that process safety deficiencies existed at some of the plants, or did not effectively respond to any information it did receive.

The Baker panel made several safety recommendations for BP, including the following.

1. The company's corporate management must provide leadership on process safety.
2. The company should establish a process safety management system that identifies, reduces, and manages the process safety risks of the refineries.
3. The company should make sure its employees have an appropriate level of process safety knowledge and expertise.
4. The company should involve "relevant stakeholders" in developing a positive, trusting, and open process safety culture at each refinery.
5. BP should clearly define expectations and strengthen accountability for process safety performance.
6. BP should better coordinate its process safety support for the refining line organization.
7. BP should develop an integrated set of leading and lagging performance indicators for effectively monitoring process safety performance.
8. BP should establish and implement an effective system to audit process safety performance.
9. The company's board should monitor the implementation of the panel's recommendations and the ongoing process safety performance of the refineries.
10. BP should transform itself into a recognized industry leader in process safety management.[1]

[1] These findings and the following suggestions are based on "BP Safety Report Finds Company's Process Safety Culture Ineffective," *Global Refining & Fuels Report*, January 17, 2007.

In making its recommendations, the panel singled out the company's chief executive at the time, Lord Browne, by saying, "In hindsight, the panel believes if Browne had demonstrated comparable leadership on and commitment to process safety [as he did for responding to climate change] that would have resulted in a higher level of safety at refineries."

Overall, the Baker panel found that BP's top management had not provided "effective leadership" on safety. It found that the failings went to the very top of the organization, to the company's chief executive, and to several of his top lieutenants. The Baker panel emphasized the importance of top management commitment, saying, for instance, that "it is imperative that BP leadership set the process safety tone at the top of the organization and establish appropriate expectations regarding process safety performance." It also said BP "has not provided effective leadership in making certain its management and U.S. refining workforce understand what is expected of them regarding process safety performance."

Lord Browne, the chief executive, stepped down about a year after the explosion. About the same time, some BP shareholders were calling for the company's executives and board directors to have their bonuses more closely tied to the company's safety and environmental performance in the wake of Texas City. In October 2009, OSHA announced it was filing the largest fine in its history for this accident, for $87 million, against BP. One year later, BP's Horizon oil rig in the Gulf of Mexico exploded, taking 11 lives. In September 2014, the U.S. District judge presiding over negligence claims in the ensuing case found BP guilty of gross negligence, basically reckless and extreme behavior; the company will appeal his ruling.

Questions

22. The text defines ethics as "the principles of conduct governing an individual or a group," and specifically as the standards one uses to decide what his or her conduct should be. To what extent do you believe that what happened at BP is as much a breakdown in the company's ethical systems as it is in its safety systems, and how would you defend your conclusion?

23. Are the Occupational Safety and Health Administration's standards, policies, and rules aimed at addressing problems like the ones that apparently existed at the Texas City plant? If so, how would you explain the fact that problems like these could have continued for so many years?

24. Since there were apparently at least three deaths in the year prior to the major explosion, and an average of about one employee death per 16 months for the previous 10 years, how would you account for the fact that mandatory OSHA inspections missed these glaring sources of potential catastrophic events?

25. The text lists numerous suggestions for "how to prevent accidents." Based on what you know about the Texas City explosion, what do you say Texas City tells you about the most important three steps an employer can take to prevent accidents?

26. Based on what you learned in Chapter 16, would you make any additional recommendations to BP over and above those recommendations made by the Baker panel and the CSB? If so, what would those recommendations be?

27. Explain specifically how strategic human resource management at BP seems to have supported the company's broader strategic aims. What does this say about the advisability of always linking human resource strategy to a company's strategic aims?

Source: Notes for BP Texas City: Sheila McNulty, "BP Knew of Safety Problems, Says Report," *Financial Times*, October 31, 2006, p. 1 "CBS: Documents Show BP Was Aware of Texas City Safety Problems," *World Refining & Fuels Today*, October 30, 2006; "BP Safety Report Finds Company's Process Safety Culture Ineffective," *Global Refining & Fuels Report*, January 17, 2007; "BP Safety Record Under Attack," *Europe Intelligence Wire*, January 17, 2007; Mark Hofmann, "BP Slammed for Poor Leadership on Safety, Oil Firm Agrees to Act on Review Panel's Recommendations," *Business Intelligence*, January 22, 2007, p. 3 "Call for Bonuses to Include Link with Safety Performance," *Guardian*, January 18, 2007, p. 24 www.bp.com/genericarticle.do?categoryId=9005029&contentId=7015905, accessed July 12, 2009; Steven Greenhouse, "BP Faces Record Fine for '05 Blast,"

The New York Times, October 30, 2009, pp. 1, 6; Kyle W. Morrison, "Blame to Go Around," *Safety & Health*, 183, no. 3, March 2011, p. 40 Ed Crooks, "BP Had Tools to End Spill Sooner, Court Told," www.ft.com/cms/s/0/40d7b076-2ae8-11e3-8fb8-00144feab7de.html?ftcamp=published_links%2Frss%2Fhome_uk%2Ffeed%2F%2Fproduct#axzz2gZshHFOc, accessed October 2, 2013; Daniel Gilbert and Justin Scheck, "Judge Hammers BP for Gulf Disaster," *The Wall Street Journal*, September 5, 2014, pp. B1, B2.

GLOSSARY

4/5ths rule Federal agency rule that a minority selection rate less than 80% (4/5ths) of that for the group with the highest rate is evidence of adverse impact.

401(k) plan A defined contribution plan based on section 401(k) of the Internal Revenue Code.

action learning A training technique by which management trainees are allowed to work full-time analyzing and solving problems in other departments.

adaptability screening A process that aims to assess the assignees' (and spouses') probable success in handling a foreign transfer.

adverse impact The overall impact of employer practices that result in significantly higher percentages of members of minorities and other protected groups being rejected for employment, placement, or promotion.

affirmative action Steps that are taken for the purpose of eliminating the present effects of past discrimination.

Age Discrimination in Employment Act of 1967 (ADEA) The act prohibiting arbitrary age discrimination and specifically protecting individuals over 40 years old.

agency shop A form of union security in which employees who do not belong to the union must still pay union dues on the assumption that union efforts benefit all workers.

alternation ranking method Ranking employees from best to worst on a particular trait, choosing highest, then lowest, until all are ranked.

alternative dispute resolution or ADR program Grievance procedure that provides for binding arbitration as the last step.

alternative staffing The use of nontraditional recruitment sources.

Americans with Disabilities Act (ADA) The act requiring employers to make reasonable accommodations for disabled employees; it prohibits discrimination against disabled persons.

analytics Using tools like statistical techniques to examine data, in order to draw cause–effect conclusions from that data.

annual bonus Plans that are designed to motivate short-term performance of managers and that are tied to company profitability.

applicant tracking systems (ATS) Online systems that help employers attract, gather, screen, compile, and manage applicants.

application form The form that provides information on education, prior work record, and skills.

appraisal interview An interview in which the supervisor and subordinate review the appraisal and make plans to remedy deficiencies and reinforce strengths.

apprenticeship training A structured process by which people become skilled workers through a combination of classroom instruction and on-the-job training.

arbitration The most definitive type of third-party intervention, in which the arbitrator usually has the power to determine and dictate the settlement terms.

artificial intelligence Using technology (particularly computers) to carry out tasks in a way that we would consider "human" or "smart".

authority The right to make decisions, direct others' work, and give orders.

authorization cards In order to petition for a union election, the union must show that at least 30% of employees may be interested in being unionized. Employees indicate this interest by signing authorization cards.

bargaining unit The group of employees the union will be authorized to represent.

behavior-based safety Identifying the worker behaviors that contribute to accidents and then training workers to avoid these behaviors.

behavior modeling A training technique in which trainees are first shown good management techniques in a film, are asked to play roles in a simulated situation, and are then given feedback and praise by their supervisor.

behavior modification Using contingent rewards or punishment to change behavior.

behavioral interview A series of job-related questions that focus on how the candidate reacted to actual situations in the past.

behaviorally anchored rating scale (BARS) An appraisal method that aims at combining the benefits of narrative critical incidents and quantified ratings by anchoring a quantified scale with specific narrative examples of good and poor performance.

benchmark job A job that is used to anchor the employer's pay scale and around which other jobs are arranged in order of relative worth.

benefits Indirect financial and nonfinancial payments employees receive for continuing their employment with the company.

bias The tendency to allow individual differences such as age, race, and sex to affect the appraisal ratings employees receive.

bona fide occupational qualification (BFOQ) Requirement that an employee be of a certain religion, sex, or national origin where that is reasonably necessary to the organization's normal operation. Specified by the 1964 Civil Rights Act.

boycott The combined refusal by employees and other interested parties to buy or use the employer's products.

broadbanding Consolidating salary grades and ranges into just a few wide levels or "bands," each of which contains a relatively wide range of jobs and salary levels.

burnout The total depletion of physical and mental resources caused by excessive striving to reach an unrealistic work-related goal.

business process reengineering Redesigning business processes, usually by combining steps, so that small multifunction process teams using information technology do the jobs formerly done by a sequence of departments.

cafeteria benefits plan Individualized tax-qualified plans allowed by employers to accommodate employee preferences for benefits.

candidate-order (or contrast) error An error of judgment on the part of the interviewer due to interviewing one or more very good or very bad candidates just before the interview in question.

career The occupational positions a person has had over many years.

career development The lifelong series of activities that contribute to a person's career exploration, establishment, success, and fulfillment.

career management The process for enabling employees to better understand and develop their career skills and interests, and to use these skills and interests more effectively.

career planning The deliberate process through which someone becomes aware of personal skills, interests, knowledge, motivations, and other characteristics and establishes action plans to attain specific goals.

case study method A development method in which the manager is presented with a written description of an organizational problem to diagnose and solve.

cash balance plans Plans under which the employer contributes a percentage of employees' current pay to employees' pension plans every year, and employees earn interest on this amount.

central tendency A tendency to rate all employees the same way, such as rating them all average.

citation Summons informing employers and employees of the regulations and standards that have been violated in the workplace.

Civil Rights Act of 1991 (CRA 1991) The act that places the burden of proof back on employers and permits compensatory and punitive damages.

classes Grouping jobs based on a set of rules for each group or class, such as amount of independent judgment, skill, physical effort, and so forth, required. Classes usually contain similar jobs.

closed shop A form of union security in which the company can hire only union members. This was outlawed in 1947 but still exists in some industries (such as printing).

coaching Educating, instructing, and training subordinates.

codetermination Employees have the legal right to a voice in setting company policies.

collective bargaining The process through which representatives of management and the union meet to negotiate a labor agreement.

college recruiting Sending an employer's representatives to college campuses to prescreen applicants and create an applicant pool from the graduating class.

compa ratio Equals an employee's pay rate divided by the pay range midpoint for his or her pay grade.

comparable worth The concept by which women who are usually paid less than men can claim that men in comparable rather than in strictly equal jobs are paid more.

compensable factor A fundamental, compensable element of a job, such as skills, effort, responsibility, and working conditions.

competency-based job analysis Describing the job in terms of measurable, observable, behavioral competencies (knowledge, skills, and/or behaviors) that an employee doing that job must exhibit to do the job well.

competency-based pay Where the company pays for the employee's range, depth, and types of skills and knowledge, rather than for the job title he or she holds.

competency model A graphic model that consolidates, usually in one diagram, a precise overview of the competencies (the knowledge, skills, and behaviors) someone would need to do a job well.

competitive advantage Any factors that allow an organization to differentiate its product or service from those of its competitors to increase market share.

competitive strategy A strategy that identifies how to build and strengthen the business's long-term competitive position in the marketplace.

compressed workweek Schedule in which employee works fewer but longer days each week.

construct validity A test that is construct valid is one that demonstrates that a selection procedure measures a construct and that construct is important for successful job performance.

content validity A test that is content valid is one that contains a fair sample of the tasks and skills actually needed for the job in question.

controlled experimentation Formal methods for testing the effectiveness of a training program, preferably with before-and-after tests and a control group.

corporate campaign An organized effort by the union that exerts pressure on the corporation by pressuring the company's other unions, shareholders, directors, customers, creditors, and government agencies, often directly.

corporate-level strategy Type of strategy that identifies the portfolio of businesses that, in total, comprise the company and the ways in which these businesses relate to each other.

criterion validity A type of validity based on showing that scores on the test (predictors) are related to job performance (criterion).

critical incident method Keeping a record of uncommonly good or undesirable examples of an employee's work-related behavior and reviewing it with the employee at predetermined times.

cross training Training employees to do different tasks or jobs than their own; doing so facilitates flexibility and job rotation.

Davis-Bacon Act (1931) A 1931 law that sets wage rates for laborers employed by contractors working for the federal government.

decertification Legal process for employees to terminate a union's right to represent them.

deferred profit-sharing plan A plan in which a certain amount of profits is credited to each employee's account, payable at retirement, termination, or death.

defined benefit pension plan A plan that contains a formula for determining retirement benefits.

defined contribution pension plan A plan in which the employer's contribution to employees' retirement savings funds is specified.

diary/log Daily listings made by workers of every activity in which they engage along with the time each activity takes.

digital dashboard Presents the manager with desktop graphs and charts, and shows a computerized picture of where the company stands on all those metrics from the HR scorecard process.

direct financial payments Pay in the form of wages, salaries, incentives, commissions, and bonuses.

discrimination Taking specific actions toward or against a person based on the person's group.

dismissal Involuntary termination of an employee's employment with the firm.

disparate rejection rates A test for adverse impact in which it can be demonstrated that there is a discrepancy between rates of rejection of members of a protected group and of others.

distributive justice Refers to a system of distributing rewards and discipline in which the actual results or outcomes are evenhanded and fair.

diversity The variety or multiplicity of demographic features that characterize a company's workforce, particularly in terms of race, sex, culture, national origin, handicap, age, and religion.

downsizing The process of reducing, usually dramatically, the number of people employed by a firm.

early retirement window A type of offering by which employees are encouraged to retire early, the incentive being liberal pension benefits plus perhaps a cash payment.

earnings-at-risk pay plan Plan that puts some portion of employees' normal pay at risk if they don't meet their goals, in return for possibly obtaining a much larger bonus if they exceed their goals.

economic strike A strike that results from a failure to agree on the terms of a contract that involves wages, benefits, and other conditions of employment.

Electronic Communications Privacy Act (ECPA) The ECPA is a federal law intended to help restrict interception and monitoring of oral and wire communications.

electronic performance monitoring (EPM) Having supervisors electronically monitor the amount of computerized data an employee is processing per day, and thereby his or her performance.

electronic performance support systems (EPSS) Sets of computerized tools and displays that automate training, documentation, and phone support; integrate this automation into applications; and provide support that's faster, cheaper, and more effective than traditional methods.

employee assistance program (EAP) A formal employer program for providing employees with counseling and/or treatment programs for problems such as alcoholism, gambling, or stress.

employee compensation All forms of pay or rewards going to employees and arising from their employment.

employee orientation A procedure for providing new employees with basic background information about the firm.

employee recruiting Finding and/or attracting applicants for the employer's open positions.

employee relations The activity that involves establishing and maintaining the positive employee–employer relationships that contribute to satisfactory productivity, motivation, morale, and discipline, and to maintaining a positive, productive, and cohesive work environment.

Employee Retirement Income Security Act (ERISA) The 1974 law that provides government protection of pensions for all employees with company pension plans. It also regulates vesting rights (employees who leave before retirement may claim compensation from the pension plan); signed into law by President Ford to require that pension rights be vested and protected by a government agency, the PBGC.

employee stock ownership plan (ESOP) A qualified, tax deductible stock bonus plan in which employers contribute stock to a trust for eventual use by employees. The corporation contributes shares of its own stock to a trust in which additional contributions are made annually. The trust distributes the stock to employees on retirement or separation from service.

employment engagement The extent to which an organization's employees are psychologically involved in, connected to, and committed to getting their jobs done.

Equal Employment Opportunity Commission (EEOC) The commission, created by Title VII, empowered to investigate job discrimination complaints and sue on behalf of complainants.

Equal Pay Act of 1963 The act requiring equal pay for equal work, regardless of sex; specifically, a 1963 amendment to the Fair Labor Standards Act designed to require equal pay for women doing the same work as men.

ethics The principles of conduct governing an individual or a group; specifically, the standards you use to decide what your conduct should be; the study of standards of conduct and moral judgment; also the standards of right conduct.

ethnocentric Here the company staffs its positions abroad with employees from its headquarters—with parent-country nationals, in other words.

ethnocentrism The tendency to view members of other social groups less favorably than members of one's own group.

executive coach An outside consultant who questions the executive's associates in order to identify the executive's strengths and weaknesses, and then counsels the executive so he or she can capitalize on those strengths and overcome the weaknesses.

exit interviews Interviews with employees who are leaving the firm, conducted for obtaining information about the job or related matters, to give the employer insight about the company.

expatriates (expats) Noncitizens of the countries in which employees are working.

expectancy chart A graph showing the relationship between test scores and job performance for a group of people.

expectancy A person's expectation that his or her effort will lead to performance.

fact finder A neutral party who studies the issues in a dispute and makes a public recommendation for a reasonable settlement.

fair day's work Output standards devised based on careful, scientific analysis.

Fair Labor Standards Act (1938) This 1938 act provides for minimum wages, maximum hours, overtime pay, and child labor protection. The law, amended many times, covers most employees.

fair treatment Reflects concrete actions, such as "employees are treated with respect," and "employees are treated fairly."

family-friendly (or work–life) benefits Benefits such as child care that make it easier for employees to balance their work and family responsibilities.

Federal Violence Against Women Act of 1994 The act that provides that a person who commits a crime of violence motivated by gender shall be liable to the party injured.

financial incentives Financial rewards paid to workers whose production exceeds some predetemined standard.

flextime A work schedule in which employees' workdays are built around a core of midday hours, and employees determine, within limits, what other hours they will work.

forced distribution method Similar to grading on a curve; predetermined percentages of ratees are placed in various performance categories.

foreign service premiums Financial payments over and above regular base pay, typically ranging between 10% and 30% of base pay.

functional strategy A strategy that identifies the broad activities that each department will pursue in order to help the business accomplish its competitive goals.

gainsharing plan An incentive plan that engages employees in a common effort to achieve productivity objectives and share the gains.

gender-role stereotypes The tendency to associate women with certain (frequently nonmanagerial) jobs. On the other hand, diversity can be an engine of performance, as the following feature shows.

global The global company aims to attract the best candidates globally, including freely using third-country nationals to staff its positions around the world with the best people available.

golden parachute A payment companies make in connection with a change in ownership or control of a company.

good faith bargaining Both parties are making every reasonable effort to arrive at agreement; proposals are being matched with counterproposals.

good-faith effort strategy An affirmative action strategy that emphasizes identifying and eliminating the obstacles to hiring and promoting women and minorities, and increasing the minority or female applicant flow.

grade definition Written descriptions of the level of, say, responsibility and knowledge required by jobs in each grade. Similar jobs can then be combined into grades or classes.

grades A job classification system like the class system, although grades often contain dissimilar jobs, such as secretaries, mechanics, and firefighters. Grade descriptions are written based on compensable factors listed in classification systems.

graphic rating scale A scale that lists a number of traits and a range of performance for each. The employee is then rated by identifying the score that best describes his or her level of performance for each trait.

graphology The use of handwriting analysis to determine the writer's personality characteristics and moods, and even illnesses, such as depression.

grievance procedure Formal process for addressing any factor involving wages, hours, or conditions of employment that is used as a complaint against the employer.

group life insurance Provides lower rates for the employer or employee and includes all employees, including new employees, regardless of health or physical condition.

halo effect In performance appraisal, the problem that occurs when a supervisor's rating of a subordinate on one trait biases the rating of that person on other traits.

hardship allowances Payments that compensate expatriates for exceptionally hard living and working conditions at certain locations.

health maintenance organization (HMO) A prepaid health-care system that generally provides routine round-the-clock medical services as well as preventive medicine in a clinic-type arrangement for employees, who pay a nominal fee in addition to the fixed annual fee the employer pays.

high-performance work system (HPWS) A set of human resource management policies and practices that promote organizational effectiveness.

HR audit An HR audit is an analysis of the completeness, efficiency, and effectiveness of the organization's HR functions, including its HR policies, practices, processes, and relevant metrics.

HR scorecard A process for assigning financial and nonfinancial goals or metrics to the human resource management–related chain of activities required for achieving the company's strategic aims and for monitoring results.

human resource management (HRM) The process of acquiring, training, appraising, and compensating employees, and of attending to their labor relations, health and safety, and fairness concerns.

human resource metrics The quantitative gauge of a human resource management activity, such as employee turnover, hours of training per employee, or qualified applicants per position.

illegal bargaining items Items in collective bargaining that are forbidden by law; for example, a clause agreeing to hire "union members exclusively" would be illegal in a right-to-work state.

impasse Collective bargaining situation that occurs when the parties are not able to move further toward settlement, usually because one party is demanding more than the other will offer.

in-house development center A company-based method for exposing prospective managers to realistic exercises to develop improved management skills.

indirect financial payments Pay in the form of financial benefits such as insurance.

injunction A court order compelling a party or parties either to resume or to desist from a certain action.

inside games Union efforts to convince employees to impede or to disrupt production—for example, by slowing the work pace.

instrumentality The perceived relationship between successful performance and obtaining the reward.

insubordination Willful disregard or disobedience of the boss's authority or legitimate orders; criticizing the boss in public.

interest arbitration Arbitration enacted when labor agreements do not yet exist or when one or both parties are seeking to change the agreement.

interest inventory A personal development and selection device that compares the person's current interests with those of others now in various occupations so as to determine the preferred occupation for the individual.

international human resource management (IHRM) The human resource management concepts and techniques employers use to manage the human resource aspects of their international operations, including acquiring, training, appraising, and compensating employees, and attending to their labor relations, health and safety, and fairness concerns.

intrinsic motivation Motivation that derives from the pleasure someone gets from doing the job or task.

job aid A set of instructions, diagrams, or similar methods available at the job site to guide the worker.

job analysis The procedure for determining the duties and skill requirements of a job and the kind of person who should be hired for it.

job classification (or job grading) A method for categorizing jobs into groups.

job descriptions A list of a job's duties, responsibilities, reporting relationships, working conditions, and supervisory responsibilities—one product of a job analysis.

job enlargement Assigning workers additional same-level activities.

job enrichment Redesigning jobs in a way that increases the opportunities for the worker to experience feelings of responsibility, achievement, growth, and recognition.

job evaluation A systematic comparison done in order to determine the worth of one job relative to another.

job hazard analysis A systematic approach to identifying and eliminating workplace hazards before they occur.

job instruction training (JIT) Listing each job's basic tasks, along with key points, in order to provide step-by-step training for employees.

job posting Publicizing an open job to employees (often by literally posting it on bulletin boards) and listing its attributes, like qualifications, supervisor, working schedule, and pay rate.

job-related interview A series of job-related questions that focus on relevant past job-related behaviors.

job-requirements matrix A more complete description of what the worker does and how and why he or she does it; it clarifies each task's purpose and each duty's required knowledge, skills, abilities, and other characteristics.

job rotation A management training technique that involves moving a trainee from department to department to broaden his or her experience and identify strong and weak points; systematically moving workers from one job to another.

job sharing Allows two or more people to share a single full-time job.

job specifications A list of a job's "human requirements," that is, the requisite education, skills, personality, and so on—another product of a job analysis.

Landrum–Griffin Act of 1959 Also known as the *Labor Management Reporting and Disclosure Act*, this law aimed at protecting union members from possible wrongdoing on the part of their unions.

layoff An employer sending employees home due to a lack of work; this is typically a temporary situation.

lifelong learning Provides employees with continuing learning experiences over their tenure with the firm, with the aims of ensuring they have the opportunity to learn the skills they need to do their jobs and to expand their occupational horizons.

line authority Traditionally gives managers the right to issue orders to other managers or employees.

line manager A manager who is authorized to direct the work of subordinates and is responsible for accomplishing the organization's tasks.

locals Citizens of the countries in which employees are working; also called *host-country nationals*.

lockout A refusal by the employer to provide opportunities to work.

machine learning Software that can improve its own performance and learn on its own.

management assessment center A simulation in which management candidates are asked to perform realistic tasks in hypothetical situations and are scored on their performance. It usually also involves testing and the use of management games.

management development Any attempt to improve current or future management performance by imparting knowledge, changing attitudes, or increasing skills.

management game A development technique in which teams of managers compete by making computerized decisions regarding realistic but simulated situations.

management process The five basic functions of planning, organizing, staffing, leading, and controlling.

manager Someone who is responsible for accomplishing the organization's goals, and who does so by managing the efforts of the organization's people.

managing To perform five basic functions: planning, organizing, staffing, leading, and controlling.

managing diversity Maximizing diversity's potential benefits while minimizing its potential barriers.

mandatory bargaining items Items in collective bargaining that a party must bargain over if they are introduced by the other party—for example, pay.

market-competitive pay plan Pay plan where pay rates are equitable both internally (based on each job's relative value) and externally (in other words when compared with what other employers are paying).

market-competitive pay system A pay system in which the employer's actual pay rates are competitive with those in the relevant labor market.

mass interview A panel interviews several candidates simultaneously.

mediation Intervention in which a neutral third party tries to assist the principals in reaching agreement.

mentoring Advising, counseling, and guiding.

merit pay (merit raise) Any salary increase awarded to an employee based on his or her individual performance.

miniature job training and evaluation Training candidates to perform several of the job's tasks, and then evaluating the candidates' performance prior to hire.

mission statement Summarizes the answer to the question, "What business are we in?"

"mixed-motive" case A discrimination allegation case in which the employer argues that the employment action taken was motivated not by discrimination, but by some nondiscriminatory reason such as ineffective performance.

mobility premiums Typically, lump-sum payments to reward employees for moving from one assignment to another.

national emergency strikes Strikes that might "imperil the national health and safety."

National Labor Relations (or Wagner) Act This law banned certain types of unfair practices and provided for secret-ballot elections and majority rule for determining whether a firm's employees want to unionize.

National Labor Relations Board (NLRB) The agency created by the Wagner Act to investigate unfair labor practice charges and to provide for secret-ballot elections and majority rule in determining whether a firm's employees want a union.

negligent hiring Hiring workers with questionable backgrounds without proper safeguards.

negligent training A situation where an employer fails to train adequately, and the employee subsequently harms a third party.

Norris–LaGuardia Act of 1932 This law marked the beginning of the era of strong encouragement of unions and guaranteed to each employee the right to bargain collectively "free from interference, restraint, or coercion."

occupational illness Any abnormal condition or disorder caused by exposure to environmental factors associated with employment.

Occupational Safety and Health Act of 1970 The law passed by Congress in 1970 "to assure so far as possible every working man and woman in the nation safe and healthful working conditions and to preserve our human resources."

Occupational Safety and Health Administration (OSHA) The agency created within the Department of Labor to set safety and health standards for almost all workers in the United States.

Office of Federal Contract Compliance Programs (OFCCP) This office is responsible for implementing the executive orders and ensuring compliance of federal contractors.

on-demand recruiting services (ODRS) Services that provide short-term specialized recruiting to support specific projects without the expense of retaining traditional search firms.

on-the-job training (OJT) Training a person to learn a job while working on it.

operational safety reviews Reviews conducted by agencies to ascertain whether units under their jurisdiction are complying with all the applicable safety laws, regulations, orders, and rules.

organization A group consisting of people with formally assigned roles who work together to achieve the organization's goals.

organization chart A chart that shows the organizationwide distribution of work, with titles of each position and interconnecting lines that show who reports to and communicates with whom.

organization-wide incentive plan Incentive plan in which all or most employees can participate.

organizational climate The perceptions a company's employees share about the firm's psychological environment, for instance, in terms of things like concern for employees' well-being, supervisory behavior, flexibility, appreciation, ethics, empowerment, political behaviors, and rewards.

organizational culture The characteristic values, traditions, and behaviors a company's employees share.

organizational development A special approach to organizational change in which employees themselves formulate and implement the change that's required.

outplacement counseling A formal process by which a terminated person is trained and counseled in the techniques of self-appraisal and securing a new position.

paired comparison method Ranking employees by making a chart of all possible pairs of the employees for each trait and indicating which is the better employee of the pair.

panel interview An interview in which a group of interviewers questions the applicant.

parent or home-country nationals Citizens of the country in which the multinational company has its headquarters.

pay (or rate) ranges A series of steps or levels within a pay grade, usually based upon years of service.

pay (or wage) grade A pay grade is composed of jobs of approximately equal difficulty.

pay-for-performance Any plan that ties pay to some measure of performance, such as productivity or profitability.

Pension Benefits Guarantee Corporation (PBGC) Established under ERISA to ensure that pensions meet vesting obligations; also insures pensions should a plan terminate without sufficient funds to meet its vested obligations.

pension plans Plans that provide a fixed sum when employees reach a predetermined retirement age or when they can no longer work due to disability.

performance analysis Verifying that there is a performance deficiency and determining whether that deficiency should be corrected through training or through some other means (such as transferring the employee).

performance appraisal Evaluating an employee's current and/or past performance relative to his or her performance standards.

performance appraisal process A three-step appraisal process involving (1) setting work standards, (2) assessing the employee's actual performance relative to those standards, and (3) providing feedback to the employee with the aim of helping him or her to eliminate performance deficiencies or to continue to perform above par.

performance management The *continuous* process of identifying, measuring, and developing the performance of individuals and teams and *aligning* their performance with the organization's *goals*.

personnel replacement charts Company records showing present performance and promotability of inside candidates for the most important positions.

picketing Having employees carry signs announcing their concerns near the employer's place of business.

piecework A system of pay based on the number of items processed by each individual worker in a unit of time, such as items per hour or items per day.

point method The job evaluation method in which a number of compensable factors are identified and then the degree to which each of these factors is present on the job is determined.

polycentric Here the company staffs positions abroad with local or host-country employees.

polygraph A device that measures physiological changes like increased perspiration, on the assumption that such changes reflect lying.

portability Instituting policies that enable employees to easily take their accumulated pension funds when they leave an employer.

portfolio careers Careers based on using one's skills to create a livelihood from multiple income sources, often from a several jobs paying different rates.

position analysis questionnaire (PAQ) A questionnaire used to collect quantifiable data concerning the duties and responsibilities of various jobs.

position replacement card A card prepared for each position in a company to show possible replacement candidates and their qualifications.

preferential shop Union members get preference in hiring, but the employer can still hire nonunion members.

Pregnancy Discrimination Act An amendment to Title VII of the Civil Rights Act that prohibits sex discrimination based on "pregnancy, childbirth, or related medical conditions."

problem-solving teams Teams that identify and research work processes and develop solutions to work-related problems.

procedural justice Refers to just procedures in the allocation of rewards or discipline, in terms of the actual procedures being evenhanded and fair.

process chart A workflow chart that shows the flow of inputs to and outputs from a particular job.

productivity The ratio of outputs (goods and services) divided by the inputs (resources such as labor and capital).

profit-sharing plan A plan whereby employees share in the company's profits.

programmed learning A systematic method for teaching job skills, involving presenting questions or facts, allowing the person to respond, and giving the learner immediate feedback on the accuracy of his or her answers.

promotion Advancement to a position of increased responsibility.

protected class Persons such as minorities and women protected by equal opportunity laws, including Title VII.

qualified individuals Under ADA, those who can carry out the essential functions of the job.

quality circle A special type of formal problem-solving team, usually composed of 6 to 12 specially trained employees who meet once a week to solve problems affecting their work area.

ranking method The simplest method of job evaluation that involves ranking each job relative to all other jobs, usually based on overall difficulty.

ratio analysis A forecasting technique for determining future staff needs by using ratios between, for example, sales volume and number of employees needed.

reality shock Results of a period that may occur at the initial career entry when the new employee's high job expectations confront the reality of a boring or otherwise unattractive work situation.

recruiting yield pyramid The historical arithmetic relationships between recruitment leads and invitees, invitees and interviews, interviews and offers made, and offers made and offers accepted.

reliability The consistency of scores obtained by the same person when retested with the identical tests or with alternate forms of the same test.

restricted policy Another test for adverse impact, involving demonstration that an employer's hiring practices exclude a protected group, whether intentionally or not.

reverse discrimination Claim that due to affirmative action quota systems, white males are discriminated against.

right to work A term used to describe state statutory or constitutional provisions banning the requirement of union membership as a condition of employment.

rights arbitration Arbitration that interprets existing contract terms, for instance, when an employee questions the employer's right to take some disciplinary action.

role-playing A training technique in which trainees act out parts in a realistic management situation.

safety awareness program Program that enables trained supervisors to orient new workers arriving at a job site regarding common safety hazards and simple prevention methods.

salary survey A survey aimed at determining prevailing wage rates. A good salary survey provides specific wage rates for specific jobs. Formal written questionnaire surveys are the most comprehensive, but telephone surveys and newspaper ads are also sources of information.

savings and thrift plan Plan in which employees contribute a portion of their earnings to a fund; the employer usually matches this contribution in whole or in part.

Scanlon plan An incentive plan developed in 1937 by Joseph Scanlon and designed to encourage cooperation, involvement, and sharing of benefits.

scatter plot A graphical method used to help identify the relationship between two variables.

scientific management movement Management approach based on improving work methods through observation and analysis.

self-managing/self-directed work team A small (usually 8 to 10 members) group of carefully selected, trained, and empowered employees who basically run themselves with little or no outside supervision, usually for the purpose of accomplishing a specific task or mission.

severance pay A one-time payment some employers provide when terminating an employee.

sexual harassment Harassment on the basis of sex that has the purpose or effect of substantially interfering with a person's work performance or creating an intimidating, hostile, or offensive work environment.

sick leave Provides pay to an employee when he or she is out of work because of illness.

situational interview A series of job-related questions that focus on how the candidate would behave in a given situation.

situational test A test that requires examinees to respond to situations representative of the job.

social responsibility Refers to the extent to which companies should and do channel resources toward improving one or more segments of society other than the firm's owners or stockholders.

Social Security Federal program that provides three types of benefits: retirement income at the age of 62 and thereafter, survivor's or death benefits payable to the employee's dependents regardless of age at time of death, and disability benefits payable to disabled employees and their dependents. These benefits are payable only if the employee is insured under the Social Security Act.

staff authority Gives a manager the right to advise other managers or employees.

staff manager A manager who assists and advises line managers.

standard hour plan A plan by which a worker is paid a basic hourly rate but is paid an extra percentage of his or her rate for production exceeding the standard per hour or per day. Similar to piecework payment but based on a percent premium.

Standard Occupational Classification (SOC) Classifies all workers into one of 23 major groups of jobs that are subdivided into minor groups of jobs and detailed occupations.

stereotyping Ascribing specific behavioral traits to individuals based on their apparent membership in a group.

stock option The right to purchase a stated number of shares of a company stock at today's price at some time in the future.

straight piecework An incentive plan in which a person is paid a sum for each item he or she makes or sells, with a strict proportionality between results and rewards.

strategic human resource management Formulating and executing human resource policies and practices that produce the employee competencies and behaviors the company needs to achieve its strategic aims.

strategic management The process of identifying and executing the organization's strategic plan by matching the company's capabilities with the demands of its environment.

strategic plan The company's plan for how it will match its internal strengths and weaknesses with external opportunities and threats in order to maintain a competitive advantage.

strategy A course of action the company can pursue to achieve its strategic aims.

strategy-based metrics Metrics that specifically focus on measuring the activities that contribute to achieving a company's strategic aims.

strategy map A strategic planning tool that shows the "big picture" of how each department's performance contributes to achieving the company's overall strategic goals.

stress interview An interview in which the applicant is made uncomfortable by a series of often rude questions. This technique helps identify hypersensitive applicants and those with low or high stress tolerance.

strictness/leniency The problem that occurs when a supervisor has a tendency to rate all subordinates either high or low.

strike A withdrawal of labor.

structured (or directive) interview An interview following a set sequence of questions.

structured sequential interview An interview in which the applicant is interviewed sequentially by several persons; each rates the applicant on a standard form.

structured situational interview A series of job-relevant questions with predetermined answers that interviewers ask of all applicants for the job.

succession planning The ongoing process of systematically identifying, assessing, and developing organizational leadership to enhance performance.

suggestion teams Temporary teams whose members work on specific analytical assignments, such as how to cut costs or raise productivity.

supplemental pay benefits Benefits for time not worked such as unemployment insurance, vacation and holiday pay, and sick pay.

supplemental unemployment benefits Provide for a "guaranteed annual income" in certain industries where employers must shut down to change machinery or due to reduced work. These benefits are paid by the company and supplement unemployment benefits.

sympathy strike A strike that takes place when one union strikes in support of the strike of another.

Taft–Hartley Act of 1947 Also known as the *Labor Management Relations Act*, this law prohibited unfair union labor practices and enumerated the rights of employees as union members. It also enumerated the rights of employers.

talent management The goal-oriented and integrated process of planning, recruiting, developing, managing, and compensating employees.

task analysis A detailed study of a job to identify the specific skills required.

task statement Written item that shows *what* the worker does on one particular job task; *how* the worker does it; the *knowledge, skills, and aptitudes required* to do it; and the *purpose of the task*.

team (or group) incentive plan A plan in which a production standard is set for a specific work group, and its members are paid incentives if the group exceeds the production standard.

terminate at will In the absence of a contract, either the employer or the employee can terminate at will the employment relationship.

termination interview The interview in which an employee is informed of the fact that he or she has been dismissed.

test validity The accuracy with which a test, interview, and so on, measures what it purports to measure or fulfills the function it was designed to fill.

the cloud Refers to placing software programs and services on vendors' remote servers, from which they can then deliver these programs and services seamlessly to employees' digital devices.

third-country nationals Citizens of a country other than the parent or the host country.

Title VII of the 1964 Civil Rights Act The section of the act that says an employer cannot discriminate on the basis of race, color, religion, sex, or national origin with respect to employment; specifically, it makes it unlawful for employers to discriminate against any individual with respect to hiring, compensation, terms, conditions, or privileges of employment because of race, color, religion, sex, or national origin.

tokenism When a company appoints a small group of women or minorities to high-profile positions, rather than more aggressively seeking full representation for that group.

training The process of teaching new or current employees the basic skills they need to perform their jobs.

transfers Reassignments to similar positions in other parts of the firm.

trend analysis Study of a firm's past employment needs over a period of years to predict future needs.

unclear standards An appraisal that is too open to interpretation.

unemployment insurance (or compensation) Provides benefits if a person is unable to work through some fault other than his or her own.

unfair labor practice strike A strike aimed at protesting illegal conduct by the employer.

Uniform Guidelines Guidelines issued by federal agencies charged with ensuring compliance with equal employment federal legislation explaining recommended employer procedures in detail.

union salting A union organizing tactic by which workers who are in fact employed full-time by a union as undercover organizers are hired by unwitting employers.

union shop A form of union security in which the company can hire nonunion people, but they must join the union after a prescribed period of time and pay dues. (If they do not, they can be fired.)

unsafe conditions The mechanical and physical conditions that cause accidents.

unstructured (or nondirective) interview An unstructured conversational-style interview in which the interviewer pursues points of interest as they come up in response to questions.

unstructured sequential interview An interview in which each interviewer forms an independent opinion after asking different questions.

valence The perceived value a person attaches to the reward.

variable pay Any plan that ties pay to productivity or profitability, usually as one-time lump payments.

video-based simulation A situational test in which examinees respond to video simulations of realistic job situations.

virtual classroom Teaching method that uses special collaboration software to enable multiple remote learners, using their PCs or laptops, to participate in live audio and visual discussions, communicate via written text, and learn via content such as PowerPoint slides.

virtual teams Groups of geographically dispersed and generally same-level coworkers who meet and interact using information technologies to accomplish an organizational task.

vision statement A general statement of the firm's intended direction; it shows, in broad terms, "what we want to become."

Vocational Rehabilitation Act of 1973 The act requiring certain federal contractors to take affirmative action for disabled persons.

voluntary (or permissible) bargaining items Items in collective bargaining over which bargaining is neither illegal nor mandatory—neither party can be compelled against its wishes to negotiate over those items.

wage curve Shows the relationship between the value of the job and the average wage paid for this job.

Walsh-Healey Public Contract Act (1936) A 1936 law that requires minimum wage and working conditions for employees working on any government contract amounting to more than $10,000.

Web 2.0 learning Training that uses online technologies such as social networks, virtual worlds (such as Second Life), and systems that blend synchronous and asynchronous delivery with blogs, chat rooms, bookmark sharing, and tools such as 3-D simulations.

wildcat strike An unauthorized strike occurring during the term of a contract.

work samples Actual job tasks used in testing applicants' performance.

work sampling technique A testing method based on measuring performance on actual basic job tasks.

work sharing Refers to a temporary reduction in work hours by a group of employees during economic downturns as a way to prevent layoffs.

workers' compensation Provides income and medical benefits to work-related accident victims or their dependents regardless of fault.

workflow analysis A detailed study of the flow of work from job to job in a work process.

workforce (or employment or personnel) planning The process of deciding what positions the firm will have to fill, and how to fill them

works councils Formal, employee-elected groups of worker representatives.

NAME/ORGANIZATION INDEX

Note: Page numbers with *f* indicate figures; those with *n* indicate endnotes; those with *t* indicate tables

E

F

M

T

U

V

SUBJECT INDEX

Note: Page numbers with *f* indicate figures; those with *n* indicate endnotes; those with *t* indicate tables

Y

Z